1-6.
21-28
47-54
85-92
113-122
133-140
165-172
29-43
209-220
243-254
313-347

The Canon
of American Legal Thought

EDITED BY

David Kennedy

and

William W. Fisher III

Illustrated by Doug Mayhew

PRINCETON UNIVERSITY PRESS

PRINCETON AND OXFORD

Copyright © 2006 by Princeton University Press
Published by Princeton University Press, 41 William Street, Princeton, New Jersey 08540
In the United Kingdom: Princeton University Press,
3 Market Place, Woodstock, Oxfordshire OX20 1SY

All Rights Reserved

ISBN-13: 978-0-691-12001-0
ISBN-10: 0-691-12001-3

ISBN-13 (pbk.): 978-0-691-12000-3
ISBN-10 (pbk): 0-691-12000-5

Library of Congress Control Number: 2006930959

British Library Cataloging-in-Publication Data is available

This book has been composed in Sabon

Printed on acid-free paper. ∞

pup.princeton.edu

Printed in the United States of America

1 3 5 7 9 10 8 6 4 2

For our teachers

CONTENTS

PREFACE

This volume contains the twenty most important works of American legal thought. We have brought together the full texts of these classic writings with a number of aims in mind. Most directly, we hope the collection will be useful to teachers and students of law, for whom the ideas will be familiar, but who may benefit from seeing them in their original context. Put another way, these are the texts that every legal scholar and teacher is presumed to have read at some point—but will likely have encountered only in short excerpts, often in single sentences or paragraphs, among the readings assembled for various basic courses. For students, we hope these articles will serve as a kind of decoder ring for the modes of reasoning their law professors are urging them to adopt in law school. We present each contribution with a short introduction and bibliography highlighting the main ideas developed in the article and situating it in the context of the author's broader intellectual projects, the scholarly debates of his or her time, and the reception the article received.

For lawyers, we hope this collection will take them back to their best days in law school—offering the chance this time to look behind the curtain at the ideas their professors were developing and teaching, and to test them against their own experiences in practice. Many of the tools of legal analysis that judges, lawyers, and policymakers use every day and take for granted originated in these texts as dramatic intellectual innovations. In that sense, the articles will be both familiar and surprising. In returning to the texts themselves, the two of us were struck by the richness, the nuance, and the intellectual sophistication with which so many of the cliches of everyday legal argument were originally formulated. We hope that legal professionals will share our experience that encountering familiar ideas in their original context can give them new life.

In a broader way, we bring these articles together as an argument for the existence of a vigorous intellectual tradition *within* the field of law. Scholars in political theory, social theory, literary and cultural studies, philosophy, economics, public administration all refer to law, and each of these disciplines has its own—outsider's—idea about what law is and how it works. The experience of lawyers and legal scholars reading the work of colleagues in other fields is often a frustrating one. "If only they had a better sense of how law worked from the *inside*," we often think, or "if only they had gone to law school." If they had, much of what they would have learned about how to think, analyze, or reason about governance and politics is to be found in these articles.

In assembling and introducing these materials, we have received the generous advice of numerous friends and colleagues. Over the last decade, we have taught these texts to hundreds of American and foreign law students at Harvard, countless of whom have shed light on their contemporary resonance in ways which enriched our interpretation. We are particularly grateful to Arnulf Becker, Brenda Cossman, Dan Danielsen, Janet Halley, Christine Jolls, Duncan Kennedy, Catharine Mackinnon, Ian Malcolm, Martha Minow, David Shapiro, Steven Shavell, and David Trubek, for their comments on our introductory essays, and for invaluable bibliographic suggestions. Our deep appreciation also to our illustrator, Mr. Doug Mayhew, an artist and writer who lives in New York. Mr. Mayhew is represented by literary agents at Glitterati Incorporated, New York.

Introduction

The Subject: "Legal Thought"

This canon traces the history of writing about legal reasoning and legal decision making. These authors seek to clarify and reform the way legal professionals think about the law: the way lawyers interpret legal rules and judicial decisions when advising clients, the way judges reason about cases, the way legal professionals in a wide variety of settings—civil servants, administrators, judges, legislators, teachers, businesspeople, humanitarian advocates, and more—think about the policy objectives and implications of legal rules, and the way legal scholars understand the workings of the legal system. Taken together, these texts tell the history of American legal thought.

That history is different from the history of American law. A general history of American law would need to relate the work of American legal institutions and legal professionals to America's political, social, economic, and intellectual development. The history of legal thought itself would have been only a minor theme. Moreover, American legal history began long before Oliver Wendell Holmes wrote the first article reproduced here. It is also true, of course, that people thought and wrote about legal reasoning before Holmes. There were great jurists, judges, and legal scholars from the country's earliest days who reflected on how judges and legal professionals should reason. But the modes of legal thought that they developed before and directly after the Civil War have largely fallen out of use. Indeed, our authors initially developed the ideas about legal reasoning contained in these texts as a revolt against what they understood to be the dominant modes of legal thought in post–Civil War America. Their revolt was largely successful—these are the ideas about legal reasoning that have endured, and that continue to be taught in America's law schools and deployed by America's lawyers and judges. Holmes represents a watershed—the emergence of a self-consciously American and modern sensibility for legal professionals.

Reading these articles, you will catch fleeting glimpses of changes in the content and context of the American legal system. Here we catch sight of the New Deal, there the postwar expansion of America's internal market, later still the Civil Rights Movement, the growth of the welfare state, the politics of 1968, the Vietnam war, and the rise of identity politics in American life. A history of American law would foreground the impact of such changes on law, and the law's own influence on the course of these large dramas. The authors here were often aware—passionately aware—of the broader political and social context within which they worked, but their immediate goal was to clarify and reform the way legal minds—lawyers, judges, scholars—thought about law itself.

It is a commonplace in American legal education that law school aims not to teach "the law" but to teach how to "think like a lawyer." Throughout the first year, students struggle to make sense of this bromide. What about the law am I *not* supposed to be learning? Don't I have to remember the doctrines? What *is* thinking like a lawyer, beyond thinking clearly, logically, dispassionately? It turns out that "thinking like a lawyer" has a history. In different periods, learning to think like a lawyer has meant acquiring a different set of reasoning skills—argumentative set pieces and classic errors to be avoided. Each of these elements had to be invented, explained, and defended. The articles collected here have each played a major role in the development of what it means to "think like a lawyer" in America today.

To a large extent, in other words, these articles are works of method. A collection of the most significant articles in various substantive fields—taxation, administrative law, constitutional law, and so forth—would look quite different. The articles here were written by legal scholars to address general methodological issues of significance for law students and teachers. They are less concerned with the outcomes of legal reasoning than with the techniques jurists use to reason—have we relied too much or too little on deduction, on principle, on policy? How should we reason from general rules to specific outcomes? How should we identify principles, what should we make of claims for "rights"? How should we reason about policy and purpose? Most of these texts criticize aspects of the way American jurists routinely reason, and most propose one or another new way of thinking for lawyers and judges. The authors identify common reasoning "mistakes"—the same mistakes law students make in their first-year classrooms—and instruct us in how they might be avoided. Of course, the authors differ a great deal about what counts as a mistake, and about how legal reasoning ought to be conducted. There is debate, and there is a history, to the *way* lawyers have been taught to reason.

The story told here is also distinct from the history of American *jurisprudence*, sometimes called "philosophy of law" or "legal theory." There is a lively history of thinking about what law is, how it differs from politics or morality, how its normative claims can and should be sustained, or how law relates to justice and power. Scholars have developed arguments about these questions in all sorts of ways, drawing on materials from philosophy, sociology, anthropology, linguistics, history, ethics, religion, political or social theory, and more. Legal scholars who study the nature of law and participate in these jurisprudential debates form a sophisticated subspecialty within the legal academy. They cannot help looking at law from a certain distance, developing the best theory they can to account for what law is and should be. Jurisprudence asks questions about the nature of "law"—as an institution, as a social or political form, even as a form of speech. They are not first and foremost concerned to describe or reform the modes of reasoning legal professionals use in their everyday work. Of course, debates about legal theory often do affect the reasoning tools used by lawyers and judges. When a "theory of law" becomes common sense among working jurists, it can affect the arguments they find persuasive, useful, or professional. But an excellent legal theory can also remain simply an excellent theory, tested only by the academic standards and professional judgments of the field of jurisprudence itself.

Many of the authors whose work is collected here have also been participants in debates about jurisprudence. But these articles have also, and more significantly, had an impact on the modes of reasoning, on the shared background assumptions and broad consciousness or intellectual style of lawyers, judges, and other jurists. The phrase "modes of reasoning" may be a bit narrow. Legal professionals in each historical period also share a broad set of background assumptions about law, economics, society, or ethics. Their work betrays a shared consciousness about professional work and a shared intellectual style. Many of these articles reflect moments when a theory of law stopped being simply a good theory and crossed over into common sense. Theoretical propositions became shared background assumptions about society. The twists and turns of theoretical debate came to be used by professionals in everyday argument, and what once counted as a shrewd or nuanced theoretical move became as well a persuasive professional thrust or parry.

These articles have had a decisive impact on the modes of argument that seem persuasive to legal professionals. Where they have invented new modes for reasoning about what to do if you are a judge, you will not be a professionally proficient judge if you are not familiar with their arguments. Where they advance criticisms of existing modes of legal reasoning, you will not be a proficient practitioner unless you understand that your professional audience will be skeptical of the arguments these authors have criticized. As a result, these articles chart the rise and fall of faith in modes of argument among American legal professionals.

Writing about legal theory is a far less reliable guide to the methodological faith of legal professionals. Although it can sometimes happen, ordinarily there is little reason to expect that an argument which has been decisively criticized in the legal theory literature will stop seeming persuasive to legal professionals. The criticisms advanced are different, the coherence demanded of legal theory will be different. These articles remain significant not because they mark changes in the popularity of various legal theories in the academy, but because their authors have invented and destroyed methods for legal analysis.

The Narrative Lines

The book tells two stories. The first focuses on the emergence of specific arguments and analytic moves, all of which remain in the eclectic toolkit of contemporary legal reasoning. In this story, nothing is lost—each article contributed a methodological tidbit to a shared professional legal consciousness that has become ever more diverse in its specific elements. For this story, the interest in returning to the texts that first proposed these analytic moves lies in making what has become familiar new again. It is fascinating to see the force, sophistication, and nuance of these ideas before they became simple argumentative gambits.

The second story would be more familiar to the protagonists themselves. It traces the passionate effort by succeeding generations of legal scholars to reform and improve the practice of legal reasoning by displacing the analytic methods of their predecessors with new thinking. This is a dramatic story of the repeated establishment and collapse of professional consensus. It is a story of methodological rivalry and generational rebellion expressed with polemic force. Both narratives are true. We might say that legal reasoning today is an eclectic practice built from the methodological sediment laid down in successive projects of wholesale criticism and reform.

The First Story: A Collage of Methods

Each of the articles in this volume promotes some modes of legal reasoning and criticizes others. Thus, for example, Holmes warns against reasoning from history or deducing what to do from what was done in England. He urges judges to focus instead on developing rules and interpretations that are sensible, solve problems, and reflect the latest in statistical and economic analysis. He warns lawyers advising clients about what the law *is* not to get caught up in the law's abstractions, mistaking deductions from principle for predictions about what courts will actually decide. And he offers a famous heuristic—to know what the law actually is, think about it from the point of view of a "bad man," who is only concerned to know when the state will bring force to bear upon him. All these ideas continue to be taught to lawyers today. And so it goes, throughout this Canon. Many of the articles focus on possible errors of deduction. Hohfeld argues against the loose usage of words like "right" or "freedom," from which too much can be deduced by sloppy reasoning. Properly understood, legal terms like "right" should only be used with reference to their logical correlatives—a "right," he argues, exists only to the extent the law establishes a corresponding "duty," and it would be a mistake to deduce any obligations from the right *other* than those reflected in the corresponding duties. Generations of law students have been taught, and continue to be taught, to avoid the Hohfeldian errors of loose deduction, to keep their minds focused on the existence of duties when they speak of rights, and to recognize that the law protects interests—in property, say—through a limited set of legal relations, by establishing rights and duties, or privileges. The errors of overdeduction, and the correlative virtues of a focus on consequences, on enforcement, on remedies and duties, on the social and distributive effects of legal analysis are developed in different ways throughout the Canon.

Other articles are preoccupied with developing and illustrating modes of legal analysis *other* than deduction through which lawyers and judges can legitimately embrace Holmes's insistence on formulating practical policy to manage the clash of social and economic interests that lie behind legal decisions. Law students struggle to understand the relationship between "the rules" and the vague arguments that lawyers call "policy." Should "policy" begin only in the exception—when legal deduction runs out—or should it be a routine part of legal analysis? If the latter, how should lawyers reason about policy? What should go into reasoning about "policy"—how much ethics, how much empiricism, how much economics? Which of the arguments laypeople use count as professionally acceptable arguments of "policy" and which do not? Which mark one as naïve, an outsider to the professional consensus? What is it about policy argument that makes it seem more professional, more analytical, more persuasive, than talking about "mere politics"?

Fuller, Hart and Sacks, Coase, Calabresi, Galanter each proposed specific types of policy argument that have become routine methods of judicial reasoning. Law students are drilled in making Fullerian arguments about the "functions" of formal rules, and Hart and Sacksian arguments about "institutional competence." They learn from Coase to attend to the *reactions* of market actors to background rules, which may well affect, even reverse, their impact. They learn to argue, alongside Macaulay and Galanter, in ways that foreground the gap between "law in the books and law in action," and the different impact of legal norms on differently situated parties. And so on. Each new method of professional policy argument was proposed—and continues to be taught—as a corrective to common errors and misunderstandings in the ways lawyers typically reason about policy. Each resolves the tension between deduction and policy reasoning differently—and each of their resolutions has found its way into the background consciousness of today's legal professional. Thinking like a lawyer is not only the mastery of the legal reasoning techniques of deduction and policy developed by these authors. One must also be adept at criticizing the reasoning of other legal professionals. Law teachers drill first-year students to recognize specific errors in deductive reasoning and policy analysis—errors identified by these authors. For example, as we will see, Coase criticizes policy arguments rooted in the welfare economics of Pigou, particularly arguments for the "internalization" by economic actors of the "social costs" of their activities, requiring railroads, for example, to pay for the damage sparks from their wheels cause to crops along the tracks. He argues that there is no way to tell, a priori, whether the railroad's sparks or the farmers' proximity "caused" the cost to be incurred. Rather than focusing on cause, we should focus on allocating the joint costs of rail transport and crop raising in such a way as to maximize social welfare. He offers a series of tantalizing suggestions for understanding when and how legal liability might or might not affect the efficient allocation of resources. When analyzing a case in first-year contracts, tort, or property class, when one student argues that the defendant should be made to internalize the costs of his or her activity, the other students will have been trained, if all goes well, to counter with an argument from Coase.

Most of the authors represented here focus on the legal reasoner as a *ruler*—the modes of analysis are oriented to figuring out what to do when you have to decide, on the basis of legal materials, on actions that will affect others, for good and ill. Interestingly, these articles tend not to focus on the reasoning of legislatures, or on the routine reasoning of trial court judges or juries. The focus, and the paradigmatic case of "thinking like a lawyer", remains the appellate judge. We might say that legal professionals learn to "think like rulers" by learning to think like appellate judges. And for most of these authors, the paradigmatic work of the appellate judge is the interpretation of private common-law rules. For most, legal reasoning means the work of finding, enunciating, and applying private rules of common law on the basis of argument—deductive argument and policy argument.

Treating the private-law reasoning of appellate judges as the paradigmatic mode of rulership is puzzling. Even lawyers do all sorts of other things in their professional lives—they counsel clients, work in administrative agencies, advise legislatures—sit as legislators. Much, even most, professional legal work concerns statutes and administrative rules. Even appellate judging is at least as often about statutes, or the Constitution, as it is about private-law rules. It turns out that modes of legal reasoning developed for common-law appellate work influence the ways legal professionals do all these other activities. Whether this is a good thing or simply a professional deformation, it arises in part from the preoccupations of the authors of these canonical works. Professional modes of reasoning have developed by focusing on the appellate private-law site, and this setting has influenced the professional expertise that has emerged.

Only late in the Canon—Wechsler, Michelman, Crenshaw—do we find public-law, largely constitutional-law, adjudication in the foreground. Even here, the focus remains largely on the appellate judge. As a result, it continues to be true that "thinking like a lawyer" means thinking like an appellate judge, and American legal thought is the collection of arguments, techniques, and common sense the profession has developed for appellate judicial work.

At first glance, the diversity of arguments aggregated in the tradition of American legal thought seems a professional virtue—the mature legal professional today is adept at a wide range of different reasoning methodologies. Yet it is safe to say that none of the authors who developed these ideas would have celebrated this kind of diversity. For each, the *choice* among modes of reasoning was enormously important. In part, the eclecticism they spawned may result from a shared disinterest in dogmatic general theories about law. Few of the authors argued that the reasoning modes they preferred were entailed by a general theory—about law, or justice, or American society. They tended not to say: "If you think this, you must reason like this." They did not develop general theories of law or society to ground exclusive claims for their own reasoning inventions.

Rather, these authors seemed far more interested in criticizing modes of reasoning they found unpersuasive than in establishing their own dogmatic method. These works tend to be *critical* in tone, castigating legal professionals for specific analytic errors. They propose modes of legal reasoning as an antidote, sometimes almost as an afterthought. Similarly, although many of the articles criticize methods of legal reasoning—associated, say, with deduction—they usually offer no general theoretical account of the limits of deductive reasoning, and no coherent ethical or instrumental theory to ground the alternatives they propose. Rather, they criticize specific types and examples of deductive reasoning, and propose other reasoning techniques as more persuasive, useful, professional. For the paradigmatic work of judicial reasoning, each article offers thoughts about what has turned out not to be persuasive, and some ideas for argumentative styles that might work in the future. The eclecticism of American legal thought is the hard-won virtue of a skeptical, rather than a dogmatic, tradition. The diverse strength of modern American legal reasoning grows as it assimilates criticisms and proposals, the more the merrier. If some of these authors can be used to criticize others, so much the better—where the criticism turns out to be persuasive, one will have corrected for the blind spot of another. The result for American legal thought is an eclectic set of deductive and policy arguments and errors, rather than a coherent single theory about law or legal method.

The relative absence of dogmatism in these materials is refreshing. But it is not clear that a relentlessly skeptical and critical tradition supports methodological pluralism this smoothly. Across the last century, the Canon reflects a growing awareness of eclecticism and of the difficulty of knitting together so many diverse modes of legal argument and criticism in a logically coherent or theoretically satisfying way. Some authors respond explicitly to this challenge, proposing modes of reasoning to accommodate, even celebrate, the increasing diversity of legal argument. The Hart and Sacks "legal process" approach is perhaps the most well-developed effort at synthesis. Thereafter, it seemed more difficult to contain the methodological diversity. By the time we get to Kennedy's semiotic analysis of legal rhetoric, the emergence of contradictory modes of professional argument is presented as a narrative about the "death of reason." For other authors, the eclecticism of contemporary legal reasoning seems problematic for other reasons—because it threatens a rising tide of instrumental styles of policy argument, a loss of ethical moorings, or a loss of legal autonomy from other professional disciplines. Several of the later articles propose antidotes—reviving the language of principle and right, or of morality, or of political or social theory to buttress the specificity of legal reasoning against instrumentalisms imported from other disciplines.

For all this diversity, we might still group the legal methods developed in the Canon in bunches. One convenient way to do that would be to focus on the "schools of thought" which have emerged in the American legal academy over the last century. It is difficult to make sense of "schools of thought" in American law by reference to their *beliefs* or legal *theories*. It may be true that supporters of "Law and Economics" or "Critical Legal Studies" or "Legal Process" share some beliefs or adhere to a common theory of law, but in our experience efforts to state the theory cleanly seem unpersuasive explanations for what holds scholars together in such schools. Rather, it seems that schools of thought emerge among people who are focused on a particular set of common methodological mistakes, and on the promise of a particular set of innovative reasoning moves. Schools of thought in American law are less cults of belief than congregations practicing a common set of critical and reconstructive methods. American legal thought as a whole has managed simply to incorporate the critical and constructive insights that preoccupy each of the schools.

Looking back, we might divide the Canon loosely into eight schools: Legal Realism, Legal Process, Law and Economics, Law and Society, Critical Legal Studies, Modern Liberalism, Feminist Legal Thought, and Critical Race Theory, each associated with a specific argumentative style that remains part of the modern repertoire. Some of the authors are polemicists for their school; more often, however, the school label has come later, an attribution by others seeking to organize the legal field. The term *legal realism*, for example, was used by some authors in the 1930s to describe methodological affinities in their work. It was also used by their enemies, often in a quite different sense. The term remains in the legal vernacular to refer to those debates and affinities, and also to denote a series of loose reasoning tendencies—a heightened awareness of deductive errors in doctrinal analysis, the routine use of criticisms of analytic positivism, enthusiasm for purposive and functional styles of reasoning, and efforts to tolerate and affirm legal pluralism and social custom. In a similar fashion, the *Legal Process* school refers to a set of authors, their allies and opponents, as well as to specific modes for arguing about the purposes of law, the principles and policy considerations that should guide legal analysis and that foreground the importance of procedures and the priority of institutional competence and legitimacy in a plural legal system. The *Law and Economics Movement* was a self-conscious school of thought and an academic movement, seeking adherents, promoting and organizing its ideas in the legal academy. For most lawyers, the term is associated with the broad tendency to bring modes of reasoning from the field of microeconomics—about efficiency, market failures, transactions cost management and more—into mainstream legal argument. The argumentative styles developed by legal realists were picked up and extended in various ways by the *Law and Society* and *Critical Legal Studies* movements. *Modern Liberalism* is associated with the use of quite general Kantian ideas in legal argument, with the reinvigoration of argument about "rights," with the development of acceptable ways to bring ethical argument and argument about substantive conceptions of the good life into legal argument. *Feminism* and *Critical Race Theory* are associated with bringing arguments about identity politics into conventional legal analysis, and with criticisms of more mainstream legal analysis, including civil rights, for responding inadequately to claims for gender and racial justice.

For nonlawyers, what it means to "think like a lawyer" in the eclectic vocabulary developed here may seem strange. The particular methods of reasoning drilled into law students are likely to be only partially familiar. It may be surprising to see legal thinkers paying so much attention to the *limits* of deduction and to see them integrating such a wide range of specific policy arguments into legal reasoning. For those who think of law as the institutional enactment of a theory—a political theory or moral theory perhaps—the unstable eclecticism of legal argument may itself be surprising. That legal thinkers worry more about becoming comfortable with multiple, overlapping modes of analysis than with rooting out contradiction or promoting fealty to a comprehensive theory may be unexpected. It often comes as a surprise to those outside the law that lawyers by and large treat legal pluralism—a multiplicity of rules, arguments, institutional and normative solutions—not only as an obvious fact, but as a virtue rather than a vice. The voracious interdisciplinarity appetite of legal analysis, importing all manner of arguments from neighboring disciplines, often deploying them in unfamiliar ways, may also startle. Legal reasoning is not a matter of beliefs or theories implemented, nor is law a world of ethical commitments or sovereign commands mechanically made real. Law turns out to be a professional practice—a practice of arguments learned, made, developed over time, accepted, and rejected.

This way of understanding the Canon, however, has limits. For one thing, the authors of these articles did not generally write as if they meant simply to add a few new criticisms and a few new reconstructive moves to the list of arguments one might plausibly make. As we will see, these articles generally have a far more messianic tone. Still, it tends not to be the tone of self-confident and proselytizing general theory. These are not fancy theoretical castles with consequences. Each author identifies a set of specific argumentative mistakes in the everyday professional practice of the day, and treats the discovery of these errors as a revolutionary insight for legal reasoning. To *avoid these errors* (not to "apply this theory") will change everything. New repertoires of legal argument arise as wholesale efforts to avoid past error. Our author's passion about professional method can be hard to understand, but often, lying just beneath or even breaking through the surface are sharp political commitments. To reason *that* way is politically unacceptable. The method errors of the profession invalidate the political tendencies of its rulership. Rulers with different political affinities, be they progressive, liberal, conservatives, or simply the views of sensible people of the establishment, should reason differently. It is these broader political claims and this apocalyptic tone that give the Canon its drama as a terrain of intellectual struggle.

The Second Story: The Fall, Rise, and Fall of Methodological Consensus

This story takes up the historical drama of the Canon's formulation. In general terms, we might say that these materials reflect two moments of consensus in American legal thought, punctuated by periods of intense criticism and diverse invention: a late nineteenth-century consensus of "classical legal thought," the criticisms and reform proposals of Holmes, Hohfeld, and the legal realists, a second postwar "legal process" consensus, and the emergence during the late 1960s and afterward of divergent critiques of the legal process, each associated with proposals for new modes of legal reasoning—law and economics, law and society, modern liberalism, critical legal studies, and, somewhat later, feminism and critical race theory.

The first period of late nineteenth-century consensus among American legal professionals is reflected in the Canon only retrospectively, as the mode of legal reasoning *against which* all of the articles from Holmes to Llewellyn were written. The predominant mode of thinking from about 1860 through the First World War was denounced as "formalism" or "mechanical jurisprudence" by the legal realists in the first half of the twentieth century. This mode of thought is now routinely labeled "classical legal thought," a term originally proposed by our colleague, Duncan Kennedy. Classical legal thought was the product of collaborative intellectual effort and real innovation among legal scholars and judges. It combined ideas about the nature of law and legal authority with propositions about how to conduct doctrinal analysis and legal interpretation. Legal professionals working in its shadow shared a loose but recognizable common sense. Jurists working in the classical mode tended to see legal authority fragmented among diverse entities—legislature and judiciary, state and individual—each exercising absolute powers within the sphere of its authority. The job of legal analysis was to police the boundaries. It was an era of sharp analytic boundaries—between public and private, law and politics or law and morality, between state and civil society. Diverse legal institutions and instruments reflected the logic of their specific place in this scheme. Doctrinal reasoning meant interpretation of the boundaries between authorities and of the nature of differing legal institutions—private law, contract, equity, public law, and so forth.

At the same time, classical legal scholars proposed to unify, modernize, and simplify the doctrinal corpus of the common law by careful scholarly analysis. Preclassical legal reasoning seemed an unruly hodgepodge of ideas about the public good, equity, and the utilitarian value of precedent. Efforts by classical legal jurists to replace the preclassical style of legal analysis with something more analytically tight and orderly were "formal" in several senses. Classical jurists seemed to imagine that specific legal rules and case outcomes could be reliably deduced from a relatively small number of basic principles which themselves reflected the nature of various legal authorities. They also aspired to link the principles guiding various legal areas into a single unified system, rooted in a small set of fundamental concepts—in particular, the "will" or "autonomy" of legal authorities, including private contracting parties or property holders, acting legitimately within their respective spheres.

The first articles in the Canon attack this consensus. They do so on numerous grounds. For Holmes, classical legal scholars' attempts to achieve conceptual unification made things more mysterious, not less. In "The Path of the Law," the first article in the Canon, Holmes argues that the classical claim that the decisions of rulers should be based on a search for principles in historical precedent is an impractical, even absurd, basis for sound decision making. Rulers should be attentive to consequences rather than concepts. For Hohfeld, who shared the aspiration for analytic rigor and systematization in the use of legal terminology, the problem with legal reasoning in the classical period was an overwhelming tendency to deductive error. Classical efforts to deduce rights from principles, or results from rights, misunderstood the correlative nature of rights and duties. Rights could only be found where a decision had been made to impose a duty, a decision which would need to be made on grounds *other* than deduction from the right. At the same time, efforts to deduce rights and duties from the broad principles of liberty, autonomy, or freedom ignored the fact that law could protect liberty in various ways—with rights and duties, but also with privileges. Again, the decision maker faced a choice which could not be resolved by deduction. For Dewey, the difficulty was that classical legal descriptions of judicial decision making misrepresented the way practical people reason—and the way they should reason—when solving problems. All of these attacks supported a broad argument for the inevitability of argument about what came to be termed "policy" within the law and the need for modes of legal reasoning that could guide policy analysis.

Across the first half of the twentieth century, the modes of legal reasoning associated with classical legal thought were also associated with the politics of laissez-faire. This association resulted from the development by courts of the idea that the "right to property" and "freedom of contract" were constitutionally protected principles derived from the autonomy of property holders and private citizens, which could not constitutionally be limited by legislative regulation of the economy. At least within the judiciary and among legal academics, much of the energy behind the effort to root out the classical style of legal reasoning came from this political association. Scholars and judges who wished to promote or uphold social legislation found themselves motivated to criticize the reasoning of judges operating in the common sense of classical legal thought. Hale, Cohen, and Llewellyn illustrate the passion with which legal realists attacked the methods of classical legal reasoning.

The result was a wholesale assault on the jurisprudence of forms, concepts, and rules. Canonical texts written in the decades prior to the Second World War develop the idea that decisions about "policy" pervade judicial reasoning—the result, they argue, of circularities, contradictions, gaps, conflicts, and ambiguities in the legal materials—prior cases, statutes, available legal principles, and rules—available to the judge facing a decision. The canonical articles of the period develop numerous analytic moves for identifying conflicts and ambiguities in what seemed perfectly plausible and conventional examples of legal reasoning. Once identified, these inner conflicts, and the resulting indeterminacy of conventional legal reasoning, provide the opportunity for the introduction of policy. The legal realists proposed a variety of modes of legal reasoning to supplement formal rules, fill gaps, resolve conflicts and ambiguities, and replace deduction from broad principles like "will" or "autonomy." Judges should look to social realities, to the changing nature of the industrial workplace, to the facts of social interdependence. They should expand the use of broad standards, like "good faith" or "reasonableness." They should think purposively, attentive to the social purposes and functions of legal rules, replacing deduction from the principle of autonomy with functional attentiveness to the realities of social interdependence. The legal realists were enthusiastic about interdisciplinary borrowings from political science, statistics, sociology, and economics—legal oughts could be wrought from facts. They were generally more deferential to the technical expert than to the judge.

By the Second World War, the intensely critical impulses of Legal Realism had faded from American legal thought. Although they had been successful in eliminating "classical legal thought" as the established common sense of the legal establishment, the legal arguments associated with the classical style remain vigorous in American legal thought today. Deduction is alive and well, there remain as many rules as standards, and the principle of autonomy and the distinctions between public and private or state and society, from which classical legal thought developed a unified, will-based theory of everything, all remain. In another sense, however, after the realist period, it was widely accepted that there was no going back to the "formalism" of the classical era. Legal norms did not fit together in a coherent system, nor were they distinct from other social, customary, and ethical norms. The question of the relationship between legal and other norms needed to be resolved in policy terms.

Two central ideas made classical legal thought seem obsolete as a mode of consciousness, however resilient many of its specific legal arguments and modes of reasoning have remained. Those two ideas were legal pluralism and policy. By the 1950s, it had become common sense that legal materials did not generate unique solutions to individual cases. The materials conflicted, were vague, had significant gaps, and would be interpreted differently—and equally legitimately—by different legal actors. Moreover, the official legal system coexisted alongside a range of other normative social and customary orders, which gave a uniform official norm any number of diverse possible meanings on the ground. Lawyers would need reasoning tools which would permit them to be comfortable and effective in a world of legal pluralism. At the same time, it had become obvious that routine legal work involved a great deal of policymaking. It was not all deduction—you needed some way to talk and think about consequences, ethics, statistics, and more. Neighboring disciplines of sociology, economics, or psychology seemed impossible to ignore. Lawyers would need to become adept at policy argument, and at determining when policy and when rule.

The canonical materials from the 1940s and 1950s address these issues. Fuller, for example, proposes a method for reinterpreting legal rules, including the most formal of rules, "consideration" doctrine, as expressions of underlying policies. In doing so, he brings policy analysis in from the cold. No longer is it just for the exceptions or the gaps, it has become integrated into quotidian legal reasoning. At the same time, he models a method of legal reasoning which interprets legal questions to fall not on one side or the other of a line, but on a continuum between two or more opposing policies. He transforms the paradigmatic activity of legal reasoning from *distinguishing* to *balancing*. Also during this period, Hart and Sacks embrace legal pluralism and policy analysis by developing methods of reasoning about the requirements of process and the priority of respect for legitimate institutional settlements that permit the judge to cultivate an agnosticism about substantive outcomes. Over the twenty years following the Second World War, these ideas were consolidated as a second moment of broad consensus in the American legal establishment about how legal professionals should reason.

The "Legal Process" consensus was in turn itself shattered by the emergence of an array of methodologies associated variously with economics, sociology, liberal theory, and the work of critical legal studies scholars. Although the pathbreaking articles—Coase, Macaulay—that would lay the intellectual groundwork for the Law and Economics or Law and Society assaults on the Legal Process consensus were written in the 1950s, their effect was felt most sharply in the late 1960s and early 1970s. Moreover, like classical legal thought, the Legal Process School did not disappear; the modes of analysis associated with it remain alive. Nevertheless, in the few years around 1968 it lost its claim to be the dominant mode of analysis—to be what it meant, and all of what it meant, to "think like a lawyer." Scholars launched a variety of different method bundles to displace it, each intensely critical of the Legal Process consensus, each committed to its own new mode of legal analysis. As in the Legal Realist period, these new methodological proposals were launched with fury, even contempt, for the common sense of the Legal Process period. First, like classical legal thought before it, the Legal Process consensus suddenly seemed riddled with unsatisfactory argument—circularities, elisions, contradictions. Something more rigorous seemed necessary. Second, we find again, only just barely beneath the surface, a conviction that the Legal Process methods were associated with politics that had become objectionable, in this case the complacent politics of the Eisenhower center-right.

In the name of intellectual rigor and new politics, the sixties generation launched a series of quite different new methods for legal work and new proposals for professional common sense. Some were plainly more instrumental than the legal process—rooted in empirical science, sociological insight, or economic analysis—and less committed to the continuity of existing institutions and procedures. These new methods came to have political associations of their own—sociology became the domain of the left, economics of the right and right-center—although these methodological ideas might easily have been used to express other political commitments. Meanwhile, for others, new developments in philosophy, political and social theory, linguistics, anthropology, and literary criticism made it possible to reinvent the vocabulary of liberalism to reflect the reality of legal pluralism and the inevitability of judicial policymaking. For critical legal studies scholars, and later for feminists and critical race theorists, the collapse of the Legal Process consensus opened the door to a range of new inquiries into the blind spots and biases of the legal order. Scholars interested in developing self-consciously leftist or progressive modes of legal thought felt free to separate themselves both from the heritage of Marxist political thought about law and from the tradition of social reform begun by the New Deal and continued by liberal legal professionals through the Civil Rights Movement and the Great Society programs of the 1960s.

We end the Canon in the early 1990s, but of course, efforts by legal scholars to invent new methods and propose new common sense for legal professionals have not ended. Much of the new work of the last decade, however, continues to till already well-ploughed methodological fields. Within the tradition of Law and Economics, a generation of more liberal scholars has emerged, focusing on the possibility that regulation might be efficient, that market failures and transaction costs are more prevalent than Calabresi and Melamed—or Posner—had imagined, and that "culture and human frailty," in Robert Elickson's words, might be of central importance. Within the sociological tradition, we find a new interest in the social and communicative effects of norms. Empirical work testing the effects of policy and the impact of rules has become more rigorous. Rational choice and public choice models have been imported from the social sciences. A school of "neoformalists" has emerged, rebuilding many of the argumentative moves of classical legal thought. Critical work analyzing the rhetorical structures of legal argument and the social or political biases of conventional forms of legal knowledge has moved outward from private law into legal history, international law, labor law, family law, local government law, public and constitutional law, criminal law, study of the legal profession and more. The traditions of feminist and critical race theory continue to be the sites of intense productivity.

All of this work has affected the repertoire of legal reasoning techniques and common-sense arguments. Some of these works may well turn out to have been canonical—to have proposed modes of legal reasoning which mark a sharp and significant break in method, or which give rise to a new school of thought. But it remains too soon to say which those will be. This, of course, raises the question of what makes the articles collected here "canonical."

IN WHAT SENSE ARE THESE WORKS "CANONICAL"?

It is not surprising, if American legal thought has a history, that the history would be traced in a set of canonical materials. If American jurists reason in a limited set of specific ways, those ways would need to have been developed and promoted. The Canon collects moments of methodological innovation which have left lasting traces in the legal reasoning practices of American lawyers and judges. If American legal professionals have lived through moments of shared consensus and methodological dispute, the Canon preserves texts that best exemplify moments of consensus or were most significant in disrupting them in favor of something new. Working closely with these texts, we have increasingly come to the view that these articles have endured not only because they were innovative or exemplary, but also because of their quality. Indeed, it is hard not to conclude that many ideas now common in American legal reasoning were developed in more sophisticated and nuanced terms by those who first proposed them than by those of us in the profession who now use them routinely. These are landmark works of scholarship. Each was methodologically innovative, and the innovations of each gave rise to further productive work. Their authors were protagonists in the most significant debates of the twentieth century about the direction for American legal thought.

We included these articles in the Canon after wide consultation among colleagues in the legal academy. We began to compile the list more than a decade ago, for use in a summer workshop series for new law teachers. At that time, we canvassed our colleagues at Harvard Law School for their views on what were the dozen most important works of legal scholarship, works with which every law teacher should be familiar. We compiled responses, sent our tentative list around again, shared it with friends and colleagues at numerous other schools. The list inevitably grew. Over the last decade, we have taught these materials to dozens of law teachers and hundreds of law students, and sought their comments on the selection. The articles we selected were those that garnered the most consensus for inclusion in our informal collegial consultations, those which have consistently taught most successfully, and those that seem to stand most clearly for particular methodological innovations. Our sense is that these are the articles legal scholars would name if asked to list the articles they imagined a majority of their colleagues would also name as canonical. Although citation frequency is one useful measure of significance, we have not relied heavily on it in making our selections. Citation fashions change, and citation practices travel in packs. Most legal citation is not directed at methodological precursors. Nevertheless, in one well-known 1996 study of recent legal citation, articles included here comprised five of the ten most cited articles, seven of the top fifteen.[1] Authors included here were represented twenty-six times in the top hundred articles.

The remarkable thing has been the degree of consensus about the list. Certainly, others would have substituted one or another article, and there were judgment calls. We might well have gone beyond the Hart and Sacks and Wechsler pieces to include any number of significant legal process classics—by Henry Friendly, Paul Bator, Henry Wellington, Alexander Bickel, or Felix Frankfurter. Owen Fiss might well have displaced Abram Chayes to represent liberal innovations in the procedural field, just as he might have displaced Robert Cover to represent liberal engagement with ideas about interpretation. Cass Sunstein might have displaced Frank Michelman to represent the turn to republicanism in liberal political theory. We might well have included Derrick Bell's article "Serving Two Masters" to mark the inauguration of critical race scholarship, rather than the introduction to the critical race canon. There were plenty of legal realists to choose from; we settled on Felix Cohen and Karl Llewellyn only with difficulty. Fran Olsen's "The Family and the Market: A Study in Ideology and Legal Reform" might have replaced Catharine MacKinnon's *Signs* articles. In our introductions to each canonical article, we have tried to indicate the *also-rans* and to sketch the reasoning which lay behind the judgments we made about whom to include.

Many fields of legal scholarship are absent—legal history, international law, criminal law, family law, administrative law, local government law. Public law generally is underrepresented—we have not included Ely, Tribe, Bickel, Monaghan, Bork, Amsterdam, Brest, or Gunther, whose work largely went unmentioned in our search for the canonical works of American legal thought more generally. Had we sought to represent particular substantive fields, there would have been a good argument for including Richard Stewart's "The Reformation of American Administrative Law," or any of several Supreme Court forewords in the *Harvard Law Review* which shaped thinking about constitutional law. Corporate law might have suggested Henry Manne's "Mergers and the Market for Corporate Control"; local government law, Jerry Frug's "The City as a Legal Concept"; alternative dispute resolution, Mnookin and Kornhauser's "Bargaining in the Shadow of the Law"; negotiation, Fisher and Ury's "Getting to Yes."

Some innovations that once seemed crucial, but were not sustained, were understandably no longer on the tips of tongues. We were sorry, for example, to find little mention of Charles Reich's 1964 essay "The New Property" among colleagues today. For many of the authors we did include, it would have been possible to settle on different texts. For many, Fuller's "The Forms and Limits of Adjudication" or "Reliance Interest in Contract Damages" or "Morality of Law" will have been more significant—the first for legal process scholars, the second for contract law scholars interested in the move to make contract doctrine more responsive to social interdependence and bargaining power differentials, the latter for those interested in rebuilding a liberal ethical posture for legal reasoning. We have included "Consideration and Form" because it most clearly marks Fuller as a broad methodological innovator, illustrating a new way to think about policy analysis in legal reasoning that would become dominant across all fields of law in the ensuing years. We made similar judgments about other scholars, often inflected by our experience teaching the materials. For example, Llewellyn's "Some Realism About Realism" might well have been replaced by "A Realistic Jurisprudence—The Next Step," "On the Good, the True, the Beautiful, in Law," or "What Price Contract—An Essay in Perspective," each of which would also have a claim to canonical status.

WHAT MAKES THIS LEGAL THOUGHT "AMERICAN"?

For many years, this Canon was taught to foreign lawyers in the Harvard Law School's LLM program, as a way of introducing the ideas that undergird the classroom experiences these foreign lawyers were having in various substantive subjects. Reading these articles with foreign lawyers and legal scholars inevitably raises the question, in what sense are these ideas, legal reasoning techniques, and common-sense assumptions American? These articles represent the course of methodological innovation among lawyers and legal scholars in the United States over the last century. As far as we can determine, they were all written by American citizens working in the United States, so in that simple sense, of course, they are "American." But that leaves unanswered a number of significant questions: were these developments unique to legal thought in the United States? Were these American authors influenced by ideas developed elsewhere? Have the legal reasoning techniques and common-sense ideas developed in the Canon had an influence elsewhere? And, perhaps most important, if also the most difficult to answer, are these ideas linked in any way to other aspects of the American legal system that seem unique?

Work on comparative *legal thought* has only recently begun. Perhaps the availability of this Canon will be a spur to further work exploring the history of influences—from elsewhere on American legal thought, and of American legal thought on other legal regimes. In a very preliminary way, however, it does appear that the developments traced by this Canon were not unique to the United States. Before the Second World War, they were often derivative of developments elsewhere. Thereafter, we find more evidence of the influence of American legal thought in legal systems around the world.

The authors in the Canon wrote about American legal method for an American audience—many had little exposure to ideas developed elsewhere and little opportunity to export their own methodological innovations abroad. For some, Holmes perhaps most significantly, the significance of an *American* approach to law, independent of the methods of old Europe—and in particular of common-law England—was paramount. It is easy to find the roots for Holmes's practical sense in the pragmatism he shared with William James and Charles Pierce in the Cambridge "Metaphysical Club." Dewey, the most influential American philosopher before 1945, seems emblematic of the roots for canonical legal methods in the traditions of American pragmatism.

Yet even Holmes was an avid reader of British and continental (particularly German) legal theory, and his thought reflected the efforts by von Ihering and others to break through the analytic paradigm of nineteenth-century legal thought. Although "classical legal thought" had elements that were uniquely American, as a general set of legal methods and basic ideas, it was the common project of jurists across the globe, with roots in continental Europe—particularly in Germany, and to a certain extent France. American scholars were not alone in repudiating its methods; indeed, many of the specific criticisms developed by Pound and the legal realists had their roots in the sociological jurisprudence of France and Germany. These ideas were taken up differently, and had different life cycles in the United States, but much of the opposition to classical legal thought in the United States ran parallel to developments in Europe of the same period. After the Second World War, the influences of European legal thought on the American Canon are less pronounced. The United States was no longer a net importer of legal methods; indeed, there is some evidence of the reverse. Modes of argument associated here with "policy analysis," with economics, sociology, and empirical study have all migrated into other legal systems.

The pattern of influences from and toward American legal thought, even once documented, will provide only a starting point for the far more difficult inquiry into the relationship between these modes of legal reasoning and aspects of the American legal system which seem to make it distinct. Throughout the history of American legal thought, it has seemed evident that modes of argument and analysis were linked to specific political interests or positions. Classical legal thought seemed inseparable from laissez-faire, legal realism the expression of the New Deal's social democracy, the legal process embedded in postwar American complacency, and so forth. But these associations, in our view, have been consistently overstated. The techniques of classical legal thought have been appropriated for all manner of political projects. There has been a sociological jurisprudence of the right, a legal process of the left, a law and economics of center-left liberalism.

The difficulty of associating modes of legal thought with political commitments makes us wary of the further step of associating them with the particular institutions and substantive preoccupations of the American legal system. If you ask a group of foreign lawyers encountering these materials what makes the American legal system unique, they will develop something like the following list: the role of juries; federalism; the prominence of the legal profession in economic and political life; the interdisciplinarity of legal reasoning; the resolution of social and political conflicts in the judiciary; the porous boundaries between law and the worlds of morality, commerce, or political debate; or the litigiousness of American society generally. As they read the Canon, it is not uncommon for them to find the origins for these stereotypes. The attention paid in these materials to legal pluralism—the presence of multiple legitimate legal resolutions within the materials of law, and of multiple legitimate legal jurisdictions and modes of resolution within the legal order—is easy to interpret as an effect of federalism, or a cause for the fuzzy line between law and other fields of inquiry. The attention paid to policy within law, to the need for policy analysis and to the modes of its exercise, is easy to associate with the prominence of judges in political and social conflict, or the interdisciplinarity of legal reasoning.

Tempting as this sort of association may seem, we remain agnostic on this score. What we can say is that these materials reflect the methodological preoccupations and common sense of the American legal establishment. And that knowing these techniques for reasoning—thinking like a lawyer—has given generations of lawyers confidence in their suitability to govern. Whether that is cause, or effect, of institutional or cultural particularities of the American legal system or American society, we leave to our readers' imagination. We offer these materials as a window into the consciousness and sensibility of America's lawyers, judges, and legal scholars about how to rule.

NOTE

1. See Fred Shapiro, The Most Cited Law Review Articles Revisited," 71 *Chicago Kent Law Review* 751, 1996. In Shapiro's study, the Coase and Wechsler pieces included here are the two most cited articles; Holmes, Chayes, Kennedy, Calabresi, and Melamed make the top ten, while Galanter and Macaulay come in at thirteen and fifteen. Shapiro excluded "older articles" from his top list; the dozen most cited older pieces include the contributions from Hohfeld, Fuller, and Llewellyn, and Canon authors account for six of the twelve.

PART I

Attacking the Old Order: 1900–1940

Oliver Wendell Holmes

Oliver Wendell Holmes

OLIVER WENDELL HOLMES, Jr., was born in 1841 into a famous Boston family. His father was both a doctor and a well-known man of letters—the author of, among other things, *The Autocrat of the Breakfast Table* (1858). His mother, Amelia Lee Jackson, was a prominent figure in Boston society. Among the eminent visitors to the household during his youth was Ralph Waldo Emerson, from whom, Holmes would later report, he learned a passion for philosophy. He attended private schools and Harvard College (from 1857 to 1861). When the Civil War broke out, he volunteered for the Massachusetts militia, serving for three years, first as a lieutenant and then as a captain, suffering serious wounds. After the war, Holmes enrolled in Harvard Law School, receiving his degree in 1866. He practiced law briefly in Boston, then sought for a time to establish himself as a man of letters—editing James Kent's *Commentaries on American Law* and writing essays, reviews, and poetry. Unable to earn enough money thereby to sustain himself and his new wife, childhood friend Fanny Dixwell, he joined a Boston law firm and for a decade practiced commercial and admiralty law. As he became more skilled as a practitioner, he began during his leisure hours to write legal scholarship—most notably, the series of essays that became *The Common Law*, published in 1881, just before he turned forty. The deserved success of the book enabled Holmes to leave practice for good. In 1882, he was appointed to the faculty of Harvard Law School. A few months later, he was appointed to the Massachusetts Supreme Judicial Court, on which he served for the next twenty years. While a judge, he wrote a few pieces of scholarship, of which the most original was "Privilege, Malice, and Intent," published in the *Harvard Law Review* in 1894, in which he argued, among other things, that the law of torts ought to be shaped more consciously and rigorously by analyses of the "policy" implications of alternative rules. But, for the most part, he contented himself with his judicial responsibilities.

The year 1897 thus found Holmes a well-regarded state appellate judge, an experienced practitioner, and the author of a few provocative articles and what would later come to be seen as a seminal book in legal scholarship—a man of considerable repute, but still overshadowed by his father. This was soon to change. In January of that year, he was asked to give a lecture at the dedication of a new building at Boston University Law School. The setting was inauspicious. In a letter written four days later, he recounted: "The room was crowded the air not too good—and I was preceded by more than an hour of prayer and discourse on the finance of the institution . . . and summaries of the little glories achieved by graduates until I saw the listeners' eyes begin to roll with poisoned slumber." Nevertheless, the speech was a considerable success. "[T]o my great satisfaction," he reported, "I had them all awake pretty soon and kept them so." In March, the text was published as "The Path of the Law" in the *Harvard Law Review*. It quickly became, and has since remained, one of the best-known essays in American law.

Its notoriety and enduring power derive in large part from the piquancy of three passages. The first comes near the beginning (and most likely served to perk up his listeners):

> Take the fundamental question, What constitutes the law? You will find some text writers telling you that it is something different from what is decided by the courts of Massachusetts or England, that it is a system of reason, that it is a deduction from principles of ethics or admitted axioms or what not, which may or may not coincide with the decisions. But if we take the view of our friend the bad man we shall find that he does not care two straws for the axioms or deductions, but that he does want to know what the Massachusetts or English courts are likely to do in fact. I am much of his mind. The prophecies of what the courts will do in fact, and nothing more pretentious, are what I mean by the law.

The second comes midway through:

> The rational study of law is still to a large extent the study of history. History must be a part of the study, because without it we cannot know the precise scope of rules which it is our business to know. It is a part of the rational study, because it is the first step toward an enlightened scepticism, that is, toward a deliberate reconsider- ation of the worth of those rules. When you get the dragon out of his cave on to the plain and in the daylight, you can count his teeth and claws, and see just what is his strength. But to get him out is only the first step. The next is either to kill him, or to tame him and make him a useful animal. For the rational study of the law the black-letter man may be the man of the present, but the man of the future is the man of statistics and the master of economics. It is revolting to have no better reason for a rule of law than that so it was laid down in the time of Henry IV. It is still more revolting if the grounds upon which it was laid down have vanished long since, and the rule simply persists from blind imitation of the past.

The last is the peroration:

> We cannot all be Descartes or Kant, but we all want happiness. And happiness, I am sure from having known many successful men, cannot be won simply by being counsel for great corporations and having an income of fifty thousand dollars. An intellect great enough to win the prize needs other food beside success. The remoter and more general aspects of the law are those which give it universal interest. It is through them that you not only become a great master in your calling, but connect your subject with the universe and catch an echo of the infinite, a glimpse of its unfathomable process, a hint of the universal law.

The central ideas expressed in these three passages were far from new. The proposition from which the first excerpt springs is that we must differentiate sharply the question of what the law is (an issue of fact) from the question of what the law ought to be (an issue of value). Holmes did not (and did not pretend to) invent this notion; it was a staple of nineteenth-century English legal positivism. The thesis of the second passage—that the fact that a legal rule has been long established does little to commend it; that a rule should be preserved and enforced if it is socially advantageous and discarded if it is not—is merely a strong version of the "instrumentalist" style of judicial reasoning that, as Willard Hurst and

Morton Horwitz have shown, many American judges had been practicing since roughly 1800. The final passage interweaves two ideas—that positive law may be connected in some way with natural ("universal") law, and that legal practice is at least potentially noble and enlightening. The former had been in circulation for millennia; the latter, as Robert Gordon has shown, was a familiar component of the "republican" ideal of advocacy.

To be sure, to each well-worn theme, Holmes added something new. With respect to the first, Thomas Grey points out that Holmes "shift[ed] the emphasis of positive legal analysis from the legislature to the courts." A definition of law that focused on predictions of what *judges* "will do in fact," rather than on the exercise of sovereign power by legislatures, was novel. With respect to the second, Holmes seemed (at least in this passage) to break with the majority of his antebellum predecessors in renouncing interest in matters of "equity"—suggesting that analysts, or judges, when assessing the merits of extant legal rules, should focus exclusively on their impact upon net social welfare and not seek simultaneously to promote "fairness." Finally, Holmes's notion of how legal practice might raise one's spirit was somewhat different from that of the typical nineteenth-century Fourth-of-July orator—less political in orientation, more philosophical, even religious. But probably more important than these innovations, at least for the fame of the essay, was the way in which the familiar themes were expressed. Each passage was (and is) arresting.

Putting aside their novelty and mnemonic power, what most strikes modern readers of these three passages are the differences, in both tone and substance, among them. The first two are realist, even cynical, in outlook; the third is romantic, even mystical. The first sees law as fixed, something whose force is to be predicted and either harnessed or avoided; the second sees law as malleable, something to be modified in order to serve contemporary social needs; the third sees law as embodying—and perhaps yearning to embody more fully—superhuman values. It is hard to discern how such disparate notions hang together.

Once one looks beyond these three passages to the larger arguments in which they are set, even deeper tensions become apparent. For example, as Grey points out, the early portions of the article sing in the key of moral skepticism; Holmes appears to take the position that "might makes legal right." By the end, however, he has aligned himself with Progressive moralism, reflecting with "hope and optimism about the possibilities of rational legal reform in the service of the public interest." G. Edward White emphasizes a different "dialectic" in the article: several portions contain "approving images of the materialist, commercial world and of those who people it," while other portions "criticize that world and its inhabitants." Perhaps the deepest of the divides lies between sections in which Holmes assumes the stance of an aloof, bemused observer and analyst of legal and social affairs—a "spectator," to use Yosal Rogat's term—and sections in which he seems invested, engaged, outraged. One is reminded of Whitman's lines in *Song of Myself*: "Looking with side-curved head curious what will come next / Both in and out of the game and watching and wondering at it."

What are we to make of such tensions and inconsistencies? A simple explanation would be that Holmes was merely suggesting how the legal system could and should be seen by different sorts of viewers. In the first section of the article, he assumes the stance of a client asking for advice concerning how to plan a course of conduct, or a lawyer attempting to provide it. In the second section, he asks his listeners to imagine themselves as judges, or perhaps as scholars advising judges concerning how cases should be decided. In the third, he is speaking to the law students in the audience, providing them inspiration and suggesting how they might plan their careers. In short, the article is not incoherent. Rather, to appropriate a metaphor later employed by Calabresi and Melamed in their contribution to the Canon, it offers readers several alternative "views of the cathedral."

A variation on this interpretation, offered by Gordon, imagines that Holmes was doing what law professors commonly do—strongly advocating extreme positions in order to "shock[ ] his audience out of complacency into an enquiring state of mind." On this view, Holmes didn't actually believe any of the arguments he was making. He certainly didn't think that law was reducible to the "predictions" made by lawyers advising purely self-interested "bad men." Indeed, elsewhere in the essay, he acknowledges that "[l]aw is the witness and external deposit of our moral life." Nor was he sincere in suggesting that all legal doctrines should be dragged from the cave of tradition and either killed or refashioned to suit contemporary social needs. As a judge, he was conservative, often enforcing common-law rules he acknowledged had outlived their usefulness. More broadly, he elsewhere frequently expressed doubt concerning the efficacy of the kind of instrumental policy-driven law reform that the metaphor of the dragon seems to commend. Finally, the sentimental, eyes-skyward peroration is distinctly out of character. In short, all of the arguments were disingenuous. Their purpose was to awaken, prod, challenge his listeners and readers.

A radically different account, offered by Grey, sees "the contrast[s] between and among the separate parts" of the essay as intentional, part of a rhetorical strategy whose ultimate aim was "to enliven his potentially bland pragmatist approach to legal theory, and so to strengthen his jurisprudence in its rhetorical competition with more simple and extreme (and therefore exciting) theories, particularly the classical legal science of Langdell." For that purpose, Holmes deliberately chose to organize the article as a "quest narrative," a venerable literary form exemplified by Dante's *Divine Comedy* and the traditional Protestant sermon, in which:

> The hero . . . begins in the middle of things, as an apparently ordinary person, sometimes marked by portents of special potential. He is then thrown or deliberately descends into misfortune or degradation. Finally, by virtue of what he learns in this fall out of the ordinary, he is able to attain stature far above his beginning point, in true knowledge or self-realization.

Following this line, Holmes begins "The Path of the Law" by immersing the reader in conventional Blackstonian jurisprudence, in which law is understood as "an impressive 'mystery' that somehow manages at the same time to direct state power, embody common morality, and operate according to its own internal logic." Then, in the famous bad-man passage, he plunges the reader into a grimmer world, in which amoral advocates use the law solely to guide purely self-interested clients. "After this drastic reduction, Holmes constructs the rest of the essay as a long ascent, by way of a series of steps each of which elevates the portrayal of his subject matter," first, by restoring a sense of the social and historical contexts in which law operates, next by recovering a moral compass in the form of utilitarianism, and ultimately in the conclusion by drawing listeners heavenward.

Yet another approach would eschew the aspiration to make the essay coherent and instead see in its disparate parts manifestations of the various dimensions of Holmes's complex personality. On this view, the cynical, bad-man conception of the law grows out of his dark side—the side accentuated by the physical and psychic wounds he sustained in the Civil War, the side that drew him toward Social Darwinism and eugenics, the side that prompted Grant Gilmore to depict him as "savage, harsh, and cruel, a bitter and lifelong pessimist who saw in the course of human life nothing but a continuing struggle in which the rich and powerful impose their will on the poor and weak." The middle portions, by contrast, capture his at least occasional belief that law, in the right hands, could be an instrument of social good—a belief that drew him toward Mugwumpery and Progressivism in politics and, as Grey has convincingly shown, toward one variant of Pragmatism in philosophy. The lyrical closing hints at the aspect of Holmes that we know least—lonely; vulnerable; hungry for companionship, affirmation, and perhaps love. The best clues we have that there was in fact such a dimension to Holmes can be found in the letters he wrote during the period in which he was drafting "The Path of the Law" to Lady Clare Castletown, a married Irish noblewoman he met during one of his many trips to Britain and with whom he subsequently became infatuated. We know very little of his relationship with her, in part because he destroyed the letters she wrote to him. But his letters to her survive (despite his wishes), and seem to have been written by a person radically different from the one sketched by Gilmore. With Clare, he purports to have lowered his guard altogether: "Oh my dear what joy it is to feel the inner chambers of one's soul open for the other to walk in and out at will." The trust suggested by this passage enabled him to speak with her more honestly than was his wont of his professional aspirations and anxieties—expressing hope, for example, that she could appreciate that his "scheme of life . . . might be noble and great without the accessories of conspicuous position and immediate power . . . I should be in despair did I not have a timid confidence that I am worth it—but oh my dear despair is always so near at hand." Such sentiments suggest that Holmes was being genuine when he contended, at the end of the essay, that "happiness" was only attainable if one could, in one's work, catch "an echo of the infinite" and that the practice of law might indeed make that possible.

Despite, or perhaps because of, its ambiguities, "The Path of the Law" has inspired a remarkably large and diverse array of subsequent legal theorists. Those who acknowledged the deepest debt to Holmes were the legal realists. As we will see, several of his themes—the predictive theory of law, his insistence on the need to separate law and morals, his sensitivity to the ways in which law both expresses and figures in class conflict—were elaborated in much greater detail in their writings. Scholars associated with the Law and Society movement shared Holmes's impatience with ignorance concerning the actual impact of legal rules— "What have we better than a blind guess to show that the criminal law in its present form does more good than harm?"—and took to heart his contention that sensible legal reform depended on, among other things, serious empirical work. Scholars associated with Law and Economics were buoyed by his prediction that "the man of the future is the man of statistics and the master of economics," agreed with him that (in Richard Posner's words) "[t]here is a lot of needlessly solemn and obfuscatory moralistic and traditional blather in judicial decision-making and legal thought generally," and, most importantly, found compelling his contention that every legal rule must be evaluated in light of its net social advantages. Scholars seeking to revive Pragmatism in modern legal scholarship found Holmes's writings inspirational. And some feminist legal theorists, though repelled by aspects of Holmes's writings and personality, found congenial his critique of formalism, his awareness of the extent to which common-law rules are rooted in power differentials, and his "appreciation of the situatedness or contingent character of law."

After writing "The Path of the Law," Holmes went on to glory, ultimately fully realizing his aspiration to greatness. A concatenation of circumstances – among them the assassination of McKinley, and Holmes's well-known imperialistic views, which endeared him to Theodore Roosevelt – enabled him in 1902 to secure a position on the United States Supreme Court. His extraordinary longevity allowed him to make the most of the opportunity. He served for almost thirty years—from age sixty to age ninety—and wrote more opinions that any other justice before or since. Many are deservedly famous (or infamous), among them, his ringing denunciations of the theory of substantive due process in *Lochner v. New York* and *Coppage v. Kansas*; his impassioned plea in *Abrams v. United States* for generous interpretation of the free-speech clause of the First Amendment; his establishment in *Pennsylvania Coal v. Mahon* of the foundations of modern "takings" jurisprudence; and his harsh declaration in *Buck v. Bell*, in the course of upholding against a constitutional challenge a state statute permitting involuntary sterilization of mentally defective women, that "three generations of imbeciles are enough." The pithiness of the language in which these opinions were delivered helps ensure that Holmes's fame and influence will not soon fade.

WILLIAM FISHER

Bibliography

Primary Sources

Holmes's principal scholarly writings are contained in *Collected Legal Papers* (New York: Harcourt, Brace and Howe, 1920; reprinted by P. Smith, New York, 1952), and *The Common Law* (Boston: Little, Brown, 1923). Other useful collections, which include some of his opinions as well as his articles, are Sheldon M. Novick, ed., *The Collected Works of Justice Holmes: Complete Public Writings and Selected Judicial Opinions of Oliver Wendell Holmes* (Chicago: University of Chicago Press, 1995); and Richard A. Posner, ed., *The Essential Holmes: Selections from the Letters, Speeches, Judicial Opinions, and Other Writings of Oliver Wendell Homes, Jr.* (Chicago: University of Chicago Press, 1992).

The citations for the judicial opinions mentioned at the end of the introductory essay are *Lochner v. New York*, 198 U.S. 45, 65 (1905); *Coppage v. Kansas*, 236 U.S. 1, 26 (1915); *Abrams v. United States*, 250 U.S. 616, 624 (1919); *Pennsylvania Coal v. Mahon*, 260 U.S. 393 (1922); and *Buck v. Bell*, 274 U.S. 200 (1927).

The best windows into Holmes's mind are provided by his letters, many of which have now been published. The most illuminating collections are Mark DeWolfe Howe, ed., *Holmes-Pollock Letters, The Correspondence of Mr. Justice Holmes and Sir Frederick Pollock, 1874–1932* (Cambridge, Mass.: Harvard University Press, 1941); Mark DeWolfe Howe, ed., *The Holmes-Laski Letters* (Cambridge, Mass.: Harvard University Press, 1963); David H. Burton, ed., *Progressive Masks: Letters of Oliver Wendell Homes, Jr., and Franklin Ford*

(Newark: University of Delaware Press; London: Associated University Presses, 1982); David H. Burton, ed., *The Holmes-Sheehan Correspondence: Letters of Justice Oliver Wendell Holmes, Jr. and Canon Patrick Augustine Sheehan* (New York: Fordham University Press, 1993); Robert M. Mennel and Christine L. Compston, eds., *Holmes and Frankfurter: Their Correspondence, 1912–1934* (Hanover, N.H.: University Press of New England, 1996); and James Bishop Peabody, ed., *The Holmes-Einstein Letters; Correspondence of Mr. Justice Holmes and Lewis Einstein, 1903–1935* (New York: St. Martin's Press, 1964).

Secondary Sources

The literature on Holmes is enormous. We can identify here only a few of the better treatments.

Excellent biographies, each of which blends in some way a study of Holmes the man with a study of Holmes the judge and scholar, include: Mark DeWolfe Howe, *Justice Oliver Wendell Holmes: The Shaping Years 1841–1870* (Cambridge, Mass.: Belknap Press of Harvard University Press, 1957); id., *Justice Oliver Wendell Holmes: The Proving Years 1870–1882* (Cambridge, Mass.: Belknap Press of Harvard University Press, 1963); G. Edward White, *Justice Oliver Wendell Holmes: Law and the Inner Self* (New York: Oxford University Press, 1993); Sheldon Novick, *Honorable Justice: The Life of Oliver Wendell Holmes* (Boston: Little, Brown, 1989); and Albert W. Alschuler, *Law without Values: The Life, Work, and Legacy of Justice Holmes* (Chicago: University of Chicago Press, 2000).

A set of brief interpretations of "The Path of the Law" can be found in the symposium issue of the *Harvard Law Review*, published a century after its original release. In this Introduction, we have drawn especially heavily from Robert W. Gordon, "The Path of the Lawyer," *Harvard Law Review* 110 (1997): 1013 (quotations taken from pages 1015–16); Tracy Higgins, "Straying from the Path," *Harvard Law Review* 110 (1997): 1019 (quotations taken from page 1019); Martha Minow, "The Path as Prologue," *Harvard Law Review* 110 (1997): 1023; Sheldon Novick, "Holmes's Path; Holmes's Goal," *Harvard Law Review* 110 (1997): 1028; Richard Posner, "The Path Away from the Law," *Harvard Law Review* 110 (1997): 1039 (quotation taken from page 1042); and G. Edward White, "Investing in Holmes at the Millennium," *Harvard Law Review* 110 (1997): 1049.

Other insightful analyses of the essay, and of Holmes more generally, can be found in Thomas C. Grey, "Plotting the Path of the Law," *Brooklyn Law Review* 63 (1997): 19 (quotations taken from pages 27–8); id., "Holmes and Legal Pragmatism," *Stanford Law Review* 41 (1989): 787; Grant Gilmore, *The Ages of American Law* (New Haven: Yale University Press, 1977) (quotation from page 49); Robert W. Gordon, "Holmes' *Common Law* as Legal and Social Science," *Hofstra Law Review* 10 (1982): 719; Robert W. Gordon, ed., *The Legacy of Oliver Wendell Holmes, Jr.* (Stanford: Stanford University Press, 1992); Morton Horwitz, *The Transformation of American Law, 1870–1960* (New York: Oxford University Press, 1992), 109–44; Benjamin Kaplan, Patrick Atiyah, and Jan Vetter, *Holmes and the Common Law: A Century Later* (Cambridge, Mass.: Harvard Law School, 1983); H. L. Pohlman, *Justice Oliver Wendell Holmes: Free Speech and the Living Constitution* (New York: New York University Press, 1991); id., *Justice Oliver Wendell Holmes and Utilitarian Jurisprudence*

(Cambridge, Mass.: Harvard University Press, 1984); Thomas A. Reed, "Holmes and the Paths of the Law," *American Journal of Legal History* 37 (1993): 273; Yosal Rogat, "The Judge as Spectator," *University of Chicago Law Review* 31 (1964): 213; David Rosenberg, *The Hidden Holmes: His Theory of Torts in History* (Cambridge, Mass.: Harvard University Press, 1995); Saul Touster, "Holmes a Hundred Years Ago: *The Common Law* and Legal Theory," *Hofstra Law Review* 10 (1982): 673; G. Edward White, "The Integrity of Holmes' Jurisprudence," *Hofstra Law Review* 10 (1982): 633; and id., "The Canonization of Holmes and Brandeis: Epistemology and Judicial Reputations," *New York University Law Review* 70 (1995): 576.

Holmes's relationship with Lady Castletown is chronicled and analyzed in Horwitz, *Transformation*, pages 142–3; Daniel J. Kornstein, "Justice Holmes in Love," *New York State Bar Journal* 64 (1992): 10; John S. Monagan, *The Grand Panjandrum: Mellow Years of Justice Holmes* (Lanham, Md.: University Press of America, 1988); Novick, *Honorable Justice*, Chap. 15; and White, *Law and the Inner Self*, pages 230–49. The quotations in the text from his letters to her are derived from White, pages 240–41.

"The Path of the Law"

10 Harvard Law Review 457 (1897)

When we study law we are not studying a mystery but a well-known profession. We are studying what we shall want in order to appear before judges, or to advise people in such a way as to keep them out of court. The reason why it is a profession, why people will pay lawyers to argue for them or to advise them, is that in societies like ours the command of the public force is intrusted to the judges in certain cases, and the whole power of the state will be put forth, if necessary, to carry out their judgments and decrees. People want to know under what circumstances and how far they will run the risk of coming against what is so much stronger than themselves, and hence it becomes a business to find out when this danger is to be feared. The object of our study, then, is prediction, the prediction of the incidence of the public force through the instrumentality of the courts.

The means of the study are a body of reports, of treatises, and of statutes, in this country and in England, extending back for six hundred years, and now increasing annually by hundreds. In these sibylline leaves are gathered the scattered prophecies of the past upon the cases in which the axe will fall. These are what properly have been called the oracles of the law. Far the most important and pretty nearly the whole meaning of every new effort of legal thought is to make these prophecies more precise, and to generalize them into a thoroughly connected system. The process is one, from a lawyer's statement of a case, eliminating as it does all the dramatic elements with which his client's story has clothed it, and retaining only the facts of legal import, up to the final analyses and abstract universals of theoretic jurisprudence. The reason why a lawyer does not mention that his client wore a white hat when he made a contract, while Mrs. Quickly would be sure to dwell upon it along with the parcel gilt goblet and the sea-coal fire, is that he forsees that the public force will act in the same way whatever his client had upon his head. It is to make the prophecies easier to be remembered and to be understood that the teachings of the decisions of the past are put into general propositions and gathered into text-books, or that statutes are passed in a general form. The primary rights and duties with which jurisprudence busies itself again are nothing but prophecies. One of the many evil effects of the confusion between legal and moral ideas, about which I shall have something to say in a moment, is that theory is apt to get the cart before the horse, and to consider the right or the duty as something existing apart from and independent of the consequences of its breach, to which certain sanctions are added afterward. But, as I shall try to show, a legal duty so called is nothing but a

An Address delivered by Mr. Justice Holmes, of the Supreme Judicial Court of Massachusetts, at the dedication of the new hall of the Boston University School of Law, on January 8, 1897. Copyrighted by O. W. Holmes, 1897.

prediction that if a man does or omits certain things he will be made to suffer in this or that way by judgment of the court;—and so of a legal right.

The number of our predictions when generalized and reduced to a system is not unmanageably large. They present themselves as a finite body of dogma which may be mastered within a reasonable time. It is a great mistake to be frightened by the ever increasing number of reports. The reports of a given jurisdiction in the course of a generation take up pretty much the whole body of the law, and restate it from the present point of view. We could reconstruct the corpus from them if all that went before were burned. The use of the earlier reports is mainly historical, a use about which I shall have something to say before I have finished.

I wish, if I can, to lay down some first principles for the study of this body of dogma or systematized prediction which we call the law, for men who want to use it as the instrument of their business to enable them to prophesy in their turn, and, as bearing upon the study, I wish to point out an ideal which as yet our law has not attained.

The first thing for a business-like understanding of the matter is to understand its limits, and therefore I think it desirable at once to point out and dispel a confusion between morality and law, which sometimes rises to the height of conscious theory, and more often and indeed constantly is making trouble in detail without reaching the point of consciousness. You can see very plainly that a bad man has as much reason as a good one for wishing to avoid an encounter with the public force, and therefore you can see the practical importance of the distinction between morality and law. A man who cares nothing for an ethical rule which is believed and practised by his neighbors is likely nevertheless to care a good deal to avoid being made to pay money, and will want to keep out of jail if he can.

I take it for granted that no hearer of mine will misinterpret what I have to say as the language of cynicism. The law is the witness and external deposit of our moral life. Its history is the history of the moral development of the race. The practice of it, in spite of popular jests, tends to make good citizens and good men. When I emphasize the difference between law and morals I do so with reference to a single end, that of learning and understanding the law. For that purpose you must definitely master its specific marks, and it is for that that I ask you for the moment to imagine yourselves indifferent to other and greater things.

I do not say that there is not a wider point of view from which the distinction between law and morals becomes of secondary or no importance, as all mathematical distinctions vanish in presence of the infinite. But I do say that that distinction is of the first importance for the object which we are here to consider,—a right study and mastery of the law as a business with well understood limits, a body of dogma enclosed within definite lines. I have just shown the practical reason for saying so. If you want to know the law and nothing else, you must look at it as a bad man, who cares only for the material consequences which such knowledge enables him to predict, not as a good one, who finds his reasons for conduct, whether inside the law or outside of it, in the vaguer sanctions of conscience. The theoretical importance of the distinction is no less, if you would reason on your subject aright. The law is full of phraseology drawn from morals, and by the mere force of language continually invites us to pass from one domain to the other without perceiving it, as we are sure to do unless we have the boundary constantly before our minds. The law talks about rights, and duties, and malice, and intent, and negligence, and so forth, and nothing is easier, or, I may say, more common in legal reasoning, than to take these words in their moral sense, at some stage of the argument, and so to drop into fallacy. For instance, when we speak of the rights of man in a moral sense, we mean to mark the limits of interference with individual freedom which we think are prescribed by conscience, or by our ideal, however reached. Yet it is certain that many laws have been enforced in the past, and it is likely that some are enforced now, which are condemned by the most enlightened opinion of the time, or which at all events pass the limit of interference as many consciences would draw it. Manifestly, therefore, nothing but confusion of thought can result from assuming that the rights of man in a moral sense are equally rights in the sense of the Constitution and the law. No doubt simple and extreme cases can be put of imaginable laws which the statute-making power would not dare to enact, even in the absence of written constitutional prohibitions, because the community would rise in rebellion and fight; and this gives some plausibility to the proposition that the law, if not a part of morality, is limited by it. But this limit of power is not coextensive with any system of morals. For the most part it falls far within the lines of any such system, and in some cases may extend beyond them, for reasons drawn from the habits of a particular people at a particular time. I once heard the late Professor Agassiz say that a German population would rise if you added two cents to the price of a glass of beer. A statute in such a case would be empty words, not because it was wrong, but because it could not be enforced. No one will deny that wrong statutes can be and are enforced, and we should not all agree as to which were the wrong ones.

The confusion with which I am dealing besets confessedly legal conceptions. Take the fundamental question, What constitutes the law? You will find some text writers telling you that it is something different from what is decided by the courts of Massachusetts or England, that it is a system of reason, that it is a deduction from principles of ethics or admitted axioms or what not, which may or may not coincide with the decisions. But if we take the view of our friend the bad man we shall find that he does not care two straws for the axioms or deductions, but that he does want to know what the Massachusetts or English courts are likely to do in fact. I am much of his mind. The prophecies of what the courts will do in fact, and nothing more pretentious, are what I mean by the law.

Take again a notion which as popularly understood is the widest conception which the law contains;—the notion of legal duty, to which already I have referred. We fill the word with all the content which we draw from morals. But what does it mean to a bad man? Mainly, and in the first place, a prophecy that if he does certain things he will be subjected to disagreeable consequences by way of imprisonment or compulsory payment of money. But from his point of view, what is the difference between being fined and being taxed a certain sum for doing a certain thing? That his point of view is the test of legal principles is shown by the many discussions which have arisen in the courts on the very question whether a given statutory liability is a penalty or a tax. On the answer to this question depends the decision whether conduct is legally wrong or right, and also whether a man is under compulsion or free. Leaving the criminal law on one side, what is the difference between the liability under the mill acts or statutes authorizing a taking by eminent domain and the liability for what we call a wrongful conversion of property where restoration is out of the question? In both cases the party taking another man's property has to pay its fair value as assessed by a jury, and no more. What significance is there in calling one taking right and another wrong from the point of view of the law? It does not matter, so far as the given consequence, the compulsory payment, is concerned, whether the act to which it is attached is described in terms of praise or in terms of blame, or whether the law purports to prohibit it or to allow it. If it matters at all, still speaking from the bad man's point of view, it must be because in one case and not in the other some further disadvantages, or at least some further consequences, are attached to the act by the law. The only other disadvantages thus attached to it which I ever have been able to think of are to be found in two somewhat insignificant legal doctrines, both of which might be abolished without much disturbance. One is, that a contract to do a prohibited act is unlawful, and the other, that, if one of two or more joint wrongdoers has to pay all the damages, he cannot recover contribution from his fellows. And that I believe is all. You see how the vague circumference of the notion of duty shrinks and at the same time grows more precise when we wash it with cynical acid and expel everything except the object of our study, the operations of the law.

Nowhere is the confusion between legal and moral ideas more manifest than in the law of contract. Among other things, here again the so called primary rights and duties are invested with a mystic significance beyond what can be assigned and explained. The duty to keep a contract at common law means a prediction that you must pay damages if you do not keep it,—and nothing else. If you commit a tort, you are liable to pay a compensatory sum. If you commit a contract, you are liable to pay a compensatory sum unless the promised event comes to pass, and that is all the difference. But such a mode of looking at the matter stinks in the nostrils of those who think it advantageous to get as much ethics into the law as they can. It was good enough for Lord Coke, however, and here, as in many other cases, I am content to abide with him. In *Bromage v. Genning*,[1] a prohibition was sought in the King's Bench against a suit in the marches of Wales for the specific performance of a covenant to grant a lease, and Coke said that it would subvert the intention of the covenantor, since he intends it to be at his election either to lose the damages or to make the lease. Sergeant Harris for the plaintiff confessed that he moved the matter against his conscience, and a prohibition was granted. This goes further than we should go now, but it shows what I venture to say has been the common law point of view from the beginning, although Mr. Harriman, in his very able little book upon Contracts has been misled, as I humbly think, to a different conclusion.

I have spoken only of the common law, because there are some cases in which a logical justification can be found for speaking of civil liabilities as imposing duties in an intelligible sense. These are the relatively few in which equity will grant an injunction, and will enforce it by putting the defendant in prison or otherwise punishing him unless he complies with the order of the court. But I hardly think it advisable to shape general theory from the exception, and I think it would be better to cease troubling ourselves about primary rights and sanctions altogether, than to describe our prophecies concerning the liabilities commonly imposed by the law in those inappropriate terms.

I mentioned, as other examples of the use by the law of words drawn from morals, malice, intent, and negligence. It is enough to take malice as it is used in the law of civil liability for wrongs,—what we lawyers call the law of torts,—to show you that it means something different in law from what it means in morals, and also to show how the difference has been obscured by giving to principles

[1] I Roll. Rep. 368.

which have little or nothing to do with each other the same name. Three hundred years ago a parson preached a sermon and told a story out of Fox's *Book of Martyrs* of a man who had assisted at the torture of one of the saints, and afterward died, suffering compensatory inward torment. It happened that Fox was wrong. The man was alive and chanced to hear the sermon, and thereupon he sued the parson. Chief Justice Wray instructed the jury that the defendant was not liable, because the story was told innocently, without malice. He took malice in the moral sense, as importing a malevolent motive. But nowadays no one doubts that a man may be liable, without any malevolent motive at all, for false statements manifestly calculated to inflict temporal damage. In stating the case in pleading, we still should call the defendant's conduct malicious; but, in my opinion at least, the word means nothing about motives, or even about the defendant's attitude toward the future, but only signifies that the tendency of his conduct under the known circumstances was very plainly to cause the plaintiff temporal harm.[2]

In the law of contract the use of moral phraseology has led to equal confusion, as I have shown in part already, but only in part. Morals deal with the actual internal state of the individual's mind, what he actually intends. From the time of the Romans down to now, this mode of dealing has affected the language of the law as to contract, and the language used has reacted upon the thought. We talk about a contract as a meeting of the minds of the parties, and thence it is inferred in various cases that there is no contract because their minds have not met; that is, because they have intended different things or because one party has not known of the assent of the other. Yet nothing is more certain than that parties may be bound by a contract to things which neither of them intended, and when one does not know of the other's assent. Suppose a contract is executed in due form and in writing to deliver a lecture, mentioning no time. One of the parties thinks that the promise will be construed to mean at once, within a week. The other thinks that it means when he is ready. The court says that it means within a reasonable time. The parties are bound by the contract as it is interpreted by the court, yet neither of them meant what the court declares that they have said. In my opinion no one will understand the true theory of contract or be able even to discuss some fundamental questions intelligently until he has understood that all contracts are formal, that the making of a contract depends not on the agreement of two minds in one intention, but on the agreement of two sets of external signs,—not on the parties' having *meant* the same thing but on their having *said* the same thing. Furthermore, as the signs may be addressed to one sense or another,—to sight or to hearing,—on the nature of the sign will depend the moment when the contract is made. If the sign is tangible, for instance, a letter, the contract is made when the letter of acceptance is delivered. If it is necessary that the minds of the parties meet, there will be no contract until the acceptance can be read,—none, for example, if the acceptance be snatched from the hand of the offerer by a third person.

This is not the time to work out a theory in detail, or to answer many obvious doubts and questions which are suggested by these general views. I know of none which are not easy to answer, but what I am trying to do now is only by a series of hints to throw some light on the narrow path of legal doctrine, and upon two pitfalls which, as it seems to me, lie perilously near to it. Of the first of these

[2] See Hanson *v.* Globe Newspaper Co., 159 Mass. 293, 302.

I have said enough. I hope that my illustrations have shown the danger, both to speculation and to practice, of confounding morality with law, and the trap which legal language lays for us on that side of our way. For my own part, I often doubt whether it would not be a gain if every word of moral significance could be banished from the law altogether, and other words adopted which should convey legal ideas uncolored by anything outside the law. We should lose the fossil records of a good deal of history and the majesty got from ethical associations, but by ridding ourselves of an unnecessary confusion we should gain very much in the clearness of our thought.

So much for the limits of the law. The next thing which I wish to consider is what are the forces which determine its content and its growth. You may assume, with Hobbes and Bentham and Austin, that all law emanates from the sovereign, even when the first human beings to enunciate it are the judges, or you may think that law is the voice of the Zeitgeist, or what you like. It is all one to my present purpose. Even if every decision required the sanction of an emperor with despotic power and a whimsical turn of mind, we should be interested none the less, still with a view to prediction, in discovering some order, some rational explanation, and some principle of growth for the rules which he laid down. In every system there are such explanations and principles to be found. It is with regard to them that a second fallacy comes in, which I think it important to expose.

The fallacy to which I refer is the notion that the only force at work in the development of the law is logic. In the broadest sense, indeed, that notion would be true. The postulate on which we think about the universe is that there is a fixed quantitative relation between every phenomenon and its antecedents and consequents. If there is such a thing as a phenomenon without these fixed quantitative relations, it is a miracle. It is outside the law of cause and effect, and as such transcends our power of thought, or at least is something to or from which we cannot reason. The condition of our thinking about the universe is that it is capable of being thought about rationally, or, in other words, that every part of it is effect and cause in the same sense in which those parts are with which we are most familiar. So in the broadest sense it is true that the law is a logical development, like everything else. The danger of which I speak is not the admission that the principles governing other phenomena also govern the law, but the notion that a given system, ours, for instance, can be worked out like mathematics from some general axioms of conduct. This is the natural error of the schools, but it is not confined to them. I once heard a very eminent judge say that he never let a decision go until he was absolutely sure that it was right. So judicial dissent often is blamed, as if it meant simply that one side or the other were not doing their sums right, and, if they would take more trouble, agreement inevitably would come.

This mode of thinking is entirely natural. The training of lawyers is a training in logic. The processes of analogy, discrimination, and deduction are those in which they are most at home. The language of judicial decision is mainly the language of logic. And the logical method and form flatter that longing for certainty and for repose which is in every human mind. But certainty generally is illusion, and repose is not the destiny of man. Behind the logical form lies a judgment as to the relative worth and importance of competing legislative grounds, often an inarticulate and unconscious judgment, it is true, and yet the very root and nerve of the whole proceeding. You can give any conclusion a logical form. You always can imply a condition in a contract. But why do you imply it? It is because of some belief as to the practice of the community or of a class, or because of some opinion as to policy, or, in short, because of some attitude of yours upon a matter not capable of exact quantitative measurement, and therefore not capable of founding exact logical conclusions. Such matters really are battle grounds where the means do not exist for determinations that shall be good for all time, and where the decision can do no more than embody the preference of a given body in a given time and place. We do not realize how large a part of our law is open to reconsideration upon a slight change in the habit of the public mind. No concrete proposition is self-evident, no matter how ready we may be to accept it, not even Mr. Herbert Spencer's "Every man has a right to do what he wills, provided he interferes not with a like right on the part of his neighbors."

Why is a false and injurious statement privileged, if it is made honestly in giving information about a servant? It is because it has been thought more important that information should be given freely, than that a man should be protected from what under other circumstances would be an actionable wrong. Why is a man at liberty to set up a business which he knows will ruin his neighbor? It is because the public good is supposed to be best subserved by free competition. Obviously such judgments of relative importance may vary in different times and places. Why does a judge instruct a jury that an employer is not liable to an employee for an injury received in the course of his employment unless he is negligent, and why do the jury generally find for the plaintiff if the case is allowed to go to them? It is because the traditional policy of our law is to confine liability to cases where a prudent man might have foreseen the injury, or at least the danger, while the inclination of a very large part of the community is to make certain classes of persons insure the safety of those with whom they deal. Since the last words were written, I have seen the requirement of such insurance put forth as part of the programme of one of the best known labor organizations. There is a concealed, half conscious battle on the question of legislative policy, and if any one thinks that it can be settled deductively, or once for all, I only can say that I think he is theoretically wrong, and that I am certain that his conclusion will not be accepted in practice *semper ubique et ab omnibus*.

Indeed, I think that even now our theory upon this matter is open to reconsideration, although I am not prepared to say how I should decide if a reconsideration were proposed. Our law of torts comes from the old days of isolated, ungeneralized wrongs, assaults, slanders, and the like, where the damages might be taken to lie where they fell by legal judgment. But the torts with which our courts are kept busy to-day are mainly the incidents of certain well known businesses. They are injuries to person or property by railroads, factories, and the like. The liability for them is estimated, and sooner or later goes into the price paid by the public. The public really pays the damages, and the question of liability, if pressed far enough, is really the question how far it is desirable that the public should insure the safety of those whose work it uses. It might be said that in such cases the chance of a jury finding for the defendant is merely a chance, once in a while rather arbitrarily interrupting the regular course of recovery, most likely in the case of an unusually conscientious plaintiff, and therefore better done away with. On the other hand, the economic value even of a life to the community can be estimated, and no recovery, it may be said, ought to go beyond that amount. It is conceivable that some day in certain cases we may find ourselves imitating, on a higher plane, the tariff for life and limb which we see in the *Leges Barbarorum*.

I think that the judges themselves have failed adequately to recognize their duty of weighing considerations of social advantage. The duty is inevitable, and the result of the often proclaimed judicial aversion to deal with such considerations is simply to leave the very ground and foundation of judgments inarticulate, and often unconscious, as I have said. When socialism first began to be talked about, the comfortable classes of the community were a good deal frightened. I suspect that this fear has influenced judicial action both here and in England, yet it is certain that it is not a conscious factor in the decisions to which I refer. I think that something similar has led people who no longer hope to control the legislatures to look to the courts as expounders of the Constitutions, and that in some courts new principles have been discovered outside the bodies of those instruments, which may be generalized into acceptance of the economic doctrines which prevailed about fifty years ago, and a wholesale prohibition of what a tribunal of lawyers does not think about right. I cannot but believe that if the training of lawyers led them habitually to consider more definitely and explicitly the social advantage on which the rule they lay down must be justified, they sometimes would hesitate where now they are confident, and see that really they were taking sides upon debatable and often burning questions.

So much for the fallacy of logical form. Now let us consider the present condition of the law as a subject for study, and the ideal toward which it tends. We still are far from the point of view which I desire to see reached. No one has reached it or can reach it as yet. We are only at the beginning of a philosophical reaction, and of a reconsideration of the worth of doctrines which for the most part still are taken for granted without any deliberate, conscious, and systematic questioning of their grounds. The development of our law has gone on for nearly a thousand years, like the development of a plant, each generation taking the inevitable next step, mind, like matter, simply obeying a law of spontaneous growth. It is perfectly natural and right that it should have been so. Imitation is a necessity of human nature, as has been illustrated by a remarkable French writer, M. Tarde, in an admirable book, *Les Lois de l'Imitation*. Most of the things we do, we do for no better reason than that our fathers have done them or that our neighbors do them, and the same is true of a larger part than we suspect of what we think. The reason is a good one, because our short life gives us no time for a better, but it is not the best. It does not follow, because we all are compelled to take on faith at second hand most of the rules on which we base our action and our thought, that each of us may not try to set some corner of his world in the order of reason, or that all of us collectively should not aspire to carry reason as far as it will go throughout the whole domain. In regard to the law, it is true, no doubt, that an evolutionist will hesitate to affirm universal validity for his social ideals, or for the principles which he thinks should be embodied in legislation. He is content if he can prove them best for here and now. He may be ready to admit that he knows nothing about an absolute best in the cosmos, and even that he knows next to nothing about a permanent best for men. Still it is true that a body of law is more rational and more civilized when every rule it contains is referred articulately and definitely to an end which it subserves, and when the grounds for desiring that end are stated or are ready to be stated in words.

At present, in very many cases, if we want to know why a rule of law has taken its particular shape, and more or less if we want to know why it exists at all, we go to tradition. We follow it into the Year Books, and perhaps beyond them to the customs of the Salian Franks, and somewhere in the past, in the German forests, in the needs of Norman kings, in the assumptions of a dominant class, in the absence of generalized ideas, we find out the practical motive for what now best is justified by the mere fact of its acceptance and that men are accustomed to it. The rational study of law is still to a large extent the study of history. History must be a part of the study, because without it we cannot know the precise scope of rules which it is our business to know. It is a part of the rational study, because it is the first step toward an enlightened scepticism, that is, toward a deliberate reconsideration of the worth of those rules. When you get the dragon out of his cave on to the plain and in the daylight, you can count his teeth and claws, and see just what is his strength. But to get him out is only the first step. The next is either to kill him, or to tame him and make him a useful animal. For the rational study of the law the black-letter man may be the man of the present, but the man of the future is the man of statistics and the master of economics. It is revolting to have no better reason for a rule of law than that so it was laid down in the time of Henry IV. It is still more revolting if the grounds upon which it was laid down have vanished long since, and the rule simply persists from blind imitation of the past. I am thinking of the technical rule as to trespass *ab initio*, as it is called, which I attempted to explain in a recent Massachusetts case.[3]

Let me take an illustration, which can be stated in a few words, to show how the social end which is aimed at by a rule of law is obscured and only partially attained in consequence of the fact that the rule owes its form to a gradual historical development, instead of being reshaped as a whole, with conscious articulate reference to the end in view. We think it desirable to prevent one man's property being misappropriated by another, and so we make larceny a crime. The evil is the same whether the misappropriation is made by a man into whose hands the owner has put the property, or by one who wrong-fully takes it away. But primitive law in its weakness did not get much beyond an effort to prevent violence, and very naturally made a wrongful taking, a trespass, part of its definition of the crime. In modern times the judges enlarged the definition a little by holding that, if the wrongdoer gets possession by a trick or device, the crime is committed. This really was giving up the requirement of a trespass, and it would have been more logical, as well as truer to the present object of the law, to abandon the requirement altogether. That, however, would have seemed too bold, and was left to statute. Statutes were passed making embezzlement a crime. But the force of tradition caused the crime of embezzlement to be regarded as so far distinct from larceny that to this day, in some jurisdictions at least, a slip corner is kept open for thieves to contend, if indicted for larceny, that they should have been indicted for embezzlement, and if indicted for embezzlement, that they should have been indicted for larceny, and to escape on that ground.

Far more fundamental questions still await a better answer than that we do as our fathers have done. What have we better than a blind guess to show that the criminal law in its present form does more good than harm? I do not stop to refer to the effect which it has had in degrading prisoners and in plunging them further into crime, or to the question whether fine and imprisonment do not fall more heavily on a criminal's wife and children than on himself. I have in mind more far-reaching questions. Does punishment deter? Do we deal with criminals on proper principles? A modern school of Continental criminalists plumes itself on the formula, first suggested, it is said, by Gall, that we must consider the criminal rather than the crime. The formula does not carry us very far, but the inquiries which

---

[3] Commonwealth *v.* Rubin, 165 Mass. 453.

have been started look toward an answer of my questions based on science for the first time. If the typical criminal is a degenerate, bound to swindle or to murder by as deep seated an organic necessity as that which makes the rattlesnake bite, it is idle to talk of deterring him by the classical method of imprisonment. He must be got rid of; he cannot be improved, or frightened out of his structural reaction. If, on the other hand, crime, like normal human conduct, is mainly a matter of imitation, punishment fairly may be expected to help to keep it out of fashion. The study of criminals has been thought by some well known men of science to sustain the former hypothesis. The statistics of the relative increase of crime in crowded places like large cities, where example has the greatest chance to work, and in less populated parts, where the contagion spreads more slowly, have been used with great force in favor of the latter view. But there is weighty authority for the belief that, however this may be, "not the nature of the crime, but the dangerousness of the criminal, constitutes the only reasonable legal criterion to guide the inevitable social reaction against the criminal."[4]

The impediments to rational generalization, which I illustrated from the law of larceny, are shown in the other branches of the law, as well as in that of crime. Take the law of tort or civil liability for damages apart from contract and the like. Is there any general theory of such liability, or are the cases in which it exists simply to be enumerated, and to be explained each on its special ground, as is easy to believe from the fact that the right of action for certain well known classes of wrongs like trespass or slander has its special history for each class? I think that there is a general theory to be discovered, although resting in tendency rather than established and accepted. I think that the law regards the infliction of temporal damage by a responsible person as actionable, if under the circumstances known to him the danger of his act is manifest according to common experience, or according to his own experience if it is more than common, except in cases where upon special grounds of policy the law refuses to protect the plaintiff or grants a privilege to the defendant.[5] I think that commonly malice, intent, and negligence mean only that the danger was manifest to a greater or less degree, under the circumstances known to the actor, although in some cases of privilege malice may mean an actual malevolent motive, and such a motive may take away a permission knowingly to inflict harm, which otherwise would be granted on this or that ground of dominant public good. But when I stated my view to a very eminent English judge the other day, he said: "You are discussing what the law ought to be; as the law is, you must show a right. A man is not liable for negligence unless he is subject to a duty." If our difference was more than a difference in words, or with regard to the proportion between the exceptions and the rule, then, in his opinion, liability for an act cannot be referred to the manifest tendency of the act to cause temporal damage in general as a sufficient explanation, but must be referred to the special nature of the damage, or must be derived from some special circumstances outside of the tendency of the act, for which no generalized explanation exists. I think that such a view is wrong, but it is familiar, and I dare say generally is accepted in England.

[4] Havelock Ellis, "The Criminal," 41, citing Garofalo. See also Ferri, "Sociologie Criminelle," *passim.* Compare Tarde, "La Philosophie Pénale."

[5] An example of the law's refusing to protect the plaintiff is when he is interrupted by a stranger in the use of a valuable way, which he has travelled adversely for a week less than the period of prescription. A week later he will have gained a right, but now he is only a trespasser. Examples of privilege I have given already. One of the best is competition in business.

Everywhere the basis of principle is tradition, to such an extent that we even are in danger of making the rôle of history more important than it is. The other day Professor Ames wrote a learned article to show, among other things, that the common law did not recognize the defence of fraud in actions upon specialties, and the moral might seem to be that the personal character of that defence is due to its equitable origin. But if, as I have said, all contracts are formal, the difference is not merely historical, but theoretic, between defects of form which prevent a contract from being made, and mistaken motives which manifestly could not be considered in any system that we should call rational except against one who was privy to those motives. It is not confined to specialties, but is of universal application. I ought to add that I do not suppose that Mr. Ames would disagree with what I suggest.

However, if we consider the law of contract, we find it full of history. The distinctions between debt, covenant, and assumpsit are merely historical. The classification of certain obligations to pay money, imposed by the law irrespective of any bargain as quasi contracts, is merely historical. The doctrine of consideration is merely historical. The effect given to a seal is to be explained by history alone. Consideration is a mere form. Is it a useful form? If so, why should it not be required in all contracts? A seal is a mere form, and is vanishing in the scroll and in enactments that a consideration must be given, seal or no seal. Why should any merely historical distinction be allowed to affect the rights and obligations of business men?

Since I wrote this discourse I have come on a very good example of the way in which tradition not only overrides rational policy, but overrides it after first having been misunderstood and having been given a new and broader scope than it had when it had a meaning. It is the settled law of England that a material alteration of a written contract by a party avoids it as against him. The doctrine is contrary to the general tendency of the law. We do not tell a jury that if a man ever has lied in one particular he is to be presumed to lie in all. Even if a man has tried to defraud, it seems no sufficient reason for preventing him from proving the truth. Objections of like nature in general go to the weight, not to the admissibility, of evidence. Moreover, this rule is irrespective of fraud, and is not confined to evidence. It is not merely that you cannot use the writing, but that the contract is at an end. What does this mean? The existence of a written contract depends on the fact that the offerer and offeree have interchanged their written expressions, not on the continued existence of those expressions. But in the case of a bond the primitive notion was different. The contract was inseparable from the parchment. If a stranger destroyed it, or tore off the seal, or altered it, the obligee could not recover, however free from fault, because the defendant's contract, that is, the actual tangible bond which he had sealed, could not be produced in the form in which it bound him. About a hundred years ago Lord Kenyon undertook to use his reason on this tradition, as he sometimes did to the detriment of the law, and, not understanding it, said he could see no reason why what was true of a bond should not be true of other contracts. His decision happened to be right, as it concerned a promissory note, where again the common law regarded the contract as inseparable from the paper on which it was written, but the reasoning was general, and soon was extended to other written contracts, and various absurd and unreal grounds of policy were invented to account for the enlarged rule.

I trust that no one will understand me to be speaking with disrespect of the law, because I criticise it so freely. I venerate the law, and especially our system of law, as one of the vastest products of the human mind. No one knows better than I do the countless number of great intellects that have spent themselves in making some addition or improvement, the greatest of which is trifling when compared with the mighty whole. It has the final title to respect that it exists, that it is not a Hegelian dream, but a part of the lives of men. But one may criticise even what one reveres. Law is the business to which my life is devoted, and I should show less than devotion if I did not do what in me lies to improve it, and, when I perceive what seems to me the ideal of its future, if I hesitated to point it out and to press toward it with all my heart.

Perhaps I have said enough to show the part which the study of history necessarily plays in the intelligent study of the law as it is today. In the teaching of this school and at Cambridge it is in no danger of being undervalued. Mr. Bigelow here and Mr. Ames and Mr. Thayer there have made important contributions which will not be forgotten, and in England the recent history of early English law by Sir Frederick Pollock and Mr. Maitland has lent the subject an almost deceptive charm. We must beware of the pitfall of antiquarianism, and must remember that for our purposes our only interest in the past is for the light it throws upon the present. I look forward to a time when the part played by history in the explanation of dogma shall be very small, and instead of ingenious research we shall spend our energy on a study of the ends sought to be attained and the reasons for desiring them. As a step toward that ideal it seems to me that every lawyer ought to seek an understanding of economics. The present divorce between the schools of political economy and law seems to me an evidence of how much progress in philosophical study still remains to be made. In the present state of political economy, indeed, we come again upon history on a larger scale, but there we are called on to consider and weigh the ends of legislation, the means of attaining them, and the cost. We learn that for everything we have to give up something else, and we are taught to set the advantage we gain against the other advantage we lose, and to know what we are doing when we elect.

There is another study which sometimes is undervalued by the practical minded, for which I wish to say a good word, although I think a good deal of pretty poor stuff goes under that name. I mean the study of what is called jurisprudence. Jurisprudence, as I look at it, is simply law in its most generalized part. Every effort to reduce a case to a rule is an effort of jurisprudence, although the name as used in English is confined to the broadest rules and most fundamental conceptions. One mark of a great lawyer is that he sees the application of the broadest rules. There is a story of a Vermont justice of the peace before whom a suit was brought by one farmer against another for breaking a churn. The justice took time to consider, and then said that he had looked through the statutes and could find nothing about churns, and gave judgment for the defendant. The same state of mind is shown in all our common digests and text-books. Applications of rudimentary rules of contract or tort are tucked away under the head of Railroads or Telegraphs or go to swell treatises on historical subdivisions, such as Shipping or Equity, or are gathered under an arbitrary title which is thought likely to appeal to the practical mind, such as Mercantile Law. If a man goes into law it pays to be a master of it, and to be a master of it means to look straight through all the dramatic incidents and to discern the true basis for prophecy. There-fore, it is well to have an accurate notion of what you mean by law, by a right, by a duty, by malice, intent, and negligence, by ownership, by possession, and so forth. I have in my mind cases in which the highest courts seem to me to have floundered because they

Oliver Wendell Holmes

had no clear ideas on some of these themes. I have illustrated their importance already. If a further illustration is wished, it may be found by reading the Appendix to Sir James Stephen's *Criminal Law* on the subject of possession, and then turning to Pollock and Wright's enlightened book. Sir James Stephen is not the only writer whose attempts to analyze legal ideas have been confused by striving for a useless quintessence of all systems, instead of an accurate anatomy of one. The trouble with Austin was that he did not know enough English law. But still it is a practical advantage to master Austin, and his predecessors, Hobbes and Bentham, and his worthy successors, Holland and Pollock. Sir Frederick Pollock's recent little book is touched with the felicity which marks all his works, and is wholly free from the perverting influence of Roman models.

The advice of the elders to young men is very apt to be as unreal as a list of the hundred best books. At least in my day I had my share of such counsels, and high among the unrealities I place the recommendation to study the Roman law. I assume that such advice means more than collecting a few Latin maxims with which to ornament the discourse,—the purpose for which Lord Coke recommended Bracton. If that is all that is wanted, the title *De Regulis Juris Antiqui* can be read in an hour. I assume that, if it is well to study the Roman law, it is well to study it as a working system. That means mastering a set of technicalities more difficult and less understood than our own, and studying another course of history by which even more than our own the Roman law must be explained. If any one doubts me, let him read Keller's *Der Römische Civil Process und die Actionen*, a treatise on the prætor's edict, Muirhead's most interesting *Historical Introduction to the Private Law of Rome*, and, to give him the best chance possible, Sohm's admirable *Institutes*. No. The way to gain a liberal view of your subject is not to read something else, but to get to the bottom of the subject itself. The means of doing that are, in the first place, to follow the existing body of dogma into its highest generalizations by the help of jurisprudence; next, to discover from history how it has come to be what it is; and, finally, so far as you can, to consider the ends which the several rules seek to accomplish, the reasons why those ends are desired, what is given up to gain them, and whether they are worth the price.

We have too little theory in the law rather than too much, especially on this final branch of study. When I was speaking of history, I mentioned larceny as an example to show how the law suffered from not having embodied in a clear form a rule which will accomplish its manifest purpose. In that case the trouble was due to the survival of forms coming from a time when a more limited purpose was entertained. Let me now give an example to show the practical importance, for the decision of actual cases, of understanding the reasons of the law, by taking an example from rules which, so far as I know, never have been explained or theorized about in any adequate way. I refer to statutes of limitation and the law of prescription. The end of such rules is obvious, but what is the justification for depriving a man of his rights, a pure evil as far as it goes, in consequence of the lapse of time? Sometimes the loss of evidence is referred to, but that is a secondary matter. Sometimes the desirability of peace, but why is peace more desirable after twenty years than before? It is increasingly likely to come without the aid of legislation. Sometimes it is said that, if a man neglects to enforce his rights, he cannot complain if, after a while, the law follows his example. Now if this is all that can be said about it, you probably will decide a case I am going to put, for the plaintiff; if you take the view which I shall suggest, you possibly will decide it for the defendant. A man is sued for trespass upon land, and justifies under a right of way. He proves that he has used the way openly and adversely for twenty years, but it turns out that the plaintiff had granted a license to a person whom he reasonably supposed to be the defendant's agent, although not so in fact, and therefore had assumed that the use of the way was permissive, in which case no right would be gained. Has the defendant gained a right or not? If his gaining it stands on the fault and neglect of the landowner in the ordinary sense, as seems commonly to be supposed, there has been no such neglect, and the right of way has not been acquired. But if I were the defendant's counsel, I should suggest that the foundation of the acquisition of rights by lapse of time is to be looked for in the position of the person who gains them, not in that of the loser. Sir Henry Maine has made it fashionable to connect the archaic notion of property with prescription. But the connection is further back than the first recorded history. It is in the nature of man's mind. A thing which you have enjoyed and used as your own for a long time, whether property or an opinion, takes root in your being and cannot be torn away without your resenting the act and trying to defend yourself, however you came by it. The law can ask no better justification than the deepest instincts of man. It is only by way of reply to the suggestion that you are disappointing the former owner, that you refer to his neglect having allowed the gradual dissociation between himself and what he claims, and the gradual association of it with another. If he knows that another is doing acts which on their face show that he is on the way toward establishing such an association, I should argue that in justice to that other he was bound at his peril to find out whether the other was acting under his permission, to see that he was warned, and, if necessary, stopped.

I have been speaking about the study of the law, and I have said next to nothing of what commonly is talked about in that connection,—text-books and the case system, and all the machinery with which a student comes most immediately in contact. Nor shall I say anything about them. Theory is my subject, not practical details. The modes of teaching have been improved since my time, no doubt, but ability and industry will master the raw material with any mode. Theory is the most important part of the dogma of the law, as the architect is the most important man who takes part in the building of a house. The most important improvements of the last twenty-five years are improvements in theory. It is not to be feared as unpractical, for, to the competent, it simply means going to the bottom of the subject. For the incompetent, it sometimes is true, as has been said, that an interest in general ideas means an absence of particular knowledge. I remember in army days reading of a youth who, being examined for the lowest grade and being asked a question about squadron drill, answered that he never had considered the evolutions of less than ten thousand men. But the weak and foolish must be left to their folly. The danger is that the able and practical minded should look with indifference or distrust upon ideas the connection of which with their business is remote. I heard a story, the other day, of a man who had a valet to whom he paid high wages, subject to deduction for faults. One of his deductions was, "For lack of imagination, five dollars." The lack is not confined to valets. The object of ambition, power, generally presents itself nowadays in the form of money alone. Money is the most immediate form, and is a proper object of desire. "The fortune," said Rachel, "is the measure of the intelligence." That is a good text to waken people out of a fool's paradise. But, as Hegel says,[6] "It is in the end not the appetite, but the opinion, which has to be satisfied." To an imagination of any

[6] Phil. des Rechts, § 190.

scope the most far-reaching form of power is not money, it is the command of ideas. If you want great examples read Mr. Leslie Stephen's *History of English Thought in the Eighteenth Century*, and see how a hundred years after his death the abstract speculations of Descartes had become a practical force controlling the conduct of men. Read the works of the great German jurists, and see how much more the world is governed to-day by Kant than by Bonaparte. We cannot all be Descartes or Kant, but we all want happiness. And happiness, I am sure from having known many successful men, cannot be won simply by being counsel for great corporations and having an income of fifty thousand dollars. An intellect great enough to win the prize needs other food beside success. The remoter and more general aspects of the law are those which give it universal interest. It is through them that you not only become a great master in your calling, but connect your subject with the universe and catch an echo of the infinite, a glimpse of its unfathomable process, a hint of the universal law.

Wesley Hohfeld

Wesley Hohfeld

WESLEY HOHFELD's taxonomy of legal concepts and relations is so central to our understanding of what it means to "think like a lawyer" that we have forgotten these ideas once needed to be thought up. Indeed, Hohfeld's name has largely faded from memory.

Hohfeld was born in 1879 in Oakland, California and attended the University of California, graduating in 1901. He graduated cum laude in 1904 from Harvard Law School, where he worked as an assistant to Professor John Chipman Gray. Hohfeld began work as a lawyer in San Francisco at Morrison, Cope and Brobeck, and in 1905 moved on to an academic career as an instructor in law at Stanford. After nine years at Stanford, Hohfeld moved to Yale Law School, where he taught until his death from endocarditis in 1918 at the age of thirty-nine. In his thirteen years as a legal academic, Hohfeld published an astonishing series of articles on corporate law, conflict of laws, the relationship between law and equity, and legal education. The article reprinted here, "Some Fundamental Legal Conceptions," pulls together the main ideas and analytic framework for all his other work.

The article is addressed to law students, and purports simply to clarify the proper use of a set of common legal terms, such as "right" and "duty," by reference to their use in a range of judicial opinions. But the article is also a manifesto for a new way of conceptualizing the "legal relations" these terms describe. The law, he argues, recognizes eight types of legal relations: rights, duties, powers, liabilities, immunities, disabilities, privileges, and what Hohfeld terms "no-rights."

The opening pages are a salvo against some of the most significant legal thinkers of Hohfeld's day—Langdell, Maitland, Ames, Austin, Hart, Salmond, Pollock, and Whitlock. All of their "discussions and analyses" of the nature of equitable trusts are "inadequate," Hohfeld claims. Their use of legal terminology is sloppy, but worse, they seek to explain different equitable institutions and arrangements differently, as if they followed different logics, rested on different foundations, or were distinct in some other fundamental way from one another. In fact, Hohfeld argues, "all possible kinds of jural interests, legal as well as equitable,—and that too, whether we are concerned with 'property,' 'contracts,' 'torts,' or any other title of the law," should be understood to be composed of the same limited set of "fundamental legal conceptions that are involved in practically every legal problem."

Hohfeld's claim is audacious—all legal instruments and arrangements reinterpreted as being composed of a single set of simple logical relationships among what turn out to be eight precisely defined terms. Legal theorists in the classical tradition had sought to unify the common law in a formal structure by organizing doctrines *substantively* as deductions from a few basic principles—most significantly, the principle of individual autonomy (and its substantive corollary, a will theory of legal obligation) and the "police power" of the state (the authority of the government to regulate interactions among private parties to preserve "the public health, safety, morals, or general welfare"). Hohfeld seeks to unify the law *analytically* rather than substantively.

In lay parlance, one often speaks of "rights" as if they were the legal translation of broader ethical or moral principles. The law offers, most fundamentally, a list of these substantive ideas, from which people reason to conclusions in particular cases as best they can. This was not Hohfeld's view. For him, law is held together by the modes of reasoning lawyers use, not by the list of substantive principles to which that reasoning refers. Moreover, legal reasoning is reasoning about the relationships among a series of terms—including "right"—that are best understood in relationship to *one another* rather than to any underlying substantive commitments. These legal relations provide the key to the legal system's unity and coherence. What ties law together is neither historical accident nor substantive principle, but a mode of thought.

For Hohfeld, as for many of the analytic jurists who preceded him, the pursuit of analytic clarity about how legal thought operates was itself a project of legal reform. In his view, sloppy thinking had led to the obscurity and unnecessary complexity for which laymen rightly criticize the legal system. Only by reforming its own house, Hohfeld argues, could the legal system stave off radical populist efforts to recall judges or limit their terms. More rigorous *legal reasoning* is the key to simplifying and unifying the law.

Hohfeld develops his technical scheme of definitions by reading judicial opinions that have used them, and he presents his analysis as a precise account of the best practices of the common law. But he is doing much more than cataloguing the usages of judges. In Hohfeld's day, no less than in our own, terms like *right* or *power* were used in all sorts of vague ways by legal professionals and laymen alike. Hohfeld proposes to limit sharply the ways in which these terms are used.

Crucially, Hohfeld proposes to use these legal terms only *in relationship to one another*. For example, he proposes to use the term *right* to describe a person's legal interest only where another person has a *duty*, and vice versa. In lay parlance, it was (and is) common to describe all sorts of interests as "rights." In Hohfeld's view, by contrast, one has a *legal right* only where the law imposes a *duty* on someone else. The right and the duty, moreover, will be parallel—each will define the scope of the other. For Hohfeld, the term *right* simply means that another person has a *duty*, while the term *duty* means that another person has a *right*.

Hohfeld's relational or correlative approach to the definition of legal rights and duties has consequences. His terminology encourages us to disaggregate "property ownership" into a list of "legally protected interests." A word like "property," Hohfeld insists, is used by laymen and lawyers with "no definite or stable connotation." Broad lay assertions—"I own this land"—should be broken down into specific rights, duties, privileges and so forth. Moreover, each Hohfeldian *right*, for example, the right to exclude others from one's premises, will have a correlative Hohfeldian *duty*, in this case, the duty of others not to trespass. Property "rights" can be extended only by creating new duties. In first-year classrooms, this insight is used to undermine all sorts of loose deductions from general assertions of ownership, to force discussion about the precise rights which are contemplated, and the desirability of creating the necessary correlative duty. "Ms. Jones, you speak eloquently about a general 'right' to freedom of speech, but who precisely is under what duty? Rights are easy to defend—but how would you define and justify the duties they entail? Who is harmed by the right you propose, what interests injured, and how do you justify that?"

Wesley Hohfeld

In a similar fashion, Hohfeld attacks the vague and general use of terms like "freedom" and "liberty." If others have an enforceable "duty" to respect a legally protected interest of yours, you have a "right" correlative to their duty of noninterference. In the absence of such a duty to respect your interest, however, they have a "privilege" to intrude upon your interest, and you have what Hohfeld calls a "no-right." Hohfeld's recognition of their privilege *as a legal interest* is profoundly significant. Imagine two property owners side by side: each may have a *privilege* to play loud music, but neither may have a *right* to insist that the other turn his music down. Such a state of affairs might be undesirable from a policy standpoint—perhaps it will lead to an arms race in volume. Nevertheless, for Hohfeld, from a legal standpoint the situation is analytically coherent. In his view, it is one thing for the law to grant a privilege, and something altogether different to corroborate that privilege with a right. Doing so requires the creation of a new duty. Using Hohfeld's terminology, it is simply wrong to deduce duties of noninterference from Hohfeldian privileges.

For Hohfeld, moreover, the legal institution we call "property" is a combination of *duty-right* pairs and *privilege-no right* pairs. Sometimes the law protects a property owner by placing a duty on others. But the law is more than a collection of rights and duties alone. Sometimes the law gives the property owner a "no right," and gives to others a "privilege" to interfere. For example, ordinarily, the owner of a field may insist that travelers on an adjacent road not enter upon her land (and the travelers thus have a corresponding duty not to enter). If the road is blocked by a snowdrift or other obstruction, however, travelers have a privilege to evade the obstacle by crossing the field, and the landowner has a "no-right" to exclude them. With this idea, Hohfeld formalized an emerging focus on the range of situations in which injury is legally permitted without compensation. Hohfeld insists on the legal nature of rules that *permit* uncompensated injuries, and focuses attention on the role of the state, not only in defining rights and enforcing duties, but also in defining privileges and permitting injury. "A rule of law that *permits* is just as real as a rule of law that *forbids*," Hohfeld writes in footnote 59, opening the door to conceptualizing inaction as a legislative and policy choice. A Hohfeldian privilege, moreover, permits injury whether it is express or not—when the injured party has no right to compel you not to injure, when you are under no duty not to injure, your injuring acts are legally privileged.

By placing "privilege/no-right" situations on a par with "right/duty" situations, Hohfeld further unsettled the idea, central to classical legal thought, that property law could be developed by unfolding the internal logic of a fundamental "right to property." First, Hohfeld insists that each additional right requires a new duty, which must be justified, and cannot simply be deduced from a general institution of property ownership. More significantly, however, by identifying two logics of property—a logic of rights and duties, and a logic of privileges and "no-rights"— Hohfeld makes clear that the enumeration of property law requires a choice. For any new legal interest or type of property, we must decide whether to protect the claims of the putative owner by placing *duties* on others, or to give those others *privileges* which could be used to interfere with the owner. This decision cannot be made through deduction from the "nature" of property—property has, if you like, two different natures. Sometimes it is a right, protected by enforceable duties, and sometimes it is "no-right," threatened by the privileges of others. The choice cannot be made by reference to the logic of property itself, it will need to be made on other grounds. Those other grounds might well be matters of social principle, ethics, or policy. For Hohfeld's followers, however, policy seemed the most significant—deduction from principle had too often been abused to suggest that the outcome lay inherent in the nature of property or autonomy. Hohfeld's analytics focused on the necessity of *choice*.

Nineteenth-century analytic jurists had proposed to unify the common law by identifying its basic analytic components. Hohfeld was not the first mover here; in one sense, Hohfeld completes their project. In another sense, Hohfeld moves American legal thought beyond their project, closing the door on efforts to render the legal system coherent and self-contained through more precise analysis. For Hohfeld, more precise analysis reveals a series of choices whose resolution requires reference to criteria beyond the legal terms themselves. What "rights" and "duties" should property contain, and what "privileges" and "no-rights"?

John Austin had focused attention on the idea that legal institutions, like property, were relations between people, not relations between people and things. In Hohfeld's scheme, this relational dimension—one person's right is another's duty, one person's privilege is another's no-right—takes on a further significance. Since one person's right is another's duty, and one person's privilege is another's no-right, the policy questions raised by developments in the institution of property are also *distributive questions*—extending privileges, rights, or any of his other six legal interests will create losers as well as winners.

Commentators quickly found use for Hohfeld's distinction between right/duty and privilege/no-right. Hohfeld indicated the direction in his comments on *Quinn v. Leathem* which introduce his discussion of "privileges." That case concerned a threat by a labor union to strike against an employer who dealt with another employer with whom the union had an ongoing labor dispute. To determine whether the union's strike should be enjoined, the Court focused on the broad "liberty" of the target employer to earn a living as he wished and deal with whatever other persons he wished. But can one deduce from these liberties a *duty* on the union not to interfere with the contractual relations of the target? Not if, as Hohfeld claims, the liberty "considered as a legal relation . . . must mean, if it have any definite content at all, precisely the same thing as *privilege*." Hohfeld continues:

> such a privilege or liberty to deal with others at will might very conceivably exist without any peculiar concomitant rights against "third parties" as regards certain kinds of interference. Whether there should be such concomitant rights (or claims) is ultimately a question of justice or policy, and it should be considered as such, on its merits. . . . It would therefore be a *non-sequitur* to conclude from the mere existence of such liberties that "third parties" are under a *duty* not to interfere, etc."
> (pp. 36–7)

Walter Wheeler Cook and other legal realists extended Hohfeld's analysis to criticize judicial expansion of a general "right to property" and "right to freedom of contract" in ways which overruled protective social legislation or restricted labor organizing. Cook, for example, argued that it was a logical error, a Hohfeldian mistake, to conclude anything about what union organizers might do from a factory owner's general "freedom to contract." Factory owners can exclude organizers only if "freedom to contract" contains a *right* to exclude and a corresponding *duty* not to interfere. But such a right must be made—it cannot be deduced. Freedom to contract, like property, will be composed of both duty/right pairs and privilege/no-right pairs. As a result, one might argue that in the absence of an explicit right to exclude, union organizers will have a correlative privilege.

Of course, one might equally well argue, in Hohfeld's terms, that a "privilege" for the union would also need to be created; there is no reason to assume that the "privilege/no-right" pair is the default. It would be more accurate to say that one must decide whether to create a duty not to interfere and a correlative right to exclude *or* to create a privilege to organize and a corresponding no-right to exclude. Hohfeld's analytic scheme offers no assistance here—this is a question for policy. All sorts of moral, political, economic, or institutional considerations might well push a decision maker to decide it one way or the other. But Hohfeld left it to others to speak about how such questions of "justice or policy" should be analyzed and decided.

Hohfeld's apparent agnosticism about questions of policy helped critics of judicial behavior who relied on his ideas to sound like nonpartisan observers, interested only in clarity and analytic rigor. Judges who deduced too much from general ideas like "property" or "freedom of contract" could be accused of *ignoring* significant questions of judgment, or of deciding them *implicitly*, by prejudice or habit. Judges could be criticized for errors of logic or for failing to come to face the need for a defensible conclusion of policy, or for deciding important social questions by default, without offering justification, rather than for reaching the wrong policy conclusion.

Unlike Holmes, Hohfeld was disinterested in the sociological effects of rights and duties. Holmes had linked rights to the *enforcement* of duties. For the "bad man," law is but a prediction of future enforcement. A statement of a "right" is a prediction of the duties which would *in fact* be enforced by judges. For Hohfeld, by contrast, rights are analytically, not sociologically, correlative with duties; whether the duties are ultimately enforced is altogether a different question.

Commentators have often pointed out that judges do not, in fact, use Hohfeldian terms with anything like the precision he proposed. Hohfeldian deductive errors continue to litter the case reports. But Hohfeld's legacy was less the elimination of the reasoning errors that troubled him than the establishment of a mode of legal reasoning that can be used to put analytic pressure on the reasoning of judges, lawyers, and law students who speak of rights without reference to their correlative duties, or power without reference to correlative liabilities. Hohfeld's article has become canonical not as a grammatical rule book for correct usage, but as the origin for a style of critical analysis which has become central to American legal thought.

DAVID KENNEDY

BIBLIOGRAPHY

Wesley Hohfeld

The article reprinted here was the first of two articles on judicial reasoning; the second, expanding and applying his system of jural relations, is Wesley Hohfeld, "Fundamental Legal Conceptions as Applied in Judicial Reasoning," 26 *Yale Law Journal* 710 (1916–1917). Hohfeld's most significant legal scholarship was posthumously collected and republished by his colleague, Walter Wheeler Cook, in Cook, ed., *Fundamental Legal Conceptions as Applied in Judicial Reasoning and Other Legal Essays by Wesley Newcomb Hohfeld* (New Haven, Conn.: Yale Press, 1923), a collection that also included the article reprinted here. The argument sketched in the opening paragraphs of *Fundamental Legal Conceptions* placing law and equity in a single analytic frame was developed in Hohfeld, "The Relations Between Equity and Law," 11 *Michigan Law Review* 537 (1912–1913).

Hohfeld applied his thinking in the field of corporate law. The image of the corporation as a "legal person" posed a challenge to Hohfeld's idea that at bottom, all legal relations were between natural persons. Hohfeld treated the idea that a corporation was a legal "person" precisely as he treated the notion that "property" could be a legal status greater than the sum of the rights of property owners and the duties of others toward them. The result was an articulation of the corporation as a nexus of relations between people, rather than as a sui generis legal entity. See Hohfeld, "Nature of Stockholders' Individual Liability for Corporation Debts," 9 *Colombia Law Review* 285 (1909), as well as a series of pieces on the relationship between the individual liability of stockholders and the conflict of law in the 1909 and 1910 (vol. 9, 1909, p. 492, and vol. 10, 1910, p. 238) volumes of the *Columbia Law Review*, which are reprinted in Cook's collection of Hohfeld's work. For a survey and analysis of the intellectual history of the private corporation, in which Hohfeld's writings play a part, see Morton Horwitz, *1870–1960: The Crisis of Legal Orthodoxy* (New York: Oxford University Press, 1992), chap. 3, "Santa Clara Revisited: The Development of Corporate Theory," p. 65.

Hohfeld also offered a bold proposal for reimagining legal education, anticipating themes pursued by legal realists and other reformers in the ensuing decades. His proposal was delivered as an address to the December 28–30, 1914 meeting of the Association of American Law Schools in Chicago and later published as "A Vital School of Jurisprudence and Law: Have American Universities Awakened to the Enlarged Opportunities and Responsibilities of the Present Day?" The address is also reprinted in Cook's edition of Hohfeld's work. He advocated a dramatic reorganization of professional education to train "jurists" who could do the intellectual work necessary to reform the legal system from within. For this task, they would need historical, interdisciplinary, comparative, and functional training, as well as more advanced work in analytic reasoning. Attention should be focused on public law, legislation, and the actual operation of the courts and administrative agencies—and lawyers should be trained to think dynamically, critically, and ethically.

Secondary Literature

Hohfeld's effort to analyze legal terminology in systematic terms built on the work of earlier analytic jurists, including Austin, Salmond, and many others. Hohfeld's relationship to his precursors is analyzed in Joseph Singer, "The Legal Rights Debate in Analytical Jurisprudence from Bentham to Hohfeld," 1982 *Wisconsin Law Review* 975 (1982), which also contains a compelling description and analysis of Hohfeld's central contributions.

Hohfeld's most significant immediate impact was felt in the work of Walter Wheeler Cook and Arthur Corbin, both colleagues at Yale. Cook promoted Hohfeld's work, both by republishing his papers and in the essay Cook, "Hohfeld's Contribution to the Science of Law," 28 *Yale Law Journal* 721 (1918–1919). He was among the first to apply Hohfeld's analysis to criticize judicial opinions which deduced too much from property rights and contractual freedom in the area of labor regulation. See Walter Wheeler Cook, "Privileges of Labor Unions in the Struggle for Life," 27 *Yale Law Journal* 779 (1917–1918).

Arthur Corbin both criticized and developed Hohfeld's terminology, extending it to issues of contract law. See Corbin, "Offer and Acceptance, and Some of the

Resulting Legal Relations," 26 *Yale Law Journal* 169 (1916–1917); id., "Conditions in the Law of Contracts," 28 *Yale Law Journal* 739 (1918–1919); id., "Legal Analysis and Terminology," 29 *Yale Law Journal* 163 (1919–1920); and id., "Jural Relations and Their Classification," 30 *Yale Law Journal* 226 (1920–1921).

It would be difficult to overstate the significance of Hohfeld's central analytic insights for the legal realists in general, all of whom borrowed from his framework. Realist focus on the role of the state in constructing and maintaining property relations was perhaps particularly indebted to Hohfeld.

Hohfeld had his share of critics. Some criticized his particular terminology, but accepted his analytic framework. Others were more sceptical about the idea of binary correlative links between legal terms. Pound was famously critical of Hohfeld's effort to restrict the term "right" to bilateral relations. For example, in "Fifty Years of Jurisprudence," 50 *Harvard Law Review* 557 (1936–1937) at 573, Pound argued:

> Moreover, Hohfeld's scheme presupposes that there can only be one opposite and one correlative and that there must be an opposite and a correlative. But there may be many contrasts and there are sometimes two correlatives. For example, correlative to one's right as owner of Blackacre is his neighbor's duty not to trespass and his liability for trespass by his servant, trespass by his cow, and (in England) for breaking loose of his ponded water and invasion of the land.

In response, Julius Stone argued that Pound had made precisely the reasoning error Hohfeld set out to correct. See Julius Stone, *The Province and Function of Law: Law as Logic, Justice and Social Control, A Study in Jurisprudence* (London; Stevens and Sons, 1947) at 131.

Hohfeld's work fell from view by the Second World War, in part because his analytic methods had been so thoroughly absorbed by the legal professoriat. In the methodological disputes which followed the war, Hohfeld's scheme was revived. After 1970, scholars influenced by the Critical Legal Studies movement and seeking to revive and extend the realist tradition of doctrinal criticism returned to Hohfeld, promoted his work as precursor to their own. Significant works in this tradition include Joseph Singer, above, and Duncan Kennedy and Frank Michelman, "Are Property and Contract Efficient?" 8 *Hofstra Law Review* (1979–1980), 711. Duncan Kennedy's own contribution to the Canon, "Form and Substance in Private Law Adjudication," 89 *Harvard Law Review* 1685 (1975–1976) also shows the influence of Hohfeld.

In the ensuing years, scholars analyzing the rhetoric of legal argument also began with Hohfeld. The most well-articulated methodological synthesis and bibliography of this work remains Duncan Kennedy, "A Semiotics of Legal Argument," 42 *Syracuse Law Review* 75 (1991). See also Jack Balkin, "The Crystalline Structure of Legal Thought," 39 *Rutgers Law Review* 1 (1986–1987) and Balkin, "The Hohfeldian Approach to Law and Semiotics," 44 *University of Miami Law Review* 1119 (1989–1990). Balkin develops a parallel between Hohfeld's relational conception of legal terms and the contemporaneous work of Ferdinand de Saussure in linguistics.

Finally, an extremely clear and useful demonstration of Hohfeld's ideas deployed by law teachers in the classroom is provided by Curtis Nyquist, "Teaching Wesley Hohfeld's Theory of Legal Relations," 52 *Journal of Legal Education* 238 (2002).

Contemporary scholars of analytic jurisprudence developing more formal models of legal reasoning, often with a view to computer simulations of legal thought, have also returned to Hohfeld. See, for example: Kevin Saunders, "A Formal Analysis of Hohfeldian Relations", 23 *Akron Law Review* 465 (1989–1990); Layman E. Allen, "Formalizing Hohfeldian Analysis to Clarify the Multiple Senses of 'Legal Right': A Powerful Lens for the Electronic Age", 48 *Southern California Law Review* 428 (1974–1975); Alan Ross Anderson, "The Logic of Hohfeldian Propositions," 33 *University of Pittsburgh Law Review* 29 (1971–1972); or Mark Andrews, "Hohfeld's Cube," 16 *Akron Law Review* 471 (1982–1983).

"Some Fundamental Legal Conceptions as Applied in Judicial Reasoning"

23 Yale Law Journal 16 (1913)

From very early days down to the present time the essential nature of trusts and other equitable interests has formed a favorite subject for analysis and disputation. The classical discussions of Bacon[1] and Coke are familiar to all students of equity, and the famous definition of the great chief justice (however inadequate it may really be) is quoted even in the latest textbooks on trusts.[2] That the subject has had a peculiar fascination for modern legal thinkers is abundantly evidenced by the well known articles of Langdell[3] and Ames,[4] by the oft-repeated observations of

---

[1] Bacon on Uses (Circa 1602; Rowe's ed. 1806), pp. 5–6: "The nature of an use is best discerned by considering what it is not, and then what it is. * * * First, an use is no right, title, or interest in law; and therefore master attorney, who read upon this statute, said well, that there are but two rights: *Jus in re: Jus ad rem*.

"The one is an estate, which is *jus in re;* the other a demand, which is *jus ad rems* but an use is neither. * * * So as now we are come by negatives to the affirmative, what an use is. * * * *Usus est dominium fiduciarium*: Use is an ownership in trust.

"So that *usus & status, sive possessio, potius differunt secundum rationem fori, quam secundum naturam rei,* for that one of them is in court of law, the other in court of conscience. * * *"

[2] Co. Lit. (1628) 272 b: "*Nota,* an use is a trust or confidence reposed in some other, which is not issuing out of the land, but as a thing collaterall, annexed in privitie to the estate of the land, and to the person touching the land, *scilicet,* that *cesty que use* shall take the profit, and that the terre-tenant shall make an estate according to his direction. So as *cesty que use* had neither *jus in re,* nor *jus ad rem,* but only a confidence and trust for which he had no remedie by the common law, but for the breach of trust, his remedie was only by *subpoena* in chancerie. * * *"

This definition is quoted and discussed approvingly in Lewin, Trusts (12th ed., 1911), p. 11. It is also noticed in Maitland, Lectures on Equity (1909), pp. 43, 116.

[3] See Langdell, Classification of Rights and Wrongs (1900), 13 Harv. L. Rev., 659, 673: "Can equity then create such rights as it finds to be necessary for the purposes of justice? As equity wields only physical power, it sems to be impossible that it should actual'y create anything. * * * It seems, therefore, that equitable rights exist only in contemplation of equity, *i.e.,* that they are a *fiction* invented by equity for the promotion of justice. * * *

"Shutting our eyes, then, to the fact that equitable rights are a fiction, and assuming them to have an actual existence, what is their nature, what their extent, and what is the field which they occupy? * * * They must not violate the law. * * * Legal and equitable rights must, therefore, exist side by side, and the latter cannot interfere with, or in any manner affect, the former."

See also (1887) 1 Harv. L. Rev., 55, 60: "Upon the whole, it may be said that equity could not create rights *in rem* if it would, and that it would not if it could." Compare *Ibid*. 58; and Summary of Eq. Plead. (2nd ed., 1883) secs. 45, 182–184.

[4] See Ames, "Purchase for Value Without Notice" (1887), 1 Harv. L. Rev., 1, 9: "The trustee is the owner of the land, and, of course, two persons with adverse interests cannot be owners of the same thing. What the *cestui que trust* really owns is the obligation of the trustee; for an obligation is as truly the subject matter of property as any physical *res*. The most striking difference between property in a thing and property in an obligation is in the mode of enjoyment. The owner of a house or a horse enjoys the fruits of ownership without the aid of any other person. The only way in which the owner of an obligation can realize his ownership is by compelling its performance by the obligor. Hence, in the one case, the owner is said to have a right *in rem,* and in the other, a right *in personam*. In other respects the common rules of property apply equally to ownership of things and ownership of obligations. For example, what may be called the passive rights of ownership are the same in both cases. The general duty resting on all mankind not to destroy the property of another, is as cogent in favor of an obligee as it is in favor of the owner of a horse. And the violation of this duty is as pure a tort in the one case as in the other."

Maitland in his Lectures on Equity,[5] by the very divergent treatment of Austin in his Lectures on Jurisprudence,[6] by the still bolder thesis of Salmond in his volume on Jurisprudence,[7] and by the discordant utterances of Mr. Hart[8] and Mr. Whitlock[9] in their very recent contributions to our periodical literature.

It is believed that all of the discussions and analyses referred to are inadequate. Perhaps, however, it would have to be admitted that even the great intrinsic interest of the subject itself and the noteworthy divergence of opinion existing among thoughtful lawyers of all times would fail to afford more than a comparatively slight excuse for any further discussion considered as a mere end in itself. But, quite apart from the presumably practical consideration of endeavoring to "think straight" in relation to all legal problems, it is apparent that the true analysis of trusts and other equitable interests is a matter that should appeal to even the most extreme pragmatists of the law. It may well be that one's view as to the correct analysis of such interests would control the decision of a number of specific questions. This is obviously true as regards the solution of many difficult and delicate problems in constitutional law and in the conflict of laws.[10] So, too, in certain questions in the law of perpetuities, the intrinsic nature of equitable interests is of great significance, as attested by the well-known *Gomm* case[11] and others more or less similar. The same thing is apt to be true of a number of special questions relating to the subject of *bona fide* purchase for value. So on indefinitely.[12]

But all this may seem like misplaced emphasis; for the suggestions last made are not peculiarly applicable to equitable interests: the same points and the same

---

[5] Lect. on Eq. (1909), 17, 18, 112: "The thesis that I have to maintain is this, that equitable estates and interests are not *jura in rem*. For reasons that we shall perceive by and by, they have come to look very like *jura in rem;* but just for this very reason it is the more necessary for us to observe that they are essentially *jura in personam,* not rights against the world at large, but rights against certain persons."

See also Maitland, Trust and Corporation (1904), reprinted in 3 Collected Papers, 321, 325.

[6] (5th ed.) Vol. I, p. 378: "By the provisions of that part of the English law which is called equity, a contract to sell at once vests *jus in rem* or ownership in buyer, and the seller has only *jus in re aliena.* * * * To complete the transaction the legal interest of the seller must be passed to the buyer, in legal form. To this purpose the buyer has only *jus in personam*: a right to compel the seller to pass his legal interest; but speaking generally, he has *dominium* or *jus in rem,* and the instrument is a conveyance."

[7] (2nd ed., 1907) p. 230: "If we have regard to the essence of the matter rather than to the form of it, a trustee is not an owner at all, but a mere agent, upon whom the law has conferred the power and imposed the duty of administering the property of another person. In legal theory, however, he is not a mere agent, but an owner. He is a person to whom the property of someone else is fictitiously attributed by the law, to the intent that the rights and powers thus rested in a *nominal* owner shall be used by him on behalf of the real owner."

[8] See Walter G. Hart (author of "Digest of Law of Trusts"), The Place of Trust in Jurisprudence (1912), 28 Law Quart. Rev., 290, 296. His position is substantially that of Ames and Maitland.

At the end of this article Sir Frederick Pollock, the editor, puts the query: "Why is Trust not entitled to rank as a head *sui generis?*"

[9] See A. N. Whitlock, Classification of the Law of Trusts (1913), 1 Calif. Law Rev., 215, 218: "It is submitted," says the writer, "that the *cestui* has in fact something more than a right *in personam,* that such a right might be more properly described as a right *in personam ad rem,* or, possibly, a right *in rem per personam.*"

Surely such nebulous and cumbrous expressions as these could hardly fail to make "confusion worse confounded."

[10] See Beale, Equitable Interests in Foreign Property, 20 Harv. L. Rev. (1907), 382; and compare the important cases, *Fall v. Eastin* (1905), 75 Neb., 104; S. C. (1909), 215 U. S., 1, 14–15 (especially concurring opinion of Holmes, J.); *Selover, Bates & Co. v. Walsh* (1912), 226 U. S., 112; *Bank of Africa Limited v. Cohen* (1909), 2 Ch. 129, 143.

[11] (1882) 20 Ch. D. 562, 580, per Sir George Jessel, M. R.: "If then the rule as to remoteness applies to a covenant of this nature, this covenant clearly is bad as extending beyond the period allowed by the rule. Whether the rule applies or not depends upon this, as it appears to me, does or does not the covenant give *an interest in the land?* * * * If it is a mere personal contract it cannot be enforced against the assignee. Therefore the company must admit that somehow it *binds the land.* But if it binds the land, it creates *an equitable interest in the land.*"

[12] Compare *Ball v. Milliken* (1910), 31 R. I., 36; 76 Atl., 789, 793, involving a point other than perpetuities, but quoting in support of the decision reached Sir George Jessel's language as to "equitable interests in land." See preceding note.

examples seem valid in relation to all possible kinds of jural interests, legal as well as equitable,—and that too, whether we are concerned with "property," "contracts," "torts," or any other title of the law. Special reference has therefore been made to the subject of trusts and other equitable interests only for the reason that the striking divergence of opinion relating thereto conspicuously exemplifies the need for dealing somewhat more intensively and systematically than is usual with the nature and analysis of all types of jural interests. Indeed, it would be virtually impossible to consider the subject of trusts at all adequately without, at the very threshold analyzing and discriminating the various fundamental conceptions that are involved in practically every legal problem. In this connection the suggestion may be ventured that the usual discussions of trusts and other jural interests seem inadequate (and at times misleading) for the very reason that they are not founded on a sufficiently comprehensive and discriminating analysis of jural relations in general. Putting the matter in another way, the tendency—and the fallacy—has been to treat the specific problem as if it were far less complex than it really is; and this commendable effort to treat as simple that which is really complex has, it is believed, furnished a serious obstacle to the clear understanding, the orderly statement, and the correct solution of legal problems. In short, it is submmitted that the right kind of simplicity can result only from more searching and more discriminating analysis.

If, therefore, the title of this article suggests a merely philosophical inquiry as to the nature of law and legal relations,—a discussion regarded more or less as an end in itself,—the writer may be pardoned for repudiating such a connotation in advance. On the contrary, in response to the invitation of the editor of this journal, the main purpose of the writer is to emphasize certain oft-neglected matters that may aid in the understanding and in the solution of practical, every-day problems of the law. With this end in view, the present article and another soon to follow will discuss, as of chief concern, the basic conceptions of the law,—the legal elements that enter into all types of jural interests. A later article will deal specially with the analysis of certain typical and important interests of a complex character,—more particularly trusts and other equitable interests. In passing, it seems necessary to state that both of these articles are intended more for law school students than for any other class of readers. For that reason, it is hoped that the more learned reader may pardon certain parts of the discussion that might otherwise seem unnecessarily elementary and detailed. On the other hand, the limits of space inherent in a periodical article must furnish the excuse for as great a brevity of treatment as is consistent with clearness, and for a comparatively meager discussion—or even a total neglect—of certain matters the intrinsic importance of which might otherwise merit greater attention. In short, the emphasis is to be placed on those points believed to have the greatest practical value.

LEGAL CONCEPTIONS CONTRASTED WITH NONLEGAL CONCEPTIONS.

At the very outset it seems necessary to emphasize the importance of differentiating purely legal relations from the physical and mental facts that call such relations into being. Obvious as this initial suggestion may seem to be, the arguments that one may hear in court almost any day and likewise a considerable number of judicial opinions afford ample evidence of the inveterate and unfortunate tendency to confuse and blend the legal and the non-legal quantities in a given problem. There are at least two special reasons for this.

For one thing, the association of ideas involved in the two sets of relations—the physical and the mental on the one hand, and the purely legal on the other—is in the very nature of the case, extremely close. This fact has necessarily had a marked influence upon the general doctrines and the specific rules of early systems of law. Thus, we are told by Pollock and Maitland:

"Ancient German law, like ancient Roman law, sees great difficulties in the way of an assignment of a debt or other benefit of a contract * * * men do not see how there can be a transfer of a right unless that right is embodied in some corporeal thing. The history of the incorporeal things has shown us this; they are not completely transferred until the transferee has obtained seisin, has turned his beasts onto the pasture, presented a clerk to the church or hanged a thief upon the gallows. A covenant or a warranty of title may be so bound up with land that the assignee of the land will be able to sue the covenantor or warrantor."[13]

In another connection, the same learned authors observe:

"The realm of mediæval law is rich with incorporeal things. Any permanent right which is of a transferable nature, at all events if it has what we may call a territorial ambit, is thought of as a thing that is very like a piece of land. Just because it is a thing it is transferable. This is no fiction invented by the speculative jurists. For the popular mind these things are things. The lawyer's business is not to make them things but to point out that they are incorporeal. The layman who wishes to convey the advowson of a church will say that he conveys the church; it is for Bracton to explain to him that what he means to transfer is not that structure of wood and stone which belongs to God and the saints, but a thing incorporeal, as incorporeal as his own soul or the *anima mundi*."[14]

A second reason for the tendency to confuse or blend non-legal and legal conceptions consists in the ambiguity and looseness of our legal terminology. The word "property" furnishes a striking example. Both with lawyers and with laymen this term has no definite or stable connotation. Sometimes it is employed to indicate the physical object to which various legal rights, privileges, etc., relate; then again—with far greater discrimination and accuracy—the word is used to denote the legal interest (or aggregate of legal relations) appertaining to such physical object. Frequently there is a rapid and fallacious shift from the one meaning to the other. At times, also, the term is used in such a "blended" sense as to convey no definite meaning whatever.

For the purpose of exemplifying the looser usage just referred to, we may quote from *Wilson v. Ward Lumber Co.*:[15]

"The term 'property', as commonly used denotes any external object *over which* the *right* of property is exercised. In this sense it is a very wide term, and includes every class of acquisitions which a man can own or have an interest in."

Perhaps the ablest statement to exemplify the opposite and more accurate usage is that of Professor Jeremiah Smith (then Mr. Justice Smith) in the leading case of *Eaton v. B. C. & M. R. R. Co.*:[16]

[13] 2 Hist. Eng. Law (2nd ed., 1905), 226.

[14] *Ibid.*, 124.

[15] (1895) 67 Fed. Rep., 674, 677. For a somewhat similar, and even more confusing, form of statement, see *In re Fixen* (1900), 102 Fed. Rep., 295, 296.

[16] 51 N. H., 504, 511. Se also the excellent similar statements of Comstock, J., in *Wynehamer v. People* (1856), 13 N. Y., 378, 396; Selden J., S. C., 13 N. Y., 378, 433–434; Ryan, C., in *Law v. Rees Printing Co.* (1894), 41 Neb., 127, 146; Magruder, J., in *Dixon v. People* (1897), 168 Ill., 179, 190.

"In a strict legal sense, land is not 'property', but the subject of property. The term 'property', although in common parlance frequently applied to a tract of land or a chattel, in its legal signification 'means only the rights of the owner in relation to it'. 'It denotes a right over a determinate thing'. 'Property is the right of any person to possess, use, enjoy, and dispose of a thing'. Selden, J., in *Wynehamer v. People,* 13 N. Y., 378, p. 433; 1 Blackstone's com., 138; 2 Austin's *Jurisprudence,* 3rd ed., 817, 818. * * * The right of indefinite user (or of using indefinitely) is an essential quality of absolute property, without which absolute property can have no existence. * * * This right of user necessarily includes the right and power of excluding others from using the land. See 2 *Austin on Jurisprudence,* 3rd ed., 836; Wells, J., in *Walker v. O. C. W. R. R.,* 103 Mass., 10, p. 14."

Another useful passage is to be found in the opinion of Sherwood, J., in *St. Louis v. Hall:*[17]

"Sometimes the term is applied to the thing itself, as a horse, or a tract of land; these things, however, though the subjects of property, are, when coupled with possession, but the *indicia,* the visible manifestation of invisible rights, 'the evidence of things not seen.'

"Property, then, in a determinate object, is composed of certain constituent elements, to wit: The unrestricted right of use, enjoyment, and disposal, of that object."

In connection with the ambiguities latent in the term "property", it seems well to observe that similar looseness of thought and expression lurks in the supposed (but false) contrast between "corporeal" and "incorporeal" property. The second passage above quoted from Pollock and Maitland exhibits one phase of this matter. For further striking illustration, reference may be made to Blackstone's well-known discussion of corporeal and incorporeal hereditaments. Thus, the great commentator tells us:

"But an hereditament, says Sir Edward Coke, is by much the largest and most comprehensive expression; for it includes not only lands and tenements, but whatsoever *may be inherited,* be it corporeal or incorporeal, real, personal, or mixed."[18]

It is clear that only *legal interests* as such can be inherited; yet in the foregoing quotation there is inextricable confusion between the physical or "corporeal" objects and the corresponding legal interests, all of which latter must necessarily be "incorporeal," or "invisible," to use the expression of Mr. Justice Sherwood. This ambiguity of thought and language continues throughout Blackstone's discussion; for a little later he says:

"Hereditaments, then, to use the largest expression, are of two kinds, corporeal and incorporeal. Corporeal consist of such as affect the senses, such as may be seen and handled by the body; incorporeal are not the objects of sensation, can neither be seen nor handled; are creatures of the mind, and exist only in contemplation."

Still further on he says:

"An incorporeal hereditament is a right issuing out of a thing corporate (whether real or personal), or concerning, or annexed to, or exercisable within, the same. * * *

---

[17] (1893) 116 Mo., 527, 533–534. That the last sentence quoted is not altogether adequate as an analysis of property will appear, it is hoped, from the latter part of the present discussion.

See also, as regards the term, "property," the opinion of Doe, C. J., in *Smith v. Fairloh* (1894), 68 N. H., 123, 144–145. ("By considering the property *dissolved* into the *legal rights* of which it consists" etc.)

[18] 2 Black. Com. (1765), 16–43.

"Incorporeal hereditaments are principally of ten sorts: advowsons, tithes, commons, ways, offices, dignities, franchises, corodies or pensions, annuities, and rents."

Since all legal interests are "incorporeal"—consisting, as they do, of more or less limited aggregates of *abstract* legal relations—such a supposed contrast as that sought to be drawn by Blackstone can but serve to mislead the unwary. The legal interest of the fee simple owner of land and the comparatively limited interest of the owner of a "right of way" over such land are alike so far as "incorporeality" is concerned; the true contrast consists, of course, primarily in the fact that the fee simple owner's aggregate of legal relations is far more extensive than the aggregate of the easement owner.

Much of the difficulty, as regards legal terminology, arises from the fact that many of our words were originally applicable only to physical things;[19] so that their use in connection with legal relations is, strictly speaking, figurative or fictional. The term, "transfer," is a good example. If X says that he has transferred his watch to Y, he may conceivably mean, quite literally, that he has physically handed over the watch to Y; or, more likely, that he has "transferred" his *legal interest,* without any delivery of possession,—the latter, of course, being a relatively figurative use of the term. This point will be reached again, when we come to treat of the "transfer" of legal interests. As another instance of this essentially metaphorical use of a term borrowed from the physical world, the word "power" may be mentioned. In legal discourse, as in daily life, it may frequently be used in the sense of physical or mental capacity to do a thing; but, more usually and aptly, it is used to indicate a *"legal power,"* the connotation of which latter term is fundamentally different. The same observations apply, *mutatis mutandis,* to the term "liberty."

Passing to the field of contracts, we soon discover a similar inveterate tendency to confuse and blur legal discussions by failing to discriminate between the mental and physical facts involved in the so-called "agreement" of the parties, and the legal "contractual obligation" to which those facts give rise. Such ambiguity and confusion are peculiarly incident to the use of the term "contract." One moment the word may mean *the agreement* of the parties; and then, with a rapid and unexpected shift, the writer or speaker may use the term to indicate the *contractual obligation* created by law as a result of the agrement. Further instances of this sort of ambiguity will be noticed as the discussion proceeds.

OPERATIVE FACTS CONTRASTED WITH EVIDENTIAL FACTS.

For the purpose of subsequent convenient reference, it seems necessary at this point to lay emphasis upon another important distinction inherent in the very nature of things. The facts important in relation to a given jural transaction may be either *operative* facts or *evidential* facts. Operative, constitutive, causal, or "dispositive" facts are those which, under the general legal rules that are applicable, suffice to change legal relations, that is, either to create a new relation, or to extinguish an

[19] Compare Poll. & Maitl. Hist. Eng. Law (2nd ed., 1905), Vol. II, p. 31: "Few, if any, of the terms in our legal vocabulary have always been technical terms. The license that the man of science can allow himself of coining new words is one which by the nature of the case is denied to lawyers. They have to take their terms out of the popular speech; gradually the words so taken are defined; sometimes a word continues to have both a technical meaning for lawyers and a different and vaguer meaning for laymen; sometimes the word that lawyers have adopted is abandoned by the laity." Compare also *Ibid.,* p. 33.

old one, or to perform both of these functions simultaneously.[20] For example, in the creation of a contractual obligation between A and B, the *affirmative* operative facts are, *inter alia,* that each of the parties is a human being, that each of them has lived for not less than a certain period of time, (is not "under age"), that A has made an "offer," that B has "accepted" it, etc. It is some-times necessary to consider, also, what may, from the particular point of view, be regarded as *negative* operative facts. Thus, *e.g.,* the fact that A did not wilfully misrepresent an important matter to B, and the fact that A had not "revoked" his offer, must really be included as parts of the totality of operative facts in the case already put.

Taking another example,—this time from the general field of torts—if X commits an assault on Y by putting the latter in fear of bodily harm, this particular group of facts immediately create in Y the privilege of self-defense,—that is, the privilege of using sufficient force to repel X's attack; or, correlatively, the other-wise existing duty of Y to refrain from the application of force to the person of X is, by virtue of the special operative facts, immediately terminated or extinguished.

In passing, it may not be amiss to notice that the term, "facts in issue," is sometimes used in the present connection. If, as is usual, the term means "facts put in issue by the *pleadings,*" the expression is an unfortunate one. The operative facts alleged by the pleadings are more or less *generic* in character; and if the pleadings be sufficient, only such *generic* operative facts are "put in issue." The operative facts of real life are, on the other hand, very specific. That being so, it is clear that the *real* and *specific* facts finally relied on are comparatively seldom put in issue by the pleadings. Thus, if, in an action of tort, the declaration of A alleges that he was, through the carelessness, etc., of B, bitten by the latter's dog, the fact alleged is generic in character, and it matters not whether it was dog Jim or dog Dick that did the biting. Even assuming, therefore, that the biting was done by Jim, (rather than by Dick), it could not be said that this specific fact was put in issue by the pleadings. Similarly, and more obviously, the pleading in an ordinary action involving so-called negligence, is usually very generic in character,[21] so that any one of various possible groups of specific operative facts would suffice, so far as the defendant's obligation *ex delicto* is concerned. It therefore could not be said that any one of such groups had been put in issue by the pleadings. A common fallacy in this connection is to regard the *spe-*

[20] Compare Waldo, C. J., in *White v. Multonomah Co.* (1886), 13 Ore., 317, 323: "A 'right' has been define dby [sic] Mr. Justice Holmes to be the legal consequence which attaches to certain facts. (The Common Law, 214). Every fact which forms one of the group of facts of which the right is the legal consequence appertains to the substance of the right."

The present writer's choice of the term "operative" has been suggested by the following passage from Thayer, Prelim. Treat. Evid. (1898), p. 393: "Another discrimination to be observed is that between documents which constitute a contract, fact, or transaction, and those which merely certify and evidence something outside of themselves,—a something valid and *operative,* independent of the writing."

Compare also Holland, Jurisp. (10th ed., 1906), 151: "A fact giving rise to a right has long been described as a 'title'; but no such well-worn equivalent can be found for a fact through which a right is transferred, or for one by which a right is extinguished. A new nomenclature was accordingly invented by Bentham, which is convenient for scientific use, although it has not found its way into ordinary language. He describes this whole class of facts as 'Dispositive'; distinguishing as 'Investitive' those by means of which a right comes into existence, as 'Divestitive' those through which it terminates, and as 'Translative' those through which it passes from one person to another."

The word "ultimate," sometimes used in this connection, does not seem to be so pointed and useful a term as either "operative" or "constitutive."

[21] Compare, however, *Illinois Steel Co. v. Ostrowski* (1902), 194 Ill., 376, 384, correctly sustaining a declaration alleging the operative facts *specifically* instead of *generically,* as required by the more approved forms of pleading.

The rules of pleading determining whether allegations must be generic or specific—and if the latter, to what degree—are, like other rules of law, based on considerations of policy and convenience. Thus the facts constituting *fraud* are frequently required to be alleged in comparatively specific form; and similarly as regards *cruelty* in an action for divorce based on that ground. The reasons of policy are obvious in each case.

cific operative facts established in a given case as being but "evidence" of the *generic* (or "ultimate") operative facts alleged in the pleadings.[22]

An evidential fact is one which, on being ascertained, affords some logical basis—not conclusive—for inferring some other fact. The latter may be either a constitutive fact or an intermediate evidential fact. Of all the facts to be ascertained by the tribunal, the operative are, of course, of primary importance; the evidential are subsidiary in their functions.[23] As a rule there is little danger of confusing evidential facts with operative facts. But there is one type of case that not infrequently gives rise to this sort of error. Suppose that in January last a contractual obligation was created by written agreement passing between A and B. In an action now pending between these parties, the physical *instrument* is offered for inspection by the tribunal. If one were thoughtless, he would be apt to say that this is a case where part of the operative facts creating the original obligation are directly presented to the senses of the tribunal. Yet a moment's reflection will show that such is not the case. The document, in its then existing shape, had, as regards its operative effect, spent its force as soon as it was delivered in January last. If, therefore, the unaltered document is produced for inspection, the facts thus ascertained must, as regards the alleged contractual agreement, be purely evidential in character. That is to say, the present existence of the piece of paper, its specific tenor, etc., may, along with other evidential facts (relating to absence of change) tend to prove the various operative facts of last January,—to wit, that such paper existed at that time; that its tenor was then the same as it now is; that it was delivered by A to B, and so forth.

It now remains to observe that in many situations a single convenient term is employed to designate (generically) certain miscellaneous groups of operative facts which, though differing widely as to their individual "ingredients," have, as regards a given matter, the same *net* force and effect. When employed with discrimination, the term "possession" is a word of this character; so also the term "capacity," the term "domicile," etc. But the general tendency to confuse legal and non-legal quantities is manifest here as elsewhere; so that only too frequently these words are used rather nebulously to indicate legal relations as such.[24]

FUNDAMENTAL JURAL RELATIONS CONTRASTED WITH ONE ANOTHER.

One of the greatest hindrances to the clear understanding, the incisive statement, and the true solution of legal problems frequently arises from the express or tacit

---

[22] Compare *McCaughey v. Schuette* (1897), 117 Cal., 223. While the decision in this case can be supported, the statement that the specific facts pleaded were "evidentiary" seems inaccurate and misleading.

There are, of course, genuine instances of the fatally erroneous pleading of strictly evidential facts instead of either generic or specific operative facts. See *Rogers v. Milwaukee*, 13 Wis., 610; and contrast *Illinois Steel Co. v. Ostrowski, supra,* note 21.

[23] Both operative and evidential facts must, under the law, be *ascertained* in some one or more of four possible modes: 1. By judicial admissions (what is not disputed); 2. By judicial notice, or knowledge (what is known or easily knowable); 3. By judicial perception (what is ascertained directly through the senses; cf. "real evidence"); 4. By judicial inference (what is ascertained by reasoning from facts already ascertained by one or more of the four methods here outlined).

[24] As an example of this, compare Lord Westbury, in *Bell v. Kennedy* (1868); L. R. 1 H. L. (Sc.), 307: "Domicile, therefore, is an idea of the law. It is the *relation* which the *law creates* between an individual and a particular locality or country."

Contrast the far more accurate language of Chief Justice Shaw, in *Abington v. Bridgewater* (1840), 23 Pick, 170: "The *fact* of domicile is often one of the highest importance to a person; it *determines* his civil and political rights and privileges, duties and obligations. * * *"

assumption that all legal relations may be reduced to "rights" and "duties," and that these latter categories are therefore adequate for the purpose of analyzing even the most complex legal interests, such as trusts, options, escrows, "future" interests, corporate interests, etc. Even if the difficulty related merely to inadequacy and ambiguity of terminology, its seriousness would nevertheless be worthy of definite recognition and persistent effort toward improvement; for in any closely reasoned problem, whether legal or non-legal, chameleon-hued words are a peril both to clear thought and to lucid expression.[25] As a matter of fact, however, the above mentioned inadequacy and ambiguity of terms unfortunately reflect, all too often, corresponding paucity and confusion as regards actual legal conceptions. That this is so may appear in some measure from the discussion to follow.

The strictly fundamental legal relations are, after all, *sui generis*; and thus it is that attempts at formal definition are always unsatisfactory, if not altogether useless. Accordingly, the most promising line of procedure seems to consist in exhibiting all of the various relations in a scheme of "opposites" and "correlatives," and then proceeding to exemplify their individual scope and application in concrete cases. An effort will be made to pursue this method:

Jural Opposites	rights no-rights	privilege duty	power disability	immunity liability

Jural Correlatives	right duty	privilege no-right	power liability	immunity disability

Rights and Duties. As already intimated, the term "rights" tends to be used indiscriminately to cover what in a given case may be a privilege, a power, or an immunity, rather than a right in the strictest sense; and this looseness of usage is occasionally recognized by the authorities. As said by Mr. Justice Strong in *People v. Dikeman*:[26]

"The word 'right' is defined by lexicographers to denote, among other things, *property, interest, power, prerogative, immunity, privilege* (Walker's Dict. word

---

[25] In this connection, the words of one of the great masters of the common law are significant. In his notable Preliminary Treatise on Evidence (1898), p. 190, Professor James Bradley Thayer said:

"As our law develops it becomes more and more important to give definiteness to its phraseology; discriminations multiply, new situations and complications of fact arise, and the old outfit of ideas, discriminations, and phrases has to be carefully revised. Law is not so unlike all other subjects of human contemplation that clearness of thought will not help us powerfully in grasping it. If terms in common legal use are used exactly, it is well to know it; if they are used inexactly, it is well to know that, and to remark just how they are used."

Perhaps the most characteristic feature of this author's great constructive contribution to the law of evidence is his constant insistence on the need for clarifying our legal terminology, and making careful "discriminations" between conceptions and terms that are constantly being treated as if they were one and the same. See, *e.g., Ibid.,* pp. vii, 183, 189–190, 278, 306; 351, 355, 390–393. How great the influence of those discriminations has been is well known to all students of the law of evidence.

The comparatively recent remarks of Professor John Chipman Gray, in his Nature and Sources of the Law (1909), Pref. p. viii, are also to the point:

"The student of Jurisprudence is at times troubled by the thought that he is dealing not with things, but with words, that he is busy with the shape and size of counters in a game of logomachy, but when he fully realizes how these words have been passed and are still being passed as money, not only by fools and on fools, but by and on some of the acutest minds, he feels that there is work worthy of being done, if only it can be done worthily."

No less significant and suggestive is the recent and charactistic utterance of one of the greatest jurists of our time, Mr. Justice Holmes. In *Hyde v. United States* (1911), 225 U. S., 347, 391, the learned judge very aptly remarked: "It is one of the misfortunes of the law that ideas become encysted in phrases and thereafter for a long time cease to provoke further analysis."

See also, Field, J., in *Morgan v. Louisiana* (1876), 93 U. S., 217, 223, and Peckham, J. in *Phoenix Ins. Co. v. Tennessee* (1895), 161 U. S., 174, 177, 178.

[26] (1852) 7 How. Pr., 124, 130.

'Right'). In law it is most frequently applied to property in its restricted sense, but it is often used to designate *power, prerogative,* and *privilege, * * *.*"

Recognition of this ambiguity is also found in the language of Mr. Justice Jackson, in *United States v. Patrick*:[27]

"The words 'right' or 'privilege' have, of course, a variety of meanings, according to the connection or context in which they are used. Their definition, as given by standard lexicographers, include 'that which one has a *legal claim to do,' 'legal power,' 'authority,' 'immunity* granted by authority,' 'the investiture with special or peculiar rights.'"

And, similarly, in the language of Mr. Justice Sneed, in *Lonas v. State*:[28]

"The state, then, is forbidden from making and enforcing any law which shall abridge the *privileges* and *immunities* of citizens of the United States. It is said that the words *rights, privileges* and *immunities,* are abusively used, as if they were synonymous. The word *rights* is generic, common, embracing whatever may be lawfully claimed."[29]

It is interesting to observe, also, that a tendency toward discrimination may be found in a number of important constitutional and statutory provisions. Just how accurate the distinctions in the mind of the draftsman may have been it is, of course, impossible to say.[30]

Recognizing, as we must, the very broad and indiscriminate use of the term, "right," what clue do we find, in ordinary legal discourse, toward limiting the word in question to a definite and appropriate meaning. That clue lies in the correlative "duty," for it is certain that even those who use the word and the conception "right" in the broadest possible way are accustomed to thinking of "duty" as the invariable correlative. As said in *Lake Shore & M. S. R. Co. v. Kurtz*:[31]

"A duty or a legal obligation is that which one ought or ought not to do. 'Duty' and 'right' are correlative terms. When a right is invaded, a duty is violated."[32]

In other words, if X has a right against Y that he shall stay off the former's land, the correlative (and equivalent) is that Y is under a duty toward X to stay

---

[27] (1893) 54 Fed. Rep., 338, 348.

[28] (1871) 3 Heisk. (Tenn.), 287, 306–307.

[29] See also, for similar judicial observations, *Atchison & Neb. R. Co. v. Baty* (1877), 6 Neb., 37, 40. (The term *right* in civil society is defined to mean that which a man is entitled *to have,* or *to do,* or *to receive* from others within the limits prescribed by law."); *San Francisco v. S. V. Water Co.* ( ), 48 Cal., 531 ("We are to ascertain the *rights, privileges, powers, duties* and *obligations* of the Spring Valley Water Co., by reference to the general law."). Compare also Gilbert, Evid. (4th ed., 1777), 126: "The men of one county, city, hundred, town, corporation, or parish are evidence in relation to the *rights privileges, immunities* and affairs of such town, city, etc."

[30] See *Kearns v. Cordwainers' Co.* (1859), 6 C. B. N. S., 388, 409 (construing The Thames Conservancy Act, 1857, 20 and 21 Vict. c. cxlvii., s. 179: "None of the powers by this act conferred * * * shall extend to, take away, alter or abridge any right, claim, privilege, franchise, exemption, or immunity to which any owners * * * of any lands * * * are now by law entitled."); *Fearon v. Mitchell* (1872), L. R. 7 Q. B., 690, 695 ("The other question remains to be disposed of, as to whether the case comes within the proviso of s. 50 of 21 and 22 Vict. c. 98, that 'no market shall be established in pursuance of this section so as to interfere with any rights, powers, or privileges enjoyed within the district by any person without his consent.'"); Cal. Civ. Code, sec. 648a: "Building and loan associations may be formed under this title with or without guarantee or other capital stock, with all the rights, powers, and privileges, and subject to all the restrictions and liabilities set forth in this title."); Tenn. Const. of 1834, Art. 9, sec. 7: "The legislature shall have no power to pass any law granting to any individual or individuals, rights, privileges and immunities or exemptions, other than * * *").

[31] (1894) 10 Ind. App., 60; 37 N. E., 303, 304.

[32] See also *Howley Park Coal, etc., Co. v. L. & N. W. Ry.* (1913), A. C. 11, 25, 27 (per Viscount Haldane, L. C.: "There is an obligation (of lateral support) on the neighbor, and in that sense there is a correlative right on the part of the owner of the first piece of land;" per Lord Shaw: "There is a reciprocal right to lateral support for their respective lands and a reciprocal obligation upon the part of each owner. * * * No diminution of the right on the one hand or of the obligation on the other can be effected except as the result of a plain contract. * * *"). Compare, to similar effect, *Galveston, etc. Ry. Co. v. Harrigan* (1903), 76 S. W., 452, 453 (Tex. Civ. App.).

off the place. If, as seems desirable, we should seek a synonym for the term "right" in this limited and proper meaning, perhaps the word "claim" would prove the best. The latter has the advantage of being a monosyllable. In this connection, the language of Lord Watson in *Studd v. Cook*[33] is instructive:

"Any words which in a settlement of moveables would be recognized by the law of Scotland as sufficient to create a right *or claim* in favor of an executor * * * must receive effect if used with reference to lands in Scotland."

Privileges and "No-Rights." As indicated in the above scheme of jural relations, a privilege is the opposite of a duty, and the correlative of a "no-right." In the example last put, whereas X has a *right* or *claim* that Y, the other man, should stay off the land, he himself has the *privilege* of entering on the land; or, in equivalent words, X does not have a duty to stay off. The privilege of entering is the negation of a duty to stay off. As indicated by this case, some caution is necessary at this point, for, always, when it is said that a given privilege is the mere negation of a *duty,* what is meant, of course, is a duty having a content or tenor precisely *opposite* to that of the privilege in question. Thus, if, for some special reason, X has contracted with Y to go on the former's own land, it is obvious that X has, as regards Y, both the privilege of entering and the *duty of entering.* The privilege is perfectly consistent with this sort of duty,—for the latter is of the *same* content or tenor as the privilege;— but it still holds good that, as regards Y, X's privilege of entering is the precise negation of a duty *to stay off.* Similarly, if A has not contracted with B to perform certain work for the latter, A's privilege of *not* doing so is the very negation of a duty of *doing* so. Here again the duty contrasted is of a content or tenor exactly opposite to that of the privilege.

Passing now to the question of "correlatives," it will be remembered, of course, that a duty is the invariable correlative of that legal relation which is most properly called a right or claim. That being so, if further evidence be needed as to the fundamental and important difference between a right (or claim) and a privilege, surely it is found in the fact that the correlative of the latter relation is a "no-right," there being no single term available to express the latter conception. Thus, the correlative of X's right that Y shall not enter on the land is Y's duty not to enter; but the correlative of X's privilege of entering himself is manifestly Y's "no-right" that X shall not enter.

In view of the considerations thus far emphasized, the importance of keeping the conception of a right (or claim) and the conception of a privilege quite distinct from each other seems evident; and more than that, it is equally clear that there should be a separate term to represent the latter relation. No doubt, as already indicated, it is very common to use the term "right" indiscriminately, even when the relation designated is really that of privilege;[34] and only too often this identity of terms has involved for the particular speaker or writer a confusion or blurring of ideas. Good instances of this may be found even in unexpected places. Thus Professor Holland, in his work on Jurisprudence, referring to a different and well known sort of ambiguity inherent in the Latin *"Ius,"* the German *"Recht,"* the

[33] (1883) 8 App. Cas., at p. 597.
[34] For merely a few out of numberless judicial instances of this loose usage, see *Pearce v. Scotcher* (1882), L. R. 9 Q. B., 162, 167; *Quinn v. Leathem* (1901), A. C. 495 (*passim*); *Allen v. Flood* (1898), A. C. 1 (*passim*); *Lindley v. Nat. Carbonic Acid Gas Co.* (1910), 220 U. S., 61, 75; *Smith v. Cornell Univ.* (1894), 45 N. Y. Supp., 640, 643; *Farnum v. Kern Valley Bk.* (1910), 107 Pac., 568. See also *post,* n. 38.

Italian *"Diritto,"* and the French *"Droit,"*—terms used to express "not only 'a right,' but also 'Law' in the abstract,"—very aptly observes:

"If the expression of widely different ideas by one and the same term resulted only in the necessity for * * * clumsy paraphrases, or obviously inaccurate paraphrases, no great harm would be done; but unfortunately the identity of terms seems irresistibly to suggest an identity between the ideas expressed by them."[35]

Curiously enough, however, in the very chapter where this appears,—the chapter on "Rights,"—the notions of right, privilege and power seem to be blended, and that, too, although the learned author states that "the correlative of * * * legal right is legal duty," and that "these pairs of terms express * * * in each case the same state of facts viewed from opposite sides." While the whole chapter must be read in order to appreciate the seriousness of this lack of discrimination a single passage must suffice by way of example:

"If * * * the power of the State will protect him in so carrying out his wishes, and will compel such acts or forbearances on the part of other people as may be necessary in order that his wishes may be so carried out, then he has a 'legal right' so to carry out his wishes."[36]

The first part of this passage suggests privileges, the middle part rights (or claims), and the last part privileges.

Similar difficulties seem to exist in Professor Gray's able and entertaining work on The Nature and Sources of Law. In his chapter on "Legal Rights and Duties" the distinguished author takes the position that a right always has a duty as its correlative;[37] and he seems to define the former relation substantially according to the more limited meaning of "claim." Legal privileges, powers, and immunities are *prima facie* ignored, and the impression conveyed that all legal relations can be comprehended under the conceptions, "right" and "duty." But, with the greatest hesitation and deference, the suggestion may be ventured that a number of his examples seem to show the inadequacy of such mode of treatment. Thus, *e.g.,* he says:

"The eating of shrimp salad is an interest of mine, and, if I can pay for it, the law will protect that interest, and it is therefore a right of mine to eat shrimp salad which I have paid for, although I know that shrimp salad always gives me the colic."[38]

This passage seems to suggest primarily two classes of relations: *first,* the party's respective privileges, as against A, B, C. D and others in relation to eating the salad, or, correlatively, the respective "no-rights" of A. B. C. D and others that the party should not eat the salad; *second,* the party's respective rights (or claims) as against A. B. C. D and others that they should not interfere with the physical act of eating the salad, or, correlatively, the respective duties of A, B, C, D and others that they should not interfere.

These two groups of relations seem perfectly distinct; and the privileges could, in a given case exist even though the rights mentioned did not. A. B. C. and D, being the owners of the salad, might say to X: "Eat the salad, if you can; you have our license to do so, but we don't agree not to interfere with you." In such a case the privileges exist, so that if X succeeds in eating the salad, he has violated no rights of any of the parties. But it is equally clear that if A had succeeded in holding so

---

[35] El. Jurisp. (10th ed.), 83.
[36] *Ibid.,* 82.
[37] See Nat. and Sources of Law (1909), secs. 45, 184.
[38] *Ibid.,* sec. 48.

fast to the dish that X couldn't eat the contents, no right of X would have been violated.[39]

Perhaps the essential character and importance of the distinction can be shown by a slight variation of the facts. Suppose that X, being already the legal owner of the salad, contracts with Y that he (X) will never eat this particular food. With A, B, C, D and others no such contract has been made. One of the relations now existing between X and Y is, as a consequence, fundamentally different from the relation between X and A. As regards Y, X has no privilege of eating the salad; but as regards either A or any of the others, X has such a privilege. It is to be observed incidentally that X's right that Y should not eat the food persists even though X's own privilege of doing so has been extinguished.[40]

On grounds already emphasized, it would seem that the line of reasoning pursued by Lord Lindley in the great case of *Quinn v. Leathem*[41] is deserving of comment:

"The plaintiff had the ordinary *rights* of the British subject. He was *at liberty* to earn his living in his own way, provided he did not violate some special law prohibiting him from so doing, and provided he did not infringe the rights of other people. This *liberty* involved *the liberty* to deal with other persons who were willing to deal with him. *This liberty* is a *right* recognized by law; its *correlative* is the general *duty* of every one not to prevent the free exercise of this *liberty* except so far as his own liberty of action may justify him in so doing. But a person's *liberty* or *right* to deal with others is nugatory unless they are at liberty to deal with him if they choose to do so. Any interference with their liberty to deal with him affects him."

A "liberty" considered as a legal relation (or "right" in the loose and generic sense of that term) must mean, if it have any definite content at all, precisely the same thing as *privilege*,[42] and certainly that is the fair connotation of the term as used the first three times in the passage quoted. It is equally clear, as already indicated, that such a privilege or liberty to deal with others at will might very conceivably exist without any peculiar concomitant rights against "third parties" as regards certain kinds of interference.[43] Whether there should be such concomitant rights (or claims) is ultimately a question of justice and policy; and it should be considered, as such, on its merits. The only correlative logically implied by the privileges or liberties in question are the "no-rights" of "third parties" It would therefore be a *non sequitur* to conclude from the mere existence of such liberties that "third parties" are under a

---

[39] Other instances in Professor Gray's work may be noted. In sec. 53, he says: "So again, a householder has the right to eject by force a trespasser from his 'castle.' That is, if sued by the trespasser for an assault, he can call upon the court to refuse the plaintiff its help. In other words, a man's legal rights include not only the power effectually to call for aid from an organized society against another, but also the power to call effectually upon the society to abstain from aiding others."

This, it is respectfully submitted, seems to confuse the householder's privilege of ejecting the trespasser (and the "no-right" of the latter) with a complex of *potential* rights, privileges, powers and immunities relating to the supposed action at law.

In sec. 102, the same learned author says: "If there is an ordinance that the town constable may kill all dogs without collars, the constable may have a legal right to kill such dogs, but the dogs are not under a legal duty to wear collars."

It would seem, however, that what the ordinance did was to create a privilege—the absence of the duty not to kill which otherwise would have existed in favor of the owner of the dog. Moreover, that appears to be the most natural connotation of the passage. The latter doesn't except very remotely, call up the idea of the constable's accompanying rights against all others that they shouldn't interfere with his actual killing of the dog.

See, also, secs. 145, 186.

[40] It may be noted incidentally that a statute depriving a party of privileges as such may raise serious constitutional questions under the Fourteenth Amendment. Compare, *e.g., Lindley v. Nat. Carbonic Gas Co.* (1910), 220 U. S., 61.

[41] (1901) A. C., 495, 534.

[42] See *post*, pp. 38–44.

[43] Compare *Allen v. Flood* (1898), A. C., 1.

duty not to interfere, etc. Yet in the middle of the above passage from Lord Lindley's opinion there is a sudden and question-begging shift in the use of terms. First, the "liberty" in question is transmuted into a "right," and then, possibly under the seductive influence of the latter word, it is assumed that the "correlative" must be "the general duty of every one not to prevent," etc.

Another interesting and instructive example may be taken from Lord Bowen's oft-quoted opinion in *Mogul Steamship Co. v. McGregor.*[44]

"We are presented in this case with an apparent conflict or antinomy between two rights that are equally regarded by the law—the right of the plaintiffs to be protected in the legitimate exercise of their trade, and the right of the defendants to carry on their business as seems best to them, provided they commit no wrong to others."

As the learned judge states, the conflict or antinomy is only apparent; but this fact seems to be obscured by the very indefinite and rapidly shifting meanings with which the term "right" is used in the above quoted language. Construing the passage as a whole, it seems plain enough that by "the right of the plaintiffs" in relation to the defendants a legal right or claim in the strict sense must be meant; whereas by "the right of the defendants" in relation to the plaintiffs a legal privilege must be intended. That being so, the "two rights" mentioned in the beginning of the passage, being respectively claim and privilege, could not be in conflict with each other. To the extent that the defendants have privileges the plaintiffs have no rights; and conversely, to the extent that the plaintiffs have rights the defendants have no privileges ("no-privilege" equals duty of opposite tenor).[45]

Thus far it has been assumed that the term "privilege" is the most appropriate and satisfactory to designate the mere negation of duty. Is there good warrant for this?

In Mackeldey's Roman Law[46] it is said:

"Positive laws either contain general principles embodied in the rules of law * * * or for especial reasons they establish something that differs from those general principles. In the first case they contain a common law (*jus commune*), in the second a special law (*jus singulare s. exorbitans*). The latter is either favorable or unfavorable * * * according as it enlarges or restricts, in opposition to the common rule, the rights of those for whom it is established. The favorable special law (*jus singulare*) as also the right created by it * * * in the Roman law is termed benefit of the law (*bencficium juris*) or privilege (*privilegium*) * * *"[47]

First a special law, and then by association of ideas, a special advantage conferred by such a law. With such antecedents, it is not surprising that the English

---

[44] (1889) 23 Q. B. D., 59.

[45] Cases almost without number might be cited to exemplify similar blending of fundamental conceptions and rapid shifting in the use of terms;—and that, too, even when the problems involved have been such as to invite close and careful reasoning. For a few important cases of this character, see *Allen v. Flood* (1898), A. C, 1, (Hawkins. J., p. 16: "I know it may be asked, 'What is the legal right of the plaintiffs which is said to have been invaded?' My answer is, that right which should never be lost sight of, and which I have already stated—the right freely to pursue their lawful calling;" Lord Halsbury, p. 84: "To dig into one's own land under the circumstances stated requires no cause or excuse. He may act from mere caprice, but his right on his own land is absolute, so long as he does not interfere with the rights of others;" Lord Ashbourne, p. 112: "The plaintiff had, in my opinion, a clear right to pursue their lawful calling. * * * It would be. I think, an unsatisfactory state of the law that allowed the wilful invader of such a right without lawful leave or justification to escape from the consequences of his action."); *Quinn v. Leathem* (1901), A. C., 495, 533; *Lindsley v. Natural Carbonic Gas Co* (1910), 220 U. S., 61, 74; *Robertson v. Rochester Folding Box Co.* (1902), 171 N. Y., 538 (Parker, C. J., p. 544: "The so-called right of privacy is, as the phrase suggests, founded upon the claim that a man has the right to pass through this world. if he wills, without having his picture published."); *Wabash, St. L. & P. R. Co. v. Shacklet* (1883), 105 Ill., 364, 389.

In *Purdy v. State* (1901), 43 Fla., 538, 540, the anomalous expression "right of privilege" is employed.

[46] (Dropsie Tr.) secs. 196–197.

[47] The same matter is put somewhat less clearly in Sohm's Institutes (Ledlies Tr., 3rd ed.), 28.

Wesley Hohfeld

word "privilege" is not infrequently used, even at the present time, in the sense of a special or peculiar legal advantage (whether right, privilege, power or immunity) belonging either to some individual or to some particular class of persons.[48] There are, indeed, a number of judicial opinions recognizing this as one of the meanings of the term in question.[49] That the word has a wider signification even in ordinary non-technical usage is sufficiently indicated, however, by the fact that the term *special privileges* is so often used to indicate a contrast to ordinary or general privileges. More than this, the dominant specific connotation of the term as used in popular speech seems to be more *negation of duty*. This is manifest in the terse and oft-repeated expression, "That is your privilege,"—meaning, of course, "You are under no duty to do otherwise."

Such being the case, it is not surprising to find, from a wide survey of judicial precedents, that the *dominant* technical meaning of the term is, similarly, negation of *legal duty*.[50] There are two very common examples of this, relating respectively to "privileged communications" in the law of libel and to "privileges against self-crimination" in the law of evidence. As regards the first case, it is elementary that if a certain group of operative facts are present, a privilege exists, which, without such facts, would not be recognized.[51] It is, of course, equally clear that even though all such facts be present as last supposed, the superadded fact of malice will, in cases of so-called "conditional privilege," extinguish the privilege that otherwise would exist. It must be evident also, that whenever the privilege does exist, it is not special in the sense of arising from a special law, or of being conferred as a special favor on a particular individual. The same privilege would exist, by virtue of general rules, for any person whatever under similar circumstances. So, also, in the law of evidence, the privilege against self-crimination signifies the mere negation of a duty, to testify,—a duty which rests upon a witness in relation to all ordinary matters; and, quite obviously, such privilege arises, if at all, only by virtue of general laws.[52]

As already intimated, while both the conception and the term "privilege" find conspicuous exemplification under the law of libel and the law of evidence, they

---

See also *Rector, etc. of Christ Church v. Philadelphia* (1860), 24 How., 300, 301, 302.

[48] According to an older usage, the term "privilege" was frequently employed to indicate a "franchise." the latter being really a miscellaneous complex of special rights, privileges, powers, or immunities, etc. Thus, in an early book, *Termes de la Ley,* there is the following definition: "'Privileges' are liberties and franchises granted to an office, place, towne, or manor by the King's great charter, letters patent, or Act of Parliament, as toll, sake, socke, infangstheefe, outfangstheefe, turne, or delfe, and divers such like."

Compare *Blades v. Higgs* (1865), 11 H. L. Cas., 621, 631, per Lord Westbury: "Property *ratione privilegii* is the right which by a peculiar franchise anciently granted by the Crown, by virtue of prerogative, one may have of taking animals *ferae naturae* on the land of another; and in like manner the game when taken by virtue of the privilege becomes the absolute property of the owner of the franchise."

[49] See *Humphrey v. Pegues* (1872), 16 Wall., 244, 247, per Hunt, J.: "All the 'privileges' as well as powers and rights of the prior company. were granted to the latter. A more imporant or more comprehensive privilege than a perpetual immunity from taxation can scarcely be imagined. It contains the essential idea of a peculiar benefit or advantage, of a special exemption from a burden falling upon others."

See also *Smith v. Floyd* (1893), 140 N. Y., 337, 342; *Lonas v. State* (1871). 3 Heisk., 287, 306,307; *Territory v. Stokes* (1881), 2 N. M., 161, 169, 170; *Ripley v. Knight* (1878), 123 Mass., 515, 519; *Dike v. State* (1888), 38 Minn., 366; *Re Miller* (1893), 1 Q. B., 327.

Compare *Wisener v. Burrell* (1911), 28 Okla., 546.

[50] Compare *Louisville & N. R Co. v. Gaines* (1880), 3 Fed. Rep., 266, 278, per Baxter, Asso. J.: "Paschal says (the term privilege) is a special right belonging to an individual or class; *properly,* an *exemption* from some *duty.*"

[51] For apt use of the terms, "privilege" and "privileged" in relation to libel, see Hawkins, J., in *Allen v. Flood* (1898), A. C. 1, 20–21.

[52] As regards the general duty to testify, specific performance may usually be had under duress of potential or actual contempt proceedings; and, apart from that, failure to testify might subject the wrongdoer either to a statutory liability for a penalty in favor of the injured party litigant or, in case of actual damage, to a common law action on the case.

nevertheless have a much wider significance and utility as a matter of judicial usage. To make this clear, a few miscellaneous judicial precedents will now be noticed. In Dowman's Case,[53] decided in the year 1583, and reported by Coke, the court applied the term to the subject of waste:

"And as to the objection which was made, that the said privilege to be without impeachment of waste cannot be without deed, etc. To that it was answered and resolved, that if it was admitted that a deed in such case should be requisite, yet without question all the estates limited would be good, although it is admitted, that the clause concerning the said privilege would be void."

In the great case of *Allen v. Flood*[54] the opinion of Mr. Justice Hawkins furnishes a useful passage for the purpose now in view:

"Every person has a privilege * * * in the interests of public justice to put the criminal law in motion against another whom be *bona fide,* and upon reasonable and probable cause, believes to have been guilty of a crime. * * * It must not, however, be supposed that hatred and ill-will existing in the mind of a prosecutor must of necessity *destroy* the *privilege,* for it is not impossible that such hatred and ill-will may have very natural and pardonable reasons for existing. * * *"

Applying the term in relation to the subject of property, Mr. Justice Foster, of the Supreme Court of Maine, said in the case of *Pulitzer v. Lumgston:*[55]

"It is contrary to the policy of the law that there should be any outstanding titles, estates, or powers, by the existence, operation or exercise of which, at a period of time beyond lives in being and twenty-one years and a fraction thereafter, the complete and unfettered enjoyment of an estate, *with all the rights, privileges and powers incident to ownership,* should be qualified or impeded."

As a final example in the present connection, the language of Baron Alderson in *Hilton v. Eckerley*[56] may be noticed:

"*Prima facie* it is the privilege of a trader in a free country, in all matters not contrary to law, to regulate his own mode of carrying them on according to his discretion and choice."[57]

The closest synonym of legal "privilege" seems to be legal "liberty." This is sufficiently indicated by an unusually discriminating and instructive passage in Mr. Justice Cave's opinion in *Allen v. Flood:*[58]

"The personal rights with which we are most familiar are: 1. Rights of reputation; 2. Rights of bodily safety and freedom; 3. Rights of property; or, in other words, rights relating to mind, body and estate, * * *

The subject of witnesses is usually thought of as a branch of the so-called *adjective* law, as distinguished, from the so-called *substantive* law. But, as the writer has had occasion to emphasize on another occasion (The Relations betwen [sic] Equity and Law, 11 Mich. L. Rev., 537, 554, 556, 569), there seems to be no intrinsic or essential difference between those jural relations that relate to the "substantive" law and those that relate to the "adjective" law. This matter will be considered more fully in a later part of the discussion.

[53] (1583) 9 Coke, 1.

[54] (1898) A. C., 1, 19.

[55] (1896) 89 Me., 359.

[56] (1856) 6 E. & B., 47. 74.

[57] For other examples of apt use of the term in question, see *Borland v Boston* (1882), 132 Mass., 89 ("municipal rights, privileges, powers or duties"); *Hamilton v. Graham* (1871), L. R. 2 H. L. (Sc.), 167, 169, per Hatherley, L. C.; *Jones v. De Moss* (1911), 151 Ia., 112, 117; *Kripp v. Curtis* (1886), 71 Cal., 62, 63; *Lamer v. Booth* (1874), 50 Miss., 411, 413; *Weller v. Brown* (1911), Cal., ; 117 Pac., 517; *Mathews v. People* (1903), 202 Ill., 389, 401; *Abington v. North Bridgewater* (1840), 23 Pick., 170.

[58] (1898) A. C., 1, 29.

"In my subsequent remarks the word 'right' will, as far as possible, always be used in the above sense; and it is the more necessary to insist on this as during the argument at your Lordship's bar it was frequently used in a much wider and more indefinite sense. Thus it was said that a man has a perfect right to fire off a gun, when all that was meant, apparently, was that a man has a *freedom* or *liberty* to fire off a gun, so long as he does not violate or infringe any one's rights in doing so, which is a very different thing from a right, the violation or disturbance of which can be remedied or prevented by legal process."[59]

While there are numerous other instances of the apt use of the term "liberty," both in judicial opinions[60] and in conveyancing documents,[61] it is by no means so common or definite a word as "privilege." The former term is far more likely to be used in the sense of physical or personal freedom (*i.e.*, absence of physi*cal* restraint), as distinguished from a legal relation; and very frequently there is the connotation of *general* political liberty, as distinguished from a particular relation between two definite individuals. Besides all this, the term "privilege" has the

---

[59] For the reference to Mr. Justice Cave's opinion, the present writer is indebted to Salmond's work on Jurisprudence. Citing this case and one other, *Starey v. Graham* (1899), 1 Q. B., 406, 411, the learned author adopts and uses exclusively the term "liberty" to indicate the opposite of "duty," and apparently overlooks the importance of *privilege* in the present connection. Curiously enough, moreover, in his separate Treatise on Torts, his discussion of the law of defamation gives no explicit intimation that *privilege* in relation to that subject represents merely *liberty*, or "*no-duty*."

Sir Frederick Pollock, in his volume on Jurisprudence (2nd ed., 1904), 62, seems in effect to deny that legal liberty represents any true legal relation as such. Thus, he says, *inter alia*: "The act may be right in the popular and rudimentary sense of not being forbidden, but freedom has not the character of legal right until we consider the risk of unauthorized interference. It is the duty of all of us not to interfere with our neighbors' lawful freedom. This brings the so-called primitive rights into the sphere of legal rule and protection. *Sometimes it is thought that lawful power or liberty is different from the right not to be interfered with; but for the reason just given this opinion, though plausible, does not seem correct.*" Compare also Pollock, Essays in Jurisp. & Ethics (1882), Ch. I.

It is difficult to see, however, why, as between X and Y, the "privilege + no-right" situation is not just as real a jural relation as the precisely opposite "duty + right" relation betwen any two parties. Perhaps the habit of recognizing exclusively the latter as a jural relation springs more or less from the traditional tendency to think of the law as consisting of "commands," or imperative rules. This, however, seems fallacious. A rule of law that *permits* is just as real as a rule of law that *forbids;* and, similarly,s aying [sic] that the law *permits* a given act to X as between himself and Y predicates just as genuine a legal relation as saying that the law *forbids* a certain act to X as between himself and Y. That this is so seems, in some measure, to be confirmed by the fact that the first sort of act would ordinarily be pronounced "lawful," and the second "unlawful." Compare *Thomas v. Sorrel* (1673), Vaughan, 331, 351.

[60] Compare *Dow v. Newborough* (1728), Comyns, 242 ("For the use is only a liberty to take the profits, but two cannot severally take the profits of the same land, therefore there cannot be an use upon a use." It should be observed that in this and the next case to be cited, along with the liberty or privilege there are associated powers and rights, etc.: for instance, the *power* to acquire a title to the things severed from the realty); *Bourne v. Taylor* (1808), 10 East., 189 (Ellenborough, C. J.): "The second question is whether the replication ought to have traversed the liberty of working the mines. * * * The word *liberty*, too, implies the same thing. It imports, *ex vi termini*, that it is a *privilege* to be exercised over another man's estates"); *Wickham v. Hawkes* (1840), 7 M. & W., 63, 78–79; *Quinn v. Leathem* (1901), A. C. 495, 534 (per Lord Lindley: see quotation *aent*, p.); *Pollock v. Farmers' Loan & Trust Co.* (1895), 157 U. S., 429, 652 (per White, J., "rights and liberties"); *Mathews v. People* (1903), 202 Ill., 389, 401 (Magruder, C. J.: "It is now well settled that the privilege of contracting is both a liberty, and a property right.").

For *legislative* use of the term in question, see the Copyright Act, 8 Anne (1709) c. 19 ("Shall have the sole right and liberty of printing each book and books for the term of * * *").

Like the word "privilege" (see *ante* p. 38, n. 48), the term "liberty" is occasionally used, especially in the older books, to indicate a franchise, or complex of special rights, privileges, powers, or immunities. Thus in Noy's Maxims (1641) there is this definition: "Liberty is a royal privilege in the hands of a subject;" and, similarly, Blackstone (2 Com. 37) says: "Franchise and liberty are used as synonymous terms; and their definition is, a royal privilege, or branch of the king's prerogative, subsisting in the hands of a subject."

This definition is quoted in *S. F. Waterworks v. Schottler* (1882), 62 Cal. 69, 106, and *Central R. & Banking Co. v. State* (1875), 54 Ga., 401, 409. Compare also *Rex v. Halifax & Co.* (1891), 2 Q. B., 263.

[61] Compare *Pond v. Bates,* 34 L. J. (N. S.), 406 ("With full power and free liberty to sink for, win and work the same, with all liberties, privileges, etc., necessary and convenient," etc.); *Hamilton v. Graham* (1871), L. R. 2 H. L. (Sc.), 166, 167; *Attersoll v. Stevens* (1808), 1 Taunt., 183; *Wickham v. Hawker* (1840), 7 M. & W., 63, 78–79.

advantage of giving us, as a variable, the adjective "privileged." Thus, it is frequently convenient to speak of a privileged act, a privileged transaction, a privileged conveyance, etc.

The term "license," sometimes used as if it were synonymous with "privilege," is not strictly appropriate. This is simply another of those innumerable cases in which the mental and physical facts are so frequently confused with the legal relation which they create. Accurately used, "license" is a generic term to indicate a group of *operative* facts required to create a particular privilege,—this being especially evident when the word is used in the common phrase "leave and license." This point is brought out by a passage from Mr. Justice Adams' opinion in *Clifford v. O'Neill*:[62]

"A license is merely a *permission* to do an act which, *without such permission,* would amount to a trespass * * * nor will the continuous enjoyment of the privilege *conferred,* for any period of time cause it to ripen into a tangible interest in the land affected."[63]

Powers and Liabilities. As indicated in the preliminary scheme of jural relations, a legal power (as distinguished, of course, from a mental or physical power) is the opposite of legal disability, and the correlative of legal liability. But what is the intrinsic nature of a legal power as such? Is it possible to analyze the conception represented by this constantly employed and very important term of legal discourse? Too close an analysis might seem metaphysical rather than useful; so that what is here presented is intended only as an approximate explanation sufficient for all practical purposes.

A change in a given legal relation may result (1) from some superadded fact or group of facts not under the volitional control of a human being (or human beings); or (2) from some superadded fact or group of facts which are under the volitional control of one or more human beings. As regards the second class of cases, the person (or persons) whose volitional control is paramount may be said to have the (legal) power to effect the particular change of legal relations that is involved in the problem.

The second class of cases—powers in the technical sense—must now be further considered. The nearest synonym for any ordinary case seems to be (legal) "ability,"[64]—the latter being obviously the opposite of "inability," or "disability." The term "right," so frequently and loosely used in the present connection, is an unfortunate term for the purpose,—a not unusual result being confusion of thought as well as ambiguity of expression.[65] The term "capacity" is equally unfortunate; for,

---

[62] (1896) 12 App. Div., 17; 42 N. Y. Sup., 607, 609.

[63] See, in accord, the oft-quoted passage from *Thomas v. Sorrell* (1673), Vaughan, 331, 351 ("A dispensation or license properly passes no interest, nor alters or transfers property in anything, but only makes an action lawful, which without it had been unlawful. As a license to go beyond the seas, to hunt in a man's park, to come into his house, are only actions, which without license, had been unlawful.").

Compare also *Taylor v. Waters* (1817), 7 Taunt., 374, 384 ("Those cases abundantly prove that a license to enjoy a beneficial privilege in land may be granted, and, notwithstanding the statue of frauds, without writing." In this case the license (operative facts) is more or less confused with privileges (the legal relation created); *Heap v. Hartley* (1889), 42 Ch. D., 461, 470.

[64] Compare *Remington v. Parkins* (1873), 10 R. I., 550, 553, per Durfee, J.: "A power is an ability to do."

[65] See *People v. Dikeman* (1852), 7 Howard Pr., 124, 130; and *Lonas v. State* (1871), 3 Heisk. (Tenn.), 287, 306–307.

See also *Mabre v. Whittaker* (1906), 10 Wash., 656, 663 (Washington Laws of 1871 provided in relation to community property: "The husband shall have the management of all the common property, but shall not have the *right* to sell or encumber real estate except he shall be joined in the sale or encumbrance by the wife. * * *" Per Scott, J.: "'Right' in the sense used there means power").

as we have already seen, when used with discrimination, this word denotes a particular group of operative facts, and not a legal relation of any kind.

Many examples of legal powers may readily be given. Thus, X, the owner of ordinary personal property "in a tangible object" has the power to extinguish his own legal interest (rights, powers, immunities, etc.) through that totality of operative facts known as abandonment; and—simultaneously and correlatively— to create in other persons privileges and powers relating to the abandoned object,—e.g., the power to acquire title to the later by appropriating it.[66] Similarly, X has the power to transfer his interest to Y,—that is, to extinguish his own interest and concomitantly create in Y a new and corresponding interest.[67] So also X has the power to create contractual obligations of various kinds. Agency cases are likewise instructive. By the use of some *metaphorical* expression such as the Latin, *qui facit per alium, facit per se,* the true nature of agency relations is only too frequently obscured. The creation of an agency relation involves, *inter alia,* the grant of legal powers to the so-called agent, and the creation of correlative liabilities in the principal.[68] That is to say, one party P has the power to create agency powers in another party A,—for example, the power to convey X's property, the power to impose (so-called) contractual obligations on P, the power to discharge a debt, owing to P, the power to "receive" title to property so that it shall vest in P, and so forth. In passing, it may be well to observe that the term "authority," so frequently used in agency cases, is very ambiguous and slippery in its connotation. Properly employed in the present connection, the word seems to be an abstract or qualitative term corresponding to the concrete "authorization,"—the latter consisting of a particular group of operative facts taking place between the principal and the agent. All too often, however, the term in question is so used as to blend and confuse these operative facts with the powers and privileges thereby created in the agent.[69] A careful discrimination

Compare also *St. Joseph Fire & Marine Ins. Co. v. Hanck* (1876), 63 Mo., 112. 118.

Numberless additional instances might be given of the use of the term "right," where the legal quantity involved is really a power rather than a right in the sense of claim.

[66] It is to be noted that abandonment would leave X himself with precisely the same sort of privileges and powers as any other person.

[67] Compare *Wynehamer v. People* (1856), 13 N. Y., 378, 396 (Comstock, J.: "I can form no notion of property which does not include the essential characteristics and attributes with which it is clothed by the laws of society * * * among which are, fundamentally the right of the occupant or owner to use and enjoy (the objects) exclusively, and his *absolute power to sell and dispose of them*"); *Bartemeyer v. Iowa* (1873), 18 Wall., 129, 137 (Field, J.: "The right of property in an article involves the *power to sell and dispose* of such articles as well as to use and enjoy it"); *Low v. Rees Printing Co.* (1894), 41 Neb., 127, 146 (Ryan, C.: "Property, in its broad sense, is not the physical thing which may be the subject of ownership, but is the right of dominion, possession, and *power of disposition* which may be acquired over it.").

Since the power of alienation is frequently one of the fundamental elements of a complex legal interest (or property aggregate), it is obvious that a statute extinguishing such power may, in a given case be unconstitutional as depriving the owner of property without due process of law. See the cases just cited.

[68] For a leading case exhibiting the nature of agency powers, especially powers "coupled with an interest," see *Hunt v. Rousmanier* (1883), 8 Wheat., 173, 201.

It is interesting to note that in the German Civil Code the provisions relating to agency are expressed in terms of powers,—e.g., sec. 168: "The expiration of the power is determined by the legal relations upon which the giving of the power is founded. The power is also revocable in the event of the continuance of the legal relation, unless something different results from the latter."

Incidentally, it may be noticed also, that as a matter of English usage, the term "power of attorney" has, by association of ideas, come to be used to designate the mere operative *instrument* creating the powers of an agent.

[69] For examples of the loose and confusing employment of the term "authority" in agency cases,—and that too, in problems of the conflict of laws requiring the closest reason,—see *Pope v. Nickerson* (1844), 3 Story, 465, 473, 476, 481, 483; *Lloyd v. Guibert* (1865), 6 B. & S., 100, 117; *King v. Sarria* (1877), 69 N. Y., 24, 28, 30–32; *Risdon, etc., Works v. Furness* (1905), 1 K. B. 304; (1906) 1 K. B. 49.

in these particulars would, it is submitted, go far toward clearing up certain problems in the law of agency.[70]

Essentially similar to the powers of agents are powers of appointment in relation to property interests. So, too, the powers of public officers are, intrinsically considered, comparable to those of agents,—for example, the power of a sheriff to sell property under a writ of execution. The power of a donor, in a gift *causa mortis,* to revoke the gift and divest the title of the donee is another clear example of the legal quantities now being considered;[71] also a pledgee's statutory power of sale.[72]

There are, on the other hand, cases where the true nature of the relations involved has not, perhaps, been so clearly recognized. Thus, in the case of a conditional sale of personality, assuming the vendee's agreement has been fully performed except as to the payment of the last installment and the time for the latter has arrived, what is the interest of such vendee as regards the property? Has he, as so often assumed, merely a contractual *right* to have title passed to him by consent of the vendor, on final payment being made; or has he, irrespective of the consent of the vendor the power to divest the title of the latter and to acquire a perfect title for himself? Though the language of the cases is not always so clear as it might be, the vendee seems to have precisely that sort of power.[73] Fundamentally considered, the typical escrow transaction in which the performance of conditions is within the volitional control of the grantee, is somewhat similar to the conditional sale of personalty; and, when reduced to its lowest terms, the problem seems easily to be solved in terms of legal powers. Once the "escrow" is formed, the grantor still has the legal title; but the grantee has an irrevocable power to divest that title by

---

For a criticism of these cases in relation to the present matter, see the writer's article The Individual Liability of Stockholders and the Conflict of Laws (1909). 9 Columb. L. Rev., 492, 512, n. 46, 521, n. 71; 10 Columb. L. Rev., 542–544.

[70] The clear understanding and recognition of the agency relation as involving the creation of legal powers may be of crucial importance in many cases,—especially, as already intimated, in regard to problems in the conflict of laws. Besides the cases in the preceding note, two others may be referred to, *Milliken v. Pratt* (1878), 125 Mass., 374, presenting no analysis of the agency problem; and, on the other hand, Freeman's Appeal (1897), 68 Conn., 533, involving a careful analysis of the agency relation by Baldwin, J. Led by this analysis to reach a decision essentially opposite to that of the Massachusetts case, the learned judge said, *inter alia*:

"Such was, in effect, the act by which Mrs. Mitchell undertook to do what she had no legal capacity to do, by making her husband her agent to deliver the guaranty to the bank. He had no more power to make it operative by delivery in Chicago to one of his creditors in Illinois, than he would have had to make it operative by delivery here, had it been drawn in favor of one of his creditors in Connecticut. It is not the place of delivery that controls, but the power of delivery."

[71] See *Emery v. Clough* (1885), 63 N. H., 552 ("right or power of defeasance").

[72] See *Hudgens v. Chamberlain* (1911), 161 Cal., 710, 713, 715. For another instance of statutory powers, see *Capital, etc., Bk. v. Rhodes* (1903), 1 Ch. 631, 655 (powers under registry acts.).

[73] Though the nebulous term "rights" is used by the courts, it is evident that powers are the actual quantities involved.

Thus, in the instructive case of *Carpenter v. Scott* (1881), 13 R. I., 477, 479, the court said, by Matteson, J.: "Under it (the conditional sale) the vendee acquires not only the right of possession and use, but the right to become the absolute owner upon complying with the terms of the contract. These are rights of which no act of the vendor can divest him, and which, in the absence of any stipulation in the contract restraining him, he can transfer by sale or mortgage. Upon performance of the conditions of the sale, the title to the property vests in the vendee, or in the event that he has sold, or mortgaged it, in his vendee, or mortgagee, without further bill of sale. * * * These rights constitute an actual, present interest in the property, which, as we have seen above, is capable of transfer by sale or mortgage."

It is interesting to notice that in the foregoing passage, the term "right" is first used to indicate *privileges* of possession and use; next the term is employed primarily in the sense of legal power, though possibly there is a partial blending of this idea with that of legal claim, or right (in the narrowest connotation); then the term (in plural form) is used for the third time so as to lump together the vendee's privileges, powers and claims.

For another case indicating in substance the true nature of the vendee's interest, see *Christensen v. Nelson* (1901), 38 Or. 473. 477, 479, indicating, in effect, that the vendee's powers as well as privileges may be transferred to another, and that a proper tender constitutes "the equivalen [sic] of payment."

performance of certain conditions (*i.e.*, the addition of various operative facts), and concomitantly to vest title in himself. While such power is outstanding, the grantor is, of course, subject to a correlative liability to have his title divested.[74] Similarly, in the case of a conveyance of land in fee simple subject to condition subsequent, after the condition has been performed, the original grantor is commonly said to have a "*right* of entry." If, however, the problem is analyzed, it will be seen that, as of primary importance, the grantor has two legal quantities, (1) the privilege of entering, and (2) the power, by means of such entry, to divest the estate of the grantee.[75] The latter's estate endures, subject to the correlative liability of being divested, until such power is actually exercised.[76]

Passing now to the field of contracts, suppose A mails a letter to B offering to sell the former's land, Whiteacre, to the latter for ten thousand dollars, such letter being duly received. The operative facts thus far mentioned have created a power as regards B and a correlative liability as regards A. B, by dropping a letter of acceptance in the box, has the power to impose potential or inchoate[77] obligation *ex contractu* on A and himself; and, assuming that the land is worth fifteen thousand dollars, that particular legal quantity—the "power *plus* liability" relation between A and B—seems to be worth about five thousand dollars to B. The liability of A will continue for a reasonable time unless, in exercise of his power to do so, A previously extinguishes it by that series of operative facts known as "revocation." These last matters are usually described by saying that A's "offer" will "continue" or "remain open" for a reasonable time, or for the definite time actually specified, unless A previously "withdraws" or "revokes" such offer.[78] While no doubt, in the great majority of cases no harm results from the use of such expressions, yet these forms of statement seem to represent a blending of non-legal and legal quantities which, in any problem requiring careful reasoning, should preferably be kept distinct. An offer, considered as a series of physical and mental operative facts, has spent its force as soon as such series has been completed by the "offeree's receipt." The real question is therefore as to the *legal effect,* if any, at that moment of time. If the latter consist of B's power and A's correlative liability, manifestly it is those *legal relations* that "continue" or "remain open" until modified by revocation or other operative facts. What has thus far been said concerning contracts completed by mail would seem to apply, *mutatis mutandis,* to every type of contract. Even where the parties are in the

[74] See *Davis v. Clark* (1897), 58 Kan. 100; 48 Pac., 563, 565; *Leiter v. Pike* (1889), 127 Ill., 287, 326; *Welstur v. Trust Co.* (1895), 145 N. Y., 275, 283; *Furley v. Palmer* (1870), 20 Oh. St., 223, 225.

The proposition that the grantee's power is irrevocable is subject to the qualification that it might possibly be extinguished (or modified *pro tanto*) as the result of a transaction between the grantor and one having the position of *bona fide purchaser,* or the equivalent.

It is hardly necessary to add that the courts, instead of analyzing the problem of the escrow in terms of powers, as here indicated, are accustomed to stating the question and deciding it in terms of "delivery," "relation back," "performance of conditions," etc.

[75] In this connection it is worthy of note that Sugden, in his work on Powers (8th ed., 1861) 4, uses, contrary to general practice, the expression, "*power* of entry for condition broken."

[76] For miscellaneous instances of powers, see the good opinions in *Bk. of S. Australia v. Abrahams,* L. R. P. C., 265; *Barlow v. Ross* (1890), 24 Q. B. D., 381, 384.

[77] As to "inchoate" obligations, see *Frost v. Knight* (1872) L. R. 7 Ex. 111, per Cockburn, C. J. This matter will receive further attention in a later part of the discussion.

[78] Compare *Boston R. Co. v. Bartlett* (1849), 3 Cush., 225: "Though the writing signed by the defendant was but an offer, and an offer which might be revoked, yet while it remained in force and unrevoked, it was a continuing offer, during the time limited for acceptance, and during the whole of the rest of the time it was an offer every instant; but as soon as it was accepted, it ceased to be an offer merely."

Compare also the forms of statement in Ashley, Contr. (1911), 16 *et. seq.*

presence of each other, the offer creates a liability against the offerer, together with a correlative power in favor of the offeree. The only distinction for present purposes would be in the fact that such power and such liability would expire within a very short period of time.

Perhaps the practical justification for this method of analysis is somewhat greater in relation to the subject of options. In his able work on Contacts,[79] Langdell says:

"If the offerer stipulates that his offer shall remain open for a specified time, the first question is whether such stipulation constitutes a binding contract. * * * When such a stipulation is binding, the further question arises, whether it makes the offer irrevocable. It has been a common opinion that it does, but that is clearly a mistake. * * * An offer is merely one of the elements of a contract; and it is indispensable to the making of a contract that the wills of the contracting parties do, in legal contemplation, concur at the moment of making it. An offer, therefore, which the party making it has no power to revoke, is a legal impossibility. Moreover, if the stipulation should make the offer irrevocable, it would be a contract incapable of being broken; which is also a legal impossibility. The only effect, therefore, of such a stipulation is to give the offeree a claim for damages if the stipulation be broken by revoking the offer."[80]

The foregoing reasoning ignores the fact that an ordinary offer *ipso facto* creates a legal relation—a legal power and a legal liability,—and that it is this relation (rather than the physical and mental facts constituting the offer) that "remains open." If these points be conceded, there seems no difficulty in recognizing an unilateral option agreement supported by consideration or embodied in a sealed instrument as creating in the optionee an irrevocable power to create, at any time within the period specified, a bilateral obligation as between himself and the giver of the option. Correlatively to that power, there would, of course, be a liability against the option-giver which he himself would have no power to extinguish. The courts seem to have no difficulty in reaching precisely this result as a matter of substance; though their explanations are always in terms of "withdrawal of offer," and similar expressions savoring of physical and mental quantities.[81]

In connection with the powers and liabilities created respectively by an ordinary offer and by an option, it is interesting to consider the liabilities of a person engaged in a "public calling"; for, as it seems, such a party's characteristic position is, one might almost say, intermediate between that of an ordinary contractual offerer and that of an option-giver. It has indeed been usual to assert that such a party is (generally speaking) under a present *duty* to all other parties; but

Wesley Hohfeld

[79] Langdell, Sum. Contr. (2nd ed., 1880), sec. 178.

[80] Langdell's *a priori* premises and specific conclusions have been adopted by a number of other writers on the subject. See, for example, Ashley, Contr. (1911), 25 *et seq.,* R. L. McWilliams, Enforcement of Option Agreements (1913), 1 Calif. Law Rev., 122.

[81] For a recent judicial expression on the subject, see *W. G. Reese Co. v. House* (1912), 162 Cal., 740, 745 per Sloss J.: "Where there is a consideration, the option cannot be withdrawn during the time agreed upon for its duration, while, if there be no consideration the party who has given the option may revoke it at any time before acceptance, even though the time limited has not expired * * * such offer, duly accepted, constitutes a contract binding upon both parties and enforceable by either."

See, to the same effect, *Linn v. McLean* (1885), 80 Ala., 360, 364; *O'Brien v. Boland* (1896), 166 Mass., 481, 483 (sealed offer).

Most of the cases recognizing the irrevocable power of the optionee have arisen in equitable suits for specific performance; but there seems to be no reason for doubting that the same doctrine should be applied in a common law action for damages. See, in accord, *Baker v. Shaw* (1912), 68 Wash., 99 103 (*dicta* in an action for damages).

this is believed to be erroneous. Thus, Professor Wyman, in his work on Public Service Companies,[82] says:

"The duty placed upon every one exercising a public calling is primarily a duty to serve every man who is a member of the public. * * * It is somewhat difficult to place this exceptional duty in our legal system. * * * The truth of the matter is that the obligation resting upon one who has undertaken the performance of public duty is *sui generis*."[83]

It is submitted that the learned writer's difficulties arise primarily from a failure to see that the innkeeper, the common carrier and others similarly "holding out" are under present *liabilities* rather than present *duties*. Correlatively to those liabilities are the respective powers of the various members of the public. Thus, for example, a travelling member of the public has the legal power, by making proper application and sufficient tender, to impose a duty on the innkeeper to receive him as a guest. For breach of the duty *thus* created an action would of course lie. It would therefore seem that the innkeeper is, to some extent, like one who had given an option to every travelling member of the public. He differs, as regards net legal effect, only because he can extinguish his present liabilities and the correlative powers of the travelling members of the public *by going out of business*. Yet, on the other hand, his liabilities are more onerous than that of an ordinary contractual offerer, for he cannot extinguish his liabilities by any simple performance akin to revocation of offer.

As regards all the "legal powers" thus far considered, possibly some caution is necessary. If, for example, we consider the ordinary property owner's power of alienation, it is necessary to distinguish carefully between the *legal* power, the *physical* power to do the things necessary for the "exercise" of the legal power, and, finally, the *privilege* of doing these things—that is, if such privilege does really exist. It may or may not. Thus, if X, a landowner, has contracted with Y that the former will not alienate to Z, the acts of X necessary to exercise the power of alienating to Z are privileged as between X and every party other than Y; but, obviously, as between X and Y, the former has no privilege of doing the necessary acts; or conversely, he is under a duty to Y not to do what is necessary to exercise the power.

In view of what has already been said, very little may suffice concerning a *liability* as such. The latter, as we have seen, is the correlative of power, and the opposite of immunity (or exemption). While no doubt the term "liability" is often loosely used as a synonym for "duty," or "obligation," it is believed, from an extensive survey of judicial precedents, that the connotation already adopted as most appropriate to the word in question is fully justified. A few cases tending to indicate this will now be noticed. In *McNeer v. McNeer*,[84] Mr. Justice Magruder balanced the conceptions of power and liability as follows:

"So long as she lived, however, his interest in her land lacked those *elements of property*, such as *power of disposition* and *liability to sale on* execution which had formerly given it the character of a vested estate."

In *Booth v. Commonwealth*,[85] the court had to construe a Virginia statute providing "that all free white male persons who are twenty-one years of age and not over sixty, shall be *liable* to serve as jurors, except as hereinafter provided." It is plain that this enactment imposed only a *liability* and not a *duty*. It is a liability

---

[82] Secs. 330–333.
[83] Compare, to the same effect, Keener, Quasi-Contr. (1893), p. 18.
[84] (1892) 142 Ill., 388, 397.
[85] (1861) 16 Grat., 519, 525.

to have a duty created. The latter would arise only when, in exercise of their powers, the parties litigant and the court officers, had done what was necessary to impose a specific duty to perform the functions of a juror. The language of the court, by Moncure, J., is particularly apposite as indicating that liability is the opposite, or negative, of immunity (or exemption):

"The word both expressed and implied is 'liable,' which has a very different meaning from 'qualified' * * *. Its meaning is 'bound' or 'obliged' * * *. A person exempt from serving on juries is not liable to serve, and a person not liable to serve is exempt from serving. The terms seem to be convertible."

A further good example of judicial usage is to be found in *Emery v. Clough*.[86] Referring to a gift *causa mortis* and the donee's liability to have his already vested interest divested by the donor's exercise of his power of revocation, Mr. Justice Smith said:

"The title to the gift *causa mortis* passed by the delivery, defeasible only in the lifetime of the donor, and his death perfects the title in the donee by terminating the donor's right or *power of defeasance*. The property passes from the donor to the donee directly * * * and after his death it is *liable* to be divested only in favor of the donor's creditors. * * * His right and power ceased with his death."

Perhaps the nearest synonym of "liability" is "subjection" or "responsibility." As regards the latter word, a passage from Mr. Justice Day's opinion in *McElfresh v. Kirkendall*[87] is interesting:

"The words 'debt' and 'liability' are not synonymous, and they are not commonly so understood. As applied to the pecuniary relations of the parties, liability is a term of broader significance than debt. * * * Liability is responsibility."

While the term in question has the broad generic connotation already indicated, no doubt it very frequently indicates that specific form of liability (or complex of liabilities) that is correlative to a power (or complex of powers)[88] vested in a party litigant and the various court officers. Such was held to be the meaning of a certain California statute involved in the case of *Lattin v. Gillette*.[89] Said Mr. Justice Harrison:

"The word 'liability' is the condition in which an individual is placed after a breach of his contract, or a violation of any obligation resting upon him. It is defined by Bouvier to be responsibility."[90]

Immunities and Disabilities. As already brought out, immunity is the correlative of disability ("no-power"), and the opposite, or negation, of liability. Perhaps it will also be plain, from the preliminary outline and from the discussion down to

[86] (1885) 63 N. H., 552.

[87] (1873) 36 Ia., 224, 226.

[88] Compare *Attorney General v. Sudeley* (1896), 1 Q. B., 354, 359 (per Lord Esher: "What is called a 'right of action' is not the *power* of bringing an action. Anybody can bring an action though he has no right at all."); *Kroessin v. Keller* (1895), 60 Minn., 372 (per Collins, J.: "The power to bring such actions").

[89] (1892) 95 Cal., 317, 319.

[90] We are apt to think of liability as exclusively an onerous relation of one party to another. But, in its broad technical significance, this is not necessarily so. Thus X, the owner of a watch, has the power to abandon his property—that is, to extinguish his existing rights, powers, and immunities relating thereto (not, however, his privileges, for until someone else has acquired title to the abandoned watch, X would have the same privileges as before); and correlatively to X's power of abandonment there is a liability in every other person. But such a liability instead of being onerous or unwelcome, is quite the opposite. As regards another person M, for example, it is a *liability to have created in his favor (though against his will) a privilege and a power* relating to the watch,—that is, the privilege of taking possession and the power, by doing so, to vest a title in himself. See *Dougherty v. Creary* (1866), 30 Cal., 290, 298. Contrast with this agreeable form of liability the *liability to have a duty created*—for example the liability of one who has made or given an option in a case where the value of the property has greatly risen.

this point, that a power bears the same general contrast to an immunity that a right does to a privilege. A right is one's affirmative claim against another, and a privilege is one's freedom from the right or claim of another. Similarly, a power is one's affirmative "control" over a given legal relation as against another; whereas an immunity is one's freedom from the legal power or "control" of another as regards some legal relation.

A few examples may serve to make this clear. X, a land-owner, has, as we have seen, power to alienate to Y or to any other ordinary party. On the other hand, X has also various immunities as against Y, and all other ordinary parties. For Y is under a disability (*i.e.*, has no power) so far as shifting the legal interest either to himself or to a third party is concerned; and what is true of Y applies similarly to every one else who has not by virtue of special operative facts acquired a power to alienate X's property. If, indeed, a sheriff has been duly empowered by a writ of execution to sell X's interest, that is a very different matter: correlative to such sheriff's power would be the *liability* of X,—the very opposite of immunity (or exemption). It is elementary, too, that as against the sheriff, X might be immune or exempt in relation to certain parcels of property, and be liable as to others. Similarly, if an agent has been duly appointed by X to sell a given piece of property, then, as to the latter, X has, in relation to such agent, a liability rather than an immunity.

For over a century there has been, in this country, a great deal of important litigation involving immunities from powers of taxation. If there be any lingering misgivings as to the "practical" importance of accuracy and discrimination in legal conceptions and legal terms, perhaps some of such doubts would be dispelled by considering the numerous cases on valuable taxation exemptions coming before the United States Supreme Court. Thus, in *Phoenix Ins. Co. v. Tennessee*,[91] Mr. Justice Peckham expressed the views of the court as follows:

"In granting to the De Sota Company 'all the rights, privileges, and immunities' of the Bluff City Company, all words are used which could be regarded as necessary to carry the exemption from taxation possessed by the Bluff City Company; while in the next following grant, that of the charter of the plaintiff in error, the word 'immunity' is omitted. Is there any meaning to be attached to that omission, and if so, what? We think some meaning is to be attached to it. The word 'immunity' expresses more clearly and definitely an intention to include therein an exemption from taxation than does either of the other words. Exemption from taxation is more accurately described as an 'immunity' than as a privilege, although it is not to be denied that the latter word may sometimes and under some circumstances include such exemptions."

In *Morgan v. Louisiana*,[92] there is an instructive discussion from the pen of Mr. Justice Field. In holding that on a foreclosure sale of the franchise and property of a railroad corporation an immunity from taxation did not pass to the purchaser, the learned Judge said:

"As has been often said by this court, the whole community is interested in retaining the power of taxation undiminished * * *. The exemption of the property of the company from taxation, and the exemption of its officers and servants from jury and military duty, were both intended for the benefit of the company, and its benefit alone. In their personal character they are analogous to

---

[91] (1895) 161 U. S., 174, 177.
[92] (1876) 93 U. S., 217, 222.

exemptions from execution of certain property of debtors, made by laws of several of the states."[93]

So far as immunities are concerned, the two judicial discussions last quoted concern respectively problems of interpretation and problems of alienability. In many other cases difficult constitutional questions have arisen as the result of statutes impairing or extending various kinds of immunities. Litigants have, from time to time, had occasion to appeal both to the clause against impairment of the obligation of contracts and to the provision against depriving a person of property without due process of law. This has been especially true as regards exemptions from taxation[94] and exemptions from execution.[95]

If a word may now be permitted with respect to mere terms as such, the first thing to note is that the word "right" is over-worked in the field of immunities as elsewhere.[96] As indicated, however, by the judicial expressions already quoted, the best synonym is, of course, the term "exemption."[97] It is instructive to note, also, that the word "impunity" has a very similar connotation. This is made evident by the interesting discriminations of Lord Chancellor Finch in *Skelton v. Skelton*,[98] a case decided in 1677:

"But this I would by no means allow, that equity should enlarge the restraints of the disabilities introduced by act of parliament; and as to the granting of injunctions to stay waste, I took a distinction where the tenant hath only *impunitatem*, and where he hath *jus in arboribus*. If the tenant have only a bare indemnity or

[93] See, in accord, *Picard v. Tennessee, etc., R. Co.* (1888), 130 U. S., 637, 642, (Field, J.); *Rochester Railway Co. v. Rochester* (1906) 205 U. S., 236, 252 (Moody, J., reviewing the many other cases on the subject).

In *Internat. & G. N. Ry. Co. v. State* (1899), 75 Tex., 356, a different view was taken as to the *alienability* of an immunity from taxation. Speaking by Stayton, C. J., the court said:

"Looking at the provisions of the Act of March 10, 1875, we think there can be no doubt the exemption from taxation given by it, instead of being a right vesting only in appellant, is a right which inheres in the property to which it applies, and follows it into the hands of whosoever becomes the owner. * * * The existence of this right enhances the value of the property to which it applies. Shareholders and creditors must be presumed to have dealt with the corporation on the faith of the contract which gave the exemption, and it cannot be taken away by legislation, by dissolution of the corporation, or in any other manner not sufficient to pass title to any other property from one person to another. The right to exemption from taxation is secured by the same guaranty which secures titles to those owning lands granted under the act, and though the corporation may be dissolved, will continue to exist in favor of persons owning the property to which the immunity applies. Lawful dissolution of a corporation will destroy all its corporate franchises or privileges vested by the act of incorporation; but if it holds rights, privileges, and franchises in the nature of property, secured by contract based on valuable consideration, these will survive the dissolution of the corporation, for the benefit of those who may have a right to or just claim upon its assets."

Compare, as regard homestead exemptions, Sloss, J., in *Smith v. Bougham* (1909), 156 Cal., 359, 365: "A declaration of homestead * * * attaches certain privileges and immunities to such title as may at the time be held."

[94] See *Choate v. Trapp* (1912), 224 U. S., 665.

[95] See *Brearly School, Limited v. Ward* (1911), 201 N. Y., 358; 94 N. E., 1001 (an interesting decision, with three judges dissenting). The other cases on the subject are collected in Ann. Cas., 1912 B, 259.

[96] See *Brearly School, Limited v. Ward,* cited in preceding note; also *Internat. & G. N. Ry. Co. v. State* (1899), 75 Tex., 356, quoted from, *ante,* n. 91.

[97] Compare also *Wilson v. Gaines* (1877), 9 Baxt. (Tenn.), 546, 550–551, Turney, J.: "The use in the statutes of two only of the words of the constitution, *i.e.,* 'rights' and 'privileges,' and the omission to employ either of the other two following in immediate succession, viz., 'immunities' and 'exemptions,' either of which would have made clear the construction claimed by complainant, evidence a purposed intention on the part of the legislature not to grant the benefit claimed by the bill.

Only very rarely is a court found seeking to draw a subtle distinction between an immunity and an exemption. Thus, in a recent case, *Strahan v. Wayne Co.* (June, 1913), 142 N. W., 678, 680 (Neb.), Mr. Justice Barnes said: "It has been held by the great weight of authority that dower is not immune (from the inheritance tax) because it is dower, but because it * * * belonged to her unchoately during (the husband's) life. * * * Strictly speaking, the widow's share should be considered as immune, rather than exempt, from an inheritance tax. It is free, rather than freed, from such tax."

[98] (1677) 2 Swanst., 170.

exemption from an action (at law), if he committed waste, there it is fit he should be restrained by injunction from committing it."[99]

In the latter part of the preceding discussion, eight conceptions of the law have been analyzed and compared in some detail, the purpose having been to exhibit not only their intrinsic meaning and scope, but also their relations to one another and the methods by which they are applied, in judicial reasoning, to the solution of concrete problems of litigation. Before concluding this branch of the discussion a general suggestion may be ventured as to the great practical importance of a clear appreciation of the distinctions and discriminations set forth. If a homely metaphor be permitted, these eight conceptions,—rights and duties, privileges and no-rights, powers and liabilities, immunities and disabilities,—seem to be what may be called "the lowest common denominators of the law." Ten fractions (1-3, 2-5, etc.) may, *superficially*, seem so different from one another as to defy comparison. If, however, they are expressed in terms of their lowest common denominators (5-15, 6-15, etc.), comparison becomes easy, and fundamental similarity may be discovered. The same thing is of course true as regards the lowest generic conceptions to which any and all "legal quantities" may be reduced.

Reverting, for example, to the subject powers, it might be difficult at first glance to discover any essential and fundamental similarity between conditional sales of personalty, escrow transactions, option agreements, agency relations, powers of appointment, etc. But if all these relations are reduced to their lowest generic terms, the conceptions of legal power and legal liability are seen to be dominantly, though not exclusively, applicable throughout the series. By such a process it becomes possible not only to discover essential similarities and illuminating analogies in the midst of what appears superficially to be infinite and hopeless variety, but also to discern common principles of justice and policy underlying the various jural problems involved. An indirect, yet very practical, consequence is that it frequently becomes feasible, by virtue of such analysis, to use as persuasive authorities judicial precedents that might otherwise seem altogether irrelevant. If this point be valid with respect to powers, it would seem to be equally so as regards all of the other basic conceptions of the law. In short, the deeper the analysis, the great become one's perception of fundamental unity and harmony in the law.[100]

WESLEY NEWCOMB HOHFELD
Stanford University, California

---

[99] In *Skelton v. Skelton,* it will be observed, the word "*impunity*" and the word "*exemption*" are used as the opposite of *liability* to the powers of a plaintiff in an action at law.

For similar recent instances, see *Vacher & Sons, Limited v. London Society of Compositors* (1913), A. C. 107, 118, 125 (per Lord Macnaghten: "Now there is nothing absurd in the notion of an association or body enjoying immunity from actions at law;" per Lord Atkinson: "Conferring on the trustees immunity as absolute," etc.).

Compare also *Baylies v. Bishop of London* (1913), 1 Ch., 127, 139, 140, per Hamilton, L. J.

For instances of the apt use of the term "disability" as equivalent to the negation of legal power, see *Poury v. Hordern* (1900), 1 Ch., 492, 495; *Sheridan v. Elden* (1862), 24 N. Y., 281, 384.

[100] The next article in the present series will discuss the distinctions between legal and equitable jural relations; also the contrast between rights, etc., *in rem*, and rights, etc., *in personam*. The supposed distinctions between substantive and adjective jural relations will also be considered,—chiefly with the purpose of showing that, so far as the intrinsic and essential nature of those relations is concerned, the distinctions commonly assumed to exist are imaginary rather than real. Finally, some attention will be given to the nature and analysis of complex legal interests, or aggregates of jural relations.

Robert Hale

Robert Hale

We all know now, though the thought was once generally considered
a heresy, that courts legislate in the process of developing the common law.[1]

HOLMES set the tone for much twentieth-century American legal thought by
focusing attention on the pragmatic consequences of judicial decisions and the
"considerations of social advantage" that would—and should—animate legal
decision making. Robert Hale provides a first analytic framework for distinguishing good and bad legal arguments about these social consequences. Hale's
approach to policy argument rests on Hohfeld's approach to legal doctrine.
Hohfeld's system of jural correlatives foregrounded the inescapable choices that
arose from the limits of deduction as a tool for interpreting legal entitlements.
If you decide to protect a property interest by giving the owner a right, you
will have placed someone else under a correlative duty. Should you decline to
do so, you will have granted the neighbor a privilege to injure the owner, who
will have no right to recompense. Both arrangements, Hohfeld recognized, are
compatible with ownership—neither can be deduced from the "nature" of property. As faith in the deductive analytics of classical legal thought eroded, it
became evident, in light of Hohfeld's analysis, that judges were making policy—
choosing among alternative legal arrangements that would benefit different
groups in society—as they interpreted the law, whether Constitution, statute, or
common-law precedent.

But if judges were to make policy, how should they do so—how should they
reason about policy choices? A great deal of twentieth-century American legal
thought, and a great deal of the first year of law school, is concerned with developing and criticizing the reasoning tools used by jurists to analyze policy questions. On the one hand, "thinking like a lawyer" requires mastery of a vernacular
for doctrinal analysis rooted in Hohfeld's correlative pairs that is sensitive to the
limits of deduction and versatile in criticizing arguments whose deductive chains
seem to be overly long. Thinking like a lawyer in twentieth-century America is also
to share a set of standard arguments for proposing and criticizing the policy
choices that inform or justify legal decisions about doctrinal alternatives. It is these
"policy arguments" that give American legal thought its interdisciplinary feel, for
they often borrow ideas from economics, sociology, psychology, and other neighboring disciplines.

Nineteenth-century jurists had also argued in general terms, and had developed broad principled justifications for the choices judges made, often rooted in general ideas about the virtues of American society, American politics, and American economic life. Before the civil war, these arguments combined diverse moral and practical considerations. During the late nineteenth-century heyday of classical legal thought, the range of arguments had narrowed considerably as faith in formal deduction had grown. Policy argument, if we can call it that, often took the form of deduction from very broad principles—freedom, liberty, autonomy—or from what were regarded as the absolute powers of various actors, particularly from the police power of the state. Judicial reasoning presented itself as the straightforward consequence of respecting these principles and powers, rather than as the working out of analytic choices among *alternative* modes of respecting "liberty" or "property" or "plenary power."

In the same way that the breakup of nineteenth-century doctrinal legal reasoning opened the door to a series of doctrinal choices—rights or privileges?—the emergence of a twentieth-century policy vernacular to inform these choices was only possible after the erosion of the principled certainty of nineteenth-century justificatory argument. This required both criticism of what came to seem naive nineteenth-century justificatory arguments, and the development of new tools to make choices among competing principles and social objectives. Standing between nineteenth-century deductive certainty and a cacophony of twentieth-century policy arguments, Robert Hale plays the role for policy that Wesley Hohfeld played for doctrine.

Robert Hale was born in 1884, attended private school in New York and Connecticut, and spent the 1901–02 academic year at the Neues Gymnasium in Brunswick, Germany before entering Harvard College. At Harvard, he majored in economics, and worked as an assistant to Frank Taussig. Although more conservative and a more orthodox economist than Hale, Taussig imparted an interest in the role of power hierarchies—including monopolies—in market-based economic arrangements, and focused Hale's attention on the role of the state in the distribution of wealth. Hale received his AB and LLB from Harvard, and worked for a year with the Chicago firm of Rosenthal and Hammill and then as a legal clerk with AT&T in New York before returning to the study of economics at Columbia. He received his PhD in 1918 with a dissertation on the public regulation of utilities. He immediately began teaching in the Columbia economics department. In 1919, Columbia law school dean Harlan Fiske Stone asked Hale to offer courses in the law faculty, where Hale received a joint appointment in 1922. He transferred full time to the Columbia law faculty in 1928, where he taught until his retirement in 1949, and with which he was associated as a Professor Emeritus until his death in 1969.

Hale's teaching and scholarly work focused on the intersection between economics and law. He was well known as a specialist in the regulation of utilities, and wrote prodigiously about the appropriate—and inappropriate—methods through which judges and administrators should think about rate regulation. He wrote numerous articles criticizing judicial efforts to narrow the scope of the government's authority to regulate utilities, and was well known for his criticism of judicial formulations used in the oversight of utility regulators. At Columbia, Hale taught an influential general course on "Legal Factors in Economic Society" for many years that developed his overall legal and economic ideas. He also taught and wrote in the field of utilities regulation—a key testing ground for ideas about the appropriate role of government in economic management for the public good. He was perhaps most well known for his criticism of the "fair-return-on-fair-value" approach to utility price regulation propounded in *Symth v. Ames* (169 U.S. 466 (1898)) and for his attacks on the idea that the "utility" is a formally delimitable category of economic activity. In condensed form, his argument was that since "value" was itself a product of social struggle in a context structured by legal entitlements, to deduce those entitlements from the idea of "fair return on fair value" was to argue in a circle.

In political terms, Hale was influenced by the Progressive movement and supported an increasing government role in the nation's economic and social life to improve the conditions of life for citizens and to reduce income inequality. He would become a supporter of Roosevelt's New Deal, and has often been associated with democratic social reformers of the period, like John Dewey or Walter Lippmann. He seems to have been particularly influenced by the functionalist approach to property he found in the works of L.T. Hobhouse and Herbert Croly. Along with other progressives, Hale was interested in the use of price controls and taxation to finance a broad welfare state. He was particularly attracted to the idea that surplus or "scarcity rents" earned by some owners in well-functioning markets—which he in turn saw as the consequence of their legal entitlements—could provide the basis for redistributive policy.

Hale was never a public figure, but he associated himself, at least behind the scenes, with a number of activist causes while at Columbia. He joined a committee of lawyers and professors seeking to reverse the conviction of Sacco and Vanzetti, and corresponded avidly with Lawrence Lowell, head of a commission appointed to review the convictions, urging reversal. He assisted in the litigation of several early desegregation cases, and saw his expanded conception of state action as the basis for civil rights decisions such as *Shelley v. Kramer*. He was critical of union-busting and a strong advocate of the free speech rights of political radicals.

As an economist, Hale was an institutionalist, influenced by the work of Thorstein Veblen and John Commons, with whom he corresponded. He worked alongside John Maurice Clark, Walton Hamilton, and Rexford Tugwell, and shared with all these economists an aversion to the formal and deductive side of neoclassical economics and an interest in the role of institutions, social arrangements, and income distribution in the habits of markets. In law, Wesley Hohfeld's analysis of jural correlatives was a profound influence. Hale had also been influenced by Joseph Beale and Roscoe Pound; he credited Beale with the idea that the enforcement of contract and property rights might be thought of as "state action," in the sense that it required a delegation of public power to private hands. Hale was acquainted with a number of modernizing judicial figures of the period, including Justices Stone, Holmes, Cardozo, Brandeis, and Frankfurther.

Hale is usually seen as a legal realist, and he shared with the realists an appetite for functionalist modes of analysis, a skepticism about deductive and formal modes of reasoning, an appreciation for a disaggregated style of contextualized reasoning and for a more fluid understanding of the relationship between law and politics. Hale had been brought to Columbia by the legal realists Walter Wheeler Cook and Underhill Moore, who were enthusiastic about the potential for a scientific and economic approach to law. At Columbia, Hale was close to many leading legal realists, including Karl Llewellyn and Jerome Frank.

Hale's most significant contribution to American legal thought was his criticism of nineteenth-century modes for defending a laissez-faire separation of political and economic life that relied on a simple proposition that the government should govern by the pole star of promoting "liberty" or "freedom" and reducing "coercion."

These are the arguments for which his canonical 1923 article is remembered. Thomas Carver's 1921 *Principles of National Economy* provide the grist for Hale's argument. According to Hale, where Carver errs, so erred the broader justificatory tradition of nineteenth-century judicial policy analytics.

For Hale, the problem is not that Carver is a libertarian and individualist absolutist. Hale is clear that Carver does not believe our economic system can be managed *without* coercion: "he is conscious of a certain amount of restriction of liberty in the scheme he advocates" (P. 470). The problem, for Hale, lies in the mode of reasoning Carver uses to analyze the more specific questions that arise in managing a market economy. For Hale, Carver repeatedly short-circuits his analysis of the policy choices available by imagining that one could decide what to do by simple reference to the ideal of promoting liberty and reducing coercion—by deduction from the broad principle of "freedom."

Carver's error arises, Hale argues, from a misunderstanding of the role of the state in private legal arrangements. It had been conventional to think of public law—criminal law, administrative law, regulatory statutes—as the vertical imposition of state power, or "coercion," on individuals in society, and to see private law—property, contract, and tort—as the horizontal defense of individual autonomy. This, for Hale, radically underestimates the role of coercion in private law.

> What is the government doing when it "protects a property right"? Passively, it is abstaining from interference with the owner when he deals with the thing owned; actively, it is forcing the non-owner to desist from handling it, unless the owner consents. (p. 471)

In the design and enforcement of private-law entitlements, the state makes choices about precisely on whom and in what circumstances to bring the state's coercive force to bear. For Hale, Hohfeld's identification of the "privilege" as a legal interest is particularly significant in this analysis—the state may decide to permit one party to injure another's property or contract interest without recompense, just as it may defend a party's property or contract right by enforcing a duty to pay damages. In making these decisions, it would be more accurate to think of the state *distributing coercion* in different ways, rather than deciding whether or not to coerce.

By imagining that a broad preference for "freedom" over "coercion" can guide policy making, Carver, to Hale's mind, simply avoids the most interesting policy question—how should we decide *whom* to coerce to do what? How should coercion be distributed? Hale does not provide a framework in this article—or elsewhere—for answering this question. Rather, by discrediting a naïve justificatory rhetoric for defense of nineteenth-century laissez-faire, he opened the door for a century of efforts to develop more useful modes of policy analysis, ranging from efforts to deduce action from the sociological context rather than from principles like "freedom" to more complex analytics rooted in welfare economics.

In doing so, Hale develops a set of themes that have recurred in American legal thought for a century. Hale deploys his central theme—the hidden element of coercion in apparently voluntary arrangements—to upend a series of doctrinal distinctions that depend in one or another way on the difference between active and passive agency. His analysis of the difference between "threats" and "promises" should remind every lawyer of first-year Socratic teaching, as he moves through various fact patterns not to *clarify* the distinction, but to *erode* it. Here, we can see American legal reasoning as a critical rather than an explicative practice; one learns the distinctions only through viewing their plasticity.

In Hale's critical analysis, the Hohfeldian permission to injure repeatedly plays a central role. Thus, for example, in criticizing the idea that "vested rights" and "legitimate expectations" in property might guide the policy maker, Hale draws attention to the wide range of injury permitted property owners, and the wide range of "legitimate expectations" that others are privileged to disappoint.

> The "vested rights" of property are protected by law from some vicissitudes. But the law leaves them exposed to many others—such as competition, the constitutional exercise of the police power, the increase in the cost of operation (due perhaps to the government raising of railroad taxes) and the falling off of demand. Moreover, there are "legitimate expectations" which have not crystallized into property rights, such as personal skill acquired at great cost, or such as an ordinary job. To be deprived of these expectations may cause fully as great hardship as any destruction of a property right. These rights do not now find protection. (p. 489)

In this world of permissible injury and coercion backed up or exercised by the state, the negotiations of private parties are best thought of as reciprocal efforts to exercise power—power that can be traced to legal entitlements. For Hale, private parties negotiate against a background of legal entitlements that determine, in part, their reciprocal bargaining power. To see them as simply "exercising their rights" obscures the element of coercion that stands behind their respective offers and demands. The employee's negotiating power is a function, in part, of a legal privilege to withhold his services, even to the detriment of the employer—the employer has no right to compel him to work. The employer negotiates confident in his privilege to withhold work, or hire another—the employee has no right to a job. The factory owner does have the right to exclude the worker from use of his machinery in the absence of an agreement, just as the property owner has the right to exclude others from use of his property without payment. When private parties face one another in negotiation, they do so against the background of a wide range of legal entitlements, each of which might be more or less strong.

As a result, the prices that result from these bargains reflect the relative strength of each party's bargaining power—their legally permitted and enforced capacity to coerce. To say that the wage rate, for example, reflects the "value" or "productivity" of labor is to treat the outcome of these negotiations as if they reflected something intrinsic to the worker's contribution or effort. It is more accurate, Hale asserts, to see the wage rate as reflecting the value of the *threats* the worker can effectively make against the employer.

> The income of each person in the community depends on the relative strength of his power of coercion, offensive and defensive. In fact it appears that what Mr. Carver calls the "productivity" of each factor means no more nor less than this coercive power. It is measured not by what one actually *is* producing, which could not be determined in the case of joint production, but by the extent to which production would fall off if one left and if the marginal laborer were put in his place—by the extent, that is, to which the execution of his threat of withdrawal would damage the employer. (p. 477)

As a result, the prices of labor and commodities in a given society will reflect, in part, the scheme of legal entitlements in force in that society. "The distribution of income, to repeat, depends on the relative power of coercion which the different members of the community can exert against one another. Income is the price paid for not using one's coercive weapons" (p. 478). This insight provided the basis for Hale's criticism of the idea that "market value" could provide a stable reference point for jurists seeking to determine how "distortive" their policy interventions would be. Market prices depend, Hale argued, on the preexisting arrangement of entitlements—to use them as justification for allocating entitlements one way or the other is to argue in a circle. This idea also provided the grist for his criticism of his neo-classical economic colleagues for whom "marginal cost" represented the value that resulted from a commodity's scarcity. For Hale, marginal cost represented the value that could be coerced in payment for a commodity given scarcity *in a given system of entitlements*.

With different legal arrangements, we could expect different bargains to be struck, and different distributions of income. For Hale, the striking thing about Carver's analysis is his *disinterest* in legal entitlements as a component in income distribution. Carver does propose a "balancing program" to reduce income inequality, by reducing the supply of labor (through immigration limits) and increasing the supply of capital (by promoting savings) to alter their relative prices. Hale wonders "why, . . . does he show little interest in supplementing his program by proposing to alter the legal arrangements themselves?" (p. 481).

Here, Hale opens the door for social policy through law—arranging private-law entitlements to strengthen the bargaining power of some and reduce that of others. Decisions about how to protect property—with a right or a privilege, for example—will require decisions that cannot be deduced from the nature of property or from a broad commitment to "freedom" as opposed to "coercion." Because they will *also* affect the balance of forces in society, and the distribution of income, these decisions will need to be made by reference to some broader social objective. We might imagine a range of different market economies, based on different entitlement allocations—each might result in a different allocation of resources. One cannot avoid regulation; the point is to decide among competing possible regulatory arrangements, each of which would offer different "channels of industry" (p. 491).

Hale does not offer a method for making these decisions. He is clear that it is no more appropriate to decide by defaulting to the interests of the "community" than by deference to private freedom. He offers no a priori argument for allocating wealth to the poor rather than the rich, or for taking the surplus as tax rather than leaving it where it has been placed by the bargains among private actors. The community is itself an amalgam of group and individual interests, the government another site for the deployment of resources, also subject to the coercive powers of others. What is needed, Hale asserts, is a method for the dynamic analysis of what will happen to the surplus when allocated to different entities in society. "Until economic science has developed some method of measuring changes in human satisfaction resulting from an increase in the production of one and a decrease in the production of another article, public officials will act pretty much in the dark" (p. 493).

In the years since, numerous efforts have been made to offer just this kind of analytic tool for making the policy choices thought necessary in determining how best to arrange legal entitlements. Scholars and judges have borrowed various strands of economics, as well as political theory, sociological study, linguistics, logic, ethics, and much more. Together, Hale's central insights—the ubiquity of coercion in civil society and the social impact of private entitlements that may be allocated in a variety of ways—opened the way for the vigorous development of "policy argument" in American legal thought.

DAVID KENNEDY

1. Robert Hale, "Commissions, Rates, and Policies," 53 Harvard Law Review 1103 at 1143 (1940).

Bibliography

Robert Hale

Hale's most significant related general scholarship, in chronological order, includes the following:

"Economic Theory and the Statesman." In *The Trend of Economics*, ed. Rexford Guy Tuqewell. New York: A.A. Knopf, 1924.

"Force and the State: A Comparison of 'Political' and 'Economic' Compulsion." 35:2 *Columbia Law Review* 149 (1935).

"Bargaining, Duress and Economic Liberty." 43 *Columbia Law Review* 603 (1943).

Freedom Through Law: Public Control of Private Governing Power. New York: Columbia University Press, 1952.

Hale's writing about utility rate regulation includes the following:

"The 'Physical Value' Fallacy in Rate Cases." 30 *Yale Law Journal* 710 (1921).

"Rate Making and the Revision of the Property Concept." 22 *Columbia Law Review* 209 (1922).

"The 'Fair Value' Merry-go-Round, 1898–1938: A Forty-Year Journey from Rates-Based-On-Value to Value-Based-on-Rates." 33 *Illinois Law Review* 517 (1939).

"Commissions, Rates, and Policies." 53 *Harvard Law Review* 1103 (1940).

Hale's contribution to the Canon was a review of T. N. Carver's *Principles of National Economy* (1921).

Commentary

Barbara H. Fried, *The Progressive Assault on Laissez Faire: Robert Hale and the First Law and Economics Movement* (Cambridge, Mass.: Harvard University Press, 1998). Fried's monograph offers a complete overview of Hale's scholarly life and work, reviewing Hale's ideas about property and liberty in the context of liberal political theory, progressive politics, and institutional economics, and tracing the tradition of critical legal writing that relied on his influence.

Fried's book spawned a series of reviews praising, attacking, and otherwise evaluating Hale's contribution from various perspectives. See, for example, Richard Epstein, "The Assault that Failed: The Progressive Critique of Laissez Faire," review of *The Progressive Assault on Laissez-Faire: Robert Hale and the First Law and Economics Movement* by Barbara Fried, 97 *Michigan Law Review* 1697 (1999), stressing the weakness of Hale's positive program. See also Ian Ayres, "Discrediting the Free Market," review of *The Progressive Assault on Laissez-Faire: Robert Hale and the First Law and Economics Movement* by Barbara Fried, 66 *University of Chicago Law Review* 273 (1999), stressing the originality and significance of Hale's "distributive view of negative liberty".

Warren Samuels, "The Economy as a System of Power and Its Legal Bases: The Legal Economics of Robert Lee Hale," 27: 3–4 *University of Miami Law Review* 261 (1973), brings together an enormous quantity of useful biographic and bibliographic information, including many unpublished sources, and offers a broad summary and analysis of Hale's economic and legal ideas.

Joseph Singer, "Legal Realism Now," review of *Legal Realism at Yale: 1927–1960*, 76 *California Law Review* 465 (1988), offers an excellent overview of legal realism, analyzes Hale's contribution, and traces his influence on legal realism generally.

Neil Duxbury, "Robert Hale and the Economy of Legal Force," 53:4 *Modern Law Review* 421 (1990), includes good biographic and bibliographic information, and situates Hale in the context of institutional economics and legal realism, and comments on his revival by critical legal studies scholars.

Pavlos Eleftheriadis, "Unfreedom in a Laissez-Faire State," in 80 *Archives for Philosophy of Law and Social Philosophy* 168–190 (1994), focuses on the significance of Hale's understanding of negative liberty for contemporary liberal theory, contrasting it with the views of Max Weber, John Dewey, and Herbert Spencer.

Matther Kramer, *In the Realm of Legal and Moral Philosophy* (1999), chapter 7, provides an appreciative exposition of Hale's critique of the distinction between public and private law, arguing that Hale's analysis is consistent with theories of natural rights.

Duncan Kennedy offers a synthesis of Hale's contribution to American legal thought, contrasting his conceptions of power (unfavorably) and of law (favorably) to those of Foucault in Duncan Kennedy, "The Stakes of Law, or Hale and Foucault!" in 15:4 *Legal Studies Forum* 327 (1991), reprinted in Duncan Kennedy, *Sexy Dressing etc.* (Cambridge, Mass.: Harvard University Press, 1993). Hale's influence can be seen in Duncan Kennedy's work on law and economics, including "Are Property and Contract Efficient" (with Frank Michelman), 8 *Hofstra Law Review* 711 (1980), and Duncan Kennedy, "Distributive and Paternalistic Motives in Contract and Tort Law, with Special Reference to Compulsory Terms and Unequal Bargaining Power," 41 *Maryland Law Review* 563 (1982).

"Coercion and Distribution in a Supposedly Noncoercive State"

38 Political Science Quarterly 470 (1923)

> And while the House of Peers withholds its legislative hand,
> And noble statesmen do not itch
> To interfere with matters which
> They cannot understand,
> As bright will shine Great Britain's rays
> As in King George's glorious days.
>
> —FROM W. S. GILBERT'S *Iolanthe*

The so-called individualist would expand this philosophy to include all states-men, whether noble or not, and to include all economic matters as among those which they cannot understand. The practical function of economic theory is merely to prove to statesmen the wisdom of leaving such matters alone, not to aid them in the process of interfering. And in foreign as well as in domestic affairs, they should make no effort to control the natural working of economic events. This would seem to be the general view of Professor Thomas Nixon Carver,[1] although he likewise speaks frequently as a nationalist. But a careful scrutiny will, it is thought, reveal a fallacy in this view, and will demonstrate that the systems advocated by professed upholders of *laissez-faire* are in reality per-meated with coercive restrictions of individual freedom, and with restrictions, moreover, out of conformity with any formula of "equal opportunity" or of "pre-serving the equal rights of others." Some sort of coercive restriction of individu-als, it is believed, is absolutely unavoidable, and cannot be made to conform to any Spencerian formula. Since coercive restrictions are bound to affect the distri-bution of income and the direction of economic activities, and are bound to affect the economic interests of persons living in foreign parts, statesmen cannot avoid interfering with economic matters, both in domestic and in foreign affairs. There is accordingly a need for the development of economic and legal theory to guide them in the process.

To proceed to an examination of Professor Carver's system. His "individualism" is not entirely orthodox, for he is conscious of a certain amount of restriction of lib-erty in the scheme he advocates. Indeed his statement on page 747 is altogether too pragmatic to please the doctrinaire disciple of Spencer. In each proposed case of governmental interference, he thinks, the question is to be asked, "Are the evils to be repressed greater than those that accompany the work of repression, and are the

---

[1] *Principles of National Economy.* By Thomas Nixon Carver. New York, Ginn and Company, 1921.—vi, 773 pp.

evils to be removed by regulation greater than those that accompany the work of regulation? The method of procedure must be to consider, appraise, and compare the evils on both sides." While this test might be accepted by the so-called paternalist, as well as by the so-called individualist, Mr. Carver's final conclusions as to governmental activity do not differ materially from those of the more orthodox of the latter. The government, he thinks, should exercise sufficient constraint to prevent destruction and deception, to standardize measures, qualities and coins, to enforce contracts, to conduct certain enterprises (like lighthouses) which cannot well be carried on otherwise, to regulate monopoly prices and to control the feeble-minded and the otherwise incompetent in their own interest. It should not coerce people to work, nor should it, with rare exceptions, undertake to direct the channels into which industry should flow. It should, however, prevent any private person or group from exercising any compulsion. The government must also impose taxes; it should restrict immigration and furnish educational opportunities. Such a scheme has the appearance of exposing individuals to but little coercion at the hands of the government and to none at all at the hands of other individuals or groups. Yet it does in fact expose them to coercion at the hands of both, or at least to a kind of influence indistinguishable in its effects from coercion. This will shortly appear more clearly, it is hoped. Meanwhile, let it be kept in mind that to call an act coercive is not by any means to condemn it. It is because the word "coercion" frequently seems to carry with it the stigma of impropriety, that the coercive character of many innocent acts is so frequently denied.

What is the government doing when it "protects a property right"? Passively, it is abstaining from interference with the owner when he deals with the thing owned; actively, it is forcing the non-owner to desist from handling it, unless the owner consents. Yet Mr. Carver would have it that the government is merely preventing the non-owner from using force against the owner (pp. 104–5 and 106). This explanation is obviously at variance with the facts—for the non-owner is forbidden to handle the owner's property even where his handling of it involves no violence or force whatever. Any lawyer could have told him that the right of property is much more extensive than the mere right to protection against forcible dispossession. In protecting property the government is doing something quite apart from merely keeping the peace. It is exerting coercion wherever that is necessary to protect each owner, not merely from violence, but also from peaceful infringement of his sole right to enjoy the thing owned.

That, however, is not the most significant aspect of present-day coercion in connection with property. The owner can remove the legal duty under which the non-owner labors with respect to the owner's property. He can remove it, or keep it in force, at his discretion. To keep it in force may or may not have unpleasant consequences to the non-owner—consequences which spring from the law's creation of legal duty. To avoid these consequences, the non-owner may be willing to obey the will of the owner, provided that the obedience is not in itself more unpleasant than the consequences to be avoided. Such obedience may take the trivial form of paying five cents for legal permission to eat a particular bag of peanuts, or it may take the more significant form of working for the owner at disagreeable toil for a slight wage. In either case the conduct is motivated, not by any desire to do the act in question, but by a desire to escape a more disagreeable alternative. In the peanut case, the consequence of abstaining from a particular bag of peanuts would be, either to go without such nutriment altogether for the time being, or to conform to the terms of some other owner. Presumably at least one of these consequences would be as bad as the loss of the five cents, or the purchaser would not buy; but one of them, at least, would be no worse, or the owner would be able to compel payment of more. In the case of the labor, what would be the consequence of refusal to comply with the owner's terms? It would be either absence of wages, or obedience to the terms of some other employer. If the worker has no money of his own, the threat of any particular employer to withhold any particular amount of money would be effective in securing the worker's obedience in proportion to the difficulty with which other employers can be induced to furnish a "job". If the non-owner works for anyone, it is for the purpose of warding off the threat of at least one owner of money to withhold that money from him (with the help of the law). Suppose, now, the worker were to refuse to yield to the coercion of any employer, but were to choose instead to remain under the legal duty to abstain from the use of any of the money which anyone owns. He must eat. While there is no law against eating in the abstract, there is a law which forbids him to eat any of the food which actually exists in the community—and that law is the law of property. It can be lifted as to any specific food at the discretion of its owner, but if the owners unanimously refuse to lift the prohibition, the non-owner will starve unless he can himself produce food. And there is every likelihood that the owners will be unanimous in refusing, if he has no money. There is no law to compel them to part with their food for nothing. Unless, then, the non-owner can produce his own food, the law compels him to starve if he has no wages, and compels him to go without wages unless he obeys the behests of some employer. It is the law that coerces him into wage-work under penalty of starvation—unless he can produce food. Can he? Here again there is no law to prevent the production of food in the abstract; but in every settled country there is a law which forbids him to cultivate any particular piece of ground unless he happens to be an owner. This again is the law of property. And this again will not be likely to be lifted unless he already has money. That way of escape from the law-made dilemma of starvation or obedience is closed to him. It may seem that one way of escape has been overlooked—acquisition of money in other ways than by wage-work. Can he not "make money" by selling goods? But here again, things cannot be produced in quantities sufficient to keep him alive, except with the use of elaborate mechanical equipment. To use any such equipment is unlawful, except on the owner's terms. Those terms usually include an implied abandonment of any claim of title to the products. In short, if he be not a property owner, the law which forbids him to produce with any of the existing equipment, and the law which forbids him to eat any of the existing food, will be lifted *only* in case he works for an employer. It is the law of property which coerces people into working for factory owners—though, as we shall see shortly, the workers can as a rule exert sufficient counter-coercion to limit materially the governing power of the owners.

Not only does the law of property secure for the owners of factories their labor; it also secures for them the revenue derived from the customers. The law compels people to desist from consuming the products of the owner's plant, except with his consent; and he will not consent unless they pay him money. They can escape, of course, by going without the product. But that does not prevent the payment being compulsory, any more than it prevents the payment of the government tax on tobacco from being compulsory. The penalty for failure to pay, in each case, may be light, but it is sufficient to compel obedience in all those cases where the consumer buys rather than go without. On pages 620–621, Mr. Carver attempts to distinguish on the ground that in the case of the tax the government "did not produce the tobacco but only charges the manufacturer or the dealer for the privilege of manufacturing or selling." But this is equally true of the owner of the factory, if he is an absentee owner. Whether the owner has rendered a service or not bears only on the question of the justification of the income which he collects, not on whether the process of collecting it was coercive.

As already intimated, however, the owner's coercive power is weakened by the fact that both his customers and his laborers have the power to make matters more or less unpleasant for him—the customers through their law-given power to withhold access to their cash, the laborers through their *actual* power (neither created nor destroyed by the law) to withhold their services. Even without this power, it is true, he would have to give his laborers enough to sustain them, just as it is to his own interest to feed his horses enough to make them efficient. But whatever they get beyond this minimum is obtained either by reason of the employer's generosity and sense of moral obligation, or by his fear that they will exercise the threat to work elsewhere or not at all. If obtained through this fear, it is a case where he submits by so much to their wills. It is not a "voluntary" payment, but a payment as the price of escape from damaging behavior of others. Furnishing food to one's slaves is essentially different; the owner may do it reluctantly, but if there is any "coercion" it is the impersonal coercion by the facts of nature which account for the slaves' labor being less efficient without the food; he is not influenced by the will of any human being. In paying high wages to wage-earners, on the other hand, he is. But for their will to obtain the high wages, and their power of backing up that will, he has no reason for paying them. Yet he does. What else is "coercion"?

There is, however, a natural reluctance so to term it. This can be explained, I think, by the fact that some of the grosser forms of private coercion are illegal, and the undoubtedly coercive character of the pressure exerted by the property-owner is disguised. Hence the natural reaction to any recognized form of private coercion is, "forbid it." One who would not wish to take from the laboring man his power to quit the employer, or to deny him the wages that he gets for *not* quitting, is apt to resent the suggestion that those wages are in fact coercive. But were it once recognized that nearly all incomes are the result of private coercion, some with the help of the state, some without it, it would then be plain that to admit the coercive nature of the process would not be to condemn it. Yet popular thought undoubtedly does require special justification for any conduct, private or governmental, which is labeled "coercive," while it does not require such special justification for conduct to which it does not apply that term. Popular judgment of social problems, therefore, is apt to be distorted by the popular recognition or non-recognition of "coercion." Hence it may be worthwhile to run down into more detail the distinctions popularly made between coercion and other forms of influence over people's conduct.

"Threats" are often distinguished from "promises." If I tell a man I will do some positive act whose results will be unpleasant to him, unless he pays me money, and if as a result he pays it, I would usually be said to be collecting it by means of a "threat." If, on the other hand, I tell him I will do some positive act, whose results will be pleasant to him, *if* he pays me money, and he does, it would be said more commonly that I collected it by means of a "promise." Partly as a result of the moral connotation generally given to these terms, partly as its cause, the law more frequently interferes to prevent the doing of harmful acts than it does to compel the doing of helpful ones. Many (but not all) positive acts which are disadvantageous to others are forbidden; not so many positive acts that are advantageous to others are compelled. In other words, most torts and crimes consist of positive acts. Failure to help does not as a rule give rise to legal punishment or a right of action. Yet there are exceptions. Certain acts not in themselves actionable at law, may give rise to legal duties to perform positive acts. If I start an automobile in motion, I have committed no legal wrong; but if subsequently I fail to perform the act of stopping it when "reasonable care" would require me to do so, the victim of my failure to act can recover damages for my non-performance.[2] Again, and more significant, if I have promised to do certain things (with certain formalities or "consideration"), my act of promising was not a legal wrong. But if I subsequently fail to perform at the time specified, the promisee has a right of action for my failure to act. It is significant of the reluctance to admit the existence of positive legal duties, that in both cases language is used which makes my wrong conduct seem to consist of wrongful acts instead of wrongful *failure* to act. It is said, in the one case, that I "ran over" the victim, in the other that I "*committed* a breach of contract." Yet in neither was the wrong an act, but a failure to act: in the first case, my failure to make the requisite motions for stopping the car; in the second, my failure to perform the act promised.

Now suppose that instead of actually refraining from doing the acts which the law requires, I say to a man, "Pay me a thousand dollars, and when I meet you on the road walking I will use sufficient care to stop my car or to steer it so that it will not hit you; otherwise I will do nothing about it." Is that a "threat" or a "promise"? Or if I say, "Pay me a thousand dollars and I will perform the acts I have already contracted to perform"? I believe most people would call these statements threats rather than promises. Why? It may be partly due to the misleading language which speaks of the *act* of running over and the *act* of breaking a contract. But even were the fact recognized that payment were demanded as the price of *not abstaining*, I believe the demands would still be called threats. The reason, I believe, is partly because to abstain is contrary to legal duty, partly because it is adjudged to be contrary to moral duty. Popular speech in this case seems to apply the term coercion to demands made as a price of not violating a legal or moral duty, whether the duty consists of acting or of letting alone. But this criterion will not do, either.

If an act is called "coercion" when, and only when, one submits to demands in order to prevent another from violating a legal duty, then every legal system by very definition forbids the private exercise of coercion—it is not coercion unless the law does forbid it. And no action which the law forbids, and which could be used as a means of influencing another, can fail to be coercion—again by definition. Hence it would be idle to discuss whether any particular legal system forbids private coercion. And if an act is called "coercion" when, and only when, one submits to demands in order to prevent another from violating a *moral* duty, we get right back to the use of the term to express our conclusion as to the justifiability of the use of the pressure in question; with the ensuing circular reasoning of condemning an act because we have already designated it "coercive." One is likely, that is, to have a vague feeling against the use of a particular form of economic pressure, then to discover that this pressure is "coercive"—forgetting that coerciveness is not a ground for condemnation except when used in the sense of influence under pain of doing a morally unjustified act. And obviously to

---

[2] *Cf.* an article by Leon Green in 21 *Michigan Law Review*, 495 (March, 1923).

pronounce the pressure unjustified because it is an unjustified pressure is to reason in a circle. Hence, it seems better, in using the word "coercion," to use it in a sense which involves no moral judgment.

But popular feeling sometimes makes another distinction. If I plan to do an act or to leave something undone for no other purpose than to induce payment, that might be conceded to be a "threat." But if I plan to do a perfectly lawful act for my own good, or to abstain from working for another because I prefer to do something else with my time, then if I take payment for changing my course of conduct in either respect, it would not be called a threat. If a man pays me to keep out of a particular business, or if he pays me to work for him (when I am not legally bound by contract to do so), then it seems absurd to many to say that he paid me under threat of coercion—unless, in the first case, my sole motive in entering the business was to bring him to terms, and unless in the second I preferred working for him to any other occupation of my time, and my sole motive in abstaining was again to bring him to terms. For purposes of ordinary conversation, some other word than coercion may be preferred to describe payments made to a man who makes a sacrifice to "earn" them. But can a line be drawn? I believe the popular distinction along these lines is based on moral judgment. If a man gives up a job he likes, or if he works for another man, why shouldn't he be paid for it?—it will be asked. Perhaps he should. But unless the term "coercion" is applied only to conduct adjudged immoral, does the justifiability of the receipt of payment prevent it from being coercive?

If those distinctions are all invalid, then, which seek to remove the term "coercive" from some of the influences exerted to induce another to act against his will, it seems to follow that the income of each person in the community depends on the relative strength of his power of coercion, offensive and defensive. In fact it appears that what Mr. Carver calls the "productivity" of each factor means no more nor less than this coercive power. It is measured not by what one actually is producing, which could not be determined in the case of joint production, but by the extent to which production would fall off if one left and if the marginal laborer were put in his place—by the extent, that is, to which the execution of his threat of withdrawal would damage the employer.[3] Not only does the distribution of income depend on this mutual coercion; so also does the distribution of that power to exert further compulsion which accompanies the management of an industry. Some extremely interesting suggestions of the likelihood of control by capitalists, cooperative buyers, cooperative sellers and laborers are to be found on pages 222–225. This power is frequently highly centralized, with the result that the worker is frequently deprived, during working hours and even beyond, of all choice over his own activities.

To take this control by law from the owner of the plant and to vest it in public officials or in a guild or in a union organization elected by the workers would neither add to nor subtract from the constraint which is exercised with the aid of the government. It would merely transfer the constraining power to a different set of persons. It might result in greater or in less actual power of free initiative all round, but this sort of freedom is not to be confused with the "freedom" which means absence of governmental constraint. Mr. Carver himself points out (pp. 134–5 and 424), that the governmental constraint involved in the

[3] *Cf.* the statement on p. 530.

maintenance of traffic police results in giving the average individual *greater* "free-dom of movement." But "freedom of movement" does not mean freedom from governmental constraint, or even from constraint by private individuals. It means freedom from physical obstruction—in other words, greater physical *power* to move. Whether in other cases, too, physical power to exercise one's will is enhanced by a certain amount of legal restriction depends upon the peculiar facts of each case.[4] Whether Mr. Carver's scheme of things would be more or less "free" (in the sense of giving people greater power to express their wills) than would a state of communism, depends largely on the economic results of communism respecting the character of factory work. Neither can be said to be any "freer" than the other in the sense that it involves less coercion on the part of other human beings, official or unofficial.

The distribution of income, to repeat, depends on the relative power of coercion which the different members of the community can exert against one another. Income is the price paid for not using one's coercive weapons. One of these weapons consists of the power to withhold one's labor. Another is the power to consume all that can be bought with one's lawful income instead of investing part of it. Another is the power to call on the government to lock up certain pieces of land or productive equipment. Still another is the power to decline to undertake an enterprise which may be attended with risk. By threatening to use these various weapons, one gets (with or with out sacrifice) an income in the form of wages, interest, rent or profits. The resulting distribution is very far from being equal, and the inequalities are very far from corresponding to needs or to sacrifice. Most radical movements have as at least one of their aims the reduction of these inequalities, and the bringing of them into closer conformity with needs or sacrifices. Professor Carver has the same aim. He would accomplish it, however, primarily, not by altering the legal arrangements under which the various weapons are allotted, but by altering the effectiveness of the weapons. In explaining the distribution of wealth "our first problem," he says, is "to study the market value of each factor, or agent, of production in order to find out why the seller of each factor gets a large or a small share" (p. 471). (The study of the legal arrangements by which the seller of each comes to have control over that particular factor does not interest him.) And a nearer approach to equality is to be reached by changing the market values—i.e., the effectiveness of the weapons. He would try to bring about what he calls a better balance of factors. One man's power to withhold his unskilled labor is not a strong weapon, because unskilled labor is too plentiful, and the demand for it too weak. Therefore make it scarcer, and increase the demand for it. Capital gets a large return because capital is relatively scarce. Therefore encourage thrift, and the interest rate will drop. Land rent will fall if more bad land is made good by reclamation projects. And the increase of the scarce factors will in itself increase the demand for the less scarce and thus will work in cooperation with the thinning-out of the latter to raise their market value.

Mr. Carver's explanation of what determines the market values of capital, labor, etc., is clear and penetrating, along the lines followed in his much earlier *Distribution of Wealth*. He employs the "marginal analysis," and his conclusions

---

[4] It is this fractional freedom which must be the interest Pound has in mind when he speaks of "men's aspirations for free self-assertion."—*Interpretations of Jurisprudence*, p. 126. But it is doubtful whether even Pound recognizes that this interest does not necessarily run counter to legal restraint.

are subject to whatever qualifications recent study has necessitated in the use of that analysis. Possibly one qualification of his analysis of the benefits to be derived from an increase in the supply of capital, may be suggested. It is a qualification required by his characteristic preoccupation with long-run results, without regard to transitional consequences. With an increased supply of capital, according to his reasoning, dividends on common and preferred stock will fall, also interest offered for new bonds. But according to the same reasoning, if the process goes far, interest on old bonds will be defaulted. If bankruptcy is widespread, and results in business depression, the demand for labor will drop, since, despite the greater *physical* productive capacity, the *psychological* motives for utilizing that capacity will be paralyzed. It is the owners who determine how far to carry its utilization, and their judgment is motivated by the prospect of profits. One result is of course a fall in wages, which will restore somewhat the net earning power, but not sufficiently to give it the old motive force to induce full utilization. Despite lower labor costs, industry is still unprofitable owing to the fall in the price of the products; and this fall is not the result solely of increased supply, but also of the decreased demand ensuing upon unemployment and enforced economy. If an increase in the supply of capital brought about its lower interest rate smoothly, without causing bankruptcies and other dislocations, there might then be no paralysis of productive motives, for the hypothesis of a greater degree of thrift implies that the motive to invest will function despite a lower interest rate, and no other factors of production would be less well rewarded than before. But such smoothness in the process is not what is found in actual life; and while the dislocations which accompany it seem from the point of view of symmetrical theory to be mere qualifications, and of no great importance for explaining the central theory, yet in actual life many qualifications of theories assume great practical importance. And business depressions are not to be overlooked in considering the effects of increased thrift. Elsewhere in his book Mr. Carver considers depressions, and his explanation is in no way inconsistent with a view that increase of thrift may be one of the things which might bring them about. He traces them back to fluctuations in prices of products, which cause magnified fluctuations in the value of capital equipment (pp. 436–9). But an increase in the amount of capital equipment, with an accompanying increase in the supply of products, will doubtless be one factor causing a reduction in the price of the products. The effect on the value of the plants will be partially offset by the fact that the lower net earnings will be capitalized at a lower interest rate, but if the increase in the supply of capital is swift, there is no reason to assume that the offset will be complete. The temporary effect of thrift, then, may be quite different from the effect which Mr. Carver foresees. But this does not, of course, prove that its total effect may not be to lower the earnings of capital and to raise those of labor. For in times of prosperity it is very likely that the limiting factor in production is not the reluctance to use existing capital equipment, but its physical scarcity. What may be the net benefits to the workers from increased thrift, is a question inviting more study than Mr. Carver gives it.

His balancing program, then, consists in a greater equalization of the market values of the different factors of production. What are the concrete steps which he would take to effectuate his "balancing program"? Unskilled labor he would render scarcer, partly by thinning out its ranks through greater educational opportunities, partly by encouraging an increase in the standard of living (thus indirectly diminishing the birth rate—he does not mention birth control) and partly by restricting immigration. In refreshing contrast with many publicists, he has no fears for a "labor shortage"—in fact he would welcome one. In his out-line of "A Liberalist's Program" he suggests minimum wage laws and minimum building standards as means of raising the standard of living, but does not develop these interesting suggestions elsewhere in the book. Thrift campaigns would be another means for raising the standard. In restricting immigration, we confront two objections, which the author ignores—one, the interests of foreign workers, the other, danger to our own people from international complications which might ensue. Mr. Carver's nationalist philosophy simplifies the problem for him by permitting him to ignore the former completely. And the avoidance of war does not seem to interest him greatly.

By his "balancing program" Mr. Carver hopes to bring about greater equality in the effectiveness of the coercive weapons (though he does not express it this way); to increase the mischief which the unskilled worker can achieve by with-holding his labor (thus enabling him to collect a larger wage as the price of not causing the mischief) and to decrease the mischief which the property-owner or the possessor of business skill can cause by withholding his property or his skill. Perhaps he would achieve all that he hopes for, but he offers no quantitative proof of the result. Why, then, does he show little interest in supplementing his program by proposing to alter the legal arrangements themselves? He might con-ceivably propose to distribute the weapons anew, or to make their use conditional either on charging low prices or on paying high wages or on paying taxes which could be redistributed to those whose bargaining weapons are weak. Such pro-posals, however, receive but limited sympathy from him. He is fond of contrast-ing his "voluntaristic" balancing program with the coercive "voting programs" of socialism and communism, and the coercive "fighting programs" of Bolshevism and the I.W.W. This is attributed, I believe, to his failure to see the coercive nature of the bargaining weapons, coupled with his keenness in scenting coercion in any legal arrangements which would alter the distribution of these weapons.

He does not, however, entirely eschew a "voting program," nor are all the rea-sons he gives for not going further, tinctured with his "voluntaristic" fallacy. One prime reason he has for not tampering with the unequal incomes which flow to the owners of the various factors, is that these incomes perform the function of redressing that same uneven balance of which the unequal incomes are but symp-toms. Whatever factors have the greatest market value, and accordingly bring their owners the greatest rewards, are the factors which society has most need to have increased, and the high rewards will induce more people to produce them. There is much reason for doubting the perfect correlation between market values and society's needs. Yet there is a large element of truth in the proposition that many of the inequalities of income serve the useful function of stimulating pro-duction in such a way as to benefit others as well as the producers. And some inequalities might be defended on other grounds—for instance, on the ground that their removal would cause serious temporary dislocations. But as we have seen, Mr. Carver is not greatly interested in such temporary matters. Even his bal-ancing program is intended to remove many of the inequalities which are not needed for incentives, with a rather ruthless disregard for dislocations. What inequalities would he remove by a "voting program"?

In the first place he would have the government regulate monopoly prices. The monopoly profit is a symptom of scarcity, but far from functioning to remove its own cause, it functions to perpetuate it. The monopolist deliberately limits output. What light does Mr. Carver's theory give to the government regulator to assist him in the regulating process? The regulation of monopoly prices presents problems concerning the amount of reward which incentive necessitates— whether an increment of value, for instance, is in some cases essential to induce the taking of socially useful risks; concerning the extent to which protection should be given to the values of shares of stock already bought at prices based on monopoly power, even where such protection is not essential as an incentive; concerning the apportionment of the joint costs of the enterprise among the various classes of consumers. Suggestions on all these problems from a keen and original mind like Mr. Carver's would be most welcome. But they are not to be had. He takes the cynical view that regulators are politicians, and politicians all demagogues, and there is no hope for any really intelligent system of regulation. He favors regulation merely as a choice of evils, on the ground that the interests of politicians and of trust operators are not the same; "and, as a result of their pulling and hauling, prices will not be fixed quite so completely in the interest of the trusts but more in the interest of the trusts and the politicians" (p. 221).

Another feature of Mr. Carver's "voting program" is "the redistribution of unearned wealth" by "increased taxation of land values," and by "a graduated inheritance tax" (p. 766). Does "unearned wealth" mean all wealth which does not function as an incentive to production? And would Mr. Carver go so far as to tax all of it away for the purpose of a more equal distribution? If so, his "voting program," little as he stresses it in this book, might far outweigh in its results his "voluntaristic" program. Let us examine briefly how far such a program would indeed go, what objections to its complete realization can be found in Mr. Carver's philosophy (he is not explicit as to how far he would push it) and what other objections there might be, not voiced by him.

How far could taxation be pushed without checking the incentive to produce? Every tax, of course, diminishes somebody's real income, if not somebody's money income. In considering the effect upon incentive of the diminution of any kind of income, it is convenient to distinguish two different sorts of effects. The *prospect* of receiving an income may stimulate one to work or to save; the *past* receipt of income may induce one to save without much *prospective* income as a further inducement. The first effect depends upon the sort of income, the second upon its size. A rich man, in other words, may be induced more easily than a poor man to devote part of his wealth to the creation of capital equipment, by investing it, and consequently the concentration of wealth may conceivably result in greater production quite regardless of whether the rich man originally received his income by way of inheritance, "rent," interest or profits. Before discussing this matter, let us turn to various forms of taxation to ask whether they would be likely to lessen the *prospective* motive to work or save. No complete discussion is attempted here, merely a summary of Mr. Carver's views with brief comments thereon.

Inheritances in excess of a certain amount could be quite severely taxed, even to the point of complete confiscation of the excess amounts, apparently, without diminishing the motives which the prospect of leaving wealth furnishes to one who leaves it.[5] Income due solely to the ownership of urban land (apart from improvements) is pure surplus above incentive, and its taxation would not

[5] *Essays in Social Justice*, pp. 322–3.

diminish the supply of anything, and therefore would increase no prices (p. 634). The same is true of a tax on the net profits of a monopoly (p. 636). Here again, as in the discussion of price regulation, Mr. Carver fails to analyze the distinction between the net monopoly profits and mere competitive profits. Interest is essential to induce the saving of capital, hence any taxation of it would reduce saving, diminish the supply of capital equipment, raise prices and lower the demand for labor, and therefore lower wages. Yet by Professor Carver's own analysis (pp. 544–50, reprinted from his earlier book, *The Distribution of Wealth*), it is only the marginal savings which require the full interest now paid to call them forth. It would seem to follow that a tax on the interest received by the "intramarginal" saver would not reduce the *prospective* motive for saving; and that a *general* tax on interest would reduce the prospective motive but slightly. This last conclusion has been drawn by A. B. Wolfe,[6] but Mr. Carver thinks that "such a conclusion is of doubtful validity." One reason he gives is an assertion that "marginal saving takes place . . . along an extended line and not simply upon a single point on that line." This assertion rests on the premise that "every saver is probably a marginal saver to some extent". Whether it is a complete answer to Professor Wolfe's more extended argument to the effect that marginal saving takes place along only a short line, may be left to the judgment of the readers of both.

But Mr. Carver has another answer, which comes nearer to the *non-prospective* motive for saving. If interest were taxed away, "it would reduce the incomes of those who had shown the propensity to save, either automatically or for the deliberate purpose of getting interest. They would therefore have less from which to save. Granting that others would find their incomes correspondingly increased, still, these would necessarily be the ones who had not previously saved much capital, and the probabilities are against the assumption that they will now save enough to compensate for the diminution in the amount saved by the previous savers." It will be noted that Mr. Carver uses the argument of the non-prospective motive, not to show that the rich as such are more likely to save, but that the interest-receivers, not because they are rich but because they have shown a saving propensity, are more likely to save again than are others with the same incomes. It may be questioned to what extent the present interest-recipients are such by reason of any "propensity," to what extent it is because they started with more money; the existence of the non-interest-receiving class might perhaps be explained just as plausibly on the hypothesis that they never received enough income to permit them to save, as on the hypothesis that they lacked as much of a saving propensity as the rest.

However that may be, the non-prospective motive presents a real problem. By assisting the rich to coerce money from the poor, the government may perhaps furnish no *prospective* stimulus to induce the rich to do anything productive *in order to get* that income, yet the money so coerced may be used to direct industry into the construction of additional productive equipment, which will benefit future generations, rich and poor alike. If this money had been diverted instead into the hands of the poor it would have caused industry to be directed, not into the production of so much additional material equipment, but into the production of more goods which would have been consumed by the poor. Such is the argument for concentration. It is not Mr. Carver's—his only use of the non-prospective

[6] 1 *Quar. Jour. Eco.*, vol. 35, pp. I *et seq.* (Nov., 1920).

motive argument is in the passage quoted. In the form above he neither advances nor refutes it; yet, if valid, it would make against his own equalizing program. It is an argument which cannot be ignored in considering a reduction of the inequalities in our present distribution of wealth. It is in effect an argument that the compulsory power of government (for all property incomes are derived from the exertion of that power) should divert funds which might otherwise be turned to the poor, to the rich instead *en route* to a voluntary diversion by the rich into a capital fund; on the capital fund so provided, the rich are to be paid interest by the poor, but this interest the rich will voluntarily re-invest, and so on indefinitely. With each new addition to the productive equipment, society will be able to pay the poor more; but if it does so, less will be added than otherwise to the capital fund in the future, and the potentiality of rewarding the poor for their enforced abstinence later will not be increased so much. If this were pushed to its extreme conclusion, the poor would be kept down perpetually to the subsistence level in order to increase the potentiality of bringing them above it. In this extreme form, the policy defeats its own end, just as excessive saving by an individual defeats its own end of adding eventually to his spending power. On the other hand if no consideration at all is given to this non-prospective motive, it is possible that the poor would soon be worse off than otherwise. One would like to see the subject discussed in all its ramifications. But one will not find the discussion in this book.

But these considerations which have to do with incentive are not the only considerations which can be advanced to stay the hand of a drastic policy of equalization by taxation. Once it is settled how far taxation could be carried in an equalizing direction without checking incentive to production, other considerations may be urged against carrying it so far. At the very threshold of the discussion, it will be urged that any taxation for the deliberate purpose of equalizing wealth violates the fundamental canon of taxing "according to ability to pay", sometimes known as the "faculty" principle. Were taxation to cut down those large incomes which do not function as incentives and to leave untouched those equally large incomes which do, the recipients of the two would not seem to be taxed according to their respective "abilities", which are equal—unless, indeed, we accepted John A. Hobson's definition of "ability" as "ability to pay *without shifting the tax to the consumer*."[7] Moreover, as between a high and a low non-incentive income, the "ability" principle would require taxes which would still leave a discrepancy between the two incomes after payment of the taxes. The principle of equalization (except where incentive forbids) would wipe out both

---

[7] Of course "shifting" takes place through an increase in the price of a commodity or service and this increase, in turn, takes place either through a diminution in production or through a failure of production to increase in the face of an increasing demand. It is only a tax of the kind which diminishes the incentive to produce which would seem to be susceptible of "shifting." When taxes of this sort are imposed, however, it is the consumers of the products who really pay it. And there is no reason to suppose that the consumers of products have abilities to pay taxes proportionate to the incomes received by those who sell them the products. In other words a tax levied on the principle of "faculty," without discrimination between incomes which function as incentives and those which do not, defeats the very principle upon which it purports to be levied, for it burdens those of little "ability to pay." This fact is well expressed by one of the foremost upholders of the "faculty theory," Professor E. R. A. Seligman, (*Progressive Taxation in Theory and Practice*, second ed., 1908, pp. 299–300). In discussing the relative merits of proportional and progressive taxation, he says: "It is only in so far as we assume that so-called direct taxes remain where they are put, that the considerations of faculty or ability are of any weight. For the purpose of the theoretical discussion it may be taken for granted that the problem of progression versus proportion must be treated on the hypothesis that the assumption is true. When we come to construct a progressive scale in practice, however, we must be careful to ascertain how far the assumption conforms to reality. A progressive scale of taxation which does not reach individual faculty at all is as unnecessary as it is illogical."

incomes. More accurately, it would seize all the non-incentive incomes in excess of the average, and would distribute them to those who receive less than the average. This it would not necessarily do in the form of a money dividend; but the use of the taxes for public purposes would increase the real incomes of the public, or of some portions of it—if only of that part of the public which finds satisfaction from municipal jubilees or from the existence of large navies or costly post-office buildings. What would Mr. Carver do? In his principal discussion of taxation, he is considering it as a necessity of government, not as an instrument of equalization. Nevertheless he rejects the "ability" theory on the ground that it violates, in his opinion, the utilitarian principle of least sacrifice. Taxation of a sort which represses desirable industry should not be resorted to, he thinks, until the possibilities of non-repressive taxation have been exhausted. Confining himself to non-repressive taxation, he undertakes to demonstrate that as between two non-incentive incomes of different sizes, less sacrifice is caused by taxing the recipient of the higher income than by taxing the recipient of the lower, until the higher is reduced to the level of the lower (p. 656). That is, each dollar taken from the richer man causes less sacrifice than one taken from the poorer, as long as the untaxed portion of the former income still exceeds the latter. Mr. Carver, then, would depart from the "ability" principle, and would not necessarily leave intact a discrepancy between the higher and the next higher of various non-incentive incomes. If the government needed income as great as the difference between the two, it should all come from the top income, which would thus be reduced to the size of the next. But even if the government did not need so much for its regular expenses, Mr. Carver's logic would lead to the conclusion that as long as there are any discrepancies between non-incentive incomes, less sacrifice will be occasioned by pushing taxation still further, and using the funds for the benefit of the recipients of the lower incomes. For not only, according to this logic, would each dollar taken from the rich cause less sacrifice than a dollar taken from the poorer, but each dollar taken from the rich would cause less sacrifice than that which would be relieved in the poorer by adding a dollar to *his* income—until equalization resulted (except, always, for the incentive incomes). Yet Mr. Carver does not push his logic so far. He accepts instead the canon "that the taxes should be as little burdensome as possible" (p. 628). But if making *taxes* more burdensome results in making something else less burdensome to a greater degree, there seems no more reason for Mr. Carver's clinging to this canon than to that of "ability to pay." Whether or not one accepts Mr. Carver's grounds for rejecting the "faculty" theory, however, it must be remembered that that theory judges taxes by comparing the amounts actually paid by different individuals, without making any comparisons of the incomes remaining after the taxes are paid. If the discrepancies in the incomes remaining are to be justified, well and good; if not, why should taxation hesitate to remove them, unless some other instrument happens to be more appropriate? The payment of the taxes affects the sizes of the incomes. To leave that effect out of account, and to consider only the amount paid, instead of the amount left, as the "faculty" theory does, is to take a distorted view of the matter. It is like comparing the amount of change handed by a street-car conductor to various passengers, without taking account of how much he has left from their payments after giving them the change. The payment of $4.95 to one and of five cents to another would seem to be unjustified discrimination if we leave out of account the fact that the former had paid the conductor a five-dollar bill and the latter a dime. By similarly leaving out of account the fact that a man with a $10,000,000 non-incentive income and the man with a $10,000 one have been given these incomes by legal arrangements (i.e., by the government), the "faculty" theory makes it seem monstrous to compel the former to pay a tax of $9,990,000 and the latter of nothing. Yet as "change" for the property rights given by the government, the appearance of monstrosity disappears—unless there is some other justification for the discrepancy.

That brings up another ground for maintaining some of the inequalities, even when they do not add incentives to production. The rich man's habits may have made some things necessities for him which the poor man cares nothing for. Hence the gain to the poor man from equalization is less, psychologically, than the loss to the rich of his accustomed satisfactions. Mr. Carver admits the point as an argument against his taxation principle of reducing the rich man's income to the level of the poorer man's before starting to tax the latter. He admits it, but dismisses it, and it seems to me that both his admission and his dismissal over-simplify the problem raised. His admission is too wholesale, for while there are some wants whose non-satisfaction is particularly painful only to one who is accustomed to satisfy them, there are other wants whose non-satisfaction is painful wholly regardless of whether they have ever been satisfied. Such is intense physical pain, even when one has never been accustomed to buy the means of relieving it. On the other hand the problem cannot be dismissed by asserting, as Mr. Carter asserts, that at the end of a generation the standards of the rich and the poor would be equalized (p. 655). Such characteristic disregard of all but long considerations brings slight comfort to the man who has to wait until the passing of his generation (till his own death, in other words) before he ceases to suffer from the taking away of his accustomed satisfactions.

Another argument against leveling all those inequalities which fail to serve as incentives, is the argument known as that of "vested rights" or "legitimate expectations." One who has paid the full market value for a right to squeeze income out of the community seems to have more claim to sympathy when deprived of that right than does a man who parted with nothing for it. If we allow him to continue to get the income for that reason, even though it does not function as an incentive, we are doing it in effect on the ground that he needs it more than would one who had not paid, or at least that he "deserves" it more. The argument has weight, but seems to justify more study than is usually accorded to it. The "vested rights" of property are protected by law from some vicissitudes. But the law leaves them exposed to many others—such as competition, the constitutional exercise of the police power, the increase in the cost of operation (due perhaps to the government raising of railroad rates) and the falling off of demand. Moreover there are "legitimate expectations" which have not crystallized into property rights, such as personal skill acquired at great cost, or such as an ordinary job. To be deprived of these expectations may cause fully as great hardship as any destruction of a property right.[8] These rights do not now find protection. In fact it would be impossible to afford a complete guaranty to all of them, or even to all property rights, against all shrinkage of value. Frequently it may be true that to preserve one value (e.g. the value of railroad securities) it may be necessary to curtail another (say the property of the shipper who has to pay the higher railroad rates). As long as this is the case it may do more harm than good

---

[8] *Cf.* the very suggestive article by Professor James H. Tufts in 21 *Columbia Law Rev.* 405 (May, 1921), "Judicial Law-Making Exemplified in Industrial Arbitration."

to "legitimate expectations" themselves to protect them against certain sorts of changes, while leaving others exposed to diminution from changes of a different sort. The ones which are exposed might be partly protected by less rigidity in the protection of the unexposed. The whole problem is another of those which fails to interest Mr. Carver. It concerns only things that happen in the interval before the "long run" tendencies, with which he is concerned, have time to work themselves out. Meanwhile it may be observed that the problem is not raised by all proposals for bringing about greater equalization of incomes. It is not raised, for instance, in any of the proposals to prevent future growths of inequality—proposals to tax inheritances, or to tax future increments in land values.

In the case of inheritances, however, Mr. Carver suggests that certain grounds against drastic reductions would become apparent by "considering the family rather than the individual as the unit of society, and considering the family as a permanent unit unaffected by the brevity of individual lives" (p. 122). But obviously no amount of "considering" will make the family such a permanent unit, as long as social custom and biological law make the cooperation of members of other families essential to the reproduction of offspring. But Mr. Carver himself in 1915 considered this argument for inheritance no bar, under modern conditions, to a very drastic tax on inheritances in excess of what is needed to maintain the family in comfort.[9] And in the present book, as we have seen, he favors a distribution of "unearned wealth" by a graduated inheritance tax (amount not specified).

The owner of every dollar has, by virtue of his law-created right of ownership, a certain amount of influence over the channels into which industry shall flow. Increased buying of one product will make it worthwhile for more industry to flow into the production of that product rather than elsewhere. This is pointed out time and again by Mr. Carver. It is what he calls the "method of price persuasion" as distinguished from the "method of governmental compulsion" (p. 208). To call this "persuasion" rather than "coercion" is to use the same logic as that which would conclude that the tobacco tax is paid by persuasion rather than by compulsion. Whatever we call it, the fact remains that the business man will divert his energies into the channels where they will result in the production of goods of high market value, and out of the channels where they will produce goods of low values, if costs are the same in each. And the high value is partly a result of the demands of the owners of dollars. In producing the goods of higher value, thinks Mr. Carver, the business man is satisfying the desires of the community more completely than he would be by producing goods of lower value. The "marginal utility" of the cheap goods is lower, because the supply is already sufficiently great to satisfy the more pressing wants for it (pp. 351–2). The community may be mistaken in wanting the goods (pp. 485 and 55–57), but if not, the business man who pursues his own interest will be doing the most good, for he will be satisfying the most pressing wants. The channels of industry are governed by the "democratic voting" of those who vote with their dollars instead of with ballots;[10] and the result is the satisfaction of the most wants of the community. But what is "the community" whose wants are thus satisfied? It is not a single sentient being, but a name given to various individuals who have wants. It must be obvious that the individuals with the most dollars exercise the

107

COERCION AND DISTRIBUTION

---

[9] *Essays in Social Justice*, pp. 322–3.
[10] *Ibid*, pp. 112–25.

most control over the channels. This Mr. Carver recognizes,[11] and replies that the rich man (if deservedly rich) *ought* to have more control. This may be true; but it does not prove that the result is to satisfy the needs of the *members* of the community in the order of the intensity of those needs. A less pressing need of a rich man will have more influence over the channels than will many a more pressing need of a poor man. This may be justified on various grounds—in fact, it would be difficult to escape it altogether without complete equality of incomes—but the grounds on which it cannot be justified are that it is the result of "democratic voting" (which in ordinary discourse implies "one man one vote") and that it satisfies the more pressing wants before the less pressing.

It is not essential to Mr. Carver's case to make the arguments described above. There is much force in the contention he makes in his somewhat heated reply to Henry Clay's statement of the assumptions underlying the *laissez-faire* philosophy (pp. 741–4). Mr. Carver contends that one may quite consistently believe it harmful for the government to meddle consciously with the channels of industry, without believing that the channels taken in response to market demands are the best conceivable. One has only to believe that the channels fixed by governmental policy would probably be worse. They might be thought worse without assuming the desirability of satisfying more fully the wants of the rich, merely because it might be thought that the government, in spite of universal suffrage, would not force industry into the channels really desired by the voters, and, even if it did, would cause incidental damage and loss in the process of meddling. Yet government officials at various times have to make decisions as to the relative desirability of different channels of industry; and in making these decisions they can get no help from the market demands. It would be helpful if some study could be made of the problems involved which would furnish a more illuminating guide than Professor Carver's cynical conclusion that all public officers are politicians, and all politicians are a bad lot anyway, whose only aim is to try to catch the most votes. Decisions as to the channels of industry have to be made in the course of regulating the rates of monopolies and spending the public revenue. Many a rate case turns on the question whether a large share of the joint costs of the railroad ought to be borne by one sort of traffic and a smaller share by another, or vice versa. The answer to the question does not depend upon the market value of the respective services, since their market value will depend upon the answer given by the commission. Whenever an appropriation is made for a governmental expenditure, the question is no other than that of what sort of activity shall be promoted by the government's money demands. Since the working out of some sort of technique, if that be possible, would be helpful in answering these necessary questions, and since governments are likely to try their hands at still further control over the direction of industry, it might be well to examine somewhat more closely than does Mr. Carver the precise respects in which the "natural" channels fall short of perfection. If such a technique could be worked out, those officials who do meddle with the channels would have less excuse for guiding their actions by demagogic motives alone.

As already indicated, the rich man will always be in a position to satisfy his wants more completely than the poor man, as long as we continue to have rich and poor. But granting that a particular uneven division of income is desirable at

[11] *Essays*, p. 123; *National Economy*, p. 485.

a given time, it would be possible to divert the channels of industry to the advantage of the poor, without destroying the inequality in the money value of the relative shares. If the supply of working clothes were increased, by governmental intervention, and if their price consequently fell, while the supply of expensive evening clothes were diminished until their price increased, the workman would be able to buy more goods with his same money income, and the rich man fewer. The workman would have the same number of dollars worth of wealth, but more things. His real wealth would increase, the rich man's decrease. *How much* the wealth of either has changed we cannot say, for lack of a unit of measurement. In the abstract terms of economic theory, what has happened is that the consumer's surplus of the working man has increased, that of the rich man decreased. But again we have no way of measuring the change. That the result is to increase the sum total of human satisfaction may perhaps follow if we assume that the wants of each are equal to those of the other, since the workman's wants are less fully satisfied than the rich man's. But suppose we have a case where there is no such clear division between rich and poor. Suppose the government contemplates a diversion of industry from the production of books into the production of soap. There may be a net gain or a net loss from the change, when we take account of the conflicting interests of the two sets of consumers and of the two sets of producers, the collateral effects on the production of other things, and the loss in effort and irritation involved in the governmental process of effecting the change. Until economic science has developed some method of measuring changes in human satisfaction resulting from an increase in the production of one and a decrease in the production of another article, public officials will act pretty much in the dark. But the existence of this important economic problem is concealed by the common but fallacious doctrine of Mr. Carver and many other economists, that "the community" wants additional supplies of various goods with an intensity which varies with their market values.

The channels into which industry shall flow, then, as well as the apportionment of the community's wealth, depend upon coercive arrangements. These arrangements are put in force by various groups, some of whom derive their coercive power from control over governmental machinery, some from their own physical power to abstain from working. The arrangements are susceptible of great alteration by governmental bodies, and governments are concerning themselves more and more with them. Important interests are affected by the shape that these arrangements shall take. It is difficult to measure the interests, and even if they could be measured, there are no simple rules for determining how conflicts between them should be settled. The "principles of justice" supposed to govern courts do not suffice. Whatever accepted "principles" there may be, scarcely envisage the problems. Should they be settled on the basis of an enumeration of the persons affected? Representative government with a democratic suffrage is a crude (a very crude) device for bringing about settlements on this basis. Yet it may be doubted if the basis is a satisfactory one. Moreover the interests of vast numbers of persons outside the area where any one government holds sway may be affected by its decisions; and these interests at present obtain no representation in its councils. If the area is one rich in natural resources, it makes a great difference to many who live elsewhere how the concessions are apportioned, whether the resources are exploited at all or are locked up, how they shall be rationed (in case the supply, at the price charged, falls short of the demand), and what government shall control the disposition of any revenues derived from their taxation. Since the foreign interests have no representation in the local government, we find them bringing pressure to bear on it through the foreign offices of their respective home governments. We find attempts to formulate "principles" concerning concessions (such as the "open door"), and we find a desire for annexation. We find the foreign governments disputing with one another over these matters, which contain the most fertile seeds of modern warfare. All such problems of democracy, representative government, international economic conflicts and their adjustments, fall properly within the scope of a treatise on *The Principles of National Economy*. They are not discussed by Mr. Carver.

John Dewey

John Dewey

JOHN DEWEY[1] (1859–1952) was the most famous American philosopher of the first half of the twentieth century. Reflecting his stature, the United States issued a stamp in his honor in 1968. Dewey was born and raised in a Calvinist household in Burlington, Vermont, his father a shopkeeper, his mother a homemaker. After attending the University of Vermont, he worked as a schoolteacher before settling on an academic career in philosophy and enrolling in graduate school at Johns Hopkins University in 1882. Dewey was a prolific writer and polymath, and his academic rise was swift. His doctoral supervisor, George Morris, arranged for Dewey to have an instructorship under him at the University of Michigan in 1884. After a brief stint as a professor of philosophy at the University of Minnesota beginning in the fall of 1888, Dewey took over Michigan's philosophy department after Morris's sudden death in 1889, and in 1894 moved on to the University of Chicago to lead the philosophy department, which at that time included both psychology and pedagogy. He soon proposed creation of a separate department of education, which he was also appointed to lead. In Ann Arbor, Dewey had fallen in love with his student, Alice Chipman, whom he married, and with whom he would have seven children. She worked with him in Chicago as principal of the Laboratory School he established under the university's education department.

Dewey's early work spanned philosophy, psychology, and education. In all these fields, his work reflected an effort to develop a mode of living and thinking consistent with what seemed the insights of modern science—Darwinian science above all. His early philosophical work sought to reconcile a liberal Christianity with Darwinism and a progressive conception of science. By the late 1890s, the major themes of what would become known as his "pragmatism" were visible. At the core was a conception, familiar from William James, of the individual being as a problem solver in an environment. For Dewey, as for James, it is a central psychological fact that people attend to things so as to make use of them or put into action. We pay attention to things, and things stand out in our perception, as we find them functional; interpretation is the process of thinking about, recognizing, and attributing function. Dewey's extensive writing about democracy, psychology, education, and philosophy all returned to this central theme, and focused on ways and means by which humans do things, overcome obstacles, and solve problems.

In 1896, he attacked "stimulus-response" psychology, proposing that organisms interacting with their environment also select and affect their own stimuli.[2] The essay made his reputation in psychology, and in 1899–1900, Dewey served as president of the American Psychological Association. In the field of education, he rejected both child-centered and curriculum-centered pedagogy, promoting a learning environment keyed to problem solving and the testing of ideas through concrete experience. While at Chicago, he worked extensively in logic, building a functional and instrumental conception of logic parallel to James's emerging psychological ideas. Most famously, Dewey began his lifelong pragmatic defense of democracy and democratic decision making, starting with his 1888 *The Ethics of Democracy*.[3]

In academic matters, Dewey was a man of the middle way. We might see his pragmatic pedagogy in these terms: he rejected both child- and curriculum-centered dogmas, the one seemed romantic, the other totalitarian. He rejected vocational education—but also education in the classics—and sought to foster social relations between teachers and students conducive to problem solving as preparation for participation in democratic life. His psychology rejected both behavioral and organic conceptions of the person, his philosophical writings attacked both realists and idealists. Facts, he argued, are neither absolute nor the product of human imagination—they are those things that a person finds it useful to engage *as* facts in a specific situation, to solve a specific problem. Knowing, he argues, is a functional capacity and a purposive activity. Dewey was a consistent proponent of a social and democratic liberalism, informed—and reformed—by careful scientific and technological instrumentalism. Alongside his prodigious writing, it may well have been this moderate liberality that propelled him to academic leadership, as president of the American Philosophical Association in 1905, and as vice president of the American Association for the Advancement of Science in 1909.

Dewey was also politically active throughout his career in various progressive and liberal causes. In Chicago, he worked with Jane Addams at her Hull House mission, and, in partnership with his wife Alice, was an active proponent of educational reform. It was Chicago president Harper's decision to terminate Alice Dewey's contract with the University's Laboratory School that precipitated Dewey's departure for Columbia University in New York in 1905. In New York, he worked with the women's suffrage movement, supported the Henry Street Settlement, and participated in the struggle to found a teachers' union. He was a founder of the American Association of University Professors and the American Civil Liberties Union. He wrote numerous short essays for the *New Republic* and other popular journals, on topics ranging from school reform to American foreign policy. He disapproved of religious instruction in public schools, and was active in defending academic freedom and opposing the imposition of loyalty oaths in education. Dewey supported U.S. intervention in the First World War and thereafter wrote frequently about American foreign policy. In the 1920s, he wrote approvingly of the socialist reforms he had seen on a visit to Mexico, and called for American recognition of the Soviet government after a visit to Soviet schools in 1928. In 1937, Dewey chaired the commission investigating charges against Leon Trotsky in Mexico, exonerating him of charges brought in Moscow. Dewey defended American neutrality after the First World War and opposed American intervention in Europe until 1939, when he joined Sidney Hook in the Committee for Cultural Freedom to denounce repression in the Soviet Union, Germany, Italy, Japan, and Spain. He supported Lend-Lease. Starting with his 1927 *The Public and Its Problems*, Dewey lamented the erosion of the practice of open public debate and citizen engagement in American democratic life. After the war, Dewey was a vocal opponent of the House Committee on Un-American Activities and of efforts to remove members of the Communist Party from teaching positions.

Dewey has been the only leading American philosopher to look at legal reasoning carefully from the inside and to participate in the internal debates of the legal academy. He was, in a sense, the opposite of Ronald Dworkin, a legal insider who participated in philosophical debates.[4] In 1913, Dewey presided over a Conference on Legal and Social Philosophy at which Roscoe Pound, Morris Cohen, and others gave papers. He co-taught jurisprudence with Edwin Patterson at Columbia Law School in the 1920s. Among his voluminous writings are several significant essays about law—each of which was cited and discussed by contemporaneous legal theorists. Dewey wrote about law, aware that American legal thought had become home to competing schools of thought and methodologies, associated more or less tightly with political tendencies. He presents his own philosophy of law as a middle way, rejecting positivism and naturalism, and as a vehicle to affirm and foster law as an instrument for the progressive and evolutionary development of society.

In 1941, Dewey contributed a short essay to a collection that included essays by Morris Cohen, Walter Wheeler Cook, Lon Fuller, Karl Llewellyn, and Roscoe Pound, among others.[5] The essay rehearses a number of familiar realist themes and provides a helpful overview of Dewey's legal thinking, which he had worked out earlier in more narrowly focused papers. Dewey stresses the relationship between legal philosophy and the "movements of the period in which they are produced" and attributes differences among legal scholars to "different attitudes toward practical questions of what should be done and how best to do it."[6] He argues that "law is through and through a social phenomenon: social in origin, in purpose or end, and in application."[7] The essay focuses on the idea that the "social" is an *ongoing* process, out of which law arises, and in which it acts. "[W]hat is called *application* is not something that happens *after* a rule or law or statute is laid down but is a necessary part of them; such a necessary part indeed that in given cases we can judge what the law *is* as a matter of fact only by telling how it operates, and what are its effects in and upon the human activities that are going on."[8] The essay develops the idea that "[a] given legal arrangement *is* what it *does*"[9] into a critique of the idea that sovereignty could refer to something *outside* law, rather than to "something existing *within* social activities and relations."[10] To say that law is social, a function of society, should not, he argues, lead us to replace one obscure concept—law, with another—"society." He rejects efforts to think about the relationship between law and society as one between stable *forms* filled with changing content, in favor of the idea of *function* as a link between social and legal processes—an approach which demands, according to Dewey, that "the best scientific methods and materials available, be used, to investigate, in terms of the context of actual situations, the consequences of legal rules and of proposed legal decisions and acts of legislation."[11] Approached in this way, legal thought can contribute to the "never-ending" process of improving standards of judgment.[12]

In 1926, Dewey had worked out this approach in his one effort at doctrinal legal analysis, explaining the doctrine of "corporate legal personality"—the idea of the corporation as a "right-and-duty-bearing-unit"—in pragmatic terms.[13] The article is more useful for its theoretical elaboration of the consequences of philosophical pragmatism for legal thought than for its analysis of corporate personality doctrine. Dewey expresses his intense belief in the long-term reliability of legal reasoning as a vehicle to move useful practices into legal rules and institutions. He also elaborates the legal significance of what he termed Pierce's "pragmatistic rule" that "our conception of . . . effects is the whole of our conception of the object"[14] in terms reminiscent of Holmes, if less sharply stated. Perhaps most significantly, he uses the indeterminacy of leading legal theories about the personality of legal and natural persons to criticize the effort to resolve legal issues by reference to such theories, rather than to social and political interests:[15]

> Each theory has been used to serve the same ends, and each has been used to serve opposing ends. The doctrine of the personality of the state has been advanced to place the state above legal responsibility on the ground that such a person has no superior person—save God—to whom to answer; and in behalf of a doctrine of the responsibility of the state and its officers to law, since to be a person is to have legal powers and duties. The personality of the state has been opposed to both the personality of "natural" singular persons and to the personality of groups. In the latter connection it has been employed both to make the state the supreme and culminating personality in a hierarchy, to make it but *primus inter paros*, and to reduce it to merely one among many, sometimes more important than others and sometimes less so. These are political rather than legal considerations, but they have affected law. In legal doctrines proper, both theories have been upheld for the same purpose, and each for opposed ends. Corporate groups less than the state have had real personality ascribed to them, both in order to make them more amenable to liability, as in the case of trade-unions, and to exalt their dignity and vital power, as against external control. Their personality (p. 670) has been denied for like reasons; they have been pulverized into mere aggregates of separate persons in order to protect other laborers from them, to make more difficult their unified action in trade disputes, as in collective bargaining, and to enable union property to escape liability, the associated individuals in their severalty having no property to levy upon. The group personality theory has been asserted both as a check upon what was regarded as anarchic and dissolving individualism, to set up something more abiding and worthful than a single human being, and to increase the power and dignity of the single being as over against the state. Even the doctrine that true personality resides only in the "natural" person has been worked in opposed directions. It was first used to give church or state a short and direct road of approach which would lessen the power of the singular being over against the collective being, while lately, through being affected by "natural" in the sense of natural rights, it has been employed to exalt private, at the expense of public, interests. (Page 673) ... Nothing accurate or intelligible can be said except by specifying the interest and purpose of a writer, and his historical context of problems and issues. Thus we end where we began: with the statement that the entire discussion of personality, is needlessly encumbered with a mass of traditional doctrines and remnants of old issues.

For Dewey, the result is unfortunate: "the doctrine of 'fictitious' personality has been employed, under the influence of the 'individualistic' philosophy already referred to, in order to deny that there is any social reality at all back of or in corporate action" (p. 673).

Dewey's most important work about law remained his first—the 1924 "Logical Method and Law" included here. Dewey's focus in this essay is legal reasoning, not as it is presented to us in opinions purporting to state the reasons for a decision, but as he imagines judges actually engaging in it—as the activity of a profession. In a quite striking passage, Dewey defines logic as "an account of the procedures followed in reaching decisions . . . in those cases when subsequent experience shows that the procedures employed were the best which could have been used under the conditions" (pp. 185–6). His description of judicial thinking demotes deduction from premises ("the problem is not to draw a conclusion from given premises; that can best be done by a piece of animate machinery") in favor of a "search for principles and data" to substantiate our vague preliminary hunches about a conclusion, or to "enable us to choose intelligently between rival conclusions" (p. 190). Dewey's intense hostility to deduction leads him not to despair over the irrationality and uncertainty of the legal order, but to optimism about its usefulness and its tendency to record and evolve ever more useful results for changing social problems.

Dewey ends the essay with a denunciation of law-by-syllogism as an obstacle to progressive social change, one that sanctifies the old and widens the gap between "current social conditions and the principles used by the courts." The result, he argues, "is to breed irritation, disrespect for law, together with virtual alliance between the judiciary and the entrenched interests that correspond most nearly to the conditions under which the rules of law were previously laid down" (p. 193). Echoing his realist colleagues, he chooses as an example the "paradoxical fact that the slogans of the liberalism of one period often become the bulwarks of reaction in a subsequent era."

> There was a time in the eighteenth century when the great social need was emancipation of industry and trade from a multitude of restrictions which held over from the feudal estate of Europe. . . . The movement of emancipation expressed itself in principles of liberty in use of property, and of freedom in making contracts, which were embodied in a consistent series of legal decisions. . . . But the absolutistic logic of rigid syllogistic forms infected these ideas. It was soon forgotten that they were relative to the requirements of a particular state of affairs, needed to secure a greater measure of economic social welfare. Thus these principles became in their turn so rigid as to be almost as socially obstructive as "immutable" feudal laws had been in their day. (pp. 193–4)

To prevent the new principles of "social justice" which have replaced freedom of contract and property from becoming rigid in their own turn, Dewey exhorts us to remain attentive to the "facts of social life," and to think of legal precepts as "tools to be adapted" to the conditions in which they are employed (p. 194).

Although Dewey's "Logical Method and Law" was widely read by legal scholars, it is not clear whether legal scholars were significantly influenced by Dewey's argument. Some have argued that, for better or worse, they were. Jerome Frank, writing in 1950, asserted that "John Dewey is rightly hailed today as America's most influential philosopher," but decried what he saw as "Deweyite" influence in the work of Walter Wheeler Cook, Karl Llewellyn, Edwin Patterson, and Benjamin Cardozo.[16] Nonetheless, he presents no specific evidence of Dewey's direct influence on their work. Whether or not Dewey's analysis was persuasive, it was a powerful description of legal reasoning as it had come to be understood in the profession by the middle of the last century: as a mode of quite fluid problem solving far removed from deduction. Dewey's description of the relationship between deduction and inattention to social conditions was so widely shared in the legal academy at the time that his essay could be read then as a statement of the obvious. In the late 1930s "everyone knew" that legal principles and purposes were often in contradiction, just as everyone knew legal reasoning should become more functionally attuned to social needs and objectives.

Although Dewey refers to his own method in various terms—pragmatic, logical, instrumental, experimental, scientific, empirical—he is remembered above all as the most significant American philosophical pragmatist of the early twentieth century. He remains with us as a point of contact between American legal thought and the pragmatist tradition in American philosophy, and an opportunity to assess the relationship between them. Still, scholars have differed on the question of pragmatism's significance for the tradition of American legal thought. The word "pragmatism" itself has had numerous connotations in legal science—most quite innocent of debates within the field of philosophy about "pragmatism." It often comes up when people are asked to characterize American legal thought in general terms. In the broadest sense, the term "pragmatic" brings to mind a range of stereotypes about American legal thinking—that we are practically minded, unprincipled, results-oriented, and anti-theoretical or anti-Intellectual. In this broad sense, the term has been used as a badge of both honor and shame. American legal professionals are forward-looking problem solvers—or unprincipled slaves of their clients and political sentiments.

In a somewhat narrower sense, pragmatism might be used to suggest many of the ideas represented in the Canon so far: a preoccupation with the social functions and practical uses of the legal system, an interest in law as an instrument of policy or as a site for making policy choices, a commitment to anti-formal methodologies for interpreting legal materials, an attentiveness to the contradictions and gaps within normative materials and a search for solutions in real-world practices, a focus on outcomes rather than first principles, an openness to partnership with the social sciences, interest in empirical methods and an instrumental approach to legal doctrine, a focus on legislation and administration rather than adjudication and on the lawyer or judge as a problem solver and policy maker, and undoubtedly many more.

The men who introduced these ideas into American legal thought did not use the word pragmatism to describe them. Nor were they particularly influenced by Dewey. The legal scholars who first focused our attention on these ideas did so in the name of sound legal thinking and analytic rigor, rather than as the expression of a self-conscious "pragmatist" methodology. Some urged that American legal thought become more "modern" or "scientific." They were more specific and articulate about the methods they rejected, which they characterized derisively as "formalism," "conceptualism," "positivism," "categorical dogmatism," and associated variously with the nineteenth century, with the names Austin and Langdell, with lay thinking about law, with British legal thought, and with the analytic scholarship of their predecessors. The legal realists, who did see themselves as introducing a new *method* for thinking about law, used the words "functionalist," "sociological," or simply "realist" to describe what they had in mind.

Even so, the "pragmatism" of William James, Charles Pierce, and John Dewey is generally regarded as the most significant American contribution to philosophy, and it seems plausible to imagine that their ideas made a distinctive American contribution to legal thought. Holmes was in conversation with James and Pierce when he wrote "The Path of the Law," and his ideas seem rooted in the same Cambridge social and intellectual milieu.[17] Holmes knew James and Pierce; Dewey wrote about law and was a famous pragmatist; American legal thought seems pragmatic—it would be natural to think these phenomena were related to one another. It is not clear, however, that Dewey and Holmes remained on the same page. Michal Alberstein has argued that Dewey's lengthy analysis of Holmes's famous statement that "the whole outline of the law is the result of a conflict at every point between logic and good sense—the one striving to work fiction out to consistent results, the other restraining and at last overcoming that effort when the results become too manifestly unjust" in "Logical Method and the Law" translates what for Holmes is a tragic existential fact into a promising opportunity for pragmatic innovation against a reassuring backdrop of social stability.[18]

> What justice Holmes terms logic is formal consistency, consistency of concepts with one another, irrespective of the consequences of their application to concrete matter-of-fact. We might state the fact by saying that concepts once developed have a kind of intrinsic inertia on their own account; once developed the law of habit applies to them. It is practically economical to use a concept ready at hand rather than to take time and trouble and effort to change it or to devise a new one. The use of prior ready-made and familiar concepts also gives rise to a sense of stability, of guarantee against sudden and arbitrary changes of the rules which determine the consequences which legally attend acts. It is the nature of any concept, as it is of any habit to change more slowly than do the concrete circumstances with reference to which it is employed. Experience shows that the relative fixity of concepts affords men with a specious sense of proportion, of assurance against the troublesome flux of events.[19]

William James first used the word "pragmatism" in 1898 to describe his philosophical focus on human intelligence as an active, problem-solving function, and his commitment to the idea that the experience of such an intelligence exceeded the language used to understand it. It was this sense of pragmatism which Dewey extended to legal decision making in his contribution to the canon.

After the Second World War, pragmatism—and Dewey—fell out of favor in American philosophy departments, replaced by an interest in British analytical and linguistic philosophy and to a lesser extent, European political and social theory. Although postwar American legal thought remained focused on efforts to metabolize the ideas introduced by Holmes, Hohfeld, and the legal realists, these ideas were known variously by the terms "functionalism," "realism," or "sociological jurisprudence" rather than "pragmatism." Postwar American legal philosophers seemed altogether less preoccupied with Dewey, turning their attention to the analytic and linguistic texts most in fashion among their colleagues in philosophy departments. Dewey was forgotten, as Holmes and the realists were remembered.

Legal historian Gary Peller emphasizes the significance of Dewey's pragmatism not in relationship to Holmes and the realists, but as a precursor for the more moderate thinking of the post–World War II generation of legal process scholars—Lon Fuller, Henry Hart, Albert Sacks, Herbert Wechsler, and others.[20] Peller argues that for these later legal intellectuals, Dewey's pragmatism offered a tamed version of modernism and relativism. He writes: "John Dewey's pragmatic compromise between the traditionalist conviction that moral authority depended on belief in the objectivity of truth and ethics and the modernist assertion that such issues were necessarily contextual and relative became, by the fifties, the broad filter through which the first generation of post-War intellectuals in America would understand both their roles as intellectuals and the general legitimacy of American society."[21] For those who read Dewey, "the relativist and instrumental premises of the modernists" became a "virtue rather than a vice."[22] In particular, he argues that:

> In short, the fifties process-theorists reconceived the relationship between law and politics in a way that closely mirrored the reconceived relationship between reason and values as articulated by Dewey. Just as reason was both a source of values (in the sense that free and open inquiry would lead to at least provisional truths) and simultaneously merely instrumental and subordinate (in the sense that all reasoning was necessarily situated within a framework of values and therefore was subsidiary to that

framework), so in the Hart and Sacks conception law, conceived of as institutional procedures, was both the "source of the substantive arrangements" and, simultaneously, merely instrumental in the sense that law was subsidiary to politics. Institutional procedures were merely the "means" that could serve any content for law.[23]

The words "pragmatic" and "pragmatism" entered mainstream American legal scholarship again in the 1980s when philosophical pragmatism was enjoying a revival among liberal American philosophers, influenced strongly by Richard Rorty's embrace of the term and the tradition. But the philosophical pragmatism of the 1980s was quite different from that of the 1890s. By the 1980s, the term pragmatism was used to refer variously to American anti-foundationalism, to the priority of social experience, conversation, and open-mindedness. These themes owed as much to increased technical specialization and the discovery of apparent dead ends within postwar analytic and linguistic philosophy as to the pragmatism of Dewey, Pierce, and James—or Holmes. Nevertheless, for some liberal legal scholars of the 1980s, these themes provided a satisfying response to the threats which seemed to be posed by legal pluralism, by the indeterminacy of much legal reasoning, and by the rise of what seemed unduly instrumental legal theories on the right and unduly relativist legal theories on the left. Several prominent legal scholars began to speak of American legal thought—beginning with Holmes—as a stable series of useful "pragmatisms." This second wave of pragmatic thought was certainly interesting, but bore only a vague genealogical relationship to the Dewey of "Logical Method and the Law."

DAVID KENNEDY

NOTES

1. Published in 33 *Philosophical Review* 560 (1924), republished in 10 *Cornell Law Quarterly* 17 (1924); and in Philosophy and Civilization (New York: Minton, Balch and Company, 1931), 126–40; and in John Dewey, *The Middle Works, vol. 15: 1923–1924*, Jo Ann Boydston, ed. (Carbondale and Edwardsville: Southern Illinois University Press, 1983), 65–77.

2. John Dewey, "The Reflex Arc Concept in Psychology," 3 *Psychological Review* 357 (1896).

3. John Dewey, *The Ethics of Democracy* (Ann Arbor: Andrews & Company, 1888).

4. See pp. 551–561 infra.

5. John Dewey, Untitled, in Julius Rosenthal Foundation, Northwestern University, eds., *My Philosophy of Law: Credos of Sixteen American Scholars* (Boston: Boston Law Book Co., 1941), 73–85.

6. Id. at 75.

7. Id. at 76.

8. Id. at 77.

9. Id.

10. Id. at 81.

11. Id. at 84.

12. Id. at 85.

13. See Dewey, "The Historic Background of Corporate Legal Personality," 35 *Yale Law Journal* 655, 656 (1926).

14. Id. at 661.

15. Id. beginning at 669.

16. Jerome Frank, "Modern and Ancient Legal Pragmatism—John Dewey and Co. vs. Aristotle: I," 25 *Notre Dame Law* (1949–50).

17. See O. W. Holmes, "The Path of the Law," 10 *Harvard Law Review* 457 (1897).

18. John Dewey, "Logical Method and the Law," 10 *Cornell Law Quarterly* 17, 20 (1925), quoted in Michal Alberstein, "*Pragmatism, and American (I)Ilegal Family Ties: Obsession, Hysteria and Problem Solving*" (PhD dissertation, 2000, Harvard University), 73.

19. Id.

20. See Gary Peller, "Neutral Principles in the 1950's," 21 *Journal of Law Reform* 561 at 580 (1987–88) and following.

21. Id. at 580.

22. Id. at 583.

23. Id. at 590–91.

BIBLIOGRAPHY

A standard biography of Dewey is George Dykhuizen, *The Life and Mind of John Dewey* (Carbondale: Southern Illinois University Press, 1973). The Center for Dewey Studies at Southern Illinois University at Carbondale is a focal point for research on Dewey's life and work. Their Web site has a useful bibliography of primary and secondary sources: http://www.siu.edu/~deweyctr/. Of Dewey's many writings, perhaps *Experience and Nature* (Chicago, London: Open Court Publishing, 1925); *The Quest for Certainty* (Carbondale: Southern Illinois University Press, 1988); and *Liberalism and Social Action* (New York: G. P. Putnam's Sons, 1935) provide the most useful entry points to his thinking.

Dewey's first significant essay about law, "Anthropology and Law" (1893) reprinted in *The Early Works of John Dewey 1882–1898, Vol. 4: 1893–1894* (Carbondale and Edwardsville: Southern Illinois University Press, 1967), 37–41, interpreted Holmes's *The Common Law* as evidence for the idea that "some of the most highly developed legal ideas and practices of to-day can be traced to a beginning in the crude psychological structure of primitive man" (p. 37). Primitive customs are not the *cause*s of modern law, he argues, but the material which man selects and modifies through the "agency of natural selection" in accordance with their "practical value, the working utility, of the rules themselves" (p. 40).

Dewey's early writings on democracy touch at various points on ideas about sovereignty and the nature of political and legislative authority. His most sustained treatment is "Austin's Theory of Sovereignty," 9 *Political Science Quarterly* 31 (1894). Dewey's ideas about sovereignty and the sources of law are analyzed in Anton Donoso, "John Dewey's Philosophy of Law," 36 *University of Detroit Law Journal* 579, 584 and following (1958–59).

The most significant legal commentary on Dewey's ideas remains Jerome Frank, "Modern and Ancient Legal Pragmatism—John Dewey and Co. vs. Aristotle: I," 25 *Notre Dame Lawyer* 207 (1949–50). Frank assails Dewey's legal pragmatism—largely as represented by legal scholars whom Frank interprets as followers of Dewey—for overestimating the rationality, progressive evolution, and overall determinacy and predictability of the judicial process. For Frank, this results from an exclusive focus, in articles such as *Logical Method and Law*, on the reasoning processes of appellate courts facing "new or unusual" questions of legal interpretation. Dewey's conception of logic as an ex post description of useful habits of thought encourages the (false) idea that legal uncertainty arises only with respect to novel questions of law—and that useful habits of thought will wear themselves into the social fabric. For Frank, the common experience of trial courts belies this hopeful conclusion. The disputes about facts, interpretation, and application of rules which arise there also require judicial reasoning and open the judicial process to all sorts of discretion. The routine work of trial courts ought to disrupt Dewey's complacency about the reliability of pragmatic (appellate) legal reasoning. At the same time, Frank cites with approval Dewey's insistence "that general legal rules and principles are working hypotheses, needing to be constantly tested by the way in which they work out in application to concrete situations," and his exhortations to courts to "trust to an experimental logic" (p. 211). See also Jerome Frank, "Cardozo and the Upper-Court Myth," 13 *Law and Contemporary Problems* 369 (1948), and Jerome Frank, "A Conflict with Oblivion: Some Observations on, the Founders of Legal Pragmatism," 9 *Rutgers Law Review* 425 (1954–55).

For a fascinating intellectual history of the Cambridge milieu common to Holmes, Pierce, and James, see Louis Menand, *The Metaphysical Club: A Story of Ideas in America* (New York: Farrar, Straus, and Giroux, 2001). For a well-researched and argued analysis of the pragmatisms of Holmes and Dewey, see Mark Mendell, "Pragmatism and Legal Reasoning," PhD dissertation, University of Pennsylvania, 1989. The leading article on Holmes and pragmatism remains Thomas C. Grey, "Holmes and Legal Pragmatism," 41 *Stanford Law Review* 787 (1988–89).

The revival of pragmatism in American philosophy departments has generated an enormous literature. One might usefully begin with Louis Menand, ed., *Pragmatism: A Reader* (New York: Vintage Books, 1997); Richard Rorty, *Contingency, Irony and Solidarity* (Cambridge and New York: New York University Press, 1989); Cornel West, *The American Evasion of Philosophy: A Genealogy of Pragmatism* (Madison: University of Wisconsin Press, 1989). Secondary treatments of the phenomenon include Sandra B. Rosenthal, Carl R. Hausman, and Douglas R. Anderson, *Classical American Pragmatism: Its Contemporary Vitality* (Urbana: University of Illinois Press, 1999); and Morris Dickstein, ed., *The Revival of Pragmatism* (Durham: Duke University Press, 1998).

The relationship between philosophical and legal pragmatism was developed by E. W. Patterson, "Pragmatism as a Philosophy of Law," in Sidney Ratner, *The Philosopher of the Common Man: Essays in Honor of John Dewey to Celebrate His Eightieth Birthday* (New York: G.P. Putnam's Sons, 1940). The most compelling recent treatment of the relationship between legal and philosophical pragmatism in America is Michal Alberstein, "Pragmatism, and American (Il)legal Family Ties: Obsession, Hysteria and Problem Solving" (PhD dissertation, 2000, Harvard University). Alberstein attacks efforts by modern liberal legal scholars to read the Holmes and realist traditions in American legal thought as "pragmatism." For Alberstein, doing so requires reading the progressive and liberal baggage which pragmatism has acquired since Dewey and Rorty back onto the more agnostic and tragic position of Holmes and the realists. Alberstein stresses that Dewey's image of legal reasoning was far more complacent, rational, and hopeful about social progress than the more instrumental, irrational, and dark sides of both Holmes and the realists whom she admires. It was precisely this difference to which Jerome Frank drew attention in attacking Dewey and his followers for diluting awareness of legal uncertainty.

"Logical Method and Law"

10 Cornell Law Quarterly 17 (1924)

Human conduct, broadly viewed, falls into two sorts: Particular cases overlap, but the difference is discernible on any large scale consideration of conduct. Sometimes human beings act with a minimum of foresight, without examination of what they are doing and of probable consequences. They act not upon deliberation but from routine, instinct, the direct pressure of appetite, or a blind 'hunch.' It would be a mistake to suppose that such behavior is always inefficient or unsuccessful. When we do not like it, we condemn it as capricious, arbitrary, careless, negligent. But in other cases, we praise the marvellous [sic] rectitude of instinct or intuition; we are inclined to accept the offhand appraisal of an expert in preference to elaborately calculated conclusions of a man who is ill-informed. There is the old story of the layman who was appointed to a position in India where he would have to pass in his official capacity on various matters in controversy between natives. Upon consulting a legal friend, he was told to use his common-sense and announce his decisions firmly; in the majority of cases his natural decision as to what was fair and reasonable would suffice. But, his friend added: "Never try to give reasons, for they will usually be wrong."

In the other sort of case, action follows upon a decision, and the decision is the outcome of inquiry, comparison of alternatives, weighing of facts; deliberation or thinking has intervened. Considerations which have weight in reaching the conclusion as to what is to be done, or which are employed to justify it when it is questioned, are called 'reasons.' If they are stated in sufficiently general terms they are 'principles.' When the operation is formulated in a compact way, the decision is called a conclusion, and the considerations which led up to it are called the premises. Decisions of the first type may be reasonable: that is, they may be adapted to good results; those of the second type are reasoned or rational, increasingly so, in the degree of care and thoroughness with which inquiry has been conducted and the order in which connections have been established between the considerations dealt with.

Now I define logical theory as an account of the procedures followed in reaching decisions of the second type, in those cases in which subsequent experience shows that they were the best which could have been used under the conditions. This definition would be questioned by many authorities, and it is only fair to say that it does not represent the orthodox or the prevailing view. But it is stated at the outset so that the reader may be aware of the conception of logic which underlies the following discussion. If we take an objection which will be brought against this conception by adherents of the traditional notion, it will serve to clarify its meaning. It will be said that the definition restricts thinking to the processes antecedent to making a decision or a deliberate choice; and, thereby, in confining logical procedure to practical matters, fails to take even a glance at those cases in which true logical method is best exemplified: namely, scientific, especially mathematical, subjects.

A partial answer to this objection is that the especial topic of our present discussion is logical method in legal reasoning and judicial decision, and that such cases at least are similar in general type to decisions made by engineers, merchants, physicians, bankers, etc., in the pursuit of their callings. In law we are certainly concerned with the necessity of settling upon a course of action to be pursued, giving judgment of one sort or another in favor of adoption of one mode of conduct and against another. But the scope of the position taken will appear more clearly if we do not content ourselves with this *ad hoc* reply.

If we consider the procedure of the mathematician or of any man of science, as it concretely occurs, instead of considering simply the relations of consistent implication which subsist between the propositions in which his finally approved conclusions are set forth, we find that he, as well as an intelligent farmer or business man or physician, is constantly engaged in making decisions; and that in order to make them wisely he summons before his mental gaze various considerations, and accepts and rejects them with a view to making his decision as rational as possible. The concrete subject with which he deals, the material he investigates, accepts, rejects, employs in reaching and justifying his decision, is different from that of farmer, lawyer, or merchant, but the course of the operation, the form of the procedure, is similar. The scientific man has the advantage of working under much more narrowly and exactly controlled conditions, with the aid of symbols artfully devised to protect his procedure. For that reason it is natural and proper that we should, in our formal treatises, take operations of this type as standards and models, and should treat ordinary 'practical' reasonings leading up to decisions as to what is to be done as only approximations. But every thinker, as an investigator, mathematician, or physicist as well as 'practical man,' thinks in order to determine *his* decisions and conduct—his conduct as a specialized agent working in a carefully delimited field.

It may be replied, of course, that this is an arbitrary notion of logic, and that in reality logic is an affair of the relations and orders of relations which subsist between propositions which constitute the accepted subject-matter of a science; that relations are independent of operations of inquiry and of reaching conclusions or decisions. I shall not stop to try to controvert this position, but shall use it to point the essential difference between it and the position taken in this article. According to the latter, logical systematization with a view to the utmost generality and consistency of propositions is indispensable but is not ultimate. It is an instrumentality, not an end. It is a means of improving, facilitating, clarifying the inquiry that leads up to concrete decisions; primarily that particular inquiry which has just been engaged in, but secondarily, and of greater ultimate importance, other inquiries directed at making other decisions in similar fields. And here at least I may fall back for confirmation upon the special theme of law. It is most important that rules of law should form as coherent generalized logical systems as possible. But these logical systematizations of law in any field, whether of crime, contracts, or torts, with their reduction of a multitude of decisions to a few general principles that are logically consistent with one another while it may be an end in itself for a particular student, is clearly in last resort subservient to the economical and effective reaching of decisions in particular cases.

It follows that logic is ultimately an empirical and concrete discipline. Men first employ certain ways of investigating, and of collecting, recording and using data in reaching conclusions, in making decisions; they draw inferences and make their checks and tests in various ways. These different ways constitute the empirical raw material of logical theory. The latter thus comes into existence without any conscious thought of logic, just as forms of speech take place without conscious reference to rules of syntax or of rhetorical propriety. But it is gradually learned that some methods which are used work better than others. Some yield conclusions that do not stand the test of further situations; they produce conflicts and confusion; decisions dependent upon them have to be retracted or revised. Other methods are found to yield conclusions which are available in subsequent inquiries as well as confirmed by them. There first occurs a kind of natural selection of the methods which afford the better type of conclusion, better for subsequent usage, just as happens in the development of rules for conducting any art. Afterwards the methods are themselves studied critically. Successful ones are not only selected and collated, but the causes of their effective operation are discovered. Thus logical theory becomes scientific.

The bearing of the conception of logic which is here advanced upon legal thinking and decisions may be brought out by examining the apparent disparity which exists between actual legal development and the strict requirements of logical theory. Justice Holmes has generalized the situation by saying that "the whole outline of the law is the resultant of a conflict at every point between logic and good sense—the one striving to work fiction out to consistent results, the other restraining and at last overcoming that effort when the results become too manifestly unjust."[1] This statement he substantiates by a thorough examination of the development of certain legal notions. Upon its surface, such a statement implies a different view of the nature of logic than that stated. It implies that logic is not the method *of* good sense, that it has as it were a substance and life of its own which conflicts with the requirements of good decisions with respect to concrete subject-matters. The difference, however, is largely verbal. What Justice Holmes terms logic is formal consistency, consistency of concepts with one another irrespective of the consequences of their application to concrete matters-of-fact. We might state the fact by saying that concepts once developed have a kind of intrinsic inertia on their own account; once developed the law of habit applies to them. It is practically economical to use a concept ready at hand rather than to take time and trouble and effort to change it or to devise a new one. The use of prior ready-made and familiar concepts also give rise to a sense of stability, of guarantee against sudden and arbitrary changes of the rules which determine the consequences which legally attend acts. It is the nature of any concept, as it is of any habit to change more slowly than do the concrete circumstances with reference to which it is employed. Experience shows that the relative fixity of concepts affords men with a specious sense of protection, of assurance against the troublesome flux of events. Thus Justice Holmes says, "The language of judicial decision is mainly the language of logic. And the logical method and form flatter that longing for certainty and for repose which is in every human mind. But certainty generally is an illusion."[2] From the view of logical method here set forth, however, the undoubted facts which Justice Holmes has in mind do not concern logic but rather certain tendencies of the human creatures who use logic;

[1] Professor of Philosophy, Columbia University.
[2] *Ibid.*, p. 181.

tendencies which a sound logic will guard against. For they spring from the momentum of habit once forced, and express the effect of habit upon our feelings of ease and stability—feelings which have little to do with the actual facts of the case.

However this is only part of the story. The rest of the story is brought to light in some other passages of Justice Holmes. "The actual life of the law has not been logic: it has been experience. The felt necessities of the times, the prevalent moral and political theories, intuitions of public policy, avowed or unconscious, even the prejudices which judges share with their fellow-men, have had a good deal more to do than the syllogism in determining the rules by which men should be governed."[3] In other words, Justice Holmes is thinking of logic as equivalent with the syllogism, as he is quite entitled to do in accord with the orthodox tradition. From the standpoint of the syllogism as the logical model which was made current by scholasticism there is an antithesis between experience and logic, between logic and good sense. For the philosophy embodied in the formal theory of the syllogism asserted that thought or reason has fixed forms of its own, anterior to and independent of concrete subject-matters, and to which the latter have to be adapted whether or no. This defines the negative aspect of this discussion; and it shows by contrast the need of another kind of logic which shall reduce the influence of habit, and shall facilitate the use of good sense regarding matters of social consequence.

In other words, there are different logics in use. One of these, the one which has had greatest historic currency and exercised greatest influence on legal decisions, is that of the syllogism. To this logic the strictures of Justice Holmes apply in full force. For it purports to be a logic of rigid demonstration, not of search and discovery. It claims to be a logic of fixed forms, rather than of methods of reaching intelligent decisions in concrete situations, or of methods employed in adjusting disputed issues in behalf of the public and enduring interest. Those ignorant of formal logic, the logic of the abstract relations of ready-made conceptions to one another, have at least heard of the standard syllogism: All men are mortal; Socrates is a man; therefore, he is mortal. This is offered as the model of all proof or demonstration. It implies that what we need and must procure is first a fixed general *principle*, the so-called major premise, such as 'all men are mortal;' then in the second place, a fact which belongs intrinsically and obviously to a class of things to which the general principle applies: Socrates is a man. Then the conclusion automatically follows: Socrates is mortal. According to this model every demonstrative or strictly logical conclusion 'subsumes' a particular under an appropriate universal. It implies the prior and given existence of particulars and universals.

It thus implies that for every possible case which may arise, there is a fixed antecedent rule already at hand; that the case in question is either simple and unambiguous, or is resolvable by direct inspection into a collection of simple and indubitable facts, such as, 'Socrates is a man.' It thus tends, when it is accepted, to produce and confirm what Professor Pound has called mechanical jurisprudence; it flatters that longing for certainty of which Justice Holmes speaks; it reinforces those inert factors in human nature which make men hug as long as possible any idea which has once gained lodgment in the mind.

In a certain sense it is foolish to criticise the model supplied by the syllogism. The statements made about men and Socrates are obviously true, and the connection

[3] The Common Law, p. 1.

between them is undoubted. The trouble is that while the syllogism sets forth the *results* of thinking, it has nothing to do with the *operation* of thinking. Take the case of Socrates being tried before the Athenian citizens, and the thinking which had to be done to reach a decision. Certainly the issue was not whether Socrates was mortal; the point was whether this mortality would or should occur at a specified date and in a specified way. Now that is just what does not and cannot follow from a general principle or a major premise. Again to quote Justice Holmes, "General propositions do not decide concrete cases." No concrete proposition, that is to say one with material dated in time and placed in space, follows from any general statements or from any connection between them.

If we trust to an experimental logic, we find that general principles emerge as statements of generic ways in which it has been found helpful to treat concrete cases. The real force of the proposition that all men are mortal is found in the expectancy tables of insurance companies, which with their accompanying rates show how it is prudent and socially useful to deal with human mortality. The 'universal' stated in the major premise is not outside of and antecedent to particular cases; neither is it a selection of something found in a variety of cases. It is an indication of a single way of treating cases for certain purposes or consequences in spite of their diversity. Hence its meaning and worth are subject to inquiry and revision in view of what happens, what the consequences are, when it is used as a method of treatment.

As a matter of fact, men do not begin thinking with premises. They begin with some complicated and confused case, apparently admitting of alternative modes of treatment and solution. Premises only gradually emerge from analysis of the total situation. The problem is not to draw a conclusion from given premises; that can best be done by a piece of inanimate machinery by fingering a keyboard. The problem is to *find* statements, of general principle and of particular fact, which are worthy to serve as premises. As a matter of actual fact, we generally begin with some vague anticipation of a conclusion (or at least of alternative conclusions), and then we look around for principles and data which will substantiate it or which will enable us to choose intelligently between rival conclusions. No lawyer ever thought out the case of a client in terms of the syllogism. He begins with a conclusion which he intends to reach, favorable to his client of course, and then analyzes the facts of the situation to find material out of which to construct a favorable statement of facts, to *form* a minor premise. At the same time he goes over recorded cases to find rules of law employed in cases which can be presented as similar, rules which will substantiate a certain way of looking at and interpreting the facts. And as his acquaintance with rules of law judged applicable widens, he probably alters perspective and emphasis in selection of the facts which are to form his evidential data. And as he learns more of the facts of the case he may modify his selection of rules of law upon which he bases his case.

I do not for a moment set up this procedure as a model of scientific method; it is too precommitted to the establishment of a particular and partisan conclusion to serve as such a model. But it does illustrate, in spite of this deficiency, the particular point which is being made here: namely, that thinking actually sets out from a more or less confused situation, which is vague and ambiguous with respect to the conclusion it indicates, and that the formation of both major premise and minor proceed tentatively and correlatively in the course of analysis of this situation and of prior rules. As soon as acceptable premises are given and of course the judge and jury have eventually to do with their becoming accepted—and the conclusion is also given. In strict logic, the conclusion does not follow from premises; conclusions and premises are two ways of stating the same thing. Thinking may be defined either as a development of premises or development of a conclusion; as far as it is one operation it is the other.

Courts not only reach decisions; they expound them, and the exposition must state justifying reasons. The mental operations therein involved are somewhat different from those involved in arriving at a conclusion. The logic of exposition is different from that of search and inquiry. In the latter, the situation as it exists is more or less doubtful, indeterminate, and problematic with respect to what it signifies. It unfolds itself gradually and is susceptible of dramatic surprise; at all events it has, for the time being, two sides. Exposition implies that a definitive solution is reached, that the situation is now determinate with respect to its legal implication. Its purpose is to set forth grounds for the decision reached so that it will not appear as an arbitrary dictum, and so that it will indicate a rule for dealing with similar cases in the future. It is highly probable that the need of justifying to others conclusions reached and decisions made has been the chief cause of the origin and development of logical operations in the precise sense; of abstraction, generalization, regard for consistency of implications. It is quite conceivable that if no one had ever had to account to others for his decisions, logical operations would never have developed, but men would use exclusively methods of inarticulate intuition and impression, feeling; so that only after considerable experience in accounting for their decisions to others who demanded a reason, or exculpation, and were not satisfied till they got it, did men begin to give an account to themselves of the process of reaching a conclusion in a justified way. However this may be, it is certain that in judicial decisions the only alternative to arbitrary dicta, accepted by the parties to a controversy only because of the authority or prestige of the judge, is a rational statement which formulates grounds and exposes connecting or logical links.

It is at this point that the chief stimulus and temptation to mechanical logic and abstract use of formal concepts come in. Just because the personal element cannot be wholly excluded, while at the same time the decision must assume as nearly as possible an impersonal, objective, rational form, the temptation is to surrender the vital logic which has actually yielded the conclusion and to substitute for it forms of speech which are rigorous in appearance and which give an illusion of certitude.

Another moving force is the undoubted need for the maximum possible of stability and regularity of expectation in determining courses of conduct. Men need to know the legal consequences which society through the courts will attach to their specific transactions, the liabilities they are assuming, the fruits they may count upon in entering upon a given course of action.

This is a legitimate requirement from the standpoint of the interests of the community and of particular individuals. Enormous confusion has resulted, however, from confusion of *theoretical* certainty and practical certainty. There is a wide gap separating the reasonable proposition that judicial decisions should possess the maximum possible regularity in order to enable persons in planning their conduct to foresee the legal import of their acts, and the absurd because impossible proposition that every decision should flow with formal logical necessity from antecedently known premises. To attain the former result there are required general principles of interpreting case—rules of law—and procedures of pleading and trying cases which do not alter arbitrarily. But principles of interpretation do not signify rules so rigid that they can be stated once for all and then be literally and mechanically adhered to. For the situations to which they are to be applied do not literally repeat one another in all details, and questions of degree of this factor or that have the chief weight in determining which general rule will be employed to judge the situation in question. A large part of what has been asserted concerning the necessity of absolutely uniform and immutable antecedent rules of law is in effect an attempt to evade the really important issue of finding and employing rules of law, substantive and procedural, which will actually secure to the members of the community a reasonable measure of practical certainty of expectation in framing their courses of conduct. The mechanical ease of the court in disposing of cases and not the actual security of agents is the real cause, for example, of making rules of pleading hard and fast. The result introduces an unnecessary element of gamble into the behavior of those seeking settlement of disputes. While it affords to the judges only that factitious ease and simplicity which is supplied by any routine habit of action. It substitutes a mechanical procedure for the need of analytic thought.

There is of course every reason why rules of law should be as regular and as definite as possible. But the amount and kind of antecedent assurance which is actually attainable is a matter of fact, not of form. It is large wherever social conditions are pretty uniform, and when industry, commerce, transportation, etc., move in the channels of old customs. It is much less wherever invention is active and when new devices in business and communication bring about new forms of human relationship. Thus the use of power machinery radically modifies the old terms of association of master and servant and fellow servants; rapid transportation brings into general use commercial bills of lading; mass production engenders organization of laborers and collective bargaining; industrial conditions favor concentration of capital. In part legislation endeavors to reshape old rules of law to make them applicable to new conditions. But statutes have never kept up with the variety and subtlety of social change. They cannot at the very best avoid some ambiguity, which is due not only to carelessness but also to the intrinsic impossibility of foreseeing all possible circumstances, since without such foresight definitions must be vague and classifications indeterminate. Hence to claim that old forms are ready at hand that cover every case and that may be applied by formal syllogizing is to pretend to a certainty and regularity which cannot exist in fact. The effect of the pretension is to increase practical uncertainty and social instability. Just because circumstances are really novel and not covered by old rules, it is a gamble which old rule will be declared regulative of a particular case, so that shrewd and enterprising men are encouraged to sail close to the wind and trust to ingenious lawyers to find some rule under which they can get off scot free.

The facts involved in this discussion are commonplace and they are not offered as presenting anything original or novel. What we are concerned with is their bearing upon the logic of judicial decisions. For the implications are more revolutionary than they might at first seem to be. They indicate either that logic must be abandoned or that it must be a logic *relative to consequences rather than to antecedents*, a logic of prediction of probabilities rather than one of deduction of certainties. For the purposes of a logic of inquiry into probable consequences, general principles can only be tools justified by the work they do. They are means of intellectual survey, analysis, and insight into the factors of the situation to be dealt with. Like other tools they must be modified when they are applied to new conditions and new results have to be achieved. Here is where the great practical evil of the doctrine of immutable and necessary antecedent rules comes in. It sanctifies the old; adherence to it in practise constantly widens the gap between current social conditions and the principles used by the courts. The effect is to breed irritation, disrespect for law, together with virtual alliance between the judiciary and entrenched interests that correspond most nearly to the conditions under which the rules of law were previously laid down.

Failure to recognize that general legal rules and principles are working hypotheses, needing to be constantly tested by the way in which they work out in application to concrete situations, explains the otherwise paradoxical fact that the slogans of the liberalism of one period often become the bulwarks of reaction in a subsequent era. There was a time in the eighteenth century when the great social need was emancipation of industry and trade from a multitude of restrictions which held over from the feudal estate of Europe. Adapted well enough to the localized and fixed conditions of that earlier age, they became hindrances and annoyances as the effects of methods, use of coal and steam, showed themselves. The movement of emancipation expressed itself in principles of liberty in use of property, and freedom of contract, which were embodied in a mass of legal decisions. But the absolutistic logic of rigid syllogistic forms infected these ideas. It was soon forgotten that they were relative to analysis of existing situations in order to secure orderly methods in behalf of economic social welfare. Thus these principles became in turn so rigid as to be almost as socially obstructive as "immutable" feudal laws had been in their day.

That the remarks which have been made, commonplace as they are in themselves, have a profound practical import may also be seen in the present reaction against the individualistic formulae of an older liberalism. The last thirty years has seen an intermittent tendency in the direction of legislation, and to a less extent of judicial decision, towards what is vaguely known as "social justice," toward formulae of a collectivistic character. Now it is quite possible that the newer rules may be needed and useful at a certain juncture, and yet that they may also become harmful and socially obstructive if they are hardened into absolute and fixed antecedent premises. But if they are conceived as tools to be adapted to the conditions in which they are employed rather than as absolute and intrinsic "principles," attention will go to the facts of social life, and the rules will not be allowed to engross attention and become absolute truths to be maintained intact at all costs. Otherwise we shall in the end merely have substituted one set of formally absolute and immutable syllogistic premises for another set.

If we recur then to our introductory conception that logic is really a theory about empirical phenomena, subject to growth and improvement like any other empirical discipline, we recur to it with an added conviction: namely, that the issue is not a purely speculative one, but implies consequences vastly significant for practise. I should indeed not hesitate to assert that the sanctification of ready-made antecedent universal principles as methods of thinking is the chief obstacle to the kind of thinking which is the indispensable prerequisite of steady, secure and intelligent social reforms in general and social advance by means of law in particular. If this be so infiltration into law of a more experimental and flexible logic is a social as well as an intellectual need.

Karl Llewellyn

Karl Llewellyn

"Some Realism About Realism" was the culmination of an argument between Karl Llewellyn and Roscoe Pound over the character and scope of a new movement in legal scholarship that Llewellyn had dubbed "Legal Realism." To understand the article and the colloquy out of which it grew, it helps to know a bit about the two debaters.

Llewellyn grew up in Brooklyn, although he was born in Seattle, Washington. His father was a businessman, his mother a passionate Congregationalist and reformer, who campaigned for women's suffrage and Prohibition. When he was sixteen, midway through high school, his father decided that he would benefit from completing his secondary education in Germany. He attended the Realgymnasium in Mecklenburg for three years, became fluent in German, and acquired a lifelong admiration for German culture. Returning to the United States in 1911, Llewellyn entered Yale College, where he did well academically and learned to box. When World War I began, he unofficially joined the German Army. He sustained a serious wound in combat, spent three months in a military hospital, and was awarded the Iron Cross. Back in the United States, he quickly completed his undergraduate degree and then in 1915 entered Yale Law School, where he became friendly with Wesley Hohfeld and Arthur Corbin (whom he would subsequently refer to in private as "Dad"), and was editor-in-chief of the *Yale Law Journal*. While still pursuing his law degree he was offered a part-time position on the faculty, teaching Commercial Law and Jurisprudence. During the early 1920s, he practiced law with Shearman and Sterling in New York, where his principal client was the National City Bank. In 1924, he married Elizabeth Sanford, then a graduate student at Columbia. Declining an offer of a permanent position on the Yale faculty, he became a visiting lecturer at Columbia Law School. In 1925, he became a full-time associate professor there and, in 1927, was promoted to tenure.

At Columbia, he quickly earned a reputation as an *enfant terrible*. Brash and opinionated, he attracted some colleagues and students, but alienated others. He continued to specialize in Commercial Law and Jurisprudence, generating growing streams of scholarship in both fields. The most influential of his early works were *Cases and Materials in the Law of Sales* (1930), a revolutionary casebook that included unusually few "leading cases" and unusually many textual notes, historical materials, and digests of decisions, often deployed so as to expose inconsistencies in the law; and *The Bramble Bush* (1930), an iconoclastic advice book for first-year law students.

At the start of the 1930s, when Llewellyn was just beginning to hit his stride, Roscoe Pound was the most famous and respected law professor in the United States—author of many widely circulated books and articles on Jurisprudence, Legal History, and Comparative Law, and dean (since 1916) of the Harvard Law

School. In his youth, Pound had himself been something of a revolutionary. In 1906, while dean of the law department at the University of Nebraska, he had delivered a ground-shaking speech, entitled "The Causes of Popular Dissatisfaction with the Administration of Justice," at the annual meeting of the American Bar Association, in which he argued, among other things, that, when deciding cases, judges should be more responsive to currents of public opinion. His 1909 essay, "Liberty of Contract," contended that the Supreme Court's recent rulings declaring unconstitutional various forms of social welfare legislation reflected ignorance of actual working conditions in the United States—and then attributed that ignorance partly to the manner in which American lawyers were educated and partly to the blinders imposed on judges by the then-prevailing "mechanical" style of judicial reasoning. In "Law in Books and Law in Action" (1910), Pound went even further, insisting upon large gaps between courts' decisions and the rules that supposedly were in force, the failure of jurisprudence to keep step with developments in "social, economic and philosophical thinking," and the "backward" way in which lawmaking occurred in the United States. Thereafter, however, both the fire in his politics and the liveliness of his prose gradually diminished. By 1916, he could deliver a speech to the Pennsylvania Bar Association (subsequently published as "The Limits of Effective Legal Action"), tracing popular "dissatisfaction with law, criticism of legal and judicial institutions, and suspicion as to the purposes of the lawyer," not to the failures of the judiciary, but to excessively activist Progressive legislation, which unchecked would result in "more and more interference with every relation of life." Over time, a growing proportion of his public pronouncements took similar tacks.

In his early writings, Llewellyn happily proclaimed his fealty to Pound. The first footnote of his first major article insisted that little of his argument was truly original and indicated that he was "particularly conscious of indebtedness to Sumner, Holmes, Veblen, Commons and Pound." In an unpublished paper written in 1925, Llewellyn was more specific, insisting that "[t]he significant school of jurisprudence today is the sociological, of which Dean Pound has been the acknowledged leader and spokesman"—and that that approach "alone is vital, growing, expanding to meet new needs."

However, as N.E.H. Hull has shown, disagreement over the Sacco and Vanzetti case began to drive a wedge between the two men. Both Llewellyn and Pound were convinced that the proceedings by which the two young working-class anarchists were convicted and sentenced to death were deeply flawed. But Pound, apparently fearing for his job, limited his views to private correspondence; in public, he did nothing more than call for the appointment by the Massachusetts governor of a "disinterested board" to look into the matter. Llewellyn, by contrast, campaigned vigorously against the convictions, persuading sixty law professors from around the country (none from Harvard) to sign a petition that denounced the proceedings, and subsequently delivering a radio address on the eve of the men's execution, fiercely condemning the trial judge, the Massachusetts governor, and the appellate process as a whole—all despite that fact that he was at the time being considered for tenure. Most likely, one by-product of these events is that Llewellyn's respect for Pound dropped several notches.

In June 1927, very soon after the execution, Llewellyn and Pound began the conversation about legal theory that would eventually culminate in the publication of "Some Realism About Realism." Llewellyn made the first move, writing

Pound a letter, politely expressing skepticism concerning Pound's characterization, set forth in an article ten years earlier, of the stages through which all legal systems pass. Pound responded with a gracious five-page defense of his position but evaded Llewellyn's sharpest arguments. Two more letters failed to satisfy Llewellyn. Three years passed, during which Llewellyn continued to work on the draft essay that seems to have instigated the initial flurry—which he finally published in 1930 in the *Columbia Law Review* under the title, "A Realistic Jurisprudence—The Next Step." A rambling, disjointed article, it was noteworthy primarily for its identification and celebration of a group of "new juristic realists," its insistence upon the difference between "real rules" (descriptions of courts' behavior) and "paper rules" (black-letter doctrine), and for its dismissive reference to Pound as "a man partially caught in the traditional precept-thinking of an age that is passing"—a characterization sharpened by a footnote describing Pound's work as sometimes falling to "the level of bed-time stories for the tired bar."

Stung, Pound responded the following year with an article entitled, "A Call for a Realistic Jurisprudence," which he published, curiously, in the issue of the *Harvard Law Review* otherwise devoted exclusively to a celebration of Oliver Wendell Holmes on the occasion of his ninetieth birthday. In it, Pound praised some aspects of the body of scholarship summarized by Llewellyn, but then went on to attribute to "current juristic realism" several propositions that Pound regarded as both extreme and indefensible. For example, the realists, Pound contended, believe that "Reason is an illusion" and "are blind to the extent to which the administration of justice attains certainty through rule and form and the extent to which the economic order rests thereon." Unfortunately—but probably deliberately—Pound cited no specific essays or authors in support of his accusations.

Llewellyn, convinced that Pound's characterization of Realism was baseless, began, with Jerome Frank's help, preparing a reply. Thinking it appropriate that his response also appear in the *Harvard Law Review*, Llewellyn wrote Paul Freund, then president of the *Review*, broaching the idea. Freund responded coolly, suggesting that "Dean's Pound's article, however it may have erred in particulars, did not itself invite controversy." Enraged, Llewellyn fired off a letter to his friend, Edmund Morgan, then acting dean of Harvard Law School (while Pound was serving on the Wickersham Commission in Washington), accusing Freund of caving in to pressure from Pound and threatening to report the matter to the Association of American Law Schools. Morgan, in turn, suggested to Freund that he bear in mind that Harvard had an undeserved reputation for self-satisfaction and hostility to new ideas in legal scholarship. Freund wrote Llewellyn, offering to publish the piece.

In preparing the article, Llewellyn was hampered by the lack of citations in the crucial portion of Pound's essay. To fill the gap, Llewellyn wrote Pound several times, asking that he identify the scholars he had in mind. Pound responded graciously, even apologetically, but plainly was reluctant to name names. Exasperated, Llewellyn finally provided him a list of forty-four scholars to whom he might have meant to refer, grouped in three categories—which he labeled realists criticized as "extremists on one or another point" (p.1227, n.18), "realists who are thorough-going, but probably less extreme in their position," and "realists-in-part-of-their-work"—asking that Pound merely check the ones he had in mind. Pound again refused to be precise, but did express skepticism concerning the last of the categories: "[Y]ou might put all of us there." So, in the end, Llewellyn was obliged to determine on his own who did and did not qualify as "realists."

In the final version of his reply, he approached the task from two angles. In Part I, in which he set out to refute Pound's charges, he adopted a short list of twenty "representative men." Unfortunately, many readers subsequently treated this set as authoritative—an exhaustive identification of all legal realists as of 1931. In context, it is clear that Llewellyn's intention was merely to make his retort to Pound as strong as possible, minimizing the chance that Pound would respond by insisting that he had had in mind a narrower set of "extreme" scholars. In the second, much longer part of the article, in which he offers his own account of the views of "real realists," Llewellyn draws upon the work of a much wider array of scholars.

So much for how the article came to be. What, then, did it contain—and why did it take on the stature of a canonical essay? The short first part, the rebuttal to Pound, had little lasting value. From a distance, it resembles a cross between a high-school science report and a contribution to a law-school tenure fight—quasi-empirical, indignant, defensive, heavy-handed. The best that can be said of it is that it was wholly convincing—effectively exposing the hollowness of Pound's critique.

The second part is where the real action was. It was there that Llewellyn outlined and defended a new approach to the study and practice of law—an approach that he insisted was already being pursued by several of his contemporaries, but to which he lent both coherence and fuel. To be sure, as Llewellyn acknowledged, the approach was not *brand* new. Several of what Llewellyn identified as its foundational principles had been well developed by earlier generations of legal theorists. For example, Llewellyn's famous (or infamous) advocacy of a "temporary divorce of Is and Ought for the purposes of study" was little more than a restatement of Holmes's contention that we should strive to look at the law through the eyes of "the bad man" before considering how it should be changed. Similarly, the "distrust" that Llewellyn attributed to the Realists "of the theory that traditional prescriptive rule-formulations are *the* heavily operative factor in producing courts decisions" had long characterized the writings of many anti-formalist legal scholars—Holmes and Pound among them. Finally, the realists' "conception of law as a means to social ends and not as an end in itself; so that any part needs constantly to be examined for its purpose, and for its effect, and to be judged in the light of both and of their relation to each other" was a straightforward alloy of Holmes's instrumentalism and Hohfeld's insistence upon the need for the disaggregation of legal categories. But, in other respects, the approach that Llewellyn sketches was novel. Five stand out.

The first, buried deep in the argument, was the way in which Llewellyn handled the distinction between rights and remedies. Previously, legal scholars typically had assumed that legal remedies were derivative of legal rights. In other words, to determine whether a party is entitled to a particular remedy, one should first ascertain the scope of the right of which he or she had been deprived. Llewellyn argued that the analysis ought to run in the opposite direction:

> Related, but distinct, is the reassertion of the fundamental quality of remedy, and the general approach to restating "what the law is" (on the side of prediction) in terms not of rights, but of what can be done: Not only "no remedy, no right," but "precisely as much right as remedy."

Legal rights, in other words, are nothing more than descriptions of the availability of legal remedies. As Llewellyn intimated by placing the phrase, "what the law is," in quotation marks, this perspective might be seen as only a modest extension of Holmes's "predictive" theory of law in general. But the typical thoroughness with which Llewellyn and his fellow realists pursued the idea had major implications. For one, it prompted a radical change in the organization of law-school casebooks. Prior to Legal Realism, the typical Contracts casebook, for example, began with the doctrines governing offers and acceptances and then gradually moved through subjects in a sequence paralleling the creation, interpretation, and enforcement of a contract itself. Casebooks influenced by Realism, by contrast, typically began by exploring first the scope of the remedies available to one party when another breaches a contract—on the theory that scope of a contractual obligation is ultimately reducible to the kinds of sanctions that will be imposed when it is violated.

The second point might be called "particularism." When attempting accurately to map the ways in which cases are actually decided, Llewellyn and the other realists argued, it makes sense to lump them "into narrower categories than has been the practice in the past." This claim goes further than Hohfeld's plea for analytical disaggregation. It combines the hypotheses that a sensible legal system would organize social and economic activities into relatively small boxes, prescribing rules suitable for each one, and that in this respect judges are generally more sensible than scholars, who in their treatises tend to make larger generalizations.

The third line of innovation concerns the number and importance of gaps and conflicts within extant legal doctrine. Llewellyn's view, which he attributed in part to Walter Wheeler Cook and T. R. Powell, was that:

> [I]n any case doubtful enough to make litigation respectable the available authoritative premises—*i. e.*, premises legitimate and impeccable under the traditional legal techniques—are at least two, and . . . the two are mutually contradictory as applied to the case at hand.

The revolutionary implications of this outlook are evident. Inconsistencies this ubiquitous would make it impossible even for a judge determined to "follow the law" to do so. In most cases, not just exceptional cases, the exercise of judicial discretion is thus inevitable.

The fourth of the new ideas was captured by the term "rationalization," which Llewellyn suggested he and his colleagues had imported from the fields of psychology and anthropology. A judicial opinion ostensibly setting forth the basis of a ruling, he argued, should be regarded, not as "a description of the process of decision, or an explanation of how the decision was reached," but rather as "trained lawyers' arguments made by judges (after the decision has been reached), intended to make the decision seem plausible, legally decent, legally right, to make it seem, indeed, legally inevitable." Many ambiguities lurk here. To whom are such pronouncements addressed—i. e., who needs to be persuaded that the ruling was "legally inevitable"? The litigants? Their lawyers? Lawyers in general? The public at large? Do judges consciously misrepresent through their opinions the ways in which they make decisions, or are they engaged in self-deception? How effective is this strategy of "rationalization"? Who, if anyone, is duped? Subsequent generations of legal theorists would wrestle with such issues.

Up to this point, all of the insights collated by Llewellyn have borne primarily on the question that obsessed most previous generations of American legal theorists: How do and should appellate judges decide cases? By contrast, the fifth and last of the novel dimensions of the approach Llewellyn outlined consisted of a plea for enlargement of the subject matter of legal theory. Specifically, Llewellyn insisted that legal scholars should be concerned at least as much with predicting and understanding: the behavior of trial courts; the decisions of "administrative bodies"; "what goes into producing legislative change—or blocking it"; and the actual impacts of legal decisions of all of these sorts on "the laymen of the community." Here one finds the headwaters of several rivers of modern American legal scholarship—among them, the continuing struggle to understand, justify, and corral the conduct of administrative agencies; and the still growing body of "public choice" theory.

Unfortunately, the essay ended with a whimper. Throughout, Llewellyn had been insisting that the "divorce of Is and Ought" was "temporary"—that realists advocated postponement of normative questions only until an accurate map of the current legal landscape in a given field had been drawn, after which they would of course consider how the field should be reshaped. But, when he finally turned to the question of the criteria that the Realists relied upon when engaging in such reform, he had little to say. On only a few minor issues, he argued, were the realists in agreement—the importance of who occupies positions of legal power; "the need for courts to face squarely the policy questions in their cases"; particularism, not just (as suggested above) when describing legal rules, but also when formulating them; and the notion that "most legal problems" were most sensibly resolved by seeking to reduce "risks." The shallowness of these recommendations lends credence to the common view that the realists had a brilliant "method of attack" but an anemic "affirmative program."

The publication of "Some Realism About Realism" marked the low point in Llewellyn's relationship with Pound. Soon thereafter, they made up. In subsequent years, Llewellyn regularly acknowledged Pound's "greatness."

Llewellyn himself went on to an extraordinary career as a teacher, scholar, and law reformer. Along with Adamson Hoebel, he wrote a pioneering anthropological study of the legal system of the Cheyenne Indians, entitled *The Cheyenne Way* (1941). His greatest accomplishment was the radical reform of commercial law known as the Uniform Commercial Code (UCC), for which he served as the chief reporter. Many aspects of the content of the Code, in particular, its frequent instructions to courts to resolve disputes on the basis of standards of "reasonableness" or the "customs" and "usages of trade," plainly bear the imprint of Llewellyn's jurisprudence. And its success—by his death, it had been adopted by fifteen states; today, it is in force in forty-nine—is testimony to his brilliance, endurance, and surprising skill in managing people.

Llewellyn's personal and professional life continued to be stormy. He divorced his first wife in 1930, remarried in 1933, divorced again in 1946, and finally married Soia Mentschikoff, his former student, research assistant, and associate on the UCC. Bouts with alcoholism and increasing tension with his colleagues at Columbia may have limited his scholarly output. In 1951, he and Mentschikoff left to join the faculty of the University of Chicago Law School, where they flourished. Throughout his career, Llewellyn maintained his ties with Germany (twice serving as a visiting professor at the University of Leipzig), although he was repulsed by Nazism and responded furiously to the suggestion that his ideas could be in any way considered Fascist in character. Llewellyn's last major publication, *The Common Law Tradition: Deciding Appeals* (1960), disappointed many readers, who saw in it a regrettable retreat from the ambition and radicalism of his Realist days. After its release, he was scheduled to present a series of lectures in Germany, in which he hoped to synthesize his views on the sociology of law, but a sudden and ultimately fatal illness prevented him from doing so.

After his death, Mentschikoff became dean of the University of Miami Law School. A remarkable scholar and forceful leader in her own right, she nevertheless insisted that, as dean, her primary aspiration was to implement Llewellyn's vision of law and legal education. By most accounts, she was remarkably successful.

WILLIAM FISHER

BIBLIOGRAPHY

Primary Sources

The essays by Roscoe Pound summarized in the introduction are: "Liberty of Contract," *Yale Law Journal* 18 (1908–1909): 454; "Law in Books and Law in Action," *American Law Review* 44 (1910): 12; "The Limits of Effective Legal Action," *American Bar Association Journal* 3 (1917): 55; and "The Call for a Realist Jurisprudence," *Harvard Law Review* 44 (1930–31): 697.

Llewellyn's two contributions to the exchange with Pound are: "A Realistic Jurisprudence—The Next Step," *Columbia Law Review* 30 (1930): 431; and "Some Realism About Realism—Responding to Dean Pound," *Harvard Law Review* 44 (1930–31): 1222.

Llewellyn's other major contributions (in English) to the literature on jurisprudence (broadly defined) are: *The Bramble Bush: On Our Law and Its Study* (New York: Oceana Publications, 1960); *The Common Law Tradition: Deciding Appeals* (Boston: Little Brown, 1960); *Jurisprudence: Realism in Theory and Practice* (Chicago: University of Chicago Press, 1962); *The Case Law System in America* (Chicago: University of Chicago Press, 1989); "On Philosophy in American Law," *University of Pennsylvania Law Review* 82 (1933–34): 205; "On What is Wrong with So-Called Legal Education," *Columbia Law Review* 35 (1935): 651; D. J. Swift Teufelsdröckh, "Jurisprudence, The Crown of Civilization—Being Also the Principles of Writing Jurisprudence Made Clear to Neophytes," *University of Chicago Law Review* 5 (1937–38): 171; "The Normative, The Legal and the Law-Jobs: The Problem of Juristic Method," *Yale Law Journal* 49 (1939–40): 1355; "My Philosophy of Law," in *My Philosophy of Law: Credos of Sixteen Scholars* (A. Kocourek, ed., 1941), 181; "The American Common Law Tradition and American Democracy," *Journal of Legal and Political Science* 1 (1942): 14; and "The Place of Skills in Legal Education," *Columbia Law Review* 45 (1945): 345.

His equally influential works on commercial law include: *Cases and Materials on the Law of Sales* (Chicago: Callaghan and Company, 1930); and *Commercial Transactions* (New York: Association of American Law Schools/Practising Law Institute, 1946).

Finally, his seminal book with E. Adamson Hoebel is *The Cheyenne Way: Conflict and Case Law in Primitive Jurisprudence* (Norman: University of Oklahoma Press, 1941).

Secondary Sources

The authoritative biography of Llewellyn is William Twining, *Karl Llewellyn and the Realist Movement* (London: Weidenfeld and Nicolson, 1973). An excellent brief summary of his life, written by David Ray Papke, appears in *American National Biographies*. The best accounts of the relationship between Pound and Llewellyn, on which we have drawn heavily, are N.E.H. Hull, "Some Realism About the Llewellyn–Pound Exchange Over Realism: The Newly Uncovered Private Correspondence, 1927–1931," *Wisconsin Law Review* (1987): 921; idem, "Reconstructing the Origins of Realistic Jurisprudence: A Prequel to the Llewellyn—Pound Exchange over Legal Realism," *Duke Law Journal* 38 (1989): 1302; and idem, *Roscoe Pound and Karl Llewellyn: Searching for an American Jurisprudence* (Chicago: University of Chicago Press, 1997). Information concerning Soia Mentschikoff's service at the University of Miami, along with a more favorable assessment of Llewellyn's final scholarly project than that suggested in the text, can be found in William Twining, "The Idea of Juristic Method: A Tribute to Karl Llewellyn," *University of Miami Law Review* 48 (1993–94): 119.

Among the many fine studies of Llewellyn's contributions to the UCC are Richard Danzig, "A Comment on the Jurisprudence of the Uniform Commercial Code," *Stanford Law Review* 27 (1974–75): 621; Grant Gilmore, "In Memoriam: Karl Llewellyn," *Yale Law Journal* 71 (1961–62): 813; Allen R. Kamp, "Between-the-Wars Social Thought: Karl Llewellyn, Legal Realism, and the Uniform Commercial Code in Context," *Albany Law Review* 59 (1995–96): 325; and James Whitman, "Commercial Law and the American *Volk*: A Note on Llewellyn's German Sources for the Uniform Commercial Code," *Yale Law Journal* 97 (1987–88): 156.

Other studies of various dimensions of Llewellyn's thought and career include N.E.H. Hull, "The Romantic Realist: Art, Literature and the Enduring Legacy of Karl Llewellyn's 'Jurisprudence,'" *American Journal of Legal History* 40 (1996): 115; Henry F. Murray, Peggy M. Pschirrer, and Robert W. Whitman, "The Poetic Imagination of Karl Llewellyn," *University of Toledo Law Review* 29 (1997–98): 27; William Twining, "The Idea of Juristic Method: A Tribute to Karl Llewellyn," *University of Miami Law Review* 48 (1993–94): 119; and Leslie E. Gerwin and Paul M. Shupack, "Karl Llewellyn's Legal Method Course: Elements of Law and Its Teaching Materials," *Journal of Legal Education* 33 (1983): 64.

"Some Realism About Realism—Responding to Dean Pound"

44 Harvard Law Review 1222 (1931)

Ferment is abroad in the law. The sphere of interest widens; men become interested again in the life that swirls around things legal. Before rules, were facts; in the beginning was not a Word, but a Doing. Behind decisions stand judges; judges are men; as men they have human backgrounds. Beyond rules, again, lie effects: beyond decisions stand people whom rules and decisions directly or indirectly touch. The field of Law reaches both forward and back from the Substantive Law of school and doctrine. The sphere of interest is widening; so, too, is the scope of doubt. *Beyond rules lie effects*—but do they? Are some rules mere paper? And if effects, what effects? Hearsay, unbuttressed guess, assumption or assertion unchecked by test—can such be trusted on this matter of what law is *doing*?

The ferment is proper to the time. The law of schools threatened at the close of the century to turn into words—placid, clear-seeming, lifeless, like some old canal. Practice rolled on, muddy, turbulent, vigorous. It is now spilling, flooding, into the canal of stagnant words. It brings ferment and trouble. So other fields of thought have spilled their waters in: the stress on behavior in the social sciences; their drive toward integration; the physicists' reëxamination of final-seeming premises; the challenge of war and revolution. These stir. They stir the law. Interests of practice claim attention. Methods of work unfamiliar to lawyers make their way in, beside traditional techniques. Traditional techniques themselves are reëxamined, checked against fact, stripped somewhat of confusion. And always there is this restless questing: what *difference* does statute, or rule, or court-decision, make?

Whether this ferment is one thing or twenty is a question; if one thing, it is twenty things in one. But it is with us. It spreads. It is no mere talk. It shows results, results enough through the past decade to demonstrate its value.

And those involved are folk of modest ideals. They want law to deal, they themselves want to deal, with things, with people, with tangibles, with *definite* tangibles, and *observable* relations between definite tangibles—not with words alone; when law deals with words, they want the words to represent tangibles which can be got at beneath the words, and observable relations between those tangibles. They want to check ideas, and rules, and formulas by facts, to keep them close to facts. They view rules, they view law, as means to ends; as only means to ends; as having meaning only insofar as they are means to ends. They

---

Jerome Frank refused me permission to sign his name as joint author to this paper, on the ground that it was my fist which pushed the pen. But his generosity does not alter the fact that the paper could not have been written without his help. I therefore write the first sections, in partial recognition, as "We," meaning thereby Frank and myself. In the description of the realists, I turn to the first person singular, partly because any alignment of such diverse work is individually colored; partly because any phrasing which would seem to suggest a non-existent school would be unfortunate.

suspect, with law moving slowly and the life around them moving fast, that some law may have gotten out of joint with life. This is a question in first instance of fact: what does law *do*, to people, or for people? In the second instance, it is a question of ends: what *ought* law to do to people, or for them? But there is no reaching a judgment as to whether any specific part of present law does what it ought, until you can first answer what it is doing now. To see this, and to be ignorant of the answer, is to start fermenting, is to start trying to find out.

All this is, we say, a simple-hearted point of view, and often philosophically naïve—though it has in it elements enough of intellectual sophistication. It denies very little, except the completeness of the teachings handed down. It knows too little to care about denying much. It affirms ignorance, pitched within and without. It affirms the need to know. Its call is for intelligent effort to dispel the ignorance. Intelligent effort to cut beneath old rules, old words, to get sight of current things. It is not a new point of view; it is as old as man. But its rediscovery in any age, by any man, in any discipline, is joyous.

Speak, if you will, of a "realistic jurisprudence." And since the individual workers who are the cells of ferment cry their wares, find their result good, see the need for more workers, more results, speak, if you will (as Dean Pound has) of a *Call for a Realist Jurisprudence.*[1] If advance is insistent on advancing further, such a call there is. But it is a call which rests on work done as well as on work to do, on experience as well as on hope, on some portion of past experiment proved useful as well as on perceived need for further experiment.

Dean Pound has discussed the call and the ferment. One portion of his discussion calls in turn for our attention. He welcomed the ferment. He described it. The general terms in which he described the fermenters we seemed to recognize: "the oncoming generation of American law teachers";[2] "our younger teachers of law" who are insistent on a realistic jurisprudence;[3] "the new juristic realists";[4] "the new school . . . current juristic realism."[5] These general designations we say, we seemed to recognize (except the "school"). There were more specific attributes which also struck responsive chords: "By realism they mean fidelity to nature, accurate recording of things as they are, as contrasted with things as they are imagined to be, or wished to be."[6] "Insistent . . . on beginning with an objectively scientific gathering of facts."[7] "Psychological exposure of the role of reason in human behavior, of the extent to which so-called reasons come after action as explanations instead of before action as determining factors, has made a profound impression upon the rising generation of jurists."[8] "Looking at precepts and doctrines and institutions with reference to how they work or fail to work, and why."[9] "There is a distinct advance in their frank recognition of the alogical or non-rational element in judicial action which the legal science [philosophy?] of the nineteenth century sought to ignore."[10] If these were the attributes of the "new realists," we knew who they were. We rejoiced that a scholar of Dean Pound's standing and perspective found much in

[1] (1931) 44 HARV. L. REV. 697.
[2] *Id.* at 697.
[3] *Ibid.*
[4] *Ibid.*, and *passim.*
[5] *Id.* at 701.
[6] *Id.* at 697.
[7] *Id.* at 700.
[8] *Id.* at 705.
[9] *Id.* at 706.
[10] *Ibid.*

their fermenting to appreciate. We agreed with him that it was important for the older thinking and the newer to make contact.

But the Dean's description did not stop with the points mentioned. It continued. On bones we knew was built a flesh we knew not of. An ugly flesh. The new realists, or "most of them," had, as the Dean read them, been guilty of goodly number of things that careful thinkers would in the main not be proud to be caught doing. These intellectual offenses Dean Pound criticized. He criticized them tellingly. The question is one of fact: whether the offenses have been committed. For if they have, the Dean's rebukes are needed. Spare the rod and spoil the realist.

The question is one of fact. By fact it must be tried. And tried it must be. When Dean Pound speaks on jurisprudence, men listen. The profession has too long relied on him to discover, read, digest, classify and report on jurists foreign and ancient not to rely again when he speaks of would-be jurists modern and at home. We regret, therefore, peculiarly that he departed in this paper from a practice he has often followed,[11] of indicating, in each instance when he presented a view, precisely whose view it was, and precisely where that person had set it forth. Freed of the check of the concrete, the most learned err. And error in perceiving or describing the attributes of these new fermenters would be unfortunate. For "here is an important movement in the science of law, and it behooves us to understand it and be thinking about it."[12]

Into a series of further points in his description—points he does not approve of—we have inquired, and present the results.[13] We speak, be it noted, for ourselves alone, and for the facts alone, not for the men whose work we have canvassed. Interpretations, judgments, and responsibility are ours. We are no spokesmen for a school.

The method of the inquiry is set forth in a note. The detailed results are printed in part in an appendix. We indicate the results here in summary, to clear up some things that realists are not. There will then be set forth an interpretation of the new ferment and its bearings, by way of contrast, along lines of organization independent of the points made by the Dean.

One further preliminary needs mention. Dean Pound was careful to recognize that "one may point out work to be done in the progress of a school without implying that those engaged in the task are ignorant thereof, or that they do not intend to direct their energies thereto in due time."[14] And to recognize that "it is unfair to take any one item, or even set of items, from one or more of its adherents and assume that it may be fastened upon the formative school as characteristic dogma."[15]

Nonetheless, he states: "five items are to be found so generally *in the writings* of the new school, *that one may be justified in pronouncing them, or most of them, the ideas of current juristic realism.*"[16] The points of description here involved are taken with three exceptions from these five items or from their detailed development in his paper.

---

[11] *The End of Law as Developed in Juristic Thought* (1914) 27 HARV. L. REV. 605; (1917) 30 ID. 201; *The Progress of the Law—Analytical Jurisprudence, 1914–1927* (1927) 41 *id.* 174; LAW AND MORALS (1924); INTERPRETATIONS OF LEGAL HISTORY (1923). AN INTRODUCTION TO THE PHILOSOPHY OF LAW (1924) contains only a general bibliography.

[12] Pound, *supra* note 1, at 697.

[13] One matter we reserve for treatment in a later portion of the paper: the repeated suggestion of the Dean as to "a school" of realists.

[14] Pound, *supra* note 1, at 709.

[15] *Id.* at 700.

[16] *Id.* at 701 (our italics).

I

The trial of Dean Pound's indictment is not easy. It is a blanket indictment. It is blanket as to time and place and person of each offense. It specifies no one offender by his name.

We have the general indications above-mentioned: "new realists" and the like. We have the more specific indications also mentioned. Taken together, they narrow the class that may come in question.[17] We can, therefore, check the items against a reasonable sampling of the men whom the rest of the description fits.[18]

---

[17] We had hoped to be more precise. We wrote Dean Pound to ask whom he had had in mind when he wrote his article. The cumulation of his work at Washington and his regular work was the reason of his not going into detail. He did mention three names specifically. Bingham and Lorenzen he had had in mind. C. E. Clark he definitely had not.

[18] *The sampling of men.* We set up the following criteria: (a) those chosen must fit the general and the more specific items set forth above; (b) they must include the leading figures in the new ferment; (c) in order that we may turn up most passages supporting the items we challenge, the men chosen must include all who may be reputed to have taken extreme positions; (d) a wide range of views and positions must be included.

(1) Bingham and Lorenzen are included as of course. (2) We add those whom we believe recognized as figures of central stimulus in the new ferment: C. E. Clark, Cook, Corbin, Moore, T. R. Powell, Oliphant. (3) We add further men peculiarly vocal in advocating new or rebellious points of view: Frank, Green, Radin. (4) We stir in all others whom we have heard criticized as extremists on one or another point mentioned by the Dean: Hutcheson, Klaus, Sturges. (5) We fill out with as many more as time permits: Douglas, Francis, Patterson, Tulin, Yntema—chosen partly because their writing has explicitly touched points of theory, partly because their writing was either familiar to us or not too bulky. (6) We throw in Llewellyn, as both vociferous and extreme, but peculiarly because he and he alone has issued a "Call for a Realist Jurisprudence" under that peculiar label. *A Realistic Jurisprudence—The Next Step* (1930) 30 COL. L. REV. 431. This gives us twenty names. There are doubtless twenty more. But half is a fair sample. We check back and find that our men range from right to the four or five prevailing lefts. They are either characteristic or extreme. They are in print more fully than most on these matters. If they do not bear out Dean Pound's challenged points of description, we feel safe in saying that those points can not stand.—(Dean Pound to the contrary notwithstanding, we must include Clark. His thirst for facts and influence in procedural research force his inclusion. Corbin, *The Law and the Judges* (1914) 3 YALE REV. 234, is, we think, the first rounded presentation of the realistic attitude, except for Holmes and Bingham. Frankfurter we do not include; he has been currently considered a "sociological jurist," not a "realist." It profits little to show that one not thought a realist does not fit an alleged description of "realists.")

The sampling of writings. We selected such writings as seemed to speak most directly to points of legal theory, or most likely to contain evidence on any of the Dean's allegations. We wrote to the men, requesting from each his suggestion as to where he had expressed himself, and were thereby led to a number of papers we might otherwise have missed. Bingham, Clark, Corbin, Douglas, Green, Klaus, Patterson, Powell, Radin, and Sturges were generous enough of their time to supply such references, often to specific pertinent passages. They are in no way responsible for what we say, or for our plan of organization. In every case, moreover, we are solely responsible for including or excluding the passages they referred us to, or any others from their works, and for the classification thereof, and especially for the general judgments expressed. But their references greatly lightened our labor. A complete list of the authors and titles is given in Appendix I, *infra*.

Procedure of testing. Each paper listed, whether quoted from or not, has been read or reread entire for the present purpose, to make sure that countervailing evidence was not present, and to make sure that any passage cited was in key with the whole. If nothing to the contrary is said, passages quoted or cited *against the Dean* are offered as in substantial harmony not only with the whole of the paper in which they appeared, but also with the author's work in general. Passages cited in the Dean's favor are often unfair to the men cited, for which we tender our apologies. Judgments as to general tone or afterglow of a writing (a matter sometimes very different from its specific phrasing) are ours.

We had prepared for use in Appendix II, in Dean Pound's language, the statement of the positions here challenged, which in his view the realists, or many of them, or some of them, hold. Under each such point the evidence was arranged. (a) *All* passages we have found which support the Dean's description. (b) Such passages as might colorably be adduced in support, and our judgment as to writings whose general flavor or afterglow might be colorably adduced in support. In each such case further passages from the same author which clarify his position were adduced, if found. (c) Some of the passages which display inappropriateness in the Dean's description. These were so many that they often required to be merely cited or even disregarded. Of the passages truly supporting the Dean's description we do not believe we have missed many. They stand out, to readers of our leanings. But the "colorable, but rebutted" passages here given are probably only a fraction of those present in the materials we have canvassed. Colorable passages take color from the mind of the reader. They camouflage themselves to one who (however he tries to find them) colors them with the meaning of the whole paper in which they are found.

We have chosen twenty men and ninety-odd titles; representative men and pertinent titles. These we have canvassed in order to ascertain the extent to which the evidence supports the Dean's allegations. The results of our investigation are presented in summary under each point.

These statements of the Dean's points here set out are *in our language, not his.* We have done our best to reach and state his meaning. But we may misinterpret. We purport therefore to give *not what Dean Pound meant but what a reasonable reader may be expected to understand from his language.*[19]

Point I. Much of the realists' discussion of judges' thinking sets forth what such thinkings "must" be, under some current psychological dogma, *without investigation of what recorded judicial experience reveals.*[20]

    (a) Supporting: perhaps Bingham, Francis, Yntema: 3;
    (b) Colorable: None;
    (c) Negating: 16;
    (d) No evidence noted: 1.

Point 2. One of the most common items found in the writings of the new school is *faith in masses of figures as having significance in and of themselves.*[21]

    (a) Supporting: None;
    (b) Colorable: (i) Unrebutted: None; (ii) Rebutted: I;
    (c) Negating: 9;
    (d) No evidence noted: 10.

Point 3. Much insisted on is the *exclusive* significance of an approach to law by way of exact terminology. Some realists believe problems are solved by terminology.[22]

As indicated in Appendix II, space forbade the printing of all of this material. Its form was mainly that of Point II, there set forth, which must serve as a sample.

Each point was closed with a nose-count summary of results, under the rubrics: (a) Supporting; (b) Colorable: (i) unrebutted, (ii) rebutted; (c) Negating; (d) No evidence noted. The category "No evidence noted" is almost as significant as any other: the Dean's description is expressly rested *on the writings* of the "new realists."

Passages published after Feb. 1, 1931, were canvassed. They are significant of the newer thinkers' views, which we wish to present. Such passages can not, however, be regarded as accessible to the Dean when he wrote. They bear only on the accuracy of his diagnosis of trends of thought.

Frank is responsible for errors and omissions as to Bingham, Green, Frank, and Radin; Llewellyn as to the others.

Finally, we write, as the men whose work we are discussing wrote, for readers patient and careful enough to *read* what stands on the page. Gratuitous implications are air-castles. There is no arguing with persons who insist on building them. Realists write for the literate. We take a writer's words in first instance for what, under reasonable and careful reading, they appear to say. We attempt to take separate account of general tone and after-impression.

[19] For Dean Pound's language in points 1, 10 and 11 together with a detailed account of the results of our investigation concerning those points, see Appendix II, *infra*. To avoid misinterpretation by us, we asked Dean Pound for permission to submit our manuscript to him and have misinterpretations corrected. His time, unfortunately, did not permit. So that misinterpretation is undoubtedly present, for we have as much trouble at times in getting the Dean's meaning as he at times has in getting the meaning of realists. Which is inevitable. Words are read against the reader's background, and distorted accordingly.

[20] See p. 1260, *infra*. Since this paper was prepared Yntema has given some warrant for being shifted into the Negating column. Yntema and Jaffin, *Preliminary Analysis of Concurrent Jurisdiction* (1931) 79 U. OF PA. L. REV. 869, esp. 881–86. And the internal evidence is abundant in the same direction, as to all three men named.

[21] See Pound, *supra* note 1, at 701, lines 1–5; 703, lines 13–15.

[22] See *id.* at 702, first full paragraph.

(a) Supporting: None;

(b) Colorable: (i) perhaps Unrebutted: Cook, Moore:[23] 2; (ii) Rebutted: 1;

(c) Negating: 14;

(d) No evidence noted: 3.

Point 4. A strong group of realists expect rigidly exact and workable formulas about law to be developed in ways analogous to mathematical physics; and these formulas are expected to be workable without more as rules of what to do.[24]

(a) Supporting: None;

(b) Colorable: (i) Unrebutted: Cook: 1; (ii) Rebutted: I;

(c) Negating: (i) As to expecting any results *via* techniques closely analogous to mathematical physics: 5; (ii) As to awareness of great limitations on what may be expected from quantitative methods: 4 (one duplication).

(d) No evidence noted: 10.

Point 5. Many of the realists insist *that the rational element in law is an illusion.*[25]

(a) Supporting: Conceivably Frank: 1;

(b) Colorable: (i) Unrebutted: Green: 1; (ii) Rebutted: 4;

(c) Negating: 13;

(d) No evidence noted: 1.

Point 6. Realists usually have a presupposition that some one of the competing psychologies is the *unum necessarium* for jurisprudence.[26] (The theory of rationalization is, we believe, employed by all our subjects. It is employed by none of them as an exclusively valid attack.) We read "competing psychologies" as referring to general bodies of doctrine: *e. g.*, behaviorism or psychoanalysis in some brand. As to this:

(a) Supporting: None;

(b) Colorable: (i) Unrebutted: None; (ii) Rebutted: 2;

(c) Negating: 4;

(d) No evidence noted: 14.

Point 7. Many of the realists seek to ignore the traditional common-law technique "of application."[27]

---

[23] The colorable passages (all cited in Appendix I) are Cook, *Scientific Method and the Law* 233; *The Alienability of Choses in Action*, II 452, 461, 462, 481 (but *cf. ibid.* 484); *The Logical and Legal Bases of the Conflict of Laws* 473, 484, n.75 (but *cf. ibid.* 475, 479, n.60). Colorable from Moore is only the afterglow of such writings as *An Institutional Approach to the Law of Commercial Banking.*

[24] See Pound, *supra* note 1, at 702, lines 4–5, 25–26, last full par.; 703, lines 13–15. Cook, *The Jurisdiction of Sovereign States and the Conflict of Laws* 380: "The postulates in question contain inherently contradictory assertions, *and so can never furnish a satisfactory basis for sound doctrine* in the field of the conflict of laws." (Our italics.) Somewhat allied in implication, *Privileges of Labor Unions in the Struggle for Life* 785; and on the *descriptive* side only, *The Utility of Jurisprudence in the Solution of Legal Problems* 337; *Scientific Method and the Law* 233; *The Jurisdiction of Sovereign States and the Conflict of Laws* 371, n.12; *The Logical and Legal Bases of the Conflict of Laws* 457–58. On the *normative* side, *cf. The Utility of Jurisprudence in the Solution of Legal Problems* 365; *Scientific Method and the Law* 230–31; *The Logical and Legal Bases of the Conflict of Laws* 485–86. But compare *ibid.* at 470, defining what he means by "sound theory." And in the context even the main passage means only that Story's postulates fail *when tested by their own premises.* (Complete citations in Appendix I, *infra.*)

[25] See Pound, *supra* note 1, at 698, lines, from bottom, 7–3; 705, lines 4–6; last 5 lines; 707, last par., first three lines. Supporting: Frank, LAW AND THE MODERN MIND, the afterglow (but *cf. id.* at 37, 121, 138, 152, 169, 288, 343, 362, and esp. 155–59; Frank informally repudiates any such opinion, and denies that his writings warrant this classification). Colorable: Green, JUDGE AND JURY, *e. g.*, at 145, 146, 148, 151, and the afterglow.

[26] See Pound, *supra* note 1, at 705, first full par., first sentence; 706, same.

[27] See *id.* at 706, last par. to its end.

Examination develops that no triable issue of fact, as distinct from opinion, is joined here, since the Dean apparently conceives the traditional techniques primarily as techniques *of applying rules*, whereas the realist would include *all* the traditional techniques of deciding cases, or of the lawyer's art.

The canvass shows only that our subjects are much interested in study of the traditional techniques so far as they can get at them, and that they weight the rule-applying aspect less heavily than does Dean Pound.

Point 8. Realists are blind to how far the administration of justice *attains certainty through rule and form.*[28]

Again no triable issue of fact, as opposed to opinion, is joined. The canvass shows that our subjects are much concerned with how far justice obtains certainty, and with how far it is attained—or hindered—through rule and form. But that they tend to differ with the Dean on the "how far" in both cases.

Point 9. A characteristic of the realist is conceiving of the administration of justice rather as a mere aggregate of single determinations than as an approximation to a uniform curse of behavior.[29]

Our evidence is directed to the proposition that our subjects do not conceive of judicial (and other legal) behavior as involving uniformities.

(a) Supporting: Frank: 1;
(b) Colorable: (i) Unrebutted: Green: I; (ii) Rebutted: 4;
(c) Negating: 14;
(d) No evidence noted: None.

Point 10. Many of the realists have an exclusive interest in the business aspects of the law, and this exclusively from the standpoint of the purposes of business, rather than of society as a whole.[30]

This could, of course, apply only to the ten commercial lawyers among our subjects:

(a) Perhaps supporting: Sturges: 1;
(b) Perhaps colorable: (i) Unrebutted (in print): Moore: 1; (ii) Rebutted: None;
(c) Negating: 7;
(d) Inadequate evidence noted (in print): 1.

Point 11. By clear implication: the work of the realists is not concerned with questions of what ought to be done by way of law.[31]

(a) Supporting: None;
(b) Colorable: (i) Unrebutted: None; (ii) Rebutted: 3;
(c) Negating: 17;
(d) No evidence noted: None.

Point 12. By clear implication: the realists, *in their attempts at description*, disregard the effects of the judges' own ideal pictures of what they ought to do.[32]

---

[28] See *id.* at 707, lines 4–9.

[29] See *id.* at 707, first full par., first sentence; 708, lines 1–8. The supporting material: FRANK, *op. cit. supra* note 25. But see *ibid.* at 104, 130–32, 166–67, 251–52. GREEN, *op. cit. supra* note 25. Green insists on predictability of procedure and formula, as distinct from outcome. Both Frank and Green are focussing on the trial court.

[30] See p. 1261, *infra.*

[31] See p. 1262, *infra.*

[32] See Pound, *supra* note 1, at 700 from line 3 through the par. Colorable: Moore, *Legal and Institutional Methods Applied to the Debiting of Direct Discounts* (1931) 40 YALE L. J. 555, 563. See Pound, *supra* note 1, at 698, lines 3–7; 699, lines 1–16; 700, second par.

(a) Supporting: None;
(b) Colorable: (i) Unrebutted: Moore: 1; (ii) Rebutted: None;
(c) Negating: Passages adduced from 11; but they are not particularly significant.

What counts here is the whole tone of a man's work. We should have thought the realists' concern as to the effects of the court's ideal picture of delusive certainty would be enough to negate.—Significant in this canvass is chiefly the absence of positive support.

Point 13. By clear implication: the realists are unmindful of the relativity of significance, of the way in which preconceptions necessarily condition observation, and are not on their guard against their own preconceptions, while investigating.[33]

(a) Supporting: None;
(b) Colorable: None;
(c) Negating: 12;
(d) No evidence noted: 8.

Summary: Of eleven points on which evidence in support could be diagnosed and counted, we find such evidence as to seven—but how much? We can adduce some support for *one* point from *three of our twenty men*, for each of four further points from two of our twenty, for each of two further points from one of our twenty. *One of our twenty men* offers some support for *three of the eleven points*, three offer some support each for two of the eleven points, four offer some support each for one point. *In no instance is the support offered strong, unambiguous, or unqualified,* even on the printed record.

Let it be conceded that we have missed men or evidence which would support these points of description on which so much of the Dean's criticism of realists is based. Let it be conceded that (though aided by his lines of criticism) we have in part misinterpreted what it was that he was criticizing. We submit, nonetheless, that *any* description of what "realists" think, or what "most of them believe" or what "many of them write"—and especially any description made on the basis of criticism—will in the light of our canvass need evidence by man and chapter and verse before it can be relied on as meaning more than: *the writer has an impression that there is someone, perhaps two someones, whose writings bear this out.* We accept the implications of this statement for ourselves. What we here further say of realists is, where no evidence is cited, to be read as giving a vague and very fallible impression.

II

Real Realists[34]

What, then, *are* the characteristics of these new fermenters? One thing is clear. There is no school of realists. There is no likelihood that there will be such a school. There is no group with an official or accepted, or even with an emerging creed. There is no abnegation of independent striking out. We hope that there may

[33] See *id.* at 698–700.
[34] Both Adler (*Law and the Modern Mind—Legal Certainty* (1931) 31 COL. L. REV. 91) and Cohen (*Justice Holmes and the Nature of Law* (1931) 31 *id.* 352) have discussed "realism" adversely, Cohen addressing himself especially to Frank, Moore (uncited specifically), Bingham, and Oliphant; Adler to the same (except Moore),

never be. New recruits acquire tools and stimulus, not masters, nor over-mastering ideas. Old recruits diverge in interests from each other. They are related, says Frank, only in their negations, and in their skepticisms, and in their curiosity.[35]

There is, however, a *movement* in thought and work about law. The movement, the method of attack, is wider than the number of its adherents. It includes some or much work of many men who would scorn ascription to its banner. Individual men, then. Men more or less interstimulated—but no more than all of them have been stimulated by the orthodox tradition, or by that ferment at the opening of the century in which Dean Pound took a leading part. Individual men, working and thinking over law and its place in society. Their differences in point of view, in interest, in emphasis, in field of work, are huge. They differ among themselves well-nigh as much as any of them differs from, say, Langdell. Their number grows. Their work finds acceptance.

What one does find as he observes them is twofold. First (and to be expected) certain points of departure are common to them all. Second (and this, when one can find neither school nor striking likenesses among individuals, is startling) a cross-relevance, a complementing, an interlocking of their varied results "as if they were guided by an invisible hand." A third thing may be mentioned in passing: a fighting faith in their methods of attack on legal problems; but in these last years the battle with the facts has proved so much more exciting than any battle with traditionalism that the fighting faith had come (until the spring offensive of 1931 against the realists) to manifest itself chiefly in enthusiastic labor to get on.

But as with a description of an economic order, tone and color of description must vary with the point of view of the reporter. No other one of the men would set the picture up as I shall. Such a report must thus be individual. Each man, of necessity, orients the whole to his own main interest of the moment—as I shall orient the whole to mine: the workings of case-law in appellate courts. Maps of the United States prepared respectively by a political geographer and a student of climate would show some resemblance; each would show a coherent picture; but neither's map would give much satisfaction to the other. So here. I speak for myself of that movement which in its sum is realism; I do not speak of "the realists"; still less do I speak *for* the participants or any of them. And I shall endeavor to keep in mind as I go that the justification for grouping these men together lies not in that they are *alike* in belief or work, but in that from certain common points of departure they have branched into lines of work which seem to be

---

especially Frank, and to Cook, Yntema, and Green (all uncited) as well. Dickinson, *Legal Rules: Their Function in the Process of Decision* (1931) 79 U. OF PA. L. REV. 833, bases his criticisms (especially of Cook, Frank, Llewellyn) largely on specific citations. Radin and Yntema publish admirable papers on the matter with which I concur almost *in toto*. Radin, *Legal Realism* (1931) 31 COL. L. REV. 824; Yntema, *The Rational Basis of Legal Science* (1931) 31 *id*. 925. Citations of realists are lacking in their papers also: they speak not of or for a school, but for themselves. So far as the present paper purports to be descriptive, it sins in non-citation. (As did my controversial paper, *supra* note 18, in non-specificity as to where the views criticized might be found. *Ma maxima culpa!* And may whoever feels that he was caricatured forgive me. Preparing the present discussion has shown me that error of my ways.) I had hoped in this part to build a fair bibliography of the literature but time has not served. Felix Cohen has been kind enough to aid me in this and I include his references, marked "©."

[35] Names for them vary. I call them realists (so do Frank, Radin, and often, Yntema; Bingham also recognizes the term. And I find it used in the same sense in the work of Cook, Douglas, Frankfurter)—stressing the interest in the actuality of what happens, and the distrust of formula. Cook prefers to speak of scientific approach to law, Oliphant of objective method—stressing much the same features. Clark speaks of fact-research, Corbin of what courts do. "Functional approach" stresses the interest in, and valuation by, effects. Dickinson speaks of the skeptical movement.

building themselves into a whole, a whole planned by none, foreseen by none, and (it may well be) not yet adequately grasped by any.

The common points of departure are several.[36]

(1) The conception of law in flux, of moving law, and of judicial creation of law.

(2) The conception of law as a means to social ends and not as an end in itself; so that any part needs constantly to be examined for its purpose, and for its effect, and to be judged in the light of both and of their relation to each other.

(3) The conception of society in flux, and in flux typically faster than the law, so that the probability is always given that any portion of law needs reëxamination to determine how far it fits the society it purports to serve.

(4) The *temporary* divorce of Is and Ought for purposes of study. By this I mean that whereas value judgments must always be appealed to in order to set objectives for inquiry, yet during the inquiry itself into what Is, the observation, the description, and the establishment of relations between the things described are to remain *as largely as possible* uncontaminated by the desires of the observer or by what he wishes might be or thinks ought (ethically) to be. More particularly, this involves during the study of what courts are doing the effort to disregard the question what they ought to do. Such divorce of Is and Ought is, of course, not conceived as permanent. To men who begin with a suspicion that change is needed, a permanent divorce would be impossible. The argument is simply that no judgment of what Ought to be done in the future with respect to any part of law can be intelligently made without knowing objectively, as far as possible, what that part of law is now doing. And realists believe that experience shows the intrusion of Ought-spectacles *during the investigation of the facts* to make it very difficult to see what is being done. On the Ought side this means an insistence on informed evaluations instead of armchair speculations. Its full implications on the side of Is-investigation can be appreciated only when one follows the contributions to objective description in business law and practice made by realists whose social philosophy rejects many of the accepted foundations of the existing economic order. (*E.g.*, Handler *re* trade-marks and advertising; Klaus *re* marketing and banking; Llewellyn *re* sales; Moore *re* banking; Patterson *re* risk-bearing.)

(5) Distrust of traditional legal rules and concepts insofar as they purport to *describe* what either courts or people are actually doing. Hence the constant emphasis on rules as "generalized predictions of what courts will do." This is much more widespread as yet than its counterpart: the careful severance of rules *for* doing (precepts) from rules *of* doing (practices).

[36] As to each of the following points I have attempted to check over not only the general tone of work but several specific writings of the twenty men named and a number of others—*e. g.*, Kidd, Maggs, Breckenridge, Morse, Durfee, Bohlen, Bryant Smith and Goble—and to make sure that each point was applicable to each. Errors may have crept in. Note how closely the description fits Holmes' work as early as 1871–72: "It commands the future, a valid but imperfectly realized ideal."

On the common points of departure see especially Corbin, *The Law and the Judges*; Llewellyn, Cases and Materials on the Law of Sales, Introd.; Oliphant, *A Return to Stare Decisis*; Patterson, *Can Law Be Scientific?*, all cited in Appendix I. See also Arnold, *Criminal Attempts—The Rise and Fall of an Abstraction* (1930) 40 Yale L. J. 53; Arnold, *The Restatement of the Law of Trusts* (1931) 31 Col. L. Rev. 800; Clark, Douglas and Thomas, *The Business Failures Project—A Problem in Methodology* (1930) 39 Yale L. J. 1013; Douglas and Thomas, *The Business Failures Project—II. An Analysis of Methods of Investigation* (1931) 40 id. 1034; Burch, *The Paradoxes of Legal Science: A Review* (1929) 27 Mich. L. Rev. 637; Radin, *The Permanent Problems of the Law* (1929) 15 Corn. L. Q. 1; Yntema and Jaffin, *supra* note 20; Yntema, *supra* note 34. And see © Isaacs, *How Lawyers Think* (1923) 23 Col. L. Rev. 555; Laski, *Judicial Review of Social Policy in England* (1926) 39 Harv. L. Rev. 832.

On checking rules descriptive against the facts of the decisions, see especially Corbin, Douglas, Klaus, Tulin, *infra*, Appendix I; © Finkelstein, *Judicial Self-Limitation* (1924) 37 Harv. L. Rev. 338; Finkelstein, *Further Notes on Self Limitation* (1925) 39 id. 221; Isaacs' more recent work in general, but especially *The Promoter: A Legislative Problem* (1925) 38 id. 887; Brown, *Due Process of Law, Police Power, and the Supreme Court* (1927) 40 id. 943; Hamilton, *Affectation with a Public Interest* (1930) 39 Yale L. J. 1089.

(6) Hand in hand with this distrust of traditional rules (on the descriptive side) goes a distrust of the theory that traditional prescriptive rule-formulations are *the* heavily operative factor in producing court decisions. This involves the tentative adoption of the theory of rationalization for the study of opinions. It will be noted that "distrust" in this and the preceding point is not at all equivalent to "negation in any given instance."

(7) The belief in the worthwhileness of grouping cases and legal situations into narrower categories than has been the practice in the past. This is connected with the distrust of verbally simple rules—which so often cover dissimilar and non-simple fact situations (dissimilarity being tested partly by the way cases come out, and partly by the observer's judgment as to how they ought to come out; but a realist tries to indicate explicitly which criterion he is applying).

(8) An insistence on evaluation of any part of law in terms of its effects, and an insistence on the worthwhileness of trying to find these effects.

(9) Insistence on *sustained and programmatic attack* on the problems of law along any of these lines. None of the ideas set forth in this list is new. Each can be matched from somewhere; each can be matched from recent orthodox work in law. New twists and combinations do appear here and there. What is as novel as it is vital is for a goodly number of men to pick up ideas which have been expressed and dropped, used for an hour and dropped, played with from time to time and dropped—to pick up such ideas and set about *consistently, persistently, insistently to carry them through*. Grant that the idea or point of view is familiar—the results of steady, sustained, systematic work with it are not familiar. Not hit-or-miss stuff, not the insight which flashes and is forgotten, but sustained effort to force an old insight into its full bearing, to exploit it to the point where it laps over upon an apparently inconsistent insight, to explore their bearing on each other by the test of fact. This urge, in law, is quite new enough over the last decades to excuse a touch of frenzy among the locust-eaters.[37]

The first, second, third and fifth of the above items, while common to the workers of the newer movement, are not peculiar to them. But the other items (4, 6, 7, 8 and 9) are to me the characteristic marks of the movement. Men or work fitting those specifications are to me "realistic" whatever label they may wear. Such, and none other, are the perfect fauna of this new land. Not all the work cited below fits my peculiar definition in all points. All such work fits most of the points.

Bound, as all "innovators" are, by prior thinking, these innovating "realists" brought their batteries to bear in first instance on the work of appellate courts. Still wholly within the tradition of our law, they strove to improve on that tradition.

(a) An early and fruitful line of attack borrowed from psychology the concept of *rationalization* already mentioned. To recanvass the opinions, viewing them no longer as mirroring the process of deciding cases, but rather as trained lawyers' arguments made by the judges (after the decision has been reached), intended to make the decision seem plausible, legally decent, legally right, to make it seem, indeed, legally inevitable—this was to open up new vision. It was assumed that the deductive logic of opinions need by no means be either a *description* of the process of decision, or an *explanation* of how the decision was reached. Indeed over-enthusiasm has at times assumed that the logic of the opinion *could* be neither; and similar over-enthusiasm, perceiving case after case in which the opinion is clearly almost valueless as an indication of how that case came to

---

[37] Since everyone who reads the manuscript in this sad age finds this allusion blind, but I still like it, I insert the passage: ". . . Preaching in the wilderness of Judea, And saying, Repent ye. . . . And the same John had his raiment of camel's hair, and a leathern girdle about his loins; *and his meat was locusts* and wild honey." Matthew III, 1,2,4.

decision, has worked at times almost as if the opinion were equally valueless in predicting what a later court will do.[38]

But the line of inquiry via rationalization has come close to demonstrating that in any case doubtful enough to make litigation respectable the available authoritative premises—*i.e.*, premises legitimate and impeccable under the traditional legal techniques—are at least two, and that the two are mutually contradictory as applied to the case in hand.[39] Which opens the question of what made the court select the one available premise rather than the other. And which raises the greatest of doubts as to *how far* that supposed certainty in decision which derives merely from the presence of accepted rules really goes.

(b) A second line of attack has been to discriminate among rules with reference to their relative significance. Too much is written and thought about "law" and "rules," lump-wise. Which part of law? Which rule? Iron rules of policy, and rules "in the absence of agreement"; rules which keep a case from the jury, and rules as to the etiquette of instructions necessary to make a verdict stick—if one can get it; rules "of pure decision" for hospital cases, and rules which counselors rely on in their counseling; rules which affect many (and which many, and how?) and rules which affect few.[40] Such discriminations affect the traditional law curriculum, the traditional organization of law books and, above all, the orientation of study: to drive into the most important fields of ignorance.

(c) A further line of attack on the apparent conflict and uncertainty among the decisions in appellate courts has been to seek more understandable statement of them by grouping the facts in new—and typically but not always narrower—categories. The search is for correlations of fact-situation and outcome which (aided by common sense) may reveal *when* courts seize on one rather than another of the available competing premises. One may even stumble on the trail of *why* they do. Perhaps, *e.g.*, third party beneficiary difficulties simply fail to get applied to promises to make provision for dependents;[41] perhaps the preexisting duty rule goes by the board when the agreement is one for a marriage-settlement.[42] Perhaps, indeed, contracts in what we may broadly call family relations do not work out in general as they do in business.[43] If so, the rules—viewed as statements of the course of judicial behavior—as *predictions* of what will happen—need to be restated. Sometimes it is a question of carving out hitherto unnoticed exceptions. But sometimes the results force the worker to reclassify an area altogether.[44] Typically, as stated, the classes of situations which

[38] *E.g.*, Tulin, *The Role of Penalties in Criminal Law* (1928) 37 Yale L. J. 1048; Douglas, *Vicarious Liability and Administration of Risk* (1929) 38 *id.* 584, 720; Corbin, *Contracts for the Benefit of Third Persons* (1930) 46 L. Q. Rev. 12.

Moore and Oliphant certainly, and I think Sturges, would differ from me, to a greater or less extent, as to how far this is "over-enthusiasm." Moore's three years' quest reached for some more objective technique of prediction. Moore and Sussman, *Legal and Institutional Methods Applied to the Debiting of Direct Discounts* (1931) 40 Yale L. J. 381, 555, 752, 928. And Oliphant, *A Return to Stare Decisis* (1928) 14 A. B. A. J. 71, 159, n. 5.

[39] For a series of examples, see Cook, *The Utility of Jurisprudence in the Solution of Legal Problems* in 5 Lectures on Legal Topics, Association of the Bar of the City of New York (1923–24) 335; Powell, *Current Conflicts Between the Commerce Clause and State Police Power, 1922–1927* (1928) 12 Minn. L. Rev. 470, 491, 607, 631.

[40] Compare the work of Bohlen and Green on torts; Llewellyn on contracts, for attempts to carry this type of old insight through more consistently.

[41] Note (1931) 31 Col. L. Rev. 117.

[42] An unpublished study by Moore. Another example is Handler and Pickett, *Trade Marks and Trade Names—An Analysis and Synthesis* (1930) 30 Col. L. Rev. 168, 759.

[43] Perhaps they should not—but that is an Ought question. One will be forced to raise it, if he finds courts in their results persistently evading the consequences of what accepted doctrine declares to be the general rule. Compare Moore and Sussman, *supra* note 38, at 555, 557; Oliphant, *supra* note 38, at 159, 160.

[44] Sometimes the effort fails. Durfee and Duffy, *Foreclosure of Land Contracts in Michigan: Equitable Suite and Summary Proceeding* (1928) 7 Mich. St. B. J. 166, 221, 236. It is a grateful sign of a growing scientific spirit when *negative* results of investigation come into print.

result are narrower, much narrower than the traditional classes. The process is in essence the orthodox technique of making distinctions, and reformulating—but undertaken systematically; exploited consciously, instead of being reserved until facts which refuse to be twisted by "interpretation" force action.[45] The departure from orthodox procedure lies chiefly in distrust of, instead of search for, the widest sweep of generalization words permit.[46] Not that such sweeping general-izations are not desired–*if they can be made so as to state what judges do.*

All of these three earliest lines of attack converge to a single conclusion: *there is less possibility of accurate prediction of what courts will do than the traditional rules would lead us to suppose*[47] *(*and what possibility there is must be found in good measure outside these same traditional rules). The particular kind of certainty that men have thus far thought to find in law is in good measure an illusion. Realistic workers have sometimes insisted on this truth so hard that they have been thought pleased with it. (The danger lies close, for one thinking indiscriminately of Is and Ought, to suspect announcements of fact to reflect preferences, ethically normative judgments, on the part of those who do the announcing.)

But announcements of fact are not appraisals of worth. The contrary holds. The immediate result of the preliminary work thus far described has been a further, var-ied series of endeavors; *the focussing of conscious attack on discovering the factors thus far unpredictable, in good part with a view to their control.* Not wholly with a view to such elimination; part of the conscious attack is directed to finding where and when and how far *un*certainty has value. Much of what has been taken as insis-tence on the exclusive significance of the particular (with supposed implicit denial of the existence of valid or apposite generalizations) represents in fact a clearing of the ground for such attack. Close study of particular unpredictables may lessen unpredictability. It may increase the value of what remains. It certainly makes clearer what the present situation is. "Link by link is chain-mail made."

[45] It may not be *convenient* to draw rules *for* courts to use in terms of these narrower categories. Williston argues that the set of official formulas must not be too complex; they are for "application" by ordinary men, not intellectual giants. WILLISTON, SOME MODERN TENDENCIES IN THE LAW (1929) 127. That does not touch the present point. Even with broad formulas prevailing, as at present, one still gets better results in *describing* where courts get to if he thinks in terms of narrower classifications of the facts. But a fair portion of present unpredictability is certainly attributable to the fact that the courts are using official formulas which fit, only part of the time, what the facts seem to call for. Sometimes the facts win, sometimes the formula. See note 46, *infra.*

[46] When this procedure results in a formulation along lines strikingly unorthodox (*cf.* my own approach to title—CASES AND MATERIALS ON THE LAW OF SALES (1930)) but one which the worker finds helpful in prediction or in general-izing results, Dean Pound's query as to *how far* courts achieve certainty by traditional rule and form becomes pressing. At times Moore (chiefly in conversation), Oliphant (*supra* note 38, conversation, and theory of contracts), and Sturges (*Legal Theory and Real Property Mortgages* (1928) 37 YALE L. J. 691), seem to me to verge upon a position which escapes my understanding: that the judges' reactions to the facts in such cases are only negligibly influenced by the orthodox rules. My experience is that when measures (here "the rule") do not fit purposes (here the line of discrimina-tion discovered by the fact-issue-judgment approach) the result is *always* some inadequacy in accomplishing purposes. And my experience is that when purposes do not become conscious, there is commonly inadequacy at times in locating a measure for their adequate accomplishment. (Compare Corbin's results on the English cases: Corbin, *Contracts for the Benefit of Third Persons* (1930) 46 L. Q. REV. 12.) What one has gained by the new formulation, if it proves significant, seems to me to be a tool for clarifying the situation and the purposes; a means of bringing a hidden factor, perhaps *the* hidden factor in past uncertainty, into view; perhaps also a new insight into wise objectives, and so a key for reform. Compare Llewellyn, *What Price Contract?—An Essay in Perspective* (1931) 40 YALE L. J. 704, 732, n. 62.

[47] Partly, as I have tried to develop elsewhere (Llewellyn, *Legal Illusion* (1931) 31 COL. L. REV. 82, 87; PRÄJUDIZIENRECHT U. RECHTSPRECHUNG IN AMERIKA (1931) § 52 *et seq.*), because the "certainty" sought is conceived verbally, and in terms of lawyers, not factually and in terms of laymen. Neither can commonly be had save at the cost of the other. We get enough of each to upset the other. One effect of the realist approach is to center on certainty for laymen and improve the machinery for attaining it. The present dilemma is quickly stated: if there is no certainty in law (rules and concepts *plus* intuition *plus* lawmen's practices) why is not any layman qualified to practice or to judge? But if the certainty is what the rule-believers claim, how can two good lawyers disagree about an appealed case? *Cf. also* © Isaacs, *supra* note 36, at 890 *et seq.*; Isaacs, *infra* note 61, at 211–12.

(i) There is the question of the personality of the judge. (Little has as yet been attempted in study of the jury; Frank, *Law and the Modern Mind*, makes a beginning.) Within this field, again, attempts diverge. Some have attempted study of the particular judge[48]—a line that will certainly lead to inquiry into his social conditioning.[49] Some have attempted to bring various psychological hypotheses to bear.[50] All that has become clear is that our government is not a government of laws, but one of laws through men.

(ii) There has been some attempt to work out the varieties of interaction between the traditional concepts (the judge's "legal" equipment for thinking, seeing, judging) and the fact-pressures of the cases.[51] This is a question not—as above–of getting at results on particular facts, but of studying the effect, *e.g.*, of a series of cases in which the facts either press successively in the one direction, or alternate in their pressures and counteract each other. Closely related in substance, but wholly diverse in both method and aim, is study of the machinery by which fact-pressures can under our procedure be brought to bear upon the court.[52]

(iii) First efforts have been made to capitalize the wealth of our reported cases to make large-scale quantitative studies of facts and outcome; the hope has been that these might develop lines of prediction more sure, or at least capable of adding further certainty to the predictions based as hitherto on intensive study of smaller bodies of cases. This represents a more ambitious development of the procedure described above, under (c); I know of no published results.

(iv) Repeated effort has been made to work with the cases of single states, to see how far additional predictability might thus be gained.[53]

---

[48] *E.g.*, Powell's insistence on the particular judges in successions of decisions. *Supra* note 39; *Commerce, Congress, and the Supreme Court, 1922–1925* (1926) 26 Col. L. Rev. 396, 521; © *The Judiciality of Minimum Wage Legislation* (1924) 37 Harv. L. Rev. 545; *The Nature of a Patent Right* (1917) 17 Col. L. Rev. 663; Haines, *General Observations on the Effects of Personal, Political, and Economic Influences in the Decisions of Judges* (1922) 17 Ill. L. Rev. 96; Brown, *Police Power—Legislation for Health and Personal Safety* (1929) 42 Harv. L. Rev. 866; Cushman, *The Social and Economic Interpretation of the Fourteenth Amendment* (1922) 20 Mich. L. Rev. 737; Frankfurter and Landis, The Business of The Supreme Court (1928), and the supplementary series of articles in (1928) 42 Harv. L. Rev. 1; (1929) 43 *id.* 1; (1930) 44 *id.* 1.

To be added, especially, is the growing volume of judicial self-revelation: Cardozo's work: Hutcheson, *Infra* Appendix 1; Judge Amidon's beautiful opinion in *Great Northern Ry. v. Brousseau*, 286 Fed. 414 (D. N. D. 1923); and parts of such earlier work as Young, *The Law as an Expression of Community Ideals and the Law Making Functions of Courts* (1917) 27 Yale L. J. 1.

[49] Nelles, Book Review (1931) 40 Yale L. J. 998.

[50] Freudian: beginnings in Frank, Law and the Modern Mind (1930). Behaviorist: an attempt in Patterson, *Equitable Relief for Unilateral Mistake* (1928) 28 Col. L. Rev. 859. Semi-behaviorist, via cultural anthropology: Moore and Sussman, *supra* note 38.

[51] Llewellyn in 3 Encyclopaedia of the Social Sciences (1930) 249; Llewellyn, Cases and Materials on the Law of Sales (1930); Präjudizienrecht U. Rechtsprechung in Amerika (1931). With which last compare Pound, *A Theory of Judicial decision* (1923) 36 Harv. L. Rev. 641, 802, esp. 940; Henderson, The Position of Foreign Corporations in American Constitutional Law (1918); Cardozo, The Nature of the Judicial Process (1925); Corbin, *supra* note 37; Haines, *supra* note 48; Berle, *Investors and the Revised Delaware Corporation Act* (1929) 29 Col. L. Rev. 563; Finkelstein, *supra* note 36; Hamilton, *Judicial Tolerance of Farmers' Cooperatives* (1929) 38 YALE L. J. 936; Patterson, *infra* Appendix I.

[52] The famous Brandeis brief and its successors mark the beginning. In commercial cases both Germany and England have evolved effective machinery.

[53] Here, as throughout, one notes the contact of the realist movement with a tradition of practice (single state law, interest in procedure, "automobile jurisprudence" and the like, damage and procedure points treated in conjunction with the relevant substantive law, interest in the facts and atmosphere) which the older academic tradition was prone to scorn. But this progress backwards takes with it, and fertilizes the practical tradition with, the interest in theory, generality of outlook, and long-range thinking of the older academic tradition. Fortunate media for this type of work are the local law reviews. Such work, long continued, will force a radical revision of thought about "the common law" and, one may hope, educate the "national" reviews. See also © Kales, *An Unsolicited Report on Legal Education* (1918) 18 Col. L. Rev. 21.

(v) Study has been attempted of "substantive rules" in the particular light of the available remedial procedure; the hope being to discover in the court's unmentioned knowledge of the immediate consequences of this rule or that, in the case at hand, a motivation for decision which cuts deeper than any shown by the opinion.[54] Related, but distinct, is the reassertion of the fundamental quality of remedy, and the general approach to restating "what the law is" (on the side of prediction) in terms not of rights, but of what can be done: Not only "no remedy, no right," but "precisely as much right as remedy."[55]

(vi) The set-up of men's ways and practices and ideas on the subject matter of the controversy has been studied, in the hope that this might yield a further or even final[56] basis for prediction. The work here ranges from more or less indefinite reference to custom (the historical school), or mores (Corbin),[57] through rough or more careful canvasses[58] or business[59] practice and ideology (*e.g.*, Berle, Sturges, Isaacs, Handler, Bogert, Durfee and Duffy, Breckenridge, Turner, Douglas, Shanks, Oliphant, and indeed Holmes) to painstaking and detailed studies in which practice is much more considered than is any prevailing set of ideas about what the practices are (Klaus) or—even—to studies in which the concept of "practice" is itself broken up into behavior-sequences presented with careful note of the degree of their frequency and recurrence, and in which all reference to the actor's own ideas is deprecated or excluded (Moore and Sussman). While grouped here together, under one formula, these workers show differences in degree and manner of interest in the background-ways which range from one pole to the other. Corbin's main interest is the appellate case; most of the second group mentioned rely on semi-special information and readily available material from economics, sociology, etc., with occasional careful studies of their own, and carry a strong interest into drafting or counselling work; Klaus insists on full canvass of all relevant literature, buttressed by and viewed in the light of intensive personal investigation; Moore's canvass and study is so original and thorough in technique as to offer as vital and important a contribution to ethnology and sociology as to banking practice. This is not one "school"; here alone are the germs of many "schools."

---

[54] *E.g.*, Tulin, *supra* note 37; Pound, *supra* note 51, at 649 *et seq.* on the art of administrating justice through damages. And *cf.* the remedy canvass in Patterson, *Equitable Relief for Unilateral Mistake* (1928) 28 COL. L. REV. 859; Durfee and Duffy, *supra* note 44.

[55] *E.g.*, Klaus, *Identification of the Holder and Tender of Receipt on the Counter Presentation of Checks* (1929) 13 MINN. L. REV. 281; Handler, *False and Misleading Advertising* (1929) 39 YALE L. J. 22; Handler and Pickett, *supra* note 42; *cf.* Tulin, *infra* Appendix I; LLEWELLYN, CASES AND MATERIALS ON THE LAW OF SALES C. III.

[56] Moore, *An Institutional Approach to the Law of Commercial Banking* (1929) 38 YALE L. J. 703; Moore and Sussman, *supra* note 38, might be so read; or rather, so misread. His study of behavior is not based on a belief that it will by itself lead to final results; it is rather (as is the intelligent behaviorist program in psychology) a "Let us see how far we can get with this" approach. And it is hard to justify a quarrel with that. See Moore and Sussman, *supra* note 38, at 556–64, esp. 561. And though prediction should be achieved, there still remains the question of Ought—if in no other guise, then as a legislative matter. Compare also L. K. Frank, *An Institutional Analysis of the Law* (1924) 24 COL. L. REV. 480 (a magnificent example of what the outsider can contribute); Moore, *Rational Basis of Legal Institutions*, *infra* Appendix I; © Ketcham, *Law as a Body of Subjective Rules* (1929) 23 ILL. L. REV. 360.

[57] Recently becoming much more specific—see *Third Parties as Beneficiaries of Contractors' Surety Bonds* (1928) 38 YALE L. J. 1.

[58] Ideals here largely outstrip scholarly achievement. But most realist scholars are in their work materially ahead of what they have printed. It should be noted that Douglas' business failures study, *supra* note 36, proceeds to a level comparable to Klaus or Moore.

[59] Or practice in criminal law administration, as in the crime surveys; or on family matters: JACOBS AND ANGELL, A RESEARCH IN FAMILY LAW (1930); Powell and Looker, *Decedents' Estates—Illumination from Probate and Tax Records* (1930) 30 COL. L. REV. 919.

(vii) Another line of attack, hardly begun, is that on the effect of the lawyer on the outcome of cases, as an element in prediction. The lawyer *in litigation* has been the subject thus far only of desultory comment.[60] Groping approach has been made to the counsellor as field general, in the business field: in drafting, and in counselling (and so in the building of practices and professional understandings which influence court action later), and in the strategy of presenting cases in favorable series, settling the unfavorable cases, etc.[61]

All of the above has focussed on how to tell what appellate courts will do, however far afield any new scent may have led the individual hunter. But the interest in *effects* on laymen of what the courts will do leads rapidly from this still respectably traditional sphere of legal discussion into a series of further inquiries whose legal decorum is more dubious. They soon extend far beyond what has in recent years been conceived (in regard to the developed state) as law at all. I can not stop to consider these inquiries in detail. Space presses. Each of the following phases could be, and should be, elaborated at least into such a rough sketch as the foregoing. Through each would continue to run interest in what actually eventuates; interest in accurate description of what eventuates; interest in attempting, where prediction becomes uncertain, some conscious attack on hidden factors whose study might lessen the uncertainty; and interest in effects—on laymen. Finally, insistence that Ought-judgment should be bottomed on knowledge. And that action should be bottomed on all the knowledge that can be got in time to act.

I. *There is first the question of what lower courts and especially trial courts are doing, and what relation their doing has to the sayings and doings of upper courts and legislatures.*

Here the question has been to begin to find out, to find some way, some ways, of getting the hitherto unavailable facts, to find some significant way or ways of classifying what business is done, how long it takes, how various parts of the procedural machinery work. (*E.g.*, Warner, Sunderland, Millar, Clark, Yntema, Marshall, Oliphant, Douglas, Arnold, Morgan, Frankfurter, Greene, and Swazi.) Another attack begins by inquiry not into records, but into the processes of trial and their effects on the outcome of cases. (Frank, Green.) This, on the civil side, where we have (save for memoirs) been wholly in the dark. On the criminal side, beginnings lie further back. (Pound, Frankfurter, Moley and the Crime Surveys; where lawyers have drawn on the criminologists.) All that is really clear to date is that until we know more here our "rules" give us no remote suggestion of *what law means* to persons in the lower income brackets,[62] and give us misleading

Karl Llewellyn

[60] One exception is Sturges, *Law's Delays, Lawyers' Delays, and Forwarded Cases* (1928) 12 MINN. L. REV. 351; *cf.* Wickser, *Bar Associations* (1930) 15 CORN. L. Q. 390. Yet no more vital field exists. Consider merely the effect of skilful or dumb-skulled presentation on the growth of case-law.

[61] Something of this in Elizabeth Sanford's forthcoming THE UNIT RULE; Something in LLEWELLYN, BRAMBLE BUSH (1930) c. X; and Frederick, *The Trust Receipt as Security* (1922) 22 COL. L. REV. 395, 546, is not only itself a step in such a sequence, but esp. at 409 *et seq.* presents, in the Farmers and Mechanics Bank cases, thence to importing, and thence to the automobile line, both materials and suggestion for such a study. And see Isaacs, *Business Security and Legal Security* (1923) 37 HARV. L. REV. 201; © Isaacs, *How Lawyers Think* (1923) 23 COL. L. REV. 555.

[62] Little has been done in print to follow up REGINALD SMITH'S path-breaking JUSTICE AND THE POOR (1924); but allied is the growing literature on poor man's financing the Bradway's work.

suggestions as to the whole body of cases unappealed. Meantime, the techniques of the social sciences are being drawn upon and modified to make the work possible.[63]

II. *There is the question of administrative bodies*—not merely on the side of administrative law (itself a novel concept recently enough—but including all the action which state officials take "under the law" so far as it proves to affect people.[64] And with this we begin departing from the orthodox. To be sure, the practicing lawyer today knows his commission as he knows his court. But the trail thus broken leads into the wilds of government, and politics, and queer events in both.

III. *There is the question of legislative regulation*—in terms of what it *means in action, and to whom*, not merely in terms of what it says. And with that, the question of what goes into producing legislative change—or blocking it[65]— especially so far as the profession participates therein; legislative history on the official record; but as well the background of fact and interest and need. And, no less vital, there is the fact-inquiry into areas of life where maladjustment capable of legal remedy exists.[66]

IV. Finally, and cutting now completely beyond the tradition-bounded area of law, there is the matter not of describing or predicting the action of officials— be they appellate courts, trial courts, legislators, administrators—but of describing and predicting *the effects of their action on the laymen of the community*.[67]

---

[63] Especially useful W. Clark, Douglas and Thomas, *supra* note 36; C. E. Clark, *Fact Research in Law Administration, infra* Appendix I.

[64] One may cite generally Freund, Frankfurter, Henderson, Dickinson, Landis, Magill. Also PATTERSON, THE INSURANCE COMMISSIONER (1927); *cf.* Stason, *Judicial Review of Tax Errors—Effect of Failure to Resort to Administrative Remedies* (1930) 28 MICH. L. REV. 637. And much of the Crime Survey and criminological work fits here. So, *e.g.*, Sheldon Glueck, Fosdick.

[65] See © Berle, *supra* note 51; CHILDS, LABOR AND CAPITAL IN NATIONAL POLITICS (1930).

[66] In general *cf.* Berle and Weiner in the corporate field; FRANKFURTER AND GREENE, THE LABOR INJUNCTION (1930); Clark, *infra* Appendix I; Sunderland. In brief, who not, realist or non-realist, who has ever touched facts and found no solution in case-law? What the realist offers is only thirst for *more* facts, better gathered, more clearly interpreted. And *not* selected (though accurate) to point an argument. For which reason not all the work just mentioned, despite its value, can count as fully "realistic."

[67] I quote Felix Cohen: "In the economic analysis of judicial rules and theories much valuable work has been done by Hale, Bonbright, Richberg, Henderson, Julius Cohen, Goddard and Weiner, particularly in the field of public utility valuation. Otherwise there is simply the call for facts, *e.g.*, Weiner, *Payment of Dissenting Stockholders* (1927) 27 COL. L. REV 547." Except that the "otherwise" comes several lines too soon, I concur *in toto*. As to the point of difference, before I even open the books to search I think, *e.g.*, of Breckenridge, J. M. Clark, J. R. Commons, Douglas, Fredericks, Herman Finkelstein, Handler, Kidd, Klaus, Patterson, Radin, Ripley, Roscoe Turner, Vold, Wilbert Ward, all (save Clark and Commons) as to work inside the field of private commercial law.

Such analysis seems to be on the increase. Comparing, *e.g.*, the Cornell Law Quarterly, vols. 14–16 with vols. 4–6, and the Michigan Law Review, vols. 27–29 with vols. 17–19, one finds both reference to facts and analysis of effects of rules of private law increasing—not so much in frequency as in scope and care and objectivity, and integration into the essential framework of the papers. (On public law the older material often rivals the recent; the fact-impetus developed there earlier.) Striking in the earlier materials is Rogers, *An Account of Some Psychological Experiments on the Subject of Trade-Mark Infringement* (1919) 18 MICH. L. REV. 75; but perhaps even more striking is that in the later, Billig, *What Price Bankruptcy: A Plea for "Friendly Adjustment"* (1929) 14 CORN. L. Q. 413 (and compare Billig, *Extra-Judicial Administration of Insolvent Estates: A Study of Recent Cases* (1930) 78 U. OF PA. L. REV. 293) using figures and more systematic approach to facts and effects, does not stand alone, but stirs up prompt and competent discussion of his *data*, not merely of his conclusions: Gamer, *On Comparing "Friendly Adjustment" and Bankruptcy* (1930) 16 CORN. L. Q. 35. Competent discussion is to the single study what the incorporation of a new tool of approach into a thinker's standard working kit is to the insight which once came and then was forgotten. Compare my own use of risk-allocation as early as 1920, *Implied Warranties of Wholesomeness Again* (1920) 29 YALE L. J. 782, only to wholly overlook it in 1922 in a problem that shrieked for its use (*Certified Altered Checks Under the Negotiable Instruments Law* (1922) 31 *id.* 522) and to almost disregard it in two papers in 1923, both in fields where it yields results. *Supervening Impossibility of Performing Conditions Precedent in the Law of Negotiable Paper* (1923) 23 COL. L. REV 142; C. I. F. Contracts in American Law* (1923) 32 YALE L. J. 711. In short I did not *have* the idea in 1920; I *had had* it then—once. Contrast its consistent employment, wherever it promised help, since 1925. It is the growing *normality* of appeal to facts and of their critical use which marks the intrusion of this aspect of realism into the literature.

"Law" without effect approaches zero in its meaning. To be ignorant of its effect is to be ignorant of its meaning. To know its effect without study of the persons whom it affects is impossible. Here the antecedents of court action touch its results. To know law, then, to know *anything* of what is necessary to judge or evaluate law, we must proceed into these areas which have traditionally been conceived (save by the historical school) as not-law. Not only what courts do instead of what courts say, but also what difference it makes to anybody that they do it. And no sooner does one begin such a study than it becomes clear that there can be no broad talk of "law" nor of "the community"; but that it is a question of reaching the particular part of the community relevant to some particular part of law. There are persons sought to be affected, and persons not sought to be affected. Of the former, some are not in fact materially affected (the gangster-feud); of the latter, some are (depositors in a failing bank which the banking laws have *not* controlled).[68] There is the range of questions as to those legal "helpful devices" (corporation,[69] contract, lease) designed to make it easier for men to get where they want and what they want. There is all the information social scientists have gathered to be explored, in its bearings on the law. There is all the information they have not been interested in gathering, likewise to be explored—but first, to be gathered.

Here are the matters one or another of the new fermenters is ploughing into. Even the sketchy citations here are enough to make clear that their lines of work organize curiously into a whole.

But again rises the query: are the matters *new*? What realist knows so little of law or the ways of human thought as to make such a claim? Which of the inquires has not been made, or started, or adumbrated in the past? Which of the techniques does not rest on our prior culture? New, I repeat, is one thing only: the *systematic* effort to carry one problem through, to carry a succession of problems through, to *consistently*, not occasionally, choose the best available technique, to *consistently* keep description on the descriptive level, to *consistently* distinguish the fact basis which will feed evaluation from the evaluation which it will later feed, to *consistently* seek *all* the relevant data one can find to *add* to the haphazard single-life experience, to *add* to general common sense.

Is it not obvious that—if this be realism—realism is a mass of trends in legal work and thinking? (1) They have their common core, present to some extent wherever realistic work is done: recognition of law as means; recognition of change in society that may call for change in law; interest in what happens; interest in effects; recognition of the need for effort toward keeping perception of the facts uncolored by one's views on Ought; a distrust of the received set of rules and concepts as adequate indications of what is happening in the courts; a drive toward narrowing the categories of description. (2) They have grown out of the study of the action of appellate courts, and that study still remains their potent stimulus. Uncertainty in the action of such courts is one main problem: to find the why of it; to find means to reduce it, where it needs reduction; to find where

[68] Further developed in Llewellyn, *Law Observance and Law Enforcement infra* Appendix I.

[69] The literature here is vast. Peculiarly striking Weiner, *Conflicting Functions of the Upset Price in a Corporate Reorganization* (1927) 27 COL. L. REV. 132; Douglas and Shanks, *Insulation from Liability Through Subsidiary Corporations* (1930) 39 YALE L. J. 193; Posner, *Liability of the Trustee Under the Corporate Indenture* (1928) 42 HARV. L. REV. 198; Berle, *Corporate Powers as Powers in Trust* (1931) 44 HARV. L. REV. 1049.

it needs reduction, where expansion. (3) But into the work of lower courts, of administrative bodies, of legislatures, of the life which lies before and behind law, the ferment of investigation spreads.

Some one or other of these realistic trends takes up the whole time of many; a hundred more participate in them to various degrees who yet would scorn the appellation "realist." The trends are centered in no man, in no coherent group. There is no leader. Spokesmen are self-appointed. They speak not for the whole but for the work each is himself concerned with—at times with little or no thought of the whole, at times with the exaggeration of controversy or innovation. Yet who should know better than lawyers the exaggeration of the controversy; who should have more skill than they to limit argument and dictum to the particular issue, to read it in the light thereof. One will find, reading thus, little said by realistic spokesmen that does not warrant careful pondering. Indeed, on *careful* pondering, one will find little of exaggeration in their writing. Meantime, the proof of the pudding: are there results?

There are. They are results, primarily, on the side of the descriptive sociology of law discussed thus far. They are big with meaning for attack on the field of Ought—either on what courts ought to do with existing rules, or on what changes in rules are called for.

Already we have a series, lengthening impressively, of the *more accurate* reformulations of what appellate courts are doing and may be expected to do. We are making headway in *seeing* (not just "knowing" without inquiry) what effects their doing has on some of the persons interested. We are accumulating some *knowledge* (*i.e.*, more than guesses) on phases of our life as to which our law seems out of joint.

We have, moreover, a first attack upon the realm of the unpredictable in the actions of courts. That attack suggests strongly that one large element in the now incalculable consists in the traditional pretense or belief (sometimes the one, sometimes the other) that there is no such area of uncertainty, or that it is much smaller than it is. To *recognize* that there are limits of the certainty sought by verbalism and deduction, to seek to define those limits, is to open the door to that other and far more useful judicial procedure: *conscious* seeking, *within the limits laid down by precedent and statute*, for the wise decision. Decisions thus reached, *within those limits*, may fairly be hoped to be more certainly predictable than decisions are now— for now no man can tell when the court will, and when it will not, thus seek the wise decision, but hide the seeking under words. And not only more certain, but what is no whit less important: more just and wise (or more frequently just and wise).

Indeed, the most fascinating result of the realistic effort appears as one returns from trial court or the ways of laymen to the tradition-hallowed problem of appellate case-law. Criticized by those who refuse to disentangle Is and Ought because of their supposed deliberate neglect of the normative aspect of law, the realists prove the value, for the normative, of temporarily putting the normative aside. They return from their excursion into the purest description they can manage with a demonstration that the field of free play for Ought in appellate courts is vastly wider than traditional Ought-bound thinking ever had made clear. This, *within* the confines of precedent as we have it, *within* the limits and on the basis of our present order. Let me summarize the points of the brief:

(a) If deduction does not solve cases, but only shows the effect of a given premise; and if there is available a competing but equally authoritative premise that leads to a different conclusion—then there is a choice in the case; a choice to be justified; a choice which *can* be justified only as a question of policy—for the authoritative tradition speaks with a forked tongue.[70]

(b) If (i) the possible inductions from one case or a series of cases—even if these cases really had each a single fixed meaning—are nonetheless not single, but many; and if (ii) the standard authoritative techniques[71] of dealing with precedent range from limiting the case to its narrowest issue on facts and procedure, and even searching the record for a hidden distinguishing fact, all the way to giving it the widest meaning the rule expressed will allow, or even thrusting under it a principle which was not announced in the opinion at all—then the available leeway in *interpretation of precedent* is (relatively to what the older tradition has *consciously* conceived) nothing less than huge. And only policy considerations and the facing of policy considerations can justify "interpreting" (making, shaping, drawing conclusions from) the relevant body of precedent in one way or in another. And—the essence of all—*stare decisis* has in the past been, now is, and must continue to be, a norm of change, and a means of change, as well as a norm of staying put, and a means of staying put.[72] *The growth of the past has been achieved by "standing on" the decided cases*; rarely by overturning them. Let this be recognized, and precedent is clearly seen to be a way of change as well as a way of refusing to change. Let this be recognized, and that peculiar one of the ways of working with precedent which consists in blinding the eyes to policy loses the fictitious sanctity with which it is now enveloped *some of the time*: to wit, whenever judges for any reason do not wish to look at policy.

(c) If the classification of raw facts is largely an arbitrary process, raw facts having in most doubtful cases the possibility of ready classification along a number of lines, "certainty," even under pure deductive thinking, has not the meaning that people who have wanted certainty in law are looking for. The quest of this unreal certainty, this certainty unattained in result, is the major reason for the self-denying ordinance of judges: their refusal to look beyond words to things. Let them once see that the "certainty" thus achieved is *un*certainty for the non-law-tutored layman in his living and dealing, and the way is open to reach for *layman's* certainty-through-law, by seeking for the fair or wise outcome, so far as precedent and statute make such outcome *possible*. To see the problem thus is also to open the way to conscious discrimination—*e.g.*, between current commercial dealings and conveyancing—in which latter the *lawyer's* peculiar reliance on formulae may be assumed as of course; whereas in the former cause must be shown for making such an assumption.

Thus, as various of the self-designated realistic spokesmen have been shouting: the temporary divorce of Is and Ought brings to the reunion a sharper eye, a fuller equipment, a sounder judgment—even a wider opportunity as to that case-law

[70] Cf. Radin, *The Theory of Judicial Decision: or How Judges Think*; Cook, *The Utility of Jurisprudence in the Solution of Legal Problems*; LLEWELLYN, THE BRAMBLE BUSH CC. IV, V; FRANK, LAW AND THE MODERN MIND; GREEN, JUDGE AND JURY; CORBIN, *Contracts for the Benefit of Third Persons*; Powell, *The Logic and Rhetoric of Constitutional Law*, all *infra* Appendix I. See also Radin, *supra* note 36; © Dickinson, *The Law Behind Law* (1929) 29 COL. L. REV. 113, 285, 296–99; Brown, *supra* note 36; Waite, *Caveat Emptor and the Judicial Process* (1925) 25 COL. L. REV. 129.

[71] I mean not those approved by the schoolmen, but those *used* by authoritative courts in dealing with "authority." On this as on other matters, the rules of the schoolmen are to be subjected to the check of fact—here, of what courts do. See LLEWELLYN, BRAMBLE BUSH (1930) c. IV. Contrast Goodhart, *Determining the Ratio Decidendi of a Case* (1930) 40 YALE L. J. 161.

[72] See especially Corbin, *The Law and the Judges; Contracts for the Benefit of Third Persons*; Llewellyn, *Legal Tradition and Social Science Method*; Tulin, all *infra* Appendix I.

which tradition has painted as peculiarly ridden by the past. That on the fact side, as to the peculiar questions, the temporary divorce yields no less gratifying results is demonstrated by the literature.

When the matter of *program in the normative aspect* is raised, the answer is: *there is none.* A likeness of method in approaching Ought-questions is apparent. If there be, beyond that, general lines of fairly wide agreement, they are hardly specific enough to mean anything on any given issue. Partly, this derives from differences in temperament and outlook. Partly, it derives from the total lack of organization or desire to schoolify among the men concerned. But partly, it is due to the range of work involved. Business lawyers have some pet Oughts, each in the material he has become familiar with; torts lawyers have the like in torts; public lawyers in public law. And so it goes. Partly also, the lack of programmatic agreement derives from the time and effort consumed in getting at facts, either the facts strictly legal or the "foreign" facts bearing on the law. Specialized interests must alone spell absence of group-program. Yet some general points of view may be hazarded.

(1) There is fairly general agreement on the importance of personnel, and of court organization, as essential to making laws have meaning. This both as to triers of fact and as to triers of law. There is some tendency, too, to urge specialization of tribunals.

(2) There is very general agreement on the need for courts to face squarely the policy questions in their cases, and use the full freedom precedent affords in working toward conclusions that seem indicated. There is fairly general agreement that effects of rules, so far as known, should be taken account of in making or remaking the rules. There is fairly general agreement that we need improved machinery for making the facts about such effects—or about needs and conditions to be affected by a decision—available to courts.

(3) There is strong tendency to think it wiser to narrow rather than to widen the categories in which concepts and rules *either about judging or for judging* are made.

(4) There is a strong tendency to approach most legal problems as problems in allocation of risks,[73] and so far as possible, as problems of their reduction, and so to insist on the effects of rules on parties who not only are not in court, but are not fairly represented by the parties who are in court. To approach not only tort but business matters, in a word, as matters of *general* policy.

And so I close as I began. What is there novel here?[74] In the ideas, nothing. In the sustained attempt to make one or another of them fruitful, much. In the narrowness of fact-category together with the wide range of fact-inquiry, much. In the technique availed of, much—for lawyers. But let this be noted—for the summary

[73] E.g., Patterson, *The Apportionment of Business Risks Through Legal Devices*; Douglas, *Vicarious Liability and Administration of Risk*, both *infra* Appendix I. See also Isaacs, *supra* note 61. Contrast Breckenridge and Llewellyn (1922) 31 Yale L. J. 522 with Breckenridge, *The Negotiability of Postdated Checks* (1929) 38 Yale L. J. 1063, and Llewellyn, Cases and Materials on the Law of Sales (1930). Or Corbin's earlier work with his article *supra* note 57. Compare the work of Green, Y. B. Smith, Turner, Weiner; Brannan, Negotiable Instruments Law (Chafee's ed. 1926) 572; Clark's conception of procedural handicapping. Code Pleading (1928); Holmes, as usual, set the mark. The Common Law (1881) cc. VIII, IX.

[74] Reports Felix Cohen: "Pound can be cited for all the planks for the realistic platform—and against many of them." My unchecked memory would endorse this (save for the rigorous temporary severance of Is and Ought?). But it is also probably true (perhaps in lesser degree because they have written less) of most realists who did not happen to be laid and hatched by other realists. Our good fortune is that the world we live in is neither static, nor, as to those who people it, too consistent.

above runs so largely to the purely descriptive side: When writers of realistic inclination are writing in general, they are bound to stress the need of more accurate description, of Is and not of Ought. There lies the *common* ground of their thinking; there lies the area of new and puzzling development. There lies the point of discrimination which they must drive home. To get perspective on their stand about ethically normative matters one must pick up the work of each man in his special field of work. There one will find no lack of interest or effort toward improvement in the law. As to whether change is called for, on any *given* point of our law, and if so, how much change, and in what direction, there is no agreement. Why should there be? A *group* philosophy or program, a *group* credo of social welfare, these realists have not. They are not a group.

KARL N. LLEWELLYN
Columbia Law School

Felix Cohen

Felix Cohen

FELIX COHEN was born in 1907 in New York City. His father, Morris Cohen, a professor at City College, was a major legal theorist in his own right, the author of "Property and Sovereignty," "The Basis of Contract," and several other articles that helped lay the groundwork for Legal Realism. Until the age of eight, Felix was educated at home by his mother, Mary Ryshpan Cohen. After four years of elementary school and one year of high school, he enrolled in a seven-year joint program offered by City College and the Townsend Harris High School, earning his bachelor's degree magna cum laude just before he turned nineteen. After graduation, he was initially inclined to attend law school, but was persuaded by his father to study philosophy first. For that purpose, he went to Harvard, earning his MA in 1927 and completing the residency requirement for his PhD in 1928. While there, he audited classes taught in the law school by Roscoe Pound and Felix Frankfurter and in the Anthropology Department by Alfred Tozzer. In the fall of 1928, he entered Columbia Law School. During the next three years, he managed somehow to pursue both degrees simultaneously, passing his Harvard PhD general exams during the midyear break in his first year of law school, finishing his dissertation and receiving his PhD in 1929, and completing his LLB in 1931.

The following year, Cohen worked as a research assistant for New York Supreme Court Justice Bernard Shinetag and married Lucy Kramer, a graduate student at Columbia, with whom he subsequently had two daughters. In 1932, he joined a private law firm in New York, where he worked on a wide variety of civil suits. In 1933, he was at the tail end of a series of appointments that would change his life: President Roosevelt named Harold Ickes Secretary of the Interior; Ickes asked Nathan Margold (at the time, the staff attorney of the NAACP) to be his Solicitor; and Margold asked Cohen to come to work with him for a year, drafting legislation strengthening the rights of Native Americans and giving the tribes more control over their own affairs. Cohen accepted, and ended up staying at the Interior Department (except for a short, related stint at the Department of Justice) for the next fourteen years. While there, Cohen was in charge of or involved in a wide variety of projects, but the largest and most important group involved Native Americans. He was the principal author of the Indian Reorganization Act of 1934—a major piece of legislation that, among other things, ended the "allotment" system (which had been designed to corrode tribal ownership of land by assigning plots to individual tribe members) and encouraged the formation of tribal governments. He subsequently drafted a model constitution for use by the tribes when setting up such governments. He and his staff prepared a forty-six-volume compilation of statutes and other legal materials pertaining to Native Americans, and he fought successfully to ensure that it would function as a "safeguard" of "the rights and property of our nation's wards," rather than as a litigation manual for Justice Department lawyers. Relying on those materials, he wrote a *Handbook of Federal Indian Law*, which soon became the standard work in the field. Finally, he successfully defended the rights of Native Americans in several lawsuits.

In 1946, Ickes retired from the Interior Department. Two years later, Cohen, believing that the department had turned in a more conservative direction, resigned his position. During the next five years—until his premature death from cancer in 1953—he worked simultaneously at several jobs. He practiced law, eventually joining the firm of Reigelman, Strasser, Schwartz & Spiegelberg as head of its Washington, D.C., office. He continued his work on behalf of Native Americans, serving as general counsel to several tribes. Finally, he regularly taught a course on legislative drafting at Yale Law School and courses on philosophy at City College.

Cohen began publishing serious legal scholarship at a remarkably early age— and continued to do so throughout his career, despite his rather extraordinary array of practical responsibilities. His first major article, "The Ethical Basis of Legal Criticism," was published in the *Yale Law Journal* in 1932, when he was twenty-four years old. His Harvard doctoral dissertation, originally submitted when he was twenty-two, was published four years later under the title, *Ethical Systems and Legal Ideals*. "Transcendental Nonsense and the Functional Approach" was published in 1935, when he was twenty-eight. Amazingly, he kept up the pace for the rest of his life, ultimately leaving us a legacy of two books plus some fifty articles and twenty-five book reviews.

Of his publications, "Transcendental Nonsense," though written when he was still young, is the most penetrating and deservedly famous. It's not a breakthrough article. Most of the fields it tills had already been cleared by Holmes, Hohfeld, Dewey, Hale, and Llewellyn. But the manner in which Cohen handles the issues is more learned and, strikingly, more mature than the treatments of his predecessors.

The critique of formalism with which he begins the essay is a good example. Many writers before him had criticized courts for purporting to rely when making their decisions upon abstract principles ungrounded in either social facts or ethical values. But Cohen's image of a "heaven of legal concepts," in which one could split hairs and squeeze interpretations out of legal texts to one's heart's content, free of the distractions of "terrestrial human affairs," gives that familiar theme liveliness and bite. Also, more than his forbears, Cohen is aware of the degree to which the anti-formalist campaign in legal theory mimics analogous campaigns in other disciplines. Many of those parallels he makes explicit in the second part of the article, when he reviews and draws inspiration from recent developments in mathematics, philosophy, and physics. Others remain implicit, but help give his argument punch. For example, his mocking descriptions of "rules of law" as "theorems in an independent system" and of contemporary jurisprudence as "an autonomous system of legal concepts, rules, and arguments" tacitly invokes both the claim of non-Euclidean geometers that all geometries, far from being descriptions of the real world, are purely formal systems, and Einstein's general theory of relativity, which showed that Euclid's particular system of postulates and theorems did not in fact accurately describe physical reality.

In most respects, Cohen's particular variant of the anti-formalist argument buttressed those of his predecessors. For instance, he lent support to Karl Llewellyn's contention that formalist reasoning decreased rather than increased the certainty and predictability of judicial decision making by demonstrating that the effort by the New York Court of Appeals to decide whether a corporation chartered in state A can be sued in state B by asking whether the corporation is "in" state B led it to reach inconsistent results in very similar cases. In other respects, however, Cohen broke with the pack. For instance, nothing in the article suggests, as did Llewellyn, that judges are generally wiser than scholars, more sensitive to the policy questions presented by particular sets of facts. On the contrary, judges—even revered ones, like Benjamin Cardozo—are depicted as at least as likely to rely upon "transcendental nonsense" as their academic counterparts.

The most serious of the traps into which judges are prone to fall is circular thinking. Again, Cohen's remarks on this score are not wholly original. As early as 1918, in the famous case of *International News Service v. Associated Press*, Justices Holmes and Brandeis had chastised their formalist colleague, Justice Pitney, for contending that the "gist" of a news story (which INS had taken from AP without permission) should be recognized as a form of "property" (or at least "quasi-property") because it had "market value." Something has market value, Holmes and Brandeis pointed out, only if (among other things) it is protected by law against unauthorized appropriation. In other words, news has market value only if the legal system recognizes it as property. One therefore cannot decide *if* it constitutes property by asking if it has value.

Cohen points out that judges—and the United States Supreme Court in particular—had certainly not yet learned the lesson. Circular reasoning, of the sort exemplified by Pitney's ruling in *INS*, was everywhere. For instance, courts were permitting the developers of trademarks to prevent competitors from making use of those marks even when there was no risk that consumers would be confused thereby, ostensibly on the ground that the marks constituted "thing[s] of value." Cohen observes:

> The vicious circle inherent in this line of reasoning is plain. It purports to base legal protection upon economic value, when, as a matter of actual fact, the economic value of a sales device depends upon the extent to which it will be legally protected.

Equally indefensible, Cohen argued, was the line of Supreme Court decisions holding that a corporation is constitutionally entitled to a fair return on the "actual value" of its property—failing to recognize that the "actual value" of the assets of a business consists of "the capitalization at current market rates of the allowed and expected profit" of the enterprise. In other words, the size of the income stream to which a corporation has a constitutional right cannot be determined on the basis of the "actual value" of the business, because the "actual value" of the business depends directly upon the magnitude of the income stream that the government permits the company to earn.

The capacity to recognize and avoid such traps is one of the standard skills now taught in first-year law school classes. It remains an important technique, because courts, despite the force and fame of Cohen's argument on this topic, still with distressing frequency fall into analogous holes.

Another area in which Cohen built upon but also transcended the work of his forbears concerned the determinants of judicial decision making. Holmes, Llewellyn, and indeed most of the scholars associated with Legal Realism had already written a good deal on that subject. Many of their essays (for example, those by Jerome Frank and Joseph Hutcheson) had emphasized idiosyncratic factors: a judge's individual history, "hunches," and so forth—providing fodder for a common caricature of Legal Realism as the view that a judge's decision in a given case depends entirely on what he had for breakfast. Cohen's musings on the same theme, though modestly framed as a sketch of topics that needed further empirical research, were more subtle and balanced. Judges commonly are influenced, he suggested, by a wide variety of factors, including: "the attitudes of their own income class on social questions"; "their past legal experience as counsel for special interests"; the "skill and eloquence" of the lawyers who appear before them; "aesthetic ideals" (lawyers' and scholars' attitudes concerning what constitutes an elegant or "harmonious" opinion—a topic he explores in more detail in other articles); and finally, precedent. The last point bears emphasis. Much more than his jurisprudential compatriots, Cohen believed it was possible for a court to "follow" the decisions reached by other courts in similar cases in the past. Not that it was always a good idea. His discussion of the Supreme Court's rulings in substantive due-process cases, which he compares to the repetitive statements of the Bellman in Lewis Carroll's "The Hunting of the Snark," makes clear he thought it often was not. But that it was possible—and, indeed, often done.

A final zone in which Cohen dredged deeper channels cut previously by other scholars concerns the social roles of legal opinions and legal discourse in general. Like Llewellyn, Cohen thought that the terms in which courts explained and justified their decisions bore little relation to the forces (such as those reviewed above) that actually produced those decisions. This should not be surprising, he suggested. Drawing explicitly upon work in anthropology and linguistics, he argued that language has many functions other than communicating ideas. "Certain words and phrases are useful for the purpose of releasing pent-up emotions, or putting babies to sleep, or inducing certain emotions and attitudes in a political or judicial audience." Elsewhere in the article he is more specific. Sometimes judges and legal scholars deliberately use certain arguments to "gag . . . criticism." For example, Blackstone's notoriously ambiguous definition of law as "a rule of civil conduct, prescribed by the supreme power in a State, commanding what is right, and prohibiting what is wrong," "is very useful to legal apologists for the existing order of society"—enabling them to dismiss any given objection, either on the ground that it is "unjust, unreasonable, monstrous and, therefore, not 'sound law,'" or on the ground that it is irrelevant because "law is the command of the sovereign and not a matter of moral theory." But deliberate legitimation or obfuscation of this sort sometimes gives rise to self-delusion, as for example when judges rely so much on "vivid fictions and metaphors" that they lose sight of the fact that they are merely "poetical or mnemonic devices for formulating decisions reached on other grounds" and as a consequence "forget the social forces which mold the law and the social ideals by which the law is to be judged." Such states of affairs, though understandable, were undesirable. Judges, Cohen argued, should be forced or persuaded to state honestly the true grounds of their rulings. Why? Two kinds of benefits are mentioned in the article. First, candor would restore "lay understanding and criticism of what the courts do in fact"—in other words, enable and encourage the public at large to denounce unjust or unwise decisions. Second, the "class prejudices and uncritical moral assumptions" that truly underlie many decisions "could not survive the sunlight of free ethical controversy"; once they were exposed, judges would be "shame[d]" into repudiating them.

The issue with respect to which Cohen distances himself most from his Realist allies concerns the relationship between descriptive and normative analysis of legal systems. As we've seen, Llewellyn, building on Holmes, advocated a "temporary divorce of Is and Ought," in other words, postponing consideration of how the law should be reformed until after one had a clear idea of how it currently worked. Cohen, more deeply steeped in the pertinent philosophic literature, thought Llewellyn's strategy was naive.

> The positive task of descriptive legal science cannot . . . be entirely separated from the task of legal criticism. The collection of social facts without a selective criterion of human values produces [a] horrid wilderness of useless statistics. The relation between positive legal science and legal criticism is not a relation of temporal priority, but of mutual dependence. Legal criticism is empty without objective description of the causes and consequences of legal decisions. Legal description is blind without the guiding light of a theory of values.

This stance, of course, made all the more imperative the development of "a critical theory of social values" that could be used, among other things, to guide empirical work. Cohen did not attempt that Herculean task in "Transcendental Nonsense," but in *Ethical Systems and Legal Ideals*, he made a beginning. The bulk of the book consists of an exploration of rival "theories of ethics," which he ultimately concludes are reducible to two:

> On the one hand, there is the theory that intrinsic goodness is relative, definable, and identical with a relation to an approving individual. On the other hand, there is the theory that intrinsic goodness is absolute, indefinable, and equivalent in application to positive pleasantness.

Beset with "doubts," unable to identify any "rational basis of choice" among these alternatives, he nevertheless "fl[ies] both on the pinions of faith" and commits himself to the second of the two routes—a variant of Benthamite utilitarianism. That decision, in turn, made clear two "political task[s]": "in thought, the translation of the books of the law into the universal language of human joys and sufferings,—in practice, the struggle for the attainment of the ideals thus discovered."

To be sure, these reflections fall somewhat short of a comprehensive and compelling moral philosophy. But recall that these lines were penned when Cohen was in his mid-twenties. They proved sufficient to guide him in an admirable life of public service. Had he lived longer, he might have been able to build upon them a system of values that would have helped fill the most conspicuous gap in modern legal theory.

WILLIAM FISHER

BIBLIOGRAPHY

Primary Sources

In June 1953, a few months before his death, Cohen put together a three-volume collection of what he considered his major published and unpublished papers and gave it to his elder daughter as a graduation present. His selection and organization is probably the best of possible guides to his oeuvre:

I. LAW AND ETHICS

"Casuistry," *Encyclopedia of the Social Sciences* 3 (1930): 265.
"The Ethical Basis of Legal Criticism," *Yale Law Journal* 41 (1931): 201.
"A Factual Study of Rule 113," *Columbia Law Review* 32 (1932): 830.
"The Subject Matter of Ethical Science," *International Journal of Ethics* 4 (July 1932): 397.

Ethical Systems and Legal Ideals: An Essay on the Foundation of Legal Criticism
(New York: Harcourt, Brace, 1933).

"Modern Ethics and the Law," *Brooklyn Law Review* 4 (1934): 33.

"Transcendental Nonsense and the Functional Approach," *Columbia Law Review* 35 (1935): 809.

"The Problems of a Functional Jurisprudence," *Modern Law Review* 1 (1937): 5.

"What City College Will Contribute to the Development of the Law," *Barrister, City College of New York* 2 (1938): 4.

Combating Totalitarian Propaganda: A Legal Appraisal (Felix S. Cohen, ed.) (Washington, D.C.: Institute of Living Law, 1944).

"Holmes-Cohen Correspondence" (Felix S. Cohen, ed.) *Journal of the History of Ideas* 9 (1) (January 1948): 3.

"Field Theory and Judicial Logic," *Yale Law Journal* 59 (1950): 238.

"Judicial Ethics," *Ohio State Law Journal* 12 (1951): 3.

Readings in Jurisprudence and Legal Philosophy (In collaboration with Morris Raphael Cohen) (New York: Prentice-Hall, 1951).

"Human Rights: An Appeal to Philosophers," *The Review of Metaphysics* 4 (June 1953): 617.

"The Reconstruction of Hidden Value Judgments: Word Choices as Value Indicators," in *Symbols and Values* (New York: Harper and Brothers, 1954).

II. The Indian's Quest for Justice

"The Posers of an Indian Tribe" (mimeographed). (Washington, D.C.: U.S. Department of the Interior, 1934).

"Anthropology and the Problems of Indian Administration," *Southwestern Social Science Quarterly* 18(2) (September 1937): 171.

"How Long Will Indian Constitution Last?" *Indians at Work* 10 (June 1939): 40.

"Indian Rights and Federal Courts," *Minnesota Law Review* 24 (1940): 145.

"The Legal Status of the Indian in the United States" (mimeographed). (Washington, D.C.: U.S. Department of the Interior, 1940).

Handbook of Federal Indian Law (Washington, D.C.: U.S. Government Printing Office, 1941) (Supp. 1942; rev. 4th printing, 1945).

"The Spanish Origin of Indian Rights in the Law of the United States," *Georgetown Law Journal* 31 (1942): 1.

"Indians are Citizens," *The American Indian* 4 (Summer 1944): 12.

"Indian Claims," *The American Indian* 3 (Spring 1945): 3.

"How We Bought the United States," *Collier's* (January 19, 1946): 22.

"Original Indian Title," *Minnesota Law Review* 32 (1947): 28.

"Breaking Faith with our First Americans," *Indian Truth* 2 (March 1948): 1.

"Alaska's Nuremberg Laws," *Commentary* 6 (August 1948): 136.

"Indian Self-Government," *The American Indian* 2 (1949): 3.

"Our Country's Shame," *The Progressive* (May 1949): 9.

"Colonialism: U.S. Style," *The Progressive* (February 1951): 16.

"Americanizing the White Man," *The American Scholar* 2 (Spring 1952): 177.

"First Americans First," *The New Leader* (January 26, 1953): 15.

"The Erosion of Indian Rights, 1950–1953: A Case Study in Bureaucracy," *Yale Law Journal* 62 (1953): 348.

"Indian Wardship: The Twilight of a Myth," *The American Indian* 4 (Summer 1953): 8.

"What Is a Question?" *The Monist* (July 1929).

"Politics and Economics," in *Socialist Planning and a Socialist Program* (New York: Falcon Press, 1932), 69.

"Justice Benjamin Nathan Cardozo," *B'nai B'rith Magazine* (1933).

"The Blessing of Unemployment," *The American Scholar* 2 (1933): 203.

"The Socialization of Morality," in *American Philosophy Today and Tomorrow* (1935), 83.

"Socialism and the Myth of Legality," *American Socialist Quarterly* 3 (November 1935): 3.

"The Relativity of Philosophical Systems and the Method of Systematic Relativism," *The Journal of Philosophy* 36 (February 1939): 57.

"The Social and Economic Consequences of Exclusionary Immigration Laws," *National Lawyers Guild Quarterly* (October 1939).

"Exclusionary Immigration Laws" (condensed from articles listed above), *Contemporary Jewish Record* (March–April 1940).

"Colonialism: A Realistic Approach," *Ethics* 55 (1945): 167.

"The Myth of the Immigration Scare," *This Month* (January 1946).

"The People vs. Discrimination," *Commentary* 5 (March 1946): 17.

"The Role of Science in Government," *Social Science* 22 (Summer 1947): 195.

"Science and Politics in Plans for Puerto Rico," *Journal of Social Issues* (Fall 1947).

"The Civil Rights Report," *5 ETC: A Review of General Semantics* 3 (Spring 1948): 161.

"Americanizing Our Immigration Laws" (Prepared for American Jewish Committee Testimony before the Senate Sub-Committee on Immigration, September 1948. In collaboration.) (March 1949).

"Puerto Rico's Human Resources," *Caribbean Economic Review* (1950).

"Harold L. Ickes—Champion of the Dispossessed," *Freeland* (June 1952).

"A Student's Homage: Jerome Michael," *Columbia Law Review* 53 (1953): 312.

"The Vocabulary of Prejudice," *Fellowship Magazine* (November 1953).

Many of these papers were reprinted posthumously in *The Legal Conscience: Selected Papers of Felix S. Cohen* (New Haven: Yale University Press, 1960).

Secondary Sources

Biographies of Cohen are scant. The best, on which we have relied heavily here, is the brief sketch of his life published anonymously soon after his death in the *Rutgers Law Review* (Volume 9 [1954], 345–53) and subsequently included in the 1982 edition of the *Handbook of Federal Indian Law*. An even shorter treatment, by Thomas Clarkin, can be found in American National Biographies (3 July 1907–19 Oct. 1953), *Civil Rights Activists, Law Reporters, Lawyers*.

Analyses of Cohen's work are also sparse. For commentary on his contributions, both scholarly and practical, to Indian law, see: Jill E. Martin, "The Miner's Canary: Felix S. Cohen's Philosophy of Indian Rights," *American Indian Law Review* 23 (1998): 165; idem, "A Year and Spring of My Existence: Felix S. Cohen and the Handbook of Federal Indian Law," *Western Legal History* 8 (1995): 1; and Stephen M. Feldman, "Felix S. Cohen and His Jurisprudence: Reflections on Federal Indian Law," *Buffalo Law Review* 35 (1986): 479. Studies of his writings on legal theory include: Joel R. Cornwell, "From Hedonism to

Human Rights: Felix Cohen's Alternative to Nihilism," *Temple Law Review* 68 (1995): 197; Walter Probert, "The Lawyer as Moral Advisor: The Cohen Strategy," *Journal of the Legal Profession* 15 (1990): 53; and Martin P. Golding, "Realism and Functionalism in the Legal Thought of Felix S. Cohen," *Cornell Law Review* 66 (1981): 1032. An especially insightful treatment of Cohen's jurisprudence, along with that of other Legal Realists, can be found in chapter 3 of Edward A. Purcell, Jr., *The Crisis of Democratic Theory: Scientific Naturalism and the Problem of Value* (Lexington: University Press of Kentucky, 1973).

"Transcendental Nonsense and the Functional Approach"

35 Columbia Law Review 809 (1935)

I. THE HEAVEN OF LEGAL CONCEPTS

Some fifty years ago a great German jurist had a curious dream. He dreamed that he died and was taken to a special heaven reserved for the theoreticians of the law. In this heaven one met, face to face, the many concepts of jurisprudence in their absolute purity, freed from all entangling alliances with human life. Here were the disembodied spirits of good faith and bad faith, property, possession, *laches*, and rights *in rem*. Here were all the logical instruments needed to manipulate and transform these legal concepts and thus to create and to solve the most beautiful of legal problems. Here one found a dialectic-hydraulic-interpretation press, which could press an indefinite number of meanings out of any text or statute, an apparatus for constructing fictions, and a hair-splitting machine that could divide a single hair into 999,999 equal parts and, when operated by the most expert jurists, could split each of these parts again into 999,999 equal parts. The boundless opportunities of this heaven of legal concepts were open to all properly qualified jurists, provided only they drank the Lethean draught which induced forgetfulness of terrestrial human affairs. But for the most accomplished jurists the Lethean draught was entirely superfluous. They had nothing to forget.[1]

Von Jhering's dream has been retold, in recent years, in the chapels of sociological, functional, institutional, scientific, experimental, realistic, and neo-realistic jurisprudence. The question is raised, "How much of contemporary legal thought moves in the pure ether of Von Jhering's heaven of legal concepts?" One turns to our leading legal textbooks and to the opinions of our courts for answer. May the Shade of Von Jhering be our guide.

1. Where Is a Corporation?

Let us begin our survey by observing an exceptionally able court as it deals with a typical problem in legal procedure. In the case of *Tauza v. Susquehanna Coal Company*,[2] a corporation which had been chartered by the State of Pennsylvania was sued in New York. Summons and complaint were served upon an officer of the corporation in New York in the manner prescribed by New York law. The corporation raised the objection that it *could not* be sued in New York. The New York Court of Appeals disagreed with this contention and held that the corporation could

---

[1] VON JHERING, IM JURISTISCHEN BEGRIFFSHIMMEL, IN SCHERZ UND ERNST IN DER JURISPRUDENZ (11th ed. 1912) 245.
[2] 220 N. Y. 259, 115 N. E. 915 (1917).

be sued in that State. What is of interest for our purposes is not the particular decision of the court but the mode of reasoning by which this decision was reached.

The problem which the Court of Appeals faced was a thoroughly practical one. If a competent legislature had considered the problem of when a corporation incorporated in another State should be subject to suit, it would probably have made some factual inquiry into the practice of modern corporations in choosing their sovereigns[3] and into the actual significance of the relationship between a corporation and the state of its incorporation. It might have considered the difficulties that injured plaintiffs may encounter if they have to bring suit against corporate defendants in the state of incorporation. It might have balanced, against such difficulties, the possible hardship to corporations of having to defend actions in many states, considering the legal facilities available to corporate defendants. On the basis of *facts* revealed by such an inquiry, and on the basis of certain political or ethical *value judgments* as to the propriety of putting financial burdens upon corporations, a competent legislature would have attempted to formulate some rule as to when a foreign corporation should be subject to suit.

The Court of Appeals reached its decision without avowedly considering any of these matters. It does not appear that scientific evidence on any of these issues was offered to the court. Instead of addressing itself to such economic, sociological, political, or ethical questions as a competent legislature might have faced, the court addressed itself to the question, "Where is a corporation?" Was this corporation *really* in Pennsylvania or in New York, or could it be in two places at once?

Clearly the question of *where a corporation is*, when it incorporates in one state and has agents transacting corporate business in another state, is not a question that can be answered by empirical observation. Nor is it a question that demands for its solution any analysis of political considerations or social ideals. It is, in fact, a question identical in metaphysical status with the question which scholastic theologians are supposed to have argued at great length, "How many angels can stand on the point of a needle?" Now it is extremely doubtful whether any of the scholastics ever actually discussed this question.[4] Yet the question has become, for us, a symbol of an age in which thought without roots in reality was an object of high esteem.

Will future historians deal more charitably with such legal questions as "Where is a corporation?" Nobody has ever seen a corporation. What right have we to believe in corporations if we don't believe in angels? To be sure, some of us have seen corporate funds, corporate transactions, etc. (just as some of us have seen angelic deeds, angelic countenances, etc.). But this does not give us the right to hypostatize, to "thingify," the corporation, and to assume that it travels about from State to State as mortal men travel. Surely we are qualifying as inmates of Von Jhering's heaven of legal concepts when we approach a legal problem in these essentially supernatural terms.

Yet it is exactly in these terms of transcendental nonsense that the Court of Appeals approached the question of whether the Susquehanna Coal Company could be sued in New York State. "The essential thing," said Judge Cardozo,

---

[3] See Berle, *Investors and the Revised Delaware Corporation Act* (1929) 29 COLUMBIA LAW REV. 563; RIPLEY, MAIN STREET AND WALL STREET (1927).

[4] Several students of scholastic philosophy inform me that they have never found any evidence of such discussion more reliable than the hearsay testimony of Rabelais.

writing for a unanimous court, "is that the corporation shall have come into the State."[5] Why this journey is *essential*, or how it is *possible*, we are not informed. The opinion notes that the corporation has an office in the State, with eight sales-men and eleven desks, and concludes that the corporation is really "in" New York State. From this inference it easily follows that since a person who is in New York can be sued here, and since a corporation is a person, the Susquehanna Coal Company is subject to suit in a New York court.

The same manner of reasoning can be used by the same court to show that the Dodge Bros. Motor Corporation "cannot" be sued in New York because the corporation (as distinguished from its corps of New York employees and dealers) is not "in" New York.[6]

Strange as this manner of argument will seem to laymen, lawyers trained by long practice in believing what is impossible,[7] will accept this reasoning as rele-vant, material, and competent. Indeed, even the great protagonist of sociological jurisprudence, Mr. Justice Brandeis, has invoked this supernatural approach to the problem of actions against foreign corporations, without betraying any doubt as to the factual reference of the question, "Where is a corporation?" Thus, in the leading case of *Bank of America v. Whitney Central National Bank*,[8] the United States Supreme Court faced the question of whether a banking corporation incor-porated in Louisiana could be sued in New York, where it carried on numerous financial transactions and where its president had been served, but where it did not own any desks. The Supreme Court held that although the defendant "had what would popularly be called a large New York business," the action could not be maintained, and offered, per Brandeis, J., the following justification of this curious conclusion:[9]

> "The jurisdiction taken of foreign corporations, in the absence of statutory require-ment or express consent, does not rest upon a fiction of constructive presence, like *qui facit per alium facit per se*. It flows from the fact that the corporation itself does business in the State or district in such a manner and to such an extent that its actual presence there is established. That the defendant was not in New York, and, hence, was not found within the district, is clear."

Of course, it would be captious to criticize courts for delivering their opinions in the language of transcendental nonsense. Logicians sometimes talk as if the only function of language were to convey ideas. But anthropologists know better and assure us that "language is primarily a pre-rational function."[10] Certain words and phrases are useful for the purpose of releasing pent-up emotions, or putting babies to sleep, or inducing certain emotions and attitudes in a political or a judicial audience. The law is not a science but a practical activity, and myths may impress the imagination and memory where more exact discourse would leave minds cold.

---

[5] See 220 N. Y. at 268, 115 N. E. at 918.

[6] Holzer v. Dodge Bros. Motor Corp., 233 N. Y. 216, 135 N. E. 268 (1922).

[7] "I can't believe *that*!" said Alice.

"Can't you?" the Queen said, in a pitying tone. "Try again: draw a long breath, and shut your eyes."

Alice laughed. "There's no use trying," she said; "one can't believe impossible things."

"I dare say you haven't had much practice," said the Queen. "When I was your age I always did it for half an hour a day. Why, sometimes I've believed as many as six impossible things before breakfast." (Lewis Carroll, Through the Looking Glass, c. 5.)

[8] 261 U.S. 171 (1923).

[9] *Id.*, at 173.

[10] SAPIR, LANGUAGE (1921) 14.

Valuable as is the language of transcendental nonsense for many practical legal purposes, it is entirely useless when we come to study, describe, predict, and criticize legal phenomena. And although judges and lawyers need not be legal scientists, it is of some practical importance that they should recognize that the traditional language of argument and opinion neither explains nor justifies court decisions. When the vivid fictions and metaphors of traditional jurisprudence are thought of as reasons for decisions, rather than poetical or mnemonic devices for formulating decisions reached on other grounds, then the author, as well as the reader, of the opinion or argument, is apt to forget the social forces which mold the law and the social ideals by which the law is to be judged. Thus it is that the most intelligent judges in America can deal with a concrete practical problem of procedural law and corporate responsibility without any appreciation of the economic, social, and ethical issues which it involves.

2. When Is a Corporation?

The field of corporation law offers many illuminating examples of the traditional supernatural approach to practical legal problems. In the famous *Coronado* case,[11] the question was presented to the United States Supreme Court, whether employers whose business had been injured in the course of a strike could recover a judgment against a labor union which had "encouraged" the strike, or whether suit could be brought only against particular individuals charged with committing or inducing the injury. So far as appears from the printed record, counsel for the union defendants did not attempt to show that labor unions would be seriously handicapped by the imposition of financial responsibility for damage done in strikes, that it would be impossible for labor unions to control *agents provocateurs*, and that labor unions served a very important function in modern industrial society which would be seriously endangered by the type of liability in question. Instead of offering any such argument to support the claim of the labor union to legal immunity for the torts of its members, counsel for the union advanced the metaphysical argument that a labor union, being an unincorporated association, is not a person and, therefore, cannot be subject to tort liability. This is a very ancient and respectable argument in procedural law. Pope Innocent IV used it in the middle of the Thirteenth Century to prove that the treasuries of religious bodies could not be subject to tort liability.[12] Unfortunately, the argument that a labor union is not a person is one of those arguments that remain true only so long as they are believed.[13] When the court rejected the argument and held the union liable, the union became a person—to the extent of being suable as a legal entity—and the argument ceased to be true.

The Supreme Court argued, "A labor union can be sued because it is, in essential aspects, a person, a quasi-corporation." The realist will say, "A labor union is a person or quasi-corporation because it can be sued; to call something a person in law, is merely to state, in metaphorical language, that it can be sued."

Felix Cohen

[11] United Mine Workers of America v. Coronado Coal Co., 259 U. S. 344 (1922). The British prototype of this case, Taff-Vale Ry. Co. v. Amalg. Soc. of Railway Servants, [1901] A. C. 426, reached a similar decision, professedly upon similar transcendental grounds, but this was soon upset by special legislation. See WEBB, HISTORY OF TRADE UNIONISM (Rev. ed. 1920) 600 ff.

[12] *Cf.* DEWEY, "*Corporate Personality*" in PHILOSOPHY AND CIVILIZATION (1931), 154; and see 3 GIERKE, DAS DEUTSCHE GENOSSENSCHAFTRECHT 279–285; *cf.* 3 HOLDSWORTH, HISTORY OF ENGLISH LAW (3d ed. 1923) 470–474.

[13] Compare the case of Wild Modesty, a flower found on certain islands of the South Seas, which is really white but turns red when any one looks at it (reported in Traprock's "The Cruise of the Kawa" [1921] 10).

There is a significant difference between these two ways of describing the situation. If we say that a court acts in a certain way "because a labor union is a person," we *appear to justify the court's action*, and to justify that action, moreover, in transcendental terms, by asserting something that sounds like a proposition but which *can not be confirmed or refuted by positive evidence or by ethical argument*. If, on the other hand, we say that a labor union is a person "because the courts allow it to be sued," we recognize that the action of the courts has not been justified at all, and that the question of whether the action of the courts is justifiable calls for an answer in non-legal terms. To justify or criticize legal rules in purely legal terms is always to argue in a vicious circle.[14]

3. What's in a Trade Name?

The divorce of legal reasoning from questions of social fact and ethical value is not a product of crusty legal fictions inherited from darker ages. Even in the most modern realms of legal development one finds the thought of courts and of legal scholars trapezing around in cycles and epicycles without coming to rest on the floor of verifiable fact. Modern developments in the law of unfair competition offer many examples of such circular reasoning.

There was once a theory that the law of trade marks and tradenames was an attempt to protect the consumer against the "passing off" of inferior goods under misleading labels.[15] Increasingly the courts have departed from any such theory and have come to view this branch of law as a protection of property rights in divers economically valuable sale devices.[16] In practice, injunctive relief is being extended today to realms where no actual danger of confusion to the consumer is present, and this extension has been vigorously supported and encouraged by leading writers in the field.[17] Conceivably this extension might be justified by a demonstration that privately controlled sales devices serve as a psychologic base for the power of business monopolies, and that such monopolies are socially valuable in modern civilization. But no such line of argument has ever been put forward by courts or scholars advocating increased legal protection of trade names and similar devices. For if they advanced any such argument, it might seem that they were taking sides upon controversial issues of politics and economics. Courts and scholars, therefore, have taken refuge in a vicious circle to which no obviously extra-legal facts can gain admittance. The current legal argument runs: One who by the ingenuity of his advertising or the quality of his product has induced consumer responsiveness to a particular name, symbol, form of packaging, etc., has thereby created a thing of value; a thing of value is property; the creator of property is entitled to protection against third parties who seek to deprive him of his property.[18] This argument

---

[14] *Cf.* ROGUIN, LA RÈGLE DU DROIT (1889): "Nothing is more fallacious than to believe that one may give an account of the law by means of the law itself."

[15] See NIMS, UNFAIR COMPETITION AND TRADE-MARKS (3d ed. 1929) § 8, and cases cited.

[16] See American Washboard Co. v. Saginaw Mfg. Co., 103 Fed. 281, 285 (C. C. A. 6th, 1900).

[17] NIMS, *op. cit. supra* note 15, §9a; Handler and Pickett, *Trade-Marks and Trade Names—An Analysis and Synthesis* (1930) 30 COLUMBIA LAW REV. 168, 759; Schechter, *The Rational Basis of Trade-Mark Protection* (1927) 40 HARV. L. REV. 813.

[18] *Cf.* American Agricultural Chemical Co. v. Moore, 17 F.(2d) 196 (M. D. Ala. 1927) in which an interesting implication of the current theory is carried to its logical conclusion. A fertilizer company is granted an injunction against state officials seeking to prevent the use of a misleading trade name. The argument is: The plaintiff expected to do a large business under this trade name; such expectations are property, and must be protected against governmental interference.

may be embellished, in particular cases, with animadversions upon the selfish motives of the infringing defendant, a summary of the plaintiff's evidence (naturally uncontradicted) as to the amount of money he has spent in advertising, and insinuations (seldom factually supported) as to the inferiority of the infringing defendant's product.

The vicious circle inherent in this reasoning is plain. It purports to base legal protection upon economic value, when, as a matter of actual fact, the economic value of a sales device depends upon the extent to which it will be legally protected. If commercial exploitation of the word "Palmolive" is not restricted to a single firm, the word will be of no more economic value to any particular firm than a convenient size, shape, mode of packing, or manner of advertising, common in the trade. Not being of economic value to any particular firm, the word would be regarded by courts as "not property," and no injunction would be issued. In other words, the fact that courts did not protect the word would make the word valueless, and the fact that it was valueless would then be regarded as a reason for not protecting it. Ridiculous as this vicious circle seems, it is logically as conclusive or inconclusive as the opposite vicious circle, which accepts the fact that courts do protect private exploitation of a given word as a reason why private exploitation of that word should be protected.

The circularity of legal reasoning in the whole field of unfair competition is veiled by the "thingification" of *property*. Legal language portrays courts as examining commercial words and finding, somewhere inhering in them, *property rights*. It is by virtue of the property right which the plaintiff has acquired in the word that he is entitled to an injunction or an award of damages. According to the recognized authorities on the law of unfair competition, courts are not *creating* property, but are merely *recognizing* a pre-existent Something.

The theory that judicial decisions in the field of unfair competition law are merely recognitions of a supernatural Something that is immanent in certain trade names and symbols is, of course, one of the numerous progeny of the theory that judges have nothing to do with making the law, but merely recognize pre-existent truths not made by mortal men.[19] The effect of this theory, in the law of unfair competition as elsewhere, is to dull lay understanding and criticism of what courts do in fact.

What courts are actually doing, of course, in unfair competition cases, is to create and distribute a new source of economic wealth or power. Language is socially useful apart from law, as air is socially useful, but neither language nor air is a source of economic wealth unless some people are prevented from using these resources in ways that are permitted to other people. That is to say, property is a function of inequality.[20] If courts, for instance, should prevent a man from breathing any air which had been breathed by another (within, say, a reasonable statute of limitations), those individuals who breathed most vigorously and were quickest and wisest in selecting desirable locations in which to breathe (or made the most advantageous contracts with such individuals) would,

---

[19] See M. R. COHEN, *The Process of Judicial Legislation*, in LAW AND THE SOCIAL ORDER (1933) 112, also printed in (1914) 48 AM. L. REV. 161.

[20] See M. R. COHEN, *Property and Sovereignty*, in LAW AND THE SOCIAL ORDER (1933) 41; R. L. Hale, *Coercion and Distribution in a Supposedly Non-Coercive State* (1923) 38 Pol. Sci. Q. 470; R. L. Hale, *Rate Making and the Revision of the Property Concept* (1922) 22 COLUMBIA LAW REV. 209.

by virtue of their property right in certain volumes of air, come to exercise
and enjoy a peculiar economic advantage, which might, through various modes
of economic exchange, be turned into other forms of economic advantage,
e.g. the ownership of newspapers or fine clothing. So, if courts prevent a man
from exploiting certain forms of language which another has already begun to
exploit, the second user will be at the economic disadvantage of having
to pay the first user for the privilege of using similar language or else of having
to use less appealing language (generally) in presenting his commodities to
the public.

Courts, then, in establishing inequality in the commercial exploitation of language are creating economic wealth and property, creating property not, of
course, *ex nihilo*, but out of the materials of social fact, commercial custom, and
popular moral faiths or prejudices. It does not follow, except by the fallacy of
composition,[21] that in creating new private property courts are benefiting society.
Whether they are benefiting society depends upon a series of questions which
courts and scholars dealing with this field of law have not seriously considered.
Is there, for practical purposes, an unlimited supply of equally attractive words
under which any commodity can be sold, so that the second seller of the commodity is at no commercial disadvantage if he is forced to avoid the word or
words chosen by the first seller? If this is not the case, i.e. if peculiar emotional
contexts give one word more sales appeal than any other word suitable for the
same product, should the peculiar appeal of that word be granted by the state,
without payment, to the first occupier? Is this homestead law for the English language necessary in order to induce the first occupier to use the most attractive
word in selling his product? If, on the other hand, all words are originally alike
in commercial potentiality, but become differentiated by advertising and other
forms of commercial exploitation, is this type of business pressure a good thing,
and should it be encouraged by offering legal rewards for the private exploitation
of popular linguistic habits and prejudices? To what extent is differentiation of
commodities by trade names a help to the consumer in buying wisely? To what
extent is the exclusive power to exploit an attractive word, and to alter the quality of the things to which the word is attached, a means of deceiving consumers
into purchasing inferior goods?

Without a frank facing of these and similar questions,[22] legal reasoning on the
subject of trade names is simply economic prejudice masquerading in the cloak
of legal logic. The prejudice that identifies the interests of the plaintiff in unfair
competition cases with the interests of business[23] and identifies the interests of
business with the interests of society, will not be critically examined by courts and
legal scholars until it is recognized and formulated. It will not be recognized or
formulated so long as the hypostatization of "property rights" conceals the circularity of legal reasoning.

---

[21] "Composition is the passage from a statement about *each* or *every* member of a collection, taken severally, in one of the premises, to a statement about the collection as a whole in the conclusion." EATON, GENERAL LOGIC (1931) 340. An instance of the commission of this fallacy, in the present context, would be the statement that the court is adding to the wealth of society because it is adding to the wealth of the particular individuals whose con- trol over the sales device it protects.

[22] An example of realistic analysis of consequences in this field is Legis., The Vestal Bill for the Copyright Registration of Designs (1931) 31 COLUMBIA LAW REV. 477.

[23] See Schechter, *supra* note 17, at 831.

4. How High Is Fair Value?

Perhaps the most notorious example of circular reasoning in contemporary jurisprudence is that involved in judicial determination of the returns to which public utilities are entitled "under the Constitution."[24] What courts purport to do in rate cases is to ascertain the "value" of the utility's property and then to fix a price to the consumer which assures the utility a fair rate of return upon that value. This would be an understandable procedure if the courts meant by "value" either actual cost or replacement cost. For almost forty years, however, since the famous case of *Smyth v. Ames*,[25] the courts have insisted that it may be "unconstitutional" to allow a utility merely a fair return on the actual cost or replacement cost of its property; it must be allowed a fair return on the "actual value" of the property.

What is the actual value of a utility's property? Obviously it is the capitalization at current market rates of the allowed and expected profit. In a six per cent money market, an enterprise which is allowed to take six million dollars profit per annum will be valued at one hundred million dollars, one that is allowed three millions per annum, at fifty million dollars. *The actual value of a utility's property, then, is a function of the court's decision*, and the court's decision cannot be based in fact upon the actual value of the property. That value is created by the court; prior to the court's decision and aside from information or belief as to what the court will decide, it is not an economic fact. Nor is it avowedly an ethical fact based upon a determination of the amount which a given utility ought, in the light of social facts and social policies, to be allowed to charge its patrons. Judicial reasoning in this field is thus entirely mythical, and the actual motivation of courts in reaching given decisions is effectively concealed, from all true believers in the orthodox legal theology.

5. When Is Legal Process "Due"?

Legal reasoning carries a peculiar freight of human hopes and human suffering in that realm where the phrase "due process of law" serves as a text for judicial review of social legislation. Here, at least, one might hope that a "decent respect to the opinions of mankind" would lead courts to formulate with some clarity their own conception of what it is that they are doing. Yet in no realm does logomachy offer more stubborn resistance to realistic analysis.

What is due process of law?

One might have supposed from the language of certain cases[26] that "due process of law" meant such law as was familiar to the Founding Fathers of the Constitution. Thus conceived, the phrase would denote a fairly definite concept, and the function of the courts in applying that concept to legislation would be that of objective scholarly inquiry into legal history. It is clear, however, that the modern judicial use of the due process clauses is not based upon any such historical

Felix Cohen

---

[24] The circularity of judicial reasoning in this field is discussed in R. L. Hale, *Value and Vested Rights* (1927) 27 COLUMBIA LAW REV. 523; D. R. Richberg, *Value by Judicial Fiat* (1927) 40 HARV. L. REV. 567; J. C. Bonbright, *The Problem of Judicial Valuation* (1927) 27 COLUMBIA LAW REV. 493.

[25] 169 U. S. 466 (1898).

[26] See Murray v. Hoboken Land and Improvement Co., 18 How. 272, 280 (U. S. 1855); Robertson v. Baldwin, 165 U. S. 275 (1897), and cases cited.

inquiry. Regulation of wages and prices, against which these clauses have been directed with particular severity, finds ample historical precedent in early colonial and English legislation.[27]

Recent judicial utterances suggest a second conception of due process: Legislation falls within the "due process" clauses when it is such as rational men may approve. Taken seriously, this conception makes of our courts lunacy commissions sitting in judgment upon the mental capacity of legislators and, occasionally, of judicial brethren. Some such conception served as the major premise for the famous brief of Mr. Brandeis in the case of *Muller v. Oregon*,[28] which marshaled the favorable opinions entertained by individuals of undisputed sanity towards legislation restricting the hours of industrial labor for women. But subsequent applications of this technique have found less favor in the eyes of the courts, and when Mr. Frankfurter presented to the Supreme Court a similar anthology of opinions in favor of minimum wage legislation for women, the reply of the Supreme Court was that one might also make an impressive compilation of unfavorable opinions.[29] The fact, then, that reasonable men approve of specific legislation does not prevent it from being a violation of "due process of law."

The phrase "due process of law," then, denotes neither an historical nor a psychiatric fact. Does it, perhaps, denote a moral ideal? Whether legislation is due or undue or overdue may seem to laymen to be a question of social ethics or morality. But such a conception has been vigorously repudiated by the courts. Thus Mr. Frankfurter's analysis of the social evils which minimum wage legislation might eliminate was characterized by the United States Supreme Court as "interesting but only mildly persuasive," and the Court went on to say:

> "These are all proper enough for the consideration of the lawmaking bodies, since their tendency is to establish the desirability or undesirability of the legislation; but they reflect no legitimate light upon the question of its validity, and that is what we are called upon to decide."[30]

"Due process of law," then, can no more be defined in social ethical terms than in terms of legal history or abnormal psychology.

In practice, the Supreme Court professes to consider, in a "due process" case, primarily its own former adjudications on the subject, apparently believing, with the Bellman,[31] that what it says three times must be true. But this process of self-fertilization will scarcely account for actual decisions. And one may suspect that

---

[27] See, for instance, the New York act of April 3, 1778, "An act to regulate the wages of mechanicks and labourers, the prices of goods and commodities, and the charges of inn holders within this State, and for other purposes therein mentioned," and other statutes cited in Handler, *Constitutionality of Investigations by the Federal Trade Commission* (1928) 28 COLUMBIA LAW REV. 708, 712 n. 14; see also 2 BOUDIN, GOVERNMENT BY JUDICIARY (1932) 401, 447.

[28] 208 U.S. 412 (1908).

[29] Adkins v. Children's Hospital, 261 U. S. 525, 559 (1923).

[30] *Ibid.*

[31]
> "Just the place for a Snark!" the Bellman cried,
>   As he landed his crew with care;
> Supporting each man on the top of the tide
>   By a finger entwined in his hair.
> "Just the place for a Snark! I have said it twice:
>   That alone should encourage the crew.
> "Just the place for a Snark! I have said it thrice:
>   What I tell you three times is true."

Lewis Carroll, The Hunting of the Snark, Fit the First.

a court would not consistently hide behind a barrage of transcendental nonsense if the grounds of its decisions were such as could be presented without shame to the public.

6. *The Nature of Legal Nonsense*

It would be tedious to prolong our survey; in every field of law we should find the same habit of ignoring practical questions of value or of positive fact and taking refuge in "legal problems" which can always be answered by manipulating legal concepts in certain approved ways. In every field of law we should find peculiar concepts which are not defined either in terms of empirical fact or in terms of ethics but which are used to answer empirical and ethical questions alike, and thus bar the way to intelligent investigation of social fact and social policy. *Corporate entity, property rights, fair value, and due process* are such concepts. So too are *title, contract, conspiracy, malice, proximate cause*, and all the rest of the magic "solving words" of traditional jurisprudence. Legal arguments couched in these terms are necessarily circular, since these terms are themselves creations of law, and such arguments add precisely as much to our knowledge as Moliere's physician's discovery that opium puts men to sleep because it contains a dormitive principle.

Now the proposition that opium puts men to sleep *because* it contains a dormitive principle is scientifically useful if "dormitive principle" is defined physically or chemically. Otherwise it serves only to obstruct the path of understanding with the pretense of knowledge. So, too, the proposition that a law is unconstitutional *because* it deprives persons of property without due process of law would be scientifically useful if "property" and "due process" were defined in non-legal terms; otherwise such a statement simply obstructs study of the relevant facts.

If the foregoing instances of legal reasoning are typical, we may summarize the basic assumptions of traditional legal theory in the following terms:

Legal concepts (for example, *corporations* or *property rights*) are supernatural entities which do not have a verifiable existence except to the eyes of faith. *Rules of law*, which refer to these legal concepts, are not descriptions of empirical social facts (such as the customs of men or the customs of judges) nor yet statements of moral ideals, but are rather theorems in an independent system. It follows that a *legal argument* can never be refuted by a moral principle nor yet by any empirical fact. *Jurisprudence*, then, as an autonomous system of legal concepts, rules, and arguments, must be independent both of ethics and of such positive sciences as economics or psychology. In effect, it is a special branch of the science of transcendental nonsense.

II. The Functional Method

That something is radically wrong with our traditional legal thought-ways has long been recognized. Holmes, Gray, Pound, Brooks Adams, M. R. Cohen, T. R. Powell, Cook, Oliphant, Moore, Radin, Llewellyn, Yntema, Frank, and other leaders of modern legal thought in America, are in fundamental agreement in their disrespect for "mechanical jurisprudence," for legal magic and word-jugglery.[32] But mutual agreement is less apparent when we come to the question of what to do: How are we going to get out of this tangle? How are we going to substitute a realistic, rational, scientific account of legal happenings for the classical theological jurisprudence of concepts?

Attempts to answer this question have made persistent use of the phrase "functional approach." Unfortunately, this phrase has often been used with as little meaning as any of the magical legal concepts against which it is directed. Many who use the term "functional" intend no more than the vague connotation which the word "practical" conveys to the "practical" man. Again, the term "functional approach" is sometimes used to designate a modern form of animism, according to which every social institution or biological organ has a "purpose" in life, and is to be judged good or bad as it achieves or fails to achieve this "purpose." I shall not attempt to be faithful to these vague usages in using the term "functional." I shall use the term rather to designate certain principles or tendencies which appear most clearly in modern physical and mathematical science and in modern philosophy. For it is well to note that the problem of eliminating supernatural terms and meaningless questions and redefining concepts and problems in terms of verifiable realities is not a problem peculiar to law. It is a problem which has been faced in the last two or three centuries, and more especially in the last four or five decades, by philosophy, mathematics, and physics, as well as by psychology, economics, anthropology, and doubtless other sciences as well. Functionalism, operationalism, pragmatism, logical positivism, all these and many other terms have been used in diverse fields, with differing overtones of meaning and emphasis, to designate a certain common approach to this general task of redefining traditional concepts and traditional problems.

It may perhaps clarify the significance of the functional approach in law to trace some of the basic contributions which the functional method has made in modern science and philosophy.

1. The Eradication of Meaningless Concepts

On its negative side (naturally of special prominence in a protestant movement), functionalism represents an assault upon all dogmas and devices that cannot be translated into terms of actual experience.

In physics, the functional or operational method is an assault upon such supernatural concepts as absolute space and absolute time; in mathematics, upon supernatural concepts of real and imaginary, rational and irrational, positive and negative numbers. In psychology, William James inaugurates the functional

---

[32] See HOLMES, "The Path of the Law" (1897) 10 HARV. L. REV. 457, COLLECTED LEGAL PAPERS (1920) 167; GRAY, NATURE AND SOURCES OF THE LAW (1909) c. 4–5; Pound, Law in Books and Law in Action (1910) 44 AM. L. REV. 12; Pound, MECHANICAL JURISPRUDENCE (1908) 8 COLUMBIA LAW REV. 605; BROOKS ADAMS, Law under Inequality: Monopoly, in CENTRALIZATION AND THE LAW (1906) Lecture 2; M. R. COHEN, The Process of Judicial Legislation (1914) 48 AM. L. REV. 161, LAW AND THE SOCIAL ORDER (1933) 112; T. R. Powell, The Judiciality of Minimum Wage Legislation (1924) 37 HARV. L. REV. 545; Cook, Logical and Legal Bases of the Conflict of Laws (1924) 33 YALE L. J. 457; Oliphant, A Return to Stare Decisis (1928) 6 AM. L. SCHOOL REV. 215; U. Moore, Rational Basis of Legal Institutions (1923) 23 COLUMBIA LAW REV. 609; M. Radin, Case Law and Stare Decisis: Concerning Präjudizienrecht in Amerika (1933) 33 COLUMBIA LAW REV. 199; Llewellyn, A Realistic Jurisprudence—The Next Step (1930) 30 COLUMBIA LAW REV. 431; Llewellyn, Some Realism about Realism: Responding to Dean Pound (1931) 44 HARV. L. REV. 1222; Yntema, The Hornbook Method and the Conflict of Laws (1928) 37 YALE L. J. 468; FRANK, LAW AND THE MODERN MIND (1930).

method (of which behaviorism is an extreme form) by asking the naive question: "Does consciousness exist?"[33] Modern "functional grammar" is an assault upon grammatical theories and distinctions which, as applied to the English language, simply have no verifiable significance—such empty concepts, for instance, as that of noun syntax, with its unverifiable distinction between a nominative, an objective, and a possessive case.[34] And passing to the field of art, we find that functional architecture is likewise a repudiation of outworn symbols and functionless forms that have no meaning,—hollow marble pillars that do not support, fake buttresses, and false fronts.[35]

So, too, in law. Our legal system is filled with supernatural concepts, that is to say, concepts which cannot be defined in terms of experience, and from which all sorts of empirical decisions are supposed to flow. Against these unverifiable concepts modern jurisprudence presents an ultimatum. Any word that cannot pay up in the currency of fact, upon demand, is to be declared bankrupt, and we are to have no further dealings with it. Llewellyn has filed an involuntary petition in bankruptcy against the concept Title,[36] Oliphant against the concept Contract,[37] Haines, Brown, T. R. Powell, Finkelstein, and Cushman against Due Process, Police Power, and similar word-charms of constitutional law,[38] Hale, Richberg, Bonbright, and others against the concept of Fair Value in rate regulation,[39] Cook and Yntema against the concept of Vested Rights in the conflict of laws.[40] Each of these men has tried to expose the confusions of current legal thinking engendered by these concepts and to reformulate the problems in his field in terms which show the concrete relevance of legal decisions to social facts.

2. The Abatement of Meaningless Questions

It is a consequence of the functional attack upon unverifiable concepts that many of the traditional problems of science, law, and philosophy are revealed as pseudo-problems devoid of meaning. As the protagonist of logical positivism, Wittgenstein, says of the traditional problems of philosophy:

"Most propositions and questions, that have been written about philosophical matters, are not false, but senseless. We cannot, therefore, answer questions of this kind at all, but only state their senselessness. Most questions and propositions of the philosophers result from the fact that we do not understand the logic of our language. (They are of the same kind as the question whether the Good is more or less

---

[33] ESSAYS IN RADICAL EMPIRICISM (1912) 1. Answering this question, James asserts, "There is . . . no aboriginal stuff or quality of being, contrasted with that of which material objects are made, out of which our thoughts of them are made; but there is a function in experience which thoughts perform . . . " (pp. 3–4).

[34] See H. N. RIVLIN, FUNCTIONAL GRAMMAR (1930); and cf. L. BLOOMFIELD, LANGUAGE (1933), p. 266 et passim.

[35] See F. L. WRIGHT, MODERN ARCHITECTURE (1931).

[36] LLEWELLYN, CASES AND MATERIALS ON THE LAW OF SALES (1930).

[37] Oliphant, Mutuality of Obligation in Bilateral Contracts at Law (1925) 25 COLUMBIA LAW REV. 705; (1928) 28 COLUMBIA LAW REV. 997.

[38] C. G. Haines, General Observations on the Effects of Personal, Political and Economic Influences in the Decisions of Judges (1922) 17 ILL. L. REV. 96; R. A. Brown, Police Power—Legislation for Health and Personal Safety (1929) 42 HARV. L. REV. 866; T. R. Powell, The Judiciality of Minimum Wage Legislation (1924) 37 HARV. L. REV. 545; M. Finkelstein, Judicial Self-Limitation (1924) 37 HARV. L. REV. 338; R.E. Cushman, The Social and Economic Interpretation of the Fourteenth Amendment (1922) 20 MICH. L. REV. 737.

[39] See note 24, supra.

[40] Cook, Logical and Legal Bases of the Conflict of Laws (1924) 33 YALE L. J. 457; Yntema, The Hornbook Method and the Conflict of Laws (1928) 37 YALE L. J. 468.

identical than the Beautiful.) And so it is not to be wondered at that the deepest
problems are really no problems."[41]

The same thing may be said of the problems of traditional jurisprudence. As commonly formulated, such "problems" as, "What is the holding or *ratio decidendi* of a case?"[42] or "Which came first,—the law or the state?"[43] or "What is the essential distinction between a crime and a tort?"[44] or "Where is a corporation?" are in fact meaningless, and can serve only as invitations to equally meaningless displays of conceptual acrobatics.

Fundamentally there are only two significant questions in the field of law. One is, "How do courts actually decide cases of a given kind?" The other is, "How ought they to decide cases of a given kind?" Unless a legal "problem" can be subsumed under one of these forms, it is not a meaningful question and any answer to it must be nonsense.[45]

3. The Redefinition of Concepts

Although the negative aspect of the functional method is apt to assume peculiar prominence in polemic controversy, the value of the method depends, in the last analysis, upon its positive contributions to the advancement of knowledge. Judged from this standpoint, I think it is fair to say that the functional method has justified itself in every scientific field to which it has been actually applied, and that functional redefinition of scientific concepts has been the keynote of most significant theoretical advances in the sciences during the last half century.

The tremendous advance made in our understanding of the foundations of pure mathematics, achieved through the work of such men as Frege, Peano, Whitehead, and Russell,[46] offers an illuminating example of the functional method in action.

Mathematics, fifty years ago, contained as many unanalyzed "fictions," supernatural concepts, unreal questions, and unjustified operations as classical jurisprudence. High school students are still taught to subtract the integer seven from the integer two, which is logically impossible. An integer is the number of a class, and obviously a class of seven members cannot be contained in, or subtracted from, a class of two members. The student who refuses to believe in such supernatural subtraction is entirely justified, although he must expect scant mercy from ignorant teachers and examiners (as must the law student who refuses to answer senseless questions of law and merely points out their senselessness).

---

[41] WITTGENSTEIN, TRACTATUS LOGICO-PHILOSOPHICUS (1922) prop. 4.003. And *cf.* JAMES, PRAGMATISM (1908): "The pragmatic method is primarily a method of settling metaphysical disputes that otherwise might be interminable. . . . The pragmatic method in such cases is to try to interpret each notion by tracing its respective practical consequences. . . . If no practical differences whatever can be traced, then the alternatives mean practically the same thing, and all dispute is idle. . . . It is astonishing to see how many philosophical disputes collapse into insignificance the moment you subject them to this simple test of tracing a practical consequence." (pp. 45–49.)

[42] See Goodhart, *Determining the Ratio Decidendi of a Case* (1930) 40 YALE L. J. 161; and *cf.* LLEWELLYN, BRAMBLE BUSH (1930) 47.

[43] Fortunately there is very little literature in the English language on this problem. German jurists, however, are inordinately fond of it.

[44] See C. K. ALLEN, LEGAL DUTIES AND OTHER ESSAYS IN JURISPRUDENCE (1931) 226. And *cf.* W. W. Cook, Book Review (1932) 42 YALE L. J. 299.

[45] *Cf.* F. S. Cohen, *What Is a Question?* (1929) 39 MONIST 350.

[46] See RUSSELL, PRINCIPLES OF MATHEMATICS (1903); INTRODUCTION TO MATHEMATICAL PHILOSOPHY (1919); RUSSELL AND WHITEHEAD, PRINCIPIA MATHEMATICA (1910); FREGE, DIE GRUNDLAGEN DER ARITHMETIK (1884).

Nevertheless, the mathematical fiction, like the legal fiction (*e.g.* the spatial location of a corporation), represents a confused perception of a significant fact, and it is the province of functional analysis to untangle the confusion and find the fact. It is a fact that if you move seven units in one direction—in the direction of bankruptcy, say, or in the direction of lowered temperature—and call that direction "minus"—and then move two units in the opposite direction—"plus"—you have in effect moved five units in the first—the "minus"—direction. Undoubtedly, it is useful to invent or define mathematical terms which will describe these two *motions* or *operations* and the relation between them (as it is useful to invent legal terms to describe the corporate activities of human beings). But such mathematical terms, it is important to recognize, are not numbers, as "number" is ordinarily defined (*i.e.* they are not integers). What, then, are these novel entities? Classical mathematics conceived of these entities as integers acting, under a special dispensation, in supernatural ways. Modern mathematics shows that these entities, known as "sign numbers," are not integers at all, but rather *constructs* or *functions* of integers. The number "-7" is the operation of moving from any integer to its immediate predecessor in the series of integers, repeated seven times. The number "$+7$" is the converse operation, *i.e.*, the operation of moving from any integer to its immediate successor, repeated seven times. The number "$+7$" is therefore something quite different from the integer "7." It is, however, a logical function or construct of the integer seven, since the integer seven appears in the definition of "$+7$" as an operation repeated "seven" times.

Similarly, modern advances in mathematics have made it clear that rational and irrational, real and imaginary, numbers are not numbers at all, in the original sense of the term, but are functions of such numbers.[47] The so-called arithmetization of mathematics, and the definition of the concepts of mathematics by Whitehead and Russell, as constructs of certain simple logical terms, have stripped mathematical terms of their supernatural significations, illumined and eliminated hidden inconsistencies, and clarified the relationships of mathematical concepts not only to each other but to the material world.

A similar use of the functional method has characterized the most significant advances of modern philosophy. The attack upon transcendental conceptions of God, matter, the Absolute, essence and accident, substance and attribute, has been vigorously pressed by C. S. Peirce, James, Dewey, Russell, Whitehead, C. I. Lewis, C. D. Broad, and most recently by the Viennese School, primarily by Wittgenstein and Carnap.[48] These men fall into various schools,—pragmatism, pragmaticism (which is the word Peirce shifted to when he saw what his followers were doing to the word "pragmatism"), neo-realism, critical realism, functional realism, and logical positivism. It would be unfair to minimize the real differences between some of these schools, but in one fundamental respect they

[47] See RUSSELL, INTRODUCTION TO MATHEMATICAL PHILOSOPHY (1919) c. 7.

[48] See C. S. PEIRCE, CHANCE, LOVE AND LOGIC (1923); COLLECTED PAPERS (1931–1934), especially vol. 5; JAMES, PRAGMATISM (1908); ESSAYS IN RADICAL EMPIRICISM (1912); DEWEY, *Appearing and Appearance*, in PHILOSOPHY AND CIVILIZATION (1931) 51; RUSSELL, OUR KNOWLEDGE OF THE EXTERNAL WORLD AS A FIELD FOR SCIENTIFIC METHOD IN PHILOSOPHY (1914); MYSTICISM AND LOGIC (1918); WHITEHEAD, THE PRINCIPLES OF NATURAL KNOWLEDGE (1919); THE CONCEPT OF NATURE (1920); C. I. LEWIS, MIND AND THE WORLD-ORDER (1929); C.D. BROAD, SCIENTIFIC THOUGHT (1923); WITTGENSTEIN, TRACTATUS LOGICO-PHILOSOPHICUS (1922); Carnap, *Ueberwindung der Metaphysik durch logische Analyse der Sprache* (1932) 2 ERKENNTNIS no. 4; J. E. Boodin, *Functional Realism* (1934) 43 PHILOSOPHICAL REVIEW 147.

assume an identical position. This is currently expressed in the sentence, "A thing is what it does." More precise is the language of Peirce: "In order to ascertain the meaning of an intellectual conception one should consider what practical consequences might conceivably result by necessity from the truth of that conception; and the sum of these consequences will constitute the entire meaning of the conception."[49] The methodological implications of this maxim are summed up by Russell in these words:

"The supreme maxim in scientific philosophising is this: *Wherever possible, logical constructions are to be substituted for inferred entities.*"[50]

In other words, instead of assuming hidden causes or transcendental principles behind everything we see or do, we are to redefine the concepts of abstract thought as constructs, or functions, or complexes, or patterns, or arrangements, of the things that we do actually see or do. All concepts that cannot be defined in terms of the elements of actual experience are meaningless.

The task of modern philosophy is the salvaging of whatever significance attaches to the traditional concepts of metaphysics, through the redefinition of these concepts as functions of actual experience. Whatever differences may exist among modern philosophers in the choice of experiential terms which are to serve as the basic terms of functional analysis—"events," "sensa," and "atomic facts" are but a few of these basic terms—few would disagree with the point of view expressed by William James when he says that in our investigation of any abstract concept the central question must be: "What is its cash value in terms of particular experience? and what special differences would come into the world if it were true or false?"[51]

A similar use of the functional method characterizes recent advances in physics. Instead of conceiving of space as something into which physical things fit, but which somehow exists, unverifiably, apart from the things that fill it (as the Common Law is supposed to exist apart from and prior to actual decisions), and then assuming that there is an ether that fills space when it is empty, modern physicists conceive space as a manifold of relations between physical objects or events. The theory of relativity begins with the recognition that relations between physical objects or events involve a temporal as well as a spatial aspect. Thus it becomes convenient for certain purposes to substitute the notion of space-time for that of space, or even to substitute a notion which includes mass as well as space and time.

The parallel between the functional method of modern physics and the program of realistic jurisprudence is so well sketched by a distinguished Chinese jurist that I can only offer a quotation without comment:[52]

"Professor Eddington, in a recent book on "The Nature of the Physical World," observes: "A thing must be defined according to the way in which it is in practice recognized and not according to some ulterior significance that we suppose it to possess." So Professor Bridgman, in "The Logic of Modern Physics":
"Hitherto many of the concepts of physics have been defined in terms of their properties." But now, "in general, we mean by any concept nothing more than a set of operations; *the concept is synonymous with the corresponding set of operations.*

[49] 5 C. S. PEIRCE, COLLECTED PAPERS 6.
[50] RUSSELL, MYSTICISM AND LOGIC (1918) 155.
[51] James, *The Pragmatic Method* (1904) 1 JOUR. OF PHILOSOPHY 673.
[52] John C. H. Wu, *Realistic Analysis of Legal Concepts: A Study in the Legal Method of Mr. Justice Holmes* (1932) 5 CHINA L. REV. 1, 2.

If the concept is physical, as of length, the operations are actual physical operations, namely, those by which length is measured; or if the concept is mental, as of mathematical continuity, the operations are mental operations, namely those by which we determine whether a given aggregate of magnitudes is continuous."

Now, this way of dealing with concepts was precisely what Holmes introduced into the science of law early in the '80's. Before discussing the significance and possibilities of the new method, let me list here some of his definitions of things juridic:

Law: "The prophecies of what the courts will do in fact, and nothing more pretentious, are what I mean by the law."

"But for legal purposes a right is only the hypostasis of a prophecy—the imagination of a substance *supporting* the fact that the public force will be brought to bear upon those who do things said to contravene it—just as we talk of the force of gravitation accounting for the conduct of bodies in space."

Duty: "A legal duty so called is nothing but a prediction that if a man does or omits certain things he will be made to suffer in this or that way by judgment of the court; and so of a legal right."

Contract: "The duty to keep a contract at common law means a prediction that you must pay damages if you do not keep it and nothing else. If you commit a tort, you are liable to pay a compensatory sum. If you commit a contract, you are liable to pay a compensatory sum unless the promised event comes to pass, and that is all the difference."

"It may be conceded at the outset that all these definitions are capable of being further developed or improved upon: The important point to note is the complete departure from the way the old Classical Jurisprudence defined things. Hostile as he was to the traditional logic, Holmes touched the springs of the neo-realistic logic in his analysis of legal concepts. He departed entirely from the subject-predicate form of logic, and employed a logic of relations. He did not try to show how a legal entity possesses certain inherent properties. What he was trying everywhere to bring out is: If a certain group of facts is true of a person, then the person will receive a certain group of consequences attached by the law to that group of facts. Instead of treating a legal concept as a substance which in its nature necessarily contains certain inherent properties, we have here a logic which regards it as a mere signpost of a real relation subsisting between an antecedent and a consequent, and, as one of the New Realists so aptly puts it, all signposts must be kept up to date, with their inscriptions legible and their pointing true. In short, by turning the juristic logic from a subject-predicate form to an antecedentconsequent form, Holmes virtually created an inductive science of law. For both the antecedent and the consequent are to be proved and ascertained empirically."

In brief, Holmes and, one should add, Hohfeld[53] have offered a logical basis for the redefinition of every legal concept in empirical terms, *i.e.* in terms of

Felix Cohen

[53] See HOHFELD, FUNDAMENTAL LEGAL CONCEPTIONS (1919).

judicial decisions. The ghost-world of supernatural legal entities to whom courts delegate the moral responsibility of deciding cases vanishes; in its place we see legal concepts as patterns of judicial behavior, behavior which affects human lives for better or worse and is therefore subject to moral criticism. Of the functional method in legal science, one may say, as Russell has said of the method in contemporary philosophy, "Our procedure here is precisely analogous to that which has swept away from the philosophy of mathematics the useless menagerie of metaphysical monsters with which it used to be infested."[54]

4. The Redirection of Research

It is often easier to distinguish a school of thought by asking not, "What basic theory does it defend?" but rather, "What basic question does it propound?"

A failure to recognize that the law is a vast field, in which different students are interested in diverse problems, has the unfortunate effect of making every school of legal thought an *ex officio* antagonist of every other school. Dean Pound's classification of jurists into mutually exclusive "analytical," "historical," "philosophical," and "sociological" schools, with sub-species too numerous to mention,[55] has given a good deal of prestige to the idea that a new school of jurisprudence must offer a revolutionary threat to all existing schools. It would be unfortunate to regard "functionalism" in law as a substitute for all other "isms." Rather, we must regard functionalism, in law as in anthropology, economics, and other fields, as a call for the study of problems which have been neglected by other scientific methods of investigation.

In general, when one comes upon a strange fact and seeks to understand it, there are four inquiries he can pursue.

In the first place, our investigator can *classify* the fact—either by putting an arbitrary label upon it or by discerning in the fact to be explained the significant similarities and differences which relate it to other facts.

Again, one may seek to discover the *genesis* of the fact in question, to trace its historical antecedents.

In the third place, one may inquire into the *nature* of the fact presented, endeavoring by logical analysis to resolve it into simpler elements.

A fourth possible approach seeks to discover the *significance* of the fact through a determination of its implications or consequences in a given mathematical, physical or social context.

It is this last approach to which the term "functional" has been applied. Obviously, it is not the *only* way of gathering useful information, and obviously, it is largely dependent upon the results of classificatory or taxonomic investigation, genetic or historical research, and analytical inquiries. Finally, it must be remarked that the functional method is not a recent invention. Plato's attempt to define "justice" by assessing the activities of a just state,[56] and Aristotle's conception of the soul as the way a living body behaves[57] are illustrious examples of functional analysis. So, too, Hume's analysis of causation in terms of uniformity of succession, and Berkeley's analysis of matter in terms of its appearances, are

---

[54] RUSSELL, *loc. cit. supra* note 50.

[55] See POUND, OUTLINES OF LECTURES ON JURISPRUDENCE (4th ed. 1928) c. 1.

[56] PLATO, REPUBLIC.

[57] ARISTOTLE, DE ANIMA, I, 1; II, 1.

significant attempts to redefine supernatural concepts in natural terms,[58] to wash ideas in cynical acid (borrowing Holmes' suggestive phrase).[59]

If functional analysis seems novel in the law, this is perhaps traceable to the general backwardness of legal science, which is the product of social factors that cannot be exorcised by new slogans.

With these caveats against the notion that the functional approach is a new intellectual invention which will solve all the problems of law (or of anthropology, economics, or any other science), we may turn to the significant question: "What are the new directions which the functional method will give to our scientific research?"

In attempting to answer this question for the field of law we may find suggestive precedents in other social sciences.

Applied to the study of religion, for instance, the functional approach has meant a shift of emphasis away from the attempt to systematize and compare religious beliefs, away from concern with the genesis and evolution of religions, and towards a study of the consequences of various religious beliefs in terms of human motivation and social structure. Outstanding examples of this focus are Weber's and Tawney's studies of the influence of Protestantism in the development of modern capitalism,[60] and James' essays on the psychological significance for the individual of various religious beliefs.[61] The functional approach asks of every religious dogma or ritual: How does it work? How does it serve to mould men's lives, to deter from certain avenues of conduct and expression, to sanction accepted patterns of behavior, to produce or alleviate certain emotional stresses, to induce social solidarity, to lay a basis for culture accumulation by giving life after death to the visions, thoughts and achievements of mortal men.[62] The significance of a religious dogma is found not in a system of theological propositions but in a mode of human conduct. The functional approach demands objective description of this conduct, in which the empirical significance of the religious belief is embodied. Just so, the functional approach in physics captures the significance of a physical concept in the actual processes and operations of the physicist, rather than in the theological or metaphysical interpretations which physicists put upon their own activities. It is an application of this same approach that discovers the significance of a legal principle in the actual behavior of judges, sheriffs and litigants rather than in conventional accounts of the principles that judges, sheriffs and litigants are "supposed" to follow.

In anthropology, the functional method represents a movement away from two types of study: the naive reporting and classification of striking human peculiarities; and the more sophisticated attempt to trace the historical origin, evolution and diffusion of "complexes." Those who have embraced the functional

---

[58] *Cf.* JAMES, PRAGMATISM (1908): "There is absolutely nothing new in the pragmatic method. Socrates was an adept at it. Aristotle used it methodically. Locke, Berkeley, and Hume made momentous contributions to truth by its means" (at p. 50). See, also, James, *The Pragmatic Method* (1904) 1 JOUR. OF PHILOSOPHY 673.

[59] " . . . the vague circumference of the notion of duty shrinks and at the same time grows more precise when we wash it with cynical acid and expel everything except the object of our study, the operations of the law." Holmes, *"The Path of the Law"* (1897) 10 HARV. L. REV. 457, 462.

[60] MAX WEBER, THE PROTESTANT ETHIC AND THE SPIRIT OF CAPITALISM (tr. by Parsons, 1930); R. H. TAWNEY, RELIGION AND THE RISE OF CAPITALISM (1926).

[61] JAMES, THE VARIETIES OF RELIGIOUS EXPERIENCE (1902).

[62] *Cf.* KAPLAN, JUDAISM AS A CIVILIZATION (1934), c. 26 *(Functional Method of Interpretation)*; Elwang, THE SOCIAL FUNCTION OF RELIGIOUS BELIEF (UNIV. OF MO. STUDIES, SOCIAL SCIENCE SERIES, vol. 2, no. 1, 1908); FOSTER, THE FUNCTION OF RELIGION IN MAN'S STRUGGLE FOR EXISTENCE (1909).

approach (not all of whom have invoked the word "functional"), have been primarily concerned to trace the social consequences of diverse customs, beliefs, rituals, social arrangements, and patterns of human conduct. This approach has led to fertile fields that most earlier investigators missed. In the study of primitive art, the new focus has brought into the foreground the question of the crafts-man's motivations and purposes, the significance of art as an individualizing or socializing force, the whole problem of interplay between materials, techniques, and social needs.[63] The study of primitive social organization comes increasingly to deal with the functional significance of family, clan, and tribal groupings as social determinants in the production, distribution, and use of property, as well as in the non-economic human relationships of education, religion, play, sex, and companionship.[64] In the study of primitive law, the functional approach raises to the fore the problem of incentives to obedience and the efficacy of these incentives, the techniques of law enforcement, and the relations of rivalry or supplementation between legal sanctions and other social forces.[65]

A similar use of the functional approach is characteristic of modern political science, in which revolt against the classical supernatural conception of sovereignty is a point of agreement uniting the most diverse schools of contemporary thought. Typical is the following statement:

"By institutions we merely mean collective behavior patterns, the ways in which a community carries on the innumerable activities of social life. . . . Society achieves certain results through collective political actions. The means that it uses are the behavior patterns which we call courts, legislative bodies, commissions, electorates, administration. We idealize these institutions collectively and personify them in the State. But this idealization is pure fancy. The State as a juristic or ideal person is the veriest fiction. It is real only as a collective name for governmental institutions."[66]

Under the influence of the functional approach political theory ceases to be a science of pure forms, and comes increasingly to grips with the psychological motives and the technological forces that function through political instruments.

In economics we have witnessed a similar shift of research from the taxonomic or systematic analysis of economic "norms" to the study of the actual economic behavior of men and nations. Veblen's indictment of classical economic theory may be applied word for word to classical jurisprudence, if we merely substitute for the terms "economic" and "economist" the terms "legal" and "jurist":

"The standpoint of the classical *economists*, in their higher or definitive syntheses and generalizations, may not inaptly be called the standpoint of ceremonial adequacy. . . . In effect, this preconception imputes to things a tendency to work out what the instructed common sense of the time accepts as the adequate or worthy

[63] See BOAS, PRIMITIVE ART (1927).

[64] See Boas, *The Social Organisation and the Secret Societies of the Kwakiutl Indians* (1895) REPORT OF U. S. NAT. MUSEUM, at 315; MALINOWSKI, THE FAMILY AMONG THE AUSTRALIAN ABORIGINES (1913); LOWIE, PRIMITIVE SOCIETY (1920); GOLDENWEISER. HISTORY, PSYCHOLOGY AND CULTURE (1933) Part III *(Totemism)*; W. C. McKern, *Functional Families of the Patwin* (UNIV. OF CALIF. PUB. IN AMER. ARCHAEOLOGY AND ETHNOLOGY, vol. 13, no. 7).

[65] See MALINOWSKI, CRIME AND CUSTOM IN SAVAGE SOCIETY (1926); HOGBIN, LAW AND ORDER IN POLYNESIA (1934). In his introduction to the latter volume, Malinowski writes: "Modern anthropology concentrates, above all, on what is now usually called the function of a custom, belief or institution. By function we mean the part which is played by any one factor of a culture within the general scheme."

[66] W. J. Shepard, *Democracy in Transition* (1935) 29 AM. POL. SCI. REV. 1; *cf.* H. J. LASKI, GRAMMAR OF POLITICS (2d ed. 1929); W. Y. ELLIOTT, THE PRAGMATIC REVOLT IN POLITICS (1928).

end. of human effort. . . . This ideal of conduct is made to serve as a canon of truth. . . ."

"The metaphors are effective, both in their homiletical use and as a laborsaving device,—more effective than their user designs them to be. By their use the theorist is enabled serenely to enjoin himself from following out an elusive train of causal sequence. . . . The scheme so arrived at is spiritually binding on the behavior of the phenomena contemplated. . . . Features of the process that do not lend themselves to interpretation in terms of the formula are abnormal cases and are due to disturbing causes. In all this the agencies or forces causally at work in the economic life process are neatly avoided. The outcome of the method, at its best, is a body of logically consistent propositions concerning the normal relations of things—a system of economic taxonomy."[67]

The same "standpoint of ceremonial adequacy" has to some extent characterized the works of our classical jurists,—such masters of the law as Beale, Williston, and even Wigmore. For them, as for the classical economists, it was easy to avoid "an elusive train of causal sequence." Principles, conceived as "spiritually binding on the behavior of the phenomena contemplated," diverted their attention from the hard facts of the legal world,—the human motivations and social prejudices of judges, the stretching or shrinking of precedents in every washing, the calculations of juries, and the fact of legislation,—and at the same time diverted attention from the task of legal criticism.[68]

The age of the classical jurists is over, I think. The "Restatement of the Law" by the American Law Institute is the last long-drawn-out gasp of a dying tradition.[69] The more intelligent of our younger law teachers and students are not interested in "restating" the dogmas of legal theology. There will, of course, be imitators and followers of the classical jurists, in the years ahead. But I think that the really creative legal thinkers of the future will not devote themselves, in the manner of Williston, Wigmore, and their fellow masters, to the taxonomy of legal concepts and to the systematic explication of principles of "justice" and "reason," buttressed by "correct" cases. Creative legal thought will more and more look behind the pretty array of "correct" cases to the actual facts of judicial behavior, will make increasing use of statistical methods in the scientific description and prediction of judicial behavior, will more and more seek to map the hidden springs of judicial decision and to weigh the social forces which are represented on the bench. And on the critical side, I think that creative legal thought will more and more look behind the traditionally accepted principles of "justice" and "reason" to appraise in ethical terms the social values at stake in any choice between two precedents.

"Social policy" will be comprehended not as an emergency factor in legal argument but rather as the gravitational field that gives weight to any rule or

[67] VEBLEN, *Why Is Economics Not an Evolutionary Science?* in THE PLACE OF SCIENCE in MODERN CIVILIZATION (1919) 56, 65–67.

[68] To say this is not to deny that such legal scholars have performed yeoman service in clarifying the logical implications and inconsistencies of judicial doctrines. Such analysis is useful, but it is not the sum and substance of legal science. *Cf.* F. S. COHEN, ETHICAL SYSTEMS AND LEGAL IDEALS (1933) 235–237.

[69] See M. Franklin, *The Historic Function of the American Law Institute: Restatement as Transitional to Codification* (1934) 47 HARV. L. REV. 1367; and *cf.* Patterson, *The Restatement of the Law of Contracts* (1933) 33 COLUMBIA LAW REV. 397; E. S. Robinson, *Law—An Unscientific Science* (1935) 44 YALE L. J. 235, 261.

precedent, whether it be in constitutional law, in the law of trade-marks, or in the most technical details of legal procedure.

There is implied in this shifting of the paths of legal research a change in the equipment needs of the student of law. Familiarity with the words of past judicial opinions and skill in the manipulation of legal concepts are not enough for the student who seeks to understand the social forces that control judicial behavior, nor for the lawyer who seeks to use these forces.[70]

The vested interests of our law schools in an "independent" science of law are undermined by every advance in our knowledge of the social antecedents and consequences of judicial decision. It becomes the part of discretion, in law schools aware of such advances, to admit that legal science necessarily involves us in psychology, economics, and political theory. Courses in our more progressive law schools are beginning to treat, most gingerly, of the psychological doctrines embedded in our rules of evidence, the sociological theories assumed in our criminal law, the economic assumptions embalmed in our doctrines of constitutional law, and the psychological, sociological, and economic *facts* which give force and significance to rules and decisions in these and other fields of law. The first steps taken are clumsy and evoke smiles of sympathy or roars of laughter from critics of diverse temperaments. The will to walk persists.

For the lawyer, no less than for the legal scholar, handling of materials hitherto considered "non-legal" assumes increasing importance. And courts that shut their doors to such non-legal materials, laying the taboos of evidence law upon facts and arguments that reveal the functional social significance of a legal claim or a legal precedent, will eventually learn that society has other organs—legislatures and legislative committees and administrative commissions of many sorts—that are willing to handle, in straightforward fashion, the materials, statistical and descriptive, that a too finicky judiciary disdains.

III. THE USES OF THE FUNCTIONAL METHOD IN LAW

The significance of the functional method in the field of law is clarified if we consider the bearings of this method upon four traditional legal problems: (1) The definition of law; (2) The nature of legal rules and concepts; (3) The theory of legal decisions; and (4) The role of legal criticism.

1. The Definition of Law

The starting point of functional analysis in American jurisprudence is found in Justice Holmes' definition of law as "prophecies of what the courts will do in fact." It is in "The Path of the Law,"[71] that this realistic conception of law is first clearly formulated:

> "If you want to know the law and nothing else, you must look at it as a bad man, who cares only for the material consequences which such knowledge enables him to predict,

---

[70] The implications of the functional method for legal education are carefully traced in Keyserling, *Social Objectives in Legal Education* (1933) 33 COLUMBIA LAW REV. 437.

[71] HOLMES, *Path of the Law* (1897) 10 HARV. L. REV. 457, 459–461; COLLECTED LEGAL PAPERS (1921) p. 167, 171–173. A more precise definition, following Holmes, is given in C. J. Keyser, *On the Study of Legal Science* (1929) 38 YALE L. J. 413.

not as a good one, who finds his reasons for conduct, whether inside the law or outside of it, in the vaguer sanctions of conscience. . . . Take the fundamental question, What constitutes the law? You will find some text writers telling you that it is something different from what is decided by the courts of Massachusetts or England, that it is a system of reason, that it is a deduction from principles of ethics or admitted axioms or what not, which may or may not coincide with the decisions. But if we take the view of our friend the bad man we shall find that he does not care two straws for the axioms or deductions, but that he does want to know what the Massachusetts or English courts are likely to do in fact. I am much of his mind. The prophecies of what the courts will do in fact, and nothing more pretentious, are what I mean by the law."

A good deal of fruitless controversy has arisen out of attempts to show that this definition of law as the way courts actually decide cases is either true or false.[72] A definition of law is *useful* or *useless*. It is not *true* or *false*, any more than a New Year's resolution or an insurance policy. A definition is in fact a type of insurance against certain risks of confusion. It cannot, any more than can a commercial insurance policy, eliminate all risks. Absolute certainty is as foreign to language as to life. There is no final insurance against an insurer's insolvency. And the words of a definition always carry their own aura of ambiguity. But a definition is useful if it insures against risks of confusion more serious than any that the definition itself contains.

"What courts do" is not entirely devoid of ambiguity. There is room for disagreement as to what a *court* is, whether, for instance, the Interstate Commerce Commission or the Hague Tribunal or the Council of Tesuque Pueblo is a court, and whether a judge acting in excess of those powers which the executive arm of the government will recognize acts as a court. There may even be disagreement as to the line of distinction between what courts *do* and what courts *say*, in view of the fact that most judicial behavior is verbal. But these sources of ambiguity in Holmes' definition of law are peripheral rather than central, and easily remedied. They are, therefore, far less dangerous sources of confusion than the basic ambiguity inherent in classical definitions of law which involve a confusion between what is and what ought to be.

The classical confusion against which realistic jurisprudence is a protest is exemplified in Blackstone's classical definition of law as "a rule of civil conduct, prescribed by the supreme power in a State, commanding what is right, and prohibiting what is wrong."[73]

---

[72] For examples of such argument see Dickinson, *Legal Rules: Their Function in the Process of Decision* (1931) 79 U. OF PA. LAW REV. 833; H. Kantorowicz, *Some Rationalism about Realism* (1934) 43 YALE L. J. 1240; FRANK, LAW AND THE MODERN MIND (1930) 127–128. The vicious circle in Dickinson's attempted refutation of the realistic definition of law I have elsewhere analyzed. See F. S. COHEN, ETHICAL SYSTEMS AND LEGAL IDEALS (1933) 12, n. 16. Kantorowicz repeats the same argument, emphasizing the charge that a definition of law in terms of court decisions "puts the cart before the horse" and is as ridiculous as a definition of medicine in terms of the behavior of doctors. The parallel, though witty, is inapt: The correct analogy to a definition of the science of law as description of the behavior of judges would be a definition of the science of medicine as a description of the behavior of certain parasites, etc. Kantorowicz accepts uncritically the metaphysical assumption that definition is a one-way passage from the more general to the less general. But modern logic has demonstrated the hollowness of this assumption. It is useful for certain purposes to define points as functions of lines. For other purposes it is useful to define lines as functions of points. It is just as logical to define law in terms of courts as the other way about. The choice is a matter of convenience, not of logic or truth.

The same metaphysical fallacy vitiates the opposite argument of Frank, namely, that "primary" reality is particular and concrete, so that a definition of law must necessarily be in terms of actual decisions. To the eyes of modern logic, the world contains things *and* relations, neither of which can claim a superior grade of reality. One can start a fight or a scientific inquiry *either* with a concrete fact *or* with a general principle.

[73] BL. COMM.* 44.

In this definition we have an attempt to unite two incompatible ideas which, in the tradition of English jurisprudence, are most closely associated with the names of Hobbes and Coke, respectively.

Hobbes, the grandfather of realistic jurisprudence, saw in law the commands of a body to whom private individuals have surrendered their force. In a state of nature there is war of all against all. In order to achieve peace and security, each individual gives up something of his freedom, something of his power, and the commands of the collective power, that is the state, constitute law.

Hobbes' theory of law has been very unpopular with respectable citizens, but I venture to think that most of the criticism directed against it, in the last two and a half centuries, has been based upon a misconception of what Hobbes meant by a state of nature. So far as I know, Hobbes never refers to the state of nature as an actual historical era, at the end of which men came together and signed a social contract. The state of nature is a stage in analysis rather than a stage of history. It exists today and has always existed, to a greater or lesser degree, in various realms of human affairs. To the extent that any social relationship is exempt from governmental control it presents what Hobbes calls a state of nature.

In international relations today, at least to the extent that nations have not effectively surrendered their power through compacts establishing such rudimentary agencies of international government as the League of Nations or the Universal Postal Union, there is in fact a state of nature and a war of all against all. This war, as Hobbes insists, is present potentially before actual hostilities break out. Not only in international relations, but in industrial relations today do we find war of all against all, in regions to which governmental control has not been extended, or from which it has been withdrawn—if it existed.

Mutual concessions and delegations of power involved in an arbitration contract, an international treaty, an industrial "code," a corporate merger, or a collective labor agreement, are steps in the creation of government, and call into operation new rules of law and new agencies of law enforcement. Governments do not arise once and for all. Government is arising today in many regions of social existence, and it arises wherever individuals find the conflicts inherent in a state of nature unendurable. The process by which government is created and its commands formulated is a process of human bargaining, based upon mutual consent but weighted by the relative power of conflicting individuals or groups.

In all this conception of law, there is no appeal to reason or goodness. Law commands obedience not because of its goodness, or its justice, or its rationality, but because of the power behind it. While this power does rest to a real extent upon popular beliefs about the value of certain legal ideals, it remains true today, as Hobbes says in his *Dialogue on the Common Law*, "In matter of government, when nothing else is turned up, clubs are trump."[74]

Quite different from this realistic conception of law is the theory made famous by Coke that law is only the perfection of reason.[75] This is a notion which has had considerable force in American constitutional history, having served first as a basis for popular revolution against tyrannical violations of "natural law" and

---

[74] Hobbes, Dialogue between a Philosopher and a Student of the Common Laws of England (1681), *Of Punishments*.

[75] Co. Litt.* 976.

the "natural rights" of Englishmen, and serving more recently as a judicial ground for denying legality to statutes that judges consider "unreasonable." It would be absurd to deny the importance of this concept of natural law or justice as a standard by which to judge the acts of rulers, legislative, executive or judicial. It is clear, however, that the validity of this concept of law lies in a realm of values, which is not identical with the realm of social actualities.

The confusion and ambiguity which infest the classical conception of law, as formulated by Blackstone and implicitly accepted by most modern legal writers, arise from the attempt to throw together two inconsistent ideas. Blackstone attempts in effect to superimpose the picture of law drawn by the tender-minded hypocrite, Coke, upon the picture executed by the tough-minded cynic, Hobbes, and to give us a composite photograph. Law, says Blackstone, is "a rule of civil conduct prescribed by the supreme power in a State (Hobbes speaking) commanding what is right and prohibiting what is wrong (Coke speaking)."[76] Putting these two ideas together, we have a fertile source of confusion, which many important legal scholars since Blackstone have found about as useful in legal polemics as the ink with which a cuttlefish befuddles his enemies.

Those theorists who adhere to the Blackstonian definition of law are able to spin legal theories to the heart's content without fear of refutation. If legislatures or courts disagree with a given theory, it is a simple matter to show that this disagreement is unjust, unreasonable, monstrous and, therefore, not "sound law." On the other hand, the intruding moralist who objects to a legal doctrine on the ground that it is unjust or undesirable can be told to go back to the realm of morality he came from, since the law is the command of the sovereign and not a matter of moral theory. Perhaps the chief usefulness of the Blackstonian theory is the gag it places upon legal criticism. Obviously, if the law is something that commands what is right and prohibits what is wrong, it is impossible to argue about the goodness or badness of any law, and any definition that deters people from criticism of the law is very useful to legal apologists for the existing order of society. As a modern authority on legal reasoning declares, "Thus all things made legal are at the same time legally ethical because it is law, and the law must be deemed ethical or the system itself must perish."[77]

2. The Nature of Legal Rules and Concepts

If the functionalists are correct, the meaning of a definition is found in its consequences. The definition of a general term like "law" is significant only because it affects all our definitions of specific legal concepts.

The consequence of defining law as a function of concrete judicial decisions is that we may proceed to define such concepts as "contract," "property," "title," "corporate personality," "right," and "duty," similarly as functions of concrete judicial decisions.

The consequence of defining law as a hodge-podge of political force and ethical value ambiguously amalgamated is that every legal concept, rule or question will present a similar ambiguity.

Consider the elementary legal question: "Is there a contract?"

Felix Cohen

[76] That "right" and "wrong" are used in this definition as ethical, rather than strictly legal, terms is made clear in Blackstone's own exegesis upon his definition. COMM.* 54–55.

[77] BRUMBAUGH, LEGAL REASONING AND BRIEFING (1917), 7.

When the realist asks this question, he is concerned with the actual behavior of courts. For the realist, the contractual relationship, like law in general, is a function of legal decisions. The question of what courts *ought* to do is irrelevant here. Where there is a promise that will be legally enforced there is a contract. So conceived, any answer to the question "Is there a contract" must be in the nature of a prophecy, based, like other prophecies, upon past and present facts. So conceived, the question "Is there a contract?" or for that matter any other legal question, may be broken up into a number of subordinate questions, each of which refers to the actual behavior of courts: (1) What courts are likely to pass upon a given transaction and its consequences? (2) What elements in this transaction will be viewed as relevant and important by these courts? (3) How have these courts dealt with transactions in the past which are *similar* to the given transaction, that is, *identical in those respects which the court will regard as important?* (4) What forces will tend to compel judicial conformity to the precedents that appear to be in point (*e.g.* inertia, conservatism, knowledge of the past, or intelligence sufficient to acquire such knowledge, respect for predecessors, superiors or brothers on the bench, a habit of deference to the established expectations of the bar or the public) and how strong are these forces? (5) What factors will tend to evoke new judicial treatment for the transaction in question (*e.g.* changing public opinion, judicial idiosyncrasies and prejudices, newly accepted theories of law, society or economics, or the changing social context of the case) and how powerful are these factors?

These are the questions which a successful practical lawyer faces and answers in any case. The law, as the realistic lawyer uses the term, is the body of answers to such questions. The task of prediction involves, in itself, no judgment of ethical value. Of course, even the most cynical practitioner will recognize that the positively existing ethical beliefs of judges are material facts in any case because they determine what facts the judge will view as important and what past rules he will regard as reasonable or unreasonable and worthy of being extended or restricted. But judicial beliefs about the values of life and the ideals of society are *facts*, just as the religious beliefs of the Andaman Islanders are facts, and the truth or falsity of such moral beliefs is a matter of complete unconcern to the practical lawyer, as to the scientific observer.

Washed in cynical acid, every legal problem can thus be interpreted as a question concerning the positive behavior of judges.

There is a second and radically different meaning which can be given to our type question, "Is there a contract?" When a judge puts this question, in the course of writing his opinion, he is not attempting to predict his own behavior. He is in effect raising the question, in an obscure way, of whether or not liability *should* be attached to certain acts. This is inescapably an ethical question. What a judge ought to do in a given case is quite as much a moral issue as any of the traditional problems of Sunday School morality.[78]

It is difficult for those who still conceive of morality in other-worldly terms to recognize that every case presents a moral question to the court. But this notion has no terrors for those who think of morality in earthly terms. Morality, so conceived, is vitally concerned with such facts as human expectations based upon

---

[78] *Cf.* F. S. Cohen, *Modern Ethics and the Law* (1934) 4 BROOKLYN L. REV. 33, on the conception of "Sunday School morality."

past decisions, the stability of economic transactions, and even the maintenance of order and simplicity in our legal system. If ethical values are inherent in all realms of human conduct, the ethical appraisal of a legal situation is not to be found in the spontaneous outpourings of a sensitive conscience unfamiliar with the social context, the background of precedent, and the practices and expectations, legal and extra-legal, which have grown up around a given type of transaction.

It is the great disservice of the classical conception of law that it hides from judicial eyes the ethical character of every judicial question, and thus serves to perpetuate class prejudices and uncritical moral assumptions which could not survive the sunlight of free ethical controversy.

The Blackstonian conception of law as half-mortal and half-divine gives us a mythical conception of contract. When a master of classical jurisprudence like Williston asks the question "Is there a contract?", he has in mind neither the question of scientific prediction which the practical lawyer faces, nor the question of values which the conscientious judge faces. If he had in mind the former question, his studies would no doubt reveal the extent to which courts actually enforce various types of contractual obligation.[79] His conclusions would be in terms of probability and statistics. On the other hand, if Professor Williston were interested in the ethical aspects of contractual liability, he would undoubtedly offer a significant account of the human values and social costs involved in different types of agreements and in the means of their enforcement. In fact, however, the discussions of a Williston will oscillate between a theory of what courts actually do and a theory of what courts ought to do, without coming to rest either on the plane of social actualities or on the plane of values long enough to come to grips with significant problems. This confused wandering between the world of fact and the world of justice vitiates every argument and every analysis.

Intellectual clarity requires that we carefully distinguish between the two problems of (1) objective description, and (2) critical judgment, which classical jurisprudence lumps under the same phrase. Such a distinction realistic jurisprudence offers with the double-barreled thesis: (1) that every legal rule or concept is simply a function of judicial decisions to which all questions of value are irrelevant, and (2) that the problem of the judge is not whether a legal rule or concept actually exists but whether it *ought* to exist. Clarity on two fronts is the result. Description of legal facts becomes more objective, and legal criticism becomes more critical.

The realistic lawyer, when he attempts to discover how courts are actually dealing with certain situations, will seek to rise above his own moral bias and to discount the moral bias of the legal author whose treatise he consults.

The realistic author of textbooks will not muddy his descriptions of judicial behavior with wishful thinking; if he dislikes a decision or line of decisions, he will refrain from saying, "This cannot be the law because it is contrary to sound principle," and say instead, "This is the law, but I don't like it," or more usefully, "This rule leads to the following results, which are socially undesirable for the following reasons * * *."

Felix Cohen

[79] So hallowed is the juristic tradition of ignoring the actual facts of cases that a distinguished jurist, Professor Goodhart, can argue in all seriousness that the practice adopted by some American law libraries of putting the records of cases on file is very dangerous. Students might be distracted from the official *ratio decidendi* of the case, and might try to discover what the actual facts of the case were, which would be a death-blow to traditional jurisprudence. See Goodhart, *Determining Ratio Decidendi of a Case* (1930) 40 YALE L. J. 161, 172.

The realistic advocate, if he continues to use ritual language in addressing an unrealistic court, will at least not be fooled by his own words: he will use his "patter" to induce favorable judicial attitudes and at the same time to distract judicial attention from precedents and facts that look the wrong way (as the professional magician uses his "patter" to distract the attention of his audience from certain facts). Recognizing the circularity of conceptual argument, the realistic advocate will contrive to bring before the court the human values that favor his cause, and since the rules of evidence often stand in the way, he will perforce bring his materials to judicial attention by sleight-of-hand—through the appeal of a "sociological brief" to "judicial notice," through discussion of the background and consequences of past cases cited as precedents, through elaboration and exegesis upon admissible evidence, or even through a political speech or a lecture on economics in the summation of his case or argument.

The realistic judge, finally, will not fool himself or anyone else by basing decisions upon circular reasoning from the presence or absence of corporations, conspiracies, property rights, titles, contracts, proximate causes, or other legal derivatives of the judicial decision itself. Rather, he will frankly assess the conflicting human values that are opposed in every controversy, appraise the social importance of the precedents to which each claim appeals, open the courtroom to all evidence that will bring light to this delicate practical task of social adjustment, and consign to Von Jhering's heaven of legal concepts all attorneys whose only skill is that of the conceptual acrobat.

3. The Theory of Legal Decisions

The uses of the functional approach are not exhausted by "realistic jurisprudence." "Realistic jurisprudence," as that term is currently used,[80] is a theory of the nature of law, and therefore a theory of the nature of legal rules, legal concepts, and legal questions. Its essence is the definition of law as a function of judicial decisions. This definition is of tremendous value in the development of legal science, since it enables us to dispel the supernatural mists that envelop the legal order and to deal with the elements of the legal order in objective, scientific terms. But this process of definition and clarification is only a preliminary stage in the life of legal science. When we have analyzed legal rules and concepts as patterns of decisions, it becomes relevant to ask, "What are judicial decisions made of?"

If we conceive of legal rules and concepts as functions of judicial decisions, it is convenient, for purposes of this analysis, to think of these decisions as hard and simple facts. Just as every physical object may be analyzed as a complex of positive and negative electrons, so every legal institution, every legal rule or concept may be analyzed as a complex of plaintiff decisions and defendant decisions. But simplicity is relative to the level of analysis. For the chemist, the atom is the lowest term of analysis. But the physicist cannot stop the process of analysis with the atom or even the electron. It would be heresy to the faith of science to endow either with final simplicity and perpetual immunity from further analysis. Unfortunately, certain advocates of realistic jurisprudence, after using the functional method to break down rules and concepts into atomic decisions, refuse to

---

[80] See K. N. LLEWELLYN, *A Realistic Jurisprudence—The Next Step* (1931) 30 COLUMBIA LAW REV. 431; Pound, *The Call for a Realist Jurisprudence* (1931) 44 HARV. L. REV, 697; Llewllyn, *Some Realism; Responding to Dean Pound* (1931) 44 *Harv, L. Rev.* 1222.

go any further with the analytic process. They are willing to look upon decisions as simple unanalyzable products of judicial hunches or indigestion.

The "hunch" theory of law,[81] by magnifying the personal and accidental factors in judicial behavior, implicitly denies the relevance of significant, predictable, social determinants that govern the course of judicial decision. Those who have advanced this viewpoint have performed a real service in indicating the large realm of uncertainty in the actual law. But actual experience does reveal a significant body of predictable uniformity in the behavior of courts. Law is not a mass of unrelated decisions nor a product of judicial bellyaches. Judges are human, but they are a peculiar breed of humans, selected to a type and held to service under a potent system of governmental controls. Their acts are "judicial" only within a system which provides for appeals, rehearings, impeachments, and legislation. The decision that is "peculiar" suffers erosion—unless it represents the first salient manifestation of a new social force, in which case it soon ceases to be peculiar. It is more useful to analyze a judicial "hunch" in terms of the continued impact of a judge's study of precedents, his conversations with associates, his reading of newspapers, and his recollections of college courses, than in strictly physiological terms.

A truly realistic theory of judicial decisions must conceive every decision as something more than an expression of individual personality, as concomitantly and even more importantly a function of social forces, that is to say, as a product of social determinants and an index of social consequences. A judicial decision is a social event. Like the enactment of a Federal statute, or the equipping of police cars with radios, a judicial decision is an intersection of social forces: Behind the decision are social forces that play upon it to give it a resultant momentum and direction; beyond the decision are human activities affected by it. The decision is without significant social dimensions when it is viewed simply at the moment in which it is rendered. Only by probing behind the decision to the forces which it reflects, or projecting beyond the decision the lines of its force upon the future, do we come to an understanding of the meaning of the decision itself. The distinction between "holding" and "dictum" in any decision is not to be discovered by logical inspection of the opinion or by historical inquiry into the actual facts of the case.[82] That distinction involves us in a prediction, a prophecy of the weight that courts will give to future citations of the decision rendered. This is a question not of pure logic but of human psychology, economics and politics.

What is the meaning of a judicial decision, summed up in the words, "Judgment for the plaintiff"? Obviously, the significance of the decision, even for the parties directly involved in the case, depends upon certain predictable uniformities of official behavior, *e.g.* that a sheriff or marshall will enforce the decision, in one way or another, over a period of time, that the given decision will be respected or followed in the same court or other courts if the question at issue is relitigated, and that certain procedures will be followed in the event of an appeal, etc.

Felix Cohen

---

[81] See Hutcheson, *The Judgment Intuitive: The Function of the "Hunch" in Judicial Decisions* (1929) 14 CORN. L. Q. 274; Hutcheson, *Lawyer's Law and the Little, Small Dice* (1932) 7 TULANE L. REV. 1; FRANK, LAW AND THE MODERN MIND (1930) c. 12–13; T. Schroeder, *The Psychologic Study of Judicial Opinions* (1918) 6 CALIF. L. REV. 89.

[82] Compare the orthodox wild goose chase of Goodhart after a formula which will determine the "real" *ratio decidendi* of a case (Goodhart, *Determining the Ratio Decidendi of a Case* (1930) 40 YALE L. J. 161) with the sane description by Llewellyn of the way in which cases come to stand for propositions of narrow or wide scope. THE BRAMBLE BUSH (1930) 47, 61–66. *Cf.* also Oliphant, *A Return to Stare Decisis* (1928) 6 AM. L. SCHOOL REV. 215, 217–218; F. S. Cohen, ETHICAL SYSTEMS AND LEGAL IDEALS (1933) 33–37.

When we go beyond the merely private significance of an actual decision, we are involved in a new set of predictions concerning the extent to which other cases, similar in certain respects, are likely to receive the same treatment in the same courts or in other courts within a given jurisdiction. Except in the context of such predictions the announcement of a judicial decision is only a noise. If reasonably certain predictions of this sort could never be made, as Jerome Frank at times seems to say,[83] then all legal decisions would be simply noises, and no better grist for science than the magical phrases of transcendental jurisprudence.

If the understanding of any decision involves us necessarily in prophecy (and thus in history), then the notion of law as something that exists completely and systematically at any given moment in time is false.[84] Law is a social process, a complex of human activities, and an adequate legal science must deal with human activity, with cause and effect, with the past and the future. Legal science, as traditionally conceived, attempts to give an instantaneous snapshot of an existing and completed system of rights and duties. Within that system there are no temporal processes, no cause and no effect, no past and no future. A legal decision is thus conceived as a logical deduction from fixed principles. Its meaning is expressed only in terms of its logical consequences. A legal system, thus viewed, is as far removed from temporal activity as a system of pure geometry. In fact, jurisprudence is as much a part of pure mathematics as is algebra, unless it be conceived as a study of human behavior,—human behavior as it molds and is molded by judicial decisions. Legal systems, principles, rules, institutions, concepts, and decisions can be understood only as functions of human behavior.[85]

Such a view of legal science reveals gaps in our legal knowledge to which, I think, legal research will give increasing attention.

We are still in the stage of guesswork and accidentally collected information, when it comes to formulating the social forces which mold the course of judicial decision. We know, in a general way, that dominant economic forces play a part in judicial decision, that judges usually reflect the attitudes of their own income class on social questions, that their views on law are molded to a certain extent by their past legal experience as counsel for special interests, and that the impact of counsel's skill and eloquence is a cumulative force which slowly hammers the law into forms desired by those who can best afford to hire legal skill and eloquence; but nobody has ever charted, in scientific fashion, the extent of such economic influences.[86] We know, too, that judges are craftsmen, with aesthetic ideals,[87] concerned with the aesthetic judgments that the bar and the law schools

---

[83] See FRANK, LAW AND THE MODERN MIND (1930), 7, 53, 104–111, 132–134.

[84] In this, law is no different from other social institutions or physical objects. *Cf.* C. I. LEWIS, *op. cit. supra* note 48, c. 5.

[85] "To say that a legal institution,—private property, the federal government of the United States, Columbia University,—exists is to say that a group of persons is doing something, is acting in some way. It is to point to a particular aspect of human behavior. . . . But a legal institution is something more than the way men act on a single occasion. . . . A legal institution is the happening over and over again of the same kind of behavior." U. Moore, *loc. cit. supra* note 32.

[86] Promising first steps towards such a study have been taken in: Brooks Adams, *op. cit. supra* note 32; GUSTAVUS MYERS, HISTORY OF THE SUPREME COURT (1912); Boudin, *op. cit. supra* note 27 (1932); Walter Nelles, *Commonwealth v. Hunt* (1932) 32 COLUMBIA LAW REV. 1128; Nelles, *The First American Labor Case* (1931) 41 YALE L. J. 165; Max Lerner, *The Supreme Court and American Capitalism* (1933) 42 YALE L. J. 668; W. Hamilton, *Judicial Tolerance of Farmers' Cooperatives* (1929) 38 YALE L. J. 936; articles of Haines, Brown, and Cushman cited *supra* note 38.

[87] *Cf.* F. S. COHEN, ETHICAL SYSTEMS AND LEGAL IDEALS (1933) 56–61; *Modern Ethics and the Law* (1934) 4 BROOKLYN L. REV. 33, 48–50.

will pass upon their awkward or skillful, harmonious or unharmonious, anomalous or satisfying, actions and theories; but again we have no specific information on the extent of this aesthetic bias in the various branches of the law. We know that courts are, at least in this country, a generally conservative social force, and more like a brake than a motor in the social mechanism, but we have no scientific factual comparison of judicial, legislative, and executive organs of government, from the standpoint of social engineering. Concretely and specifically, we know that Judge So-and-so, a former attorney for a non-union shop, has very definite ideas about labor injunctions, that another judge, who has had an unfortunate sex life, is parsimonious in the fixing of alimony; that another judge can be "fixed" by a certain political "boss"; that a series of notorious kidnappings will bring about a wave of maximum sentences in kidnapping cases. All this knowledge is useful to the practicing lawyer, to the public official, to the social reformer, and to the disinterested student of society. But it is most meager, and what little of it we have, individually, is not collectively available. There is at present no publication showing the political, economic, and professional background and activities of our various judges. Such a reference work would be exceedingly valuable, not only to the practical lawyer who wants to bring a motion or try a case before a sympathetic court, but also to the disinterested student of the law. Such a Judicial Index is not published, however, because it would be disrespectable.[88] According to the classical theory, these things have nothing to do with the way courts decide cases. A witty critic of the functional approach regards it as a *reductio ad absurdum* of this approach that law schools of the future may investigate judicial psychology, teach the art of bribery, and produce graduate detectives.[89] This is far from a *reductio ad absurdum*. Our understanding of the law will be greatly enriched when we learn more about how judges think, about the exact extent of judicial corruption, and about the techniques for investigating legally relevant facts. Of course, this knowledge may be used for improper purposes, but cannot the same be said of the knowledge which traditional legal education distributes?

If we know little today of the motivating forces which mold legal decisions, we know even less of the human consequences of these decisions. We do not even know how far the appellate cases, with which legal treatises are almost exclusively concerned, are actually followed in the trial courts.[90] Here, again, the experienced practitioner is likely to have accumulated a good deal of empirical information, but the young law clerk, just out of a first-rate law school, is not even aware that such a problem exists. Likewise, the problem of the actual enforcement of judgments has received almost no critical study. Discussion of the extent to which various statutes are actually enforced regularly moves in the thin air of polemic theory. It is usually practically impossible to find out whether a given statute has ever been enforced unless its enforcement has raised a legal tangle for appellate courts.

[88] Frank reports (LAW AND THE MODERN MIND, 112–115) the discontinuance of a statistical study of the decisions of various New York magistrates which revealed startling differences in the treatment of certain offenses.

[89] Kantorowicz, *Some Rationalism about Realism* (1934) 43 YALE L. J. 1240.

[90] The Institute of Law of Johns Hopkins broke the ice in the modern study of trial court decisions. See STUDY OF CIVIL JUSTICE IN NEW YORK (1931). See also MARSHALL, STUDY OF JUDICIAL SYSTEM OF MARYLAND (1932); C. E. Clark, *Fact Research in Law Administration* (1928) 2 CONN. BAR J. 211; B. L. Shientag and F. S. Cohen, *Summary Judgments in the Supreme Court of New York* (1932) 32 COLUMBIA LAW REV. 825, and works cited therein, notes 6 and 7; Saxe, *Summary Judgments in New York—A Statistical Study* (1934) 19 CORN. L. Q. 237; B. L. Shientag, *Summary Judgment* (1935) 4 FORDHAM L. REV. 186.

When we advance beyond the realm of official conduct and seek to discover the social consequences of particular statutes or decisions, we find a few promising programs of research[91] but almost no factual studies.[92] Today the inclusion of factual annotations in a code, showing the extent and effects of law enforcement, would strike most lawyers as almost obscene. But notions of obscenity change, and every significant intellectual revolution raises to prominence facts once obscure and disrespectable. It is reasonable to expect that some day even the impudencies of Holmes and Llewellyn will appear sage and respectable.

4. Legal Criticism

It is perhaps the chief service of the functional approach that in cleansing legal rules, concepts, and institutions of the compulsive flavors of legal logic or metaphysics, room is made for conscious ethical criticism of law. In traditional jurisprudence, criticism, where it exists, is found masked in the protective camouflage of transcendental nonsense: "The law *must* (or *cannot*) be thus and so, because the *nature* of contracts, corporations or contingent remainders so requires." The functional approach permits ethics to come out of hiding. When we recognize that legal rules are simply formulae describing uniformities of judicial decision, that legal concepts likewise are patterns or functions of judicial decisions, that decisions themselves are not products of logical parthenogenesis born of pre-existing legal principles but are social events with social causes and consequences, then we are ready for the serious business of appraising law and legal institutions in terms of some standard of human values.

The importance for legal criticism of clear, objective description of judicial behavior, its causes and its consequences, is coming to be generally recognized. What is not so easily recognized is the importance for objective legal science of legal criticism.

Since the brilliant achievements of Bentham, descriptive legal science has made almost no progress in determining the consequences of legal rules.[93] This failure of scholarship, in the light of the encouraging progress of modern research into the antecedents and social context of judicial decision, calls for explanation.

Possibly this gap is to be explained in terms of an inherited assumption that statutes and decisions are self-executing, that the consequences of a law or a judgment are, therefore, clearly indicated by the language of the statute or decision

---

[91] See, for example, Pound, *The Scope and Purpose of Sociological Jurisprudence* (1911–1912) 24 Harv. L. Rev. 591, 25 *id.* 140, 489; F. K. Beutel, *Some Implications of Experimental Jurisprudence* (1934) 48 Harv. L. Rev. 169, 191–194.

[92] Notable exceptions are: McCracken, Strike Injunctions in the New South (1931); Brissenden and Swayzee, *The Use of the Labor Injunction in the New York Needle Trades* (1929) 44 Pol. Sci. Q. 548, (1930) 45 *id.* 87. In addition to these direct studies of the effects of legal rules or decisions, there is a growing literature on the social materials with which law is concerned. Examples of such work are: Pound and Frankfurter, Criminal Justice in Cleveland (1922); R. R. Powell and Looker, *Decedents' Estates: Illumination from Probate and Tax Records* (1930) 30 Columbia Law Rev. 919; Smith, Lilly and Dowling, *Compensation for Automobile Accidents: A Symposium* (1932) 32 Columbia Law Rev. 785; S. and E. T. Glueck, *Predictability in the Administration of Criminal Justice* (1929) 42 Harv. L. Rev. 297.

[93] The following spiritual exercise is recommended by Professor Kantorowicz. Let the unconverted lawyer or law student read a code of laws in the following way: "Let him ask himself with respect to each statement . . . what harms would social life undergo if instead of this statement the opposite were enacted. And then let him turn to all textbooks, commentaries, monographs and reports of decisions and see how many questions of this sort he will find answered and how many he will find even put." Rechtswissenschaft und Sociologie (1911) 8, quoted in Pound, *supra* note 91, 25 Harv. L. Rev. 489, 513.

itself, and that factual research is therefore a work of supererogation. Possibly this failure of research is to be explained in terms of the dominance of the private lawyer in our legal education. The private attorney is interested in the *causes* of judicial decisions, but his interest in consequences is likely to stop with the payment of a fee. I am inclined to think, however, that the failure of our legal scholarship in this direction may be attributed to a more fundamental difficulty. The prospect of determining the consequences of a given rule of law appears to be an infinite task, and is indeed an infinite task unless we approach it with some discriminating criterion of what consequences are *important*. Now a criterion of *importance* presupposes a criterion of values, which is precisely what modern thinkers of the "sociological" and "realistic" schools of jurisprudence have never had. Dean Pound has talked for many years of the "balancing" of interests, but without ever indicating which interests are more important than others or how a standard of weight or fineness can be constructed for the appraisal of "interests."[94] Contemporary "realists" have, in general, either denied absolutely that absolute standards of importance can exist,[95] or else insisted that we must thoroughly understand the facts as they are before we begin to evaluate them. Such a postponement of the problem of values is equivalent to its repudiation. We never shall thoroughly understand the facts as they are, and we are not likely to make much progress towards such understanding unless we at the same time bring into play a critical theory of values. In terms of such a theory, particular human desires and habits are important, and the task of research into legal consequences passes from the realm of vague curiosity to the problem form: How do these rules of law strengthen or change these important habits and satisfy or impede these important desires?

The positive task of descriptive legal science cannot, therefore, be entirely separated from the task of legal criticism. The collection of social facts without a selective criterion of human values produces horrid wilderness of useless statistics.[96] The relation between positive legal science and legal criticism is not a relation of temporal priority, but of mutual dependence.[97] Legal criticism is empty without objective description of the causes and consequences of legal decisions. Legal description is blind without the guiding light of a theory of values. It is through the union of objective legal science and a critical theory of social values that our understanding of the human significance of law will be enriched. It is loyalty to this union of distinct disciplines that will mark whatever is of lasting importance in contemporary legal science and legal philosophy.

FELIX S. COHEN
Washington, D. C.

[94] *Cf.* W. L. Grossman, *The Legal Philosophy of Roscoc Pound* (1935) 44 YALE L. J. 605, 608–611; John C. H. Wu, *The Juristic Philosophy of Roscoe Pound* (1924) 18 ILL. LAW REV. 285, 294–304.

[95] See U. Moore, *Rational Basis of Legal Institutions* (1923) 23 COLUMBIA LAW REV. 609, 612; W. Nelles, Book Review (1933) 33 COLUMBIA LAW REV. 763, 765–768.

[96] See Pound, *The Call for a Realist Jurisprudence* (1931) 44 HARV. L. REV. 697, 701.

[97] I have attempted to trace these relations in some detail in ETHICAL SYSTEMS AND LEGAL IDEALS (1933) and again, more briefly and in words of one and two syllables, in *Modern Ethics and the Law* (1934) 4 BROOKLYN L. REV. 33.

PART II

A New Order: The Legal Process, Policy, and Principle: 1940–1960

Lon L. Fuller

Lon L. Fuller

BY 1940, the realist revolt against nineteenth-century orthodoxy was complete. American jurists had lost confidence in deduction as the central tool for legal reasoning and in the ambition to unify the law by linking rules to a small set of central concepts or organizing principles. Many found this loss of confidence disturbing. It led some realists to harsh criticism of the legal establishment. Realists were in turn denounced in many quarters as nihilists, threatening to the rule of law.

Despite the discomfort, the specific criticisms of deductive reasoning developed by Holmes, Hohfeld, and the Legal Realists could not be put back in the bottle. Already in the 1930s, lawyers were routinely trained to look out for errors of deduction, for gaps, conflicts, and ambiguities in legal argument. Questions remained about what to do when a gap in the deductive chain became apparent. Through the interwar period, many legal thinkers, influenced by realist and sociological jurisprudence, continued to argue that when deduction ran out, law ran out. One should then turn things over to someone else—to the economists, or to the legislature. Others saw gaps and conflicts in the legal materials as opportunities for creativity within the legal materials—for attention by judges and jurists to social and economic realities and for pragmatic and functional thinking about the purposes of legal rules and institutions.

As lawyers made use of the specific arguments developed to unsettle the confidence of classical legal thought, the latter view prevailed—deductive gaps require juristic creativity, for which everyday legal reasoning would require new tools—tools for reasoning about what came to be called "policy," a loose umbrella for attending to social conditions, functional purposes, broad social goals, and ethical commitments. Although policy, in this broad sense, came to seem an inevitable part of American law, there was no well-developed or common repertoire of techniques for making attention to political, social, and economic purposes or functions a routine part of legal reasoning.

The most significant legal scholarship of the 1940s and 1950s sought to develop new intellectual tools for legal reasoning about policy. It did so against the background of a changed intellectual climate in the country as a whole. The pessimism about the American economic system that had marked intellectuals from the Progressive era through the Depression gave way during the Second World War to great optimism about the American marketplace and system of industrial production. At the same time, the New Deal and war experiences had given government a good name. The intellectual class had great confidence in the mixed public/private economic order that emerged from the war.

For all their skepticism about legal reasoning and attention to its internal conflicts and ambiguities, the legal realists had remained optimistic about the ability of the social sciences—particularly economics, sociology and psychology—to provide answers on questions of policy when the legal materials could not. By the end of the war, this optimism had been replaced by an intense awareness throughout the American intellectual establishment of methodological conflict and value-pluralism. The word "relativism" was suddenly everywhere, from anthropology to physics. At the same time, the realist alliance of legal skepticism and scientific faith began to seem ethically problematic. American intellectuals shared the sense that Soviet and Nazi rule had represented a new, peculiarly modern horror, facilitated, it seemed, by a politicized, instrumental, and amoral law. This new worry seemed related, if obscurely, to the attitudes of the realists: their pessimism about the American capitalist economy, their faith in science, and their enthusiastic embrace of conflict and skepticism in discussions of law and legal reasoning.

Lon Fuller's 1941 article "Consideration and Form" marks the turn both to routinize—and de-radicalize—Legal Realism, knitting it into a new mainstream way of thinking about law. The article signals the end of the methodological preoccupation with attacking the dominant "classical" legal consciousness of the late nineteenth century by foregrounding a link between the (gap-ridden) legal formalist methods of thinking and (politically retrograde) laissez-faire individualism and voluntarism. In one sense, this battle has been won. The inadequacies of deductive legal reasoning are well established, just as the New Deal's more social, solidaristic conception of American economic life had come to be accepted by the legal establishment.

At the same time, however, legal form is back. Fuller's article rehabilitates legal form—not as the antithesis of policy analysis, but as a tool for legal policymakers. In doing so, he develops a method for reasoning about even the most formal legal rules in policy terms that would become dominant in American legal thought after the Second World War.

Lon Fuller, born in 1902 in Hereford, Texas, was raised in a middle-class family in the Imperial Valley of California. His father was a bank employee who rose to become president of the El Centro National Bank. Fuller received a bachelors degree in economics from Stanford University in 1924, a JD in 1926, and immediately embarked upon an academic career as an instructor at the University of Oregon law school. He moved on to the University of Illinois in 1928, and to Duke University in 1931. After a visiting year at Harvard in 1939–40, he joined the faculty there, where he taught until his death in 1978.

Before arriving at Harvard, Fuller wrote extensively about contract law and was preoccupied with the arguments of legal realists about legal certainty. While Fuller rejected what he saw as the more extreme claims and potential consequences of legal realism, he assimilated realism's critique of legal deduction and legal conceptualism into the core of contract law doctrine. Fuller's relevance today arises from this prewar contract scholarship—"Consideration and Form" is the last piece in this series. It was here that he formulated a legal methodology for managing legal realism's transition into the mainstream of American legal thought, developing an astonishingly durable moderate sensibility and approach to legal policy.

The Harvard Law School to which Fuller moved was itself in transition, establishing itself as the site for what would become in the next decade a new mainstream consensus. Harvard Law School had long been a holdout for more formalist thinking about law—home to the tradition of Christopher Langdell, Samuel Williston, and Joseph Beale. During the 1920s and 1930s, this tradition began to soften. Roscoe Pound, who had became dean in 1916, promoted a "sociological" approach to law. James Landis and Felix Frankfurter turned the school's intellectual focus from the private common law to the expanding body of public law, federal legislation, administrative law, and regulation. But the intellectual climate remained hostile to realism—at least to what seemed the radical legal realism associated most prominently with scholars at Columbia and Yale. Pound had been a vocal critic of legal realism during the 1930s, and with Frankfurter, had made Harvard a center for resistance to realism. The result was a kind of institutional ambivalence. The Harvard faculty that hired Fuller embraced "sociological" thinking and recognized the importance of "policy," but seemed uncertain what to do with it. Fuller seemed to hold the key.

In 1934, Fuller had written an article criticizing the legal realism of Karl Llewellyn and Underhill Moore, taking issue, in particular, with Llewellyn's response to Pound's earlier criticisms of the realists. Fuller accepted a certain "scepticism" about legal rules as sensible, and saw legal certainty of various sorts as unreachable. But he warned against "carrying the crusade against 'conceptualism' too far."[1] Fuller railed against the "behavioristic psychology," "behavioristic ethical philosophy," and "positivistic" thinking he saw in realist writings. In a move reminiscent of Dewey, Fuller argued that legal concepts, laid down by legislatures or judges, may well determine situations not at all in the contemplation of those who defined and adopted them—if we think of the concept not as "a container or 'thing' at all, but an activity of the conceiving mind."[2]

For Fuller, the realists had overemphasized society and underemphasized law—precisely as their conceptualist opponents had been "too prone to think of society as mere clay in the lands of the 'Law.'"[3] Fuller argued that "most legal writers not of a particularly philosophical turn of mind" think of law as active upon an inert society—but that it is an equally "extreme view" to think that " 'society' is the active principle and that 'law' is simply a function of this principle."[4] The correct "intermediate" view—which he attributes, among others, to Cohen and Pound—is that law and society are "polar categories":

> Though we are under the necessity of opposing them to one another we must recognize that each implies the other. If we deny one, the other becomes meaningless. We may picture Law and Society as the two blades of a pair of scissors. If we watch only one blade we may conclude it does all the cutting . . . We avoid all these difficulties by the simple expedient of recognizing that both blades cut, and that neither can cut without the other.[5]

This "intermediate" position became accepted wisdom after the war—even the "pair of scissors" metaphor continued to be taught at Harvard Law School as shrewd wisdom into the 1970s. The limits of deductive reasoning and legal conceptualism were well accepted, but the crusading vision associated with legal realism had been blunted. The views which had polarized legal thought before the war no longer did so—they had been demoted to simple "positions," extremes between which wisdom would be found.

Fuller's 1934 attack on the legal realist "extremism" caught Dean Pound's attention—he termed Fuller "the coming man in jurisprudence in this country."[6] Pound wrote letters of introduction for Fuller to numerous European legal scholars when Fuller traveled to Europe in 1938, and invited him to visit Harvard after his return. When he arrived at Harvard, Fuller seemed to revel in his position betwixt and between. Although he was critical of realism's excesses, Fuller remained close to colleagues at Duke, including his good friend David Cavers, who were more directly identified with realism. He styled himself a fellow traveler to all but what he took to be the most extreme elements of the realist revolution. In 1939, he wrote a very critical review of Williston's contracts treatise, and decided to use Corbin's realist-inspired casebook instead in his Harvard classroom—and yet was pleased and surprised when Williston nevertheless welcomed him warmly to Cambridge.[7] Fuller exuberantly described his role as house-sceptic at Harvard in a 1940 letter to his former Duke colleague C. Lowndes: "I have never taught in any school where I was more free from the fear that I might lead the students too far down the paths of realism and juristic nihilism. There is not much on the other end of the scales here, and I can throw my own little counters on my end and listen to them ring with unadulterated joy."[8]

For all Fuller's ambivalence, even sympathy, with legal realism's attention to social reality and purpose, Fuller's first book-length work of jurisprudence, *The Law in Quest of Itself*, published in 1941 (written in close conversation with both David Cavers and Henry Hart), was seen as a polemic against realism, in part because it emphasized the need for a strong moral sensibility in legal reasoning. The realists had expressed their commitment to social solidarity in the language of facts—social scientific deductions from the needs and nature of an increasingly interdependent society. Fuller insisted on the inseparability of the moral "ought" from the normative "is." Law was not simply a prediction of judicial behavior, in Holmes's sense. Deduction from social facts was no more satisfying than nineteenth-century deduction from legal concepts—or positivist exegesis of a legislative text. Law was rather a complex congeries of the norms which are and the norms which ought to be. Reasoning about law must attend to the moral ought. The book was extremely well received—and criticized—as an antidote to instrumental thinking about law, at once a defense of anti-conceptual and anti-formal awareness of the limits of deduction and a brief for the importance of social values and customary normative processes.

In his prewar contracts scholarship, Fuller translated this vision into detailed doctrinal analysis. In "Consideration and Form," Fuller analyzes the doctrine of "consideration": the contracts law rule that only promises accompanied by a legal detriment to the promisee, bargained in exchange for the promise, are enforceable. Consideration doctrine was widely understood as the quintessential example of legal form: the legal detriment to the promisee could be merely formal. You can sell me your home for a peppercorn—but your promise to give me your home, absent the peppercorn, is not enforceable.

Through the lens of Legal Realism, it would be easy to see consideration doctrine as a historical vestige of the more formal nineteenth century, suitable for abolition—along with the forms of action—as the law is modernized. At the same time, consideration seemed a perfect expression of the nineteenth-century "will theory" of contract, deducible from the voluntarist commitment that contracts express party autonomy and be rooted in consent. For the realists, it would have been easy to unravel the deductive chain from party autonomy, if only because consideration doctrine had become a complex welter of specific rules whose outcome, as applied, was often precisely what the parties had not, in fact, intended.

In defending consideration doctrine, Fuller does not defend the will theory. Neither does he argue that the will theory as a whole needs be set aside as incoherent or yield in the face of more powerful social needs. He is simply not concerned to defend—or refute—the effort to identify broad concepts, like "will" or "autonomy," from which rules can be deduced. He never asks, for example, whether consideration might be part of what it "means" to have a "bargained for exchange," or of what is required by a voluntarist system of contractual freedom. Nor does he defend—or castigate—the doctrine's common-law pedigree. Indeed, the fact that consideration doctrine has been a well-established part of the common law of contracts seems irrelevant to understanding its significance. Nineteenth-century historicism and conceptualism are simply irrelevant—but legal forms need not therefore be abolished. Instead, he argues that consideration makes sense to the extent it expresses one or another of a series of underlying formal and substantive "policies."

To make this assessment in particular cases, Fuller develops a list of formal and substantive "policies" which he sees as the purposes and justification for all contract law doctrines, consideration included. To determine whether any particular detail in the elaborate edifice of consideration doctrine merits abolition or retention, one must investigate whether, on balance, that doctrinal detail furthers or impedes one or another combination of these policies. The policies Fuller lists are themselves significant, and became touchstones for understanding the social functions of contract law more generally in the ensuing years.

More significantly, however, Fuller inaugurates a new method of legal reasoning—a way of understanding what it could mean to say, after realism, that "policy" should be at the center of legal analysis. He identifies not one, but a list of related policies, immanent in the common law rather than expressed in statute or imported from the neighboring humanist or social scientific disciplines of economics, psychology, sociology, or philosophy. And he proposes that each doctrine, in each application, will represent an ad hoc amalgam of different—even conflicting—policies, whose particular significance and net direction can only be assessed on a case-by-case, doctrine-by-doctrine basis.

This approach to policy analysis was innovative in several ways. Prior legal scholars had tended to treat "policy" as a kind of trump card or exceptional gap filler. Normally, jurists could proceed by reference to precedent and by tracing the implications of broad concepts like "will" or "consent." Policy would only be needed in exceptional cases, where precedent was unclear or ran out, or where the social interests were overwhelming—where an outrageous injustice would otherwise be done. Jurists might disagree about how many gaps there were, or how often social needs should trump existing rules, but they by and large shared this "rule-exception" frame of understanding. For Fuller, this approach misunderstood the significance of legal policies.

Although Fuller had criticized Williston for failing to inquire into the underlying bases for contract liability in the "social interests they serve," he also criticized the legal realists for treating social needs and interests as *external to* and *determinative of* legal doctrine. To Fuller, policy was not something that kicked in as a limit on the scope of private-law rules, justifying exceptions, or providing an alternative source of judicial authority in cases when rules conflicted or seemed to have gaps. Policies did not come from an alternative universe; they were immanent in law, in the rules as much as in the exceptions. Moreover, policies were not at all clear—contract law served several functions, which were often in conflict. Too often, Fuller argued, legal realists had acted as if once one was in the domain of policy, it was clear what to do—social needs spoke with a single voice. For Fuller, treating the "facts" of an interdependent social life, or the "needs" and "functions" of a modern economy as requiring particular rules or judicial decisions—deducing an ought from an is—is no more satisfactory than deducing doctrines from precedent or the "will theory." Rather, he argues, policy analysis requires nuanced reasoning about the appropriate weight to be given to various policies in particular cases and when interpreting particular rules.

The most famous doctrinal argument in "Consideration and Form" was Fuller's insistence that an "objective" approach to measuring the consent of a contracting party is fully compatible with the "principle of private autonomy." In classical legal thought, the voluntarist "will theory" of contract had logically seemed to require subjective measures of consent—a "meeting of the minds"— for the enforcement of contract. An "objective" approach to contractual consent seemed a sharp departure from the will theory, imposing contractual liability where parties had not "willed" it. By the time Fuller wrote, this approach had been widely criticized both for its logical incoherence and for its departure from the needs of a socially interdependent, relational market world. Fuller shared in the already common rejection of the idea that the will theory requires a subjective approach.

Rather, Fuller replaces the will theory, which aspired to be a complete theory of all of contract, with the more modest principle or policy of "private autonomy." He acknowledges that this principle may sometimes be undercut by an objective test of a party's will, but it may also sometimes be promoted by an objective approach, which can offer a reliable method for making known one's intention. Moreover, the principle of private autonomy is but one of several policies which might bear on the decision to adopt an objective approach. Contract law serves a mix of substantive and formal policies. It might often be the case that the balance of these policies would favor an objective approach, even if at some detriment to the principle of private autonomy. At the same time, the principle of "private autonomy" cannot simply be overruled by social necessity. The social interests served by contract are represented by other policies immanent in contract law, which must be weighed, balanced, and compromised with private autonomy.

The result is not a new "theory" of consideration doctrine, let alone of contract law or the importance of "form" more generally, but a mode of thinking about the endless series of particular doctrinal choices that make up a contract law regime, one at a time. Like an objective approach to contract more generally, consideration doctrine may overrule a party's subjective intention, releasing people from intended bargains where consideration—the peppercorn—is absent or holding people to bargains where consideration is deemed to be present even where that was not what they had thought would happen. But the result is not a battle between the "will theory" and "social necessity." Rather, Fuller presents consideration as potentially serving a blend of various policies, most prominently what he terms the formal policies promoting caution in contracting, providing evidence of the transaction, and channeling private behavior. In specific cases, a judge will need to weigh these formal policies carefully, balancing them not only against one another, but also against the various substantive principles—respecting private autonomy, protecting reliance and preventing unjust enrichment—immanent in contract law as a whole. It will not be clear in advance which policies, let alone which types of policies, will prevail.

In replacing large-scale *theories* of contract, whether rooted in will or social needs, with a mode of reasoning about the applicability of various policies in particular cases, Fuller illustrates themes which become common in postwar American legal thought more generally. The particular formal policies he elaborates—providing evidence of the parties' agreement, ensuring that they pause to deliberate, and offering a channel for parties to organize their behavior—focus

Lon L. Fuller

on the communicative functions of law, and figure law as facilitative, rather than regulatory, of private social ordering. In a passage that remains frustratingly ambivalent in its import, Fuller stresses the importance of investigating whether private ordering alone is sufficient before determining what law might add, for "[w]here life has already organized itself effectively, there is no need for the law to intervene" (p. 806). The word "effectively" does a great deal of work in that sentence—should we judge the effectiveness of social organization by its outcomes or its forms? Nevertheless, it is clear that Fuller neither offers a theory of the rules which facilitate efficient contracting, in the style of some later law and economics scholars, nor insists on the necessity of making political choices about distributive justice, in the style of later progressive scholars, as well as earlier legal realists in the tradition of Robert Hale. What he has in mind is a vague set of sociological observations about how commercial life operates, and about the exceptional circumstances in which bargaining power or party sophistication may require an extra bit of "channeling" or "cautioning" from the doctrinal regime. His paradigmatic example of a situation in which social life fails to "channel" the parties effectively is the "negotiations between a house-to-house book salesman and the housewife" (p. 806).

Fuller was optimistic that reasoning about policies in the manner he illustrated in "Consideration and Form" would solve problems of interpretation that seemed to present an intractable opposition between old theories about contract and new social or economic realities. He closes the article with these words:

> What needs abolition is not the doctrine of consideration but a conception of legal method which assumes that the doctrine can be understood and applied without reference to the ends it serves. When we have come again to define consideration in terms of its underlying policies the problem of adapting it to new conditions will largely solve itself.[9]

As subsequent judicial experience and legal scholarship would reveal, the difficulties in pursuing the type of policy analysis suggested in "Consideration and Form" were legion. Policies proliferated, their ambit remained vague, "weighing and balancing" are poor metaphors for resolving conflict among commitments with significant distributive consequences, a range of significant interests and views consistently seemed excluded from the analysis, the analytics often seemed circular, conclusory, or vague. But these problems lay in the future. In 1941, Fuller was confident that once we recognized the uselessness of searching for *a* theory, and began inquiring systematically into the details of social purpose, interest, and policy, society's difficulties would be in good hands.

In April 1942, as Harvard Law School reduced its operations for the duration of the Second World War, Fuller left full-time teaching to join the Boston law firm of Ropes and Gray. He returned to full-time teaching in 1945, but the war years in practice—and the move to Harvard—marked a sharp break in Fuller's intellectual work. After the war, Fuller's attention turned from contract law to legal philosophy. Jurisprudential eclecticism and moderation were on the move, and Fuller was becoming renowned for his opposition to positivism, to the formalism of nineteenth-century American legal thought, and to the instrumentalism he associated with Legal Realism. He was coming to be associated with the words "purpose," "value," and "morality," and to be seen as a leading voice for philosophical moderation. Fuller was a central player at Harvard in the postwar years, holding a variety of administrative assignments, including chairmanship of the graduate program, and overseeing renovation of the Harvard curriculum to emphasize planning, attention to facts, and arbitration alongside the traditional focus on litigation and appellate judging. Fuller was chairman of the Committee on Legal Education at Harvard from 1944 to 1947, and oversaw the curricular modernization which expanded the elective offerings after the first year, moved legal theory into the first year more explicitly, and in general sought to shift away from the study of appellate decision making to client counseling, planning, and efforts to avoid litigation. He wrote and lectured about legal education. In 1946, Fuller described his "conception of the lawyer's task" with a parable indicative of the centrist political sympathies and belief in social compromise he sought to institutionalize through revision of the curriculum at Harvard:

> In the field of labor relations, there often seems to be an irreconcilable conflict between two interests: the interest of management in industrial efficiency (which is also an interest of society), and the interest of the worker in human dignity and the right not to be pushed around. (This interest is also one of society as well as of the worker.)
>
> . . . [W]ith patience, with insight, with hard intellectual labor, one will find that there is an arrangement what will avoid the . . . conflict . . . or reduce it to negligible propositions, without breaking the circle. The worker can be protected against indignities in ways that do not reduce, too much, industrial efficiency; there are ways of promoting industrial efficiency which do not involve pushing the worker around.
>
> This is the kind of job in which the lawyer, properly trained excels. He it is who has the detachment that is the first essential for the task. With this he combines the imagination and the capacity for analysing the factors in the situation that are equally indispensable. Lawyers representing both management and labor have made important contributions to this task.[10]

Long a Democrat—and an early enthusiast for Roosevelt's tilt toward intervention in Europe—Fuller had become increasingly sceptical about the New Deal's regulatory and administrative interventions and an advocate of private ordering. He eventually left the Democratic Party to become active in Richard Nixon's 1960 presidential campaign, perhaps nudged along by Nixon having been his student at Duke. After Nixon's defeat, he held himself increasingly aloof from national politics.

After the war, save a short reaction to Robert Hale's 1952 book *Freedom Through Law*, Fuller turned to debate with legal philosophers who he felt were unduly positivist, instrumentalist, or otherwise insensitive to the ethical purposes of law. His found his most significant opponents abroad, in Britain, most famously in a decade-long debate with H.L.A. Hart. Fuller remained an ardent proponent of the significance of "purpose" and "value" for law making and interpretation, and engaged in a series of polemical exchanges with H.L.A. Hart and others on the subject, and on the limits of positivism, through the 1950s and 1960s. By the late 1950s, Fuller's resistance to whatever he associated with positivism, behavioralism, and instrumentalism and his insistence on the moral content of law, all placed him increasingly on the defensive. His position came increasingly to be honored for its own sense of purpose and moral virtue, rather than for its persuasive power or jurisprudential significance. Nevertheless, Fuller became famous as a defender of law as a purposive and ethical endeavor, and as a secular proponent of a kind of natural law, rooted in social behavior and custom.

Throughout the postwar period, he continued his engagement with arbitration and private practice. He remained close to Henry Hart, and became a collaborator in Hart and Al Sacks's work on the legal process. His most significant independent contribution to legal process thinking was an essay widely circulated in draft among his students and published posthumously under the title "The Forms and Limits of Adjudication." In it, he developed arguments about the competence of institutions in the legal system—particularly courts—that were parallel to those he developed for various doctrines within contract law. Judicial institutions served a range of social purposes, and "the distinguishing characteristic of adjudication lies in the fact that it confers on the affected party a peculiar form of participation in the decision, that of presenting proofs and reasoned arguments for a decision in his favor."[11] He offers his own articulation of the Hart and Sacks conception of "reasoned elaboration": "Adjudication is . . . a device which gives formal and institutional expression to the influence of reasoned argument in human affairs. As such it assumes a burden of rationality not borne by any other form of social ordering. A decision which is the product of reasoned argument must be prepared itself to meet the test of reason."[12] Courts, in other words, are particularly well suited to performing the kind of balanced analysis of policy and purpose he had promoted for interpreting doctrines like consideration.

Fuller's experiences at Ropes and Gray—negotiating collective bargaining agreements, arguing before the War Labor Board, and participating in labor arbitrations—and his work as an arbitrator throughout his later academic career strengthened his interest in the legal norms that arose from social and business relations, and in the attorney's role in planning, contracting, mediating, and arbitrating rather than in litigating and legislating. He remained an enthusiast for the market as a social organizing mechanism, and for private ordering processes and the norms which emerged from customary practices and interactions. Fuller returned repeatedly to the significance of these social norms and institutions, and promoted study of the limits of social ordering when thinking about all legal processes. He coined the term "eunomics"—never picked up—to refer to the "science of social ordering." In the 1960s and 1970s, Fuller taught advanced seminars on law and social change in Africa and the sociology of law, and became increasingly interested in anthropology and law.

Fuller's most well-known contribution to jurisprudence in the 1950s and 1960s was "The Case of the Speluncean Explorers," a series of imaginary opinions by judges in a fictitious case illustrating the influence of different jurisprudential ideas on judicial decision styles. Comparing the results of various styles led the reader to appreciate the virtues of attention to purpose and intent, rather than textual exegesis. By the time of its publication, the article reflected a broad consensus among legal scholars—principle, purpose, and policy had long since replaced deduction. Although the article's empathetic presentation of a range of judicial styles seemed to reflect Fuller's own admirably eclectic mind, the range of positions would soon be made to seem narrow and Fuller's own reasoning about purpose and policy muddled and unpersuasive, by the arrival of new schools of thought influenced by economics, sociology, literature, and social theory.

DAVID KENNEDY

1. Lon L. Fuller, "American Legal Realism," 82 *University of Pennsylvania Law Review* 429 (1934), p. 443.

2. Ibid., p. 447.

3. Ibid., p. 451.

4. Ibid. p. 451–52.

5. Ibid., p. 452.

6. Quoted in Robert S. Summers, *Lon L. Fuller* (Stanford: Stanford University Press, 1984), at 5, from Harvard Law School Library, Lon L. Fuller Papers, R. Pound to Fuller, Jan. 10, 1938.

7. *Id.* at 5.

8. As quoted in Summers, *Lon L. Fuller*, at 6, from Lon L. Fuller Papers, Harvard Law School Library, letter to C. Laundes, April 15, 1940.

9. Fuller, "Consideration and Form," p. 824.

10. Lon Fuller, "Objectives of Legal Education, Remarks before the Yale Law School Forum on Legal Education, December 4, 1946," 2 *The Record of the Association of the Bar of the City of New York* 120 (1947), at 121–2.

11. Lon L. Fuller, "The Forms and Limits of Adjudication," 92 *Harvard Law Review* 353, 364 (1978).

12. Id. at 366–7.

BIBLIOGRAPHY

Lon L. Fuller

Lon Fuller's most significant early theoretical work, preceding "Consideration and Form," includes: Lon Fuller, "Legal Fictions," 25 *Illinois Law Review*, 363 (1930–31); "American Legal Realism," 82 *University of Pennsylvania Law Review* 429 (1934); and *The Law in Quest of Itself* (Evanston, Ill. Northwestern: University Press, 1940). The 1934 article on legal realism was reprinted in the *Proceedings of the American Philosophical Society* 76 (2): 1936 at 191, which awarded Fuller the "Henry M. Phillips Prize in Jurisprudence" in 1935 for his work in jurisprudence, culminating in this piece. For Roscoe Pound's own criticism of legal realism, see "The Call for a Realist Jurisprudence," 44 *Harvard Law Review* 697 (1931), to which Llewellyn responded with "Some Realism About Realism: Responding to Dean Pound," 44 *Harvard Law Review* 1222 (1931).

In the field of contracts, Fuller's other famous works were written with William Perdue: Lon Fuller and William R. Perdue, Jr., "The Reliance Interest in Contract Damages," 46 *Yale Law Journal* 52–96 and 373–420 (1936–37). These articles remain classics of contracts scholarship, a status affirmed and evaluated in Todd Rakoff, "Fuller and Perdue's *The Reliance Interest* as a Work of Legal Scholarship," 1991 *Wisconsin Law Review* 203 (1991). Rakoff praises Fuller for having made "the epistemological doubts of the twentieth century" (p. 245) compatible with legal analysis by inaugurating a style of analysis that stressed fine distinctions of "most" and "least" on a continuum rather than of absolute rights or doctrinal deductions. For Fuller's criticism of Williston's contracts treatise, see: Lon Fuller, "Williston on Contracts" 18 *North Carolina Law Review* 1 (1939).

Fuller's most significant postwar works of legal theory include: Lon Fuller, *The Morality of Law*, rev. ed. (New Haven: Yale University Press, 1964) and Lon Fuller, "The Case of the Speluncean Explorers," 62 *Harvard Law Review* 616 (1949).

Admirers of Fuller's effort have periodically sought to update the Speluncean Explorers to broaden the range of positions. See, for example, Anthony D'Amato, "The Speluncean Explorers—Further Proceedings," 32 *Stanford Law Review* 467 (1980); William Eskridge, "The Case of the Speluncean Explorers: Twentieth-Century Statutory Interpretation in a Nutshell," 61: 6 *George Washington Law Review* 1731 (1993); and Peter Suber, *The Case of the Speluncean Explorers: Nine New Opinions* (New York and London: Routledge Press, 1998).

Fuller's most significant contribution to legal process thought (see chapter *infra*) remains: Lon L. Fuller and Kenneth I. Winston, "The Forms and Limits of Adjudication," 92 *Harvard Law Review* 353 (1978). Fuller's most well-known texts about social ordering and law are: Lon Fuller, *The Principles of Social Order* (published posthumously) (Durham, N. C.: Duke University Press, 1981); "Some Unexplored Social Dimensions of the Law," in *Path of the Law from 1967*, ed. Arthur E. Sutherland (Cambridge, Mass.: Harvard University Press, 1968); "The Law's Precarious Hold on Life," 3 *Georgia Law Review* 530 (1969); "Human Interaction and the Law," 14 *American Journal of Jurisprudence* 1 (1969); and "Law as an Instrument of Social Control and Law as a Facilitation of Human Interaction," *Archiv für Rechts- und Sozialphilosophie* 8 Beilage Neue Folge (1974).

Fuller's attitudes toward the market and political liberalism are well articulated in "Some Reflections on Legal and Economic Freedoms—A Review of Robert L. Hale's 'Freedom Through Law,'" 54 *Columbia Law Review* 70 (1954); and "Freedom—A Suggested Analysis," 68 *Harvard Law Review* 1302 (1955).

Fuller essays on legal education include "Objectives of Legal Education," 2 *Record of the New York City Bar Association* 120 (1947); "What the Law Schools Can Contribute to the Making of Lawyers," 1 *Journal of Legal Education* 189 (1948); "The Place and Uses of Jurisprudence in the Law School Curriculum," 1 *Journal of Legal Education* 495 (1948); and "On Teaching Law," 3 *Stanford Law Review* 616 (1949).

Commentary

A standard, and sympathetic, biography and elaboration of Fuller's main ideas is Robert S. Summers, *Lon L. Fuller* (Stanford, Calif.: Stanford University Press, 1984).

The leading analysis of Fuller's contribution to American Legal Thought—on which we have relied heavily in this brief introduction—is by his current successor as Carter Professor of General Jurisprudence at Harvard, Duncan Kennedy. See Duncan Kennedy, "From the Will Theory to the Principle of Private Autonomy: Lon Fuller's 'Consideration and Form,'" 100 *Columbia Law Review* 94 (2000). Kennedy treats Fuller as having inaugurated what he terms the method of "conflicting considerations" jurisprudence, in which "every rule *can be understood* as representing a choice in the colloquial lawyers' sense of a 'policy question,'" in a way which can be resolved by "balancing conflicting considerations" which can be "formal, substantive, and institutional" (94). For Kennedy, twentieth-century American private law traces a tragic arc from the coherent and integrated "will theory" of late nineteenth-century "classical legal thought" to the modern disintegrated and eclectic project of ad hoc rationalization and justification. In this "death of reason" story, Fuller demotes the "will theory" to one substantive policy among many, and opens the way to a mode of legal reasoning in which diverse substantive and formal polities, including the "principle of autonomy," will be "balanced" against one another in an increasingly unsystematic fashion. Kennedy describes the different modes Fuller's predecessors had used to escape the iron grip of the will theory and invigorate policy and attention to social needs and interests—and isolates Fuller's specific contribution with precision. For an analysis of the contribution of Fuller's particular trio of substantive policies—private autonomy, protecting reliance, and preventing unjust enrichment—to the history of American thinking about the substantive basis for contract law, and an assessment of their continuing status as one among several ideas about "what is really going on" in contract law, see Duncan Kennedy, supra, note 3 at 140 and following.

For a fascinating analysis of the differences between Fuller's early private-law scholarship and his postwar jurisprudential comments on public law, as well as of the relationship between Fuller and the Legal Process school of the 1950s, see James Boyle, "Legal Realism and the Social Contract: Fuller's Public Jurisprudence of Form, Private Jurisprudence of Substance," 78 *Cornell Law Review* 371 (1993).

For a recent collection of articles "rediscovering" Fuller, see Willem J. Witteveen and Wibren van der Burg, *Rediscovering Fuller: Essays on Implicit Law and Institutional Design* (Amsterdam: Amsterdam University Press, 1999) including essays by Philip Selznick, David Dyzenhaus, Frederick Schauer, David Luban, Gerald Postema, Roderick Macdonald, Joseph Vining, and others.

An interesting interpretation of the relationship between Fuller and Dewey is Philip Selznick, review of Lon Fuller, *Anatomy of the Law* (New York: Frederick A. Praeger, 1968) in 83 *Harvard Law Review* 1474 (1970).

For commentary on Fuller's contribution to contract law, see Philip Atiyah, "Book Review: The Principles of Social Order: Selected Essays of Lon L. Fuller edited with an Introduction by Kenneth I. Winston," in 1983 *Duke Law Journal* 669; Todd D. Rakoff, "Fuller and Perdue's *The Reliance Interest* as a Work of Legal Scholarship," 1991 *Wisconsin Law Review* 203 (1991).

For an excellent general treatment of the reaction to realism, see Edward A. Purcell, Jr., *The Crisis of Democratic Theory: Scientific Naturalism and the Problem of Value* (Lexington: University Press of Kentucky, 1973).

Fuller was not the only scholar seeking to improve the vocabulary used to analyze law as an instrument of "policy." Among others, Harold Lasswell and Myres McDougal at Yale Law School were developing an elaborate framework for rethinking law as a set of policy commitments. See generally, Lasswell and McDougal, "Legal Education and Public Policy: Professional Training in the Public Interest," 52 *Yale Law Journal* 203 (1943). See also the legal process scholars cited after Hart & Sacks' chapter.

"Consideration and Form"

41 Columbia Law Review 799 (1941)

§ 1. *Introduction.*—What is attempted in this article is an inquiry into the rationale of legal formalities, and an examination of the common-law doctrine of consideration in terms of its underlying policies. That such an investigation will
reveal a significant relationship between consideration and form is a proposition
not here suggested for the first time; indeed the question has been raised (and
sometimes answered affirmatively) whether consideration cannot in the end be
reduced entirely to terms of form.

That consideration may have both a "formal" and a "substantive" aspect is
apparent when we reflect on the reasons which have been advanced why promises
without consideration are not enforced. It has been said that consideration is "for
the sake of evidence" and is intended to remove the hazards of mistaken or perjured testimony which would attend the enforcement of promises for which nothing is given in exchange.[1] Again, it is said that enforcement is denied gratuitous
promises because such promises are often made impulsively and without proper
deliberation.[2] In both these cases the objection relates, not to the content and effect
of the promise, but to the manner in which it is made. Objections of this sort, which
touch the form rather than the content of the agreement, will be removed if the
making of the promise is attended by some formality or ceremony, as by being
under seal. On the other hand, it has been said that the enforcement of gratuitous
promises is not an object of sufficient importance to our social and economic order
to justify the expenditure of the time and energy necessary to accomplish it.[3] Here
the objection is one of "substance" since it touches the significance of the promise
made and not merely the circumstances surrounding the making of it.

The task proposed in this article is that of disentangling the "formal" and "substantive" elements in the doctrine of consideration. Since the policies underlying the
doctrine are generally left unexamined in the decisions and doctrinal discussions, it
will be necessary to postpone taking up the common-law requirement itself until we
have examined in general terms the formal and substantive bases of contract liability.

A number of friends and colleagues read the manuscript of this article at various stages of its preparation and
made valuable criticisms and suggestions. I am especially indebted to Karl Llewellyn, Benno Schmidt, Malcolm
Sharp, Daniel Boorstin, Douglas Maggs, and David Cavers.

[1] Mansfield, C. J., in Pillans v. Van Mierop, 3 Burr. 1663, 1669, 97 Eng. Rep. 1035, 1038 (K.B. 1765);
Sharington v. Strotton, 1 Plow. 297a, 302, 75 Eng. Rep. 454, 459–60 (K.B. 1565) (argument of counsel);
Whittier, *The Restatement of Contracts and Consideration* (1930) 18 CALIF. L. REV. 611, 613.

[2] Wilmot, J., in Pillans v. Van Mierop, 3 Burr. 1663, 1670, 97 Eng. Rep. 1035, 1038 (K. B. 1765); Sharington
v. Strotton, 1 Plow. 297a, 308, 75 Eng. Rep. 454, 469 (K.B. 1565) (argument of counsel); Davis v. Morgan, 117
Ga. 504, 507, 43 S.E. 732, 733 (1903); Ames, *Two Theories of Consideration* (1899) 13 HARV. L. REV. 29, 42;
Ballantine, *The Source of Obligation in Bilateral Contracts* (1916) 3 VA. L. REV. 432, 437; Whittier, *The
Restatement of Contracts and Consideration* (1930) 18 CALIF. L. REV. 611, 613.

[3] Ballantine, *Mutuality and Consideration* (1914) 28 HARV. L. REV. 121; Willis, *Rationale of the Law of
Contracts* (1936) 11 IND. L. J. 227, 230; Davis v. Morgan, 117 Ga. 504, 507, 43 S.E. 732, 733 (1903).

I. The Functions Performed by Legal Formalities[4]

§2. *The Evidentiary Function.*—The most obvious function of a legal formality is, to use Austin's words, that of providing "evidence of the existence and purport of the contract, in case of controversy." The need for evidentiary security may be satisfied in a variety of ways: by requiring a writing, or attestation, or the certification of a notary. It may even be satisfied, to some extent, by such a device as the Roman *stipulatio,* which compelled an oral spelling out of the promise in a manner sufficiently ceremonious to impress its terms on participants and possible bystanders.

§3. *The Cautionary Function.*—A formality may also perform a cautionary or deterrent function by acting as a check against inconsiderate action. The seal in its original form fulfilled this purpose remarkably well. The affixing and impressing of a wax wafer—symbol in the popular mind of legalism and weightiness—was an excellent device for inducing the circumspective frame of mind appropriate in one pledging his future. To a less extent any requirement of a writing, of course, serves the same purpose, as do requirements of attestation, notarization, etc.

§4. *The Channeling Function.*—Though most discussions of the purposes served by formalities go no further than the analysis just presented, this analysis stops short of recognizing one of the most important functions of form. That a legal formality may perform a function not yet described can be shown by the seal. The seal not only insures a satisfactory memorial of the promise and induces deliberation in the making of it. It serves also to mark or signalize the enforceable promise; it furnishes a simple and external test of enforceability. This function of form Ihering described as "the facilitation of judicial diagnosis," and he employed the analogy of coinage in explaining it.

> Form is for a legal transaction what the stamp is for a coin. Just as the stamp of the coin relieves us from the necessity of testing the metallic content and weight—in short, the value of the coin (a test which we could not avoid if uncoined metal were offered to us in payment), in the same way legal formalities relieve the judge of an inquiry *whether* a legal transaction was intended, and—in case different forms are fixed for different legal transactions—*which* was intended.[5]

In this passage it is apparent that Ihering has placed an undue emphasis on the utility of form for the judge, to the neglect of its significance for those transacting

Lon L. Fuller

---

[4] On the general problem of the rationale of legal formalities see Austin, *Fragments-On Contracts,* printed in 2 LECTURES ON JURISPRUDENCE (4ᵗʰ ed. 1879) 939–944; Llewellyn, *What Price Contract?* (1931) 40 YALE L. J. 704; Mechem, *The Requirement of Delivery in Gifts of Chattels* (1926–1927) 21 ILL. L. REV. 341, 457, 568; Bentham, *The Rationale of Judicial Evidence,* printed in 6 WORKS, (Bowring's ed. 1839) 64–86, 508–585; Chafee, *Acceleration Provisions in Time Paper* (1919) 32 HARV. L. REV. 747, 750; Sharp, *Promissory Liability, II.* (1940) 7 UNIV. OF CHI. L. REV. 250, 252 and *passim;* 3 SAVIGNY, SYSTEM DES HEUTIGEN RÖMISCHEN RECHTS (1840) § 130; 2 *Savigny,* OBLIGATIONENRECHT (1853) § 74; II² IHERING, GEIST DES RÖMISCHEN RECHTS (8ᵗʰ ed. 1923) §§ 45–47d; 3 GÉNY, SCIENCE ET TECHNIQUE (1921) §§ 202–206; DEMOGUE, LES NOTIONS FONDAMENTALES DU DROIT PRIVÉ (1911) 63–87; 1 DEMOGUE, TRAITÉ DES OBLIGATIONS EN GÉNÉRAL (1923) §§ 191–212; 1 KOHLER, LEHRBUCH DES BÜRGERLICHEN RECHTS (1906) §§ 235–237; Huber, *Formen im schweizerischen Privatrecht* (1911); in Heft 58, GMÜR, ABHANDLUNGEN ZUM SCHWEIZERISCHEN RECHT (1914) 79–126.

[5] II² GEIST DES RÖMISCHEN RECHTS (8ᵗʰ ed. 1923) 494. Cf., "In all legal systems the effort is to find definite marks which shall at once include the promises which ought to be enforceable, exclude those which ought not to be, and signalize those which will be." Llewellyn, *What Price Contract?* (1931) 40 YALE L. J. 704, 738.

business out of court. If we look at the matter purely from the standpoint of the convenience of the judge, there is nothing to distinguish the forms used in legal transactions from the "formal" element which to some degree permeates all legal thinking. Even in the field of criminal law "judicial diagnosis" is "facilitated" by formal definitions, presumptions, and artificial constructions of fact. The thing which characterizes the law of contracts and conveyances is that in this field forms are deliberately used, and are intended to be so used, by the parties whose acts are to be judged by the law. To the businessman who wishes to make his own or another's promise binding, the seal was at common law available as a device for the accomplishment of his objective. In this aspect form offers a legal framework into which the party may fit his actions, or, to change the figure, it offers channels for the legally effective expression of intention. It is with this aspect of form in mind that I have described the third function of legal formalities as "the channeling function."

In seeking to understand this channeling function of form, perhaps the most useful analogy is that of language, which illustrates both the advantages and dangers of form in the aspect we are now considering. One who wishes to communicate his thoughts to others must force the raw material of meaning into defined and recognizable channels; he must reduce the fleeting entities of wordless thought to the patterns of conventional speech. One planing to enter a legal transaction faces a similar problem. His mind first conceives an economic or sentimental objective, or, more usually, a set of overlapping objectives. He must then, with or without the aid of a lawyer, cast about for the legal transaction (written memorandum, sealed contract, lease, conveyance of the fee, etc.) which will most nearly accomplish these objectives. Just as the use of language contains dangers for the uninitiated, so legal forms are safe only in the hands of those who are familiar with their effects. Ihering explains that the extreme formalism of Roman law was supportable in practice only because of the constant availability of legal advice, *gratis*.

The ideal of language would be the word whose significance remained constant and unaffected by the context in which it was used. Actually there are few words, even in scientific language, which are not capable of taking on a nuance of meaning because of the context in which they occur. So in the law, the ideal type of formal transaction would be the transaction described on the Continent as "abstract," that is, the transaction which is abstracted from the causes which gave rise to it and which has the same legal effect no matter what the context of motives and lay practices in which it occurs. The seal in its original form represented an approach to this ideal, for it will be recalled that extra-formal factors, including even fraud and mistake, were originally without effect on the sealed promise. Most of the formal transactions familiar to modern law, however, fall short of the "abstract" transaction; the channels they cut are not sharply and simply defined. The Statute of Frauds, for example, has only a kind of negative canalizing effect in the sense that it indicates a way by which one may be sure of *not* being bound. On the positive side, the outlines of the channel are blurred because too many factors, including consideration, remain unassimilated into the form.

As a final and very obvious point of comparison between the forms of law and those of language, we may observe that in both fields the actual course of history is determined by a continuous process of compromise between those who wish to preserve the existing patterns and those who wish to rearrange them. Those who are responsible for what Ihering called "the legal alphabet"—our judges, legislators, and textwriters—exercise a certain control over the usages of business, but there are times when they, like the lexicographer, must acquiesce in the innovations of the layman. The mere fact that the forms of law and language are set by a balance of opposing tensions does not, of course, insure the soundness of the developments which actually occur. If language sometimes loses valuable distinctions by being too tolerant, the law has lost valuable institutions, like the seal, by being too liberal in interpreting them. On the other hand, in law, as in language, forms have at times been allowed to crystallize to the point where needed innovation has been impeded.

§5. *Interrelations of the Three Functions.*—Though I have stated the three functions of legal form separately, it is obvious that there is an intimate connection between them. Generally speaking, whatever tends to accomplish one of these purposes will also tend to accomplish the other two. He who is compelled to do something which will furnish a satisfactory memorial of his intention will be induced to deliberate. Conversely, devices which induce deliberation will usually have an evidentiary value. Devices which insure evidence or prevent inconsiderateness will normally advance the desideratum of channeling, in two different ways. In the first place, he who is compelled to formulate his intention carefully will tend to fit it into legal and business categories. In this way the party is induced to canalize his own intention. In the second place, wherever the requirement of a formality is backed by the sanction of the invalidity of the informal transaction (and this is the means by which requirements of form are normally made effective), a degree of channeling results automatically. Whatever may be its legislative motive, the formality in such a case tends to effect a categorization of transactions into legal and non-legal.

Just as channeling may result unintentionally from formalities directed toward other ends, so these other ends tend to be satisfied by any device which accomplishes a channeling of expression. There is an evidentiary value in the clarity and definiteness of contour which such a device accomplishes. Anything which effects a neat division between the legal and the non-legal, or between different kinds of legal transactions, will tend also to make apparent to the party the consequences of his action and will suggest deliberation where deliberation is needed. Indeed, we may go further and say that some minimum satisfaction of the desideratum of channeling is necessary before measures designed to prevent inconsiderateness can be effective. This may be illustrated in the holographic will. The necessity of reducing the testator's intention to his own handwriting would seem superficially to offer, not only evidentiary safeguards, but excellent protection against inconsiderateness as well. Where the holographic will fails, however, is as a device for separating the legal wheat from the legally irrelevant chaff. The courts are frequently faced with the difficulty of determining whether a particular document—it may be an informal family letter which happens to be entirely in the handwriting of the sender—reveals the requisite "testamentary intention." This difficulty can only be eliminated by a formality which performs adequately the channeling function, by some external mark which will signalize the testament and distinguish it from non-testamentary expressions of intention. It is obvious that by a kind of reflex action the deficiency of the holographic will from the standpoint of channeling operates to impair its efficacy as a device for inducing deliberation.

Despite the close interrelationship of the three functions of form, it is necessary to keep the distinctions between them in mind since the disposition of borderline cases of compliance may turn on our assumptions as to the end primarily sought by a particular formality. Much of the discussion about the parol evidence rule, for example, hinges on the question whether its primary objective is channeling or evidentiary. Furthermore, one or more of the ends described may enter in a subsidiary way into the application of requirements primarily directed to another end. Thus there is reason to think that a good deal of the law concerning the suretyship section of the Statute of Frauds is explainable on the ground that courts have, with varying degrees of explicitness, supposed that this section served a cautionary and channeling purpose in addition to the evidentiary purpose assumed to be primarily involved in the Statute as a whole.[6]

§6. *When are Formalities Needed? The Effect of an Informal Satisfaction of the Desiderata Underlying the Use of Formalities.*—The analysis of the functions of legal form which has just been presented is useful in answering a question which will assume importance in the later portion of this discussion when a detailed treatment of consideration is undertaken. That question is: In what situations does good legislative policy demand the use of a legal formality? One part of the answer to the question is clear at the outset. Forms must be reserved for relatively important transactions. We must preserve a proportion between means and end; it will scarcely do to require a sealed and witnessed document for the effective sale of a loaf of bread.

But assuming that the transaction in question is of sufficient importance to support the use of a form if a form is needed, how is the existence of this need to be determined? A general answer would run somewhat as follows: *The need for investing a particular transaction with some legal formality will depend upon the extent to which the guaranties that the formality would afford are rendered superfluous by forces native to the situation out of which the transaction arises*—including in these "forces" the habits and conceptions of the transacting parties.

Whether there is any need, for example, to set up a formality designed to induce deliberation will depend upon the degree to which the factual situation, innocent of any legal remolding, tends to bring about the desired circumspective frame of mind. An example from the law of gifts will make this point clear. To accomplish an effective gift of a chattel without resort to the use of documents,

---

[6] In the leading case of Davis v. Patrick, 141 U.S. 479, 487, 488 (1891), the Court, in defining the purposes of the suretyship section of the Statute, speaks of the danger that the creditor may "torture mere words of encouragement and confidence into an absolute promise." It is clear that this danger exists not so much because of a lack of satisfactory proof of what was in fact said, but because of the lack of some device which will perform what I have called the channeling function of form. Though the receipt of a benefit by the surety, which was held in *Davis v. Patrick* to make his oral promise binding, may have some significance from an evidentiary standpoint, its primary significance would seem to be from the standpoint of the other two functions of form.

In Germany the promise of a surety is required by §766 of the Civil Code to be in writing. The purpose of this requirement has been explained as follows: "The basis of this requirement of form is that oral suretyships are often entered incautiously and in haste, and that it is often difficult to decide in the case of oral ërecommendations' whether the alleged surety really intended to bind himself or only intended to recommend the principal debtor without obligation to himself." I COSACK UND MITTEIS, LEHRBUCH DES BÜRGERLICHEN RECHTS (8ᵗʰ ed. 1927) §221. The more usual explanation speaks only of a cautionary or deterrent purpose. See 2 STAUDINGER, KOMMENTAR ZUM BGB (9ᵗʰ ed. 1929) §766 (1). An interesting parallel to the "main-purpose rule" in America is presented by the fact that §350 of the German Commercial Code exempts the suretyship undertakings of "merchants" in commercial transactions from the requirement of a writing.

delivery of the chattel is ordinarily required and mere donative words are ineffective. It is thought, among other things, that mere words do not sufficiently impress on the donor the significance and seriousness of his act. In an Oregon case,[7] however, the donor declared his intention to give a sum of money to the donee and at the same time disclosed to the donee the secret hiding place where he had placed the money. Though the whole donative act consisted merely of words, the court held the gift to be effective. The words which gave access to the money which the donor had so carefully concealed would presumably be accompanied by the same sense of present deprivation which the act of handing over the money would have produced. The situation contained its own guaranty against inconsiderateness.

So far as the channeling function of a formality is concerned it has no place where men's activities are already divided into definite, clear-cut business categories. Where life has already organized itself effectively, there is no need for the law to intervene. It is for this reason that important transactions on the stock and produce markets can safely be carried on in the most "informal" manner. At the other extreme we may cite the negotiations between a house-to-house book salesman and the housewife. Here the situation may be such that the housewife is not certain whether she is being presented with a set of books as a gift, whether she is being asked to trade her letter of recommendation for the books, whether the books are being offered to her on approval, or whether—what is, alas, the fact—a simple sale of the books is being proposed. The ambiguity of the situation is, of course, carefully cultivated and exploited by the canvasser. Some "channeling" here would be highly desirable, though whether a legal form is the most practicable means of bringing it about is, or course, another question.

What has been said in this section demonstrates, I believe, that the problem of "form," when reduced to its underlying policies, extends not merely to "formal" transactions in the usual sense, but to the whole law of contracts and conveyances. Demogue has suggested that even the requirement, imposed in certain cases, that the intention of the parties be express, rather than implied or tacit, is in essence a requirement of form.[8] If our object is to avoid giving sanction to inconsiderate engagements, surely the case for legal redress is stronger against the man who has spelled out his promise than it is against the man who has merely drifted into a situation where he appears to hold out an assurance for the future.

II. The Substantive Bases of Contract Liability

§7. *Private Autonomy.*—Among the basic conceptions of contract law the most pervasive and indispensable is the principle of private autonomy. This principle simply means that the law views private individuals as possessing a power to effect, within certain limits, changes in their legal relations. The man who conveys property to another is exercising this power; so is the man who enters a contract. When a court enforces a promise it is merely arming with legal sanction a

Lon L. Fuller

[7] Waite v. Grubbe, 43 Ore. 406, 73 Pac. 206 (1903). The analysis of the case presented in the text is taken from Mechem, *The Requirement of Delivery in Gifts of Chattels* (1926–1927) 21 ILL. L. REV. 357, 486.
[8] 1 TRAITÉ DES OBLIGATIONS EN GÉNÉRAL (1923) 280.

rule or *lex* previously established by the party himself.[9] This power of the individual to effect changes in his legal relations with others is comparable to the power of a legislature. It is, in fact, only a kind of political prejudice which causes us to use the word "law" in one case and not in the other, a prejudice which did not deter the Romans from applying the word *lex* to the norms established by private agreement.

What has just been stated is not presented as an original insight; the conception described is at least as old as the Twelve Tables. But there is need to reaffirm it, because the issue involved has been obfuscated through the introduction into the discussion of what is called "the will theory of contract." The obfuscation has come partly from the proponents of that theory, but mostly from those who have undertaken to refute it and who, in the process of refutation, have succeeded in throwing the baby out with the bath.[10]

The principle of private autonomy may be translated into terms of the will theory by saying that this principle merely means that the will of the parties sets their legal relations. When the principle is stated in this way, certain consequences may seem to follow from it: (1) that the law must concern itself solely with the actual inner intention of the promisor; (2) that the minds of the parties must "meet" at one instant of time before a contract can result; (3) that the law has no power to fill gaps in an agreement and is helpless to deal with contingencies unforeseen by the parties; and even (4) that the promisor must be free to change his mind at any time, since it is his will which sets the rule. Since these consequences of the will theory are regarded as unacceptable, the theory is assumed to be refuted by the fact that it entails them.

If we recognize that the will theory is only a figurative way of expressing the principle of private autonomy, we see to what an extent this "refutation" of the will theory really obscures the issues involved. In our country a law-making power is vested in the legislature. This fact is frequently expressed by saying that the will of the legislature is the law. Yet from this hackneyed metaphor we do not feel compelled to draw a set of conclusions paralleling those listed above as deriving from the will theory of contract. Specifically, we do not seek the "actual, inner" intention of individual legislators; we do not insist, except in a very formal way, on proof that a majority of the legislators were actually of one mind at one instant of time; we do not hesitate to fill gaps in defective statutes; and, finally, we do not permit a majority of those who voted for a particular law to nullify it by a later informal declaration that they have changed their minds.

---

[9] What I have called "the principle of private autonomy" is more commonly assumed than discussed in the Anglo-American literature. See, however, SALMOND, JURISPRUDENCE (9th ed. 1937) §23, heading *Conventional law*; and VINOGRADOFF, COMMON-SENSE IN LAW (1914) 101–115. The problem generally discussed in this country under the heading "freedom of contract" is the problem of the limits on private autonomy. Cf., HECK, GRUNDRISS DES SCHULDRECHTS (1929) §41.

Cohen's discussion of *Contract and Sovereignty,* and Gardner's discussion of the *Specialty Principle* and *Bargain Principle* appear in effect to deal with the principle of private autonomy without using that term. See Cohen, *The Basis of Contract* (1933) 46 HARV. L. REV. 553, 585–592; Gardner, *An Inquiry into the Principles of the Law of Contracts* (1932) 46 HARV. L. REV. 1, 23, 25.

The principle of private autonomy has nothing to do with the ancient controversy whether the binding effect of a contract derives from "the law" or "the contract." Acceptance of it as a basis of contract liability in no way involves adherence to Marshall's view that "obligation is not conferred on contracts by positive law, but is intrinsic, and is conferred by the act of the parties." Ogden v. Saunders, 12 Wheat. 213, 345 (dissenting opinion) (U.S. 1827). As even Windscheid recognized, the problem is not *where* the obligation comes from, but *why* it is imposed.

[10] Duguit and Pound in particular seem to me to have rejected too much in their repudiation of the will theory.

The principle of private autonomy, properly understood, is in no way inconsistent with an "objective" interpretation of contracts. Indeed, we may go farther and say that the so-called objective theory of interpretation in its more extreme applications becomes understandable only in terms of the principle of private autonomy. It has been suggested that in some cases the courts might properly give an interpretation to a written contract inconsistent with the actual understanding of either party.[11] What justification can there be for such a view? We answer, it rests upon the need for promoting the security of transactions. Yet security of transactions presupposes "transactions," in other words, acts of private parties which have a law-making and right-altering function. When we get outside the field of acts having this kind of function as their *raison d' être*, for example, in the field of tort law, any such uncompromisingly "objective" method of interpreting an act would be incomprehensible.

A legitimate criticism of the principle of private autonomy may be that it is phrased too narrowly, and excludes by implication private heteronomy. If we look at the matter realistically, we see that men not only make private laws for themselves, but also for their fellows. I do not refer here simply to the frequent existence of a gross inequality of bargaining power between contracting parties, nor to the phenomenon of the standardized contract established by one party for a series of routine transactions. Even without excursion into the social reality behind juristic conceptions, a principle of private heteronomy is visible in legal theory itself, as, for example, where it is laid down as a rule of law that the servant is bound to obey the reasonable commands of his master. Here the employer, within the framework of the agreement and subject to judicial veto, is making a part of "the law" of the relation between himself and his employee.

§8. *What Matters Shall be Left to Private Autonomy?*—From the fact that a principle of private autonomy is recognized it does not follow that this principle should be given an unlimited application. Law-making by individuals must be kept within its proper sphere, just as, under our constitutional system, law-making by legislatures is kept within its field of competence by the courts. What is the proper sphere of the rule of private autonomy?

In modern society the most familiar field of regulation by private autonomy is that having to do with the exchange of goods and services. Paradoxically, it is when contract is performing this most important and pervasive of its functions that we are least apt to conceive of it as a kind of private legislation. If *A* and *B* sign articles of partnership we have little difficulty in seeing the analogy between their act and that of a legislature. But if *A* contracts to buy a ton of coal from *B* for eight dollars, it seems absurd to conceive of this act as species of private lawmaking. This is only because we have come to view the distribution of goods through private contract as a part of the order of nature, and we forget that it is only one of several possible ways of accomplishing the same general objective. Coal does not have to be bought and sold; it can be distributed by the decrees of a dictator, or of an elected rationing board. When we allow it to be bought and sold by private agreement, we are, within certain limits, allowing individuals to set their own legal relations with regard to coal.[12]

Lon L. Fuller

[11] 1 WILLISTON, CONTRACTS (rev. ed. 1936) §95.

[12] "Bargain is then the social and legal machinery appropriate to arranging affairs in any specialized economy which relies on exchange rather than tradition (the manor) or authority (the army, the U.S.S.R.) for apportionment of productive energy and of product." Llewellyn, *What Price Contract?* (1931) 40 YALE L. J. 704, 717.

The principle of private autonomy is not, however, confined to contracts of exchange, and historically it perhaps found its first applications outside the relationship of barter or trade.[13] As modern instances of the exercise of private autonomy outside the field of exchange we may cite gratuitous promises under seal, articles of partnership, and collective labor agreements. In all these cases there may be an element of exchange in the background, just as the whole of society is permeated by a principle of reciprocity. But the fact remains that these transactions do not have as their immediate objective the accomplishment of an exchange of values.

When the principle of private autonomy is extended beyond exchange, where does it stop? The answer to this question is by no means simple, even if it be attempted in terms of some particular system of positive law. I shall not attempt to give such an answer here. One question must, however, be faced. When the principle of private autonomy is extended beyond exchange, can it legitimately be referred to as a "substantive basis of contract liability"? When we say that the contracting parties set the law of their relationship are we not giving a juristic construction of their act rather than a substantive reason for judicial intervention to enforce their agreement? It must be admitted that in one aspect the principle of private autonomy is a theory of enforcement rather than a reason for enforcement. But in another aspect the principle always implies at least one broad substantive reason for enforcement, which is identical with that underlying government generally. Though occasional philosophers may seem to dispute the proposition, most of us are willing to concede that some kind of regulation of men's relations among themselves is necessary. It is this general desideratum which underlies the principle of private autonomy. Whenever we can reinforce this general need for regulation by a showing that in the particular case private agreement is the best or the only available method of regulation, then in such a case "the principle of private autonomy" may properly be referred to as a "substantive" basis of contract liability.

§9. *Reliance*.[14]—A second substantive basis of contract liability lies in a recognition that the breach of a promise may work an injury to one who has changed his position in reliance on the expectation that the promise would be fulfilled. Reliance as a basis of contract liability must not be identified with reliance as a measure of the promisee's recovery. Where the object of the court is to reimburse detrimental reliance, it may measure the loss occasioned through reliance either *directly* (by looking to see what the promisee actually expended in reliance on the promise), or *contractually* (by looking to the value of the promised performance out of which the promisee presumably expected to recoup his losses through reliance). If the court's sole object is to reimburse the losses resulting from reliance, it may be expected to prefer the direct measure where that measure may

---

[13] WEBER, WIRTSCHAFT UND GESELLSCHAFT (1925) 417.

[14] On the general topic of this section see Gardner, *An Inquiry into the Principles of the Law of Contracts* (1932) 46 HARV. L. REV. 1, 22–23; Cohen, *The Basis of Contract* (1933) 46 HARV. L. REV. 553, 578–580; POUND, AN INTRODUCTION TO THE PHILOSOPHY OF LAW (1922) 269–284; HARRIMAN, THE LAW OF CONTRACTS (2d ed. 1901) §§646–652; Fuller and Perdue, *The Reliance Interest in Contract Damages* (1936–1937) 46 YALE L. J. 52, 373; Mason, *A Theory of Contract Sanctions* (1938) 38 COLUMBIA LAW REV. 775. "It may fairly be argued that the fundamental basis of simple contract historically was action in justifiable reliance on a promise." 1 WILLISTON, CONTRACTS (rev. ed. 1936) §139.

be applied conveniently. But there are various reasons, too complicated for discussion here, why a court may find that measure unworkable and hence prefer the contractual measure, even though its sole object remains that of reimbursing reliance.[15]

What is the relation between reliance and the principle of private autonomy? Occasionally reliance may appear as a distinct basis of liability, excluding the necessity for any resort to the notion of private autonomy. An illustration may be found in some of the cases coming under Section 90 of the Restatement of Contracts. In these cases we are not "upholding transactions" but healing losses caused through broken faith. In another class of cases the principle of reimbursing reliance comes into conflict with the principle of private autonomy. These are the cases where a promisee has seriously and, according to ordinary standards of conduct, justifiably relied on a promise which the promisor expressly stipulated should impose no legal liability on him.[16] In still other cases, reliance appears not as an independent or competing basis of liability but as a ground supplementing and reinforcing the principle of private autonomy. For example, while it remains executory, a particular agreement may be regarded as too vague to be enforced; until it has been acted on, such an agreement may be treated as a defective exercise of the power of private autonomy. After reliance, however, the court may be willing to incur the hazards involved in enforcing an indefinite agreement where this is necessary to prevent serious loss to the relying party.[17] The same effect of reliance as reinforcing the principle of private autonomy may be seen in much of the law of waiver. Finally, in some branches of contract law reliance and the principle of private autonomy appear not as reinforcing one another so as to justify judicial intervention where neither alone would be sufficient, but as alternative and independently sufficient bases for imposing liability in the same case. This is perhaps the situation in those cases where the likelihood that reliance will occur influences the court to impose liability on the promisor.[18] On the one hand, we may say that the likelihood of reliance demonstrates that the parties themselves viewed their transaction as an exercise of private autonomy, that they considered that it set their rights and were prepared to act accordingly. On this view, the law simply acquiesces in the parties' conception that their transaction determined their legal relations. On the other hand, we may say that the likelihood that reliance will occur is a sufficient reason for dispensing with proof that it occurred

[15] See Fuller and Perdue, *The Reliance Interest in Contract Damages* (1936–1937) 46 YALE L. J. 52, 66–67 and *passim*.

[16] In a number of recent cases of this sort, involving promises of bonuses to employees, recovery has been permitted. In these cases the principle of reimbursing reliance is regarded as overriding the principle of private autonomy. See Tilbert v. Eagle Lock Co., 116, Conn. 357, 165 Atl. 205 (1933); Psutka v. Michigan Alkali Co., 274 Mich. 318, 264 N. W. 385 (1936), 36 Columbia Law Rev. 996; Wellington v. Curran Printing Co., 216 Mo. App. 358, 268 S. W. 396 (1925); Mabley & Carew Co. v. Borden, 129 Ohio St. 375, 195 N. E. 697 (1935), 49 HARV. L. REV. 148, 149. As tending in this direction, see also George A. Fuller Co. v. Brown, 15 F. (2d) 672 (C.C.A. 4th, 1926).

[17] Morris v. Ballard, 16 F. (2d) 175 (App. D. C. 1926) (specific performance granted); Kearns v. Andree, 107 Conn. 181, 139 Atl. 695 (1928) (damages measured by the reliance interest granted).

[18] Though there are few decisions where the likelihood of reliance is explicitly made a ground for decision, there is reason to suppose that this factor is a potent influence in shaping the law of contracts. See Fuller and Perdue, *The Reliance Interest in Contract Damages* (1936–1937) 46 YALE L. J. 52, 60–61. *Cf.* Rutgers v. Lucet, 2 Johns. 92, 95 (N.Y. 1800): "The confidence placed in him [the promisor], and his undertaking to execute the trust, raise a sufficient consideration." The factor of likely reliance may explain why the rejection of an offer, without proof of actual reliance thereon by the offeror, terminates the power of acceptance, and perhaps affords a clue to the rules laid down in connection with the problem of election between inconsistent remedies.

in fact, since where reliance takes negative and intangible forms it may be difficult to prove. On this theory enforcement of the promise is viewed either as protecting an actual reliance which has probably occurred, or as a kind of prophylactic measure against losses through reliance which will be difficult to prove if they occur.

§10. Unjust Enrichment.[19]—In return for B's promise to give him a bicycle, A pays B five dollars; B breaks his promise. We may regard this as a case where the injustice resulting from breach of a promise relied on by the promisee is aggravated. The injustice is aggravated because not only has A lost five dollars but B has gained five dollars unjustly. If, following Aristotle, we conceive of justice as being concerned with maintaining a proper proportion of goods among members of society, we may reduce the relations involved to mathematical terms. Suppose A and B have each initially ten units of goods. The relation between them is then one of equivalence, 10:10. A loses five of his units in reliance on a promise by B which B breaks. The resulting relation is 5:10. If, however, A paid these five units over to B, the resulting relation would be 5:15.[20] This comparison shows why unjust enrichment resulting from breach of contract presents a more urgent case for judicial intervention than does mere loss through reliance not resulting in unjust enrichment.

Since unjust enrichment is simply an aggravated case of loss through reliance,[21] all of what was said in the last section is applicable here. When the problem is the quantum of recovery, unjust enrichment may be measured either *directly*, (by the value of what the promisor received), or *contractually*, (by the value of the promised equivalent). So too, the prevention of unjust enrichment may sometimes appear openly as a distinct ground of liability (as in suits for restitution for breach of an oral promise "unenforceable" under the Statute of Frauds), and at other times may appear as a basis of liability supplementing and reinforcing the principle of private autonomy (as where the notion of waiver is applied "to prevent forfeiture," and in cases where the inference of a tacit promise of compensation is explained by the court's desire to prevent unjust enrichment).

§11. *Substantive Deterrents to Legal Intervention to Enforce Promises.*—I have spoken of "the substantive bases of contract liability." It should be noted that the enforcement of promises entails certain costs which constitute substantive objections to the imposition of contract liability. The first of these costs is the obvious one involved in the social effort expended in the legal procedure necessary to enforcement. Enforcement involves, however, another less tangible and more important cost. There is a real need for a field of human intercourse

---

[19] Concerning the role of unjust enrichment in contract law see Havighurst, *Services in the Home—A Study of Contract Concepts in Domestic Relations* (1932) 41 YALE L. J. 386, 390; Gardner, *An Inquiry into the Principles of the Law of Contracts* (1932) 46 HARV. L. REV. 1, 34–35; and Fuller and Perdue, *The Reliance Interest in Contract Damages* (1936–1937) 46 YALE L. J. 52, 373, esp. at pp. 53–57, 66–75, 396–397, 405, 409.

[20] *Cf.,* ARISTOTLE, NICOMACHEAN ETHICS, 1132a–1132b.

[21] It is possible to conceive of cases where a defendant would be enriched through the breach of his promise though this enrichment did not result from reliance on the promise by the party impoverished. Such a case would be presented, for example, where after the plaintiff had voluntarily described a secret formula to the defendant, the defendant, for a consideration then paid him, promised not to use the formula in his business, and then later broke his promise. Normally, however, where a man secures a benefit for himself through the breaking of a promise it is because the promise has induced someone else to give up something.

freed from legal restraints, for a field where men may without liability withdraw assurances they have once given.[22] Every time a new type of promise is made enforceable, we reduce the area of this field. The need for a domain of "free-remaining" relations is not merely spiritual. Business deals can often emerge only from a converging series of negotiations, in which each step contains enough assurance to make worthwhile a further exchange of views and yet remains flexible enough to permit a radical readjustment to new situations. To surround with rigid legal sanctions even the first exploratory expressions of intention would not only introduce an unpleasant atmosphere into business negotiations, but would actually hamper commerce. The needs of commerce in this respect are suggested by the fact that in Germany, where the code makes offers binding without consideration, it has become routine to stipulate for a power of revocation.

§12. *The Relation of Form to the Substantive Bases of Contract Liability.*—Form has an obvious relationship to the principle of private autonomy. Where men make laws for themselves it is desirable that they should do so under conditions guaranteeing the desiderata described in our analysis of the functions of form. Furthermore, the greater the assurance that these desiderata are satisfied, the larger the scope we may be willing to ascribe to private autonomy. A constitution might permit a legislature to pass laws relating to certain specified subjects in an informal manner, but prescribe a more formal procedure for "extraordinary" enactments, by requiring, for example, successive readings of the bill before it was put to a vote. So, in the law of contracts, we may trust men in the situation of exchange to set their rights with relative informality. Where they go outside the field of exchange, we may require a seal, or appearance before a notary, for the validity of their promises.

When we inquire into the relevance of form to liability founded on reliance or unjust enrichment, it becomes necessary to discriminate between the three functions of form. As to the desiderata implied in the evidentiary and cautionary functions it is clear that they do not lose their significance simply because the basis of liability has shifted. Even in the law of torts we are concerned with the adequacy of the proof of what occurred in fact, and (sometimes, at least) with the degree of deliberation with which the defendant acted. It is true that in the law of torts these considerations are not usually effectuated in the same way that they are in contract law. This is due to the fact that the channeling function of form becomes, in this field, largely irrelevant, for this function is intimately connected with the principle of private autonomy and loses its significance in fields where that principle has no application. To the extent, then, that the basis of promissory liability shifts from the principle of private autonomy to the reimbursement of reliance or the prevention of unjust enrichment, to that extent does the relevance of the channeling function of form decrease. This function loses its relevance altogether at that indefinite point at which it ceases to be appropriate to refer to the acts upon which liability is predicated as a "transaction."

Lon L. Fuller

[22] Cf., Cohen, *The Basics of Contract* (1933) 46 HARV. L. REV. 553, 573; Willis, *Rationale of the Law of Contracts* (1936) II IND. L. J. 227, 230; Richard's Ex'r v. Richards, 46 Pa. 78, 82 (1863).

§13. *Reasons for Refusing to Enforce the Gratuitous and Unrelied-on-Promise.*—A promises to give *B* $100; *B* has in no way changed his position in reliance on this promise, and he has neither given nor promised anything in return for it. In such a situation enforcement of the promise is denied both in the common law and in the civil law. We give as our reason, "lack of consideration"; the civilians point to a failure to comply with statutory formalities. In neither case, of course, does the reason assigned explain the policies which justify excluding this promise from enforcement. An explanation in terms of underlying policies can, however, be worked out on the basis of the analysis just completed.

Looking at the case from the standpoint of the substantive bases of contractual liability we observe, first of all, that there is here neither reliance nor unjust enrichment. Furthermore, gratuities such as this one do not present an especially pressing case for the application of the principle of private autonomy, particularly if we bear in mind the substantive deterrents to judicial intervention. While an exchange of goods is a transaction which conduces to the production of wealth and the division of labor, a gift is, in Bufnoir's words, a "sterile transmission."[23] If on "substantive" grounds the balance already inclines away from judicial intervention, the case against enforcement becomes stronger when we draw into account the desiderata underlying the use of formalities. That there is in the instant case a lack of evidentiary and cautionary safeguards is obvious. As to the channeling function of form, we may observe that the promise is made in a field where intention is not naturally canalized. There is nothing here to effect a neat division between tentative and exploratory expressions of intention, on the one hand, and legally effective transactions, on the other. In contrast to the situation of the immediate gift of a chattel (where title will pass by the manual tradition), there is here no "natural formality" on which the courts might seize as a test of enforceability.

§14. *The Contractual Archetype—The Half-Completed Exchange.*—A delivers a horse to *B* in return for *B*'s promise to pay him ten dollars; *B* defaults on his promise, and *A* sues for the agreed price. In this case are united all of the factors we have previously analyzed as tending in the direction of enforcement of a promise. On the substantive side, there is reliance by *A* and unjust enrichment of *B*. The transaction involves an exchange of economic values, and falls therefore in a field appropriately left to private autonomy in an economy where no other provision is made for the circulation of goods and the division of labor, or where (as perhaps in primitive society) an expanding economy makes the existing provision for those ends seem inadequate. On the side of form, the delivery and acceptance of the horse involve a kind of natural formality, which satisfies the evidentiary, cautionary, and channeling purposes of legal formalities.

Describing this situation as "the contractual archetype,"[24] we may take it as our point of departure, dealing with other cases in terms of the degree of their

[23] PRIORUÉTÉ ET CONTRAT (2d ed. 1924) 487. This remark of Bufnoir's cannot be taken too literally; the element of exchange is a variable one, and there are few human relationships which do not involve a degree of reciprocity. It should be recalled that the practice of exchanging goods has commonly emerged in primitive societies out of a system of donations with, as Llewellyn says, "a felt obligation to reciprocate."

[24] *Cf.* Fuller and Perdue, *The Reliance Interest in Contract Damages* (1936) 46 YALE L. J. 52, 67 and references there cited.

deviation from it. Naturally, all kinds of nuances are here possible, and some minor departures from the pattern were the occasion for dispute in the early history of the action of debt. We are concerned here, however, chiefly with two major deviations from the archetype: the situation of the executory exchange, and the situation of reliance without exchange.

§15. *The Wholly Executory Exchange.*—B promises to build a house for *A*, and *A*, in return, promises to pay *B* $5,000 on the completion of the house. *B* defaults on his promise, and *A*, without having had occasion to pay anything on the contract, sues *B* for damages. Judicial intervention in this kind of case apparently began in England toward the end of the sixteenth century. This development we describe by saying that after *Strangborough v. Warner*[25] and related cases the bilateral contract as such became for the first time enforceable. It is now generally assumed that so far as consideration is concerned the executory bilateral contract is on a complete parity with the situation where the plaintiff has already paid the price of the defendant's promised performance. Yet if we examine the executory bilateral contract in terms of the policies underlying consideration, it will become apparent that this assumption is unjustified, and that Lord Holt in reality overshot the mark in his assertion that "where the doing a thing will be a good consideration, a promise to do that thing will be so too."[26]

Where a bilateral contract remains wholly executory the arguments for judicial intervention have been considerably diminished in comparison with the situation of the half-completed exchange. There is here no unjust enrichment. Reliance may or may not exist, but in any event will not be so tangible and direct as where it consists in the rendition of the price of the defendant's performance. On the side of form, we have lost the natural formality involved in the turning over of property or the rendition and acceptance of services. There remains simply the fact that the transaction is an exchange and not a gift. This fact alone does offer some guaranty so far as the cautionary[27] and channeling functions of form are concerned, though, except as the Statute of Frauds interposes to supply the deficiency, evidentiary safeguards are largely lacking. This lessening of the factors arguing for enforcement not only helps to explain why liability in this situation was late in developing, but also explains why even today the executory bilateral contract cannot be put on complete parity with the situation of the half-completed exchange.

In the situation of the half-completed exchange, the element of exchange is only one factor tending toward enforcement. Since that element is there reinforced by reliance, unjust enrichment, and the natural formality involved in the surrender and acceptance of a tangible benefit, it is unnecessary to analyze the concept of exchange closely, and it may properly be left vague. In the executory bilateral contract, on the other hand, the element of exchange stands largely alone[28] as a basis of liability and its definition becomes crucial. Various definitions are possible. We may define exchange vaguely as a transaction from which

Lon L. Fuller

---

[25] 4 Leo. 3, 74 ENG. REP. 685 (K.B. 1589).

[26] Thorp v. Thorp, 12 Mod. 455, 459, 88 ENG. REP. 1448, 1450 (K.B. 1702).

[27] "In *Bilateral Contracts* [inconsiderateness] . . . is supposed to be prevented by the mutuality: each party contracting for his own pecuniary advantage; contemplating a *quid pro quo*; and therefore, being in that circumspective frame of mind, which a man who is only thinking of such advantage naturally assumes." Austin, *Fragments—On Contracts*, printed in 2 LECTURES ON JURISPRUDENCE (4th ed. 1873) 939, 940.

[28] I say "largely alone" because there is always the possibility that the court will be influenced by actual reliance on the bargain or by the probability that reliance has taken place or will occur.

each participant derives a benefit, or, more restrictively, as a transaction in which the motives of the parties are primarily economic rather than sentimental. Following Adam Smith, we may say that it is a transaction which, directly or indirectly, conduces to the division of labor. Or we may take Demorgue's notion that the most important characteristic of exchange is that it is a situation in which the interests of the transacting parties are opposed, so that the social utility of the contract is guaranteed in some degree by the fact that it emerges as a compromise of those conflicting interests.[29] The problem of choosing among these varying conceptions may seem remote and unimportant yet it underlies some of the most familiar problems of contract law. For example, suppose a nephew promises his uncle that he will not smoke until he is twenty-one, and the uncle promises him $5,000 as a reward if he will keep his promise. Where the nephew sues after having earned the reward by following the prescribed line of conduct recovery has been permitted.[30] But would such an agreement be enforced as an executory bilateral contract? Could the uncle, for example, sue the nephew for smoking a cigarette? In answering this question it is at once apparent that we are faced with the necessity of defining the particular kind of exchange which is essential to the enforcement of a bilateral contract. A similar problem underlies many of the cases involving "illusory promises."

Like consideration, exchange is a complex concept. To the problem of the executory exchange we may, within a narrower compass, apply the same general approach that we have applied to the problem of consideration as a whole. Here our "archetype" is the business trade of economic values in the form of goods, services, or money. To the degree that a particular case deviates from this archetype, the incentives to judicial intervention decrease, until a point is reached where relief will be denied altogether unless the attenuated element of exchange is reinforced, either on the formal side by some formal or informal satisfaction of the desiderata, underlying the use of legal formalities, or of the substantive side by a showing of reliance or unjust enrichment, or of some special need for a regulation of the relations involved by private autonomy.

§16. *Transactions Aucillary to Exchanges.*—There are various transactions which, though they are not themselves immediately directed toward accomplishing an exchange, are necessary preliminary steps toward exchanges, or are ancillary to exchanges in process of realization. Among these we may mention offers, promises of unpaid sureties, and what Llewellyn has described as "going-transaction adjustments" such as are involved in unilateral concessions or promises of extra compensation granted during performance of a bilateral contract.

Because of their connection with exchanges, these transactions, in varying degrees, participate in the underlying grounds, both "formal" and "substantive," which justify the enforcement of exchanges. Thus, for example, if it were thought that exchanges could in practice only be arranged through the device of preliminary offers and that offers could be effective only if made irrevocable, then the substantive grounds for enforcing bilateral contracts of exchange would extend to offers. Again, a promise of extra compensation to a man already under contract to build a house at a fixed price participates to some extent in the "formal"

---

[29] 1 TRAITÉ DES OBLIGATIONS (1923) 31; 2 *id*, 130–131.
[30] Hammer v. Sidway, 124 N.Y. 538, 27 N.E. 256 (1891); Lindell v. Rokes, 60 Mo. 249 (1875); Talbott v. Stemmons, 89 Ky. 222 (1889).

guaranties which justify the enforcement of exchanges. From the standpoint of the "channeling" function, for example, such a promise receives a certain canalization from being related to an existing business deal. There is not here to the same degree as in purely gratuitous promises a shadowy no-man's land in which it is impossible to distinguish between the binding promise and the tentative or exploratory expressions of intention.

How far legal sanction ought to be extended to these transactions bordering on and surrounding exchanges is a legislative question which cannot be discussed here, though it may be observed that it is precisely in this field that the greatest difference between the common law and the civil law exists. Probably our own law is in need of some reform. The written promise of a surety who guarantees the performance of one party to an exchange, for example, probably ought to be made enforceable without consideration. As to offers, the problem is more difficult, and probably some distinction between kinds of offers is in order.

§17. *Unbargained-for Reliance.*—An uncle promises to give his nephew one thousand dollars; in reliance on this promise the nephew incurs an indebtedness he would not otherwise have incurred. In this case we have a change of position which is not bargained for as the price of the uncle's promise. Where the element of exchange is removed from a case, the appeal to judicial intervention decreases both in terms of form and of substance. The appeal is diminished substantively because we are no longer in the field which is in modern society the most obviously appropriate field for the rule of private autonomy. From the formal standpoint, when we lose exchange, we lose the formal guaranties which go with the situation of exchange. (See §§14 and 15, *supra.*)

Section 90 of the Contracts Restatement provides in effect that a promise which has given rise to unbargained-for reliance may or may not be enforced, depending on the circumstances of the case. The section makes explicit only two criteria bearing on the question whether relief should be granted, namely, the seriousness of the promisee's reliance and its foreseeability by the promisor. On the basis of the analysis presented in this article, the following additional inquiries would be relevant: (1) Was the promise prompted wholly by generosity, or did it emerge out of a context of tacit exchange? (See §15 and 16, *supra.*) (2) Were the desiderata underlying the use of formalities satisfied in any degree by the circumstances under which the promise was made? (See §6, *supra.*) As bearing on the second question, we may ask whether the promise was express or implied, and whether after the promise was made the promisee declared to the promisor his intention of acting on it.[31]

---

[31] In this sense, the "acceptance" of the promise of a gratuity may be significant, even though the Restatement of Contracts in §85 exempts promises made enforceable under §90 from the requirement of mutual assent. On the Continent the requirement of some expression of acceptance, which is often applied even to purely unilateral promises, operates to some extent as a kind of surrogate for consideration, and many of the criticisms which in this country are directed against the requirement of consideration are there directed against the rule that the unaccepted promise cannot be binding. See HECK, GRUNDRISS DES SCHULDRECHTS (1929) §41; 1 DEMOGUE, TRAITÉ DES OBLIGATIONS (1923) 51–63. In France the principal doubt concerning the binding effect of an offer arises not from the lack of consideration but from the lack of acceptance by the offeree of the proposition to keep the offer open for a certain period. See 2 DEMOGUE, TRAITÉ 17. That there may be a certain overlapping in the function of consideration and mutual assent is apparent in the following passage from Austin, "*Why a promise is binding* . . . It binds, on account of the expectation excited in the promisee. For which reason a mere pollicitation (that is, a promise made but not accepted) is not binding; for a promise not accepted could excite no expectation." *Fragments—On Contracts*, printed in 2 JURISPRUDENCE (4th ed. 1873) 939.

§18. *Nominal Consideration.*—It has been held that a promise to make a gift may be made binding through the payment of a "nominal" consideration, such as a dollar or a cent. The proper ground for upholding these decisions would seem to be that the desiderata underlying the use of formalities are here satisfied by the fact that the parties have taken the trouble to cast their transaction in the form of an exchange. The promise supported by nominal consideration then becomes enforceable for reasons similar to those which justify the enforcement of the promise under seal. (See §12, *supra.*) From the standpoint of such an analysis such distinction as is taken in *Schnell v. Nell*[32] and Section 76(c) of the Contracts Restatement is wholly out of place.

§19. *Release of Claims.*—There is in our law a noticeable, though not consistently expressed tendency to treat the surrender of rights differently from the creation of rights.[33] The same tendency may be observed in foreign systems.[34] In general it may be said that it is easier to give up a right than to create one. Words like "renunciation," "surrender," "extinction," and "waiver" are associated in the lawyer's mind with laxness, with a letting down of the bars. What is the explanation for this tendency? This is a question which has not, so far as I am aware, been answered at all. I believe that the analysis presented in §6, *supra,* may give at least a part of the answer.

If when a creditor releases his debtor the desiderata underlying the use of formalities are satisfied by the circumstances surrounding the informal transaction, then we have an explanation for the observed relaxing of "formal" requirements in this situation. An analogy from the law of gifts will again be helpful. Ordinarily the effective gift of a chattel requires either some document of transfer or a delivery of the chattel itself. It has been held, however, that where the chattel is already in the possession of the donee, mere words of donation are sufficient. This is partly because in such a situation donative words are accompanied by a sense of present deprivation which is absent where the chattel remains in the donor's hands.[35] The cautionary function of form is thus satisfied in this situation without the imposition of form. So, I believe, if we look at the problem now under discussion from the standpoint of the cautionary function of form it will be apparent that there is a difference between releasing a claim and creating a claim by a promise. The release of a claim, even if made orally, carries with it normally a sense of deprivation which is lacking in the case of a promise. Where words have this effect, where they tend to produce a psychological wrench on the speaker, they satisfy the desideratum of inducing deliberation as well as a writing or a seal. On the side of "substance," it may be observed that releases are normally transactions ancillary to a relationship of exchange. (See §16, *supra.*)

What has just been said is not presented as an adequate analysis of the whole problem of waiver and renunciation. Such an analysis could be made, I believe, in terms of the factors outlined in this article, but it would have to take into account the nuances and complexities to which these factors are subject in this field. Among the counter-currents which pull in a direction opposite from the

---

[32] 17 Ind. 29 (1861).

[33] See 6 WILLISTON, CONTRACTS (rev. ed. 1938) §§1820–1833.

[34] See, *e.g.,* the Swiss Code of Obligations §115; the German Civil Code §397; Raynaud, La renonciation à un droit (France 1936) 35 REV. TRIM, DE DR CIV. 763.

[35] See Mechem, *The Requirement of Delivery in Gifts of Chattels* (1926) 21 ILL. LAW REV. 341, 365.

tendency just discussed are the rule of *Foakes v. Beer,*[36] and the peculiar background surrounding the surrender of personal-injury claims.

§20. *Moral Obligations as Consideration.*—Courts have frequently enforced promises on the simple ground that the promisor was only promising to do what he ought to have done anyway. These cases have either been condemned as wanton departures from legal principle, or reluctantly accepted as involving the kind of compromise logic must inevitably make at times with sentiment. I believe that these decisions are capable of rational defense. When we say the defendant was morally obligated to do the thing he promised, we in effect assert the existence of a substantive ground for enforcing the promise. In a broad sense, a similar line of reasoning justifies the special status accorded by the law to contracts of exchange. Men *ought* to exchange goods and services; therefore when they enter contracts to that end, we enforce those contracts. On the side of form, concern for formal guaranties justifiably diminishes where the promise is backed by a moral obligation to do the thing promised. What does it matter that the promisor may have acted without great deliberation, since he is only promising to do what he should have done without a promise? For the same reason, can we not justifiably overlook some degree of evidentiary insecurity?

In refutation of the notion of "moral consideration" it is sometimes said that a moral obligation plus a mere promise to perform that obligation can no more create legal liability than zero plus zero can have any other sum than zero. But a mathematical analogy at least equally appropriate is the proposition that one-half plus one-half equals one. The court's conviction that the promisor ought to do the thing, plus the promisor's own admission of his obligation, may tilt the scales in favor of enforcement where neither standing alone would be sufficient. If it be argued that moral consideration threatens certainty, the solution would seem to lie, not in rejecting the doctrine, but in taming it by continuing the process of judicial exclusion and inclusion already begun in the cases involving infants' contracts, barred debts, and discharged bankrupts.

§21. *Performance of Legal Duty as Consideration.*—The analysis presented in this article is not sufficient for a comprehension of the factors underlying all the situations where courts have talked about "consideration." For example, cases where courts have said that illegal agreements are void for lack of consideration (since the law must close its eyes to an illegal consideration)[37] obviously involve policies going beyond those analysed in this paper. It is for a similar reason that I have not drawn into the discussion cases laying down the rule that the performance of a legal duty cannot be consideration. These cases involve factors extrinsic to the problems under discussion here. Among those factors are the effects of improper coercion, and the need for preserving the morale of professions, like that of policeman, jockey, and sailor, which involve activities impinging directly on the interests of others.[38] These cases touch the present discussion

[36] L. R. 9 App. Cas. 605 (1884).
[37] *See, e.g., Branch v. Haas, 16 Fed. 53,55 (1883).*
[38] See the analysis of this problem in Whittier, *The Restatement of Contracts and Consideration (1930)* 18 CALIF. L. REV. 611, 616–624; and Sharp, *Pacta Sunt Servanda, supra* page 787. The problem of the enforceability of a promise to pay the promisee for doing his legal duty has been much discussed in French law. See, e.g., 2 DEMOGUE, TRAITÉ DES OBLIGATIONS (1923) 603. Where such promises are denied enforcement, the doctrinal dispute has hinged about the question whether the proper ground is lack of cause or illicit cause.

only in the sense that there is some relation between coercion and the desiderata underlying the use of formalities; whatever tends to guarantee deliberateness in the making of a promise tends in some degree to protect against the milder forms of coercion.

§22. *The Future of Form.*—Despite an alleged modern tendency toward "informality," there is little reason to believe that the problem of form will disappear in the future. The desiderata underlying the use of formalities will retain their relevance as long as men make promises to one another. Doubt may legitimately be raised, however, whether there will be any place in the future for what may be called the "blanket formality," the formality which, like the seal, suffices to make any kind of promise, not immoral or illegal, enforceable. It is not that there is no need for such a device. The question is whether with our present-day routinized and institutionalized ways of doing business a "blanket formality" can achieve the desiderata which form is intended to achieve. The net effect of a reform like the Uniform Written Obligations Act, for example, will probably be to add a line or two to unread printed forms and increased embarrassment to the task of judges seeking a way to let a man off from an oppressive bargain without seeming to repudiate the prevailing philosophy of free contract. Under modern conditions perhaps the only devices which would be really effective in achieving the formal desiderata would be that of a nominal consideration actually handed over, or a requirement that the promise be entirely in the handwriting of the promisor. As the holographic will show, even the second of these devices would be inadequate from the standpoint of the "channeling" function.

§23. *The Future of Consideration.*—The future of consideration is tied up to a considerable extent with the future of the principle of private autonomy. If the development of our society continues along the lines it is now following, we may expect, I believe, that private contract as an instrument of exchange will decrease in importance. On the other hand, with an increasing interdependence among the members of society we may expect to see reliance (unbargained-for, or half-bargained-for) become increasingly important as a basis of liability. We may also see an expansion of the principle of private (or semi-private) autonomy to fields outside that of exchange. We get some hint of this second development in the expanding importance of the collective labor agreement. It appears also in the increasing use by business of revocable dealer and distributor agencies, and standing offers, devices which have their *raison d'être* in furnishing a kind of frame-work or private constitution for future dealings. These changes in business practice will inevitably bring with them in time modifications of the doctrine of consideration. For example, the relationship involved in dealer and jobber agencies is one which calls increasingly for some kind of judicial regulation to prevent hardship and oppression. If the assumption that the relationship is "contractual" coupled with existing definitions of consideration operates to exclude judicial intervention, then legal doctrine should be modified so as to permit bringing this relationship within the control of the law.

It has sometimes been proposed that the doctrine of consideration be "abolished." Such a step would, I believe, be unwise, and in a broad sense even impossible. The *problems* which the doctrine of consideration attempts to solve cannot be abolished. There can be little question that some of these problems do not receive a proper solution in the complex of legal doctrine now grouped under the rubric "consideration." It is equally clear that an original attack on these problems would arrive at some conclusions substantially equivalent to those which result from the doctrine of consideration as now formulated. What needs abolition is not the doctrine of consideration but a conception of legal method which assumes that the doctrine can be understood and applied without reference to the ends it serves. When we have come again to define consideration in terms of its underlying policies the problem of adapting it to new conditions will largely solve itself.

LON L. FULLER
Harvard Law School

Henry M. Hart, Jr., and Albert M. Sacks

Henry M. Hart, Jr., and Albert M. Sacks

FOR ROUGHLY twenty years—from the Second World War to the mid-1960s—American legal elites shared a broad consensus about legal institutions, legal reasoning, and the work of the legal profession. This postwar consensus is most directly identified with a set of teaching materials prepared by Albert Sacks and Henry Hart at the Harvard Law School for a course they called "The Legal Process." The words "legal process" have become synonymous with the calm, more optimistic and moderate mode of legal analysis that followed the more turbulent debates over legal realism in the years after the war. Although the Hart and Sacks teaching materials were published only posthumously, in 1994, the course for which they were prepared was taught to a generation of law students at dozens of law schools. The opening pages of the materials, included here, introduce the main themes of the Legal Process approach to legal reasoning and the authors' broader vision of the legal system through an elaborate case study—"the case of the spoiled cantaloupes"—long the most celebrated and remembered piece of legal process scholarship.

Hart and Sacks were not alone—many hands contributed to the Legal Process consensus. In the 1940s and 1950s, at Harvard alone, Lon Fuller, Herbert Wechsler, Julius Stone, Paul Freund, and Louis Jaffe were all involved in the development of the materials. John Chipman Gray's prewar writing on judging was a significant precursor, as were the judicial opinions and other writings of Benjamin Cardozo and Louis Brandeis. Felix Frankfurter and James Landis's work on administrative law and agency regulation paved the way for a more overt focus on public law in the postwar years. Through the 1950s and 1960s, the legal process analytic was elaborated by a wide range of influential scholars, including Alexander Bickel, Harry Wellington, Walter Dellinger, Norman Dorsen, and Thomas Ehrlich. It is the Hart and Sacks materials, however, that continue to epitomize the legal thought of the era.

Henry Hart, born in Butte, Montana, in 1904, graduated from Harvard Law School in 1930, where he had been a student of Felix Frankfurter, and joined the faculty there two years later, after clerking for Justice Louis Brandeis. He remained on the faculty until his death in 1969, with two significant exceptions. In 1937–38, he went to Washington to serve as Head Attorney in the office of the Solicitor General. During the Second World War, he worked for the U.S. Attorney General as a special assistant for immigration and naturalization before serving as Associate General Counsel for the Office of Price Administration (1942–45), and General Counsel of the Office of Economic Stabilization (1945–46). These experiences in public administration left Hart with an optimism about government and administration, and an interest in public law and the processes of its elaboration.

Albert Sacks, sixteen years younger than Hart, was born into a middle-class Jewish family in New York City. His first language was Yiddish, and he attended public schools in the Bronx before attending City College of New York. After graduation, he worked briefly as a bookkeeper until he was drafted. During the Second World War he was trained as a personnel psychologist and tutor for illiterate draftees. After the war, he attended Harvard Law School, where he met Hart in the classroom, as a student in his seminar on legislation. President of the *Law Review*, Sacks graduated in 1948 and clerked for Augustus Hand of the Second Circuit and then for Felix Frankfurter on the Supreme Court. After two further years in practice with Covington and Burling, he returned to Harvard as an Assistant Professor in 1952, where he would remain until his retirement in 1981, having served as Associate Dean and Dean from 1968 to 1981.

Hart and Sacks are the first scholars included in the Canon whose intellectual sensibility was formed after the New Deal. Hart's academic career had been interrupted by years of prominent public service, before and during the war. Whereas earlier writers remembered the struggles of the early Roosevelt years to prevent the Supreme Court from overruling New Deal legislation in the name of "freedom of contract," Hart was able to take for granted the massive expansions of federal power that came with the later years of the New Deal and the Second World War, on the basis of his own experience. Sacks learned about the New Deal in law school and while practicing with a private Washington firm.

As a result, the legal process materials responded to a new set of professional concerns. Law schools struggled to adapt their curriculum to the marked expansion of federal legislative and regulatory authority that had accompanied the New Deal and the Second World War. The first-year curriculum remained focused on the private-law subjects of common law, as upper-level courses were added in the expanding fields of public law. Hart had taught courses in "legislation" before the war, focusing on the legislative process, statutory drafting and interpretation, as well as surveying the substantive fields within which the federal government was now legislating. At the same time, "administrative law" became a central focus of the upper-level curriculum, concentrating on the role and authority of executive agencies in rule making and interpretation.

An expanding public law raised new challenges. What should be the appropriate law-making role for agencies? How should the plethora of new statutes be interpreted where their terms were left vague, or conflicted? How should we think about judicial review in the face of expanding legislative and regulatory power? At the same time, a more integrated national market and a more diverse federal governmental structure increased the incidence of jurisdictional conflicts, as well as substantive issues decided differently by different courts and agencies. How should we think about the diversity of norms, outcomes, and institutions in the American legal system? For a generation of lawyers, the legal process materials offered a framework for thinking about such questions and for understanding an American legal system with expanding federal power and public regulation.

By 1950, moreover, the intellectual debates of the 1930s seemed remote. Holmes, Hohfeld, and the legal realists had won their struggle against classical legal thought. Their criticisms of formalism, conceptualism, and deduction had become routine tools of legal argument. Policy, social functions, facts, and purposes had all become accepted parts of legal analysis. Roscoe Pound and Lon Fuller, among others, had developed modes of legal reasoning to assimilate policy into legal reasoning and encourage attention to the relationship between the legal order and social or commercial life, while resisting any more critical or radical implications of legal realist skepticism about deduction.

The mainstreaming of policy analysis also raised new challenges. The realists had encouraged judges to break free of conceptualism and formalism with some confidence that they would be able to find reliable guidance by focusing on social purposes and needs, and by listening to policy experts from other social sciences. By the 1940s, this confidence seemed misplaced. The widespread triumph of more skeptical, even relativist, modes of thinking throughout the social sciences, alongside the practical experience of dueling experts and open-ended policy arguments, made purposive legal reasoning seem a recipe for legal pluralism and unpredictable outcomes. At the same time, the realists had persuaded the legal establishment that there was no going back to formal deduction—its results were also multiple and unpredictable. But how should one think about the apparently unavoidable diversity of the legal order?

The "legal process" was always more a collection of ideas, focal points for inquiry, and characteristic attitudes than a tight method or disciplined school of thought. The central "legal process" vision, a loose set of observations about the nature of law, is stated in the opening pages. Law is a purposive activity, crucial to the cooperation necessary in human society to satisfy human needs. "Law," they write, "is a doing of something, a purposive activity, a continuous striving to solve the basic problems of social living."[1] Consequently, norms should be interpreted in purposive terms—by imputing a social purpose to the specific norm, to the institution which promulgated it, or to the legal order of which it was but a part, and then asking how that purpose might best be furthered by the interpreting institution.

It was crucial to the legal process idea that attention to purpose not be mistaken for a simple instrumentalism or consequentialism. Nor should it be confused with the functionalism or pragmatism of the realist period, which sought to extract normative propositions from the facts and context. For the legal process jurist, law was a policy instrument *with a particular institutional structure*. The legal order's substantive norms are less significant to the broad project of human coordination than the *"constitutive or procedural* understandings" which become institutionalized "procedures for the settlement of questions of group concern."[2] Just as an economic division of labor in an open market results in a decentralized cooperation to satisfy needs, so an institutional division of labor in a decentralized legal order will promote the satisfaction of human needs. Each institution exercises a competence appropriate to its particular expertise and capability. The role of law in the broadest sense is to set, monitor, and enforce the procedural arrangements determining who does what. As a result, interpretation required attention first to the legal institutional context, rather than the social context.

> These institutionalized procedures and the constitutive arrangements establishing and governing them are obviously more fundamental than the substantive arrangements in the structure of a society, if not in the realization of its ultimate aims, since they are at once the source of the substantive arrangements and the indispensable means of making them work effectively.[3]

The idea reflects an agnosticism about the substance of both policy analysis and doctrinal interpretation. Legal professionals will need to work with an increasing array of often conflicting legal materials, whose interpretation will require an open-ended inquiry into policy and purpose. From the systemic perspective, however, we should not worry too much about the many different results, some of them surely mistaken, which will result. It matters less which way a controversy is resolved than *that* it is resolved.

This conviction suggested a viewpoint for legal elites throughout the legal order—in administrative agencies, local authorities, Congress, the courts. They should by and large defer to one another's substantive judgments, as long as these were legitimately the product of appropriate procedures. Hart and Sacks called this idea "the principle of institutional settlement."[4] They elaborated it in various ways in the materials. In the opening pages, they put it like this: "decisions which are the duly arrived at result of duly established procedures of this kind 'ought' to be accepted as binding upon the whole society unless and until they are duly changed."[5]

This perspective seemed particularly important for appellate judges and scholars evaluating the work of diverse legal institutions. As mandarins of the legal order, they should strive for an attitude of detachment from substantive differences, and orient themselves to the ongoing legitimacy of the procedural and institutional regime. They are encouraged to respect the outcomes of "duly constituted" institutional actors, and to focus on whether a decision was taken by the appropriate institution in the prescribed way and on the basis of the appropriate process, rather than on the outcome or the substantive principle or policy involved.

The Hart and Sacks materials often celebrate the dispersion and decentralization of decision making. In a sense, the Cantaloupe Case offers a nightmare of legal pluralism. The underlying transaction was a simple commercial dispute— a buyer disappointed to find the cantaloupes he had ordered spoiled on arrival, a seller in turn disappointed not to be paid. In their search for redress, the parties navigate a lengthy and convoluted path through numerous institutions, and receive decisions pointing in various directions. The author's benign attitude, even pleasure, as a quotidian struggle over what one would have thought the simplest question of contract law plods through decision after decision, is striking. Hart and Sacks seem not only indifferent to who wins, but perfectly content with the legal system's protracted indecisiveness. In part, this attitude arose from the conviction that most social ordering is private, that both public regulation and state enforcement of common-law obligations was far less important than private arrangements, and that law should be careful to remain "suppletive" to and "facilitative" of private ordering. Here is Hart:

> But disputes about social relations being the exception rather than the rule, intricacies in the remedial law, large though they may bulk in the professional concerns of lawyers, are of relatively minor concern in the system generally. In a well-operating society the overwhelming mass of actions and transactions never come into question— in court or elsewhere.[6]

In this sense, despite their engagement with an expanding public law, the legal process materials treat public norms and institutions as secondary to private social ordering. Unlike the New Dealers who had promoted the expansion of administrative, federal, and public law capacity before the war, or the law and society reformers who would follow in the 1960s, the legal process generation did not associate a purposive conception of law with a large-scale urge for social planning or reform. In their view, the law emerges from social understandings and practices and is designed to facilitate private social understandings and promote cooperation among individuals in society. In this sense, Hart and Sacks bring a kind of private- or common-law sensibility to a new public-law world. The common law is not simply another regulatory regime—more the reverse.

It will not always be clear, of course, which institution is, in fact, most appropriate and legitimate for particular decisions. This will often be determined simply by the formal limits of their legitimate authority, but interpretation will often be necessary. Indeed, a great deal of appellate work will concern the optimum allocation of authority among possible decision makers. To guide this work, Hart and Sacks offer a range of thoughts about the comparative advantages of various institutions, on the common-sense idea that each institution should focus on what it does best. Institutional comparative advantage seemed largely to be determined by the particular legal and practical competence and experience of each institution, as well as its unique modes of decision making. Regulatory agencies, they suggest, are particularly well suited for tasks requiring expertise, legislatures for those that require an ability to harness diverse social interests to a general social purpose. Appellate courts are particularly suited for monitoring these questions of institutional competence.

In thinking about the institutional advantages of courts, Hart and Sacks pay particular attention to the *types of reasoning* specific to them. Like legislatures and administrative agencies, judges will need to think purposively about matters of policy as well as principle. But when all goes well, they will do so in a very specific way. Unlike agencies or legislatures, courts decide disputes between parties, on the basis of evidence and argument presented to them by those parties. They must offer decisions that bear the mark of "reasoned elaboration"— explanatory statements which fulfill the "obligation of reasoned decision and elaboration." The Cantaloupe Case says little about "reasoned elaboration," but the materials as a whole include a number of short essays on aspects of judicial reasoning—on the nature and appropriate use of "rules and standards" or the meaning of "discretion"—that together form something of a catalog of appropriate and inappropriate judicial styles.

Hart and Sacks are remarkably catholic about the elements that go into legal analysis—policy considerations about the nature and functioning of the legal system, legal principles, social purposes. Rules and standards, whether of statutory or common law, should be interpreted purposively and equitably. Policy was no longer an alien realm, supplementing or trumping legal reasoning. Following the Lon Fuller of "Consideration and Form," legal rules should be analyzed in terms of the principles, purposes, and policies immanent in them. Hart and Sacks write:

> Underlying every rule and standard, in other words, is at the least a policy and in most cases a principle. This principle or policy is always available to guide judgment in resolving uncertainties about the arrangement's meaning.[7]

Of course, principles and policies may also be vague and conflicting. Here, legal process jurists relied heavily on the metaphor of "weighing and balancing" to evoke the need for careful reasoning about the application of principles and policies in specific contexts. By and large, however, Hart and Sacks were at ease with a mode of reasoning certain to produce diverse results—so long as they are the result of an appropriate deliberation.

The function of the judicial opinion is to make that deliberation visible, justifying the deference due it by the quality of the "reasoned elaboration" on display.

> Obviously, more than one solution of a problem which bristles with uncertainties like these is possible, and different magistrates are likely to come out with different solutions. It may even be said that more than one answer is permissible, in the sense that if one answer had been conscientiously reached and generally accepted a reviewing court might well think it ought not to be upset, even though its own answer would have been different as an original matter.
>
> In these circumstances there may be thought to be a justification for describing the act of interpretation as one of discretion, even within the definition which has been given. But this would be to obscure what seems to be the vital point—namely, the effort, and the importance of the effort, of each individual deciding officer to reach what *he* thinks is *the* right answer.
>
> Arrangements which call for this effort in their elaboration, it is suggested, should be distinguished from arrangements which do not.[8]

Reasoned elaboration would place a decision maker's reasons before the world, and could act as a check on judicial discretion—some opinions just "wouldn't write." The adversarial structure of adjudication, placing arguments and facts before the judge in open court, would prepare judges well for this sort of careful reasoning and increase the pressure for a well-elaborated judgment.

Judicial decisions which elaborate the most careful reasoning are due deference not only because they may persuade us, but because they demonstrate that the court followed the decision-making procedure that gives courts their comparative advantage, and justifies deference in the first place. The most compelling judicial reasoning, moreover, will concern not substantive results, but questions of institutional competence themselves. It is here that appellate courts are of most significance for the broader legal order—policing rules of decision and ensuring that outcomes are, in fact, the result of appropriate deliberation. This will also require delicate judgments. To whom should one defer when legal competences overlap or conflict? This is the sort of deliberation courts are most well suited to engage in, and where they are likely to be able to reason most persuasively to a decision. They write, "[e]ven though the substance of decision cannot be planned in advance in the form of rules and standards, the procedure of decision commonly can be."[9]

Neil Duxbury has argued that one result was a new role for legal scholars: monitoring the monitors.

> Different organs have different tasks to perform within the legal process; and it is for students and scholars not only to identify those tasks, but also to ascertain whether or not they are being performed properly. Jurisprudence, in other words, is conceived as quality control. From the late 1940s through to the 1960s, process jurisprudence flourished as many academic lawyers took it upon themselves to act as quality assessors.[10]

As they pursued this new role, legal process intellectuals disagreed, often sharply, about precisely how judges should best carry out their interpretive work. Some emphasized the priority of the law's immanent "purposes," reflecting a society's values, others stressed "policies" linked more instrumentally to social objectives, while for others, as we will see in the next selection from Herbert Wechsler, principles—"neutral principles"—were key. These differences would fuel intense debates within the legal academy across several decades.

Scholars have speculated about the political and psychological backdrop to the legal process mind-set. The legal process coincided with the emergence of a national marketplace and with the remarkable transformations wrought by the Fordist model of production and distribution first implemented on a national scale during the war. Legal process jurists were optimistic about the American market, and a sense of awe about America's productive capacity pervades the Cantaloupe Case. So many actors, so many decisions, so complex a legal and economic order—and yet how efficiently cantaloupes seem to be produced, distributed, and sold. In the last pages, students are encouraged to look at the Cantaloupe Case from an "Olympian" point of view. If they are skeptical about the wisdom of so complex a legal order, they are asked whether they think things might be better organized in a Soviet-style planned economy. In the 1960s and '70s, legal process intellectuals seemed to share the complacency and moderation of Eisenhower-era elites more generally. Their thinking seemed to reflect the moderate sensibility and consensus politics of white male decision makers ambling unwittingly into the social, racial, and sexual turmoil of the 1960s. It is surprising how little legal process scholars questioned the capacity of the American political process to resolve conflicts and aggregate interests among divergent political groups.

The confidence—even complacency—of the legal process elites may have made it easier to assimilate a growing skepticism about the determinacy of deductive reasoning, an awareness of value relativism and of legal pluralism. A functional and stable legal order, conducive to economic growth, individual freedom, and institutional pluralism, could nevertheless be assured if the elites managing American institutions would embrace an agnosticism about substantive outcome, a tolerance for value differences, and a determination to think carefully, rationally, elaborating one's reasons in public, while respecting established procedures and deferring to the decisions of society's legitimate institutions. Indeed, the *absence* of substantive agreement and the *impossibility* of predictable bureaucratic deductive rationality could be seen as virtues, protecting American market democracy and the primacy of private ordering from efforts to impose social planning or control. Indeed, the legal process might be seen as a reaction against what at the time seemed the only alternative consequence of skepticism and relativism—the amoral positivism of Nazi and Soviet totalitarianism.

Although the legal process materials are marked by the political and social mood of the postwar period, it remains difficult to link them much more concretely with particular political outcomes. Many legal process scholars greeted the activism of the Warren Court—and the *Brown v. Board of Education* decision in particular— with skepticism, as we will see in the next selection from Herbert Wechsler. But other legal process scholars became avid defenders of Brown, and of the emerging Civil Rights Movement. Although legal process themes have always been most common among the mainstream center of postwar American legal thought— whether that center was largely conservative, as in the Eisenhower years, or more liberal, as in the Johnson and Nixon years—legal process ideas have also been picked up by scholars, judges, and advocates of the left and the right.

In the 1960s and '70s, the legal process would lose its dominant grip on the legal establishment. If reasoned elaboration had once seemed the epitome of "rigor" for students and judges alike, it came increasingly to seem a collection of vague generalities and unworkable distinctions. Legal academics trained in sociology and economics—even literature and linguistics—seemed to bring more rigorous tools of analysis to the table. A range of more sharply focused modes of instrumental reasoning became canonical. Legal process arguments become but some among many. Nevertheless, the Cantaloupe Case offers a window into a frame of mind and approach to the legal order that was once the predominant consciousness of the American legal establishment.

DAVID KENNEDY

NOTES

1. Hart and Sacks, *The Legal Process: Basic Problems in the Making and Application of Law* (Westbury, N.Y.: Foundation Press, 1994), 148.
2. Id., p. 3, emphasis in original.
3. Ibid., pp. 3–4.
4. Ibid., p. 4.
5. Ibid., p. 4.
6. Henry M. Hart, Jr., "The Relations between State and Federal Law," 54:4 *Columbia Law Review* 489 (1954) at 491.
7. Hart and Sacks, *The Legal Process*, 148. (1994).
8. Hart and Sacks, Foundation Press 1994 ed., pp. 149–150. Emphasis in original.
9. Foundation Press 1994 edition, p. 154.
10. Neil Duxbury, "Faith in Reason: The Process Tradition in American Jurisprudence," 15 *Cardozo Law Review* 601 (1993) at 636.

BIBLIOGRAPHY

Neither Hart nor Sacks wrote extensively—indeed, their reluctance to publish, particularly the legal process materials, has been the object of much speculation, treated as symbolic of their modesty and moderation—or of their intellectual uncertainty. Hart famously gave the Holmes Lectures in 1963, as told in Hart and Sacks, *The Legal Process* (Eskridge, 1994), p. xcviii, interrupting himself midway through the last lecture to confess that he had been unable to bring his argument to a successful conclusion and sitting down.

Hart and Sacks contracted with Foundation Press to publish their materials in 1956, but never completed the project. The "Tentative" 1958 edition was published by Foundation in 1994, edited by William Eskridge and Philip Frickey, with an extensive analytic and historical introduction, on which our account here has relied heavily. Henry M. Hart, Jr., and Albert M. Sacks, *The Legal Process: Basic Problems in the Making and Application of Law* (Westbury, N.Y: Foundation Press, 1994), William N. Eskridge, Jr., and Philip P. Frickey, editors. Eskridge and Frickey provide a valuable and exhaustive account of the reception of the Legal Process Materials at law schools and among members of the American judiciary. In addition to "The Cantaloupe Case," sections of the materials on legal reasoning, and the ubiquitous potential for indeterminacy, remain of significance. See, e.g., "The Degrees of Specificity of Directions: Herein of Rules and Standards and of Principles and

Policies" at 138–43; or "The Processes of Official Judgment Involved in the Administration of General Directive Arrangements," pp. 143–58, in which Hart and Sacks contrast the "Reasoned Elaboration of Purportedly Determinate Directions" (p. 145), which may well have more than one right result, with the "Reasoned Elaboration of Avowedly Indeterminate Directions," (p. 150), which surely will.

Hart's other significant contribution to the legal process literature was his foreword to the 1958 Supreme Court issue of the *Harvard Law Review*: Henry M. Hart, Jr., *The Supreme Court: 1958 Term. Foreword: The Time Chart of the Justices*, 73 Harvard Law Review 84 (1959). See also, Henry M. Hart, Jr., "The Relations Between State and Federal Law," 54:4 *Columbia Law Review* 489 (1954), focusing on the relation between private ordering and official law, and elaborating a view of "government as more significantly a facility than a control" while applauding "the existence of varied facilities, providing alternative means of working out by common action, through various groupings of interest, solutions of problems which cannot be settled unilaterally" as "an enrichment of equipment for successful social life." Id. at 490.

With Herbert Wechsler, Hart wrote extensively about federal-state relations and the workings of the federal court system, most famously in a treatise and casebook that became canonical in the field of federal courts. Henry M. Hart, Jr., and Herbert Wechsler, *The Federal Courts and the Federal System* (1950) (Brooklyn, N.Y.: Foundation Press, 1953) which subsequently went through multiple editions and remains, under the editorship of Richard Fallon, the classic text in the field.

Precursors, Collaborators, and Followers

The idea of legal pluralism—that a given legal system, whether advanced or primitive, may contain multiple conflicting legal institutions and normative authorities—had been articulated by legal realists and scholars of sociological jurisprudence before the war and picked up by many in the field of law and anthropology. See Eugen Ehrlich, *Grundlegung der Soziologie des Rechts* (Munich: Duncker and Humboldt, 1913).

For important early contributors to the legal process tradition, see, e.g., Roscoe Pound, "The Scope and Purpose of Sociological Jurisprudence," 24 *Harvard Law Review* 591 (1911) and 25 *Harvard Law Review* 140, 489 (1911–12); John Chipman Gray, *The Nature and Sources of the Law* (New York: Columbia University Press, 1909, and 2d ed., New York: MacMillan, 1921); Benjamin Cardozo, *The Nature of the Judicial Process* (New Haven: Yale University Press, 1921). Secondary literature on these figures includes: Leonard Baker, *Brandeis and Frankfurter: A Dual Biography* (New York: New York University Press, 1984) and Thomas K. McCraw, *Prophets of Regulation: Charles Francis Adams, Louis D. Brandeis, James M. Landis, Alfred E. Kahn* (Cambridge, Mass.: Belkmap Press of Harvard University Press, 1984). In defending agency rule-making, Pound had focused on the legitimacy of legislative delegation. Landis and Frankfurter added an analysis of the special competences of expert agencies. See Roscoe Pound, "The Growth of Administrative Justice," 2 *Wisconsin Law Review* 321 (1924); James M. Landis, *The Administrative Process* (New Haven: Yale University Press, 1938); Louis L. Jaffe, "James Landis and the Administrative Process," 78 *Harvard Law Review* 319 (1964–65); Felix Frankfurter, *The Public and Its Government* (New Haven: Yale

University Press, 1930); Felix Frankfurter, "The Task of Administrative Law," 75 *University of Pennsylvania Law Review* 614 (1926–27); Louis L. Jaffe, *Administrative Law: Cases and Materials* (New York: Prentice-Hall, 1953). For a survey of the statutory interpretation literature of the late 1930s, see Eskridge and Frickey, *infra*, lxvii, note 74. William Eskridge and Philip Frickey identify more than thirty professors who participated in a "Legal Philosophy Discussion Group" at Harvard during the 1956–57 academic year during the development of the 1958 edition of the Legal Process Materials. Eskridge and Frickey, supra, at page 213.

Other important "legal process" texts by authors from the Canon include Lon L. Fuller, "The Forms and Limits of Adjudication," 92 *Harvard Law Review* 353 (1978) (also published posthumously after wide circulation among students and scholars); and Henry M. Hart, Jr., and Herbert Wechsler, eds., *The Federal Courts and the Federal System* (Mineola, N.Y.: Foundation Press, 1973). This casebook has been published in numerous editions in the years since.

Eskridge and Frickey provide an excellent summary of the development of legal process ideas among students of Henry Hart and Al Sacks (*infra*, at cxiii–cxxv). Significant second-generation legal process scholars included Gary Bellow, "The Lawyering Process: Materials for Critical Study in Law, Cambridge Law School, Harvard Univ., 1974; Alexander M. Bickel, *The Least Dangerous Branch; The Supreme Court at the Bar of Politics* (Indianapolis: Bobbs-Merrill, 1962); Derek Bok, *Reflections on the Distinctive Character of American Labor Laws* 5:84 HARV. L. REV. 1394 (1970–1971); Abram Chayes, "The Role of the Judge in Public Law Litigation," 89 *Harvard Law Review* 1281 (1976); Abram Chayes, Thomas Ehrlich, and Andreas F. Lowenfeld, *International Legal Process* (Boston: Little, Brown, 1968); Archibald Cox, Derek C. Bok et al, *Labour Law: Cases and Materials* (FOUNDATION PRESS 13TH Ed., 2001); Jack Davies and Robery Lawry, *Institutions and Methods of the Law* (St. Paul, Minn.: West Publishing, 1982); Melvin A. Eisenberg, *The Nature of the Common Law* (Cambridge, Mass.: Harvard University Press, 1988); John Hart Ely, *Democracy and Distrust: A Theory of Judicial Review* (Cambridge, Mass.: Harvard University Press, 1980); David L. Shapiro, "The Choice of Rulemaking or Adjudication in the Development of Administrative Policy," 78 *Harvard Law Review* 921 (1965); and Harry H. Wellington, *Labor and the Legal Process* (New York: Yale University Press, 1968). For additional works, see Eskridge and Frickey at notes 284–91, pp. cxiv–cxv.

The significance of legal pluralism was expanded by the law and society scholars of the 1970s and 1980s. For an example by another author from the Canon, see Marc Galanter, "Justice in Many Rooms: Courts, Private Ordering and Indigenous Law," 19 *Journal of Legal Pluralism* 1 (1981). For a good overview of the later literature on legal pluralism, see John Griffith's "What Is Legal Pluralism?" 24 *Journal of Legal Pluralism and Unofficial Laws* 1–56 (1986).

Commentary

A recent symposium issue of the *Vanderbilt Law Review* contains an excellent series of articles commenting on the Hart and Wechsler tradition in federal courts. Hart's successor as a federal courts teacher at Harvard, Richard Fallon, contributed a fascinating retrospective analysis (on which we have relied heavily here) of the relationship between the intellectual method inaugurated by Hart and Wechsler for thinking about the powers of courts and the doctrinal field of federal courts in the United States in the ensuing years. Richard H. Fallon, Jr., "Reflections on the Hart and Wechsler Paradigm," 47 *Vanderbilt Law Review* 953 (1994). See also Ann Althouse, *Late Night Confessions in the Hart and Wechsler Hotel* 47 *Vanderbilt Law Review* 993 (1994); and Judith Resnick, "Rereading 'The Federal Courts': Revising the Domain of Federal Courts Jurisprudence at the End of the Twentieth Century'" 47:4 *Vanderbilt Law Review* 1021 (1994).

For an overview of the legal process tradition, see Neil Duxbury, "Faith in Reason: The Process Tradition in American Jurisprudence," 15 *Cardozo Law Review* 601 (1993). For a fascinating interpretation of the political, social, and psychological background to legal process thinking, on which we have also relied, see Gary Peller, "The Metaphysics of American Law," 73 *California Law Review* 1151 (1985) and Gary Peller, "Neutral Principles in the 1950's," 21 *University of Michigan Journal of Law Reform* 561 (1987–88).

The legal process approach was strongly criticized in the late 1960s and early 1970s, and fell from dominance. The legal realist Thurman Arnold had criticized the legal process idea in "Professor Hart's Theology," 73 *Harvard Law Review* 1298 (1960). The legal process materials were sharply criticized by scholars associated with the critical legal studies movement, most significantly by Duncan Kennedy, "*Form and Substance in Private Law Adjudication,*" 89 *Harvard Law Review* 1685 (1975); Richard Davies Parker, "The Past of Constitutional Theory—And Its Future," 42 *Ohio State Law Journal* 223 (1981); Mark Tushnet, "*Truth, Justice, and the American Way: An Interpretation of Public Law Scholarship in the Seventies,*" 57 *Texas Law Review* 1307 (1979); Morton J. Horwitz, *The Transformation of American Law 1870–1960: The Crisis of Legal Orthodoxy* (New York: Oxford University Press, 1992); Paul Brest, "The Substance of Process," 42 *Ohio State Law Journal* 131 (1981); Paul Brest, "Interpretation and Interest," 34 *Stanford Law Review* 765 (1981–1982); and Laurence H. Tribe, "The Puzzling Persistence of Process-Based Constitutional Theories," 89 *Yale Law Journal* 1063 (1979–80).

Scholars associated with the law and economics movement were also critical of the legal process approach. Judicial attribution of purposes to legal rules seemed a vague cover for discretion, and reasoned elaboration a poor substitute for either enforcement of a rule's plain meaning or the rigorous analysis of the requirements of market efficiency. Richard Posner, for example, criticized Hart and Sacks for presuming that legislators could aggregate interests sensibly: "the spectrum of respectable opinion on political and social questions has widened so enormously that even if we could assume that legislators intended to bring about reasonable results in all cases, the assumption would not generate specific legal concepts." Richard A. Posner, "Legal Formalism, Legal Realism, and the Interpretation of Statutes and the Constitution," 37 *Case Western Reserve Law Review*, 179 at 193 (1986–87). See also Richard Posner, "The Problems of Jurisprudence 1990" at 294; Posner, *The Federal Courts: Crisis and Reform* 286–93 (1985); Frank H. Easterbrook, "Statutes' Domains," 50 *University of Chicago Law Review* 533 (1983); William M. Landes and Richard A. Posner, "The Independent Judiciary in an Interest-Group Perspective," 18 *Journal of*

Law and Economics 875 (1975). Public choice scholars have focused their criticism on Hart and Sacks' optimism about an "expanding pie," and the potential for consensus outcomes to distributional conflicts. See, e.g., Daniel A. Farber and Philip P. Frickey, *Law and Public Choice: A Critical Introduction* (1991).

In the late 1980s and 1990s, interest in the legal process revived, leading to the publication of the materials in 1994. Eskridge and Frickey include a useful bibliography of this revival literature, *infra*, notes 324–27.

The Legal Process: Basic Problems in the Making and Application of Law

Problem No. 1 (unpublished manuscript, 1958)

An Introduction to the Nature and Function of Law
Section 1. Two Examples of the Law in Operation
Introductory Note on the Principle of Institutional Settlement

A. *The Basic Conditions of Human Existence*

In 1789 when the American republic was established some 800 million people inhabited the globe. Today, there are about 2,500 millions, and the number is steadily increasing. These human beings have a great variety of wants, ranging from the common urge to secure the simple necessities of physical existence to the most subtle of desires to achieve some sense of oneness with the universe. The more basic wants are clearly apprehended and relatively fixed. Others often are only dimly felt, and are subject to change by many complex processes both of external suggestion and of internal reflection. But whatever for the time being each individual's wants may be, human life is an unceasing process of fixing upon those on which time and effort are to be expended, and trying to satisfy them.

Here enters the most fundamental of the conditions of human society. In the satisfaction of all their wants, people are continuously and inescapably dependent upon one another. This is obviously true of wants which are in conflict. A one-sided solution, even if otherwise feasible, can prevail only if the other person lacks the means or the disposition to challenge it effectively. It is most significantly true of the great range of wants which depend for their satisfaction upon the division of labor. What then is required of others is not indulgence and inaction but affirmative and knowledgeable cooperation.

The coexistence on the face of the same planet of these ever-changing and increasing millions of people, having these wants and such abilities to satisfy the wants under these conditions of interdependence, are the basic facts of social science, and pose its basic problems.

How, if at all, are these people even to maintain their existence? Among those who have succeeded in surviving for the time being, whose wants, taken as they are at any given time, and which of them, are to be satisfied, and how? To the extent that presently existing wants are subject to change by external suggestion, which wants are to be encouraged and which discouraged? These are all questions which in some fashion or other *must* be answered—by events if not by conscious choice. Law being a pervasive aspect of social science, the questions pose problems which are basic also for lawyers.

B. The Recognition of a Community of
Interest by Groups of Human Beings

The starting point of the response which human beings seem invariably to make to the basic conditions of human existence is to recognize the fact of their interdependence with other human beings and the community of interest which grows out of it. So recognizing, people form themselves into groups for the protection and advancement of their common interests, or they accept membership in groups formed by others.

The challenge is only partly met by the many kinds of special groups which people form—such as the family in simple societies, or clubs, churches, labor unions, business associations, and the like in complex societies. There is, in addition, an invariably felt need for an overriding, general purpose group to protect and further the overriding, basic interests which the members of a community have in common and which must be protected and furthered if they are to survive and to prosper and if their various special-purpose groups are to be able to exist and to function.

These master groupings may be large or small, and well or ill adapted to their purposes. The common interests acknowledged may be minimal or extensive. The acknowledgement may be whole-hearted or grudging—or even, as to some matters by some members, withheld altogether. But whatever the variations, the facts remain that human beings do form themselves into groups of this kind and that they do so in recognition of their interdependence and of the common interests which, because of that interdependence, transcend necessarily their points of difference.

Study of the problems of satisfying human wants thus becomes the study of the problems of people living together in such general-interest groups, or communities. This calls, first of all, for an understanding of the conditions which make such community living possible at all.

C. The Institutionalization of Procedures for
the Settlement of Questions of Group Concern

Foremost among the minimal conditions are two which cut to the heart of the need for law, and come close to describing the essence of it.

People who are living together under conditions of interdependence must obviously have a set of understandings or arrangements of some kind about the terms upon which they are doing so. This necessarily follows from the fact that interdependent living is collaborative, cooperative living. People need understandings about the kinds of conduct which must be avoided if cooperation is to be maintained. Even more importantly, they need understandings about the kinds of affirmative conduct which is required if each member of the community is to make his due contribution to the common interest.

Abstract understandings of these kinds, however, are not enough. For however such understandings may have come about—whether by the development of customary patterns of behavior, or express agreement, or both—they will necessarily be indeterminate in many respects. They will therefore require to be clarified from time to time as points of dispute or uncertainty arise, and some means of securing resolution or clarification will accordingly be needed. Moreover, human beings do not invariably do what they ought to do, so that there will necessarily be occasions when perfectly clear understandings are violated, or are claimed to have been violated. Means will accordingly be needed for determining whether an asserted violation has in fact occurred, and, if so, what is to be done about it. Finally, as people gain in experience and social conditions change, existing understandings will prove from time to time to be inadequate, or at least will be thought to be inadequate by some members of the community. Demands will arise both for changes in the existing group understandings and for additional arrangements, and some means will be needed for dealing with these demands.

To put the central point of the last paragraph somewhat differently, *substantive* understandings or arrangements about how the members of an interdependent community are to conduct themselves in relation to each other and to the community necessarily imply the existence of what may be called *constitutive or procedural* understandings or arrangements about how questions in connection with arrangements of both types are to be settled. The constitutive arrangements serve to establish and to govern the operation of regularly working—that is, *institutionalized*—procedures for the settlement of questions of group concern. These institutionalized procedures and the constitutive arrangements establishing and governing them are obviously more fundamental than the substantive arrangements in the structure of a society, if not in the realization of its ultimate aims, since they are at once the source of the substantive arrangements and the indispensable means of making them work effectively.

In a very small community, it might be possible to have a single community organ, such as a council of elders, with undifferentiated authority to settle every kind of question of community concern. But in a complex modern society the questions demanding settlement are too numerous for any single individual or group of individuals to handle. Moreover, different procedures and personnel of different qualifications invariably prove to be appropriate for deciding different kinds of questions. So it is that every modern society differentiates among social questions, accepting one mode of decision for one kind and other modes for others—*e.g.*, courts for "judicial" decisions and legislatures for "legislative" decisions. Thus, a system of institutionalized procedures is developed. An organized society is one which has an interconnected system of procedures adequate, or claiming to be adequate, to deal with every kind of question affecting the group's internal relations, and every kind of question affecting its external relations which the group can establish competence to deal with.

D. *The Principle Implicit in the Procedures*

Implicit in every such system of procedures is the central idea of law—an idea which can be described as *the principle of institutional settlement*. The principle builds upon the basic and inescapable facts of social living which have been stated: namely, the fact that human societies are made up of human beings striving to satisfy their respective wants under conditions of interdependence, and the fact that this common enterprise inevitably generates questions of common concern which have to be settled, one way or another, if the enterprise is to maintain itself and to continue to serve the purposes which it exists to serve. To leave decision of these questions to the play of raw force would defeat these purposes. The alternative to disintegrating resort to violence is the establishment of regularized and peaceable methods of decision. The principle of institutional settlement expresses the judgment that decisions which are the duly arrived at result of duly established procedures of this kind ought to be accepted as binding upon the whole society unless and until they are duly changed.

Many of the mysteries about the nature of law and of legal concepts disappear in the light of a clear understanding of the principle of institutional settlement and of the reasons which entitle it to acceptance. Thus, countless pages of paper and gallons of printer's ink have been expended in debate about whether law is something which "is," like the data of the physical sciences, or something which involves elements of what "ought" to be, resting upon moral or other prudential considerations. The external facts of physical existence and human behavior and attitudes with which the law must deal are, of course, matters of what "is," or of what "will be." But apart from these limiting conditions which the law must recognize as fixed by the nature of its subject matter, the only important elements of "is" in the law are consequences simply of the principle of institutional settlement.

The enactment of a statute or the handing down of a judicial decision, to be sure, are historical facts. But these facts get their significance in the law only from the doctrines which say that they should be taken as settling something for the future and which guide judgment in deciding what that something is. When the principle of institutional settlement is plainly applicable, we say that the law "is" thus and so, and brush aside further discussion of what it "ought" to be. Yet the "is" is not really an "is" but a special kind of "ought"—a statement that, for the reasons just reviewed, a decision which is the duly arrived at result of a duly established procedure for making decisions of that kind "ought" to be accepted as binding upon the whole society unless and until it has been duly changed.

Whenever a particular settlement or asserted settlement is involved, moreover, the "ought" proves on analysis to rest on more complex grounds than the broad considerations, simply, which demand that there be some settling procedures and that determinations arrived at in accordance with those procedures be accepted. For a particular settlement will be the product of a particular kind of procedure. There will be involved, therefore, the special considerations which aid in determining the effect to be given decisions arrived at in accordance with that procedure.

"Ought" this precedent to be followed, or may the case be distinguished or overruled? "Ought" this statute to be read as reaching this situation which its words literally cover but its apparent purpose does not? "Ought" the court to give weight to prior determinations by the administrative agency charged with primary responsibility in this matter, or is it free to examine the matter *de novo*? The answers to questions such as these call always for a perceptive understanding of the role which the particular processes of decision involved play in the total complex of decisional processes which make up the institutional system as a whole.

Recognition of the significance of the principle of institutional settlement and of the various institutionalized procedures through which it operates carries with it three corollaries of vital practical importance in the study of society.

The first corollary is of concern not only to lawyers but to students of society generally. The institutions which can be devised for the settlement of social questions vary endlessly. To be sure, every society faces many of the same basic types of questions. Naturally, therefore, there are similarities between some of the institutions of one society and those of another—between courts in the United States, for example, and the tribunals for the administration of justice among the Barotse of Northern Rhodesia,[1] or between the Congress of the United States and the English Parliament. But the possible variations in particular types of procedures are endless. So also are the variations in the relationships between each type of procedure and the system as a whole. At least in its combination of procedures, therefore, every society's system is more or less distinctive and in some respects unique. Yet each system, whatever it may be, provides the indispensable framework of living within the society in question. Short of a violent reconstitution of the system, it provides the means, and the only means, by which the problems of *that* society can be resolved. It follows that no social question can be intelligently studied without a sensitive regard to the distinctive character of the institutional system within which the particular question arises.

The second corollary is of special although not exclusive concern to lawyers. The lawyer's business in any given institutional system is to help in seeing that the principle of institutional settlement operates not merely as a principle of necessity but as a principle of justice. This means attention to the constant improvement of all of the procedures which depend upon the principle in the effort to assure that they yield decisions which are not merely preferable to the chaos of no decision but are calculated as well as may be affirmatively to advance the larger purposes of the society.

The third corollary is of special concern to students of law. Knowledge of the procedures by which particular types of decisions are made and of the doctrines which determine their settling effect is root knowledge, with a ramifying and pervasive bearing on legal problems of every kind. Moreover, it is attainable knowledge. The mass of the substantive law in the United States is beyond the capacity of any lawyer or law student to master, even as it exists at any one time. And it is constantly changing—periodically in major respects in some of its parts, and constantly in minor respects in all of its parts. In contrast, any law student or practitioner can reasonably set himself the goal of mastering the main outlines, and the respective functions and interrelationships, of the various procedures of official and private settlement, and the principal doctrines and practices which govern their operation and determine their effect. In the long run, these procedures and their accompanying doctrines and practices will come to be seen as the most significant and enduring part of the whole legal system, because they are the matrix of everything else.

E. The Interplay of Private and Official Procedures of Decision

The procedures of decision of questions of group concern which are most readily thought of as institutionalized, or regularized, are those which are manned by *officials*—that is, by individuals designated to act and acting, formally and avowedly, in behalf of the society. Among these are the procedures of public prosecution, of judicial decision, of legislative enactment, of executive and administrative action, and the like—together with the procedure of public election in which, in a just analysis, the voter acts in an essentially official capacity. For many purposes, as will be seen, official procedures are distinctive, and need to be distinguished from the other procedures which make up the whole institutional system of any organized society.

---

[1] See the illuminating study by Professor Gluckman, *The Judicial Process Among the Barotse of Northern Rhodesia* (1955), reviewed in 69 Harv. L. Rev. 780 (1956).

Not every question of group concern, however, can be decided by officials, and certainly not every such question in the first instance. Every society necessarily assigns many kinds of questions to private decision, and then backs up the private decision, if it has been duly made, when and if it is challenged before officials. Thus, private persons are empowered, by observance of a prescribed procedure, to oblige themselves to carry out certain contractual undertakings, and, if dispute arises, to settle their differences for themselves. So may a host of other matters be settled which are immediately of private, but potentially of public, concern. In a genuine sense, these procedures of private decision, too, become institutionalized. An understanding of how they work is vital to an understanding of the institutional system as a whole.

The processes of private and official decision constantly interact. How they interact a few illustrations will show.

Consider, first, some simple but typical problems of human life as they present themselves to the individual in his private and individual capacity. Shall I sing while I am taking a shower? Shall I pray now? Shall I go hunting today? Shall I ask my neighbor for a job? Shall I marry this girl? Shall I leave all my worldly goods to her after I die? And so on, *ad infinitum*.

Problems of this kind must be decided by the individual himself in the first instance, although, of course, he may have to associate someone else with him in his own final decision, as in the case of the marriage and many others. But the individual himself, acting alone or in concert with other private individuals, is in the front line of decision, and this fact is of far-reaching importance in the whole theory of social ordering.

First, virtually any decision of this kind which can be mentioned may be made the basis of an appeal to the group, either by the individual himself or by someone else. If you work for your neighbor and do not get paid, you may want to complain about the non-payment or he about the way the work was done. Even in matters which seem most plainly private, others may assert an interest. Singing in the shower too loud, or too far off key, or at the wrong hour, may seem to your neighbors to be a nuisance; and they may want to have the racket stopped. Prayers may start a civil war if they are thought to be addressed to the wrong deity.

Secondly, every conceivable decision of a private individual is of concern to the group in which he lives, if not with reference to the specific character or consequences of a particular decision, at least with reference to the question whether *that kind of decision* is a proper one for an individual to make, and what its effects should be.

This is illustrated by the fact that every one of the quite ordinary problems that have been mentioned has been the subject of group consideration and action in almost every contemporary society. Indeed, the whole shape of the problem as it presents itself to the individual is affected by this prior group action.

Shall I "marry" this girl? The very question presupposes the institution of marriage with all its manifold consequences in personal and property relationships. Shall I leave her all my worldly goods after I die? What are "my" goods? The answer implicates the entire institution of private property. What have I to say about who gets my property when I die? The problem would not exist if it were not for the statute of wills. Shall I go hunting today? Where may I hunt? What kinds of birds or animals may I kill? Must I do it with a bow and arrow or may I bear a firearm? Do I need a hunting license? On all these questions, in most modern societies, the group has something to say to the individual which bears on the decision he makes.

What the individual decides will in turn affect the questions which later confront the group. This may happen in either of the two ways already indicated. A question may arise with respect to the particular things that one or more individuals have done or left undone. Or the decisions which individuals make—including not only completed acts but futile efforts and frustrated inaction—may generate a demand for a generalized decision as to how similar problems are to be handled in the future.

Both these latter kinds of decisions have to be made for the group as a whole and in such a way as to bind the group. As already indicated, if it is impossible or thought undesirable for all the members of the group to assemble together, the only recourse is the designation of a representative to act in their behalf, namely, officials.

At any given time in a going society the problems which present themselves both to its private members and to its officials will be affected by the decisions previously made in behalf of the society. In turn current decisions both of private persons and of officials will determine the shape of the problems which present themselves thereafter.

There are elements of a chicken-and-egg relationship between private decisions and official decisions in the flow of social living which defy any facile description of the process. Two broad conclusions, however, seem warranted.

First. The structure of official institutions is immensely significant in shaping the general character and direction of private activity, since it determines both the permissible range of private decision and the conditions under which the decisions are made.

Second. Within this general framework, the mass of private decisions are the primary motive force which determine the direction of the society from day to day. It is useful to think of the working apparatus of official procedures, taken as a whole, as engaged in a continuous review of these private decisions, and in continuous revision of the terms and conditions under which similar decisions will be made in the future.

The organization of these materials is based on this analysis.

Following this introductory chapter, the second chapter examines a series of problems of private decision as they present themselves within the context of the existing set of prior official and private decisions and the existing structure of procedures for future decision. The succeeding chapters examine, in succession, the major types of procedures of official decision as they attempt to deal, in their respective ways, with typical problems of social living which have theretofore failed of private solution.

F. The Two Introductory Problems

The introductory problems which follow are designed to exhibit concretely the operation of a particular system of institutional procedures in relation to a definite set of events, and to pose some characteristic questions about the appropriate scope of the principle of institutional settlement in resolving the controversies to which the events gave rise.

1. The first of the two problems grows out of a private understanding or arrangement—in a just sense, a private law—made by the parties for the governance of certain aspects of their future conduct in relation to each other. But

it will quickly be apparent that this agreement, or law, cannot be thought about in isolation from its context. The practices, attitudes, and expectations in similar situations of members of the industry to which the parties belong are part of this context. So also are a whole complex of prior institutional settlements arrived at over the years by various official agencies—state courts, state legislatures, the Congress of the United States, the Secretary of Agriculture, and various federal courts. Included among these prior settlements are various constitutive arrangements providing means for the settlement in the future of controversies growing out of agreements of this kind.

In considering how the problem should be solved, three points should especially be noticed.

(a) Observe how the prior settlements bearing upon the matter in controversy shape the questions to be decided, in the sense of making clear what is fairly open to difference of opinion and what is not.

(b) Think about the significance of the principle of institutional settlement as one of the ingredients of justice in the ultimate disposition of the specific controversy. In what, if any, sense could a decision which disregarded prior settlements and treated every aspect of the matter as *res integra* be said to be "just"?

(c) To what extent does justice require or permit account to be taken not only of the equities as between the two immediate parties to the dispute but of the effect which one or another decision will have upon the successful functioning of the institutional system as a whole in the future?

2. The second of the two problems again illustrates, as indeed all legal problems do, the complex interplay of past institutional settlements and of existing procedures for the settlement of current questions. It focuses attention on the difficulties involved in deciding when an arrangement previously formulated in general terms is to be taken as having "settled" a particular question not clearly envisaged in the formulation. More specifically, it asks the pervasive and constantly recurring question whether it makes a difference, in resolving such difficulties, if the arrangement is one which has been embodied in a statute formally enacted by a legislature or if it is one which has simply been announced by the courts as a ground of decision of litigated cases.

Problem No. 1. The Significance of an Institutional System: The Case of the Spoiled Cantaloupes

On June 21, 1943, Joseph Martinelli & Co. of Springfield, Massachusetts, a wholesaler of fresh fruits and vegetables, agreed to buy from L. Gillarde Company of Chicago, Illinois, a primary distributor, a carload of cantaloupes then *en route* east from Yuma, Arizona. The arrangement was made by telegram, confirming a telephone conversation of the same day; and its terms were clarified by supplementary telegrams on June 22.

The cantaloupes, of various varieties, were stated to be all U.S. Grade No. 1. The sale was on a "rolling acceptance final" basis. The agreed price, including a $20 precooling charge, was $1,843.25, f.o.b. Yuma, Arizona.

The cantaloupes had been shipped from Yuma on June 20, after a federal inspector had inspected them there on that day and graded them U.S. No. 1. The car was delayed in transit and did not reach Springfield until July 3.

When Martinelli first saw the cantaloupes on July 5, the next business day, they appeared to be overripe. An inspection by a federal inspector in Springfield on July 6 showed decay ranging from 35 percent in some samples to 100 percent in others, averaging approximately 85 percent, mostly Cladosporium Rot.

Cladosporium Rot is a disease of field origin, not necessarily apparent in its early stages. It does not affect the edibility of the fruit, except as it causes or hastens decay. It affects the saleability of the fruit in a local market only to the extent that decay has actually taken place.

If the Springfield inspector's analysis of Cladosporium Rot was correct, the disease being of field origin, the cantaloupes must necessarily have been infected with it when they were inspected in Yuma. But whether at that time the quality of the fruit had yet deteriorated observably, Martinelli could not be certain.

1. The first of the two major questions for consideration is what Martinelli, faced with this contretemps, ought to have done.

Martinelli knew, of course, that the cantaloupes were not going to get any better sitting in the railroad yard, and would get worse fast. Thus, the immediate question confronting the company was whether to take charge of the carload and sell it for whatever it would bring, or to refuse to have anything to do with it.

This question, however, was entangled with other questions. What, if any, might be Gillarde's claim to be paid for the cantaloupes in full, spoiled though they were? Would this claim be in any way strengthened if Martinelli appeared to treat the cantaloupes as its own, by receiving and selling them? *Per contra*, even though the cantaloupes were still Gillarde's might not Martinelli be under obligation to move promptly in Gillarde's behalf to salvage whatever value they still had? Did Martinelli have a valid claim against Gillarde, either by way of offset from the agreed price or otherwise, for failure to deliver unspoiled cantaloupes? If Martinelli failed to salvage such value as the carload had, would this claim be in any way prejudiced?

It will be seen that at least three possible courses of action had to be weighed:

First. Martinelli might decide to accept the carload as its own, assuming responsibility for the purchase price, and resell it as quickly as possible to minimize its loss. Afterwards it could seek damages in compensation for the loss, if on full reflection it appeared that Gillarde had been guilty of a breach of the agreement. This latter it might do either defensively, by refusing to pay the agreed price until an appropriate deduction had been made, or offensively, by demanding the payment of money damages from Gillarde.

Second. Martinelli might disclaim responsibility for the purchase price and reject the carload but sell it promptly for Gillarde's account, with or without special authorization. Then it could remit the proceeds, less the expenses of sale, to Gillarde. At this point it might be content to let the matter drop, hoping that Gillarde would be similarly content. Or it might go on to demand incidental damages from Gillarde for the loss of anticipated profits resulting from the breach of contract.

Third. Martinelli might refuse to have anything whatever to do with the carload. After that it might, once again, take a defensive position, leaving the next move up to Gillarde, or go on the offensive and demand damages for breach of contract.

In deciding what to do, Martinelli, of course, had the benefit of long experience in the fresh fruit and vegetable business, and it had the possibility of benefit from the advice of counsel experienced in the legal aspects of the business. The background notes which follow tell about many things which Martinelli and its lawyer undoubtedly knew as a result of this experience, and also about some things which perhaps they did not know.

2. Martinelli and Gillarde, having decided upon their respective positions, eventually became involved in litigation to settle the rights and wrongs of them. The second major question for consideration is whether the United States Court of Appeals for the First Circuit disposed of this lawsuit justly. The two opinions which the court wrote are reproduced in Part IV of the background notes.

Background Notes on Fresh Fruits and Vegetables
Part I. The Trade in Fresh Fruits and Vegetables

It may help in bringing the Gillarde-Martinelli problem to life if it is thought about in its setting in the huge present-day trade in fresh fruits and vegetables.

People have been eating fresh fruits and vegetables in season and in or near the growing area since before the dawn of recorded history. But the consumption of those foods far from the growing area and in or out of season is a relatively recent phenomenon. Despite occasional differences of opinion from small children, the consensus of view seems to be that the development is a good thing.

The extent of the consumption and the conditions which have made it possible deserve attention.

Fresh fruits and vegetables account for about three cents out of every dollar that American consumers spend. The Consumer Price Index of the United States Bureau of Labor Statistics assigns these foods a weighting of 2.91% in the cost of living as a whole.[2]

A very large proportion of fresh fruits and vegetables in the United States are eaten in a different state from that in which they were grown, as the Gillarde cantaloupes were supposed to have been.

The technological developments that have made possible this tremendous consumption of fresh but out-of-the-area-of-production and often out-of-season produce are obvious enough. Two crucial ones were the construction in the second half of the nineteenth century of a nationwide network of railroads operating on standard-gauge tracks, and the development beginning about 1880 of methods of making artificial ice.[3] Beyond these were a host of improvements in methods of cultivating, harvesting, and handling crops, all helping to satisfy the demands of the markets thus opened up.

Less obvious, because more often taken for granted, are the institutional arrangements under which the efforts of the millions of people engaged in the trade are elicited and their activities coordinated.

[2] See U.S. Bureau of Labor Statistics, Dep't of Labor, Bull. No. 1168, Techniques of Preparing Major BLS Statistical Series, Ch. 9, Table No. 2 (1951). In addition to the 2.91% weighting for fresh fruits and vegetables, canned fruits and vegetables have a weighting of 1.20%; frozen fruits and vegetables, 0.27%; and dried fruits and vegetables, 0.17%. Thus, the weighting for all fruits and vegetables is 4.55%.

[3] See New State Ice Co v. Liebmann, 285 U.S. 262, 287–91 (1932).

The basic activities, of course, are those of growers. The trade depends upon the existence of millions of acres of tillable soil. It presupposes individuals in a position to determine the use to which the soil is to be put, and able and willing to devote it to the production of wanted varieties of fruits and vegetables, both for the fresh market and for the allied canned, frozen, and dried markets.

Such decisions call for advance planning. It takes at least the length of a growing season to produce any seed crop. It takes about four years to get a producing asparagus bed and from fifteen to twenty years for a producing orchard. The preparation of land for cultivation may take even longer. Such decisions depend accordingly upon the existence of political and social conditions which will make advance planning meaningful and feasible.

Among the conditions are the existence of dependable facilities for getting crops from the farm to the market. This calls for more than a physically adequate system of transportation. It calls also for great numbers of dealers willing and able to handle the produce. In the United States only about 1% of total sales of fresh fruits and vegetables are made directly from the farmer to the consumer, and only another 1% directly from the farmer to an ordinary retailer. Most of the remaining 98% goes through a characteristic four-step process: from grower to primary receiver; from primary receiver to wholesaler; from wholesaler to retailer; and from retailer to consumer.[4]

As of June 30, 1955, there were 26,822 persons, firms, and corporations authorized, like Gillarde and Martinelli, to be intermediaries in the handling of interstate shipments of fresh produce.[5] The number of fruit and vegetable counters and stands throughout the country, to whom these intermediaries sell, must run into the hundreds of thousands. The very existence of all these enterprises bespeaks advance planning, and interdependencies for the fulfillment of plans, comparable to those of farmers.

Beyond the handlers of fresh fruits and vegetables lie, of course, the 160-odd million consumers of them. Their wants and their collective ability to satisfy them are the two main determinants of the activities of the growers and handlers. Their ability to buy what they want is a function of the economic health of the society as a whole—an expression of the interdependence which pervades the entire social order.

Every American industry involves interrelationships of the kind which have been described, and mechanisms of coordination of the kind which these interrelationships imply. The perishable nature of fresh fruits and vegetables, however, gives a special turn to the relationships in this trade, which deserves brief notice.

Shipments have to be routed promptly and surely, and can seldom be rerouted if the market to which they are first sent proves glutted. If disputes about shipments arise, the goods have to be disposed of first and the disputes settled afterwards if unnecessary losses are to be avoided.

The necessity both of prompt shipment, when produce is ready for marketing, and of prompt sale, in the market ordinarily of first arrival, results in great fluctuations in supply and corresponding fluctuations in price. Between the years 1936–40, for example, the price of fresh tomatoes had an average monthly variation

[4] See U.S. Department of Agriculture, *Marketing Channels for Fresh Fruits and Vegetables Based on Estimated Percentage of Total Sales* (1939), reproduced in Brunk & Darrah, *Marketing of Agricultural Products* 358 (1953).

[5] Letter of November 21, 1955, to Mr. Robert L. Larson, of the Class of 1956 in the Harvard Law School, from W.G. Lensen, Acting Chief, Regulatory Branch, Fruit and Vegetable Division, Agricultural Marketing Service, Department of Agriculture, Washington, D.C.

of 30% whereas the price of canned tomatoes varied only about 1%. To these risks of price variation is added the risk of spoilage, which at best is high. Thus, a survey in Washington, D.C., during the months of August and September, 1951, showed losses on cantaloupes of 21.7% of the total shipped into the market.[6]

The risks which the handlers of fresh fruits and vegetables bear, and the high costs of guarding against them, are reflected in the extraordinarily high proportion of the sales dollar which they receive. On the average only 32% of what the consumer pays is returned to the producer. Assembly takes 6.8%; transportation, 19.7%; wholesaling, 9.5%; and retailing 32%. In contrast the producer of livestock, for example, receives 65% of the final sales price with only 35% going for distribution.[7]

Despite these difficulties, the interstate trade in fresh fruits and vegetables proceeds with a remarkable absence of friction—an absence of friction which will seem remarkable, at least, to anyone with a lively sense of the potentialities for disorganization and controversy in society. An accurate measure of the number of disputes of any seriousness is provided by the informal complaints filed with the United States Department of Agriculture, which average only about 2,500 a year.[8] Of these, some 90% are settled informally and more or less amicably. Virtually all of the remainder are disposed of by formal proceedings within the Department of Agriculture. Only a handful of cases reach the courts each year.

The carload of spoiled cantaloupes which Martinelli got from Gillarde gave rise to one of these rare lawsuits. In following the course of the controversy, it is important to be aware that it *was* exceptional, and to keep steadily in mind the question of what kind of settlement will serve best to prevent the recurrence of similar controversies in the future.

Part II. What Prior Settlements Said to Martinelli

As will soon appear, a host of prior official settlements had a bearing on the problem which Martinelli confronted on July 5 and 6, 1943: state judicial decisions, state statutes, an act of Congress, prior decisions of federal courts, regulations of the Secretary of Agriculture in specific controversies of this kind in the past. Martinelli should and must have realized that, as a result of these settlements, various officials were in effect looking over its shoulder—ready to examine thereafter what it did and to direct unpleasant consequences if the things done were disapproved.

It is important to observe at the outset, however, that even if this last were not true—even if there had been no possibility that any aspect of the transaction would ever in the future come under official scrutiny—the answer to Martinelli's problem would not have been easy. It would have been easy only in a world in which Martinelli could simply forget about its agreement to pay for the cantaloupes and about the railroad's claim for the freight, and then, swallowing its disappointment over the loss of its anticipated profit on resale and ignoring the complaints of disappointed sub-purchasers, if any, go on sweetly buying and selling carloads of fresh fruits and vegetables as before.

Officials entirely aside, this, of course, is not that kind of world. Martinelli had to worry about the effect which its action and attitude would have not only upon Gillarde and any sub-purchasers but upon other suppliers and subpurchasers

---

[6] See Brunk & Darrah, *supra* note 3, at 210.

[7] *Id.* at 380, 381.

[8] U.S. Department of Agriculture, *Yearbook of Agriculture* 278–79 (1954).

with whom it might want to have dealings in the future. In other words, it had at least to worry about trade customs and accepted ideas about fair ways of doing business—about trade ethics—even if not about "law." In relation to Gillarde, specifically, if Martinelli wanted to negotiate a reasonable settlement of the impasse, it had to consider whether the nuisance of having to dispose of distress merchandise might not be outweighed by the prejudice to its negotiating position if it failed to minimize the loss by a prompt disposition.

Trade understandings and expectations, however, do not develop in a vacuum. As pointed out in the opening note of this chapter, they grow up in a context of official settlements and understandings, and are shaped by them. This aspect of the problem, therefore, will be appraised below, at pp. 43–45, after the relevant official settlements have been considered.

A. Martinelli's Own Agreement

At the base of the problem was Martinelli's own agreement with Gillarde. It had not had to buy the cantaloupes at all. Certainly it had not had to buy them on the terms it did. They were supposed to be "U.S. Grade No. 1." What did that mean? And as of what time—purchase or delivery? It had bought them "f.o.b., Yuma, rolling acceptance final." In particular, what did this mean?

If neither of these terms had ever been formally defined, the only resort would have been to inquire into the parties' understanding of them, or trade understanding, or both. It happened, however, that both terms had been defined in regulations issued by the United States Department of Agriculture. It is appropriate now to turn to those regulations for whatever information they can give, reserving until later the question of the precise authority and effect which they had—considering them for the time being as if, say, they had been issued simply by a trade association to which both dealers belonged.

1. "U.S. GRADE NO. 1."

The federal grades for fresh fruits and vegetables are an outgrowth of the Federal Government's first entry into the fruit and vegetable field during World War I.[9] They serve as facilities for private traders, saving the parties the trouble

---

[9] By the Food Control Act of August 10, 1917, 40 Stat. 276, 65th Cong., 1st Sess., Congress vested in the President wide powers of control over these and other foods. Acting in the light of a pre-war study of the fresh fruits and vegetables industry by the Department of Agriculture, in cooperation with representatives of growers, shippers, and receivers, the Food Administration issued regulations on December 1, 1917, instituting a comprehensive scheme of control. The plan included standardized grades, an inspection service, prohibitions of undesirable business practices, and the requirement of a license for all handlers.

With the end of the war this plan lapsed. But it served as a prototype of later peacetime regulation. And two of its features—federal grades and federal inspection—were continued by authority of various appropriation acts and other legislation. They have remained in effect almost without interruption ever since.

The grades for cantaloupes are among a large number of grades for many kinds of raw agricultural commodities and processed food products which the United States has promulgated.

Standards such as these are, of course, drawn from pre-existing industry practices, or more accurately, from what are thought to be the generally prevailing or most acceptable practices. They are adopted only after extensive consultation with industry representatives, and ordinarily only after formal hearing. From time to time they are amended by a similar process.

The federal standards in turn have been adopted by many of the states. Through official publications, publication and discussion in trade papers and magazines, and word of mouth, knowledge of the standards is spread throughout the trade.

The standards for fresh fruits and vegetables are contained in Part 51 of Title 7 of the Code of Federal Regulations, and occupy some 154 double-column pages in small print.

of spelling out for themselves what it is they are buying and selling, or the uncertainty of having to depend upon unwritten trade understanding or official interpretations of it. They are facilities in the literal sense. Gillarde and Martinelli did not have to refer to a federal grade in their agreement. Nor having done so did they have to ask federal inspectors to apply it. That could have been done by a state or private inspector.[10]

The federal standards for cantaloupes are reproduced in a footnote.[11] As will be seen, they make it perfectly plain that the Gillarde-Martinelli cantaloupes had ceased to be U.S. No. 1 on July 5 in Springfield, if they ever had been. But whether a latent infection in Yuma not yet visible or affecting the skin or flesh would disqualify them as of the time of shipment the regulations leave obscure. And, of course, they do not answer the question whether it was the grade

[10] In point of fact, there not being enough federal inspectors to meet the need, the standards often are applied through state or private inspection services.

The present regulations governing the federal inspection service appear in 7 C.F.R. § 51.4–51, occupying about six printed pages. These regulations state that federal inspection is available in certain designated markets, and elsewhere "to the extent permitted by the time of the nearest inspector." The time, both in and out of the principal markets, by no means suffices to supply the demand. Recently, for example, there were only seven federal inspectors stationed in Boston, and they were responsible for the entire northeastern market area.

[11] 7 C.F.R. Part 51, §§ 51.475–51.485:

SUBPART—UNITED STATES STANDARDS FOR CANTALOUPS

Grades

§ 51.475 *U.S. No. 1.* U.S. No. 1 shall consist of cantaloups of one type which are well formed, well netted, mature but not overripe, soft, or wilted; and which are free from sunscald and decay, and free from damage caused by aphis honey dew, bruises, cracks, loose seeds, dirt, hail, insects, scars, sunburn, or mechanical or other means.

(a) In order to allow for variations incident to proper grading and handling, not more than a total of 10 percent, by count, of the cantaloups in any one lot may fail to meet the requirements of this grade, but not more than one-half of this amount, or 5 percent, shall be allowed for defects causing serious damages, including not more than 1 percent for cantaloups affected by soft rot.

§ 51.476 *U.S. Commercial.* U.S. Commercial shall consist of cantaloups which meet the requirements of U.S. No. 1 grade except that the cantaloups need be only fairly well netted and except for the increased tolerance for defects specified below:

(a) In order to allow for variations incident to proper grading and handling, not more than a total of 20 percent, by count, of the cantaloups, in any lot may fail to meet the requirements of this grade, but not more than one-fourth of this amount, or 5 percent, shall be allowed for defects causing serious damage, including not more than 1 percent for cantaloups affected by soft rot.

Unclassified

§ 51.477 *Unclassified.* Unclassified shall consist of cantaloups which have not been classified in accordance with either of the foregoing grades. The term "unclassified" is not a grade within the meaning of these standards but is provided as a designation to show that no definite grade has been applied to the lot.

Application of Tolerance

§ 51.478 *Application of tolerances to individual packages.* (a) The contents of individual packages in the lot, based on sample inspection, are subject to the following limitations, provided the averages for the entire lot are within the tolerances specified for the grade:

(1) For a tolerance of 10 percent or more, individual packages in any lot may contain not more than one and one-half times the tolerance specified, except that when the package contains 15 specimens or less, individual packages may contain not more than double the tolerance specified.
(2) For a tolerance of less than 10 percent, individual packages in any lot may contain not more than double the tolerance specified, provided at least one specimen which does not meet the requirements shall be allowed in any one package.

Definitions

§ 51.479 *One type.* "One type" means that the cantaloups in any container are similar in shape and color of flesh.

§ 51.480 *Well formed.* "Well formed" means that the cantaloup has the shape characteristic of the variety.

§ 51.481 *Well netted.* "Well netted" means that the cantaloup has good netting characteristic of the variety.

§ 51.482 *Mature.* "Mature" means that the cantaloup has reached the stage of maturity which will insure the proper completion of the normal ripening process.

in Yuma or the grade in Springfield which was to be taken as decisive in the actual case.[12]

2. "Rolling Acceptance Final"

A formal definition of "rolling acceptance final" is contained, by implication, in regulations which the Secretary of Agriculture issued under the Perishable Agricultural Commodities Act of 1930.[13] These regulations define three possible methods of selling fresh produce, each with a different allocation of obligation and risk as between seller and buyer.

Each of the three methods is a special one, in the sense that it undertakes to vary the relationship from what it would be if the parties bought and sold *simpliciter*, without specifying the defined term. The methods do not purport to be exhaustive. Like the grades, moreover, the methods are entirely optional; the parties are free to choose any of the three they wish or any other. Thus, like the grades, they operate simply as facilities, which might, indeed, have been provided by a trade association rather than by the Government of the United States.

As applied to the situation in which a car is sold before it leaves the point of origin, say, Yuma, Arizona, the three methods are: "f.o.b., Yuma," "f.o.b. acceptance, Yuma," and "f.o.b. acceptance final, Yuma." It seems plain that the same three

---

§ 51.483 *Damage.* "Damage" means any injury or defect which materially affects the appearance, or edible or shipping quality of the cantaloup. Any one of the following defects, or any combination of defects, the seriousness of which exceeds the maximum allowed for any one defect shall be considered as damage:

(a) Aphis honey dew, when more than slightly sticky, or when showing discoloration which more than slightly affects the appearance of the cantaloup.
(b) Cracks or wounds, when unhealed or deep, or when materially affecting the appearance of the cantaloup. Slight healed cracks around the ends or in the sutures of the cantaloup shall not be considered as damage.
(c) Hail injury, when unhealed or deep, or when materially affecting the appearance of the cantaloup.
(d) Scars which are healed, shallow, smooth and light colored and aggregate more than 1 1/2 inches in diameter. Healed scars which are deep, rough or dark colored are considered as damaged if their appearance is more objectionable than the amount of healed, shallow, smooth and light colored scars permitted.
(e) Sunburn, when the appearance of the cantaloup is materially affected by dark yellow or brownish discoloration, or when it causes the rind to be flattened, thin or hard.

§ 51.484 *Serious damage.* "Serious damage" means any injury or defect which seriously affects the appearance, or edible or shipping quality of the cantaloup. Cantaloups which are over ripe, wilted, immature or have unhealed cracks shall be considered as being seriously damaged.

§ 51.485 *Fairly well netted.* "Fairly well netted" means that the cantaloup has fairly good netting characteristic of the variety.

[12] In the eventual litigation, the United States District Court concluded that a merely latent infection at the point of shipment disqualified the cantaloupes from being U.S. Grade No. 1, as the seller had represented them to be. This would seem to have been incorrect. In other cases the Secretary has insisted that the grades are concerned only with qualities and defects which are apparent upon visual inspection, since otherwise the value of the inspection system would be seriously impaired. *Cf.* PACA 4686, 4688, 7 A.D. 486, 492 (1948). The wording of the grades seem to support this view.

Nevertheless, neither the seller, Gillarde, nor the Secretary of Agriculture appears to have made an effort to establish that the cantaloupes were U.S. Grade No. 1 at Yuma. This seems on first impression to be strange, since only if they were not U.S. Grade No. 1 at Yuma did Martinelli, under its agreement, have any ground of complaint at all against Gillarde—or any excuse for refusing to accept the carload.

The explanation seems to lie in the testimony of an expert in the administrative proceeding that cantaloupes showing the advanced state of decay which this shipment did on July 6 must have shown sufficient decay even as early as June 20 to preclude their being graded No. 1. This testimony, amounting to an assertion that the Yuma inspector had not done his job properly, might have given rise to an issue of fact, but Gillarde saw fit not to dispute it.

For the purposes of the present problem Gillarde's concession should be accepted, and the cantaloupes assumed *not* to have been U.S. No. 1 at Yuma.

[13] 7 U.S.C.A. § 499(e).

methods apply, in parallel fashion, when the car is sold after it is already under way, although the regulations define only "rolling acceptance" and not either "rolling" or "rolling acceptance final."[14]

The definitions are reproduced in a footnote.[15] They require close study to extract their meaning. After such study, the reader may judge for himself whether the following summary is an accurate one. It is contained in a brief *amicus curiae* filed in behalf of the United States in the court of appeals in the Gillarde-Martinelli litigation:

> It will be observed that the "f.o.b." form of contract gives a maximum of protection to the buyer. Since the seller warrants that the product not only meets contract requirements but is also in "suitable shipping condition", the buyer may either reject the shipment or accept it and recover damages from the seller if the produce arrives in an abnormally deteriorated condition. If the produce deteriorated abnormally in transit because of a latent defect, such as field or orchard diseases, the buyer is protected.
>
> The "acceptance" form of contract gives the buyer the protection of "suitable shipping condition" but imposes the requirement that the buyer cannot reject the shipment.
>
> The "acceptance final" form of contract is definitely favorable to the seller. Not only must the buyer accept the shipment but he cannot claim damages from the seller on the ground that the produce was not in "suitable shipping condition." The buyer thus has no protection against latent defects which cause abnormal deterioration in transit, although he may "recover from the seller for damages

---

[14] See Schoenberg Price & Co. v. Lewis D. Goldstein Fruit & Produce Corp., 2 A.D. 772, 775 (1943).

[15] 7 C.F.R. § 46.24 (i), (k), (l), (m), and (s). The text is as follows:

Unless otherwise defined, the following terms when included in a contract or communication involved in any investigation made or hearing held pursuant to the act shall be construed, respectively, as follows:

(i) "F.o.b." (for example, "f.o.b. Laredo, Tex.", or even "f.o.b. California") means that the produce quoted or sold is to be placed free on board the boat, car, or other agency of the through land transportation at shipping point, in suitable shipping condition (see definitions of "suitable shipping condition", paragraphs (j) and (k) of this section), and that the buyer assumes all risk of damage and delay in transit not caused by the shipper, irrespective of how the shipment is billed. The buyer shall have the right of inspection at destination before the goods are paid for, but only for the purpose of determining that the produce shipped complied with the terms of the contract or order at time of shipment, subject to the provisions covering suitable shipping condition. Such right of inspection shall not convey or imply any right of rejection by the buyer because of any loss, damage, deterioration, or change which has occurred in transit.

(j) "Suitable shipping condition", in relation to direct shipments, means that the commodity, at time of billing, is in a condition which, if the shipment is handled under normal transportation service and conditions, will assure delivery without abnormal deterioration at the destination specified in the contract of sale.

(k) "Suitable shipping condition", in connection with reconsigned rolling or tramp cars, means that the commodity, at time of sale, meets the requirements of this phrase as defined in paragraph (j) of this section, relating to direct shipment.

(l) "F.o.b. acceptance" means the same as "f.o.b.", except that the buyer assumes full responsibility for the goods at shipping point and has no right of rejection on arrival, nor has he any recourse against the shipper because of any change in condition of the produce in transit, unless the produce when shipped was not in suitable shipping condition (see definitions paragraphs (j) and (k) of this section). The buyer's remedy under this method of purchase is by recovery of damages from the shipper and not by rejection of the shipment.

(m) "F.o.b. acceptance final" means that the buyer accepts the produce f.o.b. cars at shipping point without recourse.

(s) "Rolling acceptance" means that the buyer accepts at time of purchase produce which is in the possession of the transportation company and under movement from shipping point, under the terms and conditions described in paragraphs (q) and (r) of this section [pertaining to routing and various shipping charges] except that the buyer assumes full responsibility for transportation of the goods from time of purchase, has no recourse against the seller because of any change in condition after time of purchase unless the goods when shipped were not in suitable shipping condition, and has no right of rejection on arrival. The buyer's remedy under this method of purchase is by recovery of damages from the shipper and not by rejection of shipment. By agreement between the parties, however, the purchase may be made subject to inspection at any specified point while the car is rolling or in transit and the point at which the buyer will assume transportation charges may be specified without affecting the time of acceptance of the commodity.

caused by the latter's failure to comply with the contract as to the character of the goods, the time of shipment or other material provision of the agreement." *LeRoy Dyal Co., Inc. v. Allen*, 4 Cir., 1947, 161 F. 2d 152, 158.

Is the qualification in the quoted phrase from the *LeRoy Dyal* opinion supported by the text of the regulation?[16] If so, it will be seen, the crucial question under an "acceptance final" form of contract, when the produce arrives in deteriorated condition, is whether the defect had broken out at the time of purchase, in which event the buyer is not foreclosed from claiming damages, or whether it was then still latent, in which event he takes the loss.

B. The Background of State Law

Obviously, the Gillarde-Martinelli agreement was something less then completely determinate with respect to all the details of the relationship it created, in the contingency which developed. If the cantaloupes were not U.S. Grade No. 1 when the agreement was made, as Gillarde had said they were, did the purchase "rolling acceptance final" really mean that Martinelli was supposed nevertheless to accept and dispose of them, making its claim for damages against Gillarde afterwards? If that was the correct interpretation of the agreement, was an agreement of that kind valid and effectual? If it were valid and effectual, what would happen if Martinelli violated its agreement and rejected the carload?

These questions, if they came into dispute, would have to be settled by some court or other tribunal. And that tribunal would have to settle them in accordance with some general arrangement or law. If Gillarde and Martinelli had made their agreement at any time before the effective date of the mandatory provisions of the Perishable Agricultural Commodities Act of 1930, and otherwise than during the World War I interlude already mentioned,[17] the questions would have had to have been settled under state law—that is, under the law of some one or more of the states. It is relevant now to inquire what the situation would have been in this event.

The situation under state law is worth considering for three distinct reasons.

First. In appraising the soundness of the solution of the specific Gillarde-Martinelli problem which was eventually reached under federal law, it is helpful to consider, by way of comparison, what the result would probably have been if state law alone had been determinative.

---

[16] The Secretary had so held in an opinion in a reparation proceeding which has been repeatedly cited and followed. D.B. Bruno & Co., Inc. v. S. Goldsamt, Inc., 1 A.D. 605, 608–09 (1942). The opinion said in part:

It [this conclusion] is based upon the established rule that all of the provisions of a contract must be considered in determining the intention of the parties. A trade term employed in a contract does not in and of itself restrict the effect of the agreement to the meaning of that term where additional provisions are also made in the contract. In the instant case, the buyer was not tendered at shipping point the quality of goods specified in the contract. The parties had agreed not only as to the stipulation "f.o.b. acceptance final," but as to the added specification "U.S. No. 1." While under the first stipulation the buyer had no right of rejection upon arrival, the term "without recourse" does not mean that it is without recourse if the goods did not comply at shipping point with other specifications of the contract. The additional specification "U.S. No. 1" was not met, since it is established by the appeal inspection at destination that the goods when tendered for shipment did not meet the grade. In other words, the specification "f.o.b. acceptance final" should not be so construed as to nullify the specification "U.S. No. 1". The respondent is accordingly entitled to reparation to compensate it for damages suffered by reason of the breach of warranty as to grade. Had the shipper been desirous of protecting itself against the risk of reversal on an appeal inspection, it could have sold the tomatoes subject to the term "shipping point inspection final" (7 CFR 46.29; 6 F.R. 3500).

[17] See *supra* note 8.

Second. For the academic purposes of these materials, the Perishable Agricultural Commodities Act of 1930 provides an instructive example of a once contested question of federal intervention in a sphere theretofore controlled by the states. Most federal powers, although not all of them, are powers simply in reserve. In the case of these reserve powers, federal authority does not become operative unless Congress, reviewing what the states have been doing, decides that their laws need to be supplemented or superseded by some form of federal action. When it is wise and when it is not for the United States thus to assert its dormant powers is one of the major problems of American federalism. To judge whether this was wise in the case of the interstate trade in fresh fruits and vegetables, it is necessary to consider what the situation would have been if Congress had not acted.

Third. Even after Congress has intervened, state law often continues to be of importance, as in fact it was in the interstate trade in fresh fruits and vegetables. Here we encounter a recurrent and pervasive phenomenon of the American legal system, which will be seen to be an outgrowth of the principle last stated:

> Federal law is generally interstitial in its nature. It rarely occupies a legal field completely, totally excluding all participation by the legal systems of the states. This was plainly true at the beginning when the federal legislative product (including the Constitution) was extremely small. It is significantly true today, despite the volume of Congressional enactments, and even within areas where Congress has been very active. Federal legislation, on the whole, has been conceived and drafted on an *ad hoc* basis to accomplish limited objectives. It builds upon legal relationships established by the states, altering or supplanting them only so far as necessary for the special purpose. Congress acts, in short, against the background of the total *corpus juris* of the states in much the way that a state legislature acts against the background of the common law, assumed to govern unless changed by legislation.[18]

This is conspicuously true of the Perishable Agricultural Commodities Act of 1930. The Act omits to deal with many aspects of interstate transactions in fresh fruits and vegetables, leaving these to be governed by state law as it then existed or might from time to time be changed. And Section 5(b) [7 U.S.C.A. § 499e(b)], after providing that the liabilities it creates may be enforced "either (1) by complaint to the Secretary as hereinafter provided, or (2) by suit in any court of competent jurisdiction," goes on to declare expressly that "this section shall not in any way abridge or alter the remedies now existing at common law or by statute, and the provisions of this chapter are in addition to such remedies." In speaking of remedies "at common law or by statute," the Act, of course, refers to remedies under the laws of the various states.

As one court has put it, "[w]hile additional protection and additional remedies are thus afforded to shippers of perishable commodities, the statute was not intended to repeal the law of sales [of the various states] or to destroy the rights and liabilities of the contracting parties thereunder." *LeRoy Dyal Co. v. Allen*, 161 F.2d 152, 157 (4th Cir. 1947). Study of the *Allen* case will carry the reward of a more precise understanding of the sense in which this statement is to be taken.

[18] Hart & Wechsler, *The Federal Courts and the Federal System* 435 (1953).

Hart and Sacks

Obviously, it was important to Martinelli, as soon as it found out about the condition of the cantaloupes, to be able to tell what prior official settlements were binding on it, so that it could make its various decisions about what to do in accordance with them. This was also important to the community—to the Illinois community as well as the Massachusetts community, and, indeed, to the American community as a whole. For, other things being equal, speedy, orderly, and amicable adjustments of private affairs are always to be preferred to controversy. Avoidable litigation never serves to maximize the satisfactions of human wants, or to promote the common good in any other way.

But, on the present assumption that there was no uniform federal law with a controlling voice in the matter, to what body of official settlements was Martinelli to look for guidance? To the law of Massachusetts, where it did business? To the law of Illinois, where Gillarde had its principal office? Or, conceivably, to the law of the state through which the car happened to be rolling when the agreement was made?

(a) These questions would have been of concern to one in Martinelli's position, of course, only to the extent that there were material and definite divergences in the law of two or more of the states having a possible claim to govern the transaction. In point of fact there seem not to have been any such clearly defined divergences in the actual Gillarde-Martinelli situation. How this may come about in such cases is worth noticing.

In the first place, the courts of the different states draw upon a common pool of ideas in the decision of cases—except to the extent that their own legislature has directed or their own past decisions require a distinctive mode of disposition. This pool of ideas was, in the first instance, largely although not exclusively an inheritance from England. Putting aside the special case of Louisiana, American courts all looked predominantly to the English common law, or so much of it as they believed to be adaptable to American conditions, in shaping their own decisional rules. Over the years, of course, the rules of the courts in different states have developed many points of divergence. But the common pool of ideas has been maintained and refreshed by the teaching of law schools, by the writings of legal scholars, and by cogent opinions of able judges which have won acceptance in courts of other states. This common pool constitutes always a powerful force for homogeneity of legal thought in opposition to the many forces making for heterogeneity.

In the second place, various state legislatures have adopted identical or nearly identical statutes in certain fields of law in which the need for uniformity has seemed most pressing. The most important of these statutes have been the fruit of the efforts of the Commissioners on Uniform State Laws, a body of officials representing each of the forty-eight (and presumably now forty-nine) states. One of the more widely adopted of the statutes recommended by the Commissioners is the Uniform Sales Act, which governs transactions of the Gillarde-Martinelli type. In 1943 this act was in force in both Massachusetts and Illinois.[19]

The various uniform acts in the field of commercial law are largely codifications of the decisional rules previously developed by the courts without benefit of statute. The Commissioners have not often invented new rules of law. In respects in which the rules of different courts were in conflict, they have usually been

---

[19] See Mass. Ann. Laws Vol. 3A, ch. 106; Smith-Hurd Ann. Stat. Ill., ch. 121 1/2.

content, instead, to choose the one deemed preferable, and then to reduce the whole to what was thought to be the more convenient form of an enactment. In this enterprise, they have been vastly aided, of course, by the generally homogeneous legal tradition of the various states. The same tradition has helped also to secure uniformity in the interpretation of the acts. But, as these materials recurrently illustrate, statutes are inescapably indeterminate in many of their applications. When there is room for choice, there is room for divergence of interpretive result.

(b) Suppose that in the situation confronting Martinelli these means of securing homogeneity of state law had failed, as they often do, and the company had been faced with conflicting interpretations of a material provision of the Uniform Sales Act by, say, the highest courts of Massachusetts and Illinois.

If such a situation had arisen in Australia, the company would have been able to say to itself, "one of these two interpretations must be wrong, and we have only to decide which is right and to act accordingly, secure in the knowledge that we can appeal to a higher court if the other interpretation is applied to us." Unlike the High Court of Australia, however, the Supreme Court of the United States has no jurisdiction to review and reverse a decision by the highest court of a state in a matter of state law.[20] The American system tolerates discrepancies in the substantive law of the various states, and provides no institutionalized procedure for ironing them out.

To prevent these discrepancies from working hardship or injustice to people who are faced with uncertainty as to whether one or another of two conflicting rules of law will be applied to them, the American system puts its reliance primarily on a separate body of doctrine known as the conflict of laws, which undertakes to answer the preliminary question of which state's law is applicable in a situation in which more than one state may claim a concern. To the extent that the courts of the several states follow the same rules for the choice among possibly applicable but conflicting systems of law, this body of doctrine enables people in the position of Martinelli to determine the applicable law with the same assurance that it would have if every state followed the same substantive rules of decision.

The difficulty is that questions of the conflict of laws are regarded as primarily matters of state law in which divergence of rule is permissible rather than as matters of uniform federal law. To be sure, the Supreme Court of the United States has extracted from the Full Faith and Credit Clause of the Federal Constitution and the Due Process Clause of the Fourteenth Amendment certain limitations upon extreme departures by the state courts from generally accepted principles of the common law. Within the scope of this overriding federal regulation there exists an institutionalized procedure for the resolution of differences of opinion about the choice of law among state courts and a resulting body of principle for determining with some basis for assurance which state's law is applicable. But these constitutional limitations still permit the state courts a wide latitude for the enforcement of unorthodox or divergent views of the conflict of laws.[21] To the extent that the state courts take advantage of this latitude,

---

[20] See Hart, *The Relations Between State and Federal Law*, 54 Colum. L. Rev. 489, 499–506 (1954).

[21] See, *e.g.,* Pink v. A.A.A. Highway Express, Inc., 314 U.S. 201 (1941). See generally Cheatham, *Federal Control of Conflict of Laws*, 6 Vand. L. Rev. 581 (1953); Jackson, *Full Faith and Credit—The Lawyer's Clause of the Constitution*, 45 Colum. L. Rev. 1, 17, 26–27 (1945).

a confident prediction about which state's law will be applied is impossible unless it is known in which state's courts litigation will take place.

In the actual Gillarde-Martinelli situation, one may hazard the guess that if the conflicts question had become important the law of Massachusetts would have been applied, even by a court outside Massachusetts. But this, once again, would have been the result of the tendency toward uniformity of doctrine resulting from a common body of legal thought rather than of any mandatorily applicable federal law. Moreover, the guess is only a guess, for there is no real consensus of view among either courts or commentators even in this simple and frequently recurring type of situation in which one would have supposed that the applicable rules of the conflict of laws would long since have been settled.[22]

Had there been divergences both of substantive law and of conflicts doctrine as between Massachusetts and Illinois, Martinelli would have had to take into account still another body of law in its effort to locate the rules which should guide its course of action—namely, the body of law determining which states' courts would have jurisdiction to settle the controversy if it were brought before them. This would depend in the first instance on which party chose to initiate litigation and so to propose a forum, for it is only a defendant who can object to a court's competence to adjudicate. Without attempting to explore the niceties of the matter, it seems reasonably clear that if Martinelli (1) was content to await the initiation of litigation by Gillarde, (2) was doing business only in Massachusetts, and (3) was able to keep its principal officers out of Illinois, it could count upon being sued only in Massachusetts. In this event, it could count also upon being judged by the rules of substantive law made applicable by the Massachusetts rule of the conflict of laws. If, on the other hand, Martinelli wanted to remain free to bring action against Gillarde, it would have to reckon also with the rules of substantive law made applicable by the rule of the conflict of laws of the state or states in which Gillarde could be sued. If Gillarde was doing business only in Illinois and was able to keep its principal officers out of Massachusetts, this would be the conflict of laws rule of the Illinois courts.

2. THE QUESTION OF THE EXISTENCE OF A BINDING PRIVATE SETTLEMENT

Embedded in the Gillarde-Martinelli controversy, although heretofore ignored, was a question whether the original oral telephonic agreement had been sufficiently reduced to writing by the later exchange of telegrams so as to make it enforceable against either party.

Oral agreements, ordinarily, are just as enforceable as written ones, although the problems of proof may differ. However, the English Statute of Frauds of 1677 introduced the requirement of a writing with respect to a variety of special types of transactions. Among them were sales, or contracts of sale, of goods of more than a stated value. The Statute of Frauds has been almost universally copied, with adaptations, in the various American states; and the sales provision of it was included in the Uniform Sales Act, which, as already noted, was in force in 1943 in both Massachusetts and Illinois.

---

[22] On the problem generally, see Lorenzen, *Validity and Effects of Contracts in the Conflict of Law*, 30 Yale L.J. 655 (1921); Cook, *'Contracts' and the Conflict of Laws*, 31 Nw. U. L. Rev. 143 (1936); Cook, *'Contracts' and the Conflict of Laws: Intention of the Parties*, 32 Nw. U. L. Rev. 899 (1938); Nussbaum, *Conflict Theories of Contracts: Cases Versus Restatement*, 51 Yale L. J. 893 (1942).

The Massachusetts provision is as follows:

> (1) A contract to sell or a sale of any goods or choses in action of the value of five hundred dollars or more shall not be enforceable by action unless the buyer shall accept part of the goods or choses in action so contracted to be sold, or sold, and actually receive the same, or give something in earnest to bind the contract, or in part payment, or unless some note or memorandum in writing of the contract or sale be signed by the party to be charged or his agent in that behalf.[23]

Martinelli's claim of an escape from its difficulties by way of this provision was so tenuous, in the actual situation, that it has not been thought worth while even to reproduce the evidence about the contents of the telephonic conversation and the texts of the ensuing telegrams which would be needed to appraise it with precision. The claim would almost certainly have failed in the courts of either Massachusetts or Illinois. See *Roach v. Lane*, 226 Mass. 598, 116 N.E. 470 (1917); *Western Metals Co. v. Hartman Ingot Metal Co.*, 303 Ill. 479, 135 N.E. 744 (1922). As will be seen, it failed in the end when it was advanced in a federal district court.

The provision nevertheless has a general academic interest here, since it illustrates an important type of official settlement governing the making of binding private settlements, and suggests the kinds of questions which may become entangled in the ultimate solution of a problem such as Martinelli's.

Arrangements which confer power to make binding settlements, whether upon officials or private persons, commonly attach formal or other procedural conditions for the due exercise of the power. Commonly also, hard problems are presented when there has been a failure of exact compliance with these conditions, and expectations engendered by the assumption that a power was duly exercised are threatened with disappointment. To deal with these problems, the courts frequently develop, without benefit of any further act of the legislature, *curative doctrines* to take care of situations in which the failure does not seem to touch the essential purpose of the requirement.

Precisely this happened with the Statute of Frauds. As originally enacted, the only "unless" clause in the statute was the final one requiring a note or memorandum in writing. The three earlier ones in the version above quoted were judicially developed, and then later incorporated into the statute. As a result Martinelli had express warning that it might lose any defense which the statute gave it if it "accepted" any part of the goods and "actually received" them, although they were still uncertainties as to just what would constitute "acceptance" and "actual receipt." For some further intricacies of the problem in the event of litigation in a federal rather than a state court, see *Rothenberg v. H. Rothstein & Sons*, 183 F.2d 524 (3d Cir. 1950).

3. THE EFFECT OF THE AGREEMENT, IF IT WAS VALID, UNDER THE UNIFORM SALES ACT

For centuries sellers have been shipping goods to buyers which the buyers on occasion thought were not up to snuff. Hosts of the resulting controversies have been brought to court. In the traditional analysis of such problems which the courts developed and which the Commissioners on Uniform State Laws sought to incorporate in the Uniform Sales Act, a crucial question is "Whose goods are

[23] See § 6 of statute cited *supra* note 18.

they?" Or, in other words, "When did title pass?" Martinelli thus had to ask itself, "Are these cantaloupes ours or are they still Gillarde's?" This is not to say that the answer to the question of "whose property?" gives the final answers to every question of disputed legal relationships in transactions of sale. It merely tends to fix the channels within which the further answers are to be found.

The normal inference in a transaction of the Gillarde-Martinelli type would be that the cantaloupes belonged to the buyer as soon as the seller had completed the final act which it had agreed to do. The purchase related to a specific, described carload. The buyer had agreed to pay the freight. Gillarde's final responsibility was to direct the rerouting of the car to Springfield. If at the time it did this Gillarde was in compliance with the agreement, it could fairly be concluded that the cantaloupes thenceforth were Martinelli's. It would follow that Martinelli bore the risk of subsequent spoilage.[24]

As indicated, however, this conclusion would depend upon the assumption that Gillarde had done what it was supposed to do under the agreement, or substantially so.[25] If by reason of infection with Cladosporium Rot the cantaloupes were not of U.S. Grade No. 1 when sold, as they had been represented to be, then Gillarde had not done this. In this event it could be concluded that the setting aside was unauthorized, and the carload might be treated as belonging still to Gillarde. Moreover, Gillarde would be guilty of what the traditional law calls a breach of warranty.

But even if Martinelli could be sure that Gillarde *had* been guilty of a breach of warranty, the law of sales left it with some hard problems of what to do about it. Section 69(1) of the Uniform Sales Act specifies four possible remedies of a buyer in such a situation,[26] and Section 69 (2) says that "[w]hen the buyer has claimed and been granted a remedy in any of these ways, no other remedy shall thereafter be granted."

If Martinelli pursued either of the first pair of remedies specified, it would, in effect, treat the cantaloupes as its own and depend for being made whole upon a claim against Gillarde for damages for breach of warranty, to be asserted either defensively or offensively.[27] The damages, "in the absence of special circumstances showing proximate damages of a greater amount," would be "the difference between the value of the goods at the time of delivery to the buyer and the value they would have had if answering to the warranty."[28]

---

[24] See Steel City Fruit Co. v. Monheim's Wholesale Produce Co., 64 F. Supp. 275 (W.D. Pa. 1946).

[25] For a discussion of the defense of substantial performance and a nice analysis of when it should be available, see LeRoy Dyal Co. v. Allen, 161 F.2d 152 (4th Cir. 1947).

[26] Mass. Ann. Laws, Vol. 3A, ch. 106, § 58:

(1) If there is a breach of warranty by the seller, the buyer may, at his election—

    (a) Accept or keep the goods and set up against the seller the breach of warranty by way of recoupment in diminution or extinction of the price.

    (b) Accept or keep the goods and maintain an action against the seller for damages for such breach.

    (c) Refuse to accept the goods, if the property therein has not passed, and maintain an action against the seller for damages for such breach.

    (d) Rescind the contract to sell or the sale and refuse to receive the goods, or if they have already been received, return or offer to return them to the seller and recover the price or any part thereof which has been paid.

[27] For a case in which a buyer succeeded in maintaining a claim for damages in such a situation, see A. J. Conroy, Inc. v. Weyl-Zuckerman Co., 39 F. Supp. 784, 786 (N.D. Cal. 1941).

[28] The quoted language is from Section 69(7), which applies "[i]n the case of breach of warranty of quality." Section 69(6) provides in more general terms that "[t]he measure of damages for breach of warranty shall be the loss directly and naturally resulting, in the ordinary course of events, from such breach."

By following either of these courses, Martinelli, it will be observed, would assume responsibility for payment of the purchase price. As against this fixed obligation on the debit side of the ledger, it would have on the credit side the net proceeds of sale plus whatever uncertain, additional amount it might be able to establish was called for by the statutory measure of damages. This would involve not only the annoyance of a distress sale of merchandise but the assumption of the burden of proving both the adequacy of the price realized and the price that might have been realized from unspoiled merchandise. If the market for cantaloupes had fallen, Martinelli might have been left with a net loss.

If Martinelli pursued either of the second pair of statutory remedies, Martinelli would, in effect, treat the cantaloupes as still belonging to Gillarde. Thus, it would escape responsibility for paying the agreed purchase price. If it chose to do more than this, and pursue a remedy for breach of warranty, it might end up with a credit on the ledger reflecting any profit which it lost because the goods were not as warranted.[29]

But if refusing to accept the cantaloupes and rescinding the contract of sale meant having nothing whatever to do with them, there were serious difficulties in the way.

In the first place, Martinelli had to ask itself whether it would be conscionable for a buyer to invoke the remedy of rejection in such a way as to increase the seller's loss in a case in which the seller had acted in good faith and without negligence and was not himself in a position to salvage rapidly spoiling goods. A few pre-Sales Act cases, exemplifying the flexibility of unwritten law, suggested that it was not, even in the absence of any agreement between the parties about the matter.[30] To be sure, Section 69 of the Sales Act seemed to give the aggrieved buyer the remedy of rejection in unqualified terms. But in other situations courts had found ways around this language.[31] Moreover, it is interesting to observe that at the time Martinelli faced its problem there was in existence a proposed revision of the Uniform Sales Act modifying the sweeping language of Section 69 so as to impose a qualified duty of salvage upon the buyer. This provision, now embodied in Section 2–603 of the Uniform Commercial Code, is reproduced in a footnote.[32]

[29] See *supra* note 27.

[30] See Hitchcock v. The Griffin & Skelley Co., 99 Mich. 447, 454, 58 N.W. 373 (1894); Rubin v. Sturtevant, 80 Fed. 930, 932 (2d Cir. 1897).

[31] See the illuminating discussion of the equities and practicalities of rejection in Honnold, *The Buyer's Right of Rejection*, 97 U. Pa. L. Rev. 457 (1949).

[32] As contained in the 1956 recommendations of the American Law Institute and the National Conference of Commissioners on Uniform State Laws, the provision is as follows:

Section 2–603. *Merchant Buyer's Duties as to Rightfully Rejected Goods.*

(1) Subject to any security interest in the buyer * * *, when the seller has no agent or place of business at the market of rejection a merchant buyer is under a duty after rejection of goods in his possession or control to follow any reasonable instructions received from the seller with respect to the goods *and in the absence of such instructions to make reasonable efforts to sell them for the seller's account if they are perishable or threaten to decline in value speedily.* Instructions are not reasonable if on demand indemnity for expenses is not forthcoming.

(2) When the buyer sells goods under subsection (1), he is entitled to reimbursement from the seller or out of the proceeds for reasonable expenses of caring for and selling them, and if the expenses include no selling commission then to such commission as is usual in the trade or if there is none to a reasonable sum not exceeding ten per cent on the gross proceeds.

(3) In complying with this section the buyer is held only to good faith and good faith conduct hereunder is neither acceptance nor conversion nor the basis of an action for damages.

(Emphasis added.)

In the second place, Martinelli had to ask itself whether its own agreement with Gillarde did not in any event debar it from exercising the remedy of rejection. If Section 69 were read by itself, it would seem to give the remedy in spite of any agreement to the contrary. But Section 69, as well as all the other provisions of the Sales Act, needs to be read in the light of Section 71, which says:

> If any right, duty or liability would arise under a contract to sell or a sale by implication of law, it may be negatived or varied by express agreement or by course of dealing between the parties, or by custom, if the custom be such as to bind both parties to the sale.

We touch here upon an aspect of the law of sales (and, indeed, of commercial law generally as well as of much other law) which is of immense significance and which deserves a moment's digression.

The doctrines which the English and American courts built up in defining the respective obligations of seller and buyer and the respective remedies of each in the event of default by the other were designed to reflect the general understanding of the commercial world. But hardly any of them were hard and fast. They embodied, rather, what the courts believed to be the *usual* and *fair* understanding of parties in a situation of the kind in question. For those who were willing to accept them, therefore, they operated, as so much of the law does, as a facility, saving the parties themselves the trouble of spelling out all the details of their arrangements for themselves. At the same time, those who did not wish to accept them remained free within broad limits expressly to stipulate contrary provisions. The courts, moreover, thought of themselves as free to infer a contrary provision either from a prior course of dealing between the same parties or from a special custom or usage in the trade or locality with reference to which the particular parties could fairly be taken to have contracted.

Doctrines of this kind are described hereafter in these materials as *suppletive, optional,* or *filling-in* terms of private settlements, as opposed to *constructive* or *mandatory* terms.

The draftsmen of the Uniform Sales Act, seeking to reduce the flexible decisional doctrines of the courts to a single authoritative set of words, had to deal with this phenomenon of merely suppletive terms of private settlements. This they did, for the most part, by stating the usual incidents of a sale or contract to sell in the main body of the statute as if they were mandatory and invariable, and then branding them all as suppletive by the overriding provision of Section 71.

Section 71 thus removes any doubt as to the validity under the Sales Act of an advance disclaimer of the remedy of rejection, leaving only the question whether that is what the "rolling acceptance final" clause meant. If the trade understood that one who bought "rolling acceptance final" had no right of rejection, Section 71 could be relied upon as a basis for holding the particular parties to that understanding.

On the question of what would happen if a buyer who had agreed not to reject nevertheless rejected and so increased the loss to the seller, neither the pre-Sales Act nor the Sales Act cases cast any light. Such agreements have been uncommon, and the question seems not to have been presented. Even the Uniform Commercial Code is silent as to what happens if a buyer violates the constructive obligation to the same effect imposed by Section 2–603.

Torn between the disadvantages of assuming responsibility for the purchase price, and then claiming damages for breach of warranty, and the doubts about its right to reject, Martinelli might well have considered a middle course. Why not reject the cantaloupes and so escape responsibility for the purchase price but at the same time take charge of them and sell them in Gillarde's behalf? Could it do this?

The well-known case of *White v. Schweitzer*, 221 N.Y. 461, 117 N.E. 941 (1917), would have warned Martinelli's counsel of the danger that action of this kind by its client might be taken as constituting in fact or law an acceptance cancelling out any merely verbal rejection. But there the buyer sold at once, after wiring notice of intention to do so, without giving the seller a chance to take over.[33]

Suppose that Martinelli avoided this pitfall but that Gillarde, after notice, refused to do anything?

In partial reflection of the doctrine of *White v. Schweitzer*, Section 48 of the Sales Act states that "[t]he buyer is deemed to have accepted the goods when," among other things, "he does any act in relation thereto which is inconsistent with the seller's ownership." To be sure, Section 49 makes clear that the accepting buyer in such a case does not thereby lose his claim against the seller for breach of warranty, if he notifies the seller of the breach within a reasonable time. But the buyer, if Section 48 applies, is forced to travel the road of liability for the purchase price minus whatever damages can be proved rather than the often more attractive road of no responsibility for the price at all.

In *Baker v. J.C. Watson Co.*, 64 Idaho 573, 134 P.2d 613 (1943), two of the five justices thought that a sale in the seller's behalf, even after full warning to him and his refusal to do anything on his own account, constituted an acceptance by the doing of an act inconsistent with the seller's ownership within the meaning of Section 48. But the majority of the court held to the contrary, ruling that the buyer in such circumstances does not become liable for the purchase price. Other decisions, both before and after the Sales Act, have supported this result.[34]

Whatever may be the equities of the *Baker* ruling where the buyer has not expressly disclaimed the remedy of rejection, however, is it not plain that the buyer who is under the duty of taking charge of the goods ought not to be penalized for doing his duty? Notice that the draftsmen of Section 2–603 of the Uniform Commercial Code thought so.[35]

C. What the Act of Congress Said to Martinelli

1. THE CRUCIAL PROVISIONS

It is now time to consider the bearing of the Perishable Agricultural Commodities Act of 1930.

The main bearing of that Act is that it declares it to be "unlawful" as a matter of federal law, among other things, "[f]or any dealer to reject or fail to deliver

---

[33] The unfortunate buyer in *White v. Schweitzer*, standing on his attempted rejection, failed to make any cross claim for damages for breach of warranty, and was exposed to the possibility of a jury verdict for the full price. Whether a cross claim would have been successful the opinion does not consider.

[34] For pre-Sales Act cases, see Descalzi v. William S. Sweet & Son, 30 R.I. 320, 75 A. 308, 27 L.R.A., N.S. 932 (1910), and cases cited. See also *supra* note 29. For a case under the Sales Act, see Wilson & Co. v. Werk Co., 104 Ohio St. 507, 136 N.E. 202, 24 A.L.R. 1438 (1922). As the Ohio court points out, the question seems to be controlled by the provisions of Section 69(5) giving the rescinding buyer a power of sale on the seller's behalf.

[35] See *supra* note 31 for Paragraph (3) of the section.

in accordance with the terms of the contract without reasonable cause any perishable agricultural commodity bought or sold or contracted to be bought, sold, or consigned in interstate or foreign commerce by such dealer." Section 2(2), 7 U.S.C.A. § 499b(2).

Here, in the characteristic fashion already described, federal law appears to superimpose itself on state law without displacing it. The private duty established is a federal duty. But the statute itself says nothing about what action is and what is not "in accordance with the terms of the contract." In the absence of further authoritative federal action pursuant to the statute, therefore, it says simply that there is a federal duty to comply with the state law which has just been described.

But in addition to declaring this general federal duty of observance of contracts in accordance with state law, the statute sets up a whole battery of federal remedies or sanctions for breach of the duty, and it institutionalizes new procedures for settling questions about the remedies.

The statute says, first of all, that "[i]f any * * * dealer violates any provision of" Section 2 "he shall be liable to the person or persons injured thereby for the full amount of damages sustained in consequence of such violation." Section 5(a), 7 U.S.C.A. § 499e(a).

In paragraph (b) of the same section, in a provision already quoted on p. 23, above, the statute goes on to say that "[s]uch liability may be enforced either (1) by complaint to the Secretary as hereinafter provided, or (2) by suit in any court of competent jurisdiction." The two following sections specify certain details of the procedure for complaint to the Secretary; investigation and hearing; issuance when appropriate of a reparation order; and judicial enforcement or review of the order. Sections 6 and 7, 7 U.S.C.A. § 499f and § 499g.

Secondly, the statute requires dealers in the position of Gillarde and Martinelli to secure a license from the Secretary, subject to a heavy civil penalty for doing business without a license. Section 3, 7 U.S.C.A. 499c. It then brings up its heaviest artillery:

Section 8(a), 7 U.S.C.A. § 499h(a), provides that "Whenever * * * the Secretary determines, as provided in section 499f of this title, that any commission merchant, dealer, or broker has violated any of the provisions of section 499b of this title [which includes the provision on observance of contracts], the Secretary may publish the facts and circumstances of such violation and/or, by order suspend the license of such offender for a period not to exceed ninety days, except that, if the violation is flagrant or repeated, the Secretary may, by order revoke the license of the offender * * *."

Another provision of the statute, moreover, authorizes the Secretary to suspend the license of any dealer who fails to pay promptly any reparation order issued against him, after the order has become final. Section 7(d), 7 U.S.C.A. § 499g(d).

In the first twenty-five years under the Act, the Secretary has actually revoked a dealer's license in only 103 cases, and suspended a license in only 116.[36] Nevertheless, by virtue of the statute Martinelli's decision was in some sense a matter of business life or death.

---

[36] The figures come from the letter cited in note 4, *supra*. In addition, licenses were denied in the first instance in 94 cases under the provisions of 7 U.S.C.A. § 499d(b) and in 24 cases under § 499d(d). *Ibid.*

The general history of the Perishable Agricultural Commodities Act of 1930 was common knowledge in the fresh fruit and vegetable trade, and some of the high points of it might have illuminated for Martinelli or its counsel the bare words of the statute.

(a) The Abortive Voluntary Plan of 1925. The federal government's initial entry into the field of fresh fruits and vegetables as a war measure during World War I has already been mentioned.[37] In the agricultural depression after the war, complaints of unfair dealings on the part of receivers of perishable agricultural commodities, and counter-complaints by receivers against shippers, persisted and multiplied. Memories of the war-time mode of regulation prompted many suggestions for its reintroduction.

In 1925 the Department of Agriculture, on its own initiative and without benefit of Congressional authorization, adopted a plan of voluntary registration and self-regulation by growers, shippers, and receivers. Those who registered agreed to arbitrate their disputes, the arbitrators to be officials of the Department. By 1926, a total of 788 persons and firms handling about half a million cars of produce a year had volunteered to become part of this system. The next year, however, the plan was abandoned, before it had come into full operation, upon the enactment of the Produce Agency Act.

(b) The Produce Agency Act of 1927. Congress' first effort at coercive control in peacetime of the abuses of the fresh fruit and vegetable trade followed the classic pattern of unthinking, unscientific legislation: "If you want to stop something from happening, make it a crime."

The Act still remains on the books. 44 Stat. 1355, 7 U.S.C.A. §§ 491–97. Its main provision is as follows:

> **§ 491. Destruction or dumping of farm produce received in interstate commerce by commission merchants, etc; penalty**
>
> After June 30, 1927, any person, firm, association, or corporation receiving any fruits, vegetables, melons, dairy, or poultry products or any perishable farm products of any kind or character, referred to in this section and section 492 of this title as produce, in interstate commerce, or in the District of Columbia, for or on behalf of another, who without good and sufficient cause therefor, shall destroy or abandon, discard as refuse or dump any produce directly or indirectly, or through collusion with any person, or who shall knowingly and with intent to defraud make any false report or statement to the person, firm, association or corporation from whom any produce was received, concerning the handling, condition, quality, quantity, sale, or disposition thereof, or who shall knowingly and with intent to defraud fail truly and correctly to account therefor shall be guilty of a misdemeanor and upon conviction shall be punished by a fine of not less than $100 and not more than $3,000, or by imprisonment for a period of not exceeding one year, or both, at the discretion of the court. Mar. 3, 1927, ch. 309, § 1, 44 Stat. 1355.

It will be observed that the Act applies only to persons receiving produce "for or on behalf of another"—that is, as commission agents. In the debate over the bill that became the 1930 Act, it was stated that one of the reasons for the

[37] See *supra* note 8.

failure of the measure was that large numbers of commission merchants had simply changed their way of doing business, and were buying produce on their own account, thus escaping the impact of the Act altogether.

But the Act had other shortcomings, too. The meaning of its basic commands was by no means free from doubt.[38] Even more important was the dilemma which its enforcement posed of either swinging the big club of criminal prosecution or doing nothing. As always, choice fell usually on inaction in cases of doubt. Closely related was the fact that as a criminal measure the Act was dependent for its enforcement upon the various United States district attorneys, and to compete for their interest and attention with the whole body of federal criminal laws.

Whatever the reason, enforcement activity under the Act has been minimal,[39] and Martinelli need not have been greatly concerned about being prosecuted under it.

(c) The Legislative History of the 1930 Act. The bill which became the Perishable Agricultural Commodities Act of 1930 was introduced in an earlier and more drastic form in the previous Congress by Senator Borah of Idaho. The original bill not only provided for the licensing of commission merchants, dealers and agents receiving interstate shipments but required the licensees to put up a bond for the fulfillment of their obligations. Without holding hearings, the Senate Committee on Agriculture and Forestry reported the bill, S. Rep. No. 825, 70th Cong., 1st Sess. (1928), but it got no further. In the second session of the same Congress, the House Committee on Agriculture held hearings on a similar bill introduced by Congressman Summers of Washington; but the bill never reached the floor.

Both Senator Borah and Congressman Summers pressed their proposals with amendments, in the Seventy-first Congress. The Senate acted first, and in form it was Senator Borah's bill (S. 108) which was enacted. But the House amended the Borah bill by substituting the Summers bill (H.R. 5663), and the substitution prevailed in conference.[40]

---

[38] See Sellers & Goodrich, *Administrative Procedure and Practice Under the Perishable Agricultural Commodities Act, 1930*, at 8 n.18 (1939).

[39] The annual reports of the Attorney General and of the Solicitor of the Department of Agriculture yield the following figures:

Year	Cases referred	Convictions	Dropped	Pending
1929	9	1	2	6
1930	34	4	7	39
1931	38	5	10	not stated
1932	24	15	9	" "
1933	not stated	12	9	" "
1934	—— no report given ——			
1935	not stated	3	not stated	" "
1936	" "	3	7	" "

Later reports on activity under the Act are even spottier. In 1950 the Solicitor's annual report said that there were two prosecutions under the Act and a backlog of 150 cases pending.

[40] The student will find it worthwhile to trace the legislative history of these measures in detail, since the process is one which is recurrently necessary in dealing with legal problems arising out of federal statutes. The first step in doing this is to get the number of the bill which was enacted—here S.108, 71st Congress. This number is reported in the margin of the United States Statutes at Large. Or, if the name of the sponsor is known, it can be found by looking up the sponsor's name in the general index of the appropriate volume of the Congressional Record. Alternatively, it and the numbers of related bills can be found through the appropriate subject heading in the same index.

Given the number, the floor history of the bill can be traced through the History of Bills and Resolutions which is appended in each volume of the Congressional Record Index. This history, however, does not tell what happened to the bill in committee, except for giving the fact and number of any committee report. Printed transcripts of committee hearings must be found, if any, by searching the bound volumes of hearings of the appropriate committee for the session in question. Committee reports can be found by searching the bound volumes of Senate or House Committee reports, as the case may be, for that session.

Given the number, the floor history of the bill can be traced through the History of Bills and Resolutions which is appended in each volume of the Congressional Record Index. This history, however, does not tell what happened to the bill in committee, except for giving the fact and number of any committee report. Printed transcripts of committee hearings must be found, if any, by searching the bound volumes of hearings of the appropriate committee for the session in question. Committee reports can be found by searching the bound volumes of Senate or House Committee reports, as the case may be, for that session.

The Senate Committee on Agriculture and Forestry held hearings on the bill, but these were not printed. The Committee's report on the bill, with amendments, was favorable but short, consisting chiefly of an approving letter from the Secretary of Agriculture. S. Rep. No. 6, 71st Cong., 1st Sess. The House Committee on Agriculture held more extensive hearings, which were printed. The part of the committee's report which sums up the case made in favor of the bill was as follows:

The general purpose of the bill is to regulate in interstate and foreign commerce the marketing of fresh fruits and vegetables, live and dressed poultry, and eggs.[41] After rather extensive hearings it was developed before the committee that each year the shippers and growers of such commodities suffer severe losses due to unfair practices on the part of commission merchants, dealers, and brokers. The practice on the part of irresponsible dealers of rejecting purchases of such commodities on a declining market is reported to the committee as causing heavy losses to the grower and shipper annually, particularly in the fruit and vegetable industry. In the years 1923, 1924 and 1925 the apple shippers of one State alone were compelled to take a loss on their apples of $813,000, $435,000, and $235,000, respectively, on account of such unfair practices. The high perishability of fresh fruits and vegetables and poultry and eggs enhances the opportunity for such practices. It subjects shippers to an unnecessary marketing hazard, retards distribution, interrupts and restricts the flow of commerce, and impairs the confidence that should prevail in the marketing of products of such importance to the entire country.

Unfair practice has also been charged against the seller of such perishable commodities. Many instances have arisen where the shipper, after having previously signed a contract to deliver the commodity on a certain date in the future, fails to do so when delivery would be to his disadvantage and he sells to some one else at a higher price. Such a practice at the point of shipment is as unfair as the unjustifiable rejection of shipments in the receiving markets. The bill treats buyer and seller in interstate transactions of perishable commodities alike with respect to the unwarranted repudiation of contracts.

The problem of effectively dealing with unfair trade practices in the marketing of farm products, particularly the highly perishable products covered by this bill, has been a subject of study and discussion for many years. The unjustifiable rejection on a declining market of shipments by buyers in the city markets is one of the outstanding problems in the fruit and vegetable industry.

The effective control of this and other unfair and unethical practices, such as false accounting and failure to pay on the part of commission merchants for produce intrusted to them for disposition, the circulation of fictitious and misleading market quotations in connection with the soliciting of consignments, making false

[41] Poultry and eggs were later deleted from the bill.

reports concerning the quality and condition of products, and the making of fraudulent charges in connection with marketing services by commission merchants, dealers, and brokers are problems of long standing. These problems are of equal interest and seriousness to the farmer, the honest dealer, and the cooperative marketing association.

While recourse can be had to the courts for most, if not all, of the practices declared to be unfair by this bill, litigation is but seldom resorted to except in cases involving large sums. Litigation is frequently unsatisfactory as a practical matter. The commodities are highly perishable. In case of dispute immediate disposition must be made of them. Buyers and sellers are often hundreds and frequently thousands of miles apart. In such circumstances litigation is expensive.

The farmer, small shipper, or the manager of a small cooperative association does not have the time or money to conduct the necessary investigation for successful prosecution. Long delays occur in the adjudication of complaints, and frequently judgments can not be collected when awarded. In many cases the amount of the loss suffered from the unfair practice does not warrant the cost of litigation, but taken in the aggregate, these losses are a tremendous burden upon these industries. It is believed that the regulation of interstate commerce transactions of commission merchants, dealers, and brokers as provided in this bill will provide an effective means of suppression and control of the fraudulent practices of which so much complaint is made. The honest commission merchant, dealer, and broker who now, individually or through his trade association, vigorously condemns these sharp practices will welcome the protection afforded by this bill. The dishonest and unscrupulous operator will be required to conduct his business according to long-established principles of honesty and fair dealing or engage in some other calling.

Among the many points of interest in the debates on the bill in the two Houses, the following are worthy of special note:

1. Senators and representatives from the producing areas spoke again and again of the volume and bitterness of the complaints by growers against commission men in the big city markets. Patently the statute was a response to a situation which was a serious practical problem not only for farm constituents but for their representatives in Congress as well.

2. In the period between the Seventieth and the Seventy-first Congress both Senator Borah and Representative Summers had evidently done a great deal of knowledgeable legislative spade work among the various groups interested in the measure. In the effort to meet objections Senator Borah, in particular, had made a great many changes in his original proposal. As a result most of the important organizations not only of shippers but of receivers of produce had been brought around in support of the measure. One of the dramatic episodes, apparently, was the approval given to the Summers bill by the National League of Commission Merchants in their annual convention in Detroit on January 16 to 18, 1930, where as one of the opponents of the bill said with some bitterness, "the commission men of America * * * had a conversion equal to that of Saul of Tarsus." 72 Cong. Rec. 8539. Both Senator Borah and the bill's supporters in the House were thus enabled repeatedly to meet technical objections by replying that the provision must be all right because it had been agreed to by all those who knew most about the practical problems involved. The underlying agreement was, of

course, even more important in dealing with basic opposition. In this aspect the Act illustrated one of the major features of American legislation—the extent to which the legislature acts as a ratifying agency giving effect to agreements arrived at outside the legislature.

3. The bills also had the support of the Administration and, in particular, of the Secretary of Agriculture and the Chairman of the Farm Board. In the midst of depression, facing a burgeoning political revolt of farmers, and fighting more extreme panaceas of farm leaders, the Administration, it may be gathered, welcomed one proposal for relief which it could find acceptable. Recurrent fears were expressed that the bill was inconsistent with the then-current program of the Farm Board for helping farmers by encouragement of cooperative marketing. If the government were going to act as a collection agency for the farmers, Congressman Aswell of Tennessee insisted, for example, the farmer would never join cooperatives. An approving letter from Chairman Legge of the Farm Board, quoted in the House report, was influential in dissipating these criticisms.

4. The question of the constitutionality of the measure was raised several times, particularly in an exchange between Senator Borah and Senator Wheeler of Montana. 71 Cong. Rec. 2163, 2167–68. Senator Wheeler thought *Hopkins v. United States*, 171 U.S. 578 (1898), indicated its unconstitutionality and was unpersuaded by Senator Borah's citation of *Stafford v. Wallace*, 258 U.S. 495 (1922). The discussion, however, was dropped, and the only judgment ever expressed by the Senate on the question was that which was implicit in passage of the bill. It is interesting to observe that the constitutionality of the statute seems never to have been squarely attacked in litigation. Cf. *Krueger v. Acme Fruit Co.*, 75 F.2d 67 (5th Cir. 1935). But see *Abe Rafaelson Co. v. Tugwell*, 79 F.2d 653 (7th Cir. 1935).

5. The cry that the bill would create a huge federal bureaucracy was raised in both houses, in accents that were to become increasingly familiar during the next quarter of a century. Whether this objection had as much or less force in this instance than it has had in others is worth consideration.

6. Actually, the principal evils in the trade, such as unfair and unreasonable rejection of produce, the making of fraudulent charges for marketing services, the making of false and misleading statements about the condition, quality, quantity, and disposition of produce, the circulation of fictitious and false market reports, the falsifying of accounts, and the like were all violations of contract or torts for which an injured party could seek a remedy in the courts under existing state law. The proponents of the bill fully recognized this. But again and again they emphasized that a lawsuit was not a satisfactory answer. Individual losses were small. Buyer and seller were often thousands of miles apart. The commodities were highly perishable. Litigation was expensive and slow and the hope of recovery often clouded with doubt. What was needed, the proponents argued, was a better means of preventing abuses from occurring, and of discouraging unscrupulous dealers from taking advantage of reluctance to litigate. In this view, prime emphasis was placed upon the prophylactic value of a licensing system.

7. There was a great deal of discussion in general terms about "the rejection evil." But little attention was given to reparation proceedings as such. And none

of the discussion came close to touching the specifics of the *Gillarde* problem. This lay wholly in the future, below the consciousness of the 1930 Congress.

D. *What Prior Settlements by the Secretary of Agriculture Said to Martinelli*

Like all statutes, the 1930 Act emerged from the legislative process as a bare skeleton. Muscle and flesh and blood have since been put on the skeleton through a variety of processes of growth. Congress itself has amended the Act with rather unusual frequency, although the amendments have been relatively minor perfecting changes rather than major structural alterations. Most important, however, have been the regulations issued and the decisions made by the Secretary of Agriculture in the course of the Act's administration.

The Act itself contemplated that it would grow in this fashion. Section 15 (7 U.S.C.A. § 499o) provides in broad terms that "[t]he Secretary may make such rules, regulations, and orders as may be necessary to carry out the provisions of this chapter * * *."

Pursuant to this authorization, the Secretary has issued elaborate procedural regulations for the conduct of administrative proceedings under the Act—regulations which in their present form reflect the concern about federal administrative procedure which developed in the thirties and culminated in the enactment of the Administrative Procedure Act in 1946.[42]

Of primary importance for present purposes are, first, the substantive regulations of the Secretary defining certain trade terms and, second, various prior decisions in reparations proceedings.

1. THE REGULATIONS DEFINING TRADE TERMS

The Secretary's definitions of trade terms have already been considered from the point of view both of the fair import of Martinelli's own agreement, if it is read as referring to them,[43] and of the effect of Section 71 of the Uniform Sales Act in putting the authority of the state law behind them.[44] Now the regulations need to be viewed as directly applicable to the transaction by authority of federal law.

It is relevant to point out in this connection that the definitions in the regulations were not the brainchildren simply of the Secretary and his staff. On the contrary, they were the product of an elaborate series of conferences with members of the industry. As promulgated, they conformed, with only minor editorial changes, with the formal recommendations of industry representatives. See the brief *amicus curiae* filed in behalf of the United States in the Gillarde-Martinelli litigation.

The definitions, including those of "rolling acceptance" and "acceptable final," do not purport to apply if the terms have been "otherwise defined." On their face, in other words, they are suppletive. But the clause introducing the definitions says that "[u]nless otherwise defined, the following terms when included

---

[42] 60 Stat. 237. The procedure in reparation proceedings and in disciplinary (license suspension or revocation) proceedings is dealt with in two separate bodies of rules contained in Part 57 of Title 7 of the Code of Federal Regulations. These rules occupy some 23 pages of the Code. Procedure on applications for licenses is dealt with rather scantily in Part 46 of the same title. These proceedings, however, seem infrequently to involve contests, and license refusals are extremely rare.

[43] See pp. 19–21, above.

[44] See p. 31, above.

in a contract or communication involved in any investigation made or hearing held pursuant to the act *shall* be construed, respectively, as follows: * * *." 7 C.F.R. § 46.24. (Emphasis added.)

Is it not then plain that, if the regulations are authorized by the Act, Martinelli, having used the term "acceptance final" in a contract without otherwise defining it, is bound by the provision of the definition that "[t]he buyer's remedy under this method of purchase is by recovery of damages from the shipper and not by rejection of the shipment?" Can any solid argument be made that the definitions are *not* authorized by Section 15 of the Act?

Can the obligation thus declared be satisfied by physical acceptance and disposition of the produce? Or is it an obligation also to accept the property in the goods and the basic responsibility for payment of the purchase price? Is this important?

2. THE ADMINISTRATIVE DECISIONS ON THE EFFECT OF A WRONGFUL REJECTION

The Secretary's regulations themselves say nothing about the effect of a wrongful rejection. Nor was the question discussed in the report, just mentioned, of the industry conference which approved the regulations.

However, the Act itself contains some general language about remedies. Section 5(a) declares that any dealer who violates Section 2 (prohibiting rejection or failure to deliver in accordance with the terms of the contract without reasonable cause) "shall be liable to the person or persons injured for the *full amount* of damages sustained in consequence of such violation." (Emphasis added.) Section 7(a) tells the Secretary, when he finds in a reparation proceeding that Section 2 has been violated, "to determine the amount of damage, if any, to which such person is entitled as a result of such violation."

These provisions were seemingly drafted with the normal situation in mind in which only one party to the contract has been guilty of a violation. But in the case now being considered both parties would be guilty—the seller through innocent breach of warranty, and the buyer through deliberate failure to take charge of the shipment as agreed, and to salvage what it could. The question is how the provisions should be applied in such a situation of mutual fault.

This question the Secretary undertook to answer not in any formal regulation but in the course of disposing of individual claims for reparation. In a series of decisions beginning in 1937 the Secretary held that a buyer who wrongfully rejects a shipment is not only responsible for the loss in value of the goods resulting from his failure to take charge of them and sell them promptly but also forfeits any claim for damages against the seller which he might otherwise have had. In result, the buyer is liable for the full contract price just as he would have been if the goods had answered the contract description.

The Secretary's two earliest decisions on the point are not officially reported. *Nash Corrigan Company v. W.H. Dotson and G.C. Ross, partners doing business as Dotson-Ross Produce Company*, PACA Docket No. 2038, S. 1528, decided April 5, 1937; and *Puget Sound Vegetable Growers Association v. A. Reich & Sons, Inc.*, PACA Docket No. 2530, S. 1955, decided July 23, 1938. But these rulings were followed in later published decisions. *Mark Owen & Co. v. Joseph Rothenberg & Co. and Simon Siegel Co.*, 3 A.D. 1100 (1944); *Nick Argondelis v. Senter Bros., Inc.*, 4 A.D. 420 (1945); *Battistini Bros. v. Senter Bros., Inc. and/or C. Comella, Inc.*, 4 A.D. 571 (1945); *L. Gillarde Co. v. Ritter & Company and*

C. Comella, Inc., 4 A.D. 594 (1945); *Mexican Produce Co. v. Lewis D. Goldstein Fruit & Produce Corporation*, 4 A.D. 946 (1945). Of these last cited cases, however, none had yet been decided at the time when Martinelli had to make its decision.

None of the published opinions contains any explanation of the reasons for the Secretary's position, all of them seeming to assume that the result necessarily follows from the breach of the agreement. The opinion in the *Mark Owen* case is typical. It simply says (p. 1103):

> It is not necessary to determine whether the lettuce was in suitable shipping condition since Joseph Rothenberg & Company purchased the car on the basis of "rolling acceptance." Under the terms "rolling acceptance" the rejection by Joseph Rothenberg of the car was without reasonable cause since under the applicable regulations (7 Com. Supp., 46.24 (s)), a buyer's remedy under such a contract is by recovery of damages from the shipper and not by rejection of the shipment. Complainant should be awarded reparation against the respondent Joseph Rothenberg & Company, for the purchase price of the lettuce, with interest * * *. The facts and circumstances of this case should be published.

E. Trade Practice and Understanding

To what extent the various official settlements that have been described were in fact known to Martinelli on July 5 and 6, 1943, it is, of course, impossible to discover. How important is this?

The applicable settlements *had* been officially printed to the extent indicated by the citations which have been given. Moreover, convenient pamphlets describing the provisions of the Act and the Secretary's regulations (although not the administrative decisions) had been got up and distributed to the trade by the Department of Agriculture. In addition, two regular trade newspapers—the *Packer*, a nationwide weekly newspaper, and the *Produce News*, specializing in the east coast markets—regularly print reports of official actions and proceedings of all kinds, together with other trade information. In these circumstances, an official of the department says, speaking as of 1955:

> The Act has been in existence since 1930 and it would seem that by this time, those affected thereby should be quite familiar with their rights and liabilities under the terms of their contracts, including "rolling acceptance final." In fact, we rarely find a situation where they could honestly plead ignorance.[45]

It should be noted, however, that in one respect the anticipations of those who attended the 1931 trade conference which approved the Secretary's definitions of trade terms seem not to have been fulfilled. The explanation of the conference recommendations concluded with the statement that "[n]aturally in most cases prices would rule commensurate with the risk."[46] This suggests the expectation that produce of the same variety and grade would be selling in the same market at the same time at three or more different prices, depending on the terms of sale.

Information from Boston produce dealers indicates that this is not what happens. A single price prevails within a given market. But supply and demand

---

[45] From letter cited in note 4, *supra*.
[46] See the brief *amicus curiae* filed in behalf of the United States in the Gillarde-Martinelli litigation.

factors affect the terms on which dealers are able to buy. In a glutted market they may be able to get a carload simply on consignment, assuming no risk at all. With ample but not glutted supplies, they may be able to buy on the relatively favorable terms of "f.o.b., shipping point." In a tight market they may have to buy "f.o.b., or rolling, acceptance final" or even "shipping point inspection final."

If this is correct, Martinelli did not have the direct warning of the special responsibility it was assuming which would have been given by an openly lower price for a purchase on a "rolling acceptance final" basis.

It is worthy of note also that buyers who are confident of their trade position may on occasion reject carloads when they know they have no right to do so. The representative of one large Boston firm told of getting two bad carloads in succession from a small supplier and rejecting the second, although it had been bought on an "acceptance" basis, "just to teach them a lesson."

Whatever else Martinelli knew, however, it must have known that if it rejected the cantaloupes and Gillarde refused to absorb the "lesson," it would be exposed to the risk of publication throughout the trade of the facts of what it had done. And in the event of a reparation order against it, it would be exposed to formidable unofficial as well as official sanctions to compel payment. There are two publications in the trade of the "Dun and Bradstreet" type, called *The Red Book* and *The Blue Book*. These publications encourage licensees to have their firms listed. To do so brings in business, for these are nationwide publications. The books give ratings to each listed produce dealer in accordance with his amount of capital and what sort of business he runs. After the name of the dealer there may be a notation which, on reference to the index, shows that there is an unpaid reparation award outstanding against this firm. This, of course, affects business. As Mr. Jimmy Giovino of the Boston firm of Giovino Brothers put it, "[i]t would be like cutting my leg off to lose my 4X rating."

Part III. Martinelli's Decision

Between July 5 and July 8, 1943, the following telegrams were sent:
Springfield Mass Jul 5 1943 1:01 p.m.
    Pat Gillarde Jr.
    L Gillarde Co.
Pat tried to get you on phone car lopes FGE 52764 arrived overripe mouldy stems rejected to railroad took count on last car from you on account same thing no more tried to get inspection nobody available
    Jos Martinelli Co.

Chicago Ill July 6, 1943 9:20 a.m.
    Jos Martinelli Co.
Springfield Mass
Answering reference FGE 52764 how can you reject this car when you bought it FOB shipping point on Federal Grade of USONE at shipping point. We are not liable for railroad delays deterioration and other damages beyond our control. Car was sold to you rolling acceptance final with no transit hazards assumed by us. We must request you accept this car in accordance with your contract. Otherwise referring matter to Department Agriculture immediately. For your information we hold government inspection defects average within grade tolerance of USONE grade.

This car purchased by our own salaried buyer at Yuma and cost us J45 6.00 J36 5.50 STD 45s 5.00 PONY 54s 4.00 precooling 15.00 wire answer immediately
   L Gillarde Co.

———————

Springfield Mass Jul 5 1943 2:06 p.m.
   L Gillarde
We are refusing car FGE 52764
   Joseph Martinelli and Co.

———————

Springfield Mass Jul 5 1943 2:06 p.m.
   L. Gillarde Co.
Yuma Arizona to Springfield Mass waybill 1199 June 20 refused by Jos Martinelli CANA///
Cantaloupes account overripe stems moldy FGE 52764 advise disposition at once file one C
   J E Callahan Agt.

———————

Chicago Ill July 7 1943 9:20 a.m.
   J.E. Callahan Agent
B and A Railroad
Springfield Mass
FGE 52764 is the property of Joe Martinelli Company. You secure disposition from his as car sold to them FOB shipping point. We are not liable for damages.
   L Gillarde Co.

———————

Springfield Mass Jul 8 1943 11:38 a.m.
   L. Gillarde Co.
Your wire seventh FGE 52764 cantaloupes will not be accepted by Martinelli will sell for account of owner to prevent further loss
   J E Callahan B and A RR

PART IV. THE OFFICIAL DECISIONS

A. *The Problem in the Department of Agriculture*

True to its threat, Gillarde on August 19, 1943, filed an informal complaint against Martinelli in what was then the War Food Administration, later returned to the Department of Agriculture. As already pointed out (p. 15, above), most complaints under the Act are disposed of by informal negotiation under the aegis of the Department. Thus the complainant, if he is willing to trust the Department, is spared the necessity of employing counsel. The Gillarde-Martinelli controversy, however, failed to yield to this method of settlement, after dragging out for more than a year.

Gillarde was accordingly forced to take the next step of filing a formal complaint, which it did on October 11, 1944. Time passed, and on February 17, 1945, Martinelli filed a formal answer, together with a request for a formal hearing. More time passed, and on September 18, 1945, a hearing was held before an examiner of the Department, sitting in Springfield, the proceedings being very much in the form of a litigation in court. Still more time passed, and on July 3, 1946, the Judicial Officer of the Department of Agriculture, acting in the Secretary's behalf, announced the following decision.

L. Gillarde Co. v. Joseph Martinelli & Co., Inc.

PACA Docket No. 4457, 5 A.D. 555 (1946)

Preliminary Statement

On October 11, 1944, the complainant, L. Gillarde Company, filed a formal complaint under the Perishable Agricultural Commodities Act, 1930 (7 U.S.C. 1940 ed. 499a *et seq.*) against Joseph Martinelli & Company, Inc., respondent, for damages sustained because of respondent's rejection of a carload of U.S. No. 1 cantaloups allegedly sold to respondent under the terms "Rolling Acceptance Final."

Respondent denied that the cantaloups were U.S. No. 1 quality at shipping point, due to the fact that the cantaloups were infected with Cladosporium Rot.

A formal hearing was held in Springfield, Massachusetts, on September 18, 1945, both parties being represented by counsel.

The evidence on behalf of the complainant consists of exhibits attached to the complaint, the depositions of L. Gillarde, Jr., President of the complainant company and Harry G. Wickman, owner of the Wickman Traffic Service of Chicago, Illinois. Respondent's evidence consisted of answers to cross-interrogatories taken from the abovenamed deponents, the testimony of Louis E. Martinelli, President of the respondent company, and Dr. Hein L. von Goehde.

Complainant's evidence showed that it confirmed by wire of June 21, 1943, the sale to respondent of a car FGE 52764 of Jo Jo Brand Cantaloups f.o.b. Yuma, rolling acceptance final, the wire disclaiming any responsibility for railroad delays or in-transit hazards. The respondent replied by wire of June 22, 1943, asking for assurance that the cantaloupes graded U.S. No. 1 at shipping point, and on June 22, the complainant replied by wire that the car did carry that grade at shipping point. The car arrived in Springfield, Massachusetts, on July 3, 1943, and on July 5, 1943, respondent wired complainant that the car was being rejected on account of being overripe, with the stems mouldy. The evidence showed further that the car graded U.S. No. 1 at shipping point according to an official inspection one June 20, 1943, but a similar inspection at the destination in Springfield on July 6, 1943, showed many overripe and soft melons, and indicated decay ranging from 35 per cent to 100 per cent, averaging 85 per cent, mostly Cladosporium Rot. The car was disposed of by the railroad company for the sum of $300.00. The testimony of Dr. von Goehde was to the effect that the cantaloups could not have been U.S. No. 1 at shipping point and still show the advance state of decay found at the destination, assuming that the cantaloups were properly iced in transit.

The evidence showed that the complainant through Mr. Harry G. Wickman filed a claim against the railroad on August 31, 1943, for the sum of $1,759.50, being the invoice cost to the complainant, which was settled on the basis of 50 per cent of the cost, for the sum of $879.75 from which was deducted collection costs of $175.95 and the net proceeds of $703.80 were paid to the complainant.

1. The complainant, L. Gillarde Company, is a corporation whose post office address is 79 South Water Market, Chicago, Illinois.

2. The respondent, Joseph Martinelli & Company, Inc. is a corporation whose post office address is 157 Lyman Street, Springfield, Massachusetts, and during all of the times mentioned in the complaint was licensed under the Perishable Agricultural Commodities Act of 1930, as amended.

3. On or about June 21, 1943, the complainant sold the respondent in interstate commerce a carload, FGE 52764, of U.S. No. 1 Jo Jo Cantaloups containing 60 crates J-45s at $6.25 per crate, 225 crates J-36s at $5.75 per crate, 18 crates S-45s at $5.75 per crate and 12 crates ponies at $4.25 per crate, f.o.b., Yuma, Arizona, plus $20 precooling, for a total sum of $1,843.25 on a rolling acceptance final basis. These cantaloups were inspected at shipping point on June 20, 1943, the date of shipment, and graded U.S. No. 1.

4. The car arrived in Springfield, Massachusetts, on July 3, 1943, at 3:00 p.m.; July 4 was a holiday and on the 5th of July the respondent wired the complainant that it was rejecting the shipment.

5. An inspection by an agent of the United States Department of Agriculture, on July 6, 1943, in Springfield, Massachusetts, showed many overripe and soft melons and that these cantaloups contained decay ranging from 35 per cent in some samples to 100 per cent in others, averaging approximately 85 per cent, mostly Cladosporium Rot.

6. The cantaloups were abandoned to the railroad company which sold the shipment to the United Fruit Company of Springfield, Massachusetts, for the sum of $300.

7. The cantaloups did not move under normal transportation service and conditions, and a claim was filed against the Southern Pacific Railroad Company, on behalf of the Complainant by Harry G. Wickman of the Wickman Traffic Service, 216 South Water Market, Chicago, Illinois, on August 31, 1943, for the sum of $1,759.50, being the invoice cost to complainant, which claim was settled on the basis of 50 per cent of the invoice cost or $879.75, from which was deducted $175.95 collection costs. The balance of $703.80 was paid to the complainant.

8. Respondent was not consulted in the making of the claim against the railroad nor did it take any affirmative action toward collecting from the railroad.

9. Respondent has paid no part of the contract price to complainant.

10. The informal complaint was filed on August 19, 1943, and within 9 months from the time the cause of action accrued.

Conclusions

Since the sale to respondent was on a "rolling acceptance final" basis, respondent had no right of rejection, but was limited to the recovery of damages from the seller for a breach of contract, if such could be shown. *Battistini Bros. v. Senter Bros. Inc. and/or C. Comella, Inc.*, 4 A.D. 571. Therefore, respondent's rejection of the car of cantaloups was without reasonable cause and was in violation of section 2 of the act.

Respondent's defense in this proceeding is based on the proposition that the cantaloups in question were not in fact U.S. No. 1 cantaloups at shipping point on June 20, 1945, as called for by its contract with complainant. But respondent waived its right to make that defense by rejecting the shipment. Respondent's contentions in this regard are therefore not considered. *Mark Owen & Company v. Joseph Rothenberg & Company and Simon Siegel Company*, 3 A.D. 1100.

The only other point in issue in the case was whether the action of the complainant in making and collecting a claim against the railroad amounted to such an election as to preclude its proceeding against the respondent buyer for the balance of the purchase price. It was argued by the respondent that the complainant had claimed to be the owner of the cantaloups in making its claim against the railroad and, therefore, it could not now collect from the purchaser on the ground that the purchaser became the title holder. The complainant's attorney on the other hand urged that since the statute of limitations runs on claims against the railroad in nine months from the time of the loss, and since that time expired before the hearing was held, the respondent ought to be grateful to the complainant for mitigating the damages.

While it might have been preferable for the complainant to have notified the respondent when the claim against the railroad was filed, offering the respondent an opportunity to participate in the negotiations, we do not think that the failure to do this is a sufficient cause to hold that the complainant is barred from pursuing the respondent to collect the balance of the contract price of the melons, particularly since the respondent evinced no interest in the transaction after rejecting the car. There was nothing in respondent's attitude or actions which would indicate that it recognized any obligation in the matter or had any intention of filing a claim against the railroad. It was fairly obvious that respondent wanted nothing more to do with the cantaloups. While the record indicates that many claims of a similar nature were settled on the basis of 50 per cent of the damage claimed, because of a possibility that in the event of litigation the railroads would establish a strong defense by contending that war emergency prevented normal functioning by carriers, there is nothing in the evidence or the record to show that the amount paid by the railroad to the complainant in damages was actually less than its liability in this case. Respondent cannot, therefore, logically contend that it was, in fact, damaged by complainant's settlement of the claim against the railroad.

It is concluded that complainant is entitled to reparation in the sum of $1,843.25, the contract price, less the net recovery on the damage claim against the carrier, $703.80, or the net sum of $1,139.45, with interest, and the facts should be published.

Order

Within 30 days from the date of this order, respondent shall pay to the complainant, as reparation, the sum of $1,139.45, with interest thereon at 5 per cent per annum from July 5, 1943, until paid.

The facts and circumstances as set forth herein shall be published.

Copies hereof shall be served upon the parties by registered mail or in person, and, except as to the date of payment and as to service on the parties, this order shall become effective 20 days after its date.

B. *The Problem in the United States District Court*

Martinelli was not happy about the Secretary's decision, and on July 3, 1946, it filed a notice of appeal in the United States District Court for the District of Massachusetts, pursuant to its statutory right under Section 7(c) of the Act (7 U.S.C.A. § 499g(c)).

On September 9, 1946, Gillarde filed a motion to dismiss the appeal on technical grounds, which Judge Ford denied on November 14, 1946. After various continuances the case came on for trial in Springfield on June 5, 1947, before Judge Healey, sitting without a jury. Judge Healey took the case under advisement, and on August 27, 1947, entered a judgment in favor of Martinelli, accompanied by the following memorandum opinion.

JOSEPH MARTINELLI & CO. v. L. GILLARDE CO.

United States District Court for the District of Massachusetts, 1947 73 F. Supp. 293
    HEALEY, District Judge.

The appellant, Joseph Martinelli & Company, Inc., brings this appeal in accordance with the Perishable Agricultural Commodities Act, 7 U.S.C.A. § 499a *et seq.*, to set aside a reparation award order of the Secretary of Agriculture. The Act provides for a trial *de novo* which "shall proceed in all respects like other civil suits for damages, except that the findings of fact and order or orders of the Secretary shall be *prima-facie* evidence of the facts therein stated." 7 U.S.C.A. § 499g(c).

[Here the memorandum opinion copies the ten findings of fact from the Department opinion, and recites the Secretary's order.]

The appellant's appeal is based on the following grounds:

"1. The order is against the evidence and the weight of the evidence in the case.
"2. The order is against the law in the case.
"3. The cantaloups which were shipped to the petitioner were not in fact of U.S. No. 1 grade as called for by the contract.
"4. The respondent is estopped to claim damages from the petitioner by reason of the fact that respondent made a claim for damages against the railroad for improper icing of the carload of cantaloups in question and settled the claim for much less than the amount thereof, all without any authority from the petitioner and all without the knowledge or assent of the petitioner."

At the hearing in this court, Louis A. Martinelli, president of the appellant corporation, testified as to the negotiations for the purchase, the conditions of the cantaloups on arrival at Springfield, and his subsequent notice of rejection of the shipment by wire to the appellee. The only other witness for the appellant was an expert food chemist.

The appellee introduced in evidence the "Preliminary Statement, Findings of Fact, Conclusions, and Order of the Secretary of Agriculture, dated July 3, 1946, issued by the Judicial Officer," the deposition of one Harry G. Wickman, and 13 exhibits formerly introduced at the hearing before the Examiner for the Department of Agriculture. The appellee then rested.

Appellant contends that the statute of frauds is a complete defense to the action because there was not a sufficient memorandum of the oral contract signed by its representative. The pertinent part of the statute of frauds contained in the Uniform Sales Act is as follows:

> "(1) A contract to sell or a sale of any goods or choses in action of the value of five hundred dollars or more shall not be enforceable by action . . . unless some note or memorandum in writing of the contract or sale by signed by the party to be charged or his agent in that behalf." Annotated Laws of Massachusetts, Ch. 106, § 6.

In my opinion, the telegram of June 22, 1943, signed Joseph Martinelli & Co. (appellee's exhibit 6) was under the circumstances a sufficient memorandum to satisfy the statute of frauds. *Schmoll Fils & Co., Inc. v. Wheeler*, 242 Mass. 464, 136 N.E. 164. Certainly that telegram incorporated by reference the terms of appellee's telegram of June 21, 1943, (appellee's exhibit 3). The acceptance, wired in appellee's reply telegram of June 22, 1943, (appellee's exhibit 7), would have been sufficient also to establish a written contract, if such were the intent of the parties.

Under the terms of the contract, title to the cantaloups in question, shipped "f.o.b., rolling acceptance final," passed to the appellant at the point of shipment. From that point also, all risk of normal deterioration and damage in transit fell upon the appellant. However, the appellee remained liable for any inherent or latent defects which would render the cantaloups non-conformable to the expressed or implied warranties of the contract.

Based on the examination by the destination inspector of the United States Department of Agriculture, the Secretary of Agriculture has found that on arrival, the cantaloups "contained decay . . . averaging approximately 85 per cent, mostly Cladosporium Rot." Cladosporium Rot was described by appellant's expert witness as a disease of field origin which is not apparent to the naked eye when melons are in a green ripe or hard ripe stage, but which develops as the melons ripen, causing them to decay. The witness further testified that melons infected with the disease were not, in fact, U.S. No. 1 grade, even though an inspector of the United States Department of Agriculture, who did not discover its presence, so graded them. No finding of the Secretary of Agriculture and no testimony adduced at the trial, contradicted this statement.

It is evident, therefore, that at the point of shipment, before title to the cantaloups in question passed to the appellant, they were not in fact U.S. No. 1 grade melons, as required by the terms of the contract, but were inherently defective in that they were infected with this disease of field origin. They, therefore, did not meet the implied warranties of description and quality.

While it is true that under a contract of sale f.o.b., all subsequent risks of normal deterioration or damage in transit fall on the buyer, risk of latent or inherent defects in the goods falls on the seller. *A.J. Conroy, Inc. v. Weyl-Zuckerman & Company*, 39 F. Supp. 784, and cases cited therein; *Agoos Kid Company, Inc. v. Blumenthal Import Corporation*, 282 Mass. 1.

Since the cantaloups did not correspond to the implied warranties of quality and description at the time they were shipped to the appellant, the appellant was justified, under the Uniform Sales Act, in rejecting them.

It has been held that "the P.A.C.A. does not remove the applicability of the law of sales; it merely gives an additional remedy to growers, who were previously forced to resort to expensive trials in all cases in which dealers and commission men failed to live up to the provisions of their contracts." *A.J. Conroy, Inc. v. Weyl-Zuckerman & Co., supra.*

It is, therefore, apparent that on all the facts, including the "Findings of Fact" made by the Secretary of Agriculture, which I adopt and incorporate as part of my findings of fact, the appellant was justified in refusing to accept the cantaloups on their arrival.

The Secretary's order was, therefore, erroneous and must be overruled.

The Clerk will prepare an order for judgment for the appellant.

C. The Problem in the United States Court of Appeals

It was now Gillarde's turn to be unhappy. Under what is now 28 U.S.C. § 1291 (1948), it had a right of appeal from the district court's decision to the United States Court of Appeals for the First Circuit, which sits in Boston. Gillarde filed its notice of appeal on October 21, 1947, together with a "statement of points of error asserted and intended to be urged." Both parties in due course filed printed briefs, Gillarde's occupying a little more than ten printed pages and Martinelli's only four. There was an oral argument, and on May 17, 1948, the court handed down the following opinion.

L. GILLARDE CO. v. JOSEPH MARTINELLI & CO. INC.

United States Court of Appeals for the First Circuit, 1948 168 F.2d 276

Before MAHONEY and WOODBURY, Circuit Judges, and PETERS, District Judge.

MAHONEY, Circuit Judge.

This is a proceeding under the Perishable Agricultural Commodities Act of 1930, § 1 et seq., 7 U.S.C.A. § 499a et seq. The case is before us on appeal from a judgment of the district court which reversed a reparation order issued by the Secretary of Agriculture. The facts are undisputed.

[The opinion here summarizes the facts, the relevant provisions of the statute, and the earlier proceedings in the case.]

The only important issue which is raised before us is whether the respondent violated Section 2 of the Act which makes it unlawful for any dealer to reject without reasonable cause any perishable agricultural commodity bought or contracted to be bought by it in interstate commerce. The regulations which have been issued by the Secretary of Agriculture under the authority of Section 15 of the Act define "reject with reasonable cause" to mean:

"* * * the act of any person, who has purchased or offered to handle on consignment or otherwise, for or on behalf of another, produce in commerce, (1) of refusing or failing to accept such produce within a reasonable time, or (2) of advising the seller or shipper or his agent that such produce will not be received in accordance with the contract or offer, or (3) of indicating an intention not to accept such produce through an act or failure to act inconsistent with the contract." 7 Code Fed. Reg. § 46.2(q) (Cum.Supp. 1943).

If the buyer's action in rejecting was not in accord with the contract, it was not a rejection for reasonable cause. We thus turn to a consideration of the contract.

The Secretary of Agriculture and the district court both found that the terms of the sale were "rolling acceptance final." Terms which are commonly used in contracts involving perishable agricultural commodities have been defined in the regulations[.]

[Judge Mahoney here quotes the provisions of the regulations which are set forth in note 14, *supra*.]

Although rolling acceptance is defined in the regulations, rolling acceptance final is not. But in regard to the rights of the buyer, it has substantially the same meaning as f.o.b. acceptance final. L. Gillarde Co. v. Ritter & Co., 1945, 4 A.D. 594; Battistini Bros. v. Senter Bros., Inc., 1945, 4 A.D. 571; Schoenburg Price & Co. v. Lewis D. Goldstein Fruit & Produce Corp., 1943, 2 A.D. 772. The relationship between rolling acceptance and rolling acceptance final is the same as between f.o.b. acceptance and f.o.b. acceptance final. Under an f.o.b. acceptance final contract there can be no rejection by the buyer. LeRoy Dyal Co. v. Allen, 4 Cir. 1947, 161 F.2d 152; Nick Argondelis v. Senter Bros., Inc., 1945, 4 A.D. 420. Rolling acceptance final has been similarly defined in a long line of Agricultural Department decisions. Under this type of contract the buyer has no recourse if the produce was up to the contract requirements at the time of shipment. He has no recourse for defects of quality or condition at the destination point. There is no implied warranty of suitable shipping condition. There can be no rejection. The buyer's only remedy is to sue for damages if specifications of the contract, such as grade or quality at the time of shipment, have not been complied with. L. Gillarde Co. v. Ritter & Co., supra; Battistini Bros. v. Senter Bros., Inc., supra; Schoenburg, Price & Co. v. Lewis D. Goldstein Fruit & Produce Corp., supra. Whether the terms of the contract are rolling acceptance or rolling acceptance final, there is no right of rejection. The only difference between the two terms is that under the former, there is a warranty of suitable shipping condition. Under the latter, there is no such warranty and the buyer is not entitled to recover damages for change in condition during transit. Of course under either form of contract the buyer may recover damages for the seller's failure to comply with the contract as to the character of the goods or any other material provision. Cf. LeRoy Dyal Co. v. Allen, supra at 158 of 161 F.2d.

It is clear that under the express terms of the contract there was no right to reject. The respondent, however, maintains that it has a right to reject if the goods were not in suitable condition. It relies on the Uniform Sales Act which has been enacted in Massachusetts[47] and which provides that a buyer may reject goods if there has been a breach of warranty. Uniform Sales Act § 69; Mass. Gen. Laws (Ter. Ed.) c. 106, § 58 (1932). The district court agreed with the respondent. In so doing, we think it was in error. The terms used in the contract were words that have been given a definite meaning by the regulations and decisions under the Perishable Agricultural Commodities Act. The respondent is licensed under the Act. The melons were sold in interstate commerce. When terms which have been given a definite meaning under the Act are used by licensees, in transactions governed by the Act, it can not later be maintained that a different meaning was

---

[47] No question of conflict of laws has been raised. It has been assumed by all that Massachusetts law governs the contract.

intended. The Uniform Sales Act as adopted in Massachusetts contains nothing to the contrary but in fact provides:

> "If any right, duty or liability would arise under contract to sell or a sale by implication of law, it may be negatived or varied by express agreement or by the course of dealing between the parties, or by custom, if the custom be such as to bind both parties to the contract or sale." Uniform Sales Act § 71; Mass. Gen. Laws (Ter. Ed.) c. 106 § 60 (1932).

The Sales Act only provides rules for interpretation of contracts and states what rights arise if not otherwise provided. Here the contract definitely states that there is no right of rejection and that the only recourse is for damages if the goods did not meet the specifications of the contract when shipped. Nothing in the Sales Act purports to prevent such a contract or to override such express terms. Cf. Sharples Separator Co. v. Domestic Electric Refrigerator Corp., 3 Cir., 1932, 61 F.2d 499.

The cause must therefore be remanded to the district court since that court erroneously held that there was a right to reject. On remand, however, the respondent's defense that the cantaloups were not U.S. No. 1 when shipped may be considered by way of recoupment of damages. As stated above, under a rolling acceptance final contract, there is no warranty of suitable shipping condition but the seller is liable for a breach of specifications of the contract. The district court found that there was an express term of the contract that the cantaloups were U.S. No. 1. Since the district court found that they were not, the buyer is entitled to recoup for the breach by the seller the difference between the value of what was furnished and the value of what was contracted for. Cf. United Fruit & Produce Co. v. Mailloux Fruit & Produce Co., 1945, 4 A.D. 578; D.B. Bruno & Co. v. S. Goldsamt, Inc., 1942, 1 A.D. 605.

That this is so appears fairly evident to us, but the Agricultural Department held that there was a waiver of this defense by the rejection of the shipment. We see no reason why the buyer's mistake as to its remedy should cause it to forfeit a remedy it would otherwise have. Of course, the buyer must bear any loss that results from its wrongful rejection. Thus it may well be that if the respondent had to accept but had taken the car and promptly disposed of it, there would not have been such a great loss. If this be so, of course the respondent must bear that loss. But we do not see why the respondent's wrongful rejection should cause a complete forfeiture of its claim for breach of contract. * * *

The judgment of the district court is vacated and the cause remanded for further proceedings.

Gillarde still was less than completely satisfied, and filed a petition with the court for a rehearing. Somewhat unusually, the United States, in behalf of the Department of Agriculture, sought and obtained permission to file the brief *amicus curiae*, already mentioned, in support of the petition for rehearing. The petition cited the departmental decisions earlier discussed, and others, and said:

> The department's construction is based on a number of considerations, all of which appear to lead to the conclusion reached. Under the specific wording of the regulation, which became a part of the contract between the parties, it was agreed that rejection is not a remedy available to the buyer. To allow a buyer to reject and still

claim damages for the shipper's breach is to allow the buyer a remedy which the contract provides he shall not have. The parties must be held to have contemplated that actual receipt and disposition of the produce by the buyer would be a condition precedent to any claim by the buyer based on breach of the contract by the seller. * * *

* * * Rejection of perishable produce by a buyer is a serious matter. The fact of rejection becomes known in the trade with surprising rapidity. The value of rejected produce is considerably reduced at once, merely because of the rejection. The shipper is usually at a distant point from which it is difficult for him to make satisfactory disposition of the rejected shipment. The so-called rejection evil was one of the principal factors which led to the enactment of the Perishable Agricultural Commodities Act * * *.

With the nature of the commodity and the problem of rejection clearly in mind, the drafters of the regulation undertook to provide contract terms (*e.g.*, "acceptance" and "acceptance final") that would effectively prevent rejections. One effective way of preventing a rejection is to condition the buyer's right to claim damages upon his having accepted the goods. The language of the regulation imposes such a condition. There is nothing harsh or inequitable in such a contract since the buyer can always protect his right to claim damages by accepting the shipment. Furthermore, it was contemplated that "in most cases prices would rule commensurate with the risk" (Appendix A, p. 3). That is to say, where the buyer assumes additional risks, as under the "acceptance" or "acceptance final" forms of contract, a lower price presumably would be paid for the commodity. It is also to be borne in mind that the regulation retained the "f.o.b." form of contract for buyers who are unwilling to bargain away any right they might otherwise have to reject.

It is also respectfully submitted that this term, in its application to facts similar to those of the instant case, has been frequently interpreted since 1937 by the Department of Agriculture, as indicated by the cases mentioned previously, and that the Department's interpretation is entitled to considerable weight. In *Bowles v. Seminole Rock & Sand Co.*, 325 U.S. 410 (1945), the Court stated:

> Since this involves an interpretation of an administrative regulation a court must necessarily look to the administrative construction of the regulation if the meaning of the words used is in doubt. The intention of Congress or the principles of the Constitution in some situations may be relevant in the first instance in choosing between various constructions. But the ultimate criterion is the administrative interpretation, which becomes of controlling weight unless it is plainly erroneous or inconsistent with the regulations * * *.

On July 8, 1948, the court handed down the following opinion on rehearing.

L. Gillarde co. v. Joseph Martinelli & Co., Inc.

United States Court of Appeals for the First Circuit, 1948 169 F.2d 60
Before MAHONEY and WOODBURY, Circuit Judges and PETERS, District Judge.
MAHONEY, Circuit Judge.
The complainant has petitioned for rehearing in regard to that part of our decision of May 17, 1948, 1 Cir., 168 F.2d 276, in which we held that upon remand to the district court the respondent's defense that the cantaloups were not U.S. No. 1 when shipped might be considered by way of recoupment of damages,

and filed a brief in support thereof. The United States, which has not previously participated in this case, has submitted a brief as amicus curiae in support of the petition. The respondent in response to our invitation filed a brief in opposition thereto. The only question is, as stated by the United States in its brief, does the buyer who rejects—even though he has no right to reject—an "acceptance" or "acceptance final" shipment have a right to recover damages for a breach of the contract by the shipper, assuming that there has been a breach for which damages could have been recovered if the shipment has been accepted? Both the United States and the complainant urge that to allow recoupment of damages even though there has been a wrongful rejection would defeat the policy of the Perishable Agricultural Commodities Act of 1930, 7 U.S.C.A. § 499a et seq. They contend that buyers would not be discouraged from rejecting if they knew that they would still be able to recoup damages in a suit against them for the purchase price. The United States points out that for a period of over ten years the Department of Agriculture has interpreted the regulations promulgated by the Department as not allowing recovery of damages where there has been a wrongful rejection. It states that our opinion in this case changes the principle under which the Department and the trade have operated for many years.

The Act was intended to prevent produce from becoming a distress merchandise and to protect sellers who often were at a great distance from the buyer. In our original opinion we stated that even though the buyer should be allowed to recoup for the breach by the seller, the buyer would have to bear any loss resulting from its wrongful rejection. It appeared to us that the seller would be protected from any loss caused by rejection in this way. But it is now called to our attention that the Department of Agriculture, which administers the Act and which is familiar with the evils the Act was intended to prevent, believes that to allow a buyer who rejects wrongfully to recoup would drastically reduce the effectiveness of the Act by removing much of the sanction against wrongful rejection. Upon consideration of the petition for rehearing and the briefs submitted, we think that since the Department has interpreted its regulation in a manner which it thinks necessary to carry out the purposes of the Act, and since the interpretation has been adhered to for over ten years, it should not be disregarded. Under these circumstances we hold that we should not substitute our interpretation merely because our original thought was that such a drastic interpretation is not needed to carry out the intention of the Act. The Department's interpretation is not plainly erroneous; it is a possible and reasonable interpretation of the regulation, even if not the only possible one. We therefore think it should be followed, cf. Bowles v. Seminole Rock & Sand Co., 1945, 325 U.S. 410, 65 S. Ct. 1215, 89 L. Ed. 1700, and the opinion amended by striking out the two paragraphs preceding the final paragraph.

The judgment of this court entered May 17, 1948, is vacated; and the judgment of the district court of August 27, 1947, is vacated and the case is remanded to that court for the entry of judgment in accordance with the opinion of May 17, 1948, 168 F.2d 276, as hereby amended.

D. The Problem in the Supreme Court of the United States

Martinelli was not yet ready to give up. Represented by new counsel, it filed in the Supreme Court of the United States, within the ninety days permitted by law, a petition for a writ of certiorari to review the decision of the court of appeals. See 28 U.S.C. §§ 1254 (1), 2101(c).

The petition and supporting brief were short. The gist of them is contained in the following passages:

> The petitioner submits that the power of the Secretary of Agriculture to make rules, regulations and orders is limited by the provisions of section 15 of the Act itself. [7 U.S.C.A. § 499o.] He can make only such as "may be necessary to carry out the provisions of this chapter." He has no power to enlarge the Act itself. * * *
>
> There is nothing in the body of the Act itself which requires such a result [the loss of the buyer's right to recoup damages from the seller]. Such a conclusion is at variance with the spirit of the Act taken as a whole. The Secretary of Agriculture has no authority by rule, regulation or order to deprive the petitioner of such an important right. The respondent in this case is attempting to compel the petitioner to pay the contract price for merchandise which the respondent failed to ship or deliver. * * *
>
> The petitioner submits that there is nothing in the Act itself which requires a conclusion that the rejection under such circumstances is without reasonable cause. * * * The petitioner further submits that the Secretary of Agriculture had no authority to promulgate any rules, regulations or orders which would have the effect of preventing the petitioner from rejecting the shipment pursuant to the provisions of the Uniform Sales Act * * *.

How persuasive was this argument?

Was the draftsman of the petition wise in urging also that the rejection had been rightful, instead of sticking simply to the recoupment point?

"A review on writ of certiorari is not a matter of right, but of sound judicial discretion, and will be granted only where there are special and important reasons therefor." Rule 19, Revised Rules of the Supreme Court of the United States (1954). Denial of the writ accordingly imports no judgment upon the merits of a controversy.

Rule 19 does not indicate "the character of reasons which will be considered" by the Court in deciding whether to exercise its discretion in favor of review. Among those applicable to court of appeals decisions, the two which induce a grant most frequently are a showing of a probable conflict either with a decision of another court of appeals or with a prior decision of the Supreme Court itself. But Martinelli could make no such showing. It had to satisfy the Court that the court of appeals either had "decided an important question of federal law which has not been, but should be settled by this court" or had "so far departed from the accepted and usual course of judicial proceedings * * * as to call for an exercise of this court's power of supervision."

Martinelli failed to do this. On December 6, 1948, five years, five months, and fifteen days after Martinelli agreed to buy the cantaloupes, a curt memorandum order, "certiorari denied," wrote finis to the litigation. 335 U.S. 885. Under Section 7(d) of the Act, 7 U.S.C.A. § 449g(d), Martinelli had ten days from the date on which this order became final to pay the reparation award. Presumably it did so.

PART V. SOME NOTES AND QUERIES

A. The Problem Through Martinelli's Eyes

1. What *exactly* ought Martinelli to have done on that morning of July 5, 1943, when it found out about the condition of the cantaloupes? Draft the telegram which you think it should have sent Gillarde.

2. Did Martinelli have a good reason to believe that it was legally free to abandon the carload to the railroad? An even plausible reason? Was it ethical for it do so? Does the answer to this third question have any relation to the answer to the first two?

3. Assuming that Martinelli either knew or had reason to know that the abandonment of the carload to the railroad would be a breach of its agreement with Gillarde, did it have reason also to know that the breach would entail the harsh consequence of forfeiture of any claim for breach of warranty that it might have against Gillarde? What bearing does the answer to this question have upon the question whether it was just to apply the forfeiture rule to Martinelli? Does justice require that people be told in advance exactly what will happen to them if they do wrong so that they will be better able to judge whether to do right?

4. Assuming that Martinelli was obliged to take charge of the cantaloupes promptly and sell them for whatever they would bring, was it obliged also to assume responsibility for the purchase price, relying on its claim for breach of warranty only as a basis for recoupment? If it had salvaged for Gillarde whatever value the cantaloupes had, but at the same time had disclaimed responsibility for the purchase price, would the Secretary have been warranted in holding that it had forfeited its claim for breach of warranty?

5. Martinelli's lawyer, if any, had at most only a few hours in which to formulate his advice to the company before the telegram of rejection was sent. Is it reasonable to expect the lawyer in this time to have gone through the process of analysis you have just gone through and to have come out seeing the problem the same way?

B. The Problem Through the Secretary's Eyes

1. How would you have advised the Secretary of Agriculture to dispose of Gillarde's complaint? In the way in which he did? Or in some other way? What, if any, additional things would you have needed to know in order to advise him with satisfying assurance?

2. Suppose that in an ordinary contract for the sale of durable goods the buyer had agreed expressly not to reject a shipment if it proved defective, but had nevertheless rejected. Would a court in an ordinary lawsuit be warranted in applying a rule of complete forfeiture of the buyer's claim against the seller for breach of warranty rather than in trying to make the consequences to the buyer as nearly as possible proportional to his wrong? Would a court have been warranted in doing so, in the absence of statute or administrative determination, if the goods were perishables? Would the Uniform Sales Act permit it?

3. If the questions in the last paragraph were all answered in the negative, would it follow that the Secretary ought to have been advised not to decide as he did? Or does it make a difference that a special statute was involved embodying known and special purposes, including the elimination of "the rejection evil"? Does it make a difference that an administrative agency rather than a court had to settle the controversy in the first instance?

Suppose that the marketing specialists on the Secretary's staff had urged upon him the following considerations: *first*, that any rejection, and particularly a rejection for defect of quality, always tends to reduce the market value of a shipment to a greater extent than its actual condition would warrant, and thus causes economic waste; *second*, that to force the seller to gather evidence in a remote market of the precise amount of loss attributable to a wrongful rejection is to subject him at best to expense and inconvenience and at worst to an impossible burden; *third*, that the difficulties which have been mentioned are the very ones against which the Act and the "rolling acceptance final" form of clause were supposed to protect the seller; and, *finally*, that the added penalty of forfeiture is not only fair for the reasons stated but necessary if wrongful rejections are to be effectually deterred. Would you have considered these contentions to be persuasive if satisfactorily substantiated in point of market fact? What would you have considered satisfactory substantiation?

4. Would you have advised the Secretary that the decision proposed by the marketing specialists could not be reconciled with the language of the Act, even if the asserted market facts *were* substantiated? Recall the provision of Section 5(a) that any dealer who violates Section 2 "shall be liable to the person or persons injured thereby for *the full amount of damages* sustained in consequence of such violation" (emphasis added). See p. 34, above. Gillarde, we are assuming, also violated the Act. Yet the proposed decision would exempt *it* from any liability for the resulting damages to Martinelli.

Before yielding to the line of reasoning just suggested, observe that it treats Congress as having, in effect, decided the present controversy way back in 1930. Is this sensible? Necessary, even though not sensible?

5. Does it help in resolving any of the doubts that have been raised to reflect that the Secretary was not engaged in imposing his own regime of order upon dealers in fresh fruits and vegetables, willy nilly, but only in defining the consequences of arrangements into which dealers were free to enter or not to enter as they pleased—that he was engaged, in other words, in suppletive rather than constructive lawmaking?

6. Does it help in quieting any misgivings on the score of unfair surprise to Martinelli to reflect that Martinelli was quite clearly advised about what its basic duty was—namely, to accept the cantaloupes and promptly salvage what it could—and that the surprise, if any, related only to the consequences of breach of this known or knowable duty?

Does this same consideration help also to quiet misgivings on the score of the Secretary's authority? Is it proper to read the statute as according the Secretary somewhat greater freedom in the development of remedial law than in the statement of basic, primary obligations?

Note that there may be thought to be a justification for this in the development of the general, unwritten law. In dealing with questions of basic, primary obligation—that is, with normal activity not involving controversy—the courts have on the whole sought to stick close to established custom and general understanding. But people do not usually develop customs or understandings about what happens when basic obligations are violated. Historically, for the most part, remedial doctrines have been molded by the tribunals that settle the exceptional cases of controversy from time to time arising, or else by the legislature.

7. What weight should be given to such understanding as Gillarde might have had that Martinelli's obligation to take charge of the carload would be enforced by application of the forfeiture sanction?

8. Would you feel more comfortable about the Secretary's decision if the remedial doctrine of forfeiture on which it rests had been embodied in a formal regulation instead of being announced in the form of grounds of decision in reparation proceedings? Why do you suppose the Secretary did not mention the doctrine in his regulation defining the meaning of "rolling acceptance" and "rolling acceptance final"?

Is this point of sufficient weight to warrant the conclusion that the actual decision was unjustified, in the absence of a regulation announcing the forfeiture doctrine in effect at the time Martinelli acted?

Lacking a prior regulation, would you have advised the Secretary to embody the doctrine in an amended regulation at the time Gillarde's complaint was disposed of? Would doing this have helped to justify the actual decision? Or would you have urged that the amendment be applied with prospective effect only? If the amendment were applied retrospectively to the *Gillarde* case, would this have implied that the earlier decisions made without benefit of regulation were erroneous?

Would the situation have been helped if, instead of embodying the forfeiture rule in a formal regulation, the Secretary had used another of his resources for publicity and had fully and rationally explained and justified the doctrine in the initial reparations decision announcing it? Or, at least, if he had given a satisfactory although belated explanation in the *Gillarde* case itself? Would this kind of warning have been the equivalent of a formal regulation?

Does the gist of the difficulty in the case, in other words, lie not in the substance of the decision but in the way in which the governing doctrine was formulated and promulgated? Is there any good excuse for the way the Secretary did it?

C. The Problem Through the Courts' Eyes

1. How, if at all, did the considerations which were relevant to the decision of the case by the courts differ from the considerations which were relevant to the Secretary's decision? Are there points on which you would have advised the Secretary to act differently as an original matter but with respect to which nevertheless the Secretary's failure to accept your advice would not in your opinion have warranted a reversal of his decision by a court?

2. How is it possible to account for Judge Healey's opinion in the district court? That opinion would have represented an accurate application of the conventional law of sales, would it not, if it had not been for the "rolling acceptance final" clause, Section 71 of the Uniform Sales Act, the various applicable provisions of the Perishable Agricultural Commodities Act of 1930, and the regulations and decisions thereunder? What explanation can be given for Judge Healey's failure to deal with these aspects of his problem?

3. Was justice at length done in the *Gillarde* case? What are the relevant criteria of justice?

(a) Would the court of appeals have acted justly if it had relied solely upon an intuitive *ad hoc* sense of what is fair when a carload of cantaloupes turns out to be spoiled like that? Or is it an essential ingredient of justice that due respect be paid to prior institutional settlements which have a claim to be accepted as authoritative?

(b) To what extent were the prior settlements indeterminate? The account of the episode which has been given has emphasized the vagueness and uncertainty, for many purposes, of many of the legal arrangements involved. But is it not defensible to conclude that this complex of "loose artificialities" nevertheless articulates tightly when brought to bear upon the concrete facts of an actual situation, leaving only a single question which is fairly open to a reasonable difference of opinion—namely, the question on which the court of appeals changed its mind on rehearing? If you think this is true, consider its implications with respect to the nature of the legal process.

(c) Was this single debatable question really very difficult? Could you have written an opinion satisfactory even to yourself holding, in the teeth of the representations in behalf of the Department of Agriculture, that the forfeiture doctrine was *not* authorized by the statute? That it was unauthorized in any form? Or that it was unauthorized, at least, unless embodied in a formal regulation?

On the other hand, it would have been easy, would it not, to have written an opinion holding that the reasons advanced by the Secretary in support of the doctrine in the present and earlier decisions were insufficient to overcome the presumption in favor of making damages proportional to the wrong, that these reasons could not be supplemented by *ex parte* arguments advanced in briefs of counsel, and that accordingly the case should be remanded to the Secretary for reconsideration and redetermination? Do you think the case *should* have been disposed of in this way?

D. Some Cognate Problems in the Courts

1. Some twenty-seven months after Martinelli rejected the cantaloupes it rejected a carload of grapes which it had brought from another Chicago distributor "f.o.b. shipping point acceptance final." The Secretary in due course issued another reparation order against Martinelli, and this case, too, eventually came before Judge Healey. Meanwhile the court of appeals had decided the *Gillarde* case, and Judge Healey took this as requiring him to affirm the departmental order.

It turned out, however, that the judge was wrong a second time. There was evidence, which he had refused to consider, that in making the agreement the Chicago distributor had deliberately withheld from Martinelli the important fact that the grapes had been previously sold to another purchaser and rejected because partly decayed. Judge Healey thought this was irrelevant because Martinelli had not known about it at the time of the rejection.

The court of appeals reversed, holding that the buyer's right of rejection for fraud is unaffected by the Act of Congress. *Joseph Martinelli & Co., Inc. v. Simon Siegel Co.*, 176 F.2d 98, 101 (1st Cir. 1949). It said:

> * * * This is for the reason that the technique adopted by Congress to prevent wrongful rejection by unscrupulous buyers was not to prohibit rejection entirely, but to provide for the definition of certain terms which might be employed in contracts to limit a buyer's right of rejection. And this method of regulation presupposes a valid contract, not one which may be avoided with the result that the entire contract is relegated to the discard, including limiting provisions therein such as "acceptance final" as defined by the Secretary of Agriculture pursuant to the authority conferred upon him by the Act.

In effect, the court was saying, was it not, that the protection of the "acceptance final" form of contract and the enforcement mechanisms of the Act are facilities available only to sellers who use them in good faith?

Is this sound? By what reasoning can it be said that the court was free to override the Secretary's judgment in *Siegel* but not in *Gillarde*?

2. In 1948 a Chicago distributor sold a carload of lettuce to a dealer in Johnstown, Pennsylvania. The contract of sale contained the clause "f.o.b. acceptance final," and provided for "open" billing. The seller notified the buyer of shipment pursuant to the contract, and that the billing was "advise." "Open" billing permits the buyer to receive or divert the car before payment, but "advise" billing requires him to be prepared to pay before either receipt or diversion. The buyer promptly notified the seller, two days before the car's arrival, that he objected to the change in credit terms and would consider the contract at an end unless the billing was made "open." The seller refused any change. Eventually, the buyer having stuck to his position, the car was abandoned to the railroad at an almost total loss.

On the seller's complaint, the Secretary of Agriculture entered a reparation order against the buyer for the full contract price. The district court affirmed. 122 F. Supp. 497 (W.D. 1954). However, the court of appeals reversed, holding that, although the buyer's right of rejection is limited under an "acceptance final" form of contract, the disability relates only to rejections "for causes affecting the condition or quality of the goods." Finding that the buyer had thus not surrendered his right to reject in all cases, the court concluded that the seller's alteration of the credit terms was a substantial and material breach of the contract and, under the applicable state law as determined by resort to conflicts doctrine, was a sufficient ground for rejection. *Schuman Co. v. Nelson*, 219 F.2d 627 (3d Cir. 1955).

The court reasoned that "[t]he obligation to accept must necessarily be restricted by some standard." It pointed out that, "[f]or example, it is undoubtedly true that the buyer would be relieved of any responsibility under the contract if prior to shipment the seller notified him of an increase in the price and the buyer refused to accede." It went on:

> And yet, nowhere in these proceedings has there been suggested any such limitation. We do not conceive it to be our function to choose among the various standards that could be formulated in delineating the right to reject. The courts cannot attempt to fill in the interstices of legislation when an administrative agency empowered by statute to perform this very function has issued valid regulations. The meaning to be given trade terms is a matter peculiarly within the competence of the administrative agency. Since that agency has exercised its power by issuing regulations, we can seek only to place a reasonable construction upon them, bearing in mind that the parties to this contract have presumably relied upon the regulation in issue.

"Accepting the foregoing as a premise for decision," the court pointed out that the definitions in question "speak only of risk of loss and the rights of the buyer for damage or deterioration in the merchandise. It would be anomalous indeed to hold that while these sections refer only to recovery for damage or deterioration, they nevertheless prohibit rejection for all causes. Since no other limitation on the right to reject is supplied by the regulation, we must assume that this right is to be interpreted in the light of the general subject matter covered by the regulation."

Is this sound?

3. The problem of the *Siegel* case can be solved by resort to ethical considerations as well as to established legal doctrines with respect to the vitiation of

transactions by fraud. As to such matters a court is at least as competent as an administrative agency. But the problem of the *Schuman* case may be thought to implicate other kinds of considerations. Was there any business excuse for the seller's change in credit terms? How seriously was the buyer disadvantaged thereby? Does the practical need for the protection against economic waste afforded by the buyer's obligation to take charge extend to situations in which the dispute arises out of matters other than those concerning the quality and condition of the produce?

As the court of appeals in the *Schuman* case so obviously felt, a satisfying answer to these questions requires some analysis of the theory and practical bases of the Secretary's forfeiture doctrine. Neither the original opinions of the Secretary announcing the doctrine nor any opinions which have been found in later cases contain such analysis.

Is there any escape from the conclusion that the Secretary's staff has shown itself in this matter to be professionally incompetent? If this is right, how is such incompetence to be explained?

4. Do the *Gillarde, Siegel*, and *Schuman* cases, taken together, suggest a distinctive and socially useful function for courts in the ultimate settlement of problems which are committed in the first instance to administrative determination? Did the district courts in those cases evince an adequate understanding of this function? If not, how do you explain the inadequacy?

E. The Problem Through the Eyes of Congress

Is the Congress which enacted the Perishable Agricultural Commodities Act of 1930 open to criticism for having failed to foresee the *Gillarde* problem and to make definite provision for its solution? The *Siegel* and *Schuman* problems? All the thousands of other problems which experience under the Act has turned up?

Were later Congresses remiss in failing to deal with these problems after they *had* turned up and begun to trouble the Department and the courts?

If you answer these questions in the negative, think about what the answer means. It means, does it not, that a legislature is inescapably dependent upon other agencies of decision—that in the solution of problems such as those with which the Act deals a whole system of institutionalized procedures is needed?

F. The Problem from an Olympian Point of View

An adequate supply of fresh fruits and vegetables is one of the least debatable of human wants. Is the complex of arrangements illustrated in the *Gillarde* case and these background notes well conceived to the end of maximizing human satisfactions in this regard, without undue sacrifice of other satisfactions? If not, what improvements might be made?

In the United States, winter fruits and vegetables come to the inhabitants of the industrial north mainly from the three southern prongs of Florida, Texas, and California. Observe the similarity of the geographical relationship of Greece, Italy, and Spain to northern Europe. Do the differences in political and legal arrangements have a significant bearing on the differences in the extent of the movement of winter fruits and vegetables on the two continents? Would it be possible to find out?

Consider whether the opportunities for the supply of winter fruits and vegetables within the Soviet Union, with its single national market governed by a single institutional system, are comparable to those in the United States. Is the Soviet system better adapted to securing a good supply?

Think, in particular, about the various assignments of legal power as well as the distribution of practical ability to make effective decisions which the law governing the interstate trade in fresh fruits and vegetables in the United States exhibits. Notice the role of private determinations. Notice the role, past and present, of state law, including not only the general state law of contract and sales but state legislative and administrative powers. Notice the role of the federal government, including Congress, the Department of Agriculture, and the federal courts.

Are these various assignments of powers and liberties undesirably complex and confusing? Or do they result on the whole in giving each agency of decision or action the opportunity to decide and to act in the fashion which it is best equipped to do?

In what, if any, sense can the process of social ordering exemplified in the Gillarde-Martinelli episode be described as "scientific"?

All the rest of these materials are designed to cast light on the questions under this last subheading. The questions are put at this point to invite reflection and not with any thought that what has so far been presented makes possible a confident answer.

Many other questions might be put. First and last, it will come to be seen, the problems under the Perishable Agricultural Commodities Act of 1930 exemplify an extraordinary proportion of the significant aspects of the legal process and of the American legal system.

Herbert Wechsler

Herbert Wechsler

THE LEGAL PROCESS provided a framework for addressing the practical and professional challenges that followed both the New Deal expansion of federal public law and the methodological revolution associated with Legal Realism. More laws, more agencies, and more sites for lawmaking and interpretation in an increasingly integrated national political and economic system heightened the complexities of operating in America's multijurisdictional legal order. American legal professionals had lost faith in deduction as an exclusive or reliable tool of legal interpretation and in the ideal of a rationally coherent and formally unified normative regime. They increasingly took it for granted that conflicts, gaps, and ambiguities throughout the legal materials would make what became known as "policy" analysis a necessary and desirable part of routine legal work. Lon Fuller, among others, had demonstrated how policy considerations immanent in legal rules might be used in doctrinal analysis and interpretation. Hart and Sacks had built their "legal process" vision on the virtues of disaggregated decision making in a pluralistic legal system with potentially indeterminate legal materials.

At the time, however, most legal theorists worried less about legal pluralism or intellectual skepticism than about the role of judicial review in the American constitutional order. In part, this preoccupation reflects the tendency among legal theorists to focus on the exceptional workings of elite institutions—the Supreme Court overruling Congress—rather than on more quotidian encounters with multiple jurisdictions and conflicting rules illustrated by the Cantaloupe Case. In the post–New Deal era, moreover, the opportunities for judicial review of legislation or executive rule-making expanded. Just how much deference should courts give to rule-making by agencies, as opposed to legislation? How should judges review the discretion of administrative "experts" as opposed to the decisions of legislatures?

The broad question of what made courts well suited and entitled to review the constitutionality of acts by the other branches of government had long been a vexed issue in American legal theory. Although we remember Justice Marshall's 1803 opinion in *Marbury v. Madison* as the origin of the judicial power to review the constitutionality of legislative and executive action, the idea remained controversial at least through the Civil War. Indeed, the Supreme Court did not strike down a federal statute again until the 1856 Dred Scott case, declaring unconstitutional the 1820 "Missouri compromise" legislation restricting the extension of slavery in new territories—hardly a propitious start for the legitimate exercise of judicial oversight. As classical legal thought developed in the decades following the Civil War, jurists remade American public law, borrowing ideas from a private law increasingly organized around the idea of absolute powers exercised within spheres demarcated by clear rights. It would be the task of judges to police the boundaries between absolute authorities, an idea that seemed as applicable to public as to private law. Judicial review could seem relatively unremarkable so long as judges could be understood to be policing formal boundaries between powers that remained absolute within their spheres, rather than substituting their own judgments for the decisions of other branches.

As they developed this idea, judges transformed private-law rights to property and freedom of contract into constitutional rights marking a sphere of private autonomy that could not be violated by public legislative authority. The result was a constitutional mandate to strike down progressive social legislation, most famously in the 1905 Lochner case declaring a New York statute regulating the hours bakers could work an unconstitutional interference with the general right to make a contract, itself a liberty protected by the Fourteenth Amendment. The Court stated clearly that

> This is not a question of substituting the judgment of the court for that of the legislature. If the act be within the power of the State it is valid, although the judgment of the court might be totally opposed to the enactment of such a law. But the question would still remain: Is it within the police power of the State? and that question must be answered by the court.

Although the Court eventually reversed course under extreme political pressure, for postwar jurists the Lochner era remained a sharp reminder of how judicial review might go awry. The problem was not only the background conviction that courts were likely to be more conservative, both politically and professionally, than the legislative and executive branches. Postwar jurists had also lost faith that judges could review legislative action by policing the boundary between the "police power" of the state and the "liberty" of private actors without engaging in substantive policy judgments of their own.

The legal realist assault on classical legal thought had rendered earlier thinking about the distinctiveness of judicial work obsolete. If Holmes was right that judges should embrace statistics, economics, and other tools for the weighing "considerations of social advantage," it was unclear how judicial reasoning differed from that of legislators whether judges were exercising powers of judicial review or simply interpreting and applying statutes or common-law precedent. How could judges review legislative action other than by substituting their own views for that of the people's elected representatives?

This "counter-majoritarian" problem came to seem ever more difficult to resolve as jurists lost faith in deduction as a distinctive and decisive mode of judicial reasoning. Holmes's aphorism that "the life of the law is not logic but experience" was sharpened by the legal realist claims that judges interpreting general liberties—the freedom to contract or own property—could not rely on being compelled toward one clear answer by the impersonal dictates of logic. They would need to make messy choices. As Hohfeld had shown, for example, judges could recognize an owner's interest in property either by granting the owner a "right" and imposing a corresponding "duty" on those who would interfere, or by granting the owner no such right, leaving potential trespassers "privileged" to interfere. Dewey's description of judges reasoning as problem solvers, searching as much for premises to justify their conclusions as vice versa, sounded reasonable and pragmatic but made judicial review more difficult to swallow. If routine judicial work interpreting statutes and common-law precedent was suffused with policy choices, it was more difficult to explain why judicial interpretation of the constitution should take precedence over the interpretations of the legislature or executive.

In one sense this problem seemed more difficult to the postwar generation than it had to the legal realists. Like the realists, postwar jurists were convinced the genie of

policy could not be returned to the bottle—there was no going back to a world of
confidence in formal deduction as a mode of judicial reasoning. For many realists,
however, the turn to policy had not seemed to threaten to make judicial reasoning
subjective or open-ended. The realists criticized judges for making unacknowledged
policy choices, for disguising policy choices beneath unpersuasive deductive reasoning from the broad legal concepts, for covering conflicts, gaps, and ambiguities in the
legal materials with specious reasoning rather than state-of-the-art social science. On
the whole, realists had been confident that judges could find relatively clear answers
by looking to the best social science. Properly instructed, judges could read the
requirements of social and economic conditions as reliably—more reliably—than
they could read statutes and cases. As a result, they felt no tension between decrying
Lochner and urging judges to re-interpret contract, tort, and property law to expand
protections for consumers, tenants, workers, or debtors to recognize social interdependence and ameliorate the effects of unequal bargaining power.

As it became increasingly clear that people understood "new social realities" in
quite different ways, and that social science spoke with many different voices, it
no longer seemed possible to transform a sociological is into a normative ought.
By the late 1930s, it was clear that "policy" analysis would require judges to deal
with competing social purposes and equally valid, but conflicting, legal principles.
Holmes had said as much, but the message had gotten lost under enthusiasm for
newly professional social sciences. One result was the emergence of ideas about
policy reasoning that stressed the need to balance competing policy considerations
in the evaluation of specific doctrinal interpretations. Social science could clarify
such a balance, but it would only very rarely clearly resolve it.

It remained difficult to explain why judges should not be replaced either by more
knowledgeable administrative experts or by more politically accountable legislators. For Hart and Sacks, the answer lay in the different structures of each institution. The legislature was conducive to the aggregation of divergent social interests,
and agencies were particularly suited to the mobilization of expertise, while the
judiciary was particularly suited to the adjudication of conflicts between parties on
the basis of adversarial argument and reasoned elaboration. All were involved in
policy work, but their different institutional structures and procedures led them to
have heightened competence for particular types of disputes—in a complex and disaggregated legal order, each institution should be careful to defer to others whose
competence was greater. Indeed, judges might well be better suited than either legislatures or administrative agencies to balance competing considerations in the way
necessary to reasoned policymaking, particularly at the cutting edge of social developments. The appellate opinion presented a "reasoned elaboration" of the basis for
decisions, guaranteeing a level of both transparency and reasoning care. Although
agency decision making might be preferable when scientific expertise settled a matter, this was rarely the case. Legislatures were better at aggregating multiple interests, but the statutes that resulted were often vague and only able to be clarified by
the light of adversarial proceedings between interested parties. In short, for Hart
and Sacks, judicial review lay on a continuum with other judicial work interpreting statutes or administrative decisions, offering an occasion for deference where
decisions had been arrived at in accordance with the appropriate procedures and
for deployment of the judiciary's own institutional comparative advantage.

Although Hart and Sacks seemed confident that attention to institutional competence and structure would yield a satisfactory settlement between the branches,
particularly if legal elites shared their agnosticism about substantive outcomes

and optimism about legal pluralism in a diversified legal system, not all postwar legal process scholars were convinced. For one thing, the Supreme Court would always be a special case—its decisions would not be as easily checked by legal pluralism as the diverse courts whose different opinions Hart and Sacks reported in the Cantaloupe Case. Many legal process scholars who were comfortable with judicial reasoning about policy and purpose in the interpretation of statutes or common-law precedent found it more difficult to accept an expansive exercise of judicial review. The Supreme Court could easily become the ally or enemy of one or another political force—the memory of Lochner remained a traumatic one, and it was difficult to be confident it could not happen again.

In 1954, in *Brown v. Board of Education*, the Supreme Court ruled that segregated schools were unconstitutional. It was a watershed for the legal process generation. Was this the apogee of judicial attention to social justice, social science, and social policy? Or was this a federal judicial usurpation of authority more appropriately lodged with the legislature and the states? The emergence of the Warren Court as an ally in the struggle for civil rights and the perception that it would be an "activist" court in many fields, placed the question of the appropriate limits for judicial policymaking at the top of the scholarly agenda. Although each of the legal process scholars had something to say about this set of issues, by far the most significant article on judicial review in the postwar period was Herbert Wechsler's "Toward Neutral Principles of Constitutional Law," delivered as a series of Holmes Lectures at Harvard Law School in 1959. It gave voice to the anxiety of many legal process scholars that the Warren Court had gone too far.

Wechsler, born in 1909, was raised in Manhattan. His father was a lawyer. After graduating from City College with a degree in French, Wechsler sought employment as a French teacher, but his father successfully prevailed upon the head of the French department not to hire him, on the grounds that he should become a lawyer. At Columbia Law School, Wechsler studied with Karl Llewellyn, and remembered the school as a place of "great tension." In 1928, the year Wechsler arrived, a group of empirically minded realists—William Underhill Moore, Herman Oliphant, and Walter Wheeler Cook—departed for the newly founded Institute of Law at Johns Hopkins University. Gary Peller describes the intellectual division in the law schools of the period this way:

> Like the rupture between traditionalists and modernists in the more general intellectual culture, the opposition between the realists and the traditionalists proceeded within polar terms of argument that appeared to reflect a threshold impasse between two diametrically conflicting views of law and social life: where the traditionalists saw rules, the realists saw standards. Where the traditionalists saw private choice, the realists saw public power. The traditionalist conviction that law consisted of neutral, background principles was challenged by the realist demonstration that the law was rooted in social policy. The traditionalist dedication to essential form was opposed by the realist focus on observable function. The traditionalist invocation of law as protecting private rights was challenged by the realist vision of law as distributing public power.

Wechsler, like Fuller, Hart, and Sacks, grew up with this polarity, and he had joined the realists in rejecting the "traditional" approach associated with Langdell. He was part of a generation of legal intellectuals that felt it was carrying on an intellectual revolution—partisans of a new approach to law personified by Holmes, Benjamin Cardozo, and Louis Brandeis. In 1993, Wechsler remembered Cardozo's central idea this way:

> This continuity and stability were illusory—that even if you wanted it to be a closed system, you couldn't have it, because the sources were too inconsistent. They led in opposite directions, and an element of reasoned choice was essential if the judge was to know what he was doing.

Wechsler took it for granted that the "concept of the common law as a closed system" was wrong, that legislation and administrative action should be treated sympathetically by the courts, that the Supreme Court should refrain from blocking governmental action to "order the economy" to counteract the "dislocation incident to the development of an industrial society," and that law should be understood to be more than rules and doctrines.

But Wechsler never saw himself as a realist—a group he thought too radical in their rejection of legal tradition for social science. Asked in 1993 if he was influenced by the cultural relativism of 1930s anthropology to be "something of a legal realist," he responded this way:

> Well, certainly in the literal sense, yes. That is to say, in the sense that one approaches law not with the feeling that all the answers were dictated to Moses on Mount Sinai, or that some equivalent prescription occurred, but that you want to enrich your mind by anything that experience has to offer. In that sense, yes. But that, of course, is the broadest and least specific meaning of the term "Legal Realism." If, on the other hand, you're turning to what Karl Llewellyn meant by realistic jurisprudence, in his article entitled "The Call for a Realist Jurisprudence [Karl Llewellyn, A Realistic Jurisprudence—The Next Step," 30 *Columbia Law Review* 431 (1930)] then I become a little more doubtful, because the propagandists of a realist jurisprudence were all over the lot in terms of what they were for. They tended to be united only in terms of what they were against. They were against what I have called, in speaking to you, the closed system.

Wechsler became editor-in-chief of the *Law Review* and was invited to return to the Columbia faculty immediately after graduation in 1931. He took a leave to clerk with Justice Harlan Stone in 1932, and Stone quickly became a hero and role model for Wechsler, who would himself later be appointed the Harlan Stone Professor of Constitutional Law at Columbia. Stone had been dean at Columbia in the early 1920s, had served as Attorney General, and had been appointed by President Coolidge to the Supreme Court in 1925. Wechsler identified Stone as a "middle of the roader" because "precedent was important to him, continuity was important, and people who would change things had to carry the burden of persuasion that change was desirable. He was interested in legislation, not hostile to legislation. He wasn't a madman about the closed system, but he was a conservative." Just after the war, Wechsler had written an essay celebrating Stone's approach to constitutional adjudication—his vigorous defense of judicial review, his embrace of a robust and flexible approach to interpreting the constitution as an "organic whole" whose import would change with time and place, his participation in the decade-long realignment of the Court to uphold the bulk of Roosevelt's New Deal legislation and administrative delegation against the backdrop of the political threat to remake the Court. Wechsler celebrated the Court's refusal to allow an outdated approach to the constitution to invalidate newly expansive federal power. But Wechsler was equally impressed by the Court's "self-limitation" during the Roosevelt era, expressed in Stone's insistence that the Court intrude "in the constitutional process only when the need for their participation is acute." Wechsler's admiration for what he viewed as Stone's record of principled decision making through more than twenty politically tumultuous years on the Court would later lead Wechsler to doubts about what he took to be the more hastily fashioned and less principled jurisprudence of the Warren Court.

In 1937 and 1938, Wechsler worked part-time for the New York State Democratic Party leader at the New York Constitutional Convention on the provision of housing and other benefits to low-income people, and on strengthening the state's bill of rights. He returned to Washington in 1940 to work in the Solicitor General's office. During the war years, Wechsler screened lawyers seeking employment with the Executive branch, and worked with Attorney General Francis Biddle, ultimately as Assistant Attorney General in charge of the War Division. He developed the legal framework to permit the ten million American citizens overseas with the war effort to vote, against Republican opposition. His responsibilities with the war department included the Japanese internments and the management of martial law in Hawaii. He oversaw development of the American legal framework for the trials of Nazi war criminals, and accompanied Biddle to Nuremberg for the trials, serving as chief technical adviser to the American judges. Wechsler played a significant role in rejecting efforts to convict individuals on the basis of their membership in "criminal organizations" alone.

After the war, Wechsler returned to Columbia, where he remained until his death in 2000. He was known for his work—primarily with Henry Hart—in the field of federal courts, as well as for his work in criminal law. He served as reporter at the American Law Institute for the Model Penal Code. A proponent of law reform through restatement and legislative codification, Wechsler was Executive Director of the American Law Institute from 1963 to 1984. The ALI was established in 1923 as the preeminent professional association dedicated to addressing the uncertainties in the common law through restatement. Over time, its emphasis shifted from private-law restatement to law reform. As director, Wechsler moved the Institute to adopt a more open approach to its restatement projects, weighing all the various considerations that judges would appropriately weigh in their own assessments— and doing so by majority vote rather than consensus, on the grounds that judges would also give weight to the preponderance of authority. During his directorship, the Institute completed the Second Restatement of Torts and of Contracts. Wechsler had something of a parallel career as an appellate advocate, having argued a number of significant cases for the government before and during the war, including the Korematsu case defending Japanese internment. Most famously, he represented the *New York Times* in *The New York Times v. Sullivan* in 1962.

For our purposes, however, it is Wechsler's 1959 contribution to constitutional law that endures. The article resulted from Wechsler's Holmes Lectures at Harvard Law School in 1959, which were intended as a response to Judge Learned Hand's Holmes Lectures of the preceding year. Hand had argued that judicial review, while necessary, was essentially an extrajudicial invention, and had suggested that the bill of rights was too open-ended to be judicially enforceable. In response, Wechsler offered a defense of judicial review and of the judicial enforcement of constitutional rights. However significant Wechsler may have felt it was to respond to Hand, these points were no longer controversial. Wechsler's insistence in his lectures that judicial review and judicial enforcement of rights should be exercised only on the basis of neutral principles—and his criticism of the Brown decision—were.

What makes judicial decision making distinctive, and entitles courts to exercise judicial review, is more than the practice of reasoned elaboration or the judiciary's particular institutional structure and competence. Wechsler accepts the legal process notion that courts cannot be formally precluded from "political" questions: "all the [political question] doctrine can defensibly imply is that the courts are called upon to judge whether the Constitution has committed to another agency of government the autonomous determination of the issue raised, a finding that itself requires an interpretation" (pp. 7–8). Wechsler's focus, rather, is on the appropriate "standards" to be used to interpret the constitution when "courts cannot escape the duty of deciding whether actions of the other branches . . . are consistent with the Constitution" (p. 10). Like Hart and Sacks, Wechsler stresses the significance of a written articulation of reasons—a "reasoned elaboration"—for judicial decision making, particularly when courts exercise their powers of judicial review. But he also means to restrict the types of reasons which can be part of the elaboration. When evaluating exercises of judicial review, we should not focus on the interests or values served by the decision. We should focus rather on the method of decision, the types of reasons used to justify the decision. Justice Ginsburg restated the idea in a posthumous tribute to Wechsler in these terms: "His point was that the way we decide things is very often— he'd say always, I'd say often—as important as what we decide."

Wechsler recognized that the routine work of courts engaged in common-law decision making, or the interpretation of statutes and administrative rules will involve purposive and policy-driven reasoning. But judicial review is different— the counter-majoritarian difficulty is more pronounced. For Wechsler, judicial review is only legitimate to the extent it is grounded in "neutral principles." At one level, the proposition sounds obvious and commonsensical:

> I put it to you that the main constituent of the judicial process is precisely that it must be genuinely principled, resting with respect to every step that is involved in reaching judgment on analysis and reasons quite transcending the immediate result that is achieved.

In this broad sense, at least, Wechsler succeeded in redeeming the use of "principles" from legal realist assaults on deduction from the "heaven of legal concepts" by linking principled reasoning to the specific institutional legitimacy and competence of courts, somewhat as Lon Fuller had redeemed "form" by linking it to a series of policies.

The difficulty arises in being more concrete about precisely what counts as principled reasoning. Wechsler offers several definitions for the principles he has in mind, and the type of reasoning they compel. A repeated theme is the ability—and the judicial willingness—to apply the standard across a range of cases, in situations that would affect different interests, or affect interests differently. Wechsler seems to have used the word neutral to suggest that the principle be applied generally— in the same way—to all interests to whom it could reasonably be applied. The word nevertheless generated a great deal of controversy—Wechsler was often thought to have proposed that principles must be neutral among social interests. Kent Greenawalt offers this reformulation of Wechsler's neutral principle: "A person gives a neutral reason, in Wechsler's sense, if he states a basis for a decision that he would be willing to follow in other situations to which it applies."

Despite the controversy and misunderstanding, Wechsler stood by the term "neutral," writing in 1961 that "as to the choice of adjective, my case is simply that I could discover none that better serves my purpose."

> The demand of neutrality is that a value and its measure be determined by a general analysis that gives no weight to accidents of application, finding a scope that is

acceptable whatever interest, group of person may assert the claim. So too, when there is conflict among values having constitutional protection, calling for their ordering or their accommodation, I argue that the principle of resolution must be neutral in a comparable sense (both in the definition of the individual competing values and in the approach that it entails to value competition).[1]

It is easier to see how the demand for reasoning grounded in neutral principles might be used to criticize judicial decisions than how it might serve as a program of action. Although Wechsler offered examples of principled arguments, the article is far clearer when he analyzes judicial reasoning that is not rooted in neutral principles. In this, the piece inaugurates a mode of criticism that remained a potent component of American Legal Thought after the more affirmative legal process conception of the broader institutional scheme fell out of fashion.

Wechsler's criticism of the Supreme Court's *Brown v. Board of Education* decision remains the most remembered application of this idea. Wechsler argues that the Court failed to articulate a justification for its opinion rooted in neutral principles. He dismisses the principle of "discrimination" as insufficiently neutral, and finds himself unable to work out a satisfactory defense of the decision in terms of the acceptably neutral principle of "freedom to associate." It remains difficult to grasp precisely how Wechsler understood "freedom to associate" to be a more neutral principle than "freedom from discrimination." Whether Wechsler's skepticism about *Brown v. Board of Education* should shape our evaluation of his broader call for a judicial review rooted in neutral principles remains an open question. In the years after the article was published, Wechsler's insistence on principled adjudication was much admired as a professional posture, but much criticized as legal theory and politics. He wrote as enthusiasm for an activist judiciary was growing among legal scholars, and as faith in the availability of "neutral principles" coherent enough to determine judicial outcomes was falling. Many years later, Wechsler reflected on the context for his ambivalence about an activist exercise of judicial review in these terms:

> I suppose you could say that my views on constitutional law generally date me very definitely as somebody who began to deal with these problems in the era of the Taft Court, or the early Hughes Court—the era when decisions seemed to be a road block to legislative developments that I and many others thought to be necessary for the decent humanization of American capitalism. And so we spent the first years of our lives preaching against the judicial veto of legislation of a type that we considered to be desirable. When the constitutional revolution came, as we indicated when we were talking about Roosevelt's court-packing plan . . . the problems for all of us became: How can we defend a judicial veto in areas where we thought it helpful in American life—civil liberties area, personal freedom, First Amendment—and at the same time condemn it in the areas where we considered it unhelpful? And an awful lot of the seminal thinking of my generation went into the confrontation of that antithesis, producing such things as the Carolene Products footnote and other efforts to develop a theoretical support for a civil-liberties-protective court and an active legislative function in the area of the economy. We may have grossly oversimplified the matter by drawing that antithesis as we did, but anyhow we did tend to draw it that way. Having learned through that experience of the consequences of judicial excess, we became highly sensitive to it, and on the whole, I should say, eager to develop the type of critique that would contribute to avoiding it. Now somebody who started off his thinking on these matters as an enthusiast for judicial activism is likely to think differently about such problems. If you look at a book like Laurence Tribe's treatise, you'll see what I mean.[2]

Wechsler's article was both the highpoint of postwar constitutional legal theory and the end of the legal process as a consensus in American legal thought. The 1960s and '70s would bring ever more insistent calls for the substitution of the sort of vague and indeterminate professional reasoning in which Wechsler put so much faith with one or another more instrumental modes of analysis, inspired by economics and other social sciences. At the same time, it would be a time of intense criticism of the intellectual coherence of the legal process school as a whole. When liberal legal scholars returned to principled adjudication, and eventually also to the legal process idea in the 1970s and after, they did so with far more attention to the problems of language and the instability of interpretation.

DAVID KENNEDY

NOTES

1. Herbert Wechsler, Principles, Politics, and Fundamental Law (Cambridge, Mass.: Harvard University Press, 1961).
2. Laurence Tribe, *American Constitutional Law*. Mineola, N.Y.: Foundation Press, 1978. Tribe is a well-known liberal constitutional law scholar, a generation younger than Wechsler, whom Wechsler saw as offering an unapologetic defense of Warren Court "judicial activism" in his 1978 treatise.

BIBLIOGRAPHY

Wechsler

For a bibliography of Wechsler's works and numerous commendations upon his retirement, see 78 *Columbia Law Review* N. 5 (June 1978) at 947 and following; bibliography at pages 969–72. A fascinating oral history interview with Wechsler, filled out with well-researched biographical detail, is Norman Silber and Geoffrey Miller, "Toward 'Neutral Principles' in Law: Selections from the Oral History of Herbert Wechsler," 93 *Columbia Law Review* 854 (1993). The oral history contains useful material on Wechsler's early intellectual influences, at Columbia and more generally, as well as material on his government experience, including a good discussion of Wechsler's role in arguing *Korematsu v. United States* 323 US 214 (1944) and an assessment of his claims to have toned down the War Department's factual record (pages 884 and following).

Wechsler reprinted his 1959 article with other related works in *Principles, Politics and Fundamental Law: Selected Essays* (Cambridge, Mass.: Harvard University Press, 1961). The book includes the essay "Mr. Justice Stone and the Constitution" (at 83–137), originally published as "Stone and the Constitution," 46 *Columbia Law Review* 764 (1946). Wechsler elaborated his defense of judicial review and the judicial enforcement of constitutional rights in Wechsler, "*The Courts and the Constitution,*" 65 *Columbia Law Review* 1001 (1965). The Holmes lectures of Justice Learned Hand to which Wechsler responded in his contribution to the Canon were published as *Hand, The Bill of Rights* (Cambridge, Mass.: Harvard University Press, 1958).

In the field of federal courts, Wechsler is best known as the co-author, with Henry Hart, of the leading casebook and treatise in the field, *The Federal Courts and the Federal System* (Brooklyn: Foundation Press, 1953). Wechsler wrote about his work with the American Law Institute Restatements, in Wechsler, "The Course of the Restatements," 55 *American Bar Association Journal* 147 (1969) and Herbert Wechsler, "Annual Report of the Director," 44 *American Law Institute Proceedings* 16 (1967).

Wechsler wrote about criminal law from the early stages of his career. His best known work in the field was the Model Penal Code itself and the American Law Institute commentary which accompanied it. He delivered a number of speeches defending the Code, and in particular its approach to sentencing, and published several essays on the subject. See Herbert Wechsler, "The Challenge of a Model Penal Code," 65 *Harvard Law Review* 1097 (1952); Wechsler, "Sentencing, Correction and the Model Penal Code," 109 *University of Pennsylvania Law Review* 465 (1961); Wechsler, "Codification of Criminal Law in the United States: The Model Penal Code," 68 *Columbia Law Review* 1425 (1968). Wechsler remained an opponent of more recent efforts to develop sentencing "guidelines" through the end of his career, convinced that the criminal justice system relied too heavily on imprisonment as a convenient default punishment. He developed a criminal law casebook parallel to his work with Henry Hart on federal courts, which was also well received initially, but was not extended to further editions. Jerome Michael and Herbert Wechsler, *Criminal Law and its Administration: Cases, Statutes and Commentaries* (Chicago: Foundation Press, 1940). Wechsler wrote about the legal issues involved in the Nuremberg trials in "The Issues of the Nuremberg Trial," in *Principles, Politics and Fundamental Law: Selected Essays* (Cambridge, Mass.: Harvard University Press, 1961, pp. 138–58).

Commentary

The "Neutral Principles" article drew an immediate response. See, for example, Louis H. Pollak, Jr., "Racial Discrimination and Judicial Integrity: A Reply to Professor Wechsler," 108 *University of Pennsylvania Law Review* 1 (1959) and Charles Black, "The Lawfulness of the Segregation Decisions," 69 *Yale Law Journal* 421 (1960). It remained one of the most cited law review articles for decades. Fred Shapiro, "The Most-Cited Law Review Articles Revisited," 71 *Chicago-Kent Law Review* 751 (1996) indicates that between 1956 and 1995, the piece was cited 968 times in judicial opinions and law review articles. By 2000, the piece had slipped from the second to sixth most cited law review article. Shapiro, "The Most Cited Legal Scholars," 29 *Journal of Legal Studies* 409 (2000).

The long-term impact of Wechsler's "principles" is more difficult to judge. Alexander Bickel and Harry Wellington were the most enthusiastic in continuing Wechsler's reticence about Warren Court activism. Alexander M. Bickel and Harry H. Wellington, "Legislative Purpose and the Judicial Process: The Lincoln Mills Case," 71 *Harvard Law Review* 1 (1957). Bickel continued the attack on the Court in "The Supreme Court, 1960 Term, Foreword: The Passive Virtues," 75 *Harvard Law Review* 40 (1961); Alexander Bickel, *Politics and the Warren Court* (New York: Harper & Row, 1965); and in Bickel, *The Least Dangerous Branch: The Supreme Court at the Bar of Politics* (New Haven: Yale University Press, 1986).

On the distinction between the neutral application of principles and principles which are neutral between different social interests, see Henry Paul Monaghan, "A Legal Giant is Dead," 100 *Columbia Law Review* 1370 at 1372–73 (2000). For an extension of Wechsler's argument to the interpretation of statutes, see Louis Jaffe, "Judicial Review: Question of Law," 69 *Harvard Law Review* 239 (1955).

Louis Henkin sympathetically analyzes the legal process idea of "balancing" in constitutional adjudication in relationship to Wechsler's conception of "principled" adjudication in Louis Henkin, "Infallibility Under Law: Constitutional Balancing," 78 *Columbia Law Review* 1022 (1978).

There are certainly echoes of Wechsler's approach in the jurisprudence of liberal constitutional law scholars and theorists of the 1970s and 1980s—such as Ronald Dworkin. But for Dworkin, a judge's principles must be rooted in a political morality and philosophy, of which there may well be more than one. See, for example, Dworkin, *Freedom's Law: The Moral Reading of the American Constitution* (Cambridge, Mass.: Harvard University Press, 1996) at 343 (constitutional adjudication of civil liberties involves "fundamental questions of political morality and philosophy"). Theories of judicial review after Wechsler were more likely to focus on matters of institutional structure (see Bickel, *The Least Dangerous Branch*), and take the plurality of conflicting principles and purposes more overtly as a starting point for analysis. See Tribe, "The Puzzling Persistence of Process-Based Constitutional Theories," 89 *Yale Law Journal* 1063 (1980).

The most cited criticisms of Wechsler's approach remain Mark V. Tushnet, "Following the Rules Laid Down: A Critique of Interpretivism and Neutral Principles," 96 *Harvard Law Review* 781 (1983) and Gary Peller, "Neutral Principles in the 1950s," 21 *University of Michigan Journal of Law Reform* 561, 1988, 561; Richard Parker, "The Past of Constitutional Theory—And Its Future," 42 *Ohio State Law Journal* 223 (1981); and Morton Horwitz, *The Transformation of American Law, 1780–1860* (Cambridge, Mass.: Harvard University Press, 1977); and *The Transformation of American Law, 1870–1960: The Crisis of Legal Orthodoxy* (New York: Oxford University Press, 1992). See also Martin Shapiro, "The Supreme Court and Constituitonal Adjudication: Of Politics and Neutral Principles," 31 *George Washington Law Review* 587 (1963); Arthur S. Miller and Ronald F. Howell, "The Myth of Neutrality in Constitutional Adjudication," 27 *University of Chicago Law Review* 661 (1960).

Peller credits Wechsler with having "defined the centrist position in constitutional law for some three decades"(p. 561). He stresses that "Wechsler was part of a community of white, male legal scholars who actually represented a liberal and progressive force in academia" (p. 563) and asks how their approach could seem as dated and as conservative in its import as it did by 1988. He situates Wechsler in an "intellectual setting within which . . . defending freedom also required defending the legality of racial domination" (p. 565). Peller's explanation is that legal process scholars of the 1950s came to terms with the disintegration of nineteenth-century intellectual paradigms "by means of an intense and overriding distinction between controversial issues of value and noncontroversial questions of framework and structure within which substantive conflict would take place. On that distinction rested their conviction that their own work, and intellectual work generally, transcended ideology and politics" (p. 565.) At first blush, this seems a more plausible description of Hart and Sacks than of Wechsler—he is, after all, searching precisely for principles rather than procedures to differentiate judicial from legislative work. For Wechsler, however, the distinction between the procedure used to make a decision and the values or interests reflected in it was crucial.

Morton Horwitz concludes his critical assessment of Wechsler this way:

> Wechsler seems to have believed that only something approaching unanimous agreement—that is, consensus – constituted a sufficiently general and neutral basis for making a value choice. Discrimination analysis entailed choosing between victims

and victimizers—in other words, being forced to choose between conflicting moral positions. . . . Like the consensus theory from which it was drawn, the neutral principles school sought to avoid ever having to decide whether one group was victimizing another, since that inevitably involved substantive evaluation of the justice of their respective claims. The emphasis on generality foreclosed any intervention to reform unjust social practices in precisely those cases in which the dominant groups had the greatest stake in justifying the status quo. By abstracting the question of segregation from its concrete historical meaning in order to avoid being accused of having a result orientation, Wechsler achieved neutrality through formalism—that is, by simple [sic] assuming the equal legitimacy of both groups' desire to choose freely with whom to associate. In its unhistorical abstractness, neutral principles analysis combined with ethical positivism to produce a new conservative formulation in orthodox legal thought. (*The Transformation of American Law 1870–1960*, pp. 267–68)

Wechsler is vigorously defended by Kent Greenawalt, "The Enduring Significance of Neutral Principles," 78 *Columbia Law Review* 982 (1978). See also Cass Sunstein, "Neutrality in Constitutional Law" (with special reference to Pornography, Abortion and Surrogacy) 92 *Columbia Law Review* 1 (1992).

A useful overview of Wechsler's contributions to the field of criminal law, both as a scholar and through his American Law Institute work on the Model Penal Code, is Harold Edgar, "In Memoriam: Herbert Wechsler and the Criminal Law: A Brief Tribute," 100 *Columbia Law Review* 1347 (2000). Edgar describes Wechsler's general approach to law reform and codification, and in particular, "how much the reform effort could be advanced by examining with rigorous logic the social interests a branch of law sought to serve" (pp. 1349–50). See also Geoffrey C. Hazard, Jr., "Tribute in Memory of Herbert Wechsler," 100 *Columbia Law Review* 1362 (2000). For a list of "leading" ALI projects published under Wechsler's Direction, see Silber and Miller, *supra* at 854, note 4. For commentary on Wechsler's role in *New York Times Co. v. Sullivan* 376 U.S. 254 (1964), see Henry Monaghan, "A Legal Giant is Dead," 100 *Columbia Law Review* 1370 at 1375 and following (2000), accrediting him with responsibility for theorizing the free speech limitation on libel actions by public figures and government officials. See also Anthony Lewis, *Make No Law: The Sullivan Case and the First Amendment* (New York: Random House, 1991) at 103 and following.

The Hart and Wechsler casebook—and the authors' contribution to the field of federal courts jurisprudence—has generated much commentary. The leading modern commentary on the book, linking its approach to the broader legal process paradigm, is Richard H. Fallon, Jr., "Reflections on the Hart and Wechsler Paradigm," 47 *Vanderbilt Law Review* 953 (1994). For other retrospective looks at the Hart and Wechsler approach to federal courts, see Judith Resnick, "Rereading 'The Federal Courts': Revising the Domain of Federal Courts Jurisprudence at the End of the Twentieth Century," 47 *Vanderbilt Law Review* 1021 (1994), and Ann Althouse, "Late Night Confessions in the Hart and Wechsler Hotel," 47 *Vanderbilt Law Review* 993 (1994). See also Akhil Reed Amar, "Law Story, Review of Hart and Wechsler, The Federal Courts and the Federal System, by Paul Bator, Daniel Meltzer, Paul Mishken, David Shapiro," 102 *Harvard Law Review* 688 (1989); Henry P. Monaghan, "Hart and Wechsler's The Federal Courts and the Federal System," 87 *Harvard Law Review* 889 (1974), and book review of the aforementioned book, 83 *Harvard Law Review* 1753 (1970).

HERBERT WECHSLER*

"Toward Neutral Principles of Constitutional Law"**

73 Harvard Law Review 1 (1959)

Professor Wechsler, disagreeing with Judge Learned Hand as to the justification for judicial review of legislative action, argues that courts have the power, and duty, to decide all constitutional cases in which the jurisdictional and procedural requirements are met. The author concludes that in these cases decisions must rest on reasoning and analysis which transcend the immediate result, and discusses instances in which he believes the Supreme Court has not been faithful to this principle.

On three occasions in the last few years Harvard has been hospitable to the discussion of that most abiding problem of our public law: the role of courts in general and the Supreme Court in particular in our constitutional tradition; their special function in the maintenance, interpretation and development of the organic charter that provides the framework of our government, the charter that declares itself the "supreme law."

I have in mind, of course, Mr. Justice Jackson's undelivered Godkin lectures,[1] the papers and comments at the Marshall conference,[2] and Judge Learned Hand's addresses from this very rostrum but a year ago.[3] It does not depreciate these major contributions if I add that they comprise only a fragment of the serious, continuous attention that the subject is receiving here as well as elsewhere in the nation, not to speak of that less serious attention that is not without importance to a university community, however uninstructive it may be.

I should regard another venture on a theme so fully ventilated as a poor expression of appreciation for the hospitality accorded me, were I not persuaded that there is a point to make and an exercise to be performed that will not constitute mere reiteration; and that the point and exercise have special relevancy to the most important of our current controversies. Before I put my point and undertake the exercise it is appropriate, however, that I make clear where I stand upon the larger, underlying questions that have been considered on the previous occasions I have noted, particularly by Judge Hand last year. They have a bearing, as will be apparent, on the thesis that I mean to put before you later on.

---

* This paper was delivered on April 7, 1959, as the Oliver Wendell Holmes Lecture at the Harvard Law School. It is reproduced without substantial change, except for the addition of the footnotes. The reader is asked to bear in mind that it was written for the ear and not the eye.

** Harlan Fiske Stone Professor of Constitutional Law, Columbia University School of Law. A.B., College of the City of New York, 1928; LL.B., Columbia, 1931.

[1] JACKSON, THE SUPREME COURT IN THE AMERICAN SYSTEM OF GOVERNMENT (1955).

[2] GOVERNMENT UNDER LAW (Sutherland ed. 1956).

[3] HAND, THE BILL OF RIGHTS (1958).

Let me begin by stating that I have not the slightest doubt respecting the legitimacy of judicial review, whether the action called in question in a case which otherwise is proper for adjudication is legislative or executive, federal or state. I must address myself to this because the question was so seriously mooted by Judge Hand; and though he answered it in favor of the courts' assumption of the power of review, his answer has overtones quite different from those of the answer I would give.

Judge Hand's position was that "when the Constitution emerged from the Convention in September, 1787, the structure of the proposed government, if one looked to the text, gave no ground for inferring that the decisions of the Supreme Court, and *a fortiori* of the lower courts, were to be authoritative upon the Executive and the Legislature"; that "on the other hand it was probable, if indeed it was not certain, that without some arbiter whose decision should be final the whole system would have collapsed, for it was extremely unlikely that the Executive or the Legislature, having once decided, would yield to the contrary holding of another 'Department,' even of the courts"; that "for centuries it has been an accepted canon in interpretation of documents to interpolate into the text such provisions, though not expressed, as are essential to prevent the defeat of the venture at hand"; that it was therefore "altogether in keeping with established practice for the Supreme Court to assume an authority to keep the states, Congress, and the President within their prescribed powers"; and, finally and explicitly, that for the reason stated "it was not a lawless act to import into the Constitution such a grant of power."[4]

Though I have learned from past experience that disagreement with Judge Hand is usually nothing but the sheerest folly, I must make clear why I believe the power of the courts is grounded in the language of the Constitution and is not a mere interpolation. To do this you must let me quote the supremacy clause,[5] which is mercifully short:

> This Constitution, and the Laws of the United States which shall be made, under the Authority of the United States, shall be the supreme Law of the Land; and the Judges in every State shall be bound thereby, any Thing in the Constitution or Laws of any State to the Contrary notwithstanding.

Judge Hand concedes that under this clause "state courts would at times have to decide whether state laws and constitutions, or even a federal statute, were in conflict with the federal constitution" but he adds that "the fact that this jurisdiction was confined to such occasions, and that it was thought necessary specifically to provide such a limited jurisdiction, looks rather against than in favor of a general jurisdiction."[6]

Are you satisfied, however, to view the supremacy clause in this way, as a grant of jurisdiction to state courts, implying a denial of the power and the duty to all others? This certainly is not its necessary meaning; it may be construed as a mandate to all of officialdom including courts, with a special and emphatic admonition that it binds the judges of the previously independent states. That the latter

[4] *Id.* at 27, 29, 14, 15, 29.
[5] U.S. CONST. art. VI, § 2.
[6] HAND, *op. cit. supra* note 3, at 28.

is the proper reading seems to me persuasive when the other relevant provisions of the Constitution are brought into view.

Article III, section 1 declares that the federal judicial power "shall be vested in one supreme Court, and in such inferior Courts as the Congress may from time to time ordain and establish." This represented, as you know, one of the major compromises of the Constitutional Convention and relegated the establishment *vel non* of lower federal courts to the discretion of the Congress.[7] None might have been established, with the consequence that, as in other federalisms, judicial work of first instance would all have been remitted to state courts.[8] Article III, section 2 goes on, however, to delineate the scope of the federal judicial power, providing that it "shall extend [*inter alia*] to all Cases, in Law and Equity, arising under this Constitution . . ." and, further, that the Supreme Court "shall have appellate jurisdiction" in such cases "with such Exceptions, and under such Regulations as the Congress shall make." Surely this means, as section 25 of the Judiciary Act of 1789[9] took it to mean, that if a state court passes on a constitutional issue, as the supremacy clause provides that it should, its judgment is reviewable, subject to congressional exceptions, by the Supreme Court, in which event that Court must have no less authority and duty to accord priority to constitutional provisions than the court that it reviews.[10] And such state cases might have encompassed every case in which a constitutional issue could possibly arise, since, as I have said, Congress need not and might not have exerted its authority to establish "inferior" federal courts.

If you abide with me thus far, I doubt that you will hesitate upon the final step. Is it a possible construction of the Constitution, measured strictly as Judge Hand admonishes by the test of "general purpose,"[11] that if Congress opts, as it has opted, to create a set of lower courts, those courts in cases falling within their respective jurisdictions and the Supreme Court when it passes on their judgments are less or differently constrained by the supremacy clause than are the state courts, and the Supreme Court when it reviews their judgments? Yet I cannot escape, what is for me the most astonishing conclusion, that this is the precise result of Judge Hand's reading of the text, as distinct from the interpolation he approves on other grounds.

It is true that Hamilton in the seventy-eighth *Federalist* does not mention the supremacy clause in his argument but rather urges the conclusion as implicit in the concept of a written constitution as a fundamental law and the accepted function of the courts as law interpreters. Marshall in *Marbury v. Madison* echoes these general considerations, though he also calls attention to the text, including the judiciary article, pointing only at the end to the language about supremacy, concerning which he says that it "confirms and strengthens the principle, supposed to be essential to all written constitutions, that a law repugnant to the constitution is void; and that *courts*, as well as other departments, are bound by that

---

[7] See 1 FARRAND, THE RECORDS OF THE FEDERAL CONVENTION 104–05, 119, 124–25 (1911), summarized in HART & WECHSLER, THE FEDERAL COURTS AND THE FEDERAL SYSTEM 17 (1953).

[8] See, *e.g.*, the position in Australia, described in Bailey, *The Federal Jurisdiction of State Courts*, 2 RES JUDICATAE 109 (1940); WHEARE, FEDERAL GOVERNMENT 68–72 (2d ed. 1951). The slow statutory development of federal-question jurisdiction in our lower federal courts is traced in HART & WECHSLER, *op. cit. supra* note 7, at 727–33, 1019–21, 1107–08, 1140–50.

[9] Act of Sept. 24, 1789, ch. 20, § 25, 1 Stat. 85.

[10] This too I think Judge Hand does not deny, though this concession appears only in the course of his description of the Jeffersonian position. See HAND, *op. cit. supra* note 3, at 5.

[11] *Id.* at 19.

instrument."[12] Much might be said on this as to the style of reasoning that was deemed most persuasive when these documents were written but this would be irrelevant to my concern about the meaning that Judge Hand insists he cannot find within the words or structure of the Constitution, even with the aid of the historical material that surely points in the direction I suggest.[13]

You will not wonder now why I should be concerned about the way Judge Hand has read the text, despite his view that the judicial power was a valid importation to preserve the governmental plan. Here as elsewhere a position cannot be divorced from its supporting reasons; the reasons are, indeed, a part and most important part of the position. To demonstrate I quote Judge Hand:

> [S]ince this power is not a logical deduction from the structure of the Constitution but only a practical condition upon its successful operation, it need not be exercised whenever a court sees, or thinks that it sees, an invasion of the Constitution. It is always a preliminary question how importunately the occasion demands an answer. It may be better to leave the issue to be worked out without authoritative solution; or perhaps the only solution available is one that the court has no adequate means to enforce.[14]

If this means that a court, in a case properly before it, is free—or should be free on any fresh view of its duty—either to adjudicate a constitutional objection to an otherwise determinative action of the legislature or executive, national or state, or to decline to do so, depending on "how importunately" it considers the occasion to demand an answer, could anything have more enormous import for the theory and the practice of review? What showing would be needed to elicit a decision? Would anything suffice short of a demonstration that judicial intervention is essential to prevent the government from foundering—the reason, you recall, for the interpolation of the power to decide? For me, as for anyone who finds the judicial power anchored in the Constitution, there is no such escape from the judicial obligation; the duty cannot be attenuated in this way.

The duty, to be sure, is not that of policing or advising legislatures or executives, nor even, as the uninstructed think, of standing as an ever-open forum for the ventilation of all grievances that draw upon the Constitution for support. It is the duty to decide the litigated case and to decide it in accordance with the law, with all that that implies as to a rigorous insistence on the satisfaction of procedural and jurisdictional requirements; the concept that Professor Freund reminds us was so fundamental in the thought and work of Mr. Justice Brandeis.[15] Only when the standing law, decisional or statutory, provides a remedy to vindicate the interest that demands protection against an infringement of the kind that is alleged, a law of remedies that ordinarily at least is framed in reference to rights and wrongs in general, do courts have any business asking what the Constitution may require or forbid, and only then when it is necessary for decision of the case that is at hand. How was it Marshall put the questions to be faced in *Marbury*?

[12] Marbury v. Madison, 5 U.S. (1 Cranch) 137, 180 (1803). (Emphasis in original.)

[13] See HART; WECHSLER, *op. cit. supra* note 7, at 14–16; Hart, Book Review, *Professor Crosskey and Judicial Review*, 67 HARV. L. REV. 1456 (1954).

[14] HAND, *op. cit. supra* note 3, at 15.

[15] See FREUND, ON UNDERSTANDING THE SUPREME COURT 64–65 (1949); Freund, *Mr. Justice Brandeis: A Centennial Memoir*, 70 HARV. L. REV. 769, 787–88 (1957). See also BICKEL, THE UNPUBLISHED OPINIONS OF MR. JUSTICE BRANDEIS 1–20 (1957).

1st. Has the applicant a right to the commission he demands?

2dly. If he has a right, and that right has been violated, do the laws of his country afford him a remedy?

3dly. If they do afford him a remedy, is it a mandamus issuing from this court?[16]

It was because he thought, as his opponents also thought,[17] that the Constitution had a bearing on the answers to these questions, that he claimed the right and duty to examine its commands.

As a legal system grows, the remedies that it affords substantially proliferate, a development to which the courts contribute but in which the legislature has an even larger hand.[18] There has been major growth of this kind in our system[19] and I dare say there will be more, increasing correspondingly the number and variety of the occasions when a constitutional adjudication may be sought and must be made. Am I not right, however, in believing that the underlying theory of the courts' participation has not changed and that, indeed, the very multiplicity of remedies and grievances makes it increasingly important that the theory and its implications be maintained?

It is true, and I do not mean to ignore it, that the courts themselves regard some questions as "political," meaning thereby that they are not to be resolved judicially, although they involve constitutional interpretation and arise in the course of litigation. Judge Hand alluded to this doctrine which, insofar as its scope is undefined, he labeled a "stench in the nostrils of strict constructionists."[20] And Mr. Justice Frankfurter, in his great paper at the Marshall conference, avowed "disquietude that the line is often very thin between the cases in which the Court felt compelled to abstain from adjudication because of their 'political' nature, and the cases that so frequently arise in applying the concepts of 'liberty' and 'equality'."[21]

The line is thin, indeed, but I suggest that it is thinner than it needs to be or ought to be; that all the doctrine can defensibly imply is that the courts are called upon to judge whether the Constitution has committed to another agency of government the autonomous determination of the issue raised, a finding that itself requires an interpretation. Who, for example, would contend that the civil courts may properly review a judgment of impeachment when article I, section 3 declares that the "sole Power to try" is in the Senate? That any proper trial of an impeachment may present issues of the most important constitutional dimension, as Senator Kennedy reminds us in his moving story of the Senator whose vote saved Andrew Johnson,[22] is simply immaterial in this connection.

[16] 5 U.S. (1 Cranch) at 154.

[17] It will be remembered that the Jeffersonian objections to the issuance of a mandamus to the Secretary rested on constitutional submissions with respect to the separation of judicial and executive authority. See 1 WARREN, THE SUPREME COURT IN UNITED STATES HISTORY 232 (1937); Kendall v. United States, 37 U.S. (12 Pet.) 524, 610 (1838); Lee, *The Origins of Judicial Control of Federal Executive Action*, 36 GEO. L. J. 287 (1948).

[18] See, *e.g.*, *Developments in the Law—Remedies Against the United States and Its Officials*, 70 HARV. L. REV. 827 (1957).

[19] Decisions that entail such growth do not always confront the underlying problem. See, *e.g.*, Harmon v. Brucker, 355 U.S. 579 (1958). Compare the opinion of Judge Prettyman below, 243 F.2d 613 (D.C. Cir. 1957).

[20] HAND, *op. cit. supra* note 3, at 15.

[21] Frankfurter, *John Marshall and the Judicial Function*, 69 HARV. L. REV. 217, 227–28 (1955), in GOVERNMENT UNDER LAW 6, 19 (Sutherland ed. 1956).

[22] See KENNEDY, PROFILES IN COURAGE 126 (1956).

What is explicit in the trial of an impeachment or, to take another case, the seating or expulsion of a Senator or Representative[23] may well be found to be implicit in others. So it was held,[24] and rightly it appears to me, respecting the provision that the "United States shall guarantee to every State in this Union a Republican Form of Government . . . "This guarantee appears, you will recall, in the same clause as does the duty to protect the states against invasion;[25] it envisages the possible employment of the military force and bears an obvious relationship to the autonomous authority of the Houses of Congress in seating their respective members.[26]

It also may be reasonable to conclude, or so it seems to me, though there are arguments the other way,[27] that the power of Congress to "make or alter" state regulations of the "Manner of holding Elections for Senators and Representatives,"[28] implying as it does a power to draw district lines or to prescribe the standards to be followed in defining them, excludes the courts from passing on a constitutional objection to state gerrymanders,[29] even if the Constitution can be thought to speak to this kind of inequality and the law of remedies gives disadvantaged voters legal standing to complain, which are both separate questions to be faced.[30]

If I may put my point again, I submit that in cases of the kind that I have mentioned, as in others that I do not pause to state,[31] the only proper judgment that may lead to an abstention from decision is that the Constitution has committed the determination of the issue to another agency of government than the courts. Difficult as it may be to make that judgment wisely, whatever factors may be rightly weighed in situations where the answer is not clear, what is involved is in itself an act of constitutional interpretation, to be made and judged by standards that should govern the interpretive process generally. That, I submit, is *toto caelo* different from a broad discretion to abstain or intervene.

The Supreme Court does have a discretion, to be sure, to grant or to deny review of judgments of the lower courts in situations in which the jurisdictional statute permits certiorari but does not provide for an appeal.[32] I need not say that this is an entirely different matter. The system rests upon the power that the Constitution vests in Congress to make exceptions to and regulate the Court's appellate jurisdiction; it is addressed not to the measure of judicial duty in

[23] U.S. CONST. art. I, § 5 provides, "Each House shall be the Judge of the Elections, Returns and Qualifications of its own Members . . . Each House may determine the Rules of its Proceedings, punish its Members for disorderly Behaviour, and, with the Concurrence of two thirds, expel a Member."

For a constitutional challenge to the sufficiency of primary irregularities as ground for the refusal to seat a United States Senator, see BECK, MAY IT PLEASE THE COURT 265 (1930).

[24] Pacific States Tel. & Tel. Co. v. Oregon, 223 U.S. 118 (1912); Luther v. Borden, 48 U.S. (7 How.) 1, 42 (1849).

[25] U.S. CONST. art. IV, § 4: "The United States shall guarantee to every State in this Union a Republican Form of Government, and shall protect each of them against Invasion; and on Application of the Legislature, or of the Executive (when the Legislature cannot be convened) against domestic Violence."

[26] *Cf.* Luther v. Borden, 48 U.S. (7 How.) 1, 42 (1849): "And when the senators and representatives of a State are admitted into the councils of the Union, the authority of the government under which they are appointed, as well as its republican character, is recognized by the proper constitutional authority."

[27] See, *e.g.*, Lewis, *Legislative Apportionment and the Federal Courts*, 71 HARV. L. REV. 1057 (1958).

[28] U.S. CONST. art. I, § 4.

[29] See Colegrove v. Green, 328 U.S. 549, 554 (1946) (Frankfurter, J.); Professor Freund's comment in SUPREME COURT AND SUPREME LAW 46–47 (Cahn ed. 1954).

[30] For an effort to face these questions, see Lewis, *supra* note 27, at 1071–98.

[31] See HART & WECHSLER, *op. cit. supra* note 7, at 192–97, 207–09; POST, THE SUPREME COURT AND POLITICAL QUESTIONS (1936).

[32] 28 U.S.C. §§ 1254–57 (1952). The major steps in the statutory substitution of discretionary for obligatory Supreme Court review are traced in HART & WECHSLER, *op. cit. supra* note 7, at 400–03, 1313–21. The classic detailed account appears in FRANKFURTER & LANDIS, THE BUSINESS OF THE SUPREME COURT (1927).

adjudication of a case but rather to the right to a determination by the highest as distinguished from the lower courts. Even here, however, it is well worth noting that the Court by rule has defined standards for the exercise of its discretion,[33] standards framed in neutral terms, like the importance of the question or a conflict of decisions. Only the maintenance and the improvement of such standards[34] and, of course, their faithful application[35] can, I say with deference, protect the Court against the danger of the imputation of a bias favoring claims of one kind or another in the granting or denial of review.

Indeed, I will go further and assert that, necessary as it is that the Court's docket be confined to manageable size, much would be gained if the governing statutes could be revised to play a larger part in the delineation of the causes that make rightful call upon the time and energy of the Supreme Court.[36] Think of the protection it gave Marshall's court that there was no discretionary jurisdiction, with the consequence that he could say in *Cohens v. Virginia*:[37]

> It is most true that this Court will not take jurisdiction if it should not: but it is equally true, that it must take jurisdiction if it should. The judiciary cannot, as the legislature may, avoid a measure because it approaches the confines of the constitution. We cannot pass it by because it is doubtful. With whatever doubts, with whatever difficulties, a case may be attended, we must decide it, if it be brought before us. We have no more right to decline the exercise of jurisdiction which is given, than to usurp that which is not given. The one or the other would be treason to the constitution.

II. The Standards of Review

If courts cannot escape the duty of deciding whether actions of the other branches of the government are consistent with the Constitution, when a case is properly before them in the sense I have attempted to describe, you will not doubt the relevancy and importance of demanding what, if any, are the standards to be followed in interpretation. Are there, indeed, any criteria that both the Supreme Court and those who undertake to praise or to condemn its judgments are morally and intellectually obligated to support?

Whatever you may think to be the answer, surely you agree with me that I am right to state the question as the same one for the Court and for its critics. An attack upon a judgment involves an assertion that a court should have decided otherwise than as it did. Is it not clear that the validity of an assertion of this kind depends upon assigning reasons that should have prevailed with the tribunal; and that any other reasons are irrelevant? That is, of course, not only true of a critique of a decision of the courts; it applies whenever a determination is in

---

[33] U.S. SUP. CT. R. 19.

[34] It is regrettable, in my view, that when the Court revised its rules in 1954 it determined not to attempt an improved articulation of the statement of "considerations governing review on certiorari." *But see* Wiener, *The Supreme Court's New Rules*, 68 HARV. L. REV. 20, 60–63 (1954).

[35] See, *e.g.*, Note, *Supreme Court Certiorari Policy in Cases Arising Under the FELA*, 69 HARV. L. REV. 1441 (1956).

[36] The present distribution of obligatory and discretionary jurisdiction derives largely, though not entirely, from the Judiciary Act of 1925, ch. 229, 43 Stat. 936, the architects of which were a committee of the Court. See Taft, *The Jurisdiction of the Supreme Court Under the Act of February 13, 1925*, 35 YALE L. J. 1 (1925); FRANKFURTER & LANDIS, *op. cit. supra* note 32, at 255–94. For major changes since 1925, see HART & WECHSLER, *op. cit. supra* note 7, at 1317.

[37] 19 U.S. (6 Wheat.) 264, 404 (1821).

question, a determination that it is essential to make either way. Is it the irritation of advancing years that leads me to lament that our culture is not rich with critics who respect these limitations of the enterprise in which they are engaged?

You may remind me that, as someone in the ancient world observed—perhaps it was Josephus—history has little tolerance for any of those reasonable judgments that have turned out to be wrong. But history, in this sense, is inscrutable, concealing all its verdicts in the bosom of the future; it is never a contemporary critic.

I revert then to the problem of criteria as it arises for both courts and critics—by which I mean criteria that can be framed and tested as an exercise of reason and not merely as an act of willfulness or will. Even to put the problem is, of course, to raise an issue no less old than our culture. Those who perceive in law only the element of fiat, in whose conception of the legal cosmos reason has no meaning or no place, will not join gladly in the search for standards of the kind I have in mind. I must, in short, expect dissent *in limine* from anyone whose view of the judicial process leaves no room for the antinomy Professor Fuller has so gracefully explored.[38] So too must I anticipate dissent from those more numerous among us who, vouching no philosophy to warranty, frankly or covertly make the test of virtue in interpretation whether its result in the immediate decision seems to hinder or advance the interests or the values they support.

I shall not try to overcome the philosophic doubt that I have mentioned, although to use a phrase that Holmes so often used—"it hits me where I live." That battle must be fought on wider fronts than that of constitutional interpretation; and I do not delude myself that I can qualify for a command, great as is my wish to render service. The man who simply lets his judgment turn on the immediate result may not, however, realize that his position implies that the courts are free to function as a naked power organ, that it is an empty affirmation to regard them, as ambivalently he so often does, as courts of law. If he may know he disapproves of a decision when all he knows is that it has sustained a claim put forward by a labor union or a taxpayer, a Negro or a segregationist, a corporation or a Communist—he acquiesces in the proposition that a man of different sympathy but equal information may no less properly conclude that he approves.

You will not charge me with exaggeration if I say that this type of *ad hoc* evaluation is, as it has always been, the deepest problem of our constitutionalism, not only with respect to judgments of the courts but also in the wider realm in which conflicting constitutional positions have played a part in our politics.

Did not New England challenge the embargo that the South supported on the very ground on which the South was to resist New England's demand for a protective tariff?[39] Was not Jefferson in the Louisiana Purchase forced to rest on an expansive reading of the clauses granting national authority of the very kind that he had steadfastly opposed in his attacks upon the Bank?[40] Can you square his disappointment about Burr's acquittal on the treason charge and his subsequent

[38] See Fuller, *Reason and Fiat in Case Law*, 59 HARV. L. REV. 376 (1946).

[39] See 4 ADAMS, HISTORY OF THE UNITED STATES OF AMERICA DURING THE SECOND ADMINISTRATION OF THOMAS JEFFERSON 267 (1890): "If Congress had the right to regulate commerce for such a purpose in 1808, South Carolina seemed to have no excuse for questioning, twenty years later, the constitutionality of a protective system."

[40] See 2 ADAMS, HISTORY OF THE UNITED STATES OF AMERICA DURING THE FIRST ADMINISTRATION OF THOMAS JEFFERSON 90 (1889): "[T]he Louisiana treaty gave a fatal wound to 'strict construction,' and the Jeffersonian theories never again received general support. In thus giving them up, Jefferson did not lead the way, but he allowed his friends to drag him in the path they chose." See also 3 WILSON, A HISTORY OF THE AMERICAN PEOPLE 182–83 (1902).

request for legislation[41] with the attitude towards freedom and repression most enduringly associated with his name? Were the abolitionists who rescued fugitives and were acquitted in defiance of the evidence able to distinguish their view of the compulsion of a law of the United States from that advanced by South Carolina in the ordinance that they despised?[42]

To bring the matter even more directly home, what shall we think of the Harvard records of the Class of 1829, the class of Mr. Justice Curtis, which, we are told,[43] praised at length the Justice's dissent in the *Dred Scott* case but then added, "Again, *and seemingly adverse to the above,* in October, 1862, he prepared a legal opinion and argument, which was published in Boston in pamphlet form, to the effect that President Lincoln's Proclamation of prospective emancipation of the slaves in the rebellious States is *unconstitutional.*"

Of course, a man who thought and, as a Justice, voted and maintained[44] that a free Negro could be a citizen of the United States and therefore of a state, within the meaning of the constitutional and statutory clauses defining the diversity jurisdiction; that Congress had authority to forbid slavery within a territory, even one acquired after the formation of the Union; and that such a prohibition worked emancipation of a slave whose owner brought him to reside in such a territory— a man who thought all these things detracted obviously from the force of his positions if he also thought the President without authority to abrogate a form of property established and protected by state law within the states where it was located, states which the President and his critic alike maintained had not effectively seceded from the Union and were not a foreign enemy at war.

How simple the class historian could make it all by treating as the only thing that mattered whether Mr. Justice Curtis had, on the occasions noted, helped or hindered the attainment of the freedom of the slaves.

I have cited these examples from the early years of our history since time has bred aloofness that may give them added force. What a wealth of illustration is at hand today! How many of the constitutional attacks upon congressional investigations

---

[41] In his annual message of October 27, 1807, Jefferson said:

I shall think it my duty to lay before you the proceedings and the evidence publicly exhibited on the arraignment of the principal offenders before the circuit court of Virginia. You will be enabled to judge whether the defect was in the testimony, in the law, or in the administration of the law; and wherever it shall be found, the Legislature alone can apply or originate the remedy. The framers of our Constitution certainly supposed that they had guarded as well their Government against destruction by treason as their citizens against oppression under pretense of it, and if these ends are not attained it is of importance to inquire by what means more effectual they may be secured.

I RICHARDSON, MESSAGES AND PAPERS OF THE PRESIDENT 429 (1896). The trial proceedings were transmitted to the Senate on November 23, 1807. See 17 ANNALS OF CONG. APP. 385–778 (1807).

Jefferson's conception of the "remedy" not only involved legislation overcoming Marshall's strict construction of the treason clause but also a provision for the removal of judges on the address of both Houses of Congress. See 3 RANDALL, THE LIFE OF THOMAS JEFFERSON 246–47 (1865); 1 WARREN, THE SUPREME COURT IN UNITED STATES HISTORY 311–15 (1937).

On the former point, different bills were introduced in the Senate and the House. The Senate bill by Giles undertook to define "levying war" for purposes of treason. The proposed definition included "assembling themselves together with intent forcibly to overturn or change the Government of the United States, or any one of the Territories thereof . . . or forcibly to resist the general execution of any public law thereof . . . or if any person or persons shall traitorously aid or assist in the doing any of the acts aforesaid, although not personally present when any such act is done . . ." 17 ANNALS OF CONG. 108–09 (1808). For discussion of the measure in the Senate, see 17 *id.* at 109–27, 135–49. The House bill by Randolph defined a separate offense, "conspiracy to commit treason against the United States . . ." 18 *id.* at 1717–18.

[42] See South Carolina Ordinance of Nullification, 1 S.C. Stat. 329 (1832).

[43] See 1 CURTIS, A MEMOIR OF BENJAMIN ROBBINS CURTIS 354–55 n.1 (1879).

[44] See Scott v. Sandford, 60 U.S. (19 How.) 393, 564–633 (1857).

of suspected Communists have their authors felt obliged to launch against the inquiries respecting the activities of Goldfine or of Hoffa or of others I might name? How often have those who think the Smith Act, as construed, inconsistent with the first amendment made clear that they also stand for constitutional immunity for racial agitators fanning flames of prejudice and discontent? Turning the case around, are those who in relation to the Smith Act see no virtue in distinguishing between advocacy of merely abstract doctrine and advocacy which is planned to instigate unlawful action,[45] equally unable to see virtue in the same distinction in relation, let us say, to advocacy of resistance to the judgments of the courts, especially perhaps to judgments vindicating claims that equal protection of the laws has been denied? I may live a uniquely sheltered life but am I wrong in thinking I discerned in some extremely warm enthusiasts for jury trial a certain diminution of enthusiasm as the issue was presented in the course of the debate in 1957 on the bill to extend federal protection of our civil rights?

All I have said, you may reply, is something no one will deny, that principles are largely instrumental as they are employed in politics, instrumental in relation to results that a controlling sentiment demands at any given time. Politicians recognize this fact of life and are obliged to trim and shape their speech and votes accordingly, unless perchance they are prepared to step aside; and the example that John Quincy Adams set somehow is rarely followed.

That is, indeed, all I have said but I now add that whether you are tolerant, perhaps more tolerant than I, of the *ad hoc* in politics, with principle reduced to a manipulative tool, are you not also ready to agree that something else is called for from the courts? I put it to you that the main constituent of the judicial process is precisely that it must be genuinely principled, resting with respect to every step that is involved in reaching judgment on analysis and reasons quite transcending the immediate result that is achieved. To be sure, the courts decide, or should decide, only the case they have before them. But must they not decide on grounds of adequate neutrality and generality, tested not only by the instant application but by others that the principles imply? Is it not the very essence of judicial method to insist upon attending to such other cases, preferably those involving an opposing interest, in evaluating any principle avowed?

Here too I do not think that I am stating any novel or momentous insight. But now, as Holmes said long ago in speaking of "the unrest which seems to wonder vaguely whether law and order pay," we "need education in the obvious."[46] We need it more particularly now respecting constitutional interpretation, since it has become a commonplace to grant what many for so long denied: that courts in constitutional determinations face issues that are inescapably "political"—political in the third sense that I have used that word—in that they involve a choice among competing values or desires, a choice reflected in the legislative or executive action in question, which the court must either condemn or condone.

I should be the last to argue otherwise or to protest the emphasis upon the point in Mr. Justice Jackson's book, throughout the Marshall conference, and in the lectures by Judge Hand. I have, indeed, insisted on the point myself.[47] But what is crucial, I submit, is not the nature of the question but the nature of the answer that may validly be given by the courts. No legislature or executive is

[45] See Yates v. United States, 354 U.S. 298, 318 (1957).

[46] HOLMES, *Law and the Court*, in COLLECTED LEGAL PAPERS 291, 292 (1920).

[47] See, *e.g.*, Wechsler, *Comment* on Snee, *Leviathan at the Bar of Justice*, in GOVERNMENT UNDER LAW 134, 136–37 (Sutherland ed. 1956).

obligated by the nature of its function to support its choice of values by the type of reasoned explanation that I have suggested is intrinsic to judicial action—however much we may admire such a reasoned exposition when we find it in those other realms.

Does not the special duty of the courts to judge by neutral principles addressed to all the issues make it inapposite to contend, as Judge Hand does, that no court can review the legislative choice—by any standard other than a fixed "historical meaning" of constitutional provisions[48]—without becoming "a third legislative chamber"?[49] Is there not, in short, a vital difference between legislative freedom to appraise the gains and losses in projected measures and the kind of principled appraisal, in respect of values that can reasonably be asserted to have constitutional dimension, that alone is in the province of the courts? Does not the difference yield a middle ground between a judicial House of Lords and the abandonment of any limitation on the other branches—a middle ground consisting of judicial action that embodies what are surely the main qualities of law, its generality and its neutrality? This must, it seems to me, have been in Mr. Justice Jackson's mind when in his chapter on the Supreme Court "as a political institution" he wrote[50] in words that I find stirring, "Liberty is not the mere absence of restraint, it is not a spontaneous product of majority rule, it is not achieved merely by lifting underprivileged classes to power, nor is it the inevitable by-product of technological expansion. It is achieved only by a rule of law." Is it not also what Mr. Justice Frankfurter must mean in calling upon judges for "allegiance to nothing except the effort, amid tangled words and limited insights, to find the path through precedent, through policy, through history, to the best judgment that fallible creatures can reach in that most difficult of all tasks: the achievement of justice between man and man, between man and state, through reason called law"?[51]

You will not understand my emphasis upon the role of reason and of principle in the judicial, as distinguished from the legislative or executive, appraisal of conflicting values to imply that I depreciate the duty of fidelity to the text of the Constitution, when its words may be decisive—though I would certainly remind you of the caution stated by Chief Justice Hughes: "Behind the words of the constitutional provisions are postulates which limit and control."[52] Nor will you take me to deny that history has weight in the elucidation of the text, though it is surely subtle business to appraise it as a guide. Nor will you even think that I deem precedent without importance, for we surely must agree with Holmes that "imitation of the past, until we have a clear reason for change, no more needs justification than appetite."[53] But after all, it was Chief Justice Taney who declared his willingness "that it be regarded hereafter as the law of this court, that its opinion upon the construction of the Constitution is always open to discussion when it is supposed to have been founded in error, and that its judicial authority should hereafter depend altogether on the force of the reasoning by which it is supported."[54] Would any of us have it otherwise, given the nature of the problems that confront the courts?

[48] HAND, op. cit. supra note 3, at 65.
[49] Id. at 42.
[50] JACKSON, THE SUPREME COURT IN THE AMERICAN SYSTEM OF GOVERNMENT 76 (1955).
[51] FRANKFURTER, Chief Justices I Have Known, in OF LAW AND MEN 138 (Elman ed. 1956).
[52] Principality of Monaco v. Mississippi, 292 U.S. 313, 322 (1934).
[53] HOLMES, Holdsworth's English Law, in COLLECTED LEGAL PAPERS 285, 290 (1920).
[54] Passenger Cases, 48 U.S. (7 How.) 283, 470 (1849).

At all events, is not the relative compulsion of the language of the Constitution, of history and precedent—where they do not combine to make an answer clear—itself a matter to be judged, so far as possible, by neutral principles—by standards that transcend the case at hand? I know, of course, that it is common to distinguish, as Judge Hand did, clauses like "due process," cast "in such sweeping terms that their history does not elucidate their contents,"[55] from other provisions of the Bill of Rights addressed to more specific problems. But the contrast, as it seems to me, often implies an overstatement of the specificity or the immutability these other clauses really have—at least when problems under them arise.

No one would argue, for example, that there need not be indictment and a jury trial in prosecutions for a felony in district courts. What made a question of some difficulty was the issue whether service wives charged with the murders of their husbands overseas could be tried there before a military court.[56] Does the language of the double-jeopardy clause or its preconstitutional history actually help to decide whether a defendant tried for murder in the first degree and convicted of murder in the second, who wins a reversal of the judgment on appeal, may be tried again for murder in the first or only murder in the second?[57] Is there significance in the fact that it is "jeopardy of life or limb" that is forbidden, now that no one is in jeopardy of limb but only of imprisonment or fine? The right to "have the assistance of counsel" was considered, I am sure, when the sixth amendment was proposed, a right to defend by counsel if you have one, contrary to what was then the English law.[58] That does not seem to me sufficient to avert extension of its meaning to imply a right to court-appointed counsel when the defendant is too poor to find such aid[59]—though I admit that I once urged the point sincerely as a lawyer for the Government.[60] It is difficult for me to think the fourth amendment freezes for all time the common law of search and of arrest as it prevailed when the amendment was adopted, whatever the exigencies of police problems may now be or may become. Nor should we, in my view, lament the fact that "the" freedom of speech or press that Congress is forbidden by the first amendment to impair is not determined only by the scope such freedom had in the late eighteenth century, though the word "the" might have been taken to impose a limitation to the concept of that time—a time when, President Wright has recently reminded us, there was remarkable consensus about matters of this kind.[61]

Even "due process," on the other hand, might have been confined, as Mr. Justice Brandeis urged originally,[62] to a guarantee of fair procedure, coupled perhaps with prohibition of executive displacement of established law—the analogue for us of what the barons meant in Magna Carta. Equal protection could be taken as no

---

[55] HAND, *op. cit. supra* note 3, at 30.

[56] See Reid v. Covert, 354 U.S. 1 (1957), *reversing on rehearing* 351 U.S. 487(1956).

[57] See Green v. United States, 355 U.S. 184 (1957).

[58] "Throughout the eighteenth century counsel were allowed to speak in cases of treason and misdemeanour only." 1 STEPHEN, A HISTORY OF THE CRIMINAL LAW OF ENGLAND 453 (1883). See also ASSOCIATION OF THE BAR OF THE CITY OF NEW YORK & NATIONAL LEGAL AID & DEFENDERS ASS'N, EQUAL JUSTICE FOR THE ACCUSED 40–42 (1959).

[59] See Johnson v. Zerbst, 304 U.S. 458 (1938).

[60] Walker v. Johnston, 312 U.S. 275 (1941).

[61] WRIGHT, CONSENSUS AND CONTINUITY, 1776–1787 *passim* (1958). See also CHAFEE, HOW HUMAN RIGHTS GOT INTO THE CONSTITUTION (1952). For the suggestion that political consensus has been the abiding characteristic of American democracy, see HARTZ, THE LIBERAL TRADITION IN AMERICA 139–42 (1955).

[62] "Despite arguments to the contrary which had seemed to me persuasive, it is settled that the due process clause of the Fourteenth Amendment applies to matters of substantive law as well as to matters of procedure." Whitney v. California, 274 U.S. 357, 373 (1927)(concurring opinion).

more than an assurance that no one may be placed beyond the safeguards of the law, outlawing, as it were, the possibility of outlawry, but nothing else. Here too I cannot find it in my heart to regret that interpretation did not ground itself in ancient history but rather has perceived in these provisions a compendious affirmation of the basic values of a free society, values that must be given weight in legislation and administration at the risk of courting trouble in the courts.

So far as possible, to finish with my point, I argue that we should prefer to see the other clauses of the Bill of Rights read as an affirmation of the special values they embody rather than as statements of a finite rule of law, its limits fixed by the consensus of a century long past, with problems very different from our own. To read them in the former way is to leave room for adaptation and adjustment if and when competing values, also having constitutional dimension, enter on the scene.

Let me repeat what I have thus far tried to say. The courts have both the title and the duty when a case is properly before them to review the actions of the other branches in the light of constitutional provisions, even though the action involves value choices, as invariably action does. In doing so, however, they are bound to function otherwise than as a naked power organ; they participate as courts of law. This calls for facing how determinations of this kind can be asserted to have any legal quality. The answer, I suggest, inheres primarily in that they are—or are obliged to be—entirely principled. A principled decision, in the sense I have in mind, is one that rests on reasons with respect to all the issues in the case, reasons that in their generality and their neutrality transcend any immediate result that is involved. When no sufficient reasons of this kind can be assigned for overturning value choices of the other branches of the Government or of a state, those choices must, of course, survive. Otherwise, as Holmes said in his first opinion for the Court, "a constitution, instead of embodying only relatively fundamental rules of right, as generally understood by all English-speaking communities, would become the partisan of a particular set of ethical or economical opinions . . ."[63]

The virtue or demerit of a judgment turns, therefore, entirely on the reasons that support it and their adequacy to maintain any choice of values it decrees, or, it is vital that we add, to maintain the rejection of a claim that any given choice should be decreed. The critic's role, as T. R. Powell showed throughout so many fruitful years, is the sustained, disinterested, merciless examination of the reasons that the courts advance, measured by standards of the kind I have attempted to describe. I wish that more of us today could imitate his dedication to that task.

III. Some Appraisals of Review

One who has ventured to advance such generalities about the courts and constitutional interpretation is surely challenged to apply them to some concrete problems—if only to make clear that he believes in what he says. A lecture, to be sure, is a poor medium for such an undertaking, for the statement and analysis of cases inescapably takes time. Nonetheless, I feel obliged to make the effort and I trust that I can do so without trespassing on the indulgence you already have displayed.

Needless to say, I must rely on you to understand that in alluding to some areas of constitutional interpretation, selected for their relevancy to my thesis,

---

[63] Otis v. Parker, 187 U.S. 606, 609 (1903).

I do not mean to add another capsulated estimate of the performance of our highest court to those that now are in such full supply. The Court in constitutional adjudications faces what must surely be the largest and the hardest task of principled decision-making faced by any group of men in the entire world. There is a difference worthy of articulation between purported evaluations of the Court and comments on decisions or opinions.

(I).—I start by noting two important fields of present interest in which the Court has been decreeing value choices in a way that makes it quite impossible to speak of principled determinations or the statement and evaluation of judicial reasons, since the Court has not disclosed the grounds on which its judgments rest.

The first of these involves the sequel to the *Burstyn* case,[64] in which, as you recall, the Court decided that the motion picture is a medium of expression included in the "speech" and "press" to which the safeguards of the first amendment, made applicable to the states by the fourteenth, apply. But *Burstyn* left open, as it was of course obliged to do, the extent of the protection that the movies are accorded, and even the question whether any censorship is valid, involving as it does prior restraint. The judgment rested, and quite properly, upon the vice inherent in suppression based upon a finding that the film involved was "sacrilegious"—with the breadth and vagueness that that term had been accorded in New York. "[W]hether a state may censor motion pictures under a clearly drawn statute designed and applied to prevent the showing of obscene films" was said to be "a very different question" not decided by the Court.[65] In five succeeding cases, decisions sustaining censorship of different films under standards variously framed have been reversed, but only by per curiam decisions. In one of these,[66] in which I should avow I was of counsel, the standard was undoubtedly too vague for any argument upon the merits. I find it hard to think that this was clearly so in all the others.[67] Given the subtlety and difficulty of the problem, the need and opportunity for clarifying explanation, are such unexplained decisions in a new domain of constitutional interpretation consonant with standards of judicial action that the Court or we can possibly defend? I realize that nine men often find it easier to reach agreement on result than upon reasons and that such a difficulty may be posed within this field. Is it not preferable, however, indeed essential, that if this is so the variations of position be disclosed?[68]

[64] Joseph Burstyn, Inc. v. Wilson, 343 U.S. 495 (1952).

[65] *Id.* at 506.

[66] Gelling v. Texas, 343 U.S. 960, *reversing per curiam* 157 Tex. Crim. 51, 247 S.W.2d 95 (1952)(ordinance prohibited exhibition of picture deemed by Censorship Board "of such character as to be prejudicial to the best interests of the people" of Marshall, Texas, "if publicly shown").

[67] See Times Film Corp. v. City of Chicago, 355 U.S. 35, *reversing per curiam* 244 F.2d 432 (7th Cir. 1957); Holmby Prods., Inc. v. Vaughn, 350 U.S. 870, *reversing per curiam* 177 Kan. 728, 282 P.2d 412 (1955); Superior Films, Inc. v. Department of Educ., 346 U.S. 587 (1954), *reversing per curiam* 159 Ohio St. 315, 112 N.E.2d 311 (1953); Superior Films, Inc. v. Department of Educ., *supra, reversing per curiam* Commercial Pictures Corp. v. Board of Regents of the Univ. of N.Y., 305 N.Y. 336, 113 N.E.2d 502 (1953).

[68] Attention should be called to Kingsley Int'l Pictures Corp. v. Regents of the Univ. of N.Y., 360 U.S. 684 (1959), decided with full opinions since the present paper was delivered. The Court was unanimous in holding invalid New York's refusal to license the exhibition of a film based on D. H. Lawrence's *Lady Chatterley's Lover.* The opinion of the Court by Mr. Justice Stewart, deeming the censorship order to rest solely on the ground that the picture portrays an adulterous relationship as an acceptable pattern of behavior, held the statute so construed an unconstitutional impairment of freedom to disseminate ideas. Justices Black and Douglas joined in the opinion but in brief concurrences expressed their view that any prior restraint on motion pictures is as vulnerable as the censorship of newspapers or books. Mr. Justice Frankfurter in one opinion and Mr. Justice Harlan in another, joined by Justices Frankfurter and Whittaker, conceived of the New York statute as demanding some showing of obscenity or of incitement to immorality and thought, therefore, that it escaped the condemnation of the majority opinion. In their view, however, the film could not be held to have embodied either obscenity or incitement. Hence, the statute was invalid as applied.

The second group of cases to which I shall call attention involves what may be called the progeny of the school-segregation ruling of 1954. Here again the Court has written on the merits of the constitutional issue posed by state segregation only once;[69] its subsequent opinions on the form of the decree[70] and the defiance in Arkansas[71] deal, of course, with other matters. The original opinion, you recall, was firmly focused on state segregation in the public schools, its reasoning accorded import to the nature of the educational process, and its conclusion was that separate educational facilities are "inherently unequal."

What shall we think then of the Court's extension of the ruling to other public facilities, such as public transportation, parks, golf courses, bath houses, and beaches, which no one is obliged to use—all by per curiam decisions?[72] That these situations present a weaker case against state segregation is not, of course, what I am saying. I am saying that the question whether it is stronger, weaker, or of equal weight appears to me to call for principled decision. I do not know, and I submit you cannot know, whether the per curiam affirmance in the *Dawson* case, involving public bath houses and beaches, embraced the broad opinion of the circuit court that all state-enforced racial segregation is invalid or approved only its immediate result and, if the latter, on what ground. Is this "process of law," to borrow the words Professor Brown has used so pointedly in writing of such unexplained decisions upon matters far more technical[73]—the process that alone affords the Court its title and its duty to adjudicate a claim that state action is repugnant to the Constitution?

Were I a prudent man I would, no doubt, confine myself to problems of this order, involving not the substance but the method of decision—for other illustrations might be cited in the same domain. I shall, however, pass beyond this to some areas of substantive interpretation which appear to me to illustrate my theme.

(2).—The phase of our modern constitutional development that I conceive we can most confidently deem successful inheres in the broad reading of the commerce, taxing, and related powers of the Congress, achieved with so much difficulty little more than twenty years ago—against restrictions in the name of state autonomy to which the Court had for a time turned such a sympathetic ear.

Why is it that the Court failed so completely in the effort to contain the scope of national authority and that today one reads decisions like *Hammer v. Dagenhart*,[74] or *Carter Coal*,[75] or the invalidation of the Agricultural Adjustment Act[76] with eyes that disbelieve? No doubt the answer inheres partly in the simple facts of life and the consensus they have generated on the powers that a modern nation needs. But is it not a feature of the case as well—a feature that has real importance—that the Court could not articulate an adequate analysis of the restrictions it imposed on Congress in favor of the states, whose representatives—upon an equal footing

---

[69] Brown v. Board of Educ., 347 U.S. 483 (1954). See also Bolling v. Sharpe, 347 U.S. 497 (1954), dealing with segregation in the District of Columbia.

[70] Brown v. Board of Educ., 349 U.S. 294 (1955).

[71] Cooper v. Aaron, 358 U.S. 1 (1958).

[72] New Orleans City Park Improvement Ass'n v. Detiege, 358 U.S. 54, *affirming per curiam* 252 F.2d 122 (5th Cir. 1958); Gayle v. Browder, 352 U.S. 903, *affirming per curiam* 142 F. Supp. 707 (M.D. Ala. 1956); Holmes v. City of Atlanta, 350 U.S. 879, *reversing per curiam* 223 F.2d 93 (5th Cir. 1955); Mayor & City Council v. Dawson, 350 U.S. 877, *affirming per curiam* 220 F.2d 386 (4th Cir. 1955); Muir v. Louisville Park Theatrical Ass'n, 347 U.S. 971 (1954), *reversing per curiam* 202 F.2d 275 (6th Cir. 1953).

[73] Brown, *Foreword: Process of Law, The Supreme Court, 1957 Term*, 72 HARV. L. REV. 77 (1958).

[74] 247 U.S. 251 (1918).

[75] Carter v. Carter Coal Co., 298 U.S. 238 (1936).

[76] United States v. Butler, 297 U.S. 1 (1936).

in the Senate—controlled the legislative process and had broadly acquiesced in the enactments that were subject to review?

Is it not also true and of importance that some of the principles the Court affirmed were strikingly deficient in neutrality, sustaining, for example, national authority when it impinged adversely upon labor, as in the application of the Sherman Act, but not when it was sought to be employed in labor's aid? On this score, the contrast in today's position certainly is striking. The power that sustained the Wagner Act is the same power that sustains Taft-Hartley—with its even greater inroads upon state autonomy but with restraints on labor that the Wagner Act did not impose.

One of the speculations that I must confess I find intriguing is upon the question whether there are any neutral principles that might have been employed to mark the limits of the commerce power of the Congress in terms more circumscribed than the virtual abandonment of limits in the principle that has prevailed. Given the readiness of President Roosevelt to compromise on any basis that allowed achievement of the substance of his program, might not the formulae of coverage employed in the legislation of the Thirties have quite readily embraced any such principles the Court had then been able to devise before the crisis became so intense—principles sustaining action fairly equal to the need? I do not say we would or should be happier if that had happened and the Court still played a larger part within this area of our federalism, given the attention to state interests that is so inherent in the Congress and the constitutional provisions governing the selection and the composition of the Houses, which make that attention very likely to endure.[77] I say only that I find such speculation interesting. You will recall that it was Holmes who deprecated argument of counsel the logic of which left "no part of the conduct of life with which on similar principles Congress might not interfere."[78]

(3).—The poverty of principled articulation of the limits put on Congress as against the states before the doctrinal reversal of the Thirties was surely also true of the decisions, dealing with the very different problem of the relationship between the individual and government, which invoked due process to maintain *laissez faire*. Did not the power of the great dissents inhere precisely in their demonstrations that the Court could not present an adequate analysis, in terms of neutral principles, to support the value choices it decreed? Holmes, to be sure, saw limits beyond which "the contract and due process clauses are gone"; and his insistence on the need for compensation to sustain a Pennsylvania prohibition of the exploitation of subsurface coal, threatening subsidence of a dwelling belonging to the owner of the surface land, indicates the kind of limit he perceived.[79] Am I simply voicing my own sympathies in saying that his analysis of those limits has a thrust entirely lacking in the old and now forgotten judgments striking down minimum-wage and maximum-hour laws?

If I am right in this it helps to make a further point that has more bearing upon current issues, that I believe it misconceives the problem of the Court to state it as the question of the proper measure of judicial self-restraint, with the resulting issue whether such restraint is only proper in relation to protection of a purely

Herbert Wechsler

---

[77] See Wechsler, *The Political Safeguards of Federalism: The Role of the States in the Composition and Selection of the National Government*, 54 COLUM. L. REV. 543 (1954), in FEDERALISM MATURE AND EMERGENT 97 (MacMahon ed. 1955).

[78] Northern Sec. Co. v. United States, 193 U.S. 197, 403 (1904) (dissenting opinion).

[79] Pennsylvania Coal Co. v. Mahon, 260 U.S. 393, 412 (1922).

economic interest or also in relation to an interest like freedom of speech or of religion, privacy, or discrimination (at least if it is based on race, origin, or creed). Of course, the courts ought to be cautious to impose a choice of values on the other branches or a state, based upon the Constitution, only when they are persuaded, on an adequate and principled analysis, that the choice is clear. That I suggest is all that self-restraint can mean and in that sense it always is essential, whatever issue may be posed. The real test inheres, as I have tried to argue, in the force of the analysis. Surely a stronger analysis may be advanced against a particular uncompensated taking as a violation of the fifth amendment than against a particular limitation of freedom of speech or press as a violation of the first.

In this view, the "preferred position" controversy hardly has a point—indeed, it never has been really clear what is asserted or denied to have a preference and over what.[80] Certainly the concept is pernicious if it implies that there is any simple, almost mechanistic basis for determining priorities of values having constitutional dimension, as when there is an inescapable conflict between claims to free press and a fair trial. It has a virtue, on the other hand, insofar as it recognizes that some ordering of social values is essential; that all cannot be given equal weight, if the Bill of Rights is to be maintained.

Did Holmes mean any less than this when he lamented the tendency "toward underrating or forgetting the safeguards in bills of rights that had to be fought for in their day and that still are worth fighting for"?[81] Only in that view could he have dissented in the *Abrams* and the *Gitlow* cases[82] and have struggled so intensely to develop a principled delineation of the freedom that he voted to sustain. Even if one thinks, as I confess I do, that his analysis does not succeed if it requires that an utterance designed to stimulate unlawful action must be accorded an immunity unless it is intended to achieve or creates substantial danger of immediate results,[83] can anyone deny it his respect? Is not the force of a position framed in terms of principles of the neutrality and generality that Holmes achieved entirely different from that of the main opinion, for example, in the *Sweezy* case,[84] resting at bottom as it does, on principles of power separation among the branches of state government that never heretofore have been conceived to be a federal requirement and that, we safely may predict, the Court will not apply to any other field?[85]

(4).—Finally, I turn to the decisions that for me provide the hardest test of my belief in principled adjudication, those in which the Court in recent years has vindicated claims that deprivations based on race deny the equality before the law that the fourteenth amendment guarantees. The crucial cases are, of course, those

[80] See, *e.g.*, Kovacs v. Cooper, 336 U.S. 77, 88 (1949).

[81] 2 HOLMES-POLLOCK LETTERS 25 (Howe ed. 1941); see 1 HOLMES-LASKI LETTERS 203, 529–30 (Howe ed. 1953); *cf.* 2 *id.* at 888.

[82] Abrams v. United States, 250 U.S. 616, 624 (1919); Gitlow v. New York, 268 U.S. 652, 672 (1925).

[83] "I do not doubt for a moment that by the same reasoning that would justify punishing persuasion to murder, the United States constitutionally may punish speech that produces or is intended to produce a clear and imminent danger that it will bring about forthwith certain substantive evils that the United States constitutionally may seek to prevent." Abrams v. United States, 250 U.S. 616, 627 (1919). Is it possible, however, that persuasion to murder is only punishable constitutionally if the design is that the murder be committed "forthwith"? *Cf.* HAND, *op. cit. supra* note 3, at 58–59.

[84] Sweezy v. New Hampshire, 354 U.S. 234 (1957).

[85] See Uphaus v. Wyman, 360 U.S. 72, 77 (1959), decided after the present paper was delivered: "[S]ince questions concerning the authority of the committee to act as it did are questions of state law, . . . we accept as controlling the New Hampshire Supreme Court's conclusion that '[t]he legislative history makes it clear beyond a reasonable doubt that it [the Legislature] did and does desire an answer to these questions'."

involving the white primary,[86] the enforcement of racially restrictive covenants,[87] and the segregated schools.[88]

The more I think about the past the more skeptical I find myself about predictions of the future. Viewed a priori would you not have thought that the invention of the cotton gin in 1792 should have reduced the need for slave labor and hence diminished the attractiveness of slavery? Brooks Adams tells us that its consequences were precisely the reverse; that the demand for slaves increased as cotton planting became highly lucrative, increased so greatly that Virginia turned from coal and iron, which George Washington envisaged as its future, into an enormous farm for breeding slaves—forty thousand of whom it exported annually to the rest of the South.[89] Only the other day I read that the Japanese evacuation, which I thought an abomination when it happened, though in the line of duty as a lawyer I participated in the effort to sustain it in the Court,[90] is now believed by many to have been a blessing to its victims, breaking down forever the ghettos in which they had previously lived.[91] But skeptical about predictions as I am, I still believe that the decisions I have mentioned—dealing with the primary, the covenant, and schools—have the best chance of making an enduring contribution to the quality of our society of any that I know in recent years. It is in this perspective that I ask how far they rest on neutral principles and are entitled to approval in the only terms that I acknowledge to be relevant to a decision of the courts.

The primary and covenant cases present two different aspects of a single problem—that it is a state alone that is forbidden by the fourteenth amendment to deny equal protection of the laws, as only a state or the United States is precluded by the fifteenth amendment from denying or abridging on the ground of race or color the right of citizens of the United States to vote. It has, of course, been held for years that the prohibition of action by the state reaches not only an explicit deprivation by a statute but also action of the courts or of subordinate officials, purporting to exert authority derived from public office.[92]

I deal first with the primary. So long as the Democratic Party in the South excluded Negroes from participation, in the exercise of an authority conferred by statute regulating political parties, it was entirely clear that the amendment was infringed; the exclusion involved an application of the statute.[93] The problem became difficult only when the states, responding to these judgments, repealed the statutes, leaving parties free to define their membership as private associations, protected by the state but not directed or controlled or authorized by law. In this position the Court held in 1935 that an exclusion by the party was untouched by the amendment, being action of the individuals involved, not of the state or its officialdom.[94]

Then came the *Classic* case[95] in 1941, which I perhaps should say I argued for the Government. *Classic* involved a prosecution of election officials for depriving

---

[86] Smith v. Allwright, 321 U.S. 649 (1944).

[87] Shelley v. Kraemer, 334 U.S. 1 (1948); Barrows v. Jackson, 346 U.S. 249 (1953).

[88] Brown v. Board of Educ., 347 U.S. 483 (1954).

[89] See B. Adams, *The Heritage of Henry Adams*, in H. ADAMS, THE DEGRADATION OF THE DEMOCRATIC DOGMA 22, 31 (1919).

[90] Korematsu v. United States, 323 U.S. 214 (1944).

[91] See Newsweek, Dec. 29, 1958, p. 23.

[92] See, *e.g.*, *Ex parte* Virginia, 100 U.S. 339, 347 (1880); HALE, FREEDOM THROUGH LAW ch. xi (1952).

[93] See Nixon v. Condon, 286 U.S. 73 (1932); Nixon v. Herndon, 273 U.S. 536 (1927).

[94] Grovey v. Townsend, 295 U.S. 45 (1935).

[95] United States v. Classic, 313 U.S. 299 (1941).

a voter of a right secured by the Constitution in willfully failing to count his vote as it was cast in a Louisiana Democratic primary. In holding that the right of a qualified voter to participate in choosing Representatives in Congress, a right conferred by article I, section 2,[96] extended to participating in a primary which influenced the ultimate selection, the Court did not, of course, deal with the scope of party freedom to select its members. The victim of the fraud in *Classic* was a member of the Democratic Party, voting in a primary in which he was entitled to participate, and the only one in which he could.[97] Yet three years later *Classic* was declared in *Smith v. Allwright*[98] to have determined in effect that primaries are a part of the election, with the consequence that parties can no more defend racial exclusion from their primaries than can the state, a result reaffirmed in 1953.[99] This is no doubt a settled proposition in the Court. But what it means is not, as sometimes has been thought, that a state may not escape the limitations of the Constitution merely by transferring public functions into private hands. It means rather that the constitutional guarantee against deprivation of the franchise on the ground of race or color has become a prohibition of party organization upon racial lines, at least where the party has achieved political hegemony. I ask with all sincerity if you are able to discover in the opinions thus far written in support of this result—a result I say again that I approve—neutral principles that satisfy the mind. I should suppose that a denial of the franchise on religious grounds is certainly forbidden by the Constitution. Are religious parties, therefore, to be taken as proscribed? I should regard this result too as one plainly to be desired but is there a constitutional analysis on which it can be validly decreed? Is it, indeed, not easier to project an analysis establishing that such a proscription would infringe rights protected by the first amendment?

The case of the restrictive covenant presents for me an even harder problem. Assuming that the Constitution speaks to state discrimination on the ground of race but not to such discrimination by an individual even in the use or distribution of his property, although his freedom may no doubt be limited by common law or statute, why is the enforcement of the private covenant a state discrimination rather than a legal recognition of the freedom of the individual? That the action of the state court is action of the state, the point Mr. Chief Justice Vinson emphasizes in the Court's opinion[100] is, of course, entirely obvious. What is not obvious, and is the crucial step, is that the state may properly be charged with the discrimination when it does no more than give effect to an agreement that the

---

[96] "The House of Representatives shall be composed of Members chosen every second Year by the People of the several States, and the Electors in each State shall have the Qualifications requisite for Electors of the most numerous Branch of the State Legislature."

The seventeenth amendment contains similar provisions for the choice of Senators.

[97] The Government brief in Classic stated with respect to *Grovey*:

Moreover, what Article I, Section 2 secures is the right to choose. The implicit premise of the *Grovey* decision is that the negroes excluded from the Democratic primary were legally free to record their choice by joining an opposition party or by organizing themselves. In the present case the voters exercised the right to choose in accordance with the contemplated method; and the wrong alleged deprived them of an opportunity to express their choice in any other way.

Brief for the United States, pp. 34–35, United States v. Classic, 313 U.S. 299 (1941).

[98] 321 U.S. 649 (1944). Mr. Justice Frankfurter concurred only in the result. Mr. Justice Roberts alone dissented.

[99] Terry v. Adams, 345 U.S. 461 (1953). See also Rice v. Elmore, 165 F.2d 387 (4th Cir. 1947), *cert. denied*, 333 U.S. 875 (1948). There is no opinion of the Court in *Terry*. Justices Douglas and Burton joined in an opinion by Justice Black. Justice Frankfurter, saying that he found the case "by no means free of difficulty," wrote for himself. Chief Justice Vinson and Justices Reed and Jackson joined in an opinion by Justice Clark. Justice Minton dissented.

[100] See Shelley v. Kraemer, 334 U.S. 1, 14–23 (1948).

individual involved is, by hypothesis, entirely free to make. Again, one is obliged to ask: What is the principle involved? Is the state forbidden to effectuate a will that draws a racial line, a will that can accomplish any disposition only through the aid of law, or is it a sufficient answer there that the discrimination was the testator's and not the state's?[101] May not the state employ its law to vindicate the privacy of property against a trespasser, regardless of the grounds of his exclusion, or does it embrace the owner's reasons for excluding if it buttresses his power by the law? Would a declaratory judgment that a fee is determinable if a racially restrictive limitation should be violated represent discrimination by the state upon the racial ground?[102] Would a judgment of ejectment?

None of these questions has been answered by the Court nor are the problems faced in the opinions.[103] Philadelphia, to be sure, has been told that it may not continue to administer the school for "poor male white orphans," established by the city as trustee under the will of Stephen Girard, in accordance with that racial limitation.[104] All the Supreme Court said, however, was the following: "The Board which operates Girard College is an agency of the State of Pennsylvania. Therefore, even though the Board was acting as a trustee, its refusal to admit Foust and Felder to the college because they were Negroes was discrimination by the State. Such discrimination is forbidden by the Fourteenth Amendment." When the Orphans' Court thereafter dismissed the city as trustee, appointing individuals in substitution, its action was sustained in Pennsylvania.[105] Further review by certiorari was denied.[106]

One other case in the Supreme Court has afforded opportunity for reconsidering the basis and scope of the *Shelley* principle, *Black v. Cutter Labs*.[107] Here a collective-bargaining agreement was so construed that Communist Party membership was "just cause" for a discharge. In this view, California held that a worker was lawfully dismissed upon that ground. A Supreme Court majority concluded that this judgment involved nothing but interpretation of a contract, making irrelevant the standards that would govern the validity of a state statute that required the discharge. Only Mr. Chief Justice Warren and Justices Douglas and Black, dissenting, thought the principle of *Shelley v. Kraemer* was involved when the state court sustained the discharge.[108]

Many understandably would like to perceive in the primary and covenant decisions a principle susceptible of broad extension, applying to the other power aggregates in our society limitations of the kind the Constitution has imposed on government.[109] My colleague A. A. Berle, Jr., has, indeed, pointed to the large

[101] *Cf. Gordon v. Gordon*, 332 Mass. 197, 210, 124 N.E.2d 228, 236, *cert. denied*, 349 U.S. 947 (1955).

[102] See *Charlotte Park & Recreation Comm'n v. Barringer*, 242 N.C. 311, 88 S.E.2d 114 (1955), *cert. denied*, 350 U.S. 983 (1956).

[103] Mr. Chief Justice Vinson, dissenting in *Barrows v. Jackson*, 346 U.S. 249, 260 (1953), urged a distinction between enforcement of the covenant by injunction, the problem in *Shelley*, and an action for damages against a defaulting covenantor by a co-covenantor. He was alone in his dissent.

[104] *Pennsylvania v. Board of Directors*, 353 U.S. 230, 231 (1957).

[105] *Girard College Trusteeship*, 391 Pa. 434, 441–42, 138 A.2d 844, 846 (1958).

[106] *Pennsylvania v. Board of Directors*, 357 U.S. 570 (1958).

[107] 351 U.S. 292 (1956).

[108] Attention also should be called to *Dorsey v. Stuyvesant Town Corp.*, 299 N.Y. 512, 87 N.E.2d 541 (1949), holding state action not involved in racial discrimination in the selection of tenants by the owner corporation, although the housing development involved had been constructed with the aid of New York City which, pursuant to a contract authorized by statute, had condemned the land for the corporation and granted substantial tax exemptions. Certiorari was denied, 339 U.S. 981 (1950), Justices Black and Douglas noting their dissent.

[109] See, *e.g.*, *Ming, Racial Restrictions and the Fourteenth Amendment: The Restrictive Covenant Cases*, 16 U. CHI. L. REV. 203, 235–38 (1949).

business corporation, which after all is chartered by the state and wields in many areas more power than the government, as uniquely suitable for choice as the next subject of such application.[110] I doubt that the courts will yield to such temptations; and I do not hesitate to say that I prefer to see the issues faced through legislation, where there is room for drawing lines that courts are not equipped to draw. If this is right the two decisions I have mentioned will remain, as they now are, *ad hoc* determinations of their narrow problems, yielding no neutral principles for their extension or support.

Lastly, I come to the school decision, which for one of my persuasion stirs the deepest conflict I experience in testing the thesis I propose. Yet I would surely be engaged in playing Hamlet without Hamlet if I did not try to state the problems that appear to me to be involved.

The problem for me, I hardly need to say, is not that the Court departed from its earlier decisions holding or implying that the equality of public educational facilities demanded by the Constitution could be met by separate schools. I stand with the long tradition of the Court that previous decisions must be subject to reexamination when a case against their reasoning is made. Nor is the problem that the Court disturbed the settled patterns of a portion of the country; even that must be accepted as a lesser evil than nullification of the Constitution. Nor is it that history does not confirm that an agreed purpose of the fourteenth amendment was to forbid separate schools or that there is important evidence that many thought the contrary;[111] the words are general and leave room for expanding content as time passes and conditions change. Nor is it that the Court may have miscalculated the extent to which its judgment would be honored or accepted; it is not a prophet of the strength of our national commitment to respect the judgments of the courts. Nor is it even that the Court did not remit the issue to the Congress, acting under the enforcement clause of the amendment. That was a possible solution, to be sure, but certainly Professor Freund is right[112] that it would merely have evaded the claims made.

The problem inheres strictly in the reasoning of the opinion, an opinion which is often read with less fidelity by those who praise it than by those by whom it is condemned. The Court did not declare, as many wish it had, that the fourteenth amendment forbids all racial lines in legislation, though subsequent per curiam decisions may, as I have said, now go that far. Rather, as Judge Hand observed,[113] the separate-but-equal formula was not overruled "in form" but was held to have "no place" in public education on the ground that segregated schools are "inherently unequal," with deleterious effects upon the colored children in implying their inferiority, effects which retard their educational and mental development. So, indeed, the district court had found as a fact in the Kansas case, a finding which the Supreme Court embraced, citing some further "modern authority" in its support.[114]

Does the validity of the decision turn then on the sufficiency of evidence or of judicial notice to sustain a finding that the separation harms the Negro children

---

[110] See, *e.g.*, Berle, *Constitutional Limitations on Corporate Activity—Protection of Personal Rights From Invasion Through Economic Power*, 100 U. PA. L. REV. 933, 948–51 (1952); BERLE, ECONOMIC POWER AND THE FREE SOCIETY 17–18 (Fund for the Republic 1957).

[111] See Bickel, *The Original Understanding and the Segregation Decision*, 69 HARV. L. REV. 1 (1955).

[112] See Freund, *Storm Over the American Supreme Court*, 21 MODERN L. REV. 345, 351 (1958).

[113] HAND, *op. cit. supra* note 3, at 54.

[114] For a detailed account of the character and quality of research in this field, see Note, *Grade School Segregation: The Latest Attack on Racial Discrimination*, 61 YALE L. J. 730 (1952).

who may be involved? There were, indeed, some witnesses who expressed that opinion in the Kansas case,[115] as there were also witnesses in the companion Virginia case, including Professor Garrett of Columbia,[116] whose view was to the contrary. Much depended on the question that the witness had in mind, which rarely was explicit. Was he comparing the position of the Negro child in a segregated school with his position in an integrated school where he was happily accepted and regarded by the whites; or was he comparing his position under separation with that under integration where the whites were hostile to his presence and found ways to make their feelings known? And if the harm that segregation worked was relevant, what of the benefits that it entailed: sense of security, the absence of hostility? Were they irrelevant? Moreover, was the finding in Topeka applicable without more to Clarendon County, South Carolina, with 2,799 colored students and only 295 whites? Suppose that more Negroes in a community preferred separation than opposed it? Would that be relevant to whether they were hurt or aided by segregation as opposed to integration? Their fates would be governed by the change of system quite as fully as those of the students who complained.

I find it hard to think the judgment really turned upon the facts. Rather, it seems to me, it must have rested on the view that racial segregation is, in principle, a denial of equality to the minority against whom it is directed; that is, the group that is not dominant politically and, therefore, does not make the choice involved. For many who support the Court's decision this assuredly is the decisive ground. But this position also presents problems. Does it not involve an inquiry into the motive of the legislature, which is generally foreclosed to the courts?[117] Is it alternatively defensible to make the measure of validity of legislation the way it is interpreted by those who are affected by it? In the context of a charge that segregation *with equal facilities* is a denial of equality, is there not a point in *Plessy* in the statement that if "enforced separation stamps the colored race with a badge of inferiority" it is solely because its members choose "to put that construction upon it"?[118] Does enforced separation of the sexes discriminate against females merely because it may be the females who resent it and it is imposed by judgments predominantly male? Is a prohibition of miscegenation a discrimination against the colored member of the couple who would like to marry?

For me, assuming equal facilities, the question posed by state-enforced segregation is not one of discrimination at all. Its human and its constitutional dimensions lie entirely elsewhere, in the denial by the state of freedom to associate, a denial that impinges in the same way on any groups or races that may be involved. I think, and I hope not without foundation, that the Southern white also pays heavily for segregation, not only in the sense of guilt that he must carry but also in the benefits he is denied. In the days when I was joined with Charles H. Houston in a litigation in the Supreme Court, before the present building was constructed, he did not suffer more than I in knowing that we had to go to Union Station to lunch together during the recess. Does not the problem of miscegenation show most clearly that it is

Herbert Wechsler

[115] See Record, pp. 125–26, 132 (Hugh W. Speer), Brown v. Board of Educ., 347 U.S. 483 (1954); *Id.* at 164–65 (Wilbur B. Brookover); *id.* at 170–71 (Louisa Holt); *id.* at 176–79 (John J. Kane).

[116] See Record, pp. 548–55, 568–72 (Henry E. Garrett), Davis v. County Bd. of Educ., 347 U.S. 483 (1954).

[117] Motive is open to examination when executive action is challenged as discriminatory, but there the purpose is to show that an admitted inequality of treatment was not inadvertent. See, *e.g.*, Snowden v. Hughes, 321 U.S. 1 (1944). Even in such a case, invidious motivation alone has not been held to establish the inequality.

[118] Plessy v. Ferguson, 163 U.S. 537, 551 (1896).

the freedom of association that at bottom is involved, the only case, I may add, where it is implicit in the situation that association is desired by the only individuals involved? I take no pride in knowing that in 1956 the Supreme Court dismissed an appeal in a case in which Virginia nullified a marriage on this ground, a case in which the statute had been squarely challenged by the defendant, and the Court, after remanding once, dismissed per curiam on procedural grounds that I make bold to say are wholly without basis in the law.[119]

But if the freedom of association is denied by segregation, integration forces an association upon those for whom it is unpleasant or repugnant. Is this not the heart of the issue involved, a conflict in human claims of high dimension, not unlike many others that involve the highest freedoms—conflicts that Professor Sutherland has recently described.[120] Given a situation where the state must practically choose between denying the association to those individuals who wish it or imposing it on those who would avoid it, is there a basis in neutral principles for holding that the Constitution demands that the claims for association should prevail? I should like to think there is, but I confess that I have not yet written the opinion. To write it is for me the challenge of the school-segregation cases.

Having said what I have said, I certainly should add that I offer no comfort to anyone who claims legitimacy in defiance of the courts. This is the ultimate negation of all neutral principles, to take the benefits accorded by the constitutional system, including the national market and common defense, while denying it allegiance when a special burden is imposed. That certainly is the antithesis of law.

I am confident I have said much with which you disagree—both in my basic premises and in conclusions I have drawn. The most that I can hope is that the effort be considered worthy of a rostrum dedicated to the memory of Mr. Justice Holmes. Transcending all the lessons that he teaches through the years, the most important one for me has come to this: Those of us to whom it is not given to "live greatly in the law" are surely called upon to fail in the attempt.

---

[119] See Ham Say Naim v. Naim, 197 Va. 80, 87 S.E.2d 749, *vacated*, 350 U.S. 891 (1955), on remand, 197 Va. 734, 90 S.E.2d 849, *appeal dismissed*, 350 U.S. 985 (1956).

[120] See SUTHERLAND, THE LAW AND ONE MAN AMONG MANY 35–62 (1956).

PART III

The Emergence of Eclecticism: 1960–2000

Policy and Economics

Ronald H. Coase

Ronald H. Coase

RONALD COASE'S 1960 essay, "The Problem of Social Cost," is one of the most frequently cited works in legal scholarship. Along with a few other papers, it earned Coase a Nobel Prize in Economics. Its insights permeate contemporary legal education. In short, of all the articles reprinted in this book, it perhaps can with least controversy be described as canonical.

An unusual series of accidents placed Coase in a position to write it. As a child in suburban London, he was diagnosed, apparently mistakenly, with weak legs and sent to a school for "physical defectives"—an assignment that reduced the likelihood that he, like his parents, would center his life on sports. A quirk of his subsequent educational schedule left him without the training in Latin essential to a grammar-school degree in history, his first love—prompting him to turn his attention first to chemistry and then, after discovering that the associated courses in mathematics were not to his taste, to commerce. He was admitted to the London School of Economics, where he pursued a Bachelor's degree in Commerce. While he was there, the gifted economist, Arnold Plant, joined the LSE faculty, enabling Coase to attend Plant's seminar a few months before taking his final examinations. That experience, Coase later wrote, "was to change my view of the working of the economic system, or perhaps more accurately was to give me one. What Plant did was to introduce me to Adam Smith's 'invisible hand.' He made me aware of how a competitive economic system could be coordinated by the pricing mechanism. But he did not merely influence my ideas. My encountering him changed my life." An oddity in the LSE degree requirements required Coase to continue his studies for another year after passing his exams. He intended to study Industrial Law, which would likely have led to a career as a practicing lawyer, but through Plant's influence he was instead awarded a Traveling Fellowship, which enabled him to spend the year visiting factories and businesses in the United States. The data gathered during that period provided the raw material for his first major article. Serendipity of this sort prompted Coase to write, upon the occasion of receiving his Nobel Prize, "My life has been interesting, concerned with academic affairs and on the whole successful. But, on almost all occasions, what I have done has been determined by factors which were no part of my choosing. I have had 'greatness thrust upon me.'"

Coase's "greatness" derives, not from the size of his oeuvre, but from the originality and power of a few related, fundamental insights. The first was contained in "The Theory of the Firm" (1937), the essay just mentioned that grew out of his visit to the United States. Why do business enterprises exist? he asked. Why don't workers and the owners of capital simply combine their respective resources through series of ad-hoc contracts? The answer, Coase contended, is that contracts are costly. Determining the prices at which goods and services should be exchanged is often difficult; anticipating and providing for ways in which deals can go awry is hard; and enforcing bargains when parties seek to escape from them is expensive. A business firm avoids many of these costs by gathering together semi-permanently the owners of many resources, substituting the "bureaucratic" decisions of managers for the coordinating mechanisms of prices and markets. In short, firms emerge (and grow) when the costs associated with organizing people and materials through them are less than the costs associated with the market transactions they replace.

This is not to suggest that Coase was skeptical of the power of the private market to coordinate economic activity. On the contrary, his second major paper, "The Federal Communications Commission" (1959), celebrated it. The central argument of that essay was that the then-standard way of allocating shares of the "scarce" electromagnetic spectrum was misguided. Why is allocation of any sort necessary? Why not just let broadcasters broadcast at whatever frequencies and power levels they please? The conventional answer was that the number of frequencies suitable for broadcasting was limited, and left to their own devices broadcasters would interfere with each other's operations. The only solution, it was said, was for the government (in the United States, in the form of the Federal Communications Commission) to assign to specific broadcasters inalienable rights to use specific frequencies on the basis of the relative merits of the programming the broadcasters proposed to provide the public. Coase agreed with the conventional characterization of the underlying problem, but offered a different solution: the government could define appropriate segments of the spectrum, allocate them to private parties, and then permit those parties to trade them. So long as the segments were freely transferable, the government could choose any method for making the initial assignments—for example, a public auction, or even a random distribution. It wouldn't matter; subsequent transactions would cause broadcast rights to end up in the hands of the organizations best able to put them to profitable use.

The foregoing point, Coase soon realized, could be generalized. In a wide variety of circumstances, he began to argue, the initial allocation of entitlements by a government was less durable and thus less important than most people (and indeed, most economists) thought. This insight had some surprisingly far-reaching implications. The most revolutionary concerned the appropriate response to a divergence between what were said to be the "social" and "private" costs and benefits of an enterprise. A simple example: suppose that it costs (in labor, materials, upkeep, etc.) $700 per day to run a factory that, in turn, generates $1,000 per day in revenue. Smoke produced by the factory's operations inflict during each day $500 in damage upon the neighbors. If the factory is not legally responsible for that harm, it will continue in operation. That's good for the factory owner (she earns a profit of $300 per day) but bad for society at large (it suffers an overall loss of $200 per day). How might we make the factory owner behave in a more socially responsible way? The standard response, advocated most forcefully by the famous economist Arthur Pigou, was in some fashion to use the power of government to alter her incentives. For example, she might be subjected to a tax equivalent to the harm she was causing the neighbors. Zoning rules might be employed to forbid her to use her property in this fashion. Or tort law might be adjusted to make her liable for the neighbors' injuries. Any one of these strategies, if employed with precision, would prompt the owner either to shut down her operations or, if smoke-eliminating filters were available for an amortized cost of less than $300 per day, to purchase and install such devices. In either event, society at large would be better off.

The first and perhaps most important implication of Coase's insight concerning the alienability of legal entitlements was that the factory owner might be induced to take into account the neighbors' interests without changing the legal rule. Suppose that the neighbors could easily negotiate with the factory owner. (As we will see, this is a crucial supposition.) Then the neighbors, even in the absence of any alteration in the pertinent legal norm, could persuade the owner either to shut down or to install filters by offering to pay her between $300 and $500 per day. The owner should accept such an offer, because her net profits would increase. The neighbors should make it, because they would be able to avoid thereby an even larger loss from smoke damage. And society at large would benefit from the deal just as much as it would from a change in the tax, zoning, or tort system.

Arguments of the sort just outlined are now commonplace in law-school classrooms. (Ordinarily, they provide starting points for the exploration of series of complications.) But, in the late 1950s, Coase's claim was heresy. At the time, he was teaching at the University of Virginia. A group of economists at the University of Chicago, believing his argument to be mistaken, invited him to defend his views one evening at the home of Professor Aaron Director. Those present included Milton Friedman, Al Harberger, Harry Johnson, and George Stigler. At the start of the session, the group took a vote. Twenty of the attendees thought that Pigou was right; one (apparently Coase himself) thought Coase was right. Over the next few hours, Coase stoutly defended his position. One by one, the others came round. But the end of the evening, all were convinced. George Stigler later described the discussion as "one of the most exciting intellectual events of my life." The host, Aaron Director, asked Coase to write up his views for publication in the *Journal of Law and Economics*. Coase accepted, and drafted what became "The Problem of Social Cost."

In the article, Coase makes four intertwined claims. First, the Pigouvian formulation of the problem to be solved in cases like the smoky factory is too narrow. Instead of attempting in some way to make the "private costs" faced by the factory owner match the "social costs" of her activity, the legal system ought to strive, "in all cases of harmful effects[,] . . . to maximize the value of production"— taking into account the welfare and conduct of all affected parties. Failure to adopt such a global perspective was likely to lead to analytical and lawmaking errors, Coase contended. For example, efforts by government to influence the conduct of the factory owner ignored the possibility that the neighbors might be able to avoid the damage to their properties more easily than the factory owner (perhaps by purchasing air conditioners) or might prompt the neighbors to behave in ways that decreased overall social welfare (for example, by constructing more houses immediately adjacent to the factory).

Second, Coase argued that it was misleading in cases of this sort to view one party as solely responsible for harm suffered by another. "[B]oth parties cause the damage" (18). The decision of the neighbors to locate or maintain their houses in the vicinity of the factory is as much a cause of the smoke damage as the factory owner's decision to operate without filters. To pick another famous example, while it is true that if locomotives did not emit sparks, the crops growing on a parcel of land adjacent to a railroad would not be incinerated, it is equally true that the damage would not arise if the farmer did not choose to plants his crops so close to the tracks. In all such cases, both parties "are responsible and *both* should be forced to include the loss . . . as a cost in deciding whether to continue the activity which gives rise to" the injury.

Third, Coase insisted that, in cases of the sort we have been considering, if "there were no costs involved in carrying out market transactions," "the decision of the courts concerning liability for damage would be without effect on the allocation of resources." This proposition, which George Stigler later dubbed, "the Coase Theorem," is by far the most famous of the claims made in the article. In the first twenty pages of the essay, Coase offers myriad illustrations in an effort to drive the point home. The central lesson of each is that, if the law imposes responsibility for a particular sort of harm on party A, but party B could avoid or reduce that harm more cheaply, then, in the absence of transaction costs, A will pay B to assume the legal burden, and the parties' subsequent conduct will be the same as it would have been had the law imposed responsibility on B in the first instance. "[A] rearrangement of rights will always take place if it would lead to an increase in the value of production."

To be sure, it makes a difference whether A or B is legally responsible. Specifically, the party who initially bears the burden will end up poorer than he or she would if the rule were otherwise. Such "wealth effects," Coase acknowledged, will sometimes be crucial when choosing among rules on what he called "ethical" grounds. But, if one focuses exclusively on the allocation of resources, the choice of legal rule will be irrelevant.

Coase hastened to remind readers that rearrangement of legal entitlements is virtually never costless; transaction costs of various sorts almost always get in the way. It is at this point in his argument that one sees most clearly the influence of "The Theory of the Firm."

> In order to carry out a market transaction it is necessary to discover who it is that one wishes to deal from, to inform people that one wishes to deal with and on what terms, to conduct negotiations leading up to the bargain, to draw up the contract, to undertake the inspection needed to make sure that the terms of the contract are being observed, and so on.

When such impediments exist, the choice of legal rule *will* affect the allocation of resources. But (and this is Coase's fourth major claim) one should not jump too quickly to the conclusion that the government must intervene in some way to correct misallocations—in other words, to compel parties to take into account the adverse effects of their actions on others. Instead, sensible analysis of such situations requires consideration of the relative costs of a wide variety of mechanisms by which the harm might be mitigated or avoided. These include the emergence of firms and the intervention by "brokers" to facilitate market transactions in addition to the more obvious options: the adjustment of tort rules, land-use controls, and criminal sanctions. None of these devices is perfect; "[a]ll solutions have costs." The goal should be to choose the solution whose costs are least. That cannot be done on the basis of theory. Instead, it "has to come from a detailed investigation of the actual results of handling the problem in different ways."

On each of these four issues, the article is crystal clear. On one other matter, however, it is ambiguous. Are controversies exemplified by the smoky factory and fire-spewing train best handled with clear, predictable rules or flexible standards? Early in the paper, Coase seems to prefer the former. To facilitate sensible rearrangement of entitlements, he argued, it was crucial "to know whether the damaging

business is liable or not for damage caused since without the establishment of this
initial delimitation of rights there can be no market transactions to transfer and
recombine them." To the same effect is his insistence later in the paper that "the
rights of the various parties should be well-defined and the results of legal actions
easy to forecast." However, in the second half of the essay he seems to suggest that
"rigid rules" are too clumsy to provide sensible resolutions of complex, idiosyncratic problems—for example, cases involving competing uses of land—and
that flexible standards, such as "the ordinary law of nuisance[,] would seem likely
to give economically more satisfactory results" (52). It is possible to reconcile these
disparate statements by assuming that Coase meant the former to apply only to a
world of zero transaction costs, while the latter applied to more realistic situations.
But Coase himself does not make that association clear. As we will see, subsequent
theorists of many stripes struggled over the question whether (or when) rules or
standards are superior.

Most of the criticism of "The Problem of Social Cost"—of which there has
been a great deal—has focused on Coase's third point. A variety of economists
and lawyers have sought to identify circumstances in which, even in the absence
of transaction costs, the choice of legal rule will affect the allocation of resources.
For example, several scholars have argued that "strategic behavior" will prevent
some of the efficiency-enhancing bargains that Coase predicted. Negotiating
parties often conceal their true preferences, in hopes of obtaining strategic advantages, and sometimes strive to establish reputations as hard bargainers, in hopes
of enhancing their power in future negotiations. Especially in situations characterized by "bilateral monopoly"—in other words, where each party has only one
possible trading partner—such behavior will often prevent legal entitlements
from being rearranged optimally.

Other scholars have chastised Coase for neglecting the indirect impacts of
"wealth effects" upon the allocation of resources. Assignments of legal entitlements are often "sticky," they point out, because, if initially denied a legal right,
many people will be too poor to buy it, whereas if they are initially given the
right, they will refuse to sell it. Stewart Schwab provides an illustration:

> As an example, compare a Civil-War-type draft, which lets draftees buy their way
> out for, say, $40,000 per period, with a volunteer army paying $40,000 per period.
> The question is whether, as the invariance thesis claims, the same people will be in
> the army in either case. Some people, unwilling or unable to pay $40,000 to escape
> the draft, would reject the lure of a volunteer army paying $40,000. People
> are wealthier when the army has to bribe them in, and this directly increases their
> willingness and ability to pay for civilian life.

But a wealth effect of the sort exemplified by this scenario is not the only reason why a person will commonly offer to pay less for a legal right he currently
lacks than he will demand in return for surrendering a right he already enjoys. A
host of empirical studies have confirmed the existence of this so-called "endowment effect" in many settings even when the value of the object or entitlement in
question is tiny in comparison to the actor's net worth. What accounts for it?
Hypotheses include the following:

- People experience losses more acutely than they experience foregone gains.
- People form emotional attachments to objects and legal entitlements, and the
  breaking of those bonds causes them pain.

- Under some circumstances, people are uneasy engaging in market transactions, and that unease both causes sellers of entitlements to increase the prices they demand (to offset their discomfort) and causes buyers to lower the prices they offer (for the same reason).
- People are reluctant to sell entitlements, especially those whose value is uncertain, because they fear later coming to regret their choices.
- The gap between offer and asking prices may reflect (in Mark Kelman's words) "the peculiar nature of consumption in a class society where exogenous needs, which are presumably either met or unmet at fixed levels of absolute income regardless of whether that level reflects a rise or fall in income, are subordinated to ever-expandable addictive needs to maintain a current standard of living."

There appear to be some contexts in which people are largely immune to all of these various psychological and cultural dynamics. For example, recent work by Jennifer Arlen, Matthew Spitzer, and Eric Talley suggests that the endowment effect is minimal when people make decisions in their capacities as agents for other people or organizations. But in settings in which one or another of the dynamics is at work, Coase's prediction that legal rights, no matter how they are originally assigned, will eventually end up in the hands of the parties who value them most highly can be expected to fail. That prediction is borne out by the way in which people have in fact behaved in some real situations closely approximating Coase's imaginary universe of zero-transaction costs. For example, as Harold Demsetz acknowledged, if Coase were right, then abolition of the "reserve clause" in professional baseball—which bound a player to the team that originally "signed" him or to the team to which he was subsequently traded—should have had no effect on the frequency with which players are transferred from one team to another. (Why? Because, market transactions should move players to the teams that value their services most highly, regardless of whether those services are "owned" by the teams or by the players themselves.) But, as Richard Thaler pointed out, the abolition of the clause had a huge impact. Similarly, the Coasean argument suggests that it wouldn't matter in the long run whether a "bonus" awarded by the state when an unemployed worker found a new job were payable to the new employer or to the worker; the employer and worker would adjust other terms in their contract in a fashion that would make the original assignment irrelevant. But, as John Donohue discovered, the initial allocation of the right to receive the check made a large difference in practice.

In an addendum to a collection of his essays published in 1988, Coase responded to some of these criticisms. The first critique (the charge that strategic behavior will prevent some of the bargains he predicted) he might have deflected in the manner chosen by some of his followers—namely, by simply defining "transaction costs" broadly to include such impediments to voluntary reassignments of entitlements. But, perhaps sensing that that response, if generalized, would make his argument excessively tautological, he chose a harder route. Admitting that strategic behavior might occasionally disrupt the market for entitlements, he insisted that game theorists had exaggerated the frequency and height of the barriers to efficient bargains. Parties have good (selfish) reasons to cooperate, he claimed. His response to the charge that he had neglected the impact upon parties' behavior of "wealth effects" was similar. In a world without transaction costs, he argued, even a substantial change in the pertinent legal rules should have no effect on the parties' wealth and thus their use of resources because they could

Ronald H. Coase

anticipate such contingencies and write contracts to cover them. In short, for the most part, Coase continued to defend his argument against all comers.

One ambiguous aspect of Coase's legacy concerns the political valence of his insights. Some commentators—most notably, Kelman and Morton Horwitz—have described Coase as deeply conservative, one of the creators of the "Chicago school" of law and economics, which is generally hostile to efforts by government to regulate the conduct of private actors. There are certainly aspects of "The Problem of Social Cost" that are consistent with that characterization. "It is my belief," Coase announced broadly, "that economists, and policy-makers generally, have tended to over-estimate the advantages which come from governmental regulation." And several of the examples he deploys in the second half of the paper of governmental involvement in economic affairs are distinctly negative in tone. But other aspects of the essay suggest that it is misleading to depict Coase as an unqualified defender of an unregulated market. Largely ignored in the intense debate over the accuracy of the Coase Theorem is the fact that Coase himself was adamant that impediments to market transactions are ubiquitous, and that selecting a sensible way of reducing social costs is much harder in real situations than would be true in the absence of such impediments. He was thus right to object, in his 1988 essay: "The world of zero transaction costs has often been described as a Coasian world. Nothing could be further from the truth. It is the world of modern economic theory, one which I was hoping to persuade economists to leave." On balance, it seems proper, as do some later commentators, to differentiate Coase and "the Coasians"—the economists and legal scholars who have followed in his wake, most of whom have indeed been sharply critical of regulatory activities.

And what has become of Coase himself? After the climactic intervention of "The Problem of Social Cost," Coase remained in Chicago, where his stature and influence continued to grow. After a brief period in which he held joint appointments in the Business School and the Law School, he gave up the former. He retired in 1982, but remains intellectually active.

WILLIAM FISHER

BIBLIOGRAPHY

The best source of biographical information about Ronald Coase is the brief essay he himself wrote at the time he was awarded the Nobel Prize. It is available at http://www.nobel.se/economics/laureates/1991/coase-autobio.html. Also helpful are Harold Demsetz's entry on "Ronald Coase" in *The New Palgrave Dictionary of Economics and the Law* (London: Macmillan, 1998): 1:262; and the first chapter of Steven Medema, *Ronald H. Coase* (New York: St. Martin's Press, 1994).

Coase's principal works are: "The Nature of the Firm," *Economica* 4 (1937): 386–405; "The Marginal Cost Controversy," *Economica* 13 (1946): 169–82; "The Federal Communications Commission," *Journal of Law and Economics* 2 (1959): 1–40; "The Problem of Social Cost," *Journal of Law and Economics* 3 (1960): 1–44; and *The Firm, the Market, and the Law* (Chicago: University of Chicago Press, 1988). Most are reprinted, along with several other essays extending or commenting upon Coase's arguments, in Steven Medema, ed., *The Legacy of Ronald Coase in Economic Analysis* (Aldershot, UK: Edward Elgar Publishing, 1995).

A large body of work in institutional economics grew out of "The Nature of the Firm." Among the major essays are Armen A. Alchian and Harold Demsetz, "Production, Information Costs, and Economic Organization," *American Economic Review* 62 (1972): 777–95; and Oliver E. Williamson, "Transaction-Cost Economics: The Governance of Contractual Relations," *Journal of Law and Economics* 22 (1979): 233–61.

Coase's recommendations concerning sensible ways of allocating portions of the electromagnetic spectrum proved highly influential several decades after the publication of his paper on "The Federal Communications Commission." For a description of the impact of Coase's ideas, and for an argument that his underlying conception of the problem to be solved has been superseded by technological advances, see Yochai Benkler, "Overcoming Agoraphobia: Building the Commons of the Digitally Networked Environment," *Harvard Journal of Law and Technology* 11 (1998): 287.

In a lesser known essay, Coase criticized the conventional view that navigational aids, such as lighthouses, are public goods and thus will not be produced in optimal numbers by private parties in the absence of governmental intervention. See "The Lighthouse in Economics," *Journal of Law and Economics* 17 (1974): 357–76. Coase's interpretation of the pertinent history is criticized in David E. Van Zandt, "The Lessons of the Lighthouse: 'Government' or 'Private' Provision of Goods," *Journal of Legal Studies* 22 (1993): 47–72; and Steven Shavell, "The History of Lighthouses as Public Goods" (unpublished paper, February 1996).

The argument by Arthur Pigou with which Coase took issue is set forth in *The Economics of Welfare* (London: Macmillan, 1920), chapter 9.

The first major criticism of the Coase Theorem—that it fails to take into account "strategic behavior"—is developed in Paul Samuelson, "Modern Economic Realities and Indvidualism," *Texas Quarterly* (1963): 128; Donald Regan, "The Problem of Social Cost Revisited," *Journal of Law and Economics* 15 (1972): 427; and Robert Cooter, "The Cost of Coase," *Journal of Legal Studies* 11 (1982): 1.

The leading essay contending that "wealth effects" will prevent some of the bargains that Coase predicted is C. Edwin Baker, "The Ideology of the Economic Analysis of Law," *Journal of Philosophy and Public Affairs* 5 (1975): 3. Stewart Schwab's use of the Civil War draft to illustrate the same point is taken from "Coase Defends Coase: Why Lawyers Listen and Economists Do Not," *Michigan Law Review* 87 (1989): 1171, 1182.

The literature exploring (either theoretically or empirically) reasons unrelated to the wealth effect why "offer" and "asking" prices will diverge is immense. For pioneering essays, see Richard Thaler, "Toward a Positive Theory of Consumer Choice," *Journal of Economic Behavior and Organization* 1 (1980): 39; Mark Kelman, "Consumption Theory, Production Theory, and Ideology in the Coase Theorem," *Southern California Law Review* 52 (1979): 669; Duncan Kennedy, "Cost-Benefit Analysis of Entitlement Problems: A Critique," *Stanford Law Review* 33 (1981): 387; Jack L. Knetsch and J. A. Sinden, "Willingness To Pay and Compensation Demanded: Experimental Evidence of an Unexpected Disparity in Measures of Value," *Quarterly Journal of Economics* 99 (1984): 507; Jack L. Knetsch, "The Endowment Effect and

Evidence of Nonreversible Indifference Curves," *American Economic Review* 79 (1989): 1277; Daniel Kahneman, Jack L. Knetsch, and Richard Thaler, "Experimental Tests of the Endowment Effect and the Coase Theorem," *Journal of Political Economy* 98 (1990): 1325; Jennifer Arlen, Matthew Spitzer, and Eric Talley, "Endowment Effects within Corporate Agency Relationships," *Journal of Legal Studies* 31 (2002): 1. For a thorough survey of the literature growing out of these studies, see Christine Jolls, Cass R. Sunstein, and Richard Thaler, "A Behavioral Approach to Law and Economics," *Stanford Law Review* 50 (1998): 1471. The catalogue set forth in the text of the leading hypotheses concerning the origins of the endowment effect is derived primarily from Russell Korobkin, "The Endowment Effect and Legal Analysis," *Northwestern University Law Review* 97 (2003): 1227. The final hypothesis comes from Kelman, *supra*, at page 691. The essay mentioned in the text by John Donohue is "Diverting the Coasean River: Incentive Schemes to Reduce Unemployment," *Yale Law Journal* 99 (1989): 549. Other efforts to determine whether people behave in a fashion consistent with the Coase Theorem include Harrison and McKee, "Experimental Evaluation of the Coase Theorem," *Journal of Law and Economics* 28 (1965): 653; Vogel, "The Coase Theorem and California Animal Trespass Law," *Journal of Legal Studies* 16 (1987): 149; and Robert Ellickson, "Of Coase and Cattle: Dispute Resolution Among Neighbors in Shasta County," *Stanford Law Review* 38 (1986): 623.

Coase's responses to his critics are set forth in *The Firm, the Market, and the Law, supra*. Efforts to defend Coase on other grounds include Guido Calabresi and Douglas Melamed, "Property Rules, Liability Rules, and Inalienability," *Harvard Law Review* 85 (1972): 1089 (discussed in the next chapter); and Richard Posner, *Economic Analysis of Law* (3d ed., 1986), 42–57.

Essays emphasizing the politically conservative implications of "The Problem of Social Cost" include Kelman, "Consumption Theory," *supra*; and Morton Horwitz, "Law and Economics: Science or Politics," *Hofstra Law Review* 8 (1980): 905, 906. Depictions of Coase as less hostile toward governmental regulation of private economic activity and more of a Pragmatist include Daniel A. Farber, "Parody Lost/Pragmatism Regained: The Ironic History of the Coase Theorem," *Virginia Law Review* 83 (1997): 397; Simon Johnson and Andrei Shleifer, "Coase v. The Coasians," NBER Working Paper 7447 (December 1999); and Pierre Schlag, "An Appreciative Comment on Coase's *The Problem of Social Cost*: A View from the Left," *Wisconsin Law Review* (1986): 919.

RONALD H. COASE

"The Problem of Social Cost"

3 Journal of Law and Economics 1 (1960)

I. The Problem to Be Examined[1]

THIS paper is concerned with those actions of business firms which have harmful effects on others. The standard example is that of a factory the smoke from which has harmful effects on those occupying neighbouring properties. The economic analysis of such a situation has usually proceeded in terms of a divergence between the private and social product of the factory, in which economists have largely followed the treatment of Pigou in *The Economics of Welfare*. The conclusions to which this kind of analysis seems to have led most economists is that it would be desirable to make the owner of the factory liable for the damage caused to those injured by the smoke, or alternatively, to place a tax on the factory owner varying with the amount of smoke produced and equivalent in money terms to the damage it would cause, or finally, to exclude the factory from residential districts (and presumably from other areas in which the emission of smoke would have harmful effects on others). It is my contention that the suggested courses of action are inappropriate, in that they lead to results which are not necessarily, or even usually, desirable.

II. The Reciprocal Nature of the Problem

The traditional approach has tended to obscure the nature of the choice that has to be made. The question is commonly thought of as one in which A inflicts harm on B and what has to be decided is: how should we restrain A? But this is wrong. We are dealing with a problem of a reciprocal nature. To avoid the harm to B would inflict harm on A. The real question that has to be decided is: should A be allowed to harm B or should B be allowed to harm A? The problem is to avoid the more serious harm. I instanced in my previous article[2] the case of a confectioner the noise and vibrations from whose machinery disturbed a doctor in his work. To avoid harming the doctor would inflict harm on the confectioner. The problem posed by this case was essentially whether it was worth while, as a result of restricting the methods of production which could be used by the confectioner, to secure more doctoring at the cost of a reduced supply of confectionery

---

[1] This article, although concerned with a technical problem of economic analysis, arose out of the study of the Political Economy of Broadcasting which I am now conducting. The argument of the present article was implicit in a previous article dealing with the problem of allocating radio and television frequencies (The Federal Communications Commission, 2 J. Law & Econ. [1959]) but comments which I have received seemed to suggest that it would be desirable to deal with the question in a more explicit way and without reference to the original problem for the solution of which the analysis was developed.

[2] Coase, The Federal Communications Commission, 2 J. Law & Econ. 26–27 (1959).

products. Another example is afforded by the problem of straying cattle which destroy crops on neighbouring land. If it is inevitable that some cattle will stray, an increase in the supply of meat can only be obtained at the expense of a decrease in the supply of crops. The nature of the choice is clear: meat or crops. What answer should be given is, of course, not clear unless we know the value of what is obtained as well as the value of what is sacrificed to obtain it. To give another example, Professor George J. Stigler instances the contamination of a stream.[3] If we assume that the harmful effect of the pollution is that it kills the fish, the question to be decided is: is the value of the fish lost greater or less than the value of the product which the contamination of the stream makes possible. It goes almost without saying that this problem has to be looked at in total *and* at the margin.

III. The Pricing System with Liability For Damage

I propose to start my analysis by examining a case in which most economists would presumably agree that the problem would be solved in a completely satisfactory manner: when the damaging business has to pay for all damage caused *and* the pricing system works smoothly (strictly this means that the operation of a pricing system is without cost).

A good example of the problem under discussion is afforded by the case of straying cattle which destroy crops growing on neighbouring land. Let us suppose that a farmer and a cattle-raiser are operating on neighbouring properties. Let us further suppose that, without any fencing between the properties, an increase in the size of the cattle-raiser's herd increases the total damage to the farmer's crops. What happens to the marginal damage as the size of the herd increases is another matter. This depends on whether the cattle tend to follow one another or to roam side by side, on whether they tend to be more or less restless as the size of the herd increases and on other similar factors. For my immediate purpose, it is immaterial what assumption is made about marginal damage as the size of the herd increases.

To simplify the argument, I propose to use an arithmetical example. I shall assume that the annual cost of fencing the farmer's property is $9 and that the price of the crop is $1 per ton. Also, I assume that the relation between the number of cattle in the herd and the annual crop loss is as follows:

Number in Herd (Steers)	Annual Crop Loss (Tons)	Crop Loss per Additional Steer (Tons)
1	1	1
2	3	2
3	6	3
4	10	4

Given that the cattle-raiser is liable for the damage caused, the additional annual cost imposed on the cattle-raiser if he increased his herd from, say, 2 to 3 steers is $3 and in deciding on the size of the herd, he will take this into account along with his other costs. That is, he will not increase the size of the herd unless the value of the additional meat produced (assuming that the cattle-raiser slaughters the cattle), is greater than the additional costs that this will entail, including

[3] G. J. Stigler, The Theory of Price 105 (1952).

Ronald H. Coase

the value of the additional crops destroyed. Of course, if, by the employment of dogs, herdsmen, aeroplanes, mobile radio and other means, the amount of damage can be reduced, these means will be adopted when their cost is less than the value of the crop which they prevent being lost. Given that the annual cost of fencing is $9, the cattle-raiser who wished to have a herd with 4 steers or more would pay for fencing to be erected and maintained, assuming that other means of attaining the same end would not do so more cheaply. When the fence is erected, the marginal cost due to the liability for damage becomes zero, except to the extent that an increase in the size of the herd necessitates a stronger and therefore more expensive fence because more steers are liable to lean against it at the same time. But, of course, it may be cheaper for the cattle-raiser not to fence and to pay for the damaged crops, as in my arithmetical example, with 3 or fewer steers.

It might be thought that the fact that the cattle-raiser would pay for all crops damaged would lead the farmer to increase his planting if a cattle-raiser came to occupy the neighbouring property. But this is not so. If the crop was previously sold in conditions of perfect competition, marginal cost was equal to price for the amount of planting undertaken and any expansion would have reduced the profits of the farmer. In the new situation, the existence of crop damage would mean that the farmer would sell less on the open market but his receipts for a given production would remain the same, since the cattle-raiser would pay the market price for any crop damaged. Of course, if cattle-raising commonly involved the destruction of crops, the coming into existence of a cattle-raising industry might raise the price of the crops involved and farmers would then extend their planting. But I wish to confine my attention to the individual farmer.

I have said that the occupation of a neighbouring property by a cattle-raiser would not cause the amount of production, or perhaps more exactly the amount of planting, by the farmer to increase. In fact, if the cattle-raising has any effect, it will be to decrease the amount of planting. The reason for this is that, for any given tract of land, if the value of the crop damaged is so great that the receipts from the sale of the undamaged crop are less than the total costs of cultivating that tract of land, it will be profitable for the farmer and the cattle-raiser to make a bargain whereby that tract of land is left uncultivated. This can be made clear by means of an arithmetical example. Assume initially that the value of the crop obtained from cultivating a given tract of land is $12 and that the cost incurred in cultivating this tract of land is $10, the net gain from cultivating the land being $2. I assume for purposes of simplicity that the farmer owns the land. Now assume that the cattle-raiser starts operations on the neighbouring property and that the value of the crops damaged is $1. In this case $11 is obtained by the farmer from sale on the market and $1 is obtained from the cattle-raiser for damage suffered and the net gain remains $2. Now suppose that the cattle-raiser finds it profitable to increase the size of his herd, even though the amount of damage rises to $3; which means that the value of the additional meat production is greater than the additional costs, including the additional $2 payment for damage. But the total payment for damage is now $3. The net gain to the farmer from cultivating the land is still $2. The cattle-raiser would be better off if the farmer would agree not to cultivate his land for any payment less than $3. The farmer would be agreeable to not cultivating the land for any payment greater than $2. There is clearly room for a mutually satisfactory bargain which would lead to the abandonment of cultivation.[4] But the same argument applies not only to the whole tract cultivated by the farmer but also to any subdivision of it. Suppose, for example, that the cattle have a well-defined route, say, to a brook or to a shady area. In these circumstances, the amount of damage to the crop along the route may well be great and if so, it could be that the farmer and the cattle-raiser would find it profitable to make a bargain whereby the farmer would agree not to cultivate this strip of land.

But this raises a further possibility. Suppose that there is such a well-defined route. Suppose further that the value of the crop that would be obtained by cultivating this strip of land is $10 but that the cost of cultivation is $11. In the absence of the cattle-raiser, the land would not be cultivated. However, given the presence of the cattle-raiser, it could well be that if the strip was cultivated, the whole crop would be destroyed by the cattle. In which case, the cattle-raiser would be forced to pay $10 to the farmer. It is true that the farmer would lose $1. But the cattle-raiser would lose $10. Clearly this is a situation which is not likely to last indefinitely since neither party would want this to happen. The aim of the farmer would be to induce the cattle-raiser to make a payment in return for an agreement to leave this land uncultivated. The farmer would not be able to obtain a payment greater than the cost of fencing off this piece of land nor so high as to lead the cattle-raiser to abandon the use of the neighbouring property. What payment would in fact be made would depend on the shrewdness of the farmer and the cattle-raiser as bargainers. But as the payment would not be so high as to cause the cattle-raiser to abandon this location and as it would not vary with the size of the herd, such an agreement would not affect the allocation of resources but would merely alter the distribution of income and wealth as between the cattle-raiser and the farmer.

I think it is clear that if the cattle-raiser is liable for damage caused and the pricing system works smoothly, the reduction in the value of production elsewhere will be taken into account in computing the additional cost involved in increasing the size of the herd. This cost will be weighed against the value of the additional meat production and, given perfect competition in the cattle industry, the allocation of resources in cattle-raising will be optimal. What needs to be emphasized is that the fall in the value of production elsewhere which would be taken into account in the costs of the cattle-raiser may well be less than the damage which the cattle would cause to the crops in the ordinary course of events. This is because it is possible, as a result of market transactions, to discontinue cultivation of the land. This is desirable in all cases in which the damage that the cattle would cause, and for which the cattle-raiser would be willing to pay, exceeds the amount which the farmer would pay for use of the land. In conditions of perfect competition, the amount which the farmer would pay for the use of the land is equal to the difference between the value of the total production when the factors are employed on this land and

---

[4] The argument in the text has proceeded on the assumption that the alternative to cultivation of the crop is abandonment of cultivation altogether. But this need not be so. There may be crops which are less liable to damage by cattle but which would not be as profitable as the crop grown in the absence of damage. Thus, if the cultivation of a new crop would yield a return to the farmer of $1 instead of $2, and the size of the herd which would cause $3 damage with the old crop would cause $1 damage with the new crop, it would be profitable to the cattle-raiser to pay any sum less than $2 to induce the farmer to change his crop (since this would reduce damage liability from $3 to $1) and it would be profitable for the farmer to do so if the amount received was more than $1 (the reduction in his return caused by switching crops). In fact, there would be room for a mutually satisfactory bargain in all cases in which a change of crop would reduce the amount of damage by more than it reduces the value of the crop (excluding damage)—in all cases, that is, in which a change in the crop cultivated would lead to an increase in the value of production.

the value of the additional product yielded in their next best use (which would be what the farmer would have to pay for the factors). If damage exceeds the amount the farmer would pay for the use of the land, the value of the additional product of the factors employed elsewhere would exceed the value of the total product in this use after damage is taken into account. It follows that it would be desirable to abandon cultivation of the land and to release the factors employed for production elsewhere. A procedure which merely provided for payment for damage to the crop caused by the cattle but which did not allow for the possibility of cultivation being discontinued would result in too small an employment of factors of production in cattle-raising and too large an employment of factors in cultivation of the crop. But given the possibility of market transactions, a situation in which damage to crops exceeded the rent of the land would not endure. Whether the cattle-raiser pays the farmer to leave the land uncultivated or himself rents the land by paying the land-owner an amount slightly greater than the farmer would pay (if the farmer was himself renting the land), the final result would be the same and would maximise the value of production. Even when the farmer is induced to plant crops which it would not be profitable to cultivate for sale on the market, this will be a purely short-term phenomenon and may be expected to lead to an agreement under which the planting will cease. The cattle-raiser will remain in that location and the marginal cost of meat production will be the same as before, thus having no long-run effect on the allocation of resources.

IV. The Pricing System with No Liability for Damage

I now turn to the case in which, although the pricing system is assumed to work smoothly (that is, costlessly), the damaging business is not liable for any of the damage which it causes. This business does not have to make a payment to those damaged by its actions. I propose to show that the allocation of resources will be the same in this case as it was when the damaging business was liable for damage caused. As I showed in the previous case that the allocation of resources was optimal, it will not be necessary to repeat this part of the argument.

I return to the case of the farmer and the cattle-raiser. The farmer would suffer increased damage to his crop as the size of the herd increased. Suppose that the size of the cattle-raiser's herd is 3 steers (and that this is the size of the herd that would be maintained if crop damage was not taken into account). Then the farmer would be willing to pay up to $3 if the cattle-raiser would reduce his herd to 2 steers, up to $5 if the herd were reduced to 1 steer and would pay up to $6 if cattle-raising was abandoned. The cattle-raiser would therefore receive $3 from the farmer if he kept 2 steers instead of 3. This $3 foregone is therefore part of the cost incurred in keeping the third steer. Whether the $3 is a payment which the cattle-raiser has to make if he adds the third steer to his herd (which it would be if the cattle-raiser was liable to the farmer for damage caused to the crop) or whether it is a sum of money which he would have received if he did not keep a third steer (which it would be if the cattle-raiser was not liable to the farmer for damage caused to the crop) does not affect the final result. In both cases $3 is part of the cost of adding a third steer, to be included along with the other costs. If the increase in the value of production in cattle-raising through increasing the size of the herd from 2 to 3 is greater than the additional costs that have to be incurred (including the $3 damage to crops), the size of the herd will be increased. Otherwise, it will not. The size of the herd will be the same whether the cattle-raiser is liable for damage caused to the crop or not.

It may be argued that the assumed starting point—a herd of 3 steers—was arbitrary. And this is true. But the farmer would not wish to pay to avoid crop damage which the cattle-raiser would not be able to cause. For example, the maximum annual payment which the farmer could be induced to pay could not exceed $9, the annual cost of fencing. And the farmer would only be willing to pay this sum if it did not reduce his earnings to a level that would cause him to abandon cultivation of this particular tract of land. Furthermore, the farmer would only be willing to pay this amount if he believed that, in the absence of any payment by him, the size of the herd maintained by the cattle-raiser would be 4 or more steers. Let us assume that this is the case. Then the farmer would be willing to pay up to $3 if the cattle-raiser would reduce his herd to 3 steers, up to $6 if the herd were reduced to 2 steers, up to $8 if one steer only were kept and up to $9 if cattle-raising were abandoned. It will be noticed that the change in the starting point has not altered the amount which would accrue to the cattle-raiser if he reduced the size of his herd by any given amount. It is still true that the cattle-raiser could receive an additional $3 from the farmer if he agreed to reduce his herd from 3 steers to 2 and that the $3 represents the value of the crop that would be destroyed by adding the third steer to the herd. Although a different belief on the part of the farmer (whether justified or not) about the size of the herd that the cattle-raiser would maintain in the absence of payments from him may affect the total payment he can be induced to pay, it is not true that this different belief would have any effect on the size of the herd that the cattle-raiser will actually keep. This will be the same as it would be if the cattle-raiser had to pay for damage caused by his cattle, since a receipt foregone of a given amount is the equivalent of a payment of the same amount.

It might be thought that it would pay the cattle-raiser to increase his herd above the size that he would wish to maintain once a bargain had been made, in order to induce the farmer to make a larger total payment. And this may be true. It is similar in nature to the action of the farmer (when the cattle-raiser was liable for damage) in cultivating land on which, as a result of an agreement with the cattle-raiser, planting would subsequently be abandoned (including land which would not be cultivated at all in the absence of cattle-raising). But such manoeuvres are preliminaries to an agreement and do not affect the long-run equilibrium position, which is the same whether or not the cattle-raiser is held responsible for the crop damage brought about by his cattle.

It is necessary to know whether the damaging business is liable or not for damage caused since without the establishment of this initial delimitation of rights there can be no market transactions to transfer and recombine them. But the ultimate result (which maximises the value of production) is independent of the legal position if the pricing system is assumed to work without cost.

V. The Problem Illustrated Anew

The harmful effects of the activities of a business can assume a wide variety of forms. An early English case concerned a building which, by obstructing currents of air, hindered the operation of a windmill.[5] A recent case in Florida concerned a

---

[5] See Gale on Easements 237–39 (13th ed. M. Bowles 1959).

building which cast a shadow on the cabana, swimming pool and sunbathing areas of a neighbouring hotel.[6] The problem of straying cattle and the damaging of crops which was the subject of detailed examination in the two preceding sections, although it may have appeared to be rather a special case, is in fact but one example of a problem which arises in many different guises. To clarify the nature of my argument and to demonstrate its general applicability, I propose to illustrate it anew by reference to four actual cases.

Let us first reconsider the case of *Sturges v. Bridgman*[7] which I used as an illustration of the general problem in my article on "The Federal Communications Commission." In this case, a confectioner (in Wigmore Street) used two mortars and pestles in connection with his business (one had been in operation in the same position for more than 60 years and the other for more than 26 years). A doctor then came to occupy neighbouring premises (in Wimpole Street). The confectioner's machinery caused the doctor no harm until, eight years after he had first occupied the premises, he built a consulting room at the end of his garden right against the confectioner's kitchen. It was then found that the noise and vibration caused by the confectioner's machinery made it difficult for the doctor to use his new consulting room. "In particular . . . the noise prevented him from examining his patients by auscultation[8] for diseases of the chest. He also found it impossible to engage with effect in any occupation which required thought and attention." The doctor therefore brought a legal action to force the confectioner to stop using his machinery. The courts had little difficulty in granting the doctor the injunction he sought. "Individual cases of hardship may occur in the strict carrying out of the principle upon which we found our judgment, but the negation of the principle would lead even more to individual hardship, and would at the same time produce a prejudicial effect upon the development of land for residential purposes."

The court's decision established that the doctor had the right to prevent the confectioner from using his machinery. But, of course, it would have been possible to modify the arrangements envisaged in the legal ruling by means of a bargain between the parties. The doctor would have been willing to waive his right and allow the machinery to continue in operation if the confectioner would have paid him a sum of money which was greater than the loss of income which he would suffer from having to move to a more costly or less convenient location or from having to curtail his activities at this location or, as was suggested as a possibility, from having to build a separate wall which would deaden the noise and vibration. The confectioner would have been willing to do this if the amount he would have to pay the doctor was less than the fall in income he would suffer if he had to change his mode of operation at this location, abandon his operation or move his confectionery business to some other location. The solution of the problem depends essentially on whether the continued use of the machinery adds more to the confectioner's income than it subtracts from the doctor's.[9] But now consider the situation if the confectioner had won the case. The confectioner would then have had the right to continue operating his noise and vibration-generating machinery without having to pay anything to the doctor. The boot would have been on the other foot: the doctor would have had to pay the

---

[6] See Fontainebleu Hotel Corp. v. Forty-Five Twenty-Five, Inc., 114 So. 2d 357 (1959).

[7] 11 Ch. D. 852 (1879).

[8] Auscultation is the act of listening by ear or stethoscope in order to judge by sound the condition of the body.

[9] Note that what is taken into account is the change in income after allowing for alterations in methods of production, location, character of product, etc.

confectioner to induce him to stop using the machinery. If the doctor's income would have fallen more through continuance of the use of this machinery than it added to the income of the confectioner, there would clearly be room for a bargain whereby the doctor paid the confectioner to stop using the machinery. That is to say, the circumstances in which it would not pay the confectioner to continue to use the machinery and to compensate the doctor for the losses that this would bring (if the doctor had the right to prevent the confectioner's using his machinery) would be those in which it would be in the interest of the doctor to make a payment to the confectioner which would induce him to discontinue the use of the machinery (if the confectioner had the right to operate the machinery). The basic conditions are exactly the same in this case as they were in the example of the cattle which destroyed crops. With costless market transactions, the decision of the courts concerning liability for damage would be without effect on the allocation of resources. It was of course the view of the judges that they were affecting the working of the economic system—and in a desirable direction. Any other decision would have had "a prejudicial effect upon the development of land for residential purposes," an argument which was elaborated by examining the example of a forge operating on a barren moor, which was later developed for residual purposes. The judges' view that they were settling how the land was to be used would be true only in the case in which the costs of carrying out the necessary market transactions exceeded the gain which might be achieved by any rearrangement of rights. And it would be desirable to preserve the areas (Wimpole Street or the moor) for residential or professional use (by giving non-industrial users the right to stop the noise, vibration, smoke, etc., by injunction) only if the value of the additional residential facilities obtained was greater than the value of cakes or iron lost. But of this the judges seem to have been unaware.

Another example of the same problem is furnished by the case of *Cooke v. Forbes*.[10] One process in the weaving of cocoa-nut fibre matting was to immerse it in bleaching liquids after which it was hung out to dry. Fumes from a manufacturer of sulphate of ammonia had the effect of turning the matting from a bright to a dull and blackish colour. The reason for this was that the bleaching liquid contained chloride of tin, which, when affected by sulphuretted hydrogen, is turned to a darker colour. An injunction was sought to stop the manufacturer from emitting the fumes. The lawyers for the defendant argued that if the plaintiff "were not to use . . . a particular bleaching liquid, their fibre would not be affected; that their process is unusual, not according to the custom of the trade, and even damaging to their own fabrics." The judge commented: " . . . it appears to me quite plain that a person has a right to carry on upon his own property a manufacturing process in which he uses chloride of tin, or any sort of metallic dye, and that his neighbour is not at liberty to pour in gas which will interfere with his manufacture. If it can be traced to the neighbour, then, I apprehend, clearly he will have a right to come here and ask for relief." But in view of the fact that the damage was accidental and occasional, that careful precautions were taken and that there was no exceptional risk, an injunction was refused, leaving the plaintiff to bring an action for damages if he wished. What the subsequent developments were I do not know. But it is clear that the situation is essentially the same as that found in *Sturges v. Bridgman*, except that the cocoa-nut fibre matting manufacturer could not secure an injunction but would have to seek

Ronald H. Coase

[10] L. R. 5 Eq. 166 (1867–1868).

damages from the sulphate of ammonia manufacturer. The economic analysis of the situation is exactly the same as with the cattle which destroyed crops. To avoid the damage, the sulphate of ammonia manufacturer could increase his precautions or move to another location. Either course would presumably increase his costs. Alternatively, he could pay for the damage. This he would do if the payments for damage were less than the additional costs that would have to be incurred to avoid the damage. The payments for damage would then become part of the cost of production of sulphate of ammonia. Of course, if, as was suggested in the legal proceedings, the amount of damage could be eliminated by changing the bleaching agent (which would presumably increase the costs of the matting manufacturer) and if the additional cost was less than the damage that would otherwise occur, it should be possible for the two manufacturers to make a mutually satisfactory bargain whereby the new bleaching agent was used. Had the court decided against the matting manufacturer, as a consequence of which he would have had to suffer the damage without compensation, the allocation of resources would not have been affected. It would pay the matting manufacturer to change his bleaching agent if the additional cost involved was less than the reduction in damage. And since the matting manufacturer would be willing to pay the sulphate of ammonia manufacturer an amount up to his loss of income (the increase in costs or the damage suffered) if he would cease his activities, this loss of income would remain a cost of production for the manufacturer of sulphate of ammonia. This case is indeed analytically exactly the same as the cattle example.

Bryant v. Lefever[11] raised the problem of the smoke nuisance in a novel form. The plaintiff and the defendants were occupiers of adjoining houses, which were of about the same height.

Before 1876 the plaintiff was able to light a fire in any room of his house without the chimneys smoking; the two houses had remained in the same condition some thirty or forty years. In 1876 the defendants took down their house, and began to rebuild it. They carried up a wall by the side of the plaintiff's chimneys much beyond its original height, and stacked timber on the roof of their house, and thereby caused the plaintiff's chimneys to smoke whenever he lighted fires.

The reason, of course, why the chimneys smoked was that the erection of the wall and the stacking of the timber prevented the free circulation of air. In a trial before a jury, the plaintiff was awarded damages of £40. The case then went to the Court of Appeals where the judgment was reversed. Bramwell, L.J., argued:

> ... it is said, and the jury have found, that the defendants have done that which caused a nuisance to the plaintiff's house. We think there is no evidence of this. No doubt there is a nuisance, but it is not of the defendant's causing. They have done nothing in causing the nuisance. Their house and their timber are harmless enough. It is the plaintiff who causes the nuisance by lighting a coal fire in a place the chimney of which is placed so near the defendants' wall, that the smoke does not escape, but comes into the house. Let the plaintiff cease to light his fire, let him move his chimney, let him carry it higher, and there would be no nuisance. Who then, causes it? It would be very clear that the plaintiff did, if he had built his house or chimney after the defendants had put up the timber on theirs, and it is really the same though he did so before the timber was there. But (what is in truth the same answer), if the defendants cause

---

[11] 4 C.P.D. 172 (1878–1879).

the nuisance, they have a right to do so. If the plaintiff has not the right to the passage of air, except subject to the defendants' right to build or put timber on their house, then his right is subject to their right, and though a nuisance follows from the exercise of their right, they are not liable.

And Cotton, L.J., said:

> Here it is found that the erection of the defendants' wall has sensibly and materially interfered with the comfort of human existence in the plaintiff's house, and it is said this is a nuisance for which the defendants are liable. Ordinarily this is so, but the defendants have done so, not by sending on to the plaintiff's property any smoke or noxious vapour, but by interrupting the egress of smoke from the plaintiff's house in a way to which . . . the plaintiff has no legal right. The plaintiff creates the smoke, which interferes with his comfort. Unless he has . . . a right to get rid of this in a particular way which has been interfered with by the defendants, he cannot sue the defendants, because the smoke made by himself, for which he has not provided any effectual means of escape, causes him annoyance. It is as if a man tried to get rid of liquid filth arising on his own land by a drain into his neighbour's land. Until a right had been acquired by user, the neighbour might stop the drain without incurring liability by so doing. No doubt great inconvenience would be caused to the owner of the property on which the liquid filth arises. But the act of his neighbour would be a lawful act, and he would not be liable for the consequences attributable to the fact that the man had accumulated filth without providing any effectual means of getting rid of it.

I do not propose to show that any subsequent modification of the situation, as a result of bargains between the parties (conditioned by the cost of stacking the timber elsewhere, the cost of extending the chimney higher, etc.), would have exactly the same result whatever decision the courts had come to since this point has already been adequately dealt with in the discussion of the cattle example and the two previous cases. What I shall discuss is the argument of the judges in the Court of Appeals that the smoke nuisance was not caused by the man who erected the wall but by the man who lit the fires. The novelty of the situation is that the smoke nuisance was suffered by the man who lit the fires and not by some third person. The question is not a trivial one since it lies at the heart of the problem under discussion. Who caused the smoke nuisance? The answer seems fairly clear. The smoke nuisance was caused both by the man who built the wall *and* by the man who lit the fires. Given the fires, there would have been no smoke nuisance without the wall; given the wall, there would have been no smoke nuisance without the fires. Eliminate the wall *or* the fires and the smoke nuisance would disappear. On the marginal principle it is clear that *both* were responsible and *both* should be forced to include the loss of amenity due to the smoke as a cost in deciding whether to continue the activity which gives rise to the smoke. And given the possibility of market transactions, this is what would in fact happen. Although the wall-builder was not liable legally for the nuisance, as the man with the smoking chimneys would presumably be willing to pay a sum equal to the monetary worth to him of eliminating the smoke, this sum would therefore become for the wall-builder, a cost of continuing to have the high wall with the timber stacked on the roof.

The judges' contention that it was the man who lit the fires who alone caused the smoke nuisance is true only if we assume that the wall is the given factor. This

374

is what the judges did by deciding that the man who erected the higher wall had a legal right to do so. The case would have been even more interesting if the smoke from the chimneys had injured the timber. Then it would have been the wall-builder who suffered the damage. The case would then have closely paralleled *Sturges v. Bridgman* and there can be little doubt that the man who lit the fires would have been liable for the ensuing damage to the timber, in spite of the fact that no damage had occurred until the high wall was built by the man who owned the timber.

Judges have to decide on legal liability but this should not confuse economists about the nature of the economic problem involved. In the case of the cattle and the crops, it is true that there would be no crop damage without the cattle. It is equally true that there would be no crop damage without the crops. The doctor's work would not have been disturbed if the confectioner had not worked his machinery; but the machinery would have disturbed no one if the doctor had not set up his consulting room in that particular place. The matting was blackened by the fumes from the sulphate of ammonia manufacturer; but no damage would have occurred if the matting manufacturer had not chosen to hang out his matting in a particular place and to use a particular bleaching agent. If we are to discuss the problem in terms of causation, both parties cause the damage. If we are to attain an optimum allocation of resources, it is therefore desirable that both parties should take the harmful effect (the nuisance) into account in deciding on their course of action. It is one of the beauties of a smoothly operating pricing system that, as has already been explained, the fall in the value of production due to the harmful effect would be a cost for both parties.

Bass v. Gregory[12] will serve as an excellent final illustration of the problem. The plaintiffs were the owners and tenant of a public house called the Jolly Anglers. The defendant was the owner of some cottages and a yard adjoining the Jolly Anglers. Under the public house was a cellar excavated in the rock. From the cellar, a hole or shaft had been cut into an old well situated in the defendant's yard. The well therefore became the ventilating shaft for the cellar. The cellar "had been used for a particular purpose in the process of brewing, which, without ventilation, could not be carried on." The cause of the action was that the defendant removed a grating from the mouth of the well, "so as to stop or prevent the free passage of air from [the] cellar upwards through the well . . . " What caused the defendant to take this step is not clear from the report of the case. Perhaps "the air . . . impregnated by the brewing operations" which "passed up the well and out into the open air" was offensive to him. At any rate, he preferred to have the well in his yard stopped up. The court had first to determine whether the owners of the public house could have a legal right to a current of air. If they were to have such a right, this case would have to be distinguished from *Bryant v. Lefever* (already considered). This, however, presented no difficulty. In this case, the current of air was confined to "a strictly defined channel." In the case of *Bryant v. Lefever*, what was involved was "the general current of air common to all mankind." The judge therefore held that the owners of the public house could have the right to a current of air whereas the owner of the private house in *Bryant v. Lefever* could not. An economist might be tempted to add "but the air moved all the same." However, all that had been decided at this stage of the argument was that there could be a legal right, not that the owners of the public house

[12] 25 Q.B.D. 481 (1890).

possessed it. But evidence showed that the shaft from the cellar to the well had existed for over forty years and that the use of the well as a ventilating shaft must have been known to the owners of the yard since the air, when it emerged, smelt of the brewing operations. The judge therefore held that the public house had such a right by the "doctrine of lost grant." This doctrine states "that if a legal right is proved to have existed and been exercised for a number of years the law ought to presume that it had a legal origin."[13] So the owner of the cottages and yard had to unstop the well and endure the smell.

The reasoning employed by the courts in determining legal rights will often seem strange to an economist because many of the factors on which the decision turns are, to an economist, irrelevant. Because of this, situations which are, from an economic point of view, identical will be treated quite differently by the courts. The economic problem in all cases of harmful effects is how to maximise the value of production. In the case of *Bass v. Gregory* fresh air was drawn in through the well which facilitated the production of beer but foul air was expelled through the well which made life in the adjoining houses less pleasant. The economic problem was to decide which to choose: a lower cost of beer and worsened amenities in adjoining houses or a higher cost of beer and improved amenities. In deciding this question, the "doctrine of lost grant" is about as relevant as the colour of the judge's eyes. But it has to be remembered that the immediate question faced by the courts is *not* what shall be done by whom *but* who has the legal right to do what. It is always possible to modify by transactions on the market the initial legal delimitation of rights. And, of course, if such market transactions are costless, such a rearrangement of rights will always take place if it would lead to an increase in the value of production.

VI. THE COST OF MARKET TRANSACTIONS TAKEN INTO ACCOUNT

The argument has proceeded up to this point on the assumption (explicit in Sections III and IV and tacit in Section V) that there were no costs involved in carrying out market transactions. This is, of course, a very unrealistic assumption. In order to carry out a market transaction it is necessary to discover who it is that one wishes to deal with, to inform people that one wishes to deal and on what terms, to conduct negotiations leading up to a bargain, to draw up the contract, to undertake the inspection needed to make sure that the terms of the contract are being observed, and so on. These operations are often extremely costly, sufficiently costly at any rate to prevent many transactions that would be carried out in a world in which the pricing system worked without cost.

In earlier sections, when dealing with the problem of the rearrangement of legal rights through the market, it was argued that such a rearrangement would

Ronald H. Coase

---

[13] It may be asked why a lost grant could not also be presumed in the case of the confectioner who had operated one mortar for more than 60 years. The answer is that until the doctor built the consulting room at the end of his garden there was no nuisance. So the nuisance had not continued for many years. It is true that the confectioner in his affidavit referred to "an invalid lady who occupied the house upon one occasion, about thirty years before" who "requested him if possible to discontinue the use of the mortars before eight o'clock in the morning" and that there was some evidence that the garden wall had been subjected to vibration. But the court had little difficulty in disposing of this line of argument: ". . . this vibration, even if it existed at all, was so slight, and the complaint, if it can be called a complaint, of the invalid lady . . . was of so trifling a character, that . . . the Defendant's acts would not have given rise to any proceeding either at law or in equity" (11 Ch.D. 863). That is, the confectioner had not committed a nuisance until the doctor built his consulting room.

be made through the market whenever this would lead to an increase in the value of production. But this assumed costless market transactions. Once the costs of carrying out market transactions are taken into account it is clear that such a rearrangement of rights will only be undertaken when the increase in the value of production consequent upon the rearrangement is greater than the costs which would be involved in bringing it about. When it is less, the granting of an injunction (or the knowledge that it would be granted) or the liability to pay damages may result in an activity being discontinued (or may prevent its being started) which would be undertaken if market transactions were costless. In these conditions the initial delimitation of legal rights does have an effect on the efficiency with which the economic system operates. One arrangement of rights may bring about a greater value of production than any other. But unless this is the arrangement of rights established by the legal system, the costs of reaching the same result by altering and combining rights through the market may be so great that this optimal arrangement of rights, and the greater value of production which it would bring, may never be achieved. The part played by economic considerations in the process of delimiting legal rights will be discussed in the next section. In this section, I will take the initial delimitation of rights and the costs of carrying out market transactions as given.

It is clear that an alternative form of economic organisation which could achieve the same result at less cost than would be incurred by using the market would enable the value of production to be raised. As I explained many years ago, the firm represents such an alternative to organising production through market transactions.[14] Within the firm individual bargains between the various cooperating factors of production are eliminated and for a market transaction is substituted an administrative decision. The rearrangement of production then takes place without the need for bargains between the owners of the factors of production. A landowner who has control of a large tract of land may devote his land to various uses taking into account the effect that the interrelations of the various activities will have on the net return of the land, thus rendering unnecessary bargains between those undertaking the various activities. Owners of a large building or of several adjoining properties in a given area may act in much the same way. In effect, using our earlier terminology, the firm would acquire the legal rights of all the parties and the rearrangement of activities would not follow on a rearrangement of rights by contract, but as a result of an administrative decision as to how the rights should be used.

It does not, of course, follow that the administrative costs of organising a transaction through a firm are inevitably less than the costs of the market transactions which are superseded. But where contracts are peculiarly difficult to draw up and an attempt to describe what the parties have agreed to do or not to do (e.g. the amount and kind of a smell or noise that they may make or will not make) would necessitate a lengthy and highly involved document, and, where, as is probable, a long-term contract would be desirable;[15] it would be hardly surprising if the emergence of a firm or the extension of the activities of an existing firm was not the solution adopted on many occasions to deal with the problem of harmful effects. This solution would be adopted whenever the administrative

---

[14] See Coase, The Nature of the Firm, 4 Economica, New Series, 386 (1937). Reprinted in Readings in Price Theory, 331 (1952).

[15] For reasons explained in my earlier article, see Readings in Price Theory, n. 14 at 337.

costs of the firm were less than the costs of the market transactions that it supersedes and the gains which would result from the rearrangement of activities greater than the firm's costs of organising them. I do not need to examine in great detail the character of this solution since I have explained what is involved in my earlier article.

But the firm is not the only possible answer to this problem. The administrative costs of organising transactions within the firm may also be high, and particularly so when many diverse activities are brought within the control of a single organisation. In the standard case of a smoke nuisance, which may affect a vast number of people engaged in a wide variety of activities, the administrative costs might well be so high as to make any attempt to deal with the problem within the confines of a single firm impossible. An alternative solution is direct Government regulation. Instead of instituting a legal system of rights which can be modified by transactions on the market, the government may impose regulations which state what people must or must not do and which have to be obeyed. Thus, the government (by statute or perhaps more likely through an administrative agency) may, to deal with the problem of smoke nuisance, decree that certain methods of production should or should not be used (e.g. that smoke preventing devices should be installed or that coal or oil should not be burned) or may confine certain types of business to certain districts (zoning regulations).

The government is, in a sense, a super-firm (but of a very special kind) since it is able to influence the use of factors of production by administrative decision. But the ordinary firm is subject to checks in its operations because of the competition of other firms, which might administer the same activities at lower cost and also because there is always the alternative of market transactions as against organisation within the firm if the administrative costs become too great. The government is able, if it wishes, to avoid the market altogether, which a firm can never do. The firm has to make market agreements with the owners of the factors of production that it uses. Just as the government can conscript or seize property, so it can decree that factors of production should only be used in such-and-such a way. Such authoritarian methods save a lot of trouble (for those doing the organising). Furthermore, the government has at its disposal the police and the other law enforcement agencies to make sure that its regulations are carried out.

It is clear that the government has powers which might enable it to get some things done at a lower cost than could a private organisation (or at any rate one without special governmental powers). But the governmental administrative machine is not itself costless. It can, in fact, on occasion be extremely costly. Furthermore, there is no reason to suppose that the restrictive and zoning regulations, made by a fallible administration subject to political pressures and operating without any competitive check, will necessarily always be those which increase the efficiency with which the economic system operates. Furthermore, such general regulations which must apply to a wide variety of cases will be enforced in some cases in which they are clearly inappropriate. From these considerations it follows that direct governmental regulation will not necessarily give better results than leaving the problem to be solved by the market or the firm. But equally there is no reason why, on occasion, such governmental administrative regulation should not lead to an improvement in economic efficiency. This would seem particularly likely when, as is normally the case with the smoke nuisance, a large number of people are involved and in which therefore the costs of handling the problem through the market or the firm may be high.

There is, of course, a further alternative, which is to do nothing about the problem at all. And given that the costs involved in solving the problem by regulations issued by the governmental administrative machine will often be heavy (particularly if the costs are interpreted to include all the consequences which follow from the Government engaging in this kind of activity), it will no doubt be commonly the case that the gain which would come from regulating the actions which give rise to the harmful effects will be less than the costs involved in Government regulation.

The discussion of the problem of harmful effects in this section (when the costs of market transactions are taken into account) is extremely inadequate. But at least it has made clear that the problem is one of choosing the appropriate social arrangement for dealing with the harmful effects. All solutions have costs and there is no reason to suppose that government regulation is called for simply because the problem is not well handled by the market or the firm. Satisfactory views on policy can only come from a patient study of how, in practice, the market, firms and governments handle the problem of harmful effects. Economists need to study the work of the broker in bringing parties together, the effectiveness of restrictive covenants, the problems of the large-scale real-estate development company, the operation of Government zoning and other regulating activities. It is my belief that economists, and policy-makers generally, have tended to over-estimate the advantages which come from governmental regulation. But this belief, even if justified, does not do more than suggest that government regulation should be curtailed. It does not tell us where the boundary line should be drawn. This, it seems to me, has to come from a detailed investigation of the actual results of handling the problem in different ways. But it would be unfortunate if this investigation were undertaken with the aid of a faulty economic analysis. The aim of this article is to indicate what the economic approach to the problem should be.

VII. The Legal Delimitation of Rights and the Economic Problem

The discussion in Section V not only served to illustrate the argument but also afforded a glimpse at the legal approach to the problem of harmful effects. The cases considered were all English but a similar selection of American cases could easily be made and the character of the reasoning would have been the same. Of course, if market transactions were costless, all that matters (questions of equity apart) is that the rights of the various parties should be well-defined and the results of legal actions easy to forecast. But as we have seen, the situation is quite different when market transactions are so costly as to make it difficult to change the arrangement of rights established by the law. In such cases, the courts directly influence economic activity. It would therefore seem desirable that the courts should understand the economic consequences of their decisions and should, insofar as this is possible without creating too much uncertainty about the legal position itself, take these consequences into account when making their decisions. Even when it is possible to change the legal delimitation of rights through market transactions, it is obviously desirable to reduce the need for such transactions and thus reduce the employment of resources in carrying them out.

A thorough examination of the presuppositions of the courts in trying such cases would be of great interest but I have not been able to attempt it.

Nevertheless it is clear from a cursory study that the courts have often recognized the economic implications of their decisions and are aware (as many economists are not) of the reciprocal nature of the problem. Furthermore, from time to time, they take these economic implications into account, along with other factors, in arriving at their decisions. The American writers on this subject refer to the question in a more explicit fashion than do the British. Thus, to quote Prosser on Torts, a person may

> make use of his own property or . . . conduct his own affairs at the expense of some harm to his neighbors. He may operate a factory whose noise and smoke cause some discomfort to others, so long as he keeps within reasonable bounds. It is only when his conduct is unreasonable, *in the light of its utility and the harm which results* [italics added], that it becomes a nuisance. . . . As it was said in an ancient case in regard to candle-making in a town, "Le utility del chose excusera le noisomeness del stink."
>
> The world must have factories, smelters, oil refineries, noisy machinery and blasting, even at the expense of some inconvenience to those in the vicinity and the plaintiff may be required to accept some not unreasonable discomfort for the general good.[16]

The standard British writers do not state as explicitly as this that a comparison between the utility and harm produced is an element in deciding whether a harmful effect should be considered a nuisance. But similar views, if less strongly expressed, are to be found.[17] The doctrine that the harmful effect must be substantial before the court will act is, no doubt, in part a reflection of the fact that there will almost always be some gain to offset the harm. And in the reports of individual cases, it is clear that the judges have had in mind what would be lost as well as what would be gained in deciding whether to grant an injunction or award damages. Thus, in refusing to prevent the destruction of a prospect by a new building, the judge stated:

I know no general rule of common law, which . . . says, that building so as to stop another's prospect is a nuisance. Was that the case, there could be no great towns; and I must grant injunctions to all the new buildings in this town. . . .[18]

In *Webb v. Bird*[19] it was decided that it was not a nuisance to build a schoolhouse so near a windmill as to obstruct currents of air and hinder the working of the mill. An early case seems to have been decided in an opposite direction. Gale commented:

> In old maps of London a row of windmills appears on the heights to the north of London. Probably in the time of King James it was thought an alarming circumstance,

---

[16] See W. L. Prosser, The Law of Torts 398–99, 412 (2d ed. 1955). The quotation about the ancient case concerning candle-making is taken from Sir James Fitzjames Stephen, A General View of the Criminal Law of England 106 (1890). Sir James Stephen gives no reference. He perhaps had in mind *Rex. v. Ronkett*, included in Seavey, Keeton and Thurston, Cases on Torts 604 (1950). A similar view to that expressed by Prosser is to be found in F. V. Harper and F. James, The Law of Torts 67–74 (1956); Restatement, Torts §§826, 827, and 828.

[17] See Winfield on Torts 541–48 (6th ed. T. E. Lewis 1954); Salmond on the Law of Torts 181–90 (12th ed. R.F.V. Heuston 1957); H. Street, The Law of Torts 221–29 (1959).

[18] Attorney General v. Doughty, 2 Ves. Sen. 453, 28 Eng. Rep. 290 (Ch. 1752). Compare in this connection the statement of an American judge, quoted in Prosser, op. cit. supra n. 16 at 413 n. 54: "Without smoke, Pittsburgh would have remained a very pretty village," Musmanno, J., in Versailles Borough v. McKeesport Coal & Coke Co., 1935, 83 Pitts. Leg. J. 379, 385.

[19] 10 C.B. (N.S.) 268, 142 Eng. Rep. 445 (1861); 13 C.B. (N.S.) 841, 143 Eng. Rep. 332 (1863).

as affecting the supply of food to the city, that anyone should build so near them as to take the wind out from their sails.[20]

In one of the cases discussed in section V, *Sturges v. Bridgman*, it seems clear that the judges were thinking of the economic consequences of alternative decisions. To the argument that if the principle that they seemed to be following were carried out to its logical consequences, it would result in the most serious practical inconveniences, for a man might go—say into the midst of the tanneries of *Bermondsey*, or into any other locality devoted to any particular trade or manufacture of a noisy or unsavoury character, and by building a private residence upon a vacant piece of land put a stop to such trade or manufacture altogether, the judges answered that

> whether anything is a nuisance or not is a question to be determined, not merely by an abstract consideration of the thing itself, but in reference to its circumstances; What would be a nuisance in *Belgrave Square* would not necessarily be so in *Bermondsey;* and where a locality is devoted to a particular trade or manufacture carried on by the traders or manufacturers in a particular and established manner not constituting a public nuisance, Judges and juries would be justified in finding, and may be trusted to find, that the trade or manufacture so carried on in that locality is not a private or actionable wrong.[21]

That the character of the neighborhood is relevant in deciding whether something is, or is not, a nuisance, is definitely established.

> He who dislikes the noise of traffic must not set up his abode in the heart of a great city. He who loves peace and quiet must not live in a locality devoted to the business of making boilers or steamships.[22]

What has emerged has been described as "planning and zoning by the judiciary."[23] Of course there are sometimes considerable difficulties in applying the criteria.[24]

An interesting example of the problem is found in *Adams v. Ursell*[25] in which a fried fish shop in a predominantly working-class district was set up near houses of "a much better character." England without fish-and-chips is a contradiction in terms and the case was clearly one of high importance. The judge commented:

> It was urged that an injunction would cause great hardship to the defendant and to the poor people who get food at his shop. The answer to that is that it does not follow that the defendant cannot carry on his business in another more suitable place somewhere in the neighbourhood. It by no means follows that because a fried fish shop is a nuisance in one place it is a nuisance in another.

In fact, the injunction which restrained Mr. Ursell from running his shop did not even extend to the whole street. So he was presumably able to move to other premises near houses of "a much worse character," the inhabitants of which would no doubt consider the availability of fish-and-chips to outweigh the pervading odour and "fog or mist" so graphically described by the plaintiff. Had there been no other "more suitable place in the neighbourhood," the case would

---

[20] See Gale on Easements 238, n. 6 (13th ed. M. Bowles 1959).

[21] 11 Ch.D. 865 (1879).

[22] Salmond on the Law of Torts 182 (12th ed. R.F.V. Heuston 1957).

[23] C. M. Haar, Land-Use Planning, A Casebook on the Use, Misuse, and Re-use of Urban Land 95 (1959).

[24] See, for example, Rushmer v. Polsue and Alfieri, Ltd. [1906] 1 Ch. 234, which deals with the case of a house in a quiet situation in a noisy district.

[25] [1913] 1 Ch. 269.

have been more difficult and the decision might have been different. What would "the poor people" have had for food? No English judge would have said: "Let them eat cake."

The courts do not always refer very clearly to the economic problem posed by the cases brought before them but it seems probable that in the interpretation of words and phrases like "reasonable" or "common or ordinary use" there is some recognition, perhaps largely unconscious and certainly not very explicit, of the economic aspects of the questions at issue. A good example of this would seem to be the judgment in the Court of Appeals in *Andreae v. Selfridge and Company Ltd.*[26] In this case, a hotel (in Wigmore Street) was situated on part of an island site. The remainder of the site was acquired by Selfridges which demolished the existing buildings in order to erect another in their place. The hotel suffered a loss of custom in consequence of the noise and dust caused by the demolition. The owner of the hotel brought an action against Selfridges for damages. In the lower court, the hotel was awarded £4,500 damages. The case was then taken on appeal.

The judge who had found for the hotel proprietor in the lower court said:

> I cannot regard what the defendants did on the site of the first operation as having been commonly done in the ordinary use and occupation of land or houses. It is neither usual nor common, in this country, for people to excavate a site to a depth of 60 feet and then to erect upon that site a steel framework and fasten the steel frames together with rivets. . . . Nor is it, I think, a common or ordinary use of land, in this country, to act as the defendants did when they were dealing with the site of their second operation—namely, to demolish all the houses that they had to demolish, five or six of them I think, if not more, and to use for the purpose of demolishing them pneumatic hammers.

Sir Wilfred Greene, M.R., speaking for the Court of Appeals, first noted

> that when one is dealing with temporary operations, such as demolition and re-building, everybody has to put up with a certain amount of discomfort, because operations of that kind cannot be carried on at all without a certain amount of noise and a certain amount of dust. Therefore, the rule with regard to interference must be read subject to this qualification . . .

He then referred to the previous judgment:

> With great respect to the learned judge, I take the view that he has not approached this matter from the correct angle. It seems to me that it is not possible to say . . . that the type of demolition, excavation and construction in which the defendant company was engaged in the course of these operations was of such an abnormal and unusual nature as to prevent the qualification to which I have referred coming into operation. It seems to me that, when the rule speaks of the common or ordinary use of land, it does not mean that the methods of using land and building on it are in some way to be stabilised for ever. As time goes on new inventions or new methods enable land to be more profitably used, either by digging down into the earth or by mounting up into the skies. Whether, from other points of view, that is a matter which is desirable for humanity is neither here nor there; but it is part of the normal use of land, to make use upon your land, in the matter of construction, of what particular type and what particular depth of foundations and particular

Ronald H. Coase

---

[26] [1938] 1 Ch. 1.

height of building may be reasonable, in the circumstances, and in view of the developments of the day. . . . Guests at hotels are very easily upset. People coming to this hotel, who were accustomed to a quiet outlook at the back, coming back and finding demolition and building going on, may very well have taken the view that the particular merit of this hotel no longer existed. That would be a misfortune for the plaintiff; but assuming that there was nothing wrong in the defendant company's works, assuming the defendant company was carrying on the demolition and its building, productive of noise though it might be, with all reasonable skill, and taking all reasonable precautions not to cause annoyance to its neighbors, then the planitiff might lose all her clients in the hotel because they have lost the amenities of an open and quiet place behind, but she would have no cause of complaint. . . . [But those] who say that their interference with the comfort of their neighbors is justified because their operations are normal and usual and conducted with proper care and skill are under a specific duty . . . to use that reasonable and proper care and skill. It is not a correct attitude to take to say: 'We will go on and do what we like until somebody complains!' . . . Their duty is to take proper precautions and to see that the nuisance is reduced to a minimum. It is no answer for them to say: 'But this would mean that we should have to do the work more slowly than we would like to do it, or it would involve putting us to some extra expense.' All these questions are matters of common sense and degree, and quite clearly it would be unreasonable to expect people to conduct their work so slowly or so expensively, for the purpose of preventing a transient inconvenience, that the cost and trouble would be prohibitive. . . . In this case, the defendant company's attitude seems to have been to go on until somebody complained, and, further, that its desire to hurry its work and conduct it according to its own ideas and its own convenience was to prevail if there was a real conflict between it and the comfort of its neighbors. That . . . is not carrying out the obligation of using reasonable care and skill. . . . The effect comes to this . . . the plaintiff suffered an actionable nuisance; . . . she is entitled, not to a nominal sum, but to a substantial sum, based upon those principles . . . but in arriving at the sum . . . I have discounted any loss of custom . . . which might be due to the general loss of amenities owing to what was going on at the back. . . .

The upshot was that the damages awarded were reduced from £4,500 to £1,000.

The discussion in this section has, up to this point, been concerned with court decisions arising out of the common law relating to nuisance. Delimitation of rights in this area also comes about because of statutory enactments. Most economists would appear to assume that the aim of governmental action in this field is to extend the scope of the law of nuisance by designating as nuisances activities which would not be recognized as such by the common law. And there can be no doubt that some statutes, for example, the Public Health Acts, have had this effect. But not all Government enactments are of this kind. The effect of much of the legislation in this area is to protect businesses from the claims of those they have harmed by their actions. There is a long list of legalized nuisances.

The position has been summarized in *Halsbury's Laws of England* as follows:

Where the legislature directs that a thing shall in all events be done or authorises certain works at a particular place for a specific purposes or grants powers with the intention that they shall be exercised, although leaving some discretion as to the mode of exercise, no action will lie at common law for nuisance or damage which is the inevitable result of carrying out the statutory powers so conferred. This is so whether the act causing the damage is authorised for public purposes or private profit. Acts done under powers granted by persons to whom Parliament has delegated authority to grant such powers, for example, under provisional orders of the Board of Trade, are regarded as having been done under statutory authority. In the absence of negligence it seems that a body exercising statutory powers will not be liable to an action merely because it might, by acting in a different way, have minimised an injury.

Instances are next given of freedom from liability for acts authorized:

An action has been held not to be against a body exercising its statutory powers without negligence in respect of the flooding of land by water escaping from water-courses, from water pipes, from drains, or from a canal; the escape of fumes from sewers; the escape of sewage: the subsidence of a road over a sewer; vibration or noise caused by a railway; fires caused by authorised acts; the pollution of a stream where statutory requirements to use the best known method of purifying before discharging the effluent have been satisfied; interference with a telephone or telegraph system by an electric tramway; the insertion of poles for tramways in the subsoil; annoyance caused by things reasonably necessary for the excavation of authorised works; accidental damage caused by the placing of a grating in a roadway; the escape of tar acid; or interference with the access of a frontager by a street shelter or safety railings on the edge of a pavement.[27]

The legal position in the United States would seem to be essentially the same as in England, except that the power of the legislatures to authorize what would otherwise be nuisances under the common law, at least without giving compensation to the person harmed, is somewhat more limited, as it is subject to constitutional restrictions.[28] Nonetheless, the power is there and cases more or less identical with the English cases can be found. The question has arisen in an acute form in connection with airports and the operation of aeroplanes. The case of *Delta Air Corporation v. Kersey, Kersey v. City of Atlanta*[29] is a good example. Mr. Kersey bought land and built a house on it. Some years later the City of Atlanta constructed an airport on land immediately adjoining that of Mr. Kersey. It was explained that his property was "a quiet, peaceful and proper location for a home before the airport was built, but dust, noises and low flying of airplanes caused by the operation of the airport have rendered his property unsuitable as a home," a state of affairs which was described in the report of the case with a wealth of distressing detail. The judge first referred to an earlier case, *Thrasher v. City of Atlanta*[30] in which it was noted that the City of Atlanta had been expressly authorized to operate an airport.

By this franchise aviation was recognised as a lawful business and also as an enterprise affected with a public interest . . . all persons using [the airport] in the manner contemplated by law are within the protection and immunity of the franchise granted by the municipality. An airport is not a nuisance per se, although it might become such from the manner of its construction or operation.

[27] See 30 Halsbury, Law of England 690–91 (3d ed. 1960), Article on Public Authorities and Public Officers.
[28] See Prosser, op. cit. supra n. 16 at 421; Harper and James, op. cit. supra n. 16 at 86–87.
[29] Supreme Court of Georgia. 193 Ga. 862, 20 S.E. 2d 245 (1942).
[30] 178 Ga. 514, 173 S.E. 817 (1934).

Ronald H. Coase

Since aviation was a lawful business affected with a public interest and the construction of the airport was autorized [sic] by statute, the judge next referred to *Georgia Railroad and Banking Co. v. Maddox*[31] in which it was said:

> Where a railroad terminal yard is located and its construction authorized, under statutory powers, if it be constructed and operated in a proper manner, it cannot be adjudged a nuisance. Accordingly, injuries and inconveniences to persons residing near such a yard, from noises of locomotives, rumbling of cars, vibrations produced thereby, and smoke, cinders, soot and the like, which result from the ordinary and necessary, therefore proper, use and operation of such a yard, are not nuisances, but are the necessary concomitants of the franchise granted.

In view of this, the judge decided that the noise and dust complained of by Mr. Kersey "may be deemed to be incidental to the proper operation of an airport, and as such they cannot be said to constitute a nuisance." But the complaint against low flying was different:

> . . . can it be said that flights . . . at such a low height [25 to 50 feet above Mr. Kersey's house] as to be imminently dangerous to . . . life and health . . . are a necessary concomitant of an airport? We do not think this question can be answered in the affirmative. No reason appears why the city could not obtain lands of an area [sufficiently large] . . . as not to require such low flights . . . For the sake of public convenience adjoining-property owners must suffer such inconvenience from noise and dust as result from the usual and proper operation of an airport, but their private rights are entitled to preference in the eyes of the law where the inconvenience is not one demanded by a properly constructed and operated airport.

Of course this assumed that the City of Atlanta could prevent the low flying and continue to operate the airport. The judge therefore added:

> From all that appears, the conditions causing the low flying may be remedied; but if on the trial it should appear that it is indispensable to the public interest that the airport should continue to be operated in its present condition, it may be said that the petitioner should be denied injunctive relief.

In the course of another aviation case, *Smith v. New England Aircraft Co.*,[32] the court surveyed the law in the United States regarding the legalizing of nuisances and it is apparent that, in the broad, it is very similar to that found in England:

> It is the proper function of the legislative department of government in the exercise of the police power to consider the problems and risks that arise from the use of new inventions and endeavor to adjust private rights and harmonize conflicting interests by comprehensive statutes for the public welfare. . . . There are . . . analogies where the invasion of the airspace over underlying land by noise, smoke, vibration, dust and disagreeable odors, having been authorized by the legislative department of government and not being in effect a condemnation of the property although in some measure depreciating its market value, must be borne by the landowner without compensation or remedy. Legislative sanction makes that lawful which otherwise might be a nuisance. Examples of this are damages to adjacent land arising from smoke, vibration and noise in the operation of a railroad . . . ; the noise of ringing

[31] 116 Ga. 64, 42 S.E. 315 (1902).
[32] 270 Mass. 511, 523, 170 N.E. 385, 390 (1930).

factory bells . . . ; the abatement of nuisances . . . ; the erection of steam engines and furnaces . . . ;unpleasant odors connected with sewers, oil refining and storage of naphtha. . . .

Most economists seem to be unaware of all this. When they are prevented from sleeping at night by the roar of jet planes overhead (publicly authorized and perhaps publicly operated), are unable to think (or rest) in the day because of the noise and vibration from passing trains (publicly authorized and perhaps publicly operated), find it difficult to breathe because of the odour from a local sewage farm (publicly authorized and perhaps publicly operated) and are unable to escape because their driveways are blocked by a road obstruction (without any doubt, publicly devised), their nerves frayed and mental balance disturbed, they proceed to declaim about the disadvantages of private enterprise and the need for Government regulation.

While most economists seem to be under a misapprehension concerning the character of the situation with which they are dealing, it is also the case that the activities which they would like to see stopped or curtailed may well be socially justified. It is all a question of weighing up the gains that would accrue from eliminating these harmful effects against the gains that accrue from allowing them to continue. Of course, it is likely that an extension of Government economic activity will often lead to this protection against action for nuisance being pushed further than is desirable. For one thing, the Government is likely to look with a benevolent eye on enterprises which it is itself promoting. For another, it is possible to describe the committing of a nuisance by public enterprise in a much more pleasant way than when the same thing is done by private enterprise. In the words of Lord Justice Sir Alfred Denning:

> . . . the significance of the social revolution of today is that, whereas in the past the balance was much too heavily in favor of the rights of property and freedom of contract, Parliament has repeatedly intervened so as to give the public good its proper place.[33]

There can be little doubt that the Welfare State is likely to bring an extension of that immunity from liability for damage, which economists have been in the habit of condemning (although they have tended to assume that this immunity was a sign of too little Government intervention in the economic system). For example, in Britain, the powers of local authorities are regarded as being either absolute or conditional. In the first category, the local authority has no discretion in exercising the power conferred on it. "The absolute power may be said to cover all the necessary consequences of its direct operation even if such consequences amount to nuisance." On the other hand, a conditional power may only be exercised in such a way that the consequences do not constitute a nuisance.

> It is the intention of the legislature which determines whether a power is absolute or conditional. . . . [As] there is the possibility that the social policy of the legislature may change from time to time, a power which in one era would be construed as being conditional, might in another era be interpreted as being absolute in order to further the policy of the Welfare State. This point is one which should be borne in mind when considering some of the older cases upon this aspect of the law of nuisance.[34]

[33] See Sir Alfred Denning, Freedom Under the Law 71 (1949).
[34] M. B. Cairns, The Law of Tort in Local Government 28–32 (1954).

Ronald H. Coase

It would seem desirable to summarize the burden of this long section. The problem which we face in dealing with actions which have harmful effects is not simply one of restraining those responsible for them. What has to be decided is whether the gain from preventing the harm is greater than the loss which would be suffered elsewhere as a result of stopping the action which produces the harm. In a world in which there are costs of rearranging the rights established by the legal system, the courts, in cases relating to nuisance, are, in effect, making a decision on the economic problem and determining how resources are to be employed. It was argued that the courts are conscious of this and that they often make, although not always in a very explicit fashion, a comparison between what would be gained and what lost by preventing actions which have harmful effects. But the delimitation of rights is also the result of statutory enactments. Here we also find evidence of an appreciation of the reciprocal nature of the problem. While statutory enactments add to the list of nuisances, action is also taken to legalize what would otherwise be nuisances under the common law. The kind of situation which economists are prone to consider as requiring corrective Government action is, in fact, often the result of Government action. Such action is not necessarily unwise. But there is a real danger that extensive Government intervention in the economic system may lead to the protection of those responsible for harmful effects being carried too far.

VIII. Pigou's Treatment in "The Economics of Welfare"

The fountainhead for the modern economic analysis of the problem discussed in this article is Pigou's *Economics of Welfare* and, in particular, that section of Part II which deals with divergences between social and private net products which come about because one person A, in the course of rendering some service, for which payment is made, to a second person B, incidentally also renders services or disservices to other persons (not producers of like services), of such a sort that payment cannot be exacted from the benefited parties or compensation enforced on behalf of the injured parties.[35]

Pigou tells us that his aim in Part II of *The Economics of Welfare* is

> to ascertain how far the free play of self-interest, acting under the existing legal system, tends to distribute the country's resources in the way most favorable to the production of a large national dividend, and how far it is feasible for State action to improve upon "natural" tendencies.[36]

To judge from the first part of this statement, Pigou's purpose is to discover whether any improvements could be made in the existing arrangements which determine the use of resources. Since Pigou's conclusion is that improvements could be made, one might have expected him to continue by saying that he proposed to set out the changes required to bring them about. Instead, Pigou adds a phrase which contrasts "natural" tendencies with State action, which seems in some sense to equate the present arrangements with "natural" tendencies and to

---

[35] A. C. Pigou, The Economics of Welfare 183 (4th ed. 1932). My references will all be to the fourth edition but the argument and examples examined in this article remained substantially unchanged from the first edition in 1920 to the fourth in 1932. A large part (but not all) of this analysis had appeared previously in Wealth and Welfare (1912).

[36] *Id.* at xii.

imply that what is required to bring about these improvements is State action (if feasible). That this is more or less Pigou's position is evident from Chapter I of Part II.[37] Pigou starts by referring to "optimistic followers of the classical economists"[38] who have argued that the value of production would be maximised if the Government refrained from any interference in the economic system and the economic arrangements were those which came about "naturally." Pigou goes on to say that if self-interest does promote economic welfare, it is because human institutions have been devised to make it so. (This part of Pigou's argument, which he develops with the aid of a quotation from Cannan, seems to me to be essentially correct.) Pigou concludes:

> But even in the most advanced States there are failures and imperfections . . . there are many obstacles that prevent a community's resources from being distributed . . . in the most efficient way. The study of these constitutes our present problem. . . . its purposes is essentially practical. It seeks to bring into clearer light some of the ways in which it now is, or eventually may become, feasible for governments to control the play of economic forces in such wise as to promote the economic welfare, and through that, the total welfare, of their citizens as a whole.[39]

Pigou's underlying thought would appear to be: Some have argued that no State action is needed. But the system has performed as well as it has because of State action. Nonetheless, there are still imperfections. What additional State action is required?

If this is a correct summary of Pigou's position, its inadequacy can be demonstrated by examining the first example he gives of a divergence between private and social products.

> It might happen . . . that costs are thrown upon people not directly concerned, through, say, uncompensated damage done to surrounding woods by sparks from railway engines. All such effects must be included—some of them will be positive, others negative elements—in reckoning up the social net product of the marginal increment of any volume of resources turned into any use or place.[40]

The example used by Pigou refers to a real situation. In Britain, a railway does not normally have to compensate those who suffer damage by fire caused by sparks from an engine. Taken in conjunction with what he says in Chapter 9 of Part II, I take Pigou's policy recommendations to be, first, that there should be State action to correct this "natural" situation and, second, that the railways should be forced to compensate those whose woods are burnt. If this is a correct interpretation of Pigou's position, I would argue that the first recommendation is based on a misapprehension of the facts and that the second is not necessarily desirable.

Let us consider the legal position. Under the heading "Sparks from engines," we find the following in Halsbury's Laws of England:

> If railway undertakers use steam engines on their railway without express statutory authority to do so, they are liable, irrespective of any negligence on their part, for

---

[37] *Id.* at 127–30.

[38] In Wealth and Welfare, Pigou attributes the "optimism" to Adam Smith himself and not to his followers. He there refers to the "highly optimistic theory of Adam Smith that the national dividend, in given circumstances of demand and supply, tends 'naturally' to a maximum" (p. 104).

[39] Pigou, op. cit. supra n. 35 at 129–30.

[40] *Id.* at 134.

fires caused by sparks from engines. Railway undertakers are, however, generally given statutory authority to use steam engines on their railway; accordingly, if an engine is constructed with the precautions which science suggests against fire and is used without negligence, they are not responsible at common law for any damage which may be done by sparks. . . . In the construction of an engine the undertaker is bound to use all the discoveries which science has put within its reach in order to avoid doing harm, provided they are such as it is reasonable to require the company to adopt, having proper regard to the likelihood of the damage and to the cost and convenience of the remedy; but it is not negligence on the part of an undertaker if it refuses to use an apparatus the efficiency of which is open to bona fide doubt.

To this general rule, there is a statutory exception arising from the Railway (Fires) Act, 1905, as amended in 1923. This concerns agricultural land or agricultural crops.

In such a case the fact that the engine was used under statutory powers does not affect the liability of the company in an action for the damage. . . . These provisions, however, only apply where the claim for damage . . . does not exceed £ 200, [£ 100 in the 1905 Act] and where written notice of the occurrence of the fire and the intention to claim has been sent to the company within seven days of the occurrence of the damage and particulars of the damage in writing showing the amount of the claim in money not exceeding £200 have been sent to the company within twenty-one days.

Agricultural land does not include moorland or buildings and agricultural crops do not include those led away or stacked.[41] I have not made a close study of the parliamentary history of this statutory exception, but to judge from debates in the House of Commons in 1922 and 1923, this exception was probably designed to help the smallholder.[42]

Let us return to Pigou's example of uncompensated damage to surrounding woods caused by sparks from railway engines. This is presumably intended to show how it is possible "for State action to improve on 'natural' tendencies." If we treat Pigou's example as referring to the position before 1905, or as being an arbitrary example (in that he might just as well have written "surrounding buildings" instead of "surrounding woods"), then it is clear that the reason why compensation was not paid must have been that the railway had statutory authority to run steam engines (which relieved it of liability for fires caused by sparks). That this was the legal position was established in 1860, in a case, oddly enough, which concerned the burning of surrounding woods by a railway,[43] and the law on this point has not been changed (apart from the one exception) by a century of railway legislation, including nationalisation. If we treat Pigou's example of "uncompensated damage done to surrounding woods by sparks from railway engines" literally, and assume that it refers to the period after 1905, then it is clear that the reason why compensation was not paid must have been that the damage was more than £100 (in the first edition of *The Economics of Welfare*) or more than £200 (in later editions) or that the owner of the wood failed to notify the railway in writing within seven days of the fire or

[41] See 31 Halsbury, Laws of England 474–75 (3d ed. 1960), Article on Railways and Canals, from which this summary of the legal position, and all quotations, are taken.
[42] See 152 H.C. Deb. 2622–63 (1922); 161 H.C. Deb. 2935–55 (1923).
[43] Vaughan v. Taff Vale Railway Co., 3 H. and N. 743 (Ex. 1858) and 5 H. and N. 679 (Ex. 1860).

did not send particulars of the damage, in writing, within twenty-one days. In the real world, Pigou's example could only exist as a result of a deliberate choice of the legislature. It is not, of course, easy to imagine the construction of a railway in a state of nature. The nearest one can get to this is presumably a railway which uses steam engines "without express statutory authority." However, in this case the railway would be obliged to compensate those whose woods it burnt down. That is to say, compensation would be paid in the absence of Government action. The only circumstances in which compensation would not be paid would be those in which there had been Government action. It is strange that Pigou, who clearly thought it desirable that compensation should be paid, should have chosen this particular example to demonstrate how it is possible "for State action to improve on 'natural' tendencies."

Pigou seems to have had a faulty view of the facts of the situation. But it also seems likely that he was mistaken in his economic analysis. It is not necessarily desirable that the railway should be required to compensate those who suffer damage by fires caused by railway engines. I need not show here that, if the railway could make a bargain with everyone having property adjoining the railway line and there were no costs involved in making such bargains, it would not matter whether the railway was liable for damage caused by fires or not. This question has been treated at length in earlier sections. The problem is whether it would be desirable to make the railway liable in conditions in which it is too expensive for such bargains to be made. Pigou clearly thought it was desirable to force the railway to pay compensation and it is easy to see the kind of argument that would have led him to this conclusion. Suppose a railway is considering whether to run an additional train or to increase the speed of an existing train or to install spark-preventing devices on its engines. If the railway were not liable for fire damage, then, when making these decisions, it would not take into account as a cost the increase in damage resulting from the additional train or the faster train or the failure to install spark-preventing devices. This is the source of the divergence between private and social net products. It results in the railway performing acts which will lower the value of total production—and which it would not do if it were liable for the damage. This can be shown by means of an arithmetical example.

Consider a railway, which is *not* liable for damage by fires caused by sparks from its engines, which runs two trains per day on a certain line. Suppose that running one train per day would enable the railway to perform services worth $150 per annum and running two trains a day would enable the railway to perform services worth $250 per annum. Suppose further that the cost of running one train is $50 per annum and two trains $100 per annum. Assuming perfect competition, the cost equals the fall in the value of production elsewhere due to the employment of additional factors of production by the railway. Clearly the railway would find it profitable to run two trains per day. But suppose that running one train per day would destroy by fire crops worth (on an average over the year) $60 and two trains a day would result in the destruction of crops worth $120. In these circumstances running one train per day would raise the value of total production but the running of a second train would reduce the value of total production. The second train would enable additional railway services worth $100 per annum to be performed. But the fall in the value of production elsewhere would be $110 per annum; $50 as a result of the employment of additional factors of production and $60 as a result of the destruction of crops. Since it would be better if the second train were not run and since it would not run if the railway were liable for damage caused to crops, the conclusion that the railway should be made liable for the damage seems irresistable. Undoubtedly it is this kind of reasoning which underlies the Pigovian position.

The conclusion that it would be better if the second train did not run is correct. The conclusion that it is desirable that the railway should be made liable for the damage it causes is wrong. Let us change our assumption concerning the rule of liability. Suppose that the railway is liable for damage from fires caused by sparks from the engine. A farmer on lands adjoining the railway is then in the position that, if his crop is destroyed by fires caused by the railway, he will receive the market price from the railway; but if his crop is not damaged, he will receive the market price by sale. It therefore becomes a matter of indifference to him whether his crop is damaged by fire or not. The position is very different when the railway is *not* liable. Any crop destruction through railway-caused fires would then reduce the receipts of the farmer. He would therefore take out of cultivation any land for which the damage is likely to be greater than the net return of the land (for reasons explained at length in Section III). A change from a regime in which the railway is *not* liable for damage to one in which it *is* liable is likely therefore to lead to an increase in the amount of cultivation on lands adjoining the railway. It will also, of course, lead to an increase in the amount of crop destruction due to railway-caused fires.

Let us return to our arithmetical example. Assume that, with the changed rule of liability, there is a doubling in the amount of crop destruction due to railway-caused fires. With one train per day, crops worth $120 would be destroyed each year and two trains per day would lead to the destruction of crops worth $240. We saw previously that it would not be profitable to run the second train if the railway had to pay $60 per annum as compensation for damage. With damage at $120 per annum the loss from running the second train would be $60 greater. But now let us consider the first train. The value of the transport services furnished by the first train is $150. The cost of running the train is $50. The amount that the railway would have to pay out as compensation for damage is $120. It follows that it would not be profitable to run any trains. With the figures in our example we reach the following result: if the railway is not liable for fire-damage, two trains per day would be run; if the railway is liable for fire-damage, it would cease operations altogether. Does this mean that it is better that there should be no railway? This question can be resolved by considering what would happen to the value of total production if it were decided to exempt the railway from liability for fire-damage, thus bringing it into operation (with two trains per day).

The operation of the railway would enable transport services worth $250 to be performed. It would also mean the employment of factors of production which would reduce the value of production elsewhere by $100. Furthermore it would mean the destruction of crops worth $120. The coming of the railway will also have led to the abandonment of cultivation of some land. Since we know that, had this land been cultivated, the value of the crops destroyed by fire would have been $120, and since it is unlikely that the total crop on this land would have been destroyed, it seems reasonable to suppose that the value of the crop yield on this land would have been higher than this. Assume it would have been $160. But the abandonment of cultivation would have released factors of production for employment elsewhere. All we know is that the amount by which the value of production elsewhere will increase will be less than $160. Suppose that it is $150. Then the gain from operating the railway would be $250 (the value of the transport services) minus $100 (the cost of the factors of production) minus $120 (the value of crops destroyed by fire) minus $160 (the fall in the value of crop production due to the abandonment of cultivation) plus $150 (the value of production elsewhere of the released factors of production). Overall, operating the railway will increase the value of total production by $20. With these figures it is clear that it is better that the railway should not be liable for the damage it causes, thus enabling it to operate profitably. Of course, by altering the figures, it could be shown that there are other cases in which it would be desirable that the railway should be liable for the damage it causes. It is enough for my purpose to show that, from an economic point of view, a situation in which there is "uncompensated damage done to surrounding woods by sparks from railway engines" is not necessarily undesirable. Whether it is desirable or not depends on the particular circumstances.

How is it that the Pigovian analysis seems to give the wrong answer? The reason is that Pigou does not seem to have noticed that his analysis is dealing with an entirely different question. The analysis as such is correct. But it is quite illegitimate for Pigou to draw the particular conclusion he does. The question at issue is not whether it is desirable to run an additional train or a faster train or to install smoke-preventing devices; the question at issue is whether it is desirable to have a system in which the railway has to compensate those who suffer damage from the fires which it causes or one in which the railway does not have to compensate them. When an economist is comparing alternative social arrangements, the proper procedure is to compare the total social product yielded by these different arrangements. The comparison of private and social products is neither here nor there. A simple example will demonstrate this. Imagine a town in which there are traffic lights. A motorist approaches an intersection and stops because the light is red. There are no cars approaching the intersection on the other street. If the motorist ignored the red signal, no accident would occur and the total product would increase because the motorist would arrive earlier at his destination. Why does he not do this? The reason is that if he ignored the light he would be fined. The private product from crossing the street is less than the social product. Should we conclude from this that the total product would be greater if there were no fines for failing to obey traffic signals? The Pigovian analysis shows us that it is possible to conceive of better worlds than the one in which we live. But the problem is to devise practical arrangements which will correct defects in one part of the system without causing more serious harm in other parts.

I have examined in considerable detail one example of a divergence between private and social products and I do not propose to make any further examination of Pigou's analytical system. But the main discussion of the problem considered in this article is to be found in that part of Chapter 9 in Part II which deals with Pigou's second class of divergence and it is of interest to see how Pigou develops his argument. Pigou's own description of this second class of divergence was quoted at the beginning of this section. Pigou distinguishes between the case in which a person renders services for which he receives no payment and the case in which a person renders disservices and compensation is not given to the injured parties. Our main attention has, of course, centred on this second case. It is therefore rather astonishing to find, as was pointed out to me by Professor Francesco Forte, that the problem of the smoking chimney—the "stock instance"[44] or "classroom example"[45] of the second case—is used by Pigou as an example of the first case (services rendered without payment) and is never mentioned, at any rate explicitly, in connection with the second case.[46] Pigou points out that factory owners who devote resources to preventing their chimneys from smoking render services for which they receive no payment. The implication, in the light of Pigou's discussion later in the chapter, is that a factory owner with a smokey chimney should be given a bounty to induce him to install smoke-preventing devices. Most modern economists would suggest that the owner of the factory with the smokey chimney should be taxed. It seems a pity that economists (apart from Professor Forte) do not seem to have noticed this feature of Pigou's treatment since a realisation that the problem could be tackled in either of these two ways would probably have led to an explicit recognition of its reciprocal nature.

In discussing the second case (disservices without compensation to those damaged), Pigou says that they are rendered "when the owner of a site in a residential quarter of a city builds a factory there and so destroys a great part of the amenities of neighbouring sites; or, in a less degree, when he uses his site in such a way as to spoil the lighting of the house opposite; or when he invests resources in erecting buildings in a crowded centre, which by contracting the air-space and the playing room of the neighbourhood, tend to injure the health and efficiency of the families living there."[47] Pigou is, of course, quite right to describe such actions as "uncharged disservices." But he is wrong when he describes these actions as "anti-social."[48] They may or may not be. It is necessary to weigh the harm against the good that will result. Nothing could be more "anti-social" than to oppose any action which causes any harm to anyone.

The example with which Pigou opens his discussion of "uncharged disservices" is not, as I have indicated, the case of the smokey chimney but the case of the over-running rabbits: ". . . incidental uncharged disservices are rendered to third parties when the game-preserving activities of one occupier involve the overrunning of a neighbouring occupier's land by rabbits . . ." This example is of extraordinary interest, not so much because the economic analysis of the case is essentially any different from that of the other examples, but because of the peculiarities of the legal position and the light it throws on the part which economics can play in what is apparently the purely legal question of the delimitation of rights.

The problem of legal liability for the actions of rabbits is part of the general subject of liability for animals.[49] I will, although with reluctance, confine my discussion to rabbits. The early cases relating to rabbits concerned the relations

[44] Sir Dennis Robertson, I Lectures on Economic Principles 162 (1957).

[45] E. J. Mishan, The Meaning of Efficiency in Economics, 189 The Bankers' Magazine 482 (June 1960).

[46] Pigou, op. cit. supra n.35 at 184.

[47] Id. at 185–86.

[48] Id. at 186 n.1. For similar unqualified statements see Pigou's lecture "Some Aspects of the Housing Problem" in B. S. Rowntree and A. C. Pigou, Lectures on Housing, in 18 Manchester Univ. Lectures (1914).

[49] See G. L. Williams, Liability for Animals—An Account of the Development and Present Law of Tortious Liability for Animals, Distress Damage Feasant and the Duty to Fence, in Great Britain, Northern Ireland and the Common Law Dominions (1939). Part Four, "The Action of Nuisance, in Relation to Liability for Animals," 236–62, is especially relevant to our discussion. The problem of liability for rabbits is discussed in this part, 238–47. I do not know how far the common law in the United States regarding liability for animals has diverged from that in Britain. In some Western States of the United States, the English common law regarding the duty to fence has not been followed, in part because "the considerable amount of open, uncleared land made it a matter of public policy to allow cattle to run at large" (Williams, op. cit. supra 227). This affords a good example of how a different set of circumstances may make it economically desirable to change the legal rule regarding the delimitation of rights.

between the lord of the manor and commoners, since, from the thirteenth century on, it became usual for the lord of the manor to stock the commons with conies (rabbits), both for the sake of the meat and the fur. But in 1597, in *Boulston*'s case, an action was brought by one landowner against a neighbouring landowner, alleging that the defendant had made coney-burrows and that the conies had increased and had destroyed the plaintiff's corn. The action failed for the reason that

> . . . so soon as the coneys come on his neighbor's land he may kill them, for they are ferae naturae, and he who makes the coney-boroughs has no property in them, and he shall not be punished for the damage which the coneys do in which he has no property, and which the other may lawfully kill.[50]

As *Boulston*'s case has been treated as binding—Bray, J., in 1919, said that he was not aware that *Boulston*'s case has ever been overruled or questioned[51]— Pigou's rabbit example undoubtedly represented the legal position at the time *The Economics of Welfare* was written.[52] And in this case, it is not far from the truth to say that the state of affairs which Pigou describes came about because of an absence of Government action (at any rate in the form of statutory enactments) and was the result of "natural" tendencies.

Nonetheless, *Boulston*'s case is something of a legal curiousity and Professor Williams makes no secret of his distaste for this decision:

> The conception of liability in nuisance as being based upon ownership is the result, apparently, of a confusion with the action of cattle-trespass, and runs counter both to principle and to the medieval authorities on the escape of water, smoke and filth. . . . The prerequisite of any satisfactory treatment of the subject is the final abandonment of the pernicious doctrine in *Boulston*'s case. . . . Once *Boulston*'s case disappears, the way will be clear for a rational restatement of the whole subject, on lines that will harmonize with the principles prevailing in the rest of the law of nuisance.[53]

The judges in *Boulston*'s case were, of course, aware that their view of the matter depended on distinguishing this case from one involving nuisance:

> This cause is not like to the cases put, on the other side, of erecting a lime-kiln, dye-house, or the like; for there the annoyance is by the act of the parties who make them; but it is not so here, for the conies of themselves went into the plaintiff's land, and he might take them when they came upon his land, and make profit of them.[54]

Professor Williams comments:

> Once more the atavistic idea is emerging that the animals are guilty and not the landowner. It is not, of course, a satisfactory principle to introduce into a modern law of nuisance. If A. erects a house or plants a tree so that the rain runs or drips from it on to B.'s land, this is A.'s act for which he is liable; but if A. introduces rabbits into his land so that they escape from it into B.'s, this is the act of the rabbits for which A. is not liable—such is the specious distinction resulting from *Boulston*'s case.[55]

[50] 5 Coke (Vol. 3) 104 b. 77 Eng. Rep., 216, 217.
[51] See Stearn v. Prentice Bros. Ltd., (1919) 1 K.B., 395, 397.
[52] I have not looked into recent cases. The legal position has also been modified by statutory enactments.
[53] Williams, op. cit. supra n. 49 at 242, 258.
[54] Boulston v. Hardy, Cro. Eliz., 547, 548, 77 Eng. Rep. 216.
[55] Williams, op. cit. supra n. 49 at 243.

It has to be admitted that the decision in *Boulston*'s case seems a little odd. A man may be liable for damage caused by smoke or unpleasant smells, without it being necessary to determine whether he owns the smoke or the smell. And the rule in *Boulston*'s case has not always been followed in cases dealing with other animals. For example, in *Bland v. Yates*,[56] it was decided that an injunction could be granted to prevent someone from keeping an *unusual and excessive* collection of manure in which flies bred and which infested a neighbour's house. The question of who owned the flies was not raised. An economist would not wish to object because legal reasoning sometimes appears a little odd. But there is a sound economic reason for supporting Professor Williams' view that the problem of liability for animals (and particularly rabbits) should be brought within the ordinary law of nuisance. The reason is not that the man who harbours rabbits is solely responsible for the damage; the man whose crops are eaten is equally responsible. And given that the costs of market transactions make a rearrangement of rights impossible, unless we know the particular circumstances, we cannot say whether it is desirable or not to make the man who harbours rabbits responsible for the damage committed by the rabbits on neighbouring properties. The objection to the rule in *Boulston*'s case is that, under it, the harbourer of rabbits can *never* be liable. It fixes the rule of liability at one pole: and this is as undesirable, from an economic point of view, as fixing the rule at the other pole and making the harbourer of rabbits always liable. But, as we saw in Section VII, the law of nuisance, as it is in fact handled by the courts, is flexible and allows for a comparison of the utility of an act with the harm it produces. As Professor Williams says: "The whole law of nuisance is an attempt to reconcile and compromise between conflicting interests. . . ."[57] To bring the problem of rabbits within the ordinary law of nuisance would not mean *inevitably* making the harbourer of rabbits liable for damage committed by the rabbits. This is not to say that the sole task of the courts in such cases is to make a comparison between the harm and the utility of an act. Nor is it to be expected that the courts will always decide correctly after making such a comparison. But unless the courts act very foolishly, the ordinary law of nuisance would seem likely to give economically more satisfactory results than adopting a rigid rule. Pigou's case of the overrunning rabbits affords an excellent example of how problems of law and economics are interrelated, even though the correct policy to follow would seem to be different from that envisioned by Pigou.

Pigou allows one exception to his conclusion that there is a divergence between private and social products in the rabbit example. He adds: ". . . unless . . . the two occupiers stand in the relation of landlord and tenant, so that compensation is given in an adjustment of the rent."[58] This qualification is rather surprising since Pigou's first class of divergence is largely concerned with the difficulties of drawing up satisfactory contracts between landlords and tenants. In fact, all the recent cases on the problem of rabbits cited by Professor Williams involved disputes between landlords and tenants concerning sporting rights.[59] Pigou seems to make a distinction between the case in which no contract is possible (the second class) and that in which the contract is unsatisfactory (the first

[56] 58 Sol. J. 612 (1913–1914).
[57] Williams, op. cit. supra n. 49 at 259.
[58] Pigou, op. cit. supra n. 35 at 185.
[59] Williams, op. cit. supra n. 49 at 244–47.

class). Thus he says that the second class of divergences between private and social net product

> cannot, like divergences due to tenancy laws, be mitigated by a modification of the contractual relation between any two contracting parties, because the divergence arises out of a service or disservice rendered to persons other than the contracting parties.[60]

But the reason why some activities are not the subject of contracts is exactly the same as the reason why some contracts are commonly unsatisfactory—it would cost too much to put the matter right. Indeed, the two cases are really the same since the contracts are unsatisfactory because they do not cover certain activities. The exact bearing of the discussion of the first class of divergence on Pigou's main argument is difficult to discover. He shows that in some circumstances contractual relations between landlord and tenant may result in a divergence between private and social products.[61] But he also goes on to show that Government-enforced compensation schemes and rent-controls will also produce divergences.[62] Furthermore, he shows that, when the Government is in a similar position to a private landlord, e.g. when granting a franchise to a public utility, exactly the same difficulties arise as when private individuals are involved.[63] The discussion is interesting but I have been unable to discover what general conclusions about economic policy, if any, Pigou expects us to draw from it.

Indeed, Pigou's treatment of the problems considered in this article is extremely elusive and the discussion of his views raises almost insuperable difficulties of interpretation. Consequently it is impossible to be sure that one has understood what Pigou really meant. Nevertheless, it is difficult to resist the conclusion, extraordinary though this may be in an economist of Pigou's stature, that the main source of this obscurity is that Pigou had not thought his position through.

IX. The Pigovian Tradition

It is strange that a doctrine as faulty as that developed by Pigou should have been so influential, although part of its success has probably been due to the lack of clarity in the exposition. Not being clear, it was never clearly wrong. Curiously enough, this obscurity in the source has not prevented the emergence of a fairly well-defined oral tradition. What economists think they learn from Pigou, and what they tell their students, which I term the Pigovian tradition, is reasonably clear. I propose to show the inadequacy of this Pigovian tradition by demonstrating that both the analysis and the policy conclusions which it supports are incorrect.

I do not propose to justify my view as to the prevailing opinion by copious references to the literature. I do this partly because the treatment in the literature is usually so fragmentary, often involving little more than a reference to Pigou plus some explanatory comment, that detailed examination would be inappropriate. But the main reason for this lack of reference is that the doctrine, although based on Pigou, must have been largely the product of an oral tradition. Certainly

Ronald H. Coase

---

[60] Pigou, op. cit. supra n. 35 at 192.
[61] Id. 174–75.
[62] Id. 177–83.
[63] Id. 175–77.

economists with whom I have discussed these problems have shown a unanimity of opinion which is quite remarkable considering the meagre treatment accorded this subject in the literature. No doubt there are some economists who do not share the usual view but they must represent a small minority of the profession.

The approach to the problems under discussion is through an examination of the value of physical production. The private product is the value of the additional product resulting from a particular activity of a business. The social product equals the private product minus the fall in the value of production elsewhere for which no compensation is paid by the business. Thus, if 10 units of a factor (and no other factors) are used by a business to make a certain product with a value of $105; and the owner of this factor is not compensated for their use, which he is unable to prevent; and these 10 units of the factor would yield products in their best alternative use worth $100; then, the social product is $105 minus $100 or $5. If the business now pays for one unit of the factor and its price equals the value of its marginal product, then the social product rises to $15. If two units are paid for, the social product rises to $25 and so on until it reaches $105 when all units of the factor are paid for. It is not difficult to see why economists have so readily accepted this rather odd procedure. The analysis focusses on the individual business decision and since the use of certain resources is not allowed for in costs, receipts are reduced by the same amount. But, of course, this means that the value of the social product has no social significance whatsoever. It seems to me preferable to use the opportunity cost concept and to approach these problems by comparing the value of the product yielded by factors in alternative uses or by alternative arrangements. The main advantage of a pricing system is that it leads to the employment of factors in places where the value of the product yielded is greatest and does so at less cost than alternative systems (I leave aside that a pricing system also eases the problem of the redistribution of income). But if through some God-given natural harmony factors flowed to the places where the value of the product yielded was greatest without any use of the pricing system and consequently there was no compensation, I would find it a source of surprise rather than a cause for dismay.

The definition of the social product is queer but this does not mean that the conclusions for policy drawn from the analysis are necessarily wrong. However, there are bound to be dangers in an approach which diverts attention from the basic issues and there can be little doubt that it has been responsible for some of the errors in current doctrine. The belief that it is desirable that the business which causes harmful effects should be forced to compensate those who suffer damage (which was exhaustively discussed in section VIII in connection with Pigou's railway sparks example) is undoubtedly the result of not comparing the total product obtainable with alternative social arrangements.

The same fault is to be found in proposals for solving the problem of harmful effects by the use of taxes or bounties. Pigou lays considerable stress on this solution although he is, as usual, lacking in detail and qualified in his support.[64] Modern economists tend to think exclusively in terms of taxes and in a very precise way. The tax should be equal to the damage done and should therefore vary with the amount of the harmful effect. As it is not proposed that the proceeds of the tax should be paid to those suffering the damage, this solution is not the same as that which would force a business to pay compensation to those damaged by

---

[64] *Id.* 192–4, 381 and Public Finance 94–100 (3d ed. 1947).

its actions, although economists generally do not seem to have noticed this and tend to treat the two solutions as being identical.

Assume that a factory which emits smoke is set up in a district previously free from smoke pollution, causing damage valued at $100 per annum. Assume that the taxation solution is adopted and that the factory owner is taxed $100 per annum as long as the factory emits the smoke. Assume further that a smoke-preventing device costing $90 per annum to run is available. In these circumstances, the smoke-preventing device would be installed. Damage of $100 would have been avoided at an expenditure of $90 and the factory-owner would be better off by $10 per annum. Yet the position achieved may not be optimal. Suppose that those who suffer the damage could avoid it by moving to other locations or by taking various precautions which would cost them, or be equivalent to a loss in income of, $40 per annum. Then there would be a gain in the value of production of $50 if the factory continued to emit its smoke and those now in the district moved elsewhere or made other adjustments to avoid the damage. If the factory owner is to be made to pay a tax equal to the damage caused, it would clearly be desirable to institute a double tax system and to make residents of the district pay an amount equal to the additional cost incurred by the factory owner (or the consumers of his products) in order to avoid the damage. In these conditions, people would not stay in the district or would take other measures to prevent the damage from occurring, when the costs of doing so were less than the costs that would be incurred by the producer to reduce the damage (the producer's object, of course, being not so much to reduce the damage as to reduce the tax payments). A tax system which was confined to a tax on the producer for damage caused would tend to lead to unduly high costs being incurred for the prevention of damage. Of course this could be avoided if it were possible to base the tax, not on the damage caused, but on the fall in the value of production (in its widest sense) resulting from the emission of smoke. But to do so would require a detailed knowledge of individual preferences and I am unable to imagine how the data needed for such a taxation system could be assembled. Indeed, the proposal to solve the smoke-pollution and similar problems by the use of taxes bristles with difficulties: the problem of calculation, the difference between average and marginal damage, the interrelations between the damage suffered on different properties, etc. But it is unnecessary to examine these problems here. It is enough for my purpose to show that, even if the tax is exactly adjusted to equal the damage that would be done to neighboring properties as a result of the emission of each additional puff of smoke, the tax would not necessarily bring about optimal conditions. An increase in the number of people living or of business operating in the vicinity of the smoke-emitting factory will increase the amount of harm produced by a given emission of smoke. The tax that would be imposed would therefore increase with an increase in the number of those in the vicinity. This will tend to lead to a decrease in the value of production of the factors employed by the factory, either because a reduction in production due to the tax will result in factors being used elsewhere in ways which are less valuable, or because factors will be diverted to produce means for reducing the amount of smoke emitted. But people deciding to establish themselves in the vicinity of the factory will not take into account this fall in the value of production which results from their presence. This failure to take into account costs imposed on others is comparable to the action of a factory-owner in not taking into account the harm resulting from his emission of smoke. Without the tax, there may be too much smoke and too few people in the vicinity of the factory; but with the tax there may be too little smoke and too many people in the vicinity of the factory. There is no reason to suppose that one of these results is necessarily preferable.

I need not devote much space to discussing the similar error involved in the suggestion that smoke producing factories should, by means of zoning regulations, be removed from the districts in which the smoke causes harmful effects. When the change in the location of the factory results in a reduction in production, this obviously needs to be taken into account and weighed against the harm which would result from the factory remaining in that location. The aim of such regulation should not be to eliminate smoke pollution but rather to secure the optimum amount of smoke pollution, this being the amount which will maximise the value of production.

X. A CHANGE OF APPROACH

It is my belief that the failure of economists to reach correct conclusions about the treatment of harmful effects cannot be ascribed simply to a few slips in analysis. It stems from basic defects in the current approach to problems of welfare economics. What is needed is a change of approach.

Analysis in terms of divergencies between private and social products concentrates attention on particular deficiencies in the system and tends to nourish the belief that any measure which will remove the deficiency is necessarily desirable. It diverts attention from those other changes in the system which are inevitably associated with the corrective measure, changes which may well produce more harm than the original deficiency. In the preceding sections of this article, we have seen many examples of this. But it is not necessary to approach the problem in this way. Economists who study problems of the firm habitually use an opportunity cost approach and compare the receipts obtained from a given combination of factors with alternative business arrangements. It would seem desirable to use a similar approach when dealing with questions of economic policy and to compare the total product yielded by alternative social arrangements. In this article, the analysis has been confined, as is usual in this part of economics, to comparisons of the value of production, as measured by the market. But it is, of course, desirable that the choice between different social arrangements for the solution of economic problems should be carried out in broader terms than this and that the total effect of these arrangements in all spheres of life should be taken into account. As Frank H. Knight has so often emphasized, problems of welfare economics must ultimately dissolve into a study of aesthetics and morals.

A second feature of the usual treatment of the problems discussed in this article is that the analysis proceeds in terms of a comparison between a state of laissez faire and some kind of ideal world. This approach inevitably leads to a looseness of thought since the nature of the alternatives being compared is never clear. In a state of laissez faire, is there a monetary, a legal or a political system and if so, what are they? In an ideal world, would there be a monetary, a legal or a political system and if so, what would they be? The answers to all these questions are shrouded in mystery and every man is free to draw whatever conclusions he likes. Actually very little analysis is required to show that an ideal world is better than a state of laissez faire, unless the definitions of a state of laissez faire and an ideal world happen to be the same. But the whole discussion is largely irrelevant for questions of economic policy since whatever we may have in mind as our ideal world, it is clear that we have not yet discovered how to get to it from where we are. A better approach would seem to be to start our analysis with a situation approximating that which actually exists, to examine the effects of a proposed policy change and to attempt to decide whether the new situation would be, in total, better or worse than the original one. In this way, conclusions for policy would have some relevance to the actual situation.

A final reason for the failure to develop a theory adequate to handle the problem of harmful effects stems from a faulty concept of a factor of production. This is usually thought of as a physical entity which the business-man acquires and uses (an acre of land, a ton of fertiliser) instead of as a right to perform certain (physical) actions. We may speak of a person owning land and using it as a factor of production but what the land-owner in fact possesses is the right to carry out a circumscribed list of actions. The rights of a land-owner are not unlimited. It is not even always possible for him to remove the land to another place, for instance, by quarrying it. And although it may be possible for him to exclude some people from using "his" land, this may not be true of others. For example, some people may have the right to cross the land.

Furthermore, it may or may not be possible to erect certain types of buildings or to grow certain crops or to use particular drainage systems on the land. This does not come about simply because of Government regulation. It would be equally true under the common law. In fact it would be true under any system of law. A system in which the rights of individuals were unlimited would be one in which there were no rights to acquire.

If factors of production are thought of as rights, it becomes easier to understand that the right to do something which has a harmful effect (such as the creation of smoke, noise, smells, etc.) is also a factor of production. Just as we may use a piece of land in such a way as to prevent someone else from crossing it, or parking his car, or building his house upon it, so we may use it in such a way as to deny him a view or quiet or unpolluted air. The cost of exercising a right (of using a factor of production) is always the loss which is suffered elsewhere in consequence of the exercise of that right—the inability to cross land, to park a car, to build a house, to enjoy a view, to have peace and quiet or to breathe clean air.

It would clearly be desirable if the only actions performed were those in which what was gained was worth more than what was lost. But in choosing between social arrangements within the context of which individual decisions are made, we have to bear in mind that a change in the existing system which will lead to an improvement in some decisions may well lead to a worsening of others. Furthermore we have to take into account the costs involved in operating the various social arrangements (whether it be the working of a market or of a government department), as well as the costs involved in moving to a new system. In devising and choosing between social arrangements we should have regard for the total effect. This, above all, is the change in approach which I am advocating.

Guido Calabresi and Douglas Melamed

Guido Calabresi and Douglas Melamed

AFTER THE PUBLICATION of "The Problem of Social Cost," a rapidly growing group of scholars began to explore potential applications of economics to law. One of the most important of the pioneers was Guido Calabresi. Born in Italy in 1932, Calabresi came to the United States at the age of six, when his family fled Fascism. Diverse intellectual tastes prompted him to obtain a BS in Analytical Economics from Yale (where he studied with James Tobin), a BA in Politics, Philosophy, and Economics from Oxford (where he was a Rhodes Scholar and had as tutors sir John Hicks and Lawrence Klein), and a law degree from Yale (where he graduated first in his class). In 1959, after serving for a year as a law clerk to Supreme Court Justice Hugo Black, Calabresi joined the Yale Law School faculty.

During the 1960s, Calabresi wrote several groundbreaking essays applying economic theory to tort law. Their central theme was that the goal of the legal system should not be eliminate accidents altogether, but rather to create a pattern of incentives that would induce both people who cause accidents and the victims of those accidents to behave in socially optimal ways.

Calabresi spent most of his adult life at Yale, but during the 1969–1970 academic year, he served as a visiting professor at Harvard Law School. Invited by the editors of the *Harvard Law Review* to submit an article for publication, Calabresi, collaborating closely with a promising law student, Douglas Melamed, began work on a manuscript that would both extend the arguments of his papers on accident law and apply them to other doctrinal fields. The end result was one of the most influential essays of twentieth-century legal scholarship. As Carol Rose notes, "*One View of the Cathedral* is now so much a part of the legal canon that it is widely known simply by the joined names of its authors, 'Calabresi and Melamed.'"

Three aspects of the article were eye-opening. First, like Hohfeld, Calabresi and Melamed proposed a novel taxonomy of legal entitlements. The primary doctrinal field they employed to illustrate their proposed schema was the law of nuisance—the set of common-law rules that govern the extent to which landowners are permitted to engage in activities that annoy their neighbors (generating pollution or noise; conducting noxious or frightening enterprises; etc.). Judges and scholars had traditionally assumed that there were only three possible responses to a case in which one landowner asserted a nuisance claim against another: (1) the plaintiff could be granted an injunction; (2) the plaintiff could be denied an injunction but granted damages to compensate her for the injuries she sustained as a result of the defendant's past and future activities; or (3) the plaintiff could be denied both an injunction and damages. Calabresi and Melamed argued that the range of options available to a judge (or other legal decision maker) in such a case could be clarified by differentiating two questions: which party should be granted "the entitlement" (in other words, which party should be "favored"); and what type of "rule" should be employed to "protect" that entitlement. In answering the latter question, the judge could choose among at least three options: a "property rule," under which the favored party could continue to enjoy and exercise the entitlement unless and until the disfavored party persuaded him to surrender it voluntarily (typically, by paying him a sufficient amount of money); a "liability rule," under which the disfavored party could force the favored party to surrender the entitlement by paying him a sum of money determined by the judge or by some other government official; and an "inalienability rule," under which the favored party would be forbidden to transfer the entitlement to the disfavored party (or anyone else).

Analyzing the issue this way made clear that there were at least six possible responses to a nuisance case:

	Assignment of Initial Entitlement	
	Plaintiff	Defendant
Property Rule	Option #1	Option #3
Liability Rule	Option #2	Option #4
Inalienability Rule	Option #5	Option #6

Method of Protecting the Entitlement

The first three options mapped nicely onto the traditional array of possible remedies. Option #1 (giving the plaintiff an entitlement protected by a property rule) meant granting the plaintiff an injunction against the defendant's activity; if the defendant wished to continue engaging in the challenged conduct, he would have to purchase from the plaintiff the right to do so. Option #2 (giving the plaintiff an entitlement protected by a liability rule) meant initially granting the plaintiff a right not to be subjected to the noxious activity, but permitting the defendant to override that entitlement without the plaintiff's consent by paying her a specified sum of money. (In the most traditional variant of this option, exemplified by the case of *Boomer v. Atlantic Cement Company*, the sum of money consisted of "permanent damages.") Option #3 (giving the defendant an entitlement protected by a property rule) meant denying the plaintiff all relief; if the plaintiff wished to stop the noxious activity, she would have to pay the defendant enough money to persuade him to desist.

So far, Calabresi and Melamed seem to have contributed to the traditional understanding of the nuisance problem nothing more than a somewhat counterintuitive vocabulary. The real payoff of their approach consisted of the exposure of Option #4. Hidden by the traditional approach was the possibility that the defendant could be granted an entitlement to engage in the challenged activity, but that the plaintiff could be empowered to force the defendant to desist by paying a specified sum. Calabresi and Melamed acknowledged that the oddity of requiring the plaintiff to "purchase" an injunction, plus the difficulty of determining the price thereof, made it unlikely that judges would choose this option frequently. But, they argued, other government agencies already employed this device routinely, and judges in appropriate circumstances (to be considered shortly) might consider employing it more often.

Options #5 and #6 completed the array. Under the former, the plaintiff would be granted an entitlement not to be subjected to the defendant's annoying activity and forbidden to sell that entitlement no matter how much the defendant offered. Under the latter, the defendant would be empowered to engage in the annoying activity and forbidden to surrender that right no matter how much the plaintiff offered.

Thus far, we, following Calabresi's and Melamed's lead, have been using nuisance law to illustrate their taxonomy. But a crucial claim of the article was that the same schema could be applied to virtually any field of law. As Carol Rose subsequently pointed out, many of their most evocative illustrations were derived from accident law, Calabresi's original specialty. Thus, for example, the negligence standard that governs most unintentional injuries is an example of Option #2. (The law assigns to each pedestrian an entitlement to bodily integrity, but authorizes an automobile driver to override that entitlement by negligently [not deliberately] running the pedestrian over, provided that the driver pays the pedestrian judicially determined damages to compensate him for his injuries.) Other illustrations were derived from contract law, criminal law, and the law of eminent domain.

The second major contribution of the article was a taxonomy of normative considerations that a judge or other lawmaker might rely upon when deciding which of the six options reviewed above would be the best way to resolve a particular dispute or respond to a particular doctrinal problem. In this respect, Calabresi and Melamed were surely not writing on a blank slate; there already existed a substantial literature—in economics, political theory, and philosophy as well as law—that sought to identify considerations of this sort. But the manner in which Calabresi and Melamed mapped the constellation of values was unusual and proved influential.

They divided the set of pertinent considerations into three baskets. The most coherent, and the one that occupied most of their attention, was "economic efficiency." This of course was a familiar ideal. Among legal scholars, Ronald Coase, Richard Posner, Frank Michelman, and Calabresi himself had explicated and applied it in prior essays. Calabresi's and Melamed's particular formulation was relatively conventional:

> Economic efficiency asks that we choose the set of entitlements which would lead to that allocation of resources which could not be improved in the sense that a further change would not so improve the condition of those who gained by it that they could compensate those who lost from it and still be better off than before.

But in one respect, their interpretation of this familiar standard—variously known as the "Kaldor-Hicks criterion" and "potential Pareto superiority"—was unusual: they emphasized that, when determining the magnitude of the benefits and losses caused by a legal change, one need not rely exclusively upon the self-understandings or behavior of the affected individuals; "the state, for paternalistic reasons," might be a better judge of the magnitude of those gains and losses. In other words, in Calabresi's and Melamed's view, the efficiency criterion was not necessarily tied to the principle of consumer sovereignty.

The second basket consisted of "distributional" considerations. At stake here was not the net impact of a legal decision or rule upon aggregate social welfare, but rather who was helped and who was hurt and by how much. Again, Calabresi's and Melamed's formulation of this familiar criterion was unusually encompassing. They urged lawmakers, under this heading, to take into account not only traditional considerations of "distributive justice" (such as whether a particular decision would ameliorate or exacerbate inequality of wealth) but also considerations of "corrective justice" (such as whether a person or group, because of his or its conduct or needs, *deserved* a benefit or detriment).

In Calabresi's and Melamed's judgment, efficiency and distributional values, thus capaciously defined, pretty much exhausted the set of considerations that a lawmaker might want to take into account. But, to ensure that nothing fell through the cracks, they also identified a third, residual basket, which they called "other justice considerations." What might it contain? The authors were hard pressed to offer anything. Their one example was nondistributional religious commitments.

The last of the major contributions of the article was a set of reflections upon how the taxonomy of norms and the taxonomy of values might be put together. This portion of the analysis was meant to be suggestive rather than exhaustive; the authors' aspiration was merely to identify some circumstances in which, measured by some normative standards, some types of rules would seem better than others. Some examples:

If the judge confronted with a two-party nuisance dispute (a) were concerned primarily with the maximization of economic efficiency and (b) knew which of the parties could more cheaply avoid the costs associated with the challenged activity, he or she should simply assign the entitlement to the other party; the choice of property rule or liability rule would be irrelevant. In situations in which the identity of the "least cost avoider" is unclear, but transaction costs are low, and thus the parties can rearrange entitlements easily if the initial allocation is inefficient, property rules make the most sense. By contrast, when transaction costs are high (such as when the existence of multiple affected parties gives rise to "holdout" or "freeloader" problems), and thus voluntary rearrangements are impracticable, liability rules may be superior from the standpoint of economic efficiency.

When one introduces distributional considerations into the equation, things get more complex. For example, in a situation in which high transaction costs point toward liability rules, the choice between Option #2 or Option #4 might properly be determined by which of the parties (or which of the groups whose welfare is tied to that of each of the parties) is the more deserving or, perhaps, the more wealthy.

And what about inalienability rules? When might it make sense to establish patterns of entitlements that cannot be rearranged at all? Perhaps when necessary to prevent directly affected parties from striking deals that neglect "moralisms"— psychic impacts upon third parties. Perhaps when a group wishes to "tie itself to the mast"—i.e., to advance its long-term interests by preventing it from succumbing to "momentary temptations." Or perhaps in situations characterized by "true paternalism"—in which the state knows better than the people affected by a given legal rule what's in their best interest.

Calabresi's and Melamed's purpose, in making such recommendations (and many more of this general sort), was surely not to provide a comprehensive guide to lawmakers confronted in the future with novel problems. Their goal, rather, was to enlarge and organize the array of considerations lawmakers might wish to consider when addressing particular problems and, by highlighting the variety of rules from which they might choose, to increase their ability to achieve and reconcile those objectives.

The brilliance of "One View of the Cathedral" was not immediately obvious to everyone. Indeed, Calabresi later reported, the editors of the *Harvard Law Review* almost refused to publish it, relenting only after he "explain[ed] to them face-to-face what the piece was about." But quite quickly, it began to attract fans, interpreters, and critics.

The credibility of the essay was much enhanced by a nearly simultaneous ruling by the Arizona Supreme Court in an unusual nuisance dispute. At issue in *Spur Industries v. Del E. Webb Development Company* was a demand by the developer of a rapidly expanding retirement community that a preexisting cattle feedlot be shut down because it generated odors and flies that annoyed the community residents. Trying to balance several competing considerations— the seriousness of the harm; the fact that the developer, by building houses in close proximity to the feedlot, had "come to the nuisance"; and the innocence of the community residents—the court granted an injunction against the continued operation of the feedlot, but required the developer to indemnify the feedlot operator "for a reasonable amount of the cost of moving or shutting down." Such a composite ruling, it should be apparent, is an example of Calabresi's and Melamed's Option #4. The court seems to have been unaware of their as yet unpublished article, but its ruling provided strong support for the authors' contention that a purchased injunction might make it possible to reconcile seemingly incompatible "distributional and efficiency goals."

Scholars of various stripes also soon began to take note of the essay. Many found it persuasive and applied its central insights to fields of law other than those addressed in the article itself. In a 1973 essay, for example, Robert Ellickson relied upon Calabresi's and Melamed's taxonomy of entitlements when considering the relative merits of zoning ordinances, the common law of nuisance, servitudes, and fines as ways of resolving disputes among adjacent landowners. And a large group of scholars, led by Richard Posner, invoked "One View of the Cathedral" for the proposition that liability rules were more likely than property rules to lead to economically efficient outcomes in situations in which transaction costs were high—often neglecting, unfortunately, the efforts of Calabresi and Melamed to qualify that judgment.

As one might imagine, many scholars sought to identify ways in which Calabresi's and Melamed's deliberately "simple" framework might be elaborated or improved. The large majority of these essays focused exclusively (to Calabresi's dismay) on the question of which sorts of rules were most economically efficient under particular circumstances.

One of the earliest and most important interventions was made by A. Mitchell Polinsky. In three articles published during the 1970s and in the various editions of his widely read primer, *An Introduction to Economic Analysis of Law*, Polinsky argued (among many other things) that liability rules are not necessarily better than property rules in situations where a combination of high transaction costs and uncertainty concerning the identity of the least cost avoider render the latter potentially inefficient. Why? Because a liability rule requires a judge or some other official to estimate the injury that the party to whom the entitlement is initially assigned will suffer if the initially disfavored party overrides that entitlement without permission. Making such an estimate is costly, and that cost must be taken into account when determining the merits of a liability rule. More seriously, if the estimate is too high or too low, then the disfavored party will "punch and pay" (i.e., override the entitlement and pay damages) either inefficiently seldom or inefficiently often. In short, whether a liability rule is superior from an economic standpoint to a property rule depends in part upon the expense and accuracy of the determination of damages.

Ian Ayres and Eric Talley identified a different potential advantage of liability rules. Central to their argument was the observation that, in some situations, parties can through voluntary transactions rearrange entitlements protected only by liability rules, just as they can rearrange entitlements protected by property rules. Suppose, for example, that, after the ruling just mentioned by the Arizona Supreme Court, the feedlot operator (Spur Industries) concluded that the amount of damages the court (or a lower court on remand) ordered the retirement community builder (Del Webb) to pay was significantly less than the actual harm that Spur would suffer as a result of being forced to cease operations. Spur could try to persuade Del not to exercise its option by offering it a sum of money (less than the difference between the cost to Spur of shutting down and the court-ordered damages). If that sum exceeded the difference between the value to Del of an odor-free environment and the court-ordered damages, then Del should accept the offer (or at least haggle for a larger share of the mutual benefit to the parties of allowing the feedlot to remain in business). Consummation of such a deal would benefit both parties and society at large. Up to this point, Ayres and Talley were on solid ground. Their next step was more controversial: They argued that a liability rule, which forces the parties to bargain over such unusual and complex terms, may be more likely to result in an efficiency-enhancing bargain than a property rule, which assigns to one or the other party a simple entitlement (either an absolute right to clean air or an absolute right to operate a feedlot). Why? Because the liability rule compels the party whose entitlement may be overridden (in this case, Spur) to reveal—by offering (or not offering) to bribe the other party not to exercise its option—the value that the former places upon the endangered entitlement. In short, Ayres and Talley claimed, liability rules are "information forcing"; they are thus more likely than property rules to overcome certain kinds of transactions costs and thus "may" facilitate efficient bargaining.

Louis Kaplow and Steven Shavell disagreed sharply with Ayres' and Talley's argument on this score and offered a different analysis of the relative abilities of property rules and liability rules to maximize social welfare in various circumstances. In their view, the critical distinction was between situations in which the law seeks to regulate the incidence of "harmful externalities" (undesirable impacts upon third parties of presumptively legitimate activities) and situations in which the law seeks to protect "possessory interests" (i.e., to prevent "the unwanted transfer of possession of a physical object to a taker"). In most cases of the first type, such as nuisance disputes and automobile accidents, transaction costs of various types prevent the parties from negotiating with one another. Polinsky, you will recall, had contended that liability rules could work well in such situations, but only if the courts could accurately estimate that magnitude of the injury that the plaintiff had suffered or would suffer as a result of the defendant's conduct. Kaplow and Shavell went further, contending that "there is a strong prima facie case favoring liability rules over property rules for controlling harmful externalities" even when the courts are not able to measure accurately the injuries suffered by individual plaintiffs, so long as the courts can and do "set damages equal to . . . the average harm for cases" of the general type at issue. (To that generalization, there are various exceptions—such as when the victims of externalities may be able to avoid the harm more cheaply than the perpetrators, or when defendants' limited resources render them "judgment proof.") By contrast, when the law seeks to protect possessory interests, Kaplow and Shavell argued, property rules are most often superior. One reason was that, unlike liability rules, they

Calabresi and Melamed

408

prevent endless rounds of "reciprocal takings" (A seizes B's car, paying a judicially determined fee for it; B retakes the car, returning the money; etc.). Another was that, under a liability rule, the owner of an object who considered it more valuable than the judicially determined sum would be obliged, in order to keep it, either (a) to pay a virtually unlimited number of potential takers not to seize it or (b) to resort to socially wasteful self-help measures (locks, secrecy, spring guns, etc.).

In a contemporaneous article, James Krier and Stewart Schwab expressed skepticism concerning one critical portion of Kaplow and Shavell's argument—their suggestion that reliable estimates of the "average harm" associated with a particular type of externality could be obtained at modest cost. In Krier and Schwab's view, determination of the relative merits of a property rule or a liability rule in handling a particular kind of dispute should hinge on the following inquiry:

> [M]arket bargaining [of the sort required by property rules] entails transaction costs[,] and judicial valuation [required by liability rules] entails assessment costs. Each is a species of what we can call *valuation costs*. Since both methods of valuing entitlements, through the market or in the courts, are ordinarily costly, either can be wrong, resulting in *error costs*. Hence the (efficiency) issue in any given case is this: Which kind of rule, property or liability, promises to minimize the sum of valuation and error costs?

Answering that question, unfortunately, will often be very difficult, because many of the same factors (collective action problems, strategic behavior, etc.) that increase in some contexts the various costs associated with bargaining also in those same contexts make judicial valuation more costly. So can we identify any general guidelines that might help lawmakers decide which type of rule is optimal? At least one, Krier and Schwab suggested: The transaction costs associated with property rules may prove more mutable than the valuation costs associated with liability rules. Specifically, judges might find that, if they refuse "to intervene by way of damages when bargainers might balk," then the parties or their successors will be forced to acquire the skills or build the institutions that will enable them to negotiate voluntary deals. In a subsequent essay, Robert Merges relied upon a similar, though more elaborate, argument for the superiority of property rules over liability rules in the context of intellectual-property systems.

Carol Rose's response to this cacophonous debate was to suggest that everyone may be partly right. Each commentator had identified factors highly relevant to controversies of a particular sort; each went wrong in extrapolating his insights to radically dissimilar types of disputes:

> By using examples that implicitly claim too much, liability rule scholars lose an important opportunity to consider that there could be genuine differences among the historic domains of tort, contract, and property. Since Calabresi and Melamed's pioneering work, it is not a great stretch to opine that the dominating issues of tort may be the externalities that accompany [the kind of] transaction costs [that] arise where large numbers of persons or vaguely specified rights impede actors from bargaining with one another directly. Perhaps more unexpectedly, it could be that in the areas of the law usually classed as contract, the dominating issues are to force the information that overcomes the [kind of] transaction costs [that] arise where bargaining parties can locate each other and identify their respective rights, but where their deals may nevertheless falter because of strategic bargaining and "adverse

selection." Finally, it could be that the dominating concerns of what we designate as property law are rather different: to create the conditions that induce people to work hard and to invest in things.

Note the parallelism between Rose's response to the synthetic impulses of Calabresi, Melamed, and their successors and the Legal Realists' response to the synthetic impulse of Classical Legal Thought.

While the battle raged over the relative merits of property rules and liability rules from the standpoint of economic efficiency, a smaller group of scholars began to explore a less prominent dimension of Calabresi's and Melamed's original analysis: their suggestion that, in some circumstances, inalienability rules might be the best way to protect a particular type of entitlement. In a 1985 article, Susan Rose Ackerman argued that inalienability rules came in many shapes and sizes—prohibitions on sales of entitlements, prohibitions on gifts of entitlements, limitations on the set of persons empowered to surrender their entitlements, limitations on the set of persons to whom entitlements could be transferred, etc. Then, relying on the normative taxonomy first outlined by Calabresi and Melamed, she mapped and assessed a wide variety of efficiency and distributive arguments that might be deployed to justify one or another type of restriction. The gist of her argument is as follows:

> The efficiency rationales for inalienability rules are second-best responses to market failures that arise because of externalities, imperfections in information, or difficulties of coordination. The straightforward responses of internalizing the externality through fees or taxes, of subsidizing the provision of information, and of facilitating joint action may, for one reason or another, be costly. In such cases, the alternative of restricting market trades becomes a realistic possibility. . . .
>
> [T]he distributive case for inalienability is more narrowly focused. If policymakers wish to benefit a particular sort of person but cannot easily identify these people ex ante, they may be able to impose restrictions on the entitlement that are less onerous for the worthy group than for others who are nominally eligible. For example, the coercive conditions imposed on the use of land under the Homesteading Acts can be justified as a means of ensuring that the resource was transferred only to worthy recipients—in this case, formerly landless people willing to live on and farm the property for several years.

Finally, Rose-Ackerman explored a variety of circumstances in which prohibitions on transfers of particular entitlements (such as the right to vote or obligations of military service) were essential to the realization of certain conceptions of citizenship.

In a 1987 article, Margaret Jane Radin examined more deeply one type of inalienability rule, under which a designated entitlement may be given away but not sold, which she called "market-inalienability." In Radin's view, neither traditional Liberalism (which regards the rights to life, liberty, and property as inalienable, but sees property rights themselves as fully alienable) nor the methodology of economic analysis (which presumes that entitlements of all sorts should be transferable and views all impediments to compensated exchanges as problematic, in need of special justification) provided satisfactory understandings of or guides to market-inalienability. A better approach, she contended, would begin with a theory of human flourishing, which would encompass rich conceptions of "three main, overlapping aspects of personhood: freedom, identity, and contextuality."

The freedom aspect of personhood focuses on will, or the power to choose for one-self. In order to be autonomous individuals, we must at least be able to act for ourselves through free will in relation to the environment of things and other people. The identity aspect of personhood focuses on the integrity and continuity of the self required for individuation. In order to have a unique individual identity, we must have selves that are integrated and continuous over time. The contextuality aspect of personhood focuses on the necessity of self-constitution in relation to the environment of things and other people. In order to be differentiated human persons, unique individuals, we must have relationships with the social and natural world.

In an ideal world, Radin argued, markets would still exist, but market-inalienability rules would prevent the commodification of all things important to the dimensions of personhood just identified. In our current, nonideal world, such sweeping restrictions on sales of entitlements would have to be tempered somewhat in order to avoid exacerbating inequalities of wealth and power.

It is likely that debate along these and other lines will continue for the foreseeable future. As Calabresi pointed out on the twenty-fifth anniversary of "One View of the Cathedral," the emergence of new legal issues—such as the proliferation of various ways of "splitting" the costs associated with injuries and the troublesome question of the appropriate scope of property rights in bodily parts—will provide fresh occasions to invoke, complicate, and contest the taxonomies that he and Melamed provided us.

In the now thirty-five years since the publication of the article, its authors have continued to flourish. Calabresi went on to an illustrious career as a scholar (writing, for example, a provocative book on the ways in which courts in the modern era should interpret older statutes), as dean of the Yale Law School, and as a judge on the Second Circuit Court of Appeals. Melamed has had an equally prominent career in legal practice, serving in such capacities as Acting Assistant Attorney General in the Antitrust Division of the Justice Department and as co-chair of the Antitrust and Competition Department of the law firm, Wilmer Cutler Pickering Hale and Dorr.

WILLIAM FISHER

BIBLIOGRAPHY

Short biographies of Guido Calabresi can be found on the Web sites of Yale Law School and of some of the institutions where he has been honored: http://www.law.yale.edu/outside/html/faculty/gc3/profile.htm; http://www.virginia.edu/insideuva/2000/11/jefferson.html; http://www.gmu.edu/departments/law/currnews/calabresi.html. Information concerning Douglas Melamed's education and career can be found on the Web site for his law firm: http://www.wilmerhale.com/ doug_melamed.

Calabresi's principal articles during the 1960s on accident law are: "Some Thoughts on Risk Distributions and the Law of Torts," *Yale Law Journal* 70 (1961): 499; "The Decision for Accidents: An Approach to Non-Fault Allocation of Costs," *Harvard Law Review* 78 (1965): 713; "Fault, Accidents, and the Wonderful World of Blum and Kalven," *Yale Law Journal* 75 (1965): 216; and "Transaction Costs, Resource Allocation and Liability Rules," *Journal of Law and*

Economics 11 (1968): 67. (The last, in particular, contains several arguments that appeared in fuller form in "One View of the Cathedral.") The culmination of this line of argument was *The Costs of Accidents: A Legal and Economic Analysis* (New Haven: Yale University Press, 1970).

The three best intellectual histories of "One View of the Cathedral" are James E. Krier and Stewart Schwab, "Property Rules and Liability Rules: The Cathedral in Another Light," *New York University Law Review* 70 (1995): 440; Carol M. Rose, "The Shadow of *The Cathedral*," *Yale Law Journal* 106 (1997): 2175; and Calabresi's own comments looking back on the article twenty-five years after its publication, "The Simple Virtues of The Cathedral," *Yale Law Journal* 106 (1997): 2201.

Robert Ellickson's early explication and invocation of "One View of the Cathedral" can be found in "Alternatives to Zoning: Covenants, Nuisance Rules, and Fines as Land Use Controls," *University of Chicago Law Review* 40 (1973): 681. Richard Posner's invocation of the article to support the claim that liability rules are superior to property rules when transaction costs are high appears in the first edition of *Economic Analysis of Law* (1972), 29, and the accompanying Teacher's Manual. In "The Cathedral in Another Light," cited above, Krier and Schwab document (and criticize) the consensus that emerged during the 1970s and '80s concerning the superiority of liability rules in situations characterized by high transaction costs.

A. Mitchell's Polinsky's argument—and many other refinements of the Calabresi and Melamed thesis—are set forth in "Controlling Externalities and Protecting Entitlements: Property Right, Liability Rule, and Tax-Subsidy Approaches," *Journal of Legal Studies* 8 (1979): 1; "On the Choice Between Property Rules and Liability Rules," *Economic Inquiry* 18 (1980): 233; "Resolving Nuisance Disputes: The Simple Economics of Injunctive and Damage Remedies," *Stanford Law Review* 32 (1980): 1075; and *An Introduction to Law and Economics*, (Boston: Little, Brown, 1983), 11–49.

The primary paper by Ian Ayres and Eric Talley is "Solomonic Bargaining: Dividing a Legal Entitlement to Facilitate Coasean Trade," *Yale Law Journal* 104 (1995): 1027. Their argument was criticized by Louis Kaplow and Steven Shavell in "Do Liability Rules Facilitate Bargaining? A Reply to Ayres and Talley," *Yale Law Journal* 105 (1995): 221. In response, Ayres and Talley modified their position in "Distinguishing Between Consensual and Nonconsensual Advantages of Liability Rules," *Yale Law Journal* 105 (1995): 235. The essay by Kaplow and Shavell setting forth their own analysis of the relative merits in various circumstances of norms of different sorts is "Property Rules Versus Liability Rules: An Economic Analysis," *Harvard Law Review* 109 (1996): 713.

The contributions of James Krier and Stewart Schwab to this debate are set forth in "The Cathedral in Another Light," cited above. Toward the end of that article, Krier and Schwab proposed an addition to the set of six options that Calabresi and Melamed had originally outlined, which they illustrated by suggesting an alternative remedy to the *Spur Industries* case: "First, have the judge estimate as damages the residents' social costs. . . . Next, have the judge enter the following peculiar order: If Spur Industries moves, the residents must pay Spur Industries the residents' damages set by the judge; if Spur Industries stays, it will get nothing." The paper by Robert Merges, building on the argument of Krier and Schwab, is "Contracting into Liability Rules: Intellectual Property Rights and Collective Rights Organizations," *California Law Review* 84 (1996): 1293.

The two cases to which almost all scholars refer when debating the relative merits, from an efficiency standpoint, of liability rules and property rules are *Boomer v. Atlantic Cement Company*, 257 N.E.2d 870 (N.Y. 1970); and *Spur Industries v. Del E. Webb Development Company*, 494 P.2d 700 (Ariz. 1972).

The two major essays exploring inalienability rules are Susan Rose-Ackerman, "Inalienability and the Theory of Property Rights," *Columbia Law Review* 85 (1985): 931; and Margaret Jane Radin, "Market-Inalienability," *Harvard Law Review* 100 (1987): 1849.

Since "One View of the Cathedral," Calabresi has written nearly one hundred articles and three books: *Tragic Choices* (with Philip Bobbit) (New York: Norton, 1978); *A Common Law for the Age of Statutes* (Cambridge, Mass.: Harvard University Press, 1982); and *Ideals, Beliefs, and the Law: Private Law Perspectives on a Public Law Problem* (Syracuse, N.Y.: Syracuse University Press, 1985).

GUIDO CALABRESI[*] AND DOUGLAS MELAMED[**]

"Property Rules, Liability Rules, and Inalienability: One View of the Cathedral"

85 Harvard Law Review 1089 (1972)

I. INTRODUCTION

Only rarely are Property and Torts approached from a unified perspective. Recent writings by lawyers concerned with economics and by economists concerned with law suggest, however, that an attempt at integrating the various legal relationships treated by these subjects would be useful both for the beginning student and the sophisticated scholar.[1] By articulating a concept of "entitlements" which are protected by property, liability, or inalienability rules, we present one framework for such an approach.[2] We then analyze aspects of the pollution problem and of criminal sanctions in order to demonstrate how the model enables us to perceive relationships which have been ignored by writers in those fields.

The first issue which must be faced by any legal system is one we call the problem of "entitlement." Whenever a state is presented with the conflicting interests of two or more people, or two or more groups of people, it must decide which side to favor. Absent such a decision, access to goods, services, and life itself will be decided on the basis of "might makes right"—whoever is stronger or shrewder will win.[3] Hence the fundamental thing that law does is to decide which of the conflicting parties will be entitled to prevail. The entitlement to make noise versus the entitlement to have silence, the entitlement to pollute versus the

[*] John Thomas Smith Professor of Law, Yale University. B.S. Yale, 1953; B.A. Oxford, 1955; LL.B. Yale, 1958; M.A. Oxford, 1959.

[**] Member of the District of Columbia Bar. B.A. Yale University, 1967; J.D. Harvard University, 1970.

[1] *See, e.g.*, Michelman, P*ollution as a Tort: A Non-Accidental Perspective on Calabresi's Costs*, 80 Yale L. J. 647 (1971) (analysis of three alternative rules in pollution problems); Demsetz, *Toward a Theory of Property Rights*, 57 Am. Econ. Rev. 347 (1967) (Vol. 2—Papers and Proceedings) (analysis of property as a means of cost internalization which ignores liability rule alternatives).

[2] Since a fully integrated approach is probably impossible, it should be emphasized that this article concerns only one possible way of looking at and analyzing legal problems. Thus we shall not address ourselves to those fundamental legal questions which center on what institutions and what procedures are most suitable for making what decisions, except insofar as these relate directly to the problems of selecting the initial entitlements and the modes of protecting these entitlements. While we do not underrate the importance, indeed perhaps the primacy, of legal process considerations, *see* pp. 1116–17 *infra*, we are merely interested in the light that a rather different approach may shed on problems frequently looked at primarily from a legal process point of view.

As Professor Harry Wellington is fond of saying about many discussions of law, this article is meant to be only *one* of Monet's paintings of the Cathedral at Rouen. To understand the Cathedral one must see all of them. See G. Hamilton, Claude Monet's Paintings of Rouen Cathedral 4–5, 19–20, 27 (1960).

[3] One could of course look at the state as simply a larger coalition of friends designed to enforce rules which merely accomplish the dominant coalition's desires. Rules of law would then be no more than "might makes right" writ large. Such a view does not strike us as plausible if for no other reason than that the state decides too many issues in response to too many different coalitions. This fact, by itself, would require a different form of analysis from that which would suffice to explain entitlements resulting from more direct and decentralized uses of "might makes right."

entitlement to breathe clean air, the entitlement to have children versus the entitlement to forbid them—these are the first order of legal decisions.

Having made its initial choice, society must enforce that choice. Simply setting the entitlement does not avoid the problem of "might makes right"; a minimum of state intervention is always necessary.[4] Our conventional notions make this easy to comprehend with respect to private property. If Taney owns a cabbage patch and Marshall, who is bigger, wants a cabbage, he will get it unless the state intervenes.[5] But it is not so obvious that the state must also intervene if it chooses the opposite entitlement, communal property. If large Marshall has grown some communal cabbages and chooses to deny them to small Taney, it will take state action to enforce Taney's entitlement to the communal cabbages. The same symmetry applies with respect to bodily integrity. Consider the plight of the unwilling ninety-eight-pound weakling in a state which nominally entitles him to bodily integrity but will not intervene to enforce the entitlement against a lustful Juno. Consider then the plight—absent state intervention—of the ninety-eight-pounder who desires an unwilling Juno in a state which nominally entitles everyone to use everyone else's body. The need for intervention applies in a slightly more complicated way to injuries. When a loss is left where it falls in an auto accident, it is not because God so ordained it. Rather it is because the state has granted the injurer an entitlement to be free of liability and will intervene to prevent the victim's friends, if they are stronger, from taking compensation from the injurer.[6] The loss is shifted in other cases because the state has granted an entitlement to compensation and will intervene to prevent the stronger injurer from rebuffing the victim's requests for compensation.

The state not only has to decide whom to entitle, but it must also simultaneously make a series of equally difficult second order decisions. These decisions go

---

[4] For an excellent presentation of this general point by an economist, see Samuels, *Interrelations Between Legal and Economic Processes*, 14 J. LAW & ECON. 435 (1971).

We do not intend to imply that the state relies on force to enforce all or most entitlements. Nor do we imply that absent state intervention only force would win. The use by the state of feelings of obligation and rules of morality as means of enforcing most entitlements is not only crucial but terribly efficient. Conversely, absent the state, individuals would probably agree on rules of behavior which would govern entitlements in whole series of situations on the basis of criteria other than "might makes right." That these rules might themselves reflect the same types of considerations we will analyze as bases for legal entitlements is, of course, neither here nor there. What is important is that these "social compacts" would, no less than legal entitlements, give rise to what may be called obligations. These obligations in turn would cause people to behave in accordance with the compact in particular cases regardless of the existence of a predominant force. In this article we are not concerned as much with the workings of such obligations as with the reasons which may explain the rules which themselves give rise to the obligations.

[5] "Bigger" obviously does not refer simply to size, but to the sum of an individual's resources. If Marshall's gang possesses superior brain and brawn to that of Taney, Marshall's gang will get the cabbages.

[6] Different cultures deal with the problem in different ways. Witness the following account:

"Life Insurance" Fee is 4 Bulls and $1200. Port Moresby, New Guinea. Peter Howard proved that he values his life more than four bulls and $1200. But he wants $24 and one pig in change.

Mr. Howard gave the money and livestock to members of the Jiga tribe, which had threatened to kill him because he killed a tribe member in an auto accident last October 29.

The police approved the extortion agreement after telling the 38 year old Mr. Howard they could not protect him from the sworn vengeance of the tribe, which lives at Mt. Hagen, about 350 miles Northeast of Port Moresby.

Mr. Howard, of Cambridge, England, was attacked and badly beaten by the tribesmen after the accident.

They said he would be killed unless the payment of money and bulls was made according to the tribal traditions. It was the first time a white man in New Guinea had been forced to bow to tribal laws.

After making the payment, Mr. Howard demanded to be compensated for the assault on him by the tribesmen. He said he wanted $24 and one pig. A Jiga spokesman told him the tribe would "think about it." New York Times, Feb. 16, 1972, at 17, col. 6.

to the manner in which entitlements are protected and to whether an individual is allowed to sell or trade the entitlement. In any given dispute, for example, the state must decide not only which side wins but also the kind of protection to grant. It is with the latter decisions, decisions which shape the subsequent relationship between the winner and the loser, that this article is primarily concerned. We shall consider three types of entitlements—entitlements protected by property rules, entitlements protected by liability rules, and inalienable entitlements. The categories are not, of course, absolutely distinct; but the categorization is useful since it reveals some of the reasons which lead us to protect certain entitlements in certain ways.

An entitlement is protected by a property rule to the extent that someone who wishes to remove the entitlement from its holder must buy it from him in a voluntary transaction in which the value of the entitlement is agreed upon by the seller. It is the form of entitlement which gives rise to the least amount of state intervention: once the original entitlement is decided upon, the state does not try to decide its value.[7] It lets each of the parties say how much the entitlement is worth to him, and gives the seller a veto if the buyer does not offer enough. Property rules involve a collective decision as to who is to be given an initial entitlement but not as to the value of the entitlement.

Whenever someone may destroy the initial entitlement if he is willing to pay an objectively determined value for it, an entitlement is protected by a liability rule. This value may be what it is thought the original holder of the entitlement would have sold it for. But the holder's complaint that he would have demanded more will not avail him once the objectively determined value is set. Obviously, liability rules involve an additional stage of state intervention: not only are entitlements protected, but their transfer or destruction is allowed on the basis of a value determined by some organ of the state rather than by the parties themselves.

An entitlement is inalienable to the extent that its transfer is not permitted between a willing buyer and a willing seller. The state intervenes not only to determine who is initially entitled and to determine the compensation that must be paid if the entitlement is taken or destroyed, but also to forbid its sale under some or all circumstances. Inalienability rules are thus quite different from property and liability rules. Unlike those rules, rules of inalienability not only "protect" the entitlement; they may also be viewed as limiting or regulating the grant of the entitlement itself.

It should be clear that most entitlements to most goods are mixed. Taney's house may be protected by a property rule in situations where Marshall wishes to purchase it, by a liability rule where the government decides to take it by eminent domain, and by a rule of inalienability in situations where Taney is drunk or incompetent. This article will explore two primary questions: (1) In what circumstances should we grant a particular entitlement? and (2) In what circumstances should we decide to protect that entitlement by using a property, liability, or inalienability rule?

---

[7] A property rule requires less state intervention only in the sense that intervention is needed to decide upon and enforce the initial entitlement but not for the separate problem of determining the value of the entitlement. Thus, if a particular property entitlement is especially difficult to enforce—for example, the right to personal security in urban areas—the actual amount of state intervention can be very high and could, perhaps, exceed that needed for some entitlements protected by easily administered liability rules.

What are the reasons for deciding to entitle people to pollute or to entitle people to forbid pollution, to have children freely or to limit procreation, to own property or to share property? They can be grouped under three headings: economic efficiency, distributional preferences, and other justice considerations.[8]

A. *Economic Efficiency*

Perhaps the simplest reason for a particular entitlement is to minimize the administrative costs of enforcement. This was the reason Holmes gave for letting the costs lie where they fall in accidents unless some clear societal benefit is achieved by shifting them.[9] By itself this reason will never justify any result except that of letting the stronger win, for obviously that result minimizes enforcement costs. Nevertheless, administrative efficiency may be relevant to choosing entitlements when other reasons are taken into account. This may occur when the reasons accepted are indifferent between conflicting entitlements and one entitlement is cheaper to enforce than the others. It may also occur when the reasons are not indifferent but lead us only slightly to prefer one over another and the first is considerably more expensive to enforce than the second.

But administrative efficiency is just one aspect of the broader concept of economic efficiency. Economic efficiency asks that we choose the set of entitlements which would lead to that allocation of resources which could not be improved in the sense that a further change would not so improve the condition of those who gained by it that they could compensate those who lost from it and still be better off than before. This is often called Pareto optimality.[10] To give two examples, economic efficiency asks for that combination of entitlements to engage in risky activities and to be free from harm from risky activities which will most likely lead to the lowest sum of accident costs and of costs of avoiding accidents.[11] It asks for that form of property, private or communal, which leads to the highest product for the effort of producing.

---

[8] *See generally* G. CALABRESI, THE COSTS OF ACCIDENTS 24–33 (1970) [hereinafter cited as COSTS].

[9] *See* O.W. HOLMES, JR., THE COMMON LAW 76–77 (Howe ed. 1963). For a criticism of the justification as applied to accidents today, see COSTS 261–63. *But cf.* Posner, *A Theory of Negligence*, 1 J. LEGAL STUD. 29 (1972).

[10] We are not here concerned with the many definitional variations which encircle the concept of Pareto optimality. Many of these variations stem from the fact that unless compensation actually occurs after a change (and this itself assumes a preexisting set of entitlements from which one makes a change to a Pareto optimal arrangement), the redistribution of wealth implicit in the change may well make a return to the prior position also seem Pareto optimal. There are any number of variations on this theme which economists have studied at length. Since in the world in which lawyers must live, anything close to Pareto efficiency, even if desirable, is not attainable, these refinements need not detain us even though they are crucial to a full understanding of the concept.

Most versions of Pareto optimality are based on the premise that individuals know best what is best for them. Hence they assume that to determine whether those who gain from a change could compensate those who lose, one must look to the values the individuals themselves give to the gains and losses. Economic efficiency may, however, present a broader notion which does not depend upon this individualistic premise. It may be that the state, for paternalistic reasons, see pp. 1113–14 *infra*, is better able to determine whether the total gain of the winners is greater than the total loss of the losers.

[11] The word "costs" is here used in a broad way to include all the disutilities resulting from an accident and its avoidance. As such it is not limited to monetary costs, or even to those which could in some sense be "monetizable," but rather includes disutilities or "costs"—for instance, the loss to an individual of his leg—the very expression of which in monetary terms would seem callous. One of the consequences of not being able to put monetary values on some disutilities or "costs" is that the market is of little use in gauging their worth, and this in turn gives rise to one of the reasons why liability, or inalienability rules, rather than property rules may be used.

Recently it has been argued that on certain assumptions, usually termed the absence of transaction costs, Pareto optimality or economic efficiency will occur regardless of the initial entitlement.[12] For this to hold, "no transaction costs" must be understood extremely broadly as involving both perfect knowledge and the absence of any impediments or costs of negotiating. Negotiation costs include, for example, the cost of excluding would-be freeloaders from the fruits of market bargains.[13] In such a frictionless society, transactions would occur until no one could be made better off as a result of further transactions without making someone else worse off. This, we would suggest, is a necessary, indeed a tautological, result of the definitions of Pareto optimality and of transaction costs which we have given.

Such a result would not mean, however, that the same allocation of resources would exist regardless of the initial set of entitlements. Taney's willingness to pay for the right to make noise may depend on how rich he is; Marshall's willingness to pay for silence may depend on his wealth. In a society which entitles Taney to make noise and which forces Marshall to buy silence from Taney, Taney is wealthier and Marshall poorer than each would be in a society which had the converse set of entitlements. Depending on how Marshall's desire for silence and Taney's for noise vary with their wealth, an entitlement to noise will result in negotiations which will lead to a different quantum of noise than would an entitlement to silence.[14] This variation in the quantity of noise and silence can be viewed as no more than an instance of the well accepted proposition that what is a Pareto optimal, or economically efficient, solution varies with the starting distribution of wealth. Pareto optimality is optimal given a distribution of wealth, but different distributions of wealth imply their own Pareto optimal allocation of resources.[15]

All this suggests why distributions of wealth may affect a society's choice of entitlements. It does not suggest why *economic efficiency* should affect the choice, if we assume an absence of any transaction costs. But no one makes an

---

[12] This proposition was first established in Coase's classic article, *The Problem of Social Cost*, 3 J. LAW & ECON. 1 (1960), and has been refined in subsequent literature. *See, e.g.*, Calabresi, *Transaction Costs, Resource Allocation and Liability Rules—A Comment*, 11 J. LAW & ECON. 67 (1968); Nutter, *The Coase Theorem on Social Cost: A Footnote*, 11 J. LAW & ECON. 503 (1968). *See also* G. STIGLER, THE THEORY OF PRICE 113 (3d ed. 1966); Mishan, *Pareto Optimality and the Law*, 19 OXFORD ECON. PAPERS 255 (1967).

[13] The freeloader is the person who refuses to be inoculated against smallpox because, given the fact that almost everyone else is inoculated, the risk of smallpox to him is less than the risk of harm from the inoculation. He is the person who refuses to pay for a common park, though he wants it, because he believes that others will put in enough money to make the park available to him. *See* COSTS 137 n.4. The costs of excluding the freeloader from the benefits for which he refused to pay may well be considerable as the two above examples should suggest. This is especially so since these costs may include the inefficiency of pricing a good, like the park once it exists, above its marginal cost in order to force the freeloader to disclose his true desire to use it—thus enabling us to charge him part of the cost of establishing it initially.

It is the capacity of the market to induce disclosure of individual preferences which makes it theoretically possible for the market to bring about exchanges leading to Pareto optimality. But the freeloader situation is just one of many where no such disclosure is achieved by the market. If we assume perfect knowledge, defined more broadly than is normally done to include knowledge of individual preferences, then such situations pose no problem. This definition of perfect knowledge, though perhaps implicit in the concept of no transaction costs, would not only make reaching Pareto optimality easy through the market, it would make it equally easy to establish a similar result by collective fiat.

For a further discussion of what is implied by a broad definition of no transaction costs, see note 59 *infra*. For a discussion of other devices which may induce individuals to disclose their preferences, see note 38 *infra*.

[14] *See* Mishan, *Pareto Optimality and the Law*, 19 OXFORD ECON. PAPERS 255 (1967). Unless Taney's and Marshall's desires for noise and silence are totally unaffected by their wealth, that is, their desires are totally income inelastic, a change in their wealth will alter the value each places on noise and silence and hence will alter the outcome of their negotiations.

[15] There should be no implication that a Pareto optimal solution is in some sense better than a non-Pareto optimal solution which results in a different wealth distribution. The implication is only that given the *same* wealth distribution Pareto optimal is in some meaningful sense preferable to non-Pareto optimal.

assumption of no transaction costs in practice. Like the physicist's assumption of no friction or Say's law in macro-economics, the assumption of no transaction costs may be a useful starting point, a device which helps us see how, as different elements which may be termed transaction costs become important, the goal of economic efficiency starts to prefer one allocation of entitlements over another.[16]

Since one of us has written at length on how in the presence of various types of transaction costs a society would go about deciding on a set of entitlements in the field of accident law,[17] it is enough to say here: (1) that economic efficiency standing alone would dictate that set of entitlements which favors knowledgeable choices between social benefits and the social costs of obtaining them, and between social costs and the social costs of avoiding them; (2) that this implies, in the absence of certainty as to whether a benefit is worth its costs to society, that the cost should be put on the party or activity best located to make such a cost-benefit analysis; (3) that in particular contexts like accidents or pollution this suggests putting costs on the party or activity which can most cheaply avoid them; (4) that in the absence of certainty as to who that party or activity is, the costs should be put on the party or activity which can with the lowest transaction costs act in the market to correct an error in entitlements by inducing the party who can avoid social costs most cheaply to do so;[18] and (5) that since we are in an area where by hypothesis markets do not work perfectly—there are transaction costs—a decision will often have to be made on whether market transactions or collective fiat is most likely to bring us closer to the Pareto optimal result the "perfect" market would reach.[19]

[16] See Demsetz, When Does the Rule of Liability Matter?, 1 J. LEGAL STUD. 13, 25–28 (1972); Stigler, The Law and Economics of Public Policy: A Plea to the Scholars, 1 J. LEGAL STUD. 1, 11–12 (1972).

The trouble with a term like "no transaction costs" is that it covers a multitude of market failures. The appropriate collective response, if the aim is to approach Pareto optimality, will vary depending on what the actual impediments to full bargaining are in any given cases. Occasionally the appropriate response may be to ignore the impediments. If the impediments are merely the administrative costs of establishing a market, it may be that doing nothing is preferable to attempting to correct for these costs because the administrative costs of collective action may be even greater. Similarly, if the impediments are due to a failure of the market to cause an accurate disclosure of freeloaders' preferences it may be that the collective can do no better.

[17] See COSTS 135–97.

[18] In The Costs of Accidents, the criteria here summarized are discussed at length and broken down into subcriteria which deal with the avoidance of different types of externalization and with the finding of the "best briber." Such detailed analysis is necessary to the application of the criteria to any specific area of law. At the level of generality of this article it did not seem to us necessary.

[19] In accident law this election takes the form of a choice between general or market deterrence and specific deterrence, in which the permitted level and manner of accident causing activities is determined collectively. For example, society may decide to grant an entitlement to drive and an entitlement to be compensated for accidents resulting from driving, and allow decisions by individual parties to determine the level and manner of driving. But a greater degree of specific deterrence could be achieved by selecting a different set of initial entitlements in order to accord with a collective cost-benefit analysis—by, for example, prohibiting cars of more than a certain horsepower.

The primary disadvantage of specific deterrence, as compared with general deterrence, is that it requires the central decisionmaker not only to determine the costs of any given activity, but also to measure its benefits, in order to determine the optimum level of activity. It is exceedingly difficult and exceedingly costly for any centralized decisionmaker to be fully informed of the costs and benefits of a wide range of activities. The irony is that collective fiat functions best in a world of costless perfect information; yet in a world of costless transactions, including costless information, the optimum allocation would be reached by market transactions, and the need to consider the alternative of collective fiat would not arise. One could, however, view the irony conversely, and say that the market works best under assumptions of perfect knowledge where collective fiat would work perfectly, rendering the market unnecessary. The fact that both market and collective determinations face difficulties in achieving the Pareto optimal result which perfect knowledge and no transaction costs would permit does not mean that the same difficulties are always as great for the two approaches. Thus, there are many situations in which we can assume fairly confidently that the market will do better than a collective decider, and there are situations where we can assume the opposite to be true. See COSTS 103–13.

Complex though this summary may suggest the entitlement choice to be, in practice the criteria it represents will frequently indicate which allocations of entitlements are most likely to lead to optimal market judgments between having an extra car or taking a train, getting an extra cabbage and spending less time working in the hot sun, and having more widgets and breathing the pollution that widget production implies. Economic efficiency is not, however, the sole reason which induces a society to select a set of entitlements. Wealth distribution preferences are another, and thus it is to distributional grounds for different entitlements to which we must now turn.

B. Distributional Goals

There are, we would suggest, at least two types of distributional concerns which may affect the choice of entitlements. These involve distribution of wealth itself and distribution of certain specific goods, which have sometimes been called merit goods.

All societies have wealth distribution preferences. They are, nonetheless, harder to talk about than are efficiency goals. For efficiency goals can be discussed in terms of a general concept like Pareto optimality to which exceptions—like paternalism—can be noted.[20] Distributional preferences, on the other hand, cannot usefully be discussed in a single conceptual framework. There are some fairly broadly accepted preferences—caste preferences in one society, more rather than less equality in another society. There are also preferences which are linked to dynamic efficiency concepts—producers ought to be rewarded since they will cause everyone to be better off in the end. Finally, there are a myriad of highly individualized preferences as to who should be richer and who poorer which need not have anything to do with either equality or efficiency—silence lovers should be richer than noise lovers because they are worthier.[21]

Difficult as wealth distribution preferences are to analyze, it should be obvious that they play a crucial role in the setting of entitlements. For the placement of entitlements has a fundamental effect on a society's distribution of wealth. It is not enough, if a society wishes absolute equality, to start everyone off with the same amount of money. A financially egalitarian society which gives individuals the right to make noise immediately makes the would-be noisemaker richer than the silence loving hermit.[22] Similarly, a society which entitles the person with brains to keep what his shrewdness gains him implies a different distribution of wealth from a society which demands from each according to his relative ability but gives to each according to his relative desire. One can go further and consider

[20] For a discussion of paternalism, see pp. 1113–14 *infra.*

[21] The first group of preferences roughly coincides with those notions which writers like Fletcher, following Aristotle, term distributive justice. The second and third groups, instead, presumably deal with Fletcher's "corrective" justice—rewards based on what people do rather than what they are. *See* Fletcher, *Fairness and Utility in Tort Theory*, 85 HARV. L. REV. 537, 547 n.40 (1972).

Within the "corrective" justice category our second and third groupings distinguish those preferences which are transparently linked to efficiency notions from those whose roots are less obvious. If there were a generally accepted theory of desserts, one could speak in general terms about the role the third group plays just as one tends to speak about the role of either the first or second group. We do not believe that an adequate theory of desserts—even if possible—is currently available. See also pp. 1102–05 *infra.*

[22] This assumes that there is not enough space for the noisemaker and the silence lover to coexist without intruding upon one another. In other words, this assumes that we are dealing with a problem of allocation of scarce resources; if we were not, there would be no need to set the initial entitlement. *See generally* Mishan, *supra* note 12.

that a beautiful woman or handsome man is better off in a society which entitles individuals to bodily integrity than in one which gives everybody use of all the beauty available.

The consequence of this is that it is very difficult to imagine a society in which there is complete equality of wealth. Such a society either would have to consist of people who were all precisely the same, or it would have to compensate for differences in wealth caused by a given set of entitlements. The former is, of course, ridiculous, even granting cloning. And the latter would be very difficult; it would involve knowing what everyone's tastes were and taxing every holder of an entitlement at a rate sufficient to make up for the benefits the entitlement gave him. For example, it would involve taxing everyone with an entitlement to private use of his beauty or brains sufficiently to compensate those less favorably endowed but who nonetheless desired what beauty or brains could get.

If perfect equality is impossible, a society must choose what entitlements it wishes to have on the basis of criteria other than perfect equality. In doing this, a society often has a choice of methods, and the method chosen will have important distributional implications. Society can, for instance, give an entitlement away free and then, by paying the holders of the entitlement to limit their use of it, protect those who are injured by the free entitlement. Conversely, it can allow people to do a given thing only if they buy the right from the government. Thus a society can decide whether to entitle people to have children and then induce them to exercise control in procreating, or to require people to buy the right to have children in the first place. A society can also decide whether to entitle people to be free of military service and then induce them to join up, or to require all to serve but enable each to buy his way out. Which entitlement a society decides to sell, and which it decides to give away, will likely depend in part on which determination promotes the wealth distribution that society favors.[23]

If the choice of entitlements affects wealth distribution generally, it also affects the chances that people will obtain what have sometimes been called merit goods.[24] Whenever a society wishes to maximize the chances that individuals will have at least a minimum endowment of certain particular goods—education, clothes, bodily integrity—the society is likely to begin by giving the individuals an entitlement to them. If the society deems such an endowment to be essential regardless of individual desires, it will, of course, make the entitlement

---

[23] Any entitlement given away free implies a converse which must be paid for. For all those who like children, there are those who are disturbed by children; for all those who detest armies, there are those who want what armies accomplish. Otherwise, we would have no scarce resource problem and hence no entitlement problem. Therefore, one cannot simply say that giving away an entitlement free is progressive while selling it is regressive. It is true that the more "free" goods there are the less inequality of wealth there is, if everything else has stayed the same. But if a free entitlement implies a costly converse, entitlements are not in this sense free goods. And the issue of their progressivity and regressivity must depend on the relative desire for the entitlement as against its converse on the part of the rich and the poor.

Strictly speaking, even this is true only if the money needed to finance the alternative plans, or made available to the government as a result of the plans, is raised and spent in a way that is precisely neutral with respect to wealth distribution. The point is simply this: even a highly regressive tax will aid wealth equality if the money it raises is all spent to benefit the poorest citizens. And even a system of outdoor relief for the idle rich aids wealth equality if the funds it requires are raised by taxing only the wealthiest of the wealthy. Thus whenever one speaks of a taxing program, spending program, or a system of entitlements as progressive or regressive, one must be assuming that the way the money is spent (if it is a tax) or the way it is raised (if it is a spending program) does not counter the distributive effect of the program itself.

[24] *Cf.* R. MUSGRAVE, THE THEORY OF PUBLIC FINANCE 13–14 (1959).

inalienable.[25] Why, however, would a society entitle individuals to specific goods rather than to money with which they can buy what they wish, unless it deems that it can decide better than the individuals what benefits them and society; unless, in other words, it wishes to make the entitlement inalienable?

We have seen that an entitlement to a good or to its converse is essentially inevitable.[26] We either are entitled to have silence or entitled to make noise in a given set of circumstances. We either have the right to our own property or body or the right to share others' property or bodies. We may buy or sell ourselves into the opposite position, but we must start somewhere. Under these circumstances, a society which prefers people to have silence, or own property, or have bodily integrity, but which does not hold the grounds for its preference to be sufficiently strong to justify overriding contrary preferences by individuals, will give such entitlements according to the collective preference, even though it will allow them to be sold thereafter.

Whenever transactions to sell or buy entitlements are very expensive, such an initial entitlement decision will be nearly as effective in assuring that individuals will have the merit good as would be making the entitlement inalienable. Since coercion is inherent because of the fact that a good cannot practically be bought or sold a society can choose only whether to make an individual have the good, by giving it to him, or to prevent him from getting it by giving him money instead.[27] In such circumstances society will pick the entitlement it deems favorable to the general welfare and not worry about coercion or alienability; it has increased the chances that individuals will have a particular good without increasing the degree of coercion imposed on individuals.[28] A common example of this may occur where the good involved is the present certainty of being able to buy a future benefit and where a futures market in that good is too expensive to be feasible.[29]

[25] The commonly given reasons why a society may choose to do this are discussed *infra* at pp. 1111–15. All of them are, of course, reasons which explain why such goods are often categorized as merit goods. When a society subsidizes a good it makes a similar decision based on similar grounds. Presumably, however, in such cases the grounds only justify making possession of the good less costly than would be the case without government intervention, rather than making possession of the good inevitable.

[26] This is true unless we are prepared to let the parties settle the matter on the basis of might makes right, which itself may also be viewed as a form of entitlement.

[27] For a discussion of this inevitable, and therefore irrelevant degree of coercion in the accident context, see COSTS 50–55, 161–73.

[28] The situation is analogous to that which involves choosing between systems of allocation of accident costs which minimize rapid changes in wealth, through spreading, and those that do not. Indeed, if the avoidance of rapid changes in wealth is, itself, viewed as a merit good, the analogy is complete. In the accident field a great deal of attention has been devoted to the problem of rapid changes in wealth. *See, e.g.,* Morris & Paul, *The Financial Impact of Automobile Accidents*, 110 U. PA. L. REV. 913, 924 (1962). *But see* W. BLUM & H. KALVEN, PUBLIC LAW PERSPECTIVES ON A PRIVATE LAW PROBLEM—AUTO COMPENSATION PLANS (1965).

[29] A full discussion of this justification for the giving of goods in "kind" is well beyond the scope of this article. An indication of what is involved may be in order, however. One of the many reasons why the right to vote is given in kind instead of giving individuals that amount of money which would assure them, in a voteless society, of all the benefits which having the vote gives them, is that at any given time the price of those benefits in the future is totally uncertain and, therefore, virtually no amount of money would assure individuals of having those future benefits. This would not be the case if an entrepreneur could be counted on to guarantee those future benefits in exchange for a present money payment. That is what happens in a futures market for, say, sow's bellies. The degree of uncertainty in the cost of the future benefits of the vote is such, however, that a futures market is either not feasible, or, what is the same thing, much too costly to be worthwhile. In such circumstances the nonmarket alternative of giving of the good in kind seems more efficient. Many of the merit goods which are, in fact, given in kind in our society—for example, education—share this characteristic of involving present rights to future benefits in circumstances where a futures market does not exist and at first glance seems very difficult to organize cheaply. We do not suggest that this is the sole explanation for the way voting is handled in our society. For instance, it does not explain why the vote cannot be sold. (An explanation for that may be found in the fact that Taney's benefit from the vote may depend on Marshall's not having more of it than he.) It does, however, add another, not frequently given, explanation for the occasional allocation of goods rather than money to individuals.

C. Other Justice Reasons

The final reasons for a society's choice of initial entitlements we termed other justice reasons, and we may as well admit that it is hard to know what content can be poured into that term, at least given the very broad definitions of economic efficiency and distributional goals that we have used. Is there, in other words, a reason which would influence a society's choice of initial entitlements that cannot be comprehended in terms of efficiency and distribution? A couple of examples will indicate the problem.

Taney likes noise; Marshall likes silence. They are, let us assume, inevitably neighbors. Let us also assume there are no transaction costs which may impede negotiations between them. Let us assume finally that we do not know Taney's and Marshall's wealth or, indeed, anything else about them. Under these circumstances we know that Pareto optimality—economic efficiency—will be reached whether we choose an entitlement to make noise or to have silence. We also are indifferent, from a general wealth distribution point of view, as to what the initial entitlement is because we do not know whether it will lead to greater equality or inequality. This leaves us with only two reasons on which to base our choice of entitlement. The first is the relative worthiness of silence lovers and noise lovers. The second is the consistency of the choice, or its apparent consistency, with other entitlements in the society.

The first sounds appealing, and it sounds like justice. But it is hard to deal with. Why, unless our choice affects other people, should we prefer one to another?[30] To say that we wish, for instance, to make the silence lover relatively wealthier because we prefer silence is no answer, for that is simply a restatement of the question. Of course, if the choice does affect people other than Marshall and Taney, then we have a valid basis for decision. But the fact that such external effects are extremely common and greatly influence our choices does not help us much. It does suggest that the reaching of Pareto optimality is, in practice, a very complex matter precisely because of the existence of many external effects which markets find hard to deal with. And it also suggests that there often are general distributional considerations between Taney-Marshall and the rest of the world which affect the choice of entitlement. It in no way suggests, however, that there is more to the choice between Taney-Marshall than Pareto optimality and distributional concerns. In other words, if the assumptions of no transaction costs and indifference as to distributional considerations, made as between Taney and Marshall (where they are unlikely), could be made as to the world as a whole (where they are impossible), the fact that the choice between Taney's noise or Marshall's silence might affect other people would give us no guidance. Thus what sounds like a justice standard is simply a handy way of importing efficiency

---

[30] The usual answer is religious or transcendental reasons. But this answer presents problems. If it means that Chase, a third party, suffers if the noise-maker is preferred, because Chase's faith deems silence worthier than noise, then third parties *are* affected by the choice. Chase suffers; there is an external effect. But that possibility was excluded in our hypothetical. In practice such external effects, often called moralisms, are extremely common and greatly complicate the reaching of Pareto optimality. *See* pp. 1112–13 *infra*.

Religious or transcendental reasons may, however, be of another kind. Chase may prefer silence not because he himself cares, not because he suffers if noise-makers get the best of it when his faith deems silence lovers to be worthier, but because he believes God suffers if such a choice is made. No amount of compensation will help Chase in this situation since he suffers nothing which can be compensated, and compensating God for the wrong choice is not feasible. Such a reason for a choice is, we would suggest, a true nonefficiency, nondistribution reason. Whether it actually ever plays a role may well be another matter.

and distributional notions too diverse and general in their effect to be analyzed fully in the decision of a specific case.

The second sounds appealing in a different way since it sounds like "treating like cases alike." If the entitlement to make noise in other people's ears for one's pleasure is viewed by society as closely akin to the entitlement to beat up people for one's pleasure, and if good efficiency and distributional reasons exist for not allowing people to beat up others for sheer pleasure, then there may be a good reason for preferring an entitlement to silence rather than noise in the Taney-Marshall case. Because the two entitlements are apparently consistent, the entitlement to silence strengthens the entitlement to be free from gratuitous beatings which we assumed was based on good efficiency and distributional reasons.[31] It does so by lowering the enforcement costs of the entitlement to be free from gratuitous beatings; the entitlement to silence reiterates and reinforces the values protected by the entitlement to be free from gratuitous beatings and reduces the number of discriminations people must make between one activity and another, thus simplifying the task of obedience.

The problem with this rationale for the choice is that it too comes down to efficiency and distributional reasons. We prefer the silence maker because *that* entitlement, even though it does not of itself affect the desired wealth distribution or lead us away from efficiency in the Taney-Marshall case, helps us to reach those goals in other situations where there are transaction costs or where we do have distributional preferences. It does this because people do not realize that the consistency is only apparent. If we could explain to them, both rationally and emotionally, the efficiency and distributional reasons why gratuitous beating up of people was inefficient or led to undesirable wealth distribution, and if we could also explain to them why an entitlement to noise rather than silence in the Taney-Marshall case would not lead to either inefficiency or maldistribution, then the secondary undermining of the entitlement to bodily integrity would not occur. It is only because it is expensive, even if feasible, to point out the difference between the two situations that the apparent similarity between them remains. And avoiding this kind of needless expense, while a very good reason for making choices, is clearly no more than a part of the economic efficiency goal.[32]

Still we should admit that explaining entitlements solely in terms of efficiency and distribution, in even their broadest terms, does not seem wholly satisfactory. The reasons for this are worth at least passing mention. The reason that we have so far explained entitlements simply in terms of efficiency and distribution is ultimately tautological. We defined distribution as covering *all* the reasons, other than efficiency, on the basis of which we might prefer to make Taney *wealthier* than Marshall. So defined, there obviously was no room for any other reasons. Distributional grounds covered broadly accepted ideas like "equality" or, in some societies, "caste preference," and highly specific ones like "favoring the silence lover." We used this definition because there is a utility in lumping together all those reasons for preferring Taney to Marshall which cannot be explained in

[31] The opposite would be true if noisemaking were thought to be akin to industry, and drive and silence to lethargy and laziness, and we had good efficiency or distributional reasons for preferring industry to lethargy.

[32] We do not mean to underestimate the importance of apparent consistency as a ground for entitlements. Far from it, it is likely that a society often prefers an entitlement which even leads to mild inefficiencies or maldistribution of wealth between, say, Taney and Marshall, because that entitlement tends to support other entitlements which are crucial in terms of efficiency or wealth distribution in the society at large and because the cost of convincing people that the situations are, in fact, different is not worth the gain which would be obtained in the Taney-Marshall case.

terms of a desire to make everyone better off, and in contrasting them with efficiency reasons, whether Paretian or not, which can be so explained.

Lumping them together, however, has some analytical disadvantages. It seems to assume that we cannot say any more about the reasons for some distributional preferences than about others. For instance, it seems to assume a similar universality of support for recognizing silence lovers as relatively worthier as there is for recognizing the relative desirability of equality. And that, surely, is a dangerous assumption. To avoid this danger the term "distribution" is often limited to relatively few broad reasons, like equality. And those preferences which cannot be easily explained in terms of these relatively few broadly accepted distributional preferences, or in terms of efficiency, are termed justice reasons. The difficulty with this locution is that it sometimes is taken to imply that the moral gloss of justice is reserved for these residual preferences and does not apply to the broader distributional preferences or to efficiency based preferences. And surely this is wrong, for many entitlements that properly are described as based on justice in our society can easily be explained in terms either of broad distributional preferences like equality or of efficiency or of both.

By using the term "*other* justice reasons" we hope to avoid this difficulty and emphasize that justice notions adhere to efficiency and broad distributional preferences as well as to other more idiosyncratic ones. To the extent that one is concerned with contrasting the difference between efficiency and other reasons for certain entitlements, the bipolar efficiency-distribution locution is all that is needed. To the extent that one wishes to delve either into reasons which, though possibly originally linked to efficiency, have now a life of their own, or into reasons which, though distributional, cannot be described in terms of broad principles like equality, then a locution which allows for "other justice reasons" seems more useful.[33]

III. Rules for Protecting and Regulating Entitlements

Whenever society chooses an initial entitlement it must also determine whether to protect the entitlement by property rules, by liability rules, or by rules of inalienability. In our framework, much of what is generally called private property can be viewed as an entitlement which is protected by a property rule. No one can take the entitlement to private property from the holder unless the holder sells it willingly and at the price at which he subjectively values the property. Yet a nuisance with sufficient public utility to avoid injunction has, in effect, the right to take property with compensation. In such a circumstance the entitlement to the property is protected only by what we call a liability rule: an external, objective standard of value is used to facilitate the transfer of the entitlement from the holder to the nuisance.[34] Finally, in some instances we will not allow the sale of the property at all, that is, we will occasionally make the entitlement inalienable.

This section will consider the circumstances in which society will employ these three rules to solve situations of conflict. Because the property rule and the liability rule are closely related and depend for their application on the shortcomings of each other, we treat them together. We discuss inalienability separately.

[33] *But see* Fletcher, *supra* note 21, at 547 n.40.

[34] *See, e.g.*, Boomer v. Atlantic Cement Co., 26 N.Y.2d 219, 309 N.Y.S.2d 312, 257 N.E.2d 870 (1970) (avoidance of injunction conditioned on payment of permanent damages to plaintiffs).

Why cannot a society simply decide on the basis of the already mentioned criteria who should receive any given entitlement, and then let its transfer occur only through a voluntary negotiation? Why, in other words, cannot society limit itself to the property rule? To do this it would need only to protect and enforce the initial entitlements from all attacks, perhaps through criminal sanctions,[35] and to enforce voluntary contracts for their transfer. Why do we need liability rules at all?

In terms of economic efficiency the reason is easy enough to see. Often the cost of establishing the value of an initial entitlement by negotiation is so great that even though a transfer of the entitlement would benefit all concerned, such a transfer will not occur. If a collective determination of the value were available instead, the beneficial transfer would quickly come about.

Eminent domain is a good example. A park where Guidacres, a tract of land owned by 1,000 owners in 1,000 parcels, now sits would, let us assume, benefit a neighboring town enough so that the 100,000 citizens of the town would each be willing to pay an average of $100 to have it. The park is Pareto desirable if the owners of the tracts of land in Guidacres actually value their entitlements at less than $10,000,000 or an average of $10,000 a tract. Let us assume that in fact the parcels are all the same and all the owners value them at $8,000. On this assumption, the park is, in economic efficiency terms, desirable—in values foregone it costs $8,000,000 and is worth $10,000,000 to the buyers. And yet it may well not be established. If enough of the owners hold-out for more than $10,000 in order to get a share of the $2,000,000 that they guess the buyers are willing to pay over the value which the sellers in actuality attach, the price demanded will be more than $10,000,000 and no park will result. The sellers have an incentive to hide their true valuation and the market will not succeed in establishing it.

An equally valid example could be made on the buying side. Suppose the sellers of Guidacres have agreed to a sales price of $8,000,000 (they are all relatives and at a family banquet decided that trying to hold-out would leave them all losers). It does not follow that the buyers can raise that much even though each of 100,000 citizens *in fact* values the park at $100. Some citizens may try to free-load and say the park is only worth $50 or even nothing to them, hoping that enough others will admit to a higher desire and make up the $8,000,000 price. Again there is no reason to believe that a market, a decentralized system of valuing, will cause people to express their true valuations and hence yield results which all would *in fact* agree are desirable.

Whenever this is the case an argument can readily be made for moving from a property rule to a liability rule. If society can remove from the market the valuation of each tract of land, decide the value collectively, and impose it, then the holdout problem is gone. Similarly, if society can value collectively each individual citizen's desire to have a park and charge him a "benefits" tax based upon it, the freeloader problem is gone. If the sum of the taxes is greater than the sum of the compensation awards, the park will result.

Of course, one can conceive of situations where it might be cheap to exclude all the freeloaders from the park, or to ration the park's use in accordance with original willingness to pay. In such cases the incentive to free-load might be eliminated. But such exclusions, even if possible, are usually not cheap. And the same

---

[35] The relationship between criminal sanctions and property entitlements will be examined *infra* pp. 1124–27.

may be the case for market methods which might avoid the holdout problem on the seller side.

Moreover, even if holdout and freeloader problems can be met feasibly by the market, an argument may remain for employing a liability rule. Assume that in our hypothetical, freeloaders can be excluded at the cost of $1,000,000 and that all owners of tracts in Guidacres can be convinced, by the use of $500,000 worth of advertising and cocktail parties, that a sale will only occur if they reveal their true land valuations. Since $8,000,000 plus $1,500,000 is less than $10,000,000, the park will be established. But if collective valuation of the tracts and of the benefits of the prospective park would have cost less than $1,500,000, it would have been inefficient to establish the park through the market—a market which was not worth having would have been paid for.[36]

Of course, the problems with liability rules are equally real. We cannot be at all sure that landowner Taney is lying or holding out when he says his land is worth $12,000 to him. The fact that several neighbors sold identical tracts for $10,000 does not help us very much; Taney may be sentimentally attached to his land. As a result, eminent domain may grossly undervalue what Taney would actually sell for, even if it sought to give him his true valuation of his tract. In practice, it is so hard to determine Taney's true valuation that eminent domain simply gives him what the land is worth "objectively," in the full knowledge that this may result in over or under compensation. The same is true on the buyer side. "Benefits" taxes rarely attempt, let alone succeed, in gauging the individual citizen's relative desire for the alleged benefit. They are justified because, even if they do not accurately measure each individual's desire for the benefit, the market alternative seems worse. For example, fifty different households may place different values on a new sidewalk that is to abut all the properties. Nevertheless, because it is too difficult, even if possible, to gauge each household's valuation, we usually tax each household an equal amount.

The example of eminent domain is simply one of numerous instances in which society uses liability rules. Accidents is another. If we were to give victims a property entitlement not to be accidentally injured we would have to require all who engage in activities that may injure individuals to negotiate with them before an accident, and to buy the right to knock off an arm or a leg.[37] Such pre-accident

---

[36] It may be argued that, given imperfect knowledge, the market is preferable because it places a limit—the cost of establishing a market—on the size of the possible loss, while the costs of coercion cannot be defined and may be infinite. This may be true in some situations but need not always be the case. If, for example, we know that the holdouts would sell for $500,000 more than is offered, because they recently offered the land at that higher price, coercing them to sell at an objectively determined price between the seller's offer and the purchaser's offer cannot result in more than $500,000 in harm. Thus, the costs of coercion would also not be infinite. Nor is it an answer to say that the man who would sell for a higher price but is coerced for a lower one suffers an indefinite nonmonetary cost in addition to the price differential simply because he is coerced and resents it. For while this may well be true, the same nonmonetary resentment may also exist in those who desire the park and do not get it because the market is unable to pay off those who are holding out for a greater than actual value. In other words, unascertainable resentment costs may exist as a result of either coercion or market failure.

[37] Even if it were possible, it should be clear that the good which would be sold would not be the same as the good actually taken. If Taney waives for $1,000 the right to recover for the loss of a leg, should he ever lose it, he is negotiating for a joint product which can be described as his "desire or aversion to gamble" and "his desire to have a leg." The product actually taken, however, is the leg. That the two goods are different can be seen from the fact that a man who demands $1,000 for a 1 in 1,000 chance of losing a leg may well demand more than $100,000 for a 1 in 10 chance of losing it, and more than $1,000,000 for the sale of his leg to someone who needs it for a transplant. *See generally* COSTS 88–94. This does not mean that the result of such transactions, if feasible, would *necessarily* be worse than the result of collective valuations. It simply means that the situation, even if feasible, is different from the one in which Taney sells his house for a given price.

negotiations would be extremely expensive, often prohibitively so.[38] To require them would thus preclude many activities that might, in fact, be worth having. And, after an accident, the loser of the arm or leg can always very plausibly deny that he would have sold it at the price the buyer would have offered. Indeed, where negotiations after an accident do occur—for instance pretrial settlements—it is largely because the alternative is the collective valuation of the damages.

It is not our object here to outline all the theoretical, let alone the practical, situations where markets may be too expensive or fail and where collective valuations seem more desirable. Economic literature has many times surrounded the issue if it has not always zeroed in on it in ways intelligible to lawyers.[39] It is enough for our purposes to note that a very common reason, perhaps the most common one for employing a liability rule rather than a property rule to protect an entitlement is that market valuation of the entitlement is deemed inefficient, that is, it is either unavailable or too expensive compared to a collective valuation.

We should also recognize that efficiency is not the sole ground for employing liability rules rather than property rules. Just as the initial entitlement is often decided upon for distributional reasons, so too the choice of a liability rule is often made because it facilitates a combination of efficiency and distributive results which would be difficult to achieve under a property rule. As we shall see in the pollution context, use of a liability rule may allow us to accomplish a measure of redistribution that could only be attained at a prohibitive sacrifice of efficiency if we employed a corresponding property rule.

More often, once a liability rule is decided upon, perhaps for efficiency reasons, it is then employed to favor distributive goals as well. Again accidents and eminent domain are good examples. In both of these areas the compensation given has clearly varied with society's distributive goals, and cannot be readily explained in terms of giving the victim as nearly as possible, an objectively determined equivalent of the price at which he would have sold what was taken from him.

---

[38] Such preaccident negotiations between potential injurers and victims are at times not too costly. Thus in a typical products liability situation the cost of negotiation over a potential injury need not be prohibitive. The seller of a rotary lawn mower may offer to sell at a reduced price if the buyer agrees not to sue should he be injured. Nevertheless, society often forbids such negotiations because it deems them undesirable. This may occur because of the reasons suggested in note 37 *supra*, or for any of the other reasons which cause us to make some entitlements wholly or partly inalienable, *see infra* pp. 1111–15.

Attempts have been made to deal with situations where ex ante negotiations are not feasible by fiscal devices designed to cause people to reveal their preferences. One of these contemplates requiring individuals to declare a value on their properties, or even limbs, and paying a tax on the self assessed value. That value would be the value of the good if it were taken in an accident or by eminent domain. *See generally* N. Tideman, Three Approaches to Improving Urban Land Use, ch. III (1969) (unpublished Ph.D. dissertation submitted to U. of Chicago Economics Department, on file in Yale Law Library). Of course, if the good is only taken as a result of an accident or eminent domain, the problem of gambling described in note 37 *supra* would remain. If, instead, the property or limb could be taken at will at the self assessed value, serious problems would arise from the fact that there are enormous nonmonetizable, as well as monetizable, costs involved in making people put money values on all their belongings and limbs.

An additional, though perhaps solvable, problem with self assessed taxes is the fact that the taking price would exclude any consumer surplus. This may have no significance in terms of economic efficiency, but if the existence of consumer surplus in many market transactions is thought to have, on the whole, a favorable wealth distribution effect, it might well be a reason why self assessed taxes are viewed with skepticism. *Cf.* Little, Self-Assessed Valuations: A Critique (1972) (unpublished paper, on file in Harvard Law School Library). The reader might reasonably wonder why many individuals who view self assessed taxes with skepticism show no similar concerns for what may be a very similar device, optional first party insurance covering pain and suffering damages in automobile injuries. *See, e.g.*, Calabresi, *The New York Plan: A Free Choice Modification*, 71 COLUM. L. REV. 267, 268 n.6 (1971).

[39] For a good discussion of market failure which is intelligible to lawyers, see Bator, *The Anatomy of Market Failure*, 72 Q. J. ECON. 351 (1985).

It should not be surprising that this is often so, even if the original reason for a liability rule is an efficiency one. For distributional goals are expensive and difficult to achieve, and the collective valuation involved in liability rules readily lends itself to promoting distributional goals.[40] This does not mean that distributional goals are always well served in this way. Ad hoc decisionmaking is always troublesome, and the difficulties are especially acute when the settlement of conflicts between parties is used as a vehicle for the solution of more widespread distributional problems. Nevertheless, distributional objectives may be better attained in this way than otherwise.[41]

B. Inalienable Entitlements

Thus far we have focused on the questions of when society should protect an entitlement by property or liability rules. However, there remain many entitlements which involve a still greater degree of societal intervention: the law not only decides who is to own something and what price is to be paid for it if it is taken or destroyed, but also regulates its sale—by, for example, prescribing preconditions for a valid sale or forbidding a sale altogether. Although these rules of inalienability are substantially different from the property and liability rules, their use can be analyzed in terms of the same efficiency and distributional goals that underlie the use of the other two rules.

While at first glance efficiency objectives may seem undermined by limitations on the ability to engage in transactions, closer analysis suggests that there are instances, perhaps many, in which economic efficiency is more closely approximated by such limitations. This might occur when a transaction would create significant externalities—costs to third parties.

For instance, if Taney were allowed to sell his land to Chase, a polluter, he would injure his neighbor Marshall by lowering the value of Marshall's land. Conceivably, Marshall could pay Taney not to sell his land; but, because there are many injured Marshalls, freeloader and information costs make such transactions practically impossible. The state could protect the Marshalls and yet facilitate the sale of the land by giving the Marshalls an entitlement to prevent Taney's sale to Chase but only protecting the entitlement by a liability rule. It might, for instance, charge an excise tax on all sales of land to polluters equal to its estimate of the external cost to the Marshalls of the sale. But where there are so many injured Marshalls that the price required under the liability rule is likely to be high enough so that no one would be willing to pay it, then setting up the machinery for collective valuation will be wasteful. Barring the sale to polluters will be the most efficient result because it is clear that avoiding pollution is cheaper than paying its costs—including its costs to the Marshalls.

Another instance in which external costs may justify inalienability occurs when external costs do not lend themselves to collective measurement which is

[40] Collective valuation of costs also makes it easier to value the costs at what the society thinks they should be valued by the victim instead of at what the victim would value them in a free market if such a market were feasible. The former kind of valuation is, of course, paternalism. This does not mean it is undesirable; the danger is that paternalism which is not desirable will enter mindlessly into the cost valuation because the valuation is necessarily done collectively. *See* pp. 1113–14 *infra.*

[41] For suggestions that at times systematic distributional programs may cause greater misallocation of resources than ad hoc decisions, see Ackerman, *Regulating Slum Housing Markets on Behalf of the Poor: Of Housing Codes, Housing Subsidies and Income Redistribution Policy*, 80 YALE L. J. 1093, 1157–97 (1971); Calabresi, *supra* note 12.

acceptably objective and nonarbitrary. This nonmonetizability is characteristic of one category of external costs which, as a practical matter, seems frequently to lead us to rules of inalienability. Such external costs are often called moralisms.

If Taney is allowed to sell himself into slavery, or to take undue risks of becoming penniless, or to sell a kidney, Marshall may be harmed, simply because Marshall is a sensitive man who is made unhappy by seeing slaves, paupers, or persons who die because they have sold a kidney. Again Marshall could pay Taney not to sell his freedom to Chase the slaveowner; but again, because Marshall is not one but many individuals, freeloader and information costs make such transactions practically impossible. Again, it might seem that the state could intervene by objectively valuing the external cost to Marshall and requiring Chase to pay that cost. But since the external cost to Marshall does not lend itself to an acceptable objective measurement, such liability rules are not appropriate.

In the case of Taney selling land to Chase, the polluter, they were inappropriate because we *knew* that the costs to Taney and the Marshalls exceeded the benefits to Chase. Here, though we are not certain of how a cost-benefit analysis would come out, liability rules are inappropriate because any monetization is, by hypothesis, out of the question. The state must, therefore, either ignore the external costs to Marshall, or if it judges them great enough, forbid the transaction that gave rise to them by making Taney's freedom.[42]

Obviously we will not always value the external harm of a moralism enough to prohibit the sale.[43] And obviously also, external costs other than moralisms may be sufficiently hard to value to make rules of inalienability appropriate in certain circumstances; this reason for rules of inalienability, however, does seem most often germane in situations where moralisms are involved.[44]

There are two other efficiency reasons for forbidding the sale of entitlements under certain circumstances: self paternalism and true paternalism. Examples of the first are Ulysses tying himself to the mast or individuals passing a bill of rights so that they will be prevented from yielding to momentary temptations which they deem harmful to themselves. This type of limitation is not in any real sense paternalism. It is fully consistent with Pareto efficiency criteria, based on the notion that over the mass of cases no one knows better than the individual what is best for him or her. It merely allows the individual to choose what is best in the long run rather than in the short run, even though that choice entails giving up some short run freedom of choice. Self paternalism may cause us to require certain conditions to exist before we allow a sale of an entitlement; and it may

---

[42] Granting Taney an inalienable right to be free is in many respects the same as granting most of the people a property entitlement to keep Taney free. The people may bargain and decide to surrender their entitlement, *i.e.*, to change the law, but there are limits on the feasibility of transactions of this sort which make the public's entitlements virtually inalienable.

[43] For example, I am allowed to buy and read whatever books I like, or to sell my house to whomever I choose, regardless of whether my doing so makes my neighbors unhappy. These entitlements could be a form of self paternalism on the part of the neighbors who fear a different rule would harm them more in the long run, or they could be selected because they strengthen seemingly similar entitlements. *See* pp. 1103–04 *supra*. But they may also reflect a judgment that the injury suffered by my neighbors results from a moralism shared by them but not so widespread as to make more efficient their being given an entitlement to prevent my transaction. In other words, people who are hurt by my transaction are the cheapest cost avoiders, *i.e.*, the cost to them of my being allowed to transact freely is less than the cost to me and others similarly situated of a converse entitlement.

[44] The fact that society may make an entitlement inalienable does not, of course, mean that there will be no compensation to the holder of the entitlement if it is taken from him. Thus even if a society forbids the sale of one's kidneys it will still probably compensate the person whose kidney is destroyed in an auto accident. The situations are distinct and the kidney is protected by different rules according to which situation we are speaking of.

help explain many situations of inalienability, like the invalidity of contracts entered into when drunk, or under undue influence or coercion. But it probably does not fully explain even these.[45]

True paternalism brings us a step further toward explaining such prohibitions and those of broader kinds—for example the prohibitions on a whole range of activities by minors. Paternalism is based on the notion that at least in some situations the Marshalls know better than Taney what will make Taney better off.[46] Here we are not talking about the offense to Marshall from Taney's choosing to read pornography, or selling himself into slavery, but rather the judgment that Taney was not in the position to choose best for himself when he made the choice for erotica or servitude.[47] The first concept we called a moralism and is a frequent and important ground for inalienability. But it is consistent with the premises of Pareto optimality. The second, paternalism, is also an important economic efficiency reason for inalienability, but it is not consistent with the premises of Pareto optimality: the most efficient pie is no longer that which costless bargains would achieve, because a person may be better off if he is prohibited from bargaining.

Finally, just as efficiency goals sometimes dictate the use of rules of inalienability, so, of course, do distributional goals. Whether an entitlement may be sold or not often affects directly who is richer and who is poorer. Prohibiting the sale of babies makes poorer those who can cheaply produce babies and richer those who through some nonmarket device get free an "unwanted" baby.[48] Prohibiting exculpatory clauses in product sales makes richer those who were injured by a product defect and poorer those who were not injured and who paid more for the product because the exulpatory clause was forbidden.[49] Favoring the specific group that has benefited may or may not have been the reason for the prohibition on bargaining. What is important is that, regardless of the reason for barring a contract, a group did gain from the prohibition.

This should suffice to put us on guard, for it suggests that direct distributional motives may lie behind asserted nondistributional grounds for inalienability,

---

[45] As a practical matter, since it is frequently impossible to limit the effect of an inalienable rule to those who desire it for self paternalistic reasons, self paternalism would lead to some restraints on those who would desire to sell their entitlements. This does not make self paternalism any less consistent with the premises of Pareto optimality; it is only another recognition that in an imperfect world, Pareto optimality can be approached more closely by systems which involve some coercion than by a system of totally free bargains.

[46] This locution leaves open the question whether Taney's future well-being will ultimately be decided by Taney himself or the many Marshalls. The latter implies a further departure from Paretian premises. The former, which may be typical of paternalism towards minors, implies simply that the minors do not know enough to exercise self paternalism.

[47] Sometimes the term paternalism is used to explain use of a rule of inalienability in situations where inalienability will not make the many Marshalls or the coerced Taney any better off. Inalienability is said to be imposed because the many Marshalls believe that making the entitlement inalienable is doing God's will, that is, that a sale or transfer of the entitlement would injure God. Assuming this situation exists in practice, we would not term it paternalism, because that word implies looking after the interests of the coerced party. *See* note 30 *supra*.

[48] This assumes that a prohibition on the sale of unwanted babies can be effectively enforced. If it can, then those unwanted babies which are produced are of no financial benefit to their natural parents and bring an increase in well-being to those who are allowed to adopt them free and as a result of a nonmarket allocation. Should the prohibition on sales of babies be only partially enforceable, the distributional result would be more complex. It would be unchanged for those who could obtain babies for adoption legally, *i.e.*, for those who received them without paying bribes, as it would for the natural parents who obeyed the law, since they would still receive no compensation. On the other hand, the illegal purchaser would probably pay, and the illegal seller receive, a higher price than if the sale of babies were legal. This would cause a greater distributive effect within the group of illegal sellers and buyers than would exist if such sales were permitted.

[49] *See* note 37 *supra*.

whether they be paternalism, self paternalism, or externalities.[50] This does not mean that giving weight to distributional goals is undesirable. It clearly is desirable where on efficiency grounds society is indifferent between an alienable and an inalienable entitlement and distributional goals favor one approach or the other. It may well be desirable even when distributional goals are achieved at some efficiency costs. The danger may be, however, that what is justified on, for example, paternalism grounds is really a hidden way of accruing distributional benefits for a group whom we would not otherwise wish to benefit. For example, we may use certain types of zoning to preserve open spaces on the grounds that the poor will be happier, though they do not know it now. And open spaces may indeed make the poor happier in the long run. But the zoning that preserves open space also makes housing in the suburbs more expensive and it may be that the whole plan is aimed at securing distributional benefits to the suburban dweller regardless of the poor's happiness.[51]

IV. The Framework and Pollution Control Rules

Nuisance or pollution is one of the most interesting areas where the question of who will be given an entitlement, and how it will be protected, is in frequent issue.[52] Traditionally, and very ably in the recent article by Professor Michelman, the nuisance-pollution problem is viewed in terms of three rules.[53] First, Taney may not pollute unless his neighbor (his only neighbor let us assume), Marshall, allows it (Marshall may enjoin Taney's nuisance).[54] Second, Taney may pollute but must compensate Marshall for damages caused (nuisance is found but the remedy is limited to damages).[55] Third, Taney may pollute at will and can only

[50] As a practical matter, it is often impossible to tell whether an entitlement has been made partially inalienable for any of the several efficiency grounds mentioned or for distributional grounds. Do we bar people from selling their bodies for paternalistic, self paternalistic, or moralistic cost reasons? On what basis do we prohibit an individual from taking, for a high price, one chance in three of having to give his heart to a wealthy man who needs a transplant? Do we try to avoid a market in scarce medical resources for distributional or for some or all of the efficiency reasons discussed?

[51] There is another set of reasons which causes us to prohibit sales of some entitlements and which is sometimes termed distributional; this set of reasons causes us to prohibit sales of some entitlements because the underlying distribution of wealth seems to us undesirable. These reasons, we would suggest, are not true distributional grounds. They are, rather, efficiency grounds which become valid because of the original maldistribution. As such they can once again be categorized as due to externalities, self paternalism, and pure paternalism: (1) Marshall is offended because Taney, due to poverty, sells a kidney, and therefore Marshall votes to bar such sales (a moralism); (2) Taney, seeking to avoid temporary temptation due to his poverty, votes to bar such sales (self paternalism); and (3) the law prohibits Taney from the same sale because, regardless of what Taney believes, a majority thinks Taney will be better off later if he is barred from selling than if he is free to do so while influenced by his own poverty (pure paternalism). We do not mean to minimize these reasons by noting that they are not strictly distributional. We call them nondistributional simply to distinguish them from the more direct way in which distributional considerations affect the alienability of entitlements.

[52] It should be clear that the pollution problem we discuss here is really only a part of a broader problem, that of land use planning in general. Much of this analysis may therefore be relevant to other land use issues, for example exclusionary zoning, restrictive covenants, and ecological easements. *See* note 58 *infra*.

[53] Michelman, *supra* note 1, at 670. *See also* Restatement (Second) of Torts §§ 157–215 (1965). Michelman also discusses the possibility of inalienability. Michelman, *supra*, at 684. For a discussion of the use of rules of inalienability in the pollution context, see pp. 1123–24 *infra*.

[54] *See, e.g.*, Department of Health & Mental Hygiene v. Galaxy Chem. Co., 1 ENVIR. REP. 1660 (Md. Cir. Ct. 1970) (chemical smells enjoined); Ensign v. Walls, 323 Mich. 49, 34 N.W. 2d 549 (1948) (dog raising in residential neighborhood enjoined).

[55] *See, e.g.*, Boomer v. Atlantic Cement Co., 26 N.Y.2d 219, 309 N.Y.S.2d 312, 257 N.E.2d 870 (1970) (avoidance of injunction conditioned on payment of permanent damages to plaintiffs).

be stopped by Marshall if Marshall pays him off (Taney's pollution is not held to be a nuisance to Marshall).[56] In our terminology rules one and two (nuisance with injunction, and with damages only) are entitlements to Marshall. The first is an entitlement to be free from pollution and is protected by a property rule; the second is also an entitlement to be free from pollution but is protected only by a liability rule. Rule three (no nuisance) is instead an entitlement to Taney protected by a property rule, for only by buying Taney out at Taney's price can Marshall end the pollution.

The very statement of these rules in the context of our framework suggests that something is missing. Missing is a fourth rule representing an entitlement in Taney to pollute, but an entitlement which is protected only by a liability rule. The fourth rule, really a kind of partial eminent domain coupled with a benefits tax, can be stated as follows: Marshall may stop Taney from polluting, but if he does he must compensate Taney.

As a practical matter it will be easy to see why even legal writers as astute as Professor Michelman have ignored this rule. Unlike the first three it does not often lend itself to judicial imposition for a number of good legal process reasons. For example, even if Taney's injuries could practically be measured, apportionment of the duty of compensation among many Marshalls would present problems for which courts are not well suited. If only those Marshalls who voluntarily asserted the right to enjoin Taney's pollution were required to pay the compensation, there would be insuperable freeloader problems. If, on the other hand, the liability rule entitled one of the Marshalls alone to enjoin the pollution and required all the benefited Marshalls to pay their share of the compensation, the courts would be faced with the immensely difficult task of determining who was benefited how much and imposing a benefits tax accordingly, all the while observing procedural limits within which courts are expected to function.[57]

The fourth rule is thus not part of the cases legal scholars read when they study nuisance law, and is therefore easily ignored by them. But it is available, and may sometimes make more sense than any of the three competing approaches. Indeed,

---

[56] *See, e.g.*, Francisco v. Department of Institutions & Agencies, 13 N.J. Misc. 663, 180 A. 843 (Ct. Ch. 1935) (plaintiffs not entitled to enjoin noise and odors of adjacent sanitarium); Rose v. Socony-Vacuum Corp., 54 R.I. 411, 173 A. 627 (1934) (pollution of percolating waters not enjoinable in absence of negligence).

[57] This task is much more difficult than that which arises under rule two, in which the many Marshalls would be compensated for their pollution injuries. Under rule two, each victim may act as an individual, either in seeking compensation in the first instance or in electing whether to be a part of a class seeking compensation. If he wishes to and is able to convince the court (by some accepted objective standard) that he has been injured, he may be compensated. Such individual action is expensive, and thus may be wasteful, but it presents no special problems in terms of the traditional workings of the courts. But where the class in question consists, not of those with a right to enjoin, but of those who must pay to enjoin, freeloader problems require the court to determine that an unwilling Marshall has been benefited and should be required to pay. The basic difficulty is that if we begin with the premise which usually underlies our notion of efficiency—namely, that individuals know what is best for them—we are faced with the anomaly of compelling compensation from one who denies he has incurred a benefit but whom we require to pay because *the court* thinks he has been benefited.

This problem is analogous to the difficulties presented by quasi-contracts. In terms of the theory of our economic efficiency goal, the case for requiring compensation for unbargained for (often accidental) benefits is similar to the argument for compensating tort victims. Yet courts as a general rule require compensation in quasi-contract only where there is both an indisputable benefit (usually of a pecuniary or economic nature) and some affirmative acknowledgment of subjective benefit (usually a subsequent promise to pay). *See* A. CORBIN, CONTRACTS §§ 231–34 (1963). This hesitancy suggests that courts lack confidence in their ability to distinguish real benefits from illusions. Perhaps even more importantly, it suggests that the courts recognize that what may clearly be an objective "benefit" may, to the putative beneficiary, not be a subjective benefit—if for no other reason than that unintended changes from the status quo often exact psychological costs. If that is the case, there has been no benefit at all in terms of our efficiency criterion.

in one form or another, it may well be the most frequent device employed.[58] To
appreciate the utility of the fourth rule and to compare it with the other three
rules, we will examine why we might choose any of the given rules.

We would employ rule one (entitlement to be free from pollution protected by
a property rule) from an economic efficiency point of view if we believed that the
polluter, Taney, could avoid or reduce the costs of pollution more cheaply than
the pollutee, Marshall. Or to put it another way, Taney would be enjoinable if he
were in a better position to balance the costs of polluting against the costs of not
polluting. We would employ rule three (entitlement to pollute protected by a
property rule) again solely from an economic efficiency standpoint, if we made
the converse judgment on who could best balance the harm of pollution against
its avoidance costs. If we were wrong in our judgments and if transactions
between Marshall and Taney were costless or even very cheap, the entitlement
under rules one or three would be traded and an economically efficient result
would occur in either case.[59] If we entitled Taney to pollute and Marshall valued
clean air more than Taney valued the pollution, Marshall would pay Taney to
stop polluting even though no nuisance was found. If we entitled Marshall to
enjoin the pollution and the right to pollute was worth more to Taney than freedom from pollution was to Marshall, Taney would pay Marshall not to seek an
injunction or would buy Marshall's land and sell it to someone who would agree
not to seek an injunction. As we have assumed no one else was hurt by the pollution. Taney could now pollute even though the initial entitlement, based on a
wrong guess of who was the cheapest avoider of the costs involved, allowed the
pollution to be enjoined. Wherever transactions between Taney and Marshall are
easy, and wherever economic efficiency is our goal, we could employ entitlements
protected by property rules even though we would not be sure that the entitlement chosen was the right one. Transactions as described above would cure the
error. While the entitlement might have important distributional effects, it would
not substantially undercut economic efficiency.

The moment we assume, however, that transactions are not cheap, the situation changes dramatically. Assume we enjoin Taney and there are 10,000 injured
Marshalls. Now *even if* the right to pollute is worth more to Taney than the right
to be free from pollution is to the sum of the Marshalls, the injunction will probably stand. The cost of buying out all the Marshalls, given holdout problems, is
likely to be too great, and an equivalent of eminent domain in Taney would be
needed to alter the initial injunction. Conversely, if we denied a nuisance remedy,

---

[58] *See* A. KNEESE & B. BOWER, MANAGING WATER QUALITY: ECONOMICS, TECHNOLOGY,
INSTITUTIONS 98–109 (1968); Krier, *The Pollution Problem and Legal Institutions: A Conceptual Overview*,
18 U.C.L.A.L. REV. 429, 467–75 (1971).

Virtually all eminent domain takings of a nonconforming use seem to be examples of this approach.
Ecological easements may be another prime example. A local zoning ordinance may require a developer to
contribute a portion of his land for purposes of parkland or school construction. In compensation for taking
the developer's entitlement, the locality will pay the developer "damages": it will allow him to increase the
normal rate of density in his remaining property. The question of damage assessment involved in ecological
easements raises similar problems to those raised in the benefit assessment involved in the question of quasi-
contract. *See* note 57 *supra*.

[59] For a discussion of whether efficiency would be achieved in the long, as well as the short, run, see Coase,
supra note 12; Calabresi, *supra* note 12 (pointing out that if "no transaction costs" means no impediments to
bargaining in the short or long run, and if Pareto optimality means an allocation of resources which cannot be
improved by bargains, assumptions of no transaction costs and rationality necessarily imply Pareto optimality);
Nutter, *supra* note 12 (a technical demonstration of the applicability of the Coase theorem to long run problems).
See also Demsetz, *supra* note 16, at 19–22.

the 10,000 Marshalls could only with enormous difficulty, given freeloader problems, get together to buy out even one Taney and prevent the pollution. This would be so even if the pollution harm was greater than the value to Taney of the right to pollute.

If, however, transaction costs are not symmetrical, we may still be able to use the property rule. Assume that Taney can buy the Marshalls' entitlements easily because holdouts are for some reason absent, but that the Marshalls have great freeloader problems in buying out Taney. In this situation the entitlement should be granted to the Marshalls unless we are sure the Marshalls are the cheapest avoiders of pollution costs. Where we do not know the identity of the cheapest cost avoider it is better to entitle the Marshalls to be free of pollution because, even if we are wrong in our initial placement of the entitlement, that is, even if the Marshalls are the cheapest cost avoiders, Taney will buy out the Marshalls and economic efficiency will be achieved. Had we chosen the converse entitlement and been wrong, the Marshalls could not have bought out Taney. Unfortunately, transaction costs are often high on both sides and an initial entitlement, though incorrect in terms of economic efficiency, will not be altered in the market place.

Under these circumstances—and they are normal ones in the pollution area—we are likely to turn to liability rules whenever we are uncertain whether the polluter or the pollutees can most cheaply avoid the cost of pollution. We are only likely to use liability rules where we are uncertain because, if we are certain, the costs of liability rules—essentially the costs of collectively valuing the damages to all concerned plus the cost in coercion to those who would not sell at the collectively determined figure—are unnecessary. They are unnecessary because transaction costs and bargaining barriers become irrelevant when we are certain who is the cheapest cost avoider; economic efficiency will be attained without transactions by making the correct initial entitlement.

As a practical matter we often are uncertain who the cheapest cost avoider is. In such cases, traditional legal doctrine tends to find a nuisance but imposes only damages on Taney payable to the Marshalls.[60] This way, if the amount of damages Taney is made to pay is close to the injury caused, economic efficiency will have had its due; if he cannot make a go of it, the nuisance was not worth its costs. The entitlement to the Marshalls to be free from pollution unless compensated, however, will have been given not because it was thought that polluting was probably worth less to Taney than freedom from pollution was worth to the Marshalls, nor even because on some distributional basis we preferred to charge the cost to Taney rather than to the Marshalls. It was so placed *simply because we did not know* whether Taney desired to pollute more than the Marshalls desired to be free from pollution, and the only way we thought we could test out the value of the pollution was by the only liability rule we thought we had. This was rule two, the imposition of nuisance damages on Taney. At least this would be the position of a court concerned with economic efficiency which believed itself limited to rules one, two, and three.

---

[60] *See, e.g.*, City of Harrisonville v. W.S. Dickey Clay Mfg. Co., 289 U.S. 334 (1933) (damages appropriate remedy where injunction would prejudice important public interest); Madison v. Ducktown Sulphur, Copper & Iron Co., 113 Tenn. 331, 83 S.W. 658 (1904) (damages appropriate because of plaintiff's ten year delay in seeking to enjoin fumes).

Rule four gives at least the possibility that the opposite entitlement may also lead to economic efficiency in a situation of uncertainty. Suppose for the moment that a mechanism exists for collectively assessing the damage resulting to Taney from being stopped from polluting by the Marshalls, and a mechanism also exists for collectively assessing the benefit to each of the Marshalls from such cessation. Then—assuming the same degree of accuracy in collective valuation as exists in rule two (the nuisance damage rule)—the Marshalls would stop the pollution if it harmed them more than it benefited Taney. If this is possible, then even if we thought it necessary to use a liability rule, we would still be free to give the entitlement to Taney or Marshall for whatever reasons, efficiency or distributional, we desired.

Actually, the issue is still somewhat more complicated. For just as transaction costs are not necessarily symmetrical under the two converse property rule entitlements, so also the liability rule equivalents of transaction costs—the cost of valuing collectively and of coercing compliance with that valuation—may not be symmetrical under the two converse liability rules. Nuisance damages may be very hard to value, and the costs of informing all the injured of their rights and getting them into court may be prohibitive. Instead, the assessment of the objective damage to Taney from foregoing his pollution may be cheap and so might the assessment of the relative benefits to all Marshalls of such freedom from pollution. But the opposite may also be the case. As a result, just as the choice of which property entitlement may be based on the asymmetry of transaction costs and hence on the greater amenability of one property entitlement to market corrections, so might the choice between liability entitlements be based on the asymmetry of the costs of collective determination.

The introduction of distributional considerations makes the existence of the fourth possibility even more significant. One does not need to go into all the permutations of the possible tradeoffs between efficiency and distributional goals under the four rules to show this. A simple example should suffice. Assume a factory which, by using cheap coal, pollutes a very wealthy section of town and employs many low income workers to produce a product purchased primarily by the poor; assume also a distributional goal that favors equality of wealth. Rule one—enjoin the nuisance—would possibly have desirable economic efficiency results (if the pollution hurt the homeowners more than it saved the factory in coal costs), but it would have disastrous distribution effects. It would also have undesirable efficiency effects if the initial judgment on costs of avoidance had been wrong and transaction costs were high. Rule two—nuisance damages—would allow a testing of the economic efficiency of eliminating the pollution, even in the presence of high transaction costs, but would quite possibly put the factory out of business or diminish output and thus have the same income distribution effects as rule one. Rule three—no nuisance—would have favorable distributional effects since it might protect the income of the workers. But if the pollution harm was greater to the homeowners than the cost of avoiding it by using a better coal, and if transaction costs—holdout problems—were such that homeowners could not unite to pay the factory to use better coal, rule three would have unsatisfactory efficiency effects. Rule four—payment of damages to the factory after allowing the homeowners to compel it to use better coal, and assessment of the cost of these damages to the homeowners—would be the only one which would accomplish both the distributional and efficiency goals.[61]

An equally good hypothetical for any of the rules can be constructed. Moreover, the problems of coercion may as a practical matter be extremely severe under rule four. How do the homeowners decide to stop the factory's use of low grade coal? How do we assess the damages and their proportional allocation in terms of benefits to the homeowners? But equivalent problems may often be as great for rule two. How do we value the damages to each of the many homeowners? How do we inform the homeowners of their rights to damages? How do we evaluate and limit the administrative expenses of the court actions this solution implies?

The seriousness of the problem depends under each of the liability rules on the number of people whose "benefits" or "damages" one is assessing and the expense and likelihood of error in such assessment. A judgment on these questions is necessary to an evaluation of the possible economic efficiency benefits of employing one rule rather than another. The relative ease of making such assessments through different institutions may explain why we often employ the courts for rule two and get to rule four—when we do get there—only through political bodies which may, for example, prohibit pollution, or "take" the entitlement to build a supersonic plane by a kind of eminent domain, paying compensation to those injured by these decisions.[62] But all this does not, in any sense, diminish the importance of the fact that an awareness of the possibility of an entitlement to

[61] Either of the liability rules may also be used in another manner to achieve distributional goals. For example, if victims of pollution were poor, and if society desired a more equal distribution of wealth, it might intentionally increase "objective" damage awards if rule two were used; conversely, it might decrease the compensation to the factory owners, without any regard for economic efficiency if rule four were chosen. There are obvious disadvantages to this ad hoc method of achieving distributional goals. *See* p. 1110 *supra*.

[62] Of course, variants of the other rules may be administered through political institutions as well. Rule three, granting a property entitlement to a polluter, may be effectuated by tax credits or other incentives such as subsidization of nonpolluting fuels offered for voluntary pollution abatement. In such schemes, as with rule four, political institutions are used to effect comprehensive benefit assessment and overcome freeloader problems which would be encountered in a more decentralized market solution. However, this centralization—to the extent that it replaces voluntary payments by individual pollution victims with collective payments not unanimously agreed upon—is a hybrid solution. The polluter must assent to the sale of his entitlement, but the amount of pollution abatement sought and the price paid by each pollution victim is not subjectively determined and voluntarily assented to by each.

The relationship of hybrids like the above to the four basic rules can be stated more generally. The buyer of an entitlement, whether the entitlement is protected by property or liability rules, may be viewed as owning what is in effect a property right not to buy the entitlement. But when freeloader problems abound, that property right may instead be given to a class of potential buyers. This "class" may be a municipality, a sewer authority, or any other body which can decide to buy an entitlement and compel those benefited to pay an objective price. When this is done, the individuals within the class have themselves only an entitlement not to purchase the seller's entitlement protected by a liability rule.

As we have already seen, the holder of an entitlement may be permitted to sell it at his own price or be compelled to sell it at an objective price: he may have an entitlement protected by a property or liability rule. Since, therefore, in any transaction the buyer may have a property or liability entitlement not to buy and the seller may have a property or a liability entitlement not to sell, there are, in effect, four combinations of rules for each possible original location of the entitlement: voluntary seller and voluntary buyer; voluntary seller and compelled buyer; compelled seller and voluntary buyer; compelled seller and compelled buyer. Moreover, since the entitlement to that which is being bought or sold could have been originally given to the opposite party, there are, in effect, eight possible rules rather than four.

We do not mean by the above to suggest that political institutions are used only to allocate collectively held property rights. Quite the contrary, rule two, for instance, gives pollution victims an entitlement protected by a liability rule to be free from pollution. This rule could be administered by decentralized damage assessment as in litigation, or it could be effected by techniques like effluent fees charged to polluters. The latter type of collective intervention may be preferred where large numbers are involved and the costs of decentralized injury valuation are high. Still, under either system the "sale price" is collectively determined, so the basic character of the victims' entitlement is not changed.

pollute, but one protected only by a liability rule, may in some instances allow us best to combine our distributional and efficiency goals.

We have said that we would say little about justice, and so we shall. But it should be clear that if rule four might enable us best to combine efficiency goals with distributional goals, it might also enable us best to combine those same efficiency goals with other goals that are often described in justice language. For example, assume that the factory in our hypothetical was using cheap coal *before* any of the wealthy houses were built. In these circumstances, rule four will not only achieve the desirable efficiency and distributional results mentioned above, but it will also accord with any "justice" significance which is attached to being there first. And this is so whether we view this justice significance as part of a distributional goal, as part of a long run efficiency goal based on protecting expectancies, or as part of an independent concept of justice.

Thus far in this section we have ignored the possibility of employing rules of inalienability to solve pollution problems. A general policy of barring pollution does seem unrealistic.[63] But rules of inalienability can appropriately be used to limit the levels of pollution and to control the levels of activities which cause pollution.[64]

One argument for inalienability may be the widespread existence of moralisms against pollution. Thus it may hurt the Marshalls—gentleman farmers—to see Taney, a smoke-choked city dweller, sell his entitlement to be free of pollution. A different kind of externality or moralism may be even more important. The Marshalls may be hurt by the expectation that, while the present generation might withstand present pollution levels with no serious health dangers, future generations may well face a despoiled, hazardous environmental condition which they are powerless to reverse.[65] And this ground for inalienability might be strengthened if a similar conclusion were reached on grounds of self paternalism. Finally, society might restrict alienability on paternalistic grounds. The Marshalls might feel that although Taney himself does not know it, Taney will be better off if he really can see the stars at night, or if he can breathe smogless air.

Whatever the grounds for inalienability, we should reemphasize that distributional effects should be carefully evaluated in making the choice for or against inalienability. Thus the citizens of a town may be granted an entitlement to be free of water pollution caused by the waste discharges of a chemical factory; and the entitlement might be made inalienable on the grounds that the town's citizens really would be better off in the long run to have access to clean beaches. But the entitlement might also be made inalienable to assure the maintenance of a beautiful resort area for the very wealthy, at the same time putting the town's citizens out of work.[66]

---

[63] *See* Michelman, *supra* note 1, at 667.

[64] This is the exact analogue of specific deterrence of accident causing activities. *See* COSTS at 95–129.

Although it may seem fanciful to us, there is of course the possibility that a state might wish to grant a converse entitlement—an inalienable entitlement to pollute in some instances. This might happen where the state believed that in the long run everyone would be better off by allowing the polluting producers to make their products, regardless of whether the polluter thought it advantageous to accept compensation for stopping his pollution.

[65] *See* Michelman, *supra* note 1, at 684.

[66] *Cf.* Frady, *The View from Hilton Head*, HARPER'S, May, 1970, at 103–112 (conflict over proposed establishment of chemical factory that would pollute the area's beaches in economically depressed South Carolina community; environmental groups that opposed factory backed by developers of wealthy resorts in the area, proponents of factory supported by representatives of unemployed town citizens).

Obviously we cannot canvass the relevance of our approach through many areas of the law. But we do think it beneficial to examine one further area, that of crimes against property and bodily integrity. The application of the framework to the use of criminal sanctions in cases of theft or violations of bodily integrity is useful in that it may aid in understanding the previous material, especially as it helps us to distinguish different kinds of legal problems and to identify the different modes of resolving those problems.

Beginning students, when first acquainted with economic efficiency notions, sometimes ask why ought not a robber be simply charged with the value of the thing robbed. And the same question is sometimes posed by legal philosophers.[67] If it is worth more to the robber than to the owner, is not economic efficiency served by such a penalty? Our answers to such a question tend to move quickly into very high sounding and undoubtedly relevant moral considerations. But these considerations are often not very helpful to the questioner because they depend on the existence of obligations on individuals not to rob for a fixed price and the original question was why we should impose such obligations at all.

One simple answer to the question would be that thieves do not get caught every time they rob and therefore the costs to the thief must at least take the unlikelihood of capture into account.[68] But that would not fully answer the problem, for even if thieves were caught every time, the penalty we would wish to impose would be greater than the objective damages to the person robbed.

A possible broader explanation lies in a consideration of the difference between property entitlements and liability entitlements. For us to charge the thief with a penalty equal to an objectively determined value of the property stolen would be to convert all property rule entitlements into liability rule entitlements.

The question remains, however, why *not* convert all property rules into liability rules? The answer is, of course, obvious. Liability rules represent only an approximation of the value of the object to its original owner and willingness to pay such an approximate value is no indication that it is worth more to the thief than to the owner. In other words, quite apart from the expense of arriving collectively at such an objective valuation, it is no guarantee of the economic efficiency of the transfer.[69] If this is so with property, it is all the more so with bodily integrity, and we would not presume collectively and objectively to value the cost of a rape to the victim against the benefit to the rapist even if economic efficiency is our sole motive. Indeed when we approach bodily integrity we are getting close to areas where we do not let the entitlement be sold at all and where economic efficiency enters in, if at all, in a more complex way. But even where the items taken or destroyed are things we do allow to be sold, we will not without special reasons impose an objective selling price on the vendor.

---

[67] One of the last articles by Professor Giorgio Del Vecchio came close to asking this question. See Del Vecchio, *Equality and Inequality in Relation to Justice*, 11 NAT. LAW FORUM 36, 43–45 (1966).

[68] *See, e.g.*, Becker, *Crime and Punishment: An Economic Approach*, 76 J. POL. ECON. 169 (1968).

[69] One might also point out that very often a thief will not have the money to meet the objectively determined price of the stolen object; indeed, his lack of resources is probably his main motivation for the theft. In such cases society, if it insists on a liability rule, will have to compensate the initial entitlement holder from the general societal coffers. When this happens the thief will not feel the impact of the liability rule and hence will not be sufficiently deterred from engaging in similar activity in the future. *Cf.* COSTS at 147–48.

Once we reach the conclusion that we will not simply have liability rules, but that often, even just on economic efficiency grounds, property rules are desirable, an answer to the beginning student's question becomes clear. The thief not only harms the victim, he undermines rules and distinctions of significance beyond the specific case. Thus even if in a given case we can be sure that the value of the item stolen was no more than X dollars, and even if the thief has been caught and is prepared to compensate, we would not be content simply to charge the thief X dollars. Since in the majority of cases we cannot be sure of the economic efficiency of the transfer by theft, we must add to each case an undefinable kicker which represents society's need to keep all property rules from being changed at will into liability rules.[70] In other words, we impose criminal sanctions as a means of deterring future attempts to convert property rules into liability rules.[71]

The first year student might push on, however, and ask why we treat the thief or the rapist differently from the injurer in an auto accident or the polluter in a nuisance case. Why do we allow liability rules there? In a sense, we have already answered the question. The only level at which, before the accident, the driver can negotiate for the value of what he might take from his potential victim is one at which transactions are too costly. The thief or rapist, on the other hand, could have negotiated without undue expense (at least if the good was one which we allowed to be sold at all) because we assume he knew what he was going to do and to whom he would do it. The case of the accident is different because knowledge exists only at the level of deciding to drive or perhaps to drive fast, and at that level negotiations with potential victims are usually not feasible.

The case of nuisance seems different, however. There the polluter knows what he will do and, often, whom it will hurt. But as we have already pointed out, freeloader or holdout problems may often preclude any successful negotiations between the polluter and the victims of pollution; additionally, we are often uncertain who is the cheapest avoider of pollution costs. In these circumstances a liability rule, which at least allowed the economic efficiency of a proposed transfer of entitlements to be tested, seemed appropriate, even though it permitted the

---

[70] If we were not interested in the integrity of property rules and hence we were not using an indefinable kicker, we would still presumably try to adjust the amount of damages charged to the thief in order to reflect the fact that only a percentage of thieves are caught; that is, we would fix a price-penalty which reflected the value of the good and the risk of capture.

[71] A problem related to criminal sanctions is that of punitive damages in intentional torts. If Taney sets a spring gun with the purpose of killing or maiming anyone who trespasses on his property, Taney has knowledge of what he is doing and of the risks involved which is more akin to the criminal than the negligent driver. But because Taney does not know precisely which one of many Marshalls will be the victim of his actions, ex ante negotiations seem difficult. How then do we justify the use of criminal sanctions and of more than compensatory damages? Probably the answer lies in the fact that we assume that the benefits of Taney's act are not worth the harm they entail if that harm were fully valued. Believing that this fact, in contrast with what is involved in a simple negligence case, should be, and in a sense can be, made known to the actor at the time he acts, we pile on extra damages. Our judgment is that most would act differently if a true cost-benefit burden could be placed. Given that judgment and given the impossibility of imposing a true cost-benefit burden by collective valuations—because of inadequate knowledge— we make sure that if we err we will err on the side of overestimating the cost.

There may be an additional dimension. Unlike fines or other criminal sanctions, punitive damages provide an extra compensation for the victim. This may not be pure windfall. Once the judgment is made that injuries classified as intentional torts are less desirable than nonintentional harms—either because they are expected to be less efficient or because there is less justification for the tort-feasor's not having purchased the entitlement in an ex ante bargain—then it may be that the actual, subjective injury to the victim from the tort is enhanced. One whose automobile is destroyed accidentally suffers from the loss of his car; one whose automobile is destroyed intentionally suffers from the loss of the car, and his injury is made greater by the knowledge that the loss was intentional, willful [sic], or otherwise avoidable.

nonaccidental and unconsented taking of an entitlement. It should be emphasized, however, that where transaction costs do not bar negotiations between polluter and victim, or where we are sufficiently certain who the cheapest cost avoider is, there are no efficiency reasons for allowing intentional takings, and property rules, supported by injunctions or criminal sanctions, are appropriate.[72]

VI. Conclusion

This article has attempted to demonstrate how a wide variety of legal problems can usefully be approached in terms of a specific framework. Framework or model building has two shortcomings. The first is that models can be mistaken for the total view of phenomena, like legal relationships, which are too complex to be painted in any one picture. The second is that models generate boxes into which one then feels compelled to force situations which do not truly fit. There are, however, compensating advantages. Legal scholars, precisely because they have tended to eschew model building, have often proceeded in an ad hoc way, looking at cases and seeing what categories emerged. But this approach also affords only one view of the Cathedral. It may neglect some relationships among the problems involved in the cases which model building can perceive, precisely because it does generate boxes, or categories. The framework we have employed may be applied in many different areas of the law. We think its application facilitated perceiving and defining an additional resolution of the problem of pollution. As such we believe the painting to be well worth the oils.

[72] *Cf.* pp. 1111–13.

We have not discussed distributional goals as they relate to criminal sanctions. In part this is because we have assumed the location of the initial entitlement—we have assumed the victim of a crime was entitled to the good stolen or to his bodily integrity. There is, however, another aspect of distributional goals which relates to the particular rule we choose to protect the initial entitlement. For example, one might raise the question of linking the severity of criminal sanctions to the wealth of the criminal or the victim. While this aspect of distributional goals would certainly be a fruitful area of discussion, it is beyond the scope of the present article.

The Law and Society Movement

Stewart Macaulay

Stewart Macaulay

ALTHOUGH THE PROFESSIONAL consciousness illustrated by the legal process materials remained dominant in American legal thinking for a generation after the war, even as it was being articulated legal scholars were at work on alternatives. When the consensus slipped, it would be replaced by an eclectic range of approaches to law and methods for legal scholarship, most of which were incubated during the legal process period, in self-conscious alliance with or rebellion against the paradigm developed by Fuller, Wechsler, and Hart and Sacks. The first significant departure came from Wisconsin. Willard Hurst encouraged the Wisconsin law school to launch a program on law and the behavioral sciences, and worked to found a professional association bringing scholars working on the relationship between "law and society" from various disciplines into contact with one another. In 1963, Stewart Macaulay, a professor at Wisconsin who had been mentored by Hurst, published "Non-Contractual Relations in Business: a Preliminary Study." For thirty years, the article would remain a touchstone for those seeking to bring social science to legal scholarship, under the banners of the "law and society movement," "socio-legal studies," and "empiricism."

American legal thought had regularly appealed to the social sciences—it was Holmes in "The Path of the Law" who wrote "the man of the future is the man of statistics and the master of economics." Pragmatism had its roots in statistics and fostered an instrumental conception of legal work—problem solving—for which social science techniques would often seem useful. Before the Second World War, the social sciences were routinely enlisted in projects to reconstruct legal doctrine in the wake of assaults on the formal doctrinal structures of nineteenth-century law, and to provide the expertise for an expanding legislative and public regulatory authority. The expanding administrative agencies of the New Deal made extensive use of the social sciences in rule-making. Reconstructive projects of restatement and codification routinely relied on social customs and business practices as a source for reform of legal rules. As reasoning about policy came to be seen as a necessary and desirable part of routine legal work—for judges as well as administrative agencies and legislatures—the social sciences were often invoked as a kind of answer machine for the instrumental, functional, and purposive lawmaker. In concrete cases, the call for modernization often took the form of an insistence that contextual considerations—the degree of reliance on a promise, the severity of fault, the bargaining power of the parties—influence the interpretation of both common-law precedent and statute.

These developments in the profession influenced, and were influenced by, changes in the academic study of law. Early on, a number of prominent realists had left legal scholarship to engage in empirical study—most famously by joining the Institute for Legal Study at Johns Hopkins University. Through the 1930s and '40s, knowledge from sociology, anthropology, psychology, and economics came to seem indispensable in a range of legal disciplines, most notably criminal law. Reformers urged judges to pay attention to what seemed the new social realities of modern industrial capitalism when they interpreted legal rules—social realities they felt could be understood through social science. Indeed, reformist legal scholars often promoted induction from sociologically perceived facts as a substitute for the doctrinal deduction in which they had lost faith.

In appellate litigation, the introduction of social science information remained controversial at least until the war, although Louis Brandeis had pioneered its use in his 1908 brief to the Supreme Court in *Muller v. Oregon* (208 US 412, 1908), which used social science research demonstrating the deleterious effects of working long hours on women and girls to support his argument for the constitutionality of social welfare legislation limiting such work to ten hours per day. For traditionalists, "facts" were for the trial court, not for introduction at the appellate level. By the war, however, the introduction of evidence of "legislative" as opposed to "adjudicative" facts at the appellate level had become widely accepted. After the war, the most famous use of sociological material before the Supreme Court was in *Brown v. Board of Education* to demonstrate that separate schools could not be equal in their impact on black children.

For all this, prewar legal scholars had practiced social science less often than they had invoked its virtues and potential. At precisely the moment legal scholars were turning to the social sciences, those sciences were undergoing their own revolution, coming to understand social knowledge to be itself conflicting and relative. Moreover, prewar legal scholars urging use of the social sciences remained ambivalent on several crucial points. Was attention to social conditions and social science meant to *substitute* for more routine modes of legal interpretation, or only to supplement law when "normal" interpretive techniques ran out? When law turned to social science, should it continue to think of itself standing apart from the world as judge and regulator, or should law *itself* be understood as part of the social terrain? And how precisely should the social "is" be transformed into a legal "ought"? Should the law restate social norms—or intervene to compensate for deficient or absent social norms? Should law articulate social consensus, or do something altogether different—something procedural or formal, perhaps—to encourage the formation of social norms?

Postwar legal process scholars largely sidestepped the social sciences. The legal process conviction that law was best understood as an external supplement to social life—"channeling," "cautioning," "evidencing" to use Fuller's examples—when social and commercial practices could not do so for themselves, made it less appealing to fill in the gaps in legal materials by reference to social practices. One would need rather to decide whether it was better to leave the social practice—and the gap—alone, or to seek to fill the gap in such a way as to reorient the social practice. Moreover, legal process scholars' focus on institutional considerations and procedures sustained an agnosticism about substantive outcomes and rationales that made the need for social science investigation seem less urgent. Many legal realists had seen social science as a supplement for the deductive reasoning in which they had lost faith—at least where deduction hit a conflict, gap, or ambiguity. For the legal process scholars, moreover, faith in a determinative social science seemed almost as misplaced as faith in a determinative doctrinal deduction. Social science was itself riven by methodological debate, and the most advanced thinking in every field seemed to stress the relativity of knowledge and the pluralism of multiple perspectives.

At the same time, policy reasoning no longer seemed a supplement or exception to legal interpretation. Policy had been brought inside the legal field—policy reasoning was part of legal reasoning. The style of "policy" analysis illustrated by Fuller's "Consideration and Form" was quite removed from social science. Fuller found the "policies" served by the doctrine of consideration neither by studying social custom to see how the doctrine operated, nor by interpreting the precedents articulating the doctrine. He found them through reflection on the social purpose and function of contract law more generally, of formal rules more generally, and of consideration doctrine itself. For Fuller, policies were immanent in the materials—closer to moral values than social facts. Moreover, the point about the relationship between rules and policies is that rules serve a host of different purposes that will need to be balanced against one another through careful reasoning and judgment—not by appeal to science.

Stewart Macaulay began his scholarly work very much in the legal process idiom, his first articles heavily influenced by the Fuller of "Consideration and Form." Indeed, in the evolution of Macaulay's work leading up to the 1963 article included here, we can see the fault line between the legal process mainstream consensus and what would become the "law and society" approach to law and legal scholarship.

Stewart Macaulay was born in 1931 and raised in California. He studied law at Stanford, graduating in 1954. After clerking for Judge Denman of the 9th Circuit, Macaulay joined the University of Chicago law faculty as an instructor in 1956. While there, Willard Hurst encouraged him to read widely outside law in the social sciences and funded a year of leave for him to do so, after which Macaulay joined Hurst at the Wisconsin law school, where he continues to teach. Macaulay established himself early as a scholar and teacher of contracts—alongside contracts, he teaches dispute resolution and "law and social science." Very much a man of the fifties, Macaulay likes jazz, wants people to know that he reads spy novels and mysteries, is an avid sports fan, and thinks of himself as a liberal. He has a soft and self-deprecating sense of humor, and a broadly humanist, if often tragic, sensibility and outlook.

Macaulay's first major article, "Justice Traynor and the Law of Contracts," analyzed the contract law opinions of Justice Roger Traynor of the California Supreme Court, a liberal justice widely regarded at the time as forward thinking and influential. He undertook to distill from Traynor's diverse opinions a set of goals and purposes with which to characterize his jurisprudence. Like Fuller, he did so by rumination, imaginatively reconstructing a list of purposes and policies Traynor may have been attempting to further in particular opinions. Macaulay developed a matrix of policies served by contract law, and, like Fuller, treated each opinion as expressing a compromise among two or more opposing policies. To determine where each opinion should be placed on a continuum between contrasting policies, Macaulay analyzed the language of the opinions themselves—not their effects in the world.

The terms Macaulay used to describe judicial work would have been familiar to Hart and Sacks. Macaulay imagined Traynor balancing an array of conflicting objectives, reasoning his way to a legal rule, and then to an application of that rule in a particular case. Traynor's opinions, in turn, could then be interpreted as the expression of a tendency in Traynor's jurisprudence to pursue some objectives at the expense of others. Academic work, like judicial work, required careful reasoning and judgment about the relationships between rules and the social purposes immanent in them. Macaulay cites Frank Knight approvingly:

> The right principle is to respect all principles, take them fully into account, and then use *good judgment* as to how far to follow one or another in the case in hand. All principles are false, because all are true—in a sense and to a degree; hence, none is true in a sense and to a degree which would deny to others a similarly qualified truth. There is always a principle, plausible and even sound within limits, to justify any possible course of action and, of course, the opposite one. The truly right course is a matter of the best compromise or the best or "least worse" combination of good and evil.[1]

In such a situation, all one can do is reason. Again quoting Knight: "ideals are not unitary, they conflict; and the problem is to secure the 'best' balance and compromise, for which there is no single formula; it is a matter of *judgment*."[2] As a result, social scientific evidence was not on the front burner when purposes were being assessed—nor could social science substitute for the *judgment* of judges about the resolution of conflicts among policies. Macaulay writes: "classification does not tell anyone when one policy ought to prevail over another. This remains in the realm of value judgments."[3]

> Justice Traynor's contracts decisions must be evaluated in terms of the balance he strikes between seeking the goal of market support and that of social control, and the proportions in which he makes use of the policies designed to carry out these goals.[4]

In the end, Macaulay gives Traynor high marks: "in sum, Justice Traynor's balance between supporting the market and carrying out social control ideas seems excellent in the limited context of the cases he has decided. He shows caution but is willing to act when not all the danger signals are up."[5]

The specific taxonomies Macaulay developed for analyzing Traynor's opinions well illustrate legal process assumptions about the relationship between legal rules and immanent social policies. In broad terms, Fuller had associated what he termed formal and substantive rules of contract with different sets of policies. Formal doctrines, like consideration, functioned to caution the parties, provide evidence for the deal, or channel the behavior of private parties. Substantive doctrines, by contrast, functioned to reinforce the principle of private autonomy, avoid unjust enrichment, and protect reliance. Legal process scholars developed numerous category schemes of this type, linking types of norms with social purposes or functions. Hart and Sacks had cataloged the different social functions performed by norms that took the form of broad "standards" and by those that took the form of more precise and narrowly tailored "rules." Macaulay stressed that different *modes of judicial reasoning* expressed different policy objectives. Macaulay distinguished what he termed "transactional" and "functional" policies. He describes the difference this way: "[t]he transactional policy calls for courts to support the market by taking action to carry out the *particular* transaction" while "the functional policy calls for lawmakers to create generally applicable rules which facilitate bargaining by producing a system or structure in which exchanges can take place." In Macaulay's mind, the transactional policy is expressed when judges reason on a "case by case" approach, seeking to "carry out the particular transaction." To pursue the functional policy, by contrast, "courts should not seek the best result case-by-case since predictable law is a more important means of supporting the market." Rather, they should pursue "the creation of generally applicable rules."[6] With this distinction in mind, Macaulay could read through Traynor's opinions, allocating those proceeding "case by case" to the transactional policy, those articulating rules of general applicability to the "functional" policy.

For law and society scholars, such speculative association between modes of reasoning and policy objectives were pure inventions, which might or might not be borne out in the real world. For critical legal studies scholars, led by Duncan Kennedy in "Form and Substance in Private Law Adjudication," the difficulty was rather the intellectual looseness of these associations. It seemed as plausible to imagine "form" serving or failing to serve Fuller's substantive policies as those Fuller associated with form. In Macaulay's case, it is hard to understand why carrying out the particular transaction would not sometimes require implementation of a general rule, or why the market might not be as supported by a judiciary attuned to particular cases as to the enunciation of broad rules.

The first lever used to open legal process assumptions about the links between rules and polities to scrutiny was, in fact, itself a key legal process idea—law was supplemental, rather than central, to the operations of the market. This idea had given Hart and Sacks confidence that even a pattern of judicial and administrative judgment as diverse and inconclusive as that on display in the Cantaloupe Case would do little harm to the national market in vegetables. The law and society milieu that Macaulay entered by moving to Wisconsin was preoccupied with understanding the distance between the mandarin expression of legal rules and the behavior of people in markets and bureaucracies. If Hart and Sacks were right about the supplemental character of law, they reasoned, it was hard to accept that Fuller and the others could be so confident about the policy implications of different types of rules without exploring their actual effects. Policies and purposes were not immanent in rules or modes of reasoning—they were realized, or they were not realized, on the ground.

Macaulay strikes out in precisely this new direction in "Non-Contractual Relations in Business: A Preliminary Study." Macaulay was not the first modern American legal scholar to study contracts in context—John Dawson's famous studies of the effects of inflation on contracts in Germany and the United States may have that distinction. Llewellyn had also written about the sociological limits of contract, and Friedrich Kessler's 1957 study of automobile dealer franchising was also influential. But Macaulay's article was not only a study of the effects of contract—it also proposed that we think of "contract" as a social rather than a legal institution. As such, the piece was both an innovation in the field of contracts, a model for sociological legal work more generally, and signaled a new approach in Macaulay's own thinking.

Macaulay wrote as sociology was becoming an increasingly visible and popular intellectual discipline for understanding American life. Hurst had introduced Macaulay to Talcot Parsons and Robert Merton. It is now difficult to recapture the significance of such sociology classics as Parson's *The Social System* (1951), Merton's *Social Theory and Social Structure* (1949), or David Riesman's *The Lonely Crowd/A Study of the Changing American Character* (1950). Riesman, a graduate of Harvard Law School, Brandeis clerk, and professor at Buffalo Law School, saw his book become the first sociological bestseller after appearing on the cover of *Life* magazine. These were the years in which books like Riesman's, C. Wright Mills's *The Power Elite* (1956), William Whyte's *The Organization Man* (1956), or Gunnar Myrdal's *An American Dilemma: The Negro Problem and Modern Democracy* (1944) were widely discussed in intellectual circles and in the popular press. Sociology seemed to offer a way to grasp a rapidly changing American culture, economy, and society whole.

Macaulay begins with this definition of contracts:

> Contract, as I use the term here, involves two distinct elements: (a) Rational planning of the transaction with careful provision for as many future contingencies as can be foreseen, and (b) the existence or use of actual or potential legal sanctions to induce performance of the exchange or to compensate for non-performance.[7]

The absence of doctrinal desiderata from Macaulay's definition is as odd as Fuller's disinterest in the authority of precedent in his effort to offer justifications for the doctrine of consideration. Macaulay does not begin with a doctrinal definition—with "offer and acceptance," say. Still less does he begin with conceptual abstractions like "bargained for exchange" or "meeting of the minds." With this definitional paragraph we have taken a sharp step away from Fuller and legal process. Where Fuller assessed the functions of contract rules for society, Macaulay focuses on the functions contracts serve in society for those who use them: planning and sanctioning. Contract is whatever fulfills those functions—regardless of whether it would legally or philosophically be treated by some external observer *as* a contract.

In this, Macaulay's contractor's-eye-view also differs from the Holmes of the "bad man." The bad man was a heuristic—lawyers seeking to know what the *rules really were* should ask, as would a bad man, when state force will be brought to bear upon the client. Macaulay is interested in the functions *in fact served* by the *social institution* of contract, whether through the enforcement of legal rules, or by other means. Doctrinal analysis of whether a legal contract exists (has there been an offer and an acceptance?) and how it will likely be enforced (what remedies are available to the nonbreaching party?) are but subordinate elements in Macaulay's second condition. We have contracts where we have planning and the existence of "actual or potential" legal sanctions to induce performance or compensate for nonperformance.

By defining contract as a social institution, Macaulay gave Fullerian policy analysis an altogether different complexion—it was no longer sensible to consider the policies embedded in legal doctrine *as if* that doctrine were central to the world the policies were meant to affect. Indeed, it would be foolish to think about the "policies" underlying a doctrine like consideration *as if* contracts made became contracts enforced. Reflecting on his relationship with Fuller in 1991, Macaulay sharpens the ideological significance of Fuller's inattention to the "gap between the law on the books and the law in action."[8] For Macaulay, to suggest, as Fuller repeatedly had, that contract law doctrines express a policy of protecting expectation when "[o]ur legal system seldom puts aggrieved parties where they would have been had breaching parties performed," serves the "ideolog[ical]" function of suggesting "to business lawyers and judges that the law is reasonable."[9] By this point, the political stakes in the debate between the legal process and the Law and Society movement were clearly drawn.

Contracts in the real world, moreover, are phenomena with multiple pieces, any one of which might be useful, the rest disregarded. For example, "it must be recognized that the existence of a legal sanction has no necessary relationship to the degree of rational planning" (*infra*, p. 56) so parties may plan in a contractual fashion, but never resolve disputes in this way, and vice versa. It is difficult to assess the policies embedded in contract law if the institution of contract is disaggregated by its users, treated as a bundle of individual doctrines, procedures, institutions, arguments, and professional services to be mobilized as needed.

Looking to the uses made of contract by businessmen in Wisconsin, Macaulay discovered that they paid little attention to contract law—that lawyers routinely signed off on contracts they knew to be unenforceable, that businessmen regularly forewent assertion of their rights to preserve ongoing business relationships, that disputes were only very rarely resolved legally, that contracts were often drafted more for the internal purposes of one of the parties—communication between marketing and production—than to structure the relationship with another party, that disputes which were pursued legally were as often the product of irrational revenge as calculation for recovery of expectation.

These discoveries challenged not only the significance of contract law, but also much of how it was substantively and institutionally understood. As Macaulay put it in 1985: "[t]he 1963 article challenges a model of contract law's functions, explicit or implicit in the work of contracts scholars and social theorists."[10] The market is not a miracle of cooperation among disconnected strangers at all—commercial actors are already in relationships, relationships that transcend the specific transactions that sometimes become the focus of contracts. Obligations arise in the context of relations and change over time, whatever may have been memorialized in a contract. People contract to signify commitment to cooperate, rather than to allocate risks, they write down their plans to communicate with their own organizations, rather than to secure their rights in a later dispute. The relationships among commercial actors, moreover, are generally not relations among equals, enforced by the state, but among unequals, for any one of whom the state may be an ally or an obstacle in an ongoing negotiation which began before the contract was written and will continue as long as both remain in business. Negotiation between the parties does not end with the signature of a contract; it continues, and may well be most intense, when disputes arise. In such a struggle, the law—its norms, institutions, procedures, and professionals—are a set of strategies which might be mobilized by one or the other party. The function of a legal "form"—like the requirement of consideration—is to enhance or impede one or the other side's bargaining power in a struggle over performance.

In short, the legal process would simply look different if we studied the Cantaloupe Case as aberration rather than apotheosis. In what may well be the most well developed counterpoint to the Cantaloupe Case, Macaulay wrote a gripping study of "how people can perform complex commitments without formal planning and even implicit threats to use legal sanctions" analyzing the relationship between the architect Frank Lloyd Wright and his client, S.C. Johnson and Son, in the design and construction of the Johnson Administration Building. Attention to the marginality of law and to the ubiquity of ongoing social relations and social struggle brought to the foreground aspects of commercial life that had been treated as exceptional. Macaulay's focus on law as a possible, if often marginal, terrain of struggle offered a vision of the legal system far less optimistic and harmonious than the legal process consensus. Study of the *use* made of legal institutions in society offered a new model for what legal scholars might do to understand not only what the rules *were*, but how they operated, who they helped and who they hindered.

In the years after Macaulay wrote, these strands were taken up quite differently by various groups of scholars. In the field of contract law, Macaulay's article remains foundational for those developing a "relational" approach to the field, although relatively few scholars have pursued the sociological implications of Macaulay's approach. The piece has been more significant for those seeking to study law as a social phenomenon using the techniques of social science. The Law and Society Association, founded earlier by Hurst and others, would lend its name to what became a broad scholarly movement pursuing the themes illustrated in Macaulay's article. The Law and Society movement was the first of what would be a wide range of such academic movements, launched from the disintegrating postwar legal process consensus. Eventually, their ranks would include Law and Economics, various strands of Modern Liberalism, Critical Legal Studies, and numerous others.

The Law and Society movement looked back to the great sociologists and political theorists—Karl Marx, Emile Durkheim, and most particularly Max Weber—who had written about the place of law in society. In legal thought, the most significant precursors were Roscoe Pound and the German scholar Eugen Ehrlich. The Wisconsin law faculty contained a number of key figures in the early Movement, most notably Willard Hurst, who had been a student of Felix Frankfurter at Harvard, graduating in 1935. After working for a year with Frankfurter and clerking for Brandeis, he joined the Wisconsin faculty in 1937, and mentored a generation of younger colleagues exploring the relationship between law and the social sciences, including Macaulay. He urged legal scholars to consider law a dependent rather than an independent variable, and to focus on the economic and social forces affecting it. In the 1938–39 academic year, Hurst and Dean Lloyd Garrison had taught a series of materials to first-year students called "law in society."

The Law and Society movement took institutional form in professional association and research centers at various law schools and universities. In the 1960s and 1970s, the most important of these were at Wisconsin and Berkeley—thereafter, the American Bar Foundation, Amherst College, and a number of smaller law school and university programs emerged as participants. The movement remained heavily dependent upon foundation grants to fund both its research and its academic conferences—particularly the Ford Foundation, the Russell Sage Foundation and, in the early years, the Meyer Institute.

There is no question that participants in the Law and Society movement understood themselves to share a political outlook as "liberals" or "progressives," and saw the legal process consensus they associated with the East Coast legal establishment as conservative. They saw themselves as allies of the Warren Court, of the Civil Rights Movement, and of the Great Society projects of the Johnson administration. David Trubek described their politics in these terms:

> To be a liberal in the late 1950s and early 1960s meant favoring a stronger role for the state in the economy, moderate redistribution of income, state action to improve the lot of the disadvantaged, legal protection for the accused and mentally ill, and legal bans on racial discrimination. If you were a man and thought about the issue (which was rare), you probably wanted to improve the status of women: If you were a woman (and there were a few female scholars among the founders of law and society), you certainly did.[11]

The scholarly work generated by law and society scholars pursued different strands present in Macaulay's 1963 article. Macaulay's emphasis on the "gap" between contract law and the commercial life of Wisconsin businessmen spawned a number of studies of the "gap" between "law in the books and law in action" and the "penetration" of legal rules into commercial life. Macaulay's definition of contract envisioned a complex interaction between social behavior and the "existence or use of actual or potential legal sanctions." Efforts to think more systematically about that interaction were pioneered by Lawrence Friedman, a contemporary of Macaulay at Wisconsin now teaching at Stanford Law School who became known for his work on "legal culture." He uses the term to stress the importance of understanding law as a system, a product, source, and conduit for social forces. His work developing a theoretical input-output model for understanding law was itself influenced by the work of systems theorist Niklas Luhmann, and has focused attention on the social forces, including background ideas and opinions, that alter the effectiveness and influence of legal norms. Simultaneously, a number of post-realist scholars, often influenced by the Legal Process school, looked to anthropology, rather than sociology, as a source of methodological inspiration for understanding the legal system in operation.

Macaulay's treatment of law as background to ongoing commercial negotiations foreshadowed later efforts to understand how legal norms effected the bargains made in their shadow, pioneered by scholars like Robert Mnookin and more influenced by Coase and Posner than by Macaulay. Much of this literature, however, assumed a far closer relationship between legal rules and the calculations of negotiating parties than Macaulay came to consider realistic: "Perhaps bargaining in the shadow of the law implements those values explicit or implicit in contract doctrine to some degree. This cannot be assumed but must be established by investigation."[12] Where Macaulay had used empirical work to test and criticize a prevailing theoretical consensus in legal scholarship, many in the Law and Society movement thereafter sought to use empirical work to fine-tune and evaluate the social policy programs of the Great Society. Law and society scholars were particularly attentive to the costs and strategic uses of litigation—and were often enthusiastic about alternative modes of dispute resolution. The most significant piece to emerge from this interest is Marc Galanter's "Why the Haves Come Out Ahead," next in the Canon.

As in other movements that emerged from the disintegration of the legal process, the Law and Society movement was home to a variety of strands whose differences often became points of contestation. Some were more interested in accurate scientific description, others in problem solving, some in work with long-term critical impact, others sought more immediate impact on governmental policymaking, some were attracted by quantitative and positivist methods, others by softer, more interpretive approaches, and so forth. If the Law and Society movement of the 1960s and '70s at Wisconsin was bringing social science to law, during the same years, a variant emerged on the West Coast at Berkeley, led by Phillip Selznick and Phillippe Nonet, dedicated to bringing legal theory to the social sciences.

For all these differences, law and society scholars shared a commitment to the idea that society, including law, was a system, whose operations could be understood by social scientific study. They were committed to objectivism in that study, and shared an intuition that the commanding heights of law were less central to the organization of the social system than they were generally given credit for being. These ideas can all be found in Macaulay's 1963 article, but it was also a manifesto for a more disaggregated and internally conflicted idea of law, itself embedded in ongoing political and social conflict.

The early members of the Law and Society movement may have had their greatest impact as participants in efforts to export American style legal education and modes of analysis to various locations in the Third World during the late 1960s and early 1970s, when the Law and Society idea became the basis for Third World law reform efforts in the hands of those pursuing "law and modernization or "law and development." Many leading law and society scholars went abroad, often supported by the Ford Foundation. In 1970 and 1971, Macaulay directed the Chile Law Program of the International Legal Center in Santiago. Marc Galanter went to India, David Trubek went to Brazil. Friedman, Galanter, Macaulay, and Trubek served on the Ford Foundation's steering committee on law and development research. Friedman directed a "law and development" program at Stanford Law School. The United States Agency for International Development supported much of this work, establishing a Program in Law and Modernisation at Yale Law School that supported the work of Trubek, Richard Abel, William Felstiner, Laura Nadar, Barbara Yngvesson, and Donald Black, among others. The effort led, among other things, to the spread of Law and Society methods to scholars in widespread locations. Among the most notable are Boaventura Santos in Brazil, Rogelio Perez Perdomo in Venezuela, Upendra Baxi in England, and Rajiv Dhavan in India.

By the 1970s, it was clear that the Law and Society movement had not succeeded in replacing the legal process as a new methodological consensus for legal scholars. It had become one school of thought among many, and was rapidly being eclipsed by both the law and economics movement and the emerging efforts by liberal scholars to breathe life back into the ethical and jurisprudential elaboration of rights and constitutional principles. As a critical project, it was being displaced by Critical Legal Studies—indeed, many of the most prominent law and society scholars were early participants in the Critical Legal Studies movement. In 1980, Richard Abel, a longtime participant in the movement, wrote a combination manifesto and epitaph that stated the shortcomings at that stage as he saw them. He criticized almost every strand of Law and Society research then being undertaken, concluding "the original paradigm is exhausted."[13] His essay marked a turning point. During the ensuing years, the Law and Society movement was riven (alongside much of the American academy) by methodological disagreements. As participants turned inward, an increasing number wrote retrospective accounts of the movement itself, and offered their own polemics for new directions. During this period, several conferences celebrating the early articles—including Macaulay's—offered the opportunity for introspection. A new generation of leaders appeared, most prominently at Amherst College, who sought to ally Law and Society at least loosely with Critical Legal Studies and other interdisciplinary work appearing in an increasingly academic American legal professoriat.

Although many academics, in both sociology and law, continue to work in the paradigm developed by the Law and Society movement, the movement has been more significant for bringing a series of propositions about the relationship between social and legal norms to the attention of legal scholars working in many other styles. In the 1990s, the brief for empirical legal work was largely carried by scholars associated, often quite loosely, with the law and economics movement, and by scholars interested in "rational choice" and "public choice" methods. This work proceeds from individualistic premises altogether at odds with the web of social relations and legal culture premises of the Law and Society movement. At the same time, interest in "social norms" and in the partnership between social and legal forces determining social behavior has emerged among liberal scholars in several fields, including constitutional law and criminal law. Although often liberal in orientation, these scholars have not, by and large, shared Macaulay's critical agenda. Indeed, many have sought to reinstate the legal process conception for which Macaulay's 1963 piece had offered an alternative.

Macaulay continued his criticism of the prevailing legal process contract law paradigm at the doctrinal level, arguing that "American doctrine is not clear and easy to apply. Rather it is contradictory, uncertain, and offers arguments rather than answers."[14] His most significant contribution to this line of criticism, "Private Legislation and the Duty to Read—Business Run by IBM Machine, the Law of Contracts and Credit Cards," is more continuous with Fullerian policy style than with Macaulay's own 1963 contribution to the Canon—but with a difference. The matrix of policies has become far more sophisticated—and persistently contradictory. Policy analysis seems to present choices that can only be made "in context," on a "case-by-case basis"—and yet, Macaulay insists, doing so is *also* a policy. Choices about policy will reflect both substantive attitudes about contract and procedural attitudes about the legal system itself—and both fields will require choices between conflicting and attractive alternative policies. The legal system, moreover, will itself affect and be affected by a range of other actors—the media, private parties, official actors and many others. In method, the piece is an important precursor to Duncan Kennedy's "Form and Substance in Private Law Adjudication." Indeed, it remains striking how closely the broad policy alternatives Macaulay read in Traynor's work track the analytic scheme developed by Kennedy in his contribution to the Canon. Macaulay contrasted support for the market with social control to achieve economic welfare, then subdivided each into subordinate policies ("transactional and functional" and "relief-of-hardship and economic planning"), each in turn able to be interpreted broadly or narrowly and expressed in both particular rules and general standards.

In 1966, Macaulay developed his intuition about the significance of unequal relationships of dependency for contract in a study of automotive manufacturers and dealers. He recounts evolving efforts by dealers to improve their bargaining power vis-à-vis manufacturers—at various stages, they turn to law in quite different ways, bringing individual lawsuits, organizing themselves for bargaining in unison with manufacturers, lobbying states and federal agencies for favorable rules, and passing legislation in Congress—and the efforts of manufacturers to defend and blunt these initiatives. He demonstrates the disconnection between the vocabulary used in appellate litigation over these issues and the interests and circumstances that actually gave rise to the litigation. Marc Galanter, author of the next article in the Canon, reviewed Macaulay's book and was influenced by his attention to the strategies of parties—unequal parties—using elements of the legal system in their struggles with one another.

DAVID KENNEDY

1. Frank Knight, "The Role of Principles in Economics and Politics," 41 *American Economic Review* 1 in *On the History and Method of Economics* 251, 256 (1956), quoted in Stewart Macaulay, *Justice Traynor and the Law of Contracts,* 13 *Stanford Law Review* 812, footnote 127, p. 856 (1961).

2. Knight, Review of *Freedom Through Law* by Robert Hale (New York: Columbia University Press, 1952) in 39 *Virginia Law Review* 871, 875–6 (1953) [italics in the original].

3. Macaulay, *supra* note 1, at 817.

4. Ibid., p. 856.

5. Ibid., p. 860.

6. Ibid., p. 814.

7. Macaulay, "Non-Contractual Relations in Business: A Preliminary Study," *American Sociological Review* 28: 1 (February 1963), starts at p. 55, cite at p. 56.

8. Macaulay, "*The Reliance Interest* and the World Outside the Law Schools' Doors," 1991 *Wisconsin Law Review* 247, 249, commenting on L. L. Fuller and William R. Perdue, Jr.'s, 1936 article "The Reliance Interest in Contract Damages, 46 *Yale Law Journal* 52. (1936).

9. Ibid., p. 250 and 253.

10. Macaulay, "An Empirical View of Contract," 1985 *Wisconsin Law Review* 465, 466.

11. Trubek, "The Short, Happy Life of the Law and Society Movement," 18 *Florida State University Law Review* 4, 8 (1990).

12. Macaulay, "An Empirical View of Contract," *supra* note 10, at 477.

13. Richard Abel, "Redirecting Social Studies of Law," 14 *Law and Society Review* 805, 826 (1980), and Abel "Taking Stock," 14 *Law and Society Review* 429 (1980).

14. Macaulay, "An Empirical View of Contract," *supra* note 10, at 469.

BIBLIOGRAPHY

Macaulay

See also Stewart Macaulay, "Justice Traynor and the Law of Contracts," 13 *Stanford Law Review* 812 (1961); Macaulay, "Private Legislation and the Duty to Read—Business Run by IBM Machine, the Law of Contracts and Credit Cards," 19 *Vanderbilt Law Review* 1051 (1966); Stewart Macaulay, *Law and the Balance of Power: The Automobile Manufacturers and Their* Dealers (New York: Russell Sage Foundation, 1966); reviewed by Marc Galanter in *American Journal of Sociology* 74, 6 (May 1969): 748–9. Macaulay's answer to the Cantaloupe Case was Stewart Macaulay, "Organic Transactions: Contract, Frank Lloyd Wright and the Johnson Building," 1996 *Wisconsin Law Review* 75.

Macaulay wrote his own assessment of the 1963 piece for a symposium organized for the 25th anniversary of its publication: Stewart Macaulay, "An Empirical View of Contract," 1985 *Wisconsin Law Review* 465. Macaulay reflected on the Law and Society movement in "Law and the Behavioral Sciences: Is There Any There There?" 6 *Law & Policy* 149 (1984).

Commentary

The best short statement of the distinct perspective represented by Macaulay and others is Robert Gordon, "Symposium: Law, Private Governance and Continuing Relationships: Relational Contract: Comment: Macaulay, Macneil, and the Discovery of Solidarity and Power in Contract Law," 1985 *Wisconsin Law Review* 565, on which we have relied here.

Macaulay is often cited for the proposition that the use of contract has declined in the United States. For many, the canonical cite remains the 1974 essay by Grant Gilmore, "The Death of Contract," who also cites Macaulay to this effect. Gilmore argued that with the disappearance of a self-contained and logically consistent body of contract doctrine, contract law was being merged into the looser doctrinal world of torts, a shift that coincided with a sharp decline in contracts litigation and a rise in the use of the courts to pursue tort claims. On the basis of new data about contracts litigation, Marc Galanter revisits Gilmore's argument with skepticism, and differentiates it from Stewart Macaulay's claims in Marc Galanter, "Contracts Symposium: Contract in Court; or Almost Everything you May or May Not Want to Know About Contract Litigation," 2001 *Wisconsin Law Review* 577 (2001). Galanter also reviews statistics showing a boom in business-to-business contracts litigation in light of Macaulay's earlier findings.

Law and Society

The best collection of material from the Law and Society movement remains the collection assembled by Stewart Macaulay, Lawrence Friedman, and John Stookey as teaching materials: Macaulay, Friedman, and Stookey, eds., *Law and Society: Readings on the Social Study of Law* (New York: W.W. Norton, 1995). Macaulay and Friedman also developed materials on law and society: Freidman and Macaulay, *Law and the Behavioral Sciences* (Indianapolis: Bobbs-Merrill, 1969).

Significant precursors to Macaulay's article include: John Dawson, "Effects of Inflation on Private Contracts: Germany 1914–1924," 33 *Michigan Law Review* 171 (1934); Dawson and F. E. Cooper, "The Effect of Inflation on Private Contracts: United States, 1861–1879," 33 *Michigan Law Review* 706, 1935. See also Friedrich Kessler, "Automobile Dealer Franchises: Vertical Integration by Contract," 66 *Yale Law Journal* 1135 (1957). Llewellyn had also written about the limits of contract: Llewellyn, "What Price Contract?—An Essay in Perspective," 40 *Yale Law Journal* 704 (1931).

Precursors to the Law and Society movement included Roscoe Pound, "Law in Books and Law in Action," 44 *American Law Review* 12 (1910); Pound, "The Scope and Purpose of Sociological Jurisprudence" (in three parts), 24 *Harvard Law Review* 591 (1911); 25 *Harvard Law Review* 140 (1911); 25 *Harvard Law Review* 489 (1912); Eugen Ehrlich, *Fundamental Principles of the Sociology of Law*, translated by Walter L. Moll (Cambridge, Mass.: Harvard University Press, 1936); and James Willard Hurst, *Law and Economic Growth: The Legal History of the Lumber Industry in Wisconsin, 1836–1915* (Cambridge: Belknap Press of Harvard University Press, 1964); Hurst, *The Growth of American Law: The Law Makers* (Boston: Little, Brown, 1980). Macaulay credits Hurst with the idea that each subpolicy must itself be pursued in a way that reflects a balance between policies "reflecting the particular and those the general." See James Willard Hurst, "Law and Social Process in United States History; 5 lectures delivered at the University of Michigan, November 9, 10, 11, 12 and 12, 1959," Ann Arbor: University of Michigan Law School (1960) 133–4, on the role of the general and the particular in social policymaking. For an analysis of the Garrison-Hurst materials on "law in society" see

Frickey and Eskridge, particularly at notes 84 and 85. For comment on the precursors to law and society, see David Trubek, "Max Weber's Tragic Modernism and the Study of Law in Society," 20 *Law and Society Review* 573 (1986).

The story of legal realists who left the legal academy to pursue empirical study at Johns Hopkins is well told by John Henry Schlegel, "American Legal Realism and Empirical Social Science: The Singular Case of Underhill Moore," 29 *Buffalo Law Review* 195 (1980). See also Schlegel, "American Legal Realism and Empirical Social Science: From the Yale Experience," 28 *Buffalo Law Review* 459 (1979). The distinction between legislative and adjudicative facts introduced to accommodate the use of sociological data in the style of the "Brandeis brief" was developed by Kenneth Culp Davis in "An Approach to Problems of Evidence in the Administrative Process," 55 *Harvard Law Review* 364, 1942.

A useful short introduction to the institutional and funding history of the Law and Society movement, and of its relationship to the parallel British movement for "sociolegal studies," is Bryant Garth, "Law and Society: Sociolegal Studies," in *International Encyclopedia of the Social & Behavioral Sciences*, 2004, 8484–89.

Good overviews of the Law and Society movement and its accomplishments include: David Trubek, "Back to the Future: The Short Happy Life of the Law and Society Movement," 18 *Florida State University Law Review* 4 (1990); Frank Munger, "Mapping Law and Society," in Austin Sarat, Marianne Constable, David Engel, Valerie Hans, Susan Lawrence, *Crossing Boundaries: Traditions and Transformations in Law and Society Research* (Evanston: Northwestern University Press and The American Bar Foundation, 1998, at 21–80, with good bibliography, and description of the impact of the method wars of the 1980s and 1990s on the Movement); Felice Levine, "Goose Bumps and 'The Search for Signs of Intelligent Life' in Sociolegal Studies: After Twenty-Five Years," 24: 1 *Law and Society Review* 7 (1990) (particularly on the work of the Law and Society Association itself and the role of foundations in its growth); Lee E. Teitelbaum, "An Overview of Law and Social Research," 35 *Journal of Legal Education* 465 (1985); and Donald J. Black, "The Boundaries of Legal Sociology," 81 *Yale Law Journal* 1086 (1972).

Macaulay's effort to redefine the institution of contract in sociological rather than doctrinal terms was followed by numerous efforts to give the social definition of law more theoretical precision. See, in particular, Lawrence Friedman, *The Legal System: A Social Science Perspective* (New York: Russell Sage Foundation, 1975). Friedman's term "legal culture" has been picked up by numerous law and society scholars to describe the object of their study. See, for example, David Nelken, ed., *Comparing Legal Cultures* (Brookfield, Vt.: Dartmouth, 1997). Like Macaulay, Friedman has also written extensively about contract law. See Lawrence Friedman, *Contract Law in America: A Social and Economic Case Study* (Madison: University of Wisconsin Press, 1965). See also Donald Black, "The Boundaries of Legal Sociology," 81 *Yale Law Journal* 1086 (1972).

Numerous retrospective pieces on the Law and Society movement provide an author's list of the "most significant" studies to have emerged from several decades of social study of law. A fascinating retrospective defense of the Law and Society Association's work is the Presidential Address delivered at the 1989 annual meeting of the Law and Society Association in Madison by Felice Levine. See Felice Levine, "Goose Bumps and 'The Search for Signs of Intelligent Life' in Sociolegal Studies: After Twenty Five Years," 24:1 *Law and Society Review* 7 (1990). Levine

Stewart Macaulay

offers eight favorites, including the Macaulay and Galanter pieces from the
Canon. She responds to the doubts raised by David Trubek's own retrospective
participant observer account: "Law and Society: Does It Deserve A Future?" published as "Back to the Future: The Short Happy Life of the Law and Society
Movement," 18 *Florida State University Law Review* 4 (1990). Trubek had provided his own program for the Law and society movement in Trubek, "Where the
Action Is: Critical Legal Studies and Empiricism," 36 *Stanford Law Review* 575
(1984). Marc Galanter, also as president of the Association, had delivered his verdict in Galanter, "The Legal Malaise; Or, Justice Observed," 19 *Law and Society
Review* 537 (1985). Lawrence Friedman's own affirmative account of the Law
and Society movement omits most of Macaulay's more critical project, while
lamenting the turn by Law and Society scholars to description disconnected from
"problem-solving": "The Law and Society Movement," 38 *Stanford Law Review*
763 (1986). One of the most interesting epitaphs for the movement linked its
decline to the disappearance of interest in "the social" in the American intelligentsia more generally during the Reagan/Thatcher years; Jonathan Simon, "'Law
After Society,' Review of Stewart Macaulay, Lawrence M. Friedman, John
Stookey, *Law and Society: Readings on the Social Study of Law,*" 24 *Law and
Social Inquiry* 143 (1999).

The Law and Society movement has been home to a range of diverse strands.
For work in the Law and Society tradition aimed at fine-tuning the social pro-
grams of the Great Society, see Bryant Garth and Joyce Sterling, "From Legal
Realism to Law and Society: Reshaping Law For the Last Stages of the Social
Activist State," 32 *Law and Society Review* 409 (1998). Significant works in this
tradition included: Jerome E. Carlin, Jan Howard, and Sheldon L. Messinger,
"Civil Justice and the Poor: Issues for Sociological Research," 1 *Law and Society
Review* 9 (1966); Joel Handler and Ellen Jane Hollingsworth, The *"Deserving
Poor": A Study of Welfare Administration* (Chicago: Markham Publishing, 1971).
In a classic application of Macaulay's approach to Law and Society research,
Handler criticized the idea—associated with Charles Reich—that creating "new
property" interests in welfare and due process hearings for welfare recipients
would improve their situation as an overestimation of the power of formal law.
Joel Handler, "Controlling Official Behavior in Welfare Administration," 54
California Law Review 479 (1966).

Numerous studies were carried out under the influence of the Wisconsin Law
and Society ideas. In consumer protection, see William L. Whitford, "Law and
the Consumer Transaction: A Case Study of the Automobile Warranty," 1968
Wisconsin Law Review 1006 (1968), Charles W. Grau and William L. Whitford,
"The Impact of Judicializing Repossession: The Wisconsin Consumer Act
Revisited," 1978 *Wisconsin Law Review* 983 (1978). The fields of criminal law
and criminal justice remain home to numerous scholars, in both law and sociology, influenced by the Law and Society movement. Two classic examples remain
Donald Black, "The Social Organization of Arrest," 23 *Stanford Law Review*
1087 (1971), which focused on the role of citizens in the mobilization of the
police, as well as Albert J. Reiss, Jr.'s 1971 study *The Police and the Public*
(New Haven: Yale University Press, 1971). A number of law and society scholars, including Donald Black, Lloyd Ohlin, Albert Reiss, Rita James Simon, and
Alfred Blumstein, were involved in producing President Johnson's special commission study on crime and criminal justice. For an excellent analysis of the
empirical basis used to develop and justify "community policing" initiatives in

the 1990s, see Bernard Harcourt, *Illusion of Order: the False Promise of Broken Windows Policing* (Cambridge, Mass.: Harvard University Press, 2001). Much attention was devoted to plea bargaining: see, for example, Malcolm Feeley, *The Process is the Punishment: Handling Cases in a Lower Criminal Court* (New York: Russell Sage Foundation, 1992). In the field of torts, Laurence Ross demonstrated the effect of routine claim processing procedures on recovery in *Settled Out of Court: The Social Process of Insurance Claims Adjustments* (Chicago: Aldine Publishing, 1970). Most of the studies in this tradition adopt the viewpoint of the external social science observer, measuring the effectiveness of state policy. Some scholars sought to recast Law and Society work from the point of view of the lawyer or judge, teaching law students to see social science as part of their legal skill set. A casebook illustrating this approach is John Monahan and Laurens Walker, *Social Science in Law: Cases and Materials* (Mineola, N.Y.: Foundation Press, 1985).

Work on the costs of litigation, and alternative dispute resolution, included David M. Trubek, Austin Sarat, William L. F. Felstiner, Herbert M. Kritzer, and Joel B. Grossman, "The Cost of Ordinary Litigation," 31 *UCLA Law Review* 72 (1983); Herbert Jacob, *Justice in America: Courts, Lawyers and the Judicial Process* (Boston: Little, Brown, 1965); Frank Munger, "Introduction: Longitudinal Research on Trial Courts," 24(2) *Law and Society Review* 227 (1990); Frank Munger, "Afterword: Studying Litigation and Social Change," 24(2) *Law and Society Review* 595 (1990). A great deal of attention was devoted to the study of juries; see, for example, Harry Kalven and Hans Zeisel, *The American Jury* (Boston: Little, Brown, 1966). See also: William L. F. Felstiner, Richard L. Abel, and Austin Sarat, "The Emergence and Transformation of Disputes: Naming, Blaming, Claiming . . . ,"15 *Law and Society Review* 631 (1980–81); and Robert Ellickson, "Of Coase and Cattle: Dispute Resolution Among Neighbors in Shasta County," 38 *Stanford Law Review* 623 (1986) Classic texts of the Alternative Dispute Resolution movement include Robert Bush and Joseph Folger, *The Promise of Mediation: Responding to Conflict through Empowerment and Recognition* (San Francisco: Jossey Bass Press, 1994); Roger Fisher and William Ury, *Getting to Yes: Negotiating Agreement Without Giving In* (Boston: Houghton Mifflin, 1981).

The key figures in the Berkeley branch of the Law and Society movement were Phillip Selznick and Phillippe Nonet. See Selznick, *TVA and the Grass Roots: A Study in the Sociology of Formal Organization* (Berkeley: University of California Press, 1949); and Phillip Selznick and Philippe Nonet, *Law and Society in Transition: Toward Responsive Law* (New York: Octagon Books, 1978). The Berkeley school's focus on jurisprudential issues is well represented by the collaborative project of Phillip Selznick, Philippe Nonet, and Howard Vollmer, *Law, Society and Industrial Justice* (New York: Russell Sage Foundation, 1969). On the differences between the two branches of Law and Society, see: Bryant Garth, "Law and Society: Sociolegal Studies," at 8485–86.

Austin Sarat reviewed the need for rejuvenation of the Law and Society movement in "Legal Effectiveness and Social Studies of Law: On the Unfortunate Persistence of a Research Tradition," 9 *Legal Studies Forum* 23 (1985). For the new direction the Amherst group proposed, see: Susan Silbey and Austin Sarat, "Critical Traditions in Law and Society Research," 21 *Law and Society Review* 165 (1987). The Amherst group included Silbey and Sarat, as well as John

Stewart Macaulay

Brigham, Christine Harrington, Lynn Mather, Sally Merry, Brinkley Messick, Ron Pipkin, Adelaide Villmoare, and Barbara Yngvessen. A different idea for rejuvenation was proposed by David Trubek and John Esser, "'Critical Empiricism' in American Legal Studies: Paradox, Program, or Pandora's Box?" 14 *Law and Social Inquiry* 3 (1989).

On "law and modernization" or "law and development" see, e.g.: Marc Galanter, "The Modernization of Law," in *Modernization: The Dynamics of Growth*, ed. Myron Weiner (New York: Basic Books, 1966); Trubek, "Toward a Social Theory of Law: An Essay on the Study of Law and Development," 82 *Yale Law Journal* 1 (1972); Roberto Unger, *Law and Modernisation* (New York: Free Press 1977). The best retrospective on these efforts remains David Trubek and Marc Galanter's "Scholars in Self Estrangement; Some Reflections on the Crisis in Law and Development Studies in the United States," 1974 *Wisconsin Law Review* 1062 (1974).

The law and anthropology movement had its own institutional forums and scholarly genealogy; for predecessors they looked to Maine, Malinowski, and Boas. The most famous early work of legal scholarship to examine law's tacit and active engagement with everyday social life on the basis of anthropological work had been Karl Llewellyn and Adamson Hoebel's 1941 *The Cheyenne Way: Conflict and Case Law in Primitive Jurisprudence* (Norman: University of Oklahoma Press, 1941). Exactly what the relationship between law and society is remained a matter of intense dispute among legal anthropologists. Hoebel's image of a law as a tacit and explicit ordering device contrasted sharply, for example, with Paul Bohannan's vision of law as the institutionalization of customary practices. Paul Bohannan, Law and Legal Institutions 1968, *International Encyclopedia of the Social Sciences* 9 (New York: Macmillan); David Sells and Paul Bohannan, eds. *Justice and Judgment Among the Tiv of Nigeria* (London: Oxford University Press, 1957). Significant early contributors to the law and anthropology tradition included Max Gluckman, *The Judicial Process Among the Barotse of Northern Rhodesia* (Manchester: Manchester University Press, 1955); Leopold Pospisil, *Anthropology of Law, A Comparative Theory* (New York: Harper & Row, 1971); Laura Nader, *Law in Culture and Society* (Chicago: Aldine, 1969); Sally Falk Moore, *Law as Process: An Anthropological Approach* (London: Routledge, 1978) (reflecting the influence of the legal process materials); and Sally Falk Moore, "Law and Social Change: The Semi-Autonomous Social Field as an Appropriate Subject of Study," 7 *Law and Society Review* 719 (1973); Moore, "Law and Anthropology," 1969 *Biennial Review of Anthropology 252*. For an intellectual history of the law and anthropology movement see: June Starr, *Practicing Ethnography in Law: New Dialogues, Enduring Methods* (New York: Palgrave Macmillan, 2002); Annelise Riles, "Anthropology, Human Rights and Legal Knowledge: Culture in the Iron Age," *American Anthropologist* 108, Issue Q (2006): 52–65; and Laura Nader, *The Life of the Law: Anthropological Projects* (Berkeley: University of California Press, 2002).

The most prominent work on relational contracts is that of Ian Macneil. See Ian Macneil, *The New Social Contract: An Inquiry into Modern Contractual Relations* (New Haven: Yale University Press, 1980); Macneil, "Economic Analysis of Contractual Relations: Its Shortfalls and the Need for a 'Rich Classificatory Apparatus,'" 75 *Northwestern University Law Review* 1018 (1981); Macneil, "Values in Contract: Internal and External," 78 *Northwestern University Law Review* 340 (1983). For a good introduction and retrospective evaluation, see Ian Macneil, "Relational Contract: What We Do and Do Not Know," 1985 *Wisconsin Law Review* 483. Macaulay reviewed work in the field in the context of analyzing doctrines relating to "relational contracts" in Macaulay, "Relational Contracts Floating on a Sea of Custom? Thoughts about the Ideas of Ian Macneil and Lisa Bernstein," 94 *Northwestern University Law Review* 775 (2000). See also Giddon Gottlieb, "Relationism: Legal Theory for a Relational Society," 50 *University of Chicago Law Review* 567 (1983). These relational themes have been taken up by liberal law and economics scholars in the last twenty years as well, under the influence of Oliver Williamson's landmark effort to link transactions cost economics to law: Williamson, "Transaction Cost Economics: The Governance of Contractual Relations," 22 *Journal of Law and Economics* 233 (1979); Oliver E. Williamson, "The Organization of Work: A Comparative Institutional Assessment," 1 *Journal of Economic Behavior and Organization* 5 (1980).

Leading examples of recent work on "social norms" include: Lawrence Lessig, "The Regulation of Social Meaning," 62 *University of Chicago Law Review* 943 (1995) and Lessig, "The New Chicago School," 27 *Journal of Legal Studies* 661 (1998); Cass Sunstein, "Social Norms and Social Roles," 96 *Columbia Law Review* 903 (1996); Dan Kahan and Tracey Meares, "Law and Norms of Order in the Inner City," 32 *Law and Society Review* 805 (1998). This work often harks back to Lon Fuller, rather than Macaulay. See Lon L. Fuller, "Human Interaction and the Law," 14 *American Journal of Jurisprudence* 1 (1969).

The classic article focusing on the impact of norms on bargaining remains Robert Mnookin and Lewis Kornhauser, "Bargaining in the Shadow of the Law: The Case of Divorce," 88 *Yale Law Journal* 950 (1979).

"Non-Contractual Relations in Business: A Preliminary Study"

28 *American Sociological Review* 55 (1963)

What good is contract law? who uses it? when and how? Complete answers would require an investigation of almost every type of transaction between individuals and organizations. In this report, research has been confined to exchanges between businesses, and primarily to manufacturers.[1] Futhermore, this report will be limited to a presentation of the findings concerning when contract is and is not used and to a tentative explanation of these findings.[2]

This research is only the first phase in a scientific study.[3] The primary research technique involved interviewing 68 businessmen and lawyers representing 43 companies and six law firms. The interviews ranged from a 30-minute brush-off where not all questions could be asked of a busy and uninterested sales manager to a six-hour discussion with the general counsel of a large corporation. Detailed notes of the interviews were taken and a complete report of each interview was dictated, usually no later than the evening after the interview. All but two of the companies had plants in Wisconsin; 17 were manufacturers of machinery but none made such items as food products, scientific instruments,

---

Revision of a paper read at the annual meeting of the Americal Sociological Association, August, 1962. An earlier version of the paper was read at the annual meeting of the Midwest Sociological Society, April, 1962. The research has been supported by a Law and Policy Research Grant to the University of Wisconsin Law School from the Ford Foundation. I am grateful for the help generously given by a number of sociologists including Robert K. Merton, Harry V. Ball, Jerome Carlin and William Evan.

[1] The reasons for this limitation are that (a) these transactions are important from an economic standpoint, (b) they are frequently said in theoretical discussions to represent a high degree of rational planning, and (c) manufacturing personnel are sufficiently public-relations-minded to cooperate with a law professor who wants to ask a seemingly endless number of questions. Future research will deal with the building construction industry and other areas.

[2] For the present purposes, the what-difference-does-it-make issue is important primarily as it makes a case for an empirical study by a law teacher of the use and nonuse of contract by businessmen. First, law teachers have a professional concern with what the law ought to be. This involves evaluation of the consequences of the existing situation and of the possible alternatives. Thus, it is most relevant to examine business practices concerning contract if one is interested in what commercial law ought to be. Second, law teachers are supposed to teach law students something relevant to becoming lawyers. These business practices are facts that are relevant to the skills which law students will need when, as lawyers, they are called upon to create exchange relationships and to solve problems arising out of these relationships.

[3] The following things have been done. The literature in law, business, economics, psychology, and sociology has been surveyed. The formal systems related to exchange transactions have been examined. Standard form contracts and the standard terms and conditions that are found on such business documents as catalogues, quotation forms, purchase orders, and acknowledgment-of-order forms from 850 firms that are based in or do business in Wisconsin have been collected. The citations of all reported court cases during a period of 15 years involving the largest 500 manufacturing corporations in the United States have been obtained and are being analyzed to determine why the use of contract legal sanctions was thought necessary and whether or not any patterns of "problem situations" can be delineated. In addition, the informal systems related to exchange transactions have been examined. Letters of inquiry concerning practices in certain situations have been answered by approximately 125 businessmen. Interviews, as described in the text, have been conducted. Moreover, six of my students have interviewed 21 other businessmen, bankers and lawyers. Their findings are consistent with those reported in the text.

textiles or petroleum products. Thus the likelihood of error because of sampling bias may be considerable.[4] However, to a great extent, existing knowledge has been inadequate to permit more rigorous procedures—as yet one cannot formulate many precise questions to be asked a systematically selected sample of "right people." Much time has been spent fishing for relevant questions or answers, or both.

Reciprocity, exchange or contract has long been of interest to sociologists, economists and lawyers. Yet each discipline has an incomplete view of this kind of conduct. This study represents the effort of a law teacher to draw on sociological ideas and empirical investigation. It stresses, among other things, the functions and dysfunctions of using contract to solve exchange problems and the influence of occupational roles on how one assesses whether the benefits of using contract outweigh the costs.

To discuss when contract is and is not used, the term "contract" must be specified. This term will be used here to refer to devices for conducting exchanges. Contract is not treated as synonymous with an exchange itself, which may or may not be characterized as contractual. Nor is contract used to refer to a writing recording an agreement. Contract, as I use the term here, involves two distinct elements: (a) Rational planning of the transaction with careful provision for as many future contingencies as can be foreseen, and (b) the existence or use of actual or potential legal sanctions to induce performance of the exchange or to compensate for non-performance.

These devices for conducting exchanges may be used or may exist in greater or lesser degree, so that transactions can be described relatively as involving a more contractual or a less contractual manner (a) of creating an exchange relationship or (b) of solving problems arising during the course of such a relationship. For example, General Motors might agree to buy all of the Buick Division's requirements of aluminum for ten years from Reynolds Aluminum. Here the two large corporations probably would plan their relationship carefully. The plan probably would include a complex pricing formula designed to meet market fluctuations, an agreement on what would happen if either party suffered a strike or a fire, a definition of Reynolds' responsibility for quality control and for losses caused by defective quality, and many other provisions. As the term contract is used here, this is a more contractual method of creating an exchange relationship than is a home-owner's casual agreement with a real estate broker giving the broker the exclusive right to sell the owner's house which fails to include provisions for the consequences of many easily foreseeable (and perhaps even highly probable) contingencies. In both instances, legally enforceable contracts may or may not have been created, but it must be recognized that the existence of a legal sanction has no necessary relationship to the degree of rational planning by the parties, beyond certain minimal legal requirements of certainty of obligation. General Motors and Reynolds might never sue or even refer to the written record of their agreement to answer questions which come up during their ten-year relationship, while the real estate broker might sue, or at least threaten to sue, the owner of the house. The broker's method of *dispute*

Stewart Macaulay

---

[4] However, the cases have not been selected because they *did* use contract. There is as much interest in, and effort to obtain, cases of nonuse as of use of contract. Thus, one variety of bias has been minimized.

settlement then would be more contractual than that of General Motors and Reynolds, thus reversing the relationship that existed in regard to the "contractualness" of the *creation* of the exchange relationships.

Tentative Findings

It is difficult to generalize about the use and nonuse of contract by manufacturing industry. However, a number of observations can be made with reasonable accuracy at this time. The use and nonuse of contract in creating exchange relations and in dispute settling will be taken up in turn.

The Creation of Exchange Relationships. In creating exchange relationships, businessmen may plan to a greater or lesser degree in relation to several types of issues. Before reporting the findings as to practices in creating such relationships, it is necessary to describe what one can plan about in a bargain and the degrees of planning which are possible.

People negotiating a contract can make plans concerning several types of issues: (1) They can plan what each is to do or refrain from doing; e.g., S might agree to deliver ten 1963 Studebaker four-door sedan automobiles to B on a certain date in exchange for a specified amount of money. (2) They can plan what effect certain contingencies are to have on their duties; e.g., what is to happen to S and B's obligations if S cannot deliver the cars because of a strike at the Studebaker factory? (3) They can plan what is to happen if either of them fails to perform; e.g., what is to happen if S delivers nine of the cars two weeks late? (4) They can plan their agreement so that it is a legally enforceable contract—that is, so that a legal sanction would be available to provide compensation for injury suffered by B as a result of S's failure to deliver the cars on time.

As to each of these issues, there may be a different degree of planning by the parties. (1) They may carefully and explicitly plan; e.g., S may agree to deliver ten 1963 Studebaker four-door sedans which have six cylinder engines, automatic transmissions and other specified items of optional equipment and which will perform to a specified standard for a certain time. (2) They may have a mutual but tacit understanding about an issue; e.g., although the subject was never mentioned in their negotiations, both S and B may assume that B may cancel his order for the cars before they are delivered if B's taxi-cab business is so curtailed that B can no longer use ten additional cabs. (3) They may have two inconsistent unexpressed assumptions about an issue; e.g., S may assume that if any of the cabs fails to perform to the specified standard for a certain time, all S must do is repair or replace it. B may assume S must also compensate B for the profits B would have made if the cab had been in operation. (4) They may never have thought of the issue; e.g., neither S nor B planned their agreement so that it would be a legally enforceable contract. Of course, the first and fourth degrees of planning listed are the extreme cases and the second and third are intermediate points. Clearly other intermediate points are possible; e.g., S and B neglect to specify whether the cabs should have automatic or conventional transmissions. Their planning is not as careful and explicit as that in the example previously given.

The following diagram represents the dimensions of creating an exchange relationship just discussed with "X's" representing the example of S and B's contract for ten taxi-cabs.

	Definition of Performances	Effect of Contingencies	Effect of Defective Performances	Legal Sanctions
Explicit and careful	X			
Tacit agreement		X		
Unilateral assumptions			X	
Unawareness of the issue				X

Most larger companies, and many smaller ones, attempt to plan carefully and completely. Important transactions not in the ordinary course of business are handled by a detailed contract. For example, recently the Empire State Building was sold for $65 million. More than 100 attorneys, representing 34 parties, produced a 400 page contract. Another example is found in the agreement of a major rubber company in the United States to give technical assistance to a Japanese firm. Several million dollars were involved and the contract consisted of 88 provisions on 17 pages. The 12 house counsel—lawyers who work for one corporation rather than many clients—interviewed said that all but the smallest businesses carefully planned most transactions of any significance. Corporations have procedures so that particular types of exchanges will be reviewed by their legal and financial departments.

More routine transactions commonly are handled by what can be called standardized planning. A firm will have a set of terms and conditions for purchases, sales, or both printed on the business documents used in these exchanges. Thus the things to be sold and the price may be planned particularly for each transaction, but standard provisions will further elaborate the performances and cover the other subjects of planning. Typically, these terms and conditions are lengthy and printed in small type on the back of the forms. For example, 24 paragraphs in eight point type are printed on the back of the purchase order form used by the Allis Chalmers Manufacturing Company. The provisions: (1) describe, in part, the performance required, e.g., "DO NOT WELD CASTINGS WITHOUT OUR CONSENT"; (2) plan for the effect of contingencies, e.g., ". . . in the event the Seller suffers delay in performance due to an act of God, war, act of the Government, priorities or allocations, act of the Buyer, fire, flood, strike, sabotage, or other causes beyond Seller's control, the time of completion shall be extended a period of time equal to the period of such delay if the Seller gives the Buyer notice in writing of the cause of any such delay within a reasonable time after the beginning thereof"; (3) plan for the effect of defective performances, e.g., "The buyer, without waiving any other legal rights, reserves the right to cancel without charge or to postpone deliveries of any of the articles covered by this order which are not shipped in time reasonably to meet said agreed dates"; (4) plan for a legal sanction, e.g., the clause "without waiving any other legal rights," in the example just given.

In larger firms such "boiler plate" provisions are drafted by the house counsel or the firm's outside lawyer. In smaller firms such provisions may be drafted by the industry trade association, may be copied from a competitor, or may be found on forms purchased from a printer. In any event, salesmen and purchasing agents, the operating personnel, typically are unaware of what is said in the fine print on the back of the forms they use. Yet often the normal business patterns will give effect to this standardized planning. For example, purchasing agents may have to use a purchase order form so that all transactions receive a number under the firm's accounting system. Thus, the required accounting record will carry the necessary planning of the exchange relationship printed on its reverse side. If the seller does not object to this planning and accepts the order, the buyer's "fine print" will control. If the seller does object, differences can be settled by negotiation.

This type of standardized planning is very common. Requests for copies of the business documents used in buying and selling were sent to approximately 6,000 manufacturing firms which do business in Wisconsin. Approximately 1,200 replies were received and 850 companies used some type of standardized planning. With only a few exceptions, the firms that did not reply and the 350 that indicated they did not use standardized planning were very small manufacturers such as local bakeries, soft drink bottlers and sausage makers.

While businessmen can and often do carefully and completely plan, it is clear that not all exchanges are neatly rationalized. Although most businessmen think that a clear description of both the seller's and buyer's performances is obvious common sense, they do not always live up to this ideal. The house counsel and the purchasing agent of a medium size manufacturer of automobile parts reported that several times their engineers had committed the company to buy expensive machines without adequate specifications. The engineers had drawn careful specifications as to the type of machine and how it was to be made but had neglected to require that the machine produce specified results. An attorney and an auditor both stated that most contract disputes arise because of ambiguity in the specifications.

Businessmen often prefer to rely on "a man's word" in a brief letter, a handshake, or "common honesty and decency"—even when the transaction involves exposure to serious risks. Seven lawyers from law firms with business practices were interviewed. Five thought that businessmen often entered contracts with only a minimal degree of advance planning. They complained that businessmen desire to "keep it simple and avoid red tape" even where large amounts of money and significant risks are involved. One stated that he was "sick of being told, 'We can trust old Max,' when the problem is not one of honesty but one of reaching an agreement that both sides understand." Another said that businessmen when bargaining often talk only in pleasant generalities, think they have a contract, but fail to reach agreement on any of the hard, unpleasant questions until forced to do so by a lawyer. Two outside lawyers had different views. One thought that large firms usually planned important exchanges, although he conceded that occasionally matters might be left in a fairly vague state. The other dissenter represents a large utility that commonly buys heavy equipment and buildings. The supplier's employees come on the utility's property to install the equipment or construct the buildings, and they may be injured while there. The utility has been sued by such employees so often that it carefully plans purchases with the assistance of a lawyer so that suppliers take this burden.

Moreover, standardized planning can break down. In the example of such planning previously given, it was assumed that the purchasing agent would use his company's form with its 24 paragraphs printed on the back and that the seller would accept this or object to any provisions he did not like. However, the seller may fail to read the buyer's 24 paragraphs of fine print and may accept the buyer's order on the seller's own acknowledgment-of-order form. Typically this form will have ten to 50 paragraphs favoring the seller, and these provisions are likely to be different from or inconsistent with the buyer's provisions. The seller's acknowledgment form may be received by the buyer and checked by a clerk. She will read the *face* of the acknowledgment but not the fine print on the back of it because she has neither the time nor ability to analyze the small print on the 100 to 500 forms she must review each day. The face of the acknowledgment—where the goods and the price are specified—is likely to correspond with the face of the purchase order. If it does, the two forms are filed away. At this point, both buyer and seller are likely to assume they have planned an exchange and made a contract. Yet they have done neither, as they are in disagreement about all that appears on the back of their forms. This practice is common enough to have a name. Law teachers call it "the battle of the forms."

Ten of the 12 purchasing agents interviewed said that frequently the provisions on the back of their purchase order and those on the back of a supplier's acknowledgment would differ or be inconsistent. Yet they would assume that the purchase was complete without further action unless one of the supplier's provisions was really objectionable. Moreover, only occasionally would they bother to read the fine print on the back of suppliers' forms. On the other hand, one purchasing agent insists that agreement be reached on the fine print provisions, but he represents the utility whose lawyer reported that it exercises great care in planning. The other purchasing agent who said that his company did not face a battle of the forms problem, works for a division of one of the largest manufacturing corporations in the United States. Yet the company may have such a problem without recognizing it. The purchasing agent regularly sends a supplier both a purchase order and another form which the supplier is asked to sign and return. The second form states that the supplier accepts the buyer's terms and conditions. The company has sufficient bargaining power to force suppliers to sign and return the form, and the purchasing agent must show one of his firm's auditors such a signed form for every purchase order issued. Yet suppliers frequently return this buyer's form *plus* their own acknowledgment form which has conflicting provisions. The purchasing agent throws away the supplier's form and files his own. Of course, in such a case the supplier has not acquiesced to the buyer's provisions. There is no agreement and no contract.

Sixteen sales managers were asked about the battle of the forms. Nine said that frequently no agreement was reached on which set of fine print was to govern, while seven said that there was no problem. Four of the seven worked for companies whose major customers are the large automobile companies or the large manufacturers of paper products. These customers demand that their terms and conditions govern any purchase, are careful generally to see that suppliers acquiesce, and have the bargaining power to have their way. The other three of the seven sales managers who have no battle of the forms problem, work for manufacturers of special industrial machines. Their firms are careful to reach complete agreement with their customers. Two of these men stressed that they could take no chances because such a large part of their firm's capital is tied up in making any one machine. The other sales manager had been influenced by a law suit against one of his competitors for over a half million dollars. The suit was brought by a customer when the competitor had been unable to deliver a machine and put it in operation on time. The sales manager interviewed said his firm could not guarantee that its machines would work perfectly by a specified time because they are designed to fit the customer's requirements, which may present difficult engineering problems. As a result, contracts are carefully negotiated.

A large manufacturer of packaging materials audited its records to determine how often it had failed to agree on terms and conditions with its customers or had failed to create legally binding contracts. Such failures cause a risk of loss to this firm since the packaging is printed with the customer's design and cannot be salvaged once this is done. The orders for five days in four different years were reviewed. The percentages of orders where no agreement on terms and conditions was reached or no contract was formed were as follows:

1953	75.0%
1954	69.4%
1955	71.5%
1956	59.5%

It is likely that businessmen pay more attention to describing the performances in an exchange than to planning for contingencies or defective performances or to obtaining legal enforceability of their contracts. Even when a purchase order and acknowledgment have conflicting provisions printed on the back, almost always the buyer and seller will be in agreement on what is to be sold and how much is to be paid for it. The lawyers who said businessmen often commit their firms to significant exchanges too casually, stated that the performances would be defined in the brief letter or telephone call; the lawyers objected that nothing else would be covered. Moreover, it is likely that businessmen are least concerned about planning their transactions so that they are legally enforceable contracts.[5] For example, in Wisconsin requirements contracts—contracts to supply a firm's requirements of an item rather than a definite quantity—probably are not legally enforceable. Seven people interviewed reported that their firms regularly used requirements contracts in dealings in Wisconsin. None thought that the lack of legal sanction made any difference. Three of these people were house counsel who knew the Wisconsin law before being interviewed. Another example of a lack of desire for legal sanctions is found in the relationship between automobile manufacturers and their suppliers of parts. The manufacturers draft a carefully planned agreement, but one which is so designed that the supplier will have only minimal, if any, legal rights against the manufacturers. The standard contract used by manufacturers of paper to sell to magazine publishers has a pricing clause which is probably sufficiently vague to make the contract legally unenforceable. The house counsel of one of the largest paper producers said that everyone in the industry is aware of this because of a leading New York case concerning the contract, but that no one cares. Finally, it seems likely that planning for contingencies and defective performances are in-between cases—more likely to occur than planning for a legal sanction, but less likely than a description of performance.

Thus one can conclude that (1) many business exchanges reflect a high degree of planning about the four categories—description, contingencies, defective performances and legal sanction—but (2) many, if not most, exchanges reflect no planning, or only a minimal amount of it, especially concerning legal sanctions

---

[5] Compare the findings of an empirical study of Connecticut business practices in Comment, "The Statute of Frauds and the Business Community: A Re-Appraisal in Light of Prevailing Practices," *Yale Law Journal*, 66 (1957), pp. 1038–1071.

and the effect of defective performances. As a result, the opportunity for good faith disputes during the life of the exchange relationship often is present.

The Adjustment of Exchange Relationships and the Settling of Disputes. While a significant amount of creating business exchanges is done on a fairly noncontractual basis, the creation of exchanges usually is far more contractual than the adjustment of such relationships and the settlement of disputes. Exchanges are adjusted when the obligations of one or both parties are modified by agreement during the life of the relationship. For example, the buyer may be allowed to cancel all or part of the goods he has ordered because he no longer needs them; the seller may be paid more than the contract price by the buyer because of unusual changed circumstances. Dispute settlement involves determining whether or not a party has performed as agreed and, if he has not, doing something about it. For example, a court may have to interpret the meaning of a contract, determine what the alleged defaulting party has done and determine what, if any, remedy the aggrieved party is entitled to. Or one party may assert that the other is in default, refuse to proceed with performing the contract and refuse to deal ever again with the alleged defaulter. If the alleged defaulter, who in fact may not be in default, takes no action, the dispute is then "settled."

Business exchanges in non-speculative areas are usually adjusted without dispute. Under the law of contracts, if B orders 1,000 widgets from S at $1.00 each, B must take all 1,000 widgets or be in breach of contract and liable to pay S his expenses up to the time of the breach plus his lost anticipated profit. Yet all ten of the purchasing agents asked about cancellation of orders once placed indicated that they expected to be able to cancel orders freely subject to only an obligation to pay for the seller's major expenses such as scrapped steel.[6] All 17 sales personnel asked reported that they often had to accept cancellation. One said, "You can't ask a man to eat paper [the firm's product] when he has no use for it." A lawyer with many large industrial clients said,

> Often businessmen do not feel they have "a contract"—rather they have "an order."
> They speak of "cancelling the order" rather than "breaching our contract." When
> I began practice I referred to order cancellations as breaches of contract, but
> my clients objected since they do not think of cancellation as wrong. Most clients,
> in heavy industry at least, believe that there is a right to cancel as part of the buyer-
> seller relationship. There is a widespread attitude that one can back out of any deal
> within some very vague limits. Lawyers are often surprised by this attitude.

Disputes are frequently settled without reference to the contract or potential or actual legal sanctions. There is a hesitancy to speak of legal rights or to threaten to sue in these negotiations. Even where the parties have a detailed and carefully planned agreement which indicates what is to happen if, say, the seller fails to deliver on time, often they will never refer to the agreement but will negotiate a solution when the problem arises apparently as if there had never been any original contract. One purchasing agent expressed a common business attitude when he said,

> if something comes up, you get the other man on the telephone and deal with the
> problem. You don't read legalistic contract clauses at each other if you ever want to

---

[6] See the case studies on cancellation of contracts in *Harvard Business Review*, 2 (1923–24), pages 238–40, 367–70, 496–502.

do business again. One doesn't run to lawyers if he wants to stay in business because one must behave decently.

Or as one businessman put it, "You can settle any dispute if you keep the lawyers and accountants out of it. They just do not understand the give-and-take needed in business." All of the house counsel interviewed indicated that they are called into the dispute settlement process only after the businessmen have failed to settle matters in their own way. Two indicated that after being called in house counsel at first will only advise the purchasing agent, sales manager or other official involved; not even the house counsel's letterhead is used on communications with the other side until all hope for a peaceful resolution is gone.

Law suits for breach of contract appear to be rare. Only five of the 12 purchasing agents had ever been involved in even a negotiation concerning a contract dispute where both sides were represented by lawyers; only two of ten sales managers had ever gone this far. None had been involved in a case that went through trial. A law firm with more than 40 lawyers and a large commercial practice handles in a year only about six trials concerned with contract problems. Less than 10 per cent of the time of this office is devoted to any type of work related to contracts disputes. Corporations big enough to do business in more than one state tend to sue and be sued in the federal courts. Yet only 2,779 out of 58,293 civil actions filed in the United States District Courts in fiscal year 1961 involved private contracts.[7] During the same period only 3,447 of the 61,138 civil cases filed in the principal trial courts of New York State involved private contracts.[8] The same picture emerges from a review of appellate cases.[9] Mentschikoff has suggested that commercial cases are not brought to the courts either in periods of business prosperity (because buyers unjustifiably reject goods only when prices drop and they can get similar goods elsewhere at less than the contract price) or in periods of deep depression (because people are unable to come to court or have insufficient assets to satisfy any judgment that might be obtained). Apparently, she adds, it is necessary to have "a kind of middle-sized depression" to bring large numbers of commercial cases to the courts. However, there is little evidence that in even "a kind of middle-sized depression" today's businessmen would use the courts to settle disputes.[10]

At times relatively contractual methods are used to make adjustments in ongoing transactions and to settle disputes. Demands of one side which are deemed unreasonable by the other occasionally are blocked by reference to the terms of the agreement between the parties. The legal position of the parties can influence negotiations even though legal rights or litigation are never mentioned in their discussions; it makes a difference if one is demanding what both concede to be a right or begging for a favor. Now and then a firm may threaten to turn matters over to its attorneys, threaten to sue, commence a suit or even litigate and carry

---

[7] *Annual Report of the Director of the Administrative Office of the United States Courts*, 1961, p. 238.

[8] State of New York, The Judicial Conference, Sixth Annual Report, 1961, pp. 209–11.

[9] My colleague Lawrence M. Friedman has studied the work of the Supreme Court of Wisconsin in contracts cases. He has found that contracts cases reaching that court tend to involve economically-marginal-business and family-economic disputes rather than important commercial transactions. This has been the situation since about the turn of the century. Only during the Civil War period did the court deal with significant numbers of important contracts cases, but this happened against the background of a much simpler and different economic system.

[10] New York Law Revision Commission, *Hearings on the Uniform Code Commercial Code*, 2 (1954), p. 1391.

an appeal to the highest court which will hear the matter. Thus, legal sanctions, while not an everyday affair, are not unknown in business.

One can conclude that while detailed planning and legal sanctions play a significant role in some exchanges between businesses, in many business exchanges their role is small.

TENTATIVE EXPLANATIONS

Two questions need to be answered: (A) How can business successfully operate exchange relationships with relatively so little attention to detailed planning or to legal sanctions, and (B) Why does business ever use contract in light of its success without it?

Why Are Relatively Non-contractual Practices So Common? In most situations contract is not needed.[11] Often its functions are served by other devices. Most problems are avoided without resort to detailed planning or legal sanctions because usually there is little room for honest misunderstandings or good faith differences of opinion about the nature and quality of a seller's performance. Although the parties fail to cover all foreseeable contingencies, they will exercise care to see that both understand the primary obligation on each side. Either products are standardized with an accepted description or specifications are written calling for production to certain tolerances or results. Those who write and read specifications are experienced professionals who will know the customs of their industry and those of the industries with which they deal. Consequently, these customs can fill gaps in the express agreements of the parties. Finally, most products can be tested to see if they are what was ordered; typically in manufacturing industry we are not dealing with questions of taste or judgment where people can differ in good faith.

When defaults occur they are not likely to be disastrous because of techniques of risk avoidance or risk spreading. One can deal with firms of good reputation or he may be able to get some form of security to guarantee performance. One can insure against many breaches of contract where the risks justify the costs. Sellers set up reserves for bad debts on their books and can sell some of their accounts receivable. Buyers can place orders with two or more suppliers of the same item so that a default by one will not stop the buyer's assembly lines.

Moreover, contract and contract law are often thought unnecessary because there are many effective non-legal sanctions. Two norms are widely accepted. (1) Commitments are to be honored in almost all situations; one does not welsh on a deal. (2) One ought to produce a good product and stand behind it. Then, too, business units are organized to perform commitments, and internal sanctions will induce performance. For example, sales personnel must face angry customers when there has been a late or defective performance. The salesmen do not enjoy this and will put pressure on the production personnel responsible for the default. If the production personnel default too often, they will be fired. At all levels of

Stewart Macaulay

---

[11] The explanation that follows emphasizes a *considered* choice not to plan in detail for all contingencies. However, at times it is clear that businessmen fail to plan because of a lack of sophistication; they simply do not appreciate the risk they are running or they merely follow patterns established in their firm years ago without reexamining these practices in light of current conditions.

the two business units personal relationships across the boundaries of the two
organizations exert pressures for conformity to expectations. Salesmen often
know purchasing agents well. The same two individuals occupying these roles
may have dealt with each other from five to 25 years. Each has something to give
the other. Salesmen have gossip about competitors, shortages and price increases
to give purchasing agents who treat them well. Salesmen take purchasing agents
to dinner, and they give purchasing agents Christmas gifts hoping to improve the
chances of making sale. The buyer's engineering staff may work with the seller's
engineering staff to solve problems jointly. The seller's engineers may render great
assistance, and the buyer's engineers may desire to return the favor by drafting
specifications which only the seller can meet. The top executives of the two firms
may know each other. They may sit together on government or trade committees.
They may know each other socially and even belong to the same country club.
The interrelationships may be more formal. Sellers may hold stock in corporations which are important customers; buyers may hold stock in important
suppliers. Both buyer and seller may share common directors on their boards.
They may share a common financial institution which has financed both units.

The final type of non-legal sanction is the most obvious. Both business units
involved in the exchange desire to continue successfully in business and will avoid
conduct which might interfere with attaining this goal. One is concerned with both
the reaction of the other party in the particular exchange and with his own general
business reputation. Obviously, the buyer gains sanctions insofar as the seller wants
the particular exchange to be completed. Buyers can withhold part or all of their
payments until sellers have performed to their satisfaction. If a seller has a great
deal of money tied up in his performance which he must recover quickly, he will
go a long way to please the buyer in order to be paid. Moreover, buyers who are
dissatisfied may cancel and cause sellers to lose the cost of what they have done up
to cancellation. Furthermore, sellers hope for repeat for orders, and one gets few of
these from unhappy customers. Some industrial buyers go so far as to formalize
this sanction by issuing "report cards" rating the performance of each supplier. The
supplier rating goes to the top management of the seller organization, and these
men can apply internal sanctions to salesmen, production supervisors or product
designers if there are too many "D's" or "F's" on the report card.

While it is generally assumed that the customer is always right, the seller may
have some counterbalancing sanctions against the buyer. The seller may have
obtained a large downpayment from the buyer which he will want to protect. The
seller may have an exclusive process which the buyer needs. The seller may be
one of the few firms which has the skill to make the item to the tolerances set by
the buyer's engineers and within the time available. There are costs and delays
involved in turning from a supplier one has dealt with in the past to a new supplier. Then, too, market conditions can change so that a buyer is faced with shortages of critical items. The most extreme example is the post World War II gray
market conditions when sellers were rationing goods rather than selling them.
Buyers must build up some reserve of good will with suppliers if they face the risk
of such shortage and desire good treatment when they occur. Finally, there is reciprocity in buying and selling. A buyer cannot push a supplier too far if that supplier also buys significant quantities of the product made by the buyer.

Not only do the particular business units in a given exchange want to deal
with each other again, they also want to deal with other business units in the
future. And the way one behaves in a particular transaction, or a series of trans-

actions, will color his general business reputation. Blacklisting can be formal or informal. Buyers who fail to pay their bills on time risk a bad report in credit rating services such as Dun and Bradstreet. Sellers who do not satisfy their customers become the subject of discussion in the gossip exchanged by purchasing agents and salesmen, at meetings of purchasing agents' associations and trade associations, or even at country clubs or social gatherings where members of top management meet. The American male's habit of debating the merits of new cars carries over to industrial items. Obviously, a poor reputation does not help a firm make sales and may force it to offer great price discounts or added services to remain in business. Furthermore, the habits of unusually demanding buyers become known, and they tend to get no more than they can coerce out of suppliers who choose to deal with them. Thus often contract is not needed as there are alternatives.

Not only are contract and contract law not needed in many situations, their use may have, or may be thought to have, undesirable consequences. Detailed negotiated contracts can get in the way of creating good exchange relationships between business units. If one side insists on a detailed plan, there will be delay while letters are exchanged as the parties try to agree on what should happen if a remote and unlikely contingency occurs. In some cases they may not be able to agree at all on such matters and as a result a sale may be lost to the seller and the buyer may have to search elsewhere for an acceptable supplier. Many businessmen would react by thinking that had no one raised the series of remote and unlikely contingencies all this wasted effort could have been avoided.

Even where agreement can be reached at the negotiation stage, carefully planned arrangements may create undesirable exchange relationships between business units. Some businessmen object that in such a carefully worked out relationship one gets performance only to the letter of the contract. Such planning indicates a lack of trust and blunts the demands of friendship, turning a cooperative venture into an antagonistic horse trade. Yet the greater danger perceived by some businessmen is that one would have to perform his side of the bargain to its letter and thus lose what is called "flexibility." Businessmen may welcome a measure of vagueness in the obligations they assume so that they may negotiate matters in light of the actual circumstances.

Adjustment of exchange relationships and dispute settlement by litigation or the threat of it also has many costs. The gain anticipated from using this form of coercion often fails to outweigh these costs, which are both monetary and non-monetary. Threatening to turn matters over to an attorney may cost no more money than postage or a telephone call; yet few are so skilled in making such a threat that it will not cost some deterioration of the relationship between the firms. One businessman said that customers had better not rely on legal rights or threaten to bring a breach of contract law suit against him since he "would not be treated like a criminal" and would fight back with every means available. Clearly actual litigation is even more costly than making threats. Lawyers demand substantial fees from larger business units. A firm's executives often will have to be transported and maintained in another city during the proceedings if, as often is the case, the trial must be held away from the home office. Top management does not travel by Greyhound and stay at the Y.M.C.A. Moreover, there will be the cost of diverting top management, engineers, and others in the organization from their normal activities. The firm may lose many days work from several key people. The non-monetary costs may be large too. A breach of

Stewart Macaulay

contract law suit may settle a particular dispute, but such an action often results in a "divorce" ending the "marriage" between the two businesses, since a contract action is likely to carry charges with at least overtones of bad faith. Many executives, moreover, dislike the prospect of being cross-examined in public. Some executives may dislike losing control of a situation by turning the decision-making power over to lawyers. Finally, the law of contract damages may not provide an adequate remedy even if the firm wins the suit; one may get vindication but not much money.

Why Do Relatively Contractual Practices Ever Exist? Although contract is not needed and actually may have negative consequences, businessmen do make some carefully planned contracts, negotiate settlements influenced by their legal rights and commence and defend some breach of contract law suits or arbitration proceedings. In view of the findings and explanation presented to this point, one may ask why. Exchanges are carefully planned when it is thought that planning and a potential legal sanction will have more advantages than disadvantages. Such a judgment may be reached when contract planning serves the internal needs of an organization involved in a business exchange. For example, a fairly detailed contract can serve as a communication device within a large corporation. While the corporation's sales manager and house counsel may work out all the provisions with the customer, its production manger will have to make the product. He must be told what to do and how to handle at least the most obvious contingencies. Moreover, the sales manager may want to remove certain issues from future negotiation by his subordinates. If he puts the matter in the written contract, he may be able to keep his salesmen from making concessions to the customer without first consulting the sales manager. Then the sales manager may be aided in his battles with his firm's financial or engineering departments if the contract calls for certain practices which the sales manager advocates but which the other departments resist. Now the corporation is obligated to a customer to do what the sales manager wants to do; how can the financial or engineering departments insist on anything else?

Also one tends to find a judgment that the gains of contract outweigh the costs where there is a likelihood that significant problems will arise.[12] One factor leading to this conclusion is complexity of the agreed performance over a long period. Another factor is whether or not the degree of injury in case of default is thought to be potentially great. This factor cuts two ways. First, a buyer may want to commit a seller to a detailed and legally binding contract, where the consequences of a default by the seller would seriously injure the buyer. For example, the airlines are subject to law suits from the survivors of passengers and to great adverse publicity as a result of crashes. One would expect the airlines to bargain for carefully defined and legally enforceable obligations on the part of the airframe manufacturers when they purchase aircraft. Second, a seller may want to limit his liability for a buyer's damages by a provision in their contract. For example, a manufacturer of air conditioning may deal with motels in the South and Southwest. If this equipment fails in the hot summer months, a motel may lose a

---

[12] Even where there is little chance that problems will arise, some businessmen insist that their lawyer review or draft an agreement as a delaying tactic. This gives the businessman time to think about making a commitment if he has doubts about the matter or to look elsewhere for a better deal while still keeping the particular negotiations alive.

great deal of business. The manufacturer may wish to avoid any liability for this type of injury to his customers and may want a contract with a clear disclaimer clause.

Similarly, one uses or threatens to use legal sanctions to settle disputes when other devices will not work and when the gains are thought to outweigh the costs. For example, perhaps the most common type of business contracts case fought all the way through to the appellate courts today is an action for an alleged wrongful termination of a dealer's franchise by a manufacturer. Since the franchise has been terminated, factors such as personal relationships and the desire for future business will have little effect; the cancellation of the franchise indicates they have already failed to maintain the relationship. Nor will a complaining dealer worry about creating a hostile relationship between himself and the manufacturer. Often the dealer has suffered a great financial loss both as to his investment in building and equipment and as to his anticipated future profits. A cancelled automobile dealer's lease on his showroom and shop will continue to run, and his tools for servicing, say, Plymouths cannot be used to service other makes of cars. Moreover, he will have no more new Plymouths to sell. Today there is some chance of winning a law suit for terminating a franchise in bad faith in many states and in the federal courts. Thus, often the dealer chooses to risk the cost of a lawyer's fee because of the chance that he may recover some compensation for his losses.

An "irrational" factor may exert some influence on the decision to use legal sanctions. The man who controls a firm may feel that he or his organization has been made to appear foolish or has been the victim of fraud or bad faith. The law suit may be seen as a vehicle "to get even" although the potential gains, as viewed by an objective observer, are outweighed by the potential costs.

The decision whether or not to use contract—whether the gain exceeds the costs—will be made by the person within the business unit with the power to make it, and it tends to make a difference who he is. People in a sales department oppose contract. Contractual negotiations are just one more hurdle in the way of a sale. Holding a customer to the letter of a contract is bad for "customer relations." Suing a customer who is not bankrupt and might order again is poor strategy. Purchasing agents and their buyers are less hostile to contracts but regard attention devoted to such matters as a waste of time. In contrast, the financial control department—the treasurer, controller or or auditor—leans toward more contractual dealings. Contract is viewed by these people as an organizing tool to control operations in a large organization. It tends to define precisely and to minimize the risks to which the firm is exposed. Outside lawyers—those with many clients—may share this enthusiasm for a more contractual method of dealing. These lawyers are concerned with preventive law—avoiding any possible legal difficulty. They see many unstable and unsuccessful exchange transactions, and so they are aware of, and perhaps overly concerned with, all of the things which can go wrong. Moreover, their job of settling disputes with legal sanctions is much easier if their client has not been overly casual about transaction planning. The inside lawyer, or house counsel, is harder to classify. He is likely to have some sympathy with a more contractual method of dealing. He shares the outside lawyer's "craft urge" to see exchange transactions neat and tidy from a legal standpoint. Since he is more concerned with avoiding and settling disputes than selling goods, he is likely to be less willing to rely on a man's word as the sole sanction than is a salesman. Yet the house counsel is more a part of the organi-

zation and more aware of its goals and subject to its internal sanctions. If the
potential risks are not too great, he may hesitate to suggest a more contractual
procedure to the sales department. He must sell his services to the operating
departments, and he must hoard what power he has, expending it on only what
he sees as significant issues.

The power to decide that a more contractual method of creating relationships
and settling disputes shall be used will be held by different people at different
times in different organizations. In most firms the sales department and the purchasing department have a great deal of power to resist contractual procedures
or to ignore them if they are formally adopted and to handle disputes their own
way. Yet in larger organizations the treasurer and the controller have increasing
power to demand both systems and compliance. Occasionally, the house counsel
must arbitrate the conflicting positions of these departments; in giving "legal
advice" he may make the business judgment necessary regarding the use of contract. At times he may ask for an opinion from an outside law firm to reinforce
his own position with the outside firm's prestige.

Obviously, there are other significant variables which influence the degree that
contract is used. One is the relative bargaining power or skill of the two business
units. Even if the controller of a small supplier succeeds within the firm and creates a contractual system of dealing, there will be no contract if the firm's large
customer prefers not to be bound to anything. Firms that supply General Motors
deal as General Motors wants to do business, for the most part. Yet bargaining
power is not size or share of the market alone. Even a General Motors may need
a particular supplier, at least temporarily. Furthermore, bargaining power may
shift as an exchange relationship is first created and then continues. Even a giant
firm can find itself bound to a small supplier once production of an essential item
begins for there may not be time to turn to another supplier. Also, all of the factors discussed in this paper can be viewed as *components* of bargaining power—
for example, the personal relationship between the presidents of the buyer and
the seller firms may give a sales manager great power over a purchasing agent
who has been instructed to give the seller "every consideration." Another variable relevant to the use of contract is the influence of third parties. The federal
government, or a lender of money, may insist that a contract be made in a particular transaction or may influence the decision to assert one's legal rights under
a contract.

Contract, then, often plays an important role in business, but other factors are
significant. To understand the functions of contract the whole system of conducting exchanges must be explored fully. More types of business communities
must be studied, contract litigation must be analyzed to see why the nonlegal
sanctions fail to prevent the use of legal sanctions and all of the variables suggested in this paper must be classified more systematically.

Marc Galanter

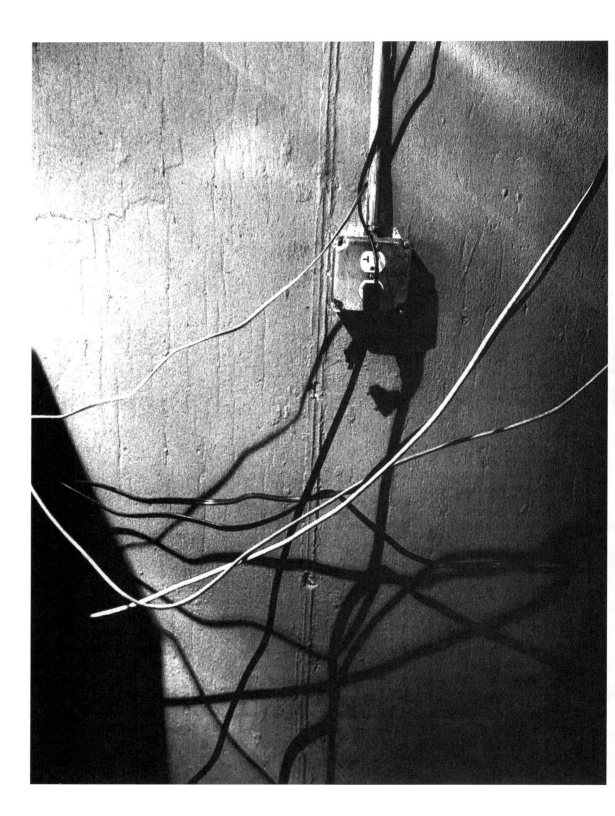

Marc Galanter

SCHOLARS PARTICIPATING in the Law and Society movement of the 1960 and '70s shared a commitment to the idea that law could and should be an instrument of social change. They rejected the more optimistic and complacent image of the American legal system and marketplace offered by the legal process materials. The legal process materials had also been rather accepting of the pluralism of American law—diverse outcomes for similar cases in different institutional settings or in competing jurisdictions did not trouble them. The legal process itself would sort things out, guided by a professional class attuned to respect for the principle of institutional settlement. Law and society scholars shared a substantive agenda of liberal and progressive reform, and evaluated the American legal system's procedural and bureaucratic structures in light of that agenda. An indeterminacy of substantive results within a stable but disaggregated and unpredictable procedural frame was precisely what they didn't want.

From the 1954 Supreme Court decision *Brown v. Board of Education* through the Great Society programs of the Johnson era, liberal and progressive lawyers focused on altering substantive legal rules to bring about social change. They proposed new statutes, administrative rules and programs in the fields of civil rights, voting rights, poverty law, welfare law, consumer protection, and environmental regulation. Indeed, the Great Society initiatives all involved statutory, constitutional, and regulatory changes. By the late 1960s and early 1970s, however, it was becoming clear that substantive rule change would not be enough. Frustrated by their own experiences with law reform as much as by the persistence of segregation and poverty almost two decades after *Brown*, liberal and progressive lawyers and scholars wrestled with precisely what in the legal system as a whole made it an unwieldy and ineffective instrument of social change.

The gap between law in action and law in the books—articulated by Macaulay—offered one explanation. Macaulay had drawn attention to this gap in order to criticize the consensus common sense among contract law scholars that the commitments of the contract law regime translated seamlessly into the behavior of businessmen. This "gap between law and action," as it became known, challenged those who sought to use law as an instrument for liberal or progressive ends. How could the gap between changes in the law and changes in society be bridged? What caused this gap—where was the resistance? Most importantly, was there a bias—were progressive initiatives *particularly* likely to be stymied in practice? The most well known effort to develop a structural account of the legal system's own resistance to being harnessed as an instrument of social change was Marc Galanter's 1974 article, "Why the 'Haves' Come Out Ahead: Speculations on the Limits of Legal Change."

Galanter, born in 1931, attended both college and law school at the University of Chicago, graduating with his JD in 1956. After a stint as a Teaching Fellow,

Galanter spent a Fulbright year in India at the University of Delhi faculty of law, before returning to Stanford as an Assistant Professor. Galanter taught at the universities of Chicago, Buffalo, and Columbia—often in Asian Studies rather than law—before joining the Wisconsin law faculty in 1977, where he remains a professor emeritus. He has been a Guggenheim Fellow, a Fellow of the National Endowment for the Humanities, a Fellow of the Center for Advanced Study in Behavioral Sciences, and has served as editor of the *Law & Society Review* and president of the Law and Society Association. Galanter is a well-regarded comparative law scholar who has focused on India throughout his career. He was an early participant in efforts to harness law as an instrument of modernization and economic development. Indeed, his studies of the difficulties of transforming the Indian caste system through legislation and constitutional guarantees set the stage for his study of the resilience of inequality in the American legal order. From 1990 to 1998, Galanter directed the University of Wisconsin's Institute for Legal Studies, one of the leading centers for empirical research on the legal system.

Like Macaulay, Galanter focuses on the *uses* made of the legal system. From the perspective of users—potential litigants, in this case—the legal system offers a set of bargaining chips and procedural possibilities which can be "played" in various ways. For Macaulay, the point had been how rarely and to what ends the legal regime's possibilities were, in fact, used by the businessmen he studied. His analysis of Wisconsin business practices had made the Hart and Sacks Cantaloupe Case seem completely anomalous. Indeed, Macaulay had concluded by asking why businessmen would *ever* turn to law—and offered a series of hypotheses: to help with internal management and planning, for spite, and so on. Macaulay stressed that if parties litigate to "enforce the contract," either through specific performance or expectation damages, they are barking up the wrong tree, for such damages, however much discussed, are rarely forthcoming from the legal system.

Galanter begins by looking at the nature of the parties who do and do not use the legal system. He asks whether some *types* of parties are more likely to use—and others to disregard—the legal system. Perhaps the disinclination of Macaulay's businessmen to use the tools of litigation is typical—but only for similarly situated commercial parties. If we look at the range of people who do and do not use the legal system, broader patterns might emerge, and Macaulay's businessmen—repeat players in ongoing commercial relationships—may turn out themselves to be anomalous. It may turn out that some potential users have more to gain by turning to law, others by staying away. It may also turn out that the operations of the legal system itself make its use easier and more advantageous for some parties than for others.

To guide the inquiry, Galanter develops a rough typology of parties, distinguishing "one-shotters" from "repeat players." To speculate about how the legal system we have might present different opportunities and advantages to parties of these two types, he identifies a series of elements in the legal system which might look different to one-shotters and repeat players. He then works his way through these variables, developing hypotheses about how they might lead parties of these types to use the system differently, and how that, in turn, might affect the legal system itself. This mode of analysis—a typology of parties, a schematic picture of the legal order, speculation about how use by different parties would affect the legal order—was new to legal scholarship, and became a model for much later work. The result was a set of arguments and hypotheses—rather than empirical claims—about how the legal order functions.

Galanter reverses the traditional relationship between rules and parties, treating the parties to litigation as the independent variable—they determine when and how to mobilize the legal system's rules and institutions.

> Most analyses of the legal system start at the rules end and work down through institutional facilities to see what effect the rules have on the parties. I would like to reverse that procedure and look through the other end of the telescope. Let's think about the different kinds of parties and the effect these differences might have on the way the system works.[1]

He describes the legal order from the parties' points of view—there are rules and institutions, some are easy, some more difficult to utilize. Some rules are clear, some less so. Using the system requires professional intermediaries and has costs, which can vary substantially. Using the system can produce a variety of results—disappointment, symbolic victory, compensatory gains in the particular case, changes in the rule structure itself.

As Galanter develops this model, he speculates that differently situated parties will use different elements in the legal order more or less often, in different circumstances and with different results, both for themselves, and for the system as a whole. One-shotters will turn to litigation with different goals, and in different circumstances, from repeat players. Moreover, he proposes, much will depend on the *relative* positions of the two parties. Repeat players may well have quite different incentives for suing one another and suing one-shotters. The differential use made of the system by different types of parties in different constellations will, Galanter argues, have the effect of biasing the rules in favor of repeat players—an outcome which may then reinforce itself over time by encouraging repeat players and discouraging one-shotters from engaging the rule system.

As a result, he argues, the fact that the judicial machinery is reactive and incremental, that judges struggle to maintain neutrality, and that rules set by the legislature and by administrative agencies often have the objective of benefiting social groups which tend to be one-shotters, the legal system may nevertheless drift toward rules and outcomes favoring repeat players. Hence, Galanter's title: "why the 'haves' come out ahead." Of course, not all "haves" are also repeat players—but many are. They have a range of advantages in "playing" the legal system, including greater access to professional expertise. They can play for long-term results—for rules, rather than outcomes in particular cases. The legal system, moreover, responds to long-term users in ways that reinforce their advantages. The system is procedurally complex and normatively uncertain, strengthening the advantages of those with access to sophisticated expertise. The judicial system is largely reactive, giving players the power to settle and avoid an adverse result—a power that is more advantageous over time to the interests of repeat players. Opinions tend to move law incrementally, allowing repeat players to consolidate gains and play for marginal rule changes in their favor. And so forth. Many of these propositions were picked up for study by scholars working in the law and economics tradition.

Galanter focuses particular attention on the role of the legal profession, which in his view accentuates rather than ameliorates the advantages of repeat players. He asks how the internal structure of the legal profession itself—the distribution of status, access, and pay—might, through the uses made of lawyers by various parties, in turn influence the substantive content of rules, the distribution of justice, or the effectiveness of legislative and administrative efforts to use law as an instrument of social change. Many later Law and Society scholars set out to measure these effects. Indeed, treating lawyers as independent variables in the legal system—as key to the operation of the legal process—generated a whole series of interesting questions which were pursued in later scholarship. Galanter went on to publish a series of well-regarded studies of litigation and the legal profession in the United States, including path-breaking studies of the growth and transformation of large law firm practice and patterns of litigation. Particularly suggestive in "Why the 'Haves' Come Out Ahead" was the idea that the legal profession's own ethical rules might have an impact on the success differently situated parties could expect from the legal system:

> What might be good strategy for an insurance company lawyer or prosecutor—trading off some cases for gains on others—is branded as unethical when done by a criminal defense or personal injury plaintiff lawyer. It is not permissible for him to play his series of OSs [one-shotters] as if they constituted a single RP [repeat- player].[2]

In analyzing the difference between parties, Galanter pays particular attention to differences in what we might call the "legal culture" of various types of players—their "rule-mindedness," their expectations about justice, about the official legal culture, and about the time horizon of the interests they pursue through the legal system. Lawrence Friedman had been the first law and society scholar to write extensively about "legal culture."[3] Later law and society scholars explored the significance of a diversity of "legal cultures" within one legal order in a wide variety of ways. Rather than either condemning diversity as a threat to the ideal of a unitary order, or simply accepting it as part of the "legal process" in a complex marketplace, scholars explored the distributional impact of specific cultural splits in a legal order—between an elite and a non-elite legal profession, for example—on differently situated social groups. Galanter's innovation was to link legal culture not to the broader political or economic system, but to the micro-expectations of parties with different relationships to the legal system. Legal culture might not only be plural, but structured—and linked to the substantive distributional outcomes of the legal system. Like the legal profession, ideas about law might serve either to sharpen or blunt the advantages of repeat players.

Galanter has relatively little to say about the substantive rules of the legal order, but what he does say bears repeating in full:

> We assume here that rules tend to favor older, culturally dominant interests. This is not meant to imply that the rules are explicitly designed to favor those interests, but rather that those groups which have become dominant have successfully articulated their operations to pre-existing rules. To the extent that rules are evenhanded or favor the "have-nots," the limited resources for their implementation will be allocated, I have argued, so as to give greater effect to those rules which protect and promote the tangible interests of organized and influential groups. Furthermore, the requirements of due process, with their barriers or protections against precipitate action, naturally tend to protect the possessor or holder against the claimant. Finally, the rules are sufficiently complex and problematic (or capable of being problematic if sufficient resources are expended to make them so) that differences in the quantity and quality of legal services will affect capacity to derive advantages from the rules.[4]

Galanter pulls together here a number of different ideas, all of which came to be widely shared by law and society scholars and those associated with Critical Legal Studies. Whatever policy "balance" a given set of rules may initially represent, that balance will be powerfully influenced by the course of the rule's use and

implementation. Use and implementation will be affected by the complexity
and indeterminacy of the legal system, both substantively and procedurally.
Differentially situated parties will make use of the system differently, and will be
served by legal professionals in different ways. Over time, the result will both
favor the vindication of claims by dominant interests in society, and favor the
development of new rules and rule interpretations that strengthen that dominance.

Galanter's model of the legal order as a whole departs significantly from the legal
process vision of Hart and Sacks. Like them, Galanter focuses on the relationship
between legal rules and other forms of dispute settlement. Legal process scholars
had praised the law's broadly "suppletive" role in society—allowing other social
forms to stabilize social relations and facilitate cooperation among commercial
actors when possible, stepping in to compensate when other mechanisms failed. By
focusing attention on the use made by parties of different parts of the legal order,
Macaulay suggested that this relationship was far less coherent—and far less in the
control of legal analysts, judges, or policymakers—than the legal process vision had
suggested. Galanter complicates the image still further. He stresses that the relationship between law and other social machinery is not only a function of what
judges or policymakers decide. The parties themselves play a significant role—
in part by exercising, or threatening to exercise, their power to settle rather than
litigate, to "lump it," to withdraw from the relationship or dispute, or to seek other
forms of settlement. Different parties, moreover, will use different pieces of the legal
order in different ways as they struggle with one another. Consensus about when
to turn to law and when to rely on social procedures is unlikely; indeed, only in the
rare cases of repeat players in ongoing relationships—Macaulay's businessmen—
will the law seem equally "suppletive" to everyone. Far more often, parties will see
different pieces of the legal order differently and engage them more or less energet-
ically and effectively. The decision to settle, for example, emerges as a key power in
the hands of repeat players, offering them immense opportunities to game disputes
with one-shotters. The system that results is far less ordered—or hierarchical—than
the Hart and Sacks legal process conception would suggest:

> Contrast the more symmetrical "great pyramid of legal order" envisioned by Hart and
> Sacks (1958:312). Where the Hart and Sacks pyramid portrays private and official
> decision-making as successive moments of an integrated normative and institutional
> order, the present 'iceberg' model suggests that the existence of disparate systems of
> settling disputes is a reflection of cultural and structural discontinuities.[5]

In such a system, what can be done to make law an effective instrument of legal
change on behalf of the "have-nots"? In many ways, Galanter's story is a pessimistic
one—like Macaulay, he is in many ways a tragic liberal, lamenting the difficulties of
legal change and uncovering impediments to progressive law reform. But Galanter
also offers a program of action which proved immensely popular among legal scholars and activists associated with the Law and Society movement in the 1970s.

In the last section of the article, Galanter suggests that those interested in using
law as an instrument of social change on behalf of "have-nots" should focus
on *restructuring the parties rather than the rules*—turning one-shotters into
repeat players—in part by changing the way legal services are made available to
one-shotters:

> Our analysis suggests that breaking the interlocked advantages of the "haves"
> requires attention not only to the level of rules, but also to institutional facilities, legal

services and organization of parties. It suggests that litigating and lobbying have to be complemented by interest organizing, provisions of services and invention of new forms of institutional facilities.[6]

For lawyers and scholars associated with the Law and Society movement, the work of organizing the "have-nots"—into unions, civic associations, and tenant's unions—and providing legal services in the "public interest" on their behalf became central law reform projects. In short, Galanter placed lawyers, activists, and legal services programs that could alter the nature of participation by "have-nots" in the legal system at the center of law reform initiatives.

Galanter's crucial innovation was to think about law and social change as a dynamic process in which the parties of different types struggled with one another in relationship to an uncertain and complex legal regime. He placed the relationship between the substantive norms and the legal system's "everyday operations" in the foreground, and sought to understand the structure of that relationship and its effect on the distribution of power and wealth in society as a whole. In the closing pages of the article, he contemplates what might result in such a dynamic system were one-shotters more successfully organized as repeat players. Galanter is not at all sanguine about what this work might achieve. He acknowledges that these new repeat players might take their long-term disputes with other repeat players out of the litigation business altogether, with consequences which were not easily foreseen. The result may well be outcomes that departed widely from the normative terms proposed in the official legal system—much would depend on the balance of power among the repeat players in the unofficial system. In particular cases, the substantive outcome might well favor the haves yet more.

Galanter holds up the possible outcomes of a reformed legal order, in which efforts had been made to spread repeat-player advantages to all parties, as a heuristic. What, he asks, is the *function*—politically, economically, ideologically— of the legal system's current "unreformed" structure? In the ruminations which follow, Galanter illustrates a style of ideological interpretive analysis which would become more common throughout the 1970s and 1980s. He imagines the legal order as a system with a purpose—but what precisely is the purpose? Hart and Sacks had proposed an answer—the legal system is a process whose purpose is the facilitation of human cooperation. Some sociologists sought to move away from such broad conceptions—the legal system is not a system, it is disaggregated, plural, a set of tools and obstacles to parties and users. As such, it doesn't have a "purpose." It just is—and it has consequences. Galanter might well have concluded that the legal system as currently structured favors the "haves" without suggesting that this was "its purpose." Promoting the interests of the "haves" is certainly a purpose for the "haves"—but it doesn't add anything to Galanter's analysis to suggest that this is also the "purpose" of the legal order itself, beyond suggesting a vague conspiracy among the insiders who constructed the system. It is very difficult, however, to imagine a group of conspiratorial policymakers coming up with the idea of a disaggregated and passive legal order which could be used over time more effectively by repeat players as a constitutional design.

Galanter does speculate that the legal order has purposes. But he does not imagine what they are by translating the system's substantive outcomes into the language of intentions. He puts it this way:

> The unreformed features of the legal system then appear as a device for maintaining the partial dissociation of everyday practice from these authoritative institutional and

normative commitments. Structurally, (by cost and institutional overload) and culturally (by ambiguity and normative overload) the unreformed system effects a massive
covert delegation from the most authoritative rule-makers to field level officials (and
their constituencies) responsive to other norms and priorities than are contained in the
"higher law." By their selective application of rules in a context of parochial understandings and priorities, these field level legal communities produce regulatory outcomes which could not be predicted by examination of the authoritative "higher law."

Thus its unreformed characted (sic) articulates the legal system to the discontinuities
of culture and social structure: it provides a way of accommodating cultural heterogeneity and social diversity while propounding universalism and unity; of
accommodating vast concentrations of private power while upholding the supremacy
of public authority; of accommodating inequality in fact while establishing equality
at law; of facilitating action by great collective combines while celebrating individualism. Thus "unreform"—that is, ambiguity and overload of rules, overloaded and
inefficient institutional facilities, disparities in the supply of legal services, and disparities in the strategic position of parties—is the foundation of the "dualism" of
the legal system. It permits unification and universalism at the symbolic legal and
diversity and particularism at the operating level.[7]

The effort to interpret the legal order's ambivalence, pluralism, inefficiency,
and institutional failure to make good on its substantive commitments as in some
sense *functional*, as part of a general cultural, political, or ideological project,
would become a staple in the legal academy in the next decades. Galanter's effort
in that direction offered a first dystopic counterpart to the optimistic stories told
by the legal process authors about the American legal system's disaggregation and
substantive agnosticism.

DAVID KENNEDY

NOTES

1. Galanter, "Why the Haves Come out Ahead," . . . *supra* , at p. 97.
2. Ibid., p. 117.
3. See *supra* , pp. 459–464.
4. Galanter, pp. 123–4 footnotes in the original eliminated.
5. Ibid., p. 134, n. 97.
6. Ibid., p. 150.
7. Ibid., pp. 147–8, notes removed.

BIBLIOGRAPHY

Marc Galanter

Marc Galanter, "Why the 'Haves' Come Out Ahead: Speculations on the Limits
of Legal Change," 9 *Law & Society Review* 95 (1974). Although the article was
initially rejected by the leading law reviews, as well as by several political science
journals, it has since been reprinted and translated into numerous languages, and
has consistently been one of the most cited of American law review articles.

A symposium on the twenty-fifth anniversary of the article's publication is "Do the 'Haves' Still Come Out Ahead?" *Law & Society Review* 33(4) 793–1131. The article is reprinted, with a selection of related essays, in Susan S. Sibley and Herbert M. Kritzer, *In Litigation: Do the 'Haves' Still Come Out Ahead?* (Stanford, Calif.: Stanford University Press, 2003).

Other work by Galanter following his contribution to the Canon includes: Galanter, "Delivering Legality: Some Proposals for the Direction of Research" 11 *Law & Society Review* 225 (1976); "The Duty *Not* to Deliver Legal Services," 30 *University of Miami Law Review* 929 (1975–76); "Legality and its Discontents: A Preliminary Assessment of Theories of Legalization and Delegalization," in Erhard Blankenburg et al., eds., "Alternative Rechtsformen und Alternativen zum Recht," 6 Jahrbuch fuer Rechtssoziologie und Rechtstheorie 11 (Opladen: Westdeutscher Verlag, 1980); Galanter, "Reading the Landscape of Disputes: What We Know and Don't Know (and Think We Know) About Our Allegedly Contentious and Litigious Society," 31 *UCLA Law Review* 4 (1983); "Adjudication, Litigation and Related Phenomena," in Leon Lipson and Stanton Wheeler, eds., *Law and the Social Sciences* (New York: Russell Sage Foundation, 1986) at 151–257; Galanter (with Mia Cahill), "Most Cases Settle: Judicial Promotion and Regulation of Settlements," 46 *Stanford Law Review* 1339 (1993–94); Galanter, "Old and In the Way: The Coming Demographic Transformation of the Legal Profession and its Implications for the Provision of Legal Services," 1999 *Wisconsin Law Review* 1081 (1999).

Galanter's work on India includes: Galanter, *Competing Equalities: Law and the Backward Classes in India* (Berkeley: University of California Press, 1984); *Law and Society in Modern India* (New Delhi and New York: Oxford Press, 1989); "Equality and 'Protective Discrimination' in India," 16 *Rutgers Law Review* 42 (1961); "Compensatory Discrimination in Political Representation: A Preliminary Assessment of India's Thirty-year Experience with Reserved Seats in Legislatures," *14 Economic and Political Weekly* 437 (1979); and numerous other articles on the role of caste, indigenous law, the judiciary, the role of Hinduism and secularism, and federalism in modern India.

Galanter has also collaborated with Macaulay and others in the field of contracts: Marc Galanter, Stewart Macaulay, John Kidwell, and William Whitford, *Contracts: Law in Action* (Charlottesville, Va.: Michie Co., 1995). See also "Contract in Court; or Almost Everything You May or May Not Want to Know About Contract Litigation," 2001 *Wisconsin Law Review* 579 (2001), which develops the "one-shotter/repeat player" model further, contrasting those engaged in "uphill" and "downhill" litigation. He concludes that:

> Cases in the uphill cluster are typically brought by individuals against organizations, are more frequently contested, take considerably longer, and end with fewer plaintiff victories. In contrast, in the much larger downhill cluster, the typical plaintiff is an organization but defendants are split, with a slight preponderance of organizational defendants, defaults are frequent, settlements are somewhat less frequent, disposition comes sooner, trials are quite rare, and plaintiffs have a very high win rate. (p. 593)

The article continues Galanter's insistence that the nature of parties matters. Macaulay comments on Galanter's article in Stewart Macaulay, "Almost Everything That I Did Want to Know About Contract Litigation: A Comment on Galanter," *Wisconsin Law Review* 629 (2001). Both Macaulay and Galanter are concerned with the ideological effects of contract scholarship and teaching which overemphasizes the availability of remedies, the significance of litigation, and the opportunities for small parties to defeat large ones in uphill litigation.

Galanter's work on the legal profession in the United States includes: Galanter (with Thomas Palay), *Tournament of Lawyers: The Growth and Transformation of the Big Law Firms* (Chicago: University of Chicago Press, 1991); "Mega-Law and Mega-Lawyering in the Contemporary United States," in Robert Dingwall and Philip Lewis, eds., *The Sociology of the Professions: Lawyers, Doctors and Others* (London: MacMillan, 1983) at 152; Galanter (with Thomas Palay), "The Transformation of the Big Law Firm," in Robert L. Nelson, David M. Trubek, and Rayman L. Solomon, eds., *Lawyers' Ideals/Lawyers' Practice*: Transformations in the American Legal Profession (Ithaca and London: Cornell University Press, 1992) at 31. Galanter analyzes the particular consequences of using the resources of enormous firms to exploit the procedural possibilities in Galanter, "Mega-Law and Mega-Lawyering in the Contemporary United States," in *The Sociology of the Professions: Lawyers, Doctors and Others*, Dingwall and Lewis, eds., 152. Galanter focuses on the ratio of lawyers to judges, arguing that the large number of lawyers in the United States does not translate into numerous cases, but into the use of legal procedures in ongoing commercial bargaining. See Galanter, "Reading the Landscape of Disputes: What we Know and Don't Know (and Think we Know) About Our Allegedly Contentious and Litigious Society," 31 *UCLA Law Review* 4, 55 (1983–84): "the ratio of lawyers to judges in the United States is . . . one of [the] highest anywhere; the private sector of the law industry is very large relative to the public institutional sector." Galanter is particularly interested in the role of judges pushing parties back into negotiations with one another toward settlement. See Galanter, "A Settlement Judge, not a Trial Judge: Judicial Mediation in the United States," 12 *Journal of Law and Society* 1 (1985); and Galanter, "The Emergence of the Judge as a Mediator in Civil Cases," 69 *Judicature* 257 (1986).

Commentary

Galanter wrote this article as part of a generational cohort of law and society scholars working in the Hurst-Macaulay tradition. A number of these are cited in Galanter's bibliography. See, for example, Richard Abel, "A Comparative Theory of Dispute Institutions in Society," 8 *Law & Society Review* 217 (1974); William L. F. Felstiner, "Influences of Social Organization on Dispute Processing," 9 *Law & Society Review* 63 (1974); Lawrence Friedman, "Legal Rules and the Process of Social Change," 19 *Stanford Law Review* 786 (1967); Lawrence Friedman, "Legal Culture and Social Development," 4 *Law & Society Review* 29 (1969); Joel F. Handler, *The Lawyer and his Community: The Practicing Bar in a Middle-sized City* (Madison: University of Wisconsin Press, 1967); Geoffrey C. Hazard, Jr., "Law Reforming in the Anti-Poverty Effort," 37 *University of Chicago Law Review* 242 (1969–70); Leon H. Mayhew, *Law and Equal Opportunity: A Study of the Massachusetts Commission Against Discrimination* (Cambridge, Mass.: Harvard University Press 1968); William Simon, "Class Actions—Useful Tool or Engine of Destruction," 55 *Federal Rules Decisions* 375 (1972); Jerome H. Skolnick, "Social Control in the Adversary System," 11 *Journal of Conflict Resolution* 52 (1967); David M. Trubek, "Toward a Social Theory of Law: An Essay on the Study of Law and Development," 82 *Yale Law Journal* 1 (1972–73); William C. Whitford, "Law and the Consumer Transaction: A Case Study of the Automobile Warranty," 1968 *Wisconsin Law Review* 1006 (1968).

The link between the relationship among parties and the uses made of litigation was also of interest to Macaulay. His study of the use of litigation in the dealership and franchise relationships highlighted the role of dependency in the turn to litigation. Stewart Macaulay, *Law and the Balance of Power: The Automobile Manufacturers and Their Dealers* (New York: Russell Sage Foundation, 1966); Macaulay, "Law Schools and the World Outside Their Doors II: Some Nots on Two Recent Studies of the Chicago Bar," 32 *Journal of Legal Education* 506 (1982).

Galanter's focus on the options of "lumping it" or "exiting" the relationship relied heavily on the work of Albert O. Hirschman, *Exit, Voice and Loyalty: Responses to Decline in Firms, Organizations and States* (Cambridge, Mass.: Harvard University Press, 1970), which would also be enormously influential on the next generation of scholars developing sociological game theory analysis of the actions of participants in the legal order.

In the years after Galanter wrote, many scholars focused on the ways in which legislative and constitutional struggle continues in implementing agencies and courts, often in ways that blunt or dilute the substantive vision. See, for example, Abram Chayes, Karl E. Klare, "Judicial De-radicalization of the Wagner Act and the Origins of Modern Legal Consciousness, 1937–41," 62 *Minnesota Law Review* 265 (1977–78). Philippe Nonet, *Administrative Justice: Advocacy and Change in a Government Agency* (New York: Russell Sage Foundation, 1969); R. Shep Melnick, "Administrative Law and Bureaucratic Reality," in Thomas O. Sargentich, ed., *Administrative Law Anthology* (Cincinnati: Anderson Publishing, 1994), 392; R. Shep Melnick, *Between the Lines: Interpreting Welfare Rights* (Washington, D.C.: Brookings Institution, 1994).

Over the last twenty years, a large body of scholarship has emerged which uses game theory models developed in political science and economics to analyze participants in the legal system. See, e.g., Tom Schelling, *The Strategy of Conflict* (New York: Oxford University Press, 1963).

Galanter's focus on the ideological or psychological function of the legal system's combination of authoritative pronouncement and indeterminate interpretive and procedural machinery was fleshed out by scholars in both the Law and Society and Critical Legal Studies tradition. See Macaulay on relational contracts; Duncan Kennedy and "Blackstone's Commentaries," arguing that "legal consciousness" had an "apologetic" and "legitimating" function. The effort to interpret the symbolic cultural effects of the legal system had begun with the legal realists. See, for example, Thurmond Arnold, *The Symbols of Government* (New Haven: Yale University Press, and London, H. Milford: Oxford University Press, 1935); and Jerome Frank, *Law and the Modern Mind* (New York: Brentano's, 1930). Patricia Ewick and Susan Silbey analyze the consequences of awareness of the legal system's "dualism" identified by Galanter's thorough empirical study of lay attitudes toward uses of the legal system in "Common Knowledge and Ideological Critique: The Significance of Knowing that the "Haves" Come Out Ahead," 33 *Law & Society Review* 1025 (1999). See also Peter Fitzpatrick, *The Mythology of Modern Law* (London, New York: Routledge, 1992); and Pierre Schlag, "Law and Phrenology," 110 *Harvard Law Review* 877 (1996–97).

A variety of law and society scholars turned their attention to the legal profession. See, for example, Joel F. Handler, *The Lawyer in his Community: The Practicing Bar in a Middle-Sized City* (Madison: University of Wisconsin Press, 1967); Jerome Edward Carlin, *Lawyers' Ethics: a Survey of the New York City*

Bar (New York: Russell Sage Foundation, 1966); Herbert Jacobs, *Justice in America: Courts, Lawyers, and the Judicial Process* (Boston: Little Brown, 1965); Abram Chayes and Antonia H. Chayes, "Corporate Counsel and the Elite Law Firm," 37 *Stanford Law Review* 277 (1984–85). A fascinating analysis of the international commercial arbitration profession in this tradition is Yves Dezalay and Bryant G. Garth, *Dealing in Virtue: International Commercial Arbitration and the Construction of a Transnational Legal Order* (Chicago: University of Chicago Press, 1996).

Law and Society scholars have debated the usefulness of the public interest legal services model steadily since Galanter wrote. See, for example, William H. Simon, *The Practice of Justice: A Theory of Lawyers' Ethics* (Cambridge, Mass.: Harvard University Press, 1998); William H. Simon, *The Community Economic Development: Law, Business, and the New Social Policy* (Durham, N.C.: Duke University Press, 2001); Louise G. Trubek and Jeremy Cooper, *Educating for Justice: Social Values and Legal Education Brookfield, Vt.: (Aldershot, Ashgate*: Dartmouth, 1997); and Louise G. Trubek and Jeremy Cooper, *Educating for Justice Around the World: Legal Education, Legal Practice, and the Community (Aldershot, Ashgate*: Dartmouth, 1999). See also Susan E. Lawrence, *The Poor in Court: The Legal Services Program and Supreme Court Decision Making* (Princeton, N.J.: Princeton University Press, 1990); Martha F. Davis, *Brutal Need: Lawyers and the Welfare Rights Movement, 1960–73* (New Haven: Yale University Press, 1993); Stuart Scheingold, *The Politics of Rights: Lawyers, Public Policy and Political Change* (New Haven: Yale University Press, 1974); Joel F. Handler, "Controlling Official Behavior in Welfare Administration," 54 *California Law Review* 479 (1966); Joel F. Handler, *Social Movements and the Legal System: A Theory of Law Reform and Social Change* (New York: Academic Press, 1978); Joel Handler, *Down from Bureaucracy: The Ambiguity of Privatization and Empowerment* (Princeton, N.J.: Princeton University Press, 1996); Jack Katz, *Poor People's Lawyers in Transition* (New Brunswick, N.J.: Rutgers University Press, 1982); Austin Sarat and Stuart Scheingold, *Cause Lawyering: Political Commitments and Professional Responsibilities* (New York: Oxford University Press, 1998).

Galanter's article led to numerous follow-up studies focusing on the viability of his typology of parties, and the nature of their respective advantages in litigation. See, for example, John Heinz and Edward Laumann's study of the differences in wealth, power, and prestige between lawyers in corporate and individual practice: John P. Heinz and Edward O. Laumann, *Chicago Lawyers: The Social Structure of the Bar* (New York: Russell Sage Foundation, 1982).

Legal pluralism had been a focal point for legal anthropologists. See, for example, Paul Bohannan, "The Differing Realms of the Law in the Ethnology of Law," in Laura Nadar, ed., "The Ethnography of Law," *The American Anthropologist* 67 (1965):33–42. Galanter's work in India led to work in the field of law and modernization, and on legal pluralism, most notably, "The Modernization of Law," in M. Weiner, ed., *Modernization: The Dynamics of Growth* (New York: Basic Books, 1966) at 153–65; Galanter (with David M. Trubek), "Scholars in Self-Estrangement: Some Reflections on the Crisis of Law and Development Studies in the United States," *Wisconsin Law Review* 1062 (1974); "Justice in Many Rooms: Courts, Private Ordering and Indigenous Law," 19 *Journal of Legal Pluralism* 1 (1981).

On the twenty-fifth anniversary of the publication of Galanter's article, the *Law & Society Review* published a symposium issue devoted to commentary on the article. See Herbert M. Kritzer and Susan Silbey, eds., "Do the 'Haves' Still Come Out

Ahead?" Symposium, 33 *Law & Society Review* 799 (1999). Some authors contributed retrospective analyses of Galanter's arguments. See, for example, Joel Grossman, Herbert M. Kritzer, and Stewart Macaulay, "Do the 'Haves' Still Come Out Ahead?" 33 *Law & Society Review* 803 (1999).

Others extended Galanter's model and argument to new contexts. See particularly, Lauren Edelman and Mark C. Suchman, "When the 'Haves' Hold Court: Speculations on the Organizational Internalization of Law," 33 *Law & Society Review* 941 (1999). Edelman and Suchman extend Galanter's analysis by analyzing the processes through which institutions internalize legal rules and legal personnel through the legalization of their own internal governance, the expansion of private dispute resolution, the rise of in-house counsel, and the emergence of private policing. They argue that these trends "transform the large bureaucratic organization from being merely a repeat player in the public legal system to being a full-fledged private legal system in its own right" (at p. 941). Their analysis of the role of the alternative dispute resolution movement is particularly instructive.

See also Kathryn Hendley, Peter Murrell, and Randi Ryterman, "Do Repeat Players Behave Differently in Russia? Contractual and Litigation Behavior of Russian Enterprises," 33 *Law & Society Review* 833 (1999) (arguing that although access to legal services and party structure is crucial to litigation in Russia, repeat players behave differently; they do not play for rules "because that is a mostly futile pursuit" and they are not particularly aggressive or sophisticated in legal strategy, perhaps reflecting the more unstable Russian commercial environment and the calculation that "future payoff of long-run relationships and established business routines is less important when survival is at issue," p. 859); Catherine Albiston, "The Rule of Law and the Litigation Process: The Paradox of Losing by Winning," 33 *Law & Society Review* 869 (1999) (analyzing litigation under the Family and Medical Leave Act to demonstrate how success for individual litigants fails to translate into substantive social change); and Beth Harris, "Representing Homeless Families: Repeat Player Implementation Strategies," 33 *Law & Society Review* 911 (1999) (analyzing efforts by public interest lawyers to act as repeat players on behalf of homeless and potentially homeless families).

"Why the 'Haves' Come Out Ahead: Speculations on the Limits of Legal Change"

9 Law and Society Review 95 (1974)

This essay attempts to discern some of the general features of a legal system like the American by drawing on (and rearranging) commonplaces and less than systematic gleanings from the literature. The speculative and tentative nature of the assertions here will be apparent and is acknowledged here wholesale to spare myself and the reader repeated disclaimers.

I would like to try to put forward some conjectures about the way in which the basic architecture of the legal system creates and limits the possibilities of using the system as a means of redistributive (that is, systemically equalizing) change. Our question, specifically, is, under what conditions can litigation[1] be redistributive, taking litigation in the broadest sense of the presentation of claims to be decided by courts (or court-like agencies) and the whole penumbra of threats, feints, and so forth, surrounding such presentation.

For purposes of this analysis, let us think of the legal system as comprised of these elements:

A body of authoritative normative learning—for short, RULES
A set of institutional facilities within which the normative learning is applied to specific cases—for short, COURTS
A body of persons with specialized skill in the above—for short, LAWYERS
Persons or groups with claims they might make to the courts in reference to the rules, etc.—for short, PARTIES

This essay grew out of a presentation to Robert Stevens' Seminar on the Legal Profession and Social Change at Yale Law School in the autumn of 1970, while the author was Senior Fellow in the School's Law and Modernization Program. It has gathered bulk and I hope substance in the course of a succession of presentations and revisions. It has accumulated a correspondingly heavy burden of obligation to my colleagues and students. I would like to acknowledge the helpful comments of Richard Abel, James Atleson, Guido Calabresi, Kenneth Davidson, Vernon Dibble, William L.F. Felstiner, Lawrence M. Friedman, Marjorie Girth, Paul Goldstein, Mark Haller, Stephen Halpern, Charles M. Hardin, Adolf Homberger, Geoffrey Hazard, Quintin Johnstone, Patrick L. Kelley, David Kirp, Arthur Leff, Stuart Nagel, Philippe Nonet, Saul Touster, David M. Trubeck and Stephen Wasby on earlier drafts, and to confer on them the usual dispensation.

The development of this essay was linked in many places to a contemporaneous project on the Deployment Process in the Implementation of Legal Policy supported by the National Science Foundation. I am grateful to the Foundation for affording me the opportunity to pursue several lines of inquiry touched on here. The Foundation bears no responsibility for the views set forth here.

An earlier version was issued as a working paper of the Law and Modernization Program; yet another version of the first part is contained in the proceedings (edited by Lawrence Friedman and Manfred Rehbinder) of the Conference on the Sociology of the Judicial Process, held at Bielefeld, West Germany in September, 1973.

[1] "Litigation" is used here to refer to the pressing of claims oriented to official rules, either by actually invoking official machinery or threatening to do so. Adjudication refers to full-dress individualized and formal application of rules by officials in a particular litigation.

Let us also make the following assumptions about the society and the legal system:

It is a society in which actors with different amounts of wealth and power are constantly in competitive or partially cooperative relationships in which they have opposing interests.

This society has a legal system in which a wide range of disputes and conflicts are settled by court-like agencies which purport to apply pre-existing general norms impartially (that is, unaffected by the identity of the parties).

The rules and the procedures of these institutions are complex; wherever possible disputing units employ specialized intermediaries in dealing with them.

The rules applied by the courts are in part worked out in the process of adjudication (courts devise interstitial rules, combine diverse rules, and apply old rules to new situations). There is a living tradition of such rule-work and a system of communication such that the outcomes in some of the adjudicated cases affect the outcome in classes of future adjudicated cases.

Resources on the institutional side are insufficient for timely full-dress adjudication in every case, so that parties are permitted or even encouraged to forego bringing cases and to "settle" cases,—that is, to bargain to a mutually acceptable outcome.

There are several levels of agencies, with "higher" agencies announcing (making, interpreting) rules and other "lower" agencies assigned the responsibility of enforcing (implementing, applying) these rules. (Although there is some overlap of function in both theory and practice, I shall treat them as distinct and refer to them as "peak" and "field level" agencies.)

Not all the rules propounded by "peak" agencies are effective at the "field level," due to imperfections in communication, shortages of resources, skill, understanding commitment and so forth. (Effectiveness at the field level will be referred to as "penetration."[2])

I. A Typology of Parties

Most analyses of the legal system start at the rules end and work down through institutional facilities to see what effect the rules have on the parties. I would like to reverse that procedure and look through the other end of the telescope. Let's think about the different kinds of parties and the effect these differences might have on the way the system works.

Because of differences in their size, differences in the state of the law, and differences in their resources, some of the actors in the society have many occasions to utilize the courts (in the broad sense) to make (or defend) claims; others do so only rarely. We might divide our actors into those claimants who have only occasional recourse to the courts (one-shotters or OS) and repeat players (RP) who are engaged in many similar litigations over time.[3] The spouse in a divorce case, the

[2] Cf. Friedman (1969:43) who defines penetration as "the number of actors and spheres of action that a particular rule . . . actually reaches."

[3] The discussion here focuses on litigation, but I believe an analogous analysis might be applied to the regulatory and rule-making phases of legal process. OSs and RPs may be found in regulatory and legislative as well as adjudicative settings. The point is nicely epitomized by the observation of one women's movement lobbyist:

By coming back week after week . . . we tell them not only that we're here, but that we're here to stay. We're not here to scare anybody. . . . The most threatening thing I can say is that we'll be back. *New York Times*, Jan. 29, 1974, p. 34, col. 7–8.

For an interesting example of this distinction in the regulatory arena, see Lobenthal's (1970:20 ff.) description of the regulation of parking near a pier, contrasting the "permanent" shipping company and longshoreman interests with the OS pier visitors, showing how regulation gravitates to the accommodation of the former. This is, of course, akin to the "capture by the regulated" that attends (or afflicts) a variety of administrative agencies. *See, e.g.*, Bernstein (1955); Edelman (1967).

auto-injury claimant, the criminal accused are OSs; the insurance company, the prosecutor, the finance company are RPs. Obviously this is an oversimplification; there are intermediate cases such as the professional criminal.[4] So we ought to think of OS-RP as a continuum rather than as a dichotomous pair. Typically, the RP is a larger unit and the stakes in any given case are smaller (relative to total worth). OSs are usually smaller units and the stakes represented by the tangible outcome of the case may be high relative to total worth, as in the case of injury victim or the criminal accused. Or, the OS may suffer from the opposite problem: his claims may be so small and unmanageable (the shortweighted consumer or the holder of performing rights) that the cost of enforcing them outruns any promise of benefit. See Finklestein (1954: 284–6).

Let us refine our notion of the RP into an "ideal type" if you will—a unit which has had and anticipates repeated litigation, which has low stakes in the outcome of any one case, and which has the resources to pursue its long-run interests.[5] (This does not include every real-world repeat player; that most common repeat player, the alcoholic derelict, enjoys few of the advantages that may accrue to the RP [see below]. His resources are too few to bargain in the short run or take heed of the long run.[6]) An OS, on the other hand, is a unit whose claims are too large (relative to his size) or too small (relative to the cost of remedies) to be managed routinely and rationally.

We would expect an RP to play the litigation game differently from an OS. Let us consider some of his advantages:

(1) RPs, having done it before, have advance intelligence; they are able to structure the next transaction and build a record. It is the RP who writes the form contract, requires the security deposit, and the like.

(2) RPs develop expertise and have ready access to specialists.[7] They enjoy economies of scale and have low startup costs for any case.[8]

(3) RPs have opportunities to develop facilitative informal relations with institutional incumbents.[9]

---

[4] Even the taxpayer and the welfare client are not pure OSs, since there is next year's tax bill and next month's welfare check. Our concept of OS conceals the difference between pure OSs—persons such as the accident victim who get in the situation only once—and those who are in a continuing series of transactions (welfare clients or taxpayers) but whose resources permit at most a single crack at litigation.

[5] Of course a Repeat Player need not engage in adjudication (or even in litigation). The term includes a party who makes or resists claims which may occupy any sector of the entire range of dispute processing mechanisms discussed in section V below. Perhaps the most successful RPs are those whose antagonists opt for resignation.

[6] In the "processing" of these parties and their limited strategic options, see Foote (1956); Spradley (1970: Chap. 6).

[7] Ironically, RPs may enjoy access to competent paraprofessional help that is unavailable to OSs. Thus the insurance company can, by employing adjusters, obtain competent and experienced help in routine negotiations without having to resort to expensive professionally qualified personnel. See Ross (1970:25) on the importance of the insurance adjuster in automobile injury settlements.

[8] An intriguing example of an RP reaping advantage from a combination of large scale operations and knowledgeability is provided by Skolnick's (1966:174 ff.) account of professional burglars' ability to trade clearances for leniency.

[9] See, for example, Jacob's (1969:100) description of creditor colonization of small claims courts:

... the neutrality of the judicial process was substantially compromised by the routine relationships which developed between representatives of frequent users of garnishment and the clerk of the court. The clerk scheduled cases so that one or two of the heavy users appeared each day. This enabled the clerk to equalize the work flow of his office. It also consolidated the cases of large creditors and made it unnecessary for them to come to court every day. It appeared that these heavy users and the clerk got to know each other quite well in the course of several months. Although I observed no other evidence of favoritism toward these creditors, it was apparent that the clerk tended to be more receptive toward the version of the conflict told by the creditor than disclosed by the debtor, simply because one was told by a man he knew and the other by a stranger.

(4) The RP must establish and maintain credibility as a combatant. His interest in his "bargaining reputation" serves as a resource to establish "commitment" to his bargaining positions. With no bargaining reputation to maintain, the OS has more difficulty in convincingly committing himself in bargaining.[10]

(5) RPs can play the odds.[11] The larger the matter at issue looms for OS, the more likely he is to adopt a minimax strategy (minimize the probability of maximum loss). Assuming that the stakes are relatively smaller for RPs, they can adopt strategies calculated to maximize gain over a long series of cases, even where this involves the risk of maximum loss[12] in some cases.[13]

(6) RPs can play for rules as well as immediate gains. First, it pays an RP to expend resources in influencing the making of the relevant rules by such methods as lobbying.[14] (And his accumulated expertise enables him to do this persuasively.)

(7) RPs can also play for rules in litigation itself, whereas an OS is unlikely to. That is, there is a difference in what they regard as a favorable outcome. Because his stakes in the immediate outcome are high and because by definition OS is unconcerned with the outcome of similar litigation in the future, OS will have little interest in that element of the outcome, which might influence the disposition of the decision-maker next time around. For the RP, on the other hand, anything that will favorably influence the outcomes of future cases is a worthwhile result. The larger the stake for any player and the lower the probability of repeat play, the less likely that he will be concerned with the rules which govern future cases

---

The opportunity for regular participants to establish relations of trust and reciprocity with courts is not confined to these lowly precincts. Scigliano (1971:183–84) observes that:

> The Government's success in the Supreme Court seems to owe something . . . to the credit which the Solicitor General's Office has built up with the Court . . . in the first place, by helping the Court manage its great and growing burden of casework. . . . He holds to a trickle what could be a deluge of Government appeals. . . . In the second place by ensuring that the Government's legal work is competently done. So much so that when the Justices or their clerks want to extract the key issues in a complicated case quickly, they turn, according to common report, to the Government's brief.

> [Third.] The Solicitor General gains further credit . . . by his demonstrations of impartiality and independence from the executive branch.

[10] See Ross (1970:156 ff.); Schelling (1963:22 ff., 41). An offsetting advantage enjoyed by some OSs deserves mention. Since he does not anticipate continued dealings with his opponent, an OS can do his damnedest without fear of reprisal next time around or on other issues. (The advantages of those who enjoy the luxury of singlemindedness are evidenced by some notorious examples in the legislative arena, for instance, the success of prohibitionists and of the gun lobby.) Thus there may be a bargaining advantage to the OS who (a) has resources to damage his opponent; (b) is convincingly able to threaten to use them. An OS can burn up his capital, but he has to convince the other side he is really likely to do so. Thus an image of irrationality may be a bargaining advantage. See Ross (1970:170n.); Schelling (1963:17). An OS may be able to sustain such an image in a way that an RP cannot. But cf. Leff (1970a:18) on the role of "spite" in collections and the externalization to specialists of "irrational" vengeance.

[11] Ross (1970:214) notes that in dealing with the injury claimant, the insurance adjuster enjoys the advantage of "relative indifference to the uncertainty of litigation . . . the insurance company as a whole in defending large numbers of claims is unaffected by the uncertainty with respect to any one claim. . . . from the claimant's viewpoint [litigation] involves a gamble that may be totally lost. By taking many such gambles in litigating large numbers of cases the insurance company is able to regard the choice between the certainty and the gamble with indifference."

[12] That is, not the whole of RPs' worth, but the whole matter at issue in a single claim.

[13] Cf. the overpayment of small claims and underpayment of large claims in automobile injury cases. Franklin, Chanin and Mark (1961); Conard, et al. (1964). If small claim overpayment can be thought of as the product of the transaction costs of the defendants (and, as Ross [1970:207] shows, organizational pressures to close cases), the large claim underpayment represents the discount for delay and risk on the part of the claimant. (Conard, et al. 1964:197–99).

[14] Olson's analysis (1965:36ff, 127) suggests that their relatively small number should enhance the capacity of RPs for coordinated action to further common interests. See note 127.

of the same kind. Consider two parents contesting the custody of their only child, the prizefighter vs. the IRS for tax arrears, the convict facing the death penalty. On the other hand, the player with small stakes in the present case and the prospect of a series of similar cases (the IRS, the adoption agency, the prosecutor) may be more interested in the state of the law.

Thus, if we analyze the outcomes of a case into a tangible component and a rule component,[15] we may expect that in case 1, OS will attempt to maximize tangible gain. But if RP is interested in maximizing his tangible gain in a series of cases 1 . . . n, he may be willing to trade off tangible gain in any one case for rule gain (or to minimize rule loss).[16] We assumed that the institutional facilities for litigation were overloaded and settlements were prevalent. We would then expect RPs to "settle" cases where they expected unfavorable rule outcomes.[17] Since they expect to litigate again, RPs can select to adjudicate (or appeal) those cases which they regard as most likely to produce favorable rules.[18] On the other hand, OSs should be willing to trade off the possibility of making "good law" for tangible gain. Thus, we would expect the body of "precedent" cases— that is, cases

---

[15] This can be done only where institutions are simultaneously engaged in rule-making and dispute-settling. The rule-making function, however, need not be avowed; all that is required is that the outcome in Case 1 influence the outcome in Case 2 in a way that RP can predict.

[16] This is not to imply that rule loss or gain is the main determinant of settlement policy. First, the RP must litigate selectively. He can't fight every case. Second, rules are themselves the subject of dispute relatively rarely. Only a small fraction of litigation involves some disagreement between the parties as to what the rules are or ought to be. Dibble (1973).

In addition, the very scale that bestows on RPs strategic advantages in settlement policy exposes them to deviations from their goals. Most RPs are organizations and operate through individual incumbents of particular roles (house counsel, claims adjuster, assistant prosecutor) who are subject to pressures which may lead them to deviate from the optimization of institutional goals. Thus Ross (1970:220–21) notes that insurance companies litigate large cases where, although settlement would be "rational" from the overall viewpoint of the company, it would create unacceptable career risk to incumbents. Newman (1966:72) makes a similar observation about prosecutors' offices. He finds that even where the probability of conviction is slim "in cases involving a serious offense which has received a good deal of publicity . . . a prosecutor may prefer to try the case and have the charge reduction or acquittal decision made by the judge or jury."

[17] The assumption here is that "settlement" does not have precedent value. Insofar as claimants or their lawyers form a community which shares such information, this factor is diminished—as it is, for example, in automobile injury litigation where, I am told, settlements have a kind of precedent value.

[18] Thus the Solicitor General sanctions appeal to the Supreme Court in one-tenth of the appealable defeats of the Government, while its opponents appeal nearly half of their appealable defeats. Scigliano points out that the Government is more selective because:

> In the first place, lower-court defeats usually mean much less to the United States than they do to other parties. In the second place, the government has, as private litigants do not, an independent source of restraint upon the desire to litigate further (1971:169).

Appellants tend to be winners in the Supreme Court—about twothirds of cases are decided in their favor. The United States govgovernment wins about 70% of the appeals it brings.

> What sets the government apart from other litigants is that it wins a much higher percentage of cases in which it is the appellee (56% in 1964–66). (1971:178).

Scigliano assigns as reasons for the government's success in the Supreme Court not only the "government's agreement with the court on doctrinal position" but the "expertise of the Solicitor General's Office" and "the credit which the Solicitor General has developed with the Court." (1971:182).
More generally, as Rothstein (1974:501) observes:

> The large volume litigant is able to achieve the most favorable forum; emphasize different issues in different courts; take advantage of difference in procedure among courts at the state and federal level; drop or compromise unpromising cases without fear of heavy financial loss; stall some cases and push others; and create rule conflicts in lower courts to encourage assumption of jurisdiction in higher courts. Cf. Hazard (1965:68).

capable of influencing the outcome of future cases—to be relatively skewed toward those favorable to RP.[19]

Of course it is not suggested that the strategic configuration of the parties is the sole or major determinant of rule-development. Rule-development is shaped by a relatively autonomous learned tradition, by the impingement of intellectual currents from outside, by the preferences and prudences of the decision-makers. But courts are passive and these factors operate only when the process is triggered by parties. The point here is merely to note the superior opportunities of the RP to trigger promising cases and prevent the triggering of unpromising ones. It is not incompatible with a course of rule-development favoring OSs (or, as indicated below, with OSs failing to get the benefit of those favorable new rules).

In stipiulating [sic] that RPs can play for rules, I do not mean to imply that RPs pursue rule-gain as such. If we recall that not all rules penetrate (i.e., become effectively applied at the field level) we come to some additional advantages of RPs.

(8) RPs, by virtue of experience and expertise, are more likely to be able to discern which rules are likely to "penetrate" and which are likely to remain merely symbolic commitments. RPs may be able to concentrate their resources on rule-changes that are likely to make a tangible difference. They can trade off symbolic defeats for tangible gains.

(9) Since penetration depends in part on the resources of the parties (knowledge, attentiveness, expert sevices [sic], money), RPs are more likely to be able to invest the matching resources necessary to secure the penetration of rules favorable to them.

It is not suggested that RPs are to be equated with "haves" (in terms of power, wealth and status) or OSs with "have-nots." In the American setting most RPs are larger, richer and more powerful than are most OSs, so these categories overlap, but there are obvious exceptions. RPs may be "have-nots" (alcoholic derelicts) or may act as champions of "have-nots" (as government does from time to time); OSs such as criminal defendants may be wealthy. What this analysis does is to

---

[19] Macaulay (1966:99–101) in his study of relations between the automobile manufacturers and their dealers recounts that the manufacturers:

> . . . had an interest in having the [Good Faith Act] construed to provide standards for their field men's conduct. Moreover they had resources to devote to the battle. The amount of money involved might be major to a canceled dealer, but few, if any cases involved a risk of significant liability to the manufacturers even if the dealer won. Thus the manufacturers could afford to fight as long as necessary to get favorable interpretations to set guidelines for the future. While dealers' attorneys might have to work on a contingent fee, the manufacturers already had their own large and competent legal staffs and could afford to hire trial and appellate specialists. . . . an attorney on a contingent fee can afford to invest only so much time in a particular case. Since the manufacturers were interested in guidelines for the future, they could afford to invest, for example, $40,000 worth of attorneys' time in a case they could have settled for $10,000. Moreover, there was the factor of experience. A dealer's attorney usually started without any background in arguing a case under the Good Faith Act. On the other hand, a manufacturer's legal staff became expert in arguing such a case as it faced a series of these suits. It could polish its basic brief in case after case and even influence the company's business practices—such as record keeping—so that it would be ready for any suit.

> . . . While individual dealers decide whether or not to file a complaint, the manufacturer, as any fairly wealthy defendant facing a series of related cases, could control the kinds of cases coming before the courts in which the Good Faith Act could be construed. It could defend and bring appeals in those cases where the facts are unfavorable to the dealer, and it could settle any where the facts favor the dealer. Since individual dealers were more interested in money than establishing precedents . . . the manufacturers in this way were free to control the cases the court would see.

The net effect . . . was to prompt a sequence of cases favorable to the manufacturers.

define a position of advantage in the configuration of contending parties and indicate how those with other advantages tend to occupy this position of advantage and to have their other advantages reinforced and augmented thereby.[20] This position of advantage is one of the ways in which a legal system formally neutral as between "haves" and "have-nots" may perpetuate and augment the advantages of the former.[21]

DIGRESSION ON LITIGATION-MINDEDNESS

We have postulated that OSs will be relatively indifferent to the rule-outcomes of particular cases. But one might expect the absolute level of interest in rule-outcomes to vary in different populations: in some there may be widespread and intense concern with securing vindication according to official rules that overshadows interest in the tangible outcomes of disputes; in others rule outcomes may be a matter of relative indifference when compared to tangible outcomes. The level and distribution of such "rule mindedness" may affect the relative strategic position of OSs and RPs. For example, the more rule minded a population, the less we would expect an RP advantage in managing settlement policy.

But such rule mindedness or appetite for official vindication should be distinguished from both (1) readiness to resort to official remedy systems in the first place and (2) high valuation of official rules as symbolic objects. Quite apart from relative concern with rule-outcomes, we might expect populations to differ in their estimates of the propriety and gratification of litigating in the first place.[22]

---

[20] Of course, even within the constraints of their strategic position, parties may fare better or worse according to their several capacities to mobilize and utilize legal resources. Nonet (1969: Chap. IV) refers to this as "legal competence"—that is, the capacity for optimal use of the legal process to pursue one's interests, a capacity which includes information, access, judgment, psychic readiness, and so forth.

An interesting example of the effects of such competence is provided by Rosenthal (1970: Chap. 2) who notes the superior results obtained by "active" personal injury plaintiffs. ("Active" clients are defined as those who express special wants to their attorneys, make follow-up demands for attention, marshall information to aid the lawyer, seek quality medical attention, seek a second legal opinion, and bargain about the fee.) He finds such "active" clients drawn disproportionately from those of higher social status (which presumably provides both the confidence and experience to conduct themselves in this active manner).

The thrust of the argument here is that the distribution of capacity to use the law beneficially cannot be attributed solely or primarily to personal characteristics of parties. The personal qualities that make up competence are themselves systematically related to social structure, both to general systems of stratification and to the degree of specialization of the parties. The emphasis here differs somewhat from that of Nonet, who makes competence central and for whom, for example, organization is one means of enhancing competence. This analysis views personal competence as operating marginally within the framework of the parties' relations to each other and to the litigation process. It is submitted that this reversal permits us to account for systematic differentials of competence and for the differences in the structure of opportunities which face various kinds of parties when personal competence is held constant.

[21] The tendency for formal equality to be compatible with domination has been noted by Weber (1954:188–91) and Ehrlich (1936:238), who noted "The more the rich and the poor are dealt with according to the same legal propositions, the more the advantage of the rich is increased."

[22] Cf. Hahm (1969); Kawashima (1963) for descriptions of cultural settings in which litigation carries high psychic costs. (For the coexistence of anti-litigation attitudes with high rates of litigation, see Kidder [1971].) For a population with a greater propensity to litigate consider the following account (*New York Times*, Oct. 16, 1966) of contemporary Yugoslavia:

> Yugoslavs often complain of a personality characteristic in their neighbors that they call inat, which translates roughly as "spite." . . . One finds countless examples of it chronicled in the press. . . the case of two neighbors in the village of Pomoravije who had been suing each other for 30 years over insults began when one "gave a dirty look" to the other's pet dog.

> Last year the second district court in Belgrade was presented with 9000 suits over alleged slanders and insults. . . . Often the cases involve tenants crowded in apartment buildings. In one building in the Street of the October Revolution tenants began 53 suits against each other. Other causes of "spite" suits . . . included

501

LIMITS OF LEGAL CHANGE

Such attitudes may affect the strategic situation of the parties. For example, the greater the distaste for litigation in a population, the greater the barriers to OSs pressing or defending claims, and the greater the RP advantages, assuming that such sentiments would affect OSs, who are likely to be individuals, more than RPs, who are likely to be organizations.[23]

It cannot be assumed that the observed variations in readiness to resort to official tribunals is directly reflective of a "rights consciousness" or appetite for vindication in terms of authoritative norms.[24] Consider the assertion that the low rate of litigation in Japan flows from an undeveloped "sense of justiciable rights" with the implication that the higher rate in the United States flows from such rights-consciousness.[25] But the high rate of settlements and the low rate of appeals in the

---

"a bent fence, a nasty look." Business enterprises are not immune and one court is handling a complaint of the Zastava Company of Knic over a debt of 10 dinars (less than 1 cent).

> In the countryside spite also appears in such petty forms as a brother who sued his sister because she gathered fruit fallen from a tree he regarded as his own. . . .

> Dr. Mirko Barjakterevic, professor of ethnology at Belgrade University . . . remarked that few languages had as many expressions for and about spite as Serbian and that at every turn one hears phrases like, "I'm going to teach him a lesson," and "I don't want to be made a fool of."

Consider, too, Frake's ("Litigation in Lipay: A Study in Subanum Law" quoted in Nader [1965:21]) account of the prominence of litigation among the Lipay of the Philippines:

> A large share, if not the majority, of legal cases deal with offenses so minor that only the fertile imagination of a Subanum legal authority can magnify them into a serious threat to some person or to society in general . . . A festivity without litigation is almost as unthinkable as one without drink. If no subject for prosecution immediately presents itself, sooner or later, as the brew relaxes the tongues and actions, someone will make a slip.

> In some respects a Lipay trial is more comparable to an American poker game than to out legal proceedings. It is a contest of skill, in this case of verbal skill, accompanied by social merry-making, in which the loser pays a forfeit. He pays for much the same reason we pay a poker debt: so he can play the game again. Even if he does not have the legal authority's ability to deal a verbalized "hand," he can participate as a defendant, plaintiff, kibitzer, singer, and drinker. No one is left out of the range of activities associated with litigation.

> Litigation nevertheless has far greater significance in Lipay than this poker-game analogy implies. For it is more than recreation. Litigation, together with the rights and duties it generates, so pervades Lipay life that one could not consistently refuse to pay fines and remain a functioning member of society. Along with drinking, feasting, and ceremonializing, litigation provides patterned means of interaction linking the independent nuclear families of Lipay into a social unit, even though there are no formal group ties of comparable extent. The importance of litigation as a social activity makes understandable its prevalence among the peaceful and, by our standards, "law-abiding" residents of Lipay.

[23] Generally, sentiments against litigation are less likely to affect organizations precisely because the division of labor within organizations means that litigation will be handled impersonally by specialists who do not have to conduct other relations with the opposing party (as customers, etc.). See Jacob (1969:78 ff.) on the separation of collection from merchandizing tasks as one of the determinants of creditor's readiness to avail of litigation remedies. And cf. the suggestion (note 16 above) that in complex organizations resort to litigation may be a way to externalize decisions that no one within the organization wants to assume responsibility for.

[24] Cf. Zeisel, Kalven & Buchholz (1959: Chap. 20). On the possibility of explaining differences in patterns of litigation by structural rather than cultural factors, see Kidder's (1971: Chap. IX) comparison of Indian and American litigation.

[25] Henderson (1968:488) suggests that in Japan, unlike America,

> . . . popular sentiment for justiciable rights is still largely absent. And, if dispute settlement is the context from which much of the growth, social meaning and political usefulness of justiciable rights derive—and American experience suggests it is—then the traditional tendency of the Japanese to rely on sublegal conciliatory techniques becomes a key obstacle in the path toward the rule-of-law envisioned by the new constitution.

He notes that

> In both traditional and modern Japan, conciliation of one sort or another has been and still is effective in settling the vast majority of disputes arising in the gradually changing social context. (1968:449).

United States suggest it should not be regarded as having a population with great interest in securing moral victories through official vindication.[26] Mayhew (1973:14, Table I) reports a survey in which a sample of Detroit area residents were asked how they had wanted to see their "most serious problem" settled. Only a tiny minority (0% of landlord-tenant problems; 2% of neighborhood problems; 4% of expensive purchase problems; 9% of public organization problems; 31% of discrimination problems) reported that they sought "justice" or vindication of their legal rights: "most answered that they sought resolution of their problems in some more or less expedient way."

Paradoxically, low valuation of rule-outcomes in particular cases may co-exist with high valuation of rules as symbolic objects. Edelman (1967: chap. 2) distinguishes between remote, diffuse, unorganized publics, for whom rules are a source of symbolic gratification and organized, attentive publics directly concerned with the tangible results of their application. Public appetite for symbolic gratification by the promulgation of rules does not imply a corresponding private appetite for official vindication in terms of rules in particular cases. Attentive RPs on the other hand may be more inclined to regard rules instrumentally as assets rather than as sources of symbolic gratification.

We may think of litigation as typically involving various combinations of OSs and RPs. We can then construct a matrix such as Figure 1 and fill in the boxes with some well-known if only approximate American examples. (We ignore for the moment that the terms OS and RP represent ends of a continuum, rather than a dichotomous pair.)

On the basis of our incomplete and unsystematic examples, let us conjecture a bit about the content of these boxes:

Box I: OS vs. OS

The most numerous occupants of this box are divorces and insanity hearings. Most (over 90 per cent of divorces, for example) are uncontested.[27] A large portion of these are really pseudo-litigation, that is, a settlement is worked out between the parties and ratified in the guise of adjudication. When we get real litigation in Box I, it is often between parties who have some intimate tie with one another, fighting over some unsharable good, often with overtones of "spite" and "irrationality." Courts are resorted to where an ongoing relationship is ruptured; they have little to do with the routine patterning of activity. The law is invoked *ad hoc* and instrumentally by the parties. There may be a strong interest in vindication, but neither party is likely to have much interest in the long-term state of the law (of, for

---

Finding that Californians resorted to litigation about 23 times as often as Japanese, he concludes (1968:453) that traditional conciliation is employed to settle most "disputes that would go to court in a country with a developed sense of justiciable right." Henderson (1968:454) seems to imply that "in modern society [people] must comport thereselves according to reasonable and enforceable principles rather than haggling, negotiating and jockeying about to adjust personal relationships to fit an ever-shifting power balance among individuals."

Cf. Rabinowitz (1968: Part III) for a "cultural" explanation for the relative unimportance of law in Japanese society. (Non-egodeveloped personality, non-rational approach to action, extreme specificity of norms with high degree of contextual differentiation.)

[26] For an instructive example of response to a claimant who wants vindication rather than a tidy settlement, see Katz (1969:1492):

When I reported my client's instructions not to negotiate settlement at the pretrial conference, the judge appointed an impartial psychiatrist to examine Mr. Lin.

[27] For descriptions of divorce litigation, see Virtue (1956); O'Gorman (1963); Marshall and May (1932).

FIGURE 1
A Taxonomy of Litigation by Strategic Configuration of Parties

Initiator, Claimant

	One-Shotter	Repeat Player
One-Shotter	Parent v. Parent (Custody)	Prosecutor v. Accused
	Spouse v. Spouse (Divorce)	Finance Co. v. Debtor
	Family v. Family Member	Landlord v. Tenant
	(Insanity Commitment)	I.R.S. v. Taxpayer
	Family v. Family	Condemnor v. Property
	(Inheritance)	Owner
	Neighbor v. Neighbor	
	Partner v. Partner	
Defendant	OS vs OS I	RP vs OS II
Repeat Player	Welfare Client v. Agency	Union v. Company
	Auto Dealer v. Manufacturer	Movie Distributor v.
	Injury Victim v. Insurance Company	Censorship Board
	Tenant v. Landlord	Developer v. Suburban
	Bankrupt Consumer v. Creditors	Municipality
	Defamed v. Publisher	Purchaser v. Supplier
		Regulatory Agency v. Firms of Regulated Industry
	OS vs RP III	RP vs RP IV

instance, custody or nuisance). There are few appeals, few test cases, little expenditure of resources on rule-development. Legal doctrine is likely to remain remote from everyday practice and from popular attitudes.[28]

Box II: RP vs. OS

The great bulk of litigation is found in this box—indeed every really numerous kind except personal injury cases, insanity hearings, and divorces. The law is used for routine processing of claims by parties for whom the making of such claims is a regular business activity.[29] Often the cases here take the form of stereotyped

---

[28] For an estimate of the discrepancy between the law and popular attitudes in a "Box I" area, see Cohn, Robson and Bates (1958).

[29] Available quantitative data on the configuration of parties to litigation will be explored in a sequel to this essay. For the moment let me just say that the speculations here fit handily with the available findings. For example, Wanner (1974), analyzing a sample of 7900 civil cases in three cities, found that business and governmental units are plaintiffs in almost six out of ten cases; and that they win more, settle less and lose

mass processing with little of the individuated attention of full-dress adjudication.
Even greater numbers of cases are settled "informally" with settlement keyed to possible litigation outcome (discounted by risk, cost, delay).

The state of the law is of interest to the RP, though not to the OS defendants. Insofar as the law is favorable to the RP it is "followed" closely in practice[30] (subject to discount for RP's transaction costs).[31] Transactions are built to fit the rules by creditors, police, draft boards and other RPs.[32] Rules favoring OSs may be less readily applicable, since OSs do not ordinarily plan the underlying transaction, or less meticulously observed in practice, since OSs are unlikely to be as ready or able as RPs to invest in insuring their penetration to the field level.[33]

Box III: OS vs. RP

All of these are rather infrequent types except for personal injury cases which are distinctive in that free entry to the arena is provided by the contingent fee.[34] In auto injury claims, litigation is routinized and settlement is closely geared to possible litigation outcome. Outside the personal injury area, litigation in Box III is not

---

less than individual plaintiffs. Individuals, on the other hand, are defendants in two thirds of all cases and they win less and lose more than do government or business units. A similar preponderance of business and governmental plaintiffs and individual defendants is reported in virtually all of the many studies of small claims courts. E.g., Pagter et al. (1964) in their study of a metropolitan California small claims court find that individuals made up just over a third of the plaintiffs and over 85% of defendants. A later survey of four small-town California small claims courts (Moulton 1969:1660) found that only 16% of plaintiffs were individuals [sic]—but over 93% of defendants.

[30] The analysis here assumes that, when called upon, judges apply rules routinely and relentlessly to RPs and OSs alike. In the event, litigation often involves some admixture of individuation, kadijustice, fireside equities, sentimentality in favor of the "little guy." (For a comparison of two small claims courts in one of which the admixture is stronger, see Yngvesson (1965)). It also involves some offsetting impurities in favor of frequent users. See Note 9 above and Note 59 below.

[31] Cf. Friedman (1967:806) on the zone of "reciprocal immunities" between, for example, landlord and tenant, afforded by the cost of enforcing their rights. The foregoing suggests that these immunities may be reciprocal, but they are not necessarily symmetrical. That is, they may differ in magnitude according to the strategic position of the parties. Cf. Vaughan's (1968:210) description of the "differential dependence" between landlord and low-income tenant. He regards this as reflecting the greater immediacy and constancy of the tenant's need for housing, the landlord's "exercise of privilege in the most elemental routines of the relationship," greater knowledge, and the fact that the landlord, unlike the tenant, does not have all his eggs in one basket (i.e., he is, in our terms, an RP).

> Whereas each tenant is dependent upon one landlord, the landlord typically diffuses his dependency among many tenants. As a result, the owner can rather easily retain an independent position in each relationship.

A similar asymmetry typically attends relations between employer and employee, franchiser and franchisee, insurer and insured, etc.

[32] See note 74 below. Cf. Skolnick's (1966:212ff) description of police adjustment to the exclusionary rule.

[33] Similarly, even OSs who have procured favorable judgments may experience difficulty at the execution stage. Even where the stakes loom large for OSs, they may be too small to enlist unsubsidized professional help in implementation. A recent survey of consumers who "won" in New York City's Small Claims Court found that almost a third were unable to collect. Marshalls either flatly refused to accept such judgments for collection or "conveyed an impression that, even if they did take a small claims case, they would regard it as an annoyance and would not put much work into it." *New York Times*, Sept. 19, 1971. A subsequent survey (Community Service Society 1974:16) of 195 successful individual plaintiffs in two Manhattan Small Claims Courts revealed that "only 50% of persons who received *judgments* were able to collect these through their own efforts or through use of sheriffs and marshals." (Plaintiffs who received settlements were more successful, collecting in 82% of the cases.) Cf. the finding of Hollingsworth, *et al.* (1973: Table 16) that of winning small claims plaintiffs in Hamilton County only 31% of individuals and unrepresented proprietorships collected half or more of the judgment amount; the corresponding figure for corporations and represented proprietorships was 55%.

[34] Perhaps high volume litigation in Box III is particularly susceptible to transformation into relatively unproblematic administrative processing when RPs discover that it is to their advantage and can secure a shift with some gains (or at least no losses) to OSs. Cf. the shift from tort to workman's compensation in the industrial accident area (Friedman and Ladinsky [1967]) and the contemporary shift to no-fault plans in the automobile injury area.

routine. It usually represents the attempt of some OS to invoke outside help to create leverage on an organization with which he has been having dealings but is now at the point of divorce (for example, the discharged employee or the cancelled franchisee).[35] The OS claimant generally has little interest in the state of the law; the RP defendant, however, is greatly interested.

Box IV: RP vs. RP

Let us consider the general case first and then several special cases. We might expect that there would be little litigation in Box IV, because to the extent that two RPs play with each other repeatedly,[36] the expectation of continued mutually benefcial interaction would give rise to informal bilateral controls.[37] This seems borne out by studies of dealings among businessmen[38] and in labor relations. Official agencies are invoked by unions trying to get established and by management trying to prevent them from getting established, more rarely in dealings between bargaining partners.[39] Units with mutually beneficial relations do not adjust their differences in courts. Where they rely on third parties in dispute-resolution, it is likely to take a form (such as arbitration or a domestic tribunal) detached from official sanctions and applying domestic rather than official rules.

However, there are several special cases. First, there are those RPs who seek not furtherance of tangible interests, but vindication of fundamental cultural commitments. An example would be the organizations which sponsor much church-state litigation.[40] Where RPs are contending about value differences (who is right) rather than interest conflicts (who gets what) there is less tendency to settle and less basis for developing a private system of dispute settlement.[41]

[35] Summers (1960:252) reports that

> more than 3/4 of the reported cases in which individuals have sought legal protection of their rights under a collective agreement have arisen out of disciplinary discharge.

The association of litigation with "divorce" is clear in Macaulay (1963, 1969) and other discussions of commercial dealings. (Bonn 1972b:573 ff.). Consumer bankruptcy, another of the more numerous species of litigation in Box III, might be thought of as representing the attempt of the OS to effectuate a "divorce."

[36] For example, Babcock (1969:53–54) observes that what gives the suburb its greatest leverage on any one issue is the builder's need to have repeated contact with the regulatory powers of the suburb on various issues.

[37] The anticipated beneficial relations need not be with the identical party but may be with other parties with whom that party is in communication. RPs are more likely to participate in a network of communication which cheaply and rapidly disseminates information about the behavior of others in regard to claims and to have an interest and capacity for acquiring and storing that information. In this way RPs can cheaply and effectively affect the business reputation of adversaries and thus their future relations with relevant others. Leff (1970a; 26 ff.); Macaulay (1963:64).

[38] . . . why is contract doctrine not central to business exchanges?

> Briefly put, private, between-the-parties sanctions usually exist, work and do not involve the costs of using contract law either in litigation or as a ploy in negotiations. . . . most importantly, there are relatively few one-shot, but significant, deals. A businessman usually cares about his reputation. He wants to do business again with the man he is dealing with and with others. Friedman and Macaulay (1967:805).

[39] Aspin (1966:2) reports that 70 to 75% of all complaints to the NLRB about the unfair labor practices of companies are under the single section [8(a)(3)] which makes it an unfair labor practice for employers to interfere with union organizing. These make up about half of *all* complaints of unfair labor practices.

[40] In his description of the organizational participants in church-state litigation, Morgan (1968:chap. 2) points out the difference in approach between value-committed "separationist purists" and their interest-committed "public schoolmen" allies. The latter tend to visualize the game as non-zero-sum and can conceive of advantages in alliances with their parochial-school adversaries. (1968:58n).

[41] Cf. Aubert's (1963:27 ff.) distinction between conflict careers based upon conflicts of interest and those arising from conflicts of value.

Second, government is a special kind of RP. Informal controls depend upon the ultimate sanction of withdrawal and refusal to continue beneficial relations.[42] To the extent that withdrawal of future association is not possible in dealing with government, the scope of informal controls is correspondingly limited. The development of informal relations between regulatory agencies and regulated firms is well known. And the regulated may have sanctions other than withdrawal which they can apply; for instance, they may threaten political opposition. But the more inclusive the unit of government, the less effective the withdrawal sanction and the greater the likelihood that a party will attempt to invoke outside allies by litigation even while sustaining the ongoing relationship. This applies also to monopolies, units which share the government's relative immunity to withdrawal sanctions.[43] RPs in monopolistic relationships will occasionally invoke formal controls to show prowess, to give credibility to threats, and to provide satisfactions for other audiences. Thus we would expect litigation by and against government to be more frequent than in other RP vs. RP situations. There is a second reason for expecting more litigation when government is a party. That is, that the notion of "gain" (policy as well as monetary) is often more contingent and problematic for governmental units than for other parties, such as businesses or organized interest groups. In some cases courts may, by proffering [sic] authoritative interpretations of public policy, redefine an agency's notion of gain. Hence government parties may be more willing to externalize decisions to the courts. And opponents may have more incentive to litigate against government in the hope of securing a shift in its goals.

A somewhat different kind of special case is present where plaintiff and defendant are both RPs but do not deal with each other repeatedly (two insurance companies, for example.) In the government/monopoly case, the parties were so inextricably bound together that the force of informal controls was limited; here they are not sufficiently bound to each other to give informal controls their bite; there is nothing to withdraw from! The large one-time deal that falls through, the marginal enterprise—these are staple sources of litigation.

Where there is litigation in the RP vs. RP situation, we might expect that there would be heavy expenditure on rule-development, many appeals, and rapid and elaborate development of the doctrinal law. Since the parties can invest to secure implementation of favorable rules, we would expect practice to be closely articulated to the resulting rules.

On the basis of these preliminary guesses, we can sketch a general profile of litigation and the factors associated with it. The great bulk of litigation is found in Box II; much less in Box III. Most of the litigation in these Boxes is mass routine

---

[42] This analysis is illuminated by Hirschman's distinction between two modes of remedial action by customers or members disappointed with the performance of organizations: (1) exit (that is, withdrawal of custom or membership); and (2) voice ("attempts at changing the practices and policies and outputs of the firm from which one buys or the organizations to which one belongs") [1970:30]. Hirschman attempts to discern the conditions under which each will be employed and will be effective in restoring performance. He suggests that the role of voice increases as the opportunities for exit decline, but that the possibility of exit increases the effectiveness of the voice mechanism. (1970:34, 83). Our analysis suggests that it is useful to distinguish those instances of voice which are "internal," that is, confined to expression to the other party, and those which are external, that is, seek the intervention of third parties. This corresponds roughly to the distinction between two-party and three-party dispute settlement. We might then restate the assertion to suggest that internal voice is effective where there is a plausible threat of sanction (including exit and external voice).

[43] The potency of the monopolistic character of ties in promoting resort to third parties is suggested by the estimate that in the Soviet Union approximately one million contract disputes were arbitrated annually in the early 1960's. (Loeber, 1965:128, 133). Cf. Scott's (1965:63–64) suggestion that restricted mobility (defined in terms of job change) is associated with the presence of formal appeal systems in business organizations.

processing of disputes between parties who are strangers (not in mutually beneficial continuing relations) or divorced[44]—and between whom there is a disparity in size. One party is a bureaucratically organized "professional" (in the sense of doing it for a living) who enjoys strategic advantages. Informal controls between the parties are tenuous or ineffective; their relationship is likely to be established and defined by official rules; in litigation, these rules are discounted by transaction costs and manipulated selectively to the advantage of the parties. On the other hand, in Boxes I and IV, we have more infrequent but more individualized litigation between parties of the same general magnitude, among whom there are or were continuing multi-stranded relationships with attendant informal controls. Litigation appears when the relationship loses its future value; when its "monopolistic" character deprives informal controls of sufficient leverage and the parties invoke outside allies to modify it; and when the parties seek to vindicate conflicting values.

II. Lawyers

What happens when we introduce lawyers? Parties who have lawyers do better.[45] Lawyers are themselves RPs. Does their presence equalize the parties, dispelling the advantage of the RP client? Or does the existence of lawyers amplify the advantage of the RP client? We might assume that RPs (tending to be larger units) who can buy legal services more steadily, in larger quantities, in bulk (by retainer) and at higher rates, would get services of better quality. They would have better information (especially where restrictions on information about legal services are present).[46] Not only would the RP get more talent to begin with, but he would on the whole get greater

---

[44] That is, the relationship may never have existed, it may have "failed" in that it is no longer mutually beneficial, or the parties may be "divorced." On the incompatibility of litigation with ongoing relations between parties, consider the case of the lawyer employed by a brokerage house who brought suit against his employer in order to challenge New York State's law requiring fingerprinting of employees in the securities industry.

> They told me, "Don, you've done a serious thing: you've sued your employer." And then they handed me [severance pay] checks. They knew I had to sue them. Without making employer a defendant, it's absolutely impossible to get a determination in court. It was not a matter of my suing them for being bad guys or anything like that and they knew it. . . . the biggest stumbling block is that I'm virtually blacklisted on Wall Street. . . .

His application for unemployment compensation was rejected on the ground that he had quit his employment without good cause, having provoked his dismissal by refusing to be fingerprinted. *New York Times,* March 2, 1970. It appears that, in the American setting at any rate, litigation is not only incompatible with the maintainance of continuing relationships, but with their subsequent restoration. On the rarity of successful reinstatement of employees ordered reinstated by the NLRB, see Aspin (1966). Bonn (1972: 262) finds this pattern even among users of arbitration, which is supposedly less lethal to continuing relations than litigation. He found that in 78 cases of arbitration in textiles, "business relations were resumed in only fourteen." Cf. Golding's (1969:90) observation that jural forms of dispute-settlement are most appropriate where parties are not involved in a continuing relationship. But the association of litigation with strangers is not invariate. See the Yugoslav and Lipay examples in note 22 above. Cf. the Indian pattern described by Kidder (1971) and by Morrison (1975:39) who recounts that his North Indian villagers "commented scornfully that GR [a chronic litigant] would even take a complete stranger to law—proof that his energies were misdirected."

[45] For example, Ross (1970:193) finds that automobile injury claimants represented by attorneys recover more frequently than unrepresented claimants; that among those who recover, represented claimants recover significantly more than do unrepresented claimants with comparable cases. Claimants represented by firms recovered considerably more than claimants represented by solo practitioners; those represented by negligence specialists recovered more than those represented by firm attorneys. Similarly, Mosier and Soble (1973:35ff) find that represented tenants fare better in eviction cases than do unrepresented ones. The advantages of having a lawyer in criminal cases are well-known. See, for instance, Nagel (1973).

[46] As it happens, the information barriers vary in their restrictiveness. The American Bar Association's Code of Professional Responsibility

continuity, better record-keeping, more anticipatory or preventive work, more experience and specialized skill in pertinent areas, and more control over counsel.

One might expect that just how much the legal services factor would accentuate the RP advantage would be related to the way in which the profession was organized. The more members of the profession were identified with their clients (i.e., the less they were held aloof from clients by their loyalty to courts or an autonomous guild) the more the imbalance would be accentuated.[47] The more close and enduring the lawyer-client relationship, the more the primary loyalty of lawyers is to clients rather than to courts or guild, the more telling the advantages of accumulated expertise and guidance in overall strategy.[48]

What about the specialization of the bar? Might we not expect the existence of specialization to offset RP advantages by providing OS with a specialist who in pursuit of his own career goals would be interested in outcomes that would be advantageous to a whole class of OSs? Does the specialist become the functional equivalent of the RP? We may divide specialists into (1) those specialized by field of law (patent, divorce, etc.), (2) those specialized by the kind of party represented (for example, house counsel), and (3) those specialized by both field of law and "side" or party (personal injury plaintiff, criminal defense, labor). Divorce lawyers do not specialize in husbands or wives,[49] nor real-estate lawyers in buyers or sellers. But labor lawyers

---

permits advertising directed at corporations, banks, insurance companies, and those who work in the upper echelons of such institutions . . . [while proscribing] most forms of dissemination of information which would reach people of "moderate means" and apprise them of their legal rights and how they can find competent and affordable legal assistants to vindicate those rights. (Burnley 1973:77).

On the disparate effect of these restrictions, cf. note 51.

[47] The tension between the lawyer's loyalties to the legal system and to his client has been celebrated by Parsons (1954:381 ff.) and Horsky (1952: chap. 3). But note how this same deflection of loyalty from the client is deplored by Blumberg (1967) and others. The difference in evaluation seems to depend on whether the opposing pull is to the autonomous legal tradition, as Parsons (1954) and Horsky (1972) have it, or to the maintanance of mutually beneficial interaction with a particular local institution whose workings embody some admixture of the "higher law" (see note 82 below) with parochial understandings, institutional maintenance needs, etc.

[48] Although this is not the place to elaborate it, let me sketch the model that underlies this assertion. (For a somewhat fuller account, see International Legal Center, 1973:4ff.). Let us visualize a series of scales along which legal professions might be ranged:

	A	B
1. Basis of Recruitment	Restricted-------------	Wide
2. Barriers to Entry	High------------------	Low
3. Division of Labor		
a. Coordination	Low-------------------	High
b. Specialization	Low-------------------	High
4. Range of Services and Functions	Narrow--------------	Wide
5. Enduring Relationships to Client	Low-------------------	High
6. Range of Institutional Settings	Narrow--------------	Wide
7. Identification with Clients	Low-------------------	High
8. Identification with Authorities	High------------------	Low
9. Guild Control	Tight------------------	Loose
10. Ideology	Legalistic------------	Problem-solving

It is suggested that the characteristics at the A and B ends of the scale tend to go together, so that we can think of the A and B clusters as means of describing types of bodies of legal professionals, for example, the American legal profession (Hurst 1950; Horsky 1952: Pt. V.; Carlin 1962, 1966; Handler 1967; Smigel 1969) would be a B type, compared to British barristers (Abel-Smith and Stevens 1967) and French *avocats* (Le Paulle 1950); Indian lawyers (Galanter 1968–69), an intermediate case. It is suggested that some characteristics of Type B professions tend to accentuate or amplify the strategic advantages of RP parties. Consideration of, for instance, the British bar, should warn us against concluding that Type B professions are necessarily more conservative in function than Type A. See text, at footnote 145.

[49] Which is not to deny the possibility that such "side" specialization might emerge. One can imagine "women's liberation" divorce lawyers—and anti-alimony ones—devoted to rule-development that would favor one set of OSs.

and tax lawyers and stockholders-derivative-suit lawyers do specialize not only in the field of law but in representing one side. Such specialists may represent RPs or OSs. Figure 2 provides some well-known examples of different kinds of specialists:

Most specializations cater to the needs of particular kinds of RPs. Those specialists who service OSs have some distinctive features:

First, they tend to make up the "lower echelons" of the legal profession. Compared to the lawyers who provide services to RPs, lawyers in these specialties tend to be drawn from lower socio-economic origins, to have attended local, proprietary or part-time law schools, to practice alone rather than in large firms, and to possess low prestige within the profession.[50] (Of course the correlation is far from perfect; some lawyers who represent OSs do not have these characteristics and some representing RPs do. However, on the whole the difference in professional standing is massive).

Second, specialists who service OSs tend to have problems of mobilizing a clientele (because of the low state of information among OSs) and encounter "ethical" barriers imposed by the profession which forbids solicitation, advertising, referral fees, advances to clients, and so forth.[51]

Third, the episodic and isolated nature of the relationship with particular OS clients tends to elicit a stereotyped and uncreative brand of legal services. Carlin and Howard (1965:385) observe that:

> The quality of service rendered poorer clients is . . . affected by the non-repeating character of the matters they typically bring to lawyers (such as divorce, criminal,

FIGURE 2
A Typology of Legal Specialists
Lawyer

		Specialized by Party	*Specialized by Field and Party*	*Specialized by Field*
Client	RP	"House Counsel" or General Counsel for Bank, Insurance Co. etc.	Prosecutor	
			Personal Injury Defendant	
		Corporation Counsel for Government Unit	Staff Counsel for NAACP	
			Tax	
			Labor/Management	
			Collections	Patent
	OS	"Poverty Lawyers"	Criminal Defense	
		Legal Aid	Personal Injury	Bankruptcy
			Plaintiff	Divorce

[50] On stratification within the American legal profession see Ladinsky (1963); Lortie (1959); Carlin (1966). But cf. Handler (1967).

[51] See Reichstein (1965); Northwestern University Law Review (1953). On the differential impact of the "Canons of Ethics" on large law firms and those lawyers who represent OSs, see Carlin (1966); Schuchman (1968); Christianson (1970:136).

personal injury): this combined with the small fees encourages a mass processing of cases. As a result, only a limited amount of time and interest is usually expended on any one case—there is little or no incentive to treat it except as an isolated piece of legal business. Moreover, there is ordinarily no desire to go much beyond the case as the client presents it, and such cases are only accepted when there is a clear-cut cause of action; i.e., when they fit into convenient legal categories and promise a fairly certain return.

Fourth, while they are themselves RPs, these specialists have problems in developing optimizing strategies. What might be good strategy for an insurance company lawyer or prosecutor—trading off some cases for gains on others—is branded as unethical when done by a criminal defense or personal injury plaintiff lawyer.[52] It is not permissible for him to play his series of OSs as if they constituted a single RP.[53]

Conversely, the demands of routine and orderly handling of a whole series of OSs may constrain the lawyer from maximizing advantage for any individual OS. Rosenthal (1970:172) shows that "for all but the largest [personal injury] claims an attorney loses money by thoroughly preparing a case and not settling it early."

For the lawyer who services OSs, with his transient clientele, his permanent "client" is the forum, the opposite party, or the intermediary who supplies clients. Consider, for example, the dependence of the criminal defense lawyer on maintaining cooperative relations with the various members of the "criminal court community."[54] Similarly, Carlin notes that among metropolitan individual practitioners whose clientele consists of OSs, there is a deformation of loyalty toward the intermediary.

> In the case of those lawyers specializing in personal injury, local tax, collections, criminal, and to some extent divorce work, the relationship with the client . . . is generally mediated by a broker or business supplier who may be either another lawyer or a layman. In these fields of practice the lawyer is principally concerned with pleasing the broker or winning his approval, more so than he is with satisfying the individual client. The source of business generally counts for more than the client, especially where the client is unlikely to return or to send in other clients. The

---

[52] " . . . the canons of ethics would prevent an attorney for a [oneshotter] . . . from trying to influence his client to drop a case that would create a bad precedent for other clients with similar cases. On the other hand, the canons of ethics do not prevent an attorney from advising a corporation that some of its cases should not be pursued to prevent setting a bad precedent for its other cases." (Rothstein 1974:502).

[53] Ross (1970:82) observes the possibility of conflict between client and

> the negligence specialist, who negotiates on a repeated basis with the same insurance companies. [H]is goal of maximizing the return from any given case may conflict with the goal of maximizing returns from the total series of cases he represents.

For a catalog of other potential conflicts in the relationship between specialists and OS clients, see O'Connell (1971:46–47).

[54] Blumberg (1967:47) observes

> [defense] counsel, whether privately retained or of the legal aid variety, have close and continuing relations with the prosecuting office and the court itself. Indeed, lines of communication, influence and contact with those offices, as well as with the other subsidiary divisions of the office of the clerk and the probation division and with the press are essential to the practice of criminal law. Accused persons come and go in the court system, but the structure and its personnel remain to carry on their respective careers, occupational, and organizational enterprises. . . . the accused's lawyer has far greater professional, economic, intellectual, and other ties to the various elements of the court system than to his own client.

Cf. Skolnick (1967); Battle (1971). On the interdependence of prosecutor and public defender, see Sudnow (1965:265, 273).

client is then expendable: he can be exploited to the full. Under these conditions, when a lawyer receives a client . . . he has not so much gained a client as a piece of business, and his attitude is often that of handling a particular piece of merchandise or of developing a volume of a certain kind of merchandise.[55]

The existence of a specialized bar on the OS side should overcome the gap in expertise, allow some economies of scale, provide for bargaining commitment and personal familiarity. But this is short of overcoming the fundamental strategic advantages of RPs—their capacity to structure the transaction, play the odds, and influence rule-development and enforcement policy.

Specialized lawyers may, by virtue of their identification with parties, become lobbyists, moral entrepreneurs, proponents of reforms on the parties' behalf. But lawyers have a cross-cutting interest in preserving complexity and mystique so that client contact with this area of law is rendered problematic.[56] Lawyers should not be expected to be proponents of reforms which are optimum from the point of view of the clients taken alone. Rather, we would expect them to seek to optimize the clients' position without diminishing that of lawyers. Therefore, specialized lawyers have an interest in a framework which keeps recovery (or whatever) problematic at the same time that they favor changes which improve their clients' position within this framework. (Consider the lobbying efforts of personal injury plaintiffs and defense lawyers.) Considerations of interest are likely to be fused with ideological commitments: the lawyers' preference for complex and finely-tuned bodies of rules, for adversary proceedings, for individualized case-by-case decision-making.[57] Just as the culture of the client population affects strategic position, so does the professional culture of the lawyers.

III. Institutional Facilities

We see then that the strategic advantages of the RP may be augmented by advantages in the distribution of legal services. Both are related to the advantages conferred by the basic features of the institutional facilities for the handling of claims: passivity and overload.

These institutions are passive, first, in the sense that Black refers to as "reactive"—they must be mobilized by the claimant—giving advantage to the claimant

---

[55] Carlin (1962:161–62). On the "stranger" relationship between accident victim client and lawyer, see Hunting and Neuwirth (1962:109).

[56] Cf. Consumer Council (1970:19). In connection with the lawyer's attachment to (or at least appreciation of) the problematic character of the law, consider the following legend, carried at the end of a public service column presented by the Illinois State Bar Association and run in a neighborhood newspaper:

No person should ever apply or interpret any law without consulting his attorney. Even a slight difference in the facts may change the result under the law. (*Woodlawn Booster*, July 31, 1963).

Where claims become insufficiently problematic they may drop out of the legal sphere entirely (such as social security). In high-volume and repetitive tasks which admit of economies of scale and can be rendered relatively unproblematic, lawyers may be replaced by entrepreneurs—title companies, bank trust departments—serving OSs on a mass basis (or even serving RPs, as do collection agencies). Cf. Johnstone and Hopson (1967:158ff).

[57] Stumpf, *et al.* (1970:60) suggest that professional responses to OEO legal services programs require explanation on ideological ("the highly individualized, case-by-case approach . . . as a prime article of faith") as well as pecuniary grounds. On the components of legalism as an ideology, see Shklar (1964:1–19). Of course this professional culture is not uniform but contains various subcultures. Brill's (1973) observations of OEO poverty lawyers suggest that crucial aspects of professional ideology (e.g., the emphasis on courts, rules and adjudication) are equally pronounced among lawyers who seek far-reaching change through the law.

with information, ability to surmount cost barriers, and skill to navigate restrictive procedural requirements.[58] They are passive in a further sense that once in the door the burden is on each party to proceed with his case.[59] The presiding official acts as umpire, while the development of the case, collection of evidence and presentation of proof are left to the initiative and resources of the parties.[60] Parties are treated as if they were equally endowed with economic resources, investigative opportunities and legal skills (Cf. Homberger [1971: 641]). Where, as is usually the case, they are not, the broader the delegation to the parties, the greater the advantage conferred on the wealthier,[61] more experienced and better organized party.[62]

The advantages conferred by institutional passivity are accentuated by the chronic overload which typically characterizes these institutions.[63] Typically there are far more claims than there are institutional resources for full dress adjudication

[58] Black (1973:141) observes the departures from the passive or "reactive" stance of legal institutions tend to be skewed along class lines:

> ... governments disproportionately adopt proactive systems of legal mobilization when a social control problem primarily involves the bottom of the social-class system. ... The common forms of legal misconduct in which upper status citizens indulge, such as breach of contract and warranty, civil negligence, and various forms of trust violation and corruption, are usually left to the gentler hand of a reactive mobilization process.

[59] The passivity of courts may be uneven. Cf. Mosier and Soble's (1973:63) description of Detroit landlord-tenant court:

> If a tenant was unrepresented, the judge ordinarily did not question the landlord regarding his claims, nor did the judge explain defenses to the tenant. The most common explanation given a tenant was that the law permitted him only ten days to move and thus the judge's hands were tied. In addition, judges often asked tenants for receipts for rent paid and corroboration of landlord-breach claims. In contrast, the court supplied complaint and notice forms to the landlords and clerks at the court helped them to fill out the forms if necessary. In addition, the in-court observers noticed during the beginning of the study that the court would not dismiss a nonappearing landlord's case until completion of the docket call, which took approximately forty-five minutes (which the tenant sat and waited), but extended no similar courtesy to tardy tenants. However, once the surprised observers questioned the court personnel about the practice, it was changed; thereafter, tenants had thirty minutes after the call within which to appear.

> The disparities in help given to landlords and tenants and the treatment of late landlords and tenants are an indication of the perhaps inevitable bias of the court toward the landlord. Most of the judges and court personnel have a middle-class background and they have become familiar with many landlords and attorneys appearing regularly in the court. The court had years of experience as a vehicle for rent collection and eviction where no defenses could be raised. The judges and clerks repeatedly hear about tenants who fail to pay rent or did damage to the premises, while they probably never have the opportunity to observe the actual condition of the housing that the landlords are renting.

[60] Homberger (1970:31–31). For a description of more "active" courts see Kaplan, *et al.* (1958:1221 ff); Homberger (1970). Our description is of courts of the relatively passive variety typical of "common law" systems, but should not be taken as implying that "civil law" systems are ordinarily or typically different in practice. Cf. Merryman (1969:124). The far end of a scale of institutional "activism" might be represented by institutions like the Soviet Procuracy (Berman 1963:238ff). And, of course, even among common law courts passivity is relative and variable. Courts vary in the extent to which they exercise initiative for the purpose of developing a branch of the law (the "Lord Mansfield Syndrome"—see Lowry 1973) or actively protecting some class of vulnerable parties.

[61] As Rothstein (1974:506) sums it up, counsel fees and

> [c]ourt costs, witness fees (especially for experts), investigation costs, court reporters fees, discovery costs, transcript costs, and the cost of any bond needed to secure opponents' damages, all make litigation an expensive task, thereby giving the advantage to those with large financial resources.

[62] A further set of institutional limitations should be mentioned here: limitations on the scope of matters that courts hear; the kind of relief that they can give; and on their capacity for systematic enforcement are discussed below. (pp. 136 ff).

[63] On the limited supply of institutional facilities, consider Saari's (1967) estimate that in the early 1960's total governmental expenditures for civil and criminal justice in the United States ran about four to five billion dollars annually. (Of this, about 60% went for police and prosecution, about 20% for corrections, and 20% for courts.) This amounted to about 2.5% of direct expenditures of American governments. In 1965–66 expenditures for the judiciary represented 1/17 of 1% of the total federal budget; 6/10 of 1% of state budgets; something less than 6% of county and 3% of city budgets.

of each. In several ways overload creates pressures on claimants to settle rather than to adjudicate:

(a) by causing delay (thereby discounting the value of recovery);
(b) by raising costs (of keeping the case alive);
(c) by inducing institutional incumbents to place a high value on clearing dockets, discouraging full-dress adjudication in favor of bargaining, stereotyping and routine processing;[64]
(d) by inducing the forum to adopt restrictive rules to discourage litigation.[65]

Thus, overload increases the cost and risk of adjudicating and shields existing rules from challenge, diminishing opportunities for rule-change.[66] This tends to favor the beneficiaries of existing rules.

Second, by increasing the difficulty of challenging going practice, overload also benefits those who reap advantage from the neglect (or systematic violation) of rules which favor their adversaries.

Third, overload tends to protect the possessor—the party who has the money or goods—against the claimant.[67] For the most part, this amounts to favoring RPs over OSs, since RPs typically can structure transactions to put themselves in the possessor position.[68]

Finally, the overload situation means that there are more commitments in the formal system than there are resources to honor them—more rights and rules "on the books" than can be vindicated or enforced. There are, then, questions of priorities in the allocation of resources. We would expect judges, police, administrators and other managers of limited institutional facilities to be responsive to the more organized, attentive and influential of their constituents.[69] Again, these tend to be RPs.

---

[64] The substitution of bargaining for adjudication need not be regarded as reflecting institutional deficiency. Even in criminal cases it may seem providential:

> It is elementary, historically and statistically, that systems of courts—the number of judges, prosecutors and courtrooms—have been based on the premise that approximately 90 percent of all [criminal] defendants will plead guilty, leaving only 10 percent, more or less, to be tried. . . . The consequences of what might seem on its face a small percentage change in the rate of guilty pleas can be tremendous. . . . in Washington, D.C. . . . the guilty plea rate dropped to 65 percent . . . [T]welve judges out of fifteen in active service were assigned to the criminal calendar and could barely keep up. . . . [T]o have this occur in the National Capital, which ought to be a model for the nation and show place for the world, was little short of disaster (Burger, 1970:931).

[65] On institutional coping with overload, see Friedman (1967:798ff).

[66] Cf. Foote (1956:645) on the rarity of appeal in vagrancy cases. Powell and Rohan (1968:177–78) observe that the ordinary week-to-week or month-to-month rental agreement

> is tremendously important sociologically in that occupancy thereunder conditions the home life of a very substantial fraction of the population. On the other hand, the financial smallness of the involved rights results in a great dearth of reported decisions from the courts concerning them. Their legal consequences are chiefly fixed in the 'over the counter' mass handling of "landlord and tenant" cases of the local courts. So this type of estate, judged sociologically is of great importance, but judged on the basis of its jurisprudential content is almost negligible.

[67] In the criminal process, too, the "possessor" (i.e., of defendant's mobility) enjoys great advantages. On the higher likelihood of conviction and of severe sentencing of those detained before trial, see Rankin (1964) and Wald (1964). Engle (1971) finds that among those convicted pre-trial status explains more of the variation in sentencing severity than any of 23 other factors tested.

[68] See Leff (1970a:22) on the tendency of RP creditors to put themselves in the possessor position, shifting the costs of "due process" to the OS debtor. There are, however, instances where OSs may use overload to advantage; for instance, the accused out on bail may benefit from delay. Cf. Engle's (1971) observation of the "weakening effect of time on the prosecutor's position." Rioters or rent-strikers may threaten to demand jury trials, but the effectiveness of this tactic depends on a degree of coordination that effectuates a change of scale.

[69] For example, the court studied by Zeisel, *et al* . (1959:7) "had chosen to concentrate all of its delay in the personal injury jury calendar and to keep its other law calendars up to date, granting blanket preferment to all commercial cases . . . and to all non-jury personal injury cases." (Recovery in the latter was about 20% lower than jury awards in comparable cases [1959:119]).

Thus, overloaded and passive institutional facilities provide the setting in which the RP advantages in strategic position and legal services can have full play.[70]

IV. RULES[71]

We assume here that rules tend to favor older, culturally dominant interests.[72] This is not meant to imply that the rules are explicitly designed to favor these interests,[73] but rather that those groups which have become dominant have successfully

FIGURE 3
Why The "Haves" Tend to Come Out Ahead

Element	Advantages	Enjoyed by
PARTIES	— ability to structure transaction	
	— specialized expertise, economies of scale	
	— long-term strategy	— repeat players large, professional*)
	— ability to play for rules	
	— bargaining credibility	
	—ability to invest in penetration	
LEGAL SERVICES	— skill, specialization, continuity	— organized professional* wealthy
INSTITUTIONAL FACILITIES	— passivity	— wealthy, experienced, organized
	— cost and delay barriers	
		— holders, possessors
		— beneficiaries of existing rules
	— favorable priorities	
		— organized, attentive
RULES	— favorable rules	— older, culturally dominant
	— due process barriers	— holders, possessors

In the Simple Sense of "Doing It for a Living"

[70] This analysis has not made separate mention of corruption, that is, the sale by incumbents of system outcomes divergent from those prescribed by authoritative norms. Insofar as such activities are analytically distinguishable from favorable priorities and "benign neglect" it should be noted that, since such enterprise on any considerable scale is confined to the organized, professional and wealthy, this provides yet another layer of advantage to some classes of "haves."

[71] I would like to emphasize that the term "rules" is used here as shorthand for all the authoritative normative learning. It is unnecessary for the purpose at hand to take a position on the question of whether all of that learning consists of rules or whether principles, policies, values, and standards are best understood as fundamentally different. It is enough for our purposes to note that this learing is sufficiently complex that the result in many cases is problematic and unknowable in advance.

[72] Even assuming that every instance of formulating rules represented a "fair" compromise among "have" and "have-not" interests, we should expect the stock of rules existing at any given time to be skewed toward those

articulated their operations to pre-existing rules.[74] To the extent that rules are evenhanded or favor the "have-nots," the limited resources for their implementation will be allocated, I have argued, so as to give greater effect to those rules which protect and promote the tangible interests of organized and influential groups. Furthermore, the requirements of due process, with their barriers or protections against precipitate action, naturally tend to protect the possessor or holder against the claimant.[75] Finally, the rules are sufficiently complex[76] and problematic (or capable of being problematic if sufficient resources are expended to make them so) that differences in the quantity and quality of legal services will affect capacity to derive advantages from the rules.[77]

Thus, we arrive at Figure 3 which summarizes why the "haves" tend to come out ahead. It points to layers of advantages enjoyed by different (but largely overlapping) classes of "haves"—advantages which interlock, reinforcing and shielding one another.

---

which favor "haves." The argument (cf. Kennedy 1973:384–5) goes like this: At the time of its formulation, each rule represents a current consensus about a just outcome as among competing interests. Over time the consensus changes, so that many rules are out of line with current understandings of fairness. Rule-makers (legislative, administrative and judicial) can attend to only some of all the possible readjustments. Which ones they will attend to depends in large measure on the initiative of those affected in raising the issue and mobilizing support to obtain a declaration of the more favorable current consensus. "Haves" (wealthy, professional, repeat players) enjoy a superior ability to elicit such declarations (cf. p. 100 ff); they are thus likely to enjoy the timely benefits of shifts of social consensus in their favor. OSs, on the other hand, will often find it difficult to secure timely changes in the rules to conform to a new consensus more favorable to them. Thus RPs will be the beneficiaries of the timelag between crystallized rules and current consensus. Thus, even with the most favorable assumptions about rule-making itself, the mere fact that rules accrue through time, and that it requires expenditure of resources to overcome the lag of rules behind current consensus, provides RPs with a relatively more favorable set of rules than the current consensus would provide.

[73] This is sometimes the case; consider, for instance, the rules of land-lord-tenant. Ohlhausen (1936) suggests that rules as to the availability of provisional remedies display a pronounced pattern of favoring claims of types likely to be brought by the "well to do" over claims of types brought by the impecunious.

[74] Thus the modern credit seller-lender team have built their operation upon the destruction of the purchaser's defenses by the holder in due course doctrine originally developed for the entirely different purpose of insuring the circulation of commercial paper. See Rosenthal (1971:377ff). Shuchman (1971:761–62) points out how in consumer bankruptcies:

> Consumer creditors have adjusted their practices so that sufficient proof will be conveniently available for most consumer loans to be excepted from discharge under section 17a (2). They have made wide use of renewals, resetting, and new loans to pay off old loans, with the result that the consumers' entire debt will often be nondischargeable. Section 17a (2) constitutes, in effect, an enabling act—a skeletal outline that the consumer creditor can fill in to create nondis-chargeable debts—that operated to defeat the consumer's right to the benefits of a discharge in bankruptcy.

Similarly, Shuchman (1969) shows how RP auto dealers and financial institutions have developed patterns for resale of repossessed automobiles that meet statutory resale requirements but which permit subsequent profitable second sale and in addition produce substantial deficiency claims. More generally, recall the often-noted adaptive powers of regulated industry which manage, in Hamilton's (1957: chap. 2) terms, to convert "regulations into liberties" and "controls into sanctions."

[75] For some examples of possessor-defendants exploiting the full panoply of procedural devices to raise the cost to claimants, see Schrag (1969); Macaulay (1966:98). Large (1972) shows how the doctrines of standing, jurisdiction and other procedural hurdles, effectively obstruct application of favorable substantive law in environmental litigation. Facing these rules in serial array, the environmentalists win many skirmishes but few battles.

[76] Cf. the observation of Tullock (1971:48–49) that complexity and detail—the "maze" quality of legal rules—in itself confers advantages on "people of above average intelligence, with literary and scholarly interests"—and by extension on those who can develop expertise or employ professional assistance.

[77] For an example of the potency of a combination of complexity and expertise in frustrating recovery, see Laufer (1970). Of course, the advantage may derive not from the outcome, but from the complexity, expense and uncertainty of the litigation process itself. Borkin (1950) shows how, in a setting of economic competition among units of disparate size and resources, patent litigation may be used as a tactic of economic struggle. Cf. Hamilton (1957:75–76).

We have been discussing resort to the official system to put forward (or defend against) claims. Actually, resort to this system by claimants (or initiators) is one of several alternatives. Our analysis should consider the relationship of the characteristics of the total official litigation system to its use *vis-à-vis* the alternatives. These include at least the following:

(1) Inaction—"lumping it," not making a claim or complaint. This is done all the time by "claimants" who lack information or access[78] or who knowingly decide gain is too low, cost too high (including psychic cost of litigating where such activity is repugnant). Costs are raised by lack of information or skill, and also include risk. Inaction is also familiar on the part of official complainers (police, agencies, prosecutors) who have incomplete information about violations, limited resources, policies about *de minimus*, schedules of priorities, and so forth.[79]

(2) "Exit"—withdrawal from a situation or relationship by moving, resigning, severing relations, finding new partners, etc. This is of course a very common expedient in many kinds of trouble. Like "lumping it," it is an alternative to invocation of any kind of remedy system—although its presence as a sanction may be important to the working of other remedies.[80] The use of "exit" options depends on the availability of alternative opportunities or partners (and information about them), the costs of withdrawal, transfer, relocation, development of new relationships, the pull of loyalty to previous arrangements—and on the availability and cost of other remedies.[81]

(3) Resort to some unofficial control system—we are familiar with many instances in which disputes are handled outside the official litigation system. Here we should distinguish (a) those dispute-settlement systems which are normatively and institutionally appended to the official system (such as settlement of auto-injuries, handling of bad checks) from (b) those settlement systems which are relatively independent in norms and sanctions (such as businessmen settling disputes *inter se*, religious groups, gangs).

What we might call the "appended" settlement systems merge imperceptibly into the official litigation system. We might sort them out by the extent to which the official intervention approaches the adjudicatory mode. We find a continuum from situations where parties settle among themselves with an eye to the official

[78] On the contours of "inaction," see Levine and Preston (1970); Mayhew and Riess (1969); Ennis (1967); Republic Research, Inc. (1970); Hallauer (1972).

[79] See Rabin (1972) and Miller (1969) (prosecutors); LaFave (1965) and Black (1971) (police); and generally, Davis (1969). Courts are not the only institutions in the legal system which are chronically overloaded. Typically, agencies with enforcement responsibilities have many more authoritative commitments than resources to carry them out. Thus "selective enforcement" is typical and pervasive; the policies that underlie the selection lie, for the most part, beyond the "higher law." On the interaction between enforcement and ruledevelopment, see Gifford (1971).

[80] On exit or withdrawal as a sanction, see note 42 and text there. For an attempt to explore propensities to choose among resignation, exit, and voice in response to neighborhood problems, see Orbell and Uno (1972). "Exit" would seem to include much of what goes under the rubric of "self-help." Other common forms of self-help, such as taking possession of property, usually represent a salvage operation in the wake of exit by the other party. Yet other forms, such as force, are probably closer to the private dispute settlement systems discussed below.

[81] There are, of course, some cases (such as divorce or bankruptcy) in which exit can be accomplished only by securing official certification or permission; that is, it is necessary to resort to an official remedy system in order to effectuate exit.

rules and sanctions, through situations where official intervention is invoked, to those in which settlement is supervised and/or imposed by officials, to full-dress adjudication. All along this line the sanction is supplied by the official system (though not always in the manner prescribed in the "higher law")[82] and the norms or rules applied are a version of the official rules, although discounted for transaction costs and distorted by their selective use for the purposes of the parties.

FIGURE 4
"Appended" Dispute-Settlement Systems

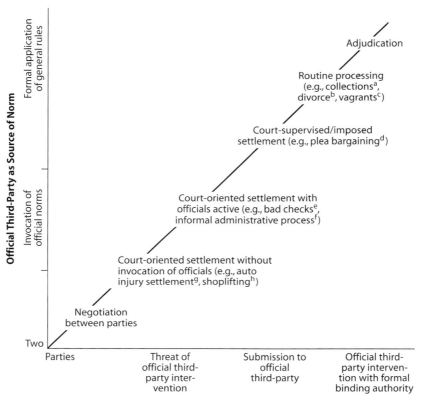

Notes:

a. Jacob (1969).
b. O'Gorman (1963); Virtue (1956).
c. Foote (1956); Spradley (1970).
d. Newman (1966: chap. 3); McIntyre and Lippman (1970).
e. Beutel (1957:287 ff.); cf. the operation of the Fraud and Complaint Department at McIntyre (1968:470–71).
f. Woll (1970); cf. the "formal informal settlement system" of the Motor Vehicles Bureau, described by Macaulay (1966:153 ff.).
g. Ross (1970).
h. Cameron (1964:32–36).

Marc Galanter

[82] This term is used to refer to the law as a body of authoritative learning (rules, doctrines, principles) as opposed to the parochial embodiments of this higher law, as admixed with local understandings, priorities, and the like.

From these "appended" systems of discounted and privatized official justice, we should distinguish those informal systems of "private justice" which invoke other norms and other sanctions. Such systems of dispute-settlement are typical among people in continuing interaction such as an organized group, a trade, or a university.[83] In sorting out the various types according to the extent and the mode of intervention of third parties, we can distinguish two dimensions: the first is the degree to which the applicable norms are formally articulated, elaborated, and exposed, that is, the increasingly organized character of the norms. The second represents the degree to which initiative and binding authority are accorded to the third party, that is, the increasingly organized character of the sanctions. Some conjectures about the character of some of the common types of private systems are presented in Figure 5.

Our distinction between "appended" and "private" remedy systems should not be taken as a sharp dichotomy but as pointing to a continuum along which we might range the various remedy systems.[84] There is a clear distinction between appended systems like automobile injury or bad check settlements and private systems like the internal regulation of the mafia (Cressey, 1969: Chaps. VIII, IX; Ianni, 1972), or the Chinese community.[85] The internal regulatory aspects of universities, churches and groups of businessmen lie somewhere in between.[86] It is as if we could visualize a scale stretching from the official remedy system through ones oriented to it through relatively independent systems based on similar values to independent systems based on disparate values.[87]

[83] "Private" dispute settlement may entail mainly bargaining or negotiation between the parties (dyadic) or may involve the invocation of some third party in the decision-making position. It is hypothesized that parties whose roles in a transaction or relationship are complementaries (husband-wife, purchaser-supplier, landlord-tenant) will tend to rely on dyadic processes in which group norms enter without specialized apparatus for announcing or enforcing norms. Precisely because of the mutual dependence of the parties, a capacity to sanction is built into the relationship. On the other hand, parties who stand in a parallel position in a set of transactions, such as airlines or stockbrokers *inter se* , tend to develop remedy systems with norm exposition and sanction application by third parties. Again, this is because the parties have little capacity to sanction the deviant directly. This hypothesis may be regarded as a reformulation of Schwartz' (1954) proposition that formal controls appear where informal controls are ineffective and explains his finding of resort to formal controls on an Israeli moshav (cooperative settlement) but not in a kibbutz (collective settlement). In this instance, the interdependence of the kibbutzniks made informal controls effective, while the "independent" moshav members needed formal controls. This echos Durkheim's (1964) notion of different legal controls corresponding to conditions of organic and mechanical solidarity. A corollary to this is suggested by re-analysis of Mentschikoff's (1961) survey of trade association proclivity to engage in arbitration. Her data indicate that the likelihood of arbitration is strongly associated with the fungibility of goods (her categories are raw, soft and hard goods). Presumably dealings in more unique hard goods entail enduring purchaser-supplier relations which equip the parties with sanctions for dyadic dispute-settlement, sanctions which are absent among dealers in fungible goods. Among the latter, sanctions take the form of exclusion from the circle of traders, and it is an organized third party (the trade association) that can best provide this kind of sanction.

[84] The distinction is not intended to ignore the overlap and linkage that may exist between "appended" and "private" systems. See, for example, Macaulay's (1966:151 ff.) description of the intricate interweaving of official, appended and private systems in the regulation of manufacturer-dealer relations; Randall's (1968: Chap. 8) account of the relation between official and industry censorship; Aker's (1968:470) observation of the interpenetration of professional associations and state regulatory boards.

[85] On internal regulation in Chinese communities in the United States, see Doo (1973); Light (1972, chap. 5, especially 89–94); Grace (1970).

[86] Cf. Mentschikoff's (1961) discussion of various species of commercial arbitration. She distinguishes casual arbitrations conducted by the American Arbitration Association which emphasize general legal norms and standards and where the "ultimate sanction . . . is the rendering of judgment on the award by a court. . . ." (1961:858) from arbitration within

> self-contained trade groups [where] the norms and standards of the group itself are being brought to bear by the arbitrators (1961:857)

and the ultimate sanction is an intra-group disciplinary proceeding.

[87] The dotted extension of the scale in Table 6 is meant to indicate the possibility of private systems which are not only structurally independent of the official system but in which the shared values comprise an oppositional

FIGURE 5
"Private" Remedy Systems

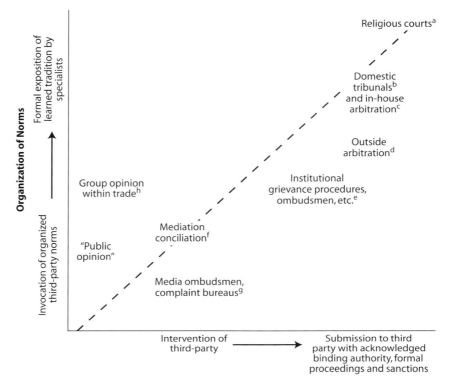

Notes:

a. Columbia J. of Law and Social Problems (1970, 1971); Shriver (1966); Ford (1970:457–79).
b. E.g., The International Air Transport Association (New York Times, Nov. 8, 1970); professional sports leagues and associations (N.Y. Times, Jan. 15, 1971).
c. Mentschikoff (1961:859).
d. Bonn (1972); Mentschikoff (1961:856–57).
e. Gellnorn, 1966; Anderson (1969:chaps IV, V).
f. E. g ., labor-management (Simkin [1971:chap. 3]); MacCallum (1967).
g. E.g., newspaper "action-line" columns, Better Business Bureaus
h. Macaulay (1963:63–64); Leff (1970a:29 ff).

Presumably it is not accidental that some human encounters are regulated frequently and influentially by the official and its appended systems while others seem to generate controls that make resort to the official and its appended systems rare. Which human encounters are we likely to find regulated at the "official" end of our scale and which at the "private" end? It is submitted that location on our

culture. Presumably this would fit, for example, internal dispute settlement among organized and committed criminals or revolutionaries. Closer to the official might be the sub-cultures of delinquent gangs. Although they have been characterized as deviant sub-cultures, Matza (1964: chap. 2, esp. 59 ff.) argues that in fact the norms of these groups are but variant readings of the official legal culture. Such variant readings may be present elsewhere on the scale; for instance, businessmen may not recognize any divergence of their notion of obligatory business conduct from the law of contract.

scale varies with factors that we might sum up by calling them the "density" of the relationship. That is, the more inclusive in life-space and temporal span a relationship between parties,[88] the less likely it is that those parties will resort to the official system[89] and more likely that the relationship will be regulated by some independent "private" system.[90] This seems plausible because we would expect inclusive and enduring relationships to create the possibility of effective sanctions;[91] and we would expect participants in such relationships to share a value consensus[92] which provided standards for conduct and legitimized such sanctions in case of deviance.

FIGURE 6
A Scale of Remedy Systems from Official to Private Remedy Systems

Official		*Appended*			*Private*	
Adjudication	Routine Processing	Structurally Interstitial (Officials Participating)	Oriented to Official	Articulated to Official	Independent	Oppositional
	Collections Divorce	Plea bargaining, bad check recovery	Auto injury settlement	Business-men	Churches, Chinese community	Gangs Mafia, Revolutionaries

Examples

[88] Since dealings between settlement specialists such as personal injury and defense lawyers may be more recurrent and inclusive than the dealings between parties themselves, one might expect that wherever specialist intermediaries are used, the remedy-system would tend to shift toward the private end of our spectrum. Cf. Skolnick (1967:69) on the "regression to cooperation" in the "criminal court community."

[89] Not only is the transient and simplex relationship more likely to be subjected to official regulation, it is apparently more amenable to formal legal control. See, for example, the greater success of antidiscrimination statutes in public accommodation than in housing and in housing than in employment (success here defined merely as a satisfactory outcome for the particular complainant). See Lockard (1968:91,122,138). Mayhew (1968:245 ff; 278 ff.) provides an interesting demonstration of the greater impact of official norms in housing than in employment transactions in spite of the greater evaluative resistance to desegregation in the latter.

[90] The capacity of continuing or "on-going" relationships to generate effective informal control has been often noted (Macaulay 1963:63–64; Yngvesson 1973). It is not temporal duration *per se* that provides the possibility of control, but the serial or incremental character of the relationship, which provides multiple choice points at which parties can seek and induce adjustment of the relationship. The mortgagor-mortgagee relationship is an enduring one, but one in which there is heavy reliance on official regulation, precisely because the frame is fixed and the parties cannot withdraw or modify it. Contrast landlord-tenant, husband-wife or purchaser-supplier, in which recurrent inputs of cooperative activity are required, the with-holding of which gives the parties leverage to secure adjustment. Schelling (1963:41) suggests a basis for this in game theory: threats intended to deter a given act can be delivered with more credibility if they are capable of being decomposed into a number of consecutive smaller threats.

[91] Conversely, the official system will tend to be used where such sanctions are unavailable, that is, where the claimee has no hope of any stream of benefits from future relations with the claimant (or those whose future relation with claimee will be influenced by his response to the claim). Hence the association of litigation with the aftermath of "divorce" (marital, commercial or organizational) or the absence of any "marriage" to begin with (e.g., auto injury, criminal). That is, government is the remedy agent of last resort and will be used in situations where one party has a loss and the other party has no expectation of any future benefit from the relationship.

[92] This does not imply that the values of the participants are completely independent of and distinct from the officially authoritative ones. More common are what we have referred to (note 87 above) as "variant readings" in which elements of authoritative tradition are re-ordered in the light of parochial understandings and priorities. For example, the understanding of criminal procedure by the police (Skolnick [1966:219 ff.]) or of air pollution laws by health departments (Goldstein and Ford [1971:20 ff.]). Thus the variant legal cultures of various legal communities at the field or operating level can exist with little awareness of principled divergence from the higher law.

The prevalence [sic] of private systems does not necessarily imply that they embody values or norms which are competing or opposed to those of the official system. Our analysis does not impute the plurality of remedy systems to cultural differences as such. It implies that the official system is utilized when there is a disparity between social structure and cultural norm. It is used, that is, where interaction and vulnerability create encounters and relationships which do not generate shared norms (they may be insufficiently shared or insufficiently specific) and/or do not give rise to group structures which permit sanctioning these norms.[93]

FIGURE 7

Relationship between Density of Social Relationships and Type of Remedy System

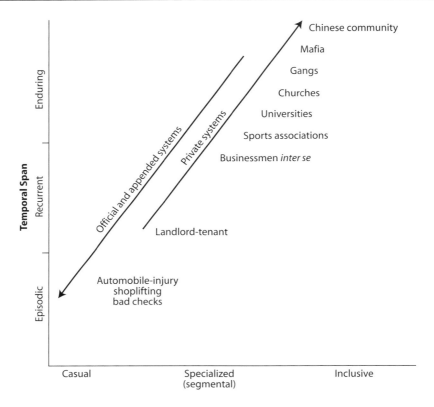

[93] This comports with Bohannon's (1965:34 ff.) notion that law comprises a secondary level of social control in which norms are re-institutionalized in specialized legal institutions. But where Bohannon implies a constant relationship between the primary institutionalization of norms and their reinstitutionalization in specialized legal institutions, the emphasis here is on the difference in the extent to which relational settings can generate self-corrective remedy systems. Thus it suggests that the legal level is brought into play where the original institutionalization of norms is incomplete, either in the norms or the institutionalization.

Bohannon elaborates his analysis by suggesting (1965:37 ff.) that the legal realm can be visualized as comprising various regions of which the "Municipal systems of the sort studied by most jurists deal with a single legal culture within a unicentric power system." (In such a system, differences between institutional practice and legal prescription are matters of phase or lag.) Divergences from unity (cultural, political, or both) define other regions of the legal realm: respectively, colonial law, law in stateless societies and international law.

The analysis here suggests that "municipal systems" themselves may be patchworks in which normative consensus and effective unity of power converge only imperfectly. Thus we might expect a single legal system to include phenomena corresponding to other regions of his schema of the legal realm. The divergence of the "law on the books" and the "law in action" would not then be ascribable solely to lag or "phase" (1965:37) but rather would give expression to the discontinuity between culture and social structure.

Figure 7 sketches out such relationships of varying density and suggests the location of various official and private remedy systems.

Life-Space Inclusiveness

It restates our surmise of a close association between the density of relationships and remoteness from the official system.[94] We may surmise further that on the whole the official and appended systems flourish in connection with the disputes between parties of disparate size which give rise to the litigation in Boxes II and III of Figure I. Private remedy systems, on the other hand, are more likely to handle disputes between parties of comparable size.[95] The litigation in Boxes I and IV of Figure 1, then, seems to represent in large measure the breakdown (or inhibited development) of private remedy systems. Indeed, the distribution of litigation generally forms a mirror image of the presence of private remedy systems. But the mirror is, for the various reasons discussed here, a distorting one.

From the vantage point of the "higher law" what we have called the official system may be visualized as the "upper" layers of a massive "legal"[96] iceberg, something like this:

Adjudication
Litigation
Appended Settlement Systems
Private Settlement Systems
Exit Remedies/Self Help
Inaction ("lumping it")

The uneven and irregular layers are distinct although they merge imperceptibly into one another.[97] As we proceed to discuss possible reforms of the official system, we will want to consider the kind of impact they will have on the whole iceberg.

---

[94] The association postulated here seems to have support in connection with a number of distinct aspects of legal process:

Presence of legal controls: Schwartz (1954) may be read as asserting that relational density (and the consequent effectiveness of informal controls) is inversely related to the presence of legal controls (defined in terms of the presence of sanction specialists).
Invocation (mobilization) of official controls: Black (1971:1097) finds that readiness to invoke police and insistence of complainants on arrest is associated with "relational distance" between the parties. Cf. Kawashima's (1962:45) observation that in Japan, where litigation was rare between parties to an enduring relationship regulated by shared ideals of harmony, resort to officials was common where such ties were absent, as in cases of inter-village and usurer-debtor disputes.
Elaboration of authoritative doctrine: Derrett (1959:54) suggests that the degree of elaboration of authoritative learned doctrine in classical Hindu law is related to the likelihood that the forums applying such doctrine would be invoked, which is in turn dependent on the absence of domestic controls.

[95] There are, of course, exceptions, such as the automobile manufacturers' administration of warranty claims described by Whitford (1968) or those same manufacturers' internal dealer relations tribunals described by Macaulay (1966).

[96] The iceberg is not properly a legal one, hence the quotation marks. That is, I do not mean to impute any characteristics that might define the "legal" (officials, coercive sanctions, specialists, general rules) to all the instances in the iceberg. It is an iceberg of potential claims or disputes and the extent to which any sector of it is legalized is problematic. Cf. Abel (1974).

[97] Contrast the more symmetrical "great pyramid of legal order" envisioned by Hart and Sacks (1958:312). Where the Hart and Sacks pyramid portrays private and official decision-making as successive moments of an integrated normative and institutional order, the present "iceberg" model suggests that the existence of disparate systems of settling disputes is a reflection of cultural and structural discontinuities.

We will look at some of the connections and flows between layers mainly from the point of view of the construction of the iceberg itself, but aware that flows and connections are also influenced fluenced by atmospheric (cultural) factors such as appetite for vindication, psychic cost of litigation, lawyers' culture and the like.

VI. STRATEGIES FOR REFORM

Our categorization of four layers of advantage (Figure 3) suggests a typology of strategies for "reform" (taken here to mean equalization—conferring relative advantage on those who did not enjoy it before). We then come to four types of equalizing reform:

(1) rule-change
(2) improvement in institutional facilities
(3) improvement of legal services in quantity and quality
(4) improvement of strategic position of have-not parties

I shall attempt to sketch some of the possible ramifications of change on each of these levels for other parts of the litigation system and then discuss the relationship between changes in the litigation system and the rest of our legal iceberg. Of course such reforms need not be enacted singly, but may occur in various combinations. However, for our purposes we shall only discuss, first, each type taken in isolation and then, all taken together.

A. Rule-change

Obtaining favorable rule changes is an expensive process. The various kinds of "have-nots" (Figure 3) have fewer resources to accomplish changes through legislation or administrative policy-making. The advantages of the organized, professional, wealthy and attentive in these forums are well-known. Litigation, on the other hand, has a flavor of equality. The parties are "equal before the law" and the rules of the game do not permit them to deploy all of their resources in the conflict, but require that they proceed within the limiting forms of the trial. Thus, litigation is a particularly tempting arena to "have-nots," including those seeking rule change.[98] Those who seek change through the courts tend to represent relatively isolated interests, unable to carry the day in more political forums.[99]

Litigation may not, however, be a ready source of rulechange for "have-nots." Complexity, the need for high inputs of legal services and cost barriers (heightened by overloaded institutional facilities) make challenge of rules expensive. OS claimants, with high stakes in the tangible outcome, are unlikely to try to obtain rule changes. By definition, a test case—litigation deliberately designed to procure rule-change—is an unthinkable undertaking for an OS. There are some departures from our ideal type: OSs who place a high value on vindication by

---

[98] Hazard (1970:246–47) suggests that the attractions of the courts include that they are open as of right, receptive to arguments based on principle and offer the advocate a forum in which he bears no responsibility for the consequences of having his arguments prevail.

[99] Dolbeare (1967:63). Owen (1971:68, 142) reports the parallel finding that in two Georgia counties "opinion leaders and influentials seldom use the court, except for economic retrieval." Cf. Howard's (1969:346) observation that ". . . adjudication is preeminently a method for individuals, small groups and minorities who lack access to or sufficient strength within the political arena to mobilize a favorable change in legislative coalitions."

official rules or whose peculiar strategic situation makes it in their interest to pursue rule victories.[100] But generally the testcase involves some organization which approximates an RP.[101]

The architecture of courts severely limits the scale and scope of changes they can introduce in the rules. Tradition and ideology limit the kinds of matters that come before them; not patterns of practice but individual instances, not "problems" but cases framed by the parties and strained through requirements of standing, case or controversy, jurisdiction, and so forth. Tradition and ideology also limit the kind of decision they can give. Thus, common law courts for example, give an all-or-none,[102] once-and-for-all[103] decision which must be justified in terms of a limited (though flexible) corpus of rules and techniques.[104] By tradition, courts cannot address problems by devising new regulatory or administrative machinery (and have no taxing and spending powers to support it); courts are limited to solutions compatible with the existing institutional framework.[105] Thus, even the most favorably inclined court may not be able to make those rule-changes most useful to a class of "have-nots."

---

[100] There are situations in which no settlement is acceptable to the OS. The most common case, perhaps, is that of the prisoner seeking post-conviction remedies. He has "infinite" costless time and nothing further to lose. Other situations may be imagined in which an OS stands only to gain by a test case and has the resources to expend on it. Consider, for example, the physician charged with ten counts of illegal abortion. Pleading guilty to one count if the state dropped the others and agreeing to a suspended sentence would still entail the loss of his license. Every year of delay is worth money, win or lose: the benefits of delay are greater than the costs of continued litigation.

When the price of alternatives becomes unacceptably high, we may find OSs swimming upstream against a clear rule and strategic disadvantage. (Cf. the explosion of selective service cases in the 1960's.) Such a process may be facilitated by, for example, the free entry afforded by the contingent fee. See Friedman and Ladinsky's (1967) description of the erosion of the fellow servant rule under the steady pounding of litigation by injured workman with no place else to turn and free entry.

[101] See Vose (1967) on the test-case strategy of the NAACP in the restrictive covenant area. By selecting clients to forward an interest (rather than serving the clients) the NAACP made itself an RP with corresponding strategic advantages over the opposite parties (neighborhood associations). The degree of such organizational support of litigation is a matter of some dispute. Participation by organized interest groups in litigation affecting municipal powers is described in Vose (1966); but Dolbeare (1967:40), in his study of litigation over public policy issues in a suburban county, found a total absence of interest-group sponsorship and participation in cases at the trial court level. Vose (1972:332) concludes a historical review by observing that:

> Most constitutional cases before the Supreme Court . . . are sponsored or supported by an identifiable voluntary association . . . [This] has been markedly true for decades.

But Hakman (1966, 1969) found management of Supreme Court litigation by organized groups pursuing coherent long-range strategies to be relatively rare. But see Casper (1970) who contends that civil liberties and civil rights litigation in the Supreme Court is increasingly conducted by lawyers who are "group advocates" (that is, have a long-term commitment to a group with whose aims they identify) or "civil libertarians" (that is, have an impersonal commitment to the vindication of broad principles) rather than advocates. He suggests that the former types of representation lead to the posing of broader issues for decision.

[102] Although judicial decisions do often embody or ratify compromises agreed upon by the parties, it is precisely at the level of rule promulgation that such splitting the difference is seen as illegitimate. On the ideological pressures limiting the role of compromise in judicial decision see Coons (1964).

[103] Cf. Kalven (1958:165). There are, of course, exceptions, such as alimony, to this "once and for all" feature.

[104] Hazard (1970:248–50) points out that courts are not well-equipped to address problems by devising systematic legal generalization. They are confined to the facts and theories presented by the parties in specific cases; after deciding the case before them, they lose their power to act; they have little opportunity to elicit commentary until after the event; and generally they can extend but not initiate legal principles. They have limited and rapidly diminishing legitimacy as devisers of new policy. Nor can courts do very much to stimulate and maintain political support for new rules.

[105] See generally Friedman (1967: esp. 821); Hazard (1970:248–50). The limits of judicial competence are by no means insurmountable. Courts do administer bankrupt railroads, recalcitrant school districts, offending election boards. But clearly the amount of such affirmative administrative re-ordering that courts can undertake is limited by physical resources as well as by limitations on legitimacy.

Rule-change may make use of the courts more attractive to "have-nots." Apart from increasing the possibility of favorable outcomes, it may stimulate organization, rally and encourage litigants. It may directly redistribute symbolic rewards to "have-nots" (or their champions). But tangible rewards do not always follow symbolic ones. Indeed, provision of symbolic rewards to "have-nots" (or crucial groups of their supporters) may decrease capacity and drive to secure redistribution of tangible benefits.[106]

Rule-changes secured from courts or other peak agencies do not penetrate automatically and costlessly to other levels of the system, as attested by the growing literature on impact.[107] This may be especially true of rule-change secured by adjudication, for several reasons:

(1) Courts are not equipped to assess systematically the impact or penetration problem. Courts typically have no facilities for surveillance, monitoring, or securing systematic enforcement of their decrees. The task of monitoring is left to the parties.[108]

(2) The built-in limits on applicability due to the piecemeal character of adjudication. Thus a Mobilization for Youth lawyer reflects:

> ... What is the ultimate value of winning a test case? In many ways a result cannot be clearcut ... if the present welfare-residency laws are invalidated, it is quite possible that some other kind of welfare-residency law will spring up in their place. It is not very difficult to come up with a policy that is a little different, stated in different words, but which seeks to achieve the same basic objective. The results of test cases are not generally self-executing ... It is not enough to have a law invalidated or a policy declared void if the agency in question can come up with some variant of that policy, not very different in substance but sufficiently different to remove it from the effects of the court order.[109]

(3) The artificial equalizing of parties in adjudication by insulation from the full play of political pressures—the "equality" of the parties, the exclusion of "irrelevant" material, the "independence" of judges—means that judicial outcomes are more likely to be at variance with the existing constellation of political forces than decisions arrived at in forums lacking such insulation. But resources that cannot be employed in the judicial process can reassert themselves at the implementation stage, especially where institutional overload requires another round of decision making (what resources will be deployed to implement which rules) and/or private expenditures to secure implementation. Even where "have-nots" secure favorable

---

[106] See Lipsky (1970:176 ff.) for an example of the way in which provision of symbolic rewards to more influential reference publics effectively substituted for the tangible reforms demanded by rentstrikers. More generally, Edelman (1967:chap. 2) argues that it is precisely unorganized and diffuse publics that tend to receive symbolic rewards, while organized professional ones reap tangible rewards.

[107] For a useful summary of this literature, see Wasby (1970). Some broad generalizations about the conditions conducive to penetration may be found in Grossman (1970:545 ff.); Levine (1970:599 ff.).

[108] Cf. Howard's (1969:365 ff.) discussion of the relative ineffectualness of adjudication in voter registration and school integration (as opposed to subsequent legislative/administrative action) as flowing from judicial reliance on party initiative.

[109] Rothwax (1969:143). An analogous conclusion in the consumer protection field is reached by Leff (1970b:356). ("One cannot think of a more expensive and frustrating course than to seek to regulate goods or 'contract' quality through repeated law-suits against inventive 'wrongdoers.'") Leff's critique of Murray's (1969) faith in good rules to secure change in the consumer marketplace parallels Handler's (1966) critique of Reich's (1964a, 1964b) prescription of judicial review to secure change in welfare administration. Cf. Black's (1973:137) observation that institutions which are primarily reactive, requiring mobilization by citizens, tend to deal with specific instances rather than general patterns and, as a consequence, have little preventive capacity.

changes at the rule level, they may not have the resources to secure the penetration of these rules.[110] The impotence of rule-change, whatever its source, is particularly pronounced when there is reliance on unsophisticated OSs to utilize favorable new rules.[111]

Where rule-change promulgated at the peak of the system does have an impact on other levels, we should not assume any isomorphism. The effect on institutional facilities and the strategic position of the parties may be far different than we would predict from the rule change. Thus, Randall's study of movie censorship shows that liberalization of the rules did not make censorship boards more circumspect; instead, many closed down and the old game between censorship boards and distributors was replaced by a new and rougher game between exhibitors and local government-private group coalitions.[112]

B. Increase in Institutional Facilities

Imagine an increase in institutional facilities for processing claims such that there is timely full-dress adjudication of every claim put forward—no queue, no delay, no stereotyping. Decrease in delay would lower costs for claimants, taking away this advantage of possessor-defendants. Those relieved of the necessity of discounting recovery for delay would have more to spend on legal services. To the extent that settlement had been induced by delay (rather than insuring against the risk of unacceptable loss), claimants would be inclined to litigate more and settle less. More litigation without stereotyping would mean more contests, including more contesting of rules and more rule change. As discounts diminished, neither side could use settlement policy to prevent rule-loss. Such reforms would for the most part benefit OS claimants, but they would also improve the position of those RP claimants not already in the possessor position, such as the prosecutor where the accused is free on bail.

This assumes no change in the kind of institutional facilities. We have merely assumed a greater quantitative availability of courts of the relatively passive variety typical of (at least) "common law" systems in which the case is "tried by the parties before the court. . . ." (Homberger, 1970:31). One may imagine institutions with augmented authority to solicit and supervise litigation, conduct investigations, secure, assemble and present proof; which enjoyed greater flexibility in devising outcomes (such as compromise or mediation); and finally which had available staff for monitoring compliance with their decrees.[113] Greater institutional "activism"

---

[110] Consider for example the relative absence of litigation about schoolroom religious practices clearly in violation of the Supreme Court's rules, as reported by Dolbeare and Hammond (1971). In this case RPs who were able to secure rule-victories were unable or unwilling to invest resources to secure the implementation of the new rules.

[111] See, for example, Mosier and Soble's (1973:61–64) study of the Detroit Landlord-Tenant Court, where even after the enactment of new tenant defenses (landlord breach, retaliation), landlords obtained all they sought in 97% of cases. The new defenses were raised in only 3% of all cases (13% of the 20% that were contested) although, the authors conclude, "many defendants doubtless had valid landlord breach defenses."

[112] Randall (1968:chap. 7). Cf. Macaulay's (1966:156) finding that the most important impact of the new rules was to provide leverage for the operation of informal and private procedures in which dealers enjoyed greater bargaining power in their negotiations with manufacturers.

[113] Some administrative agencies approximate this kind of "activist" posture. Cf. Nonet's (1969:79) description of the California Industrial Accident Commission:

When the IAC in its early days assumed the responsibility of notifying the injured worker of his rights, of filing his application for him, of guiding him in all procedural steps, when its medical bureau checked the accuracy of his medical record and its referees conducted his case at the hearing, the injured employee was able to obtain his benefits at almost no cost and with minimal demands on his intelligence and capacities.

might be expected to reduce advantages of party expertise and of differences in the quality and quantity of legal services. Enhanced capacity for securing compliance might be expected to reduce advantages flowing from differences in ability to invest in enforcement. It is hardly necessary to point out that such reforms could be expected to encounter not only resistance from the beneficiaries of the present passive institutional style, but also massive ideological opposition from legal professionals whose fundamental sense of legal propriety would be violated.[114]

C. Increase in Legal Services

The reform envisaged here is an increase in quantity and quality of legal services to "have-nots" (including greater availability of information about these services).[115] Presumably this would lower costs, remove the expertise advantage, produce more litigation with more favorable outcomes for "have-nots," perhaps with more appeals and more rule challenges, more new rules in their favor. (Public defender, legal aid, judicare, and pre-payment plans approximate this in various fashions.) To the extent that OSs would still have to discount for delay and risk, their gains would be limited (and increase in litigation might mean even more delay). Under certain conditions, increased legal services might use institutional overload as leverage on behalf of "have-nots." Our Mobilization for Youth attorney observes:

> . . . if the Welfare Department buys out an individual case, we are precluded from getting a principle of law changed, but if we give them one thousand cases to buy out, that law has been effectively changed whether or not the law as written is changed. The practice is changed; the administration is changed; the attitude to the client is changed. The value of a heavy case load is that it allows you to populate the legal process. It allows you to apply remitting pressure on the agency you are dealing with. It creates a force that has to be dealt with, that has to be considered in terms of the decisions that are going to be made prospectively. It means that you are not somebody who will be gone tomorrow, not an isolated case, but a force in the community that will remain once this particular case has been decided.
>
> As a result . . . we have been able, for the first time to participate along with welfare recipients . . . in a rule-making process itself. . . . (Rothwax, 1969:140–41).

The increase in quantity of legal services was accompanied here by increased coordination and organization on the "have-not" side, which brings us to our fourth level of reform.

D. Reorganization of Parties

The reform envisaged here is the organization of "have-not" parties (whose position approximates OS) into coherent groups that have the ability to act in a coordinated fashion, play long-run strategies, benefit from high-grade legal services, and so forth.

In the American setting, at least, such institutional activism seems unstable; over time institutions tend to approximate the more passive court model. See Nonet (1969: chaps. 6–7) and generally Bernstein (1955: chap. 7) on the "judicialization" of administrative agencies.

[114] Perhaps the expansive political role of the judiciary and the law in American society is acceptable precisely because the former is so passive and the latter so malleable to private goals. Cf. Selznick's (1969:225 ff.) discussion of the "privatization" and "voluntarization" of legal regulation in the United States.

[115] This would, of course, require the relaxation of barriers on information flow now imposed under the rubric of "professional ethics." See notes 46 and 51 above.

One can imagine various ways in which OSs might be aggregated into RPs. They include (1) the membership association bargaining agent (trade unions, tenant unions); (2) the assignee-manager of fragmentary rights (performing rights associations like ASCAP); (3) the interest group-sponsor (NAACP, ACLU, environmental action groups).[116] All of these forms involve upgrading capacities for managing claims by gathering and utilizing information, achieving continuity and persistence, employing expertise, exercising bargaining skill and so forth. These advantages are combined with enhancement of the OS party's strategic position either by aggregating claims that are too small relative to the cost of remedies (consumers, breathers of polluted air, owners of performing rights); or by reducing claims to manageable size by collective action to dispel or share unacceptable risks (tenants, migrant workers).[117] A weaker form of organization would be (4) a clearing-house which established a communication network among OSs. This would lower the costs of information and give RPs a stake in the effect OSs could have on their reputation. A minimal instance of this is represented by the "media ombudsman"—the "action line" type of newspaper column. Finally, there is governmentalization—utilizing the criminal law or the administrative process to make it the responsiblity [sic] of a public officer to press claims that would be unmanageable in the hands of private grievants.[118]

[116] For some examples of OSs organizing and managing claims collectively see Davis and Schwartz (1967) and various pieces in Burghhardt (1972) (tenant unions); McPherson (1972) (Contract Buyers League); Shover (1966) (Farmers Holiday Association—mortgagors); Finklestein (1954) (ASCAP—performing rights); Vose (1967) (NAACP); Macaulay (1966) (automobile dealers).

[117] A similar enhancement of prowess in handling claims may sometimes be provided commercially, as by collection agencies. Nonet (1969:71) observes that insurance coverage may serve as a form of organization:

> When the employer buys insurance [against workman's compensation claims], he not only secures financial coverage for his losses, but he also purchases a claims adjustment service and the legal defense he may need. Only the largest employers can adequately develop such services on their own. . . . Others find in their carrier a specialized claims administration they would otherwise be unable to avail themselves of . . . . to the employer, insurance constitutes much more than a way of spreading individual risks over a large group. One of its major functions is to pool the resources of possibly weak and isolated employers so as to provide them with effective means of self-help and legal defense.

[118] On criminalization as a mode of aggregating claims, see Friedman (1973:258). This is typically a weak form of organization, for several reasons. First, there is so much law that officials typically have far more to do than they have resources to do it with, so they tend to wait for complaints and to treat them as individual grievances. For example, the Fraud and Complaint Bureau described by McIntyre (1968) or the anti-discrimination commission described by May-hew (1968). Cf. Selznick's (1969:225) observations on a general "tendency to turn enforcement agencies into passive recipients of privately initiated complaints. . . . The focus is more on settling disputes than on affirmative action aimed at realizing public goals." Second, enforcers have a pronounced tendency not to employ litigation against established and respectable institutions. Consider, for instance, the patterns of air pollution enforcement described by Goldstein and Ford (1971) or the Department of Justice position that the penal provisions of the Refuse Act should be brought to bear only on infrequent or accidental polluters, while chronic ones should be handled by more conciliatory and protracted administrative procedures. (1 ENV. RPTR, CURDEV No. 12 at 288 [1970]). Compare the reaction of Arizona's Attorney General to the litigation initiated by the overzealous chief of his Consumer Protection Division, who had recently started an investigation of hospital pricing policies.

> I found out much to my shock and chagrin that anybody who is anybody serves on a hospital board of directors and their reaction to our hospital inquiry was one of defense and protection.

> My policy concerning lawsuits . . . is that we don't sue anybody except in the kind of emergency situation that would involve [a business] leaving town or sequestering money or records. . . . I can't conceive any reason why hospitals in this state are going to make me sue them.

(New York Times, April 22, 1973).

An organized group is not only better able to secure favorable rule changes, in courts and elsewhere, but is better able to see that good rules are implemented.[119] It can expend resources on surveillance, monitoring, threats, or litigation that would be uneconomic for an OS. Such new units would in effect be RPs.[120] Their encounters with opposing RPs would move into Box IV of Figure 1. Neither would enjoy the strategic advantages of RPs over OSs. One possible result, as we have noted in our discussion of the RP v. RP situation, is delegalization, that is, a movement away from the official system to a private system of dispute-settlement; another would be more intense use of the official system.

Many aspects of "public interest law" can be seen as approximations of this reform. (1) The class action is a device to raise the stakes for an RP, reducing his strategic position to that of an OS by making the stakes more than he can afford to play the odds on,[121] while moving the claimants into a position in which they enjoy the RP advantages without having to undergo the outlay for organizing. (2) Similarly, the "community organizing" aspect of public interest law can be seen as an effort to create a unit (tenants, consumers) which can play the RP game. (3) Such a change in strategic position creates the possibility of a test-case strategy for getting rule-change.[122] Thus "public interest law" can be thought of as a combination of community organizing, class action and test-case strategies, along with increase in legal services.[123]

VII. Reform and the Rest of the Iceberg

The reforms of the official litigation system that we have imagined would, taken together, provide rules more favorable to the "have nots." Redress according to the offficial rules, undiscounted by delay, strategic disability, disparities of legal services

[119] On the greater strategic thrust of group-sponsored complaints in the area of discrimination, see Mayhew (1968:168–73).

[120] Paradoxically, perhaps, the organization of OSs into a unit which can function as an RP entails the possibility of internal disputes with distinctions between OSs and RPs reappearing. On the reemergence of these disparities in strategic position within, for example, unions, see Atleson (1967:485 ff.) (finding it doubtful that Title I of the LMRDA affords significant protection to "single individuals"). Cf. Summers (1960); Atleson (1971) on the poor position of individual workers *vis-à-vis* unions in arbitration proceedings.

[121] As an outspoken opponent of class actions puts it:

When a firm with assets of, say, a billion dollars is sued in a class action with a class of several million and a potential liability of, say $2 billion, it faces the possibility of destruction. . . . The potential exposure in broad class actions frequently exceeds the net worth of the defendants, and corporate management naturally tends to seek insurance against whatever slight chance of success plaintiffs may have (Simon, 1972:289–90).

He then cites "eminent plaintiff's' counsel" to the effect that:

I have seen nothing so conducive to settlement of complex litigation as the establishment by the court of a class . . . whereas, if there were no class, it would not be disposed of by settlement.

[122] The array of devices for securing judicial determination of broad patterns of behavior also includes the "public interest action" in which a plaintiff is permitted to vindicate rights vested in the general public (typically by challenging exercises of government power). (Homberger, 1974). Unlike the class action, plaintiff does not purport to represent a class of particular individuals (with all the procedural difficulties of that posture) and unlike the classic test case he is not confined to his own grievance, but is regarded as qualified by virtue of his own injury to represent the interests of the general public.

[123] However, there may be tensions among these commitments. Wexler (1970), arguing for the primacy of "organizing" (including training in lay advocacy) in legal practice which aims to help the poor, points to the seductive pull of professional notions of the proper roles and concerns of the lawyer. Cf. Brill's (1973) portrayal of lawyers' professional and personal commitment to "class action" cases (in which the author apparently includes all "test cases'") as undercutting their avowed commitment to facilitate community organization. On the inherent limits of "organizing" strategies, see note 127.

and so forth could be obtained whenever either party found it to his advantage. How might we expect such a utopian upgrading of the official machinery to affect the rest of our legal iceberg?

We would expect more use of the official system. Those who opted for inaction because of information or cost barriers and those who "settled" at discount rates in one of the "appended" systems would in many instances find it to their advantage to use the official system. The appended systems, insofar as they are built on the costs of resort to the official system, would either be abandoned or the outcomes produced would move to approximate closely those produced by adjudication.[124]

On the other hand, our reforms would, by organizing OSs, create many situations in which *both* parties were organized to pursue their long-run interest in the litigation arena. In effect, many of the situations which occupied Boxes II and III of Figure 1 (RP v. OS, OS v. RP)—the great staple sources of litigation—would now be moved to Box IV (RP v. RP). We observed earlier that RPs who anticipate continued dealings with one another tend to rely on informal bilateral controls. We might expect then that the official system would be abandoned in favor of private systems of dispute-settlement.[125]

Thus we would expect our reforms to produce a dual movement: the official and its appended systems would be "legalized"[126] while the proliferation of private systems would "delegalize" many relationships. Which relationships would we expect to move which way? As a first approximation, we might expect that the less "inclusive" relationships currently handled by litigation or in the appended systems would undergo legalization, while relationships at the more inclusive end of the scale (Figure 7) would be privatized. Relationships among strangers (casual, episodic, non-recurrent) would be legalized; more dense (recurrent, inclusive) relationships between parties would be candidates for the development of private systems.

Our earlier analysis suggests that the pattern might be more complex. First, for various reasons a class of OSs may be relatively incapable of being organized. Its size, relative to the size and distribution of potential benefits, may require disproportionately large inputs of coordination and organization.[127] Its shared interest may be insufficiently respectable to be publicly acknowledged (for instance, shoplifters, homosexuals until very recently). Or recurrent OS roles may be staffed by shifting population for whom the sides of the transaction are interchangeable.[128]

[124] That is, the "reciprocal immunities" (Friedman 1967:806) built on transaction costs of remedies would be narrowed and would be of the same magnitude for each party.

[125] This is in Boxes II and III of Figure 1, where both parties are now RPs. But presumably in some of the litigation formerly in Box I, one side is capable of organization but the other is not, so new instances of strategic disparity might emerge. We would expect these to remain in the official system.

[126] That is, in which the field level application of the official rules has moved closer to the authoritative "higher law" (see note 82).

[127] Olson (1965) argues that capacity for coordinated action to further common interests decreases with the size of the group: ". . . relatively small groups will frequently be able voluntarily to organize and act in support of their common interests, and some large groups normally will not be able to do so." (1965:127). Where smaller groups can act in their common interest, larger ones are likely to be capable of so acting only when they can obtain some coercive power over members or are supplied with some additional selective incentives to induce the contribution of the needed inputs of organizational activity. (On the reliance of organizations on these selective incentives, see Salisbury [1969] and Clark and Wilson [1961].) Such selective incentives may be present in the form of services provided by a group already organized for some other purpose. Thus many interests may gain the benefits of organization only to the extent that those sharing them overlap with those with a more organizable interest (consider, for instance, the prominence of labor unions as lobbyists for consumer interests).

[128] Cf. Fuller's (1969:23) observation that the notion of duty is most understandable and acceptable in a society in which relationships are sufficiently fluid and symmetrical so that duties "must in theory and practice be reversible."

(For instance, home buyers and sellers, negligent motorists and accident victims.)[129] Even where OSs are organizable, we recall that not all RP v. RP encounters lead to the development of private remedy systems. There are RPs engaged in value conflict; there are those relationships with a governmental or other monopoly aspect in which informal controls may falter; and finally there are those RPs whose encounters with one another are non-recurring. In all of these we might expect legalization rather than privatization.

Whichever way the movement in any given instance, our reforms would entail changes in the distribution of power. RPs would no longer be able to wield their strategic advantages to invoke selectively the enforcement of favorable rules while securing large discounts (or complete shielding by cost and overload) where the rules favored their OS opponents.

Delegalization (by the proliferation of private remedy and bargaining systems) would permit many relationships to be regulated by norms and understandings that departed from the official rules. Such parochial remedy systems would be insulated from the impingement of the official rules by the commitment of the parties to their continuing relationship. Thus, delegalization would entail a kind of pluralism and decentralization. On the other hand, the "legalization" of the official and appended systems would amount to the collapse of species of pluralism and decentralization that are endemic in the kind of (unreformed) legal system we have postulated. The current prevalence of appended and private remedy systems reflects the inefficiency, cumbersomeness and costliness of using the official system. This inefficient, cumbersome and costly character is a source and shield of a kind of decentralization and pluralism. It permits a selective application of the "higher law" in a way that gives effect at the operative level to parochial norms and concerns which are not fully recognized in the "higher law" (such as the right to exclude low status neighbors,[130] or police dominance in encounters with citizens[131]). If the insulation afforded by the costs of getting the "higher law" to prevail were eroded, many relationships would suddenly be exposed to the "higher law" rather than its parochial counterparts. We might expect this to generate new pressures for explicit recognition of these "subterranean" values or for explicit decentralization.

---

[129] Curiously these relationships have the character which Rawls (1958: 98) postulates as a condition under which parties will agree to be bound by "just" rules; that is, no one knows in advance the position he will occupy in the proposed "practice." The analysis here assumes that while high turnover and unpredictable interchange of roles may approximate this condition in some cases, one of the pervasive and important characteristics of much human arranging is that the participants have a pretty good idea of which role in the arrangement they will play. Rawls (1971:136 ff.) suggests that one consequence of this "veil of ignorance" (". . . no one knows his place in society, his class position or social status; nor does he know his fortune in the distribution of natural assets and abilities, his intelligence and strength and the like") is that "the parties have no basis for bargaining in the usual sense" and concludes that without such restriction "we would not be able to work out any definite theory of justice at all." "If knowledge of particulars is allowed, then the outcome is biased by arbitrary contingencies." If we posit knowledge of particulars as endemic, we may surmise that a "definite theory of justice" will play at most a minor role in explaining the legal process.

[130] On exclusion of undesirable neighbors, see Babcock (1969); of undesirable sojourners, see the banishment policy described in Foote (1956).

[131] See the anguished discovery (Seymour 1971:9) of this by a former United States Attorney in his encounter with local justice:

When the police officer had finished his testimony and left the stand, I moved to dismiss the case as a matter of law, pointing out that the facts were exactly the same as in the case cited in the annotation to the statute. I asked the judge to please look at the statute and read the case under it. Instead he looked me straight in the eye and announced, "Motion denied."

These conjectures about the shape that a "reformed" legal system might take suggest that we take another look at our unreformed system, with its pervasive disparity between authoritative norms and everyday operations. A modern legal system of the type we postulated is characterized structurally by institutional unity and culturally by normative universalism. The power to make, apply and change law is reserved to organs of the public, arranged in unified hierarchic relations, commited to uniform application of universalistic norms.

There is, for example, in American law (that is, in the higher reaches of the system where the learned tradition is propounded) an unrelenting stress on the virtues of uniformity and universality and a pervasive distaste for particularism, compromise and discretion.[132] Yet the cultural attachment to universalism is wedded to and perhaps even intensifies diversity and particularism at the operative level.[133]

The unreformed features of the legal system then appear as a device for maintaining the partial dissociation of everyday practice from these authoritative institutional and normative commitments. Structurally (by cost and institutional overload) and culturally (by ambiguity and normative overload) the unreformed system effects a massive covert delegation from the most authoritative rule-makers to field level officials (and their constituencies) responsive to other norms and priorities than are contained in the "higher law."[134] By their selective application of rules in a context of parochial understandings and priorities, these field level legal communities produce regulatory outcomes which could not be predicted by examination of the authoritative "higher law."[135]

Thus its unreformed characted [sic] articulates the legal system to the discontinuities of culture and social structure: it provides a way of accommodating cultural heterogeneity and social diversity while propounding universalism and unity; of accommodating vast concentrations of private power while upholding the supremacy of public authority; of accommodating inequality in fact while establishing equality at law; of facilitating action by great collective combines while celebrating individualism. Thus "unreform"—that is, ambiguity and overload of rules, overloaded and inefficient institutional facilities, disparities in the supply of legal services, and disparities in the strategic position of parties—is the foundation of the "dualism"[136] of the legal system. It permits unification and universalism at the symbolic level and diversity and particularism at the operating level.[137]

---

[132] It seems hardly necessary to adduce examples of this pervasive distaste of particularism. But consider Justice Frankfurter's admonition that "We must not sit like a kadi under a tree dispensing justice according to conditions of individual expediency." *Terminiello v. Chicago*, 337 U.S. 1, 11 (1948). Or Wechsler's (1959) castigation of the Supreme Court for departing from the most fastidiously neutral principles.

[133] As Thurman Arnold observed, our law "compels the necessary compromises to be carred on *sub rosa*, while the process is openly condemned. . . . Our process attempts to outlaw the 'unwritten law.'" (1962:162). On the co-existence of stress on uniformity and rulefulness with discretion and irregularity, see Davis (1969).

[134] Cf. Black's (1973:142–43) observations on "reactive" mobilization systems as a form of delegation which perpetuates diverse moral subcultures as well as reinforces systems of social stratification (141).

[135] Some attempts at delineating and comparing such "local legal cultures'" are found in Jacob (1969); Wilson (1968); Goldstein and Ford (1971). It should be emphasized that such variation is not primarily a function of differences at the level of rules. All of these studies show considerable variation among localities and agencies governed by the same body of rules.

[136] I employ this term to refer to one distinctive style of accommodating social diversity and normative pluralism by combining universalistic law with variable application, local initiative and tolerated evasion. (Cf. the kindred usage of this term by Rheinstein [1972: chaps. 4, 10] to describe the divorce regime of contemporary western nations characterized by a gap between "the law of the books and the law in action;" and by ten Broek [1964a, 1965] to describe the unacknowledged co-existence of diverse class-specific bodies of law.) This dualistic style might be contrasted to, among others, (a) a "millet" system in which various groups are explicitly delegated broad power to regulate their own internal dealings through their own agencies (cf. Reppetto, 1970); (b) official

We have discussed the way in which the architecture of the legal system tends to confer interlocking advantages on overlapping groups whom we have called the "haves." To what extent might reforms of the legal system dispel these advantages? Reforms will always be less total than the utopian ones envisioned above. Reformers will have limited resources to deploy and they will always be faced with the necessity of choosing which uses of those resources are most productive of equalizing change. What does our analysis suggest about strategies and priorities?

Our analysis suggests that change at the level of substantive rules is not likely in itself to be determinative of redistributive outcomes. Rule change is in itself likely to have little effect because the system is so constructed that changes in the rules can be filtered out unless accompanied by changes at other levels. In a setting of overloaded institutional facilities, inadequate costly legal services, and unorganized parties, beneficiaries may lack the resources to secure implementation; or an RP may restructure the transaction to escape the thrust of the new rule. (Leff, 1970b; Rothwax, 1969:143; Cf. Grossman, 1970). Favorable rules are not necessarily (and possibly not typically) in short supply to "have-nots"; certainly less so than any of the other resources needed to play the litigation game.[138] Programs of equalizing reform which focus on rule-change can be readily absorbed without any change in power relations. The system has the capacity to change a great deal at the level of rules without corresponding changes in everyday patterns of practice[139] or distribution of tangible advantages. (See, for example, Lipsky, 1970: chap. 4, 5.) Indeed rule-change may becom a symbolic substitute for redistribution of advantages. (See Edelman, 1967:40.)

The low potency of substantive rule-change is especially the case with rule-changes procured from courts. That courts can sometimes be induced to propound rule-changes that legislatures would not make points to the limitations as well as the possibilities of court-produced change. With their relative insulation from retaliation by antagonistic interests, courts may more easily propound new rules which depart from prevailing power relations. But such rules require even greater inputs of other resources to secure effective implementation. And courts have less capacity than other rule-makers to create institutional facilities and re-allocate resources to secure implementation of new rules. Litigation then is unlikely to shape decisively the distribution of power in society. It may serve to secure or solidify symbolic commitments. It is vital tactically in securing temporary advantage or protection, providing

---

administration of disparate bodies of "special law" generated by various groups (for example, the application of their respective "personal laws'" to adherents of various religions in South Asian countries. See Galanter [1968].) Although a legal system of the kind we have postulated is closest to dualism, it is not a pure case, but combines all three. For some observations on changes in the relation of government law to other legal orderings, see Weber (1954: 16–20, 140–49).

[137] The durability of "dualism" as an adaptation is reinforced by the fact that it is "functional" not only for the larger society, but that each of its "moieties" gives support to the other: the "higher law" masks and legitimates the "operating level"; the accommodation of particularistic interests there shields the "higher law" from demands and pressures which it could not accommodate without sacrificing its universalism and semblance of autonomy. I do not suggest that this explains why some societies generate these "dual" structures.

[138] Indeed the response that reforms must wait upon rule-change is one of the standard ploys of targets of reform demands. See, for example, Lipsky's (1970: 94–96) housing officials' claim that implementation of rent-strikers' demands required new legislation, when they already had the needed power.

[139] Compare Dolbeare and Hammond's (1971:151) observation, based on their research into implementation of the school prayer decisions, that "images of change abound while the status quo, in terms of the reality of people's lives, endures."

leverage for organization and articulation of interests and conferring (or withhold-ing) the mantle of legitimacy.[140] The more divided the other holders of power, the greater the redistributive potential of this symbolic/tactical role. (Dahl, 1958:294).

Our analysis suggests that breaking the interlocked advantages of the "haves" requires attention not only to the level of rules, but also to institutional facilities, legal services and organization of parties. It suggests that litigating and lobbying have to be complemented by interest organizing, provisions of services and inven-tion of new forms of institutional facilities.[141]

The thrust of our analysis is that changes at the level of parties are most likely to generate changes at other levels. If rules are the most abundant resource for reformers, parties capable of pursuing long-range strategies are the rarest. The pres-ence of such parties can generate effective demand for high grade legal services—continuous, expert, and oriented to the long run—and pressure for institutional reforms and favorable rules. This suggests that we can roughly surmise the relative strategic priority of various rule-changes. Rule changes which relate directly to the strategic position of the parties by facilitating organization, increasing the supply of legal services (where these in turn provide a focus for articulating and organizing common interests) and increasing the costs of opponents—for instance authoriza-tion of class action suits, award of attorneys fees and costs, award of provisional remedies—these are the most powerful fulcrum for change.[142] The intensity of the opposition to class action legislation and autonomous reform-oriented legal serv-ices[143] such as California Rural Legal Assistance indicates the "haves" own esti-mation of the relative strategic impact of the several levels.[144]

The contribution of the lawyer to redistributive social change, then, depends upon the organization and culture of the legal profession. We have surmised that court-produced substantive rule-change is unlikely in itself to be a determinative element in producing tangible redistribution of benefits. The leverage provided by litigation depends on its strategic combination with inputs at other levels. The question then is whether the organization of the profession permits lawyers to develop and employ skills at these other levels. The more that lawyers view

[140] On litigation as an organizational tool, see the examples given by Gary Bellow in *Yale Law Journal* (1970:1087–88).

[141] Cf. Cahn and Cahn's (1970:1016 ff.) delineation of the "four principal areas where the investment of . . . resources would yield critically needed changes: the creation (and legitimation) of new justice-dispensing institutions, the expansion of the legal manpower supply . . . the development of a new body of procedural and substantive rights, and the development of forms of group representation as a means of enfranchisement," and the rich catalog of examples under each heading.

[142] The reformer who anticipates "legalization" (see text at note 126 above) looks to organization as a ful-crum for expanding legal services, improving institutional facilities and eliciting favorable rules. On the other hand, the reformer who anticipates "de-legalization" and the development of advantageous bargaining relation-ships/private remedy system may be indifferent or opposed to reforms of the official remedy system that would make it more likely that the official system would impinge on the RP v. RP relationship.

[143] It is, clear e.g. that what Agnew (1972:930) finds objectionable is the redistributive thrust of the legal services program:

. . . the legal services program has gone way beyond the idea of a governmentally funded program to make legal remedies available to the indigent. . . . We are dealing, in large part, with a systematic effort to redis-tribute societal advantages and disadvantages, penalties and rewards, rights and resources.

[144] Summed up neatly by the head of OEO programs in California, who, defending Governor Reagan's veto of the California Rural Legal Assistance program, said:

What we've created in CRLA is an economic leverage equal to that of a large corporation. Clearly that should not be.

Quoted at Stumpf, et al. (1971:65).

themselves exclusively as courtroom advocates, the less their willingness to undertake new tasks and form enduring alliances with clients and operate in forums other than courts, the less likely they are to serve as agents of redistributive change. Paradoxically, those legal professions most open to accentuating the advantages of the "haves" (by allowing themselves to be "captured" by recurrent clients) may be most able to become (or have room for, more likely) agents of change, precisely because they provide more license for indentification with clients and their "causes" and have a less strict definition of what are properly professional activities.[145]

References

ABEL, Richard L. (1974) "A Comparative Theory of Dispute Institutions in Society," 8 *Law & Society Review* 217.

ABEL-SMITH, Brian and Robert STEVENS (1967) *Lawyers and the Courts: A Sociological Study of the English Legal System, 1750–1965.* Cambridge: Harvard University Press.

AGNEW, Spiro (1972) "What's Wrong with the Legal Services Program," 58 *A.B.A. Journal* 930.

AKERS, Ronald L. (1968) "The Professional Association and the Legal Regulation of Practice," 2 *Law & Society Review* 463.

ANDERSON, Stanley (1969) *Ombudsman Papers: American Experience and Proposals, With a Comparative Analysis of Ombudsmen Offices by Kent M. Weeks.* Berkeley: Univ. of Cal. Inst. of Govt. Studies.

ARNOLD, Thurman (1962) *The Symbols of Government.* New York: Harcourt Brace and World (First publication, 1935).

ASPIN, Leslie (1966) *A Study of Reinstatement Under the National Labor Relations Act.* Unpublished dissertation, Mass. Inst. of Tech., Dept. of Economics.

ATLESON, James B. (1971) "Disciplinary Discharges, Arbitration and NLRB Deference," 20 *Buffalo Law Review* 355.

———. (1967) "A Union Member's Right of Free Speech and Assembly: Institutional Interests and Individual Rights," 51 *Minnesota Law Review* 403.

AUBERT, Vilhelm (1967) "Courts and Conflict Resolution," 11 *Journal of Conflict Resolution* 40.

———. (1963) "Competition and Dissensus: Two Types of Conflict Resolution," 7 *Journal of Conflict Resolution* 26.

BABCOCK, Richard S. (1969) *The Zoning Game: Municipal Practices and Policies.* Madison: University of Wisconsin Press.

BATTLE, Jackson B. (1971) "In Search of the Adversary System—The Cooperative Practices of Private Criminal Defense Attorneys," 50 *Texas Law Review* 60.

BERMAN, Harold J. (1963) *Justice in the U.S.S.R.: An Interpretation of Soviet Law.* Revised Ed., Enlarged. New York: Vintage Books.

BERNSTEIN, Marver H. (1955) *Regulating Business by Independent Commission.* Princeton: Princeton University Press.

BEUTEL, Frederick K. (1957) *Some Potentialities of Experimental Jurisprudence as a New Branch of Social Science.* Lincoln: University of Nebraska Press.

BLACK, Donald J. (1973) "The Mobilization of Law," 2 *Journal of Legal Studies* 125.

[145] Cf. Note 48 above. It is submitted that legal professions that approximate "Type B" will not only accentuate the "have" advantages, but will also be most capable of producing redistributive change.

———. (1971) "The Social Organization of Arrest," 23 *Stanford Law Review* 1087.

———. (1970) "Production of Crime Rates," 35 *American Sociological Review* 733.

BLANKENBURG, Erhard, Viola BLANKENBURG and Hellmut MORASON (1972) "Der lange Weg in die Berufung," in Rolf BENDER (ed.) *Tatsachen Forschung in der Justiz.* Tubingen: C.B. Mohr, 1972.

BLUMBERG, Abraham S. (1967a) *Criminal Justice.* Chicago: Quadrangle Books.

———. (1967b) "The Practice of Law as a Confidence Game," 1 *Law & Society Review* 15.

BOHANNON, Paul (1965) "The Differing Realms of the Law in The Ethnography of Law," in Laura NADER (ed.) *The Ethnography of Law* (=Part 2 of *American Anthropologist,* Vol. 67, No. 6.).

BONN, Robert L. (1972a) "Arbitration: An Alternative System for Handling Contract Related Disputes," 17 *Administrative Sciences Quarterly* 254.

———. (1972b) "The Predictability of Nonlegalistic Adjudication," 6 *Law & Society Review* 563.

BORKIN, Joseph (1950) "The Patent Infringement Suit—Ordeal by Trial," 17 *University of Chicago Law Review* 634.

BRILL, Harry (1973) "The Uses and Abuses of Legal Assistance," No. 31 (Spring) *The Public Interest* 38.

BRUFF, Harold H. (1973) "Arizona's Inferior Courts," 1973 *Law and the Social Order* 1.

BURGER, Warren (1970) "The State of the Judiciary—1970," 56 *A.B.A. Journal* 929.

BURGHARDT, Stephen (ed.) (1972) *Tenants and the Urban Housing Crisis.* Dexter, Mich.: The New Press.

BURNLEY, James H. IV (1973) "Comment, Solicitation by the Second Oldest Profession: Attorneys and Advertising," 8 *Harvard Civil Rights-Civil Liberties Law Review* 77.

CAHN, Edgar S. and Jean Camper CAHN (1970) "Power to the People or the Profession?—The Public Interest in Public Interest Law," 79 *Yale Law Journal* 1005.

CAMERON, Mary Owen (1964) *The Booster and the Snitch: Department Shoplifting.* New York: Free Press of Glencoe.

CARLIN, Jerome E. (1966) *Lawyers' Ethics: A Survey of the New York City Bar.* New York: Russell Sage Foundation.

———. (1962) *Lawyers on Their Own: A Study of Individual Practitioners in Chicago.* New Brunswick: Rutgers University Press.

CARLIN, Jerome E. and Jan HOWARD (1965) "Legal Representation and Class Justice," 12 *U.C.L.A. Law Review* 381.

CASPER, Jonathan D. (1970) "Lawyers Before the Supreme Court: Civil Liberties and Civil Rights, 1957–66," 22 *Stanford Law Review* 487.

CHRISTIANSON, Barlow F. (1970) *Lawyers for People of Moderate Means: Some Problems of Availability of Legal Services.* Chicago: American Bar Foundation.

CLARK, Peter B. and James Q. WILSON (1961) "Incentive Systems: A Theory of Organizations," 6 *Administrative Sciences Quarterly* 129.

COHEN, Julius, Reginald A.H. ROBSON and Alan BATES (1958) *Parental Authority: The Community and the Law.* New Brunswick: Rutgers University Press.

COHN, Bernard S. (1959) "Some Notes on Law and Change in North India," 8 *Economic Development and Cultural Change* 79.

COLUMBIA JOURNAL OF LAW AND SOCIAL PROBLEMS (1971) "Roman Catholic Ecclesiastical Courts and the Law of Marriage," 7 *Columbia Journal of Law and Social Problems* 204.

———. (1970) "Rabbinical Courts: Modern Day Solomons," 6 *Columbia Journal of Law and Social Problems* 49.

COMMUNITY SERVICE SOCIETY, Department of Public Affairs, Special Committee On Consumer Protection (1974) *Large Grievances About Small Causes: New York City's Small Claims Court—Proposals for Improving the Collection of Judgments.* New York: New York City Community Service Society.

CONRAD, Alfred F., James N. MORGAN, Robert W. PRATT, JR., Charles F. VOLTZ and ROBERT L. BOMBAUGH (1964) *Automobile Accident Costs and Payments: Studies in the Economics of Injury Reparation.* Ann Arbor: University of Michigran Press.

CONSUMER COUNCIL (1970) *Justice Out of Reach: A Case for Small Claims Courts.* London: Her Majesty's Stationery Office.

COONS, John E. (1964) "Approaches to Court-Imposed Compromise—The Uses of Doubt and Reason," 58 *Northwestern University Law Review* 750.

CRESSEY, Donald R. (1969) *Theft of the Nation: The Structure and Operations of Organized Crime in America.* New York: Harper and Row.

DAHL, Robert A. (1958) "Decision-making in a Democracy: The Supreme Court as a National Policy-maker," 6 *Journal of Public Law* 279.

DAVIS, Gordon J. and Michael W. SCHWARTZ (1967) "Tenant Unions: An Experiment in Private Law Making," 2 *Harvard Civil Rights-Civil Liberties Law Review* 237.

DAVIS, Kenneth Culp (1969) *Discretionary Justice: A Preliminary Inquiry.* Baton Rouge: Louisiana State University Press.

DERRETT, J. Duncan M. (1959) "Sir Henry Maine and Law in India," 1959 (Part I) *Juridical Review* 40.

DIBBLE, Vernon K. (1973) "What Is, and What Ought to Be: A Comparison of Certain Formal Characteristics of the Ideological and Legal Styles of Thought," 79 *American Journal of Sociology* 511.

DOLBEARE, Kenneth M. (1969) "The Federal District Courts and Urban Public Policy: An Exploratory Study (1960–1967)," in J. GROSSMAN and J. TANENHAUS (eds.) *Frontiers of Judicial Research.* New York: John Wiley.

———. (1967) *Trial Courts in Urban Politics: State Court Policy Impact and Function in a Local Political System.* New York: John Wiley.

DOLBEARE, Kenneth M. and Phillip E. HAMMOND (1971) *The School Prayer Decisions: From Court Policy to Local Practice.* Chicago: University of Chicago Press.

DOO, Leigh-Wei (1973) "Dispute Settlement in Chinese-American Communities," 21 *American Journal of Comparative Law* 627.

DURKHEIM, Emile (1964) *The Division of Labor in Society.* New York: Free Press.

EDELMAN, Murray (1967) *The Symbolic Uses of Politics.* Urbana: University of Illinois Press.

EHRLICH, Eugen (1936) *Fundamental Principles of the Sociology of Law.* New York: Russell and Russell Publishers.

ENGLE, C. Donald (1971) *Criminal Justice in the City.* Unpublished dissertation, Department of Political Science, Temple University.

ENNIS, Phillip H. (1967) *Criminal Victimization in the United States: A Report of a National Survey.* (President's Commission on Law Enforcement and Administration of Justice, Field Survey II). Washington: Government Printing Office.

FELSTINER, William L.F. (1974) "Influences of Social Organization on Dispute Processing," 9 *Law & Society Review* 63.

FINKLESTEIN, Herman (1954) "The Composer and the Public Interest—Regulation of Performing Rights Societies," 19 *Law and Contemporary Problems* 275.

FOOTE, Caleb (1956) "Vagrancy-type Law and Its Administration," 104 *University of Pennsylvania Law Review* 603.

FORD, Stephen D. (1970) *The American Legal System.* Minneapolis: West Publishing Company.

FRANK, Jerome (1930) *Law and the Modern Mind.* New York: Coward-McCann.

FRANKLIN, Marc, Robert H. CHANIN and Irving MARK (1961) "Accidents, Money and the Law. A Study of the Economics of Personal Injury Litigation," 61 *Columbia Law Review* 1.

FRIEDMAN, Lawrence M. (1973) *A History of American Law.* New York: Simon and Shuster.

————. (1969) "Legal Culture and Social Development," 4 *Law & Society Review* 29.

————. (1967) "Legal Rules and the Process of Social Change," 19 *Stanford Law Review* 786.

FRIEDMAN, Lawrence M. and Jack LADINSKY (1967) "Social Change and the Law of Industrial Accidents," 67 *Columbia Law Review* 50.

FRIEDMAN, Lawrence M. and Stewart MACAULAY (1967) "Contract Law and Contract Teaching: Past, Present, and Future," 1967 *Wisconsin Law Review* 805.

FULLER, Lon L. (1969) *The Morality of Law.* Revised ed., New Haven: Yale University Press.

GALANTER, Marc (1968–69) "Introduction: The Study of the Indian Legal Profession," 3 *Law & Society Review* 201.

————. (1968) "The Displacement of Traditional Law in Modern India," 24 *Journal of Social Issues* 65.

GELLHORN, Walter (1966) *When Americans Complain: Governmental Grievance Procedures.* Cambridge: Harvard University Press.

GIFFORD, Daniel J. (1971) "Communication of Legal Standards, Policy Development and Effective Conduct Regulation," 56 *Cornell Law Review* 409.

GOLDING, Martin P. (1969) "Preliminaries to the Study of Procedural Justice," in G. HUGHES (ed.) *Law, Reason and Justice.* New York: New York University Press.

GOLDSTEIN, Paul and Robert FORD (1971) "The Management of Air Quality: Legal Structures and Official Behavior," 21 *Buffalo Law Review* 1.

GRACE, Roger (1970) "Justice, Chinese Style," 75 *Case and Comment* 50.

GROSSMAN, Joel (1970) "The Supreme Court and Social Change: A Preliminary Inquiry," 13 *American Behavioral Scientist* 535.

HAHM, Pyong-Choon (1969) "The Decision Process in Korea," in G. SCHUBERT and D. DANELSKI (eds.) *Comparative Judicial Behavior: Cross-Cultural Studies of Political Decision-Making in the East and West.* New York: Oxford University Press.

HALLAUER, Robert Paul (1972) "Low Income Laborers as Legal Clients: Use Patterns and Attitudes Toward Lawyers," 49 *Denver Law Journal* 169.

HAKMAN, Nathan (1969) "The Supreme Court's Political Environment: The Processing of Noncommercial Litigation," in J. GROSSMAN and J. TANENHAUS (eds.) *Frontiers of Judicial Research.* New York: John Wiley and Sons.

————. (1966) "Lobbying the Supreme Court—An Appraisal of Political Science Folklore," 35 *Fordham Law Review* 15.

HANDLER, Joel (1967) *The Lawyer and his Community: The Practicing Bar in a Middlesized City.* Madison: University of Wisconsin Press.

————. (1966) "Controlling Official Behavior in Welfare Administration," in Jacobus TEN-BROEK, *et al.* (eds.) *The Law of the Poor.* San Francisco: Chandler Publishing Co.

HANDLER, Milton (1971a) "The Shift from Substantive to Procedural Innovations in Antitrust Suits," 26 *Record of N.Y.C. Bar Association* 124.

————. (1971b) "Twenty-Fourth Annual Antitrust Review," 26 *Record of N.Y.C. Bar Association* 753.

HART, Henry M., JR. and Albert M. SACKS (1958) *The Legal Process: Basic Problems in the Making and Application of Law.* Cambridge, Mass.: Harvard Law School, Tentative Edition (Mimeographed).

HAZARD, Geoffrey C., JR. (1970) "Law Reforming in the Anti-Poverty Effort," 37 *University of Chicago Law Review* 242.

————. (1965) "After the Trial Court—the Realities of Appellate Review," in Harry JONES (ed.) *The Courts, the Public and the Law Explosion.* Englewood Cliffs: Prentice Hall.

HENDERSON, Dan Fenno (1968) "Law and Political Modernization in Japan," in Robert E. WARD (ed.) *Political Development in Modern Japan.* Princeton: Princeton University Press.

HIRSCHMAN, Albert O. (1970) *Exit, Voice, and Loyalty: Responses to Decline in Firms, Organizations and States.* Cambridge: Harvard University Press.

HOLLINGSWORTH, Robert J., William B. FELDMAN and David C. CLARK (1974) "The Ohio Small Claims Court: An Empirical Study," 42 *University of Cincinnati Law Review* 469.

HOMBERGER, Adolf (1974) "Private Suits in the Public Interest in the United States of America," 23 *Buffalo Law Review* 343.

———. (1971) "State Class Actions and the Federal Rule," 71 *Columbia Law Review* 609.

———. (1970) "Functions of Orality in Austrian and American Civil Procedure," 20 *Buffalo Law Review* 9.

HORSKY, Charles (1952) *The Washington Lawyer*. Boston: Little, Brown and Co.

HOWARD, J. Woodford, JR. (1969) "Adjudication Considered as a Process of Conflict Resolution: A Variation on Separation of Powers," 18 *Journal of Public Law* 339.

HUNTIN, Roger Bryand and Gloria S. NEUWIRTH (1962) *Who Sues in New York City? A Study of Automobile Accident Claims*. New York: Columbia University Press.

HURST, James Willard (1950) *The Growth of American Law: The Law Makers*. Boston: Little, Brown and Co.

IANNI, Francis A.J. (1972) *A Family Business: Kinship and Control in Organized Crime*. New York: Russell Sage Foundation and Basic Books.

INTERNATIONAL LEGAL CENTER (1973) *Newsletter* No. 9, July 1973. New York: International Legal Center.

JACOB, Herbert (1969) *Debtors in Court: The Consumption of Government Services*. Chicago: Rand McNally.

JOHNSTONE, Quintin and Dan HOPSON, JR. (1967) *Lawyers and Their Work: An Analysis of the Legal Profession in the United States and England*. Indianapolis: Bobbs Merrill Co.

KALVEN, Harry, JR. (1958) "The Jury, the Law and the Personal Injury Damage Award," 19 *Ohio State Law Journal* 158.

KAPLAN, Benjamin, Arthur T. von MEHREN and Rudolf SCHAEFER (1958) "Phases of German Civil Procedure," 71 *Harvard Law Review* 1193–1268, 1443–72.

KATZ, Marvin (1969) "Mr. Lin's Accident Case: A Working Hypothesis on the Oriental Meaning of Face in International Relations on the Grand Scheme," 78 *Yale Law Journal* 1491.

KAWASHIMA, Takeyoshi (1963) "Dispute Resolution in Contemporary Japan," in A.T. von MEHREN (ed.) *Law in Japan: The Legal Order in a Changing Society*. Cambridge: Harvard University Press.

KENNEDY, Duncan (1973) "Legal Formality," 2 *Journal of Legal Studies* 351.

KIDDER, Robert L. (1974) "Formal Litigation and Professional Insecurity: Legal Entrepreneurship in South India," 9 *Law & Society Review* 11.

———. (1973) "Courts and Conflict in an Indian City: A Study in Legal Impact," 11 *Journal of Commonwealth Political Studies* 121.

———. (1971) *The Dynamics of Litigation: A Study of Civil Litigation in South Indian Courts*. Unpublished Dissertation, Northwestern University.

LADINSKY, Jack (1963) "Careers of Lawyers, Law Practice and Legal Institutions," 28 *American Sociological Review* 47.

LAFAVE, Wayne R. (1965) *Arrest: The Decision to Take a Suspect into Custody*. Boston: Little, Brown and Co.

LARGE, Donald W. (1972) "Is Anybody Listening? The Problem of Access in Environmental Litigation," 1972 *Wisconsin Law Review* 62.

LAUFER, Joseph (1970) "Embattled Victims of the Uninsured: In Court with New York's MVAIC, 1959–69," 19 *Buffalo Law Review* 471.

LE VAR, C. Jeddy (1973) "The Small Claims Court: A Case Study of Process, Politics, Outputs and Factors Associated with Businessmen Usage." Unpublished Paper.

LEFF, Arthur A. (1970a) "Injury, Ignorance, and Spite—The Dynamics of Coercive Collection," 80 *Yale Law Journal* 1.

———. (1970b) "Unconscionability and the Crow-Consumers and the Common-Law Tradition," 31 *University of Pittsburgh Law Review* 349.

LEPAULLE, Pierre George (1950) "Law Practice in France," 50 *Columbia Law Review* 945.

LEVINE, Felice J. and Elizabeth PRESTON (1970) "Community Resource Orientation Among Low Income Groups," 1970 *Wisconsin Law Review* 80.

LEVINE, James P. (1970) "Methodological Concerns in Studying Supreme Court Efficacy," 4 *Law & Society Review* 583.

LIGHT, Ivan H. (1972) *Ethnic Enterprise in America: Business and Welfare Among Chinese, Japanese and Blacks.* Berkeley: University of California Press.

LIPSKY, Michael (1970) *Protest in City Politics: Rent Strikes, Housing, and the Power of the Poor.* Chicago: Rand McNally and Co.

LOBENTHAL, Joseph S., JR. (1970) *Power and Put-On: The Law in America.* New York: Outerbridge and Dienstfrey.

LOCKARD, Duane (1968) *Toward Equal Opportunity: A Study of State and Local Antidiscrimination Laws.* New York: Macmillan Co.

LOEBER, Dietrich A. (1965) "Plan and Contract Performance in Soviet Law," in W. LAFAVE (ed.) *Law in the Soviet Society.* Urbana: University of Illinois Press.

LORTIE, Dan C. (1959) "Laymen to Lawmen: Law School, Careers, and Professional Socialization," 29 *Harvard Educational Review* 352.

LOWRY, S. Todd (1973) "Lord Mansfield and the Law Merchant," 7 *Journal of Economic Issues* 605.

LOWY, Michael J. (n.d.) "A Good Name is Worth More than Money: Strategies of Court Use in Urban Ghana." Unpublished paper.

MACAULAY, Stewart (1966) *Law and the Balance of Power: The Automobile Manufacturers and Their Dealers.* New York: Russell Sage Foundation.

———. (1963) "Non-Contractual Relations in Business: A Preliminary Study," 28 *American Sociological Review* 55.

MacCALLUM, Spencer (1967) "Dispute Settlement in an American Supermarket," in Paul BOHANNON (ed.) *Law and Warfare.* Garden City, N.Y.: Natural History Press for American Museum of Natural History.

MARSHALL, Leon C. and Geoffrey MAY (1932) *The Divorce Court: Volume One— Maryland.* Baltimore: The Johns Hopkins Press.

MATZA, David (1964) *Delinquency and Drift.* New York: John Wiley.

MAYHEW, Leon H. (1973) "Institutions of Representation." A paper prepared for delivery at the Conference on the Delivery and Distribution of Legal Services, State University of New York at Buffalo, October 12, 1973.

———. (1971) "Stability and Change in Legal Systems," in Alex INKELES and Bernard BARBER (eds.) *Stability and Social Change.* Boston: Little, Brown and Co.

———. (1968) *Law and Equal Opportunity: A Study of the Massachusetts Commission Against Discrimination.* Cambridge: Harvard University Press.

MAYHEW, Leon and Albert J. REISS, JR. (1969) "The Social Organization of Legal Contacts," 34 *American Sociological Review* 309.

McINTYRE, Donald M. (1968) "A Study of Judicial Dominance of the Charging Process," 59 *Journal of Criminal Law, Criminology and Police Science* 463.

McINTYRE, Donald M. and David LIPPMAN (1970) "Prosecutors and Early Disposition of Felony Cases," 56 *A.B.A. Journal* 1154.

McPHERSON, James Alan (1972) "In My Father's House There are Many Mansions, and I'm Going to Get Me Some of Them, Too! The Story of the Contract Buyers League," 229(4) *Atlantic Monthly* 51.

MENTSCHIKOFF, Soia (1961) "Commercial Arbitration," 61 *Columbia Law Review* 846.

MERRYMAN, John Henry (1969) *The Civil Law Tradition: An Introduction to the Legal Systems of Western Europe and Latin America.* Stanford, Cal.: Stanford University Press.

MILLER, Frank W. (1969) *Prosecution: the Decision to Charge a Suspect with a Crime.* Boston: Little, Brown and Co.

MORGAN, Richard S. (1968) *The Politics of Religious Conflict: Church and State in America.* New York: Pegasus.

MORRISON, Charles (1974) "Clerks and Clients: Paraprofessional Roles and Cultural Identities in Indian Litigation," 9 *Law & Society Review* 39.

MOSIER, Marilyn Miller and Richard A. SOBLE (1973) "Modern Legislation, Metropolitan Court, Miniscule Results: A Study of Detroit's Landlord-Tenant Court," 7 *University of Michigan Journal of Law Reform* 6.

MOULTON, Beatrice A. (1969) "The Persecution and Intimidation of the Low-Income Litigant as Performed by the Small Claims Court in California," 21 *Stanford Law Review* 1657.

MURPHY, Walter (1959) "Lower Court Checks on Supreme Court Power," 53 *American Political Science Review* 1017.

MURRAY, John E., JR. (1969) "Unconscionability: Unconscionability." 31 *University of Pittsburgh Law Review* 1.

NADER, Laura (1965) "The Anthropological Study of Law," in Laura NADER (ed). *The Ethnography of Law* (= Part 2 of *American Anthropologist,* Volume 67, No. 6).

NAGEL, Stuart S. (1973) "Effects of Alternative Types of Counsel on Criminal Procedure Treatment," 48 *Indiana Law Journal* 404.

NEWMAN, Donald J. (1966) *Conviction: The Determination of Guilt or Innocence Without Trial.* Boston: Little, Brown and Co.

NONET, Philippe (1969) *Administrative Justice: Advocacy and Change in a Government Agency.* New York: Russell Sage Foundation.

NORTHWESTERN UNIVERSITY LAW REVIEW (1953) "Settlement of Personal Injury Cases in the Chicago Area," 47 *Northwestern University Law Review* 895.

O'CONNELL, Jeffrey (1971) *The Injury Industry and the Remedy of No-Fault Insurance.* Chicago: Commerce Clearing House.

O'GORMAN, Hubert (1963) *Lawyers and Matrimonial Cases: A Study of Informal Pressures in Private Professional Practice.* New York: Free Press.

OHLHAUSEN, George C. (1936) "Rich and Poor in Civil Procedure," 11 *Science and Society* 275.

OLSON, Mancur, JR. (1965) *The Logic of Collective Action: Public Goods and the Theory of Groups.* Cambridge: Harvard University Press.

ORBELL, John M. and Toro UNO (1972) "A Theory of Neighborhood Problem Solving: Political Action *vs.* Residential Mobility," 66 *American Political Science Review* 471.

OWEN, Harold J., JR. (1971) *The Role of Trial Courts in the Local Political System: A Comparison of Two Georgia Counties.* Unpublished dissertation, Department of Political Science, University of Georgia.

PAGTER, C.R., R. McCLOSKEY and M. REINIS (1964) "The California Small Claims Court," 52 *California Law Review* 876.

PARSONS, Talcott (1954) "A Sociologist Looks At The Legal Profession," in *Essays in Sociological Theory.* New York: Free Press.

POWELL, Richard R. and Patrick J. ROHAN (1968) *Powell on Real Property.* One Volume Ed. New York: Mathew Bender.

RABIN, Robert L. (1972) "Agency Criminal Referrals in the Federal System: An empirical study of prosecutorial discretion," 24 *Stanford Law Review* 1036.

RABINOWITZ, Richard W. (1968) "Law and the Social Process in Japan," in *Transactions of the Asiatic Society of Japan,* Third Series, Volume X. Tokyo.

RANDALL, Richard S. (1968) *Censorship of the Movies: Social and Political Control of a Mass Medium.* Madison: University of Wisconsin Press.

RANKIN, Anne (1964) "The Effect of Pretrial Detention," 39 *N.Y.U. Law Review* 641.

RAWLS, John (1971) *A Theory of Justice.* Cambridge: Harvard University Press.

———. (1958) "Justice as Fairness," 68 *The Philosophical Review* 80.

REICH, Charles (1964a) "The New Property," 73 *Yale Law Journal* 733.

———. (1964b) "Individual Rights and Social Welfare: The Emerging Legal Issues," 74 *Yale Law Journal* 1245.

REICHSTEIN, Kenneth J. (1965) "Ambulance Chasing: A Case Study of Deviation Within the Legal Profession," 3 *Social Problems* 3.

REPPETTO, Thomas (1970) "The Millet System in the Ottoman and American Empires," 5 *Public Policy* 629.

REPUBLIC RESEARCH, INC. (1970) "Claims and Recovery for Product Injury Under the Common Law," in National Commission on Product Safety, Supplemental Studies, Vol. III: *Product Safety Law and Administration: Federal, State, Local and Common Law.* Washington: U.S. Government Printing Office, 237.

ROSENTHAL, Albert J. (1971) "Negotiability—Who Needs It?," 71 *Columbia Law Review* 375.

ROSENTHAL, Douglas E. (1970) *Client Participation in Professional Decision: the Lawyer-Client Relationship in Personal Injury Cases.* Unpublished dissertation, Yale University.

ROSS, H. Laurence (1970) *Settled Out of Court: The Social Process of Insurance Claims Adjustment.* Chicago: Aldine.

ROTHSTEIN, Lawrence E. (1974) "The Myth of Sisyphus: Legal Services Efforts on Behalf of the Poor," 7 *University of Michigan Journal of Law Reform* 493.

ROTHWAX, Harold J. (1969) "The Law as an Instrument of Social Change," in Harold H. WEISSMAN (ed.) *Justice and the Law in the Mobilization for Youth Experience.* New York: New York Association Press.

SAARI, David J. (1967) "Open Doors to Justice—An Overview of Financing Justice in America," 50 *Journal of the American Judicature Society* 296.

SALISBURY, Robert H. (1969) "An Exchange Theory of Interest Groups," 13 *Midwest Journal of Political Science* 1.

SCHELLING, Thomas C. (1963) *The Strategy of Conflict.* New York: Oxford University Press.

SCHRAG, Philip G. (1969) "Bleak House 1968: A Report on Consumer Test Litigation," 44 *N.Y.U. Law Review* 115.

SCHWARTZ, Richard D. (1954) "Social Factors in the Development of Legal Control: A Case Study of Two Israeli Settlements," 63 *Yale Law Journal* 471.

SCIGLIANO, Robert (1971) *The Supreme Court and the Presidency.* New York: Free Press.

SCOTT, William G. (1964) *The Management of Conflict: Appeal Systems in Organizations.* Homewood, Ill.: Irwin/Dorsey.

SELZNICK, Philip with the collaboration of Philippe NONET and Howard M. VOLLMER (1969), *Law, Society and Industrial Justice.* Russell Sage Foundation.

SEYMOUR, Whitney North, JR. (1974) "Frontier Justice: A Run-In With the Law," *The New York Times,* July 21, 1974.

SHKLAR, Judith N. (1964) *Legalism.* Cambridge: Harvard University Press.

SHOVER, John L. (1966) *Cornbelt Rebellion: The Farmers' Holiday Association.* Urbana: University of Illinois Press.

SHRIVER, George H. (ed.) (1966) *America's Religious Heretics: Formal and Informal Trials in American Protestantism.* Nashville: Abdingdon Press.

SHUCHMAN, Philip (1971) "The Fraud Exception in Consumer Bankruptcy," 23 *Stanford Law Review* 735.

———. (1969) "Profit on Default: an archival study of automobile repossession and resale," 22 *Stanford Law Review* 20.

———. (1968) "Ethics and Legal Ethics: The Propriety of the Canons as a Group Moral Code," 37 *George Washington Law Review* 244.

SIMKIN, William E. (1971) *Mediation and the Dynamics of Collective Bargaining.* Washington: Bureau of National Affairs.

SIMON, William (1972) "Class Actions—Useful Tool or Engine of Destruction," 55 *Federal Rules Decisions* 375.

SKOLNICK, Jerome (1967) "Social Control in the Adversary Process," 11 *Journal of Conflict Resolution* 52.

———. (1966) *Justice Without Trial: Law Enforcement in a Democratic Society.* New York: John Wiley.

SMALL CLAIMS STUDY GROUP (1972) "Little Injustices: Small Claims Courts and the American Consumer." A preliminary report to The Center for Auto Safety, Cambridge, Mass.

SMIGEL, Erwin O. (1969) *The Wall Street Lawyer: Professional Organization Man?* Bloomington: Indiana University Press.

SMITH, Regan G. (1970) *The Small Claims Court: a Sociological Interpretation.* Unpublished dissertation, Department of Sociology, University of Illinois.

SPRADLEY, James P. (1970) *You Owe Yourself a Drunk: An Ethnography of Urban Nomads.* Boston: Little, Brown and Co.

STUMPF, Harry P., Henry P. SCHROERLUKE and Forrest D. DILL (1971) "The Legal Profession and Legal Services: Explorations in Local Bar Politics," 6 *Law & Society Review* 47.

SUDNOW, David (1965) "Normal Crimes: Sociological Features of the Penal Code in a Public Defender Office," 12 *Social Problems* 255.

SUMMERS, Clyde (1960) "Individual Rights in Collective Agreements: A Preliminary Analysis," 9 *Buffalo Law Review* 239.

TANNER, Nancy (1970) "Disputing and the Genesis of Legal Principles: Examples from Minangkabau," 26 *Southwestern Journal of Anthropology* 375.

tenBROEK, Jacobus (1964–65) "California's Dual System of Family Law: Its Origin, Development and Present Status," 16 *Stanford Law Review* 257–317, 900–81; 17 *Stanford Law Review* 614-82.

TRUBEK, David M. (1972) "Toward a Social Theory of Law: An Essay on the Study of Law and Development," 82 *Yale Law Journal* 1.

TULLOCK, Gordon (1971) *Logic of the Law.* New York: Basic Books, Inc.

VAUGHAN, Ted R. (1968) "The Landlord-Tenant Relationship in a Low-Income Area," 16 *Social Problems* 208.

VIRTUE, Maxine Boord (1956) *Family Cases in Court: A Group of Four Court Studies Dealing with Judicial Administration.* Durham: Duke University Press.

VOSE, Clement E. (1972) *Constitutional Change: Amendment Politics and Supreme Court Litigation Since 1900.* Lexington, Mass.: D.C. Heath.

———. (1967) *Caucasians Only: The Supreme Court, the NAACP, and the Restrictive Covenant Cases.* Berkeley: University of California Press.

———. (1966) "Interest Groups, Judicial Review, and Local Government," 19 *Western Political Quarterly* 85.

WALD, Patricia (1964) "Foreward: Pretrial Detention and Ultimate Freedom," 39 *N.Y.U. Law Review* 631.

WANNER, Craig (1974a) "The Public Ordering of Private Relations: Part I: Initiating Civil Cases in Urban Trial Courts," 8 *Law & Society Review* 421.

———. (1974b) "The Public Ordering of Private Relations: Part II: Winning Civil Cases in Urban Trial Courts," 9 *Law & Society Review* forthcoming.

———. (1973) "A Harvest of Profits: Exploring the Symbiotic Relationship between Urban Civil Trial Courts and the Business Community," Paper prepared for delivery at the 1973 Annual Meeting of the American Political Science Association.

WASBY, Stephen L. (1970) *The Impact of the United States Supreme Court: Some Perspectives.* Homewood, Ill.: The Dorsey Press.

WEBER, Max (1954), Max RHEINSTEIN (ed.) *Max Weber on Law in Economy and Society.* Cambridge: Harvard University Press.

WECHSLER, Herbert (1959) "Toward Neutral Principles of Constitutional Law," 73 *Harvard Law Review* 1.

WEXLER, Stephen (1973) "Practicing Law for Poor People," 79 *Yale Law Journal* 1049.

WHITFORD, William C. (1968) "Law and the Consumer Transaction: A case study of the automobile warranty," 1968 *Wisconsin Law Review* 1006.

WILSON, James Q. (1968) *Varieties of Police Behavior: The Management of Law and Order in Eight Communities*. Cambridge: Harvard University Press.

WOLL, Peter (1960) "Informal Administrative Adjudication: Summary of Findings," 7 *U.C.L.A. Law Review* 436.

YALE LAW JOURNAL (1970) "The New Public Interest Lawyers," 79 *Yale Law Journal* 1069.

YNGVESSON, Barbara (1973) "Responses to Grievance Behavior: Extended Cases in a Fishing Community," Forthcoming in Michael LOWY (ed). *Choice-Making in the Law.*

———. (1965) "The Berkeley-Albany and Oakland-Piedmont Small Claims Courts: A Comparison of Role of the Judge and Social Function of the Courts." Unpublished paper.

ZEISEL, Hans, Harry KALVEN, JR., and Bernard BUCHHOLZ (1959) *Delay in the Court*. Boston: Little, Brown and Co.

*Liberalism: Interpretation and the Role
of the Judge*

Ronald Dworkin

Ronald Dworkin

IN THE YEARS after 1968, the liberal mainstream of American legal thought came under increasing pressure. It is hard to reconstruct what led legal intellectuals to translate the political anxieties of the period into legal-theoretical terms, or to feel that a better *legal theory* might strengthen the capacity or legitimacy of American political liberalism. But they did sense a link. As Ronald Dworkin put it,

> the political attitude called "liberalism," once the posture of almost all politicians, seemed to lose a great deal of its appeal. The middle-aged blamed liberalism for permissiveness and the young blamed it for rigidity, economic injustice and the war in Vietnam. Uncertainty about law reflected uncertainty about a conventional political attitude.[1]

In part, the "liberalism" with which legal academics were most familiar was the liberalism of the federal judiciary, and particularly of the Supreme Court, from the Warren Court of *Brown v. Board of Education* through *Miranda* to the decisions of the Nixon and Watergate era. The legitimacy of legal liberalism was linked to the legitimacy of an activist judiciary. The significance of the judiciary for the liberal vision was reinforced by the enhanced role judges were starting to play in the broadening field of public-law litigation analyzed by Abram Chayes in his contribution to the Canon.

The reasoning tools of the liberal judiciary remained rooted in the intellectual legacy of the legal process and the New Deal periods. But these modes of reasoning—and the centrality of adjudication itself—were increasingly under attack. The "gap" between the official pronouncements of judges and "law in action" seemed ever more visible. Liberal judicial decisions did not translate into liberal outcomes on the ground. As Mark Galanter's contribution to the Canon suggested, the periodic outcroppings of liberal rules and decisions were often worn smooth through the litigation process.

At the same time, the modes of legal reasoning through which judges had tackled broad questions of "policy" in the postwar years no longer seemed as persuasive as they once may have. Utilitarian, instrumental, and pragmatist methods, developed through the interdisciplinary borrowing of the Law and Society movement on the left, and Law and Economics scholars on the right, made the everyday judicial reasoning of liberal judges about policy matters seem sloppy, lacking in sophistication or rigor by contrast. At the same time, the first stirrings of textual neoformalism, rooted in a renewed logical positivism often supported by interdisciplinary borrowings from analytic philosophy, heightened the sense that liberal judicial interpretation was, in fact, "activist"—lacking in fealty to the texts of Constitution, statute, or precedent, an unjustified usurpation of legislative authority. From the left, the legitimacy of liberal judicial reasoning was also being challenged by the renewal of legal realist skepticism and antinomianism among post–1968 scholars associated with Critical Legal Studies. In this sense, Dworkin was right—uncertainty about the legitimacy of a conventional political attitude generated uncertainty about law.

Defending the liberal tradition seemed to require a defense of adjudication as an intellectual activity distinct from legislation—and utilitarian policymaking—while remaining open to the broad readings of legal texts and tradition favored by liberal judges. To defend adjudication in this way seemed to require a better *theory* about what judges do—a theory distinct from both positivist conceptions of fealty to text and from instrumentalist conceptions of how one should legislate. Starting in the 1970s, a wide range of theories about what judges do and ought to do were developed by scholars who saw themselves as "liberals." Indeed, it was during this period that the philosophical field of "jurisprudence"—theories about law—had the greatest impact on American legal thought. To think like a lawyer—to reason like a judge—seemed to require *theorizing about law* in the manner of a professor of jurisprudence, or at least possessing a familiarity with a range of theoretical justifications and explanations for the activist work of the liberal judiciary. Students in constitutional law courses in the 1970s, for example, studied the philosophical plausibility of various theories of adjudication and followed disputes among theorists with much the same sense of significance and engagement as they brought to the study of the Supreme Court's doctrinal reasoning in constitutional cases.

Some of those theories, of course, did seem to have implications for the way judges and lawyers should reason—if you accept theory X, you should reason this way, if theory Y seems more compelling, you should reason more like this, and so on. Many of the theories were concerned to isolate the kinds of questions judges should pose to themselves when analyzing difficult and contested issues, the sorts of arguments it was legitimate to make, the modes of discretion it was appropriate to exercise. John Rawls, for example, provided perhaps the most influential philosophical "theory of justice" during this period. His work translated rather easily, if crudely, into an idea reminiscent of Wechsler's search for "neutral principles" to guide interpretation. As taught in law schools, Rawls stood for the idea that judges should prefer reasons and interpretations that people in American society could be imagined to choose "behind a veil of ignorance" about their own stake in a particular case. In this sense, these new theories lay foursquare in the tradition of American Legal Thought. From Holmes, through the legal realists and the legal process, scholars had written about the types of arguments and forms of reasoning it was appropriate and inappropriate for judges to make. That tradition had largely focused on the persuasiveness of legal argument, developing skills to criticize modes of deductive doctrinal reasoning and policy argumentation as contradictory, inconsistent or otherwise not compelling as a matter of internal logic.

The liberal theories of the 1970s were more concerned to evaluate modes of judicial argument from an external standpoint, analyzing the forms of argument which are and are not appropriate for a judiciary in a liberal legal and political order. Theory comes into it because, of course, people differ about what a "liberal" legal and political order is and requires. Theories of liberalism had been implicit, certainly, in earlier contributions to the Canon, from Dewey's democratic pragmatism to the institutional proceduralism of the legal process. In the 1970s, liberals came increasingly to place theories of liberalism and liberal adjudication in the foreground.

Ronald Dworkin

It is not altogether clear precisely how this newly visible theoretical practice would staunch the unraveling of the liberal consensus among elite legal intellectuals. The implicit strategy seems to have been that judges would feel constrained by the judgments of their intellectual and professional peers about their own theoretical consistency and fealty to the most well articulated theory of justice. This effect would be particularly strong where those theories seemed to track, or give expression to, the most central moral and political commitments of the wider population. It is hard, looking back, to understand just how a generation of intellectuals came to feel this type of theoretical sophistication had such political and practical significance. Even if a convincing legal theory *could* be written refuting neopositivist and instrumentalist accounts of what judges do and what they should do, or outlining a theoretically defensible mode of judicial reasoning in a liberal republic, it was not clear that such a book could turn back political skepticism about the liberal endeavor or even anxiety among the liberal professorial elite about the activism of the judiciary. Even with a perfectly air-tight theoretical explanation, liberal judicial activism might not seem sensible. Even an excellent theory might not convince those who favored more instrumentalist modes of analysis, or who opposed judicial activism, or who were not liberals. Moreover, it was never clear how even a persuasive theory would cabin the actual reasoning of judges within the channels it thought appropriate—how it would connect with what judges do in fact.

Despite these difficulties, for many in the legal academy, the need for new liberal theories about law and judging seemed urgent. If judges could be understood to be doing something other than legislating when the texts of law left them room to maneuver, their role as agents of a liberal political vision might be vindicated, at least in the eyes of the theorists who shared the same theory. To that end, some developed theories of American political and legal history, in the style of Frank Michelman's contribution to the Canon, or theories of legal interpretation and ethics, in the style of Robert Cover's contribution.

In all of the liberal theories of the day, the judge was a central figure. The central thing that needed explaining was the distinct nature and legitimacy of judicial decision making in the absence of clear textual guidance. Only if it seemed possible to see judicial reasoning as different from and differently legitimate than legislation could an engaged liberal judiciary be defended.

It had been common ground in American legal thought since early in the century that judges encounter conflicts, gaps, or ambiguities in the legal materials that require judicial ingenuity. The need for new theories about what judges do in such circumstances reflected a broad erosion of confidence in the then existing ideas about how judges operate in such circumstances. Dewey's functional idea— one shuttles back and forth between possible premises and possible conclusions— seemed far too open-ended, at once open to the judge's subjective ideological preferences and to utilitarian or pragmatic calculations that would be indistinguishable from legislative or administrative action. Too "activist," in a word. One could, of course, see judicial gap-filling work as basically legislation by other means, and many significant legal intellectuals had thought just that in the years after the arrival of sociological jurisprudence and legal realism. But as the liberal political vision lost its hegemonic status in the legal establishment, it became more difficult to defend liberal judicial activism in these terms against the alternative politics of other branches and social powers.

One might imagine that judges fill the gaps by deduction from the facts of the case—but this was precisely the type of circular deduction, extracting an ought

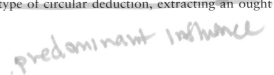

predominant influence

from an is, criticized by Felix Cohen as an open door for subjectivism. Many legal process jurists had thought judges constrained in their gap-filling work by the policies and ethical commitments immanent in the legal rules themselves, identified in the impressionistic style illustrated by Lon Fuller in his contribution to the Canon. Others influenced more by the Hart and Sacks legal process materials had simply learned to live with a degree of judicial indeterminacy and subjectivism, channeled by the institutional constraints of deference to procedural legitimacy and prior institutional settlement. These were precisely the modes of reasoning that had come to seem sloppy by the late 1960s—loose covers for who knew what political or ideological commitment.

Ronald Dworkin was the most well known of the many liberal theorists of the period who took up the challenge of offering a theory of adjudication between textual fealty and legislative policymaking. It would be fair to say that none of the particular theories offered at the time were fully persuasive, and the journals of the period are full of passionate disagreements among liberal theorists about precisely how to think about this aspect of judicial work. Dworkin's theory was no less subject to disagreement and impassioned refutation. But it remains emblematic of the work of liberal legal scholars in the period—a period in which one could not "think like a lawyer" about public law without being conversant with such theories. Dworkin's own fame as a liberal public intellectual ensured that his particular approach to these enduring questions of legal theory would enter into the background thinking of mainstream lawyers and scholars.

Ronald Dworkin was born in 1931 in Worcester, Massachusetts, and studied at Harvard College and Oxford University, receiving an AB in 1953 and a BA in 1955 respectively, before entering Harvard Law School. Upon graduation in 1957, he clerked for Judge Learned Hand, and practiced law for four years as an Associate at Sullivan and Cromwell in New York before joining the Yale law faculty in 1962, where he eventually came to hold the Wesley Hohfeld Chair of Jurisprudence. In 1969, he returned to Oxford as Professor of Jurisprudence and Fellow at University College, succeeding H.L.A. Hart, whose views on law and adjudication Dworkin had consistently disputed. In 1977, Dworkin took a joint appointment at New York University, where he continues to teach. Upon retiring from Oxford, Dworkin took a Chair at University College at the University of London, where he also lectures. Dworkin has been a prolific commentator on legal issues of the day, as well as the author of numerous philosophical and legal books and articles. He is a fellow of the British Academy and a member of the American Academy of Arts and Sciences.

The article "Hard Cases" was originally published in 1975 in the *Harvard Law Review*, and was included in Dworkin's 1977 book *Taking Rights Seriously*. The article, like the larger and influential book, situates itself as an argument against what Dworkin terms "legal positivism" and "utilitarianism." Dworkin sees the two as components of a "ruling theory of law" that understands itself to be "liberal." Dworkin aims to replace this ruling liberal theory with another.

By legal positivism, Dworkin refers to a theory of what law is and is not—only "rules that have been adopted by specific social institutions" can provide the basis for determining that a statement "is," as a matter of fact, a legal norm. Dworkin associates this idea most directly with H.L.A. Hart, and argues that it defines law far too narrowly. For Dworkin, judges are speaking and writing law even in the gaps— even when their analysis cannot be rooted in preexisting texts. For Dworkin, the key to a statement's quality as "legal" does not lie in its textual origin. There is no secret

Ronald Dworkin

book or parchment where all the background commitments and norms of the legal order are written. There are gaps, conflicts, ambiguities—judges do make law, and the propositions that emerge from adjudication, properly conducted, are properly understood as legal.

By utilitarianism, Dworkin refers to a theory about what law should be—about the purpose of law, and about what judges or other lawmakers ought to do when they make rules. Utilitarianism, according to Dworkin, "holds that law and its institutions should serve the general welfare, and nothing else" (*Taking Rights Seriously*, p. vii). For Dworkin, this is a useful theory when thinking like a legislature—legislatures do and should make law by choosing among policies aiming in different ways to improve the general welfare. When they do, they break eggs, impose costs, distribute assets and possibilities from one person to another, so as to improve the general welfare. When judges make law, however, they are doing and should be doing something altogether different—they should be respecting rights and reasoning from "principle," rather than "policy."

Dworkin wants an account of adjudication that is *neither* the implementation of *preexisting* texts, adopted by appropriate institutions, *nor* the making of new law to improve general welfare. Reasoning from "rights" provides the solution. He acknowledges that rights may not be visible in the pre-existing authoritative legal sources. To find them, the judge must develop a theory, in the context of a particular case, about what the rights are that would be coherent with, would "fit" with, the rest of the legal fabric, including its political, social, and ethical foundations. In a sense, the judge reasons as the voice of the community, looking back on its history and weaving the present case as coherently as possible into the fabric of commitments expressed by the community's prior social, political, and legal history. The idea that judges should be guided by an effort to articulate a consistency or coherence in the legal order, that they should fill gaps and resolve conflicts in the legal materials by the reasoned elaboration of propositions that seem most congruent with the broader institutional and normative framework of the legal order, was not new. Dworkin would have heard many similar ideas in his own time at the Harvard Law School from the legal process jurists.

But if theories of this general type were familiar, Dworkin's own formulation was novel in a variety of ways. The legal process scholars had treated "reasoned elaboration" and "sound judgment" as qualities of judicial reasoning and argument that would make themselves known as an opinion was written—some opinions simply would not write. Dworkin builds on this attention to argument and language. Writing after the "linguistic turn" in many of the humanities and social sciences, Dworkin saw the judicial enterprise as quintessentially one of interpretation, articulation, persuasion, and argument. Legal reasoning was a textual, linguistic exercise, having more in common with literature than economics or political science. Hercules, Dworkin's iconic judicial figure, "constructs his political theory as an argument."

Dworkin shared this interest in interpretation and language, and in the interdisciplinary potential of literature and literary or artistic criticism, with many liberal scholars of the period, including Robert Cover, who developed it in his own contribution to the Canon. Dworkin often used literary metaphors to describe judicial practice—he describes legal interpretation as an aesthetic or artistic practice, akin to writing a novel. Judges must work to develop an aesthetically satisfying arrangement of narrative components, with each judge and each case providing a further chapter in the society's autobiography. At other times, Dworkin compared legal interpretation to literary or artistic criticism, which he thought of as seeking to make of the existing materials, despite their gaps and conflicts, the "best" work of art one could. Metaphors of this type were particularly significant in liberal theories of the period, suggesting that ideological or political conflict in the legal order should be understood as a debate, a conversation, a discussion, rather than a brawl. Dworkin often used spatial and physical metaphors to describe the judicial encounter with one or another argument—arguments do not determine decision, they exert "gravitational pull" on the judge, for example.

In "hard cases," Dworkin's judge—heroically figured as "Hercules"—will often face an Augean Stables of legal pluralism, conflict, and ambiguity. He will need to develop his own theory of his community's political and social commitments. It may well happen that other judges disagree—but this does not make Hercules' theory an illegitimately subjective one, as long as he has posed himself the right questions—questions oriented to the identification and interpretation of rights, understood as the best, most coherent and consistent articulation of the society's legal, social, and ethical commitments. Dworkin's conception of Hercules as a deeply learned interpreter of a community's best historic narratives is familiar from the posture of literary theorists analyzing poetry in the "new criticism" of the 1950s and '60s.

To make this theory fly—to make the case that judges, even Herculean judges, could, in hard cases, reason in a way that was not subjective preference, but also neither utilitarian, in the manner of legislatures, nor bound to an origin in prior law, in the mode of positivism—Dworkin developed a series of more precise propositions and distinctions for which he has become known, each of which has been the subject of much debate and criticism. He distinguished "principled" arguments about "rights" from arguments of "policy" rooted in considerations of general welfare. He developed a conception of legal rights as preexisting their discovery and articulation, even where there are gaps or conflicts in the legal materials, and where people disagree about what the rights are. To defend his notion that judges reasoning in hard cases need not rely on their own subjective preferences, Dworkin argued that in principle, there was only one correct way to resolve hard cases, even where judges might well disagree in good faith about what that way is. Each of these more specific ideas makes an appearance in the "Hard Cases" essay.

Looking back, Dworkin's theory is less significant for these details, all of which have been sharply contested by other liberal theorists, than for the broad effort to develop a theory of adjudication between positivist fealty to text and Holmesian attention to statistics, economics, and considerations of general welfare. Many liberal legal scholars of the period imported their political and social theory from either philosophy or ethics, although the specific extradisciplinary influences certainly varied. For some, it was the linguistic theories of the later Wittgenstein, for others the pragmatism of Richard Rorty or the political philosophy of John Rawls. Dworkin was influenced by these interdisciplinary efforts, but he set out to construct a theory of liberalism centered in law, and on the appropriate role for the judge. The theory that resulted was remarkably fluid.

Writing from within the tradition of American legal thought, Dworkin had no illusions about the formal rigidity or determinacy of legal materials—he had absorbed the lessons of everyone in the Canon since Holmes that judicial decision is a matter of experience rather than logic. What judges do is, in a sense, ethical and political. Legal claims cannot always be objectively grounded or validated. Rights may be less than absolute, rights may involve distributional concerns, rights may emerge from considerations of general welfare, just as considerations of general welfare may guide us in comprehending what rights there are and what they mean in concrete cases. Rights do depend upon a deep political theory, about which people in a society might well disagree. In this sense, rights cannot be read in the organic history of the community as a whole—judges must struggle like Hercules to articulate a theory, perhaps an idiosyncratic one, of how to read a community's values through time. Judges may disagree in good faith about the most central commitments of the legal order, and may have quite different political theories about how their society works and should evolve, and about how the prior cases and institutional arrangements can best be made sense of.

In the latter part of the "Hard Cases" essay, the word "morality" appears ever more often, as Hercules struggles to articulate a conception of "community morality" and "political morality presupposed by the laws and institutions of the community" that can be "decisive of legal issues" (p. 126). In the almost thirty years since the "Hard Cases" essay was first published, Dworkin has by turns modified, adjusted, and vociferously defended various of the specific formulations in the essay. He has been steadfast, however, in his insistence that arguments of principle rooted in ethics and morality provide a source of universal validation for liberal legal reasoning despite the fact that judges will of necessity have reference to their own personal notions of morality in making arguments on that basis. Ultimately, Dworkin's vision of liberalism affirms that "government by adjudication" on the basis of principled ethical argument "seems better suited than the alternatives to the cultural and ethical pluralism that is so marked in modern political communities and associations."[2] His later work has articulated the principles that for him are and must be central to a liberal legal order.

DAVID KENNEDY

NOTES

1. Ronald Dworkin, *Taking Rights Seriously*, 1977 (Cambridge: Harvard University Press, vii).
2. Ronald Dworkin, "The Judge's New Role: Should Personal Convictions Count?" 1 *Journal of International Criminal Justice* 4–12 (2003) at 11.

BIBLIOGRAPHY

Ronald Dworkin

Dworkin's best known works include:

Taking Rights Seriously (Cambridge, Mass.: Harvard University Press, 1978), containing the essay "Hard Cases" originally published in 88 *Harvard Law Review* 1057 (1975). The 1978 edition contains an expanded appendix replying to seven critics (including H.L.A. Hart) of Dworkin's theory developed in a symposium issue of the *Georgia Law Review* in 1978.

A Matter of Principle (Cambridge, Mass.: Harvard University Press, 1985).

Law's Empire (Cambridge, Mass.: Harvard University Press, 1986).

Freedom's Law: The Moral Reading of the American Constitution (Cambridge, Mass.: Harvard University Press, 1996).

Natural Law and Natural Rights (Oxford: Clarendon Press, 1987).

Articles developing the themes of "Hard Cases" include:

"Judicial Discretion," 60 *Journal of Philosophy* 624 (1963).

"Does Law Have a Function? A Comment on the Two-Level Theory of Decision," 74 *Yale Law Journal* 640 (1965).

"Law as Interpretation," 9 *Critical Inquiry* 179 (1982).

"My Reply to Stanley Fish (and Walter Benn Michaels): Don't Talk About Objectivity Any More," in W.J.T. Mitchel, ed., *The Politics of Interpretation* (Chicago, University of Chicago Press, 1983).

"In Praise of Theory," 29 *Arizona State Law Journal* 353 (1997).

"Objectivity and Truth: You'd Better Believe It," 25 *Philosophy and Public Affairs* 87 (1996).

Ronald Dworkin, "The Judge's New Role: Should Personal Convictions Count?" 1 *Journal of International Criminal Justice* 4–12 (2003).

Commentary

Dworkin's writings have generated numerous collections of commentary, including Alan Hunt, ed., *Reading Dworkin Critically* (New York: Berg Press, 1992) (containing essays written from the perspective of the British tradition of critical legal studies); Marshall Cohen, ed., *Ronald Dworkin and Contemporary Jurisprudence* (Totowa, N. J.: Rowman and Allanheld, 1984)(containing essays by, among others, Philip Soper, David Lyons, Joseph Raz, Kent Greenawalt, Neil MacCormick, H.L.A. Hart, Michael Sandel, and Richard Posner, a response by Dworkin, and a short and useful bibliography of commentary on Dworkin); Justine Burley, ed., *Dworkin and His Critics: With Replies by Dworkin* (Malden, Mass.: Blackwell, 2004). Four European constitutional law scholars assess Dworkin's influence in Europe in 1 *International Journal of Constitutional Law* 555 (2003). *The Georgia Law Review* published a Jurisprudence Symposium in 1977 (11 *Ga. L. Rev.* 1976–77) containing comment on Dworkin from H.L.A. Hart, Kent Greenawalt, Stephen Munzer, David Richards, James Nickel, Edgar Bodenheimer, and Lea Brilmayer, along with a reply from Dworkin.

For interesting and useful analyses of Dworkin's work, see also:

Andrew Altman, "Legal Realism, Critical Legal Studies and Dworkin," 15 *Philosophy and Public Affairs* 205 (1986).

Raoul Berger, "Ronald Dworkin's 'The Moral Reading of the Constitution': A Critique," 72 *Indiana Law Journal* 1099 (1997).

Jules Coleman, "Book Review: *Taking Rights Seriously*," 66 *California Law Review* 885 (1978).

Stanley Fish, "Wrong Again," 62 *Texas Law Review* 299 (1983).

Paul Lawrence Gaffney, *Ronald Dworkin on Law and Interpretation,* (THESIS, Catholic University, 1990); Paul Gaffney, *Ronald Dworkin on Law as Integrity: Rights as Principles of Adjudication* (Lewiston, N.Y.: Mellon University Press, 1996).

Kenneth Einar Himma, "Trouble in Law's Empire: Rethinking Dworkin's Third Theory of Law," 23 *Oxford Journal of Legal Studies* 345 (2003) (containing a concise summary of the Dworkin/Hart debate).

Simon Honeyball and James Walter, *Integrity, Community and Interpretation: A Critical Analysis of Ronald Dworkin's Theory of Law* (Aldershot:

Ronald Dworkin

Ashgate/Dartmouth Press, 1998) (focusing on Dworkin's approach to interpretation, and comparing it to that of Gadamer).

Arthur Jacobsen, "Taking Responsibilities: Law's Relation to Justice and D'Amato's Deconstructive Practice," 90 *Northwestern University Law Review* 1755 (1996) (particularly criticizing the Hercules metaphor).

Matthew Kramer, "Also Among the Prophets: Some Rejoinders to Ronald Dworkin's Attacks on Legal Positivism" 12 *Canadian Journal of Law and Jurisprudence* 53 (1999).

Massimo La Torre, "Theories of Legal Argumentation and Concepts of Law. An Approximation," 15:4 *Ratio Juris* 377 (2002) (particularly at 390ff).

David Lyons, "Principles, Positivism and Legal Theory: A Review of *Taking Rights Seriously*," 87 *Yale Law Journal* 415 (1977–78).

John Mahoney, "Objectivity, Interpretation and Rights: A Critique of Dworkin," 23 *Law and Philosophy* 187 (2004).

Alexsander Peczenik, "Taking Law Seriously," 68 *Cornell Law Review* 660 (1982–83).

Richard Pildes, "Dworkin's Two Conceptions of Rights," 29 *Journal of Legal Studies* 309 (2000).

Michael Rosenfeld, "Dworkin and the One Law Principle: A Pluralistic Critique," *Cardozo Law* School, Legal Studies Research Paper No. 86, 2004.

Frederick Schauer, "Constitutional Invocations," 65 *Fordham Law Review* 1295 (1997).

Louis Wolcher, "Ronald Dworkin's Right Answers Thesis Through the Lens of Wittgenstein," 29 *Rutgers Law Journal* 43 (1997).

Other influential liberal theorists of the period, who disputed and distanced themselves from Dworkin's theory in a variety of ways and who were influential in the legal academy, included:

John Finnis, *Natural Law and Natural Rights* (Oxford: Clarendon Press, 1980); "On Reason and Authority in Law's Empire," 6 *Law and Philosophy* 357 (1987).

Owen Fiss, "Objectivity and Interpretation," 34 *Stanford Law Review* 739 (1982); "The Forms of Justice," 93 *Harvard Law Review* 1 (1979).

Juergen Habermas, *Between Facts and Norms: Contributions to a Discourse Theory of Law and Democracy* (Cambridge, Mass.: MIT Press, 1996) (discussing Dworkin throughout, but particularly at 210 and following).

H.L.A. Hart, "American Jurisprudence through English Eyes: The Nightmare and the Noble Dream," 11 *Georgia Law Review* 969 (1977). Hart's 1961 classic *The Concept of Law* (Oxford: Clarendon Press; New York: Oxford University Press, 1961) lays the foundation for the neopositivist position Dworkin criticizes.

Antony Kronman, "The Value of Moral Philosophy," 111 *Harvard Law Review* 1751 (1998).

Neil MacCormick, *Legal Reasoning and Legal Theory* (Oxford: Clarendon Press, 1978) (reacting to Dworkin's conceptions of "coherence" and definition of "principle" in chapter 7, at 152ff., and responding to Dworkin's criticisms of positivism in chapter 9 at 229ff.).

Alistair MacIntyre, *After Virtue: A Study in Moral Theory* (Notre Dame, Ind.: University of Notre Dame Press, 1981).

Thomas Nagel, *The Last Word* (New York: Oxford University Press, 1997).

Martha Nussbaum, *Love's Knowledge: Essays on Philosophy and Literature* (New York: Oxford University Press, 1990); *The Fragility of Goodness: Luck and Ethics in Greek Tragedy and Philosophy* (Cambridge, New York: Cambridge University Press, 1986).

Hilary Putnam, *Reason, Truth and History* (Cambridge [Cambridgeshire], New York: Cambridge University Press, 1981).

Margaret Radin, *Contested Commodities* (Cambridge, Mass.: Harvard University Press, 1996).

John Rawls, *A Theory of Justice* (Cambridge, Mass.: Belknap Press of Harvard University Press, 1971); *Political Liberalism* (New York: Columbia University Press, 1993).

Joseph Raz, "Legal Principles and the Limits of the Law," 81 *Yale Law Journal* 823 (1972); "Dworkin: A New Link In The Chain, Book review of *A Matter of Principle*," 74 *California Law Review* 1103 (1986); "The Relevance of Coherence," 72 *Boston University Law Review* 273 (1992); "Professor Dworkin's Theory of Rights," *Political Studies* 26:123 (1978); Joseph Raz, *The Authority of Law: Essays on Law and Morality* (Oxford: Clarendon Press, 1979); *Ethics in the Public Domain: Essays in the Morality of Law and Politics* (Oxford: Clarendon Press; New York: Oxford University Press, 1994); *Practical Reasons and Norms* (London: Hutchinson, 1975).

For an impassioned exchange between Rorty and Dworkin on pragmatism, see Rorty, "The Banality of Pragmatism and the Poetry of Justice" and Dworkin, "Pragmatism, Right Answers and True Banality," in *Pragmatism in Law and Society* Michael Brint and William Weaver, eds., Boulder, Co: Westview Press, 1991 at 89 and 359, respectively.

Michael Sandel, *Liberalism and the Limits of Justice* (Cambridge: Cambridge University Press, 1982); *Democracy's Discontent: America in Search of a Public Philosophy* 25–26 (Cambridge, Mass.: Belknap Press of Harvard University Press, 1996).

Thomas Scanlon, "Rights as Trumps by Ronald Dworkin: Can There be a Rights Based Moral Theory," in Jeremy Waldron, ed., *Theories of Rights* (Oxford: Oxford University Press, 1984); *What We Owe Each Other* (Cambridge, Mass.: Harvard University Press, 1971).

Cass Sunstein, *Legal Reasoning and Political Conflict* (New York: Oxford University Press, 1996); "The Supreme Court, 1995 Term: Foreword, Leaving Things Undecided," 110 *Harvard Law Review* 4 (1996); *One Case at a Time: Judicial Minimalism on the Supreme Court* (Cambridge, Mass.: Harvard University Press, 1999).

Jeremy Waldron, "The Irrelevance of Moral Objectivity," in *Natural Law Theory: Contemporary Essays* 158, Robert George, ed. (Oxford: Clarendon Press; New York: Oxford University Press, 1992); *Liberal Rights: Collected Papers 1981–1991* (Cambridge, New York: Cambridge University Press, 1993).

Lloyd Weinreb, *Natural Law and Justice* (Cambridge, Mass.: Harvard University Press, 1987) (discussing Dworkin as a natural law theorist at chapter 4).

Dworkin's position has often been compared with that of Lon Fuller's The *Morality of Law* (New Haven: Yale University Press, 1969), who carried on his own lengthy debate with H.L.A. Hart. See, for example, Lon Fuller, "Positivism and

Fidelity to Law—A Reply to Professor Hart," 71 *Harvard Law Review* 630 (1958).

Dworkin's most well known critic on the right has been Richard Posner. See Richard Posner, *The Problems of Jurisprudence* (Cambridge, Mass.: Harvard University Press, 1990) and Richard Posner, *The Problematics of Moral and Legal Theory* (Cambridge, Mass.: Harvard University Press, 1999). For a strong libertarian reaction, see Henry Veatch, "Comment: On Taking Rights Still More Seriously," 8 *Harvard Journal of Law and Public Policy.* 109 (1985). See also Michael McConnell, "The Importance of Humility in Judicial Review: A Comment on Ronald Dworkin's 'Moral Reading' of the Constitution," 65 *Fordham Law Review* 1269 (1997).

Dworkin has also been sharply criticized from the left by scholars associated with Critical Legal Studies, most notably by Duncan Kennedy in *Critique of Adjudication (fin de siecle)* (Cambridge, Mass.: Harvard University Press, 1997). See also Peter Gabel, "Book Review," 91 *Harvard Law Review* 302 (1977) (reviewing Dworkin's *Law's Empire*); Robin West, "Integrity and Universality: A Comment on Ronald Dworkin's Freedom's Law," 65 *Fordham Law Review* 1313 (1997); J. M. Balkin, "Taking Ideology Seriously: Ronald Dworkin and the CLS Critique," 55 *UMKC Law Review* 392 (1987).

"Hard Cases"

88 Harvard Law Review 1057 (1975)

This essay is a revised form of an inaugural lecture given at Oxford in June of 1971. I should like to repeat what I said then about my predecessor in the Chair of Jurisprudence. The philosophers of science have developed a theory of the growth of science; it argues that from time to time the achievement of a single man is so powerful and so original as to form a new paradigm, that is, to change a discipline's sense of what its problems are and what counts as success in solving them. Professor H.L.A. Hart's work is a paradigm for jurisprudence, not just in his country and not just in mine, but throughout the world. The province of jurisprudence is now the province he has travelled; it extends from the modal logic of legal concepts to the details of the law of criminal responsibility, and in each corner his is the view that others must take as their point of departure. It is difficult to think of any serious writing in jurisprudence in recent years, certainly in Great Britain and America, that has not either claimed his support or taken him as a principal antagonist. This essay is no exception.

His influence has extended, I might add, to form as well as substance. His clarity is famous and his diction contagious: other legal philosophers, for example, once made arguments, but now we only deploy them, and there has been a perfect epidemic of absent-mindedness in imitation of the master. How shall we account for this extraordinary influence? In him reason and passion do not contend, but combine in intelligence, the faculty of making clear what was dark without making it dull. In his hands clarity enhances rather than dissipates the power of an idea. That is magic, and it is the magic that jurisprudence needs to work.

I. INTRODUCTION

The Rights Thesis

Theories of adjudication have become more sophisticated, but the most popular theories still put judging in the shade of legislation. The main outlines of this story are familiar. Judges should apply the law that other institutions have made; they should not make new law. That is the ideal, but for different reasons it cannot be realized fully in practice. Statutes and common law rules are often vague and must be interpreted before they can be applied to novel cases. Some cases, moreover, raise issues so novel that they cannot be decided even by stretching or reinterpreting existing rules. So judges must sometimes make new law, either covertly or explicitly. But when they do, they should act as deputy to the appropriate

Professor of Jurisprudence and Fellow of University College, Oxford University. B.A., Harvard, 1953; B.A. Oxford, 1955; LL.B., Harvard, 1957.

legislature, enacting the law that they suppose the legislature would enact if seized of the problem.

That is perfectly familiar, but there is buried in this common story a further level of subordination not always noticed. When judges make law, so the expectation runs, they will act not only as deputy to the legislature but as a deputy legislature. They will make law in response to evidence and arguments of the same character as would move the superior institution if it were acting on its own. This is a deeper level of subordination because it makes any understanding of what judges do in hard cases parasitic on a prior understanding of what legislators do all the time. This deeper subordination is therefore conceptual as well as political.

In fact, however, judges neither should be nor are deputy legislators, and the familiar assumption, that when they go beyond political decisions already made by someone else they are legislating, is misleading. It misses the importance of a fundamental distinction within political theory, which I shall now introduce in a crude form. This is the distinction between arguments of principle on the one hand and arguments of policy on the other.[1]

Arguments of policy justify a political decision by showing that the decision advances or protects some collective goal of the community as a whole. The argument in favor of a subsidy for aircraft manufacturers, that the subsidy will protect national defense, is an argument of policy. Arguments of principle justify a political decision by showing that the decision respects or secures some individual or group right. The argument in favor of anti-discrimination statutes, that a minority has a right to equal respect and concern, is an argument of principle. These two sorts of argument do not exhaust political argument. Sometimes, for example, a political decision, like the decision to allow extra income tax exemptions for the blind, may be defended as an act of public generosity or virtue rather than on grounds of either policy or principle. But principle and policy are the major grounds of political justification.

The justification of a legislative program of any complexity will ordinarily require both sorts of argument. Even a program that is chiefly a matter of policy, like a subsidy program for important industries, may require strands of principle to justify its particular design. It may be, for example, that the program provides equal subsidies for manufacturers of different capabilities, on the assumption that weaker aircraft manufacturers have some right not to be driven out of business by government intervention, even though the industry would be more efficient without them. On the other hand, a program that depends chiefly on principle, like an antidiscrimination program, may reflect a sense that rights are not absolute and do not hold when the consequences for policy are very serious. The program may provide, for example, that fair employment practice rules do not apply when they might prove especially disruptive or dangerous. In the subsidy case we might say that the rights conferred are generated by policy and qualified by principle; in the antidiscrimination case they are generated by principle and qualified by policy.

It is plainly competent for the legislature to pursue arguments of policy and to adopt programs that are generated by such arguments. If courts are deputy legislatures, then it must be competent for them to do the same. Of course, unoriginal

---

[1] I discussed the distinction between principles and policies in an earlier article. *See* Dworkin, *The Model of Rules*, 35 U. CHI. L. REV. 14, 22–29 (1967). The more elaborate formulation in Part II of this essay is an improvement; among other virtues it prevents the collapse of the distinction under the (artificial) assumptions described in the earlier article.

judicial decisions that merely enforce the clear terms of some plainly valid statute are always justified on arguments of principle, even if the statute itself was generated by policy. Suppose an aircraft manufacturer sues to recover the subsidy that the statute provides. He argues his right to the subsidy; his argument is an argument of principle. He does not argue that the national defense would be improved by subsidizing him; he might even concede that the statute was wrong on policy grounds when it was adopted, or that it should have been repealed, on policy grounds, long ago. His right to a subsidy no longer depends on any argument of policy because the statute made it a matter of principle.

But if the case at hand is a hard case, when no settled rule dictates a decision either way, then it might seem that a proper decision could be generated by either policy or principle. Consider, for example, the problem of the recent Spartan Steel case.[2] The defendant's employees had broken an electrical cable belonging to a power company that supplied power to the plaintiff, and the plaintiff's factory was shut down while the cable was repaired. The court had to decide whether to allow the plaintiff recovery for economic loss following negligent damage to someone else's property. It might have proceeded to its decision by asking either whether a firm in the position of the plaintiff had a right to a recovery, which is a matter of principle, or whether it would be economically wise to distribute liability for accidents in the way the plaintiff suggested, which is a matter of policy.

If judges are deputy legislators, then the court should be prepared to follow the latter argument as well as the former, and decide in favor of the plaintiff if that argument recommends. That is, I suppose, what is meant by the popular idea that a court must be free to decide a novel case like Spartan Steel on policy grounds; and indeed Lord Denning described his own opinion in that case in just that way.[3] I do not suppose he meant to distinguish an argument of principle from an argument of policy in the technical way I have, but he in any event did not mean to rule out an argument of policy in that technical sense.

I propose, nevertheless, the thesis that judicial decisions in civil cases, even in hard cases like Spartan Steel, characteristically are and should be generated by principle not policy. That thesis plainly needs much elaboration, but we may notice that certain arguments of political theory and jurisprudence support the thesis even in its abstract form. These arguments are not decisive, but they are sufficiently powerful to suggest the importance of the thesis, and to justify the attention that will be needed for a more careful formulation.

B. Principles and Democracy

The familiar story, that adjudication must be subordinated to legislation, is supported by two objections to judicial originality. The first argues that a community should be governed by men and women who are elected by and responsible to the majority. Since judges are, for the most part, not elected, and since they are not, in practice, responsible to the electorate in the way legislators are, it seems to compromise that proposition when judges make law. The second argues that if a judge makes new law and applies it retroactively in the case before him, then the losing party will be punished, not because he violated some duty he had, but rather a new duty created after the event.

---

[2] Spartan Steel & Alley Ltd. v. Martin & Co., [1973] 1 Q.B. 27.
[3] Id. at 36.

These two arguments combine to support the traditional ideal that adjudication should be as unoriginal as possible. But they offer much more powerful objections to judicial decisions generated by policy than to those generated by principle. The first objection, that law should be made by elected and responsible officials, seems unexceptionable when we think of law as policy; that is, as a compromise among individual goals and purposes in search of the welfare of the community as a whole. It is far from clear that interpersonal comparisons of utility or preference, through which such compromises might be made objectively, make sense even in theory; but in any case no proper calculus is available in practice. Policy decisions must therefore be made through the operation of some political process designed to produce an accurate expression of the different interests that should be taken into account. The political system of representative democracy may work only indifferently in this respect, but it works better than a system that allows nonelected judges, who have no mail bag or lobbyists or pressure groups, to compromise competing interests in their chambers.

The second objection is also persuasive against a decision generated by policy. We all agree that it would be wrong to sacrifice the rights of an innocent man in the name of some new duty created after the event; it does, therefore, seem wrong to take property from one individual and hand it to another in order just to improve overall economic efficiency. But that is the form of the policy argument that would be necessary to justify a decision in Spartan Steel. If the plaintiff had no right to the recovery and the defendant no duty to offer it, the court could be justified in taking the defendant's property for the plaintiff only in the interest of wise economic policy.

But suppose, on the other hand, that a judge successfully justifies a decision in a hard case, like Spartan Steel, on grounds not of policy but of principle. Suppose, that is, that he is able to show that the plaintiff has a right to recover its damages. The two arguments just described would offer much less of an objection to the decision. The first is less relevant when a court judges principle, because an argument of principle does not often rest on assumptions about the nature and intensity of the different demands and concerns distributed throughout the community. On the contrary, an argument of principle fixes on some interest presented by the proponent of the right it describes, an interest alleged to be of such a character as to make irrelevant the fine discriminations of any argument of policy that might oppose it. A judge who is insulated from the demands of the political majority whose interests the right would trump is, therefore, in a better position to evaluate the argument.

The second objection to judicial originality has no force against an argument of principle. If the plaintiff has a right against the defendant, then the defendant has a corresponding duty, and it is that duty, not some new duty created in court, that justifies the award against him. Even if the duty has not been imposed upon him by explicit prior legislation, there is, but for one difference, no more injustice in enforcing the duty than if it had been.

The difference is, of course, that if the duty had been created by statute the defendant would have been put on much more explicit notice of that duty, and might more reasonably have been expected to arrange his affairs so as to provide for its consequences. But an argument of principle makes us look upon the defendant's claim, that it is unjust to take him by surprise, in a new light. If the plaintiff does indeed have a right to a judicial decision in his favor, then he is entitled to rely upon that right. If it is obvious and uncontroversial that he has the right, the defendant is in no position to claim unfair surprise just because the right arose in some way other than by publication in a statute. If, on the other hand, the plaintiff's claim is doubtful, then the court must, to some extent, surprise one or another of the parties; and if the court decides that on balance the plaintiff's argument is stronger, then it will also decide that the plaintiff was, on balance, more justified in his expectations. The court may, of course, be mistaken in this conclusion; but that possibility is not a consequence of the originality of its argument, for there is no reason to suppose that a court hampered by the requirement that its decisions be unoriginal will make fewer mistakes of principle than a court that is not.

C. Jurisprudence

We have, therefore, in these political considerations, a strong reason to consider more carefully whether judicial arguments cannot be understood, even in hard cases, as arguments generated by principle. We have an additional reason in a familiar problem of jurisprudence. Lawyers believe that when judges make new law their decisions are constrained by legal traditions but are nevertheless personal and original. Novel decisions, it is said, reflect a judge's own political morality, but also reflect the morality that is embedded in the traditions of the common law, which might well be different. This is, of course, only law school rhetoric, but it nevertheless poses the problem of explaining how these different contributions to the decision of a hard case are to be identified and reconciled.

One popular solution relies on a spatial image; it says that the traditions of the common law contract the area of a judge's discretion to rely upon his personal morality, but do not entirely eliminate that area. But this answer is unsatisfactory on two grounds. First, it does not elucidate what is at best a provocative metaphor, which is that some morality is embedded in a mass of particular decisions other judges have reached in the past. Second, it suggests a plainly inadequate phenomenological account of the judicial decision. Judges do not decide hard cases in two stages, first checking to see where the institutional constraints end, and then setting the books aside to stride off on their own. The institutional constraints they sense are pervasive and endure to the decision itself. We therefore need an account of the interaction of personal and institutional morality that is less metaphorical and explains more successfully that pervasive interaction.

The rights thesis, that judicial decisions enforce existing political rights, suggests an explanation that is more successful on both counts. If the thesis holds, then institutional history acts not as a constraint on the political judgment of judges but as an ingredient of that judgment, because institutional history is part of the background that any plausible judgment about the rights of an individual must accommodate. Political rights are creatures of both history and morality: what an individual is entitled to have, in civil society, depends upon both the practice and the justice of its political institutions. So the supposed tension between judicial originality and institutional history is dissolved: judges must make fresh judgments about the rights of the parties who come before them, but these political rights reflect, rather than oppose, political decisions of the past. When a judge chooses between the rule established in precedent and some new rule thought to be fairer, he does not choose between history and justice. He rather makes a judgment that requires some compromise between considerations that ordinarily combine in any calculation of political right, but here compete.

The rights thesis therefore provides a more satisfactory explanation of how judges use precedent in hard cases than the explanation provided by any theory that gives a more prominent place to policy. Judges, like all political officials, are subject to the doctrine of political responsibility. This doctrine states, in its most general form, that political officials must make only such political decisions as they can justify within a political theory that also justifies the other decisions they propose to make. The doctrine seems innocuous in this general form; but it does, even in this form, condemn a style of political administration that might be called, following Rawls, intuitionistic.[4] It condemns the practice of making decisions that seem right in isolation, but cannot be brought within some comprehensive theory of general principles and policies that is consistent with other decisions also thought right. Suppose a Congressman votes to prohibit abortion, on the ground that human life in any form is sacred, but then votes to permit the parents of babies born deformed to withhold medical treatment that will keep such babies alive. He might say that he feels that there is some difference, but the principle of responsibility, strictly applied, will not allow him these two votes unless he can incorporate the difference within some general political theory he sincerely holds.

The doctrine demands, we might say, articulate consistency. But this demand is relatively weak when policies are in play. Policies are aggregative in their influence on political decisions and it need not be part of a responsible strategy for reaching a collective goal that individuals be treated alike. It does not follow from the doctrine of responsibility, therefore, that if the legislature awards a subsidy to one aircraft manufacturer one month it must award a subsidy to another manufacturer the next. In the case of principles, however, the doctrine insists on distributional consistency from one case to the next, because it does not allow for the idea of a strategy that may be better served by unequal distribution of the benefit in question. If an official believes, for example, that sexual liberty of some sort is a right of individuals, then he must protect that liberty in a way that distributes the benefit reasonably equally over the class of those whom he supposes to have the right. If he allows one couple to use contraceptives on the ground that this right would otherwise be invaded, then he must, so long as he does not recant that earlier decision, allow the next couple the same liberty. He cannot say that the first decision gave the community just the amount of sexual liberty it needed, so that no more is required at the time of the second.

Judicial decisions are political decisions, at least in the broad sense that attracts the doctrine of political responsibility. If the rights thesis holds, then the distinction just made would account, at least in a very general way, for the special concern that judges show for both precedents and hypothetical examples. An argument of principle can supply a justification for a particular decision, under the doctrine of responsibility, only if the principle cited can be shown to be consistent with earlier decisions not recanted, and with decisions that the institution is prepared to make in the hypothetical circumstances. That is hardly surprising, but the argument would not hold if judges based their decisions on arguments of policy. They would be free to say that some policy might be adequately served by serving it in the case at bar, providing, for example, just the right subsidy to some troubled industry, so that neither earlier decisions nor hypothetical future decisions need be understood as serving the same policy.

Consistency here, of course, means consistency in the application of the principle relied upon, not merely in the application of the particular rule announced

Ronald Dworkin

[4] *See generally* Dworkin, *The Original Position*, 40 U. CHI. L. REV. 500 (1973).

in the name of that principle. If, for example, the principle that no one has the duty to make good remote or unexpected losses flowing from his negligence is relied upon to justify a decision for the defendant in Spartan Steel, then it must be shown that the rule laid down in other cases, which allows recovery for negligent misstatements, is consistent with that principle; not merely that the rule about negligent misstatements is a different rule from the rule in Spartan Steel.

D. Three Problems

We therefore find, in these arguments of political theory and jurisprudence, some support for the rights thesis in its abstract form. Any further defense, however, must await a more precise statement. The thesis requires development in three directions. It relies, first, on a general distinction between individual rights and social goals, and that distinction must be stated with more clarity than is provided simply by examples. The distinction must be stated, moreover, so as to respond to the following problem. When politicians appeal to individual rights, they have in mind grand propositions about very abstract and fundamental interests, like the right to freedom or equality or respect. These grand rights do not seem apposite to the decision of hard cases at law, except, perhaps, constitutional law; and even when they are apposite they seem too abstract to have much argumentative power. If the rights thesis is to succeed, it must demonstrate how the general distinction between arguments of principle and policy can be maintained between arguments of the character and detail that do figure in legal argument. In Part II of this essay I shall try to show that the distinction between abstract and concrete rights, suitably elaborated, is sufficient for that purpose.

The thesis provides, second, a theory of the role of precedent and institutional history in the decision of hard cases. I summarized that theory in the last section, but it must be expanded and illustrated before it can be tested against our experience of how judges actually decide cases. It must be expanded, moreover, with an eye to the following problem. No one thinks that the law as it stands is perfectly just. Suppose that some line of precedents is in fact unjust, because it refuses to enforce, as a legal right, some political right of the citizens. Even though a judge deciding some hard case disapproves of these precedents for that reason, the doctrine of articulate consistency nevertheless requires that he allow his argument to be affected by them. It might seem that his argument cannot be an argument of principle, that is, an argument designed to establish the political rights of the parties, because the argument is corrupted, through its attention to precedent, by a false opinion about what these rights are. If the thesis is to be defended, it must be shown why this first appearance is wrong. It is not enough to say that the argument may be an argument of principle because it establishes the legal, as distinguished from the political, rights of the litigants. The rights thesis supposes that the right to win a law suit is a genuine political right, and though that right is plainly different from other forms of political rights, like the right of all citizens to be treated as equals, just noticing that difference does not explain why the former right may be altered by misguided earlier decisions. It is necessary, in order to understand that feature of legal argument, to consider the special qualities of institutional rights in general, which I consider in Part III, and the particular qualities of legal rights, as a species of institutional rights, which I consider in Part IV.

But the explanation I give of institutional and legal rights exposes a third and different problem for the rights thesis. This explanation makes plain that judges must sometimes make judgments of political morality in order to decide what the legal rights of litigants are. The thesis may therefore be thought open, on that ground, to the first challenge to judicial originality that I mentioned earlier. It might be said that the thesis is indefensible because it cheats the majority of its right to decide questions of political morality for itself. I shall consider that challenge in Part V.

These, then, are three problems that any full statement of the rights thesis must face. If that full statement shows these objections to the thesis misconceived, then it will show the thesis to be less radical than it might first have seemed. The thesis presents, not some novel information about what judges do, but a new way of describing what we all know they do; and the virtues of this new description are not empirical but political and philosophical.

II. Rights and Goals

A. *Types of Rights*

Arguments of principle are arguments intended to establish an individual right; arguments of policy are arguments intended to establish a collective goal. Principles are propositions that describe rights; policies are propositions that describe goals. But what are rights and goals and what is the difference? It is hard to supply any definition that does not beg the question. It seems natural to say, for example, that freedom of speech is a right, not a goal, because citizens are entitled to that freedom as a matter of political morality, and that increased munitions manufacture is a goal, not a right, because it contributes to collective welfare, but no particular manufacturer is entitled to a government contract. This does not improve our understanding, however, because the concept of entitlement uses rather than explains the concept of a right.

In this essay I shall distinguish rights from goals by fixing on the distributional character of claims about rights, and on the force of these claims, in political argument, against competing claims of a different distributional character. I shall make, that is, a formal distinction that does not attempt to show which rights men and women actually have, or indeed that they have any at all. It rather provides a guide for discovering which rights a particular political theory supposes men and women to have. The formal distinction does suggest, of course, an approach to the more fundamental question: it suggests that we discover what rights people actually have by looking for arguments that would justify claims having the appropriate distributional character. But the distinction does not itself supply any such arguments.

I begin with the idea of a political aim as a generic political justification. A political theory takes a certain state of affairs as a political aim if, for that theory, it counts in favor of any political decision that the decision is likely to advance, or to protect, that state of affairs, and counts against the decision that it will retard or endanger it. A political right is an individuated political aim. An individual has a right to some opportunity or resource or liberty if it counts in favor of a political decision that the decision is likely to advance or protect the state of affairs in which he enjoys the right, even when no other political aim is served and some political aim is disserved thereby, and counts against that decision that it will retard or endanger that state of affairs, even when some other political aim is thereby served.[5] A goal is a nonindividuated political aim, that is, a state of affairs whose specification does not in this way call for any particular opportunity or resource or liberty for particular individuals.

Collective goals encourage trade-offs of benefits and burdens within a community in order to produce some overall benefit for the community as a whole. Economic efficiency is a collective goal: it calls for such distribution of opportunities and liabilities as will produce the greatest aggregate economic benefit defined in some way. Some conception of equality may also be taken as a collective goal; a community may aim at a distribution such that maximum wealth is no more than double minimum wealth, or, under a different conception, so that no racial or ethnic group is much worse off than other groups. Of course, any collective goal will suggest a particular distribution, given particular facts. Economic efficiency as a goal will suggest that a particular industry be subsidized in some circumstances, but taxed punitively in others. Equality as a goal will suggest immediate and complete redistribution in some circumstances, but partial and discriminatory redistribution in others. In each case distributional principles are subordinate to some conception of aggregate collective good, so that offering less of some benefit to one man can be justified simply by showing that this will lead to a greater benefit overall.

Collective goals may, but need not, be absolute. The community may pursue different goals at the same time, and it may compromise one goal for the sake of another. It may, for example, pursue economic efficiency, but also military strength. The suggested distribution will then be determined by the sum of the two policies, and this will increase the permutations and combinations of possible trade-offs. In any case, these permutations and combinations will offer a number of competing strategies for serving each goal and both goals in combination. Economic efficiency may be well served by offering subsidies to all farmers, and to no manufacturers, and better served by offering double the subsidy to some farmers and none to others. There will be alternate strategies of pursuing any set of collective goals, and, particularly as the number of goals increases, it will be impossible to determine in a piecemeal or case-by-case way the distribution that best serves any set of goals. Whether it is good policy to give double subsidies to some farmers and none to others will depend upon a great number of other political decisions that have been or will be made in pursuit of very general strategies into which this particular decision must fit.

Rights also may be absolute: a political theory which holds a right to freedom of speech as absolute will recognize no reason for not securing the liberty it requires for every individual; no reason, that is, short of impossibility. Rights may also be less than absolute; one principle might have to yield to another, or even to an urgent policy with which it competes on particular facts. We may define the weight of a right, assuming it is not absolute, as its power to withstand such competition. It follows from the definition of a right that it cannot be outweighed by all social goals. We might, for simplicity, stipulate not to call any political aim a right unless it has a certain threshold weight against collective goals in general; unless, for example, it cannot be defeated by appeal to any of the ordinary, routine goals of political administration, but only by a goal of special urgency.

---

[5] I count legal persons as individuals, so that corporations may have rights; a political theory that counts special groups, like racial groups, as having some corporate standing within the community may therefore speak of group rights.

Suppose, for example, some man says he recognizes the right of free speech, but adds that free speech must yield whenever its exercise would inconvenience the public. He means, I take it, that he recognizes the pervasive goal of collective welfare, and only such distribution of liberty of speech as that collective goal recommends in particular circumstances. His political position is exhausted by the collective goal; the putative right adds nothing and there is no point to recognizing it as a right at all.

These definitions and distinctions make plain that the character of a political aim—its standing as a right or goal—depends upon its place and function within a single political theory. The same phrase might describe a right within one theory and a goal within another, or a right that is absolute or powerful within one theory but relatively weak within another. If a public official has anything like a coherent political theory that he uses, even intuitively, to justify the particular decisions he reaches, then this theory will recognize a wide variety of different types of rights, arranged in some way that assigns rough relative weight to each.

Any adequate theory will distinguish, for example, between background rights, which are rights that provide a justification for political decisions by society in the abstract, and institutional rights, that provide a justification for a decision by some particular and specified political institution. Suppose that my political theory provides that every man has a right to the property of another if he needs it more. I might yet concede that he does not have a legislative right to the same effect; I might concede, that is, that he has no institutional right that the present legislature enact legislation that would violate the Constitution, as such a statute presumably would. I might also concede that he has no institutional right to a judicial decision condoning theft. Even if I did make these concessions, I could preserve my initial background claim by arguing that the people as a whole would be justified in amending the Constitution to abolish property, or perhaps in rebelling and overthrowing the present form of government entirely. I would claim that each man has a residual background right that would justify or require these acts, even though I concede that he does not have the right to specific institutional decisions as these institutions are now constituted.

Any adequate theory will also make use of a distinction between abstract and concrete rights, and therefore between abstract and concrete principles. This is a distinction of degree, but I shall discuss relatively clear examples at two poles of the scale it contemplates, and therefore treat it as a distinction in kind. An abstract right is a general political aim the statement of which does not indicate how that general aim is to be weighed or compromised in particular circumstances against other political aims. The grand rights of political rhetoric are in this way abstract. Politicians speak of a right to free speech or dignity or equality, with no suggestion that these rights are absolute, but with no attempt to suggest their impact on particular complex social situations.

Concrete rights, on the other hand, are political aims that are more precisely defined so as to express more definitely the weight they have against other political aims on particular occasions. Suppose I say, not simply that citizens have a right to free speech, but that a newspaper has a right to publish defense plans classified as secret provided this publication will not create an immediate physical danger to troops. My principle declares for a particular resolution of the conflict it acknowledges between the abstract right of free speech, on the one hand, and competing rights of soldiers to security or the urgent needs of defense on the other. Abstract rights in this way provide arguments for concrete rights, but the claim of a concrete right is more definitive than any claim of abstract right that supports it.[6]

B. *Principles and Utility*

The distinction between rights and goals does not deny a thesis that is part of popular moral anthropology. It may be entirely reasonable to think, as this thesis provides, that the principles the members of a particular community find persuasive will be causally determined by the collective goals of that community. If many people in a community believe that each individual has a right to some minimal concern on the part of others, then this fact may be explained, as a matter of cultural history, by the further fact that their collective welfare is advanced by that belief. If some novel arrangement of rights would serve their collective welfare better, then we should expect, according to this thesis, that in due time their moral convictions will alter in favor of that new arrangement.

I do not know how far this anthropological theory holds in our own society, or any society. It is certainly untestable in anything like the simple form in which I have put it, and I do not see why its claim, that rights are psychologically or culturally determined by goals, is a priori more plausible that the contrary claim. Perhaps men and women choose collective goals to accommodate some prior sense of individual rights, rather than delineating rights according to collective goals. In either case, however, there must be an important time lag, so that at any given time most people will recognize the conflict between rights and goals, at least in particular cases, that the general distinction between these two kinds of political aims presupposes.

The distinction presupposes, that is, a further distinction between the force of a particular right within a political theory and the causal explanation of why the theory provides that right. This is a formal way of putting the point, and it is appropriate only when, as I am now supposing, we can identify a particular political theory and so distinguish the analytical question of what it provides from the historical question of how it came to provide it. The distinction is therefore obscured when we speak of the morality of a community without specifying which of the many different conceptions of a community morality we have in mind. Without some further specification we cannot construct even a vague or abstract political theory as the theory of the community at any particular time, and so we cannot make the distinction between reasons and force that is analytically

---

[6] A complete political theory must also recognize two other distinctions that I use implicitly in this essay. The first is the distinction between rights against the state and rights against fellow citizens. The former justify a political decision that requires some agency of the government to act; the latter justify a decision to coerce particular individuals. The right to minimum housing, if accepted at all, is accepted as a right against the state. The right to recover damages for a breach of contract, or to be saved from great danger at minimum risk of a rescuer, is a right against fellow citizens. The right to free speech is, ordinarily, both. It seems strange to define the rights that citizens have against one another as political rights at all; but we are now concerned with such rights only insofar as they justify political decisions of different sorts. The present distinction cuts across the distinction between background and institutional rights; the latter distinguishes among persons or institutions that must make a political decision, the former between persons or institutions whom that decision directs to act or forbear. Ordinary civil cases at law, which are the principal subject of this essay, involve rights against fellow citizens; but I also discuss certain issues of constitutional and criminal law and so touch on rights against the state as well.

The second distinction is between universal and special rights; that is, between rights that a political theory provides for all individuals in the community, with exceptions only for phenomena like incapacity or punishment, and rights it provides for only one section of the community, or possibly only one member. I shall assume, in this essay, that all political rights are universal.

necessary to understand the concepts of principle and policy. We are therefore prey to the argument that the anthropological thesis destroys the distinction between the two; we speak as if we had some coherent theory in mind, as the community's morality, but we deny that it distinguishes principle from policy on the basis of an argument that seems plausible just because we do not have any particular theory in mind. Once we do make plain what we intend by some reference to the morality of a community, and proceed to identify, even crudely, what we take the principles of that morality to be, the anthropological argument is tamed.

There are political theories, however, that unite rights and goals not causally but by making the force of a right contingent upon its power, as a right, to promote some collective goal. I have in mind various forms of the ethical theory called rule utilitarianism. One popular form of that theory, for example, holds that an act is right if the general acceptance of a rule requiring that act would improve the average welfare of members of the community.[7] A political theory might provide for a right to free speech, for example, on the hypothesis that the general acceptance of that right by courts and other political institutions would promote the highest average utility of the community in the long run.

But we may nevertheless distinguish institutional rights, at least, from collective goals within such a theory. If the theory provides that an official of a particular institution is justified in making a political decision, and not justified in refusing to make it, whenever that decision is necessary to protect the freedom to speak of any individual, without regard to the impact of the decision on collective goals, the theory provides free speech as a right. It does not matter that the theory stipulates this right on the hypothesis that if all political institutions do enforce the right in that way an important collective goal will in fact be promoted. What is important is the commitment to a scheme of government that makes an appeal to the right decisive in particular cases.

So neither the anthropological thesis nor rule utilitarianism offers any objection to the distinction between arguments of principle and arguments of policy. I should mention, out of an abundance of caution, one further possible challenge to that distinction. Different arguments of principle and policy can often be made in support of the same political decision. Suppose that an official wishes to argue in favor of racial segregation in public places. He may offer the policy argument that mixing races causes more overall discomfort than satisfaction. Or he may offer an argument of principle appealing to the rights of those who might be killed or maimed in riots that desegregation would produce. It might be thought that the substitutibility of these arguments defeats the distinction between arguments of principle and policy, or in any case makes the distinction less useful, for the following reason. Suppose it is conceded that the right to equality between races is sufficiently strong that it must prevail over all but the most pressing argument of policy, and be compromised only as required by competing arguments of principle. That would be an empty concession if arguments of principle could always be found to substitute for an argument of policy that might otherwise be made.

But it is a fallacy to suppose that because some argument of principle can always be found to substitute for an argument of policy, it will be as cogent or as powerful as the appropriate argument of policy would have been. If some minority's claim to an antidiscrimination statute were itself based on policy, and could

Ronald Dworkin

[7] See Brandt, *Toward a Credible Form of Utilitarianism*, in MORALITY AND THE LANGUAGE OF CONDUCT 107 (H. Castenada and G. Nakhnikian, eds. 1963).

therefore be defeated by an appeal to overall general welfare or utility, then the argument that cites the majority's discomfort or annoyance might well be powerful enough. But if the claim cites a right to equality that must prevail unless matched by a competing argument of principle, the only such argument available may be, as here, simply too weak. Except in extraordinary cases, the danger to any particular man's life that flows from desegregation adequately managed and policed will be very small. We might therefore concede that the competing right to life offers some argument countervailing against the right to equality here, and yet maintain that that argument is of negligible weight; strong enough, perhaps to slow the pace of desegregation but not strong enough even to slow it very much.

C. Economics and Principle

The rights thesis, in its descriptive aspect, holds that judicial decisions in hard cases are characteristically generated by principle not policy. Recent research into the connections between economic theory and the common law might be thought to suggest the contrary: that judges almost always decide on grounds of policy rather than principle. We must, however, be careful to distinguish between two propositions said to be established by that research. It is argued, first, that almost every rule developed by judges in such disparate fields as tort, contract and property can be shown to serve the collective goal of making resource allocation more efficient.[8] It is argued, second, that in certain cases judges explicitly base their decisions on economic policy.[9] Neither of these claims subverts the rights thesis.

The first claim makes no reference to the intentions of the judges who decided the cases establishing rules that improve economic efficiency. It does not suppose that these judges were aware of the economic value of their rules, or even that they would have acknowledged that value as an argument in favor of their decisions. The evidence, for the most part, suggests the contrary. The courts that nourished the unfortunate fellow-servant doctrine, for example, thought that the rule was required by fairness, not utility, and when the rule was abolished it was because the argument from fairness, not the argument from utility, was found wanting by a different generation of lawyers.[10]

If this first claim is sound, it might seem to some an important piece of evidence for the anthropological thesis described in the last section. They will think that it suggests that judges and lawyers, reflecting the general moral attitudes of their time, thought that corporations and individuals had just those rights that an explicit rule utilitarian would legislate to serve the general welfare. But the first claim might equally well suggest the contrary conclusion I mentioned, that our present ideas of general welfare reflect our ideas of individual right. Professor Posner, for example, argues for that claim by presupposing a particular conception of efficient resource allocation. He says that the value of some scarce resource to a particular individual is measured by the amount of money he is willing to pay for it, so that community welfare is maximized when each resource is in the hands of someone who would pay more than anyone else to have it.[11] But that is hardly a self-evident or neutral conception of value. It is congenial to a political theory that celebrates competition, but far less congenial to a more egalitarian

---

[8] See, e.g., R. POSNER, ECONOMIC ANALYSIS OF LAW 10–104 (1972).

[9] See, e.g., Coase, The Problem of Social Cost, 3 J. LAW & ECON. 1, 19–28 (1960).

[10] See Posner, A Theory of Negligence, 1 J. LEGAL STUD. 29, 71 (1972).

[11] R. POSNER, supra note 8, at 4.

theory, because it demotes the claims of the poor who are willing to spend less because they have less to spend. Posner's conception of value, therefore, seems as much the consequence as the cause of a theory of individual rights. In any case, however, the anthropological thesis of the first claim offers no threat to the rights thesis. Even if we concede that a judge's theory of rights is determined by some instinctive sense of economic value, rather than the other way about, we may still argue that he relies on that theory, and not economic analysis, to justify decisions in hard cases.

The second claim we distinguished, however, may seem to present a more serious challenge. If judges explicitly refer to economic policy in some cases, then these cases cannot be understood simply as evidence for the anthropological thesis. Learned Hand's theory of negligence is the most familiar example of this explicit reference to economics. He said, roughly, that the test of whether the defendant's act was unreasonable, and therefore actionable, is the economic test which asks whether the defendant could have avoided the accident at less cost to himself than the plaintiff was likely to suffer if the accident occurred, discounted by the improbability of the accident.[12] It may be said that this economic test provides an argument of policy rather than principle, because it makes the decision turn on whether the collective welfare would have been advanced more by allowing the accident to take place or by spending what was necessary to avoid it. If so, then cases in which some test like Hand's is explicitly used, however few they might be, would stand as counterexamples to the rights thesis.

But the assumption that an economic calculation of any sort must be an argument of policy overlooks the distinction between abstract and concrete rights. Abstract rights, like the right to speak on political matters, take no account of competing rights; concrete rights, on the other hand, reflect the impact of such competition. In certain kinds of cases the argument from competing abstract principles to a concrete right can be made in the language of economics. Consider the principle that each member of a community has a right that each other member treat him with the minimal respect due a fellow human being.[13] That is a very abstract principle: it demands some balance, in particular cases, between the interests of those to be protected and the liberty of those from whom the principle demands an unstated level of concern and respect. It is natural, particularly when economic vocabulary is in fashion, to define the proper balance by comparing the sum of the utilities of these two parties under different conditions. If one man acts in a way that he can foresee will injure another so that the collective utility of the pair will be sharply reduced by his act, he does not show the requisite care and concern. If he can guard or insure against the injury much more cheaply or effectively than the other can, for example, then he does not show care and concern unless he takes these precautions or arranges that insurance.

That character of argument is by no means novel, though perhaps its economic dress is. Philosophers have for a long time debated hypothetical cases testing the level of concern that one member of a community owes to another. If one man is

[12] United States v. Carroll Towing Co., 159 F.2d 169, 173 (2d Cir. 1947). Coase, *supra* note 9, at 22–23, gives other examples, mostly of nuisance cases interpreting the doctrine that a "reasonable" interference with the plaintiff's use of his property is not a nuisance.

[13] A more elaborate argument of principle might provide a better justification for Hand's test than does this simple principle. I described a more elaborate argument in a set of Rosenthal Lectures delivered at Northwestern University Law School in March, 1975. The simple principle, however, provides a sufficiently good justification for the present point.

drowning, and another may save him at minimal risk to himself, for example, then the first has a moral right to be saved by the second. That proposition might easily be put in economic form: if the collective utility of the pair is very sharply improved by a rescue, then the drowning man has a right to that rescue and the rescuer a duty to make it. The parallel legal proposition may, of course, be much more complex than that. It may specify special circumstances in which the crucial question is not whether the collective utility of the pair will be sharply advanced, but only whether it will be marginally advanced. It might put the latter question, for example, when one man's positive act, as distinct from a failure to act, creates a risk of direct and foreseeable physical injury to the person or property of another. If the rights thesis is sound, of course, then no judge may appeal to that legal proposition unless he believes that the principle of minimal respect states an abstract legal right; but if he does, then he may cast his argument in economic form without thereby changing its character from principle to policy.

Since Hand's test, and the parallel argument about rescuing a drowning man, are methods of compromising competing rights, they consider only the welfare of those whose abstract rights are at stake. They do not provide room for costs or benefits to the community at large, except as these are reflected in the welfare of those whose rights are in question. We can easily imagine an argument that does not concede these restrictions. Suppose someone argued that the principle requiring rescue at minimal risk should be amended so as to make the decision turn, not on some function of the collective utilities of the victim and rescuer, but on marginal utility to the community as a whole, so that the rescuer must take into account not only the relative risks to himself and the victim, but the relative social importance of the two. It might follow that an insignificant man must risk his life to save a bank president, but that a bank president need not even tire himself to save a nobody. The argument is no longer an argument of principle, because it supposes the victim to have a right to nothing but his expectations under general utility. Hand's formula, and more sophisticated variations, are not arguments of that character; they do not subordinate an individual right to some collective goal, but provide a mechanism for compromising competing claims of abstract right.

Negligence cases are not the only cases in which judges compromise abstract rights in defining concrete ones. If a judge appeals to public safety or the scarcity of some vital resource, for example, as a ground for limiting some abstract right, then his appeal might be understood as an appeal to the competing rights of those whose security will be sacrificed, or whose just share of that resource will be threatened if the abstract right is made concrete. His argument is an argument of principle if it respects the distributional requirements of such arguments, and if it observes the restriction mentioned in the last section: that the weight of a competing principle may be less than the weight of the appropriate parallel policy. We find a different sort of example in the familiar argument that certain sorts of law suits should not be allowed because to do so would "swamp" the courts with litigation. The court supposes that if it were to allow that type of suit it would lack the time to consider promptly enough other law suits aiming to vindicate rights that are, taken together, more important than the rights it therefore proposes to bar.

This is an appropriate point to notice a certain limitation of the rights thesis. It holds in standard civil cases, when the ruling assumption is that one of the parties has a right to win; but it holds only asymmetrically when that assumption cannot be made. The accused in a criminal case has a right to a decision in his favor if he is innocent, but the state has no parallel right to a conviction if he is guilty. The court may therefore find in favor of the accused, in some hard case testing rules of evidence, for example, on an argument of policy that does not suppose that the accused has any right to be acquitted. The Supreme Court in Linkletter v. Walker[14] said that its earlier decision in Mapp v. Ohio[15] was such a decision. The Court said it had changed the rules permitting the introduction of illegally obtained evidence, not because Miss Mapp had any right that such evidence not be used if otherwise admissible, but in order to deter policemen from collecting such evidence in the future. I do not mean that a constitutional decision on such grounds is proper, or even that the Court's later description of its earlier decision was accurate. I mean only to point out how the geometry of a criminal prosecution, which does not set opposing rights in a case against one another, differs from the standard civil case in which the rights thesis holds symmetrically.

III. INSTITUTIONAL RIGHTS

The rights thesis provides that judges decide hard cases by confirming or denying concrete rights. But the concrete rights upon which judges rely must have two other characteristics. They must be institutional rather than background rights, and they must be legal rather than some other form of institutional rights. We cannot appreciate or test the thesis, therefore, without further elaboration of these distinctions.

Institutional rights may be found in institutions of very different character. A chess player has a "chess" right to be awarded a point in a tournament if he checkmates an opponent. A citizen in a democracy has a legislative right to the enactment of statutes necessary to protect his free speech. In the case of chess, institutional rights are fixed by constitutive and regulative rules that belong distinctly to the game, or to a particular tournament. Chess is, in this sense, an autonomous institution; I mean that it is understood, among its participants, that no one may claim an institutional right by direct appeal to general morality. No one may argue, for example, that he has earned the right to be declared the winner by his general virtue. But legislation is only partly autonomous in that sense. There are special constitutive and regulative rules that define what a legislature is, and who belongs to it, and how it votes, and that it may not establish a religion. But these rules belonging distinctly to legislation are rarely sufficient to determine whether a citizen has an institutional right to have a certain statute enacted; they do not decide, for example, whether he has a right to minimum wage legislation. Citizens are expected to repair to general considerations of political morality when they argue for such rights.

The fact that some institutions are fully and others partly autonomous has the consequence mentioned earlier, that the institutional rights a political theory acknowledges may diverge from the background rights it provides. Institutional rights are nevertheless genuine rights. Even if we suppose that the poor have an abstract background right to money taken from the rich, it would be wrong, not merely unexpected, for the referees of a chess tournament to award the prize money to the poorest contestant rather than the contestant with the most points. It would provide no excuse to say that since tournament rights merely describe

Ronald Dworkin

[14] 381 U.S. 618 (1965).
[15] 367 U.S. 643 (1961).

the conditions necessary for calling the tournament a chess tournament, the referee's act is justified so long as he does not use the word "chess" when he hands out the award. The participants entered the tournament with the understanding that chess rules would apply; they have genuine rights to the enforcement of these rules and no others.

Institutional autonomy insulates an official's institutional duty from the greater part of background political morality. But how far does the force of this insulation extend? Even in the case of a fully insulated institution like chess some rules will require interpretation or elaboration before an official may enforce them in certain circumstances. Suppose some rule of a chess tournament provides that the referee shall declare a game forfeit if one player "unreasonably" annoys the other in the course of play. The language of the rule does not define what counts as "unreasonable" annoyance; it does not decide whether, for example, a player who continually smiles at his opponent in such a way as to unnerve him, as the Russian grandmaster Tal once smiled at Fischer, annoys him unreasonably.

The referee is not free to give effect to his background convictions in deciding this hard case. He might hold, as a matter of political theory, that individuals have a right to equal welfare without regard to intellectual abilities. It would nevertheless be wrong for him to rely upon that conviction in deciding difficult cases under the forfeiture rule. He could not say, for example, that annoying behavior is reasonable so long as it has the effect of reducing the importance of intellectual ability in deciding who will win the game. The participants, and the general community that is interested, will say that his duty is just the contrary. Since chess is an intellectual game, he must apply the forfeiture rule in such a way as to protect, rather than jeopardize, the role of intellect in the contest.

We have, then, in the case of the chess referee, an example of an official whose decisions about institutional rights are understood to be governed by institutional constraints even when the force of these constraints is not clear. We do not think that he is free to legislate interstitially within the "open texture" of imprecise rules.[16] If one interpretation of the forfeiture rule will protect the character of the game, and another will not, then the participants have a right to the first interpretation. We may hope to find, in this relatively simple case, some general feature of institutional rights in hard cases that will bear on the decision of a judge in a hard case at law.

I said that the game of chess has a character that the referee's decisions must respect. What does that mean? How does a referee know that chess is an intellectual game rather than a game of chance or an exhibition of digital ballet? He may well start with what everyone knows. Every institution is placed by its participants in some very rough category of institution; it is taken to be a game rather than a religious ceremony or a form of exercise or a political process. It is, for that reason, definitional of chess that it is a game rather than an exercise in digital skill. These conventions, exhibited in attitudes and manners and in history, are decisive. If everyone takes chess to be a game of chance, so that they curse their luck and nothing else when a piece *en prise* happens to be taken, then chess is a game of chance, though a very bad one.

But these conventions will run out, and they may run out before the referee finds enough to decide the case of Tal's smile. It is important to see, however, that the conventions run out in a particular way. They are not incomplete, like a book

---

[16] *See generally* H.L.A. HART, THE CONCEPT OF LAW 121–32 (1961).

whose last page is missing, but abstract, so that their full force can be captured in a concept that admits of different conceptions; that is, in a contested concept.[17] The referee must select one or another of these conceptions, not to supplement the convention, but to enforce it. He must construct the game's character by putting to himself different sets of questions. Given that chess is an intellectual game, is it, like poker, intellectual in some sense that includes ability at psychological intimidation? Or is it, like mathematics, intellectual in some sense that does not include that ability? This first set of questions asks him to look more closely at the game, to determine whether its features support one rather than the other of these conceptions of intellect. But he must also ask a different set of questions. Given that chess is an intellectual game of some sort, what follows about reasonable behavior in a chess game? Is ability at psychological intimidation, or ability to resist such intimidation, really an intellectual quality? These questions ask him to look more closely at the concept of intellect itself.

The referee's calculations, if they are self-conscious, will oscillate between these two sets of questions, progressively narrowing the questions to be asked at the next stage. He might first identify, by reflecting on the concept, different conceptions of intellect. He might suppose at this first stage, for example, that physical grace of the sort achieved in ballet is one form of intelligence. But he must then test these different conceptions against the rules and practices of the game. That test will rule out any physical conception of intelligence. But it may not discriminate between a conception that includes or a conception that rejects psychological intimidation, because either of these conceptions would provide an account of the rules and practices that is not plainly superior, according to any general canons of explanation, to the account provided by the other. He must then ask himself which of these two accounts offers a deeper or more successful account of what intellect really is. His calculations, so conceived, oscillate between philosophy of mind and the facts of the institution whose character he must elucidate.

This is, of course, only a fanciful reconstruction of a calculation that will never take place; any official's sense of the game will have developed over a career, and he will employ rather than expose that sense in his judgments. But the reconstruction enables us to see how the concept of the game's character is tailored to a special institutional problem. Once an autonomous institution is established, such that participants have institutional rights under distinct rules belonging to that institution, then hard cases may arise that must, in the nature of the case, be supposed to have an answer. If Tal does not have a right that the game be continued, it must be because the forfeiture rule, properly understood, justifies the referee's intervention; if it does, then Fischer has a right to win at once. It is not useful to speak of the referee's "discretion" in such a case. If some weak sense of discretion is meant, then the remark is unhelpful; if some strong sense is meant, such that Tal no longer has a right to win, then this must be, again, because the rule properly understood destroys the right he would otherwise have.[18] Suppose we say that in such a case all the parties have a right to expect is that the referee will use his best judgment. That is, in a sense, perfectly true, because they can have no more, by way of the referee's judgment, than his best judgment. But they are

[17] See Gallie, *Essentially Contested Concepts*, 56 PROCEEDINGS OF THE ARISTOTELIAN SOCIETY 167, 167–68 (1955–56). *See also* Dworkin, *The Jurisprudence of Richard Nixon*, NEW YORK REVIEW OF BOOKS, May 4, 1972, at 27.

[18] *See* Dworkin, *The Model of Rules*, 35 U. CHI. L. REV. 14, 32–40 (1967).

nevertheless entitled to his best judgment about which behavior is, in the circumstances of the game, unreasonable; they are entitled, that is, to his best judgment about what their rights are. The proposition that there is some "right" answer to that question does not mean that the rules of chess are exhaustive and unambiguous; rather it is a complex statement about the responsibilities of its officials and participants.

But if the decision in a hard case must be a decision about the rights of the parties, then an official's reason for that judgment must be the sort of reason that justifies recognizing or denying a right. He must bring to his decision a general theory of why, in the case of his institution, the rules create or destroy any rights at all, and he must show what decision that general theory requires in the hard case. In chess the general ground of institutional rights must be the tacit consent or understanding of the parties. They consent, in entering a chess tournament, to the enforcement of certain and only those rules, and it is hard to imagine any other general ground for supposing that they have any institutional rights. But if that is so, and if the decision in a hard case is a decision about which rights they actually have, then the argument for the decision must apply that general ground to the hard case.

The hard case puts, we might say, a question of political theory. It asks what it is fair to suppose that the players have done in consenting to the forfeiture rule. The concept of a game's character is a conceptual device for framing that question. It is a contested concept that internalizes the general justification of the institution so as to make it available for discriminations within the institution itself. It supposes that a player consents not simply to a set of rules, but to an enterprise that may be said to have a character of its own; so that when the question is put—To what did he consent in consenting to that?—the answer may study the enterprise as a whole and not just the rules.

IV. LEGAL RIGHTS

A. *Legislation*

Legal argument, in hard cases, turns on contested concepts whose nature and function are very much like the concept of the character of a game. These include several of the substantive concepts through which the law is stated, like the concepts of a contract and of property. But they also include two concepts of much greater relevance to the present argument. The first is the idea of the "intention" or "purpose" of a particular statute or statutory clause. This concept provides a bridge between the political justification of the general idea that statutes create rights and those hard cases that ask what rights a particular statute has created. The second is the concept of principles that "underlie" or are "embedded in" the positive rules of law. This concept provides a bridge between the political justification of the doctrine that like cases should be decided alike and those hard cases in which it is unclear what that general doctrine requires. These concepts together define legal rights as a function, though a very special function, of political rights. If a judge accepts the settled practices of his legal system—if he accepts, that is, the autonomy provided by its distinct constitutive and regulative rules—then he must, according to the doctrine of political responsibility, accept some general political theory that justifies these practices. The concepts of legislative purpose and common law principles are devices for applying that general political theory to controversial issues about legal rights.

We might therefore do well to consider how a philosophical judge might develop, in appropriate cases, theories of what legislative purpose and legal principles require. We shall find that he would construct these theories in the same manner as a philosophical referee would construct the character of a game. I have invented, for this purpose, a lawyer of superhuman skill, learning, patience and acumen, whom I shall call Hercules. I suppose that Hercules is a judge in some representative American jurisdiction. I assume that he accepts the main uncontroversial constitutive and regulative rules of the law in his jurisdiction. He accepts, that is, that statutes have the general power to create and extinguish legal rights, and that judges have the general duty to follow earlier decisions of their court or higher courts whose rationale, as lawyers say, extends to the case at bar.

I. The Constitution. Suppose there is a written constitution in Hercules' jurisdiction which provides that no law shall be valid if it establishes a religion. The legislature passes a law purporting to grant free busing to children in parochial schools. Does the grant establish a religion?[19] The words of the constitutional provision might support either view. Hercules must nevertheless decide whether the child who appears before him has a right to her bus ride.

He might begin by asking why the constitution has any power at all to create or destroy rights. If citizens have a background right to salvation through an established church, as many believe they do, then this must be an important right. Why does the fact that a group of men voted otherwise several centuries ago prevent this background right from being made a legal right as well? His answer must take some form such as this. The constitution sets out a general political scheme that is sufficiently just to be taken as settled for reasons of fairness. Citizens take the benefit of living in a society whose institutions are arranged and governed in accordance with that scheme, and they must take the burdens as well, at least until a new scheme is put into force either by discrete amendment or general revolution. But Hercules must then ask just what scheme of principles has been settled. He must construct, that is, a constitutional theory; since he is Hercules we may suppose that he can develop a full political theory that justifies the constitution as a whole. It must be a scheme that fits the particular rules of this constitution, of course. It cannot include a powerful background right to an established church. But more than one fully specified theory may fit the specific provision about religion sufficiently well. One theory might provide, for example, that it is wrong for the government to enact any legislation that will cause great social tension or disorder; so that, since the establishment of a church will have that effect, it is wrong to empower the legislature to establish one. Another theory will provide a background right to religious liberty, and therefore argue that an established church is wrong, not because it will be socially disruptive, but because it violates that background right. In that case Hercules must turn to the remaining constitutional rules and settled practices under these rules to see which of these two theories provides a smoother fit with the constitutional scheme as a whole.

But the theory that is superior under this test will nevertheless be insufficiently concrete to decide some cases. Suppose Hercules decides that the establishment provision is justified by a right to religious liberty rather than any goal of social

[19] *See* Everson v. Board of Educ., 330 U.S. 1 (1947).

order. It remains to ask what, more precisely, religious liberty is. Does a right to religious liberty include the right not to have one's taxes used for any purpose that helps a religion to survive? Or simply not to have one's taxes used to benefit one religion at the expense of another? If the former, then the free transportation legislation violates that right, but if the latter it does not. The institutional structure of rules and practice may not be sufficiently detailed to rule out either of these two conceptions of religious liberty, or to make one a plainly superior justification of that structure. At some point in his career Hercules must therefore consider the question not just as an issue of fit between a theory and the rules of the institution, but as an issue of political philosophy as well. He must decide which conception is a more satisfactory elaboration of the general idea of religious liberty. He must decide that question because he cannot otherwise carry far enough the project he began. He cannot answer in sufficient detail the question of what political scheme the constitution establishes.

So Hercules is driven, by this project, to a process of reasoning that is much like the process of the self-conscious chess referee. He must develop a theory of the constitution, in the shape of a complex set of principles and policies that justify that scheme of government, just as the chess referee is driven to develop a theory about the character of his game. He must develop that theory by referring alternately to political philosophy and institutional detail. He must generate possible theories justifying different aspects of the scheme and test the theories against the broader institution. When the discriminating power of that test is exhausted, he must elaborate the contested concepts that the successful theory employs.

2. *Statutes.* A statute in Hercules' jurisdiction provides that it is a federal crime for someone knowingly to transport in interstate commerce "any person who shall have been unlawfully seized, confined, inveigled, decoyed, kidnapped, abducted, or carried away by any means whatsoever. . . . "Hercules is asked to decide whether this statute makes a federal criminal of a man who persuaded a young girl that it was her religious duty to run away with him, in violation of a court order, to consummate what he called a celestial marriage.[20] The statute had been passed after a famous kidnapping case, in order to enable federal authorities to join in the pursuit of kidnappers. But its words are sufficiently broad to apply to this case, and there is nothing in the legislative record or accompanying committee reports that says they do not.

Do they apply? Hercules might himself despise celestial marriage, or abhor the corruption of minors, or celebrate the obedience of children to their parents. The groom nevertheless has a right to his liberty, unless the statute properly understood deprives him of that right; it is inconsistent with any plausible theory of the constitution that judges have the power retroactively to make conduct criminal. Does the statute deprive him of that right? Hercules must begin by asking why any statute has the power to alter legal rights. He will find the answer in his constitutional theory: this might provide, for example, that a democratically elected legislature is the appropriate body to make collective decisions about the conduct that shall be criminal. But that same constitutional theory will impose on the legislature certain responsibilities: it will impose not only constraints reflecting individual rights, but also some general duty to pursue collective goals defining the

---

[20] *See* Chatwin v. United States, 326 U.S. 455 (1946).

public welfare. That fact provides a useful test for Hercules in this hard case. He might ask which interpretation more satisfactorily ties the language the legislature used to its constitutional responsibilities. That is like the referee's question about the character of a game. It calls for the construction, not of some hypotheses about the mental state of particular legislators, but of a special political theory that justifies this statute, in the light of the legislature's more general responsibilities, better than any alternative theory.[21]

Which arguments of principle and policy might properly have persuaded the legislature to enact just that statute? It should not have pursued a policy designed to replace state criminal enforcement by federal enforcement whenever constitutionally possible. That would represent an unnecessary interference with the principle of federalism that must be part of Hercules' constitutional theory. It might, however, responsibly have followed a policy of selecting for federal enforcement all crimes with such an interstate character that state enforcement was hampered. Or it could responsibly have selected just specially dangerous or widespread crimes of that character. Which of these two responsible policies offers a better justification of the statute actually drafted? If the penalties provided by the statute are large, and therefore appropriate to the latter but not the former policy, the latter policy must be preferred. Which of the different interpretations of the statute permitted by the language serves that policy better? Plainly a decision that inveiglement of the sort presented by the case is not made a federal crime by the statute.

I have described a simple and perhaps unrepresentative problem of statutory interpretation, because I cannot now develop a theory of statutory interpretation in any detail. I want only to suggest how the general claim, that calculations judges make about the purposes of statutes are calculations about political rights, might be defended. There are, however, two points that must be noticed about even this simple example. It would be inaccurate, first, to say that Hercules supplemented what the legislature did in enacting the statute, or that he tried to determine what it would have done if it had been aware of the problem presented by the case. The act of a legislature is not, as these descriptions suggest, an event whose force we can in some way measure so as to say it has run out at a particular point; it is rather an event whose content is contested in the way in which the content of an agreement to play a game is contested. Hercules constructs his political theory

---

[21] One previous example of the use of policy in statutory interpretations illustrates this form of construction. In Charles River Bridge v. Warren Bridge, 24 Mass. (7 Pick.) 344 (1830), *aff'd*, 36 U.S. (11 Pet.) 420 (1837), the court had to decide whether a charter to construct a bridge across the Charles River was to be taken to be exclusive, so that no further charters could be granted. Justice Morton of the Supreme Judicial Court held that the grant was not to be taken as exclusive, and argued, in support of that interpretation, that:

> [I]f consequences so inconsistent with the improvement and prosperity of the state result from the liberal and extended construction of the charters which have been granted, we ought, if the terms used will admit of it, rather to adopt a more limited and restricted one, than to impute such improvidence to the legislature.
>
> . . .
>
> . . . [Construing the grant as exclusive] would amount substantially to a covenant, that during the plaintiffs' charter an important portion of our commonwealth, as to facilities for travel and transportation, should remain *in statu quo*. I am on the whole irresistibly brought to the conclusion, that this construction is neither consonant with sound reason, with judicial authorities, with the course of legislation, nor with the principles of our free institutions.

Id. at 460.

as an argument about what the legislature has, on this occasion, done. The contrary argument, that it did not actually do what he said, is not a realistic piece of common sense, but a competitive claim about the true content of that contested event.

Second, it is important to notice how great a role the canonical terms of the actual statute play in the process described. They provide a limit to what must otherwise be, in the nature of the case, unlimited. The political theory Hercules developed to interpret the statute, which featured a policy of providing federal enforcement for dangerous crimes, would justify a great many decisions that the legislature did not, on any interpretation of the language, actually make. It would justify, for example, a statute making it a federal crime for a murderer to leave the state of his crime. The legislature has no general duty to follow out the lines of any particular policy, and it would plainly be wrong for Hercules to suppose that the legislature had in some sense enacted that further statute. The statutory language they did enact enables this process of interpretation to operate without absurdity; it permits Hercules to say that the legislature pushed some policy to the limits of the language it used, without also supposing that it pushed that policy to some indeterminate further point.

B. The Common Law

I Precedent. One day lawyers will present a hard case to Hercules that does not turn upon any statute; they will argue whether earlier common law decisions of Hercules' court, properly understood, provide some party with a right to a decision in his favor. Spartan Steel was such a case. The plaintiff did not argue that any statute provided it a right to recover its economic damages; it pointed instead to certain earlier judicial decisions that awarded recovery for other sorts of damage, and argued that the principle behind these cases required a decision for it as well.

Hercules must begin by asking why arguments of that form are ever, even in principle, sound. He will find that he has available no quick or obvious answer. When he asked himself the parallel question about legislation he found, in general democratic theory, a ready reply. But the details of the practices of precedent he must now justify resist any comparably simple theory.

He might, however, be tempted by this answer. Judges, when they decide particular cases at common law, lay down general rules that are intended to benefit the community in some way. Other judges, deciding later cases, must therefore enforce these rules so that the benefit may be achieved. If this account of the matter were a sufficient justification of the practices of precedent, then Hercules could decide these hard common law cases as if earlier decisions were statutes, using the techniques he worked out for statutory interpretation. But he will encounter fatal difficulties if he pursues that theory very far. It will repay us to consider why, in some detail, because the errors in the theory will be guides to a more successful theory.

Statutory interpretation, as we just noticed, depends upon the availability of a canonical form of words, however vague or unspecific, that set limits to the political decisions that the statute may be taken to have made. Hercules will discover that many of the opinions that litigants cite as precedents do not contain any special propositions taken to be a canonical form of the rule that the case lays down. It is true that it was part of Anglo-American judicial style, during the last part of the nineteenth century and the first part of this century, to attempt to compose such canonical statements, so that one could thereafter refer, for example, to the rule in *Rylands v. Fletcher*.[22] But even in this period, lawyers and textbook writers disagreed about which parts of famous opinions should be taken to have that character. Today, in any case, even important opinions rarely attempt that legislative sort of draftsmanship. They cite reasons, in the form of precedents and principles, to justify a decision, but it is the decision, not some new and stated rule of law, that these precedents and principles are taken to justify. Sometimes a judge will acknowledge openly that it lies to later cases to determine the full effect of the case he has decided.

Of course, Hercules might well decide that when he does find, in an earlier case, a canonical form of words, he will use his techniques of statutory interpretation to decide whether the rule composed of these words embraces a novel case.[23] He might well acknowledge what could be called an enactment force of precedent. He will nevertheless find that when a precedent does have enactment force, its influence on later cases is not taken to be limited to that force. Judges and lawyers do not think that the force of precedents is exhausted, as a statute would be, by the linguistic limits of some particular phrase. If Spartan Steel were a New York case, counsel for the plaintiff would suppose that Cardozo's earlier decision in *MacPherson v. Buick*,[24] in which a woman recovered damages for injuries from a negligently manufactured automobile, counted in favor of his client's right to recover, in spite of the fact that the earlier decision contained no language that could plausibly be interpreted to enact that right. He would urge that the earlier decision exerts a gravitational force on later decisions even when these later decisions lie outside its particular orbit.

This gravitational force is part of the practice Hercules' general theory of precedent must capture. In this important respect, judicial practice differs from the practice of officials in other institutions. In chess, officials conform to established rules in a way that assumes full institutional autonomy. They exercise originality only to the extent required by the fact that an occasional rule, like the rule about forfeiture, demands that originality. Each decision of a chess referee, therefore, can be said to be directly required and justified by an established rule of chess, even though some of these decisions must be based on an interpretation, rather than on simply the plain and unavoidable meaning, of that rule.

Some legal philosophers write about common law adjudication as if it were in this way like chess, except that legal rules are much more likely than chess rules to require interpretation. That is the spirit, for example, of Professor Hart's argument that hard cases arise only because legal rules have what he calls "open texture."[25] In fact, judges often disagree not simply about how some rule or principle should be interpreted, but whether the rule or principle one judge cites should be acknowledged to be a rule or principle at all. In some cases both the majority and

---

[22] L.R. I Ex. 265 (1866), *aff'd*, L.R. 3 H.L. 330 (1868).

[23] But since Hercules will be led to accept the rights thesis, *see* pp. 1091–93 *infra*, his "interpretation" of judicial enactments will be different from his interpretation of statutes in one important respect. When he interprets statutes he fixes to some statutory language, as we saw, arguments of principle or policy that provide the best justification of that language in the light of the legislature's responsibilities. His argument remains an argument of principle; he uses policy to determine what rights the legislature has already created. But when he "interprets" judicial enactments he will fix to the relevant language only arguments of principle, because the rights thesis argues that only such arguments acquit the responsibility of the "enacting" court.

[24] MacPherson v. Buick Motor Co., 217 N.Y. 382, 111 N.E. 1050 (1916).

[25] H.L.A. HART, *supra* note 18, at 121–32.

the dissenting opinions recognize the same earlier cases as relevant, but disagree about what rule or principle these precedents should be understood to have established. In adjudication, unlike chess, the argument for a particular rule may be more important than the argument from that rule to the particular case; and while the chess referee who decides a case by appeal to a rule no one has ever heard of before is likely to be dismissed or certified, the judge who does so is likely to be celebrated in law school lectures.

Nevertheless, judges seem agreed that earlier decisions do contribute to the formulation of new and controversial rules in some way other than by interpretation; they are agreed that earlier decisions have gravitational force even when they disagree about what that force is. The legislator may very often concern himself only with issues of background morality or policy in deciding how to cast his vote on some issue. He need not show that his vote is consistent with the votes of his colleagues in the legislature, or with those of past legislatures. But the judge very rarely assumes that character of independence. He will always try to connect the justification he provides for an original decision with decisions that other judges or officials have taken in the past.

In fact, when good judges try to explain in some general way how they work, they search for figures of speech to describe the constraints they feel even when they suppose that they are making new law, constraints that would not be appropriate if they were legislators. They say, for example, that they find new rules imminent in the law as a whole, or that they are enforcing an internal logic of the law through some method that belongs more to philosophy than to politics, or that they are the agents through which the law works itself pure, or that the law has some life of its own even though this belongs to experience rather than logic. Hercules must not rest content with these famous metaphors and personifications, but he must also not be content with any description of the judicial process that ignores their appeal to the best lawyers.

The gravitational force of precedent cannot be captured by any theory that takes the full force of precedent to be its enactment force as a piece of legislation. But the inadequacy of that approach suggests a superior theory. The gravitational force of a precedent may be explained by appeal, not to the wisdom of enforcing enactments, but to the fairness of treating like cases alike. A precedent is the report of an earlier political decision; the very fact of that decision, as a piece of political history, provides some reason for deciding other cases in a similar way in the future. This general explanation of the gravitational force of precedent accounts for the feature that defeated the enactment theory, which is that the force of a precedent escapes the language of its opinion. If the government of a community has forced the manufacturer of defective motor cars to pay damages to a woman who was injured because of the defect, then that historical fact must offer some reason, at least, why the same government should require a contractor who has caused economic damage through the defective work of his employees to make good that loss. We may test the weight of that reason, not by asking whether the language of the earlier decision, suitably interpreted, requires the contractor to pay damages, but by asking the different question whether it is fair for the government, having intervened in the way it did in the first case, to refuse its aid in the second.

Hercules will conclude that this doctrine of fairness offers the only adequate account of the full practice of precedent. He will draw certain further conclusions about his own responsibilities when deciding hard cases. The most important of these is that he must limit the gravitational force of earlier decisions to the extension of the arguments of principle necessary to justify those decisions. If an earlier decision were taken to be entirely justified by some argument of policy, it would have no gravitational force. Its value as a precedent would be limited to its enactment force, that is, to further cases captured by some particular words of the opinion. The distributional force of a collective goal, as we noticed earlier, is a matter of contingent fact and general legislative strategy. If the government intervened on behalf of Mrs. MacPherson, not because she had any right to its intervention, but only because wise strategy suggested that means of pursuing some collective goal like economic efficiency, there can be no effective argument of fairness that it therefore ought to intervene for the plaintiff in *Spartan Steel*.

We must remind ourselves, in order to see why this is so, of the slight demands we make upon legislatures in the name of consistency when their decisions are generated by arguments of policy.[26] Suppose the legislature wishes to stimulate the economy and might do so, with roughly the same efficiency, either by subsidizing housing or by increasing direct government spending for new roads. Road construction companies have no right that the legislature choose road construction; if it does, then home construction firms have no right, nor any principle of consistency, that the legislature subsidize housing as well. The legislature may decide that the road construction program has stimulated the economy just enough, and that no further programs are needed. It may decide this even if it now concedes that subsidized housing would have been the more efficient decision in the first place. Or it might concede even that more stimulation of the economy is needed, but decide that it wishes to wait for more evidence—perhaps evidence about the success of the road program—to see whether subsidies provide an effective stimulation. It might even say that it does not now wish to commit more of its time and energy to economic policy. There is, perhaps, some limit to the arbitrariness of the distinctions the legislature may make in its pursuit of collective goals. Even if it is efficient to build all ship-yards in southern California, it might be thought unfair, as well as politically unwise, to do so. But these weak requirements, which prohibit grossly unfair distributions, are plainly compatible with providing sizeable incremental benefits to one group that are withheld from others.

There can be, therefore, no general argument of fairness that a government which serves a collective goal in one way on one occasion must serve it that way, or even serve the same goal, whenever a parallel opportunity arises. I do not

---

[26] In Williamson v. Lee Optical Co., 348 U.S. 483 (1955), Justice Douglas suggested that legislation generated by policy need not be uniform or consistent:

> The problem of legislative classification is a perennial one, admitting of no doctrinaire definition. Evils in the same field may be of different dimensions and proportions, requiring different remedies. Or so the legislature may think. Or the reform may take one step at a time, addressing itself to the phase of the problem which seems most acute to the legislative mind. The legislature may select one phase of one field and apply a remedy there, neglecting the others. The prohibition of the Equal Protection Clause goes no further than the invidious discrimination.

Id. at 489 (citations omitted).

Of course the point of the argument here, that the demands of consistency are different in the cases of principle and policy, is of great importance in understanding the recent history of the equal protection clause. It is the point behind attempts to distinguish "old" from "new" equal protection, or to establish "suspect" classifications, and it provides a more accurate and intelligible distinction than these attempts have furnished.

mean simply that the government may change its mind, and regret either the goal or the means of its earlier decision. I mean that a responsible government may serve different goals in a piecemeal and occasional fashion, so that even though it does not regret, but continues to enforce, one rule designed to serve a particular goal, it may reject other rules that would serve that same goal just as well. It might legislate the rule that manufacturers are responsible for damages flowing from defects in their cars, for example, and yet properly refuse to legislate the same rule for manufacturers of washing machines, let alone contractors who cause economic damage like the damage of *Spartan Steel*. Government must, of course, be rational and fair; it must make decisions that overall serve a justifiable mix of collective goals and nevertheless respect whatever rights citizens have. But that general requirement would not support anything like the gravitational force that the judicial decision in favor of Mrs. MacPherson was in fact taken to have.

So Hercules, when he defines the gravitational force of a particular precedent, must take into account only the arguments of principle that justify that precedent. If the decision in favor of Mrs. MacPherson supposes that she has a right to damages, and not simply that a rule in her favor supports some collective goal, then the argument of fairness, on which the practice of precedent relies, takes hold. It does not follow, of course, that anyone injured in any way by the negligence of another must have the same concrete right to recover that she has. It may be that competing rights require a compromise in the later case that they did not require in hers. But it might well follow that the plaintiff in the later case has the same abstract right, and if that is so then some special argument citing the competing rights will be required to show that a contrary decision in the later case would be fair.

2. *The Seamless Web.* Hercules' first conclusion, that the gravitational force of a precedent is defined by the arguments of principle that support the precedent, suggests a second. Since judicial practice in his community assumes that earlier cases have a general gravitational force, then he can justify that judicial practice only by supposing that the rights thesis holds in his community. It is never taken to be a satisfactory argument against the gravitational force of some precedent that the goal that precedent served has now been served sufficiently, or that the courts would now be better occupied in serving some other goal that has been relatively neglected, possibly returning to the goal the precedent served on some other occasion. The practices of precedent do not suppose that the rationales that recommend judicial decisions can be served piecemeal in that way. If it is acknowledged that a particular precedent is justified for a particular reason; if that reason would also recommend a particular result in the case at bar; if the earlier decision has not been recanted or in some other way taken as a matter of institutional regret; then that decision must be reached in the later case.

Hercules must suppose that it is understood in his community, though perhaps not explicitly recognized, that judicial decisions must be taken to be justified by arguments of principle rather than arguments of policy. He now sees that the familiar concept used by judges to explain their reasoning from precedent, the concept of certain principles that underlie or are embedded in the common law, is itself only a metaphorical statement of the rights thesis. He may henceforth use that concept in his decisions of hard common law cases. It provides a general test for deciding such cases that is like the chess referee's concept of the character of a game, and like his own concept of a legislative purpose. It provides a question—What set of principles best justifies the precedents?—that builds a bridge between the general justification of the practice of precedent, which is fairness, and his own decision about what that general justification requires in some particular hard case.

Hercules must now develop his concept of principles that underlie the common law by assigning to each of the relevant precedents some scheme of principle that justifies the decision of that precedent. He will now discover a further important difference between this concept and the concept of statutory purpose that he used in statutory interpretation. In the case of statutes, he found it necessary to choose some theory about the purpose of the particular statute in question, looking to other acts of the legislature only insofar as these might help to select between theories that fit the statute about equally well. But if the gravitational force of precedent rests on the idea that fairness requires the consistent enforcement of rights, then Hercules must discover principles that fit, not only the particular precedent to which some litigant directs his attention, but all other judicial decisions within his general jurisdiction and, indeed, statutes as well, so far as these must be seen to be generated by principle rather than policy. He does not satisfy his duty to show that his decision is consistent with established principles, and therefore fair, if the principles he cites as established are themselves inconsistent with other decisions that his court also proposes to uphold.

Suppose, for example, that he can justify Cardozo's decision in favor of Mrs. MacPherson by citing some abstract principle of equality, which argues that whenever an accident occurs then the richest of the various persons whose acts might have contributed to the accident must bear the loss. He nevertheless cannot show that that principle has been respected in other accident cases, or, even if he could, that it has been respected in other branches of the law, like contract, in which it would also have great impact if it were recognized at all. If he decides against a future accident plaintiff who is richer than the defendant, by appealing to this alleged right of equality, that plaintiff may properly complain that the decision is just as inconsistent with the government's behavior in other cases as if MacPherson itself had been ignored. The law may not be a seamless web; but the plaintiff is entitled to ask Hercules to treat it as if it were.

You will now see why I called our judge Hercules. He must construct a scheme of abstract and concrete principles that provides a coherent justification for all common law precedents and, so far as these are to be justified on principle, constitutional and statutory provisions as well. We may grasp the magnitude of this enterprise by distinguishing, within the vast material of legal decisions that Hercules must justify, a vertical and a horizontal ordering. The vertical ordering is provided by distinguishing layers of authority; that is, layers at which official decisions might be taken to be controlling over decisions made at lower levels. In the United States the rough character of the vertical ordering is apparent. The constitutional structure occupies the highest level, the decisions of the Supreme Court and perhaps other courts interpreting that structure the next, enactments of the various legislatures the next and decisions of the various courts developing the common law different levels below that. Hercules must arrange justification of principle at each of these levels so that the justification is consistent with principles taken to provide the justification of higher levels. The horizontal ordering simply requires that the principles taken to justify a decision at one level must also be consistent with the justification offered for other decisions at that level.

Suppose Hercules, taking advantage of his unusual skills, proposed to work out this entire scheme in advance, so that he would be ready to confront litigants with an entire theory of law should this be necessary to justify any particular decision. He would begin, deferring to vertical ordering, by setting out and refining the constitutional theory he has already used. That constitutional theory would be more or less different from the theory that a different judge would develop, because a constitutional theory requires judgments about complex issues of institutional fit, as well as judgments about political and moral philosophy, and Hercules' judgments will inevitably differ from those other judges would make. These differences at a high level of vertical ordering will exercise considerable force on the scheme each judge would propose at lower levels. Hercules might think, for example, that certain substantive constitutional constraints on legislative power are best justified by postulating an abstract right to privacy against the state, because he believes that such a right is a consequence of the even more abstract right to liberty that the constitution guarantees. If so, he would regard the failure of the law of tort to recognize a parallel abstract right to privacy against fellow citizens, in some concrete form, as an inconsistency. If another judge did not share his beliefs about the connection between privacy and liberty, and so did not accept his constitutional interpretation as persuasive, that judge would also disagree about the proper development of tort.

So the impact of Hercules' own judgments will be pervasive, even though some of these will be controversial. But they will not enter his calculations in such a way that different parts of the theory he constructs can be attributed to his independent convictions rather than to the body of law that he must justify. He will not follow those classical theories of adjudication I mentioned earlier, which suppose that a judge follows statutes or precedent until the clear direction of these runs out, after which he is free to strike out on his own. His theory is rather a theory about what the statute or the precedent itself requires, and though he will, of course, reflect his own intellectual and philosophical convictions in making that judgment, that is a very different matter from supposing that those convictions have some independent force in his argument just because they are his.[27]

3. Mistakes. I shall not now try to develop, in further detail, Hercules' theory of law. I shall mention, however, two problems he will face. He must decide, first, how much weight he must give, in constructing a scheme of justification for a set of precedents, to the arguments that the judges who decided these cases attached to their decisions. He will not always find in these opinions any proposition precise enough to serve as a statute he might then interpret. But the opinions will almost always contain argument, in the form of propositions that the judge takes to recommend his decision. Hercules will decide to assign these only an initial or prima facie place in his scheme of justification. The purpose of that scheme is to satisfy the requirement that the government must extend to all the rights it supposes some to have. The fact that one officer of the government offers a certain principle as the ground of his decision may be taken to establish prima facie that the government does rely that far upon that principle.

But the main force of the underlying argument of fairness is forward-looking, not backward-looking. The gravitational force of Mrs. MacPherson's case depends not simply on the fact that she recovered for her Buick, but also on the fact that the government proposes to allow others in just her position to recover in the future. If the courts proposed to overrule the decision, no substantial argument

[27] *See* pp. 1101–09 *infra*.

of fairness, fixing on the actual decision in the case, survives in favor of the plaintiff in *Spartan Steel*. If, therefore, a principle other than the principle Cardozo cited can be found to justify MacPherson, and if this other principle also justifies a great deal of precedent that Cardozo's does not, or if it provides a smoother fit with arguments taken to justify decisions of a higher rank in vertical order, then this new principle is a more satisfactory basis for further decisions. Of course, this argument for not copying Cardozo's principle is unnecessary if the new principle is more abstract, and if Cardozo's principle can be seen as only a concrete form of that more abstract principle. In that case Hercules incorporates, rather than rejects, Cardozo's account of his decision. Cardozo, in fact, used the opinion in the earlier case of *Thomas v. Winchester*,[28] on which case he relied, in just that fashion. It may be, however, that the new principle strikes out on a different line, so that it justifies a precedent or a series of precedents on grounds very different from what their opinions propose. Brandeis' and Warren's famous argument about the right to privacy[29] is a dramatic illustration: they argued that this right was not unknown to the law but was, on the contrary, demonstrated by a wide variety of decisions, in spite of the fact that the judges who decided these cases mentioned no such right. It may be that their argument, so conceived, was unsuccessful, and that Hercules in their place, would have reached a different result. Hercules' theory nevertheless shows why their argument, sometimes taken to be a kind of brilliant fraud, was at least sound in its ambition.

Hercules must also face a different and greater problem. If the history of his court is at all complex, he will find, in practice, that the requirement of total consistency he has accepted will prove too strong, unless he develops it further to include the idea that he may, in applying this requirement, disregard some part of institutional history as a mistake. For he will be unable, even with his superb imagination, to find any set of principles that reconciles all standing statutes and precedents. This is hardly surprising: the legislators and judges of the past did not all have Hercules' ability or insight, nor were they men and women who were all of the same mind and opinion. Of course, any set of statutes and decisions can be explained historically, or psychologically, or sociologically, but consistency requires justification, not explanation, and the justification must be plausible and not sham. If the justification he constructs makes distinctions that are arbitrary and deploys principles that are unappealing, then it cannot count as a justification at all.

Suppose the law of negligence and accidents in Hercules' jurisdiction has developed in the following simplified and imaginary way. It begins with specific common law decisions recognizing a right to damages for bodily injury caused by very dangerous instruments that are defectively manufactured. These cases are then reinterpreted in some landmark decision, as they were in MacPherson, as justified by the very abstract right of each person to the reasonable care of others whose actions might injure his person or property. This principle is then both broadened and pinched in different ways. The courts, for example, decide that no concrete right lies against an accountant who has been negligent in the preparation of financial statements. They also decide that the right cannot be waived in certain cases; for example, in a standard form contract of automobile purchase. The legislature adds a statute providing that in certain cases of industrial accident,

Ronald Dworkin

[28] 6 N.Y. 397 (1852).
[29] Warren & Brandeis, *The Right of Privacy*, 4 HARV. L. REV. 193 (1890).

recovery will be allowed unless the defendant affirmatively establishes that the plaintiff was entirely to blame. But it also provides that in other cases, for example, in airplane accidents, recovery will be limited to a stipulated amount, which might be much less than the actual loss; and it later adds that the guest in an automobile cannot sue his host even if the host drives negligently and the guest is injured. Suppose now, against this background, that Hercules is called upon to decide *Spartan Steel*.

Can he find a coherent set of principles that justifies this history in the way that fairness requires? He might try the proposition that individuals have no right to recover for damages unless inflicted intentionally. He would argue that they are allowed to recover damages in negligence only for policy reasons, not in recognition of any abstract right to such damages, and he would cite the statutes limiting liability to protect airlines and insurance companies, and the cases excluding liability against accountants, as evidence that recovery is denied when policy argues the other way. But he must concede that this analysis of institutional history is incompatible with the common law decisions, particularly the landmark decision recognizing a general right to recovery in negligence. He cannot say, compatibly with the rest of his theory, that these decisions may themselves be justified on policy grounds, if he holds, by virtue of the rights thesis, that courts may extend liability only in response to arguments of principle and not policy. So he must set these decisions aside as mistakes.

He might try another strategy. He might propose some principle according to which individuals have rights to damages in just the circumstances of the particular cases that decided they did, but have no general right to such damages. He might concede, for example, a legal principle granting a right to recover for damages incurred within an automobile owned by the plaintiff, but deny a principle that would extend to other damage. But though he could in this way tailor his justification of institutional history to fit that history exactly, he would realize that this justification rests on distinctions that are arbitrary. He can find no room in his political theory for a distinction that concedes an abstract right if someone is injured driving his own automobile but denies it if he is a guest or if he is injured in an airplane. He has provided a set of arguments that cannot stand as a coherent justification of anything.

He might therefore concede that he can make no sense of institutional history except by supposing some general abstract right to recover for negligence: but he might argue that it is a relatively weak right and so will yield to policy considerations of relatively minor force. He will cite the limiting statutes and cases in support of his view that the right is a weak one. But he will then face a difficulty if, though the statute limiting liability in airplane accidents has never been repealed, the airlines have become sufficiently secure, and the mechanisms of insurance available to airlines so efficient and inexpensive, that a failure to repeal the statute can only be justified by taking the abstract right to be so weak that relatively thin arguments of policy are sufficient to defeat it. If Hercules takes the right to be that weak then he cannot justify the various common law decisions that support the right, as a concrete right, against arguments of policy much stronger than the airlines are now able to press. So he must choose either to take the failure to repeal the airline accident limitation statute, or the common law decisions that value the right much higher, as mistakes.

In any case, therefore, Hercules must expand his theory to include the idea that a justification of institutional history may display some part of that history as mistaken. But he cannot make impudent use of this device, because if he were free to take any incompatible piece of institutional history as a mistake, with no further consequences for his general theory, then the requirement of consistency would be no genuine requirement at all. He must develop some theory of institutional mistakes, and this theory of mistakes must have two parts. It must show the consequences for further arguments of taking some institutional event to be mistaken; and it must limit the number and character of the events than can be disposed of in that way.

He will construct the first part of this theory of mistakes by means of two sets of distinctions. He will first distinguish between the specific authority of any institutional event, which is its power as an institutional act to effect just the specific institutional consequences it describes, and its gravitational force. If he classifies some event as a mistake, then he does not deny its specific authority, but he does deny its gravitational force, and he cannot consistently appeal to that force in other arguments. He will also distinguish between embedded and corrigible mistakes; embedded mistakes are those whose specific authority is fixed so that it survives their loss of gravitational force; corrigible mistakes are those whose specific authority depends on gravitational force in such a way that it cannot survive this loss.

The constitutional level of his theory will determine which mistakes are embedded. His theory of legislative supremacy, for example, will insure that any statutes he treats as mistakes will lose their gravitational force but not their specific authority. If he denies the gravitational force of the aircraft liability limitation statute, the statute is not thereby repealed; the mistake is embedded so that the specific authority survives. He must continue to respect the limitations the statute imposes upon liability, but he will not use it to argue in some other case for a weaker right. If he accepts some strict doctrine of precedent, and designates some judicial decision, like the decision denying a right in negligence against an accountant, a mistake, then the strict doctrine may preserve the specific authority of that decision, which might be limited to its enactment force, but the decision will lose its gravitational force; it will become, in Justice Frankfurter's phrase, a piece of legal flotsam or jetsam. It will not be necessary to decide which.

That is fairly straightforward, but Hercules must take more pains with the second part of his theory of mistakes. He is required, by the justification he has fixed to the general practice of precedent, to compose a more detailed justification, in the form of a scheme of principle, for the entire body of statutes and common law decisions. But a justification that designates part of what is to be justified as mistaken is prima facie weaker than one that does not. The second part of his theory of mistakes must show that it is nevertheless a stronger justification than any alternative that does not recognize any mistakes, or that recognizes a different set of mistakes. That demonstration cannot be a deduction from simple rules of theory construction, but if Hercules bears in mind the connection he earlier established between precedent and fairness, this connection will suggest two guidelines for his theory of mistakes. In the first place, fairness fixes on institutional history, not just as history but as a political program that the government proposed to continue into the future; it seizes, that is, on forward-looking, not the backward-looking implications of precedent. If Hercules discovers that some previous decision, whether a statute or a judicial decision, is now widely regretted within the pertinent branch of the profession, that fact in itself distinguishes that decision as vulnerable. He must remember, second, that the argument from fairness that demands consistency is not the only argument from fairness to which government in general, or judges in particular, must respond. If he believes, quite apart from any argument of consistency, that a particular statute or decision was wrong because unfair, within the community's own concept of fairness, then that belief is sufficient to distinguish the decision, and make it vulnerable. Of course, he must apply the guidelines with a sense of the vertical structure of his overall justification, so that decisions at a lower level are more vulnerable than decisions at a higher.

Hercules will therefore apply at least two maxims in the second part of his theory of mistakes. If he can show, by arguments of history or by appeal to some sense of the legal community, that a particular principle, though it once had sufficient appeal to persuade a legislature or court to a legal decision, has now so little force that it is unlikely to generate any further such decisions, then the argument from fairness that supports that principle is undercut. If he can show by arguments of political morality that such a principle, apart from its popularity, is unjust, then the argument from fairness that supports that principle is overridden. Hercules will be delighted to find that these discriminations are familiar in the practice of other judges. The jurisprudential importance of his career does not lie in the novelty, but just in the familiarity, of the theory of hard cases that he has now created.

V. POLITICAL OBJECTIONS

The rights thesis has two aspects. Its descriptive aspect explains the present structure of the institution of adjudication. Its normative aspect offers a political justification for that structure. The story of Hercules shows how familiar judicial practice might have developed from a general acceptance of the thesis. This at once clarifies the thesis by showing its implications in some detail, and offers powerful, if special, argument for its descriptive aspect. But the story also provides a further political argument in favor of its normative aspect. Hercules began his calculations with the intention, not simply to replicate what other judges do, but to enforce the genuine institutional rights of those who came to his court. If he is able to reach decisions that satisfy our sense of justice, then that argues in favor of the political value of the thesis.

It may now be said, however, by way of rebuttal, that certain features of Hercules' story count against the normative aspect of the thesis. In the introductory part of this essay I mentioned a familiar objection to judicial originality: this is the argument from democracy that elected legislators have superior qualifications to make political decisions. I said that this argument is weak in the case of decisions of principle, but Hercules' story may give rise to fresh doubts on that score. The story makes plain that many of Hercules' decisions about legal rights depend upon judgments of political theory that might be made differently by different judges or by the public at large. It does not matter, to this objection, that the decision is one of principle rather than policy. It matters only that the decision is one of political conviction about which reasonable men disagree. If Hercules decides cases on the basis of such judgments, then he decides on the basis of his own convictions and preferences, which seems unfair, contrary to democracy, and offensive to the rule of law.

That is the general form of the objection I shall consider in this final Part. It must first be clarified in one important respect. The objection charges Hercules with relying upon his own convictions in matters of political morality. That charge is ambiguous, because there are two ways in which an official might rely upon his own opinions in making such a decision. One of these, in a judge, is offensive, but the other is inevitable.

Sometimes an official offers, as a reason for his decision, the fact that some person or group holds a particular belief or opinion. A legislator might offer, as a reason for voting for an anti-abortion statute, the fact that his constituents believe that abortion is wrong. That is a form of appeal to authority: the official who makes that appeal does not himself warrant the substance of the belief to which he appeals, nor does he count the soundness of the belief as part of his argument. We might imagine a judge appealing, in just this way, to the fact that he himself has a particular political preference. He might be a philosophical skeptic in matters of political morality. He might say that one man's opinion in such matters is worth no more than another's, because neither has any objective standing, but that, since he himself happens to favor abortion, he will hold anti-abortion statutes unconstitutional.

That judge relies upon the naked fact that he holds a particular political view as itself a justification for his decision. But a judge may rely upon his own belief in the different sense of relying upon the truth or soundness of that belief. Suppose he believes, for example, that the due process clause of the Constitution, as a matter of law, makes invalid any constraint of a fundamental liberty, and that anti-abortion statutes constrain a fundamental liberty. He might rely upon the soundness of those convictions, not the fact that he, as opposed to others, happens to hold them. A judge need not rely upon the soundness of any particular belief in this way. Suppose the majority of his colleagues, or the editors of a prominent law journal, or the majority of the community voting in some referendum, holds a contrary view about abortion. He may decide that it is his duty to defer to their judgment of what the Constitution requires, in spite of the fact that their view is, as he thinks, unsound. But in that case he relies upon the soundness of his own conviction that his institutional duty is to defer to the judgment of others in this matter. He must, that is, rely upon the substance of his own judgment at some point, in order to make any judgment at all.

Hercules does not rely upon his own convictions in the first of these two ways. He does not count the fact that he himself happens to favor a particular conception of religious liberty, for example, as providing an argument in favor of a decision that advances that conception. If the objection we are considering is pertinent, therefore, it must be an objection to his relying upon his own convictions in the second way. But in that case the objection cannot be a blanket objection to his relying upon any of his convictions, because he must, inevitably, rely on some. It is rather an objection to his relying on the soundness of certain of his own convictions; it argues that he ought to defer to others in certain judgments even though their judgments are, as he thinks, wrong.

It is difficult, however, to see which of his judgments the objection supposes he should remand to others. We would not have any such problem if Hercules had accepted, rather than rejected, a familiar theory of adjudication. Classical jurisprudence supposes, as I said earlier, that judges decide cases in two steps: they find the limit of what the explicit law requires, and they then exercise an independent discretion to legislate on issues which the law does not reach. In the recent abortion cases,[30] according to this theory, the Supreme Court justices first

[30] Roe v. Wade, 410 U.S. 113 (1973); Doe v. Bolton, 410 U.S. 179 (1973).

determined that the language of the due process clause and of prior Supreme Court decisions did not dictate a decision either way. They then set aside the Constitution and the cases to decide whether, in their opinion, it is fundamentally unfair for a state to outlaw abortion in the first trimester.

Let us imagine another judge, called Herbert, who accepts this theory of adjudication and proposes to follow it in his decisions. Herbert might believe both that women have a background right to abort fetuses they carry, and that the majority of citizens think otherwise. The present objection argues that he must resolve that conflict in favor of democracy, so that, when he exercises his discretion to decide the abortion cases, he must decide in favor of the prohibitive statutes. Herbert might agree, in which case we should say that he has set aside his morality in favor of the people's morality. That is, in fact, a slightly misleading way to put the point. His own morality made the fact that the people held a particular view decisive; it did not withdraw in favor of the substance of that view. On the other hand, Herbert might disagree. He might believe that background rights in general, or this right in particular, must prevail against popular opinion even in the legislature, so that he has a duty, when exercising a legislative discretion, to declare the statutes unconstitutional. In that case, the present objection argues that he is mistaken, because he insufficiently weighs the principle of democracy in his political theory.

In any case, however, these arguments that seem tailor-made for Herbert are puzzling as arguments against Hercules. Hercules does not first find the limits of law and then deploy his own political convictions to supplement what the law requires. He uses his own judgment to determine what legal rights the parties before him have, and when that judgment is made nothing remains to submit to either his own or the public's convictions. The difference is not simply a difference in ways of describing the same thing: we saw in Part III that a judgment of institutional right, like the chess referee's judgment about the forfeiture rule, is very different from an independent judgment of political morality made in the interstices provided by the open texture of rules.

Herbert did not consider whether to consult popular morality until he had fixed the legal rights of the parties. But when Hercules fixes legal rights he has already taken the community's moral traditions into account, at least as these are captured in the whole institutional record that it is his office to interpret. Suppose two coherent justifications can be given for earlier Supreme Court decisions enforcing the due process clause. One justification contains some principle of extreme liberality that cannot be reconciled with the criminal law of most of the states, but the other contains no such principle. Hercules cannot seize upon the former justification as license for deciding the abortion cases in favor of abortion, even if he is himself an extreme liberal. His own political convictions, which favor the more liberal justification of the earlier cases, must fall, because they are inconsistent with the popular traditions that have shaped the criminal law that his justification must also explain.

Of course, Hercules' techniques may sometimes require a decision that opposes popular morality on some issue. Suppose no justification of the earlier constitutional cases can be given that does not contain a liberal principle sufficiently strong to require a decision in favor of abortion. Hercules must then reach that decision, no matter how strongly popular morality condemns abortion. He does not, in this case, enforce his own convictions against the community's. He rather judges that the community's morality is inconsistent on this issue: its constitutional morality, which is the justification that must be given for its constitution as interpreted by its judges, condemns its discrete judgment on the particular issue of abortion. Such conflicts are familiar within individual morality; if we wish to use the concept of a community morality in political theory, we must acknowledge conflicts within that morality as well. There is no question, of course, as to how such a conflict must be resolved. Individuals have a right to the consistent enforcement of the principles upon which their institutions rely. It is this institutional right, as defined by the community's constitutional morality, that Hercules must defend against any inconsistent opinion however popular.

These hypothetical cases show that the objection designed for Herbert is poorly cast as an objection against Hercules. Hercules' theory of adjudication at no point provides for any choice between his own political convictions and those he takes to be the political convictions of the community at large. On the contrary, his theory identifies a particular conception of community morality as decisive of legal issues; that conception holds that community morality is the political morality presupposed by the laws and institutions of the community. He must, of course, rely on his own judgment as to what the principles of that morality are, but this form of reliance is the second form we distinguished, which at some level is inevitable.

It is perfectly true that in some cases Hercules' decision about the content of this community morality, and thus his decision about legal rights, will be controversial. This will be so whenever institutional history must be justified by appeal to some contested political concept, like fairness or liberty or equality, but it is not sufficiently detailed so that it can be justified by only one among different conceptions of that concept. I offered, earlier, Hercules' decision of the free busing case as an example of such a decision; we may now take a more topical example. Suppose the earlier due process cases can be justified only by supposing some important right to human dignity, but do not themselves force a decision one way or the other on the issue of whether dignity requires complete control over the use of one's uterus. If Hercules sits in the abortion cases, he must decide that issue and must employ his own understanding of dignity to do so.

It would be silly to deny that this is a political decision, or that different judges, from different subcultures, would make it differently. Even so, it is nevertheless a very different decision from the decision whether women have, all things considered, a background right to abort their fetuses. Hercules might think dignity an unimportant concept; if he were to attend a new constitutional convention he might vote to repeal the due process clause, or at least to amend it so as to remove any idea of dignity from its scope. He is nevertheless able to decide whether that concept, properly understood, embraces the case of abortion. He is in the shoes of the chess referee who hates meritocracy, but is nevertheless able to consider whether intelligence includes psychological intimidation.

It is, of course, necessary that Hercules have some understanding of the concept of dignity, even if he denigrates that concept; and he will gain that understanding by noticing how the concept is used by those to whom it is important. If the concept figures in the justification of a series of constitutional decisions, then it must be a concept that is prominent in the political rhetoric and debates of the time. Hercules will collect his sense of the concept from its life in these contexts. He will do the best he can to understand the appeal of the idea to those to whom it does appeal. He will devise, so far as he can, a conception that explains that appeal to them.

This is a process that can usefully be seen as occupying two stages. Hercules will notice, simply as a matter of understanding his language, which are the clear, settled cases in which the concept holds. He will notice, for example, that if one man is thought to treat another as his servant, though he is not in fact that man's employer, then he will be thought to have invaded his dignity. He will next try to put himself, so far as he can, within the more general scheme of beliefs and attitudes of those who value the concept, to look at these clear cases through their eyes. Suppose, for example, that they believe in some Aristotelian doctrine of the urgency of self-fulfillment, or they take self-reliance to be a very great virtue. Hercules must construct some general theory of the concept that explains why those who hold that belief, or accept that virtue, will also prize dignity; if his theory also explains why he, who does not accept the belief or the virtue, does not prize dignity, then the theory will be all the more successful for that feature.

Hercules will then use his theory of dignity to answer questions that institutional history leaves open. His theory of dignity may connect dignity with independence, so that someone's dignity is compromised whenever he is forced, against his will, to devote an important part of his activity to the concerns of others. In that case, he may well endorse the claim that women have a constitutional liberty of abortion, as an aspect of their conceded constitutional right to dignity.

That is how Hercules might interpret a concept he does not value, to reach a decision that, as a matter of background morality, he would reject. It is very unlikely, however, that Hercules will often find himself in that position; he is likely to value most of the concepts that figure in the justification of the institutions of his own community. In that case his analysis of these concepts will not display the same self-conscious air of sociological inquiry. He will begin within, rather than outside, the scheme of values that approves the concept, and he will be able to put to himself, rather than to some hypothetical self, questions about the deep morality that gives the concept value. The sharp distinction between background and institutional morality will fade, not because institutional morality is displaced by personal convictions, but because personal convictions have become the most reliable guide he has to institutional morality.

It does not follow, of course, that Hercules will even then reach exactly the same conclusions that any other judge would reach about disputed cases of the concept in question. On the contrary, he will then become like any reflective member of the community willing to debate about what fairness or equality or liberty requires on some occasion. But we now see that it is wrong to suppose that reflective citizens, in such debates, are simply setting their personal convictions against the convictions of others. They too are contesting different conceptions of a concept they suppose they hold in common; they are debating which of different theories of that concept best explains the settled or clear cases that fix the concept. That character of their debate is obscured by the fact that they do value the concepts they contest, and therefore reason intuitively or introspectively rather than in the more sociological mode that an outsider might use; but, so long as they put their claims as claims about concepts held in common, these claims will have the same structure as the outsider's. We may summarize these important points this way: the community's morality, on these issues at least, is not some sum or combination or function of the competing claims of its members; it is rather what each of the competing claims claims to be. When Hercules relies upon his own conception of dignity, in the second sense of reliance we distinguished, he is still relying on his own sense of what the community's morality provides.

It is plain, therefore, that the present objection must be recast if it is to be a weapon against Hercules. But it cannot be recast to fit Hercules better without losing its appeal. Suppose we say that Hercules must defer, not to his own judgment of the institutional morality of his community, but to the judgment of most members of that community about what that is. There are two apparent objections to that recommendation. It is unclear, in the first place, how he could discover what that popular judgment is. It does not follow from the fact that the man in the street disapproves of abortion, or supports legislation making it criminal, that he has considered whether the concept of dignity presupposed by the Constitution, consistently applied, supports his political position. That is a sophisticated question requiring some dialectical skill, and though that skill may be displayed by the ordinary man when he self-consciously defends his position, it is not to be taken for granted that his political preferences, expressed casually or in the ballot, have been subjected to that form of examination.

But even if Hercules is satisfied that the ordinary man has decided that dignity does not require the right to abortion, the question remains why Hercules should take the ordinary man's opinion on that issue as decisive. Suppose Hercules thinks that the ordinary man is wrong; that he is wrong, that is, in his philosophical opinions about what the community's concepts require. If Herbert were in that position, he would have good reason to defer to the ordinary man's judgments. Herbert thinks that when the positive rules of law are vague or indeterminate, the litigants have no institutional right at all, so that any decision he might reach is a piece of fresh legislation. Since nothing he decides will cheat the parties of what they have a right to have at his hands, the argument is plausible, at least, that when he legislates he should regard himself as the agent of the majority. But Hercules cannot take that view of the matter. He knows that the question he must decide is the question of the parties' institutional rights. He knows that if he decides wrongly, as he would do if he followed the ordinary man's lead, he cheats the parties of what they are entitled to have. Neither Hercules nor Herbert would submit an ordinary legal question to popular opinion; since Hercules thinks that parties have rights in hard cases as well as in easy ones, he will not submit to popular opinion in hard cases either.

Of course, any judge's judgment about the rights of parties in hard cases may be wrong, and the objection may try, in one final effort, to capitalize on that fact. It might concede, *arguendo*, that Hercules' technique is appropriate to Hercules, who by hypothesis has great moral insight. But it would deny that the same technique is appropriate for judges generally, who do not. We must be careful, however, in assessing this challenge, to consider the alternatives. It is a matter of injustice when judges make mistakes about legal rights, whether these mistakes are in favor of the plaintiff or defendant. The objection points out that they will sometimes make such mistakes, because they are fallible and in any event disagree. But of course, though we, as social critics, know that mistakes will be made, we do not know when because we are not Hercules either. We must commend techniques of adjudication that might be expected to reduce the number of mistakes overall based on some judgment of the relative capacities of men and women who might occupy different roles.

Hercules' technique encourages a judge to make his own judgments about institutional rights. The argument from judicial fallibility might be thought to suggest two alternatives. The first argues that since judges are fallible they should make no effort at all to determine the institutional rights of the parties before them, but should decide hard cases only on grounds of policy, or not at all. But that is perverse; it argues that because judges will often, by misadventure, produce unjust decisions they should make no effort to produce just ones. The second alternative argues that since judges are fallible they should submit questions of institutional right raised by hard cases to someone else. But to whom? There is no reason to credit any other particular group with better facilities of moral argument; or, if there is, then it is the process of selecting judges, not the techniques of judging that they are asked to use, that must be changed. So this form of skepticism does not in itself argue against Hercules' technique of adjudication, though of course it serves as a useful reminder to any judge that he might well be wrong in his political judgments, and that he should therefore decide hard cases with humility.

Abram Chayes

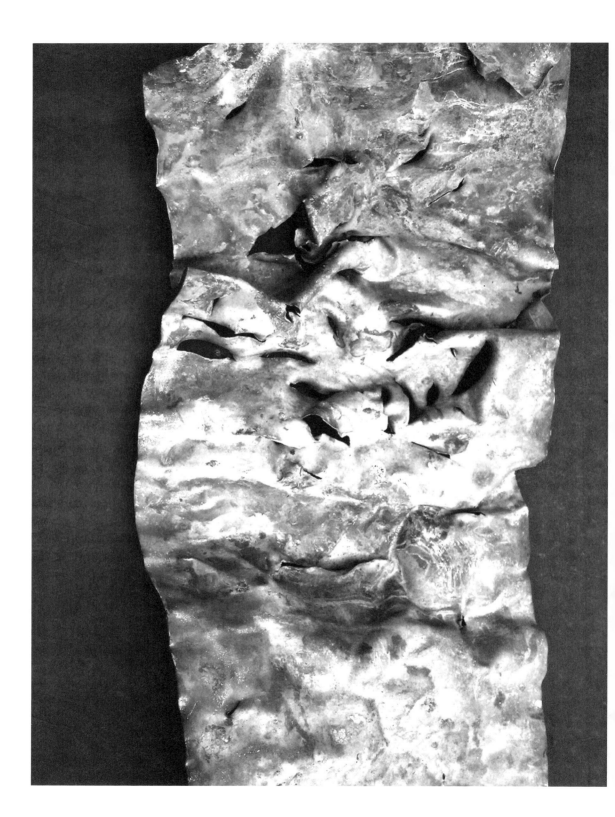

Abram Chayes

THE APPROPRIATE ROLE for the judge, and for courts in general, has consistently been a central focus for American legal thought. That courts should be different from legislatures and from the executive is, of course, central to political theories of democracy that promote a separation of powers. Judges should neither legislate nor administer. For American jurists of the late nineteenth century, it was relatively easy to say what made the judiciary a distinct form of power. Judicial decision making was thought to proceed by deduction in a scheme of logically linked principles and rules. Judicial review was limited to policing the boundaries of other powers, each absolute within its sphere—determining, for example, where the state's absolute police power ended and the individual's absolute freedom of contract began. Judicial power was passive, coercing individuals and legislatures alike only to enforce preexisting rights and recognize the preexisting limits of their power.

As we have seen, beginning with Holmes, the tradition of American legal thought is one long reaction against these late nineteenth-century ideas. The common law is not like that, judicial reasoning is not like that, deduction doesn't work that way, the "autonomy" of various powers is an inadequately determinative basis for settling doctrinal boundaries, policy is everywhere, coercion is unavoidable, judicial discretion is unavoidable.

In the context of judicial review, after *Brown v. Board* and the Warren Court, these challenges came to be focused by the words "judicial activism"—how often and on what basis is it appropriate for the unelected Supreme Court to overrule action by the other elected branches? In the years after *Lochner*, as we have seen, the problem was not conceptualized in precisely these terms. For the realists, rather, *Lochner* had represented the hand of an increasingly discredited mode of reasoning about the law, out of step with new social realities and purposes. The point was to transform how legal professionals reasoned, not how often or actively they did so. After *Brown v. Board*, as we saw in Wechsler's article, the issue began to look different. Purposive reasoning, attuned to social conditions, as proposed by the realist generation, might lead in all sorts of directions. Wechsler found it difficult to see how judicial reasoning about such matters should be thought more legitimate than that of legislatures, unless the judiciary, at least in cases of judicial review, constrained itself to judgment on the basis of "neutral principles." For Wechsler, and for many others of his generation, *Lochner* and *Brown* presented similar "counter-majoritarian" problems. For Wechsler, the solution was "neutral principles," for Hart and Sacks, respect for the principle of "institutional settlement" and for each institution's special decision-making capacities and formal competence. Both suggested the idea that attention to procedural considerations—procedures of reasoning and institutional decision making—could prevent judicial review from overspilling its banks. By the late 1960s, although these issues remained important subjects for theoretical argument, for the legal profession and academy more broadly, *Brown* had come to seem a heroic moment. For the center-liberal professional consensus, society seemed to be changing so rapidly that the danger of a court getting too far out front seemed unlikely.

We now know this consensus would not last. Even at the time, arguments used by legal process scholars to justify and limit judicial review were losing their persuasiveness. Liberal constitutional scholars, like Laurence Tribe, assailed what he termed the "strange persistence" of proceduralist approaches to judicial review. Procedural considerations blended seamlessly into substantive outcomes, and it seemed both intellectually incoherent and politically irresponsible to suggest judges pay no attention. At the same time, of course, conservative politicians were making the Warren Court's "judicial activism" a hot political issue. They would soon also have representatives in the legal academy, who would shatter the consensus favoring a forward-looking, moderately active Court.

In the context of common-law adjudication or statutory interpretation, the challenges posed for our image of the appropriate judicial role by the disintegration of classical legal thought were focused by the word "policy." Before the war, the realists had developed a hearty tradition mocking judicial pretenses to neutrality and dispassionateness and had mooted a variety of alternatives—greater judicial deference to administrative and legislative power, codification (by statute or restatement) of private-law rules, replacement of doctrinal deduction with social science expertise, judicial embrace of the needs and nature of a newly interdependent industrial world, re-imagining judges as "problem solvers," expanding the space for policy and equitable discretion when "normal" judicial reasoning ran out, and more. By the 1950s, it was well accepted that sensible judicial practice, particularly in the face of conflicts, gaps, or ambiguities in the legal materials, required judges to reason about consequences, about the distributional effects of their decisions, and to rely on a host of materials and arguments from other disciplines, including economics, sociology, or psychology. It was well understood, moreover, that doing so would require the judge to balance conflicting policies and purposes. Fuller had offered one way to re-imagine judicial reasoning in policy terms, by identifying the mix of policies or purposes immanent in legal rules and seeking to implement them in concrete cases. Hart and Sacks offered a vision of a stable legal order open to the diversity of decisions that would inevitably flow from judicial reasoning about conflicting policies. For those sharing the "legal process" consensus, judicial reasoning about "policy" presented no problem as long as judges had the intelligence and temperament necessary to engage in reasoned elaboration and an intuitive respect for the principle of institutional settlement. The unique features of the judiciary were procedural and institutional—passive, responsive to parties, deciding case-by-case, exercising "sound judgment," restricting their decision to the matter before them. These features gave the judiciary an institutional comparative advantage. As in the case of judicial review, *procedural* considerations could stabilize the legal order even as judges reasoned about matters of policy.

In the context of common-law litigation and statutory interpretation, this proceduralist consensus was most famously attacked by Abram Chayes's 1976 article, "The Role of the Judge in Public Law Litigation," which became an instant classic. Abram Chayes was born in 1922, and grew up in Chicago, the son of two lawyers. He graduated from Harvard College in 1943 and entered military service, serving with the Field Artillery in France, Holland, Germany, and Japan.

Upon his discharge, he returned to Harvard Law School, where he was president of the *Law Review* and recipient of the Fay Diploma for maintaining the highest grade point average during his three years of study. Thereafter, he worked as a legal adviser to Chester Bowles, then governor of Connecticut, before moving to Washington to serve as Associate General Counsel to the President's Materials Policy Commission in 1951, and then, with Eisenhower's victory in the 1952 elections, clerking for Felix Frankfurter on the U.S. Supreme Court. After two more years as an associate at Covington and Burling in Washington, Chayes joined the Harvard law faculty in 1955. After working on the Kennedy presidential campaign in 1960 (and serving as head draftsman for the 1960 Democratic Party platform), he joined the new administration as Legal Advisor to the State Department. After four years in Washington, he returned to Harvard, where he taught until his death in 2000.

Chayes's experiences in Washington during the Cuban Missile Crisis, the Berlin Crisis, arguing before the International Court of Justice, and in negotiations for the Limited Test Ban Treaty turned his teaching and scholarship toward international law. He became a noted specialist in the law of arms control, space exploration, and international environmental law. He remained active in international law negotiations and litigation, most notably as counsel to Nicaragua in its suit against the United States during the Reagan administration. In a sense, it is odd that Chayes should have so strongly attacked the legal process conception of judging—his most significant contribution in the international field began with course materials designed to encourage international lawyers to think of the international legal order in legal process terms, as a disaggregated system of political/legal institutions to be mobilized by various players pursuing political and other agendas. In such a system, he argued, procedures and institutional structures were more significant than substantive rules, about which there was often likely to be unresolvable disagreement. He developed and pursued this perspective across forty years of teaching and scholarship, often in collaboration with his wife, Antonia Handler Chayes, an expert in the law of national security and arms control negotiations who served as under secretary of the Air Force in the Carter administration.

Although most well known as an internationalist, Chayes taught civil procedure throughout his career, and took a particularly keen interest in the political and strategic uses of litigation. His 1976 article brings into focus a series of conceptual and institutional changes that were transforming civil litigation in the United States at the time, and, he thought, rendering the legal process vision of the appropriate judicial role obsolete. Changes in the rules of civil procedure, and in the routine uses made of trial and appellate courts had, in Chayes's view, changed the nature of litigation itself. Increasingly, he argued, litigation is about the "vindication of constitutional or statutory policies" rather than the solution of "disputes between private parties about private rights."[1] The result, he argued, was a new type of "public-law" litigation, structured by a series of procedural innovations:

> The party structure is sprawling and amorphous, subject to change over the course of the litigation. The traditional adversary relationship is suffused and intermixed with negotiating and mediating processes at every point. The judge is the dominant figure in organizing and guiding the case, and he draws for support not only on the parties and their counsel, but on a wide range of outsiders—masters, experts, and

oversight personnel. Most important, the trial judge has increasingly become the creator and manager of complex forms of ongoing relief, which have widespread effects on persons not before the court and require the judge's continuing involvement in administration and implementation.[2]

Recent changes in civil procedure had facilitated the emergence of this new mode of litigation by expanding access by interested parties to the litigation, modes of fact-finding, and the range of available remedies. It had become easier to involve more parties in one litigation on the basis of relaxed rules about standing and joinder or through the class action. Indeed, Chayes's article appeared in the *Harvard Law Review* alongside a Developments Note on the "class action," then emerging as a profoundly significant tool for litigation. The editors noted that "both pieces share the perspective that adjudication and civil procedure can usefully be analyzed as elements of a larger system of public regulation" and may therefore "profitably be read together." [3]

Often, the use of these new litigation possibilities had been pioneered in the fields of civil rights, consumer protection, tenants rights, and elsewhere by public interest lawyers working to restructure the parties to litigation, precisely as Galanter had advocated, transforming one-shotters into repeat players. For these lawyers, litigation, legislative and administrative advocacy were increasingly the subject of coordinated strategies. Among the most well known, perhaps, was Ralph Nader, whose 1965 attack on the auto industry, *Unsafe at Any Speed*, had begun as a third-year paper at Harvard. In 1982, Chayes looked back at the expansion of class action litigation in these terms:

> The availability of the class action, in my view, had not a little to do with the burgeoning of theories about groups (as opposed to individuals) as right bearers. In any case, it emphasized the vision enunciated in *NAACP v. Button* of the lawsuit as a form of political expression and a vehicle for vindicating political and social rights. And the class action device confirmed the self-image of public interest lawyers as spokesmen for large groupings toward which they had duties and responsibilities different from those of the ordinary lawyer-client relationship.[4]

These procedural innovations were linked, for Chayes, to a series of substantive changes in the American legal order. Like many of his contemporaries, Chayes felt he was living through a period of the "triumph of equity"—a broad expansion in judicial willingness to make use of equitable exceptions, broad standards, and equitable injunctive relief. In the common law, the "triumph of equity" was associated with the rise of "reliance" as a basis for enforcement of a promise, the routinization of "unjust enrichment" as a substantive policy basis for contract law interpretation, the expansion of exceptions and broad standards allowing judicial recognition of social needs and interdependence throughout the common law, and the general rise of torts and decline in contract-based litigation. Fuller's writings on the "reliance" interest in contract were seen as an important early statement of the new vision, also associated with Grant Gilmore's short 1974 essay "The Death of Contract." Social considerations were sometimes understood as background "purposes" informing judicial interpretation in cases of gaps or ambiguities in the fabric of rules, sometimes used to carve out new exceptions to existing rules of private law to recognize the vulnerabilities of weak parties, and sometimes invoked as justifications for broad standards of behavior—good faith, reasonableness—to be read into common-law obligations.

These various substantive reforms all heightened the visibility of judicial reasoning about policy, and the impression of the litigation process as a source of new substantive duties. The triumph of equity was also a triumph for forward-looking, consequentialist policy balancing by judges.

It was this combination of new procedural possibilities and more assertive, substantive judicial reasoning about policy that made legal process images of litigation seem obsolete. The most well-known legal process writing about adjudication was Fuller's unpublished manuscript, "The Forms and Limits of Adjudication," which stressed the passive role of the judge, responding to the claims and factual presentations of parties and fashioning remedies one case at a time.[5] For Chayes, judges reasoning in terms of the "new equity" were—and should be—far less passive than Fuller suggested. They would need to balance a wide range of policies and interests to make new rules affecting interests beyond the parties before them. To do so, they would often need to engage in broad fact-finding—the category of "legislative fact" was expanding, along with the use of social science data about the broad impact of rule changes. Furthermore, adjudication on the basis of a policy balance encouraged judges to relax their dependence upon a clean logical chain linking rights, duties, and remedies, to focus on the impact decisions could have on the interests of many other players. Judges would need to fashion remedies affecting people far beyond those linked by correlative Hohfeldian "rights" and "duties" who may be before them. Remedies, in the form of judicial decrees, could seek to implement policy goals and ensure a long-term balance among social or economic interests affecting numerous people who had not been parties to the litigation.

Chayes's criticisms of nineteenth-century ideas about adjudication echo legal realists like Morris Cohen and Karl Llewelyn, who had ridiculed "traditional" views of judging formed by taking appellate decisions at face value as representations of judicial reasoning, rather than focusing on underlying ideas about policy that helped judges cross logical gaps, or on the development of facts through the real practice of trial courts. Chayes is also borrowing from his colleague, Duncan Kennedy, who had been the first to term the "legal consciousness" of the late nineteenth-century "classical legal thought."

Although Chayes terms the image of adjudication he attacks "traditional," he associates it with *both* the legal process and with nineteenth-century classical legal thought. Of course, the legal process was quite self-consciously seeking to avoid being lumped together with what they agreed was nineteenth-century "formalism." The legal process scholars had learned from the realists. But Chayes was correct to see an echo of nineteenth-century ideas about judicial passivity and the judicial management of boundaries among other powers in the legal process faith in the stability of procedural considerations and the principle of institutional settlement. The legal process had re-invigorated a rather formal separation of procedure and substance, at least when discussing the proper institutional role for the judge. For Chayes, this distinction was no more stable than any of the other sharp distinctions—public and private, act and omission—criticized by the realists. As Chayes saw it, the legal process consensus had successfully embraced realist skepticism about the substantive determinacy of law and about the potential for deduction as a judicial method, but they had not succeeded in updating their image of litigation and judicial activity to account for the expansion of public law and public law–related litigation. Indeed, precisely the reverse, the legal process consensus relied on a passive and traditional view of the judicial process to stabilize their broader image of a disaggregated and yet workable legal process: litigation was—and should be—the retrospective resolution of bipolar controversies among parties seeking remedy for the violation of their rights in a party-controlled and initiated procedure which terminated with a judgment on the claim for a remedy. It is this vision that Chayes traces to the broader will and autonomy-based ideas of late nineteenth-century American legal thought:

> which assumed that the major social and economic arrangements would result from the activities of autonomous individuals. In such a setting, the courts could be seen as an adjunct to private ordering, whose primary function was the resolution of disputes about the fair implications of individual interactions. The basic conceptions governing legal liability were "intention" and "fault." . . . Government regulatory action was presumptively suspect, and was tested by what was in form a common law action against the offending official in his private person.[6] . . .
>
> The "Classical" view saw the courts as performing the objective—even "scientific"—function of deducing legal consequences from agreed first principles. The Realists, after challenging and eventually undermining their predecessors' "pretentions" to objectivity, substituted a more pliable view of judicial method: "reasoned elaboration," or "the inner morality of law" or adherence to "neutral principles." But both schools accepted the traditional conception of adjudication and the premise that the limits of proper judicial action inhered in and could be derived from it.[7]

Chayes chastises this vision as unrealistic and politically undesirable. The explosion of public law, the transformation of litigation parties, fact-finding, and remedies make it unrealistic to view courts only as the passive enforcers of private right. Thinking they are hampers the judiciary's ability to facilitate the public-law explosion and participate in the substantive triumph of equity. *Only* by expanding participants, transforming judicial reasoning and fact-finding, and inventing new forms of relief can the judiciary preserve its broader legitimacy by "responding to, indeed by stirring, the deep and durable demand for justice in our society."[8]

> I confess some difficulty in seeing how this is to be accomplished by erecting barriers of the traditional conception to turn aside, for example, attacks on exclusionary zoning and police violence, two of the ugliest remaining manifestations of official racism in American life.[9]

The traditional conception, for Chayes, not only restrained the judiciary's ability to meet these political challenges, it also served the pernicious ideological function of legitimating the results.

> The conception of litigation as a private contest between private parties with only minimal judicial intrusion confirmed the general view of government powers as stringently limited. . . . Most importantly, the formulation operated to legitimate the increasingly visible political consequences of the actions of a judiciary that was not politically accountable in the usual sense.[10]

Nevertheless, the article remains ambiguous on the significance of this criticism. On one reading, the new "public-law litigation" is simply a new form of litigation, which needs to be understood in its own terms. After the New Deal, there simply is more public law, more cases require statutory or constitutional interpretation, public policy is more prevalent in adjudication. Public interest attorneys are pursuing ever more activist litigation strategies, encouraged by changes in the rules. Visible public-law cases, at the cutting edge of this trend, are particularly significant in the struggle for social justice. To understand these developments requires a new theory—but that theory will only be applicable to the extent lawyers bring this type of case and judges make use of these new procedural possibilities. Although Chayes does not say so, one might well infer that the traditional conception of adjudication continued to be useful in understanding other, more routine, judicial work. Indeed, if the trend toward public interest litigation could itself be stemmed, a traditional image of the judiciary could also be salvaged.

By and large, the article has been read in this way. Although Chayes thought the changes he identified were increasingly significant, he tied them to *public* law, to the rise of regulation, administrative action, and constitutional litigation.

> School desegregation, employment discrimination, and prisoners' or inmates' rights cases come readily to mind as avatars of this new form of litigation. But it would be mistaken to suppose that it is confined to these areas. Antitrust, securities fraud and other aspects of the conduct of corporate business, bankruptcy and reorganizations, union governance, consumer fraud, housing discrimination, electoral reapportionment, environmental management—cases in all these fields display in varying degrees the features of public law litigation."[11]

Chayes wrote as if the rising tide of public-law litigation would not ebb—in this he expresses the confidence of liberals of his generation that history was on their side. An increasingly complex and interdependent economy simply required an expanded federal regulatory presence and exposed a variety of social injustices which demanded remedy. The combination had wrought procedural and substantive changes in the legal system—Chayes set about to chronicle the march of this progressive history in the field of civil procedure.

But the tide did ebb. As Chayes wrote, the judicial activism of the Warren Court era was already a politically controversial legacy. "Government by judges" in the fields of prison management, the desegregation of schools, environmental cleanup and numerous other fields in which judges had issued decrees exercising broad and ongoing supervisory authority was already widely criticized as inappropriate judicial intrusion unlikely to yield wise policy. Public interest lawyering was under attack, and legal services offices were being defunded. The Burger Court had already begun dismantling the procedural innovations that had made the rise of public-law litigation seem workable. Statutory initiatives to stem the "litigation explosion" and enact "tort reform" began to threaten the developments Chayes described with being just a mid-century moment of liberal innovation.

To this, Chayes offered a second argument. Public-law litigation was not simply a new, potentially narrow category of litigation, but a new and unavoidable way of thinking about law and society—a new "legal consciousness"—which places all litigation in a new light. Chayes developed this argument more strongly five years later in his review of the Burger Court's procedural jurisprudence—all of which, he argued, ran against the tide of this new consciousness.[12] Attributing the term "legal consciousness" to Duncan Kennedy, Chayes argued:

> But at a different level, the earlier article made the claim that the public law trend does not simply reflect the political or ideological coloration of a generation of

federal judges. The development is rooted in much more pervasive changes in the contemporary "legal consciousness"—our ways of thinking about law and the legal system—that are in turn related to changes in the larger social, political and cultural environment. If this claim is valid, it implies that the development in question can be affected only marginally even by sustained resistance in the Supreme Court. A fundamental reversal would require a transformation of the underlying political and legal culture as vast as that by which it was initially produced. The Supreme Court can contribute to such a transformation over time, but cannot accomplish it.[13]

After the rise of public law—and the theoretical discoveries of legal realism—awareness of the "public" nature of *all* litigation cannot be put back in the bottle.

> In such a system, enforcement and application of law is necessarily implementation of regulatory policy. Litigation inevitably becomes an explicitly political forum and the court a visible arm of the political process.[14]

The remainder of the article is devoted to a speculative defense of the inevitability—and desirability—of this development. On inevitability, Chayes argues that the doctrinal machinery deployed to *limit* the procedural transformations he describes is unpersuasive. Restricting remedies to those who have "rights" is herding cats—". . . it is never hard to find an adequately Hohfeldian plaintiff to raise the issues."[15] Doctrines limiting standing, restricting joinder, hobbling class actions, narrowing the scope of judicial remedies, all depend upon the kind of distinctions—between public law and private right most crucially—which the realists had demonstrated to be "transcendental nonsense."[16] As a result, now that people know this, there is no alternative to judicial engagement with public policy.

> One may further question whether even a conscious effort to limit judicial review of executive and administrative action can be effective except at the margin. The now-obligatory reference to de Toqueville, as well as the current suspicion of administrative agencies and the congressional propensity for private enforcement of regulatory programs, betoken a cultural commitment to judicial oversight that is not likely to yield very far to a temporary majority of the Court.[17]

Theoretical attention to the "special" functions and nature of the judiciary are simply misguided:

> In any event, I think, we have invested excessive time and energy in the effort to define—on the basis of the inherent nature of adjudication, the implications of a constitutional text, or the functional characteristics of courts—what the precise scope of judicial activity ought to be. Separation of powers comes in for a good deal of veneration in our political and judicial rhetoric, but it has always been hard to classify all government activity into three, and only three, neat and mutually exclusive categories. In practice, all governmental officials, including judges, have exercised a large and messy admixture of powers, and that is as it must be.[18]

That said, when Chayes turns to the desirability of the developments he chronicles, he argues that judges do have "important institutional advantages" for public-law litigation. He acknowledges criticism that judges are not well suited to balancing, to policymaking, to the fashioning of broad remedies, the finding of complex facts, the representation of multiple interests, which are necessary for public policymaking—and he brushes them aside. Instead, he defends the judge as a public law policymaker, on the basis of his "reflective and dispassionate analysis," the "ad hoc" nature of adjudicative policymaking, the "high degree of participation" by affected parties, the place of courts on the front line for seeing and responding to "grievances generated by the operation of public programs in a regulatory state," and more.[19] Judges, for Chayes, are peculiarly well equipped to "perform the task of balancing the importance of competing policy interests in a specific situation."[20] His assessments are impressionistic, to be sure, and he calls repeatedly for further sociological study to confirm or contradict them. They reflect Chayes's intense distrust of both administrative and legislative branches:

> . . . to retreat to the notion that the legislature itself—Congress!—is in some mystical way adequately representative of all the interests at stake, particularly on issues of policy implementation and application, is to impose democratic theory by brute force on observed institutional behavior.[21]

And they reflect Chayes's confidence that the liberal expansions of public policy of the 1960s had history on their side. "In the circumstances," he concludes, "I would concentrate not on turning the clock back (or off), but on improving the performance of public law litigation, both by practical attention to the difficulties noted in this Article and by a more systematic professional understanding of what is being done."[22]

The substantive outcomes of public-law litigation, he insists, will turn out to be more "legitimate" than results obtained through fealty to the more conventionally separated channels of legislation, administration, and adjudication. Chayes notes, for example, that "one may ask whether democratic theory really requires deference to majoritarian outcomes whose victims are prisoners, inmates of mental institutions, and ghetto dwellers":[23]

> These observations will, no doubt, fail to dispel the uneasiness that American political and legal thinkers have always felt at the power of courts to frustrate, or to order, action by elected officials. For it cannot be denied that public law litigation explicitly rejects many of the constraints of judicial method and procedure in which we have characteristically sought respite from the unease. Now, I do not deny that the law, like other creative and performing arts, encompasses a recognizable (and teachable) technique; and this technique plays an important part in the development of the medium and in the criticism and evaluation of its practitioners. But in the law, as elsewhere, technical virtuosity has never been a guarantee of acceptable performance.
>
> Moreover, an amalgam of less tangible institutional factors will continue to shape judicial performance in the public law system as in the past: general expectations as to the competence and conscientiousness of federal judges; professional traditions of conduct and performance; the accepted, often tacit canons and leeways of office. These are amorphous. They mark no sharp boundaries. Their flexibility and vagueness can be abused. But other kinds of constraint are no less vulnerable; and the historical experience is that egregious violation has invariably activated a countervailing response.
>
> In such a setting, the ability of a judicial pronouncement to sustain itself in the dialogue and the power of judicial action to generate assent over the long haul become the ultimate touchstone of legitimacy. In my view, judicial action only achieves such legitimacy by responding to, indeed by stirring, the deep and durable demand for justice in our society. . . . In practice, if not in words, the

American legal tradition has always acknowledged the importance of substantive results for the legitimacy and accountability of judicial action. . . . Perhaps the most important consequence of the inevitably exposed position of the judiciary in our contemporary regulatory state is that it will force us to confront more explicitly the qualities of wisdom, viability, responsiveness to human needs—the justice—of judicial decisions.[24]

In this defense of public-law litigation, Chayes relies on a mode of reasoning which had become ubiquitous in American Legal Thought by the 1970s, signaled by the repeated use of the word "legitimacy." The idea had multiple sources, and had long been part of armchair sociological speculation about legal institutions in the United States. In the 1970s, legitimacy came to be used almost universally as a decisive argument of last resort, and as a replacement for standards of evaluation which turned out to be subject to manipulation. Legal scholars shared an image of the legal system in which all institutions pursued their objectives under scrutiny from one another and the broader public. By its actions, each could add to or deduct from its legitimacy stockpile. Careful fealty to institutional role might seem a safe bet—but if the results were not perceived to be just, the institution would nevertheless lose legitimacy. A key point about "legitimacy" was that it could be earned by deference to majority sentiment, by scrupulous rule following—and by conformity with what turned out to be ethical or virtuous. Liberal commentators of the period often wrote as if their own historical understanding gave them access to this retrospective ethical trump card, and that over time, in an open society, institutions could strengthen their authority by pursuing liberal ends.

Chayes concludes optimistically, linking his sense for the inevitability of public-law litigation—courts can do no other once formal doctrines delimiting their institutional capacity have lost their persuasive power—with a historical/sociological prediction about the power of public-law litigation to strengthen the legitimacy of our legal system by aligning it with the requirements of social justice. In 1976, his liberal faith was still widely shared in the American legal academy.

Five short years later, Chayes wrote a lengthy analysis of the Burger Court's procedural jurisprudence as a Foreword to the *Harvard Law Review's* issue on the 1981 Supreme Court Term.[25] He acknowledged that "the long summer of social reform that occupied the middle third of the century was drawing to a close."[26] The liberal vision of public-law litigation was on the defensive. Nevertheless, he castigates the Burger Court's procedural decisions for analytic incoherence and a long-run institutional miscalculation. His argument well expresses the incredulity of the post-realist liberal generation that the revolution in legal consciousness they had witnessed would not endure. The Court, he argues, is simply unpersuasive in its efforts to limit the expansion of public law litigation. Moreover, the effort to do so has "prevented the Court from coming to grips with the underlying issues" which the public law litigation model renders visible:

Justice Rehnquist has mounted a serious effort to reimpose the right-remedy linkage as a way of limiting the power of judges, and for a time he appeared to command a majority of the Court. The Court, however, seems unable to sustain this rigid limitation. At the same time, preoccupation with the right-remedy analysis has prevented the Court from developing any other basis for effective supervision of the remedial discretion of trial courts.[27]

He predicts that the Burger Court's approach will not stand. Legal professionals will find its arguments unpersuasive, society will find its outcomes illegitimate:

> I submit that the foregoing reconnaissance, limited and fragmentary as it is, provides considerable evidence that the attributes of public law litigation are strongly resistant to conscious efforts at reversal.[28]

Perhaps Chayes will turn out to be right. In the meantime, one can hear the legal realist in his affirmation: "nor can judges escape the painful necessity of policy choice," because "judicial decisions . . . always constitute *both* the acceptance *and* the rejection of . . . public policy alternatives,"[29] and in his confidence that "even a conservative Court" will find itself "practicing public law litigation," given the ubiquity of public policy issues throughout the legal order, the inevitability that disputes between private parties will affect "the systemic effects of governmental action," and the truism that a refusal to adjudicate is no more "neutral" in its policy consequences than the most activist court.[30]

DAVID KENNEDY

NOTES

1. Chayes at 1284.
2. Ibid.
3. 89:7 HLR 1976 at 1281.
4. Abram Chayes, "Foreword: Public Law Litigation and the Burger Court, The Supreme Court 1981 Term," 96 *Harvard Law Review* 4 (1982–1983) at p. 27–28, citations omitted.
5. Fuller's manuscript was subsequently published as "The Forms and Limits of Adjudication," 92 *Harvard Law Review* 353 (1978).
6. Chayes, p. 1285, footnotes in the original omitted.
7. Ibid., pp. 1313–14, notes omitted.
8. Ibid., p. 1316.
9. Ibid. 1316.
10. Ibid. p. 1288. Interestingly, Chayes cites Morris Cohen, *Law and Social Order*, (1933) at p. 144 for this proposition.
11. Chayes, p. 1284.
12. Chayes, "Foreword."
13. Chayes, "Foreword," p. 8, citing Duncan Kennedy, "Toward a Historical Understanding of Legal Consciousness: The Core of Classical Legal Thought in America, 1850–1940," 3 *Research in Law and Sociology* 3 (S. Spitzer, ed., 1980).
14. Chayes, p. 1304.
15. Ibid. at p. 1305.
16. See Felix Cohen, *infra*, p. 163.
17. Chayes at p. 1307, notes in the original omitted.
18. Ibid.
19. Ibid. pp. 1308 ff.
20. Ibid., p. 1308.
21. Ibid., p. 1311.
22. Ibid., p. 1313.
23. Ibid., p. 1315.
24. Ibid., pp. 1315–16, notes in the original omitted.
25. Chayes, "Foreword."

26. Ibid., p. 7.
27. Ibid., p. 47.
28. Ibid., at p. 56.
29. Ibid., p. 59, quoting R. Gambitta, M. May, and J Foster, *Governing Through Courts* (1981) at p. 12.
30. "Foreword," pp. 57–58. Citing Benjamin Cardozo, *The Growth of the Law* (1924).

Bibliography

Abram Chayes

Abram Chayes, "The Role of the Judge in Public Law Litigation," 89 *Harvard Law Review* 1281 (1976).

Abram Chayes, "Foreword: Public Law Litigation and the Burger Court: The Supreme Court 1981 Term," 96 *Harvard Law Review* 4 (1982–1983).

Chayes also wrote extensively about international law. In collaboration with Thomas Ehrlich and Andreas Lowenfeld, he developed course materials extending the "legal process" method to the field of international law. See Abram Chayes, Thomas Ehrlich, and Andreas Lowenfeld, *International Legal Process* (Boston, Little Brown: 1968, 1969). In collaboration with Antonia Handler Chayes, he extended and updated this vision to explain compliance with international norms in a world of disaggregated sovereign powers, multiple public and private actors, and in which national judiciaries played an increasingly significant role in international law. See Abram Chayes and Antonia Handler Chayes, *The New Sovereignty: Compliance with International Regulatory Agreements* (Cambridge, Mass.: Harvard University Press, 1995). His short essay "A Common Lawyer Looks at International Law" also became a classic text in the re-imagination of international law to reflect legal process and legal realist ideas about law: Abram Chayes, "A Common Lawyer Looks at International Law," 78 *Harvard Law Review* 1396 (1965). For an oral history of Chayes's participation in the Kennedy administration, see Sarah Dooley Rothman, ed., "Symposium: Nuclear Weapons, the World Court, and Global Security: Living History Interview with Abram Chayes" 7 *Transnational Law and Contemporary Problems* 459 (1997). For an account of his participation in the Nicaragua case by his co-counsel, see Paul Reichler, "Holding America to Its Own Best Standards: Abe Chayes and Nicaragua in the World Court," 42 *Harvard International Law Journal* 15 (2001).

Commentary

For a fascinating review of the use made of Chayes's arguments, see Richard Marcus, "Public Law Litigation and Legal Scholarship," 21 *University of Michigan Journal of Law Reform* 647 (1988). According to Marcus, Chayes's article was repeatedly cited by judges who wrote law review articles, including Patrick Higgenbotham, Benjamin Kaplan, Frank Coffin, Richard Posner, Antonin Scalia, Roger Traynor, and Jack Weinstein. Stephen Burbank situates Chayes's perspective among other contemporary writing on procedure in a review of Richard Marcus and Edward Sherman, *Complex Ligitation: Cases and Materials on Advanced Civil Procedure* St. Paul, Minn.: West Publishing, 1985) in "1987

Survey of Books Relating to the Law," 85 *Michigan Law Review* 1463, 1987. See also Kellis Parker and Robin Stone, "Standing and Public Law Remedies," 78 *Columbia Law Review* 771 (1978); and Richard Fallon, "Of Justiciability, Remedies and Public Law Litigation: Notes on the Jurisprudence of Lyons," 59 *New York University Law Review* 1 (1984); Frank Coffin, "The Frontier of Remedies: A Call for Exploration," 67 *California Law Review* 983 (1979)(at 989, note 11); Mark Tushnet, "Truth, Justice and the American Way: An Interpretation of Public Law Scholarship in the Seventies," 57 *Texas Law Review* 1307 at 1357 (1979).

For legal realist precursors to Chayes's criticisms of traditional images of litigation, see, for example, Morris Cohen, *Law and the Social Order* (New York: Harcourt, Brace, 1933); Karl Llewelyn, *The Common Law Tradition* (Boston: Little, Brown, 1960) and Llewelyn, "Some Realism About Realism—Responding to Dean Pound." For commentary on the rise of public law cases brought by public interest lawyers, and the new roles taken on by judges in crafting remedies, see, for example; Nathan Glazer, "Towards an Imperial Judiciary?" 41 *Public Interest* 104 (1975); John Dawson, "Lawyers and Involuntary Clients in Public Interest Litigation," 88 *Harvard Law Review* 849 (1975); John Dawson, "Lawyers and Involuntary Clients: Attorney Fees from Funds," 87 *Harvard Law Review* 1597 (1974); and John Dawson, "The Self Serving Intermeddler," 87 *Harvard Law Review* 1409 (1974).

For other analyses of the more assertive role of many judges in the period, see, for example, Robert F. Peckham, "The Federal Judge as a Case Manager: The New Role in Guiding a Case from Filing to Disposition," 69 *California Law Review* 770 (1981), and Judy Resnick, "Managerial Judges", 96 *Harvard Law Review* 374 (1982). Much was written in the 1970s and '80s about the class action and the use of litigation for statutory enforcement. See, for example, John Coffee, "The Regulation of Entrepreneurial Litigation: Balancing Fairness and Efficiency in the Large Class Action," 54 *University of Chicago Law Review* 877 (1987), and Bryant Garth, Ilene Nagel, and S. Jay Plager, "The Institution of the Private Attorney General: Perspectives from an Empirical Study of Class Action Litigation," 61 *Southern California Law Review* 353 (1988). On the rise of "equity," accompanying the procedural changes that were the focus of Chayes's attention, see Fuller and Perdue, *The Reliance Interest in Contract Damages* (New Haven, Conn.: Yale Law School, 1936–37); Grant Gilmore, *The Death of Contract* (Columbus; Ohio State University Press, 1974); and Macaulay on litigation explosion. The extension of the trends Chayes associated with "public law litigation" to ever wider fields through a broad "triumph of equity" is recounted in Steve Subrin, "How Equity Conquered Common Law: The Federal Rules of Civil Procedure in Historical Perspective," 135 *University of Pennsylvania Law Review* 909 (1987). Subrin criticizes Chayes for not going far enough in recognizing the pervasiveness of equitable procedures throughout the federal rules.

The most significant parallel work was by Owen Fiss. Owen Fiss had completed a book on injunctive relief several years before; see Owen Fiss, *Injunctions* (Mineola, N.Y.: Foundation Press, 1972). See also Owen Fiss, *The Civil Rights Injunction* (Bloomington: Indiana University Press, 1978). Owen Fiss would echo Chayes's interpretation that all court decisions are in a sense public law decisions affecting public interest and public values. See Owen Fiss, "Foreword: The Forms of Justice," 93 *Harvard Law Review* 35 (1979), and Robert Cover and

Owen Fiss, *The Structure of Procedure* (Mineola, N.Y.: Foundation Press, 1979). See also Donald Horowitz, *The Courts and Social Policy* (Washington, D.C.: Brookings Institution, 1977) and Laurence Tribe, "Structural Due Process," 10 *Harvard Civil Rights Civil Liberties Law Review* 269 (1975).

A parallel transformation in administrative law tracing the consequences of administrative efforts to fashion ever broader remedies on behalf of ever more diverse and intangible interests is chronicled in Richard Stewart, "The Reformation of American Administrative Law," 88 *Harvard Law Review* 1667 (1975).

Chayes's general enthusiasm for judicial engagement in policymaking and for the role of litigation in public law implementation was picked up in the 1990s in the field of international law, most notably by two of Chayes's students, Harold Koh and Anne Marie Slaughter. See, for example, Harold Koh, "Transnational Legal Process," 75 *Nebraska Law Review* 181 (1996) and Harold Koh, "Transnational Public Law Litigation," 100 *Yale Law Journal* 2347 (1991); and Anne-Marie Slaughter, "International Law and International Relations: A Dual Agenda," 87 *American Journal of International Law* 205 (1993), and Anne-Marie Slaughter, "International Law in a World of Liberal States," 6 *European Journal of International Law* 503 (1995).

"The Role of the Judge in Public Law Litigation"

89 Harvard Law Review 1281 (1976)

Holmes admonished us in one of his most quoted aphorisms to focus our attention on "what the courts will do in fact, and nothing more pretentious."[1] Despite this fashionably empirical slogan, the revolution he instigated proceeded comfortably within an accepted intellectual conception of the nature of civil adjudication and of the judge's role in it, a conception that still remains central to the way we teach, practice, and think about the law.[2] But if, for a moment, we take Holmes' advice and look closely at what federal courts and particularly federal trial judges are doing "in fact," what we see will not easily fit our preconception of civil adjudication. We are witnessing the emergence of a new model of civil litigation and, I believe, our traditional conception of adjudication and the assumptions upon which it is based provide an increasingly unhelpful, indeed misleading framework for assessing either the workability or the legitimacy of the roles of judge and court within this model.

In our received tradition, the lawsuit is a vehicle for settling disputes between private parties about private rights.[3] The defining features of this conception of civil adjudication are:[4]

(1) The lawsuit is *bipolar*. Litigation is organized as a contest between two individuals or at least two unitary interests, diametrically opposed, to be decided on a winner-takes-all basis.[5]

(2) Litigation is *retrospective*. The controversy is about an identified set of completed events: whether they occurred, and if so, with what consequences for the legal relations of the parties.[6]

Copyright 1976 by Abram Chayes.

Professor of Law, Harvard University. A.B., Harvard, 1943; LL.B., 1949.

This Article is a sketch of work in progress. It comprises a set of preliminary hypotheses, as yet unsupported by much more than impressionistic documentation, which I hope to test, refine, and develop in the course of research over the coming year. The research on which this Article is based is supported by grants from the National Science Foundation and the New World Foundation. I should also record my debt to colleagues who critiqued an earlier draft of this paper presented to a group of them late last year and to the students in my current seminar in Contemporary Procedural Developments.

[1] Holmes, *The Path of the Law*, 10 HARV. L. REV. 457, 461 (1897). *See also* J. GRAY, THE NATURE AND SOURCES OF THE LAW 102–03 (2d ed. 1927); K. LLEWELLYN, THE BRAMBLE BUSH 3 (1930).

[2] *See, e.g.,* L. FULLER, THE PROBLEMS OF JURISPRUDENCE 706 (temp. ed. 1949); H.M. HART & A. SACKS, THE LEGAL PROCESS: BASIC PROBLEMS IN THE MAKING AND APPLICATION OF LAW 662–69 (tent. ed. 1958).

[3] *See* M. COHEN, LAW AND THE SOCIAL ORDER 251–52 (1933).

[4] *See generally* F. James, Civil Procedure § 1.2 (1965).

[5] *See, e.g., id.* §§ 1.2, 10.19; C. LANGDELL, A SUMMARY OF EQUITY PLEADING xxiii (1877); Shapiro, *Some Thoughts on Intervention Before Courts, Agencies, and Arbitrators*, 81 HARV. L. REV. 721, 721 (1968).

[6] *See* L. FULLER, *supra* note 2, at 706; H.M. HART & A. SACKS, *supra* note 2, at 185; CALIFORNIA LAW REV. COMM'N, RECOMMENDATIONS & STUD. 657–58, *quoted in* Advisory Comm. Note to FED. R. EVID. 404 ("Character evidence . . . tends to distract the trier of fact from the main question of what actually happened on the particular occasion.").

(3) *Right and remedy are interdependent.* The scope of the relief is derived more or less logically from the substantive violation under the general theory that the plaintiff will get compensation measured by the harm caused by the defendant's breach of duty—in contract by giving plaintiff the money he would have had absent the breach; in tort by paying the value of the damage caused.[7]

(4) The lawsuit is a *self-contained* episode. The impact of the judgment is confined to the parties. If plaintiff prevails there is a simple compensatory transfer, usually of money, but occasionally the return of a thing or the performance of a definite act. If defendant prevails, a loss lies where it has fallen. In either case, entry of judgment ends the court's involvement.[8]

(5) The process is *party-initiated* and *party-controlled.* The case is organized and the issues defined by exchanges between the parties.[9] Responsibility for fact development is theirs. The trial judge is a neutral arbiter of their interactions who decides questions of law only if they are put in issue by an appropriate move of a party.

This capsule description of what I have called the traditional conception of adjudication is no doubt overdrawn. It was not often, if ever, expressed so severely;[10] indeed, because it was so thoroughly taken for granted, there was little occasion to do so. Although I do not contend that the traditional conception ever conformed fully to what judges were doing in fact,[11] I believe it has been central to our understanding and our analysis of the legal system.

Whatever its historical validity, the traditional model is clearly invalid as a description of much current civil litigation in the federal district courts.[12] Perhaps the dominating characteristic of modern federal litigation is that lawsuits do not arise out of disputes between private parties about private rights. Instead, the object of litigation is the vindication of constitutional or statutory policies. The shift in the legal basis of the lawsuit explains many, but not all, facets of what is going on "in fact" in federal trial courts. For this reason, although the label is not wholly satisfactory, I shall call the emerging model "public law litigation."

[7] *See, e.g.,* Draft Opinion of Taney, C.J., Gordon v. United States, 64 U.S. (2 Wall.) 561 (1864), *printed at* 117 U.S. 697 (1886); G. PATON, A TEXT-BOOK OF JURISPRUDENCEE § 110 (3d ed. 1964); J. POMEROY, CODE REMEDIES § 2 (5th ed. 1929); Hohfeld, *Fundamental Legal Conceptions as Applied in Judicial Reasoning,* 23 YALE L. J. 16, 28–59 (1913).

[8] *See, e.g.,* R. Field & B. Kaplan, MATERIALS FOR A BASIC COURSE IN CIVIL PROCEDURE 103–05 (3d ed. 1973); G. Gilmore, The Death of Contract 51–52 (1974); C. Langdell, *supra* note 5, at xxii.

[9] *See, e.g.,* C. CLARK, HANDBOOK OF THE LAW OF CODE PLEADING § 1 (2d ed. 1947); R. FIELD & B. KAPLAN, *supra* note 8, at 12.

[10] *But see* Morgan, *Judicial Notice,* 57 HARV. L. REV. 269, 269–72 (1944); Arnold, *Trial by Combat and the New Deal,* 47 HARV. L. REV. 913, 920–21 (1934).

[11] The characteristic features of the traditional model were strongly marked in the developed common law procedure of the seventeenth and eighteenth centuries, which was inherited by the American colonies and states. It is true that procedure in equity was not constrained by any such rigid structure. It was relatively flexible and pragmatic on the questions of parties, the scope of the controversy, and the forms of relief available. And it was essentially the equitable procedure that was adopted in the reforming codes of the last half of the nineteenth century, both in this country and in England. *See* C. CLARK, *supra* note 9, § 8, at 23; *id.* §§ 56–57. But the common law outlook predominated for almost another hundred years, and, while it did, the codes did little to alter the basic structural characteristics of common law litigation. *See* pp. 1289–96 *infra. See also* Pound, *The Decadence of Equity,* 5 COLUM. L. REV. 20 (1905).

[12] For present purposes, I confine my discussion to civil litigation in the federal courts. There are, I think, corresponding departures from the traditional model in the state courts. There, litigation itself has declined in importance, and the overwhelming bulk of cases is disposed of either administratively, through the mechanism of default (as in consumer credit and landlord-tenant cases), or by manipulation of consent (as in divorce and criminal matters). *See generally* Friedman & Percival, *A Tale of Two Courts: Litigation in Alameda and San Benito Counties,* 10 LAW & SOC'Y 267 (1976); Rubenstein, *Procedural Due Process and the Limits of the Adversary System,* 11 HARV. CIV. RIGHTS-CIV. LIB. L. REV. 48, 66–70 (1976).

The characteristic features of the public law model are very different from those of the traditional model. The party structure is sprawling and amorphous, subject to change over the course of the litigation. The traditional adversary relationship is suffused and intermixed with negotiating and mediating processes at every point. The judge is the dominant figure in organizing and guiding the case, and he draws for support not only on the parties and their counsel, but on a wide range of outsiders—masters, experts, and oversight personnel. Most important, the trial judge has increasingly become the creator and manager of complex forms of ongoing relief, which have widespread effects on persons not before the court and require the judge's continuing involvement in administration and implementation. School desegregation, employment discrimination, and prisoners' or inmates' rights cases come readily to mind as avatars of this new form of litigation. But it would be mistaken to suppose that it is confined to these areas. Antitrust, securities fraud and other aspects of the conduct of corporate business, bankruptcy and reorganizations, union governance, consumer fraud, housing discrimination, electoral reapportionment, environmental management—cases in all these fields display in varying degrees the features of public law litigation.

The object of this Article is first to describe somewhat more fully the public law model and its departures from the traditional conception, and second, to suggest some of its consequences for the place of law and courts in the American political and legal system.

I. The Received Tradition

The traditional conception of adjudication reflected the late nineteenth century vision of society, which assumed that the major social and economic arrangements would result from the activities of autonomous individuals.[13] In such a setting, the courts could be seen as an adjunct to private ordering, whose primary function was the resolution of disputes about the fair implications of individual interactions.[14] The basic conceptions governing legal liability were "intention" and "fault."[15] Intentional arrangements, not in conflict with more or less universal attitudes like opposition to force or fraud, were entitled to be respected, and other private activities to be protected unless culpable. Government regulatory action was presumptively suspect, and was tested by what was in form a common law action against the offending official in his private person.[16] The predominating influence of the private law model can be seen even in constitutional litigation, which, from its first appearance in *Marbury v. Madison*,[17] was understood as an outgrowth of the judicial duty to decide otherwise-existing private disputes.[18]

---

[13] *See, e.g.,* O. HOLMES, THE COMMON LAW 77 (M. Howe ed. 1963); Pound, *Do We Need a Philosophy of Law*, 5 COLUM. L. REV. 339, 344–49 (1905).

[14] *See, e.g.,* H.M. HART & A. SACKS, *supra* note 2, at 185–86; R. POUND, AN INTRODUCTION TO THE PHILOSOPHY OF LAW 189 (1922).

[15] *See, e.g.,* L. FULLER, THE MORALITY OF LAW 167 (1964); O. HOLMES, *supra* note 13, Lecture III, at 63–103.

[16] *See, e.g., Ex parte* Young, 209 U.S. 123 (1908); United States v. Lee, 106 U.S. 196 (1882). *See also* Jaffe, *Suits Against Governments and Officers*, 77 HARV. L. REV. 1209 (1964).

[17] 5 U.S. (1 Cranch) 137, 177 (1803).

[18] *See, e.g.,* Massachusetts v. Mellon, 262 U.S. 447, 488 (1923). *See generally* Monaghan, *Constitutional Adjudication: The Who and When*, 82 YALE L. J. 1363, 1365–68 (1973).

Litigation also performed another important function—clarification of the law to guide future private actions.[19] This understanding of the legal system, together with the common law doctrine of stare decisis, focussed [sic] professional and scholarly concern on adjudication at the appellate level, for only there did the process reach beyond the immediate parties to achieve a wider import through the elaboration of generally applicable legal rules. So, in the academic debate about the judicial function, the protagonist was the appellate judge (not, interestingly enough, the appellate *court*), and the spotlight of teaching, writing, and analysis was almost exclusively on appellate decisions.[20] In practice, the circle was even more narrowly confined to the decisions of the United States Supreme Court, the English high courts (though decreasingly so in recent years), and a few "influential" federal and state appellate judges.[21] As to this tiny handful of decisions subjected to critical scrutiny, the criterion for evaluation was primarily the technical skill of the opinion in disposing of the case adequately within the framework of precedent and other doctrinal materials, so as to achieve an increasingly more systematic and refined articulation of the governing legal rules.

In contrast to the appellate court, to which the motive power in the system was allocated, the functions of the trial judge were curiously neglected in the traditional model.[22] Presumably, the trial judge, like the multitude of private persons who were supposed to order their affairs with reference to appellate pronouncements, would be governed by those decisions in disposing smoothly and expeditiously of the mine-run of cases.[23] But if only by negative implication, the traditional conception of adjudication carried with it a set of strong notions about the role of the trial judge. In general he was passive.[24] He was to decide only those issues identified by the parties, in accordance with the rules established by the appellate courts, or, infrequently, the legislature.

Passivity was not limited to the law aspects of the case. It was strikingly manifested in the limited involvement of the judge in factfinding. Indeed, the sharp distinction that Anglo-American law draws between factfinding and law declaration is itself remarkable. In the developed common law system, these were not only regarded as analytically distinct processes, but each was assigned to a different tribunal for performance. The jury found the facts. The judge was a neutral umpire, charged with little or no responsibility for the factual aspects of the case or for shaping and organizing the litigation for trial.[25]

---

[19] *See, e.g.,* Holmes, *supra* note 1, at 457–58.

[20] *See, e.g.,* K. LLEWELLYN, THE COMMON LAW TRADITION 4 (1960).

[21] Virtually all casebooks illustrate this focus. For example, see R. FIELD & B. KAPLAN, *supra* note 8; L. JAFFE & N. NATHANSON, ADMINISTRATIVE LAW: CASES & MATERIALS (3d ed. 1968); F. KESSLER & G. GILMORE, CONTRACTS: CASES & MATERIALS (2d ed. 1970).

[22] *See* M. COHEN, *supra* note 3, at 36; Wyzanski, *A Trial Judge's Freedom and Responsibility*, 65 HARV. L. REV. 1281, 1302 (1952):

> Are the usages followed by trial judges anything more than patterns of behavior? Are they law in any sense? And even if they are law, are they too disparate and detailed ever to have an honored place in the study of jurisprudence?

[23] *See id.* at 1297–301.

[24] *See, e.g.,* Arnold, *supra* note 10, at 918–19; Morgan, *supra* note 10, at 271; Pound, *supra* note 13, at 346, 349. *See also* J. GRAY, *supra* note 1, at 127.

[25] *See* K. LLEWELLYN, *supra* note 1, at 12; Frankel, *The Adversary Judge*, 54 TEX. L. REV. 465, 468 (1976). Indeed, the judge who takes too active a role may discover he has created grounds for a new trial. *See generally* J. MAGUIRE, J. WEINSTEIN, J. CHADBOURN & J. MANSFIELD, CASES & MATERIALS ON EVIDENCE 1082–1127 (6th ed. 1973).

Because the immediate impact of the judgment was confined to the parties, the traditional model was relatively relaxed about the accuracy of its factfinding.[26] If the facts were not assumed as stated in the pleadings or on the view most favorable to one of the parties or determined on the basis of burdens or presumptions, they were remitted to a kind of black box, the jury. True, some of the law of evidence reflects an active suspicion of the jury. And if the evidence adduced would not "rationally" support a finding for one party or the other, the case could be taken from the jury. But the limits of rationality are inevitably commodious. Even law application, unless there was a special verdict (never much favored in this country),[27] was left to the jury's relatively untrammeled discretion. Indeed, one of the virtues of the jury was thought to be its exercise of a rough-hewn equity, deviating from the dictates of the law where justice or changing community mores required.[28]

The emphasis on systematic statement of liability rules involved a corresponding disregard of the problems of relief. There was, to be sure, a good deal of discussion of measure of damages, as a corollary to the analysis of substantive rights and duties. Similarly, the question of the availability of specific performance and other equitable remedies came in for a share of attention. But the discussion was carried forward within the accepted framework that compensatory money damages was the usual form of relief. Prospective relief was highly exceptional in the traditional model and was largely remitted to the discretion of the trial judge.[29]

So in theory. But from another perspective, it seems remarkable that the system—and for the most part its critics as well—could attach so much importance to uniformity and consistency of doctrinal statement in appellate opinions, while at the same time displaying an almost complete lack of curiosity about actual uniformity of decision in the vast bulk of cases heard.[30] The realist analysis, which demonstrated the painful inevitability of choice for appellate judges on questions of law,[31] was equally applicable at the trial level. The uncertainties introduced by remitting factfinding and fact characterization to the jury were also ignored. Such factors as differences among potential litigants in practical access to the system or in the availability of litigating resources were not even perceived as problems. Although it was well that particular disputes should be fairly settled, there was comfort in the thought that the consequences of the settlement would be confined to the individuals involved. And since the parties controlled the litigating process, it was not unfair to cast the burden of any malfunction upon them.

Besides its inherent plausibility in the nineteenth century American setting, the traditional model of adjudication answered a number of important political and intellectual needs. The conception of litigation as a private contest between private parties with only minimal judicial intrusion confirmed the general view of government powers as stringently limited. The emphasis on the appellate function, conceived as an exercise in deduction from a few embracing principles themselves

[26] See Arnold, supra note 10, at 920; Morgan, supra note 10, at 271–72. See also Webster Eisenlohr, Inc. v. Kalodner, 145 F.2d 316, 318–19 (3d Cir. 1944), cert. denied, 325 U.S. 867 (1945). [27] See F. JAMES, supra note 4, § 7.15.

[28] See, e.g., 3 W. BLACKSTONE, COMMENTARIES *379–81 (1897); P. DEVLIN, TRIAL BY JURY 164 (1956); O. HOLMES, supra note 13, at 97–100; H. KALVEN & H. ZEISEL, THE AMERICAN JURY 8–9 (1966).

[29] See G. GILMORE, supra note 8, at 14–15.

[30] The few so-called "fact-skeptics," e.g., J. FRANK, LAW AND THE MODERN MIND (1930), were notable exceptions.

[31] See B. CARDOZO, THE GROWTH OF THE LAW 65 (1924).

induced from the data of the cases,[32] supplied the demand of the new legal academics for an intellectual discipline comparable to that of their faculty colleagues in the sciences, and for a body of teachable materials.[33] For practitioners and judges, the same conception provided a professional methodology that could be self-consciously employed. Most importantly, the formulation operated to legitimate the increasingly visible political consequences of the actions of a judiciary that was not politically accountable in the usual sense.[34]

II. THE PUBLIC LAW LITIGATION MODEL

Sometime after 1875, the private law theory of civil adjudication became increasingly precarious in the face of a growing body of legislation designed explicitly to modify and regulate basic social and economic arrangements.[35] At the same time, the scientific and deductive character of judicial lawmaking came under attack, as the political consequences of judicial review of that legislation became urgent.[36]

These developments are well known and have become an accepted part of our political and intellectual history. I want to address in somewhat greater detail the correlative changes that have occurred in the procedural structure of the lawsuit. Most discussion of these procedural developments, while recognizing that change has been far-reaching, proceeds on the assumption that the new devices are no more than piecemeal "reforms" aimed at improving the functional characteristics or the efficiency of litigation conducted essentially in the traditional mode.[37] I suggest, however, that these developments are interrelated as members of a recognizable, if changing, system and that taken together they display a new model of judicial action and the judicial role, both of which depart sharply from received conceptions.

A. *The Demise of the Bipolar Structure*

Joinder of parties, which was strictly limited at common law, was verbally liberalized under the codes to conform with the approach of equity calling for joinder of all parties having an "interest" in the controversy.[38] The codes, however, did not at first produce much freedom of joinder. Instead, the courts defined the concept of "interest" narrowly to exclude those without an independent legal right to the remedy to be given in the main dispute.[39] The definition itself illustrates the continuing power of the traditional model. The limited interpretation

[32] *See* A. SUTHERLAND, THE LAW AT HARVARD 174–75 (1967) (quoting Langdell).[33] *See* J. GRAY, *supra* note 1, at 137; A. SUTHERLAND, *supra* note 32, at 174–75.

[34] *See, e.g.,* M. COHEN, *supra* note 3, at 144; *cf.* J. GRAY, *supra* note 1, at 99–100.

[35] *See* J. HURST, LAW AND THE CONDITIONS OF FREEDOM IN NINETEENTH CENTURY UNITED STATES 88–89 (1956); Pound, *supra* note 13, at 344.

The choice of 1875 is approximate. General federal question jurisdiction was first granted in 1871. Act of March 3, 1875, c. 137, § 1, 18 Stat. 470. The Slaughter-House Cases, 83 U.S. (16 Wall.) 36 (1873), and Munn v. Illinois, 94 U.S. 113 (1877), mark the beginning of the interaction between economic regulation and the fourteenth amendment. The professional law school in the modern mode is a product of the same decade. *See* A. SUTHERLAND, *supra* note 32, ch. 6, at 162–205.

[36] *See, e.g.,* M. COHEN, *supra* note 3, at 146–47; J. GRAY, *supra* note 1, at 177–78; J. THAYER, LEGAL ESSAYS 27–30 (1908).

[37] *e.g.,* Kaplan, *Continuing Work of the Civil Committee: 1966 Amendments of the Federal Rules of Civil Procedure,* 81 HARV. L. REV. 356, 591 (1967, 1968).

[38] *See* C. CLARK, *supra* note 9, § 57, at 365; J. POMEROY, *supra* note 7, § 113.

[39] *See* C. CLARK, *supra* note 9, § 57, at 366. For joinder of defendants, see *id.* § 32, at 205.

of the joinder provisions ultimately fell before the banners of "rationality" and "efficiency." But the important point is that the narrow joinder rule could be perceived as irrational or inefficient only because of a growing sense that the effects of the litigation were not really confined to the persons at either end of the right-remedy axis.[40]

The familiar story of the attempted liberalization of pleadings under the codes is not dissimilar. Sweeping away the convolutions of the forms of action did not lead to the hoped-for elimination of technicality and formality in pleading. The immediate response was the construction of cause-of-action rules that turned out to be almost as intricate as the forms themselves.[41] The power of the right-remedy connection was at work here too, but so also was the late nineteenth century impulse toward systemization, which tended to focus attention on accurate statement of legal theory.[42] The proponents of "efficiency" argued for a more informal and flexible approach, to the end that the courts should not have to rehear the same complex of events. This argument ultimately shifted the focus of the lawsuit from legal theory to factual context—the "transaction or occurrence" from which the action arose.[43] This in turn made it easier to view the set of events in dispute as giving rise to a range of legal consequences all of which ought to be considered together.[44]

This more open-ended view of the subject matter of the litigation fed back upon party questions and especially intervention. Here, too, the sharp constraints dictated by the right-remedy nexus give way.[45] And if the right to participate in litigation is no longer determined by one's claim to relief at the hands of another party or one's potential liability to satisfy the claim, it becomes hard to draw the line determining those who may participate so as to eliminate anyone who is or might be significantly (a weasel word) affected by the outcome—and the latest revision of the Federal Rules of Civil Procedure has more or less abandoned the attempt.[46]

The question of the right to intervene is inevitably linked to the question of standing to initiate litigation in the first place. The standing issue could hardly arise at common law or under early code pleading rules, that is, under the traditional model. There the question of plaintiff's standing merged with the legal merits: On the facts pleaded, does this particular plaintiff have a right to the particular relief sought from the particular defendant from whom he is seeking it?[47] With the erosion of the tight structural integration of the lawsuit, the pressure to expand the circle of potential plaintiffs has been inexorable.[48] Today, the

---

[40] *See id.* at 366–67.

[41] *See id.* § 19, at 129–30; J. POMEROY, *supra* note 7, § § 412–13. The law review literature is voluminous, see, *e.g.*, McCaskill, *Actions and Causes of Action*, 34 YALE L. J. 614 (1925), and works cited in C. CLARK, *supra* note 9, § 19, at 141–42 nn.176–79, 144 n.185.

[42] *See, e.g.*, C. LANGDELL, *Preface* to CASES ON CONTRACTS, *quoted in* A. SUTHERLAND, *supra* note 32, at 174–75.

[43] *See, e.g.*, Fed. R. Civ. P. 13, 14, 15, 20, 24.

[44] The transaction or occurrence thus became the basis for defining the unit that ought to be litigated as one "case." *Compare* Restatement of Judgments § 61 (1942) (cause of action approach) *with* Restatement (Second) of Judgments § 61 (Tent. Draft No. 1, 1973) (transaction or occurrence).

[45] *See* Shapiro, *supra* note 5, at 722.

[46] *See* Fed. R. Civ. P. 24(a)(2), 24(b). *See also* Kaplan, *supra* note 37, at 400–07.

[47] *See* Albert, *Standing to Challenge Administrative Action: An Inadequate Surrogate for Claims for Relief*, 83 YALE L. J. 425, 426 (1974).

[48] *See, e.g.*, United States v. Students Challenging Regulatory Agency Procedures (SCRAP), 412 U.S. 669 (1973); Association of Data Processing Serv. Org's., Inc. v. Camp, 397 U.S. 150 (1970); Flast v. Cohen, 392 U.S. 83 (1968); Baker v. Carr, 369 U.S. 186 (1962).

Supreme Court is struggling manfully, but with questionable success, to establish a formula for delimiting who may sue that stops short of "anybody who might be significantly affected by the situation he seeks to litigate."[49]

"Anybody"—even "almost anybody"—can be a lot of people, particularly where the matters in issue are not relatively individualized private transactions or encounters. Thus, the stage is set for the class action, which is discussed at length in the remainder of this issue.[50] Whatever the resolution of the current controversies surrounding class actions, I think it unlikely that the class action will ever be taught to behave in accordance with the precepts of the traditional model of adjudication. The class suit is a reflection of our growing awareness that a host of important public and private interactions—perhaps the most important in defining the conditions and opportunities of life for most people—are conducted on a routine or bureaucratized basis and can no longer be visualized as bilateral transactions between private individuals. From another angle, the class action responds to the proliferation of more or less well-organized groups in our society and the tendency to perceive interests as group interests, at least in very important aspects.

The emergence of the group as the real subject or object of the litigation not only transforms the party problem, but raises far-reaching new questions.[51] How far can the group be extended and homogenized? To what extent and by what methods will we permit the presentation of views diverging from that of the group representative? When the judgment treads on numerous—perhaps innumerable—absentees, can the traditional doctrines of finality and preclusion hold? And in the absence of a particular client, capable of concretely defining his own interest, can we rely on the assumptions of the adversary system as a guide to the conduct and duty of the lawyer?

These questions are brought into sharp focus by the class action device. But it would be a mistake to think that they are confined to that procedural setting. The class action is only one mechanism for presenting group interests for adjudication, and the same basic questions will arise in a number of more familiar litigating contexts. Indeed, it may not be too much to say that they are pervasive in the new model.

B. The Triumph of Equity

One of the most striking procedural developments of this century is the increasing importance of equitable relief.[52] It is perhaps too soon to reverse the traditional maxim to read that money damages will be awarded only when no suitable form of specific relief can be devised. But surely, the old sense of equitable remedies as "extraordinary" has faded.[53]

---

[49] *See, e.g.*, Warth v. Seldin, 422 U.S. 490 (1975); Sierra Club v. Morton, 405 U.S. 727 (1972). *See generally* Scott, Standing in the Supreme Court—A Functional Analysis, 86 HARV. L. REV. 645 (1973); Stewart, *The Reformation of American Administrative Law*, 88 HARV. L. REV. 1667, 1723–47 (1975).

[50] *See Developments in the Law—Class Actions, infra* at 1318 [hereinafter cited as *Developments*].

[51] Some of these questions, as they arise in the class action context, are addressed in *id*. at 1479–82 (sub-classing); *id*. at 1394–1402 (res judicata); *id*. at 1577–1623 (professional responsibility).

[52] *See Developments in the Law—Injunctions*, 78 HARV. L. REV. 994, 996 (1965).

[53] *See* R. FIELD & B. KAPLAN, *supra* note 8, at 307–08. Even in contract law, which should be the heartland of the belief that money cures all ills, there is apparently increasing resort to equitable relief. *See* G. GILMORE, *supra* note 8, at 83 & 140 n.222.

I am not concerned here with specific performance—the compelled transfer of a piece of land or a unique thing. This remedy is structurally little different from traditional money-damages. It is a one-time, one-way transfer requiring for its enforcement no continuing involvement of the court. Injunctive relief, however, is different in kind, even when it takes the form of a simple negative order. Such an order is a presently operative prohibition, enforceable by contempt, and it is a much greater constraint on activity than the risk of future liability implicit in the damage remedy.[54] Moreover, the injunction is continuing. Over time, the parties may resort to the court for enforcement or modification of the original order in light of changing circumstances.[55] Finally, by issuing the injunction, the court takes public responsibility for any consequences of its decree that may adversely affect strangers to the action.

Beyond these differences, the prospective character of the relief introduces large elements of contingency and prediction into the proceedings. Instead of a dispute retrospectively oriented toward the consequences of a closed set of events, the court has a controversy about future probabilities. Equitable doctrine, naturally enough, given the intrusiveness of the injunction and the contingent nature of the harm, calls for a balancing of the interests of the parties. And if the immediate parties' interests were to be weighed and evaluated, it was not too difficult to proceed to a consideration of other interests that might be affected by the order.[56]

The comparative evaluation of the competing interests of plaintiff and defendant required by the remedial approach of equity often discloses alternatives to a winner-takes-all decision. An arrangement might be fashioned that could safeguard at least partially the interests of both parties, and perhaps even of others as well. And to the extent such an arrangement is possible, equity seems to require it.[57] Negative orders directed to one of the parties—even though pregnant with affirmative implications[58]—are often not adequate to this end. And so the historic power of equity to order affirmative action gradually freed itself from the encrustation of nineteenth century restraints.[59] The result has often been a decree embodying an affirmative regime to govern the range of activities in litigation and having the force of law for those represented before the court.[60]

---

[54] For example, even an erroneously issued injunction must be obeyed at the risk of contempt. *See, e.g.,* Walker v. City of Birmingham, 388 U.S. 307, 314 (1967).

[55] *See generally Developments in the Law—Injunctions, supra* note 52, at 1080–86.

[56] *See, e.g.,* Richards's Appeal, 57 Pa. 105, 112 (1868) (because iron is a "prime necessity," iron works may not be enjoined as a nuisance); McCann v. Chasm Power Co., 211 N.Y. 301, 305, 105 N.E. 416, 417 (1914):

> A court of equity can never be justified in making an inequitable decree. If the protection of a legal right even would do a plaintiff but comparatively little good and would produce great public or private hardship, equity will withhold its discreet and beneficent hand and remit the plaintiff to his legal rights and remedies.

[57] *See, e.g.,* Reserve Mining Co. v. EPA, 514 F.2d 492, 535–36 (8th Cir. 1975) (balancing social and economic harm to employees of defendant and area surrounding defendant's plant against environmental damage caused by defendant; *held,* no injunction will issue even though defendant clearly in violation of antipollution laws); *Developments in the Law—Injunctions, supra* note 52, at 1006–08.

[58] *See, e.g.,* Lumley v. Wagner, 1 De G.M. & G. 604, 42 Eng. Rep. 687 (Ch. 1852).

[59] The injunction was characteristically seen as a prohibitive or protective remedy rather than an affirmative one, *see e.g.,* F. Maitland, Equity 318 (1949); 4 J. Pomeroy, A TREATISE ON EQUITY JURISPRUDENCE § 1337, at 934 (5th ed. 1941); *id.* § 1338, at 935. For the traditional power of the Chancellor to grant affirmative relief, see Penn v. Lord Baltimore, 1 Vesey Senior *444, 27 Eng. Rep. 1132 (Ch. 1750); The Salton Sea Cases, 172 F. 792, 820 (9th Cir. 1909).

[60] Some such approach to relief is to be found in railroad and corporate reorganizations. *See, e.g.,* Arnold, *supra* note 10, at 930–31. However, the new model envisions such relief in a wide range of situations.

At this point, right and remedy are pretty thoroughly disconnected.[61] The form of relief does not flow ineluctably from the liability determination, but is fashioned ad hoc. In the process, moreover, right and remedy have been to some extent transmuted. The liability determination is not simply a pronouncement of the legal consequences of past events, but to some extent a prediction of what is likely to be in the future. And relief is not a terminal, compensatory transfer, but an effort to devise a program to contain future consequences in a way that accommodates the range of interests involved.[62]

The interests of absentees, recognized to some extent by equity's balancing of the public interest in individual suits for injunction, become more pressing as social and economic activity is increasingly organized through large aggregates of people. An order nominally addressed to an individual litigant—the labor injunction is an early example—has obvious and visible impact on persons not individually before the court. Nor must the form of the action be equitable: A suit against an individual to collect a tax, if it results in a determination of the constitutional invalidity of the taxing statute, has the same result for absentees as a grant or denial of an injunction. Statutory construction, for example of welfare[63] or housing legislation,[64] may have a similar extended impact, again even if the relief is not equitable in form. Officials will almost inevitably act in accordance with the judicial interpretation in the countless similar situations cast up by a sprawling bureaucratic program.[65] We may call this a stare decisis effect, but it is quite different from the traditional image of autonomous adjustment of individual private transactions in response to judicial decisions. In cases of this kind, the fundamental conception of litigation as a mechanism for private dispute settlement is no longer viable. The argument is about whether or how a government policy or program shall be carried out.

Recognition of the policy functions of litigation feeds the already intense pressure against limitations on standing, as well as against the other traditional limitations on justiciability—political question,[66] ripeness,[67] mootness[68] and the like. At the same time, the breadth of interests that may be affected by public law litigation raises

---

[61] The logical outcome of this development was the declaratory judgment, first authorized at the federal level in 1934. See 28 U.S.C. § § 2201–02 (1970) (enacted as Act of June 14, 1934, ch. 512, 48 Stat. 955). The traditional objection to this procedure was that it permitted the decision of legal issues "in the abstract," that is, without the constraint implicit in the availability of an established remedy. See Willing v. Chicago Auditorium Ass'n, 277 U.S. 274, 289–90 (1928). See also Draft Opinion of Taney, C.J., Gordon v. United States, 64 U.S. (2 Wall.) 561 (1864), printed at 117 U.S. 697 (1886).

[62] For example, see Steel Industry Consent Decrees, reprinted in BNA FAIR EMPL. PRAC. MANUAL 431:125 (1974). Earlier examples from the antitrust field include the motion picture and ASCAP cases, United States v. Paramount Pictures, Inc., 165 F. Supp. 643 (S.D.N.Y. 1958) (motion for injunction), 333 F. Supp. 1100 (S.D.N.Y. 1971) (motion for court approval of proposed acquisition), and United States v. ASCAP, 341 F.2d 1003 (2d Cir.), cert. denied, 382 U.S. 877 (1965).

[63] E.g., Goldberg v. Kelly, 397 U.S. 254 (1970).

[64] E.g., Thompson v. Washington, 497 F.2d 626 (D.C. Cir. 1973); Escalera v. New York City Housing Auth., 425 F.2d 853 (2d Cir.), cert. denied, 400 U.S. 853 (1970).

[65] Several courts have refused to certify as class action suits challenging government policy because if the plaintiff were successful, the government would certainly change its behavior in all instances. See, e.g., Vulcan Soc'y v. Civil Service Comm'n, 490 F.2d 387, 399 (2d Cir. 1973); Galvin v. Levine, 490 F.2d 1255, 1261 (2d Cir. 1973); McDonald v. McLucas, 371 F. Supp. 831, 833–34 (S.D.N.Y. 1974); Tyson v. New York City Housing Auth., 369 F. Supp. 513, 516 (S.D.N.Y. 1974). But see Percy v. Brennan, 8 CCH EMPL. PRAC. DEC. ¶ 9,799, at 6,347 (S.D.N.Y. 1974).

[66] E.g., Baker v. Carr, 369 U.S. 186 (1962).

[67] E.g., Abbott Laboratories v. Gardner, 387 U.S. 136 (1967).

[68] E.g., Roe v. Wade, 410 U.S. 113 (1973); Sosna v. Iowa, 419 U.S. 393, 398 (1975).

questions about the adequacy of the representation afforded by a plaintiff whose interest is narrowly traditional.[69]

Again, as in private litigation, the screw gets another turn when simple prohibitory orders are inadequate to provide relief. If a mental patient complains that he has been denied a right to treatment, it will not do to order the superintendent to "cease to deny" it. So with segregation in education, discrimination in hiring, apportionment of legislative districts, environmental management. And the list could be extended. If judicial intervention is invoked on the basis of congressional enactment, the going assumption is that the statute embodies an affirmative regulatory objective. Even when the suit is premised on constitutional provisions, traditionally regarded as constraining government power, there is an increasing tendency to treat them as embodying affirmative values, to be fostered and encouraged by judicial action.[70] In either case, if litigation discloses that the relevant purposes or values have been frustrated, the relief that seems to be called for is often an affirmative program to implement them. And courts, recognizing the undeniable presence of competing interests, many of them unrepresented by the litigants, are increasingly faced with the difficult problem of shaping relief to give due weight to the concerns of the unrepresented.[71]

C. The Changing Character of Factfinding

The traditional model of adjudication was primarily concerned with assessing the consequences for the parties of specific past instances of conduct. This retrospective orientation is often inapposite in public law litigation, where the lawsuit generally seeks to enjoin future or threatened action,[72] or to modify a course of conduct presently in train or a condition presently existing.[73] In the former situation, the question whether threatened action will materialize, in what circumstances, and with what consequences can, in the nature of things, be answered only by an educated guess. In the latter case, the inquiry is only secondarily concerned with

---

[69] For example, the plaintiffs in Wyatt v. Stickney, 344 F. Supp. 373, 344 F. Supp. 387 (M.D. Ala. 1972), *aff'd in part, remanded in part, decision reserved in part sub nom.* Wyatt v. Aderholt, 503 F.2d 1305 (5th Cir. 1974), a suit ultimately leading to the restructuring of state mental health facilities in Alabama under a "right to treatment" rationale, were originally disgruntled employees seeking to resist cuts in the mental health budget. *See* Note, *The Wyatt Case: Implementation of a Judicial Decree Ordering Institutional Change*, 84 YALE L. J. 1338 (1975). *See also* Sierra Club v. Morton, 405 U.S. 727, 759 (1972) (Blackmun, J., dissenting) (non-traditional plaintiff should have standing because ". . . any resident of the Mineral King area . . . is an unlikely adversary for this Disney governmental project [since he] will be inclined to regard the situation as one that should benefit him economically").

[70] *Compare* T. COOLEY, A TREATISE ON THE CONSTITUTIONAL LIMITATIONS WHICH REST UPON THE LEGISLATIVE POWER OF THE STATES OF THE AMERICAN UNION 5 (6th ed. 1890), *with* A. COX, THE ROLE OF THE SUPREME COURT IN AMERICAN GOVERNMENT 76–98 (1976). *See also* Monaghan, *The Supreme Court, 1974 Term—Foreword: Constitutional Common Law*, 89 HARV. L. REV. 1, 19 (1975) (". . . body of constitutionally inspired implementing rules whose only sources are constitutional provisions framed as limitations on government").

[71] The Norwalk, Connecticut school litigation illustrates the type of competing interests that often emerge in public law litigation. In that litigation black and Puerto Rican parents—who had been included in the class certified—split over the desirability of continuing an integration plan that bussed only minority pupils. *See* Norwalk CORE v. Norwalk Bd. of Educ., 298 F. Supp. 203 (denial of temporary restraining order), 298 F. Supp. 208 (D. Conn. 1968) (denial of application by black and Puerto Rican parents and students to intervene as defendants); 298 F. Supp. 210 (1969) (certification); 298 F. Supp. 213 (1969) (merits), aff'd, 423 F.2d 121 (2d Cir. 1970) (held, no violation).

[72] *See, e.g.,* Sierra Club v. Morton, 405 U.S. 727 (1972) (plaintiff sought injunction to restrain approval of planned commercial development of Mineral King Valley).

[73] *See, e.g.,* COPPAR v. Rizzo, 357 F. Supp. 1289 (E.D. Pa. 1973), *aff'd sub nom.* Goode v. Rizzo, 560 F.2d 542 (3d Cir. 1975), *rev'd*, 96 S.Ct. 598 (1976).

how the condition came about, and even less with the subjective attitudes of the actors, since positive regulatory goals are ordinarily defined without reference to such matters. Indeed, in dealing with the actions of large political or corporate aggregates, notions of will, intention, or fault increasingly become only metaphors.

In the remedial phases of public law litigation, factfinding is even more clearly prospective. As emphasized above, the contours of relief are not derived logically from the substantive wrong adjudged, as in the traditional model. The elaboration of a decree is largely a discretionary process within which the trial judge is called upon to assess and appraise the consequences of alternative programs that might correct the substantive fault. In both the liability and remedial phases, the relevant inquiry is largely the same: How can the policies of a public law best be served in a concrete case?[74]

In public law litigation, then, factfinding is principally concerned with "legislative" rather than "adjudicative" fact. And "fact evaluation" is perhaps a more accurate term than "factfinding." The whole process begins to look like the traditional description of legislation: Attention is drawn to a "mischief,"[75] existing or threatened, and the activity of the parties and court is directed to the development of on-going measures designed to cure that mischief. Indeed, if, as is often the case, the decree sets up an affirmative regime governing the activities in controversy for the indefinite future and having binding force for persons within its ambit, then it is not very much of a stretch to see it as, *pro tanto*, a legislative act.

Given these consequences, the casual attitude of the traditional model toward factfinding is no longer tolerable. The extended impact of the judgment demands a more visibly reliable and credible procedure for establishing and evaluating the fact elements in the litigation, and one that more explicitly recognizes the complex and continuous interplay between fact evaluation and legal consequence. The major response to the new requirements has been to place the responsibility for factfinding increasingly on the trial judge. The shift was in large part accomplished as a function of the growth of equitable business in the federal courts, for historically the chancellor was trier of fact in suits in equity. But on the "law side" also, despite the Supreme Court's expansion of the federal right to jury trial, there has been a pronounced decline in the exercise of the right, apart, perhaps, from personal injury cases.[76]

The courts, it seems, continue to rely primarily on the litigants to produce and develop factual materials, but a number of factors make it impossible to leave the organization of the trial exclusively in their hands. With the diffusion of the party structure, fact issues are no longer sharply drawn in a confrontation between two adversaries, one asserting the affirmative and the other the negative. The litigation is often extraordinarily complex and extended in time, with a continuous and intricate interplay between factual and legal elements. It is hardly feasible and, absent

---

[74] For characteristic examples of this approach to fact evaluation at both the liability and remedial stages, *see* Pettway v. American Cast Iron Pipe Co., 494 F.2d 211 (5th Cir. 1974) (employment discrimination), and COPPAR v. Rizzo, 357 F. Supp. 1289 (E.D. Pa. 1973), *aff'd sub nom.* Goode v. Rizzo, 506 F.2d 542 (3d Cir. 1975), *rev'd*, 96 S. Ct. 598 (1976).

[75] *See* Heydon's Case, 3 Co. Rep. 7a, 76 Eng. Rep. 637, 638 (1584).

[76] Some indication of the decline in the number of jury trials in civil cases can be derived from data of the Administrative Office of the United States Courts. In 1960, for example, 3,035 of 6,988 civil trials were jury trials. *See* 1960 ADMINISTRATIVE OFFICE OF THE UNITED STATES COURTS ANN. REP. 103. In 1974, although the total number of civil trials had almost doubled to 10,972, jury trials remained at 3,569. 1974 *id.* at 318.

a jury, unnecessary to set aside a contiguous block of time for a "trial stage" at
which all significant factual issues will be presented. The scope of the fact investigation and the sheer volume of factual material that can be exhumed by the
discovery process pose enormous problems of organization and assimilation. All
these factors thrust the trial judge into an active role in shaping, organizing and
facilitating the litigation.[77] We may not yet have reached the investigative judge of
the continental systems,[78] but we have left the passive arbiter of the traditional
model a long way behind.

D. The Decree

The centerpiece of the emerging public law model is the decree. It differs in
almost every relevant characteristic from relief in the traditional model of adjudication, not the least in that it is the centerpiece. The decree seeks to adjust
future behavior, not to compensate for past wrong. It is deliberately fashioned
rather than logically deduced from the nature of the legal harm suffered. It provides for a complex, on-going regime of performance rather than a simple, one-
shot, one-way transfer. Finally, it prolongs and deepens, rather than terminates,
the court's involvement with the dispute.

The decree is also an order of the court, signed by the judge and issued under
his responsibility (itself a shift from the classical money judgment).[79] But it cannot be supposed that the judge, at least in a case of any complexity, composes it
out of his own head. How then is the relief formulated?

The reports provide little guidance on this question. Let me nonetheless suggest a prototype that I think finds some support in the available materials. The
court will ask the parties to agree on an order or it will ask one party to prepare a draft.[80] In the first case, a negotiation is stipulated. In the second, the
dynamic leads almost inevitably in that direction. The draftsman understands
that his proposed decree will be subject to comment and objection by the other
side and that it must be approved by the court. He is therefore likely to submit
it to his opponents in advance to see whether differences cannot be resolved.
Even if the court itself should prepare the initial draft of the order, some form
of negotiation will almost inevitably ensue upon submission of the draft to the
parties for comment.

The negotiating process ought to minimize the need for judicial resolution
of remedial issues. Each party recognizes that it must make some response to

---

[77] *See generally* MANUAL FOR COMPLEX LITIGATION (1973).

[78] *See generally* Kaplan, von Mehren & Schaefer, *Phases of German Civil Procedure*, 71 HARV. L. REV.
1193, 1443 (1958).

[79] The judgment in a common law action was not an order to the defendant to pay but a recital that "'it is considered that plaintiff do recover so much from the defendant.'" R. FIELD & B. KAPLAN, *supra* note 8, at 104 n.j.

[80] *See Developments in the Law—Injunctions, supra* note 52, at 1067. Often the court will ask the defendants
to help draft the initial decree since they may be the only persons who can combine the needed technical background and detailed knowledge of the institution to be changed. *See, e.g.*, United States v. Allegheny-Ludlum
Indus., Inc., 63 F.R.D. 1 (N.D. Ala. 1974), *aff'd*, 517 F.2d 826 (5th Cir. 1975) *petition for cert. filed*, 44 U.S.L.W.
3450 (U.S. Jan. 15, 1976) (job discrimination); Butterworth v. Dempsey, 229 F. Supp. 754, 765 (D. Conn.), *aff'd
sub nom.* Pinney v. Butterworth, 378 U.S. 564 (1964) (reapportionment); Wyatt v. Stickney, 344 F. Supp. 373,
374–75, 344 F. Supp. 387 (M.D. Ala. 1972), *aff'd in part, remanded in part, decision reserved in part sub nom.*
Wyatt v. Aderholt, 503 F.2d 1305 (5th Cir. 1974) (mental health); Pennsylvania Ass'n for Retarded Children v.
Pennsylvania, 343 F. Supp. 279, 288 (E.D. Pa. 1972) (mental health); Mapp v. Board of Educ., 203 F. Supp. 843,
845 (E.D. Tenn. 1962), *modified*, 319 F.2d 571 (6th Cir. 1963) (school desegregation); Note, *Reapportionment*,
79 HARV. L. REV. 1226, 1267 (1966).

the demands of the other party, for issues left unresolved will be submitted to the court, a recourse that is always chancy and may result in a solution less acceptable than might be reached by horse-trading. Moreover, it will generally be advantageous to the demanding party to reach a solution through accommodation rather than through a judicial fiat that may be performed "in a literally compliant but substantively grudging and unsatisfactory way."[81] Thus, the formulation of the decree in public law litigation introduces a good deal of party control over the practical outcome. Indeed, relief by way of order after a determination on the merits tends to converge with relief through a consent decree or voluntary settlement. And this in turn mitigates a major theoretical objection to affirmative relief—the danger of intruding on an elaborate and organic network of interparty relationships.[82]

Nevertheless it cannot be supposed that this process will relieve the court entirely of responsibility for fashioning the remedy. The parties may fail to agree. Or the agreement reached may fail to comport with the requirements of substantive law as the judge sees them. Or the interests of absentees may be inadequately accommodated.[83] In these situations, the judge will not, as in the traditional model, be able to derive his responses directly from the liability determination, since, as we have seen, the substantive law will point out only the general direction to be pursued and a few salient landmarks to be sought out or avoided. How then is the judge to prescribe an appropriate remedy?

If the parties are simply in disagreement, it seems plausible to suppose that the judge's choice among proposals advanced by the *quondam* negotiators will be governed by his appraisal of their good faith in seeking a way to implement the constitutional or statutory command as he has construed it. The interest in a decree that will be voluntarily obeyed can be promoted by enforcing a regime of good faith bargaining among the parties.[84] Without detailed knowledge of the negotiations, however, any attempt to enforce such a regime can rest on little more than an uneasy base of intuition and impression. Where a proposed decree is agreed among the parties, but is inadequate because the interests shared by the litigants do not span the range that the court thinks must be taken into account, resubmission for further negotiation may not cure this fundamental defect. Here too, the judge will be unable to fill the gap without a detailed understanding of the issues at stake in the bargaining among the parties.

[81] Eisenberg, *Private Ordering Through Negotiation: Dispute-Settlement and Rulemaking*, 89 HARV. L. REV. 637, 676 (1976). *See generally id.* at 672–80.

[82] *See* L. Fuller, The Forms and Limits of Adjudication 32–33 (unpublished manuscript on file with the Harvard Law School Library).

[83] In the Atlanta school desegregation case, Calhoun v. Cook, 362 F. Supp. 1249 (N.D. Ga. 1973), *aff'd*, 522 F.2d 717 (5th Cir. 1975), representatives of black children, the Atlanta School Board, and a Biracial Committee appointed by the court reached agreement on a plan to implement integration in Atlanta schools. The district court affirmed this agreement, 362 F. Supp. at 1251–52, apparently relying on the wide acceptance of the decree among the plaintiff class and the fact that the plaintiff class representatives had actively participated in its negotiation and drafting. The adequacy of the decree was, however, challenged on an appeal because its provisions for pairing white students with black schools and for bussing were alleged to be inadequate. 522 F.2d at 718. The Fifth Circuit, noting that blacks controlled the school administration and that there was little further chance for segregation, *id.* at 719, rejected this challenge. *See also* note 71 *supra*.

[84] This approach appears to have been followed by Judge Gordon in implementing school desegregation in Louisville. *See* Louisville Courier-Journal, Jan. 31, 1975, at A1, col. 1 (Gordon put burden on county school board that objected to previously approved plan to come up with another, under threat to impose his own otherwise).

For these reasons, the judge will often find himself a personal participant in the negotiations on relief.[85] But this course has obvious disadvantages, not least in its inroads on the judge's time and his pretentions to disinterestedness. To avoid these problems, judges have increasingly resorted to outside help[86]—masters, amici, experts, panels, advisory committees[87]—for information and evaluation of proposals for relief. These outside sources commonly find themselves exercising mediating and even adjudicatory functions among the parties.[88] They may put forward their own remedial suggestions,[89] whether at the request of the judge or otherwise.

Once an ongoing remedial regime is established, the same procedure may be repeated in connection with the implementation and enforcement of the decree.[90] Compliance problems may be brought to the court for resolution and, if necessary, further remediation. Again, the court will often have no alternative but to resort to its own sources of information and evaluation.[91]

I suggested above that a judicial decree establishing an ongoing affirmative regime of conduct is *pro tanto* a legislative act. But in actively shaping and monitoring the decree, mediating between the parties, developing his own sources of expertise and information, the trial judge has passed beyond even the role of legislator and has become a policy planner and manager.

[85] In Louisville Judge Gordon personally drafted the decree with the aid of school officials and the plaintiff's attorney. No formal hearings were held. Instead, the judge formulated the decree in an informal working conference. *See* Louisville Courier-Journal, July 23, 1975, at A2, col. 2.

[86] For example, special masters appointed by the district court drafted the Boston School Desegregation decree. *See* Draft Report of the Masters, Morgan v. Kerrigan, Civ. No. 72-911-G (D. Mass. March 21, 1975).

[87] *See, e.g.,* Wyatt v. Stickney, 344 F. Supp. 373, 344 F. Supp. 387 (M.D. Ala. 1972), *aff'd in part, remanded in part, decision reserved in part sub nom.* Wyatt v. Aderholt, 503 F.2d 1305 (5th Cir. 1974) (advisory committees, amici); Hart v. Community School Bd., 383 F. Supp. 699, 767 (E.D.N.Y. 1974), *aff'd,* 512 F.2d 37 (2d Cir. 1975) (masters); Hamilton v. Landrieu, 351 F. Supp. 549 (E.D. La. 1972) (same); Pennsylvania Ass'n for Retarded Children v. Pennsylvania, 343 F. Supp. 279, 288 (E.D. Pa. 1972) (same); Knight v. Board of Educ., 48 F.R.D. 115 (E.D.N.Y. 1969) (same); Calhoun v. Cook, 362 F. Supp. 1249 (N.D. Ga. 1973), *aff'd,* 522 F.2d 717 (5th Cir. 1975) (Biracial Committee).

The Securities Exchange Commission often participates in review of settlements in class actions and derivative suits by filing an amicus brief or appearing at the approval hearing. *See, e.g.,* Schimmel v. Goldman, 57 F.R.D. 481 (S.D.N.Y. 1973); Norman v. McKee, 290 F. Supp. 29 (N.D. Cal. 1968). *But see* Josephson v. Campbell [1967–69 Transfer Binder] CCH FED. SEC. L. REP. ¶ 92,347 (S.D.N.Y. 1969) (SEC notified of hearing, but did not appear).

See also Developments, infra at 1536–76.

[88] *See* Note, *supra* note 69, at 1344.

[89] *See, e.g.,* Draft Report of the Masters, Morgan v. Kerrigan, Civ. No. 72-911-G (D. Mass. March 21, 1975); Wyatt v. Stickney, 344 F. Supp. 373, 375 (M.D. Ala. 1972), *aff'd in part, remanded in part, decision reserved in part sub nom.* Wyatt v. Aderholt, 503 F.2d 1305 (5th Cir. 1974) (outside experts).

[90] In Calhoun v. Cook, 362 F. Supp. 1249 (N.D. Ga. 1973), *aff'd,* 522 F.2d 717 (5th Cir. 1975), the district court ordered a Biracial Committee, originally formed to assist in drafting the decree, to oversee its implementation as well:

It is further directed that all disagreements between the parties over implementation of the plan, if any, be first presented to the Biracial Committee, or a subcommittee designated for such purpose, during said three-year period at a quarterly or special meeting for such purpose. No issue will be considered by the court until such procedure is followed and the Biracial Committee certifies to the court that it is unable to resolve the dispute.

362 F. Supp. at 1252. *See also* United States v. Allegheny-Ludlum Indus., Inc., 63 F.R.D. 1 (N.D. Ala. 1974), *aff'd,* 517 F.2d 826 (5th Cir. 1975); New York State Ass'n for Retarded Children v. Rockefeller, 357 F. Supp. 752 (E.D.N.Y. 1973). *See generally* Harris, *The Title VII Administrator: A Case Study in Judicial Flexibility,* 60 CORNELL L. REV. 53 (1974); Note, *supra* note 69, at 1338–40.

[91] *See, e.g.,* Wyatt v. Stickney, 344 F. Supp. 373, 378, 344 F. Supp. 387, 392 (M.D. Ala. 1972), *aff'd in part, remanded in part, decision reserved in part sub nom.* Wyatt v. Aderholt, 503 F.2d 1305 (5th Cir. 1974) (outside experts provide information); Pennsylvania Ass'n for Retarded Children v. Pennsylvania, 343 F. Supp. 279, 288 (E.D. Pa. 1972); Gates v. Collier, 501 F.2d 1291, 1321 (5th Cir. 1974), *aff'g* 349 F. Supp. 881 (N.D. Miss. 1972) (court appoints monitors); Stroman v. Griffin, 331 F. Supp. 226, 230 (S.D. Ga. 1971) (surprise visit by judge).

E. A Morphology of Public Law Litigation

The public law litigation model portrayed in this paper reverses many of the crucial characteristics and assumptions of the traditional concept of adjudication:

(1) The scope of the lawsuit is not exogenously given but is shaped primarily by the court and parties.

(2) The party structure is not rigidly bilateral but sprawling and amorphous.

(3) The fact inquiry is not historical and adjudicative but predictive and legislative.

(4) Relief is not conceived as compensation for past wrong in a form logically derived from the substantive liability and confined in its impact to the immediate parties; instead, it is forward looking, fashioned ad hoc on flexible and broadly remedial lines, often having important consequences for many persons including absentees.

(5) The remedy is not imposed but negotiated.

(6) The decree does not terminate judicial involvement in the affair: its administration requires the continuing participation of the court.

(7) The judge is not passive, his function limited to analysis and statement of governing legal rules; he is active, with responsibility not only for credible fact evaluation but for organizing and shaping the litigation to ensure a just and viable outcome.

(8) The subject matter of the lawsuit is not a dispute between private individuals about private rights, but a grievance about the operation of public policy.

In fact, one might say that, from the perspective of the traditional model, the proceeding is recognizable as a lawsuit only because it takes place in a courtroom before an official called a judge. But that is surely too sensational in tone. All of the procedural mechanisms outlined above were historically familiar in equity practice. It is not surprising that they should be adopted and strengthened as the importance of equity has grown in modern times.

We have yet to ask how pervasive is the new model. Is it, as was traditional equity, a supplementary weapon in the judicial armory, destined at best for a subordinate role? Is it a temporary, add-on phenomenon, more extensive perhaps, but not more significant than the railroad reorganization functions that the courts assumed (or were given) in other times?[92] Or can we say that the new form has already or is likely to become the dominant form of litigation in the federal courts, either in terms of judicial resources applied to such cases, or in its impact on society and on attitudes toward the judicial role and function?

The question is not wholly quantitative, but certainly it has a quantitative dimension. A crude index for the new model in federal civil litigation is the well-known shift from diversity to federal question cases in the federal courts. Since most of the features I have discussed derive from the fact that public law provides the basis of the action, it seems plausible that litigation in the new model would increase concomitantly with the predominance of federal

---

[92] From 1870 to 1933, federal judges, acting through equitable receivers, reorganized over 1,000 railroads. See Rodgers & Groom, *Reorganization of Railroad Corporations Under Section 77 of the Bankruptcy Act*, 33 COLUM. L. REV. 571, 571 (1933). *See generally* Chamberlain, *New-Fashioned Receivership*, 10 HARV. L. REV. 139 (1896); Fuller, *The Background and Techniques of Equity and Bankruptcy Railroad Reorganizations— A Survey*, 7 LAW & CONTEMP. PROB. 377 (1940).

question jurisdiction. But the quantitative analysis is in patent need of much further development.[93]

On the other hand, qualitatively—that is, in terms of the importance and interest of the cases and their impact on the public perception of the legal system—it seems abundantly clear that public law litigation is of massive and growing significance. The cases that are the focus of professional debate, law review and academic comment, and journalistic attention are overwhelmingly, I think, new model cases. It could hardly be otherwise, since, by hypothesis, these cases involve currently agitated questions of public policy, and their immediate consequences are to a considerable extent generalized.

I would, I think, go further and argue that just as the traditional concept reflected and related to a system in which social and economic arrangements were remitted to autonomous private action, so the new model reflects and relates to a regulatory system where these arrangements are the product of positive enactment. In such a system, enforcement and application of law is necessarily implementation of regulatory policy. Litigation inevitably becomes an explicitly political forum and the court a visible arm of the political process.

III. A First Appraisal

A. *Trial Balance*

One response to the positive law model of litigation would be to condemn it as an intolerable hodge-podge of legislative, administrative, executive, and judicial functions addressed to problems that are by their nature inappropriate for judicial resolution. Professor Lon Fuller has argued that when such functions are given to the judiciary they are parasitic, in the sense that they can be effectively carried out only by drawing on the legitimacy and moral force that courts have developed through the performance of their inherent function, adjudication according to the traditional conception.[94] A certain limited amount of such parasitism can be accommodated, but too much undermines the very legitimacy on which it depends, because the nontraditional activities of the judiciary are at odds with the conditions that ensure the moral force of its decisions.

From one perspective, the Burger Court may be seen to be embarked on some such program for the restoration of the traditional forms of adjudication. Its

---

[93] The Annual Report of the Administrative Office of the United States Courts for 1974 shows 72% of the cases filed in the district courts were federal question cases or involved the United States as a party, as opposed to 53% in 1940, when the series began. *See* 1974 ANN. REP. at 389–90; 1940 *id.* at 72–75. Even these crude figures are subject to speculative refinement. The proportion of federal cases is even larger, 81% in 1974, if personal injury cases are eliminated from the tally. This, I believe, is permissible since the impulse that accounts for the volume of personal injury litigation is not the demand of the parties for an adjudication under law, but the plaintiff's desire for access to a jury where the governing legal rules are at odds with popular sentiment. Among the federal question cases apart from personal injury, the tax cases are the only large group that look like traditional adjudications, 3.6n 1974. These cases are governed by a detailed code, and a unique relationship has grown among the administrative enforcement agency (exercising detailed rulemaking powers), a highly specialized bar, an expert and well-staffed congressional committee, and the courts (including a specialized court). These factors, and the nature of the taxpayer's claim, which looks very much like an old-fashioned individual claim of right, seem to give traditional adjudication continuing vitality both as a mode of resolving disputes and of contributing to the lawmaking process. These two categories aside, I would guess that much of the rest of the business of the federal district courts displays many of the features of public law litigation. But much statistical analysis remains to be done.

[94] *See generally* L. Fuller, *supra* note 82, at 94–101.

decisions on standing,[95] class actions,[96] and public interest attorneys' fees,[97] among others, achieve a certain coherence in this light. On the other hand, it is hard to believe that the Court is actuated by concern for jurisprudential orthodoxy. One suspects that at bottom its procedural stance betokens a lack of sympathy with the substantive results and with the idea of the district courts as a vehicle of social and economic reform. The Court's distaste for reformist outcomes is barely veiled—or so the dissenters thought—in two recent cases, *Warth v. Seldin*,[98] challenging exclusionary zoning in the suburbs of Rochester, and *Rizzo v. Goode*,[99] attacking police brutality in the city of Philadelphia. But these cases also illustrate some of the difficulties of retrenchment, if, as I believe, the new form of litigation is integrally related to the predominantly public law character of the modern legal system.

In *Warth*, with an attention to the intricacies of pleading that would have gladdened the heart of Baron Parke, the Court last year denied standing to a variety of plaintiffs to attack zoning practices detailed in the complaint.[100] But, because such practices, like others that are the subject matter of public law litigation, are characteristic, rather than occasional, it is never hard to find an adequately Hohfeldian plaintiff to raise the issues. And this year the Court will have to confront the merits of exclusionary zoning in the suburbs of Chicago at the behest of a plaintiff whose standing appears to be impeccable, even by *Warth's* standards.[101]

In the second and more disturbing sally, *Rizzo v. Goode*,[102] the Court overturned a decree mandating a procedure for handling citizen complaints against the Philadelphia police department. The case is a textbook example of public law litigation.[103] It was brought as a class action under the Civil Rights Act of 1871[104] by a number of individuals and a broad coalition of community organizations.[105] Evidence was taken as to over 40 incidents of alleged police brutality, 19 of which, the Court was willing to accept, rose to the level of deprivation of constitutional rights.[106] District Judge Fullam found that these could not be dismissed as "rare or isolated instances"[107] and ordered city police officials to draft a complaint procedure consistent with "generally recognized minimum standards."[108] Such a procedure, negotiated by plaintiffs and the police department,[109] went into effect pending appeal, and was widely greeted with satisfaction.[110]

---

[95] *E.g.*, Warth v. Seldin, 422 U.S. 490 (1975).

[96] *E.g.*, Eisen v. Carlisle & Jacquelin, 417 U.S. 156 (1974); Zahn v. International Paper Co., 414 U.S. 291 (1973).

[97] Alyeska Pipeline Serv. Co. v. Wilderness Soc'y, 421 U.S. 240 (1975)

[98] *See* 422 U.S. 490, 518 (1975) (Douglas, J., dissenting); *id.* at 520 (Brennan, J., dissenting).

[99] *See* 96 S. Ct. 598, 610, 612 (1976) (Blackmun, J., dissenting).

[100] *See* 422 U.S. at 502–18. *See generally The Supreme Court, 1974 Term*, 89 HARV. L. REV. 47, 189–95 (1975).

[101] Village of Arlington Heights v. Metropolitan Housing Dev. Corp., 517 F.2d 409 (7th Cir. 1975), *cert. granted*, 96 S. Ct. 560 (1975) (No. 75–616).

[102] 96 S. Ct. 598 (1976).

[103] The district court opinion is reported as COPPAR v. Rizzo, 357 F. Supp. 1289 (E.D. Pa. 1973), *aff'd sub nom.* Goode v. Rizzo, 506 F.2d 542 (3d Cir. 1974), *rev'd*, 96 S. Ct. 598 (1976).

[104] 42 U.S.C. § 1983 (1970).

[105] *See* 96 S.Ct. at 601 n.1.

[106] *See* 96 S.Ct. at 602–603. The district judge found three violations in the Goode case and two in the COPPAR case, but the Supreme Court was willing to concede *arguendo* that 14 additional incidents in COPPAR, as to which no express findings were made by the district court, constituted constitutional violations, *id.* at 630.

[107] 357 F. Supp. At 1319.

[108] *Id.* at 1321.

[109] 96 S.Ct. at 601.

[110] *See id.* at 610 (Balckmun J. dissenting).

Nevertheless, the Supreme Court struck it down. On the merits, the Court said that despite the 19 cases of proven police brutality before the district court, nothing by way of affirmative policy or condonation had been brought home to the official defendants.[111] Rejecting the plaintiff's argument that the Civil Rights Act provided relief from official disregard of persistent police abuses aimed at the plaintiff class,[112] the Court appeared to adopt the view that the record disclosed only 19 claims by individual minority victims against individual policemen, each apparently to be enforced in a separate suit.[113] On relief, the Court held that the decree infringed the "'latitude'" necessary for a local administration "in the 'dispatch of its own internal affairs.'"[114] At one point the opinion even seems to say that only if one of the individual plaintiffs could show that he was personally threatened with repeated acts of unconstitutional police violence would injunctive relief of any kind be appropriate.[115]

The Court's substantive prescription is, of course, an illusory redress for endemic low level police violence, which, as Judge Fullam noted, is "fairly typical . . . of police departments in major urban areas."[116] The decision is at odds with pattern and practice cases in employment discrimination, housing, school segregation, and other fields inferring official complicity from a statistically small set of similar actions together with official inaction in response.[117] Likewise, it is hard to credit the Court's position on relief, except on the assumption that no substantive violation has occurred. From reapportionment and desegregation to mental institutions and prisons, federal judicial decrees, often sanctioned by the Court, have constrained the "latitude" normally reserved for state and local officials precisely to secure constitutional rights against exercises of official discretion. The pressure of this doctrinal environment, in large part beyond the power of the Court to alter quickly, seems to me to be more than the anomalies of *Rizzo v. Goode* can withstand over the long run. One may further question whether even a conscious effort to limit judicial review of executive and administrative action can be effective except at the margin. The now-obligatory reference to deToqueville,[118] as well as the current suspicion of administrative agencies[119] and the congressional propensity for private enforcement of regulatory programs,[120] betoken a cultural commitment to judicial oversight that is not likely to yield very far to a temporary majority on the Court.

In any event, I think, we have invested excessive time and energy in the effort to define—on the basis of the inherent nature of adjudication, the implications of a constitutional text, or the functional characteristics of courts—what the precise scope of judicial activity ought to be. Separation of powers comes in for a good deal of veneration in our political and judicial rhetoric, but it has always been hard to classify all government activity into three, and only three, neat and mutually

[111] *Id.* at 604, 606.

[112] *Id.* at 606.

[113] *Id.* at 605–07.

[114] *Id.* at 608.

[115] *Id.* at 604–05.

[116] 357 F. Supp. at 1319.

[117] *See, e.g.,* Keyes v. School Dist., 413 U.S. 189 (1973); cases cited in Rizzo v. Goode, 96 S. Ct. 611 n.2 (Blackmun J., dissenting).

[118] *E.g.,* Sierra Club v. Morton, 405 U.S. 727, 740 n.16 (1972).

[119] *Compare* J. LANDIS, THE ADMINISTRATIVE PROCESS 10–16, 46–50 (1938), with Stewart, *supra* note 49, at 1676–88.

[120] *E.g.,* 15 U.S.C.A. § 1640 (West Supp. 1976) (Truth in Lending Act); 42 U.S.C. § 1857h-2 (1970) (Clean Air Act).

exclusive categories. In practice, all governmental officials, including judges, have exercised a large and messy admixture of powers, and that is as it must be. That is not to say that institutional characteristics are irrelevant in assigning governmental tasks or that judges should unreservedly be thrust directly into political battles. But such considerations should be taken as cautionary, not decisive; for despite its well rehearsed inadequacies, the judiciary may have some important institutional advantages for the tasks it is assuming:

First, and perhaps most important, is that the process is presided over by a judge. His professional tradition insulates him from narrow political pressures, but, given the operation of the federal appointive power and the demands of contemporary law practice, he is likely to have some experience of the political process and acquaintance with a fairly broad range of public policy problems. Moreover, he is governed by a professional ideal of reflective and dispassionate analysis of the problem before him and is likely to have had some experience in putting this ideal into practice.

Second, the public law model permits ad hoc applications of broad national policy in situations of limited scope. The solutions can be tailored to the needs of the particular situation and flexibly administered or modified as experience develops with the regime established in the particular case.[121]

Third, the procedure permits a relatively high degree of participation by representatives of those who will be directly affected by the decision, without establishing a liberum veto.

Fourth, the court, although traditionally thought less competent than legislatures or administrative agencies in gathering and assessing information,[122] may have unsuspected advantages in this regard. Even the diffused adversarial structure of public law litigation furnishes strong incentives for the parties to produce information. If the party structure is sufficiently representative of the interests at stake, a considerable range of relevant information will be forthcoming. And, because of the limited scope of the proceeding, the information required can be effectively focused and specified. Information produced will not only be subject to adversary review, but as we have seen, the judge can engage his own experts to assist in evaluating the evidence. Moreover, the information that is produced will not be filtered through the rigid structures and preconceptions of bureaucracies.

Fifth, the judicial process is an effective mechanism for registering and responding to grievances generated by the operation of public programs in a regulatory state. Unlike an administrative bureaucracy or a legislature, the judiciary must respond to the complaints of the aggrieved. It is also rather well situated to perform the task of balancing the importance of competing policy interests in a specific situation. The legislature, perhaps, could balance, but it cannot address specific situations. The bureaucracy deals with specific situations, but only from a position of commitment to particular policy interests.

Sixth, the judiciary has the advantage of being non-bureaucratic. It is effective in tapping energies and resources outside itself and outside the government in the exploration of the situation and the assessment of remedies. It does not work through a rigid, multilayered hierarchy of numerous officials, but through

Abram Chayes

---

[121] Thus, the court often establishes implementation committees to facilitate modification of relief as that seems necessary. *See, e.g.*, cases cited at note 90 *supra*.

[122] *See, e.g.*, Cox, The Role of Congress in Constitutional Determinations, 40 U. CIN. L. REV. 199, 228–29 (1971). *But see* Wellington, *Common Law Rules and Constitutional Double Standards: Some Notes on Adjudication*, 83 YALE L. J. 221, 240 (1973).

a smallish, representative task force, assembled ad hoc, and easily dismantled when the problem is finally resolved.

The foregoing enumeration is admittedly one-sided. It surely does not warrant unqualified endorsement of the public law litigation model in its present form. For one thing, the returns are not all in, and those we have show varying degrees of success. Legislative apportionment, although bitterly opposed as an arena of judicial intervention, seems to have worked out reasonably well. School segregation, on the other hand, seemed obviously appropriate for judicial reform under the Constitution, but the results are at best mixed. And some heralded efforts at management of state institutions may turn out to be pretty thoroughgoing failures. What experience we have with administrative resistance to intrusive court decrees is not particularly encouraging.[123]

There are also counter-instances and counter-arguments for each of the advantages of the public law model suggested above. Can the disinterestedness of the judge be sustained, for example, when he is more visibly a part of the political process? Will the consciously negotiated character of the relief ultimately erode the sense that what is being applied is law? Can the relatively unspecialized trial judge, even with the aid of the new authority and techniques being developed in public law litigation, respond adequately to the demands for legislative and predictive factfinding in the new model?[124] Against the asserted "responsiveness" of the courts, it may be argued that the insensitivity of other agencies represents a political judgment that should be left undisturbed. And although the courts may be well situated to balance competing policy interests in the particular case, if as is often true the decree calls for a substantial commitment of resources, the court has little basis for evaluating competing claims on the public purse. Each of these considerations needs exploration in much more detail—although I would hope that the discussion would proceed on the basis of what has been happening in the cases rather than a priori.

B. The Problem of Interest Representation

One issue, because it is the center of much current theoretical discussion, deserves somewhat fuller treatment, even in this preliminary effort. Public law litigation, because of its widespread impact, seems to call for adequate representation in the proceedings of the range of interests that will be affected by them. At the stage of relief in particular, if the decree is to be quasi-negotiated and party participation is to be relied upon to ensure its viability, representation at the bargaining table assumes very great importance, not only from the point of view of the affected interests but from that of the system itself. As noted above, the tendency, supported by both the language and the rationale of the Federal Rules of Civil Procedure, is to regard anyone whose interests may be significantly affected by the litigation to be presumptively entitled to participate in the suit on demand. In a public law system, persons are usually "affected" by litigation in terms of an "interest" that they share with many others similarly situated, whether organized or unorganized, that is to say, as members of an "interest group." Participation

[123] See, e.g., A. STONE, MENTAL HEALTH AND THE LAW 94 (1975); Note, supra note 69, at 1352–60.
[124] See generally Miller & Barron, The Supreme Court, The Adversary System, and the Flow of Information to the Justices: A Preliminary Inquiry, 61 VA. L. REV. 1187 (1975); The Courts, Social Science, and School Desegregation, 39 LAW & CONTEMP. PROB. 217 (1975).

of those affected by the decision has a reassuringly democratic ring, but when participation is mediated by group representatives, often self-appointed, it gives a certain pause.

Professor Richard Stewart, in a recent article, perceptively develops these misgivings about the theory and practice of interest representation.[125] Some of his objections are properly confined to the administrative agency context that was the focus of his discussion. One of these takes as its point of departure the now familiar notion of agency "capture" by the regulated interest.[126] If the agency is locked in a symbiotic relation with those it regulates, what basis is there, he asks, to suppose that merely formal representation of divergent interests will significantly affect the substance of administrative determinations?[127] The premise of "capture" does not apply in anything like the same degree, however, in the contemporary judicial setting. It may well be that, as in other eras, judges have a congenital preference for the established order. But the traditional independence and prestige of the federal judiciary, the range of subject matter with which it deals, its frequent involvement with substantive programs such as anti-discrimination laws or environmental regulation that cut across industry lines, and the relatively random pattern in which cases are presented for decision, all operate to insulate the judge from the cruder forms of "capture."[128]

Professor Stewart's main thrust, however, is that in a proceeding with broad public impacts, whether judicial or administrative, there are no very reliable criteria for identifying the affected interests, apart from the decibel level of the protest.[129] The fundamental objection, of course, is not to the participation of those who perceive themselves as affected and can make a plausible showing on that point. True, one may question whether those who do volunteer will adequately represent the larger groups for which they purport to speak. But intervention doctrine, class action rules looking toward adequate representation and subclassification,[130] and the judge's ability to draw on outside points of view all speak to this matter. There is a problem of the complexity of the proceedings if all affected parties are to be heard, but here too the judicial system has a potential for flexibility and administrative finesse that is being gradually mobilized.

The real problem that emerges from Professor Stewart's analysis is the inevitable incompleteness of the interest representation. What about those who do not volunteer—most often the weak, the poor, the unorganized? A first response is that these groups are unlikely to be better off in any other process to which the policy issue might be remitted for decision.[131] On this score, neither the judiciary nor the administrative agencies, it seems to me, need entertain feelings of inferiority to the typical bureaucratic decision or local governing board action, or even to the operation of "de-regulated" private activity. And to retreat to the notion that the legislature itself—Congress!—is in some mystical way adequately representative of all the interests at stake, particularly on issues of policy implementation and application, is to impose democratic theory by brute force on observed institutional behavior.

---

[125] Stewart, *supra* note 49.
[126] *See id.* at 1684–88.
[127] *See id.* at 1760–70.
[128] Compare the role of the trial judge with that of the administrative official described in *id.* at 1684–88.
[129] *See id.* at 1760–70.
[130] *See Developments, infra* at 1475–89.
[131] *See* Rabin, *Lawyers for Social Change: Perspectives on Public Interest Law*, 28 STAN. L. REV. 207, 230 n.75 (1976).

Moreover, a number of techniques are available to the judge to increase the breadth of interests represented in a suit, if that seems desirable. He can, for example, refuse to proceed until new parties are brought in, as in the old equity procedure, where the categories of necessary and proper parties converged.[132] In class actions, the judge may order such "notice as may be required for the protection of members of the class or otherwise for the fair conduct of the action,"[133] including "sampling notice" designed to apprise the judge of significant divisions of interest among the putative class, not brought to light by its representatives.[134] And that notice is supposed to be reasonably calculated to inform absentees of their potential interest in the litigation, which is more than can be said of notification of administrative proceedings in the Federal Register. The judge can also appoint guardians *ad litem* for unrepresented interests. And as we have seen, he can and does employ experts and amici to inform himself on aspects of the case not adequately developed by the parties. Finally, the judge can elicit the views of public officials at all levels.[135]

There is also a basis for thinking that the judge may have some success in identifying unrepresented interests that ought to be involved. The diversity of his work load may induce a certain breadth of perspective, in contrast to the specialized administrator. Courts have been somewhat more successful than some agencies in deriving policy guidance from opaque statutory provisions, a guidance that may help inform the choice of interests to be represented. The relatively defined focus even of public law litigation and its often local setting may help in identifying and defining affected interests.

The foregoing is at best a fragmentary and impressionistic response to the Stewart analysis. Moreover, most of it relates to the *potential* of the judicial system. A critical question for research is whether this potential is or can be exploited to produce a party structure that is adequately representative in light of the consequences of public law litigation without introducing so much complexity that the procedure falls of its own weight.

Even if one could be reasonably confident of the capacity of the court to construct ad hoc a kind of mini-legislature for the situation in litigation, I take it an even more fundamental query remains. In reaching a decision, what weight is to be assigned to the interests represented? A part of the answer may be found in the suggestion that the decision, or at least the remedy, involves a species of negotiation among the parties. But on this issue, the argument is familiar and powerful that Congress, whatever its makeup, is the institution authoritatively empowered in our system to balance incommensurable political values and interests. Here we confront, finally, the question of the legitimacy of judicial action in public law litigation.

[132] *See, e.g.*, J. STORY, EQUITY PLEADINGS § 72, at 83 (3d ed. 1844).

[133] Fed. R. Civ. P. 23 (d)(2).

[134] *See Developments, infra* at 1415, 1441–42 & n.254.

[135] For example, the Justice Department frequently participates in civil rights suits, e.g., Wyatt v. Stickney, 344 F. Supp. 373, 344 F. Supp. 387 (M.D. Ala. 1972), *aff'd in part, remanded in part, decision reserved in part sub nom.* Wyatt v. Aderholt, 503 F.2d 1305 (5th Cir. 1974); Lemon v. Bossier Parish School Bd., 240 F. Supp. 709 (W.D. La. 1965), *aff'd*, 370 F.2d 847 (5th Cir.), *cert. denied*, 388 U.S. 911 (1967). The Securities Exchange Commission frequently intervenes to review the adequacy of judgments reached under the securities laws. *See* cases cited at note 87 *supra*.

Despite the foregoing reservations, I am inclined, perhaps actuated by the outcome-oriented motives I ascribed earlier to the Supreme Court, to urge a hospitable reception for the developments I have described and a willingness to accept a good deal of disorderly, pragmatic institutional overlap. After all, the growth of judicial power has been, in large part, a function of the failure of other agencies to respond to groups that have been able to mobilize considerable political resources and energy. And, despite its new role, the judiciary is unlikely to displace its institutional rivals for governing power or even to achieve a dominant share of the market. In the circumstances, I would concentrate not on turning the clock back (or off), but on improving the performance of public law litigation, both by practical attention to the difficulties noted in this Article and by a more systematic professional understanding of what is being done.

IV. Some Thoughts on Legitimacy

Among the most important functions served by the traditional conception of adjudication was that of accommodating the reality of judicial power to the theory of representative government. The issue became urgent in the latter part of the 19th century as the pace of social and economic change increased and the courts, under the rubric of the fourteenth amendment, were repeatedly thrust into the charged political arena.

The two principal parties to the debate and their positions have grown familiar to the point of caricature. The "Classical" view[136] saw the courts as performing the objective—even "scientific"—function of deducing legal consequences from agreed first principles.[137] The Realists, after challenging and eventually undermining their predecessors' "pretentions" to objectivity, substituted a more pliable view of judicial method: "reasoned elaboration"[138] or "the inner morality of law"[139] or adherence to "neutral principles."[140] But both schools accepted the traditional conception of adjudication and the premise that the limits of proper judicial action inhered in and could be derived from it.[141]

As the traditional model has been displaced in recent years, therefore, questions of judicial legitimacy and accountability have reasserted themselves. Only the general direction of a response to these questions can be sketched in an Article of this compass. In so doing, we shift from more-or-less pragmatic consideration of how public law litigation works to the level of political theory: How to reconcile adjudication in the new model with the majoritarian premises of American political life.

For cases brought under an Act of Congress rather than the Constitution, the problem, formally at least, is not difficult. The courts can be said to be engaged

---

[136] The reference is to work in progress—tentatively entitled The *Rise and Fall of Classical Legal Thought*—of my colleague, Professor Duncan Kennedy, to whom I am indebted for much in this paper.

[137] *See* note 32 *supra*.

[138] H.M. HART & A. SACKS, *supra* note 2, at 161.

[139] L. FULLER, *supra* note 15, at 42–43.

[140] Wechsler, *Toward Neutral Principle of Constitutional Law*, 73 HARV. L. REV. 1. 15–16 (1959).

[141] *See id.:*

No legislature or executive is obligated by the nature of its function to support its choice of values by the type of reasoned elaboration that I have suggested is intrinsic to judicial action.

See also L. FULLER, *supra* note 15; Dworkin, *Hard Cases*, 88 HARV. L. REV. 1057 (1975).

in carrying out the legislative will, and the legitimacy of judicial action can be understood to rest on a delegation from the people's representatives. The judiciary is also, at least in theory, accountable: If Congress is dissatisfied with the execution of its charge, it can act to modify or withdraw the delegation.

But this formalistic analysis does not begin to capture the complexities of the way the legislature operates and of its relations with the courts. In enacting fundamental social and economic legislation, Congress is often unwilling or unable to do more than express a kind of general policy objective or orientation. Whether this be legislative abdication or not, the result is to leave a wide measure of discretion to the judicial delegate. The corrective power of Congress is also stringently limited in practice. Only a very few judicial aberrations will cross the threshold of political urgency needed to precipitate congressional action. In any case, a comprehensive defense of the legitimacy of public law litigation must account for its operation in the constitutional as well as the statutory field, and in truth the reality of contemporary judicial action does not differ much between them.

The fundamental ground of traditional reservations about constitutional adjudication is that the courts may be called upon to act counter to the popular will as expressed in legislation. In this respect, constitutional litigation in the new mode differs to some extent from the characteristic activity of the courts under the due process clause in the early part of the century. In the economic due process cases the courts acted to frustrate legislatures "speak[ing] the present will of the dominant forces in the state,"[142] and, beyond that, to withdraw altogether vast realms of policy from the reach of legislative action. Public law litigation is at once more and less intrusive: more, because it may command affirmative action of political officers; less, because it is ordinarily limited to adjusting the *manner* in which state and federal policy on education, prisons, mental institutions, and the like is carried forward. Its target is generally administrative rather than legislative action, action that is thus derivative rather than a direct expression of the legislative mandate. Moreover, one may ask whether democratic theory really requires deference to majoritarian outcomes whose victims are prisoners, inmates of mental institutions, and ghetto dwellers. Unlike the numerical minorities that the courts protected under the banner of economic due process, these have no alternative access to the levers of power in the system.

These observations will, no doubt, fail to dispel the uneasiness that American political and legal thinkers have always felt at the power of courts to frustrate, or to order, action by elected officials. For it cannot be denied that public law litigation explicitly rejects many of the constraints of judicial method and procedure in which we have characteristically sought respite from the unease. Now, I do not deny that the law, like other creative and performing arts, encompasses a recognizable (and teachable) technique; and this technique plays an important part in the development of the medium and in the criticism and evaluation of its practitioners. But in the law, as elsewhere, technical virtuosity has never been a guarantee of acceptable performance.

Moreover, an amalgam of less tangible institutional factors will continue to operate to shape judicial performance in the public law system as in the past: general expectations as to the competence and conscientiousness of federal judges; professional traditions of conduct and performance; the accepted, often tacit, canons and leeways of office. These are amorphous. They mark no sharp boundaries. Their

---

[142] A. BICKEL, THE LEAST DANGEROUS BRANCH 147 (1962).

flexibility and vagueness can be abused. But other kinds of constraint are no less vulnerable; and the historical experience is that egregious violation has invariably activated a countervailing response.

More fundamentally, our transformed appreciation of the whole process of making, implementing, and modifying law in a public law system points to sources other than professional method and role for the legitimacy of the new model lawsuit. As we now begin to see it, that process is plastic and fluid. Popular participation in it is not alone through the vote or by representation in the legislature. And judicial participation is not by way of sweeping and immutable statements of *the* law, but in the form of a continuous and rather tentative dialogue with other political elements—Congress and the executive, administrative agencies, the profession and the academics, the press and wider publics. Bentham's "judge and company" has become a conglomerate. In such a setting, the ability of a judicial pronouncement to sustain itself in the dialogue and the power of judicial action to generate assent over the long haul become the ultimate touchstones of legitimacy.[143]

In my view, judicial action only achieves such legitimacy by responding to, indeed by stirring, the deep and durable demand for justice in our society. I confess some difficulty in seeing how this is to be accomplished by erecting the barriers of the traditional conception to turn aside, for example, attacks on exclusionary zoning and police violence, two of the ugliest remaining manifestations of official racism in American life. In practice, if not in words, the American legal tradition has always acknowledged the importance of substantive results for the legitimacy and accountability of judicial action. Otherwise it could not praise *Marbury v. Madison*[144] as creative judicial statesmanship while condemning *Lochner v. New York*[145] as abuse of power. Perhaps the most important consequence of the inevitably exposed position of the judiciary in our contemporary regulatory state is that it will force us to confront more explicitly the qualities of wisdom, viability, responsiveness to human needs—the justice—of judicial decisions.

If we must accept that the artificial reason of the law gives no very certain guidance in these matters, we will be no worse off than other professions—and their professors.

---

[143] *See, e.g.,* A. COX, *supra* note 70, at 29–30, 99–118; Bickel, *The Supreme Court, 1960 Term—Foreword: The Passive Virtues*, 75 HARV. L. REV. 40, 47–51 (1961).

[144] 5 U.S. (1 Cranch) 137 (1803).

[145] 198 U.S. 45 (1905).

Critical Legal Studies

Duncan Kennedy

Duncan Kennedy

DUNCAN KENNEDY has had a long, productive, and extremely influential academic career. He started fast. After receiving his BA in Economics from Harvard College and his LLB from Yale Law School, he served for a year as a law clerk to Justice Potter Stewart, and then in 1971, at age twenty-nine, joined the faculty of Harvard Law School. He rapidly made a name for himself, most notably through his role, during the late 1970s and early '80s, as one of the principal organizers of the Conference on Critical Legal Studies. His influence was enhanced by his willingness to serve as a mentor for many students and younger scholars, including both of the editors of this volume. His body of writings is deep (including three books and over fifty articles) and extraordinarily broad (encompassing topics as diverse as Legal Theory, Legal Education, American Legal History, Contracts, Housing Law, Law and Economics, Feminism, and Law and Development). Of all of his works, however, the most famous and arguably the most powerful remains one of his first: "Form and Substance in Private Law Adjudication," published in the *Harvard Law Review* in 1976.

The article, Kennedy later suggested, grew out of and sought to amplify rebellion against two related bodies of thought: Liberalism and Legal Process Theory. With respect to the first, "the failure of the federal government and the 'system' as a whole to respond to the social problems of the 60s, the [Vietnam] war, the civil rights movement and the women's movement" had by the 1970s disillusioned many young political activists, himself included, in the prospects for "liberal reform" and increased their interest in more radical political projects. Within law schools, the counterpart to Liberalism (in the conventional, political sense) was Legal Process Theory, which had responded to the challenges of Legal Realism by offering a vision of how the legal system could be put back together, including, most importantly, a recipe for how adjudication, inevitably partially discretionary in character, could be practiced legitimately in a democratic society by unelected and largely unaccountable judges. That response—exemplified in this volume by the writings of Albert Sacks, Henry Hart, and Herbert Wechsler—Kennedy found wholly unconvincing, and he set out to discredit it.

That Kennedy had such iconoclastic aspirations is not obvious in early portions of the article, where he maps what he calls the "dimensions of legal form." Surveying an enormous body of legal theory, Kennedy argues that legal norms differ in the positions they occupy on three separate axes. The first he describes as "formal realizability." At one of its poles lie norms we call "rules"—sharp-edged "directives" that require judges or other officials "to respond to the presence together of each of a list of easily distinguishable factual aspects of a situation by intervening in a determinate manner." At the other pole lie "standards"—norms that make direct reference to "substantive objectives of the legal order" (such as "the best interests of the child" or the avoidance of "unjust enrichment") and leave judges or other officials considerable latitude in deciding how particular controversies should be resolved in order best to advance those goals. Few if any real norms can fairly be described as pure "rules" or pure "standards"; most if not all partake to different degrees of the qualities of "ruleness" and "standardness." The second of the three axes is "generality." Some norms are highly particular, governing few factual situations; others try "to kill many birds with one stone." The third, least obvious axis concerns norms' purposes. At one of its ends lie norms that seek to prevent people from engaging in activities deemed "morally wrong or otherwise flatly undesirable." At the other end lie "formalities"—norms designed to "facilitate private ordering," specifically by inducing parties to communicate in ways that later will give judges good evidence of what they had in mind. The penalties for murder and breaches of fiduciary duty lie near the first pole; the parol evidence rule (which renders unenforceable certain oral contracts) lies near the second; and the principle that ambiguities in a form contract (such as a standardized lease) will be resolved against the interests of the party that drafted the contract lies somewhere in between.

That the three axes are "logically independent" suggests that they might plausibly be depicted as follows:

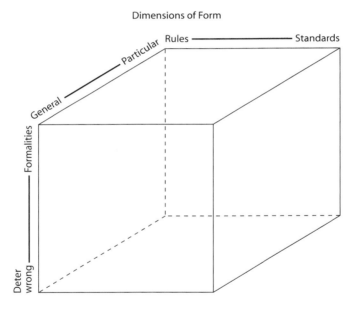

So, for example, a highly general standard intended to halt undesirable behavior (like the proposition that persons who fail to exercise reasonable care under all the circumstances are liable for injuries proximately caused by their negligence) would be located near the bottom right front corner of the box; a broadly applicable precise formality (like the requirement that a will be signed by two disinterested witnesses) would be located near the top front left corner; and so forth.

The most extensive and powerful aspect of Kennedy's discussion of these issues concerns, not the axes themselves, but the various arguments that legislators, judges, scholars, and lawyers have advanced in favor of one or another position on each of these dimensions. For example, it is often said that rules have the merits of certainty and the tendency to curb judicial arbitrariness and the demerit of imprecision in the advancement of substantive ends. Another widely held view is the claim (traceable to Max Weber and Roscoe Pound) that "property and business transactions" are more sensibly managed with mechanically applicable rules, while "human conduct and . . . the conduct of enterprises" are better handled with open-ended standards.

For almost every such argument, Kennedy suggests, there can be found within the body of legal materials a counterargument. For example, it is commonly thought that "formalities" should take the form of general rules rather than standards (i.e., that the upper left front corner of the box is superior to the upper right sector) on the theory that sharp-edged predictable norms, firmly enforced, will force parties to become fluent in the transactional language, and that the more broadly applicable those norms, the faster the parties will learn. The legal realists, however, attacked this conventional perspective on two grounds: (a) that some groups (e.g., poor consumers) will learn more slowly than others (e.g., businessmen) and thus firm enforcement of the rules will exacerbate inequalities of bargaining power; and (b) that judges, moved in part by a desire to counterbalance those inequalities, will convert seemingly crisp rules into standards (e.g., by developing "exceptions" and then choosing between the rules and the exceptions in particular cases on the basis of direct reference to substantive values). For the most part, Kennedy does not offer views concerning which of two opposed arguments of this sort is superior. His goal is to map the debates, not to resolve them.

His tour of arguments about form complete, Kennedy turns to a comparable study of arguments about the "substance" of private-law norms. Here, too, he suggests that most of the positions that appear in the case law and scholarly literature can be located on an axis between two poles. At one end is "individualism," which he describes as "the making of a sharp distinction between one's interests and those of others, combined with the belief that a preference in conduct for one's own interests is legitimate, but that one should be willing to respect the rules that make it possible to coexist with others similarly self-interested." At the other end is "altruism," which he defines as "the belief that one ought *not* to indulge a sharp preference for one's own interest over those of others, [but should] make sacrifices, . . . share, and . . . be merciful." Each outlook incorporates some elements of its rival. By insisting upon the importance of respecting the rights of others, individualism acknowledges significant limitations upon the pursuit of self-interest and thus differentiates itself from "pure egotism." Analogously, by setting limits on a person's moral obligations, altruism differentiates itself from "total selflessness or saintliness."

After defining them, Kennedy plunges into a sustained examination of the roles that these competing but intertwined outlooks have played and continue to play in American law. His historical analysis recapitulates in brief compass the story line of a book-length manuscript that in 1976 he had just completed, which traced the development of American legal thought. In that manuscript, entitled "The Rise and Fall of Classical Legal Thought," Kennedy followed earlier studies (e.g., that of Karl Llewellyn) in dividing our history into three overlapping stages—the first extending from 1800 to 1870, the second from 1850 to 1940, the third from 1900 to the present—but characterized those periods in ways radically different from his predecessors. American law during all three periods, he argued, was heavily colored by "conflict" between the visions of individualism and altruism, but the forms that conflict took varied sharply. In the first era, "morality," strongly associated with altruism, was thought to be in tension with "policy," a set of "pragmatic arguments" emphasizing the importance of shaping legal rules to promote economic development, which drew heavily on individualism. In the second, "Classical" period, individualism became the dominant position, purporting to reconcile considerations of morality and economic efficiency in a coherent vision that offered legal decisionmakers a reliable guide when defining the scope of liability. In the third, individualism fell from grace, and "policy" and "morality" were once again seen as in tension, but now each one of those terms incorporated some propositions that were individualist in character and some that were altruist in character.

One crucial effect of the collapse of the Classical synthesis during the modern era was a widespread perception among participants in the legal order of the ubiquity of fundamental contradictions. When should one person be forced "to share or make sacrifices for others"? To what extent should the law respect the outcome of deals struck by consenting adults and to what extent, conversely, should it regulate the terms of their interaction? To what extent should the law override people's choices in order to promote their own "best interests"? Questions of these sorts— each derivative of the underlying tension between individualism and altruism— emerged in countless doctrinal settings, and lawyers lacked any general theory for resolving them.

In short, Kennedy argues, two competing constellations of ideas and attitudes— one emphasizing autonomy and self-reliance, the other emphasizing community and sharing—have infused at least since 1800 the ways in which American lawyers and lawmakers have thought about the proper content of legal norms. What is the status of these constellations? At various points in the article, Kennedy addresses that question in somewhat different ways, but the short answer seems to be that they are deep, durable, and perhaps essential. At a minimum, they resonate with and draw sustenance from even larger belief systems that shape American politics and culture as a whole. Specifically, individualism "is associated with" the worldview of liberalism, most notably through their common commitment to the propositions that values are subjective and arbitrary and that governmental action in the pursuit of substantive conceptions of the good life or good society is dangerous, illegitimate, and likely futile. Conversely, altruism is associated with collectivism, a worldview that repudiates liberalism and asserts, instead, "that justice consists of order according to shared ends. Everything else is rampant or residual injustice." But the roots of individualism and altruism, Kennedy suggests, may go deeper still—through the layer of ideology, into the bedrock of human nature. They are "rhetorical modes," to be sure, but not *mere* rhetoric; rather, they "are responsive to real issues in the real world."

At this point, we reach the lynchpin of the article: the debates among American lawyers with respect to the form of legal norms and with respect to the substance of legal norms are connected. Arguments in favor of rules, Kennedy argues, are associated with arguments in favor of individualism, while arguments in favor of standards are associated with arguments in favor of altruism. He describes the character of those associations in different ways in different passages. In some, he goes so far as to claim that individualism "leads to" a preference for rules, while altruism "leads to" a preference for standards. Elsewhere, he is more tentative, suggesting that the connections between the respective pairs of arguments involve analogy or homology or resonance, rather than causation or entailment—and it is the latter set of formulations that, in retrospect, he prefers.

Resonance, he argues, operates on three distinct levels—morality, economics, and politics. The connections on the first level are the most straightforward. Individualism and "strict" enforcement of mechanical rules (even, or especially, when those rules are "mere formalities") share a sense of the virtue of self-reliance, while altruism and a willingness to "relax the rigor" of rules share a sense of the virtue of mercy.

The connections on the second level are more subtle. Structurally, individualism and a preference for rules share an implicit commitment to Social Darwinism—the belief that a posture of "tough love" will not only minimize the total number of injuries over the long haul but also maximize levels of socially valuable economic activity, while altruism and a preference for standards share skepticism concerning those assertions. Such structural parallels are confirmed by historical links: Individualism and rules-preference both found expression in the late nineteenth-century ideology (and legal theory) of laissez-faire, while altruism and standards-preference were united in criticizing that ideology.

The connections on the third level—that of "politics"—Kennedy concedes, are the most intricate and qualified. The issue, here, is what sorts of legal norms will lead to a style of adjudication that is most consistent with democracy. Kennedy begins his analysis by sketching the answers that the proponents of each type of norm *ought* to have made. In brief, both the advocates of rules and the devotees of individualism should have made essentially the same argument: that judges should strive to minimize the extent to which they make unaccountable decisions based upon inherently subjective value judgments, and that they can best do so by: (i) "eschew[ing] result orientation" when engaged in private-law adjudication; (ii) assuming a posture of judicial passivism when engaged in constitutional adjudication; and (iii) framing decisions of both sorts in the form of "formally realizable general rules." The advocates of standards and the devotees of altruism, by contrast, should have insisted upon the inevitability of value judgments both in private-law adjudication and in the exercise of judicial review and then developed a theory of how judges could make those judgments most responsibly.

Unfortunately (for the tightness of Kennedy's argument), with respect to *public* law, things did not play out quite this way historically. In the late nineteenth and early twentieth centuries, classical theorists (individualist rule-preferers) succeeded in developing a theory that, instead of pointing toward judicial passivism, justified aggressive exercises of the power of judicial review to strike down social-welfare legislation—a theory that Kennedy, drawing on his work in "The Rise and Fall of Classical Legal Thought," explicates brilliantly. In response, the legal realists (altruist standard-preferers) for "tactical" reasons sought to differentiate private law from public (constitutional) law, insisting that, while judicial decision making in the latter was inevitably political in character, judicial decision making in the former ordinarily was not. Fidelity to democracy thus required judges to avoid, through exercises of the power of judicial review, "substituting their judgments for those of the legislature," but did not constrain analogously the ways in which they shaped and applied the rules of contracts, torts, property, etc. This awkward, "intellectually dishonest" stance had the short-term advantage of enabling the realists to denounce *Lochner*ism, but in the long run deprived their platform of both radicalism and coherence. In short, in this one (major) context, Kennedy argues that the positions actually taken by the major groups of legal thinkers failed to track the structural parallels between the "real positions" of individualism and rules-preference on one hand and altruism and standards-preference on the other.

It's a delicate argument, and it stands out in the essay because of its apparent abandonment of the phenomenological methodology that infuses almost all of its other parts.

With respect to the political aspect of *private*-law adjudication, by contrast, the arguments actually deployed by the major groups of legal theorists did align reasonably well with their "real" positions. Somewhat more specifically, the classical theorists (individualist rule-preferers) contended that the resolution of private disputes was consistent with democracy only if it respected the differences among three "tiers of activity." Kennedy summarizes their conceptions of those tiers as follows:

> First, . . . private parties interact, and someone acquires a grievance. Second, the judge applies the system of Classical individualist common law rules, and either grants or denies a remedy. Third, the legislature, if it wishes, but not the judge, imposes altruistic duties that go beyond the common law system of remedies.

Critical to this picture was the conviction that decision making on the second tier could be determinate—i.e., could generate a single right answer to each controversy. And that conviction rested, in turn, on a vision of the common law as "a gapless, closed system of Classical individualist principles." The legal realists (altruist standard-preferers) mounted a massive and ultimately successful assault on that vision, demonstrating that most common-law rules incorporated to different degrees the qualities of both individualism and altruism and thus that judges, when called upon to fill in the "gaps" in the system, had no alternative but to make discretionary, "political" choices among the rival worldviews.

The success of the realists' assault, Kennedy contends, exposed anew the underlying problem: How can inevitably discretionary private-law adjudication be reconciled with democracy—specifically, with the principle that the rules by which we are governed are selected by our elected representatives rather than by unelected judges through ad-hoc decision making? Here, at last, Kennedy turns his guns on rival schools of legal theory. Since 1940, he contends, two groups of scholars have tried to answer that question—and neither has succeeded. Advocates of "law and economics" (e.g., Posner and Calabresi) argue that private-law adjudication can be both determinate and legitimate if judges frame rules and resolve cases in the ways that will most efficiently allocate scarce resources—specifically, by determining the result that would be reached by the parties themselves if they were able to bargain freely in the absence of transaction costs—leaving to the legislatures the controversial, political determinations of how those resources should be distributed. The fatal defect of this project, Kennedy argues (drawing on the work of Robert Hale, Mitchell Polinsky, Arthur Leff, and Ed Baker), is that the outcome of frictionless bargaining depends upon the initial distribution of resources among the relevant parties, which in turn is heavily affected by the shape of extant private-law rules. To attempt to determine what those rules should be by asking what bargains private actors, in the absence of friction, would make in their shadow is therefore "circular."

Legal process theorists (e.g., Henry Hart, Albert Sacks, Lon Fuller, and Harry Wellington), Kennedy argues, offer a different solution. In their judgment, there exists within the legal system a "core" set of issues with respect to which society is in general agreement. When confronted by cases arising within that core, judges can and should use the techniques of "reasoned elaboration" to identify the underlying, consensual "social values or purposes"; articulate norms (either in the form of rules or in the form of standards) that incorporate and advance those ends; and then use those norms to make decisions. Cases that implicate issues that fall outside the "core," by contrast, must be left to the legislature to resolve. The fatal defect of this alternative approach, Kennedy contends, is that there exists no such consensual "core." The legal system consists of one large "battleground" between individualism and altruism "on which no foot of ground is undisputed." Legal process theorists, in short, fail to offer "a convincing description of reality."

In sum, in Kennedy's judgment, the fundamental contradiction between individualism and altruism is ubiquitous and inescapable. The elaborate structure by which Classical theorists and judges sought to resolve it has collapsed, and neither of the two major efforts by modern theorists to fill the gap left by the fall of Classicism is persuasive. A contemporary judge, Kennedy suggests, should give up hope of "overcoming" the conflict. What then should she do? At the end of the essay, Kennedy suggests, hesitantly, that a "noble" response would be to follow the lead of Judge Skelly Wright and others in promoting, through individual private-law decisions, the cause of altruism—not because those efforts have any realistic prospect of "transform[ing] society," but because the dramatic impact of such decisions might help persuade some "adversaries" and because they contribute to "the indispensable task of imagining an altruistic order."

Several aspects of "Form and Substance" drew upon and then fueled ongoing debates within legal theory. As noted above (and as Kennedy freely acknowledged), several theorists previously had sought to map the arguments that might be made for "rules" or "standards"—in general or in particular contexts. Interest in this particular dimension of "legal form" did not dissipate after 1976; many major scholars subsequently extended or contested Kennedy's arguments. For example, in "Crystals and Mud in Property Law," Carol Rose challenged the conventional associations that Kennedy had helped systematize—namely, that rules are associated with individualism and liberalism, while standards are associated with altruism and communitarianism. Although she agreed that those are the conventional connotations of the terms, she argued that, in practice, they may operate quite differently. Rules, by facilitating commerce, may do more to foster "sociability" than standards, while standards, in contexts like the Uniform Commercial Code, may lead to more predictable outcomes, enabling private actors to plan their affairs with more confidence, than rules. More original, perhaps, was Rose's claim that, within a given field of doctrine (say, real property law), rules and standards tend to oscillate over time. Sharp-edged rules tend to deteriorate (largely because judges are too soft-hearted to enforce them rigorously forever), gradually collapsing into standards, the vagueness of which provokes resentment and a return to rules, and so forth.

In her Foreword to the 1992 Supreme Court issue of the *Harvard Law Review*, Kathleen Sullivan explored the ways in which the same themes find expression in modern constitutional law. In her judgment, the somewhat surprising pattern of decisions rendered by the Court during the previous year was partially attributable to disagreement among the Justices concerning the relative merits of rules and standards. Some of them, imbued with a "rationalist and positivist spirit," favor rules, in part because of a suspicion that "standards will enable the Court to translate raw subjective value preferences into law." Other Justices "are skeptical about the capacity of rules to constrain value choice and believe that custom and shared understandings can adequately constrain judicial deliberation in a regime of standards." Other scholars who offered divergent takes on the rules-versus-standards debate include Frank Easterbrook, Margaret Jane Radin, Antonin Scalia, Frederick Schauer, and Pierre Schlag.

Kennedy's periodization of what he called "styles of legal thought" also drew upon earlier treatments of the same subject and shaped many later ones. A crucial collaborator on this front was his colleague, Morton Horwitz. While Kennedy was working on "Form and Substance," Horwitz was writing a series of articles he would eventually gather together in *The Transformation of American Law*. In those articles, Horwitz divided the history of American private-law doctrine—and, more to the point, the history of styles of reasoning about private-law doctrine—into an antebellum era (characterized by "instrumentalism"), a postbellum era (characterized by "formalism"), and a modern era. Horwitz's description of the character of those approaches differed markedly from Kennedy's but their two accounts surely influenced one another, and their senses of the timing of the major watersheds in our legal history were identical. The same three-stage narrative can be found in many subsequent works—including Bruce Ackerman's highly influential study of constitutional law and theory, *We The People*.

The critique of "law and economics" that Kennedy briefly outlined in "Form and Substance" also blossomed in later works. Kennedy himself did a good deal of the work in two subsequent essays: "Cost-Benefit Analysis of Entitlement Problems: A Critique"; and "Are Property and Contract Efficient?" (co-authored with Frank Michelman). Lucian Bebchuk and Mark Kelman also contributed much to the analysis. Among the arguments deployed in this still-growing body of literature is that economic analysts, seeking to show courts how to resolve cases in ways that will maximize aggregate welfare, regularly stumble on the so-called "offer-asking problem"—the fact (discussed at some length in the introduction to Coase's "Problem of Social Cost") that the value a given consumer places upon a particular entitlement will often depend upon whether it is allocated to her initially (and she is thus considering whether to sell it) or it is not allocated to her initially (and she is thus considering whether to buy it). A related difficulty, foreshadowed in "Form and Substance," is the problem of "general indeterminacy"—the fact that, when seeking the efficient solutions to more than one doctrinal issue, the order in which one considers them often makes a big difference, and economic analysis offers no insight into the correct sequence. Such attacks on the claim that economic analysis can offer judges a reliable guide when resolving private-law disputes have divided economists. Some dispute the criticisms; others concede their force but argue that their practical import is modest; still others have taken the lead in developing or refining the arguments.

One of the central themes of "Form and Substance," namely, the important role played in American law by a fundamental contradiction between individualism and altruism, had similarly important aftershocks. Kennedy himself elaborated the theme in a 1979 article, "The Structure of Blackstone's Commentaries." Following his lead, Greg Alexander argued that a series of efforts to mediate a similar contradiction—specifically, between the freedom of testators to control uses of their property after their deaths and the freedom of devisees to use and dispose of bequests as they wish—explains much of the history of the law of trusts.

An analogous argument undergirds Elizabeth Mensch's study of the development of property law in the colonial era. In the 1980s, as the applications of Kennedy's original idea diverged ever further from his original intent, he renounced this aspect of this argument, insisting that it had become a "lifeless slogan." But for many scholars and students, the idea remains illuminating.

The aspect of "Form and Substance" that, today, remains most puzzling is why it proved so inspiring. It's very long. Its subject is abstruse. Its demonstration that for most arguments involving the merits of a particular legal form there exists a colorable counterargument, combined with its refusal to offer an opinion concerning which of two opposed claims is the more persuasive, leaves many readers with a sense of the "indeterminacy" of legal discourse and prompted critics to charge that it leads to either apathy or cynicism. How then did the article manage to help inspire Critical Legal Studies—an aptly named "movement" with sufficient energy and popular appeal that it prompted President Reagan to denounce it?

To some extent, the answer probably is that the article was less central to Critical Legal Studies than is conventionally supposed. CLS was a broad umbrella, sheltering an array of scholars, many of whom were uninterested in the intricacies of "Form and Substance." Kennedy's pamphlet, *Legal Education and the Reproduction of Hierarchy*, a sweeping attack on conventional legal education, had broader appeal.

But even thus tempered, the question still has bite. The answer may lie in the liberating potential of the article's comprehensive critique of American legal theory. In the judgment of many readers, Kennedy had succeeded in discrediting the efforts of all of the extant schools of legal thought to justify the legal foundations for American capitalism and democracy. Indeed, his critical arguments had implications even broader than Kennedy himself had acknowledged. For example, aspects of his assault on Law and Economics were equally damaging to the projects of many other social reformers, including the more programmatic of the legal realists and law-and-society scholars. Similarly, some of his criticisms of Legal Process Theory were equally applicable to the normative theories of other, later scholars, such as Dworkin or Cover, working within the broad tradition of Liberalism. The lesson seemed to be that nothing in the Canon provides us guidance. Rather, we face choices—choices requiring moral and political debate, not legal theory and interpretation. For many, it was at once a revelation and a call to action.

WILLIAM FISHER

BIBLIOGRAPHY

Primary Sources

Aside from "Form and Substance" and *Legal Education and the Reproduction of Hierarchy* (originally published in 1983; revised and expanded edition by NYU Press, 2004), Kennedy's most influential works are *Sexy Dressing, Etc.* (Cambridge, Mass.: Harvard University Press, 1983) (a collection of some of his best essays on feminism, legal theory, and legal education); and *A Critique of Adjudication [fin de siecle]* (Cambridge, Mass.: Harvard University Press, 1997) (in which can be found considerable discussion of other scholars' uses and misuses of his arguments in

"Form and Substance"). His other major works include: "The Structure of Blackstone's Commentaries," *Buffalo Law Review* 28 (1979): 205; "Cost-Benefit Analysis of Entitlement Problems: A Critique," *Stanford Law Review* 33 (1981): 387; "Distributive and Paternalist Motives in Contract and Tort Law, with Special Reference to Compulsory Terms and Unequal Bargaining Power," *Maryland Law Review* 41 (1982): 563; "The Stages of the Decline of the Public/Private Distinction," *University of Pennsylvania Law Review* 130 (1982): 1349; "Freedom & Constraint in Adjudication: A Critical Phenomenology," *Journal of Legal Education* 36 (1986): 518; "The Effect of the Warranty of Habitability on Low Income Housing: "Milking" and Class Violence," *Florida State Law Review* 15 (1987): 485; and "A Semiotics of Legal Argument," *Syracuse Law Review* 42 (1991): 75. A complete list of his publications, including many translations of his essays, can be found on his Web site: http://duncankennedy.net/bibliography/chrono.html.

Secondary Sources

The literature on Critical Legal Studies is formidable. Good collections of essays by scholars affiliated with the Conference include James Boyle, ed., *Critical Legal Studies* (New York: New York University Press, 1992); David Kairys, ed., *The Politics of Law: A Progressive Critique* (New York: Pantheon, 1990); and the January 1984 issue of the *Stanford Law Review*. For a comprehensive list of CLS works (as of 1984), see Duncan Kennedy and Karl Klare, "A Bibliography of Critical Legal Studies," *Yale Law Journal* 94 (1984): 461–90. The best known studies of the movement are Mark Kelman, *A Guide to Critical Legal Studies* (Cambridge, Mass.: Harvard University Press, 1977) and Roberto Unger, *The Critical Legal Studies Movement* (Cambridge, Mass.: Harvard University Press, 1986).

The essays discussed in the text that built upon Kennedy's discussion of rules and standards are: Carol Rose, "Crystals and Mud in Property Law," *Stanford Law Review* 40 (1988): 577, reprinted in *Property and Persuasion: Essays on the History, Theory and Rhetoric of Ownership* (Boulder: Westview Press, 1994), 199–232; Kathleen Sullivan, "The Supreme Court, 1991 Term—Foreword: The Justice of Rules and Standards," *Harvard Law Review* 106 (1992): 22; Frank H. Easterbrook, "The Supreme Court, 1983 Term—Foreword: The Court and the Economic System," *Harvard Law Review* 98 (1984): 4; Margaret Jan Radin, "Reconsidering the Rule of Law," *Boston University Law Review* 69 (1989): 781; Antonin Scalia, "The Rule of Law as a Law of Rules," *University of Chicago Law Review* 56 (1989): 1175; Frederick Schauer, *Playing by the Rules: A Philosophic Examination of Rule-Based Decision-making in Law and Life* (New York: Oxford University Press, 1991); and Pierre Schlag, "Rules and Standards," *UCLA Law Review* 33 (1985): 379.

Treatments of the history of American legal thought that were influenced by Kennedy's periodization include Morton Horwitz, *The Transformation of American Law, 1760–1860* (Cambridge, Mass.: Harvard University Press, 1977): Bruce Ackerman, *We the People: Foundations* (Cambridge, Mass.: Harvard University Press, 1991); and Thomas Grey, "Langdell's Orthodoxy," *Pittsburgh Law Review* 45 (1983): 1.

Criticisms of economic analysis of law that were affected by Kennedy's arguments include Mark Kelman, "Consumption Theory, Production Theory, and

Ideology in the Coase Theorem," *Southern California Law Review* 52 (1979): 669 (discussed more extensively in the introduction to Coase's "Problem of Social Cost"); and Lucian Bebchuk, "The Pursuit of a Bigger Pie: Can Everyone Expect a Bigger Slice?" *Hofstra Law Review* 8 (1980): 671.

Papers exploring the impact on legal thought and doctrine of fundamental contradictions include Gregory Alexander, "The Dead Hand and the Law of Trusts in the Nineteenth Century," *Stanford Law Review* 37 (1985): 1189; Elizabeth Mensch, "The Colonial Origins of Liberal Property Rights," *Buffalo Law Review* 31 (1982): 635. Kennedy's recantation of the idea was made in "Roll Over Beethoven," *Stanford Law Review* 84 (1984): 1, 15–16.

Kennedy's magnum opus, *A Critique of Adjudication [fin de siecle]*, has elicited considerable discussion, criticism, and praise. An excellent collection of reviews and responses can be found in the March 2001 issue of the *Cardozo Law Review*.

DUNCAN KENNEDY

"Form and Substance in Private Law Adjudication"

88 Harvard Law Review 1685 (1976)

This article is an inquiry into the nature and interconnection of the different rhetorical modes found in American private law opinions, articles and treatises. I argue that there are two opposed rhetorical modes for dealing with substantive issues, which I will call individualism and altruism. There are also two opposed modes for dealing with questions of the form in which legal solutions to the substantive problems should be cast. One formal mode favors the use of clearly defined, highly administrable, general rules; the other supports the use of equitable standards producing ad hoc decisions with relatively little precedential value.

My purpose is the rational vindication of two common intuitions about these arguments as they apply to private law disputes in which the validity of legislation is not in question. The first is that altruist views on substantive private law issues lead to willingness to resort to standards in administration, while individualism seems to harmonize with an insistence on rigid rules rigidly applied. The second is that substantive and formal conflict in private law cannot be reduced to disagreement about how to apply some neutral calculus that will "maximize the total satisfactions of valid human wants."[1] The opposed rhetorical modes lawyers use reflect a deeper level of contradiction. At this deeper level, we are divided, among ourselves and also within ourselves, between irreconcilable visions of humanity and society, and between radically different aspirations for our common future.

The discussion proceeds as follows. Sections I and II address the problem of the choice between rules and standards as the form for legal directives, collecting and organizing the wide variety of arguments that have been found persuasive in different areas of legal study. Sections III and IV develop the dichotomy of individualism and altruism, with the hope of bringing a measure of order to the chaotic mass of "policies" lawyers use in justifying particular legal rules. Sections V, VI and VII argue that the formal and substantive dichotomies are in fact aspects of a single conflict, whose history is briefly traced through a hundred and fifty years of moral, economic and political dispute. Section VIII outlines the contradictory sets of fundamental premises that underlie this conflict. Section IX is a conclusion.

Professor of Law, Harvard University.
Colleagues, friends and family too numerous to list helped me generously in the writing of this article; Philip Heymann, Morton Horwitz, Robert Nozick and Henry Steiner were especially profligate of their time and thoughts. Errors are mine alone.
[1] H. HART & A. SACKS, THE LEGAL PROCESS 113 (tent. ed. 1958).

I will use the law of contracts as a primary source of illustrations, for two reasons. I know it better than other private law subjects, and it is blessed with an extraordinary scholarly literature full of insights that seem to beg for application beyond the narrow compass within which their authors developed them. For example, much of this article simply abstracts to the level of "private law" the argument of an article by Stewart Macaulay on credit cards.[2] It may be useful to take, as a beginning text, the following passage from the Kessler and Gilmore *Contracts* casebook:[3]

> The eventual triumph of the third party beneficiary idea may be looked on as still another instance of the progressive liberalization or erosion of the rigid rules of the late nineteenth century theory of contractual obligation. That such a process has been going on throughout this century is so clear as to be beyond argument. The movement on all fronts has been in the direction of expanding the range and the quantum of obligation and liability. We have seen the development of theories of quasi-contractual liability, of the doctrines of promissory estoppel and culpa in contrahendo, of the perhaps revolutionary idea that the law imposes on the parties to a contract an affirmative duty to act in good faith. During the same period the sanctions for breach of contract have been notably expanded. Recovery of "special" or "consequential" damages has become routinely available in situations in which the recovery would have been as routinely denied fifty years ago. The once "exceptional" remedy of specific performance is rapidly becoming the order of the day. On the other hand the party who has failed to perform his contractual duty but who, in the light of the circumstances, is nevertheless felt to be without fault has been protected by a notable expansion of theories of excuse, such as the over-lapping ideas of mistake and frustration. To the nineteenth century legal mind the propositions that no man was his brother's keeper, that the race was to the swift and that the devil should take the hindmost seemed not only obvious but morally right. The most striking feature of nineteenth century contract theory is the narrow scope of social duty which it implicitly assumed. In our own century we have witnessed what it does not seem too fanciful to describe as a socialization of our theory of contract.

My purpose is to examine the relationship between the first and last sentences of the quoted passage. What is the connection between the *"erosion of the rigid rules* of the late nineteenth century theory of contractual obligation" and the "socialization of our theory of contract"? I will begin by investigating the formal concept of a rigid rule.

I. The Jurisprudence of Rules

The jurisprudence of rules is the body of legal thought that deals explicitly with the question of legal form. It is premised on the notion that the choice between standards and rules of different degrees of generality is significant, and can be

Duncan Kennedy

[2] Macaulay, Private Legislation and the Duty to Read—Business Run by IBM Machine, The Law of Contracts and Credit Cards, 19 VAND. L. REV. 1051, 1056–69 (1966).

[3] F. KESSLER & G. GILMORE, CONTRACTS, CASES AND MATERIALS 1118 (2d ed. 1970) [hereinafter cited as KESSLER & GILMORE].

analyzed in isolation from the substantive issues that the rules or standards respond to.[4]

A. Dimensions of Form

1. Formal Realizability. The first dimension of rules is that of formal realizability. I will use this term, borrowed from Rudolph von Ihering's classic *Spirit of Roman Law*, to describe the degree to which a legal directive has the quality of "ruleness." The extreme of formal realizability is a directive to an official that requires him to respond to the presence together of each of a list of easily distinguishable factual aspects of a situation by intervening in a determinate way. Ihering used the determination of legal capacity by sole reference to age as a prime example of a formally realizable definition of liability; on the remedial side, he used the fixing of money fines of definite amounts as a tariff of damages for particular offenses.[5]

At the opposite pole from a formally realizable rule is a standard or principle or policy. A standard refers directly to one of the substantive objectives of the legal order. Some examples are good faith, due care, fairness, unconscionability, unjust enrichment, and reasonableness. The application of a standard requires the judge both to discover the facts of a particular situation and to assess them in terms of the purposes or social values embodied in the standard.[6]

It has been common ground, at least since Ihering, that the two great social virtues of formally realizable rules, as opposed to standards or principles, are the restraint of official arbitrariness and certainty. The two are distinct but overlapping.

---

[4] The principal sources on the jurisprudence of form with which I am acquainted are: 6 J. BENTHAM, THE WORKS OF JEREMY BENTHAM 60–86, 508–85 (Bowring ed. 1839); 2 AUSTIN, LECTURES ON JURISPRU-DENCE § 939–44 (4th ed. 1873); 3 R. VON IHERING, DER GEIST DES ROMSICHEN RECHT § 4, at 50–55 (1883) [available in French translation as R. VON IHERING, L'ESPRIT DU DROIT ROMAIN (Meulenaere trans. 1877); future citations are to French ed.]; 2 M. WEBER, ECONOMY AND SOCIETY 656–67, 880–88 (Ross & Wittich eds. 1969); Pound, *The Theory of Judicial Decision, III*, 36 HARV. L. REV. 940 (1923); Fuller, *Consideration and Form*, 41 COLUM. L. REV. 799 (1941); von Mehren, *Civil Law Analogues to Consideration: An Exercise in Comparative Analysis*, 72 HARV. L. REV. 1009 (1959); Macaulay, *Justice Traynor and the Law of Contracts*, 13 STAN. L. REV. 812 (1961); Fried, *Two Concepts of Interests: Some Reflections on the Supreme Court's Balancing Test*, 76 HARV. L. REV. 755 (1963); Friedman, *Law, Rules and the Interpretation of Written Documents*, 59 NW. U.L. REV. 751 (1965); Macaulay, *supra* note 2; Dworkin, *The Model of Rules*, 35 U. Chi. L. Rev. 14 (1967); K. Davis, DISCRETIONARY JUSTICE: A PRELIMINARY INQUIRY (1969); P. Selznick, LAW, SOCIETY AND INDUSTRIAL JUSTICE 11–18 (1969); Kennedy, *Legal Formality*, 2 J. Leg. Stud. 351 (1973); R. Unger, LAW IN MODERN SOCIETY 203–16 (1976); A. Katz, *Vagueness and Legal Control of Children in Need of Supervision, in Studies in Boundary Theory* (unpublished manuscript on file at Harvard Law Review, 1976).

[5] *See* 1 R. VON IHERING, *supra* note 4, at 51–56.

[6] *See* H. HART & A. SACKS, *supra* note 1, at 126–29; Friedman, *supra* note 4, at 753–54; Dawson, *Unconscionable Coercion: The German Version*, 89 HARV. L. REV. 1041, 1042–47 (1976). The extent to which particular words or categories are regarded as sufficiently "factual" to serve as the basis of formally realizable rules changes through time, is subject to dispute at any particular time, and is a matter of degree. For example, the idea of competition may appear to one writer to be capable of generating precise and predictable answers to particular questions of antitrust law, while another may regard it as no more than a standard, unadministrable except though a further body of per se rules. *Compare* Bork, *The Rule of Reason and the Per Se Concept: Price Fixing and the Market Division*, 74 YALE L. J. 775 (1965), *with* Turner, *The Principles of American Antitrust Law*, in COMPARATIVE ASPECTS OF ANTITRUST LAW IN THE UNITED STATES, THE UNITED KING-DOM AND THE EUROPEAN ECONOMIC COMMUNITY 9–12 (Int'l & Comp. L.Q. Supp. Vol. 6, 1963). "Best interests of the child" has been subject to a similar dispute. *See* Mnookin, *Child Custody Adjudication: Judicial Functions in the Face of Indeterminacy*, 1975 LAW & CONTEMP. PROB. 226. The grandfather of such controversies in Anglo-American law is the "objectivism" issue. Late nineteenth century legal thought claimed that "subjective intent" was no more than a standard, and that legal directives dependent on its determination should be recast as rules referring to "external" aspects of the situation. *See* Kennedy, *supra* note 4, at 364 n.22.

Official arbitrariness means the sub rosa use of criteria of decision that are inappropriate in view of the underlying purposes of the rule. These range from corruption to political bias. Their use is seen as an evil in itself, quite apart from their impact on private activity.

Certainty, on the other hand, is valued for its effect on the citizenry: if private actors can know in advance the incidence of official intervention, they will adjust their activities in advance to take account of them. From the point of view of the state, this increases the likelihood that private activity will follow a desired pattern. From the point of view of the citizenry, it removes the inhibiting effect on action that occurs when one's gains are subject to sporadic legal catastrophe.[7]

It has also been common ground, at least since Ihering,[8] that the virtues of formal realizability have a cost. The choice of rules as the mode of intervention involves the sacrifice of precision in the achievement of the objectives lying behind the rules. Suppose that the reason for creating a class of persons who lack capacity is the belief that immature people lack the faculty of free will. Setting the age of majority at 21 years will incapacitate many but not all of those who lack this faculty. And it will incapacitate some who actually possess it. From the point of view of the purpose of the rules, this combined over- and underinclusiveness amounts not just to licensing but to requiring official arbitrariness. If we adopt the rule, it is because of a judgment that this kind of arbitrariness is less serious than the arbitrariness and uncertainty that would result from empowering the official to apply the standard of "free will" directly to the facts of each case.

2. Generality. The second dimension that we commonly use in describing legal directives is that of generality vs. particularity. A rule setting the age of legal majority at 21 is more general than a rule setting the age of capacity to contract at 21. A standard of reasonable care in the use of firearms is more particular than a standard of reasonable care in the use of "any dangerous instrumentality." Generality means that the framer of the legal directive is attempting to kill many birds with one stone. The wide scope of the rule or standard is an attempt to deal with as many as possible of the different imaginable fact situations in which a substantive issue may arise.[9]

The dimensions of generality and formal realizability are logically independent: we can have general or particular standards, and general or particular rules. But there are relationships between the dimensions that commonly emerge in practice. First, a general rule will be more over- and underinclusive than a particular rule. Every rule involves a measure of imprecision vis-à-vis its purpose (this is definitional), but the wider the scope of the rule, the more serious the imprecision becomes.

Second, the multiplication of particular rules undermines their formal realizability by increasing the number of "jurisdictional" questions. Even where the

---

[7] While certainty is now praised through the formal language of efficiency, the idea has been familiar for centuries. Montesquieu put it as follows, speaking of the peasants of the Ottoman Empire in the eighteenth century: "Ownership of land is uncertain, and the incentive for agricultural development is consequently weakened: there is neither title nor possession that is good against the caprice of the rulers." C. DE MONTESQUIEU, LETTRES PERSANES 64 (1721). *See* Kennedy, *supra* note 4, at 365–77.

[8] R. VON IHERING, *supra* note 4, at 54–55.

[9] *See generally* Friedman, *Legal Rules and the Process of Social Change*, 19 STAN. L. REV. 786, 832–35 (1967); Leff, *Contract as Thing*, 19 AMER. U.L. REV. 131, 131–37 (1970). For an illustration of how the issue arises in legal argument, *See* Meinhard v. Salmon, 249 N.Y. 458, 472, 164 N.E. 545, 549 (1928) (Andrews, J., dissenting). *See also* note 10 *infra*.

scope of each particular rule is defined in terms of formally realizable criteria, if we have a different age of capacity for voting, drinking, driving, contracting, marrying and tortfeasing, there are likely to be contradictions and uncertainty in borderline cases. One general rule of legal capacity at age 18 eliminates all these at a blow, and to that extent makes the system more formally realizable.[10]

Third, a regime of general rules should reduce to a minimum the occasions of judicial lawmaking. Generality in statement guarantees that individual decisions will have far reaching effects. There will be fewer cases of first impression, and because there are fewer rules altogether, there will be fewer occasions on which a judge is free to choose between conflicting lines of authority. At the same time, formal realizability eliminates the sub rosa lawmaking that is possible under a regime of standards. It will be clear what the rule is, and everyone will know whether the judge is applying it. In such a situation, the judge is forced to confront the extent of his power, and this alone should make him more wary of using it than he would otherwise be.[11]

Finally, the application of a standard to a particular fact situation will often generate a particular rule much narrower in scope than that standard. One characteristic mode of ordering a subject matter area including a vast number of possible situations is through the combination of a standard with an ever increasing group of particular rules of this kind. The generality of the standard means that there are no gaps: it is possible to find out something about how judges will dispose of cases that have not yet arisen. But no attempt is made to formulate a formally realizable general rule. Rather, case law gradually fills in the area with rules so closely bound to particular facts that they have little or no precedential value.[12]

3. Formalities vs. Rules Designed to Deter Wrongful Behavior. There is a third dimension for the description of legal directives that is as important as formal realizability and generality. In this dimension, we place at one pole legal institutions whose purpose is to prevent people from engaging in particular activities because those activities are morally wrong or otherwise flatly undesirable. Most of the law of crimes fits this pattern: laws against murder aim to eliminate murder. At the other pole are legal institutions whose stated object is to facilitate private ordering. Legal institutions at this pole, sometimes called formalities,[13] are supposed to help parties in communicating clearly to the judge which of various alternatives they want him to follow in dealing with disputes that may arise later in their relationship. The law of conveyancing is the paradigm here.

---

[10] This phenomenon is discussed in Surrey, *Complexity and the Internal Revenue Code: The Problem of the Management of Tax Detail*, 1969 LAW & CONTEMP. PROB. 673, 695–702; Amsterdam, *Perspectives on the Fourth Amendment*, 58 MINN. L. REV. 349, 374–77, 388–95 (1974).

[11] On the obligation to formulate rules as a check on discretionary power, *see* K. DAVIS, *supra* note 4, at 52–96; Amsterdam, *supra* note 10, at 416–28.

[12] Chief Justice Shaw gave classic expression to this view in Norway Plains Co. v. Boston & Maine R.R. Co., 67 Mass. (1 Gray) 263, 267 (1854):

It is one of the great merits and advantages of the common law, that, instead of a series of detailed practical rules, established by positive provisions, and adapted to the precise circumstances of particular cases, which would become obsolete and fail, when the practice and course of business, to which they apply, should cease or change, the common law consists of a few broad and comprehensive principles founded on reason, natural justice, and enlightened public policy modified and adapted to the circumstances of all the particular cases which fall within it.

[13] *See* generally Fuller, *supra* note 4; von Mehren, *supra* note 4.

Formalities are premised on the lawmaker's indifference as to which of a number of alternative relationships the parties decide to enter. Their purpose is to make sure, first, that the parties know what they are doing, and, second, that the judge will know what they did. These are often referred to as the cautionary and evidentiary functions of formalities.[14] Thus the statute of frauds is supposed both to make people take notice of the legal consequences of a writing and to reduce the occasions on which judges enforce non-existent contracts because of perjured evidence.

Although the premise of formalities is that the law has no preference as between alternative private courses of action, they operate through the contradiction of private intentions. This is true whether we are talking about the statute of frauds,[15] the parol evidence rule,[16] the requirement of an offer and acceptance,[17] of definiteness,[18] or whatever. In every case, the formality means that unless the parties adopt the prescribed mode of manifesting their wishes, they will be ignored. The reason for ignoring them, for applying the sanction of nullity, is to force them to be self conscious and to express themselves clearly, not to influence the substantive choice about whether or not to contract, or what to contract for.

By contrast, legal institutions aimed at wrongdoing attach sanctions to courses of conduct in order to discourage them. There is a wide gamut of possibilities, ranging from outright criminalization to the mere refusal to enforce contracts to perform acts "contrary to public policy" (*e.g.*, contracts not to marry). In this area, the sanction of nullity is adopted not to force the parties to adopt a prescribed form, but to discourage them by making it more difficult to achieve a particular objective.

While the two poles are quite clear in theory, it is often extremely difficult to decide how the concepts involved apply in practice. One reason for this is that, whatever its purpose, the requirement of a formality imposes some cost on those who must use it, and it is often unclear whether the lawmaker intended this cost to have a deterrent effect along with its cautionary and evidentiary functions. Thus the requirement that promises of bequests be in writing may have been aimed to discourage the descent of property outside of the normal family channel, as well as to decrease the probability of perjurious claims.[19]

Another source of difficulty is that there exists an intermediate category of legal institutions that partakes simultaneously of the nature of formalities and of rules designed to deter wrongdoing.[20] In this category fall a vast number of

---

[14] The limitation of the functions of formalities to the cautionary and evidentiary defies the modern trend, begun by Fuller, to multiply functions almost indefinitely. The cautionary function, as I use it, includes both making the parties think twice about what they are doing and making them think twice about the legal consequences. The evidentiary function includes both providing good evidence of the existence of a transaction and providing good evidence of the legal consequences the parties intended should follow. For our purposes, it is unnecessary to subdivide further. *See* Kennedy, *supra* note 4, at 374–76. More detailed treatment of functions of form can be found in Fuller, *supra* note 4, at 800–04; von Mehren, *supra* note 4, at 1016–17; I. MACNEIL, CASES AND MATERIALS ON CONTRACTS, EXCHANGE TRANSACTIONS AND RELATIONSHIPS 1314–19 (1971); Perillo, *The Statute of Frauds in the Light of the Functions and Dysfunctions of Form*, 43 FORD. L. REV. 39, 43–69 (1974).

[15] *See* Perillo, *supra* note 14, at 70–77.

[16] *See* note 33 *infra*.

[17] *See, e.g.*, United States v. Braunstein, 75 F. Supp. 137 (S.D.N.Y. 1947); Friedman, *supra* note 4, at 775–76.

[18] *See, e.g.*, B. CARDOZO, THE GROWTH OF THE LAW 110–11 (1924).

[19] *See* von Mehren, *supra* note 4, at 1016–17.

[20] *See generally* Calabresi & Melamed, *Property Rules, Liability Rules and Inalienability: One View of the Cathedral*, 85 Harv. L. Rev. 1089 (1972); R. Nozick, ANARCHY, STATE AND UTOPIA 54–87 (1974); E. Durkheim, THE DIVISION OF LABOR IN SOCIETY 68–69, 127–29 (Simpson trans. 1933); Wellington, *Common Law Rules and Constitutional Double Standards: Some Notes on Adjudication*, 83 Yale L.J. 221, 229–35 (1973). *See also* notes 22, 112 *infra*.

directives applied in situations where one party has injured another, but has not done something that the legal system treats as intrinsically immoral or antisocial. It is generally the case that the parties could have, but have not made an agreement that would have determined the outcome under the circumstances. In the absence of prior agreement, it is up to the court to decide what to do. The following are examples of rules of this kind:

(a) Rules defining nonconsensual duties of care to another, imposed by the law of torts, property, quasi-contract, or fiduciary relations, or through the "good faith" requirement in the performance of contractual obligations.
(b) Rules defining the circumstances in which violations of legal duty will be excused (*e.g.*, for mistake, impossibility, assumption of risk, contributory negligence, laches).
(c) Rules for the interpretation of contracts and other legal instruments, insomuch as those rules go beyond attempting to determine the actual intent of the parties (*e.g.*, interpretation of form contracts against the drafting party).
(d) The law of damages.

The ambiguity of the legal directives in this category is easiest to grasp in the cases of interpretation and excuses. For example, the law of impossibility allocates risks that the parties might have allocated themselves. Doctrines of this kind, which I will call suppletive, can be interpreted as merely facilitative. In other words, we can treat them *not* as indicating a preference for particular conduct (sharing of losses when unexpected events occur within a contractual context), but as cheapening the contracting process by making it known in advance that particular terms need not be explicitly worked out and written in. The parties remain free to specify to the contrary whenever the suppletive term does not meet their purposes.

On the other hand, it may be clear that the terms in question *are* designed to induce people to act in particular ways, and that the lawmaker is not indifferent as to whether the parties adopt them. This approach may be signalled by a requirement of "clear and unambiguous statement" of contrary intent, or by other rules of interpretation, like that in favor of bilateral rather than unilateral contracts. But it is only when the courts refuse to allow even an explicit disclaimer or modification of the term that we know that we are altogether out of the realm of formalities.[21]

The same kind of obscurity of purpose is present in the legal rules defining liability and fixing damages in tort, property and contract. *Sometimes* it is quite clear that the legal purpose is to eradicate a particular kind of behavior. By granting punitive damages or specific performance, for example, the lawmaker indicates that he is not indifferent as between the courses of action open to the parties. But where damages are merely compensatory, and perhaps even then not *fully* compensatory, there is a problem. The problem is aggravated when these damages are exacted both for breaches or torts involving some element of fault and for those that are innocent (nonnegligent injury; involuntary breach).

It is nonetheless possible to take a determinedly moralistic view of tort and breach of contract. The limitation of damages to compensation may be seen not

---

[21] *See* 3 A. CORBIN, CONTRACTS § 534 (1960); 3A id. §§ 632, 653; E. DURKHEIM, *supra* note 20, at 123–25; H. HART & A. SACKS, *supra* note 1, at 251–56; Holmes, *The Path of the Law*, 10 HARV. L. REV. 457, 466 (1897). On impossibility, *see* KESSLER & GILMORE, *supra* note 3, at 742–44; Berman, *Excuse for Nonperformance in the Light of Contract Practices in International Trade*, 63 COLUM. L. REV. 1413 (1963); Note, *The Economic Implications of the Doctrine of Impossibility*, 26 HAST. L. J. 1251 (1975).

as condoning the conduct involved, but as recognizing the deterrent effect that higher damages would have on activity in general, including innocent and desirable activity. It may also reflect qualms about windfall gains to the victims. Liability for involuntary breach and for some nonnegligent injuries are overinclusive from the moralistic point of view, but may be justified by the need to avoid hopelessly difficult factual issues.

The contrary view is that contract and tort liability reflect a decision that, so long as compensation is paid, the lawmaker is indifferent as between "wrongful" and "innocent" behavior.[22] Legal directives defining breach of contract and tortious activity, and fixing damage measures, are then in a special class situated midway between formalities and rules punishing crimes that are *mala in se*. Unlike the rules of offer and acceptance, for example, they reflect a moral objective: that private actors should internalize particular costs of their activities, and have some security that they will not have to bear the costs of the activities of others. But the moral objective is a limited one, implying no judgment about the qualities of tort or breach of contract in themselves. The wrong involved is the failure to compensate, not the infliction of damage.

Along with a limited substantive content, these legal doctrines have limited cautionary and evidentiary functions. They define in advance a tariff that the private actor must pay if he wishes to behave in a particular way. The lawmaker does not care what choice the actor makes within this structure, but has an interest in the choice being made knowingly and deliberately, and in the accuracy of the judicial processes that will assess liability to pay the tariff and determine its amount. Since he is not trying to discourage torts or breaches of contract, it is important to define liability and its consequences in such a way as to facilitate private choice.[23]

B. Relationship of the Formal Dimensions to One Another

The categorization of rules as formalities or as designed to deter wrongdoing is logically independent of the issues of formal realizability and generality. In other words, legal directives designed to deter immoral or antisocial conduct can be couched in terms of general or particular rules, general or particular standards, or some combination. This is equally true, though less obvious in the case of formalities. While it is easy to imagine formalities cast as rules (general or particular) and difficult to see them as standards, there is nothing to prevent a judge from nullifying a transaction in which the parties have failed to use a prescribed mode of communication by applying a standard. For example, Williston favored a general rule that contracts must be definite as to price and quantity, or they were not legally binding.[24] But the UCC takes the general position that an agreement is not void for indefiniteness if the parties intended a contract and there is an adequate basis for the provision of a remedy for breach.[25] The judge can still disregard the

---

[22] *See* O. HOLMES, THE COMMON LAW 233–39 (Howe ed. 1963); 2 M. HOWE, JUSTICE OLIVER WENDELL HOLMES 76–80 (1963); Calabresi & Melamed, *supra* note 20; Posner, *A Theory of Negligence*, 1 J. LEG. STUD. 29 (1972).

[23] *See, e.g.*, Note, *Once More Into the Breach: Promissory Estoppel and Traditional Damage Doctrine*, 37 U. CHI. L. REV. 559 (1970).

[24] *See* S. WILLISTON, CONTRACTS § 37 (2d ed. 1937).

[25] UNIFORM COMMERCIAL CODE [U.C.C.] § 2-204. For Williston's criticism, *see* Williston, *The Law of Sales in the Proposed Uniform Commercial Code*, 63 HARV. L. REV. 561, 576 (1950).

will of the parties, sanctioning them for failure to observe the formality, but he
does so according to criteria patently lacking in formal realizability.[26]

In spite of logical independence, there are conventional arguments pro and con
the use of general rules both in the design of formalities and in the design of directives that deter immoral or antisocial conduct. The argument about laws
designed to deter wrongdoing focuses on the "chilling" effect of standards on
those parties who will come as close to the forbidden behavior as they can without getting caught. That about formalities identifies as the crucial issue the
impact of general rules on the parties' willingness to master the language of form.

1. Directives Designed to Deter Wrongdoing.[27] The use of rules, as opposed to
standards, to deter immoral or antisocial conduct means that sometimes perfectly
innocent behavior will be punished, and that sometimes plainly guilty behavior
will escape sanction. These costs of mechanical over- and underinclusion are the
price of avoiding the potential arbitrariness and uncertainty of a standard.

As between the mechanical arbitrariness of rules and the biased arbitrariness
of standards, there is an argument that bias is preferable, because it will "chill"
behavior on the borderline of substantive obnoxiousness. For example, a measure of uncertainty about when a judge will find a representation, or a failure to
disclose, to be fraudulent may encourage openness and honesty. Rules, on the
other hand, allow the proverbial "bad man" to "walk the line," that is, to take
conscious advantage of underinclusion to perpetrate fraud with impunity.

There are three familiar counterarguments in favor of rules. First, a standard will
deter desirable as well as undesirable conduct.[28] Second, *in terrorem* general standards are likely to be paper tigers in practice. Uncertainty about whether the sanction
will in fact materialize may lead to a lower level of actual social control than would
occur if there were a well defined area within which there was a high probability of
even a mild punishment. Death is likely to be an ineffective penalty for theft.[29]

Third, where the substantively undesirable conduct can be deterred effectively
by *private* vigilance, rules alert, or should alert the potential victims to the danger.
For example, a formally realizable general rule of caveat emptor should stimulate
buyers to take all kinds of precautions against the uncommunicative seller. It is true
that the rule will also allow many successful frauds. But these may be *less* numerous in the end than those that would occur if buyers knew that there was the possibility, however uncertain, of a legal remedy to save them from their sloppiness in
inspecting the goods. Likewise, the rigid rule that twenty-one year olds are adult for
purposes of contractual capacity makes their change of status more conspicuous; it
puts them on notice in a way that a standard (*e.g.*, undue influence) would not.[30]

These arguments apply to suppletive terms and to the rules defining civil liability and damage measures, at least in so far as we regard those institutions as
designed to deter wrongdoing. For example, expectation damages should
discourage breach of contract more effectively than would a reliance recovery.

[26] For another example, see Professor Perillo's proposed revision of the Statute of Frauds in Perillo, *supra* note 14, at 71–77.

[27] For a comprehensive discussion of this general subject in the context of administrative law, see Gifford, *Communication of Legal Standards, Policy Development, and Effective Conduct Regulation*, 56 CORNELL L. REV. 409 (1971).

[28] See Note, *The Void for Vagueness Doctrine in the Supreme Court*, 109 U. PA. L. REV. 67 (1960).

[29] *See* Hay, *Property, Authority and Criminal Law*, in ALBION'S FATAL TREE 17–26 (1975).

[30] *See* Kessler, *The Protection of the Consumer under Modern Sales Law*, Part I, 74 YALE L. J. 262, 266–67 (1964); Hamilton, *The Ancient Maxim Caveat Emptor*, 40 YALE L. J. 1133, 1178–82 (1931).

Reliance is difficult to measure and to prove, whereas in many situations the expectancy can be determined almost mechanically. While our real concern may be with the promisee's out-of-pocket loss from breach, the occasional imprecision of expectation damages may be justified at least in commercial situations, on the grounds of superior deterrent power.[31]

2. Formalities. Here, as in the area of immoral or antisocial conduct, the main disadvantage of general rules is their over and underinclusiveness from the point of view of the lawmaker's purposes. In the context of formalities the problem is that general rules will lead to many instances in which the judge is obliged to disregard the real intent of the parties choosing between alternative legal relationships. For example, he will refuse to enforce contracts intended to be binding (underinclusion), and he will enforce terms in agreements contrary to the intent of one or even both parties (overinclusion).[32] Since we are dealing with formalities, this is an evil: the lawmaker has no substantive preferences about the parties' choice, and he would like to follow their wishes.

(a) The Argument for Casting Formalities as Rules. The response is that the problem of over- and underinclusiveness has a special aspect in the case of formalities because the lawmaker can enlist the energies of the parties in reducing the seriousness of the imprecision of rules. The parties have an interest in communicating their exact intentions to the judge, an interest that is absent when they are engaged in activity the legal system condemns as immoral or antisocial. But this communication has a cost and involves risks of miscarriage. The lower the cost, and the greater the probability that the judge will respond as expected, the more the parties will invest in getting the message across.

The lawmaker can take this private calculus into account in designing the formalities. He can reduce the cost of learning the language of form by making his directives as general as possible. A "technical" system composed of many different rules or standards applying to closely related situations will be difficult to master and confusing in practice. For example, Williston's formulation of the parol evidence rule involves a rule of "plain meaning of the writing on its face" to determine whether a given integration embodies the total agreement of the parties. But this is subject to exceptions for fraud and duress. Another rule applies in determining whether the integration was intended to be "final," and yet another to the problem of agreements whose enforceability was meant to be conditional on the occurrence of events not mentioned in the document. It is hard to imagine a layperson setting out to master this doctrinal tangle.[33]

If generality can reduce the cost of formal proficiency, formal realizability should reduce the risk that the exercise of judicial discretion will bring formal proficiency to naught. Standards discourage investment in two ways. The uncertainty of the outcome if the judge is at large in finding intent, rather than bound to respond mechanically to ritual acts like sealing, will reduce the payoff that can be expected from being careful. Second, the dangers of imprecision are reduced because the

[31] *See* Fuller & Perdue, *The Reliance Interest in Contract Damages*, I, 46 YALE L. J. 52, 60–63 (1936).

[32] This is the consequence of adopting an "objective" theory of contract to deal with problems like mistake and parol evidence. *Compare* Williston, *Mutual Assent in the Formation of Contracts*, 14 ILL. L. REV. 85 (1919), *with* Whittier, *The Restatement of Contracts and Mutual Assent*, 17 CALIF. L. REV. 441 (1929).

[33] *See* S. WILLISTON, CONTRACTS §§ 631–47 (2d ed. 1937); Calamari & Perillo, *A Plea for a Uniform Parol Evidence Rule and Principles of Contract Interpretation*, 42 IND. L. J. 333 (1967).

judge may bail you out if you blunder. The result *may* be a slippery slope of increasing informality that ends with the legal system treating disputes about wills as though they were automobile accidents litigated under a fault standard.

If general rules lead people to invest in formal proficiency, at least as compared to standards, the result should be the reduction of their over- and underinclusiveness. In other words, the application of the rule should only very rarely lead to the nullification of the intent of the parties. The rare cases that do occur can then be written off as a small cost to pay for the reinforcement of the sanction of nullity. People will miss fewer trains, the argument goes, if they know the engineer will leave without them rather than delay even a few seconds. Standards, by contrast, are dynamically unstable. Rather than evoking private action that compensates their inadequacies, they stimulate responses that aggravate their defects.

Finally, rules encourage transaction in general. If an actor knows that the use of a formality guarantees the execution of his intentions, he will do things that he would not do if there were a risk that the intention would be defeated. In particular, actors will rely on enforcement of contracts, trusts, and so forth, in making investments. Since we are dealing with formalities, it is a matter of definition that the legal system is anxious to encourage this kind of activity so long as private parties desire to engage in it.[34]

Suppletive rules and the general principles of tort and contract liability can be treated, as we have seen already, either as primarily aimed to suppress breach of contract and tortious injury or to structure private choice between injury *cum* compensation and no injury. If we choose to analogize the tortfeasor to a testator or a bond indenture lawyer, it is easy to argue that formally realizable general rules are as important in torts as they are in the area of pure formalities.

If the rules are clear, people will invest time and energy in finding out what they are. They will then adjust their behavior so that they commit torts only up to the point at which what they gain is equal to what they have to pay in compensation. A regime of standards, on the other hand will "chill" private activity by making its consequences less certain. At the same time uncertainty reduces the incentive to find out the nature of one's duties and then choose rationally between performing them and paying damages.

(b) The Critique of the Argument for Rules. The argument for casting formalities as rules rests on two sets of assumptions, each of which is often challenged in discussions of actual legal institutions. The first set of assumptions concerns the impact on real participants in a real legal system of the demand for formal proficiency. If the argument for rules is to work, we must anticipate that private parties will in fact respond to the threat of the sanction of nullity by learning to operate the system. But real as opposed to hypothetical legal actors may be unwilling or unable to do this.[35]

The contracts of dealers on produce exchanges are likely to use the most exquisite and most precisely manipulable formal language. Poor consumers, by contrast, are likely to be formally illiterate. Somewhere in between lie the businessmen who have a highly developed understanding of the mechanics of their deals, yet persistently—and perfectly rationally, given the money cost of lawyers and the social and business cost of legalism—fail to master legal technicalities

---

[34] *See* Fuller & Perdue, *supra* note 31, at 60–63; Kennedy, *supra* note 4, at 365–77.

[35] See the literature on contracts of adhesion collected in Leff, *supra* note 9, at 140–44; Friedman, *supra* note 4, at 759–61, 771–72, 779.

that return to plague them when things go wrong. We must take all the particular variations into account. In the end, we may decide that a particular formal system works so smoothly that a refusal to fill the gaps with general rules would be a wanton sacrifice of the parties to a judicial prima donna. But others work so badly that little is lost by riddling them with loopholes.

This problem of differing degrees of responsiveness to the sanction of nullity can be generalized to the intermediate category of rules defining tort and contract liability in the absence of party specification. It can be argued that private activity is only rarely and sporadically undertaken with a view to legal consequences. The law intervenes only when things have gone so far astray that all the private mechanisms for adjusting disputes have been tried and failed. It is therefore unwise to treat the judicial decision process as though it could or should legislate effectively for all or even most contract or tort disputes, let alone all contracts or torts. The parties have an immediate interest in a resolution that will be neither under- nor overinclusive from the point of view of the lawmaker's purposes. The countervailing interest in telling others clearly what will happen in their hypothetical future lawsuits is weak, because it is so unlikely that "others" will listen.[36]

In those situations in which some parties *are* responsive to the legal system, a regime of formally realizable general rules may intensify the disparity in bargaining power in transactions between legally skilled actors who use the legal system constantly, and unskilled actors without lawyers or prior experience.[37] At one extreme there is a kind of fraud that is extremely difficult to police effectively: one party knows that the other party does *not* know that the contract must be in writing if it is to be legally binding. At the other is the bargaining confrontation in which the party with the greater skills legitimately relies on them to obtain a result more favorable than would have occurred if everyone knew that the issue *had* to be left to the judge's discretion.

The second set of assumptions underlying the argument for rules concerns the practical possibility of maintaining a highly formal regime. A great deal of legal scholarship between the First and Second World Wars went into showing that legal directives that looked general and formally realizable were in fact indeterminate.[38] Take, for example, the "rule" that a contract will be rescinded for mutual mistake going to the "substance" or "essence" of the transaction, but not for mistakes as to a "mere quality or accident," even though the quality or accident in question was the whole reason for the transaction. We have come to see legal directives of this kind as invitations to sub rosa balancing of the equities. Such covert standards may generate more uncertainty than would a frank avowal that the judge is allocating a loss by reference to an open textured notion of good faith and fair dealing.[39]

In other situations, a "rule" that appears to dispose cleanly of a fact situation is nullified by a counterrule whose scope of application seems to be almost identical. Agreements that gratuitously increase the obligations of one contractual partner are unenforceable for want of consideration. *But*, such agreements may

---

[36] *See* Macaulay, *The Use and Non-Use of Contracts in the Manufacturing Industry*, 9 PRACTICAL LAWYER 13 (1963).

[37] *See generally* Galanter, *Why the "Haves" Come Out Ahead: Speculations on the Limits of Legal Change*, 9 LAW & SOC. REV. 95 (1974); Perillo, *supra* note 14, at 70–71.

[38] *See generally* Llewellyn, *A Realistic Jurisprudence—The Next Step*, 30 COLUM. L. REV. 431 (1930); Llewellyn, *On Reading and Using the Newer Jurisprudence*, 40 COLUM. L. REV. 581 (1940).

[39] *See* Thayer, *Unilateral Mistake and Unjust Enrichment as a Ground for the Avoidance of Legal Transactions*, in HARVARD LEGAL ESSAYS 467 (1934).

be binding if the judge can find an implied recission of the old contract and the formation of a new one incorporating the unilaterally onerous terms. The realists taught us to see this arrangement as a smokescreen hiding the skillful judge's decision as to duress in the process of renegotiation, and as a source of confusion and bad law when skill was lacking.[40]

The critic of the argument for rules can often use this sort of analysis to show that what looks like a rule is really a covert standard. It is also often possible to make a plausible claim that the reason for the "corruption" of what was supposed to be a formal regime was that the judges were simply unwilling to bite the bullet, shoot the hostages, break the eggs to make the omelette and leave the passengers on the platform. The more general and the more formally realizable the rule, the greater the equitable pull of extreme cases of over- or underinclusion. The result may be a dynamic instability as pernicious as that of standards. There will be exceptions that are only initially innocuous, playing with the facts, the invention of counterrules (*e.g.*, waiver and estoppel), the manipulation of manifestations of intent, and so forth. Each successful evasion makes it seem more unjust to apply the rule rigidly in the next case; what was once clear comes to be surrounded by a technical and uncertain penumbra that is more demoralizing to investment in form than an outright standard would be.[41]

II. TYPES OF RELATIONSHIP BETWEEN FORM AND SUBSTANCE

The jurisprudence of form presented in the last section is common to legal thinkers of many times and places. There seems no basis for disputing that the notions of rule and standard, and the idea that the choice between them will have wide-ranging practical consequences, are useful in understanding and designing legal institutions. But there is more to the matter than that.

The discussion presented a pro-rules position and a pro-standards position, but there was nothing to suggest that these were truly incompatible. A hypothetical lawmaker with undefined purposes could approach the problem of form with no bias one way or another. He could use the analysis to identify the likely benefits of using rules by applying the pro-rules position to the particular circumstances that concerned him. He could then review the opposed position to get an idea of the costs of using rules and the advantages of standards. He might make up his mind to adopt one form, or the other, or one of the infinite number of intermediate positions, by assessing the net balance of advantage in terms of his underlying legislative objective.

From this starting point of "value neutral" description of the likely consequences of adopting rules or standards, there are two quite different directions in which one might press the analysis of legal form. One alternative is to attempt to enrich the initial schema by contextualizing it. This approach involves being more specific both about the particular situations in which lawmakers operate and about the different objectives that they try to achieve in those situations. The first part of this section provides some illustrations of this line of investigation.

---

[40] See the cases and notes collected in KESSLER & GILMORE, *supra* note 3, at 478–508; U.C.C. § 2-209; Restatement (Second) of Contracts § 89D.

[41] *See, e.g.*, Gellhorn, *Contracts and Public Policy*, 35 COLUM. L. REV. 679, 683–84 (1935); C. KAYSEN & D. TURNER, ANTITRUST POLICY: AN ECONOMIC AND LEGAL ANALYSIS 235 (1959); Perillo, *Restitution in a Contractual Context*, 73 COLUM. L. REV. 1208 (1973). On the development of promissory estoppel as an alternative contract cause of action through which damages can be recovered without compliance with formal requirements, see G. GILMORE, THE DEATH OF CONTRACT 66, 90 (1974).

The second, and I think more important, approach ignores both the question of how rules and standards work in realistic settings and the question of how we can best solve the problem of fitting form to particular objectives. The purpose of the second line of investigation is to relate the pro-rules and pro-standards positions to other ideas about the proper ordering of society, and particularly to ideas about the proper substantive content of legal rules. The second part of this section describes this approach, as a preliminary to its pursuit in Section III.

A. Contextualization

There are two primary modes of contextualization, which might be called the social engineering and the social science approaches, respectively. The first aims to develop principles that will guide the legislator in deciding when to use rules and when standards. The second eschews normative judgments, preferring simply to describe the various effects, legitimate and illegitimate, that follow from the choice of form.

1. Social Engineering. It seems that the first self-conscious general statement of principles for the choice of form, at least by an American, is Pound's *Theory of Judicial Decision*, published in 1923. The thesis of the article is simple: "rules of law . . . which are applied mechanically are more adapted to property and to business transactions; standards where application proceeds upon intuition are more adapted to human conduct and to the conduct of enterprises."[42]

If we ask the criterion of "adaptedness," Pound had a ready but from today's perspective vacuous answer: "for the purposes of today our picture should be one, not . . . of a body of unchallengeable deductions from ultimate metaphysically-given data at which men arrived a century ago in seeking to rationalize the social phenomena of that time, . . . but rather a picture of a process of social engineering. Such a picture, I venture to think, would represent the social order as an organized human endeavor to satisfy a maximum of human wants with a minimum of sacrifice of other wants."[43]

Pound was explicit that "individualization" of law through the use of standards was inappropriate where "security of transaction" was the paramount value. At the same time, he made free use of the argument that the certainty of rules was often illusory. Where he favored standards, he claimed that the special nature of the circumstances made "the sacrifice of certainty . . . more theoretical than actual."[44]

---

[42] Pound, *supra* note 4, at 951.

[43] *Id.* at 954.

[44] *Id.* at 952. The following is his most complete statement:

Social engineering may not expect to meet all its problems with the same machinery. Its tasks are as varied as life and the complicated problems of a complex social order call for a complicated mechanism and a variety of legal implements. This is too large a subject for discussion in the present connection. Suffice it to say that conveyance of land, inheritance and succession, and commercial law have always proved susceptible of legislative statement, while no codification of the law of torts and no juristic or judicial defining of fraud or of fiduciary duties has ever maintained itself. In other words, the social interests in security of acquisitions and security of transactions—the economic side of human activity in civilized society—call for rule or conception authoritatively prescribed in advance and mechanically applied. These interests also call peculiarly for judicial justice. Titles to land and the effects of promissory notes or commercial contracts cannot be suffered to depend in any degree on the unique circumstances of the controversies in which they come in question. It is one of the grave faults of our present theory of judicial decision that, covering up all individualization, it sometimes allows individualized application to creep into those situations where it is anything but a wise social engineering. On the other hand, where we have to do with the social interest in the individual human life and with individual claims to free self-assertion subsumed thereunder, free judicial finding of the grounds of decision for the case in hand is the most effective way of bringing about a practicable compromise

There are few areas of law in which there has not been, since Pound's article, an attempt to generalize about what form best suits the peculiar nature of the subject matter. In family[45] and labor law,[46] in antitrust[47] and tax law,[48] in juvenile delinquency[49] and sentencing of criminals,[50] there have been fluctuations from one model to the other and back again. The same is true of administrative law,[51] civil procedure,[52] and the law of contracts.[53]

The social engineering approach has not produced convincing results beyond the confines of particular fields. Generalizations that at first seem highly plausible turn out on further examination to be false, or at least no more convincing than diametrically opposed counterprinciples. For example, Larry Tribe has recently argued, as a matter of constitutional right, that the treatment of unwed motherhood is "an area in which the need to reflect rapidly changing norms affecting important interests in liberty compels an individualized determination, one not bound by any pre-existing rule of thumb within the zone of moral change."[54] But a recent article by Heymann and Holtz takes the position that the existence of moral flux makes it overwhelmingly important that we use rigid per se rules in defining "personhood" for purposes of decisions about the treatment of severely defective newborn infants.[55] Perhaps the positions can be reconciled in terms of a more abstract principle, but none comes to mind.

The difficulty of arriving at a consensus about the optimal social role of rules is best illustrated by the case of Article 2 of the Uniform Commercial Code, which governs commercial contracts. According to a persistent line of theorizing associated with Max Weber,[56] this should be an area prototypically adapted to rules. The "social function of maintaining the market" supposedly requires a formal approach here, if anywhere. Yet the drafters of Article 2 proceeded on the conviction that general commercial law was prototypically adapted to standards. This choice was explicitly based on the claim that ideas like "reasonableness" and

---

and has always gone on in fact no matter how rigidly in theory the tribunals have been tied down by the texts of codes or statutes.

Id. at 956–57.

[45] *See* Mnookin, *supra* note 6; Katz, *supra* note 4.

[46] *See* Shulman, *Reason, Contract and Law in Labor Relations*, 68 HARV. L. REV. 999, 1016 (1955). The administration of the NLRA requirement of bargaining in good faith has also been the subject of debate. *See, e.g.,* H.K. Porter v. NLRB, 397 U.S. 99 (1970); NLRB v. General Electric, 418 F.2d 736 (2d Cir. 1969), *cert. denied,* 398 U.S. 965 (1970); H. WELLINGTON, LABOR & THE LEGAL PROCESS 52–63 (1968).

[47] *See* C. KAYSEN & D. TURNER, *supra* note 41, at 234X45; Bork, *supra* note 6; Bok, *Section 7 of the Clayton Act and the Merging of Law and Economics*, 74 HARV. L. REV. 226, 295–98 (1960); Turner, *supra* note 6, at 9–12.

[48] It has been argued that the judicial use of a general standard of "prevention of tax avoidance" in interpreting the Tax Code has rendered the Code more certain. *See* Surrey, *supra* note 10, at 694–95; 2 S. SURREY, W. WARREN, P. MCDANIEL & H. AULT, FEDERAL INCOME TAXATION 633–34 (1973).

[49] *See In re* Gault, 387 U.S. 1 (1967); McKeiver v. Pennsylvania, 403 U.S. 528 (1971); Griffiths, *Ideology in Criminal Procedure, or A Third "Model" of the Criminal Process*, 79 YALE L. J. 359, 399–404 (1970).

[50] *See* Dershowitz, *Background Paper*, in FAIR AND CERTAIN PUNISHMENT 67–100 (Report of the Twentieth Century Fund Task Force on Criminal Sentencing, 1976).

[51] *See generally* Gifford, *supra* note 27; K. DAVIS, *supra* note 4.

[52] *See* 2 F. POLLOCK & F. MAITLAND, THE HISTORY OF ENGLISH LAW BEFORE THE TIME OF EDWARD I 562–64 (Milsom ed. 1968); Chayes, *The Role of the Judge in Public Law Litigation*, 89 HARV. L. REV. 1281 (1976).

[53] *See* Friedman, *supra* note 4, at 777–79; L. FRIEDMAN, CONTRACT LAW IN AMERICA (1965); Perillo, *supra* note 14, at 41–42.

[54] Tribe, *Structural Due Process*, 10 HARV. CIV. RIGHTS—CIV. LIB. L. REV. 269, 307 (1975).

[55] Heymann & Holtz, *The Severely Defective Newborn: The Dilemma and the Decision Process*, 23 PUBLIC POLICY 381, 410–16 (1975).

[56] 2 M. WEBER, *supra* note 4; Macaulay, *supra* note 4; Friedman, *supra* note 4, at 764–77; Macaulay, *supra* note 2 at 1056–69; Friedman, *supra* note 53; Friedman, *supra* note 9.

"good faith" provide greater predictability in practice than the intricate and technical rule system they have replaced.[57]

2. *The Social Science Approach.* Efforts like those of Pound have a legislative focus and are therefore concerned with the impact of rules on generalized "social interests" or "functions" assertedly important regardless of the "partisan" or "political" objectives of particular groups. The social science approach is not restricted in this way. The "scientist" as opposed to the "engineer" can ask how the choice of form will favor the interests of some participants in a conflict and disfavor others. My aim here is simply to illustrate this perspective rather than to investigate it fully or develop it. For this purpose, it may be useful to make the following subdivision among types of conflict to which the choice of form is relevant:

(a) Conflict between lawmakers within a single institution, particularly that between "reform" and the status quo, however those may be defined.

(b) Conflict between lawmakers and a group that is supposed to execute the law (e.g., the police) or to obey it (the citizenry).

(c) Conflict between lawmakers within one institution (e.g., the courts) and those in other institutions (e.g., the legislature, the jury) which have a parallel or overlapping jurisdiction.

(a) Standards as Instruments of Change. Imagine a court with a rule that legislative interference with freedom of contract is unconstitutional. Some newly appointed judges disapprove of this policy. They *might* come up with a new rule: the question of whether or not to interfere with freedom of contract is inherently legislative, and not open to judicial review. But they might find it preferable to argue for a rule that only "unreasonable" interference is forbidden. Some reasons for such a posture have to do with the relationship between court and legislature as competing institutions, but others might be internal to the court.

First, the standard might represent a substantive compromise between all and nothing. The reformers might support it because they lacked the power to impose their ideal solution. Second, the standard could be adopted without overruling any earlier cases. Previous invalidations of statutes could simply be reinterpreted as findings of unreasonableness. Third, the reformers might themselves be unsure of how far they wanted to go. Experience under a standard might lead with time to the emergence of the knowledge necessary to formulate a more precise rule than that of blanket deference to the legislature.

Of course, the reformers might adopt other tactics, such as undermining the formal realizability of the existing rule, proposing exceptions or counterrules, or developing jurisdictional limitations on effective legal challenges to legislation. All one can say is that standards may be advocated because they fit a political strategy for dealing with conflict rather than for reasons intrinsic to the social situation in which they will be applied, or to the substantive content of the law in question.[58]

(b) Rules as a Means to Control Action. A court charged with laying down rules for police behavior in investigating crimes may be convinced that the police have a tendency to place an impermissibly low value on the rights of suspects to be

Duncan Kennedy

[57] *See* W. TWINING, KARL LLEWELLYN AND THE REALIST MOVEMENT, ch. 12 (1973); Danzig, *A Comment on The Jurisprudence of the Uniform Commercial Code*, 27 STAN. L. REV. 621 (1975).

[58] *See* McCloskey, *Economic Due Process and the Supreme Court: An Exhumation and Reburial*, 1962 SUP. CT. REV. 34, 36–40. On vagueness in contracts as the outcome of compromise, *See* Macaulay, *supra* note 36, at 14–17. On legislative standards, see Friedman, *supra* note 9, at 835–36.

secure against unreasonable searches and seizures and to refrain from testifying against themselves. This difference in valuation arises, let us suppose, both from a substantive disagreement about the content of constitutional guarantees and from inherent tendencies of large bureaucratic organizations.

In this situation, a court might believe that formally realizable general rules (notification of legal rights prior to interrogation) would function much better than standards to force the executive agency to put the court's view of the issue into practice. A standard might be much preferable to a rule if the court could itself apply it in every case, but the necessity of delegation of the application function creates an excessive danger of de facto nullification.[59]

Similar dilemmas arise in the relation of courts to juries, to legislatures, to inferior tribunals, and to private parties. In each of these relationships, there may be an unquestioned consensus that the court is the legitimate lawmaker, and that the other party has no other duty than to carry out judicial directives. But given a standard of "fair compensation" juries may habitually award punitive damages, leading judges to impose detailed rules about how damage must be measured in typical fact situations.[60] "One man, one vote" may seem the only feasible mechanism for policing reapportionment although the judges believe strongly that a standard of "fair representation" would better reflect their own and the nation's political philosophy. A court with no desire to punish innocent employers may nonetheless hesitate to read a "good faith" defense against back pay awards into an equal employment opportunity statute.[61]

But it will not always be true that the best way for the lawmaking institution to control the subordinate is through rules. The very widespread acceptance of the proposition appears to be based on implicit assumptions about the bureaucratic costs of direct control through the application of standards. Where these costs are low or non-existent, it is common to argue that the superior will prefer the ad hoc approach because it maximizes his discretion. By refusing to enunciate anything but a standard, the superior with powers of review can induce the inferior to follow its wishes with an attentiveness and submissiveness born of insecurity. If the executive agency experiences "reversal" as a serious sanction, and will try to avoid it by sensitivity to all the subtle overtones and cues provided by the reviewing institution's applications of the standard, the use of rules may be counterproductive. Indeed, rules may foster a sense of bureaucratic (or private) autonomy and provide a basis of independent executive power that would be absent under a regime of standards.[62]

---

[59] *See* Miranda v. Arizona, 384 U.S. 436, 455–70 (1966); Amsterdam, *supra* note 10, at 429–39. On the use of detailed rules by the legislature as a means to curb judicial discretion, *see* Friedman, *supra* note 4, at 752 n.4.

[60] *See* KESSLER & GILMORE, *supra* note 3, at 1016–21; Friedman, *supra* note 4, at 778; Horwitz, *The Emergence of an Instrumental Conception of American Law*, in 5 PERSPECTIVES IN AMERICAN HISTORY 287, 323 (1971).

[61] *See* Albermarle Paper Co. v. Moody, 422 U.S. 405 (1975). For a discussion of the impact of the choice of form in out-of-court settlement, *see* Macaulay, *supra* note 2, at 1065. On reapportionment, *see* Friedman, *supra* note 9, at 815–20.

[62] See the discussion of the "non-directive functions of rules" in A. GOULDNER, PATTERNS OF INDUSTRIAL BUREAUCRACY 157–81 (1955). Even the highly qualified generalization in the text is open to serious question. For example, Gifford, *supra* note 27, argues that the use of standards may be characteristic of underfunded administrative agencies that know that an accurate description of what they intend to do would reveal their weakness and encourage violators.

The idea that rules guarantee private actors an area of "autonomy" from judicial control is developed in Friedman, *supra* note 4, at 754–55, 764–74, and in Kennedy, *supra* note 4, at 366–77. Weber argues that the trend to standards in modern law reflects the desire of judges and lawyers to reassert their power and prestige relative to legislatures and private parties grown independent under the protection of a regime of rules. 2 M. WEBER, *supra* note 4, at 886.

(c) Rules and the Legitimacy of Judicial Action. In many situations that arise in our legal system, it is open to argument whether substantive norms of conduct ought to be laid down by the courts or by some other, more "democratically legitimate" institution, such as the legislature, the jury, or private parties pursuing their own objectives through institutions like contract or corporate law. Judges making law in these situations have to worry not only about conflict within the judiciary and about effectively controlling subordinate agencies but also about the question of whether they will be seen as "usurping" the jurisdiction of other institutions. In short, there may be conflict about who is the superior and who the inferior legal actor in the premises.

In disputes about the judicial role, the parties appeal to stereotyped images of what courts, legislators, juries, and private right holders "ought" to do. A very deepseated idea of the judicial function is that judges apply rules. It follows that there will often be a great tactical advantage, for a court which wants to expand its power at the expense of another institution, in casting the norms it wants to impose in the rule form. The object is to draw on the popular lay notion that "discretion" and "value judgments" are the province of legislatures, juries, and private parties, while judges are concerned with techniques of legal reasoning that are neutral and ineluctable, however incomprehensible.

There are two different ways in which the rule form shores up the legitimacy of judicial action. First, the discretionary elements in the choice of a norm to impose are obscured by the process of justification that pops a rule out of the hat of policy, precedent, the text of the Constitution, or some other source of law. Second, once the norm has been chosen, the rule form disguises the discretionary element involved in applying it to cases. A standard is often a tactically inferior weapon in jurisdictional struggle, both because it seems less plausible that it is the only valid outcome of the reasoning process and because it is often clear that its application will require or permit resort to "political" or at least non-neutral aspects of the situation.[63] For example, the Supreme Court in the 1950's adopted a "balancing test" for the interpretation of the first amendment to the Constitution. The issue was typically whether or not the Court should nullify a statute that the legislature claimed was necessary to protect "national security." The proponents of the balancing test attempted to "weigh the interest in free speech against the interest in national security" as a means to deciding whether the statute was constitutional.

The Justices who favored this procedure were quite explicitly concerned to prevent the Court from encroaching on legislative power. They argued that the use of a standard would enhance both judicial and legislative awareness of the inherently discretionary nature of the Court's jurisdiction.[64] The opposed position was that the first amendment was an "absolute," meaning that it was a rigid rule. The absolutists bottomed their claim on the very nature of legal as opposed to discretionary justice.[65] They also admitted on occasion that the trouble with balancing was that "it will be almost impossible at this late date to rid the formula of the elements of political surrender with which it has long been

Duncan Kennedy

---

[63] *See* Note, *Civil Disabilities and the First Amendment*, 78 YALE L. J. 842, 851–52 (1969).
[64] The literature on balancing is collected in Note, *supra* note 63, at 842–52. *See, e.g.*, Dennis v. United States, 342 U.S. 494, 524–25, 542–43 (1951) (Frankfurter, J., concurring); P. FREUND, THE SUPREME COURT OF THE UNITED STATES 44 (1949).
[65] *See, e.g.*, Frantz, *Is the First Amendment Law? A Reply To Professor Mendelson*, 51 CALIF. L. REV. 729 (1963).

associated. The very phrase, balancing of interests, has such a legislative ring about it that it undermines judicial self-confidence unduly."[66]

Nonetheless, there are limits to the usefulness of the rule form as a tactical weapon, as the Supreme Court has discovered in the controversies both about the one-man-one-vote decision[67] and about its specific time limits for different aspects of the regulation of abortion.[68] It seems to be the case that while judges are expected to deal in rules, the rules are not expected to be *quantitatively* precise. Like "value judgments," the choice between 30 days and 31 days is thought of as political or administrative. The reason, presumably, is that quantitatively precise rules are obviously compromises: the cases close to the line on either side have been disposed of arbitrarily in order to *have* a line. This makes it implausible that precedent or "legal reasoning" were the only elements entering into the decision.[69]

We might contextualize indefinitely. The problem of form, in this perspective, is never more than one of political tactics, analogous to the reformer's problem of choosing between gradualist and confrontational lines of attack, or between centralized and decentralized emphases in organization. Tactics are rigidly subordinate to the choice among goals, form follows function, and the main lesson to be drawn is that one should have no a priori biases in choosing among the possibilities. In assessing a proposal to change a regime of rules to standards, or vice versa, we should ignore all claims about the intrinsic merits of formal positions and demand an accounting of effects. What is the substantive objective? How does the choice of form affect the likelihood of embodying the objective in law? Who will implement the rule or standard? How can it be evaded? How will the choice of form affect the lawmaker's claim to institutional legitimacy?

B. Form as Substance

The main problem with contextualization as I have presented it thus far is that it leaves out of account the common sense that the choice of form is seldom purely instrumental or tactical. As they appear in real life, the arguments pro and con the use of rules have powerful overtones of substantive debates about what values and what visions of the universe we should adopt. In picking a form through which to achieve some goal, we are almost always making a statement that is independent or at least distinguishable from the statement we make in choosing the goal itself. What we need is a way to relate the values intrinsic to form to the values we try to achieve *through* form.

The different values that people commonly associate with the formal modes of rule and standard are conveyed by the emotive or judgmental words that the advocates of the two positions use in the course of debate about a particular issue. Here is a suggestive list drawn from the vast data bank of casual conversation. Imagine, for the items in each row, an exchange: "Rules are A." "No, they are B." "But standards are C." "On the contrary, they are D."

---

[66] M. SHAPIRO, FREEDOM OF SPEECH: THE SUPREME COURT AND JUDICIAL REVIEW 103 (1966).
[67] Reynolds v. Sims, 377 U.S. 533 (1964).
[68] Roe v. Wade, 410 U.S. 113 (1973).
[69] *See generally* Friedman, *supra* note 9, at 820–25. On abortion, see Tribe, *Supreme Court, 1972 Term—Foreword: Toward A Model of Roles in the Due Process of Life & Law*, 87 HARV. L. REV. 1, 4, 26–29 (1973); Ely, *The Wages of Crying Wolf: A Comment on Roe v. Wade*, 82 YALE L. J. 920, 924–26 (1973). On reapportionment, *see* A. BICKEL, THE SUPREME COURT AND THE IDEA OF PROGRESS 151–73 (1970).

	Rules		Standards	
Good	Bad	Bad	Good	
Neutrality	Rigidity	Bias	Flexibility	
Uniformity	Conformity	Favoritism	Individualization	
Precision	Anality	Sloppiness	Creativity	
Certainty	Compulsiveness	Uncertainty	Spontaneity	
Autonomy	Alienation	Totalitarianism	Participation	
Rights	Vested Interests	Tyranny	Community	
Privacy	Isolation	Intrusiveness	Concern	
Efficiency	Indifference	Sentimentality	Equity	
Order	Reaction	Chaos	Evolution	
Exactingness	Punitiveness	Permissiveness	Tolerance	
Self-reliance	Stinginess	Romanticism	Generosity	
Boundaries	Walls	Invasion	Empathy	
Stability	Sclerosis	Disintegration	Progress	
Security	Threatenedness	Dependence	Trust	

This list suggests something that we all know: that the preference for rules or standards is an aspect of opposed substantive positions in family life, art, psychotherapy, education, ethics, politics and economics. It is also true that everyone is to some degree ambivalent in his feelings about these substantive conflicts. There are only a few who are confident either that one side is right or that they have a set of metacategories that allow one to choose the right side for any particular situation. Indeed, most of the ideas that might serve to dissolve the conflict and make rational choice possible are claimed vociferously by both sides:

Rules		Standards	
Good	Bad	Bad	Good
Morality (playing by the rules)	Moralism (self-righteous strictness)	Moralism (self-righteousness about own intuitions)	Morality (openness to the situation)
Freedom			Freedom
Fairness	Mechanical arbitrariness	Arbitrariness of subjectivity	Fairness
Equality (of opportunity)	of right to sleep under the bridges of Paris	of subjection to other people's value judgments	Equality (in fact)
Realism	Cynicism	Romanticism	Realism

So long as we regard the debate about form as a debate only about means, it is a debate about facts, and reality can be conceived as an ultimate arbiter to whose final decision we must submit if we are rational.[70] But if the question is

---

[70] The associations and contradictions in my two lists pose no special problem for the contextualizer. First, it is sometimes possible simply to ignore the values that seem implicit in the choice of form on the ground that the people involved don't care about them, or that the substantive values at stake are vastly more important. The opponent of mechanical rules in family life may think it absurd to worry about mechanicalness when the issue is enforcing a minimum wage law. Second, and more important, we can incorporate the values that inhere in different formal arrangements into the substantive decision process. Instead of deciding first what we want and then how to get it, we can treat the "how" as an aspect of the "what." The decisionmaker formulates his objectives "subject to the constraint" that he will be able to use only acceptable means to achieve them. Or he engages in a back-and-forth process of

whether "real" equality is equality of opportunity or equality of enjoyment of the good things of life, then the situation is different. Likewise if the question is whether human nature "is" good or bad, or whether people "do" act as rational maximizers of their interests. For this kind of question, whether phrased in terms of what is or what ought to be, we accept that there is no arbiter (or that he is silent, or that the arbiter is history, which will have nothing to say until we are all long dead).[71] Thus the pro-rules and pro-standards positions are more than an invitation to a positivist investigation of reality. They are also an invitation to choose between sets of values and visions of the universe.

The great limitation of the method of contextualization is that it is useless in trying to understand the character of such a choice. The contextualizer takes values and visions of the universe as given, and investigates their implications in particular situations. Yet it is not impossible or futile to talk about the choice of goals, or about their nature and interrelationship. We do this constantly, we change in consequence, and these changes are neither random nor ineffable. The rest of this essay is an example of this sort of discussion. Its premise is that we will have a better understanding of issues of form if we can relate them meaningfully to substantive questions about what we should want and about the nature of humanity and society.[72] There are two steps to the argument. The first is to set up the substantive dichotomy of individualism and altruism, and to show that the issue of form is one of its aspects. The second is to trace historically and analytically the course of the conflict between the two larger positions.

The method I have adopted in place of contextualization might be called, in a loose sense, dialetical or structuralist or historicist or the method of contradictions.[73] One of its premises is that the experience of unresolvable conflict among our *own* values and ways of understanding the world is here to stay. In this sense it is pessimistic, one might even say defeatist. But another of its premises is that there is order and meaning to be discovered even within the sense of contradiction. Further, the process of discovering this order and this meaning is both good in itself and enormously useful. In this sense, the method of contradiction represents an attitude that is optimistic and even utopian. None of which is to say that any particular attempt will be worth the paper it is printed on.

investigating goals, then means, then returning to reformulate goals in light of the new information. Or he integrates the whole process, treating processual or formal values as indistinguishable from those relating to outcomes. *See* Tribe, *Policy Science: Analysis or Ideology*, 2 PHIL. & PUB. AFF. 66 (1972); Tribe, *Ways Not to Think About Plastic Trees: New Foundations for Environmental Law*, 83 YALE L. J. 1315, 1317–25 (1974).

[71] Two introductions to the American literature are M. WHITE, SOCIAL THOUGHT IN AMERICA: THE REVOLT AGAINST FORMALISM (2d ed. 1957), and E. PURCELL, THE CRISIS OF DEMOCRATIC THEORY: SCIENTIFIC NATURALISM AND THE PROBLEM OF VALUE (1973). For law, see Hart, *Positivism and Separation of Law and Morals*, 71 Harv. L. Rev. 593, 620–29 (1958); Hart & Sacks, *supra* note 1, at 126–29.

[72] *See* P. SELZNICK, *supra* note 4.

[73] Some important works in the tradition I am referring to are G. HEGEL, PHILOSOPHY OF RIGHT (Knox trans. 1952); K. MARX, On the Jewish Question, in EARLY WRITINGS (Benton trans. 1975); R. VON IHERING, *supra* note 4; F. POLLOCK & D. MAITLAND, *supra* note 52; Lukacs, *Reification and the Consciousness of the Proletariat*, in HISTORY AND CLASS-CONSCIOUSNESS: STUDIES IN MARXIST DIALECTICS (Livingstone trans. 1971); K. MANNHEIM, IDEOLOGY AND UTOPIA: AN INTRODUCTION TO THE SOCIOLOGY OF KNOWLEDGE (1936); H. MARCUSE, REASON AND REVOLUTION: HEGEL AND THE RISE OF SOCIAL THEORY (1941); C. LEVI-STRAUSS, THE SAVAGE MIND (1966); R. UNGER, KNOWLEDGE AND POLITICS (1975); A. KATZ, *supra* note 4. Not all of these works, or even most of them, are based on the premises about the permanence of contradictions in consciousness that are described in the text following this note. My position is closest to that of Mannheim and Levi-Strauss. It is also close to that of Griffiths, *supra* note 49, and Katz, *supra* note 4.

III. Altruism and Individualism

This section introduces the substantive dichotomy of individualism and altruism. These are two opposed attitudes that manifest themselves in debates about the content of private law rules. My assertion is that the arguments lawyers use are relatively few in number and highly stereotyped, although they are applied in an infinite diversity of factual situations. What I have done is to abstract these typical forms or rhetorical set pieces and attempt to analyze them. I believe that they are helpful in the general task of understanding why judges and legislators have chosen to enact or establish particular private law doctrines. For that reason this section and the next should be useful independently of their immediate purpose, which is to establish a substantive legal correlate for the dichotomy of rules and standards. Later sections attempt to link attitudes in the formal dimension to those in the substantive, and then to identify the contradictory sets of premises that underlie both kinds of conflict.

A. *The Content of the Ideal of Individualism*

The essence of individualism is the making of a sharp distinction between one's interests and those of others, combined with the belief that a preference in conduct for one's own interests is legitimate, but that one should be willing to respect the rules that make it possible to coexist with others similarly self-interested. The form of conduct associated with individualism is self-reliance. This means an insistence on defining and achieving objectives without help from others (*i.e.,* without being dependent on them or asking sacrifices of them). It means accepting that they will neither share their gains nor one's own losses. And it means a firm conviction that I am entitled to enjoy the benefits of my efforts without an obligation to share or sacrifice them to the interests of others.[74]

---

[74] Some interesting nineteenth century treatments of self-reliance are R. EMERSON, *Self-Reliance*, in ESSAYS, FIRST SERIES 37 (1847) and H. SPENCER, JUSTICE (1891). A judicial classic in the individualist vein is Smith v. Brady, 17 N.Y. 173 (1858).

My definition of individualism owes much to A. DICEY, LECTURES ON THE RELATION BETWEEN LAW AND PUBLIC OPINION IN ENGLAND DURING THE NINETEENTH CENTURY (1905). The American legal realists used the term extensively to describe the "spirit" of 19th century private and public law. *See, e.g.,* Hamilton, *Property—According to Locke*, 41 YALE L. J. 864 (1932). This usage is still current; *See* Dawson, *supra* note 6, at 1047.

On the intellectual history of individualism, *See* R. MCCLOSKEY, AMERICAN CONSERVATISM IN THE AGE OF ENTERPRISE (1951); R. HOFSTADTER, SOCIAL DARWINISM IN AMERICAN THOUGHT, 1860–1915 (1944); E. KIRKLAND, DREAM AND THOUGHT IN THE BUSINESS COMMUNITY, 1860–1900 (1956); S. FINE, LAISSEZ-FAIRE AND THE GENERAL-WELFARE STATE, A STUDY OF CONFLICT IN AMERICAN THOUGHT, 1865–1901 (1956); R. WIEBE, THE SEARCH FOR ORDER, 1877–1920 (1967).

The rhetoric of self-reliance is a permanent theme of American public discourse: "'We must strike a better balance in our society,' [said President Ford.] 'We must introduce a new balance in the relationship between the individual and the Government, a balance that favors a greater individual freedom and self-reliance.'" N. Y. Times, July 18, 1976, at 24, col. 2.

The individualist ethic is reflected in a perennial strain of economic theorizing that emphasizes the natural and beneficial character of economic conflict and competition. According to this view, social welfare, *over the long run*, will be maximized only if we preserve a powerful set of incentives to individual activity. The argument is that the wealth and happiness of a people depend less on natural advantages or the wisdom of rulers than on the moral fiber of the citizenry, that is, on their self-reliance. If they are self-reliant, they will overcome obstacles, adjust easily to changes in fortune, and, above all, they will generate progress through the continual quest for personal advantage within the existing structure of rights.

The classic statement of this position is J. BENTHAM, THE THEORY OF LEGISLATION 119–22 (Ogden ed. 1931). On the nineteenth century United States, *see* J. HURST, LAW AND THE CONDITIONS OF FREEDOM IN THE NINETEENTH CENTURY UNITED STATES (1956). *See also* the works of intellectual

It is important to be clear from the outset that individualism is sharply distinct from pure egotism, or the view that it is impossible and undesirable to set any limits at all to the pursuit of self-interest. The notion of self-reliance has a strong affirmative moral content, the demand for respect for the rights of others. This means that the individualist ethic is as demanding in its way as the counter-ethic of altruism. It involves the renunciation of the use of both private and public force in the struggle for satisfaction, and acquiescence in the refusal of others to behave in a communal fashion.

Individualism provides a justification for the fundamental legal institutions of criminal law, property, tort, and contract. The function of law is the definition and enforcement of rights, of those limits on the pursuit of self- interest that distinguish an individualist from a purely egotistical regime. The great preoccupation of individualist legal philosophy is to justify these restrictions, in the face of appetites that are both boundless and postulated to be legitimate.[75]

A pure egotist defends the laws against force on the sole ground that they are necessary to prevent civil war.[76] For the individualist, the rules against the use of force have intrinsic rightness, because they are identified with the ideal of self-reliance, the economic objective of security for individual effort, and the political rhetoric of free will, autonomy, and natural rights.[77] Rules against violence provide a space within which to realize this program, rather than a mere bulwark against chaos.

Some level of protection of person and property against nonviolent interference (theft, fraud, negligence) is also desirable from the point of view of self-reliance. First, the thief is violating the injunction to rely on his own efforts in pursuing his goals. Second, the self-reliant man will be discouraged if he must devote all his energies to protecting the fruits of his labor. The rationale for contract is derivative from that of property. The law creates a property in expectations. One who breaches deprives the promisee in a sense no less real than the thief.

Beyond these fundamental legal institutions, the individualist program is much less clear. Moreover, it has varied greatly even within the two hundred year history of individualism as an organizing element in American public discourse. The next section presents a synopsis of these historical variations that should give both this concept and that of altruism more concreteness.

---

history cited in this note. A representative modern statement is A. OKUN, EQUALITY AND EFFICIENCY, THE BIG TRADEOFF (1975). Economic individualism, as I am using the term, is not synonymous with nineteenth century laissez-faire. It appeals to the beneficial effects of competition and self-reliance within whatever structure of rights and regulations the state may have set up. See C.B. MACPHERSON, THE POLITICAL THEORY OF POSSESSIVE INDIVIDUALISM: HOBBES TO LOCKE 57–58 (1962); E. ROSTOW, PLANNING FOR FREEDOM 10–45 (1959).

The political expression of individualism is the concept of a regime that secures liberty within a structure of legal rights. Liberty or freedom or autonomy is conceived as a good in itself, because it is synonymous with the ability to pursue one's own conception of the good to the best of one's ability. The function of the state (its only primary and intrinsically legitimate function) is to enforce the like rights of all members of the body politic. The state guarantees that so long as one remains within the area of autonomy for the individual free will, one will receive the benefits and suffer the ill consequences of one's chosen course of action. Thus rights simultaneously protect us in the possession of the fruits of our activities and prevent us from demanding that others participate in our misfortunes.

The progenitor of American theories of this kind is J. LOCKE, TWO TREATISES OF GOVERNMENT (Laslett ed. 1960). An example of the nineteenth century version is H. SPENCER, JUSTICE 176 (1891). The modern conservative version is best represented by F. HAYEK, THE CONSTITUTION OF LIBERTY (1960). The modern civil libertarian version is all around us but has no master expositors. See Black, *The Bill of Rights*, 35 N.Y.U.L. REV. 865 (1960).

[75] On the problem and the conventional solutions, see J. RAWLS, A THEORY OF JUSTICE 3–43 (1971). See also Kennedy, *supra* note 4, at 361–62.

[76] T. HOBBES, LEVIATHAN 109–13 (Oxford ed. 1957).

[77] J. LOCKE, *supra* note 74, at § 13, §§ 123–26.

Just as there are a multitude of implications that legal thinkers of different periods have drawn from individualism, there are a number of more abstract ideas that are possible bases for adopting it as an attitude and as a guide in formulating legal rules. What this means is that the idea of the "legitimacy" of the pursuit of self-interest within a framework of rights is ambiguous, and different thinkers have given it different contents.

The simplest explanation of the legitimacy of self-interestedness is that it is a moral good in itself. When the law refuses to interfere with its pursuit, it does so because it approves of it, and disapproves of people's attempts at altruism. Since this approach seems to flatly contradict the basic precepts of the Judaeo-Christian ethic, even in its most secularized form, it is not surprising that it is more common to find social thinkers justifying individualism in more circuitous, if sometimes less convincing ways.

The first of these is the notion of the invisible hand transforming apparent selfishness into public benefit. In this view, the moral problem presented by the law's failure to interfere with unsavory instances of individualism is apparent rather than real. If we are concerned with the ultimate good of the citizenry, then individualists are pursuing it *and will achieve it*, even when they are most convinced that they care only about themselves.

A much more common justification for individualism in law might be called the "clenched teeth" idea. It is that the refusal to consult the interests of others is an evil, and an evil not redeemed by any long-term good effects. But for the *state* to attempt to suppress this evil would lead to a greater one. As soon as the state attempts to legislate an ethic more demanding than that of individualism, it runs up against two insuperable problems: the relative inability of the legal system to alter human nature, and the tendency of officials to impose tyranny behind a smoke-screen of morality. The immorality of law is therefore the necessary price for avoiding the greater immoralities that would result from trying to make law moral.

A third view is that there is a viable distinction to be made between the "right" (law) and the "good" (morals). Since the criterion for the legitimacy of state intervention is radically different from that for moral judgment, one can favor an individualist legal system while remaining opposed to the behavior that such a system permits or even encourages. This view is often associated with the claim that individuals have inalienable rights whose content can be derived from fundamental concepts like freedom or human personality. The individual can set these up in his defense when the state claims the power to make him act in the interests of others.[78]

B. The Content of the Ideal of Altruism

The rhetoric of individualism so thoroughly dominates legal discourse at present that it is difficult even to identify a counter-ethic. Nonetheless, I think there is a coherent, pervasive notion that constantly competes with individualism, and I will call it altruism. The essence of altruism is the belief that one ought not to indulge a sharp preference for one's own interest over those of others. Altruism enjoins us to make sacrifices, to share, and to be merciful. It has roots in culture, in religion, ethics and art, that are as deep as those of individualism. (Love thy neighbor as thyself.)

[78] *See* R. NOZICK, ANARCHY, STATE AND UTOPIA 149–82 (1974).

The simplest of the practices that represent altruism are sharing and sacrifice. Sharing is a static concept, suggesting an existing distribution of goods which the sharers rearrange. It means giving up to another gains or wealth that one has produced oneself or that have come to one through some good fortune. It is motivated by a sense of duty or by a sense that the other's satisfaction is a reward at least comparable to the satisfaction one might have derived from consuming the thing oneself. Sharing may also involve participation in another's losses: a spontaneous decision to shift to oneself a part of the ill fortune, deserved or fortuitous, that has befallen someone else. Sacrifice is the dynamic notion of taking action that will change an ongoing course of events, at some expense to oneself, to minimize another's loss or maximize his gain.[79]

The polar opposite concept for sharing and sacrifice is exchange (a crucial individualist notion). The difference is that sharing and sacrifice involve a vulnerability to non-reciprocity. Further, this vulnerability is undergone out of a sense of solidarity: with the hope of a return but with a willingness to accept the possibility that there will be none. Exchange, on the contrary, signifies a transfer of resources in which equivalents are defined, and the structure of the situation, legal or social, is designed in order to make it unlikely that either party will disappoint the other. If there is some chance of disappointment, then this is experienced as a risk one must run, a cost that is unavoidable if one is to obtain what one wants from the other. The difference is one of degree, and it is easy to imagine arrangements that are such a thorough mixture, or so ambiguous, that they defy characterization one way or the other.[80]

Individualism is to pure egotism as altruism is to total selflessness or saintliness. Thus the altruist is unwilling to carry his premise of solidarity to the extreme of making everyone responsible for the welfare of everyone else. The altruist believes in the necessity and desirability of a sphere of autonomy or liberty or freedom or privacy within which one is free to ignore both the plights of others and the consequences of one's own acts for their welfare.

Just as the individualist must find a justification for those minimal restraints on self-interest that distinguish him from the pure egotist, the altruist must justify stopping short of saintliness. The basic notion is that altruistic duties are the product of the interaction of three main aspects of a situation. First, there is the degree of communal involvement or solidarity or intimacy that has grown up between the parties. Second, there is the issue of moral fault or moral virtue in

---

[79] There is a large literature about altruism, much of it concerned with the question of whether the concept can have any meaning at all. If I sacrifice or share, can I be said to behave altruistically, given that presumably I preferred sacrifice or sharing to the alternatives? Wouldn't it be better to speak of "internalizing another person's utility function"? For my purposes, it makes no difference how one answers these questions. In the cases that I deal with, there is no problem in distinguishing self-interested from altruistic behavior in the rough way suggested in the text. On the "larger" issue, *see* T. NAGEL, THE POSSIBILITY OF ALTRUISM (1970).

For an example of a typically altruistic but decidedly non-socialistic program of legal reform, *See* Pound, *The New Feudalism*, 35 COMMERCIAL L. J. 397 (1930). For more typical examples of altruist thinking about economic and social life, see, *e.g.*, A. GORZ, STRATEGY FOR LABOR: A RADICAL PROPOSAL (Nicolaus & Ortiz trans. 1964); Hamilton, Competition, in 4 ENCYCLOPEDIA SOC. SCI. 141 (1931); H. GEORGE, PROGRESS AND POVERTY (1879). *See also* M. RICHTER, THE POLITICS OF CONSCIENCE, T.H. GREEN AND HIS AGE 267–91 (1964). On the conservative element in nineteenth century altruism, see Dicey, *supra* note 74, at 220–40; J. RUSKIN, UNTO THIS LAST: FOUR ESSAYS ON THE FIRST PRINCIPLES OF POLITICAL ECONOMY (1862). On the conservative aspects of modern reform, see G. KOLKO, THE TRIUMPH OF CONSERVATISM (1963); J. WEINSTEIN, THE CORPORATE IDEAL IN THE LIBERAL STATE: 1900–1918 (1968); E. HAWLEY, THE NEW DEAL AND THE PROBLEM OF MONOPOLY (1966).

[80] *See* the discussions in I. MACNEIL, *supra* note 14, at 68–79; Macneil, *The Many Futures of Contract*, 47 S. CAL. L. REV. 691, 797–800 (1974).

the conduct by A and B that gives rise to the duty. Third, there is the intensity of the deprivation that can be averted, or of the benefit that can be secured in relation to the size of the sacrifice demanded by altruism. Thus we can define a continuum. At one extreme, there is the duty to make a small effort to save a best friend from a terrible disaster that is no fault of his own. At the other, there are remote strangers suffering small injuries induced by their own folly and remediable only at great expense.

At first glance the usefulness of the concept of altruism in describing the legal system is highly problematic. A very common view alike in the lay world and within the legal profession is that law is unequivocally the domain of individualism, and that this is true most clearly of the private law of property, torts, and contract. Private legal justice supposedly consists in the respect for rights, never in the performance of altruistic duty. The state acts through private law only to protect rights, not to enforce morality.

Of course, there are institutions, like the progressive income tax, that seem to have an unmistakable altruistic basis. But these are exceptional. They are after-the-fact adjustments to a preexisting legal structure that has its own, individualist, logical coherence. Likewise, social security or the minimum wage or pure food and drug laws are often seen as designed to force people with power to have a due regard for the interests of others. Many lay people see the employer's share of social security payments as designed to redistribute income from bosses to workers. But all of this takes place against a background of private law rules whose altruistic content is invisible if it exists at all.

Nonetheless, it is easy enough to fit fundamental legal institutions into the altruist mold. The rules against violence, for example, have the effect of changing the balance of power that would exist in the state of nature into that of civil society. The strong, who would supposedly dominate everyone if there were no state, are deprived of their advantages and forced to respect the "rights" of the weak. If altruism is the sharing or sacrifice of advantages that one might have kept for oneself, then the state forces the strong to behave altruistically. Further, the argument that the prohibition of theft is based on the ethic of self-reliance is weak at best. The thief is a very paragon of self-reliance, and the property owning victim has failed to act effectively in his own defense. The point for the altruist is not that the thief is a slacker, but that he is oblivious to any interest but his own. The law, as the expression goes, "provides him a conscience."

The rules of tort law can likewise be seen as enforcing some degree of altruism. Compensation for injuries means that the interests of the injured party must be taken into account by the tortfeasor. In deciding what to do, he is no longer free to consult only his own gains and losses, since these are no longer the only gains and losses for which he is legally responsible. Likewise in contract, when I want to breach because I have found a better deal with a new partner, the law makes me incorporate into my calculation the losses I will cause to the promisee. If my breach is without fault because wholly involuntary, I may be excused for mistake or impossibility.

There are two intuitively appealing objections to this way of looking at the legal order. The first is that "rights" and "justice" are much more plausible explanations of the rules than altruism. But as we will see, in this century at least, individualists have had a hard time showing that "rights" are anything more than after-the-fact rationalizations of the actual rules. Contemporary legal thinkers tend to agree that we decide whether I have a right to performance of a contract by examining the rules, rather than deciding what rules to have by first defining and then "protecting" the right. The distinction between justice and morality has proved no less problematic.[81]

The second objection is that the rules fall so far short of imposing the outcomes required by our moral sense that there must be some other way to account for them. If the solution is not "rights" in the abstract, then perhaps it is "the social function of maintaining a market economy." Or perhaps the rules simply carry into effect the objectives of the dominant political or economic groups within society.[82]

Each of these propositions has a great deal of truth to it, but neither is a valid objection to the point of view I am suggesting. First, it is important to distinguish the use of the concept of altruism as a direction in an altruism-individualism continuum from its use as an absolute standard for judging a situation. The way I am using the term, we can say that even a very minimal legal regime, one that permitted outcomes extremely shocking to our moral sense, would impose more altruistic duty than a regime still closer to the state of nature. In this near tautological sense, virtually *all* the rules of our own legal regime impose altruistic duty, because they make us show greater regard for the interests of others than we would if there were no laws. Only rules *prohibiting* sacrifice and sharing are truly anti-altruistic, and of these there are very few.

Second, to describe a given legal regime as more altruistic than another should suggest nothing about the motives of those who impose the regime. Every change in legal rules produces a pattern of changes in benefits to different affected parties. It is often a good inference that those who seemed likely to gain were influential in bringing the change about. It may nonetheless be useful to describe the change as one increasing or decreasing the degree of legally enforced altruistic duty.

Third, the "social function of maintaining the market" or the interests of dominant groups are, as tools, simply too crude to explain the detailed content of, say, the law of contracts. The vast majority of issues that arouse sharp conflict within contract law are either irrelevant to these larger considerations or of totally

---

[81] *See* Cohen, *The Ethical Basis of Legal Criticism*, 41 YALE L. J. 201 (1931). *See also* E. DURKHEIM, *supra* note 20, at 121–22:

It is customary to distinguish carefully justice from charity; that is, simple respect for the rights of another from every act which goes beyond this purely negative virtue. We *see* in the two sorts of activity two independent layers of morality: justice, in itself, would only consist of fundamental postulates; charity would be the perfection of justice. The distinction is so radical that, according to partisans of a certain type of morality, justice alone would serve to make the functioning of social life good; generous self-denial would be a private virtue, worthy of pursuit by a particular individual, but dispensable to society. Many even look askance at its intrusion into public life. We can *see* from what has preceded how little in accord with the facts this conception is. In reality, for men to recognize and mutually guarantee rights, they must, first of all, love each other, they must, for some reason, depend upon each other and on the same society of which they are a part. Justice is full of charity, or, to employ our expressions, negative solidarity is only an emanation from some other solidarity whose nature is positive. It is the repercussion in the sphere of real rights of social sentiments which come from another source. There is nothing specific about it, but it is the necessary accompaniment of every type of solidarity. It is met with forcefully wherever men live a common life, and that comes from the division of social labor or from the attraction of like for like.

[82] The master of the social function approach is Max Weber. For an introduction, see Trubek, *Max Weber on Law and the Rise of Capitalism*, 1972 Wis. L. Rev. 720; A. Gouldner, THE COMING CRISIS OF WESTERN SOCIOLOGY 341–70 (1970). An example of the typical modern combination of the social function and class interest ideas is L. Friedman, A HISTORY OF AMERICAN LAW 14–15 (1973). *See generally* Gordon, *Introduction: J. Willard Hurst and the Common Law Tradition in American Historiography*, 10 Law & Soc. Rev. 9 (1975). The criticism offered in the text following this note is similar to that of E. THOMPSON, WHIGS AND HUNTERS: THE ORIGIN OF THE BLACK ACT 258–69 (1975).

problematic import. Take the question of the "good faith" duties of a buyer in a requirements contract when there is a sudden price increase. The buyer may be able to bankrupt the seller and make a large profit by sharply increasing his requirements, supposing that the item in question accounts for much of his own cost of manufacture, or that he can resell it without using it at all.

The buyers and sellers in these situations do not seem to line up in terms of any familiar categories of political or economic power, and the effects on "the market" of deciding one way or another are highly problematic. Yet there is clearly something important at stake. The possible solutions range from a minimal buyer's duty not to "speculate" against the seller's interests to a good faith duty to absorb some loss in order to avoid a larger loss to one's contractual partner.[83] The notion of altruism captures the court's dilemma far better than either class struggle or the needs of a market economy.[84] There are hundreds of such problems in private law.

Finally, it is a familiar fact that for about a century there has been a movement of "reform" of private law. It began with the imposition of statutory strict liability on railroads for damage to cattle and crops, and has persisted through the current redefinition of property law in the interests of the environment. In the battles and skirmishes of reform, across an enormous variety of particular issues, it has been common for conservatives to argue that liberals are consciously or unconsciously out to destroy the market system. Liberals respond that the conservative program is a cloak for the interests of big business.

Yet it is perfectly clear that all the changes of 100 years have not "destroyed the market," nor would further vast changes throughout property, torts, and contracts. It is equally clear that the nineteenth century rules the liberals have been attacking form a complex intellectual system whose vitality even in the last quarter of the twentieth century is as much or more the product of its ideological power as of the direct material dominance of particular economic or political interests. If the concepts of individualism and altruism turn out to be useful, it is because they capture something of this struggle of contradictory utopian visions. It is this dimension that the ideas of class domination and of social function cannot easily grasp. The approaches should therefore be complementary rather than conflicting.

The last objection I will consider is that to characterize fundamental legal institutions like tort or contract in terms of altruism is wrong because it is nonsense to speak of forcing someone to behave altruistically. True, the notion requires the *experience* of solidarity and the voluntary undertaking of vulnerability in consequence. It therefore implies duties that transcend those imposed by the legal order. It is precisely the refusal to take all the advantage to which one is legally, but not morally entitled that is most often offered as an example of altruism. It follows that when the law "enforces" such conduct, it can do no more than make people behave "as if" they had really experienced altruistic motives. Yet nothing could be clearer than that, in many circumstances, this is exactly what we want the law to do. One idea of justice is the organization of society so that the outcomes of interaction are equivalent to those that would occur *if* everyone behaved altruistically. I take this as a given in the rest of the discussion.[85]

Duncan Kennedy

---

[83] See the cases collected in KESSLER & GILMORE, *supra* note 3, at 337–62.

[84] Weber himself was forced to recognize this difficulty by the "case of England," which attained a high level of economic development under a legal regime which, as he saw it, was profoundly irrational. *See* 2 M. WEBER, *supra* note 4, at 890–92. *See also* Trubek, *supra* note 82, at 746–48.

[85] *See* R. UNGER, *supra* note 4, at 214–16.

There are many problems with the use of concepts like individualism and altruism. Both positions have been assembled from diverse legal, moral, economic, and political writings, and I can give no plausible description of the principle of selection at work. As a result, it is impossible to "prove" or "disprove" the validity of the two constructs. They are neither falsifiable empirical statements about a determinate mass of data, nor logically pure "models" totally abstracted from reality.

Nonetheless, I hope that the reader will find that the bits and pieces fit together into two intuitively familiar, easily recognizable wholes. Not being a systematic nominalist, I believe that there really is an altruist and an individualist mode of argument. More, I believe that the rhetorical modes are responsive to real issues in the real world. They are opposed concepts like Romanticism *vs.* Classicism, Gothic *vs.* Renaissance, toughminded *vs.* tenderminded, shame culture *vs.* guilt culture, or *Gemeinschaft vs. Gesellschaft.* As with Romanticism, we can believe in the usefulness of the notion of altruism without being able to demonstrate its existence experimentally, or show the inevitability of the association of the elements that compose it.

Methodological difficulties of this kind color all of the analysis that follows. One must keep constantly in mind that the individualist arguments are drawn from the same basic sources as the altruist ones. The same judge may, in a single opinion, provide examples of each mode. Over time, a single judge may provide complete statements of both positions. In other words, a person can use the arguments that compose the individualist set without being an "individualist character." When I speak of "altruist judges" or "altruist legislators," I mean only the proponents of particular arguments that fall within one set or the other. I have no intention of characterizing these proponents as *personalities.*

When we set out to analyze an action, and especially a judicial opinion, it is only rarely possible to make a direct inference from the rhetoric employed to the real motives or ideals that animate the judge. And it is even harder to characterize outcomes than it is personalities or opinions. It will almost always be possible to argue that, if we look hard at its actual effects on significant aspects of the real world, a particular decision will further both altruist and individualist values, or neither. I will therefore avoid talking about "altruist outcomes" as much as possible.

Given that individualism and altruism are sets of stereotyped pro and con arguments, it is hard to see how either of them can ever be "responsible" for a decision. First, each argument is applied, in almost identical form, to hundreds or thousands of fact situations. When the shoe fits, it is obviously not because it was designed for the wearer. Second, for each pro argument there is a con twin. Like Llewellyn's famous set of contradictory "canons on statutes," the opposing positions seem to cancel each other out.[86] Yet somehow this is not *always* the case in practice. Although each argument has an absolutist, imperialist ring to it, we find that we are able to distinguish particular fact situations in which one side is much more plausible than the other. The difficulty, the mystery, is that there are no available metaprinciples to explain just what it is about these particular situations that make them ripe for resolution. And there are many, many cases in which confidence in intuition turns out to be misplaced.

---

[86] *See* K. LLEWELLYN, THE COMMON LAW TRADITION: DECIDING APPEALS 521–35 (1960).

These are problems of a kind familiar in some other fields.[87] Lawyers don't usually confront them, because lawyers usually believe that their analytic skills can produce explanations of legal rules and decisions more convincing than any that employ such vague, "value laden" concepts. The typical legal argument at least pretends that it is possible to get from some universally agreed or positively enacted premise (which may be the importance of protecting a "social interest") to some particular desirable outcome through a combination of logic and "fact finding" (or, more likely, "fact asserting").

Yet most contemporary students of legal thought seem to agree that an account of adjudication limited to the three dimensions of authoritative premises, facts and analysis is incomplete.[88] One way to express this is to say that "policy" plays a large though generally unacknowledged part in decisionmaking. The problem is to find a way to describe this part. My hope is that the substantive and formal categories I describe can help in rendering the contribution of "policy" intelligible. Although individualism and altruism can be reduced neither to facts nor to logic, although they cannot be used with any degree of consistency to characterize personalities or opinions or the outcomes of lawsuits, they may nonetheless be helpful in this enterprise.

The ultimate goal is to break down the sense that legal argument is autonomous from moral, economic, and political discourse in general. There is nothing innovative about this. Indeed, it has been a premise of legal scholars for several generations that it is impossible to construct an autonomous logic of legal rules. What is new in this piece is the attempt to show an orderliness to the debates about "policy" with which we are left after abandonment of the claim of neutrality.

IV. THREE PHASES OF THE CONFLICT OF INDIVIDUALISM AND ALTRUISM

Eighteenth century common law thinking does not seem to have been afflicted with a sense of conflict between two legal ideals. Positive law was of a piece with God's moral law as understood through reason and revelation. In Blackstone, for example, there is no suggestion of recurrent conflicts either about the nature of legal morality or about which of two general utilitarian strategies the legislator had best pursue.[89] The sense of a conflict between systems of thought emerged only at the beginning of the nineteenth century. It has had three overlapping phases, corresponding roughly to the periods 1800–1870, 1850–1940, and 1900 to the present.[90]

---

[87] *See* R. UNGER, *supra* note 73, at 12–16, 106–19; A. GOULDNER, *supra* note 73, at 20–60. For an early nineteenth century attempt to deal with the problem, see Coleridge, *Essays on the Principles of Method*, 1 THE FRIEND 448–524 (Rooke ed. 1969).

[88] For a useful summary, *see* Christie, Objectivity in Law, 78 YALE L. J. 1311, 1312–26 (1969). The most striking recent formulation of the problem is Deutsch, Neutrality, Legitimacy and the Supreme Court: Some Intersections Between Law and Political Science, 20 STAN. L. REV. 169 (1968). *See also* Gordon, *supra* note 82.

[89] *See* 1 W. BLACKSTONE, COMMENTARIES *38–*61. An English judge could write the following even in 1828: "It has been argued that the law does not compel every line of conduct which humanity or religion may require; but there is no act which Christianity forbids, that the law will not reach: if it were otherwise, Christianity would not be, as it has always been held to be, part of the law of England." Bird v. Holbrook, 29 Rev. R., 657, 667 (Ct. Com. Pleas 1828).

[90] The discussion in this section is a compressed version of a larger work tentatively called *The Rise and Fall of Classical Legal Thought: 1850–1940*. Copies of the completed chapters are on file at the office of the Harvard Law Review.

Individualism was at first not an *ethic* in conflict with the ethic of altruism, but a set of pragmatic arguments perceived as in conflict with ethics in general. Antebellum judges and commentators referred to these pragmatic arguments by the generic name of "policy," and contrasted it to "morality." A crucial fact about the legal order was that it stopped short of the full enforcement of morality. Counsel in an 1817 Supreme Court case defended his client's failure to reveal crucial information to a buyer as follows:[91]

> Even admitting that his conduct was unlawful, in foro conscientiae, does that prove that it was so in the civil forum? Human laws are imperfect in this respect, and the sphere of morality is more extensive than the limits of civil jurisdiction. The maxim of caveat emptor could never have crept into the law, if the province of ethics had been co-extensive with it.

The explanation for the distinction between laws of perfect and imperfect obligation was that imposing high standards of conduct in contract and tort, and then granting large damage judgments for violating those standards, would discourage economic development.[92] This is a prototypically individualist position. The "morality" that opposed this program of limited liability was the first systematic version of common law altruism. The idea was that the purpose of law and the source of its legitimacy was that it forced people to behave toward one another in a substantively equitable fashion. The contraction of liability amounted to permitting or encouraging people to disregard the impact of their actions on those around them, and was therefore unjustifiable.

The antebellum conception of the conflict is perhaps most perfectly expressed by Parsons (1855) in his discussion of the law of fraud. He distinguished between:[93]

> that kind and measure of craft and cunning which the law deems it impossible or inexpedient to detect and punish, and therefore leaves unrecognized, and that worse kind and higher degree of craft and cunning which the law prohibits, and of which it takes away all the advantage from him by whom it is practised.
>
> The law of morality, which is the law of God, acknowledges but one principle, and that is the duty of doing to others as we would that others should do to us, and this principle absolutely excludes and prohibits all cunning; if we mean by this word any astuteness practised by any one for his own exclusive benefit. But this would be perfection; and the law of God requires it because it requires perfection; that is, it sets up a perfect standard, and requires a constant and continual effort to approach it. But human law, or municipal law, is the rule which men require each other to obey; and it is of its essence that it should have an effectual sanction, by itself providing that a certain punishment should be administered by men, or certain adverse consequences take place, as the direct effect of a breach of this law. If therefore the municipal law were identical with the law of God, or adopted all its requirements, one of three consequences must flow therefrom; either the law would become confessedly, and by a common understanding, powerless and dead as to a part of it; or society would be constantly employed in visiting all its members with punishment; or, if the law

---

[91] Laidlaw v. Organ, 15 U.S. (2 Wheat.) 178, 193 (1817).

[92] *See generally* M. HORWITZ, THE TRANSFORMATION OF AMERICAN LAW: 1780–1860, ch. 3 (forthcoming in 1977).

[93] T. PARSONS, THE LAW OF CONTRACTS *767–78 (1855).

annulled whatever violated its principles, a very great part of human transactions would be rendered void. Therefore the municipal law leaves a vast proportion of unquestionable duty to motives, sanctions, and requirements very different from those which it supplies. And no man has any right to say, that whatever human law does not prohibit, that he has a right to do; for that only is right which violates no law, and there is another law besides human law. Nor, on the other hand, can any one reasonably insist, that whatever one should do or should abstain from doing, this may properly be made a part of the municipal law, for this law must necessarily fail to do all the great good that it can do and therefore should, if it attempts to do that which, while society and human nature remain what they are it cannot possibly accomplish.

In this early nineteenth century view, the law aimed at and usually achieved the imposition of a high level of altruistic duty, but had an occasion to make concessions to individualism. Here are a few examples:

Negotiability: It was common to argue that it was immoral to force the maker of a note to pay a holder in due course after failure of the consideration: the law was requiring the maker to pay for something he never got. But the policy of encouraging transactions dictated the cutting off of defenses.[94]

Incorporation: It was a Jacksonian objection to limited corporate liability that it allowed stockholders to escape their share of the debts of the corporation. The law obliged partners to live up to their moral obligations, but allowed stockholders to behave dishonorably. The answer was the policy in favor of the pooling of resources.[95]

Consideration: The common law refused to enforce promises whose performance was dictated by the most solemn moral obligation when they lacked consideration. The reason was the policy against the multiplication of lawsuits and the legalization of family life.[96]

Breaching Plaintiff's Suit for Restitution: Most courts refused to honor the breaching plaintiff's claim for restitution even when the result was a windfall unjust enrichment of the defendant. To allow recovery would have created a dangerous incentive to lax performance.[97]

Bankruptcy: Bankruptcy laws sanctioned and even encouraged the dishonorable conduct of refusing to pay one's debts. The reason was the policy against demoralizing economic actors by eliminating the incentive of self-enrichment.[98]

Still, there was no question which of the ethics was primary: we would achieve a social order according to the law of God if we could. We can't, because the ideal is too demanding. We therefore validate a certain amount of conduct inconsistent with altruism but consistent with individualism, hoping that by accepting to this extent the imperfections of human nature we will at least forestall pure egotism, while at the same time promoting economic growth.

B. Classical Individualism (1850–1940): Free Will

Modern legal thought is preoccupied with "competing policies," conflicting "value judgments" and the idea of a purposive legal order, and to that extent has much in

Duncan Kennedy

[94] *See* M. HORWITZ, *supra* note 92, ch. 7, § 1.
[95] *See* J. HURST, THE LEGITIMACY OF THE BUSINESS CORPORATION IN THE LAW OF THE UNITED STATES: 1780–1970, at 31–32 (1970).
[96] *See, e.g.,* Mills v. Wyman, 20 Mass. (3 Pick.) 207 (1825).
[97] *Compare* Britton v. Turner, 6 N.H. 481 (1834), *with* Smith v. Brady, 17 N.Y. 173 (1858).
[98] 2 J. KENT, COMMENTARIES ON AMERICAN LAW *391 n.(a), *394 n. (a) (1826).

common with pre-Civil War thinking. One major difference is the total disappearance of religious arguments, and the fading of overtly moralistic discussion. More important for our purposes, the modern situation has been conditioned by the post-Civil War triumph of what I will call Classical individualism,[99] which represented not just a rhetorical shift away from the earlier emphasis on altruism, but the denial that altruism had anything at all to do with basic legal doctrines.

The reasons for this conceptual revolution will not concern us here. It is enough to say that they were complex, involving the triumph of particular economic interests, the desire to establish an apolitical scientific justification for the power of judges and lawyers, and autonomous movements in all the different areas of late nineteenth century thought. What does concern us is the structure of the Classical individualist position, since this structure forms the backdrop for the modern discussion.

Classical individualism rejected the idea that particular rules represented an ad hoc compromise between policy and altruist morality. Rather, the rules represented a fully principled and consistent solution *both* to the ethical and to the practical dilemmas of legal order. The contraction of liability that occurred over the course of the nineteenth century was thereby rationalized, and shielded from the charge that it represented the sacrifice of equity to expediency.

The Classical position can be reduced to three propositions concerning the proper definition of liability. First, the fundamental theory of our political and economic institutions is that there should exist an area of individual autonomy or freedom or liberty within which there is no responsibility at all for effects on others.[100] Second, the meaning of this political and economic theory for private law is that there are only two legitimate sources of liability: fault, meaning intentional or negligent interference with the property or personal rights of another, and contract. As between strangers, there are no duties of mutual assistance; there are only duties to abstain from violence and negligence. Contract adds new duties, and these are enforced as a matter of right, rather than of judicial discretion.[101] The content of contractual duty is strictly limited by the intent of the parties. The third proposition is that the concepts of fault and free will to contract can generate, through a process of deduction, determinate legal rules defining the boundaries and content of tort and contract duties.[102]

The important thing about the Classical position, from our point of view, is that it presented the choice between individualism and altruism as one of all-or-nothing commitment to a complete system. One might accept or reject the individualist claim that our institutions are based on liberty, private property and bodily security. But if one once subscribed to these ideas, a whole legal order followed inescapably. To reject the particular applications was a sign either of error or of bad faith, since they were no more than the logical implications of the abstract premises.

---

[99] The legal thought of this period is generally referred to as formal or formalist. *See* K. LLEWELLYN, THE COMMON LAW TRADITION: DECIDING APPEALS 38–40 (1960); G. GILMORE, *supra* note 41; Horwitz, *The Rise of Legal Formalism*, 19 Am. J. Leg. Hist. 251 (1975); Nelson, *The Impact of the Antislavery Movement Upon Styles of Judicial Reasoning in Nineteenth Century America*, 87 HARV. L. REV. 513, 547 (1974).

[100] For an illustration, *see* M. Fuller, Chief Justice of the United States, *Address in Commemoration of the Inauguration of George Washington*, Dec. 11, 1889 (G.P.O. 1890).

[101] For an illustration, see Ames, *Undisclosed Principal—His Rights and Liabilities*, 18 YALE L. J. 443 (1909).

[102] For an illustration, see J. BRADLEY, *Law, Its Nature and Office as the Bond and Basis of Civil Society*, in MISCELLANEOUS WRITINGS 226–66 (1901).

If one believed in the first principles and in the possibility of deducing rules from them, then it was easy to believe that the Classical regime was both morally and practically far superior to the state of nature. The restrictions on pure egotism imposed by that regime did not represent a concession to the utopian ideal of altruism. They embodied the individualist morality of self- reliance, the individualist economic theory of free competition, and the individualist political philosophy of natural rights, which set well-defined boundaries to the demand that people treat the interests of others as of equal importance with their own.

For example, the contract law of 1825 was full of protective doctrines, such as the incapacity of married women, infants, lunatics and seamen. The consideration doctrine often functioned to enforce an altruist contractual morality, as did the doctrines of fraud, mistake, duress, undue influence and unconscionability. Jury discretion in setting damages provided a further vehicle for importing community standards of fair conduct. For antebellum legal thought, there was not much difficulty in explaining all of this: the doctrines represented the legal enforcement of straightforward moral norms, but raised questions of policy in so much as an insistence on policing bargains might be harmful to the goal of economic development.[103]

During the latter part of the century, some of these doctrines were cut back, and others expanded somewhat. But all of the doctrines were recast as implications of the fundamental idea that private law rules protect individual free will. The basis of restrictions on capacity is that infants and those like them lack free will; duress is the overbearing of the will, undue influence its subversion; fraud leads to a consent that is only apparent; mistake meant that the wills of the parties had miscarried; the measure of damages was defined by the will of the parties with respect to the extent of liability.[104]

Recast in terms of will, the rules of contract law still represented a moral as well as a practical vision, but that vision was no longer perceptibly altruist. The new premise was that people were responsible for themselves unless they could produce evidence that they lacked free will in the particular circumstances. If no such evidence was available, then they were bound to look to their own resources in performing what they had undertaken. In place of a situational calculus of altruistic duty and an equally situational calculus of economic effects, there was a single individualist moral-political-economic premise from which everything else followed.

We could trace a similar process of development in torts or property or corporate law. In each case, there was a central individualist concept representing a substantial limitation on the total freedom of the state of nature. In each case, the concept defined an area of autonomy, of "absolute right," and also provided the basis for limiting the right. Since the basis of tort law, for example, was the enforcement of compensation for wrongful injury, it followed that there could be no tort liability without fault. Existing instances, such as strict liability in trespass or respondeat superior, must either be rationalized in terms of the will theory or rejected as anachronistic.[105]

It is common to equate late nineteenth century thought with conceptualism, that is with my third proposition about the possibility of a *deductive* process of defining the boundaries and content of liability. This is misleading to the extent

[103] *See* Horwitz, *Historical Foundations of Modern Contract Law*, 87 HARV. L. REV. 917 (1974).
[104] For an illustration, see S. AMOS, A SYSTEMATIC VIEW OF THE SCIENCE OF JURISPRUDENCE 85–92, 176–213 (London 1872).
[105] For an illustration, see F. POLLOCK, THE LAW OF TORTS 1–15 (1887).

that it suggests that the concepts were just "there," as arbitrary starting points for judicial reasoning. They were, on the contrary, crucial components in the larger individualist argument designed to link the very general proposition, that the American system is based on freedom, with the very concrete rules and doctrines of the legal order. "Free will" in law followed from, indeed was simply the practical application of, the freedom of individualist political, moral and economic theory.[106]

C. Modern Legal Thought (1900 to the present): The Sense of Contradiction

In private law, modern legal thought begins with the rejection of Classical individualism. Its premise is that Classical theory failed to show either that the genius of our institutions is individualist or that it is possible to deduce concrete legal rules from concepts like liberty, property or bodily security. For this reason, morality and policy reappear in modern discussions, in place of first principles and logic. The problem is that morality is no longer unequivocally altruist—there is a conflict of moralities. Nor is policy any longer unequivocally individualist—there are arguments for collectivism, regulation, the welfare state, along with the theory of economic development through laissez-faire. This conflict of morality with morality and of policy with policy pervades every important issue of private law.

1. The Critique of Classical Individualism. This is not the place for a description of the argumentative strategies by which more or less altruist thinkers, working in many different fields,[107] disintegrated the Classical individualist structure. I will make do with some flat assertions. First, modern legal thought and especially modern legal education are committed to the position that no issue of substance can be resolved merely by reference to one of the Classical concepts. This applies to liberty, free will, property, fault, proximate cause, the "subject matter of the contract," title, cause of action, privity, necessary party, "literal meaning," "strictly private activity," and a host of others.

Second, the problem with the concepts is that they assert the possibility of making clear and convincing on-off distinctions among fact situations, along the lines of free vs. coerced; proximate vs. remote cause; private vs. affected with a public interest. In modern legal thought, it is a premise that any real fact situation will contain elements from both sides of the conceptual polarity. The problem of classification is therefore that of locating the situation on a continuum. This process is not self-executing: people are certain to disagree strongly about how to classify, according to their purposes in making the distinction in the first place, and there is no "objective" or "absolute" standard of correctness for resolving these disagreements.[108]

Third, given the indeterminacy of the concepts, their inherent ambiguity as criteria of decision, it is implausible to describe the total body of legal rules as implicit in general principles like "protection of property" or "freedom of contract."

---

[106] The classic illustration is the majority opinion in Coppage v. Kansas, 236 U.S. 1 (1915).

[107] For useful treatments of American thought during the period in question, see E. PURCELL, THE CRISIS OF DEMOCRATIC THEORY: SCIENTIFIC NATURALISM AND THE PROBLEM OF VALUE (1973); White, *From Sociological Jurisprudence to Realism: Jurisprudence and Social Change in Twentieth Century America*, 58 VA. L. REV. 999 (1972).

[108] *See* Dewey, *Logical Method and Law*, 10 CORNELL L.Q. 17 (1924); Cohen, *Transcendental Nonsense and the Functional Approach*, 35 COLUM. L. REV. 809 (1935); Cohen, *On Absolutisms in Legal Thought*, 84 U. Pa. L. Rev. 681 (1936); R. Unger, *supra* note 73, at 29–144; A. Katz, *supra* note 4.

Since it is not possible to move in a deductive fashion from concept to implications, we need some other way to account for the process of judicial lawmaking. That explanation will be found in the judge's moral, political and economic views and in the idiosyncracies of his understanding of the character of the fact situation.[109]

Fourth, there are numerous issues on which there exists a judicial and also a societal consensus, so that the judge's use of his views on policy will be noncontroversial. But there are also situations in which there is great conflict. The judge is then faced with a dilemma: to impose his personal views may bring on accusations that he is acting "politically" rather than "judicially." He can respond to this with legalistic mumbo jumbo, that is, by appealing to the concepts and pretending that they have decided the case for him. Or he can take the risks inherent in acknowledging the full extent of his discretion.[110]

2. The Sense of Contradiction. The death of conceptualism has brought on a new phase of the conflict of individualism and altruism. To begin with it has reduced them to the same argumentative level. While he still believed in the Classical system, the individualist had no problem in defining and justifying his position on any given issue. He could derive everything from the concepts. The altruist, on the other hand, had no deductive system that explained where she would stop short of total collectivism. She was obliged to argue in an ad hoc manner from the injustice, immorality or irrationality of particular individualist outcomes.

But modern individualism presents itself not as a deductive system, but as a pole, or tendency or vector or bias, in the debate with altruism over the legitimacy of the system of rules that emerged in the late nineteenth century. As a consequence, altruists can argue for the establishment of legal institutions like zoning, workmen's compensation, social security, compulsory collective bargaining, products liability and no-fault automobile insurance without being vulnerable to the charge of subverting a logical structure. They admit that such institutions are anti-individualist, and also that they have no principles capable of logically determining where, short of total collectivism, they would stop the expansion of legally enforceable altruistic duty. But given the death of the concepts, the individualists no longer have any principles that determine where, short of the state of nature, *they* would stop the *contraction* of altruistic duty. They are open to the charge of dissolving society, or of stacking the rules in favor of particular blackguards.

This parity in argumentative positions is the starting point of the modern debate about what to do with the rule structure Classical individualism created through deduction from first principles. The new scepticism destroyed the presumptive legitimacy of the old system, creating a vast number of difficult legal problems, but solving none of them. Rules that referred directly to the discredited concepts (duress equals overbearing of the will) were recognized as indeterminate, and had to be replaced or reconceived as vague standards. More concrete rules that had been derived from the abstract premises (silence cannot be acceptance) had to be justified in their own right or rejected. The new, more altruistic institutions like labor law, consumer protection, social insurance and securities regulation immediately became a battleground. Their boundaries and internal structure had to be defined by the courts. A thoroughgoing individualist

---

[109] *See* Cohen, *The Basis of Contract*, 46 HARV. L. REV. 553 (1933); Cohen, Property and Sovereignty, 13 CORNELL L.Q. 8 (1927); Cohen, *The Ethical Basis of Legal Criticism*, 41 YALE L. J. 201 (1931).

[110] *See* Deutsch, *supra* note 88; A. BICKEL, *supra* note 69.

interpretation of altruist statutes might have constricted them to the point of de facto nullification.

In private law, this modern phase of conflict occurs over three main issues, which I will call, somewhat arbitrarily, community vs. autonomy, regulation vs. facilitation, and paternalism vs. self-determination.[111] Each particular debate has a stalemated quality that reflects the inability of either individualism or altruism to generate a new set of principles or metaprinciples to replace the late lamented concepts.

(a) Community vs. Autonomy. The issue here is the extent to which one person should have to share or make sacrifices in the interest of another in the absence of agreement or other manifestation of intention. At first sight this issue may seem largely confined to torts and quasi-contract, but it arises in identical form in many other areas as well. The law must define the reciprocal rights of neighboring land holders through the law of easements, and the rights of third party beneficiaries and assignees against obligors. Within consensual arrangements, it must decide how to dispose of the multitude of possible controversies not covered or ambiguously covered by the parties themselves. There is the issue of the scope and intensity of the duties of fiduciaries to beneficiaries, including duties of directors and officers of corporations to shareholders. There is the whole apparatus of interpretation, excuses and damage measures in the law of contracts. And there is the borderline area of pre- or extra-contractual liability represented by the doctrine of promissory estoppel.

The conflict of community and autonomy is the modern form of the early nineteenth century debate about the impact on economic growth of extending or contracting nonconsensual altruistic duties. The legal institutions involved are those that I characterized in Section I as intermediate between pure formalities (where the law is indifferent as to which of a number of courses of action the parties undertake) and rules designed to deter wrongdoing. We noted there that this category could be regarded either as designed to deter tort and breach of contract as wrongful in themselves, or, in the more common mode, as designed to offer a choice between no injury and injury *cum* compensation.

The adoption of the second view represents a decision to place *general* limits on the ability of the legal system to enforce altruistic duty. If damages are a tariff, the "wrongdoer" is authorized to consult his own interest exclusively, so long as he is willing to make the payment that secures the other party's rights. This may well involve two distinct breaches of altruistic duty.

First, even if compensation is perfect, the injuring party is forcing the injured party to take compensation, rather than specific performance or freedom from tortious interference. Second, the injuring party is under no obligation to share the excess over the compensation payment that he may derive from inflicting the injury. Once I have paid the expectation damage measure, *all* the windfall profits from breach of contract go to me.[112]

Given the decision to regard contract and tort law as compensatory rather than punitive, the altruist and individualist have disagreements at three levels:

> *Scope of obligation*: Given a particular relationship or situation, is there any duty at all to look out for the interests of the other?

---

[111] The general idea of categorizing legal doctrines in the way suggested here owes much to I. MACNEIL, *supra* note 14; Macaulay, *supra* note 2; Gardner, *An Inquiry into the Principles of the Law of Contracts*, 46 HARV. L. REV. 1 (1932).

[112] *See* R. NOZICK, *supra* note 78, at 63–71; Ames, *Law and Morals*, 22 HARV. L. REV. 97, 106 (1909); Wellington, *supra* note 20, at 229–33.

Intensity of obligation: Given duty, how great is the duty on the scale from mere abstention from violence to the highest fiduciary obligation?

Extent of liability for consequences: Given breach of duty, how far down the chain of causation should we extend liability?

The individualist position is the restriction of obligations of sharing and sacrifice. This means being opposed to the broadening, intensifying and extension of liability and opposed to the liberalization of excuses once duty is established. This position is only superficially paradoxical. The contraction of initial liability leaves greater areas for people to behave in a self-interested fashion. Liberal rules of excuse have the opposite effect: they oblige the beneficiary of a duty to share the losses of the obligor when for some reason he is unable to perform. The altruist position is the expansion of the network of liability and also the liberalization of excuses.

(b) Regulation vs. Facilitation. The issue here is the use of bargaining power as the determinant of the distribution of desired objects and the allocation of resources to different uses. It arises whenever two parties with conflicting claims or interests reach an accommodation through bargaining, and the stronger party attempts to enforce it through the legal system. The judge must then decide whether the stronger party has pressed her advantage further in her own interests than is acceptable to the legal system. If she has not, then the agreement will be enforced; if she has, a sanction will be applied, ranging from the voiding of the agreement to criminal punishment of the abuse of bargaining power.[113]

There are many approaches to the control of bargaining power, including:

Incapacitation of classes of people deemed particularly likely to lack adequate bargaining power (children, lunatics, etc.) with the effect that they can void their contracts if they want to.

Outlawing particular tactics, such as the use of physical violence, duress of goods, threats to inflict malicious harm, fraudulent statements, "bargaining in bad faith," etc.

Outlawing particular transactions that are thought to involve great dangers of overreaching, such as the settlement of debts for less than the full amount or the making of unilaterally beneficial modifications in the course of performance of contracts.

Control of the competitive structure of markets, either by atomizing concentrated economic power or by creating countervailing centers strong enough to bargain equally.

Direct policing of the substantive fairness of bargains, whether by direct price fixing or quality specification, by setting maxima or minima, or by announcing a standard such as "reasonableness" or "unconscionability."

The individualist position is that judges ought not to conceive of themselves as regulators of the use of economic power. This means conceiving of the legal system as a limited set of existing restraints imposed on the state of nature, and then refusing to extend those constraints to new situations. The altruist position is that existing restraints represent an attempt to achieve distributive justice which the judges should carry forward rather than impede.

(c) Paternalism vs. Self-Determination. This issue is distinct from that of regulation vs. facilitation because it arises in situations not of conflict but of error. A party to an agreement or one who has unilaterally incurred a legal obligation seeks

Duncan Kennedy

[113] The classic treatment is Dawson, *Economic Duress—An Essay In Perspective*, 45 MICH. L. REV. 253 (1947).

to void it on the grounds that they acted against their "real" interests. The beneficiary of the agreement or duty refuses to let the obligor back out. An issue of altruistic duty arises because the obligee ought to take the asserted "real" interests into account, both at the bargaining stage, if he is aware of them, and at the enforcement stage, if he only becomes aware of them then. On the other hand, he may have innocently relied on the obligor's own definition of his objectives, so that he will have to sacrifice something of his own if he behaves mercifully.

No issue of bargaining power is necessarily involved in such situations. For example:

Liquidated damage clauses freely agreed to by both parties are often voided on grounds of unreasonableness.

Express conditions unequivocal on their face are excused on grounds of forfeiture or interpreted out of existence.

Merger clauses that would waive liability for fraudulent misrepresentations are struck down or reinterpreted.

No oral modification clauses are held to be waived by actions of the beneficiary or disallowed altogether.

Modifications of contract remedy such as disclaimers of warranty or of liability for negligence, limitations of venue, waiver of defenses, and limitations on time for complaints are policed under various standards, even where they apparently result from conscious risk allocation rather than from mere superior power.

Persons lacking in capacity are allowed to void contracts that are uncoerced and substantively fair.

Consideration doctrine sometimes renders promises unenforceable because there was no "real" exchange, as in the cases of the promissory note of a widow given in exchange for a discharge of her husband's worthless debts, or that of a contract for "conjuring."

Fraud and Unconscionability doctrine protect against "unfair surprise" in situations where a party is a victim of his own foolishness rather than of the exercise of power.

The individualist position is that the parties themselves are the best and only legitimate judges of their own interests, subject to a limited number of exceptions, such as incapacity. People should be allowed to behave foolishly, do themselves harm, and otherwise refuse to accept any other person's view of what is best for them. Other people should respect this freedom; they should also be able to rely on those who exercise it to accept the consequences of their folly. The altruist response is that the paternalist rules are not exceptions, but the representatives of a developed counterpolicy of forcing people to look to the "real" interests of those they deal with. This policy is as legitimate as that of self-determination and should be extended as circumstances permit or require.

One way of conceiving of the transition from Classical to modern legal thought is through the imagery of core and periphery. Classical individualism dealt with the issues of community vs. autonomy, regulation vs. facilitation and paternalism vs. self-determination by affirming the existence of a core of legal freedom which was equated with firm adherence to autonomy, facilitation and self-determination. The existence of countertendencies was acknowledged, but in a backhanded way. By its "very nature," freedom must have limits; these could be derived as implications *from* that nature; and they would then constitute a periphery of exceptions to the core doctrines.

What distinguishes the modern situation is the breakdown of the conceptual boundary between the core and the periphery, so that all the conflicting positions are at least potentially relevant to all issues. The Classical concepts oriented us to one ethos or the other—to core or periphery—and then permitted consistent argument within that point of view, with a few hard cases occurring at the borderline. Now, each of the conflicting visions claims universal relevance, but is unable to establish hegemony anywhere.

V. The Correspondence between Formal and Substantive Moral Arguments

This and the two following sections develop the connection between the formal dimension of rules and standards and the substantive dimension of individualism and altruism. This section deals with the issue at the level of moral discourse; those that follow deal with the economic and political issues. The three sections also have a second purpose: to trace the larger dispute between individualism/rules and altruism/standards through the series of stages that lead to the modern confrontation of contradictory premises that is the subject of Section VIII. We began this intellectual historical task in the last section, in the course of explicating the substantive conflict. The historical discussions in the next two sections are likewise designed both to illustrate the analytic arguments linking form and substance, and to fill in the background of the current situation.

One might attempt to link the substantive and formal dimensions at the level of social reality. This would involve investigating, from the points of view of individualism and altruism, the actual influence of private law decisions on economic, social, and political life. One could then ask how the form in which the judge chooses to cast his decision contributes to these effects, being careful to determine the *actual* degree of formal realizability and generality of the rule or standard in question.[114] This method is hopelessly difficult, given the current limited state of the art of assessing either actual effects of decisions or their actual formal properties. *Theories* of the practical importance of deciding private law disputes in one way or another abound, but ways to test those theories do not. This gives most legal argument a distinctly unreal, even fantastic quality that this essay will do nothing to dispel. Rather, my subject is that often unreal and fantastic rhetoric itself. This is no more than a first step, but it may be an important one.

There is a strong analogy between the arguments that lawyers make when they are defending a "strict" interpretation of a rule and those they put forward when they are asking a judge to make a rule that is substantively individualist. Likewise, there is a rhetorical analogy between the arguments lawyers make for "relaxing the rigor" of a regime of rules and those they offer in support of substantively altruist lawmaking. The simplest of these analogies is at the level of moral argument. Individualist rhetoric in general emphasizes self-reliance as a cardinal virtue. In the substantive debate with altruism, this means claiming that people *ought* to be willing to accept the consequences of their own actions. They ought not to rely on their fellows or on government when things turn out badly for them. They

---

[114] The closest thing we have to such a study is L. FRIEDMAN, *supra* note 51.

should recognize that they must look to their own efforts to attain their objectives. It is implicit in this idea that they are entitled to put others at arms length—to refuse to participate in their losses or make sacrifices for them.

In the formal dispute about rules and standards, this argument has a prominent role in assessing the seriousness of the over- and underinclusiveness of rules. Everyone agrees that this imprecision is a liability, but the proponent of rules is likely to argue that we should not feel too badly about it, because those who suffer have no one to blame but themselves. Formally realizable general rules are, by definition, knowable in advance. A person who finds that he is included in liability to a sanction that was designed for someone else has little basis for complaint. Conversely, a person who gains by the victim's miscalculation is under no obligation to forego those gains.

This argument is strongest with respect to formalities. Here the meaning of underinclusion is that because of a failure to follow the prescribed form, the law refuses to carry out a party's intention to create some special set of legal relationships (*e.g.* voiding a will for failure to sign it). Overinclusion means that a party is treated as having an intention (*e.g.* to enter a contract) when he actually intended the opposite. The advocate of rules is likely to present each of these adverse results as in some sense deserved, since there is no good reason why the victim should not have engaged in competent advance planning to avoid what has happened to him.[115]

The same argument applies to rules that are designed to enforce substantive policies rather than merely to facilitate choice between equally acceptable alternatives. Like formalities, these rules are concerned with intentional behavior in situations defined in advance. When one enters a perfectly fair contract with an infant, one has no right to complain when the infant voids it for reasons having nothing to do with the law's desire to protect him from his own folly or from overreaching.

The position of the advocate of rule enforcement is unmistakably individualist. It is the sibling if not the twin of the general argument that those who fare ill in the struggle for economic or any other kind of success should shoulder the responsibility, recognize that they deserved what they got, and refrain from demanding state intervention to bail them out. The difference is that the formal argument is interstitial. It presupposes that the state has already intervened to some extent (*e.g.*, by enforcing contracts rather than leaving them to business honor and nonlegal sanctions). It asserts that *within* this context, it is up to the parties to look out for themselves. The fact of altruistic substantive state intervention does not ipso facto wipe out the individual's duty to take care of herself.

The argument of the advocate of "relaxation," of converting the rigid rule into a standard, will include an enumeration of all the particular factors in the situation that mitigate the failure to avoid over- or underinclusion. There will be reference to the substantive purpose of the rule in order to show the arbitrariness of the result. But the ultimate point will be that there is a moral duty on the part of the private beneficiary of the over- or underinclusion to forego an advantage that is a result of the other's harmless folly. Those who take an inheritance by course of law because the testator failed to sign his will should hand the property over to those the testator wanted to receive it. A contracting party *ought not* to employ the statute of frauds to void a contract honestly made but become onerous because of a price break.

---

[115] *See* Macaulay, *supra* note 2, at 1067.

This argument smacks as unmistakably of altruism as the argument for rules smacks of individualism. The essential idea is that of mercy, here concretized as sharing or sacrifice. The ethic of self-reliance is rejected in both its branches: the altruist will neither punish the incompetent nor respect the "right" of the other party to cleave to her own interests. Again, the difference between the substantive and the formal arguments is the area of their application. It may well be that the structure of rules falls far short of requiring the level of altruistic behavior that the altruist would prefer. But within that structure, whatever it may be, there are still duties of sharing and sacrifice evoked by the very operation of the rules.

It is important to note that the altruist demand for mercy will be equally strong whether we are dealing with formalities, or with rules designed to deter substantively undesirable behavior (crimes, unconscionable contracts). The party who tries to get out of a losing contract because of failure to comply with a formality is betraying a contractual partner, someone toward whom he has assumed special duties. The infant who voids the same contract although it was neither foolish nor coerced is behaving equally reprehensibly.

VI. The Correspondence between Formal and Substantive Economic Arguments

The correspondence between the formal and substantive economic arguments is more intricate and harder to grasp than the moral debate. I have divided the discussion into two parts: an abstract statement of the structural analogy of the formal and substantive positions, and an historical synopsis of how the positions got to their present state.

A. An Abstract Statement of the Analogy

1. Nonintervention vs. Result-Orientation. Suppose a situation in which the people who are the objects of the lawmaking process can do any one of three things: X, Y and Z. The lawmaker wants them to do X, and he wants them to refrain from Y and Z. If he does not intervene at all, they will do some X, some Y and some Z. As an individualist, the lawmaker believes that it would be wrong to try to force everyone to do X all the time. He may see freedom to do Y as a natural right, or believe that if he forbids Z, most people will find themselves choosing X over Y as often as if it were legally compelled. Or he may take the view that the bad side effects of state intervention to prohibit Y outweigh the benefits.

There is still the problem of the *form* of the injunction against Z. There may be a number of tactical considerations that push in the direction either of a rule or of a standard. For example, if the law appliers are very strongly in favor of compelling X, then they may use the discretion inherent in a standard to ban both Z *and* Y, thus smuggling in the substantive policy the lawmaker had rejected. On the other hand, it may be that the nature of the Y-Z distinction defies precise formulation except in terms of rules that will lead to the arbitrary inclusion of a very large amount of Y in the Z category, so that a standard seems the only workable formal mechanism.

In spite of these contextual factors, there is a close analogy between the substantive individualist position and the argument for rules. The individualist claims that we must achieve X through a strategy that permits Y. The rule advocate claims that we can best achieve the prohibition of Z through a rule that not only permits some Z (underinclusion) but also arbitrarily punishes some Y (overinclusion).

What ties the two arguments together is that they both reject result orientation in the particular case in favor of an indirect strategy. They both claim that the attempt to achieve a total ordering in accord with the lawmaker's purpose will be counterproductive. More success will be achieved by limited interventions creating a structure that influences the pattern of private activity without pretensions to full realization of the underlying purpose. In short, the arguments for rules over standards is inherently noninterventionist, and it is for that reason inherently individualist.

The main difficulty with seeing rules as noninterventionist is that they presuppose state intervention. In other words, the issue of rules vs. standards only arises after the lawmaker has decided against the state of nature and in favor of the imposition of some level of duty, however minimal. The point is that *within this structure*, whatever it may be, rules are less result oriented than standards. As with the moral argument, the economic individualism of rules is interstitial and relative rather than absolute.

2. Tolerance of Breach of Altruistic Duty: The Sanction of Abandonment. In the economic area, the analogy between the arguments for rules and those for substantive individualism goes beyond their common noninterventionism. Both strategies rely on the sanctioning effect of nonintervention to stimulate private activity that will remedy the evils that the state refuses to attack directly.

The fundamental premise of economic individualism is that people will create and share out among themselves more wealth if the state refuses either to direct them to work or to force them to share. Given human nature and the limited effectiveness of legal intervention, the attempt to guarantee everyone a high level of welfare, regardless of their productivity, would require massive state interference in every aspect of human activity, and still could not prevent a precipitous drop in output. On the other hand, a regime which convincingly demonstrates that it will let people starve (or fall to very low levels of welfare) before forcing others to help them will create the most powerful of incentives to production and exchange.

The self-conscious use of the sanction of abandonment as an incentive to production expresses itself on two different levels of the legal system. In private law, it means that people are authorized to refuse to share their superfluous wealth with those who need it more than they do. The most elementary doctrines of property law carry out this idea: trespass and conversion are not excused by need, short of *actual* starvation, and even then subject to a duty of restitution. In public law, the individualist opposes welfare programs financed through the tax system as a form of compulsory collective altruism that endangers the wealth of society.

The advocate of rules as the proper form for private law proposes a strategy that is exactly analogous to that of substantive individualism. The sanction of abandonment consists of not adjusting legal intervention to take account of the particularities of the case. The enforcement of the rule in situations where it is plainly over- or underinclusive involves condoning a violation of altruistic duty by the beneficiary. The motive for this passivity in the face of a miscarriage of the lawmaker's goal is to stimulate those subject to the rules to invest in formal proficiency, and thereby indirectly reduce the evil tolerated in the particular case.

In the area of formalities, the sanction of nullity works in the same fashion as the sanction of starvation in the substantive debate. The parties are told that unless they use the proper language in expressing their intentions, they will fail of legal effect. The result will be that a party who thought he had a legally enforceable agreement turns out to be vulnerable to betrayal by his partner. The law will tolerate this betrayal, although the whole purpose of instituting a regime of enforceable promises was to prevent it. In the area of rules designed to deter wrongdoing, the analogue of the sanction of abandonment is reliance on a rule to alert the potential victims to their danger. Caveat emptor and the rule of full legal capacity at 21 years are supposed to reduce wrongdoing, in spite of their radical underinclusiveness, because they induce vigilance where a standard would foster a false sense of security. Again, the theory is that permitting A to injure B may be the best way to save B from injury.

For the intermediate category consisting of suppletory directives (interpretation, excuses) and directives defining liability (fault, breach, damages), the decision to use rules rather than standards has a similar justification. Here the sanction is the imposition of liability on the actor who is not morally blameworthy, as for example for a breach of contract that is involuntary, but not within the doctrine of impossibility, or for a violation of an objective rule of tort liability. The result is a gain to the other party that he has an altruistic duty to disgorge. The motive for condoning the refusal to perform this duty, for enforcing the rule, is to stimulate people to make accurate advance calculations of those impacts of their activities on others that the law regards as justifying compensation. The thesis of the advocate of rules is that people will learn to make rational choices between abstention from injury and injury *cum* compensation only under a regime that tolerates occasional over- and under-compensation.

The basic notion behind these arguments for rules is that ability to manipulate formalities, vigilance in one's interests and awareness of the legally protected rights of others are all economic goods, components of the wealth of a society. The same considerations apply to them as apply to wealth in general. The best way to stimulate their production is to sanction those who fail to acquire them, by exposing them to breach of altruistic duty by those who are more provident. The rule advocate may affirm that "this hurts me more than it does you" as she administers the sanction. But the refusal to tolerate present inequity would make everyone worse off in the long run.

3. Transaction in General. There is a third element to the abstract parallel between substantive and formal dimensions. The argument is that both rules and the substantive reduction of altruistic duty will encourage transaction in general.[116] The classic statement of the substantive position is that of Holmes:[117]

> A man need not, it is true, do this or that act,—the term act implies a choice,—but he must act somehow. Furthermore, the public generally profits by individual activity. As action cannot be avoided, and tends to the public good, there is obviously no policy in throwing the hazard of what is at once desirable and inevitable upon the actor.

[116] See pp. 1725–27 *supra*; M. HORWITZ, *supra* note 92, ch. 3. For a typical application of the theory to the case of Hadley v. Baxendale, 156 Eng. Rep. 145 (1854), *see* Patterson, *The Apportionment of Business Risks Though Legal Devices*, 24 COLUM. L. REV. 335, 342 (1924); Danzig, *Hadley v. Baxendale: A Study in the Industrialization of the Law*, 4 J. LEG. STUD. 249 (1975).

[117] O. HOLMES, *supra* note 22, at 77.

The state might conceivably make itself a mutual insurance company against accidents, and distribute the burden of its citizens' mishaps among all its members. There might be a pension for paralytics, and state aid for those who suffered in person or estate from tempest or wild beasts. As between individuals it might adopt the mutual insurance principle pro tanto, and divide damages when both were in fault, as in the rusticum judicium of the admiralty, or it might throw all loss upon the actor irrespective of fault. The state does none of these things, however, and the prevailing view is that its cumbrous and expensive machinery ought not to be set in motion unless some clear benefit is to be derived from disturbing the status quo. State interference is an evil, where it cannot be shown to be a good. Universal insurance, if desired, can be better and more cheaply accomplished by private enterprise.

This is not a simple argument. Holmes does not explain why the activity encouraged by permitting breach of altruistic duty should lead to a public good. Presumably he would not have generalized his position to cover all such duties, although a return to the state of nature would certainly stimulate a vast amount of activity now deterred by fear of legal intervention. Further, the limitation of duty should have an inhibiting effect on the activity of those subjected to uncompensated injury. Holmes simply assumes that these inhibiting effects on desirable activity (or stimulating effects on undesirable activity) do not cancel out the gains from the "liberation of energy."

The implicit premise seems to be that the aggressive action of the injurers, looked at as a class, has greater social value than the activity of the injured inhibited by the removal of protection. In Holmes's thought, this premise is linked to Social Darwinism and the belief in the desirability of conflict in general.[118] As he saw it, the outcome of bargaining under individualist background rules would be to place control of productive resources, and therefore of investment, in the hands of those most likely to use them for the long-run good of the community. Regulatory, paternalist and communitarian objectives are all less important than secular economic growth. The management of growth requires exactly those capacities for aggressive self-reliance that are rewarded under an individualist regime of contract and fault. Regulation, paternalism and communitarian obligation shift economic power from those who know how to use it to those who do not.[119]

The parallel argument about rules is that "security" encourages transaction in general. The minimization of "judicial risk" (the risk that the judge will upset a transaction and defeat the intentions of the parties) leads to a higher level of activity than would occur under a regime of standards. Of course, some people will be *deterred* from transacting by fear of the mechanical arbitrariness of a system of formally realizable general rules. But their activity is less important, less socially desirable than that of the self-reliant class of actors who will master and then rely on the rule system.

The formal argument rests on the same implicit Social Darwinism as the substantive. Security of transaction is purchased at the expense of tolerating breach of altruistic duty on the part of the beneficiary of mechanical arbitrariness. The liberation of that actor's energy is achieved through a kind of subsidy based on a long term judgment that society gains through the actions of the aggressive and competent even when those actions are directly at the expense of the weak.

---

[118] See the discussion of Holmes' overall position in R. FAULKNER, THE JURISPRUDENCE OF JOHN MARSHALL 227–68 (1968).

[119] O. HOLMES, *Economic Elements*, in COLLECTED LEGAL PAPERS 279–83 (1920).

B. Rules as an Aspect of Classical Laissez-Faire

The conclusion of the abstract consideration of the relationship of form and substance is that there is a sound analytical basis for the intuition of a connection between individualism and rules. The connection is structural rather than contextual. It is *not* a connection that is necessary in practice, or even verifiable empirically. It consists in the exact correspondence between the structures of the two arguments.

For all one can tell from the discussion so far, this structural similarity is an interesting historical accident. On the basis of the analogy we might hazard a guess that particular values or premises that make substantive nonintervention attractive will tend to make formal nonintervention attractive as well. But this would be no more than a psychological speculation (of a type which I will undertake at some length in the last section of this essay).

But there is also an historical dimension to the problem. Economic individualism was once much more tightly linked to advocacy of rules than it is today, because they were both parts of a larger intellectual entity: the Classical theory of laissez-faire. That theory asserted that economics could discover general laws about the welfare consequences of particular legal regimes looked at as wholes. The scientific study of such regimes suggested that the best was that in which the state systematically refused to intervene ad hoc to achieve particular economic results.

The study of the theory of laissez-faire has intrinsic interest, but it is also useful for our particular purposes. Modern altruism is in large part a critique of the premises on which it was based, rather than a developed countertheory. As a result of the altruist critique, the modern individualist will admit that *sometimes* rules don't work, and standards do. But because the critique is *only* a critique, the altruist will concede that rules are sometimes necessary. This pragmatic reasonableness on both sides conceals the fact that the disputants reached their similar positions by different routes.

The individualist has reached the pragmatic position after abandoning a general theory of why rules are rationally required by the laws of economic science. The altruist has arrived in the same place after abandoning a more tentative and (among legal thinkers) much less widely shared vision of a social harmony so complete as to obviate the need for any rules at all. We can ignore the existence of these divergent historical paths so long as we ourselves are interested in a purely instrumental understanding of the issue of form. But if we are interested in the values intrinsic to form, in the fundamental conflict of visions of the universe that underlies instrumental discussion, then it is dangerous to make a sharp distinction between where we are and how we got here.

1. Laissez-Faire. It is not easy to reconstruct the Classical individualist economic vision, especially if we want to understand it from the inside as plausible, rather than absurd or obviously evil. While there were several strands of argumentation, the most important seems to have been the idea that the outcome of economic activity within a common law framework of contract and tort rules mechanically applied would be a natural allocation of resources and distribution of income.

The outcome was natural because it was a reflection of the real bargaining power of the parties, given the supply and demand conditions in the market in question. No legal intervention could change it except in the direction of making everyone worse off, unless the reformer was willing to establish full collectivism.

It was simply an implication of the immutable laws of economics that piecemeal reform must be self-defeating or counterproductive.

The refusal to enforce contracts or contract terms because of disapproval of the abuse of bargaining power is a case in point. Each party was willing to exchange on the designated terms; each therefore thought he would profit. Refusal to enforce deprives each of that profit. It does *not*, however, modify their bargaining power. If we refuse to enforce a particular term, they will readjust the rest of the bargain, and the stronger will exact in the form of a higher price, or whatever, the advantage that can no longer express itself in an allocation of a risk. The net result will be to drive some of the buyers out of the market, because they cannot afford to pay the higher price imposed by regulation. The victims of exclusion from the market are likely to be precisely those poorer buyers the regulator was trying to help.

If we respond by trying to fix the price directly, the result will be an imbalance of supply and demand, since the prices we are trying to change were those necessary to clear the market. If we want to prevent the disappointment of sellers or buyers, we will have to establish rationing or compulsory contracts. These cannot be enforced without a degree of supervision of individual businesses that amounts to socialism de facto, if not de jure.[120]

The assertion of the "naturalness" of economic interaction under property and contract rules is not plausible for us. Its plausibility in 1900 was based on the combination of the belief that the substantive content of the common law rules was an embodiment of the idea of freedom with the belief that official intervention to enforce the rules was nondiscretionary. The basis of the first belief, as we have seen, was conceptualism. The second notion expressed itself through a complex of doctrines, including stare decisis, the nondelegation doctrine, the void for vagueness doctrine, objectivism in contracts, the reasonable person standard in torts, the distinction between questions of law and questions of fact, and the general idea that law tended to develop toward formally realizable general rules.

If one could believe that the common law rules were logically derived from the idea of freedom and that there was no discretionary element in their application, it made sense to describe the legal order itself as at least neutral, nonpolitical if not really "natural." The economy was regulated, if one compared it to the state of nature, but it was regulated in the interests of its own freedom. What happened to economic actors when they exercised that freedom had almost as much claim to being natural as what would have happened if there was no state at all.

2. The Altruist Attack on Laissez-Faire. The altruist attack on laissez-faire denied the neutrality of the outcomes of bargaining within the background rules. The altruists began from the proposition that outcomes are heavily conditioned by the legal order in effect at any given moment. Those who enforce that legal order must accept responsibility for the allocation of resources and distribution of income it produces. In particular, bargaining power is a function of the legal order. All the individualist rules restrain or liberate that power. Changes in the rules alter its pattern. The outcome of bargaining will therefore be radically different according to whether we allow a state of nature, enforce a much more

---

[120] *See generally* the works on laissez-faire cited in note 90 *supra*, and L. ROBBINS, THE THEORY OF ECONOMIC POLICY IN ENGLISH CLASSICAL POLITICAL ECONOMY (1952); W. SAMUELS, THE CLASSICAL THEORY OF POLITICAL ECONOMY (1966); Coppage v. Kansas, 236 U.S. 1 (1915); West Coast Hotel v. Parrish, 300 U.S. 379, 400–14 (1937) (Sutherland, J., dissenting).

regulatory individualist regime, or a still more regulatory altruist one. All the outcomes are equally "natural." The question is which one is best.

The persuasiveness of the altruist attack depended heavily on discrediting both conceptualism and the claim that the legal order is composed of rules judges merely apply. As long as one believed in these two ideas, one could distinguish easily enough between an individualist regime and either the state of nature or a more altruist welfare state. Only the individualist regime was based on freedom. Under that regime, economic actors were never subjected to political restraints or to interference based on altruism. The rules that governed conduct depended neither on legislative consensus nor on a utopian morality, but on deduction from first principles acceptable to everyone. They were applied without the exercise of discretion by judges who had no power to inject their own politics or morals into the process.

The altruists attempted to show that neither conceptualism nor the idea of law as rules had any reality at all as a basis for defining a truly individualist legal order. As we have seen, the charge against conceptualism was that it was a mystification: there simply was no deductive process by which one could derive the "right" legal answer from abstractions like freedom or property.[121] The attack on the claimed objectivity of the law-applying process covered the whole complex of doctrines that supposedly eliminated the discretionary element from official intervention.[122] The aim was to show that as a matter of fact most rules were standards. The legal order, in this view, was shot through with discretion masquerading as the rule of law.

If the judges had neither derived the common law rules from the concepts nor applied them mechanically to the facts, then what *had* they been doing? The altruist answer was that they had been legislating and then enforcing their economic *biases*. The legal order represented not a coherent individualist philosophy, but concrete individualist economic interests dressed up in gibberish.[123] This once recognized, the next target was the argument that interference with the "free market" (market regulated by conceptually derived groundrules mechanically applied) would necessarily make everyone worse off.

The altruists demonstrated that no single general analysis could predict the effects of legal intervention in the economy. Everything depended on the structure of the particular market, which in turn depended on the legal system. It was quite true that attempts to regulate the exercise of economic power by interfering with particular terms of bargains *might* be self-defeating, if the market was perfectly competitive (so that price was equal to cost), or if the stronger party could shift his exactions from one term to another. But this was not *always* the case. Compulsory standardized terms in insurance policies might reduce the bargaining power of the sellers by increasing the buyers' understanding of the transaction.

---

[121] *See* p. 1732 *supra*.

[122] On stare decisis, *see* Dewey, *supra* note 108, and the sources cited in Christie, *supra* note 88, at 1317 n. 27. On nondelegation, *see* Jaffe, *Law Making By Private Groups*, 51 Harv. L. Rev. 201 (1937); K. Davis, *supra* note 4, ch. 2. On law and fact, *see* H. Hart & A. Sacks, *supra* note 1, at 366–85. On objectivism, see Costigan, *Implied-in-Fact Contracts and Mutual Assent*, 33 Harv. L. Rev. 376 (1920). *See also* pp. 1700–01 *supra*.

[123] The single greatest statement of this position is the first: Marx's theory of the fetishism of commodities. K. MARX, CAPITAL 81–96 (Moore & Aveling transl. 1906). For a modern Marxist statement, *see* Perlman, *The Reproduction of Daily Life* in "ALL WE ARE SAYING . . .," THE PHILOSOPHY OF THE NEW LEFT 133 (Lothstein, ed. 1970). The major works in the American, non-Marxist critique of the Classical theory of economic policy as applied to law are R. ELY, PROPERTY AND CONTRACT IN THEIR RELATIONS TO THE DISTRIBUTION OF WEALTH (1914); J. COMMONS, LEGAL FOUNDATIONS OF CAPITALISM (1924). The clearest statement of the general position is Hale, *Bargaining, Duress and Economic Liberty*, 43 COLUM. L. REV. 603 (1943).

Even supposing that the result of intervention is to force most people to transact on the new set of terms at a higher price while driving the rest out of the market, this might be justified on paternalist grounds. According to the new, post-conceptual mode of analysis, the common law was already full of paternalism, that is, of rules like those of capacity, which could no longer be rationalized through the will theory. The extension of the protective policy to, say, disclaimer of warranties to consumers would not represent any radical break with common law tradition.

It was also possible to relativize the argument about direct price regulation: its impact was a function of the whole situation, rather than of any general maxim about supply and demand. For example, where sellers cannot easily withdraw from the market, a compulsory price reduction may not reduce supply, except over the long, long run. A monopolist who is forced to reduce his price may *increase* supply in order to maintain the highest possible level of profit.

Finally, there were many ways to influence economic outcomes in an altruist direction without directly regulating outcomes, and there was no reason at all to believe that these would reduce welfare. The optimizing tendencies of the market will work, within the leeways we choose to leave for them, no matter how we make the initial definition and allocation of property rights. For example, we can limit the tactics employers can use in bargaining with employees. This changes the balance of power that existed under the old rules about what people could do with their property. But it does not "impede the functioning of the market" any more or less than we impeded it by imposing the rules of property and contract in the first place.[124]

This line of altruist argument applies with exactly equal force to changes in form and to changes in substance. For example, a working class automobile buyer may be highly skilled at price bargaining but have neither the time nor the education to argue successfully about warranties. Competition may not force the seller to translate his self-interested warranty terms into a lower price, because there may be no competition.

The normal rule that parties are bound to their contracts whether or not they read and understand them has obvious advantages in many situations, but here it will allow the seller to dictate to the buyer. The judge may reduce the seller's bargaining power if he adopts a more flexible approach based on a "reasonable understanding of a prudent lay buyer in all the circumstances." The result may be that there is a net increase in protection for buyers, a change whose cost is absorbed by the seller out of his monopoly profits.

It *may* be that the judge can counteract the ill effects of the normal rule about intent through substantive doctrines about duress, fraud, unconscionability or whatever. But there will be formal problems with these doctrines as well. They may be underinclusive in ways that are desirable in general but deprive them of efficacy in this situation (*e.g.*, failure to explain the boilerplate is not fraud because there has been no false statement of fact). A series of highly particularized applications of a general standard of "reasonable understanding" may be the

---

[124] The critique of the Classical welfare propositions has two strands. One of these is institutional economics, an American outgrowth of the German rejection of Classical economics. On institutionalism, see B. SELIGMAN, MAIN CURRENTS IN MODERN ECONOMICS, PT. 1 (1962) and 3 J. DORFMAN, THE ECONOMIC MIND IN AMERICAN CIVILIZATION, 1865–1918 (1949). The second strand was the neo-classical formalization and positivization of Classical economic theory, which aimed to rob categories like value, equilibrium, competition, efficiency, and the free market of their ethical overtones. Useful discussions will be found in J. SCHUMPETER, HISTORY OF ECONOMIC ANALYSIS (1954) and E. ROLL, A HISTORY OF ECONOMIC THOUGHT (3d ed. 1954). The starting point for modern discussion is L. ROBBINS, AN ESSAY ON THE NATURE AND SIGNIFICANCE OF ECONOMIC SCIENCE (2d ed. 1935).

only effective way to deal with the problem, short of the more intrusive approach of judicially constructed compulsory terms.

The choice between the old "strict" rule, a standard of "reasonable understanding," and compulsory terms cannot be made in a neutral fashion. Each choice affects the balance of economic power, to the advantage of one side and the disadvantage of the other. Since these effects are directly attributable to the legal order, the judge must take responsibility for choosing among them. He is an "interventionist" no matter what he does.[125]

Stripped to essentials, the altruist substantive and formal arguments are identical. Legislative, administrative and judicial action based on a detailed knowledge of particular situations can achieve paternalist and regulatory objectives without paralyzing private economic energies. The state should move directly to implement "the public interest" rather than relying on the combination of property and contract rules with private activity to produce a social maximum. At the substantive level of lawmaking, the altruist rejects the individualist position that it is necessary to tolerate inequality of bargaining power and other abuses of altruistic duty as between large social groups. The economic argument for standards is the formal version of the same proposition. It is that we can sometimes enforce our substantive values in particular cases, as well as in general, without the disastrous consequences the individualist predicts.

VII. The Political Arguments about Judicial Result Orientation

Thus far, we have dealt with a moral confrontation between the ethic of self-reliance and that of sacrifice and sharing. We then took up an economic dispute that opposed equity in adjudication (defined in terms of the lawmaker's purposes) to the achievement of the general welfare through non-intervention. Here we take up the political confrontation, in which the opposed slogans are rights and powers. The advocate of rules argues that the casting of law as standards is inconsistent with the fundamental rights of a citizen of a democratic state.

There are two branches to the argument. I will call them the institutional competence and the political question gambits. The premise of the institutional competence argument is that judges do not have the equipment they would need if they were to try to determine the likely consequences of their decisions for the total pattern of social activity. In other words, rational result orientation requires factual inquiries that are at once particularized and wide-ranging. Only the legislature is competent to carry out such investigations. Judges should therefore restrict themselves to *general* prescriptions.

The premise of the political question gambit is that there is a radical distinction between the activity of following rules and that of applying standards. Standards refer directly to the substantive values or purposes of the community. They involve "value judgments." Since value judgments are inherently arbitrary and subjective, they should be made only according to majority vote. By contrast, formally realizable rules involve the finding of facts. Factfinding poses objective questions susceptible to rational discussion. So long as the rulemaking process is democratically legitimate, there is no political objection to the delegation of rule application to judges.[126]

Duncan Kennedy

[125] *See* p. 1700 & note 37 *supra*.
[126] *See* Macaulay, *supra* note 2, at 1065–69.

Of course, so long as the judge has the power to formulate a new rule rather than applying an old one, it is clear that he has a measure of political or legislative power. The argument for rules, in the form in which we will consider it, is therefore a matter of degree. But rulemaking followed by rule application should be *less* political than proceeding according to standards. Both rulemaking and rule application limit discretion, by publicizing it at the legislative stage and by providing criteria for criticizing it at the stage of application.

Together, the institutional competence and political question arguments would produce a regime in which judges did nothing but formulate and apply formally realizable general rules. This procedure would minimize both the institutionally inappropriate investigation of the likely results of decision and the inherently legislative activity of making value judgments. A regime of standards would have the opposite effect. Every case would require a detailed, open-ended factual investigation *and* a direct appeal to values or purposes.

It seems intuitively obvious that both of these gambits are prototypically individualist. Each is an argument for nonintervention, for judicial passivity in the face of breach of altruistic duty. It would therefore seem reasonable to expect that we would find an exactly parallel substantive claim that the judge should not attempt to impose a high standard of altruistic duty because he has neither the knowledge nor the democratic legitimacy required for the enterprise. Such an argument does in fact exist. It is the central thesis of the modern conservative attack on judicial activism in both public and private law.[127] Indeed, in this area the formal and substantive arguments are so close to identical that I will treat them as a unit.

Because the institutional competence and political question gambits apply so clearly both to form and to substance, they pose more sharply than the economic arguments the underlying question of the relationship of individualism and altruism in modern legal thought. But before we can take up this issue, we must deal with a difficult historical problem.

The modern forms of the institutional competence and political question gambits are the inventions of pre-World War II altruism, rather than of individualism. Their first application was to the U.S. Supreme Court's activist use of the due process clause to strike down social legislation. Men who devoted most of their lives to furthering communitarian, paternalist and regulatory goals within the legal system are responsible for the most powerful statement of the political case for judicial nonintervention in public *and* private law. One purpose of this section is to show that in private law the gambits are nonetheless "essentially" individualist. Their adoption by the altruists in the constitutional context of 1936 was an unfortunate, if perhaps necessary tactic. The long-run result has been that modern altruists spend much of their rhetorical energy defending themselves against their own analysis of forty years ago.

A. The Origins of the Institutional Competence and Political Question Gambits

1. The Classical Individualist Position on Judicial Review. We have seen already that a particular definition of the judicial role was an important component of

---

[127] *See, e.g.*, Wechsler, *Toward Neutral Principles of Constitutional Law*, 73 HARV. L. REV. 1 (1959); Leff, *Unconscionability and the Code—The Emperor's New Clause*, 115 U. PA. L. REV. 485 (1967). The connection between public and private law is made explicitly in Wellington, *supra* note 20, *passim*.

the Classical individualist vision of the nature and function of the legal order. We might call it the "rule of law" model.[128] The two operations that defined it were the deduction of legal rules from first principles, and the mechanical application of the rules to fact situations. Each operation was strictly rational or objective; the judge could and should exclude his own political or economic values from the process of judgment. Other doctrines (nondelegation, vagueness, law vs. fact, stare decisis, etc.)[129] fleshed out the model so that it could be used to describe virtually all acts of officials impinging on the rights of citizens.

This theory of the judicial role played an especially important part in the Classical theory of judicial review. In that theory, the Constitution was law like any other law, except higher. Judicial review consisted of the deductive elaboration of its principles and their application to particular statutes. As such, the task was wholly rational and objective. It made no sense to accuse the judges of usurping the political powers or functions of the legislature, because there was nothing political (prudential, discretionary) about what the judges were doing.[130]

While this much went back to Marshall,[131] the Classical individualist thinkers added a new dimension. They were possessed of the post-Civil War theory of *private* law as a set of deductions from the concept of free will, whereas in Marshall's time the dominant jurisprudence presented private law rules either as given through the forms of action or as the outcome of the conflict between morality and policy. What the Classical thinkers did was to equate the "liberty" secured by the due process clause of the federal and state constitutions with the "free will" from which they believed they could deduce the common law rules.

This bold stroke integrated public and private law. It provided a set of tests of the constitutionality of legislation that had the assumed neutrality of private law to back them up against the charge that the courts were overstepping themselves. For example, the "liberty" of the constitutions meant liberty of contract. It followed that the state *must* enforce the set of legal rules that were implicit in the very idea of contract. In particular, an injunctive remedy against union attempts to organize workers bound by "yellow dog contracts" was constitutionally required.[132] Conversely, an attempt by the legislature to expand the law of duress to ban contracts that "really" represented free will was unconstitutional and void.[133]

Applied to the hilt, this approach would have meant freezing into the legal system the whole structure of laissez-faire that the Classical individualists claimed to be able to derive deductively from the concepts. But even in the 1920's, the heyday of activist judicial review, no court attempted anything so radical. In practice, the individualist argument was as much historical and pragmatic as purely conceptual, drawing on the idea that American law had always been committed to free enterprise, which was the only policy short of socialism that accorded with the "laws of economic science."

We can take Justice Sutherland's dissenting opinion in *West Coast Hotel Co. v. Parrish*[134] as an example. The issue was the constitutionality of a statute

---

[128] On the "rule of law" *See* A. Dicey, Lectures Introductory to the Study of the Law of the Constitution 179–201 (8th ed. 1915); F. Hayek, The Constitution of Liberty 162–233 (1960); Kennedy, *supra* note 4.

[129] *See* pp. 1748–49 & note 122 *supra*.

[130] This was the position of *both* liberals and conservatives in the conflict about the constitutionality of social legislation. Compare the dissent of Harlan, J., *with* the majority opinion in Lochner v. New York, 198 U.S. 45, 52–65 (Peckham, J.), 65–74 (Harlan, J., dissenting) (1905).

[131] *See* Marbury v. Madison, 5 U.S. (1 Cranch) 137 (1803).

[132] *See* Hitchman Coal & Coke Co. v. Mitchell, 245 U.S. 229 (1917).

[133] *See* Coppage v. Kansas, 236 U.S. 1 (1915).

[134] 300 U.S. 379, 400–14 (1937).

establishing a commission with power to fix minimum wages for different cate-

gories of women workers in the District of Columbia. Sutherland argued that the due process clause made freedom of contract a constitutional right. Its enforcement against attempts at legislative abridgment was the duty of the judiciary, indistinguishable from the duty to enforce private law rules in contests between the lowliest private parties.

The right was subject to legislative control, but a control strictly limited to paternalist interventions, such as specification of the mode of payment or maximum hours. Here, by contrast, the object was regulatory: to eliminate the actual bargaining power of worker and employer as the determinant of the wage rate. Unlike earlier legislation that let the parties adjust the wage rate to reflect state imposed conditions of labor, this law threw state power into the contest on the side of the worker. It therefore amounted to forcing the employer to donate a part of his income to support the worker at a minimum level of welfare. The measure of the subsidy was the difference between the minimum wage and what the worker could have earned in the "free market."

The goal, according to Sutherland, might be laudable, but the means adopted amounted to a taking of the employer's property without compensation, combined with a violation of the employee's freedom of contract, all to the detriment of everyone involved. First, the plaintiff employee had lost her job because she was not allowed to make a contract that was satsifactory to her. She had been denied her constitutional rights with no compensating gain whatever, since the statute had impoverished her rather than guaranteeing her a minimum level of welfare. Second, where the statute succeeded in making workers better off, it did so through an arbitrary redistribution of income between particular employers and workers, allocating the burden of maintaining welfare in such a way as to have a maximum negative impact on the incentive to create wealth and employment.

2. The Altruists Accept the Individualist Theory of the Judicial Role. In retrospect, there appear to have been two plausible lines of altruist attack on the individualist attempt to constitutionalize the groundrules of laissez-faire. The road not taken was the more radical. It involved accepting the analogy of private and public law, and then arguing that *both* were inherently "political," in the sense of requiring the judge to make choices between the rival social visions of individualism and altruism. The altruists could then have argued for judicial deference to altruist social legislation either on the ground that judges are the constitutional inferiors of the legislature, or on the ground that the particular legislation in question was affirmatively just and desirable, retaining the option of striking down any future legislation that infringed fundamental human rights.

In fact, the altruist response was fragmented and evasive. There are hints of the more radical argument in some opinions,[135] and in the *Carolene Products*[136] footnote about the role of the judiciary in protecting minorities. But the dominant strain was different. It consisted of an attempt to distinguish the inescapably "political" role of the judges in reviewing legislation from more conventional aspects of the judicial function, such as private law adjudication. Nonetheless, it drew inconsistently on altruist arguments developed in the private law context.

[135] *See, e.g.*, Home Building & Loan Ass'n v. Blaisdell, 290 U.S. 398 (1934).
[136] United States v. Carolene Prods., 304 U.S. 144, 152–53 n.4 (1938).

First, the altruists pointed out that the individualist public law position was conceptualist. Individualism claimed to deduce a theory of judicial review from the mere fact that the Constitution was "law," and that the court was "judicial." It asserted that "liberty" had a single meaning from which it was possible to deduce rules of review that would distinguish in a nonpolitical fashion between regulatory statutes. In the background was the claim that common law rules could serve as a benchmark of constitutionality because they represented deductions from free will.

The altruists attacked this position on both historical and analytic grounds. Paternalist and regulatory intervention had been common throughout the ante-bellum period,[137] and no one had ever supposed that it violated the due process clause.[138] The conceptual arguments about the logical implications of the words "law," "judge" and "liberty" were meaningless. Any state intervention, however minimal, represented a step along the path toward altruism and away from the state of nature. Once one recognized this, it was clear that the courts had upheld dozens and dozens of regulatory and paternalist statutes (*e.g.*, regulation of the mode of payment) on the basis of conceptualist quibbles whose only real meaning was that the Constitution validates *both* individualist and altruist ideals.[139]

In the case of the minimum wage, for example, the altruists made the by now familiar argument that there was no way to deduce the effects of the law from first principles. There was no such thing as "natural" bargaining power or worth of labor in the "free market," since the market was already heavily regulated through private law institutions. The impact of this particular statute could be determined only through a complex, specific factual inquiry into the supply and demand conditions and competitive structure of the market for unskilled women workers in the District of Columbia in the mid-1930's.[140]

The crucial step in the altruist argument was the next one: Since the Constitution embodied both altruist and individualist ideals, and the impact of the statute on those ideals was obscure, the question of its validity was political and therefore inappropriate for judicial determination. It was not that the altruist position was correct in this case that made the statute valid. Rather, the issue of validity was inherently legislative. Judicial attempts to define rightness and wrongness in areas of legislative intervention to achieve communitarian, paternalist or regulatory objectives were inappropriate, because *any* decision required one to choose between conflicting values.[141]

The altruists thus accepted the individualist dichotomy between legislative and judicial functions. Although their purpose was to defend altruistic intervention in the economy, they cast their position in the form of an argument against intervention by the judiciary in cases that involved the conflict of individualism and altruism. The basis for the position was that judicial review of social legislation was sui generis in terms of the judicial role. The reformers were implicitly contrasting it with the unequivocally judicial task of private law adjudication when

[137] *See, e.g.,* O. & M. HANDLIN, COMMONWEALTH—A STUDY OF THE ROLE OF GOVERNMENT IN THE AMERICAN ECONOMY: MASSACHUSETTS, 1774–1861 (rev. ed. 1969).
[138] *See* Corwin, *The Doctrine of Due Process of Law Before the Civil War*, 24 HARV. L. REV. 366, 460 (1911).
[139] *See* pp. 1731–37 *supra*; R. MCCLOSKEY, THE AMERICAN SUPREME COURT 101–79 (1960).
[140] *See* pp. 1745–51 *supra*.
[141] *See* Nebbia v. New York, 291 U.S. 502 (1934); Powell, *The Judiciality of Minimum Wage Legislation*, 37 HARV. L. REV. 545 (1924).

they spoke of "inquiries for which the judiciary is ill equipped," and the "necessity for choice between rival political philosophies."[142]

3. The Inconsistency of the Altruist Distinction between Public and Private Law.

Hindsight suggests that this formulation of the distinction between public and private law was a misrepresentation of the real positions of the altruist reformers. It may have been essential in the political task of mobilizing opposition to the Nine Old Men. It permitted an appeal to the ideal of legality in defense of legislative supremacy, thereby avoiding a polarized confrontation between those who believed in the total politicization of everything and those who believed in rights as well as in democracy. But it was intellectually dishonest.

The problem was that the altruist *private law* theorists had been busy for years in showing that common law adjudication was not one whit less "political" or "value laden" than judicial review. Moreover, they had confronted the institutional competence and political question gambits as they apply to private law, and concluded that they led to a theory of the judicial role that was both false in itself and intrinsically biased toward individualist outcomes. At the very same time that their public law allies were stressing the neutrality of private law adjudication by way of contrast to the political character of judicial review, the private law theorists were undermining the basis for such a distinction and attacking its implications. It is their arguments, rather than those developed in the public law context, that are important for our purposes here.

First, Classical individualist private law was no less dependent on conceptualism than public law for its claim to neutrality and legitimacy. It was equally open to the charge that the judges had used the ambiguity of the concepts to smuggle in their biases.[143] Second, a major strand in the public law argument was precisely that common law rules of property, tort and contract represented a massive state intervention in the economy. These private law rules, rather than "natural" or "real" strength, were the basis of the bargaining power the altruists were trying to regulate. Exactly the same "choice between rival philosophies" as in public law was necessary, after the death of the concepts, in deciding how state force should be used to structure economic conflict. And the institutional competence gambit was, if anything, stronger for private than for public law.[144]

Take the case of the judge asked to declare disclaimers of power lawnmower warranties void as against public policy. To begin with, there is the question of how his action will affect the price of mowers and of how a change in price will affect demand. Then there are the "inherently political" questions: (a) should we overrule the choices of those who prefer a cheaper mower without a warranty; (b) should we drive those who can't afford the mower with a warranty out of the market; (c) supposing that we can eliminate disclaimers without causing a fully compensating price hike, is it either ethically or economically *desirable* thus to shift the balance of economic power toward the consumer at the expense of the manufacturer? Finally, can the court successfully impose its decision on the market in question, given consumer ignorance, the limited impact of the sanction of nullity, the court's inability either to publicize its view or to enforce it through continuing supervision, the decentralization of the decision process, and so forth.

---

[142] United States v. Trenton Potteries Co., 273 U.S. 392 (1927) (Stone, J.).

[143] *See* pp. 1700–01, 1731–37 *supra*.

[144] *See* Hale, *supra* note 123.

It is possible to argue that the warranty case is an exception, because it involves judicial interference with freedom of contract, and that most of contract and tort law is at least relatively nonpolitical. This is true in the sense that it is not generally *perceived* as political, but it is plainly false if the assertion is that it does not involve "value judgments" of the kind that are supposed to be inherently legislative. Much of the altruist scholarly tradition in contracts, for example, is devoted precisely to politicizing the most apparently mundane doctrinal issues, as the quotation in the Introduction to this Article sweepingly illustrates.

To take one of a series of examples that could be extended indefinitely, it is not possible to decide when a breach of contract is "substantial," and therefore justifies recission by the nonbreaching party, without taking a position on a basic individualist-altruist conflict. The judge who is not mechanically applying a rule must look to the degree of risk that the victim will undergo if forced to perform and then sue for damages, and weigh it against the reliance loss or unjust impoverishment that will befall the breaching party if the other takes his marbles and goes home. Fault will be inescapably relevant, as will the degree of involvement or intimacy of the parties prior to the mishap. The underlying issue is that of the degree of altruistic duty we want to impose on the nonbreaching party, and this can be determined "rationally" only on the basis of a detailed factual inquiry, followed by a "choice between rival philosophies."[145]

Thus there is really a single altruist critique of constitutional *and* common law judicial lawmaking. The institutional competence and political question gambits apply to both or to neither. The altruist argument can not be that some law is political while other law is neutral. If the gambits are valid in public but not in private law, it must be because we should draw different conclusions from the discovery of the political element according to whether we are dealing with the Constitution or with common law institutions.

B. The Individualist Character of the Gambits in Private Law

This is not the place to try to develop an altruist theory of judicial review. It is enough for our purposes to show that in private law, the institutional competence and political question gambits have a distinctively individualist character.

Judicial private lawmaking takes place precisely in those marginal and interstitial areas of the legal system where there is no unequivocal, or even extremely suggestive indication of legislative will. The judge is asked to add to the corpus of common law rules and standards by deciding how to fill a gap, resolve a contradiction, or harmonize an old doctrine with new perceptions. It follows that the institutional competence and political question doctrines have a special meaning. They do *not* demand deference to legislative will because there is none in the premises. Rather, they enjoin the judge to perform his lawmaking in such a way as not to usurp legislative power *by performing legislative functions.*[146]

This is a good deal more than an injunction to avoid nullifying the decisions of the elected representatives of the people. The argument is the general one that the judge will be acting both ineffectively and illegitimately if he attempts, at the margin or in the interstices, to implement the community's substantive purposes with respect to individualism and altruism. The formal corollary, that he should

---

[145] *See* Jacob & Youngs, Inc. v. Kent, 230 N.Y. 239, 129 N.E. 889 (1921).
[146] *See* International News Serv. v. Associated Press, 248 U.S. 215, 248–67 (1918) (Brandeis, J., dissenting).

cast his resolution of marginal and interstitial disputes as formally realizable general rules, follows directly from the premise that he should not behave politically.

In this individualist argument, the judge has a legitimate function as a marginal and interstitial lawmaker, and as a law applier, so long as he eschews result orientation. The problem for the individualist is to describe to him exactly how he is to decide without taking results into account. The Classical answer was that the common law is a gapless, closed system of Classical individualist principles. According to this view, it is possible to distinguish between two kinds of common law adjudication, one involving the application of these existing principles to a new situation, and the other the introduction of new principles. The activity of applying existing principles to new situations is the noncontroversial core of the judicial role. But the creation of new principles is political and therefore legislative. For example, it would be inappropriate for a judge to outlaw disclaimers of warranties on power lawnmowers, because that would require him to create a new exception to the existing common law principle of freedom of contract. Since the only basis for doing this is the political one of furthering altruism, the judge has no basis for acting.

It is implicit in this view that the judge does have a basis for enforcing the disclaimer by throwing out an injured user's suit for damages. Likewise, he would have a basis for applying the general rules of offer and acceptance to power lawnmower contracts whenever a case of first impression should arise. But he would be usurping legislative power if he were to create, on particularistic altruist grounds, special lawnmower contract doctrines. In other words, there are three tiers of activity. First, the private parties interact, and someone acquires a grievance. Second, the judge applies the system of Classical individualist common law rules, and either grants or denies a remedy. Third, the legislature, if it wishes, but not the judge, imposes altruistic duties that go beyond the common law system of remedies.[147]

The altruist response is that the three tiered system leads to deference to *private power*, rather than to the legislature. The judge is not deferring to the legislature because the legislature has said nothing. The will that the judge is enforcing when he refuses to interfere with freedom of contract is the will of the parties, or of the dominant party, if the relationship is an unequal one. Such a program is quintessentially individualist. Unless he is willing with Austin, to embrace the fiction that no sparrow falls without the legislature's tacit consent, the judge cannot claim that he has no responsibility for this "political" outcome.

Furthermore, the individualist proposal assumes that the common law system, defined in terms of some point in the past, has the qualities of internal consistency necessary to allow the judge to distinguish between usurpation and the simple extension of existing principles. The whole altruist analytic assault on conceptualism was designed to show that the real, historical common law lacked these qualities. First, the concepts that were supposedly the basis for the rules were useless as grounds of decision. Second, the actual pattern of outcomes reflected an unstable compromise somewhere in between pure egotism and total collectivism.

Once one accepts such a conception, the three tiered structure collapses. The judge, by hypothesis, cannot appeal to a legislative command, and the common law with which she is to harmonize her result points in both directions at the same time. Certainly it falls far short of imposing the altruist's vision of social

---

[147] *See, e.g.,* Roberson v. Rochester Folding Box Co., 171 N.Y. 538, 64 N.E. 442 (1902).

duties of sharing and sacrifice. Yet it is possible to argue that *all* of its doctrines point in that direction, *i.e.,* toward collectivization and away from the state of nature. The trouble is that the glass may be half empty rather than half full. It is just as plausible to see the common law, as we have inherited it, as the manifesto of individualism against feudal and mercantilist attempts to create an organic relationship between state and society. There is nothing left of the three tiers but a field of forces. In order to decide cases, the judge will have to align herself one way or the other. But there can be no justification for her choice—other than a circular statement of commitment to one or the other of the conflicting visions.

C. Two Proposed Solutions to the Political Dilemma

While in 1940 one might reasonably have asserted that the net effect of individualist-altruist conflict in private law had been to deprive the judge of any basis for deciding cases beyond personal orientation to results, there have since been two major attempts to help him out of this embarrassing situation, and to restore the prestige of law by vindicating its claim to autonomy from politics. The first of these is based on the assertion of immanent, nonpolitical rationality in the social order, or of immanent moral consensus among the citizenry. The second is based on the premise that if the judge leaves all issues of distributive justice to the legislature there will remain a rational science of resource allocation that can serve as a clear guide to marginal and interstitial lawmaking.

It is impossible to sum up these two movements in a paragraph or two, but that is what I will try to do, beginning with the more recent. The law and economics movement,[148] insomuch as it purports to offer a theory of what judges should do, is an attempt to formalize the three-tiered system while at the same time substituting the authority of economic science for that of the historical common law. The distinction between legislative and judicial questions rests squarely on the institutional competence and political question gambits, here cast in the economist's language of allocation and distribution. The point that the common law is in fact distributive is answered by the assertion that it ought not to be.

The problem with this position, even supposing that one accepts its revolutionary rejection of the common law tradition, is that efficient resource allocation cannot provide a determinate answer for the judge's dilemma as to what law to make. The theory tells him only that the outcomes of free bargaining—efficient by definition—are preferable to state-directed outcomes, because they generate gains which could make everyone better off if redistributed.

But free bargaining presupposes an existing definition and distribution of property rights. The basic insight of the critics of classical individualism was that *all* legal rules go into the definition of initial bargaining positions—*all* rules are property rules in that sense. By hypothesis, the judge is trying to decide a marginal or interstitial question concerning those rules. Whatever he decides, subsequent bargaining will produce an efficient outcome. It is therefore circular to suggest that he can decide on the basis of efficiency. Another way to put the same point is to say that the outcome of bargaining would be efficient even in the state of nature. All interventions are distributively motivated.[149]

[148] R. POSNER, ECONOMIC ANALYSIS OF LAW (1972); G. CALABRESI, THE COSTS OF ACCIDENTS (1970).

[149] See Calabresi, Transaction Costs, Resource Allocation and Liability Rules, 11 J. LAW & ECON. 67 (1968); Baker, The Ideology of the Economic Analysis of Law, 5 PHIL. & PUB. AFF. 3, 32 n.56 (1975).

Duncan Kennedy

It follows that the elimination of the effects of transaction costs on the alloca-tion of resources cannot provide an independent objective criterion for judicial lawmaking. It is only possible to decide that these effects are bad if we can estab-lish that the outcome under some initial regime of legal rules, without transaction costs, would be good. But this cannot be done through criteria of efficiency, since *all* initial regimes meet that test. Before he starts applying the transaction cost analysis, the judge must therefore decide just how altruistic the background regime ought to be. Even supposing that he has done this, the steps required before the analysis can yield a determinate result involve a whole series of "value judgments."[150]

The alternative proposal, that the judge engage in "reasoned elaboration" of the immanent social purposes of the legal order, or that he decide on the basis of a "moral discourse," rejects the dichotomy of factual judgments and value judg-ments.[151] But it also creates a three-tiered structure. There is the outcome of pri-vate activity. There is judicial intervention *via* reasoned elaboration. And there is legislative intervention in pursuit of goals that the judge must ignore. As with the Classical individualist and law and economics solutions, the judge must define his jurisdiction through the institutional competence and political question gambits to avoid usurpation. As with the other solutions, usurpation means result orien-tation, here defined as going beyond the immanent rationality or immanent social morality of the legal order.

This proposal represents the recognition that the altruist analysis of the eco-nomic and political content of common law rules led into a dilemma. If the judge could not escape a role as an autonomous lawmaker, there seemed to be only two alternatives. He might retreat into passivity, and thereby behave in an objectively individualist way by facilitating the exercise of private power. Or he might take responsibility for imposing his "subjective value judgments" on the populace.

The proposed way out is a *partial* rejection of both the institutional compe-tence and political question gambits. *Some* kinds of complex factual questions are appropriate for the judiciary; others are not. *Some* social values or purposes are capable of reasoned elaboration by judges; others are not, and must be left to the legislature. On the formal level, there is eclecticism about when we should use rules and when standards. *Sometimes* it will be true that we can trust the judge to apply the purposes of the legal order directly to the particular facts, without worrying either about arbitrariness or about the inefficiencies generated by uncertainty. Sometimes, on the other hand, we will want him to distinguish clearly between his lawmaking and law-applying roles.

This attempted compromise is a coherently incoherent response to the individ-ualist's last ditch insistence on the institutional competence and political question

---

[150] This formulation owes much to a conversation with Tom Heller of the University of Wisconsin Law School. *See generally* Polinsky, *Economic Analysis as a Potentially Defective Product: A Buyer's Guide to Posner's Economic Analysis of Law*, 87 HARV. L. REV. 1655 (1974); Leff, *Economic Analysis of Law: Some Realism About Nominalism*, 60 VA. L. REV. 451 (1974); Baker, *supra* note 149; Mishan, *Pangloss on Pollution*, 73 SWED. J. ECON. 113 (1971).

[151] *See* H. HART & A. SACKS, *supra* note 1, at 116–20; Dworkin, *supra* note 4; L. FULLER, THE MORAL-ITY OF LAW (1964); Fuller, *Positivism and Fidelity to Law—A Reply to Professor Hart*, 71 HARV. L. REV. 630 (1958); Hart, *The Supreme Court, 1958 Term, Foreword: The Time Chart of the Justices*, 73 Harv. L. Rev. 84 (1959); K. Llewellyn, *supra* note 99; P. Selznick, *supra* note 4; Wellington, *supra* note 20. For a recent piece of analysis in this mode, *see* Dawson, *supra* note 6. For criticisms of this the Common Law Tradition, 71 Yale L. J. 255 (1961); Arnold, *Professor Hart's Theology*, approach, see Clark & Trubek, *The Creative Role of the Judge: Restraint and Freedom* in 73 Harv. L. Rev. 1298 (1960); Kennedy, *supra* note 4, at 395–98.

gambits. The individualist can counter only with a reassertion of the ontological first principle that facts and values are radically distinct. It is simply *true* of all values that they are subjective and arbitrary. Immanent rationality, according to the individualist, is an illusion or a contingency based on an accidental and unstable social consensus, and the judge's role is therefore inevitably discretionary in the fullest sense.[152] The postulate of democracy then requires the judge to restrict his lawmaking to the narrowest possible compass by adopting a regime of formally realizable general rules.

But a compromise of this kind is as hostile to the altruist program of result orientation as it is to individualism. Like the other three tiered structures, it asserts that there are some effects of decision that the judge cannot take into account. To relativize the distinction between legislative and judicial questions is a very different thing from abolishing it altogether. The reasoned elaborator is the ally of the individualist in asserting that there are some values that can be enforced only through legislation.

The essence of the immanent rationality approach is that it attempts to finesse the confrontation of opposing philosophies by developing a middle ground. The strategy is predicated on the belief that individualism and altruism lead to conflict only on a fringe of disputed questions, leaving a fully judicial core within which there is consensus. Marginal and interstitial lawmaking within the core favors neither of the competing ideologies. It is only if the judge makes the mistake of moving into the "political" periphery that he will find himself obliged to make a choice between them.

There is no logical problem with this way of looking at the legal order. The question is whether it is more or less plausible than the vision, shared by individualist and altruist alike, of a battleground on which no foot of ground is undisputed. The reasoned elaborator can protest to the individualist that he has gained the principle of judicial restraint in exchange for admitting a limited number of altruist principles into the legal core. To the altruist he will point out that the sacrifice of full result orientation is well worth it, given that some altruist principles have been legitimated as a source of judicial lawmaking.

My own view is that the ideologists offer a convincing description of reality when they answer that there is no core. Every occasion for lawmaking will raise the fundamental conflict of individualism and altruism, on both a substantive and a formal level. It would be convenient, indeed providential, if there really were a core, but if one ever existed it has long since been devoured by the encroaching periphery.

If this is the case, then there is simply no way for the judge to be neutral. It is not that the concepts, liberty, equality, justice, welfare, that are supposed to motivate him are utterly without meaning or possible influence on his behavior. They are deeply ingrained in culture and for most of us it is impossible to make sense of the world without them. The problem is that they make two senses of the world, one altruist and the other individualist. This is true alike for issues of form and issues of substance. Indeed, I hope I have shown that the dimension of rules vs. standards is no more than a fourth instance of the altruist-individualist conflict of community vs. autonomy, regulation vs. facilitation and paternalism

Duncan Kennedy

---

[152] *See* Arnold, *supra* note 151; Clark & Trubek, *supra* note 151; Hart, Positivism and the Separation of Law and Morals, 71 HARV. L. REV. 593 (1958); Nagel, Fact, Value and Human Purpose, 4 NATURAL LAW FORUM 26 (1959).

vs. self-determination. What remains is to explore the level of contradiction that lies below the conflict as it manifests itself in debates about the form and substance of legal rules.

VIII. Fundamental Premises of Individualism and Altruism

Whatever their status may have been at different points over the last hundred years, individualism and altruism are now strikingly parallel in their conflicting claims. The individualist attempt at a comprehensive rational theory of the form and content of private law was a failure. But altruism has not emerged as a comprehensive rational counter theory able to accomplish the task which has defeated its adversary.

Nonetheless, the two positions live on and even flourish. The individualist who accepts the (at least temporary) impossibility of constructing a truly neutral judicial role still insists that there is a rational basis for a presumption of non-intervention or judicial passivity. The altruist, who can do no better with the problem of neutrality, is an activist all the same, arguing that the judge should accept the responsibility of enforcing communitarian, paternalist and regulatory standards wherever possible.

In this section, I will argue that the persistence of these attitudes as organizing principles of legal discourse is derived from the fact that they reflect not only practical and moral dispute, but also conflict about the nature of humanity, economy and society. There are two sets of conflicting fundamental premises that are available when we attempt to reason abstractly about the world, and these are linked with the positions that are available to us on the more mundane level of substantive and formal issues in the legal system.

Individualism is associated with the body of thought about man and society sometimes very generally described as liberalism. It is not necessary (in a logical or any other sense of necessity) for an individualist to hold to the liberal theory.[153] It is possible to believe passionately in the intrinsic moral rightness of self-reliance and in the obvious validity of the practical arguments for an individualist bias in law, and yet reject the liberal premises. It is a fact, however, that liberal theory has been an important component of individualism in our political culture at least since Hobbes. The whole enterprise of Classical individualist conceptualism was to show that a determinate legal regime could be deduced from liberal premises, as well as derived from individualist morality and practicality.

The same is true on the altruist side. The organicist premises with which the altruist responds to the liberal political argument are on another level altogether from the moral and practical assertions we have dealt with up to now. Yet, as is the case with individualism, there is both an historical connection and a powerful modern resonation between the levels of argument.

The importance of adding this theoretical dimension to the moral and practical is that it leads to a new kind of understanding of the conflict of individualism and altruism. In particular, it helps to explain what I called earlier the sticking points of the two sides—the moments at which the individualist, in his movement towards the state of nature, suddenly reverses himself and becomes an altruist, and the symmetrical moment at which the altruist becomes an advocate of rules and self-reliance rather than slide all the way to total collectivism or anarchism.

---

[153] On the methodological problem, see p. 1724 & note 87 *supra*.

A. Fundamental Premises of Individualism

The characteristic structure of individualist social order consists of two elements.[154] First, there are areas within which actors (groups or individuals) have total arbitrary discretion (often referred to as total freedom) to pursue their ends (purposes, values, desires, goals, interests) without regard to the impact of their actions on others. Second, there are rules, of two kinds: those defining the spheres of freedom or arbitrary discretion, and those governing the cooperative activities of actors—that is, their activity outside their spheres of arbitrariness. A full individualist order is the combination of (a) property rules that establish, with respect to everything valued, a legal owner with arbitrary control within fixed limits, and (b) contract rules—part supplied by the parties acting privately and part by the group as a whole acting legislatively—determining how the parties shall interact when they choose to do so.[155]

The most important characteristic of an order with this structure is that individuals encounter one another in only three situations.

(a) *A* is permitted to ignore *B* and carry on within the sphere of his discretion as though *B* did not exist. *A* can let *B* starve, or, indeed, kill him, so long as this can be accomplished without running afoul of one of the limits of discretion.

(b) *A* and *B* are negotiating, either as private contracting parties or as public legislators, the establishment of some rules to govern their future relations. These rules will be binding whether or not based on agreement between *A* and *B* about what ends they should pursue or even about what ends the rules are designed to serve. *A* and *B* are working only toward binding directives that will benefit each *according to his own view of desirable outcomes*.

(c) *A* and *B* are once again permitted to ignore one another, so long as each follows the rules that govern their cooperative behavior. Although they are working together, neither need have the slightest concern for the other's ends, or indeed for the other's person, so long as he executes the plan.

Thus an individualist social order eliminates any necessity for *A* and *B* to engage in a discussion of ends or values. They can achieve the most complex imaginable interdependence in the domains of production and consumption, without acknowledging any interdependence whatever as moral beings. If we define freedom as the ability to choose for oneself the ends one will pursue, then an individualist order maximizes freedom, within the constraints of whatever substantive regime is in force.

The creation of an order within which there are no occasions on which it is necessary for group members to achieve a consensus about the ends they are to pursue, or indeed for group members to make the slightest effort toward the achievement of other ends than their own, makes perfect sense if one operates on the premise that values, as opposed to facts, are inherently arbitrary and subjective. Like the relationship between the other components of individualism (or of Romanticism, Classicism, etc.), the link between the two sets of ideas is more complicated than one of logical implication. But it is enough for our purposes to mention briefly some of the ways in which the idea of the subjectivity and arbitrariness of values reinforces or resonates the rule/discretion structure.

---

[154] *See* K. MARX, *supra* note 73; R. UNGER, *supra* note 73; A. KATZ, *supra* note 4 for analysis of a similar kind.

[155] For a similar conception, see E. DURKHEIM, *supra* note 20, at 115–32.

The *subjectivity* of values means that it is, by postulate, impossible to verify directly another person's statement about his experience of ends. That is, when *A* asserts that for him a particular state of affairs involves particular values in particular ways, *B* must choose between accepting the statement or challenging the good faith of the report. *B* knows about the actual state of affairs only through the medium of *A's* words and actions. She cannot engage *A* in an argument about *A's* values except on the basis of that information.[156]

The postulate of the *arbitrariness* of values means that there is little basis for discussing them. Even supposing that values were objective, so that we could all agree which ones were involved in a particular situation, and how they were involved, it would still be impossible to show by any rational process how one ought to change that objective situation. Our understanding of the existence of values, according to the postulate, is not founded on rational deductive or inductive processes. Values are simply *there* in the psyche as the springs of all action. And since we cannot explain—except by appeal to behavioristic notions like those of learning theory—why or how they *are* there, we cannot expect to converse intelligently about what they ought to be or become.

Given these conditions, it seems likely that mechanisms of social order dependent on consensus about ends will run into terrible trouble. If, by providential arrangement (or perhaps by conditioning) everyone's values turn out to be identical (or to produce identical effects), then all is well; if there is disagreement, chaos ensues. This expectation is reinforced by the other major postulate of liberal theory: that people enter groups in order to achieve ends that pre-exist the group, so that the group is a means or instrument of its members considered as individuals.

Once again, this idea is *logically* connected neither with the postulate of the arbitrariness of values nor with the characteristic rule/discretion structure of an individualist social order. It merely "resonates" these allied conceptions. Thus, if the state is only an instrument each party adopts to achieve his individual purposes, it is hard to see how it would ever make sense to set up state processes founded on the notions of changing or developing values. If the state is truly only a means to values, and all values are inherently arbitrary and subjective, the only legitimate state institutions are *facilitative*. The instant the state adopts change or development of values as a purpose, we will suspect that it does so in opposition to certain members whose values other members desire to change. The state then becomes not a means to the ends of all, but an instrument of some in their struggle with others, supposing that those others desire to retain and pursue their disfavored purposes.

The individualist theory of the judicial role follows directly from these premises. In its pure form, that theory makes the judge a simple rule applier, and rules are defined as directives whose predicates are always facts and never values. So long as the judge refers only to facts in deciding the question of liability, and the remedial consequences, he is in the realm of the objective. Since facts are objective rather than subjective, they can be determined, and one can assert that the

---

[156] On this basis alone it may be easy to show that *A's* statement of his experience of values is self-contradictory, and this may cause *A* such discomfort that he will actually undertake to rectify the orderliness of his values. *B's* conduct still resolves itself into (a) rational, objective discourse about facts (showing *A's* self-contradiction) and (b) a-rational, subjective exhortation about values (urging *A* to attain consistency on the ground that consistency is "good").

judge is right or wrong in what he does. The result is both the certainty necessary for private maximization and the exclusion of arbitrary use of state power to further some ends (values) at the expense of others.

Classical late nineteenth century individualism had to deal with the argument that it was impossible to formulate a code of laws that would deal with all situations in advance through formally realizable rules. The response was that the truly common, though minimal, ends that led to the creation of the state could be formulated as concepts from which formally realizable rules could be deduced. The judge could then deal with gaps in the legal order—with new situations—by deductively elaborating new rules. The process of elaboration would be objective, because rational, just as the application of rules was objective because referring only to facts.

Modern individualism accepts that this enterprise was a failure, but it does not follow that the judge is totally at large. There is still a rational presumption in favor of nonintervention, based on the fundamental liberal premises. These have been strengthened rather than weakened by the failure of the Classical enterprise, which asserted that there was at least enough consensus about values to found an aggressive theory of the "right," if not of the good.

Nonintervention is consistent with the liberal premises because it means the refusal of the group to use the state to enforce its vision of altruistic duty against the conflicting visions of individuals pursuing their self-interest. The judge should be intensely aware of the subjectivity and arbitrariness of values, and of the instrumental character of the state he represents. He may not be able to frame a coherent theory of what it means to be neutral, and in this sense the legitimacy of everything he does is problematic. All reason can offer him in this dilemma is the injunction to respect autonomy, to facilitate rather than to regulate, to avoid paternalism, and to favor formal realizability and generality in his decisions. If nothing else, his action should be relatively predictable, and subject to democratic review through the alteration or prospective legislative overruling of his decisions.

B. *Fundamental Premises of Altruism*

The utopian counter-program of altruist justice is collectivism.[157] It asserts that justice consists of order according to shared ends. Everything else is rampant or residual injustice. The state, and with it the judge, are destined to disappear as people come to feel their brotherhood; it will be unnecessary to make them act "as if." The direct application of moral norms through judicial standards is therefore far preferable to a regime of rules based on moral agnosticism. But it still leaves us far from anything worthy of the name of altruistic order. The judge, after all, is there because we feel that force is necessary. Arbitrators are an improvement; mediators even better. But we attain the goal only when we surmount our alienation from one another and share ends to such an extent that contingency provides occasions for ingenuity but never for dispute.

Altruism denies the arbitrariness of values. It asserts that we understand our own goals and purposes and those of others to be at all times in a state of evolution, progress or retrogression, in terms of a universal ideal of human brotherhood.

Duncan Kennedy

[157] *See* K. MARX, *Economic and Philosophical Manuscripts* (1844), in EARLY WORKS 322–34, 345–58 (Benton trans. 1975); S. AVINERI, THE SOCIAL AND POLITICAL THOUGHT OF KARL MARX 65–95 (1968); E. DURKHEIM, *supra* note 20 at 193–99. For a recent attempt to develop similar notions in the context of American constitutional law, *see* Tribe, *supra* note 54, at 310–14.

The laws of this evolution are reducible neither to rules of cause and effect, nor to a logic, nor to arbitrary impulses of the actor. We do not control our own moral development in the sense that the mechanic controls his machine or legal rules control the citizen, but we do participate in it rather than simply undergoing it. It follows that we can speak meaningfully about values, perhaps even that this is the highest form of discourse.

Altruism also denies the subjectivity of values. My neighbor's experience is anything but a closed book to me. Economists make the simplifying assumption of the "independence of utility functions," by which they suppose that A's welfare is unaffected by B's welfare. This notion is at *two* removes from reality: A's utility function is not only dependent on B's, it cannot truthfully be distinguished from B's. Quite true that we suffer *for* the suffering of others; more important that we suffer directly the suffering of others.

For the altruist, it is simply wrong to imagine the state as a means to the pre-existing ends of the citizens. Ends are collective and in process of development. It follows that the purposes that form a basis for moral decision are those of man-in-society rather than those of individuals. The administration of justice is more than a means to the ends of this whole. It is a part of it. In other words, judging is not something we have to *tolerate*; it is not a *cost* unavoidable if we are to achieve the various individual benefits of living together in groups.

Good judging, in this view, means the creation and development of values, not just the more efficient attainment of whatever we may already want. The parties and the judge are bound together, because their disputes derive an integral part of their meaning from his participation, first imagined, later real. It is desirable rather than not that they should see their negotiations as part of a collective social activity from which they cannot, short of utopia, exclude a representative of the group. A theory that presents the judge as an instrument denies this. Recognizing it means accepting that private citizens do or do not practice justice. It is an illusion to think that they only submit to or evade it.

Perhaps as important, an instrumental theory of judging lies to the judge himself, telling him that he has two kinds of existence. He is a private citizen, a *subject*, a cluster of ends "consuming" the world. And he is an official, an *object*, a service consumed by private parties. As an instrument, the judge is not implicated in the legislature's exercise of force through him. Only when he chooses to make his own rules, rather than blindly apply those given him, must he take moral responsibility. And then, that responsibility is asserted to be altogether individual, his alone, and therefore fatally close to tyranny. The judge must choose alienation from his judgment (rule application) or the role of God (rule making).

By contrast, altruism denies the judge the right to apply rules without looking over his shoulder at the results. Altruism also denies that the only alternative to the passive stance is the claim of total discretion as creator of the legal universe. It asserts that we can gain an understanding of the values people have woven into their particular relationships, and of the moral tendency of their acts. These sometimes permit the judge to reach a decision, after the fact, on the basis of all the circumstances, as a person-in-society rather than as an individual.[158] Though

---

[158] Of course there must be a selection among "all the circumstances," or the judge would never get beyond the collection of his facts. And of course the selection is intimately guided by *criteria* (or concepts) of some kind. And of course those criteria in turn are closely linked to the criteria of justice to be applied (why gather facts irrelevant to the issue at hand). But it does *not* follow that because we can select a *mass* of relevant facts from among the larger mass available, we can determine how *particular* facts, capable of founding per se rules, will

these faculties do not permit him to make rules for the future, that they permit him to decide is enough to make decision his duty. He must accept that his official life is personal, just as his private life, as manipulator of the legal order and as litigant, is social. The dichotomy of the private and the official is untenable, and the judge must undertake to practice justice, rather than merely transmit or invent it.

Altruism offers its own definitions of legal certainty, efficiency, and freedom. The certainty of individualism is perfectly embodied in the calculations of Holmes' "bad man," who is concerned with law only as a means or an obstacle to the accomplishment of his antisocial ends. The essence of individualist certainty-through-rules is that because it identifies for the bad man the precise limits of toleration for his badness, it authorizes him to hew as close as he can to those limits. To the altruist this is a kind of collective insanity by which we traduce our values while pretending to define them. Of what possible benefit can it be that the bad man calculates with certainty the contours within which vice is unrestrained? Altruism proposes an altogether different standard: the law is certain when not the bad but the *good* man is secure in the expectation that if he goes forward in good faith, with due regard for his neighbor's interest as well as his own, and a suspicious eye to the temptations of greed, then the law will not turn up as a dagger in his back. As for the bad man, let him beware; the good man's security and his own are incompatible.

"Efficiency" in the resolution of disputes is a pernicious objective unless it includes in the calculus of benefits set against the costs of administering justice the moral development of society through deliberation on the problem of our apparently disparate ends. Indeed, attempts to achieve the efficiency celebrated by individualism are likely to make these true benefits of judging unattainable, and end in a cheaper and cheaper production of injustice and social disintegration.

The "freedom" of individualism is negative, alienated and arbitrary. It consists in the absence of restraint on the individual's choice of ends, and has no moral content whatever. When the group creates an order consisting of spheres of autonomy separated by (property) and linked by (contract) rules, each member declares her indifference to her neighbor's salvation—washes her hands of him the better to "deal" with him. The altruist asserts that the staccato alternation of mechanical control and obliviousness is destructive of every value that makes freedom a thing to be desired. We can achieve real freedom only collectively, through *group* self-determination. We are simply too weak to realize ourselves in isolation. True, collective self-determination, short of utopia, implies the use of force against the individual. But we experience and accept the use of physical and psychic coercion every day, in family life, education and culture. We experience it indirectly, often unconsciously, in political and economic life. The problem is the conversion of force into moral force, in the fact of the experience of moral indeterminacy. A definition of freedom that ignores this problem is no more than a rationalization of indifference, or the velvet glove for the hand of domination through rules.

Duncan Kennedy

---

define the circumstances of justice in the future. I am here asserting the existence of a grey area, a slippage, a no-man's land, between two quite clearly defined aspects of the situation. Yes, it is true that there are criteria of justice well enough defined to orient the search for relevant facts. No, it is *not* true that these are now or seem to have any tendency to become the kind of criteria that constitute a formal system. The world is intelligible, *but not intelligible enough*.

The explanation of the sticking points of the modern individualist and altruist is that both believe quite firmly in both of these sets of premises, in spite of the fact that they are radically contradictory. The altruist critique of liberalism rings true for the individualist who no longer believes in the possibility of generating concepts that will in turn generate rules defining a just social order. The liberal critique of anarchy or collectivism rings true for the altruist, who acknowledges that after all we have not overcome the fundamental dichotomy of subject and object. So long as others are, to some degree, independent and unknowable beings, the slogan of shared values carries a real threat of a tyranny more oppressive than alienation in an at least somewhat altruistic liberal state.

The acknowledgment of contradiction does not abate the moral and practical conflict, but it does permit us to make some progress in characterizing it. At an elementary level, it makes it clear that it is futile to imagine that moral and practical conflict will yield to analysis in terms of higher level concepts. The meaning of contradiction at the level of abstraction is that there is no metasystem that would, if only we could find it, key us into one mode or the other as circumstances "required."

Second, the acknowledgment of contradiction means that we cannot "balance" individualist and altruist values or rules against equitable standards, except in the tautological sense that we can, as a matter of fact, decide if we have to. The imagery of balancing presupposes exactly the kind of more abstract unit of measurement that the sense of contradiction excludes. The only kind of imagery that conveys the process by which we act and act and act in one direction, but then reach the sticking point, is that of existentialist philosophy. We make commitments, and pursue them. The moment of abandonment is no more rational than that of beginning, and equally a moment of terror.

Third, the recognition that both participants in the rhetorical struggle of individualism and altruism operate from premises that they accept only in this problematic fashion weakens the individualist argument that result orientation is dynamically unstable. Given contradiction at the level of pure theory, the open recognition of the altruist element in the legal system does not mean an irrevocable slide down the slope to totalitarianism, any more than it would lead to the definitive establishment of substantive justice in the teeth of the individualist rule structure.

Individualism, whether in the social form of private property or in that of rules, is *not* an heroically won, always precariously held symbol of man's fingernail grip on civilized behavior. That is a liberal myth. In any developed legal system, individualist attitudes, and especially the advocacy of rules, respond to a host of concrete interests having everything to lose by their erosion. Lawyers are necessary because of rules; the prestige of the judge is professional and technical, as well as charismatic and arcane, because of them; litigants who have mastered the language of form can dominate and oppress others, or perhaps simply prosper because of it; academics without number hitch their wagonloads of words to the star of technicality. Individualism is the structure of the status quo.

But there is more to it even than that. In elites, it responds to fear of the masses. In the masses, it responds to fear of the caprice of rulers. In small groups, it responds to fear of intimacy. In the psyche, it responds to the ego's primordial fear of being overwhelmed by the id. Its roots are deep enough so that one suspects an element of the paranoid in the refusal to recognize its contradictory sibling within consciousness.

Finally, the acknowledgement of contradiction makes it easier to understand judicial behavior that offends the ideal of the judge as a supremely rational being. The judge cannot, any more than the analyst, avoid the moment of truth in which one simply shifts modes. In place of the apparatus of rule making and rule application, with its attendant premises and attitudes, we come suddenly on a gap, a balancing test, a good faith standard, a fake or incoherent rule, or the enthusiastic adoption of a train of reasoning all know will be ignored in the next case. In terms of individualism, the judge has suddenly begun to act in bad faith. In terms of altruism *she has found herself*. The only thing that counts is this change in attitude, but it is hard to imagine anything more elusive of analysis.

IX. Conclusion

There *is* a connection, in the rhetoric of private law, between individualism and a preference for rules, and between altruism and a preference for standards. The substantive and formal dimensions are related because the same moral, economic and political arguments appear in each. For most of the areas of conflict, the two sides emerge as biases or tendencies whose proponents have much in common and a large basis for adjustment through the analysis of the particularities of fact situations. But there is a deeper level, at which the individualist/formalist and the altruist/informalist operate from flatly contradictory visions of the universe. Fortunately or unfortunately, the contradiction is as much internal as external, since there are few participants in modern legal culture who avoid the sense of believing in both sides simultaneously.

Even this conclusion applies only so long as it is possible to abstract from the context of compromises within the mixed economy and the bureaucratic welfare state. In practice, the choice between rules and standards is often instrumental to the pursuit of substantive objectives. We cannot assess the moral or economic or political significance of standards in a real administration of justice independently of our assessment of the substantive structure within which they operate.

It follows that the political tendency of the resort to standards, as it occurs in the real world, cannot be determined a priori. The most barbarous body of law may be rendered "human," and therefore tolerable, by their operation. Indeed, the "corruption" of formality by informality may be the greatest source of strength for an oppressive social order. Or equally plausibly, standards may be a vehicle for opposition to the dominant ideology (opposition *within* a particular judge as well as opposition among judges), keeping alive resistance in spite of the capture of the substantive order by the enemy. These currents of resistance may be reactionary or revolutionary, reformist or mildly conservative.[159] Standards may even be accepted into the predominant conception of how a rule system works, treated as an area of "inchoacy" or of "emerging rules," as though altruist justice were inevitably the prelude to a higher stage of individualism.

How should a person committed to altruism in the contradictory fashion I have been describing assess the significance of informality in our actual law of contracts, for example? I have only a little confidence in my own answer, which

[159] *See* Hay, *supra* note 29.

is that the case for standards is problematic but worth making. There is a strong argument that the altruist judges who have created the modern law of unconscionability and promissory estoppel have diverted resources available for the reform of the overall substantive structure into a dead end. There is an argument that individualist judges are restrained from working social horrors only by a mistaken faith in judicial neutrality that it would be folly to upset. It might be better to ignore contract law, or to treat it in an aggressively formal way, in order to heighten the level of political and economic conflict within our society.

Nonetheless, I believe that there is value as well as an element of real nobility in the judicial decision to throw out, every time the opportunity arises, consumer contracts designed to perpetuate the exploitation of the poorest class of buyers on credit. Real people are involved, even if there are not very many whose lives the decision can affect. The altruist judge can view himself as a resource whose effectiveness in the cause of substantive justice is to be maximized, but to adopt this attitude is to abandon the crucial proposition that altruistic duty is owed by one individual to another, without the interposition of the general category of humanity.

Further, judges like Skelly Wright are important actors in a symbolic representation of the conflict of commitments.[160] Given the present inability of altruism to transform society, it is only a dramatic production, ancillary to a hypothetical conflict that would be revolutionary. As such, the judge is a cultural figure engaged in the task of persuading adversaries, in spite of the arbitrariness of values. More, he is at work on the indispensable task of imagining an altruistic order. Contract law may be an ideal context for this labor, precisely because it presents problems of daily life, immediate and inescapable, yet deeply resistant to political understanding. It seems to me that we should be grateful for this much, and wish the enterprise what success is possible short of the overcoming of its contradictions.

---

[160] *See, e.g.,* Williams v. Walker-Thomas Furniture Co., 350 F.2d 445 (D.C. Cir. 1965).

Liberalism: Legal Philosophy and Ethics

Robert Cover

Robert Cover

ROBERT COVER's contribution to the Canon marks a turning point in the mainstream thinking of liberal legal scholars of the center and center-left who had been reacting to the disintegration of the legal process consensus. Like Chayes, Cover was an expert in civil procedure, and, like Dworkin and Michelman, he was an ardent participant in discussions about theories of interpretation and legal language. Nevertheless, he placed ethics, rather than political theory, linguistic theory, or institutional strategy at the center of liberal legal reasoning. He developed a sensibility rooted in evocation of the authenticity of suffering and victimization that would become widely influential, particularly among those seeking to bring identity politics into law and the legal academy. The essay needs to be understood against the background of liberal reactions to the decline of the postwar legal process consensus.

Since the 1960s, American legal thought has not been as unified or confident in its mode of reasoning as it had been in the heyday of the legal process vision. The disintegration of the legal process consensus left a range of diverse modes of reasoning, associated with different schools of thought, and understood to have significantly different political associations. The "Law and Economics" movement, influenced by Coase and Calabresi, and the "Law and Society" movement, influenced by Macaulay and Galanter, both sought to replace what seemed the sloppy mandarin reasoning of legal process thinkers with more rigorous policy analysis, reinforced by methods borrowed from the social sciences. Legal scholars associated with both the center and the left were interested in empirical sociology during these years, although the Law and Society movement began as a project of the left and center-left. The economic analysis of law would eventually come to be developed by scholars with liberal and progressive political leanings, although the early Law and Economics movement was firmly associated with conservative political leanings. The Critical Legal Studies movement, also initiated in the 1970s, challenged the political and social implications of the legal process school as well as the coherence and plausibility of the modes of judicial analysis with which it had become associated from a left-wing perspective.

In the 1970s, there was no gainsaying the appeal of these new movements. For law students, the legal process approach to legal thought had come to mean infinitely complex case-by-case explanations of how an expanding list of vague principles and policies somehow explained the results, with little effort to fit the pieces together in any way, or to chase down the policy connections being asserted in any rigorous sense. Legal process thinking was equally difficult to pin down in political terms. There was something status quo or establishment oriented about it all, but beyond that, the still dominant voice of legal reasoning seemed vague, even coy, about its political commitments. For many, the new methods offered by law and economics, critical legal studies, and law and society seemed appealing both because they seemed more intellectually rigorous, and because scholars working in them were more overt about their political commitments.

For many legal academics of a broadly liberal political persuasion—people like Dworkin, Michelman, or Chayes—the collapse of the legal process framework was disquieting. Intellectually, many liberal voices had participated in developing strands of what would become law and society, law and economics, or critical legal studies. They shared the general sense that the legal process consensus had become obsolete. But they had also grown up with it as a way of seeing the world of law, and although much in the legal process had come to seem oversimplified or naïve, the tide of instrumentalism, pragmatism, and critical analysis represented by the new movements seemed to sacrifice much that was valuable in American legal thought—and to flirt far too easily with anti-establishment political extremes. In political terms, liberals still represented a center to center-left mainstream in American elite political culture. In broad terms, through the 1960s, their thinking was in tune with that of the nation's judges, at least as those views were reflected in federal appellate opinions. The new movements in American legal thought were more readily associated with the left and right. Some liberal scholars worried that the center might not hold—and indeed, it did not. The legal academy became far more politically diverse, and polarized, in the 1980s and '90s.

Of course, the rising sense on law faculties that American liberalism was an embattled faith reflected the broader decline of political enthusiasm for the welfare state programs and reform efforts of the 1960s, the emergence of a judiciary considerably more conservative than the Warren Court, and the election of Ronald Reagan in 1980. Over the next twenty years, liberals struggled to develop new modes of expressing their core commitments to social justice and equality in American law. Eventually, more liberal strands of law and economics, law and society, and critical legal scholarship would be developed. In the meantime, scholars like Dworkin, Michelman, and Chayes had developed theories and institutional strategies for harnessing American law to liberal political commitments. From the mid-'60s onward, liberal voices defended the distinctiveness, if not the autonomy, of legal culture against inroads being made by economics, political science, and sociology. They articulated doctrinal and theoretical grounds for liberal opinions by liberal judges and defended the viability of legal reasoning about "rights."

Many were influenced by Dworkin's effort to elaborate a theory of rights compatible with anti-foundationalism and the experience of indeterminacy inherited from the legal realists, and felt again with the collapse of the legal process. Some, like Michelman, sought to develop political and social theories of American constitutionalism which might provide the basis for liberal judicial interpretation. Others, like John Ely, sought to revitalize the legal process tradition by developing a more rigorous procedural theory to guide judges in the interpretation of the Constitution's substantive provisions. Procedural theories of this sort would both give judges an autonomous role, as the keepers and interpreters of process, and provide the basis for liberal judges to expand civil rights protection. Some, perhaps most notably Laurence Tribe, rejected the effort to theorize a new foundation for liberal judgments in favor of strategic and tactical work to develop liberal interpretations of constitutional doctrines that might persuade an increasingly conservative judiciary in concrete contexts.

In all these efforts, the *language* of legal argument and judgment seemed central. Law, after all, was a matter of words and arguments. Seeing law as a special language provided a plausible footing for theorizing the autonomy of legal reasoning from instrumentalism. This turn to language did not occur in a vacuum. The "linguistic turn" in philosophy—begun in the 1930s—had been mainstreamed in the American academy. In the humanities, cultural practices were being reinterpreted as acts of communication in a kind of social language. In the social sciences, all manner of political and institutional behavior yielded to analysis as a kind of language—suddenly even missiles were "missives." Social systems became "discourses" among people who inhabited "interpretive communities" and whose practices could be decoded by "thick description," a term and framework popularized in the legal academy through the work of anthropologist Clifford Geertz.

Legal scholars applied this material in a variety of ways. From Richard Rorty's pragmatism, legal scholars harvested the idea that a language should be judged by its usefulness, not by its coherence. It mattered less whether arguments about "rights" or legal "principles" were logically coherent or philosophically plausible than whether they "worked." Legal scholars began to speak about "rights talk"— the practice of articulating, advocating, and claiming rights—instead of rights *per se*, and to make arguments about the opportunities and practical limits of engaging in rights talk. Martha Minow was a prominent exponent of this approach: "Rights in this sense are not 'trumps' but the language we use to try to persuade others to let us win this round."[1] She located the roots of her treatment of rights as a "language" in "Sartre's and Wittgenstein's notions of language . . . not as a set of rule-bound meanings, but as a mode of human action and creative self-expression."[2] This approach seemed to sidestep attacks on both the coherence of rights analysis and the political or philosophical foundation for rights.

At the same time, many legal scholars turned their attention to theories of *interpretation*. The open-endedness of legal argument had been exploited by critics seeking more rigorous, social-scientific methods for reasoning about legal policy, and had provided ammunition to critics revitalizing legal realist attacks on judicial reasoning as, in Felix Cohen's terms, so much "transcendental nonsense." But all language was both open to new meanings and capable of communicating and persuading. Theories of interpretation offered explanations of how this was possible—and began to fill the law journals.

A focus on the law as an interpretive practice had a number of advantages. As Dworkin had pointed out in his essay, "Law as Interpretation," conceiving law this way foregrounds the functions rather than the "validity" of legal rules. To the extent worry about the internal coherence and determinacy of legal materials cast doubt on argument about validity, these criticisms could be sidestepped. The extent to which such criticisms undermined the experience of law's persuasiveness could be settled by reference to the actual experiences of people in an "interpretive community." If "rights talk," for example, persuaded judges, one need not worry too much about the coherence or philosophical foundations of "rights." Here is Dworkin on this point:

> Interpretation is an enterprise, a public institution, and it is wrong to assume, a priori, that the propositions central to any public enterprise must be capable of validity. It is also wrong to assume much about what validity in such enterprises must be like— whether validity requires the possibility of demonstrability, for example. It seems better to proceed more empirically here. We should first study a variety of activities in which people assume that they have good reasons for what they say, which they

assume hold generally and not just from one or another individual point of view. We can then judge what standards people accept in practice for thinking that they have reasons of that kind.[3]

Thinking of law as the social practice of interpretation in a given community—a continual remaking of their history, political commitments, social purposes and values, and the meanings they give their institutions—roots law interactively in those communicative practices, rather than in any historical intention, or decisive political or ethical consensus. As we saw, Dworkin had also used the image of law as a language to secure his embrace of anti-foundationalism in his analysis of hard cases.[4]

At the same time, liberal scholars of the era easily acknowledged that the work of judges is political, both in the sense that the judge's own ideological commitments will inflect his analysis, and that the enterprise as a whole is directed to political ends. Unlike their legal process predecessors, however, they did not rely on the principle of institutional settlement, or the arrangement of divided competences among institutions to pull the sting of this admission. Instead, they relied on their theories of interpretation. Some maintained, for example, that the interactive conventions of the legal profession would provide the necessary constraint. An interpretive practice, they maintained, is a *social* production. The subjective preferences of any particular interpreter cannot alone determine what works as an interpretation for the community, and in this sense, the practice of interpretation is constrained. For others, the constraint would come from the professional posture of judges—their own fealty to the interpretive task, understood to require a kind of fealty to texts and precedents and a faithful projection of their best potential into the future. In "Law as Interpretation," Dworkin presents the interpretation of art as a struggle to make of an artifact the best work of art it can be as a useful analogy. Judges should also make of the laws they find the best laws they can be:

> I said that a literary interpretation aims to show how the work in question can be seen as the most valuable work of art, and so must attend to formal features of identity coherence and integrity as well as more substantive considerations of artistic value. A plausible interpretation of legal practice must also, in a parallel way, satisfy a test with two dimensions: it must both fit that practice and show its point or value. But point or value here cannot mean artistic value because law, unlike literature, is not an artistic enterprise. Law is a political enterprise whose general point, if it has one, lies in coordinating social and individual effort, or resolving social and individual disputes, or securing justice between citizens and between them and their government or some combination of these. . . . So an interpretation of any body or division of law, like the law of accidents, must show the value of that body of law in political terms by demonstrating the best principle or policy it can be taken to serve.[5]

Dworkin's account of interpretive constraint, plausible or not, was not alone. Owen Fiss expressed a similar thought, with reference to *Brown v. Board of Education*:

> I start with the view that the Constitution embodies a public morality, including a commitment to racial equality. But I recognize that this commitment, when applied to a particular situation, such as segregated schools, is capable of several readings, some of which may conflict with other constitutional promises, such as liberty. The

judicial task is to choose among these readings (and to harmonize the whole), and this choice is for me . . . the core of the intellectual process known as interpretation (legal or literary). Unlike Levinson, however, I do not believe that the choice is unconstrained. The judge's choice is constrained by a set of rules (or norms, standards, principles, guides, etc.) that are authorized by the professional community of which the judge is part (and that define and constitute the community). A judge might be directed, for example, to pay particular attention to the wording of a text and to the intent of the framers, while a political actor might consider the impact of segregation on the conduct of foreign affairs. Adherence to the rules authorized by the professional community imparts a measure of impersonality to a legal judgment (its objective quality) and at the same time provides the standards for evaluating the correctness of the judgment as a legal judgment. I can say *Brown* is a correct interpretation of the fourteenth amendment because it conforms to the properly authorized disciplining rules, not because I subscribe to some political or moral tenet that condemns racial segregation.[6]

Social coherence, the everyday experience of the coherence of language, the clarifying intuition of a "hermeneutic moment," the sensible collaborative effort to make of each legal artifact all it could be—all were offered as bulwarks against criticism of legal arguments from the left and the right. The idea of "law as language" remains central to American legal thought. In the field of jurisprudence, scholars continue to work on problems in analytic language philosophical terms.

Nevertheless, by the end of the 1980s, the idea that a general theory of interpretation could explain the distinctive nature of legal judgment and respond to attacks on law's methodological rigor and plausibility had waned among the nation's liberal legal scholars. It seemed increasingly clear that liberal values—and the defense of rights—would need something more. The theoretical questions that interpretive theories were designed to answer—how is the judge constrained, how can law hold back the flood of instrumental reason—seemed less urgent. In their place came worry about the accuracy and empathy of judicial representations of social life—in particular, the need to avoid stereotyping—and about the substantive moral and ethical commitments written into judicial pronouncements. Robert Cover's death from a heart attack in 1984 at the age of forty-two focused national scholarly attention on his last essays, making Cover the foremost symbol of the liberal turn from interpretation to ethics.

Cover was born in 1942 and raised in Boston. He graduated from Princeton University in 1965, and from Columbia Law School in 1968, where he immediately began teaching. He married Diane Bornstein Cover during law school, with whom he had a son, Avi, and a daughter, Leah. After a year at the Hebrew University in Jerusalem in 1971–72, he joined the Yale Law School faculty, where he taught until his sudden death in 1984. Cover was a leading figure in the Yale Jewish community, and an avid student of Jewish legal history. He taught American legal history, constitutional law, civil procedure and federal courts, and was known as a scholar of procedure. Cover was also a committed supporter of civil rights and civil liberties throughout his career. He had participated in the SNCC voting rights campaign, and remembered a three-week jail term in Georgia—during which he went on a hunger strike and was beaten by other prisoners—as a central formative event in his life. Enraged by the willingness of judges to enforce the draft during the Vietnam War, Cover wrote a scathing attack on judicial complicity, comparing it to enforcement of the fugitive slave law by abolitionist judges. The polemic became a book, *Justice Accused: Antislavery and the Judicial Process*, which explored the modes of reasoning and action other than resigning that would have been available to judges who had wished to resist. His account of judicial complicity remains a powerful evocation of the possibilities for ethical resistance within the judicial role—possibilities that he felt were all too rarely utilized. Cover participated in demonstrations throughout his career, standing atop a car in downtown Manhattan with a megaphone to protest the prosecution of radical black activists on conspiracy charges, supporting striking workers at Yale and student efforts to force divestment from South Africa. Cover seems to have been an extremely charismatic figure, popular as a teacher and mentor, who received an extraordinary round of testaments to his ethical vision and broad learning after his death.

Cover's foreword to the 1982 Supreme Court issue of the *Harvard Law Review*, "Nomos and Narrative," has been cited alongside "Violence and the Word" as a touchstone for contemporary liberal legal consciousness. The Foreword develops an ethical vision of law, affirming Lon Fuller's insistence upon the moral dimension of legal norms developed in his 1940 book, *The Law in Quest of Itself*.[7] Cover describes law as part of a "normative universe," in which "rules and principles of justice, the formal institutions of the law" blend with "the conventions of the social order" whose "narratives . . . locate it and give it meaning."[8] He proposes that we focus on the *expressive* functions of law within a broader social conversation about our shared normative universe. To understand law's own narrative force, he encourages attention to the broader cultural "narratives" with which the legal world is in conversation and struggle. In this, he shifts the focus of interdisciplinary attention among those interested in law as a language from literary theory to anthropology and cultural studies—and within literature from new critical to historicist understandings of the role and significance of literary texts. Cover was particularly interested in the cultural narratives of religious traditions, and encouraged study of religious traditions outside the mainstream of American religious life—the Amish, the Shakers, those engaging in civil disobedience, the Mormons. The bulk of "Nomos and Narrative" is devoted to placing the Supreme Court's jurisprudence in a conversation with narratives from various strands of the Jewish tradition. This focus on the narrative world of outsiders found immediate resonance in American legal scholarship exploring the "stories" of those excluded from mainstream American culture of governance—most immediately, women and racial minorities.

Cover uses these outsider narratives to highlight two roles played by official legal pronouncements in the broader normative universe. Through interactions between official law and other cultural narratives, law expresses and validates cultural narratives (a process Cover calls "jurisgenesis"). At the same time, however, law also destroys the normative worlds of some outsider cultures, an effect which Cover terms "jurispathic." Identifying the jurisgenerative and jurispathic function of legal pronouncements focused attention on how judges described the social world. A great deal of legal scholarship analyzed and criticized judicial portraits of the women and minorities, insisting that stereotypes be replaced by efforts to hear the narrative voices of excluded groups. This work seemed all the more urgent in light of Cover's analysis of the jurispathic effect of judicial decisions as a form of *violence*:

> Judges are people of violence. Because of the violence they command, judges characteristically do not create law, but kill it. Theirs is the jurispathic office. Confronting

the luxuriant growth of a hundred legal traditions, they assert that this one is law and destroy or try to destroy the rest.[9]

The violent impact of judicial interpretation on cultural meanings presented far more pressing ethical and social concerns than what seemed the excessively theoretical worries of those who had theretofore focused on legal interpretation. Cover focuses on the incommensurability of vision among different communities engaged in the process of normative development. The result is conflict—and the violent "jurispathic" elimination of some visions by others. Cover does not seem to share the aspiration for convergence or persuasion evident in the work of many other liberal legal scholars of the period, including Michelman and Dworkin—often themselves influenced by political theorists such as John Rawls or Jürgen Habermas. Cover seems to revel in the chaotic and open-ended struggle among cultural visions, rather than in the procedures for a reasoned constitutional conversation:

> For some time the jurisdictional structure of "our federalism" has struck me as comprehensible only as a blueprint for conflict and confrontation, not for cooperation and deference. . . . It is a daring system that permits tensions and conflicts of the social order to be displayed in the very jurisdictional structure of its courts. It is that view of federalism that we ought to embrace.[10]

For Cover, moreover, the liberal professoriate had devoted far too much attention to the fear that an indeterminate corpus of legal materials posed the threat of "nihilism"—a threat they associated both with the instrumentalism of law and economics and with the critical analyses of legal materials developed by the Critical Legal Studies movement. Nihilism was not the problem—the problem was the legitimacy of jurispathic coercion, and the need to ensure that the legal culture remain open to the production of new meanings:

> By posing the question as one involving a choice between the judicial articulation of values (albeit contested) and nihilism, Fiss has made too easy the answer to his question about the institutional virtue of the judiciary and of the political system of which the judiciary is a part. The real challenge presented by those whom Fiss calls "nihilists" is not a looming void in which no interpretation would take place. Even those who deny the possibility of interpretation must constantly engage in the interpretive act. The challenge presented by the absence of a single, "objective" interpretation is, instead, the need to maintain a sense of legal meaning despite the destruction of any pretense of superiority of one nomos over another. By exercising its superior brute force, however, the agency of state law shuts down the creative hermeneutic of principle that is spread throughout our communities. The question, then, is the extent to which coercion is necessary to the maintenance of minimum conditions for the creation of legal meaning in autonomous interpretive communities.[11]

"Violence and the Word" focuses on coercion—legal violence. His opening line, "Legal interpretation takes place in a field of pain and death," has become an aphorism, rebuking those who focus on interpretation for "blithely" ignoring the connection between legal interpretation and violence. In part, Cover's focus on violence is hortatory—legal scholars should not forget, should remember, should remain aware, of the violence and suffering, meted out by law. Such exhortations have become increasingly common in American legal scholarship. Martha Minow reinforces this exhortation in her introduction to Cover's collected essays: "We must acknowledge violence in the acts of judicial interpretation and we must also nurture the communities threatened by those acts: these are the themes recurring in Cover's articles."[12] Cover exhorts us not only to witness, but to action, guided by ethics. He developed his conception of ethical action most directly in his analysis of the opportunities for resistance by abolitionist judges, and by judges who did not support the Vietnam-era draft. The turn to ethics also represented a change in the interdisciplinary appetites of liberal scholars within the legal academy—for Cover, it meant a turn to religion, to the Aristotelian tradition of practical ethical reflection, to literature. In the mainstream scholarship of American liberals, Hannah Arendt, Hans Gadamer, Paul Ricoeur, Alasdair MacIntyre, Maurice Merleau Ponty, Emmanuel Levinas had suddenly replaced the diverse linguistic philosophies of Searle, Austin, and Derrida.

Cover was certainly not the first to focus our attention on law's often brutal effects. From Holmes onward, authors in the Canon had drawn attention to law's consequences, insisting that we view law as a purposive instrument. To bring about consequences will be to have distributional consequences—there will be losers as well as winners. Cover takes us back to Hale when he insists that "all law which concerns property, its use and its protection, has a similarly violent base."[13] But for Cover, the relationship between law and violence is not simply one of cause and effect. Law is *word*, a place of narration and meaning. Violence is something altogether different and incommensurate. Cover makes this point most forcefully quoting literary critic Elaine Scarry's description of the violence of torture:

> Whatever pain achieves, it achieves in part through its unshareability, and it ensures this unshareability in part through its resistance to language. . . . Prolonged pain does not simply resist language but actively destroys it, bringing about an immediate reversion to a state anterior to language, to the sounds and cries a human being makes before language is learned.[14]

Following Scarry, Cover treats the pain of torture as the archetype for other suffering inflicted by law. Law is not only the jurispathic destroyer of narrative. The goal of legal interpretation—of legal language—is to bring about a result on the "field of pain and death." The violence of that result both resists or chooses among languages *and* "destroys" language.

Here Cover departs most sharply from the "interpretive" tradition in liberal legal theory. To see law as interpretation had meant seeing it as social or interactive phenomenon, a communicative act among participants in a long chain of conversations about how to govern, about the nature of justice, and about good policy. For Cover, the image of a governing class in a long-term conversation about how to rule is not the most important conversation going on. There is also the relationship between the ruler and the ruled—which, for Cover, is not a conversation. For the condemned prisoner, the death penalty is not a communicative act—death and pain are "unshareable":

> Even the violence of weak judges is utterly real—a naive but immediate reality, in need of no interpretation, no critic to reveal it.[15]

The inexpressibility of a victim's pain, alongside the absolute reality and authenticity of a victim's perspective and experience, quickly became a standard point of reference in liberal legal scholarship. The unspeakable suffering of the marginalized became a metaphorical refutation for anti-foundationalism and a guidepost for ethical action. It was routinely presented as a baseline justification for law reform efforts emerging from the identity politics of the 1980s and '90s.

Nevertheless, in his concluding reflections, Cover draws back somewhat from the clarity of Scarry's opening description of torture, reframing his observations as limits or qualifications to the interpretive conversation among lawmakers. The tone has shifted as well—the disconnection between judge and executioner, the incommensurability of perspective between the legal order and its victims, has become "tragic" and "aching." After Cover's essay, this tone of intense ethical regret and execration increasingly replaced the self-confident posture of Dworkin's Hercules in the writings of America's liberal legal professoriate:

> There is, however, danger in forgetting the limits which are intrinsic to this activity of legal interpretation; in exaggerating the extent to which any interpretation rendered as part of the act of state violence can ever constitute a common and coherent meaning. We are left, then, in this actual world of the organization of law-as-violence with decisions whose meaning is not likely to be coherent if it is in common, and not likely to be common if it is coherent . . . [T]here will always be a tragic limit to the common meaning that can be achieved. The perpetrator and victim of organized violence will undergo achingly disparate significant experiences. For the perpetrator, the pain and fear are remote, unreal, and largely unshared. They are, therefore, almost never made part of the interpretive artifact, such as the judicial opinion. On the other hand, for those who impose the violence the justification is important, real and carefully culti-vated. Conversely, for the victim, the justification for the violence recedes in reality and significance in proportion to the overwhelming reality of the pain and fear that is suf-fered. Between the idea and the reality of common meaning falls the shadow of the violence of law, itself.[16]

For Cover, moreover, a focus on the violence which results from interpretation shifts our attention from the long chain of debate connecting one Hercules to another, toward the conversation between those who interpret the law and those who must carry out its violence. Legal interpretation is socially embedded—in an administrative apparatus first, and a broader social field more generally—which has as its object the production of violence. The emphasis here is no longer on the victim, but on the men and women, bureaucrats and administrators, who carry out the commands of the judiciary. Those who interpret the law, Cover argues, develop narratives that both distance themselves from violence and obtain the compliance of others to carry out their violent orders.

In this sense, the social conditions for effective legal interpretation are funda-mentally different from the humanities. Ideas about interpretation developed in the humanities will be helpful only in part. However socially embedded literature may be, Cover argues, and whatever their incidental political effects, the "insti-tutions that are designed to realize normative futures in part through the practice of collective violence stand on a somewhat different footing."[17] To understand this social process requires attention to the work of ideology and the conditions for the legitimation of political violence. Suddenly, Stanley Fish's "Is There a Text in this Class?" has been replaced by Fredric Jameson's "The Political Unconscious: Narrative as a Socially Symbolic Act," and Harold Bloom's "The Anxiety of Influence" has given way to Michel Foucault's "Discipline and Punish: The Birth of the Prison."[18]

At the same time, Cover has shifted the point of view from which we think about the law's ideological effects:

> The violence of the act of sentencing is most obvious when observed from the defendant's perspective. Therefore, any account which seeks to downplay the violence or elevate the interpretive character or meaning of the event within a community of shared values will tend to ignore the prisoner or defendant and focus upon the judge and the judicial interpretive act. Beginning with broad interpretive categories such as "blame" or "punishment," meaning is created for the event which justifies the judge to herself and to others with respect to her role in the acts of violence. I do not wish to downplay the significance of such ideological functions of law. But the function of ideology is much more significant in justifying an order to those who principally benefit from it and who must defend it than it is in hiding the nature of the order from those who are its victims.[19]

The victim knows the truth of the situation. Legal interpretation is not meaningfully constrained by the need to get the law's victims to accept their losses, but by the need to anaesthetize the judge against the feeling of responsibility for violence, and by the need to convince other officials to carry out the sentence. The judge thus faces two significant narrative demands—his own need not to feel implicated in violence, and his need to get someone else to feel comfortable carrying it out. Against these, other interpretive demands—of professional colleagues for argumentative plausibility, of the legal texts for fealty to the historic conversation they represent—are simply not significant:

> The legal philosopher may hold up to us a model of a hypothetical judge who is able to achieve a Herculean understanding of the full body of legal and social texts relevant to a particular case, and from this understanding to arrive at the single legally correct decision. But that mental interpretive act cannot give itself effect. The practice of interpretation requires an understanding of what others will do with such a judicial utterance and, in many instances, an adjustment to that understanding, regardless of how misguided one may think the likely institutional response will be.[20]

The key to responding to these narrative demands is "legitimacy," a term Cover does not develop in this essay, beyond suggesting that several traditions—psychology, psychiatry, sociology—may be useful in unpacking the process by "persons who act within social organizations that exercise authority [judges and executioners] act violently without experiencing the normal inhibitions or the normal degree of inhibition which regulates the behavior of those who act autonomously."[21] For Cover, the work of judging should be examined in this light:

> On one level judges may appear to be, and may in fact be, offering their understanding of the normative world to their intended audience. But on another level they are engaging a violent mechanism through which a substantial part of their audience loses its capacity to think and act autonomously."[22]

In his 1983 essay, "The Folktales of Justice," Cover credits the Critical Legal Studies movement with having inaugurated this general approach:

> The critical legal studies movement has certainly been a primary force in placing the ideological functions and the "legitimation" process at the heart of contemporary legal scholarship."[23]

He describes what he means by "legitimation" this way:

> The struggle over what is "law" is then a struggle over which social patterns can plausibly be coated with a veneer which changes the very nature of that which it covers up. There is not automatic legitimation of an institution by calling it or what it produces "law," but the label is a move, the staking out of a position in the complex social game of legitimation. The jurisdictional inquiry into the question "what is law" is an engagement at one remove in the struggle over what is legitimate.[24]

In this struggle, Cover emphasizes the social limits of legitimate judging, and the role of religious and other ethical narratives as checks on what will seem legitimate.

Throughout the 1990s, ideas about the social impact and legitimating effects of normative argument remained central themes in American legal thought. Normative judicial argument was no longer a conversation among judges and scholars with effects—it was a plea directed to the administration and to the public to bring about those effects. In such a world, the substantive terms and institutional forms of legal argument mattered a great deal—they would create the normative pull to compliance, and reinforce or undermine the legitimacy of the legal process itself. In this, Cover placed legal language in a social conversation with a broad public, and focused attention on the expressive functions of legal norms and arguments, as representations of what could be, might be, would have to be—representations whose efficacy would ultimately be vouchsafed by the regard paid them.

DAVID KENNEDY

NOTES

1. See Martha Minow, "Interpreting Rights: An Essay for Robert Cover," 96 *Yale Law Journal* 1860, 1876. Or later, "The language of rights helps people to articulate standards for judging conduct, and the nature of rights discourse as a language for expressing meaning persists even beyond its use within legal institutions." Ibid., at 1886.

2. Ibid. 106.

3. Ronald Dworkin, "Law as Interpretation," 60 *Texas Law Review* 527, 535 (1981–82).

4. See Dworkin, "Hard Cases," introduction.

5. Ronald Dworkin, "Law as Interpretation," *supra* note 3 at 543–544.

6. Owen Fiss, "Conventionalism," 58 *Southern California Law Review* 177, 183 (1985).

7. Lon Fuller, *The Law in Question of Itself: Being a Series of Three Lectures Provided by the Julius Rosenthal Foundation for General Law* (Chicago: Foundation Press, 1940).

8. Cover, "The Supreme Court, 1982 Term: Foreword: Nomos and Narrative," 97 *Harvard Law Review* 4, 4 (1983–1984).

9. Ibid., at 53. In a more expansive passage, Cover described judicial violence in these terms: "In an imaginary world in which violence played no part in life, law would indeed grow exclusively from the hermeneutic impulse—the human need to create and interpret texts. Law would develop within small communities of mutually committed individuals who cared about the text, about what each made of the text, and about one another and the common life they shared. . . . But the jurisgenerative principle by which legal meaning proliferates in all communities never exists in isolation from violence. Interpretation always takes place in the shadow of coercion. And from this fact we may come to recognize a special role for courts. Courts, at least the courts of the state, are characteristically 'jurispathic.' It is remarkable that in myth and history the origin of and justification for a court is rarely understood to be the need for law. Rather, it is understood to be the need to suppress law, to choose between two or more laws, to impose upon laws a hierarchy. It is the multiplicity of laws, the fecundity of the jurisgenerative principle, that creates the problem to which the court and the state are the solution." Ibid., at 40.

10. Cover, "The Uses of Jurisdictional Redundancy," in Martha Minow, Michael Ryan, and Austin Sarat, eds., *Narrative Violence and the Law: The Essays of Robert Cover*, 93 (Ann Arbor: University of Michigan Press, 1992).

11. Cover, "Nomos and Narrative," *supra* note 7 at p. 44.

12. Minow, Ryan, and Sarat, eds., *Narrative, Violence, and the Law*, 7.

13. Cover, "Violence and the Word," at 1607, n. 16.

14. Elaine Scarry, *The Body in Pain*, 4 (New York: Oxford University Press, 1985), quoted by Cover, "Violence and the Word," pp. 1602–3.

15. Cover, "Violence and the Word," p. 1609.

16. Ibid.," pp. 1628–9.

17. Ibid., p. 1606, n. 15.

18. See particularly Cover, "Violence and the Word," p. 1606, n. 15, and p. 1609, n. 20. Stanley Fish, *Is there a Text in this Class?: The Authority of Interpretive Communities* (Cambridge, Mass.: Harvard University Press, 1980). Fredric Jameson, *The Political Unconscious: Narrative as a Socially Symbolic Act*, (Ithac N.Y.: Cornell University Press, 1981). Harold Bloom, *The Anxiety of Influence: A Theory of Poetry*, (New York: Oxford University Press, 1973). Michel Foucault, *Discipline and Punish: The Birth of the Prison* (New York: Pantheon Books, 1977).

19. Cover, "Violence and the Word," p. 1608.

20. Ibid., p. 1612.

21. Ibid., p. 1615.

22. Ibid.

23. See Cover, "The Folktales of Justice," in Minow, Ryan, and Sarat, eds., *Narrative Violence and the Law* at 175, n. 10, crediting Roberto Unger, "The Critical Legal Studies Movement," 96 *Harvard Law Review* 561 (1983).

24. Ibid., p. 175.

25. Ausin Sarat, ed., *Law, Violence, and the Possibility of Justice* (Princeton N. J.: Princeton University Press, 2001) at 3–4.

26. Martha Minow, "Introduction: Robert Cover and Law, Judging, and Violence," in Minow, Ryan and Sarat, eds., *Narrative, Violence and the Law: The Essays of Robert Cover* (Ann Arbor: University of Michigan Press, 1992) at 2.

27. Ibid., at 6.

28. Schlegel, 14 *Law and History Review*, 125, 125–6 (1996).

Robert Cover

A full bibliography of Cover's work can be found at "Bibliography of Robert M. Cover," *Yale Law Journal* 96 (1987) at 1725–6.

Cover's most significant essays were reprinted in Martha Minow, Michael Ryan, and Austin Sarat, ed, *Narrative, Violence, and the Law: The Essays of Robert Cover* (Ann Arbor: The University of Michigan Press, 1992). The editors each contributed an essay interpreting Cover's work.

Other than "Violence and the Word," Cover is most well known for Robert Cover, "The Supreme Court, 1982 Term—Foreword: Nomos and Narrative," 97 *Harvard Law Review* 4 (1983).

With his Yale colleague Owen Fiss, Cover authored *The Structure of Procedure* (New York: Foundation Press, 1979). After Cover's death, a casebook co-authored with Fiss and Judy Resnick was published: Robert Cover, Judith Resnick, and Owen Fiss, *Procedure* (Mineola, N. Y.: Foundation Press, 1988).

For Cover's earlier work on judicial action—and inaction—to protect minorities, see: Robert Cover, *Justice Accused: Antislavery and the Judicial Process* (New Haven: Yale University Press, 1975); and "The Origins of Judicial Activism in the Protection of Minorities," 91 *Yale Law Journal* 1287 (1983).

Many of the themes in "Violence and the Word" are also developed in Robert Cover, "The Bonds of Constitutional Interpretation: Of the Word, the Deed, and the Role," 20 *Georgia Law Review* 815 (1986).

Commentary

For tributes to Cover's work and life, see 96 *Yale Law Journal*, 8 (July 1987), including tributes from Guido Calabresi, Michael Graetz, Barbara Black, Stephen Wizner, Owen Fiss, and others.

The most sustained elaboration—and interpretation—of Cover's contributions in both "Violence and the Word" and "Nomos and Narrative" remains Martha Minow, "Interpreting Rights: An Essay for Robert Cover," 96 *Yale Law Journal* 1860 (1986–87).

An excellent series of responses to Cover's work is contained in the volume *Law, Violence, and the Possibility of Justice*," edited by Austin Sarat. (Princeton, N. J.: Princeton University Press, 2001). The volume includes essays by Sarat, Jonathan Simon, Sarat and Thomas Kearns, Marianne Constable, Peter Fitzpatrick, and Shaun McVeign, Peter Rush and Alison Young. Writing a decade or more after Cover's death, all take some distance from the specific arguments of "Violence and the Word," while affirming Cover's significance. The volume illustrates the response of many in the Law and Society movement to Cover's work. Sarat focuses on Cover's attention to "law's lethal character" and the process by which state violence is legitimated when "legal theory tacitly encourages officials to ignore the bloody consequences of their authoritative acts and the pain that those acts produce,"[25] and reviews the uses made of Cover's general ideas in legal scholarship. Sarat and Kearns highlight the "crucial conceptual breakthrough" represented by Cover's insistence that the law's legitimation of violence is not complete, that the exercise of legal force remains brutal in its implementation regardless of the efforts to render that force "legitimate."

Jonathan Simon's criticisms of Cover's attitudes toward the law's violence are typical of an increasingly skeptical reception for the specifics of Cover's argument—even as the sensibility he modeled continued to influence legal scholars. Simon argues that the "violence" Cover invokes following criminal punishment remains an intensely social and interactive affair, challenging the usefulness of the absolute opposition of Elaine Scarry's description of torture. For Simon, Cover's essay remains significant as a mark in legal scholarship of a turn in the social sciences away from ideology as the dominant instrument of governance to violence and coercion. The sharp distinction between law and violence for which Cover invokes Scarry is sharply criticized by Peter Fitzpatrick, arguing that the turn to "narrative" marks a departure from the turn to "interpretation"—expressing a limit, or the wish for a limit, to social constructionism and a desire for the return of authenticity and foundationalism which seem to lie at the core of the turn to ethics.

Earlier commentary by Martha Minow, Austin Sarat and Michael Ryan is contained in their edited re-publication of Cover's main essays: *Narrative, Violence, and the Law: The Essays of Robert Cover* (Ann Arbor: University of Michigan Press, 1992). There, Minow summarizes Cover's contributions in these terms:

> Cover placed at the center of law the communal groups that would seem peripheral if the government's own worldview were the starting point. In so doing, Cover set in motion three captivating arguments: (1) government should be understood as one among many contestants for generating and implementing norms; (2) communities ignored or despised by those running the state actually craft and sustain norms with at least as much effect and worth as those espoused by the state; and (3) imposition of the state's norms does violence to communities, a violence that may be justifiable but is not to be preferred a priori.[26]

Minow stresses the significance of the judicial experience of being confronted by multiple norms, and urges attention to the process by which judges flee this experience to formality and convention. She affirms Cover's enthusiasm for legal pluralism: "the availability of multiple judicial settings offers a check against errors, a guard against bias, a challenge to ideological blinders, and an opportunity for innovation."[27] Minow also stresses Cover's commitment to social solidarity and obligation—an increasingly significant theme in legal scholarship skeptical of the individualism associated with seeking social justice through rights. See, for example, Mary Anne Glendon, *Rights Talk: The Impoverishment of Political Discourse* (New York: Free Press, 1991).

The two collections of Cover's work are reviewed by John Henry Schlegel, in 14 *Law and History Review* 125 (1996). Schlegel comments on the hagiography which followed Cover's death, and notes an asymmetry in Cover's engagement with violence:

> Had Cover . . . held that the law was visiting violence upon the parents of the white children of Little Rock when it forced integration of that city's school system, he would have invited many to stop and think about violence and procedure in new ways. But that is not exactly what Cover did. Rather, he seems to have focused on one of the more obvious forms of violence in law—the death penalty—and one of the more metaphoric forms of violence in law—the shutting off of alternative normative choices—and lamented. That is all; as if by the waters of Babylon he wept.[28]

For an interesting review of the Minow/Ryan/Sarat collection of Cover's essays which focuses on the consequences for legal scholarship of Cover's attention to "narrative," see Rebecca French, "Of Narrative in Law and Anthropology," 30 *Law and Society Review* 417 (1996).

The *Journal of Law and Religion* devoted an issue to essays commenting on Cover's work by Milner Ball, Mark Tushnet, Michael Stokes Paulsen, Christine Desan Husson, Tristan Layle Duncan, Bryan Schwartz, and Howard Vogel. 7 *The Journal of Law and Religion* 1 (1989).

Cover's concern for the limits of interpretive theories to capture the multiplicity of lived experience—not all of which will share in the narrative process—was echoed in anthropology by Renato Rosaldo, who insisted upon the extent to which culture was formed by the activities of people who were not seeking to communicate normatively—but were simply waiting, carrying on other business. See Renato Rosaldo, "While Making Other Plans," 58 *Southern California Law Review*" 19 (1985). The image of victims as authentic challenges to the possibility of social narration is explored and criticized in Gayatri Spivak's "Can the Subaltern Speak," and *Marxism and the Interpretation of Culture*, Cary Nelson and Lawrence Grossberg, eds. (Houndsmill, Barringstoke, Hampshire: MacMillan Education, 1988).

The leading scholar of "law and literature" at the time was James Boyd White, *The Legal Imagination* (Chicago: University of Chicago Press, 1985). By the 1970s and early 80s, literature departments had largely moved on to various critical and "deconstructive" methods, whose proponents were often antagonists in debates with liberal legal scholars interested in interpretation. See, most notably, Stanley Fish, *Is There a Text in This Class?: The Authority of Interpretive Communities* (Cambridge, Mass.: Harvard University Press, 1980), and his debates with Owen Fiss. See, for example, Stanley Fish, *Doing What Comes Naturally: Change, Rhetoric, and the Practice of Theory in Library and Legal Studies* (Durham, N.C.: Duke University Press, 1989).

On the related "linguistic turn" in the broader American academy, see Richard Rorty, ed., *The Linguistic Turn: Essays in Philosophical Method, with Two Retrospective Essays* (Chicago: University of Chicago Press, 1967). Many legal scholars were familiar with J. L. Austin's 1955 William James Lectures at Harvard, published as *How to Do Things With Words* (Cambridge, Mass.: Harvard University Press) in 1962. See also Stanley Cavell, *Must We Mean What We Say* (New York: Charles Scribner's and Sons, 1969). Legal scholars focusing on interpretation traced their concerns to Wittgenstein's *Philosophical Investigations*, trans. G.E.M. Anscombe (New York: Macmillan, 1953). See, for example, Owen Fiss, "Conventionalism," 58:135 *Southern California Law Review* 177 (1985) at note 1. A significant influence on legal scholarship in the 1970s and 1980s was Paul Ricoeur's *Interpretation Theory: Discourse and the Surplus of Meaning* (Fort Worth: Texas Christian University Press, 1976) and Richard Rorty's *Philosophy and the Mirror of Nature* (Princeton, N.J.: Princeton University Press, 1979).

The anthropological writings of Clifford Geertz exerted a significant influence on legal scholars during this period. See particularly, Clifford Geertz, "Thick Description: Toward an Interpretive Theory of Culture," in *The Interpretation of Cultures* 3 (1974). Also influential were R. Bernstein, *The Restructuring of Social and Political Theory* (New York: Harcourt Brace Jovanovich, 1976); Pierre Bourdieu, *Outline of a Theory of Practice*, trans. Richard Nice (Cambridge: Cambridge University Press, 1977), Victor Turner, *Dramas, Fields and Metaphors* (Ithaca, N.Y.: Cornell University Press, 1974). In the field of literary studies, numerous scholars were developing theories focused on the interpretive communities—imaginative and real—which linked authors and readers. See, for example, Jonathan Culler, *Structuralist Poetics* (London: Routledge, 1975). For some, the most significant influences came from the world of philosophy, and particularly from Alisdair MacIntyre. See, for example, MacIntyre, "Epistemological Crises, Dramatic Narrative and the Philosophy of Science," 60 *The Monist* 453 (1977), *After Virtue: A Study in Moral Theory* (Notre Dame, Ind.: University of Notre Dame Press, 1981). Perhaps no other single work had the impact of Thomas Kuhn's *The Structure of Scientific Revolutions*, originally published in 1962, but reissued in a second edition in 1970 by University of Chicago Press. These works played a role parallel to that played by classic sociological works for early Law and Society scholars. For Cover, the transition ran from Robert Merton, *Social Theory and Social Structure* (1949) through Geertz, "Ideology as a Cultural System," in *The Interpretation of Cultures: Selected Essays* (New York: Basic Books, 1973) to Foucault's *Discipline and Punish: The Birth of the Prison*, trans. Alan Sheridan (New York, Pantheon Books, 1977).

A representative selection of contemporaneous work on "law and interpretation" is contained in two law review symposia. See: "Symposium: Law and Literature," 60 *Texas Law Review* 373 (1982) and "Interpretation Symposium," 58 *Southern California Law Review* 1 (1985). Alongside Dworkin, Owen Fiss and James Boyd White were perhaps the most sophisticated liberal voices articulating a theory of legal interpretation. See Fiss, "Conventionalism," 58 *Southern California Law Review* 177 (1985); Fiss, "Objectivity and Interpretation," 34 *Stanford Law Review* 739 (1982). See also James Boyd White's *The Legal Imagination: Studies in the Nature of Legal Thought and Expression* (Boston: Little, Brown, 1973) and "Law as Language: Reading Law and Reading Literature," 60 *Texas Law Review* 415 (1982). For Dworkin, see particularly "Law as Interpretation," 60: 3 *Texas Law Review* 1982 at 527, for his most explicit effort to equate law with inquiries in literature and the humanities. Already in "Hard Cases," Dworkin focused on the problem of "articulating" consistency, rather than being consistent, and described the work of judges in terms familiar from the humanities. Minow gives an account of the influences on this interpretive movement in "Interpreting Rights," at p. 1861, note 2. Her article offers a useful retrospective account of the interpretive turn in legal scholarship—and offers a sense for its limits, influenced by her reading of Cover.

Among legal scholars, Drucilla Cornell's contemporaneous and influential work marked a similar trajectory from Derrida to Levinas, and remains a significant expression of the liberal turn to ethics. See, for example, Drucilla Cornell, *The Philosophy of the Limit* (New York: Routledge, 1992); Drucilla Cornell, "From the Lighthouse: The Promise of Redemption and the Possibility of Legal Interpretation," 11 *Cardozo Law Review* 1716 (1990); and Drucilla Cornell, "Post-Structuralism, the Ethical Relation, and the Law," 9 *Cardozo Law Review* 1587 (1988). See also Jack Balkin, "Being Just with Deconstruction," 3 *Social and Legal Studies: An International Journal* 393 (1994). Judith Butler also became interested in the process by which interpretation involved a constant forward projection of ethical possibilities. See, for example, Judith Butler, "Deconstruction and the Possibility of Justice: Comments on Bernasconi, Cornell, Miller, Wever," 11 *Cardozo Law Review* 1715 (1990). See also Jacques Derrida's own attention to ethics and violence in Derrida, "The Force of Law: The Mystical Foundation of Authority," published in translation in 11 *Cardozo Law Review* 919 (1990), and Derrida, *Specter of Marx: The State of the Debt, the Work of Mourning, and the New International,* (New York: Routledge, 1994). The "force of law" essay was republished in Drucilla Cornell,

Michel Rosenfeld, and David Carlson, *Deconstruction and the Possibility of Justice* (New York: Routledge 1992). See also Emmanuel Levinas, *Totality and Infinity: An Essay on Exteriority* (Pittsburgh: Duquesne University Press, 1969).

Cover's call for the development of more "narrative" modes of legal scholarship was taken up with particular force by those giving voice to women and minorities in legal scholarship. See, for example, Pat Williams, *The Alchemy of Race and Rights*, (Cambridge, Mass.: Harvard University Press, 1991). See also Lucie White, "Subordination, Rhetorical Survival Skills, and Sunday Shoes: Notes on the Hearing of Mrs. G.," 38 *Buffalo Law Review* 1 (1990).

The focus on the politics of expression resonated throughout the legal academy. See, for example, Martha Minow, "Interpreting Rights" at 1900 and following, analyzing the consequences of a variety of expressive and labeling practices, including the effects of racial stereotyping, designation as handicapped or mentally ill, and pornography. For example, "child pornography subjects individual children to actual violence and also uses their images to damage and devalue all children" at p. 1901.

"Violence and the Word"

95 Yale Law Journal 1601 (1986)

I. Introduction: The Violence of Legal Acts

Legal interpretation[1] takes place in a field of pain and death. This is true in several senses. Legal interpretive acts signal and occasion the imposition of violence upon others: A judge articulates her understanding of a text, and as a result, somebody loses his freedom, his property, his children, even his life. Interpretations in law also constitute justifications for violence which has already occurred or which is about to occur. When interpreters have finished their work, they frequently leave behind victims whose lives have been torn apart by these organized, social practices of violence. Neither legal interpretation nor the violence it occasions may be properly understood apart from one another. This much is obvious, though the growing literature that argues for the centrality of interpretive practices in law blithely ignores it.[2]

Chancellor Kent Professor of Law and Legal History, Yale University.

There are always legends of those who came first, who called things by their right names and thus founded the culture of meaning into which we latecomers are born. Charles Black has been such a legend, striding across the landscape of law naming things, speaking "with authority." And we who come after him are eternally grateful.

I wish to thank Harlon Dalton, Susan Koniak and Harry Wellington for having read and commented upon drafts of this essay. Some of the ideas in this essay were developed earlier, in the Brown Lecture which I delivered at the Georgia School of Law Conference on Interpretation in March, 1986. I am grateful to Milner Ball, Avi Soifer, Richard Weisberg and James Boyd White for comments made in response to that lecture which have helped me in reworking the ideas here.

I am particularly grateful to my summer research assistant, Tracy Fessenden, for research, editorial and substantive assistance of the highest order.

[1] I have used the term "legal interpretation" throughout this essay, though my argument is directed principally to the interpretive acts of judges. To this specifically judicial interpretation my analysis of institutional action applies with special force. Nonetheless, I believe the more general term "legal interpretation" is warranted, for it is my position that the violence which judges deploy as instruments of a modern nation-state necessarily engages anyone who interprets the law in a course of conduct that entails either the perpetration or the suffering of this violence.

[2] There has been a recent explosion of legal scholarship placing interpretation at the crux of the enterprise of law. A fair sampling of that work may be seen in the various articles that have appeared in two symposia. Symposium: Law and Literature, 60 TEX. L. REV. 373 (1982); Interpretation Symposium, 58 S. CALIF. L. REV. 1 (1985) (published in two issues). The intense interest in "interpretation" or "hermeneutics" in recent legal scholarship is quite a different phenomenon from the traditional set of questions about how a particular word, phrase, or instrument should be given effect in some particular context. It is, rather, the study of what I have called "a normative universe . . . held together by . . . interpretive commitments . . ." Cover, The Supreme Court, 1982 Term—Foreword: Nomos and Narrative, 97 HARV. L. REV. 4, 7 (1983). Or, in Ronald Dworkin's words, it is the study of the effort "to impose meaning on the institution . . . and then to restructure it in the light of that meaning." R. DWORKIN, LAW'S EMPIRE 47 (1986) (emphasis in original). Dworkin, in Law's Empire, has written the most elaborate and sophisticated jurisprudence which places the meaning-giving, constructive dimension of interpretation at the heart of law. James Boyd White has been another eloquent voice claiming primacy for what he has called the "culture of argument." White has raised rhetoric to the pinnacle of jurisprudence. See J. B. WHITE, WHEN WORDS LOSE THEIR MEANING (1984); J. B. WHITE, HERACLES' BOW (1985).

The violent side of law and its connection to interpretation and rhetoric is systematically ignored or underplayed in the work of both Dworkin and White. White, in chapter nine of *Heracles' Bow*, comes closest to the concerns of this essay. He launches a critique of the practice of criminal law in terms of its unintelligibility as a "system of meaning" in the absence of significant reforms. White does not see violence as central to the breakdown of the system of meaning. But he does contrast what the judge says with what he does in the saying of it. Still, White reiterates in this book his central claim that "law . . . is best regarded not as a machine for social control, but as what I call a system of

Taken by itself, the word "interpretation" may be misleading. "Interpretation" suggests a social construction of an interpersonal reality through language. But pain and death have quite other implications. Indeed, pain and death destroy the world that "interpretation" calls up. That one's ability to construct interpersonal realities is destroyed by death is obvious, but in this case, what is true of death is true of pain also, for pain destroys, among other things, language itself. Elaine Scarry's brilliant analysis of pain makes this point:

> [F]or the person, in pain, so incontestably and unnegotiably present is it that "having pain" may come to be thought of as the most vibrant example of what it is to "have certainty," while for the other person it is so elusive that hearing about pain may exist as the primary model of what it is "to have doubt." Thus pain comes unshareably into our midst as at once that which cannot be denied and that which cannot be confirmed. Whatever pain achieves, it achieves in part through its unshareability, and it ensures this unshareability in part through its resistance to language . . . Prolonged pain does not simply resist language but actively destroys it, bringing about an immediate reversion to a state anterior to language, to the sounds and cries a human being makes before language is learned.[3]

The deliberate infliction of pain in order to destroy the victim's normative world and capacity to create shared realities we call torture. The interrogation that is part of torture, Scarry points out, is rarely designed to elicit information. More commonly, the torturer's interrogation is designed to demonstrate the end of the normative world of the victim—the end of what the victim values, the end of the bonds that constitute the community in which the values are grounded. Scarry thus concludes that "in compelling confession, the torturers compel the prisoner to record and objectify the fact that intense pain is world-destroying."[4] That is why torturers almost always require betrayal—a demonstration that the victim's intangible normative world has been crushed by the material reality of pain and its extension, fear.[5]

---

constitutive rhetoric: a set of resources for claiming, resisting, and declaring significance." *Id.* at 205. I do not deny that law is all those things that White claims, but I insist that it is those things in the context of the organized social practice of violence. And the "significance" or meaning that is achieved must be experienced or understood in vastly different ways depending upon whether one suffers that violence or not. In *Nomos and Narrative,* I also emphasized the world-building character of interpretive commitments in law. However, the thrust of *Nomos* was that the creation of legal meaning is an essentially cultural activity which takes place (or *best* takes place) among smallish groups. Such meaning-creating activity is not naturally coextensive with the range of effective violence used to achieve social control. Thus, because law is the attempt to build future worlds, the essential tension in law is between the elaboration of legal meaning and the exercise of or resistance to the violence of social control. Cover, *supra,* at 18: "[T]here is a radical dichotomy between the social organization of law as power and the organization of law as meaning." This essay elaborates the senses in which the traditional forms of legal decision cannot be easily captured by the idea of interpretation understood as interpretation normally is in literature, the arts, or the humanities.

[3] E. SCARRY, THE BODY IN PAIN 4 (1985).

[4] *Id.* at 29.

[5] *Id.*

Pain and interrogation inevitably occur together in part because the torturer and the prisoner each experience them as opposites. The very question that, within the political pretense, matters so much to the torturer that it occasions his grotesque brutality will matter so little to the prisoner experiencing the brutality that he will give the answer. For the torturers, the sheer and simple fact of human agony is made invisible, and the moral fact of inflicting that agony is made neutral by the feigned urgency and significance of the question. For the prisoner, the sheer, simple, overwhelming fact of his agony will make neutral and invisible the significance of any question as well as the significance of the world to which the question refers . . . It is for this reason that while the content of the prisoner's answer is only sometimes important to the regime, the form of the answer, the fact of his answering, is always crucial . . . [I]n confession, one betrays oneself and all those aspects of the world—friend, family, country, cause—that the self is made up of.

Id. While pain is the extreme form of world destruction, fear may be as potent, even if not connected to physical pain and torture. The fact of answering and the necessity for "world destruction" through betrayal were

The torturer and victim do end up creating their own terrible "world," but this world derives its meaning from being imposed upon the ashes of another.[6] The logic of that world is complete domination, though the objective may never be realized.

Whenever the normative world of a community survives fear, pain, and death in their more extreme forms, that very survival is understood to be literally miraculous both by those who have experienced and by those who vividly imagine or recreate the suffering. Thus, of the suffering of sainted Catholic martyrs it was written:

> We must include also . . . the deeds of the saints in which their triumph blazed forth through the many forms of torture that they underwent and *their marvelous confession of the faith*. For what Catholic can doubt that they suffered more than is possible for human beings to bear, and did not endure this by their own strength, but by the grace and help of God?[7]

And Jews, each year on Yom Kippur, remember—

> Rabbi Akiba . . . chose to continue teaching in spite of the decree [of the Romans forbidding it]. When they led him to the executioner, it was time for reciting the Sh'ma. With iron combs they scraped away his skin as he recited Sh'ma Yisrael, freely accepting the yoke of God's Kingship. "Even now?" his disciples asked. He replied: "All my life I have been troubled by a verse: 'Love the Lord your God with all your heart and with all your soul,' which means even if He take your life. I often wondered if I would ever fulfill that obligation. And now I can." He left the world while uttering, "The Lord is One."[8]

Martyrdom, for all its strangeness to the secular world of contemporary American Law, is a proper starting place for understanding the nature of legal interpretation. Precisely because it is so extreme a phenomenon, martyrdom helps us see what is present in lesser degree whenever interpretation is joined with the practice of violent domination. Martyrs insist in the face of overwhelming force that if there is to be continuing life, it will not be on the terms of the tyrant's law. Law is the projection of an imagined future upon reality. Martyrs require that any future they possess will be on the terms of the law to which they are committed (God's law). And the miracle of the suffering of the martyrs is their insistence on the law to which they are committed, even in the face of world-destroying pain.[9] Their triumph—which may well be partly imaginary—is the imagined triumph of the normative universe—of Torah, Nomos,—over the material world of death and

---

also central to the reign of fear of McCarthyism. *See, e.g.*, V. NAVASKY, NAMING NAMES 346 (1980) (informer destroys "the very possibility of a community . . . for the informer operates on the principle of betrayal and a community survives on the principle of trust").

[6] On the "fiction of power" that torture creates, see E. SCARRY, *supra* note 3, at 56–58.

[7] P. BROWN, THE CULT OF THE SAINTS 79 (1981) (emphasis added) (quoting from the DECRETUM GELASIANUM, PATROLOGIA LATINA 59.171).

[8] The quotation is from the traditional Eileh Ezkerah or martyrology service of Yom Kippur. I have quoted from the translation used in MAHZOR FOR ROSH HASHANAH AND YOM KIPPUR, A PRAYER BOOK FOR THE DAYS OF AWE 555-57 (J. Harlow ed. 1972).

[9] The word "martyr" stems from the Greek root martys, "witness," and from the Aryan root *smer*, "to remember." Martyrdom functions as a *re*-membering when the martyr, in the act of witnessing, sacrifices herself on behalf of the normative universe which is thereby reconstituted, regenerated, or recreated. One of the earliest sources dealing with martyrdom as a religious phenomenon, 2 MACCABEES, stresses the characteristic of the phenomenon as an insistence on the integrity of the Law of the martyr and of obligation to it in the face of overpowering violence. At one point the book describes the horrible torture and killing of seven sons before their mother's eyes, each death more horrible than the one before. The last and youngest child, encouraged by his mother, answers the King's demand to eat pork with the words: "I will not submit to the King's command; I obey the command of the law given by Moses to our ancestors." 2 MACCABEES 7.30.

pain.[10] Martyrdom is an extreme form of resistance to domination. As such it reminds us that the normative world building which constitutes "Law" is never just a mental or spiritual act. A legal world is built only to the extent that there are commitments that place bodies on the line. The torture of the martyr is an extreme and repulsive form of the organized violence of institutions. It reminds us that the interpretive commitments of officials are realized, indeed, in the flesh. As long as that is so, the interpretive commitments of a community which resists official law must also be realized in the flesh, even if it be the flesh of its own adherents.

Martyrdom is not the only possible response of a group that has failed to adjust to or accept domination while sharing a physical space. Rebellion and revolution are alternative responses when conditions make such acts feasible and when there is a willingness not only to die but also to kill for an understanding of the normative future that differs from that of the dominating power.[11]

Our own constitutional history begins with such an act of rebellion. The act was, in form, an essay in constitutional interpretation affirming the right of political independence from Great Britain:

> We therefore the representatives of the United States of America in General Congress assembled, appealing to the supreme judge of the world for the rectitude of our intentions, do in the name, and by the authority of the good people of these colonies, solemnly publish and declare that these United Colonies are and of right ought to be free and independent states, that they are absolved from all allegiance to the British crown, and that all political connection between them and the State of Great Britain is, and ought to be, totally dissolved.[12]

But this interpretive act also incorporated an awareness of the risk of pain and death that attends so momentous an interpretive occasion:

> We mutually pledge to each other our lives, our fortunes and our sacred honour.[13]

Life, fortune, and sacred honour were, of course, precisely the price that would have been exacted from the conspirators were their act unsuccessful. We too often forget that the leaders of the rebellion had certainly committed treason from the English constitutional perspective. And conviction of treason carried with it a horrible and degrading death, forfeiture of estate, and corruption of the

---

[10] In extreme cases martyrdom may be affirmatively sought out, for it is the final proof of the capacity of the spirit to triumph over the body. That triumph may be seen as a triumph of love or of law or of both, depending upon the dominant motifs of the normative and religious world of the martyr and her community. The great jurist and mystic, Joseph Karo (1488–1578), had ecstatic dreams of martyrdom and was promised the privilege of dying a martyr by a "maggid"—a celestial messenger who spoke through his mouth and appeared to him in visions. (The promise was not fulfilled. He died of very old age.) See Z. WERBLOWSKI, JOSEPH KARO: LAWYER AND MYSTIC 151–54 (2d ed. 1977). Note also the phenomenon of communities slaughtering themselves in the face of an enemy. Compare the complex mythos of the Jewish martyrs before the crusaders, elaborated in S. SPIEGEL., THE LAST TRIAL. ON THE LEGENDS AND LORE OF THE COMMAND TO ABRAHAM TO OFFER ISSAC AS A SACRIFICE THE AKEDAH (J. Goldin trans. 1969) with the myth of the White Night enacted by Jonestown in our own day, recounted in J. SMITH, IMAGINING RELIGION: FROM BABYLON TO JONESTOWN 102–20, 126–34 (1982).

[11] The archetype for the transition from martyrdom to resistance is found in 1 MACCABEES, with the dramatic killing carried out by the Priest Matathias in Modi'in. 1 MACCABEES 2, 19–28. His act assumes dramatic significance in the work in part because it stands in marked contrast to the acts of heroic martyrdom described in 2 MACCABEES. See supra note 9.

[12] The Declaration of Independence (1776). For the senses in which the Declaration should be seen as interpretive of the constitutional position of America in the Empire, see Black, *The Constitution of Empire: The Case for the Colonists*, 124 U. PA. L. REV. 1157 (1976).

[13] The Declaration of Independence (1776).

Robert Cover

blood.[14] Great issues of constitutional interpretation that reflect fundamental questions of political allegiance—the American Revolution, the secession of the States of the Confederacy, or the uprising of the Plains Indians—clearly carry the seeds of violence (pain and death) at least from the moment that the understanding of the political texts becomes embedded in the institutional capacity to take collective action. But it is precisely this embedding of an understanding of political text in institutional modes of action that distinguishes *legal* interpretation from the interpretation of literature, from political philosophy, and from constitutional criticism.[15] Legal interpretation is either played out on the field of pain and death or it is something less (or more) than law.

Revolutionary constitutional understandings are commonly staked in blood. In them, the violence of the law takes its most blatant form. But the relationship between legal interpretation and the infliction of pain remains operative even in the most routine of legal acts. The act of sentencing a convicted defendant is among these most routine of acts performed by judges.[16] Yet it is immensely revealing of the way in which interpretation is distinctively shaped by violence. First, examine the event from the perspective of the defendant. The defendant's world is threatened. But he sits, usually quietly, as if engaged in a civil discourse. If convicted, the defendant customarily walks—escorted—to prolonged confinement, usually without significant disturbance to the civil appearance of the event. It is, of course, grotesque to assume that the civil facade is "voluntary" except in the sense that it represents the defendant's autonomous recognition of the overwhelming array of violence ranged against him, and of the hopelessness of resistance or outcry.[17]

---

[14] *See* IV BLACKSTONE'S COMMENTARIES *92–93:

> The punishment of high treason in general is very solemn and terrible. 1. That the offender be drawn to the gallows, and not be carried or walk; though usually (by connivance, at length ripened by humanity into law) a sledge or hurdle is allowed, to preserve the offender from the extreme torment of being dragged on the ground or pavement. 2. That he be hanged by the neck, and then cut down alive. 3. That his entrails be taken out, and burned, while yet he is alive. 4. That his head be cut off. 5. That his body be divided into four parts. 6. That his head and quarters be at the king's disposal.

On forfeiture and corruption of the blood, see *Id.* at *388–96. It is, therefore, not unexpected that among the few specific protections incorporated into the body of the original Constitution were those which closely defined treason, set procedural safeguards for conviction of treason, and forbade the extension of attaint and corruption of the blood as vicarious punishment upon the family or descendants of those convicted of treason.

[15] Every interpretive practice takes place in some context. Among recent critics, Stanley Fish has been as insistent as any concerning the dominance of institutional contexts even in understanding literary texts. *See generally* S. FISH, IS THERE A TEXT IN THIS CLASS? (1980); Fish, *Fish v. Fiss*, 36 STAN. L. REV. 1325, 1332 (1984) ("To be . . . 'deeply inside' a context is to be already and always thinking (and perceiving) with and within the norms, standards, definitions, routines, and understood goals that both define and are defined by that context."). I do not wish to dispute Fish's central point about literature. I do think, however, that the institutions that are designed to realize normative futures in part through the practice of collective violence stand on a somewhat different footing than do those which bear only a remote or incidental relation to the violence of society. I am prepared to entertain views such as those of Fredric Jameson, who argues for "the priority of the political interpretation of literary texts." F. JAMESON, THE POLITICAL UNCONSCIOUS: NARRATIVE AS A SOCIALLY SYMBOLIC ACT 17 (1981). But while asserting the special place of a political understanding of our social reality, such views do not in any way claim for literary interpretations what I am claiming about legal interpretation—that it is part of the *practice* of political violence.

[16] I have used the criminal law for examples throughout this essay for a simple reason. The violence of the criminal law is relatively direct. If my argument is not persuasive in this context, it will be less persuasive in most other contexts. I would be prepared to argue that all law which concerns property, its use and its protection, has a similarly violent base. But in many, perhaps most, highly visible legal transactions concerning property rights, that violent foundation is not immediately at issue. My argument does not, I believe, require that every interpretive event in law have the kind of direct violent impact on participants that a criminal trial has. It is enough that it is the case that where people care passionately about outcomes and are prepared to act on their concern, the law officials of the nation state are usually willing and able to use either criminal or violent civil sanctions to control behavior.

[17] A few defendants who have reached their own understandings of the legal order have overtly attempted to deny the fiction that the trial is a joint or communal civil event where interpretations of facts and legal concepts are tested

There are societies in which contrition or shame control defendants' behavior to a greater extent than does violence. Such societies require and have received their own distinctive form of analysis.[18] But I think it is unquestionably the case in the United States that most prisoners walk into prison because they know they will be dragged or beaten into prison if they do not walk. They do not organize force against being dragged because they know that if they wage this kind of battle they will lose—very possibly lose their lives.

If I have exhibited some sense of sympathy for the victims of this violence it is misleading. Very often the balance of terror in this regard is just as I would want it. But I do not wish us to pretend that we talk our prisoners into jail. The "interpretations" or "conversations" that are the preconditions for violent incarceration are themselves implements of violence. To obscure this fact is precisely analogous to ignoring the background screams or visible instruments of torture in an inquisitor's interrogation. The experience of the prisoner is, from the outset, an experience of being violently dominated, and it is colored from the beginning by the fear of being violently treated.[19]

The violence of the act of sentencing is most obvious when observed from the defendant's perspective. Therefore, any account which seeks to downplay the violence or elevate the interpretive character or meaning of the event within a community of shared values will tend to ignore the prisoner or defendant and focus upon the judge and the judicial interpretive act. Beginning with broad interpretive categories such as "blame" or "punishment," meaning is created for the event which justifies the judge to herself and to others with respect to her role in the acts of violence. I do not wish to downplay the significance of such ideological functions of law. But the function of ideology is much more significant in justifying an order to those who principally benefit from it and who must defend it than it is in hiding the nature of the order from those who are its victims.

The ideology of punishment is not, of course, the exclusive property of judges. The concept operates in the general culture and is intelligible to and shared by prisoners, criminals and revolutionaries as well as judges. Why, then, should we not conclude that interpretation is the master concept of law, that the interpretive work of understanding "punishment" may be seen as mediating or making sense of the opposing acts and experiences of judge and defendant in the criminal trial? Naturally, one who is to be punished may have to be coerced. And punishment, if it is "just," supposedly legitimates the coercion or violence applied. The ideology of punishment may, then, operate successfully to justify our practices of criminal law to ourselves and, possibly, even to those who are or may come to be "punished" by the law.

---

and refined. The playing out of such an overt course of action ends with the defendant physically bound and gagged. Bobby Seale taught those of us who lived through the 1960's that the court's physical control over the defendant's body lies at the heart of the criminal process. The defendant's "civil conduct," therefore, can never signify a shared understanding of the event; it may signify his fear that any public display of his interpretation of the event as "bullshit" will end in violence perpetrated against him, pain inflicted upon him. Our constitutional law, quite naturally enough, provides for the calibrated use of ascending degrees of overt violence to maintain the 'order' of the criminal trial. See, e.g., Illinois v. Allen, 397 U.S. 337 (1970); Tigar, *The Supreme Court, 1969 Term—Foreword: Waiver of Constitutional Rights: Disquiet in the Citadel*, 84 HARV. L. REV. 1, 1–3, 10–11 (1970) (commenting in part upon *Allen*).

[18] On the distinction between "shame cultures" and "guilt cultures," see generally E. DODDS, THE GREEKS AND THE IRRATIONAL (1951), and J. REDFIELD, NATURE AND CULTURE IN THE ILIAD (1975). For an analysis of a modern "shame culture," see R. BENEDICT, THE CHRYSANTHEMUM AND THE SWORD: PATTERNS OF JAPANESE CULTURE (1946).

[19] This point and others very similar to it are made routinely in the literature that comes out of prisons. *See, e.g.,* E. CLEAVER, SOUL ON ICE 128–30 (1968); J. WASHINGTON, A BRIGHT SPOT IN THE YARD: NOTES & STORIES FROM A PRISON JOURNAL 5 (1981).

There is, however, a fundamental difference between the way in which "punishment" operates as an ideology in popular or professional literature, in political debate, or in general discourse, and the way in which it operates in the context of the legal acts of trial, imposition of sentence, and execution. For as the judge interprets, using the concept of punishment, she also acts—through others—to restrain, hurt, render helpless, even kill the prisoner. Thus, any commonality of interpretation that may or may not be achieved is one that has its common meaning destroyed by the divergent experiences that constitute it. Just as the torturer and victim achieve a "shared" world only by virtue of their diametrically opposed experiences, so the judge and prisoner understand "punishment" through their diametrically opposed experiences of the punishing act. It is ultimately irrelevant whether the torturer and his victim share a common theoretical view on the justifications for torture—outside the torture room. They still have come to the confession through destroying in the one case and through having been destroyed in the other. Similarly, whether or not the judge and prisoner share the same philosophy of punishment, they arrive at the particular act of punishment having dominated and having been dominated with violence, respectively.

II. The Acts of Judges: Interpretations, Deeds and Roles

We begin, then, not with what the judges say, but with what they do. The judges deal pain and death.

That is not all that they do. Perhaps that is not what they usually do. But they *do* deal death, and pain. From John Winthrop through Warren Burger they have sat atop a pyramid of violence, dealing . . .

In this they are different from poets, from critics, from artists. It will not do to insist on the violence of strong poetry, and strong poets. Even the violence of weak judges is utterly real—a naive but immediate reality, in need of no interpretation, no critic to reveal it.[20] Every prisoner displays its mark. Whether or not the violence of judges is justified is not now the point—only that it exists in fact and differs from the violence that exists in literature or in the metaphoric characterizations of literary critics and philosophers. I have written elsewhere that judges of the state are jurispathic—that they kill the diverse legal traditions that

[20] On the violence that strong poets do to their literary ancestors, see H. BLOOM, THE ANXIETY OF INFLUENCE (1973), H. BLOOM, THE BREAKING OF THE VESSELS (1982), and much of Bloom's other work since *Anxiety*. Judges, like all readers and writers of texts, do violence to their literary—i.e., judicial—forebearers. For an interesting application of Bloom's central thesis to law, see D. Cole, *Agon and Agora: Creative Misreadings in the First Amendment Tradition*, 95 YALE L. J. 857 (1986). Cole acknowledges that the connection of law to violence distinguishes legal from literary interpretation, though he does not, unfortunately, develop the point. *Id.* at 904.

The anxiety of juridical influence was rather aptly and nicely stated somewhat earlier by Learned Hand in his tribute to Cardozo, *Mr. Justice Cardozo*, 39 COLUM. L. REV. 9 (1939). My point here is not that judges do not do the kind of figurative violence to literary parents that poets do, but that they carry out—in addition—a far more literal form of violence through their interpretations that poets do not share. It is significant, and has been much noted, that the immediacy of the connection between judge and violence of punishment has changed over the centuries. *See, e.g.*, M. FOUCAULT, DISCIPLINE AND PUNISH: THE BIRTH OF THE PRISON (A. Sheridan trans. 1977). Certainly in the United States today, the judge's obvious responsibility for the violence of punishment requires an appreciation—which all who live in this society acquire—of the organizational form of action. In that sense "naïve" reality should not be taken to signify too much. One need not be sophisticated to understand the violence of judging, but neither is it as naive a form of violence as it would be if judges carried out their own sentencing. On the implications of this point, *see infra* pp. 1626–27.

compete with the State.[21] Here, however, I am not writing of the jurispathic quality of the office, but of its homicidal potential.[22]

The dual emphasis on the *acts* of judges and on the violence of these acts leads to consideration of three characteristics of the interpretive dimension of judicial behavior. Legal interpretation is (1) a practical activity, (2) designed to generate credible threats and actual deeds of violence, (3) in an effective way. In order to explore the unseverable connection between legal interpretation and violence, each of these three elements must be examined in turn.

A. *Legal Interpretation as a Practical Activity*

Legal interpretation is a form of practical wisdom.[23] At its best it seeks to "impose *meaning* on the institution . . . and then to restructure it in the light of that meaning."[24] There is, however, a persistent chasm between thought and action. It is one thing to understand what ought to be done, quite another thing

---

[21] Cover, *supra* note 2, at 40–44.

[22] The violence of judges and officials of a posited constitutional order is generally understood to be implicit in the practice of law and government. Violence is so intrinsic to this activity, so taken for granted, that it need not be mentioned. For instance, read the Constitution. Nowhere does it state, as a general principle, the obvious—that the government thereby ordained and established has the power to practice violence over its people. That, as a general proposition, need not be stated, for it is understood in the very idea of government. It is, of course, also directly implicit in many of the specific powers granted to the general government or to some specified branch or official of it. E.g., U.S. CONST. art. I, § 8, cl. 1('Power To lay and collect Taxes . . . and provide for the common Defence'); *Id.*, cl. 6 ("To provide for the Punishment of counterfeiting"); *Id.*, cl. 10 ("To define and punish Piracies"); *Id.*, cl. 11 ('To declare War'); *Id.*, cl. 15 ("To provide for calling forth the Militia to execute the Laws of the Union, suppress Insurrections and repel Invasions;"); *Id.*, art. IV, § 2, cls. 2–3 (providing for rendition of fugitives from justice and service).

[23] On practical wisdom, see ARISTOTLE, THE NICOMACHEAN ETHICS 1140a(24) to 1140b(30).

[24] R. DWORKIN, *supra* note 2, at 47. Dworkin's opus, celebrating what he calls the "integrity" of coherent and consistent interpretation, stands within a long tradition of work elaborating on Aristotle's fundamental insight into the nature of deliberation. Aristotle assigned the broad area of normative deliberation, of which legal interpretation consists, to practical wisdom or phronesis, which he distinguished from speculative knowledge. ARISTOTLE, *supra* note 23, at 1139b(14) to 1140b(30). On *phronesis*, see also H. ARENDT, WILLING 59–62 (1977). Practical wisdom, according to Aristotle, is a form of applied understanding: it does not consist, like knowledge, or pre-existing truths. It entails deliberation—an activity which is senseless with respect to logical truth. Deliberation engages the relevance of past to present understandings through a reflexive "discovery" of what is implicit in past understanding. Technical knowledge also has applied character, but practical wisdom, being in the normative sphere, cannot be measured by an external standard such as usefulness, because it consists of the application of understanding to the shaping of self.

Hans Georg Gadamer elevated these characteristics of practical wisdom to the central place in what he called "the human sciences." H. GADAMER, TRUTH AND METHOD 5–10 and passim (G. Barden & J. Cumming eds. 2d ed. 1975). Gadamer found these interpersonal, constructive acts of understanding—hermeneutics or interpretations— most clearly exemplified in what he called "legal dogmatics." Gadamer's project may be understood in some measure as an attempt to comprehend all human understanding in terms of *phronesis*; that is, to take the category of applied thought that defines our situation as moral actors and generalize that situation to include all of life. "Understanding is, then, a particular case of the application of something universal to a particular situation." *Id.* at 278.

For Gadamer, Aristotle is the source—the one who places action and striving at the center of moral philosophy. "Aristotle's description of the ethical phenomenon and especially of the virtue of moral knowledge . . . is in fact a kind of model of the problems of hermeneutics . . . Application is neither a subsequent nor a merely occasional part of the phenomenon of understanding, but codetermines it as a whole from the beginning." *Id.* at 289. Gadamer proceeds from Aristotle by incorporating Heidegger's fundamental insight that we are always situated in the world, building the future worlds we shall inhabit. We do this through interpretation which is simultaneously a discovery of what we know and a new understanding of this "known" that enables us to discover more about what we know. Building on Heidegger, Gadamer posits the unity of all hermeneutics, all interpretive activity. Because all understanding is a building of both self and the world, it is in some measure practical and social, and therefore never divorced from ethics.

The practice of legal interpretation by the judge is no different from any other hermeneutic exercise. It exemplifies the mutually and reflexively constructive effects of text, of prior understanding of text (tradition), of present application and understanding-as-applied, and of future commitment. And legal dogmatics are for Gadamer the "model for the unity of dogmatic and historical interest and so also for the unity of hermeneutics as a whole." J. WEINSHEIMER, GADAMER'S HERMENEUTIcS, A READING OF *Truth and Method* 194 (1985).

to do it. Doing entails an act of will and may require courage and perseverance. In the case of an individual's actions, we commonly think such qualities are functions of motivation, character, or psychology.

Legal interpretation is practical activity in quite another sense, however. The judicial word is a mandate for the deeds of others. Were that not the case, the practical objectives of the deliberative process could be achieved, if at all, only through more indirect and risky means. The context of a judicial utterance is institutional behavior in which others, occupying preexisting roles, can be expected to act, to implement, or otherwise to respond in a specified way to the judge's interpretation. Thus, the institutional context ties the language act of practical understanding to the physical acts of others in a predictable, though not logically necessary, way.[25] These interpretations, then, are not only "practical," they are, themselves, practices.

Formally, on both a normative and descriptive level, there are or may be rules and principles which describe the relationship between the interpretive acts of judges and the deeds which may be expected to follow from them. These rules and principles are what H.L.A. Hart called "secondary rules."[26] At least some secondary rules and principles identify the terms of cooperation between interpretation specialists and other actors in a social organization. Prescriptive secondary materials purport to set the norms for what those relations ought to be; descriptive secondary rules and principles would generate an accurate prediction of what the terms of cooperation actually will be. Of course, in any given system there need be no particular degree of correspondence between these two sets of rules.

Secondary rules and principles provide the template for transforming language into action, word into deed. As such they occupy a critical place in the analysis of legal interpretation proposed here. The legal philosopher may hold up to us a model of a hypothetical judge who is able to achieve a Herculean understanding of the full body of legal and social texts relevant to a particular case, and from this understanding to arrive at the single legally correct decision.[27] But that mental interpretive

---

Gadamer's placement of legal dogmatics at the center of the general enterprise of understanding the human sciences represents an invitation—or perhaps a temptation—to those legal academics who conceive law as the building of a system of normative meaning. If one can begin to understand the entire world of the humanities, i.e., the many forms of interpretive activity, in terms of law, it should be possible to put this common element of interpretation at the heart of law itself. That, indeed, seems to have been the effect of the slow trickle down of ideas about interpretation to the legal academy in America.

Ronald Dworkin synthesizes these interpretativist ideas in his new work, *Law's Empire*. R. DWORKIN, *supra* note 2. *Law's Empire* is a major elaboration of the reflexive, deliberative form of practical wisdom rooted in Aristotle's *phronesis*. It also builds upon Dworkin's own earlier critique of legal positivism to render "interpretation" the central activity in the judicial act while keeping the judicial act central to law. I fully agree that the dominant form of legal thought ought to be interpretive in the extended sense of the term. However, the emergence of interpretation as a central motif does not, by itself, reflect upon the way in which the interpretive acts of judges are simultaneously performative utterances in an institutional setting for violent behavior.

[25] One might say that institutions create the context for changing the contingent to the necessary. See H. ARENDT, *supra* note 24, at 14; *see also* J. SEARLE, SPEECH ACTS (1969).

[26] H.L.A. HART, THE CONCEPT OF LAW 77–106 (1961). Dworkin has ably challenged the supposedly central role of secondary rules in a theory of law. R. DWORKIN, TAKING RIGHTS SERIOUSLY (1977). Dworkin's critique is most telling in undermining the idea that rules of recognition adequately account for certain principles which have the effect of law. *See also* Cover, *supra* note 2. However, some secondary rules of recognition are designed not to generate recognition of content of rules or principles but to recognize outcomes that are to be effectuated. That is, some secondary rules organize social cooperation in the violent deeds of the law. By and large the secondary rules that organize the law's violence are clearer and more hierarchical than those that organize the ideational content of the law. For an excellent review of the significance of Dworkin's position for the viability of legal positivism as a system, see Coleman, *Negative and Positive Positivism*, 11 J. LEG. STUD. 139 (1982).

[27] See R. DWORKIN, *supra* note 26, at 105–30; *see also infra* note 61.

act cannot give itself effect. The practice of interpretation requires an understanding of what others will do with such a judicial utterance and, in many instances, an adjustment to that understanding, regardless of how misguided one may think the likely institutional response will be. Failing this, the interpreter sacrifices the connection between understanding what ought to be done and the deed, itself. But bridging the chasm between thought and action in the legal system is never simply a matter of will. The gap between understanding and action roughly corresponds to differences in institutional roles and to the division of labor and of responsibility that these roles represent. Thus, what may be described as a problem of will with respect to the individual becomes, in an institutional context, primarily a problem in social organization. Elsewhere I have labeled the specialized understanding of this relation, between the interpretation of the judge and the social organization required to transform it into a reality, the hermeneutic of the texts of jurisdiction.[28] This specialized understanding must lie at the heart of official judging.

B. Interpretation within a System Designed to Generate Violence

The gulf between thought and action widens wherever serious violence is at issue, because for most of us, evolutionary, psychological, cultural and moral considerations inhibit the infliction of pain on other people. Of course, these constraints are neither absolute nor universal. There are some deviant individuals whose behavior is inconsistent with such inhibitions.[29] Furthermore, almost all people are fascinated and attracted by violence, even though they are at the same time repelled by it.[30] Finally, and most important for our purposes, in almost all people social cues may overcome or suppress the revulsion to violence under certain circumstances.[31] These limitations do not deny the force of inhibitions against violence. Indeed, both together create the conditions without which law would either be unnecessary or impossible. Were the inhibition against violence perfect, law would be unnecessary; were it not capable of being overcome through social signals, law would not be possible.

Because legal interpretation is as a practice incomplete without violence— because it depends upon the social practice of violence for its efficacy—it must be related in a strong way to the cues that operate to by-pass or suppress the psycho-social mechanisms that usually inhibit people's actions causing pain and death. Interpretations which occasion violence are distinct from the violent acts

[28] Cover, *supra* note 2, at 53–60.

[29] There are persons whose behavior is both violent toward others and apparently reckless in disregard of violent consequences to themselves. Moreover, this behavior is frequently accompanied by a strange lack of affect. The classification of such persons as suffering from mental illness is a matter of great dispute. Nonetheless, at the present time there are a variety of labels that may be appropriately applied on the basis of one authority or another. See, e.g., AM. PSYCHIATRIC ASSOC., DIAGNOSTIC AND STATISTICAL MANUAL OF MENTAL DISORDERS 317-21 (3d ed. 1980) (diagnosing persons similar to those described above as suffering from 'antisocial personality disorder'). For some earlier classifications, see W. McCORD & J. McCORD, THE PSYCHOPATH 39–55 (1964).

[30] See, e.g., C. FORD & F. BEACH, PATTERNS OF SEXUAL BEHAVIOR 64–65 (1951) (varying cultural responses to linking pain and sexuality). Whether there is a deeper sado-masochistic attraction to pain or violence involving more serious forms of imposition or suffering of pain that is similarly universal is a matter of dispute. The attraction to violence may also be accounted for in terms of an impulse of "aggression." See generally K. LORENZ, ON AGGRESSION (M. Wilson trans. 1966).

[31] See, e.g., S. MILGRAM, OBEDIENCE TO AUTHORITY (1974). The Milgram experiments are discussed and placed in the context of a much larger body of experimental work and anecdotal material on decisionmaking in I. JANIS & L. MANN, DECISION MAKING: A PSYCHOLOGICAL ANALYSIS OF CONFLICTS, CHOICE, AND COMMITMENT 268–71 (1977).

they occasion. When judges interpret the law in an official context, we expect a close relationship to be revealed or established between their words and the acts that they mandate. That is, we expect the judges' words to serve as virtual triggers for action. We would not, for example, expect contemplations or deliberations on the part of jailers and wardens to interfere with the action authorized by judicial words. But such a routinization of violent behavior requires a form of organization that operates simultaneously in the domains of action and interpretation. In order to understand the violence of a judge's interpretive act, we must also understand the way in which it is transformed into a violent deed despite general resistance to such deeds; in order to comprehend the meaning of this violent deed, we must also understand in what way the judge's interpretive act authorizes and legitimates it.

While it is hardly possible to suggest a comprehensive review of the possible ways in which the organization of the legal system operates to facilitate overcoming inhibitions against intraspecific violence, I do wish to point to some of the social codes which limit these inhibitions. Here the literature of social psychology is helpful. The best known study and theory of social codes and their role in overcoming normal inhibitions against inflicting pain through violence is Milgram's *Obedience to Authority*.[32] In the Milgram experiments, subjects administered what they thought were actually painful electric shocks to persons who they thought were the experimental subjects. This was done under the direction or orders of supposed experimenters. The true experimental subjects—those who administered the shocks— showed a disturbingly high level of compliance with authority figures despite the apparent pain evinced by the false experimental subjects. From the results of his experiment, Milgram has formulated a theory that is in some respects incomplete. The most developed part of the theory relies heavily on the distinction he draws between acting in an "autonomous" state and acting in an "agentic" state. Milgram posits the evolution of a human disposition to act "agentically" within hierarchies, since the members of organized hierarchies were traditionally more likely to survive than were members of less organized social groups. Concurrently, the "conscience" or "superego" evolved in response to the need for autonomous behavior or judgment given the evolution of social structures. It is this autonomous behavior which inhibits the infliction of pain on others. But the regulators for individual autonomous behavior had to be capable of being suppressed or subordinated to the characteristics of agentic behavior when individuals acted within an hierarchical structure.[33] In addition to his theories of species-specific evolutionary mechanisms, Milgram also points to the individual-specific and culture-specific forms of learning and conditioning for agentic behavior within hierarchical structures. Thus, in Milgram's explanation of the "agentic state," "institutional systems of authority" play a key role in providing the requisite cues for causing the shift from autonomous behavior to the agentic behavior cybernetically required to make hierarchies work.[34] According to Milgram, the cues for overcoming autonomous behavior or "conscience" consist of the institutionally sanctioned commands, orders, or signals of institutionally legitimated authorities characteristic of human hierarchical organization.[35]

---

[32] S. MILGRAM, *supra* note 31.

[33] *Id.* at 135–38. Milgram even suggests that there may be chemoneurological regulators of that subordination.

[34] *Id.* at 123–64.

[35] *Id.* at 125–30, 143–48. Milgram also quite properly subjects his theory to the question of whether the behavior elicited in his experiments might be better explained by postulating a general impulse or tendency to aggression which is built into the human being and which is normally suppressed by social factors. The experiments might then be understood as opportunities created by the removal of the social constraints upon violence for the pre-existing aggression to emerge. *Id.* at 165–68. It is not clear that the two theories are mutually exclusive.

There are, of course, a variety of alternative ways to conceptualize the facilitation of violence through institutional roles. One could point, for example, to the theory that human beings have a natural tendency, an instinctual drive, to aggression, and that a variety of learned behaviors keep aggression within bounds. The institutionally specified occasions for violence may then be seen as outlets for the aggression that we ordinarily would seek to exercise but for the restraints. Some scholars have, from a psychoanalytic perspective, hypothesized that formal structures for the perpetration of violence permit many individuals to deny themselves the fulfillment of aggressive wishes by "delegating" the violent activity to others.[36]

There is an enormous difference between Milgram's theory of institutionalized violence and Anna Freud's or Konrad Lorenz's, and between the assumptions about human nature which inform them. But common to all of these theories is a behavioral observation in need of explanation. Persons who act within social organizations that exercise authority act violently without experiencing the normal inhibitions or the normal degree of inhibition which regulates the behavior of those who act autonomously. When judges interpret, they trigger agentic behavior within just such an institution or social organization. On one level judges may appear to be, and may in fact be, offering their understanding of the normative world to their intended audience. But on another level they are engaging a violent mechanism through which a substantial part of their audience loses its capacity to think and act autonomously.

C. Interpretation and the Effective Organization of Violence

A third factor separates the authorization of violence as a deliberative, interpretive exercise from the deed. Deeds of violence are rarely suffered by the victim apart from a setting of domination.[37] That setting may be manifestly coercive and violent or it may be the product of a history of violence which conditions the expectations of the actors. The imposition of violence depends upon the satisfaction of the social

---

[36] Anna Freud follows Stone in calling the phenomenon "delegation." "The individual denies himself the fulfillment of aggressive wishes but concedes permission for it to some higher agency such as the state, the police, the military or legal authorities." A. Freud, *Comments on Aggression*, in PSYCHOANALYTIC PSYCHOLOGY OF NORMAL DEVELOPMENT 161 (1981) (Vol. VIII of THE WRITINGS OF ANNA FREUD). I am indebted to Diane Cover for this reference.

[37] My colleague, Harlon Dalton, reports a view among some people who have clerked for judges on the Second Circuit Court of Appeals that the judges seem reluctant to affirm convictions from the bench when they believe the defendant to be in the courtroom. Dalton suggests two reasons for the tendency to reserve decision in such cases. First, the judges desire to give the appearance of deliberation in order to minimize, to the extent possible, the loser's dissatisfaction with the outcome; second, and more important, the judges desire to avoid having a disgruntled defendant (whose inhibitions against perpetrating violence are not what they might be) decide to "approach the bench," as it were. Dalton relates the scene he witnessed when clerking for a then-quite-new district judge who made the mistake of pronouncing sentence in the small robing room behind the courtroom. (The courtroom was temporarily unavailable for one reason or another.) The defendant's request that his family be present during sentencing was of course granted. As a result, the judge had to confront a weeping wife, dejected children, a lawyer who was now able to emote on an intimate stage, and a defendant who was able to give his allocution eye-to-eye with the judge from a distance of, at most, ten feet. It was impossible, therefore, for the judge to hide or insulate himself from the violence that would flow from the words he was about to utter, and he was visibly shaken as he pronounced sentence. Even so, neither he nor Dalton was prepared for what followed. The defendant began alternately shouting and begging the judge to change his mind; his wife began sobbing loudly; the defendant lurched forward with no apparent purpose in mind except, literally, to get to the judge who was doing this awful thing to him. Because the seating in the robing room was not designed with security in mind, it took the marshall a moment or two—a long moment or two—to restrain the defendant. Then, because the room's only exit was behind where the defendant and his family had been seated, the judge had to wait until they were, respectively, forced and importuned to leave before he could make his exit, thus witnessing first hand how his words were translated into deeds. I am grateful to Harlon Dalton for these accounts.

preconditions for its effectiveness. Few of us are courageous or foolhardy enough to act violently in an uncompromisingly principled fashion without attention to the likely responses from those upon whom we would impose our wills.[38]

If legal interpretation entails action in a field of pain and death, we must expect, therefore, to find in the act of interpretation attention to the *conditions of effective domination*. To the extent that effective domination is not present, either our understanding of the law will be adjusted so that it will require only that which can reasonably be expected from people in conditions of reprisal, resistance and revenge,[39] or there will be a crisis of credibility. The law may come over time to bear only an uncertain relation to the institutionally implemented deeds it authorizes. Some systems, especially religious ones, can perpetuate and even profit from a dichotomy between an ideal law and a realiable one.[40] But such a dichotomy has immense implications *if built into* the law. In our own secular legal system, one must assume this to be an undesirable development.

D. Legal Interpretation as Bonded Interpretation

Legal interpretation, therefore, can never be "free"; it can never be the function of an understanding of the text or word alone. Nor can it be a simple function of what the interpreter conceives to be merely a reading of the "social text," a reading of all relevant social data. Legal interpretation must be capable of transforming itself into action; it must be capable of overcoming inhibitions against violence in order to generate its requisite deeds; it must be capable of massing a sufficient degree of violence to deter reprisal and revenge.

In order to maintain these critical links to effective violent behavior, legal interpretation must reflexively consider its own social organization. In so reflecting, the interpreter thereby surrenders something of his independence of mind and autonomy of judgment, since the legal meaning that some hypothetical Hercules (Hyporcules) might construct out of the sea of our legal and social texts is only one element in the institutional practice we call law. Coherent legal meaning is an element in legal interpretation. But it is an element potentially in tension with the need to generate effective action in a violent context. And neither effective action nor coherent meaning can be maintained, separately or together, without an entire structure of social cooperation. Thus, legal interpretation is a form of bonded interpretation, bound at once to practical application (to the deeds it implies) and to the ecology of jurisdictional roles (the conditions of effective domination). The bonds are reciprocal. For the deeds of social violence as we know them also require that

---

[38] It is the fantasy of so acting which accounts for the attraction of so many violent heroes. Where systems of deterrence and justice do in fact depend, or have depended, upon high risk acts of violence, there have been great temptations to avoid too high principles. In many feuding societies the principal social problem appears not to have been how to stop feuds, but how to get reluctant protagonists to act in such a manner as to protect vulnerable members or avenge them. Miller, C*hoosing the Avenger: Some Aspects of the Bloodfeud in Medieval Iceland and England*, 1 LAW AND HIST. REV. 159, 160–62, 175 (1983).

[39] See the corpus of Miller's work on the Icelandic feuds. *Id.* at 175–94. *See also* W. Miller, *Gift, Sale, Payment, Raid: Case Studies in the Negotiation and Classification of Exchange in Medieval Iceland*, 61 SPECULUM 18–50 (1986); *cf.* E. AYERS, VENGEANCE AND JUSTICE CRIME AND PUNISHMENT IN THE 19TH CENTURY AMERICAN SOUTH 18 (1984) ("Honor and legalism . . . are incompatible . . .").

[40] For example, the account of the dispute within Shi'ite legal theory as to whether it was permissible to set up an avowedly Shiah government before the advent of the Twelfth Imam reflects this dichotomy in a religious context. See R. MOTTAHEDEH, THE MANTLE OF THE PROPHET: RELIGION AND POLITICS IN IRAN 172–73 (1985). According to Shi'ite belief, only the advent of this "Imam of the age" would bring the possibility of a perfect Islamic political community. *Id.* at 92–93.

they be rendered intelligible—that they be both subject to interpretation and to the specialized and constrained forms of behavior that are "roles." And the behavior within roles that we expect can neither exist without the interpretations which explain the otherwise meaningless patterns of strong action and inaction, nor be intelligible without understanding the deeds they are designed to effectuate.

Legal interpretation may be the act of judges or citizens, legislators or presidents, draft resisters or right-to-life protesters. Each kind of interpreter speaks from a distinct institutional location. Each has a differing perspective on factual and moral implications of any given understanding of the Constitution. The understanding of each will vary as roles and moral commitments vary. But considerations of word, deed, and role will always be present in some degree. The relationships among these three considerations are created by the practical, violent context of the practice of legal interpretation, and therefore constitute the most significant aspect of the legal interpretive process.

III. Interpretation and Effective Action: The Case of Criminal Sentencing

The bonded character of legal interpretation can be better appreciated by further unpacking a standard judicial act—the imposition of a sentence in a criminal case—this time from the judge's perspective. Such an act has few of the problematic remedial and role complications that have occupied commentators on the judicial role with regard to affirmative relief in institutional reform litigation or complex "political questions" cases.[41] In imposing sentences in criminal cases, judges are doing something clearly within their province. I do not mean to suggest that there are not disagreements about how the act should be carried out—whether with much or little discretion, whether attending more to objective and quantifiable criteria or to subjective and qualitative ones. But the act is and long has been a judicial one, and one which requires no strange or new modes of interaction with other officials or citizens.

Taken for granted in this judicial act is the structure of cooperation that ensures, we hope, the effective domination of the present and prospective victim of state violence—the convicted defendant. The role of judge becomes dangerous, indeed, whenever the conditions for domination of the prisoner and his allies are absent. Throughout history we have seen the products of ineffective domination in occasional trials in our country and in many instances in other nations.[42] The imposition of a sentence thus involves the roles of police, jailers or other enforcers who will restrain the prisoner (or set him free subject to effective conditions for future restraint) upon the order of the judge, and guards who will secure the prisoner from rescue and who will protect the judge, prosecutors, witnesses and jailers from revenge.

---

[41] My argument is not simply that there are prudential considerations in some sub-class of cases that render it wise or politic or necessary for the judge to defer to supposed wishes or policies of other political actors. Rather, my point here is that in every act—even one thought to "being" to judges—there is a necessary element of deference to the requirements of transforming judicial thought into violent action.

[42] Ineffective domination has resulted, for example, in the extraordinary security precautions that take place in the more significant mafia trials in Italy. It is reflected in the failures of Weimar justice. *See* P. GAY, WEIMAR CULTURE: THE OUTSIDER AS INSIDER 20–21 (1968). We ought not to assume that our own legal system is entirely free from such problems. While judges, on the whole, have fared remarkably well given the number of people whom they injure, there are occasional instances of violence directed at judges. And the problem of protecting witnesses is a persistent and serious one for the criminal justice system.

The judge in imposing a sentence normally takes for granted the role structure which might be analogized to the "transmission" of the engine of justice. The judge's interpretive authorization of the "proper" sentence can be carried out as a deed only because of these others; a bond between word and deed obtains only because a system of social cooperation exists. That system guarantees the judge massive amounts of force—the conditions of effective domination—if necessary. It guarantees—or is supposed to—a relatively faithful adherence to the word of the judge in the deeds carried out against the prisoner.

A. Revealing Latent Role Factors

If the institutional structure—the system of roles—gives the judge's understanding its effect, thereby transforming understanding into "law," so it confers meaning on the deeds which effect this transformation, thereby legitimating them as "lawful." A central task of the legal interpreter is to attend to the problematic aspects of the integration of role, deed, and word, not only where the violence (i.e., enforcement) is lacking for meaning, but also where meaning is lacking for violence.

In a nation like ours, in which the conditions of state domination are rarely absent, it is too easy to assume that there will be faithful officials to carry out what the judges decree, and judges available to render their acts lawful. Just how crucial this taken-for-granted structure is may be appreciated by examining a case in which it is lacking. The decisions by Judge Herbert Stern in *United States v. Tiede*[43] display an unusually lucid appreciation of the significance of the institutional connections between the judicial word and the violent deeds it authorizes.

Judge Stern was (and is) a federal district judge in New Jersey. In 1979 he was appointed an Article II judge for the United States Court for Berlin. This unique event, the only convening of the Court for Berlin, was a response to the reluctance of West Germany to prosecute two skyjackers who had used a toy gun to threaten the crew of a Polish airliner en route from Gdansk to East Berlin and had forced it to land in West Berlin. The formal status of Berlin as an "occupied" city enabled the Germans to place the responsibility for prosecution of the skyjacker-refugees upon the Americans.[44]

Stern wrote a moving account of the unusual trial which ensued, including his long struggle with the United States government over the general question of whether the Constitution of the United States would govern the proceedings. After a jury trial, opposed by the prosecution, and a verdict of guilty on one of the charges, Stern was required to perform the "simple" interpretive act of imposing the appropriate sentence. As a matter of interpreting the governing materials on sentencing it might indeed have been a "simple" act—one in which relatively unambiguous German law was relatively unambiguously to be applied by virtue of American law governing a court of occupation.[45]

---

[43] 86 F.R.D. 227 (U.S. Ct. for Berlin 1979). The reported opinion encompasses only certain procedural questions that arose in the trial, primarily the question of whether the defendants were entitled to a jury trial. A comprehensive account of the trial and the various rulings made during its course can be found in H. STERN, JUDGMENT IN BERLIN (1984).

[44] H. STERN, *supra* note 43, at 3–61.

[45] There were several significant interpretive issues involved in the sentencing other than the one treated below: for example, whether an offer of a deal by the prosecution to the defendant in return for not persisting with the demand for a jury trial should operate to limit any sentence imposed to one to more severe than the proffered deal, *id.* at 344–45, and whether the judge was obligated to apply German law which carried a mandatory minimum sentence of three years for the offense of which Tiede was convicted, *id.* at 350–55.

Stern brilliantly illuminated the defects in such a chain of reasoning. The judicial interpretive act in sentencing issues in a deed—the actual performance of the violence of punishment upon a defendant. But these two—judicial word and punitive deed—are connected only by the social cooperation of many others, who in their roles as lawyers, police, jailers, wardens, and magistrates perform the deeds which judicial words authorize. Cooperation among these officials is usually simply assumed to be present, but, of course, the conditions which normally ensure the success of this cooperation may fail in a variety of ways.

This is Judge Stern's account of his sentencing of the defendant, Hans Detlef Alexander Tiede:

> Gentlemen [addressing the State Department and Justice Department lawyers], I will not give you this defendant . . . I have kept him in your custody now for nine months, nearly . . . You have persuaded me. I believe, now, that you recognize no limitations of due process . . .
>
> I don't have to be a great prophet to understand that there is probably not a great future for the United States Court for Berlin here. [Stern had just been officially "ordered" not to proceed with a civil case brought against the United States in Stern's Court. The case was a last ditch attempt in a complicated proceeding in which the West Berlin government had acquired park land—allegedly in violation of German law—for construction of a housing complex for the United States Army Command in Berlin. The American occupation officials had refused to permit the German courts to decide the case as it affected the interests of the occupation authority. American Ambassador Walter Stoessel had officially written Stern on the day before the sentencing that "your appointment as a Judge of the United States Court for Berlin does not extend to this matter."[46]]
>
> . . .
>
> Under those circumstances, who will be here to protect Tiede if I give him to you for four years? Viewing the Constitution as nonexistent, considering yourselves not restrained in any way, who will stand between you and him? What judge? What independent magistrate do you have here? What independent magistrate will you permit here?
>
> When a judge sentences, he commits a defendant to the custody—in the United States he says, "I commit to the custody of the Attorney General of the United States"— et cetera. Here I suppose he says, I commit to the custody of the Commandant, or the Secretary of State, or whatever. . . . I will not do it. Not under these circumstances. . . .
>
> I sentence this defendant to time served. You . . . are a free man right now.[47]

Herbert Stern's remarkable sentence is not simply an effective, moving plea for judicial independence, a plea against the subservience which Stern's government tried to impose. It is a dissection of the anatomy of criminal punishment in a constitutional system. As such, it reveals the interior role of the judicial word in sentencing. It reveals the necessity of a latent role structure to render the judicial utterance morally intelligible. And it proclaims the moral unintelligibility of routine judicial utterance when the structure is no longer there. Almost all judicial utterance becomes deed through the acts of others—acts embedded in roles. The judge must see, as Stern did, that the meaning of her words may change when the

[46] *Id.* at 353.
[47] *Id.* at 370.

roles of these others change. We tend overwhelmingly to assume that constitutional violence is always performed within institutionally sanctioned limits and subject to the institutionally circumscribed, role-bound action of others. Stern uncovered the unreliability of that assumption in the Berlin context and "reinterpreted" his sentence accordingly.[48]

B. The Death Sentence as an Interpretive Act of Violence

The questions of whether the death sentence is constitutionally permissible and, if it is, whether to impose it, are among the most difficult problems a judge encounters. While the grammar of the capital sentence may appear to be similar to that of any other criminal sentence, the capital sentence as interpretive act is unique in at least three ways. The judge must interpret those constitutional and other legal texts which speak to the question of the proper or permissible occasions for imposition of a capital sentence. She must understand the texts in the context of an application that prescribes the killing of another person. And she must act to set in motion the acts of others which will in the normal course of events end with someone else killing the convicted defendant. Our judges do not ever kill the defendants themselves. They do not witness the execution. Yet, they are intensely aware of the deed their words authorize.[49]

The confused and emotional situation which now prevails with respect to capital punishment in the United States is in several ways a product of what I have described as the bonded character of legal interpretation—the complex structure of relationships between word and deed. To any person endowed with the normal inhibitions against the imposition of pain and death, the deed of capital punishment entails a special measure of the reluctance and abhorrence which constitute the gulf that must be bridged between interpretation and action. Because in capital punishment the action or *deed* is extreme and irrevocable, there is pressure placed on the *word*—the interpretation that establishes the legal justification for the act.[50] At the same time, the fact that capital punishment constitutes the most plain, the most deliberate, and the most thoughtful manifestation of legal interpretation as violence makes the imposition of the sentence an especially powerful test of the

---

[48] Judge Stern confronted an unusual situation—no independent system of courts, and no explicit denial by those in control of official violence that their power was constitutionally limited. In a sense the situation was one of *de jure* lawlessness. But Stern's reasoning reaches beyond the case at hand; it may be extended to include, for example, the *de facto* state of lawlessness that attends life in many United States prisons. Institutional reform litigation— whether applied to prisons, schools, or hospitals—entails complex questions of judicial remedial power. Very often these questions are framed around problems of discretion in the administration of remedies. When deciding whether to issue an injunction, judges often "interpret" the law in light of the difficulties involved in effectuating their judgments. But Stern's decision in Tiede pursues a different path. A judge may or may not be able to change the deeds of official violence, but she may always withhold the justification for this violence. She may or may not be able to bring a good prison into being, but she can refrain from sentencing anyone to a constitutionally inadequate one. Some judges have in fact followed this course. *See, e.g.,* Barnes v. Government of the Virgin Islands, 415 F. Supp. 1218 (D.V.I. 1976).

[49] Contrast the discreet distance judges now keep from capital sentences with the pageant of capital punishment in Hay, *Property, Authority and the Criminal Law,* in ALBIONíS FATAL TREE: CRIME SOCIETY IN EIGHTEENTH-CENTURY ENGLAND 28–29 (1975).

[50] This pressure for more certain justification of the death sentence lies behind the development of the "super due process" position with regard to death penalty cases. *See, e.g.,* Radin, *Cruel Punishment and Respect for Persons: Super Due Process for Death,* 53 S. CAL. L. REV. 1143 (1980) (describing Supreme Court's Eighth Amendment procedural safeguards). No more powerful statement of the ultimate implications of this position is to be found than in C. BLACK, CAPITAL PUNISHMENT: THE INEVITABILTY OF CAPRICE AND MISTAKE (2d ed. 1981)

faith and commitment of the interpreters.[51] Not even the facade of civility, where it exists, can obscure the violence of a death sentence.

Capital cases, thus, disclose far more of the structure of judicial interpretation than do other cases. Aiding this disclosure is the agonistic character of law: The defendant and his counsel search for and exploit any part of the structure that may work to their advantage. And they do so to an extreme degree in a matter of life and death.[52]

Thus, in the typical capital case in the United States, the judge is constantly reminded of that which the defense constantly seeks to exploit: The structure of interdependent roles that Judge Stern found to be potentially lacking in Berlin in the *Tiede* case. Consider. Not only do the actors in these roles carry out the judicial decision—they await it! All of them know that the judges will be called upon, time and again, to consider exhaustively all interpretive avenues that the defense counsel might take to avoid the sentence. And they expect that no capital sentence will in fact be carried out without several substantial delays during which judges consider some defense not yet fully decided by that or other courts.[53] The almost stylized action of the drama requires that the jailers stand visibly ready to receive intelligence of the judicial act—even if it be only the act of deciding to take future action. The stay of execution, though it be nothing—literally nothing—as an act of *textual* exegesis, nonetheless constitutes an important form of constitutional interpretation. For it shows the violence of the warden and executioner to be linked to the judge's deliberative act of understanding. The stay of execution, the special line open, permits, or more accurately, requires the inference to be drawn from the failure of the stay of execution. That too is the visible tie between word and deed.[54] These wardens, these guards, these doctors, jump to the judge's turn. If the deed is done, it is a constitutional deed—one integrated to and justifiable under the proper understanding of the word. In short, it is the stay, the drama of the possibility of the stay, that renders the execution constitutional violence, that makes the deed an act of interpretation.

For, after all, executions I can find almost anywhere. If people disappear, if they die suddenly and without ceremony in prison, quite apart from any articulated justification and authorization for their demise, then we do not have constitutional interpretation at the heart of this deed, nor do we have the deed, the death, at the heart of the Constitution. The problem of incapacity or unwillingness to ensure a

---

[51] The decade-long moratorium on death sentences may quite intelligibly be understood as a failure of will on the part of a majority of the Court which had, at some point in that period, decided *both* that there was to be no general constitutional impediment to the imposition of the death sentence, *and* that they were not yet prepared to see the states begin a series of executions. Of course, throughout the period, new procedural issues were arising. But it does not seem far-fetched to suppose that there was also a certain squeamishness about facing the implications of the majority position on the constitutional issue. *See* Note, *Summary Processes and the Rule of Law: Expediting Death Penalty Cases in the Federal Courts*, 95 YALE L. J. 349, 354 (1985) (citing Court's "often uncertain and tortuous" death penalty jurisprudence during this period).

[52] *See, e.g.,* Sullivan v. Wainwright, 464 U.S. 109, 112 (1983) (Burger, C.J., concurring in denial of stay) (Chief Justice Burger accused death penalty lawyers of turning "the administration of justice into a sporting contest").

[53] The current Court (or a majority of it) is very hostile to such delays. Barefoot v. Estelle, 463 U.S. 880 (1983), Zant v. Stephens, 462 U.S. 862 (1983), California v. Ramos, 463 U.S. 992 (1983), and Barclay v. Florida, 463 U.S. 939 (1983), mark a reversal of the trend to permit or encourage a full hearing of all plausible claims or defenses. Nonetheless, even with this new impatience to be on with the execution, there are usually substantial delays at some point before execution.

[54] Consider the opinions of the various Justices in Rosenberg v. United States, 346 U.S. 273 (1953), vacating, in special term, the stay of the sentence of death that had been granted by Justice Douglas. For an analysis of the deliberations, see Parrish, *Cold War Justice: The Supreme Court and the Rosenbergs*, 82 AM. HIST. REV. 805–42 (1977).

strong, virtually certain link between judicial utterance and violent deed in this respect characterizes certain legal systems at certain times.[55] It characterized much of the American legal system well into the twentieth century; lynching, for example, was long thought to be a peculiarly American scandal.[56] It was a scandal which took many forms. Often it entailed taking the punishment of alleged offenders out of the hands of courts entirely. But sometimes it entailed the carrying out of death sentences without abiding by the ordered processes of appeals and post-conviction remedies. Such was the outcome, for example, of the notorious "Leo Frank" case.[57]

The plain fact is that we have come a good way since 1914 with respect to our expectations that persons accused of capital crimes will be given a trial, will be sentenced properly, and will live to see the appointed time of the execution of their sentence. In fact, we have come to expect near perfect coordination of those whose role it is to inflict violence subject to the interpretive decisions of the judges. We have even come to expect coordinated cooperation in securing all plausible judicial interpretations on the subject.[58]

Such a well-coordinated form of violence is an achievement. The careful social understandings designed to accomplish the violence that is capital punishment, or to refrain from that act, are not fortuitous or casual products of circumstance. Rather, they are the products of design, tied closely to the secondary rules and principles which provide clear criteria for the recognition of these and other interpretive acts as, first and foremost, *judicial* acts. Their "meaning" is always secondary to their provenance. No wardens, guards or executioners wait for a telephone call from the latest constitutional law scholar, jurisprudence or critic before executing prisoners, no matter how compelling the interpretations of these others may be. And, indeed, they await the word of judges only insofar as that word carries with it the formal indicia of having been spoken in the judicial capacity. The social cooperation critical to the constitutional form of cooperation in violence is, therefore, also predicated upon the recognition of the judicial role and the recognition of the one whose utterance performs it.

There are, of course, some situations in which the judicial role is not well-defined but is contested. Nonetheless, social cooperation in constitutional violence as we know it requires at least that it be very clear who speaks as a judge and when. The hierarchical ordering among judicial voices must also be clear or subject to clarification. We have established, then, the necessity for rules and principles that locate authoritative interpreters and prescribe action on the basis of what they say. The rules and principles that locate authoritative voices for the purposes of action point to the defect in a model of judicial interpretation that

---

[55] *See, e.g.,* R. BROWN, STRAIN OF VIOLENCE, HISTORICAL STUDIES OF AMERICAN VIOLENCE AND VIGILANTISM 144–79 (1975) (discussing legal attitudes toward American vigilantism).

[56] *See* R. Zangando, THE NAACP CRUSADE AGAINST LYNCHING, 1909–1950, at 9–11 (1980).

[57] Leo Frank was a Jewish New Yorker managing a pencil factory in Georgia. He was accused of having raped and murdered a 14-year-old employee of the factory. The trial (and conviction) took place amidst a mob atmosphere in which the Court was required to warn the defendant and his counsel not to be present in the courtroom at the rendering of the verdict lest they be violently harmed. After Frank's conviction he was forcibly removed from a prison labor gang and lynched. The case was instrumental in the formation of the B'nai Brith Anti-Defamation League. Collateral relief was denied by the Supreme Court in Frank v. Mangum, 237 U.S. 309 (1915), over the strong dissent of Justice Holmes and Justice Hughes.

[58] I am not, of course, suggesting that unauthorized violence on the part of police, jailers, etc., no longer exists. But the quasi-public position that the "justice" of the mob should supplant the ordered process of the courts is no longer prevalent. See the extraordinary article by Charles Bonaparte, *Lynch Law and its Remedy*, 8 YALE L. J. 335, 336 (1899) (arguing that underlying purpose of lynching is "not to violate, but to vindicate, the law; or, to speak more accurately, . . . its "adjective" part . . . is disregarded that its 'substantiative' [sic] part may be preserved").

centers around a single coherent and consistent mind at work. For here in the United States there is no set of secondary rules and principles more fundamental than those which make it impossible for any single judge, however Herculean her understanding of the law, ever to have the last word on legal meaning as it affects real cases. In the United States—with only trivial exceptions—no judge sitting alone on a significant legal issue is immune from appellate review. Conversely, whenever any judge sits on the court of last resort on a significant legal issue, that judge does not sit alone. A complex of secondary rules determines this situation. These rules range from the statutes which generally give a right to at least one appeal from final judgments of trial courts, to special statutes which require that there be appellate review of death sentences, to the constitutional guarantee that the writ of habeas corpus not be suspended.[59] Final appellate courts in the United States have always had at least three judges. Some state constitutions specify the number. No explicit provision in the United States Constitution defines the Supreme Court in such a way that requires that it be made up of more than a single judge. But both invariant practice and basic understandings since 1789 have made the idea of a single-Justice Supreme Court a practical absurdity. Given the clarity of the expectation that Supreme judicial bodies be plural, it seems doubtful to me whether such an imaginary Court should be held to satisfy the constitutional requirement that there be a Supreme Court.[60]

If some hypothetical Herculean judge should achieve an understanding of constitutional and social texts—an interpretation—such that she felt the death penalty to be a permissible and appropriate punishment in a particular case, she would be confronted at once with the problem of translating that conviction into a deed. Her very understanding of the constitutionality of the death penalty and the appropriateness of its imposition would carry with it—as part of the understanding—the knowledge that she could not carry out the sentence herself. The most elementary understanding of our social practice of violence ensures that a judge know that she herself cannot actually pull the switch. This is not a trivial convention. For it means that someone else will have the duty and opportunity to pass upon what the judge has done. Were the judge a trial judge, and should she hand down an order to execute, there would be another judge to whom application could be made to stay or reverse her decision. The fact that *someone else* has to carry out the execution means that this someone else may be confronted with two pieces of paper: let us say a warrant for execution of the sentence of death at a specified time and place and a stay of execution from an appellate tribunal. The someone else—the warden, for simplicity's sake—is expected to determine which of these two pieces of paper to act upon according to some highly arbitrary, hierarchical principles which have nothing to do with the relative merits or demerits of the arguments which justify the respective substantive positions.

It is crucial to note here that if the warden should cease paying relatively automatic heed to the pieces of paper which flow in from the judges according to these arbitrary and sometimes rigid hierarchical rules and principles, the judges

[59] *See, e.g.,* 28 U.S.C. § 1291 (1982) (providing for appeals as of right from final decisions of district courts); *Id.* §§ 46(b), 46(c) (providing for hearing of cases by U.S. Courts of Appeals in panels of three judges unless rehearing en banc is ordered); U.S. CONST. art. I, § 9, cl. 2 (protecting writ of habeus corpus).

[60] 28 U.S.C. § 1 (1982) (providing for Supreme Court of nine Justices, of whom six constitute a quorum). The one rather significant historical exception to the generalization in the text gives me some pause with respect to the conclusion about the constitutionality of a single-Justice Supreme Court. It is true, of course, that the Chancellor was, in form, a single-justice high court. And, while it has not been the rule, some American court systems have preserved a chancery, though often with multi-judge appellate courts in equity.

would lose their capacity to do violence. They would be left with only the opportunity to persuade the warden and his men to do violence. Conversely, the warden and his men would lose their capacity to shift to the judge primary moral responsibility for the violence which they themselves carry out. They would have to pass upon the justifications for violence in every case themselves, thereby turning the trial into a sort of preliminary hearing. There are, indeed, many prisons in this world that bear some resemblance to this hypothetical situation. There are systems in which the most significant punishment decisions are made by those who either perform or have direct supervisory authority over the performance of the violence itself.

We have done something strange in our system. We have rigidly separated the act of interpretation—of understanding what ought to be done—from the carrying out of this "ought to be done" through violence. At the same time we have, at least in the criminal law, rigidly linked the carrying out of judicial orders to the act of judicial interpretation by relatively inflexible hierarchies of judicial utterances and firm obligations on the part of penal officials to heed them. Judges are both separated from, and inextricably linked to, the acts they authorize.

This strange yet familiar attribute of judging in America has the effect of ensuring that no judge *acts* alone. Ronald Dworkin's "Judge as Hercules"[61] may appear to be a useful construct for understanding how a judge's mind ought to work. But it is misleading precisely because it suggests, if it does not require, a context which, in America, is never present. There may or may not be any sense in thinking about a judicial understanding of the law apart from its application. But one thing is near certain. The application of legal understanding in our domain of pain and death will always require the active or passive acquiescence of other judicial minds. It is possible to wear this point down to the most trite observation of professional practice. A judge who wishes to transform her understanding into deed must, if located on a trial court, attend to ensuring that her decision not be reversed. If on an appellate court, she must attend to getting at least one other judge to go along. It is a commonplace that many "majority" opinions bear the scars or marks of having been written primarily to keep the majority. Many a trial court opinion bears the scars of having been written primarily to avoid reversal.

Now the question arises, which is the true act of legal interpretation? The hypothetical understanding of a single mind placed in the admittedly hypothetical position of being able to render final judgments sitting alone? Or the actual products of judges acting under the constraint of potential group oversight of all decisions that are to be made real through collective violence? The single decision of a hypothetical Hercules is likely to be more articulate and coherent than the collective decision of many judges who may make compromises to arrive at that decision. But Hyporcules does not and cannot carry the force of collective violence. This defect is intrinsic to the definition of legal interpretation as a mental activity of a person rather than as the violent activity of an organization of people.

So let us be explicit. If it seems a nasty thought that death and pain are at the center of legal interpretation, so be it. It would not be better were there only a

---

[61] Dworkin's Hercules appears first in the article "Hard Cases." Dworkin, *Hard Cases*, 89 HARV. L. REV. 1057 (1975). Hercules lives on in LAW'S EMPIRE, *supra* note 2, at 239–75, wherein he assumes the mantle of a model judge of "integrity," which seems not to be primarily a personal quality for Dworkin but an interpretive posture which values intellectual consistency and coherence.
Id. at 164–67.

community of argument, of readers and writers of texts, of interpreters. As long as death and pain are part of our political world, it is essential that they be at the center of the law. The alternative is truly unacceptable—that they be within our polity but outside the discipline of the *collective* decision rules and the individual efforts to achieve outcomes through those rules. The fact that we require many voices is not, then, an accident or pecularity of our jurisdictional rules. It is intrinsic to whatever achievement is possible in the domesticating of violence.

CONCLUSION

There is a worthy tradition that would have us hear the judge as a voice of reason; see her as the embodiment of principle. The current academic interest in interpretation, the attention to community of meaning and commitment, is apologetic neither in its intent or effect. The trend is, by and large, an attempt to hold a worthy ideal before what all would agree is an unredeemed reality. I would not quarrel with the impulse that leads us to this form of criticism.

There is, however, danger in forgetting the limits which are intrinsic to this activity of legal interpretation; in exaggerating the extent to which any interpretation rendered as part of the act of state violence can ever constitute a common and coherent meaning. I have emphasized two rather different kinds of limits to the commonality and coherence of meaning that can be achieved. One kind of limit is a practical one which follows from the social organization of legal violence. We have seen that in order to do that violence safely and effectively, responsibility for the violence must be shared; law must operate as a system of cues and signals to many actors who would otherwise be unwilling, incapable or irresponsible in their violent acts. This social organization of violence manifests itself in the secondary rules and principles which generally ensure that no single mind and no single will can generate the violent outcomes that follow from interpretive commitments. No single individual can render any interpretation operative as law—as authority for the violent act. While a convergence of understandings on the part of all relevant legal actors is not necessarily impossible, it is, in fact, very unlikely. And, of course, we cannot flee from the multiplicity of minds and voices that the social organization of law-as-violence requires to some hypothetical decision process that would aggregate the many voices into one. We know that—aside from dictatorship—there is no aggregation rule that will necessarily meet elementary conditions for rationality in the relationships among the social choices made.[62]

While our social decision rules cannot guarantee coherence and rationality of meaning, they can and do generate violent action which may well have a distinct coherent meaning for at least one of the relevant actors. We are left, then, in this actual world of the organization of law-as-violence with decisions whose meaning is not likely to be coherent if it is common, and not likely to be common if it is coherent.

This practical, contingent limit upon legal interpretation is, however, the less important and less profound of the two kinds of limits I have presented. For if we truly attend to legal interpretation as it is practiced on the field of fear, pain,

[62] K. ARROW, SOCIAL CHOICE AND INDIVIDUAL VALUES (1951).

and death, we find that the principal impediment to the achievement of common and coherent meaning is a necessary limit, intrinsic to the activity. Judges, officials, resisters, martyrs, wardens, convicts, may or may not share common texts; they may or may not share a common vocabulary, a common cultural store of gestures and rituals; they may or may not share a common philosophical framework. There will be in the immense human panorama a continuum of degrees of commonality in all of the above. But as long as legal interpretation is constitutive of violent behavior as well as meaning, as long as people are committed to using or resisting the social organizations of violence in making their interpretations real, there will always be a tragic limit to the common meaning that can be achieved.

The perpetrator and victim of organized violence will undergo achingly disparate significant experiences. For the perpetrator, the pain and fear are remote, unreal, and largely unshared. They are, therefore, almost never made a part of the interpretive artifact, such as the judicial opinion. On the other hand, for those who impose the violence the justification is important, real and carefully cultivated. Conversely, for the victim, the justification for the violence recedes in reality and significance in proportion to the overwhelming reality of the pain and fear that is suffered.

Between the idea and the reality of common meaning falls the shadow of the violence of law, itself.

Frank Michelman

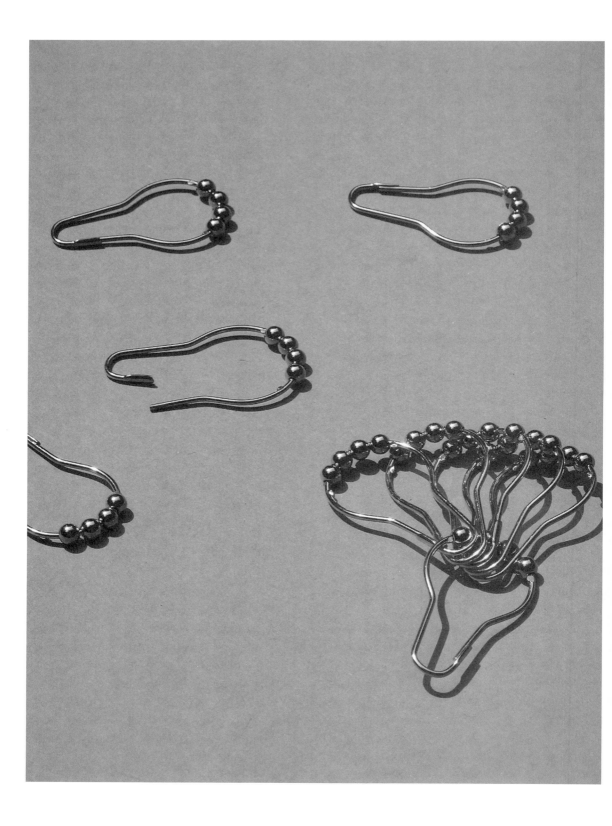

Frank Michelman

IN THE 1980s, an important group of American legal theorists, unsatisfied by the efforts of their predecessors to stabilize law through invocations of legal process or economic efficiency, began to look for guidance to "theories of the good"— philosophic traditions that hold up visions of the good life and the good society and urge that political and legal systems be structured so as to foster those visions. Of the many theories of this general sort they explored, the most influential by far was classical republicanism.

To understand the character and attraction of republicanism, one needs some historiographic background. For much of the twentieth century, the overwhelming majority of historians believed (and taught) that the American Revolution was powered by one or both of two impulses. (Simplifying a bit), either the North American colonists, influenced by the writings of John Locke and Adam Smith, became convinced that British taxation policies encroached upon their natural rights to liberty and property and thus justified a rebellion, or North American merchants, chafing under the restrictions imposed by the imperial authorities, sought through independence a way to enhance their private fortunes (and then used the federal Constitution to curb the popular uprising that they had crassly provoked). In the late 1960s, a new cohort of historians led by Bernard Bailyn, Gordon Wood, and J.G.A. Pocock ventured a dramatically different interpretation of the Revolution. Political culture in the North American colonies, they argued, was dominated, not by the liberal ideology of Locke and Smith, but by the fundamentally different ideology of republicanism. Originating in the writings of Aristotle, Machiavelli, and James Harrington, later refined by a dissident group of English politicians known as the Commonwealthmen, that ideology revolved around the notions that a good life is a virtuous life, that virtue consists partly of a willingness to subordinate one's private desires and interests to the common good, and that only through active participation in the deliberative politics of a republic can a person fully realize his self. Viewed through the lenses of those convictions, the British policies of the 1760s and 1770s seemed to the colonists irremediably "corrupt." If they wished to preserve their own republican governments and culture, the colonists became convinced, they needed to cut themselves free of the rotting British body politic.

This new interpretation gained currency quickly. Other historians soon began to excavate republican ideas from the residues of other episodes in American political history—the platforms of both the Federalist and the Antifederalist parties of the 1780s, the Jacksonian and Whig persuasions in the 1830s and '40s, antebellum working-class movements, late nineteenth-century Populism, even early twentieth-century protest movements. Republicanism, it began to appear, though little noticed previously by historians, had in fact been a major—perhaps *the* major—tradition in American politics.

In the 1980s, an important group of law professors began to take notice of this outpouring of historical scholarship and started to explore its implications for legal theory. One of the earliest and most important essays in this vein was Cass Sunstein's 1985 article, "Interest Groups in American Law." In its opening pages, Sunstein made his intentions plain:

> At the normative level, the purpose of this article is to help revive aspects of an attractive conception of governance—we may call it republican—to point out its often neglected but nonetheless prominent place in the thought of the framers, and to suggest its availability as a foundation from which judges and others might evaluate political processes and outcomes.

In the 1780s, Sunstein argued, the emergent American nation "faced a choice between two different conceptions of politics": a republican vision, centered on the ideals of civic virtue and deliberative democracy; and a "pluralist" vision, which depicted politics as a "struggle among self-interested groups for scarce social resources." In his view, the principal achievement of the Federalist Party—and of James Madison in particular—was to fashion a hybrid of these two perspectives. The Madisonian blend, encapsulated in The Federalist numbers 10 and 51, acknowledged that factionalism (the formation of groups that seek through politics to advance their own interests) was inevitable, but sought to curb it (and thus preserve a conception of democracy as the collective pursuit of the public good) through careful organization of the system of government—specifically, through an increase in the size of the polity, through electoral processes that "filtered" statesmen from the body of the citizenry, and through a system of "checks and balances." Sunstein's original contribution to this familiar story was his claim that Madison and his colleagues sought, through these arrangements, to preserve an environment in which national legislators would behave in the same selfless, virtuous fashion as did individual citizens in traditional republican ideology.

What did all this have to do with law? Sunstein claimed that several doctrines developed by the courts over two centuries of American history are best understood as efforts to prevent or at least discourage national legislators from deviating from this ideal. In constitutional law, those doctrines included the "rationality requirement" developed under the auspices of the due-process clause of the Fourteenth Amendment, the modern interpretations of the contracts clause and the "public use" requirement of the eminent-domain clause, the non-delegation doctrine, and "strict scrutiny" of certain kinds of legislation under the equal-protection clause. In administrative law, they included the "hard-look doctrine" and the requirement that administrative officials disclose all "ex parte contacts" with people or groups they are supposed to be regulating. Sunstein then argued that the courts could and should go further in these directions, intervening into legislative processes even more aggressively to ensure that legislators and officials of administrative agencies engage in genuine deliberation "instead of responding mechanically to interest-group pressures."

In three respects, Sunstein's article set the tone for what might be described as the initial wave of republican legal scholarship. First, it depicted republicanism as a coherent political theory that had influenced substantially the draftsmen of the federal Constitution. Second, it argued that republicanism had had a significant influence on a variety of legal doctrines. Third, it contended that the republican vision was commendable and convincing, and thus should be invoked and enforced even more vigorously in the future by lawmakers of various sorts.

In the late 1980s, several articles sharing all or most of these features appeared in American legal periodicals. Among the legal reforms they urged were the following: cities and organizations that afforded meaningful opportunities for the exercise of citizenship should be accorded more autonomy and power; pornography and other forms of expression corrosive of civic virtue should be curbed; group libel laws and limits on campaign contributions should not be deemed to violate the First Amendment; businesses should be discouraged from moving their factories and thereby disrupting local communities; and the Fifth Amendment's "takings" provision should be construed to incorporate the Framers' beliefs that landowners must sometimes subordinate their individual interests to the common weal.

This rapidly growing body of literature came under attack from two directions. First, historians of various stripes expressed dismay. Those who had been instrumental in the reconceptualization of the origins of the American Revolution were troubled by what they saw as the anachronistic efforts of legal scholars to lift the ideology of republicanism from its original cultural and political context and apply it to contemporary problems. Historians skeptical of the whole enterprise—who doubted that a coherent ideology of republicanism ever existed or that, if it had, that it had a significant impact on the thinking of the revolutionary generation—believed that the legal scholars were building their new edifice on sand. Second, a substantial group of legal scholars argued that republicanism was not an "attractive" belief system, worthy of greater attention, but a patriarchal, xenophobic, and reactionary outlook that, impressed on contemporary legal problems, would do more harm than good—and that, in any event, its tenets are "highly uncongenial to modern ontology and epistemology."

Frank Michelman's essay, "Law's Republic," is the premier example of what might be called the second wave of republican legal scholarship—a body of articles that sought to harness republicanism to the chariot of law in a fashion that could withstand these objections. Like Sunstein, Michelman contends that the principal theories of politics from which Americans might choose when making sense of their legal system are a pluralist vision and a republican vision. Also like Sunstein, Michelman argues that constitutional law could be improved by "serious and sympathetic (but not uncritical) reflection upon" the latter. But, in other respects, his argument is sharply different.

Most notably, Michelman acknowledges—indeed, insists—that some aspects of republicanism are repellent. For example, many of its historical manifestations have been militantly organicist, willing to extend membership in the political community only to persons who share a particular set of moral or religious commitments, deeply hostile to dissent and cultural experimentation. Other variants (for example, those associated with Rousseau and Miachiavelli) have located both virtue and wisdom in a "founding" individual or generation, assigning to all subsequent generations of citizens only the responsibility to resist the inevitable temptations to stray from the path marked out by the political Creators. Republicanisms of these sorts, he argues, offer us little guidance or assistance today. The organicist versions are "obnoxious," and the founder-centered versions diminish unacceptably the freedoms and responsibilities of citizens in the present. Fortunately, Michelman argues, the republican tradition also contains variants—or "resources"—from which can be fashioned a belief system more consistent with contemporary Americans' needs and self-understandings. Once purged of its exclusionary, hierarchical, and authoritarian tendencies, republicanism, he contends, can be a highly useful tool of political and constitutional analysis.

Next, despite these efforts to polish republicanism before putting it to work, Michelman, unlike Sunstein, does not rest his argument on the "attractiveness" of the worldview. To be sure, he conveys through his tone considerable affection for the republican conception of civic virtue and quotes with evident approval Hanna Pitken's famous definition of positive liberty, implicitly associating himself with her celebration of "a shared, collective, deliberate, active intervention in our fate." But he purports to adopt an agnostic posture toward the conceptions of the good life and the good society upon which the vision is founded:

> I am not here recommending strong republicanism. I do not know what is good for the soul. I do not know in what (if anything) personal freedom essentially consists. I do not know whether citizenship is a fundamental human good.

Finally, Michelman diverges from Sunstein in placing little weight on the historical pedigree of republicanism. Nothing in his argument hinges on the controversial contention that the members of the "founding generation" of Americans subscribed to the republican creed.

How, then, does he defend his claim that we should (indeed, we must) pay more attention to republicanism—specifically when interpreting the Constitution? Interestingly, he relies upon logic, what he describes at one point as "deduction." (Note the ironic echoes here of classical legal thought.) Central to our political heritage, he contends, are two propositions between which there is considerable tension: "first, that the American people are politically free insomuch as they are governed by themselves collectively, and, second, that the American people are politically free insomuch as they are governed by laws and not men." Our politics and law can be coherent, he contends, only if these two propositions can be reconciled. And how might that be done? Michelman argues that there are only three theories that might be capable of accomplishing the task. The first two candidates fail, leaving only one (republicanism) standing.

The first suitor is the principal rival of republicanism: pluralism. In this context, Michelman means not pluralism in the (good) sense of toleration of diverse lifestyles and beliefs, but pluralism in the narrower sense of a worldview "in which the primary interests of individuals appear as pre-political, and politics, accordingly, as a secondary instrumental medium for protecting or advancing those 'exogenous' interests"—an outlook founded upon a "deep distrust of people's capacities to communicate *persuasively* to one another their diverse normative experiences." Michelman concedes that it is not difficult, on these premises, to *justify* our constitutional system in a way that reconciles the principles of collective self-government and government by laws. Indeed, it's been done (often). The key idea is that the Constitution establishes a set of ground rules ("higher" laws) that enable self-government but also limit its scope. Such a system, arguably, is precisely what a group of citizens who both differ sharply on matters of importance and doubt their ability to persuade others concerning the merits of their own positions would, behind a "veil of ignorance" concerning the distribution of their preferences, select as the most congenial system of government. But such a familiar, liberal *justification* is not enough, Michelman contends. To provide a full, persuasive account of our constitutional regime, the pluralist vision would also need to supply a plausible narrative concerning how the

Frank Michelman

Constitution came to be drafted and ratified. That it cannot offer—or at least cannot offer without resorting to republican images of altruistic deliberations among virtuous citizens.

The second suitor is Bruce Ackerman's deservedly famous proposal that American constitutional history can be best described and justified as a series of cycles, each beginning with a short period in which large portions of the citizenry, provoked by a group of unusually far-sighted politicians, became energized and collectively refashioned the federal Constitution, followed by a long period in which the Supreme Court sought, more or less successfully, to defend the fruits of those founding moments against fluctuations in the sentiments of politicians and relatively disengaged voters. Though Michelman finds many aspects of this account attractive, it suffers, he contends, from one fundamental defect: it assigns to the judiciary an exclusively "benedictory" role, that of faithfully giving effect to the collective judgment of the People in the past, and denies to it any "prophetic," inventive responsibility. As such, Ackerman's account, Michelman claims, is incapable of making sense of such crucial acts of judicial leadership as the decision in *Brown v. Board of Education*.

How else might one generate a theory of politics in general and constitutional law in particular that accommodates Americans' shared sense of being both self-governing and governed by law? Republicanism, Michelman contends, offers us one intriguing approach. The key, he suggests, is the concept of "republican citizenship." To flesh out that concept, Michelman weaves together several analytical threads, some old, some new. In a classical republic, he argues, the exercise of citizenship might have entailed collective deliberation concerning the best way of implementing the ideals shared by all members of the community. But, in a modern, plural society, characterized by substantial differences among citizens on matters of public importance, citizenship demands something more: the willingness and ability of each member of the community to engage regularly in "a process of personal self-revision under social-dialogic stimulation." That ability and willingness, in turn, depend upon citizens regularly engaging persons with fundamentally different outlooks and orientations, not just in arenas conventionally thought of as "political," but in a wide variety of public and private settings. One important responsibility for the judiciary, Michelman contends, is preserving the conditions that foster such engagement—in which citizens frequently come into contact with identities sharply different from their own and, through such interactions, periodically re-conceive themselves in ways they do not experience as "coercive, invasive, or otherwise a violation of [their] identity or freedom." Left to their own devices, people will often shy away from such conditions, indulging their "self-enclosing tendency to assume their own moral completion as they are now." The courts can and should prevent them from doing so, partly by preventing the majority from denying, through law, full citizenship to members of minority groups, like homosexuals, whose conduct and self-conceptions might destabilize their own self-understandings.

One of the eye-opening features of this last, critical portion of Michelman's essay is the way that, like Levi-Strauss's "bricoleur," it refashions and then stitches together arguments deployed in radically different contexts by prior legal theorists: the "process theory" of constitutional law developed by John Ely; the critique of the public/private distinction developed by the legal realists; and insistence upon the ubiquity and value of "indeterminacy" in legal analysis developed both by the Realists and then more fully by the scholars affiliated with Critical Legal Studies. Integrating such disparate materials was a heroic undertaking.

Few legal scholars would be capable of such a feat; Michelman's background and extraordinarily far-ranging interests equipped him, perhaps uniquely, to attempt it. He was educated at Yale College and Harvard Law School, then served as a law clerk to Justice William Brennan of the United States Supreme Court. Since 1963, he has taught at Harvard, first as a professor in the law school, ultimately as the Robert Walmsley University Professor, an appointment that entitles him to offer courses in any department in the university. His teaching interests are remarkably diverse—ranging from Property Law, to Constitutional Theory, to Moral and Political Philosophy. His scholarship is equally adventuresome. He has written pioneering essays on the "takings" doctrine; on the relevance of Rawlsian political theory for Constitutional Law; on Habermas; on Pragmatism; on Democratic Theory; and on both the uses and the abuses of economic analysis of law. He has both applied and refined his reflections on these disparate topics through political activity on several levels—from participation in town government in Lexington, Massachusetts, to advising the Supreme Court of South Africa on the shaping and interpretation of that country's new constitution.

For a time, the synthesis he ventured in "Law's Republic" was highly influential among legal scholars and students. In 1987, roughly a thousand law professors packed a lecture hall during the annual meeting of the Association of American Law Schools to hear Michelman and Sunstein summarize their respective visions of republicanism and to defend their views against skeptics. During the next few years, explicit invocations of republicanism were common in casebooks and classrooms. Since then, the popularity of the theory has diminished a good deal, but it remains a formidable force in legal discourse, in part because no comparably evocative and integrative conception has emerged to take its place.

Substantively, how well does the argument of "Law's Republic" hold up? Answering that question is made easier by Michelman's remarkable willingness to identify the points of vulnerability in his analysis and to wrestle with them openly. He is refreshingly honest, for example, concerning the seriousness of the criticisms that might be made of the republican vision itself. And he is forthright in acknowledging the delicacy of his claim for its importance to contemporary legal issues. Based, as his thesis is, on a process of elimination, it could be toppled easily by the deployment of any other theory—less intricate, perhaps, or more obviously compatible with the shared experience of Americans—capable of reconciling what Michelman depicts as our seemingly competing commitments to the ideals of self-government and a government of laws.

One potential theory of this sort would begin by explicating the famous phrase, "a government of laws, not of men," in a fashion somewhat different from the way Michelman does. To an important group of political theorists, that slogan refers not to a state of affairs in which we are bound by rules established by our predecessors, but rather to a particular set of guidelines, sometimes referred to in the aggregate as "the rule of law," concerning the appropriate substance and form of legal norms. The most important of those guidelines are: the state should impose its will upon persons only through the promulgation (by lawmakers who do not know the identities of those who will be affected) and enforcement (by judges who are free from bias and immune to bribery or political pressure) of general, clear, well-publicized rules that are capable of being obeyed. These injunctions are said to grow out of and to help sustain several related principles that should be familiar to most Americans: like cases must be decided alike; no person is above the law; legal rules (especially criminal rules) should not be retroactive; and every person has a right to a "day in court" before legal sanctions are brought to bear upon him or her. If this is what is meant by "a government of laws," then the job of reconciling it with the ideal of popular sovereignty may be easier than Michelman believes. A polity that combined majority rule (and perhaps, though not necessarily, representative government) with fidelity to the guidelines itemized above would seem to fit the bill. The judiciary would have an important role in maintaining such a state of affairs—specifically, that of preventing the adoption or enforcement of laws inconsistent with the guidelines. But that role would be very different from the role sketched by Michelman. Republicanism, though compatible with such a solution, would not be required by it.

In short, to explain why republicanism, rather than democracy disciplined by fidelity to the "rule of law," is the best way of making sense of Americans' political ideals, proponents of this school of thought may be obliged to provide a substantive defense of the conceptions of the good life and good society around which republicanism revolves—a defense that Michelman, in this particular essay, is reluctant to offer.

WILLIAM FISHER

BIBLIOGRAPHY

The major works developing the new theory of the nature of republicanism and its impact on the American Revolution and its immediate aftermath were Bernard Bailyn, *The Ideological Origins of the American Revolution* (Cambridge, Mass.: Harvard University Press, 1967); Gordon S. Wood, *The Creation of the American Republic, 1776–1787* (Chapel Hill: University of North Carolina Press, 1969); and J.G.A. Pocock, *The Machiavellian Moment: Florentine Political Thought and the Atlantic Republican Tradition* (Princeton, N.J.: Princeton University Press, 1975). Works exploring the impact of republicanism on subsequent political and social movements in American history include: Lance Banning, *The Jeffersonian Persuasion: Evolution of a Party Ideology* (Ithaca, N.Y.: Cornell University Press, 1978); Drew R. McCoy, *The Elusive Republic: Political Economy in Jeffersonian America* (Chapel Hill, N.C.: University of North Carolina Press, 1980); Harry L. Watson, *Liberty and Power: The Politics of Jacksonian America* (New York: Noonday Press, 1990); Sean Wilentz, *Chants Democratic: New York City and the Rise of the American Working Class, 1788–1850* (New York: Oxford University Press, 1984); Thomas Brown, *Politics and Statesmanship: Essays on the American Whig Party* (New York: Columbia University Press, 1985); and Jerome Mushkat and Joseph Rayback, *Martin Van Buren: Law, Politics, and the Shaping of Republican Ideology* (DeKalb, Ill.: Northern Illinois University Press, 1997).

For studies of the "republican revival" within historical scholarship, see Robert E. Shalhope, "Toward a Republican Synthesis: The Emergence of an Understanding of Republicanism in American Historiography," *William & Mary Quarterly* 29 (1972): 49; *idem*, "Republicanism and Early American

Historiography," *William & Mary Quarterly*, 3rd series, 39 (April 1982): 334; Dorothy Ross, "The Liberal Tradition Revisited and the Republican Tradition Addressed," in *New Directions in American Intellectual History* (John Higham and Paul K. Conkin, eds., Baltimore: Johns Hopkins University Press, 1979), 116.

In addition to "Interest Groups in American Public Law," *Stanford Law Review* 38 (1985): 29 (discussed in the text), Cass Sunstein's efforts to connect this body of scholarship to legal issues include "Beyond the Republican Revival," *Yale Law Journal* 97 (1988): 1539; and "Factions, Self-Interest, and the APA: Four Lessons Since 1946," *Virginia Law Review* 72 (1986): 271. A response to some of his critics can be found in "The Idea of a Useable Past," *Columbia Law Review* 95 (1995): 601.

Other efforts by legal scholars to apply republicanism to contemporary problems include Gerald Frug, "The City as a Legal Concept," *Harvard Law Review* 93 (1980): 1057; *idem*, "Why Neutrality," *Yale Law Journal* 92 (1983): 1591; Suzanna Sherry, "Civic Virtue and the Feminine Voice in Constitutional Adjudication," *University of Virginia Law Review* 72 (1986): 543; *idem*, "Speaking of Virtue: A Republican Approach to University Regulation of Hate Speech," *Minnesota Law Review* 75 (1990): 933; William Treanor, "The Origins and Original Significance of the Just Compensation Clause of the Fifth Amendment," *Yale Law Journal* 94 (1985): 694; Morton Horwitz, "Republicanism and Liberalism in American Constitutional Thought," *William & Mary Law Review* 29 (1987): 57; Mark Tushnet, *Red, White, and Blue: A Critical Analysis of Constitutional Law* (Cambridge, Mass.: Harvard University Press 1988); Dan Kahan, "A Communitarian Defense of Group Libel Laws," *Harvard Law Review* 101 (1988): 682; Robert W. Gordon, "The Independence of Lawyers," *Boston University Law Review* 68 (1988): 1; Robert W. Gordon, "Corporate Law Practice as a Public Calling," *Maryland Law Review* 49 (1990): 255; Mark Seidenfeld, "A Civic Republican Justification for the Bureaucratic State," *Harvard Law Review* 105 (1992): 1511; Stephen M. Feldman, "Republican Revival/Interpretive Turn," *Wisconsin Law Review* (1992): 679; Nathan Alexander Sales, "Classical Republicanism and the Fifth Amendment's 'Public Use' Requirement," *Duke Law Journal* 49 (1999): 339; and John Braithwaite and Peter Drahos, *Global Business Regulation* (Cambridge: Cambridge University Press, 2000). For an essay in the same vein by a leading political theorist, see Michael Sandel, "Democrats and Community," *New Republic* (February 22, 1988): 20.

Frank Michelman's scholarship is extraordinarily wide-ranging, encompassing topics as diverse as Property Theory, the First Amendment, Constitutional Theory in general, and Law and Economics. Of his many contributions to the republican revival, the richest and deservedly the most famous is "Law's Republic," featured in this volume. The argument of that essay was foreshadowed in some of his earlier works, most notably his Foreword to the 1986 Supreme Court issue of the *Harvard Law Review*, "Traces of Self-Government," Volume 100 (1986): 4. In subsequent essays, Michelman contributed to elaborate on these themes—typically, not by urging readers simply to adopt as a solution to a modern problem a claim associated with republicanism, but rather by extracting from republicanism arguments or insights that might help illuminate some modern issue. Articles in this heuristic vein include: "Possession vs. Distribution in the Constitutional Idea of Property," *Iowa Law Review* 72 (1987): 1319;

"Conceptions of Democracy in American Constitutional Argument: Voting Rights," *Florida Law Review* 41 (1989): 443; "Conceptions of Democracy in American Constitutional Argument: The Case of Pornography Regulation," *Tennessee Law Review* 56 (1989): 291; and "Habermas on Law and Democracy: Critical Exchanges: Liberalism, Republicanism, and Constitutionalism," *Cardozo Law Review* 17 (1996): 1163.

Bruce Ackerman's constitutional theory, which Michelman criticizes in "Law's Republic" but which is sometimes considered at least consonant with the republican revival, was first outlined in "The Storrs Lectures: Discovering the Constitution," *Yale Law Journal* 93 (1984): 1013, then elaborated in *We The People: Foundations* (Cambridge, Mass.: Harvard University Press, 1991).

Criticisms by historians of the republican synthesis itself include Joyce Appleby, *Capitalism and a New Social Order: The Republican Vision of the 1790s* (New York: New York University Press, 1984); John Diggins, The *Lost Soul of American Politics: Virtue, Self-Interest, and the Foundations of Liberalism* (New York: Basic Books, 1984); Isaac Kramnick, "Republican Revisionism Revisited," *American Historical Review* 87 (1982): 629; and Daniel T. Rodgers, "Republicanism: The Career of a Concept," *Journal of American History* 79 (1992): 11.

Criticisms by historians of the efforts of legal scholars to apply republicanism to contemporary problems include Hendrik Hartog, "Imposing Constitutional Traditions," *William & Mary Law Review* 29 (1987): 75; Linda K. Kerber, "Making Republicanism Useful," *Yale Law Journal* 97 (1988): 1663; G. Edward White, "Reflections on the 'Republican Revival': Interdisciplinary Scholarship in the Legal Academy," *Yale Journal of Law and Humanities* 6 (1994): 1; Martin S. Flaherty, "History 'Lite' in Modern American Constitutionalism," *Columbia Law Review* 95 (1995): 523; and Laura Kalman, *The Strange Career of Legal Liberalism* (New Haven: Yale University Press, 1996).

Prominent among the essays by legal scholars critical of their colleagues' efforts to invoke republicanism as a guide to the resolution of modern controversies are Kathryn Abrams, "Law's Republicanism," *Yale Law Journal* 97 (1988): 1591; Derrick Bell and Preeta Bansal, "The Republican Revival and Racial Politics," *Yale Law Journal* 97 (1988): 1609; Kathleen Sullivan, "Rainbow Republicanism," *Yale Law Journal* 97 (1988): 1713; Richard Delgado, "Zero-Based Racial Politics: An Evaluation of Three Best Case Arguments on Behalf of the Nonwhite Underclass," *Georgia Law Journal* 78 (1990): 1929; and Richard H. Fallon, "What Is Republicanism and Why Is It Worth Reviving?" *Harvard Law Review* 102 (1989): 1695. An excellent account of the emergence of these criticisms, and an effort to meet them, can be found in Naomi Maya Stolzenberg, "A Book of Laughter and Forgetting: Kalman's 'Strange Career' and the Marketing of Civic Humanism," *Harvard Law Review* 111 (1998): 1025.

Major works developing or defending the ideal of the "rule of law" (discussed in the penultimate paragraph of this Introduction) include Lon Fuller, *The Morality of Law* (New Haven: Yale University Press, 1964), 33–91; Friedrich Hayek, *The Political Ideal of the Rule of Law* Cairo (1955); *idem, The Constitution of Liberty* (Chicago: University of Chicago Press, 1960), 153–54; John Rawls, *A Theory of Justice* (Cambridge, Mass.: Belknap Press of Harvard University Press, 1971), 235–43; and Joseph Raz, *The Authority of Law* (New York: Oxford University Press, 1979), 210–29. Portions of the summary offered here were derived from William Fisher, "The Jurisprudence of Justice Marshall," *Harvard Blackletter Law Journal* (Spring 1989): 131, 138–9.

FRANK MICHELMAN

"Law's Republic"

97 *Yale Law Journal* 1493 (1988)

I. INTRODUCTION: REPUBLICAN CONSTITUTIONALISM

A. *Bowers v. Hardwick: Authority vs. Freedom*

I begin with three premises: First, the Supreme Court's analysis and decision in *Bowers v. Hardwick*[1] are strikingly resistant to obvious claims of political freedom.[2] Second, judicial constitutional analysis ought to be receptive to such claims. Third, constitutional analysis is rooted in underlying, often tacit, sensibilities and understandings regarding the larger aims and methods of constitutionalism. Prompted by Hardwick's case, I will consider how contemporary American constitutional understanding and analysis might benefit from serious and sympathetic (but not uncritical) reflection upon the civic-republican strain in political thought that has been identified, traced, and analyzed in much recent writing on history,[3] social and political theory,[4] and American

---

Professor of Law, Harvard University. Many friends provided help with earlier drafts. Special thanks to Bruce Ackerman and Martha Minow.

[1] 478 U.S. 186 (1986) (upholding Georgia law criminalizing homosexual sodomy, as applied to adult defendant's conduct in his own home with consenting adult partner).

[2] *See e.g.* Richards, *Constitutional Legitimacy and Constitutional Privacy*, 61 N.Y.U. L. REV. 800, 852–57 (1986); Note, *The Supreme Court: Leading Cases*, 100 Harv. L. Rev. 210, 215–18 (1986). By "political freedom" I mean the redemption or achievement of personal freedom from or through the institutionalized social power that regulates social conflicts, given a perception of need for some form of such power. To perceive such a need, as I do, is to open oneself to the experience of "dilemma"—"either resign yourself to some established version of social order, or face the war of all against all"—that, as Roberto Unger says, prompts many to believe that legal-doctrinal practice must somehow be kept insulated from genuine "controversy over the basic terms of social life." This essay concurs in Unger's rejection of that view: An order or practice may retain its identity while undergoing transformation through a process of reflexive criticism. *See* R. Unger, THE CRITICAL LEGAL STUDIES MOVEMENT 15 (1986). Indeed, as Unger says, it is only such an expanded notion of the identity and continuity of a doctrinal order that can sustain "the validity of normative and programmatic argument itself; at least this must be true when such argument takes the standard form of working from within a tradition rather than the exceptional one of appealing to transcendent insight." *Id.* at 15–16.

[3] *See, e.g.,* J APPLEBY, CAPITALISM AND A NEW SOCIAL ORDER: THE REPUBLICAN VISION OF THE 1790'S (1984); B. BAILYN, THE IDEOLOGICAL ORIGINS OF THE AMERICAN REVOLUTION (1967); F. MacDONALD, NOVUS ORDO SECLORUM; THE INTELLECTUAL ORIGINS OF THE CONSTITUTION (1985); D. McCoy, THE ELUSIVE REPUBLIC: POLITICAL ECONOMY IN JEFFERSONIAN AMERICA (1980); J. POCOCK, THE MACHIAVELLIAN MOMENT: FLORENTINE POLITICAL THOUGHT AND THE ATLANTIC REPUBLICAN TRADITION (1975); G. WOOD, THE CREATION OF THE AMERICAN REPUBLIC, 1776–1787 (1969); Shalhope, *Republicanism and Early American Historiography*, 39 Wm & Mary Q. 334 (1982).

[4] *See, e.g.,* B. Barber, *Strong Democracy: Participatory Politics for a New Age* (1984); R. Bellah, R. Madsen, W. Sullivan, A. Swidler & S. Tipton, *Habits of the Heart: Individualism and Commitment in American Life* 28–31 & *passim* (1985) [hereinafter R. Bellah]; R. Bernstein, *Beyond Objectivism and Relativism: Science, Hermeneutics and Praxis* (1983); A. MacIntyre, *After Virtue* (1981); C. Taylor, *Kant's Theory of Freedom*, in 2 Philosophy and the Human Sciences: Philosophical Papers 318 (1985); Cornell, *Toward a Modern/Postmodern Reconstruction of Ethics*, 133 U. Pa L. Rev. 291 (1986); Herzog, *Some Questions for Republicans*, 14 Pol. Theory 473 (1986); Sandel, *The Procedural Republic and the Unencumbered Self*, 12 Pol. Theory 81 (1984).

constitutionalism.[5] My task is to explain how an examination of our constitutionalism from a republican-inspired standpoint might help invigorate a constitutional discourse that would steel judges against the desertion of claims like Hardwick's.

To many readers this may seem a lunatic undertaking. Classical republicanism, with its legacy of excluding from the political community all those whose voices would—by reason of supposed defect of understanding, foreignness of outlook, subservience of position, or corruption of interest—threaten disruption of a community's normative unity, will seem sadly consonant with the result in *Bowers.* "Republicanism" conjures up just that strain in the history of political thought that would defend a repressive and discriminatory law for which there is no justification save "majority sentiments about . . . morality," for the simple reason that "[t]he law . . . is constantly based on notions of morality."[6] Even worse, republicanism suggests justification of such a law on the frightening ground that its specific moral motivation "is firmly rooted in Judaeo-Christian moral and ethical standards"[7]—standards to which (it seems to be implied) the entire political community is forever committed by the community's history as read from a particular moral-majoritarian perspective.

I will contend, to the contrary, that republican constitutional thought is not indissolubly tied to any such static, parochial, or coercive communitarianism; that, indeed, reconsideration of republicanism's deeper constitutional implications can remind us of how the renovation of political communities, by inclusion of those who have been excluded, enhances everyone's political freedom. Republican constitutionalism, I will argue, involves a kind of normative tinkering. It involves the ongoing revision of the normative histories that make political communities sources of contestable value and self-direction for their members. This tinkering entails not only the recognition but also the kind of recognition—reconception—of those histories that will always be needed to extend political community to persons in our midst who have as yet no stakes in "our" past because they had no access to it.[8]

If republican thought does thus, as I believe, contain visionary resources of use to modern liberal constitutionalism, we need not fear drawing upon those resources because of their sometime historical connection with an obnoxiously solidaristic social doctrine.[9] Contemporary American liberals have less to fear from lurking social solidarism than from a constitutional jurisprudence that debases the community by slighting its self-transformative capacity, and abets the community's self-betrayal through lapse of commitment to extension of membership to persons who, at many historical moments, could not count themselves

Frank Michelman

---

[5] *See, e.g.,* D. EPSTEIN, THE POLITICAL THEORY OF THE FEDERALIST (1984); G. STONE, L. SEIDMAN, C. SUNSTEIN & M. TUSHNET, CONSTITUTIONAL LAW 5–13 (1986); Ackerman, *The Storrs Lectures: Discovering the Constitution,* 93 YALE L. J. 1013 (1984); Frug, *The City As a Legal Concept,* 93 HARV. L. REV. 1057 (1980); Horwitz, *Republicanism and Liberalism in American Constitutional Thought,* 29 WM & MARY L. REV. 57 (1987); Michelman, *The Supreme Court 1985 Term-Foreword: Traces of Self-Government,* 100 HARV. L. REV. 4 (1986); Sherry, *Civic Virtue and the Feminine Voice in Constitutional Adjudication,* 72 VA. L. REV. 543 (1986); Sunstein, *Beyond the Republican Revival,* 97 YALE L. J. 1539 (1988).

[6] Bowers v. Hardwick, 478 U.S. 186, 196 (1986); *see,* e.g., Herzog, *supra* note 4, at 483–86.

[7] 478 U.S. at 196 (Burger, C.J., concurring); *see* Richards, *supra* note 2, at 861; Simon, *The New Republicanism: Generosity of Spirit in Search of Something to Say,* 29 WM. & MARY L. REV. 83, 91–92 (1987).

[8] *See, e.g.,* Hirsch, *The Threnody of Liberalism: Constitutional Liberty and the Renewal of Community,* 14 POL. THEORY 423, 424–25 (1986) (warning contemporary communitarian political thought against insensitivity to issues of belonging and exclusion).

[9] *But see* Simon, *supra* note 7.

heirs to traditions whose meanings did at those times involve the exclusion or subordination of just those persons.[10]

What ought chiefly to alarm liberals about the *Bowers* decision, then, is not a judicial affection for moral majoritarianism that the justices collectively almost certainly do not hold and could not propagate if they did. Rather, it is the decision's embodiment of an excessively detached and passive judicial stance toward constitutional law. The devastating effect in *Bowers* of a judicial posture of deference to external authority appears in the majority's assumption, plain if not quite explicit in its opinion, that public values meriting enforcement as law are to be uncritically equated with either the formally enacted preferences of a recent legislative or past constitutional majority, or with the received teachings of an historically dominant, supposedly civic, orthodoxy. I will call such a looking backward jurisprudence *authoritarian* because it regards adjudicative actions as legitimate only insofar as dictated by the prior normative utterance, express or implied, of extra-judicial authority.[11]

Justice White's opinion for the Court in *Bowers* wears its positivistic constitutional theory on its sleeve: It is not for the Court to "impose" its members' "own choice of values" on the people by "announc[ing] . . . a fundamental right to engage in homosexual sodomy," contrary to both the formally legislated will of the Georgia majority and (as the Court believed[12]) "'the Nation's history and tradition'" as manifested in state legislation widely in force when both the Ninth and Fourteenth Amendments were ratified.[13] If the Court declares the existence of fundamental constitutional rights "having little or no cognizable roots in the language

---

[10] Consider Crenshaw, *Race, Reform, and Retrenchment: Transformation and Legitimation in Antidiscrimination Law*, 101 Harv. L. Rev. 1331, 1358–59 (1988) ("The most significant aspect of Black oppression seems to be what is believed *about* Black Americans, not what Black Americans believe. . . . Blacks seem to carry the stigma of 'otherness,' which effectively precludes their potentially radicalizing influence from penetrating the dominant consciousness."); *id.* at 1385 ("Optimally, the deconstruction of white race consciousness might lead to a liberated future for both Blacks and whites."). For testimony to, and accounts of, the experience of exclusion, see, e.g., D. BELL, AND WE ARE NOT SAVED 26–42 & *passim* (1987); Lopez, *The Idea of a Constitution in the Chicano Tradition*, 37 J. LEGAL ED. 162 (1987); Marshall, *Reflections on the Bicentennial of the United States Constitution*, 101 HATTV. L. REV. 1 (1987). *But cf.* Minow, *Interpreting Rights: An Essay For Robert Cover*, 96 YALE L. J. 1860, 1880 (1987) ("Some people may feel so shut out that the appeal to a communal commitment to rights makes no sense to them. Nonetheless, an interpretive conception of rights is a way to . . . promote change by reliance on inherited traditions."); Williams, *Alchemical Notes: Reconstructed Ideals From Deconstructed Rights*, 22 HARV. C.R.-C.L. L. REv. 401, 415 (1987):

> To say that blacks never fully believed in rights is true; yet it is also true that blacks believed in them so much and so hard that we gave them life where there was none before. . . . This was the resurrection of life from 400-year-old ashes; the parthenogenesis of unfertilized hope. *See also infra* text accompanying notes 117–23; *id.* 152–56.

[11] "Originalists" such as Robert Bork are one camp within authoritarianism. *See, e.g.,* Dronenburg v. Zech, 741 F.2d 1388, 1396–97 (D.C. Cir. 1984) (Bork, J.) (only fresh expression of "the moral choices of the people and their elected representatives" can justify court in "protect[ing] from regulation a form of behavior [i.e., homosexual sex] never before protected, and indeed traditionally condemned" when claimed right to protection has "little or no cognizable roots in the language or even the design of the Constitution"); Bork, *Tradition and Morality in Constitutional Law*, in AMERICAN ENTERPRISE INSTITUTE FOR PUBLIC POLICY RESEARCH, THE FRANCIS BOYER LECTURES ON PUBLIC POLICY 10 (1984) ("It is necessary to establish the propositions that the framers' intentions with respect to freedoms are the sole legitimate premise from which constitutional analysis may proceed."). Surprisingly, another authoritarian constitutional theorist is Bruce Ackerman. While Ackerman's theory is best noted for its claim that We The People can amend the Constitution in ways not recognized by Article V, *see* Ackerman, *supra* note 5, at 1055, 1057–73, that theory also insists that today's constitutional interpretations must refer to the dictates of past episodes— "transformative" moments—of popular law-making. *See* Ackerman, *Transformative Appointments*, 101 HARV. L. REV. 1164 (1988); *see also* Ackerman, *supra* note 5, at 1070–71. For a critical appreciation of Ackerman's view, see *infra* text accompanying notes 103–23.

[12] This belief was evidently based on oversimplified and misleadingly selective historical claims. *See* Goldstein, *History, Homosexuality, and Political Values: Searching for the Hidden Determinants* of Bowers v. Hardwick, 97 YALE L. J. 1073 (1988).

[13] Bowers v. Hardwick, 478 U.S. 186,192–94 (1986) (*quoting* Moore v. City of East Cleveland, 431 U.S. 494, 503 (1977) (plurality opinion of Powell, J.)).

or design of the Constitution," says the justice, it wrongly assumes power "to govern the country without express constitutional authority."[14]

The deeper premises of the *Bowers* majority, although unstated, are clear enough: Most fundamentally, the Court is the servant, not the author, of a prescriptive text. As such, it inquires into meaning—signification—not into reason or value. Justice Blackmun's plea for evaluating Hardwick's claim "in the light of the values that underlie the constitutional right of privacy"[15] thus fails, in the majority's view, because the values on which Blackmun would base protection of Hardwick's privacy against the declared will of the current legislative majority of Georgia cannot be credibly traced to any historical occasion of popular higher law-making. Even granting that the people speaking through the Ninth and Fourteenth Amendments meant to insulate a traditional regard for family privacy from the general norm of rule by contemporary majorities, it is "facetious," says justice White, to suggest that they meant that exception to cover the right to engage in homosexual sodomy.[16] The people's duly registered constitutional and legislative choices to protect certain privacies and not others is their own political matter with which the Supreme Court has nothing to do; the Court engaged in constitutional adjudication is an organ of law, and therefore not of politics.

Dare one ask: Why *ought* the Supreme Court not be an organ of politics, if that is what it takes to secure liberty and justice for Hardwick and those for whom he stands? Because—so runs the answer clearly implied by justice White's opinion and the familiar constitutional dogma that informs it—for the Court to act politically, as a law-maker and not just a law-finder, would amount to a judicial usurpation of power that belongs by right to others, to "the people" acting through their electorally accountable representatives. But again, why? Why by *right* to others? Why *ought* popular-majoritarian preference rather than judicial argument ultimately determine the question of law controlling Hardwick's liberty?

While the Court's opinion does not directly speak to this question, we already know the answer. It is, of course, democracy.[17] But that answer without more is

---

[14] *Id.* at 194–95.

[15] *Id.* at 199 (Blackmun, J., dissenting).

[16] *Id.* at 194.

[17] *See, e.g.*, Bork, *Neutral Principles and Some First Amendment Problems, 47* IND. L. J. 1, 2–4 (1971) [hereinafter Bork, *Neutral Principles*]; Boric, *supra* note 11, at 9, 11 ("Constitutional scholarship today is dominated by the creation of arguments that will encourage judges to thwart democratic choice. . . . In a constitutional democracy, the moral content of law must be given by the morality of the framer or legislator, never by the morality of the judge.").

Earl Maltz denies that the case for originalism need rest on any notion of democracy. According to Maltz, "the originalist position is . . . grounded [not] on democracy . . . but on the concept of law" and on a corresponding "view[] of the appropriate function of judges in a well-ordered society." Maltz, *The Failure of Attacks on Constitutional Originalism, 4* CONSTITUTIONAL COMMENTARY 43, 53, 56 (1987). With respect, I find Maltz's distinction puzzling. It is by now widely recognized that concepts of law, views of judicial function, and related notions of social well-orderedness are all embedded in some substantive political-moral conception, tacit or explicit, *see, e.g.*, R. DWORKIN, *The Forum of Principle, in* A MATTER OF PRINCIPLE 33, 34–57 (1985), and indeed Maltz himself acknowledges this. *See* Maltz, *Foreword: The Appeal of Originalism, 1987* UTAH L. REV. 773, 774–75. I understand that an originalist approach to constitutional adjudication might suggest itself to those holding certain notions about legality and judicial role, but I cannot see how the connection between legality and originalism could be persuasively drawn within the context of American constitutionalism without at some point appealing to a normative notion of democracy or self-government by the people. Maltz himself argues that "constitutional [like statutory] supremacy derives from the intuition that the Constitution embodies the will of a [legitimate] governmental body whose authority is superior to . . . courts. . . ." *Id.* at 789. It's true that Maltz also suggests that conventional belief in the legitimacy of these law-giving assemblies is independent of any concern about "whether [they are] democratically selected." *Id.* at 783. But if Maltz means by this that the conventional legitimacy of these bodies has nothing to do with their being perceived as

both lazy and presumptuous. It conjures with a term that rings of sovereign value, but too often does so without pausing to consider what that value is.[18] Too often, indeed, the invocation of democracy in defense of judicial restraint signifies little more than *Faute de Mieux;* too often, it means merely that if a determination of law can only, at bottom, be a matter of acceding to someone's preferences, then the people should be ruled by the sum of their own preferences (as mediated by the system of representation) rather than by the preferences of a few judges.[19] Democracy thus conveniently answers to the need for authority: When the social determination of disputed questions of value is imaginable only as a battle of preferences or as the exertion of an arbitrary, dominant will, then law—the adjudicative act—tends to be understandable only as the unquestioning and uncreative (which is not to say necessarily wooden or unintelligent) application of the prior word of some socially recognized, extra judicial authority.[20]

I believe that a close consideration of certain implications of historical republican constitutional thought can point us toward an account of the relations among law, politics, and democracy that not only would have called for the opposite result in Bowers, but that Americans also will, on reflection, recognize as truer in other respects to their most basic understandings of what constitutionalism is all about.[21] This is the republicanism I advocate.

---

representative of the people and their will(s), he has simply posited their legitimacy while repudiating the only explanation of it that the discourse of constitutionalism has ever, to my knowledge, entertained. *See, e.g.,* Bork, *Neutral Principles, supra,* at 3–4.

[18] *See* Posner, *The Constitution as an Economic Document,* 56 GEO. WASH. L. REV. 4, 21–22 (1987) (criticizing "aggressive constitutionalism" for "diminish[ing] the role of democracy" while hazarding no affirmative account of democracy's value); Bork, *Neutral Principles, supra* note 17, at 2–3 (asserting that "it is a 'given' in our society" that "in wide areas of life majorities are entitled to rule for no better reason than that they are majorities"); *cf.* Lyons, *Substance, Process, and Outcome in Constitutional Theory* 72 CORNELL L. REV. 745, 754 (1987):

> Most Constitutional Scholars see to believe . . . that a theory concerning the character of constitutional institutions must guide an interpretation of the Constitution itself. But these scholars usually limit their general theories to simple talk about "democracy" or "majoritarianism." They fail to explain what that means, in part because they do not address the question of what values a constitutional system like ours should serve.

[19] See, e.g., Bork, Neutral Principles, supra note 17, at 3.

[20] Thus, when judge Posner suggests that, in the popular understanding, our only choice lies between having judges "decide cases in accordance with law, viewed as a body of principles external to the policy preferences of the individual judges" and letting judge's decide in accordance with their own "views of public policy," Posner, *supra* note 18, at 33, many readers will rush to construe the judge's words as meaning that the only perceived alternative to illegitimate judicial self-indulgence is judicial deference to objective, determinate and determining, positive-legal authority. On that construction of it (which does not, in fact, accord with the judges view, *see* Posner, *The Jurisprudence of Skepticism,* 86 MICH. L. REV. 827 (1988)), Judge Posner's analysis would allow no space for the possibility of a judicial decision according to persuasive and disciplined argument in which the governing principles are themselves determined in the course of the argument. *See, e.g.,* Farber & Frickey, *Practical Reason and the First Amendment,* 34 UCLA L. REV. 1615, 1645–56 (1987); Michelman, *supra* note 5, at 28–29.

Owen Fiss and Robin West both draw the connection between a conception of politics as the registration of preferences (as opposed to the determination of values) and a deferential/authoritarian judicial attitude towards constitutional adjudication. *See* Fiss, *Foreword: The Form of justice,* 93 HARV. L. REV. 1, 15 (1979); West, *The Authoritarian Impulse in Constitutional Law,* 42 U. Miami L. REV. 531, 535–37, 541–45 (1988).

[21] In *Reconsidering the Rule of Law* (forthcoming 1989), Margaret Jane Radin approaches from the opposite direction the possibility of a "modern reinterpretation" of "the rule of law" that is strikingly convergent with the "republican" interpretation offered in this Article. Radin launches her inquiry from a Wittgensteinian critique of the idea that verbal rules could possibly govern us, whereas I launch mine from the conundrum of government-of-laws versus government-by-the-people. We seem to meet at a common destination, and it is easy to see why. Radin concludes that "if law cannot be formal rules its people cannot be mere functionaries." The flip side of that is that if the people are not mere functionaries (but rather are self-governing), then their law cannot be formal rules.

B. Constitutionalism: Self-Rule As Laze Rule

I take American constitutionalism—as manifest in academic constitutional theory, in the professional practice of lawyers and judges, and in the ordinary political self-understanding of Americans at large—to rest on two premises regarding political freedom:[22] first, that the American people are politically free insomuch as they are governed by themselves collectively,[23] and, second, that the American people are politically free insomuch as they are governed by laws and not men [sic].[24] I take it that no earnest, non-disruptive participant in American constitutional debate is quite free to reject either of those two professions of belief. I take them to be premises whose problematic relation to each other, and therefore whose meanings, are subject to an endless contestation that always organizes, sometimes explicitly but always implicitly, American constitutional argument.[25]

The problematic relationship between the two American constitutionalist premises—the government of the people by the people and the government of the people by laws—should be evident.[26] We ordinarily think of ourselves (qua

---

[22] For a rough definition of political freedom, see *supra* note 2.

[23] *E.g.*, THE FEDERALIST No. 39, at 240 (J. Madison) (C. Rossiter ed. 1961):

It is evident that no [nonrepublican] form [of government] would be reconcilable with the genius of the American people; with the fundamental principles of the Revolution; or with that honorable determination which animates every votary of freedom to rest all our political experiments on the capacity of mankind for self-government.

It is enough for my purposes that Madison and his fellow federalists "agreed, explicitly, that the people could create, alter, or abolish their government whenever they chose to do so," and that they did so by way of concession to the country's prevailing democratic-republican sentiment. *See* Miller, *The Ghostly Body Politic. The Federalist Papers and Popular Sovereignty*, 16 POL. THEORY 99,104 & *passim* (1988). Professor Miller goes on to urge that the Federalists made this concession only rhetorically, and only subject to the stipulation that:

for the acts of 'the people' to be valid, they had to act all at once and together. Thus the Federalists rendered the democratic vocabulary of popular sovereignty harmless by invoking a fictitious people who could not possibly act together. The Federalists ascribed all power to a mythical entity that could never meet, never deliberate, never take action. The body politic became a ghost.

Even after allowing for the obvious hyperbole of Professor Miller's reading of the framers' design with respect to popular sovereignty (how did they regard the initial ratification, then?), that reading is subject to strong contestation. *See infra* text accompanying notes 106–12 (describing Ackerman's two-track theory). Even were it not, its deepest premise would remain that of the recognized commitment of Americans to the principle of popular self-government. *See* Zuckerman, *Charles Beard and the Constitution: The Uses of Enchantment*, 56 GEO. WASH. L. REV. 81, 95, 99 (1987):

[The founders] were realists . . . in their experience of their social milieu. They moved in a world in which rhetoric bore some reasonable relation to reality, a world especially in which political language bore some substantial resemblance to political life. . . .
. . . *The Federalist Papers* were written [by the founders] precisely out of passion and necessity to take [their] acquired expertise to the people and share it with them, rather than shut them out of it.

[24] *See, e.g.*, Marbury v. Madison, 5 U.S. (1 Cranch) 137, 163 (1803); 2 J. ADAMS, PAPERS OF JOHN ADAMS 314 (R. Taylor ed. 1977); *see* Richards, *supra* note 2, at 842–43.

[25] *See* Pitkin, *The Idea of a Constitution*, 37 J. LEGAL EDUC. 167 (1987) ("[T]o understand what a Constitution is, one must look *at* the ambiguities, the specific oppositions that this specific concept helps us to hold in tension"); *cf.* Rawls, *Justice as Fairness: Political not Metaphysical*, 14 PHIL & PUB. AFF. 223, 227 (1985):

The course of democratic thought over the past two centuries . . . makes plain that there is no agreement on the way the basic institutions of a constitutional democracy should be arranged. . . . [W]e may think of [the] disagreement as a conflict within the tradition of democratic thought itself, between the tradition associated with Locke, which gives greater weight to what Constant called "the liberties of the moderns," . . . certain basic rights of the person . . . and the rule of law, and the tradition associated with Rousseau, which gives greater weight to what Constant called "the liberties of the ancients," the equal political liberties and the values of public life.

[26] *See, e.g.*, G. WOOD, *supra* note 3, at 362:

"Civil liberty" became for Americans "not 'a government of laws,' made agreeable to charters, bills of rights or compacts, but a power existing in the people at large, at any time, for any cause, or for no cause, but their own sovereign pleasure, to alter or annihilate both the mode and essence of any former government and adopt a new one in its stead."

"people") and laws as being entirely different orders of things. Yet if we are sincerely and consistently committed both to ruling ourselves and to being ruled by laws, there must be some sense in which we think of self-rule and law-rule (if not exactly of "people" and "laws") as amounting to the same thing.[27] It should be apparent that the problem is not just a verbal artifact. Each of the two constitutionalist formulas—self-government and a government of laws—seems to express a demand that we are all bound to respect as a primal requirement of political freedom: the first demands the people's determination for themselves of the norms that are to govern their social life, while the second demands the people's protection against abuse by arbitrary power. Reconciliation is not accomplished simply by regarding the people as making or consenting to their own laws. The process of popular law-making is what we call politics; and politics is, in the traditional (and healthy) American under-standing, a theater of power in which some people stand always in danger of abuse by others. If "a government of laws" stands—as surely it does—for the institutionalized discipline that would render legislative politics trustworthy, then "law" in the "government of laws" formula must stand in a circular relation with politics as both outcome and input, both product and prior condition.[28]

Perhaps we can think our way through this difficulty by taking seriously the cue we have already noticed in our constitutionalist formulas, that is, the conceptual identification (although of course not outright identity or equivalence) of "people" with "laws," which at the same time holds "people" distinct from mere "men." One possible way of making sense of this is by conceiving of politics as a process in which private—regarding "men" become public—regarding citizens and thus

---

(quoting Hichborn, *Oration, March 5th, 1777*, in PRINCIPLES AND ACTS OF THE AMERICAN REVOLUTION, 1750–76, at 47 (H. Niles ed. 1876)).

[27] Moreover, if we are serious about opposing the government of laws to that of men [sic], yet at the same time insistent upon having a government of the people by the people as well as a government of laws, then we must be using "men" in some sense opposed to that in which we use "people" when we think of people-rule as consonant with law-rule.

[28] It would be a plain misreading to reduce the American constitutionalist premise of the government of laws to the "rule of law" or *Rechtsstaat* idea concerned only with the regularity of legal administration and, derivatively, with the form of legislation. *Accord* Epstein, *Beyond the Rule of Law: Civic Virtue and Constitutional Structure*, 56 GEO. WASH. L. REV. 149, 154, 162, 169 (1987). On the *Rechtsstaat* view, the demand for a rule of law is satisfied by certain conditions of legal administration and derivatively of legal form, without regard to normative content. The rule of law then exists as long as all legislative enactments, whatever their content, are rigorously and impersonally applied to all cases falling within their terms, and those terms are sufficiently abstract and decisive ("formally realizable") to support the requisite degree of impersonality and predictability in administration. See F. HAYEK, THE CONSTITUTION OF LIBERTY 193–204 (1960) (describing *Rechtsstaat* ideal and its history). If this purely formal conception of the rule of law were all that were meant by the constitutionalist demand for a "government of laws," then that demand would be easily reconcilable with the demand for popular self-government: The people make the laws politically, subject to certain demands of formality in both the terms in which the laws are couched and the manner in which they are administered. Doubtless we do sometimes use the term in that sense, as, for example, Chief Justice Marshall may perhaps be taken to have done in *Marbury v. Madison*, when he wrote that our government would cease to deserve the name of "a government of laws, and not of men" if its "laws furnish no remedy for the violation of a vested legal right." 5 U.S. (1 Cranch) at 163 But surely it will be agreed that in American constitutional rhetoric the notion of "a government of laws" has also shared the meaning of formulas like "higher law," *see, eg.,* Corwin, *The "Higher* Law" *Background of American Constitutional Law* (pts. 1 & 2), 42 HARV. L. REV. 149, 365 (1928–29), and "limited government," *see, e.g.,* J. NEDELSKY, PRIVATE PROPERTY AND THE *LIMITS* OF AMERICAN CONSTITUTIONALISM: A VIEW FROM THE FORMATION (forthcoming 1989). Shorn of these nuances, the constitutionalist tradition would be unrecognizable. See, e.g., F. HAYEK, *supra,* at 165 (affirming, as contained in "the ideal of government by law," Aristotle's doctrine that what ought to govern is "the law," as distinguished from "the people" and "majority vote"); Brennan, The Constitution of the United States: Contemporary Ratification, 27 S. TEX. L. REV. 433, 436 (1986) ("It is the very purpose of our Constitution . . . to declare certain values transcendent, beyond the reach of temporary political majorities."); c f. S. LEVINSON, CONSTITUTIONAL FAITH 150–51 (1988) (reviewing theories of "unconstitutional constitutional amendments"). *See generally* NOMOS XX: CONSTITUTIONALISM (J. Pennock & J. Chapman eds. 1979).

members of a people. It would be by virtue of that people-making quality that the process would confer upon its law-like issue the character of law binding upon all as self-given. A political process having such a quality is one that, adapting a term of Robert Cover's, we may call jurisgenerative.[29] Reconciling the two premises of constitutionalism seems to require that we entertain the possibility of a jurisgenerative politics, capable of imbuing its legislative product with a "sense of validity" as "our" law.[30]

The idea of jurisgenerative politics is historically recognizable as an idea of republican lineage.[31] nostalgic "republican revival," but rather American constitutionalism as we have all along thought it, that we lose—or at any rate lose the ability to explain and justify—if we cannot now reclaim that idea on terms we can accept.[32] Republicanism, I mean thus to argue, is not optional with us. Whatever else the term may or may not fairly signify as a category in the history of political thought, "republicanism" does, I take it, signify the sort of belief in jurisgenerative politics that it seems must play a role in any explanation of how the constitutionalist principles of self-rule and law-rule might coincide.

C. Republicanism and Modernity

1. THE DIALOGIC TRADITION

In the strongest versions of republicanism, citizenship—participation as an equal in public affairs, in pursuit of a common good—appears as a primary, indeed constitutive, interest of the person. Political engagement is considered a positive human good because the self is understood as partially constituted by, or as coming to itself through, such engagement.[33] This view opposes the "pluralist" view in which the primary interests of individuals appear as pre-political, and politics, accordingly, as a secondary instrumental medium for protecting or advancing those "exogenous" interests.[34]

---

[29] See Cover, *The Supreme Court, 1982 Term—Foreword: Nomos and Narrative*, 97 HARV. L. REV. 4, 4–19 (1983).

[30] S. BENHABIB, CRITIQUE, NORM, AND UTOPIA 272 (1985). Benhabib apparently draws her notion of validity from her critical examination of Habermas' theory of communicative reason. Habermas has contended that only "unconstrained dialogue" conducted under certain "ideal" conditions can hope to produce socially "valid" resolutions of controversial claims—that is, resolutions consisting of "rationally motivated consensus" as distinguished from "mere compromise or . . . agreement of convenience." Benhabib draws a special connection between this idea of "discursive justification of validity claims" and "the normative self-understanding of democracies that public decisions are reached by autonomous . . . Citizens in a process of unconstrained exchange of opinions. . . . [T]he theory of communicative ethics is primarily concerned with norms of public-institutional life." *Id.* at 283; *see also id.* at 284–85 (explicating Habermas' theory of communicative competence). For a quite different—non-discursive—theory of public or social normative validation, see *infra* note 53.

[31] *See infra* text accompanying notes 37–43. Ancient and early modern republican influences and inspirations are manifest in recent evocations of variants of this idea. *See, e.g.,* H. ARENDT, THE HUMAN CONDITION (1958); B. BARBER, *supra* note 4, H. PITKIN, FORTUNE IS A WOMAN: GENDER AND POLITICS IN THE THOUGHT OF NICCOLO MACHIAVELLI (1984); Cover, *supra* note 29.

[32] See B. BARBER, *supra* note 4, at 118:

> Strong democracy has a good deal in common with the classical democratic theory of the ancient Greek polis, but it is in no sense identical with that theory. . . . [I]n practical terms it is sometimes complementary to rather than a radical alternative to the liberal argument. . . . It incorporates a Madisonian wariness about actual human nature into a more hopeful, Jeffersonian outlook on human potentialities. . . . [It is] drawn from a variety of established practices and nourished by classical theories of community, civic education, and participation. . . . It has no share in the republican nostalgia of such commentators as Hannah Arendt or Leo Strauss.

[33] *See, e.g., id.* at 132–33.

[34] *See infra* text accompanying notes 50–51.

A related opposition of ideas is that between "negative" and "positive" liberty. Negative liberty refers to absence of restraint against doing as one wants, while positive liberty implies action governed by reasons or laws that one gives to oneself.[35] The two concepts of liberty differ hugely in their implications respecting the good of citizenship. From a negative-libertarian standpoint, participation in politics is not a good (except upon the sheer accident of a given person's happening to like it). But positive liberty is hardly conceivable without citizenship.[36] Hanna Pitkin still offers the best contemporary statement of the position I know:

> What distinguishes politics, as Arendt and Aristotle said, is . . . the possibility of a shared, collective, deliberate, active intervention in our fate, in what would otherwise be the by-product of private decisions. Only in public life can we jointly, as a community, exercise the human capacity to "think what we are doing," and take charge of the history in which we are all constantly engaged by drift and inadvertence. . . . [T]he distinctive promise of political freedom re-mains the possibility of genuine collective action, an entire community consciously and jointly shaping its policy, its way of life. . . . A family or other private association can inculcate principles of justice shared in a community, but only in public citizenship can we jointly take charge of and responsibility for those principles.
>
> Kant suggests something analogous in his concept of moral autonomy: that we are not mature as moral actors until we have become self-governing, have [taken] . . . responsibility not only for our actions but also for the norms and principles according to which we act. As long as we live only by habit or tradition, unaware that they mask an implicit choice, there is something about ourselves as actors in the world that we are not seeing and for which we are not acknowledging our responsibility.[37]

I am not here recommending strong republicanism. I do not know what is good for the soul. I do not know in what (if anything) personal freedom essentially consists. I do not know whether citizenship is a fundamental human good. What I do claim is that the republican conception of politics, a conception that has apparently been motivated historically by certain convictions about those matters that we may or may not be able to share, is one that good, contemporary constitutional explanation and analysis cannot do without.

2. THE DIALOGIC CONSTITUTION: REPUBLICANISM AND JURISGENESIS

In republican thought, the normative character of politics depends on the independence of mind and judgment, the authenticity of voice, and—in some versions of republicanism—the diversity or "plurality" of views that citizens bring to "the

---

[35] See, e.g., I. BERLIN, *Two Concepts of Liberty*, in FOUR ESSAYS ON LIBERTY 118 (1969); I. BERLIN, *Introduction*, in *id.* ix; C. TAYLOR, *What's Wrong With Negative Liberty*, in C. TAYLOR, *supra* note 4, at 211.

[36] Advocates of strong republicanism have historically emphasized various kinds of reasons for tying the personal and the political so closely together. Hannah Arendt, for example, has expounded on the Aristotelian notion of civic action as good for the soul—as, indeed, the distinctively human mode of excellence or "public happiness." *See* H. ARENDT, *supra* note 31; H. ARENDT, ON REVOLUTION (1963). Others, notably Rousseau and Kant, have stressed the ethical importance of governing oneself. Motivation by pre-reflective, uncriticized inclination is, they contend, a kind of enslavement, not of freedom, and we are free only insofar as we direct our actions in accordance with reasons or ends that we, as it were, legislate to ourselves upon conscious, critical reflection. *See, e.g.,* C. TAYLOR, *supra* note 4, at 318 (discussing Rousseau as well as Kant).

[37] Pitkin, *Justice: On Relating Private and Public*, 9 POL. THEORY 327, 344–45 (1981) (citation omitted).

debate of the commonwealth."[38] Republicanism has been, *par excellence*, the strain in constitutional thought that has been sensitive to both the dependence of good politics on social and economic conditions capable of sustaining "an informed and active citizenry that would not permit its government either to exploit or dominate one part of society or to become its instrument," and the dependence of such conditions, in turn, on the legal order.[39] These perceptions irresistibly motivate a republican attachment to rights.[40] These include, most obviously, rights of speech[41] and of property.[42] They may also include privacy rights—perhaps stronger ones than many contemporary liberals would welcome.[43]

Yet republican thought is no less committed to the idea of the people acting politically as the sole source of law and guarantor of rights, than it is to the idea of law, including rights, as the precondition of good politics. Republican thought thus demands some way of understanding how laws and rights can be both the free creations of citizens and, at the same time, the normative givens that constitute and underwrite a political process capable of creating constitutive law.[44] Perfectly prefiguring the American constitutionalist dilemma I have already described, classical republican constitutional jurisprudence evidently depends on the possibility of jurisgenerative politics.

---

[38] *See* Michelman, *supra* note 5, at 41–47. We shall see below how an inclusory, plurality-protecting conception of republican citizenship can anchor justice Blackmun's account of the value of intimate association, the heart of his powerful dissenting opinion in *Bowers*. Inclusory republicanism seems especially pertinent to the opinion's evocative references to "association that promotes a way of life," Bowers v. Hardwick, 478 U.S. 186, 205 (1986) (Blackmun, J., dissenting) (quoting Griswold v. Connecticut, 381 U.S. 479, 486 (1965)), and to "self-definition" dependent upon "close ties with others," *id*. at 2851 (quoting Roberts v. United States Jaycees, 468 U.S. 609, 619 (1984)).

[39] Horwitz, *Republicanism and Liberalism in American Constitutional Thought*, 29 WM. & MARY L. REV. 57, 71–72 (1987); *see* Michelman, *supra* note 5, at 40–41; Michelman, *Possession vs. Distribution in the Constitutional Idea of Property*, 72 IOWA L. REV. 1319, 1329 (1987) [hereinafter Michelman, *Possession vs. Distribution*].

[40] *See* Sunstein, *supra* note 5. Pocock has noticed the way in which the constitution of both the republic and of citizenship—the grounding in practical imagination of the republic's external relations, its membership boundaries, and the virtuous independence of its citizens—seems to demand expression in a juristic language of law and rights that sits problematically with the "humanist" vocabulary of civic virtue:

[C]itizenship in the Italian republics was for the most part defined in jurisdictional and jurisprudential terms. . . . An Italian commune was a juristic entity, inhabited by persons subject to rights and obligations; to define these and to define the authority that protected them was to define the citizen and his city, and the practice as opposed to the principles of citizenship was overwhelmingly conducted in this language.

Pocock, *Virtues, Rights, and Manners. A Model for Historians of Political Thought*, 9 POL. THEORY 353, 355 (1981); *see id*. at 357, 360.

[41] *See, e.g.*, A MEIKLEJOHN, FREE SPEECH AND ITS RELATION To SELF-GOVERNMENT (1948); Brennan, *The Supreme Court and the Meiklejohn Interpretation of the First Amendment*, 79 HARV. L. REV. 1 (1965).

[42] *See* Michelman, *Possession vs. Distribution, supra* note 39, at 1329–34.

[43] For a discussion of Arendt's defense of familial and local-communitarian "privacy" rights, including the exclusionary rights of racial-segregationist communities, as protecting "plurality"—and hence fending off totalitarianism and visionary stasis—in civic debate at the state level, see Failinger, *Equality Versus the Right to Choose Associates. A Critique of Hannah Arendt's View of the Supreme Court's Dilemma*, 49 U. PITT. L. REV. 143, 158–62 (1987); *see also infra* text accompanying notes 134–44 (discussing value of plurality in republican constitutional theory).

[44] "Law . . . is the creation of the free citizenry. Yet law is valued for its role in protecting the public realm." Cornell, *Should a Marxist Believe in Rights?*, 4 PRAXIS INT'L 45, 50 (1984); *cf*. Pocock, *Cambridge Paradigms and Scotch Philosophers. A Study of the Relations Between the Civic Humanist and the Civic Jurisprudential Interpretation of Eighteenth Century Social Thought*, in WEALTH AND VIRTUE 235, 248–49 (I. Hont & M. Ignatieff eds. 1983) ("[I]n republican thinking . . . the rights exist for the sake of the equality and the virtue which is its expression, not the other way round.").

It is certainly true that not all historical versions of republicanism have reflected the inclusory, plurality-protecting ideal that arguably characterizes the tradition at its best. It is also true that extension of the circle of citizens to encompass genuine diversity greatly complicates republican thinking about the relation between rights (or law) and politics. For if republican jurisprudence depends on jurisgenerative politics, jurisgenerative politics in turn seems to depend on the existence of a normative consensus that can hardly survive the diversification of the political community by inclusion of persons of widely and deeply differing experiences and outlooks.[45]

What, after all can jurisgenerative politics be, if not a process of disclosing a latent, pre-existent, actual societal *consensus* respecting the right terms of social ordering?[46] What are the social conditions of such an effective, pre-existent consensus? Historically, those conditions have been conceived as devices for avoiding or denying plurality in the political sphere, usually involving some combination of political hierarchy, civic regimentation, and organicist culture.[47] Modern American political culture is militantly anti-organicist, committed to political democracy, hostile to social-role *constraint*, and broadly reconciled to deep and conflictual diversity of social experience and normative perspective.[48] If any social condition defines modern American politics, plurality does. How, then, might modern American politics be jurisgenerative? What is it, in particular, that we might think that could make a jurisgenerative virtue of plurality?

Perhaps the answer is that republican constitutionalism as I have presented it is just not possible any more, or for us: either not at all (that is, its possibility depends on false or incredible assumptions about social facts), or only on conditions of social ordering or control that are too onerous or repellent to accept.[49] Such a demonstration I would regard as neither a refutation of this essay nor a sign of its failure; if republican constitutionalism isn't possible for us then it isn't, and we may as well know plainly on what rock our ship has for some time been foundering.

If I have not grossly misread the aspirational content of American constitutional discourse, expressed in its organizing tension of self-rule and law-rule, denials of republican constitutionalism's modern possibility will at any rate not be lightly entertained. The next three parts of this essay are, accordingly, devoted to the "deduction" of a set of understandings capable of sustaining that possibility as a credible aspiration worthy of a modern, plural society. In Part II, I consider

---

[45] *See, e.g.*, Young, Polity *and Group Difference: A Critique of the Ideal of Universal Citizenship*, 99 ETHICS (forthcoming 1989); Cover, *supra* note 29, at 13–19.

[46] *Cf.* J. MANSBRIDGE, BEYOND ADVERSARY DEMOCRACY 4–6, 24–25 (1983) (explaining "unitary" as distinguished from "adversary democracy" as process of disclosing latent consensus through argument and discussion).

[47] *See, e.g.*, R. UNGER, FALSE NECESSITY: ANTI-NECESSITARIAN SOCIAL THEORY IN THE SERVICE OF RADICAL DEMOCRACY 92–95 (1987) (reviewing "dosed options" in ancient city-states).

[48] This assessment is generally borne out by R. BELLAH, *supra* note 4. But *see id.* at 277 (people realize that "though the processes of separation and individualization were necessary to free us from the tyrannical structures of the past, they must be balanced by a renewal of commitment and community if they are not to end in self-destruction").

[49] *See, e.g.*, Zuckerman, *supra* note 23, at 95–100 (arguing that specialization of life in modern "technological order" is at odds with "the human integrity at the heart of Madisonian assumptions," is "antithetical to the classical conception of self-government," and "precludes . . . the informed and active citizenry whose part in the political process the framers presupposed").

whether the republican synthesis of self-rule and law-rule is sustainable strictly within the understanding of modern pluralist political science according to which all social interaction is insuperably private-regarding or strategic; I conclude that it is not. In Part III, I consider whether the synthesis is sustainable on the classical American understanding—that of *Federalist No. 78*, as recently refurbished by Bruce Ackerman—according to which periodic, exceptional episodes of relatively public-regarding popular politics issue in higher-law declarations that become and remain fixed as constitutional-legal authority until revised by another such episode. Again, I conclude that it is not. In Part IV, I offer a more thoroughly dialogic and non-authoritarian conception of constitutionalist practice—one that responds affirmatively rather than negatively to social plurality, and also one in which courts play an active and generative role. In developing the dialogic conception I both draw upon the literature of the classical republican tradition and also trace some connections between it and contemporary work on both legal interpretation and the theory of self-government. Finally, in Part V, I return to *Bowers* v. *Hardwick* and sketch the republican-inspired argument for an opposite result in that case—an argument whose familiar feel I hope will help provide some sense of validation for the whole effort.

II. CONSTITUTIONALISM VS. PLURALIST POLITICAL SCIENCE

A. Pluralism

By "pluralism" here I don't mean the acceptance and celebration of diversity within a society. It should already be plain that nothing could be further from the aim and spirit of this essay than to question the value of pluralism in that sense. Rather, I mean by pluralism the deep mistrust of people's capacities to communicate *persuasively* to one another their diverse normative experiences: of needs and rights, values and interests, and, more broadly, interpretations of the world. Pluralism, that is, doubts or denies our ability to communicate such material in ways that move each other's views on disputed normative issues towards felt (not merely strategic) agreement without deception, coercion, or other manipulation.[50] It follows that in pure pluralist vision, good politics does not essentially involve the direction of reason and argument towards any common, ideal, or self-transcendent end. For true pluralists, good politics can only be a market-like medium through which variously interested and motivated individuals and groups seek to maximize their own particular preferences.[51] Pluralist politics, in short, seems the negation of jurisgenerative politics.

Yet the pluralist picture of politics as market cannot do without higher law. From the pluralist standpoint, constitutional law is to politics what private law is

Frank Michelman

---

[50] *See, e.g.*, S. BENHABIB, *supra* note 30, at 313–15, 320–21, 332–36 (holding open communicative possibility that pluralism denies, while noting situations—involving "those who feel that the reconciliation in social life has been achieved at their expense"—in which nature of conflict between parties is such that they cannot mutually recognize each other as "discursive partners," and thus can have no dialogue); J. BUCHANAN, FREEDOM IN CONSTITUTIONAL CONTRACT 11–24 (1977) (expressing pluralist attitude); Minow, *The Supreme Court 1986 Term—Foreword: Justice Engendered*, 101 HARV. L. REV. 10, 57–60, 70–74 (holding open communicative possibility in specific context of constitutional adjudication).

[51] *See, e.g.*, A. BENTLEY, THE PROCESS OF GOVERNMENT (1949); A. DOWNS, AN ECONOMIC THEORY OF DEMOCRACY (1957); M. OLSON, THE LOGIC OF COLLECTIVE ACTION (1965); D. TRUMAN, THE GOVERNMENTAL PROCESS (1958).

to free-market activity: a body of governing rules that stands outside the process, conferring upon the process not only its intelligibility but also its beneficence—not only its structure and order but also its promise of safety, fairness, and utility for participants.[52] I want now to consider whether pluralism unmodified can explain the origins and normative authority of the Constitution, without contravening one or the other of the underlying commitments of constitutionalism, that is, without violating either self-government or the government of laws.

B. Self-Limiting Power, Higher Laze, and Jurisgenesis

The first requirement for any such explanation is that it make sense of the centrality and constancy in American constitutional practice of the remembrance of its origins in public acts of deliberate creation; for that remembrance both deeply reflects and deeply informs American understanding of what it means for a people to be both self-governing and under law.[53] It is, accordingly, an accepted fact of American constitutional history that the founders, republicanly sensitive to the American ideology of popular self-government but also intent upon curbing popular power for the sake of liberty (or, it may be, for the sake of interests[54] conjured with the notion of popular sovereignty in order to produce the magic of power binding and limiting itself. In the most extreme account, the founders induced the popular sovereign to recognize itself for the one-time purpose of legislating its own irrevocable future disappearance from the scene.[55] Less luridly, we think of the founders envisioning the people both constituting themselves as sovereign and, by that same self-constitutive act, entrenching substantive limits on the reach of their own sovereignty, thereby demarcating spheres of private right into which they, the people acting collectively through the agency of their government, might never intrude for the duration of the entrenchment.[56]

The strategy of entrenchment thus implies—at least for pluralists—the radical separation of law from politics. Granting that the constitutionally entrenched law of a self-governing people must originate in popular politics, if that law is also to serve the idea of an effectively self-limiting political will, then that law, once enacted, must immediately abscond from politics to higher ground. It must become an autonomous force against politics, a force elaborated through its own

---

[52] *See, e.g.*, J. BUCHANAN & G. TULLOCK, THE CALCULUS OF CONSENT (1962).

[53] *See, e.g.*, S. LEVINSON, *supra* note 28, at 180–94 (on "adding one's signature to the Constitution"). Doubtless one can envision the possibility of a constitutional practice evolving without benefit of focal, human deliberation and evolving, moreover, in such a way as to satisfy the demand for a rule of law—and even also, in a certain, attenuated sense, the demand for self-government. Hayek, for example, explains law as the progressive codification of the informally originating and accumulating moral experience and practice of a successful civilization. The result could be described as a kind of behind-our-backs self-government: the law would be "ours" although we never deliberately gave it to ourselves. *See* 1 F. HAYEK, LAW, LEGISLATION AND LIBERTY: RULES AND ORDER (1973); 3 F. HAYEK, LAW, LEGISLATION, AND LIBERTY: THE POLITICAL ORDER OF A FREE PEOPLE 153–76 (1979). That is not, however, how American constitutional practice professes to understand itself. Rather, our practice insistently traces its origins to deliberate human action. *See, e.g.*, 2 J. WILSON, THE WORKS OF JAMES WILSON 762 (R. McCloskey ed. 1967) ("[T]he United States exhibit to the world the first instance . . . of a nation . . . assembling voluntarily, deliberating fully, and deciding calmly, concerning that system of government, under which they would wish that they and their posterity should live.").

[54] See, e.g., Komesar, *Paths of Influence. Beard Revisited*, 56 GEO. WASH. L. REV. 124 (1987); Tushnet, *The Constitution as an Economic Document: Beard Revisited*, 56 GEO. WASH. L. REV. 106 (1987).

[55] *See* Miller, *supra* note 23.

[56] *See* J. NEDELSKY, *supra* note 28.

nonpolitical modes of reason by its own nonpolitical, judicial organ.[57] Again we find the republican problem of law-politics circularity lying at the core of American constitutionalism.[58]

While there may be some semblance of mystery here,[59] there is none to which Publius is not equal, by the stroke of *Federalist No. 78*:[60] At the constitutional moment, We The People establish our own sovereignty by legislating to ourselves a supreme law. We thereby create and authorize certain executive and sub-legislative agencies to act, subject to that law's limitations, on various matters of concern to Us, and also certain judicial agencies to enforce those limitations on Our behalf. This Publian reconciliation of people-rule with law-rule obviously reposes on a belief that a political process—specifically, the constitution-making process of We The People—can produce a normative doctrine that commands respect as law.[61] The question now before us is whether it is possible to envision that *constitution-creating* political process strictly within the terms of pluralist political psychology, without contravening one or the other of our constitution-alist premises—either the government of laws or popular self-government. Can pluralist political science account for the possibility of jurisgenerative politics that lies at the problematic core of American constitutional thought?

C. Pluralist Higher Law. "Political" or "Metaphysical"?[62]

The question here is not whether the Constitution's *content is* well explained, in the sense of rationally justified, as having been aptly devised for a country whose future politics were expected to be pluralist in character. Instead, it is whether and how the legitimate authority—the "sense of validity"—of *the political event consisting of the Constitution's enactment* might be brought within the terms of pluralist explanation.

Pluralist-inspired rationalizations of constitutional content are certainly not unknown to the literature.[63] All such accounts have at their core a line of argu-mentation designed to show something like the following: Given the various, partly complementary but partly conflicting, pre-political aims and interests of the individuals concerned, and given also the inevitably competitive and strategic motivational realities of social (including political and economic) interaction,[64]

---

[57] *See id.*; Nedelsky, *Confining Democratic Politics: Anti-Federalists, Federalists, and the Constitution* (Book Review), 96 HARV. L. REV. 340 (1982).

[58] *See supra* text accompanying notes 25–29.

[59] *See* J. NEDELSKY, *supra* note 56, on "the irreducible problem of a government setting and enforcing its own limits" (manuscript at 1–8), and "the dilemma of self-limiting government—of the political entity requiring limits being the one to set those limits" (manuscript at 1–11).

[60] THE FEDERALIST No. 78 (A. Hamilton).

[61] "Publian" is, I believe, an Ackermanian coinage. *See* Ackerman, *supra* note 5, at 1023 n.17. For another con-temporary strong reminder of the Publian answer, see Amar, *Of Sovereignty and Federalism*, 96 YALE L. J. 1425 (1987). For the historical necessity and invention of popular sovereignty theory, see G. Wood, *supra* note 3, at 462–63, 530–32, 599–600.

[62] *Cf.* Rawls, *supra* note 25 (contrasting "political" and "metaphysical" interpretations of Rawlsian justice-as-fairness).

[63] *See, e.g.,* R. EPSTEIN, TAKINGS: PRIVATE PROPERTY AND THE THEORY OF EMINENT DOMAIN (1986); Epstein, *supra* note 28; Macey, *Competing Economic Views of the Constitution*, 56 GEO. WASH. L. REV. 50 (1987); Posner, *supra* note 18, at 5–19. Pluralistic justificatory accounts of constitutional content may also be constructed out of such large and notable (and otherwise diverse) works of political and constitutional theory as J. BUCHANAN & G. TULLOCK, *supra* note 52; J. ELY, DEMOCRACY AND DISTRUST: A THEORY OF JUDICIAL REVIEW (1980); and J. BAWLS, A THEORY OF JUSTICE (1971).

[64] *See supra* text accompanying notes 50–51.

it is rational for everyone concerned to prefer the constitution in question to the next best practically attainable alternative.[65] Such arguments are thus based on a set of characteristically pluralist premises, some of which are descriptive or social-scientific in content, while others are normative or philosophical insofar as they posit a particular notion of rationality rooted in a certain conception of the self, its ends, and its relations with others.[66]

Insofar as such an argument stands outside of actual, political history, it has a transcendental (or what Rawls calls a "metaphysical") character.[67] Taking its scientific and philosophical premises as given, the argument's gist then is that each person, whether she knows it or not, ought to accept the law in question as conformable to some assertedly objective notion of reason, nature, fairness, utility, or other criterion of rightness. For example, the contention may be that the law *ought to be* accepted by everyone because it *would be* accepted by strategically motivated, rationally self-regarding social contractors hypothetically abstracted—or imaginatively separated by a "veil of ignorance"—from their actual worldly situations and perspectives.[68]

No such purely transcendental argument can by its own force confer upon any constitution or other law the validity of self-givenness.[69] Lacking actual societal consensus on its premises both descriptive and normative, such an argument by itself does nothing, from a republican stand-point, to remove the law it rationalizes from the long list of instances of government by some "men" (those who accept the argument's premises) of others (those who reject those premises).[70] Whatever kind of authority a law may possess by force of transcendental justifiability, it is not the authority of self-government. In order to approach republican validation of a law, justificatory argument must at least begin to explain how that law might have been actually regarded by the people subject to it, in all their actual social and experiential situations, as deserving acceptance by them.[71]

---

[65] Such an account might point to (i) the overwhelming productivity advantages attributed to capitalist (competitive, market-based) economic organization; (ii) a perceived dominance (at least, or especially, in a successful capitalist society) of private-regarding political motivations over public-regarding ones; (iii) deep diversity and conflict among the values and self-perceived interests of citizens and factional groups (at least, or especially, in a modern capitalist society); and (iv) the resultant dangers of grievous oppression, exploitation and waste inherent in majoritarian politics unless effectively regulated by a protective constitution. A pluralist constitutional explanation might undertake to show that on such a set of assumptions, a chief virtue of the constitution in question is its expected effect of constraining private-regarding political motivations into simulatedly public-regarding channels, through both its structure and process rules for majoritarian legislative action, and the substantive limits it sets for such action. *See, e.g.,* Macey, *supra* note 63, at 54–59, 71–76; Epstein, *supra* note 28.

[66] The locus classicus is T. HOBBES, LEVIATHAN Chs. 1–13.

[67] *See* Rawls, *supra* note 25, at 223.

[68] To this extent, much of Rawls' argument in J. RAWLS, *supra* note 63, in support of the quasi-constitutional conception of "justice as fairness" may be construed as transcendental. *But see* Rawls, *The Idea of an Overlapping Consensus,* 7 OXFORD J. LEGAL STUD. 1 (1987) [hereinafter Rawls, *Overlapping Consensus);* Rawls, *supra* note 25; Rawls, *Kantian Constructivism in Moral Theory,* 77 J. PHIL. 515 (1980).

[69] *See* S. BENHABIB, *supra* note 30, at 94–95, 101, 103 (criticizing Hegel), 299–300 (contrasting Kantian ethics with communicative ethics); B. FAY, CRITICAL SOCIAL SCIENCE 183 (1987); Rorty, *The Priority of Democracy to Philosophy,* in THE VIRGINIA STATUTE OF RELIGIOUS FREEDOM: ITS EVOLUTION AND CONSEQUENCES IN AMERICAN HISTORY 257, 258–59, 261–65 (M. Peterson & R. Vaughan eds. 1988); Walzer, *Philosophy and Democracy,* 9 POL. THEORY 379 (1981). The distinction between a law's objective rightness and its enjoyment of a sense of validity was one that James Madison understood. Madison based his argument against frequent constitutional revision in part on the extra veneration accorded to a constitution by reason of its age, apart from its objective merit. *See* THE FEDERALIST No. 49 (J. Madison); *infra* note 97 and accompanying text.

[70] *See* S. BENHABIB, *supra* note 30, at 313–14; Rawls, *supra* note 25, at 225–26. This is not to deny that "hypothetical abstraction about what individuals could accept is [capable] of illuminating moral responsibilities or rights," Allen, *Taking Liberties: Privacy, Private Choice, and Social Contract Theory,* 56 U. CIN. L. REV. 461, 489–90 (1987), or at least of clarifying controversies about those matters.

[71] *See* S. BENHABIB, *supra* note 30, at 310–11, 341–42.

Perhaps it is possible by historicization to convert to such purposes what first appears as a transcendental justification.[72] For example, one might try to show that the actual historical conditions under which people had to decide whether to approve our Constitution approximated a hypothetical "veil of ignorance";[73] that the actual ratification procedures approximated consensual approval;[74] and that the requisite consensus was actually obtained by the use of argument to convince voters that the proposed Constitution would indeed serve their several and various, privately conceived interests better than any available alternative.[75] To show that such an account could possibly succeed would apparently be to establish the conceptual possibility, at least, of describing a jurisgenerative political process without ever stepping outside the terms of pluralist political psychology.

We have already noted, however, that the success of any such account depends on giving credible content to the notion of everyone's coming to accept, as his or her own, all the normative and scientific beliefs underlying the supposedly persuasive demonstration that this is the right or the best constitution from anyone's private-regarding standpoint. It is obvious that not nearly all Americans have ever deeply agreed on any set of beliefs capable of supporting any such demonstration. Perhaps we can imagine people being persuaded to accept the requisite beliefs *arguendo*, as suitable to the immediate, urgent, practical work of resolving upon some constitution, while continuing to doubt or deny their deep truth (or rightness, or inevitability).[76] But at just that point in our imaginings, the ethos of the ratification debates would have passed from pluralist to republican.[77] We would be envisioning some participants appealing to others to agree either that (i) the others, allowing for their differences in needs and out-looks, have what they ought for their own sakes to regard as good reasons for adopting, at least provisionally, the assumptions (however competitivistic) and norms (however calculative) presupposed by the pluralist rationalization of the constitution's merit from everyone's standpoint, or else that (ii) due consideration for the overriding interest of "the whole" requires that they do so. Participants, then, would be regarding themselves and each other as arguing sincerely on behalf of one another or of everyone, or as each adopting the interest of the whole as his own interest—an understanding that certainly seems confirmed by much of the actual rhetoric of the debates.[78]

Such a round of persuasive arguments and discussions seems inconceivable without conscious reference by those involved to their mutual and reciprocal awareness

[72] *See* Rawls, *supra* note 25, at 231 (seeking to "conceive how, given a desire for free and uncoerced agreement, a public understanding could arise consistent with the historical conditions and constraints of our social world"); Richards, *supra* note 2, at 820.

The argument I sketch here on behalf of the possibility of pluralist jurisgenesis is adapted from Macey, *supra* note 63.

[73] *See* Macey, *supra* note 63, at 72–75. Macey in effect suggests that the veil of ignorance was simulated by a combination of two factors: (i) the proposed Constitution's having been cast in the form of general-structural (as opposed to policy-specific) provisions whose long-range consequences for specifically partisan interests (as opposed to general interests in social order and prosperity) were virtually impossible to predict, and (ii) the pressure for concession to the demands of general order and prosperity, and to the vital interests of others, exerted by awareness of the super-majoritarian, quasi-consensual ratification procedure. I think that any reliance on the second of these factors would take Macey's account of the Constitution's "public-regarding" origins and character beyond the limits of strictly pluralist explanation, into republican territory. *See infra* text accompanying notes 76–78.

[74] *See* Macey, *supra* note 63, at 76, 79.

[75] *See id.* at 77–79.

[76] *See* Rawls, *supra* note 25, at 229–30, 245–46.

[77] *See* Rawls, *Overlapping Consensus*, *supra* note 68, at 9–12, 18–23; Rawls, *supra* note 25, at 247–48.

[78] *See, e.g.*, THE FEDERALIST *passim*.

of being co-participants not just in this one debate, but in a more encompassing common life, bearing the imprint of a common past, within and from which the arguments and claims arise and draw their meaning.[79] The *persuasive* character of the process depends on the normative efficacy of some context that is everyone's— of the past that is constitutively present in and for every self as language, culture, worldview, and political memory. Is this not, for example, how we almost irresistibly recall successive generations of Americans arguing to each other that "we" are already committed to religious plurality, toleration, and privacy—and by extension to some broader if still limited libertarian principle—by common narratives of refuge explaining how "we" came to be here, in this country?[80]

What we thus imagine, remember, and chronicle is republican political conversation.

D. Republican Jurisgenesis. A Politics of Law

Jurisgenerative political debate among a plurality of self-governing subjects involves the contested "re-collection" (in Drucilla Cornell's telling phrase) of a fund of public normative references conceived as narratives, analogies, and other professions of commitment.[81] Upon that fund those subjects draw both for identity and, by the same token, for moral and political freedom.[82] That fund is the matrix of their identity "as" a people or political community, that is, as individuals in effectively persuasive, dialogic relation with each other, and it is also the medium of their political freedom, that is, of their translation of past into future through the dialogic exercise of recollective "'imagination.'"[83] The republican idea of political jurisgenesis thus presupposes (in what might be called a transcendental moment of republican constitutional thought) that such a fund of normatively effective material—publicly cognizable, persuasively recollectible and contestable—is always already available.[84]

Interestingly, the idea of such a fund, together with that of the persuasive process of its contested recollection, seems all but indistinguishable from one of our most influential contemporary conceptions not of politics but of law. Ronald Dworkin's linked notions of law "as integrity," of law as the medium of the community's constitutive

---

[79] *See* R. BELLAH, *supra* note 4, at 281–82; B. FAY, *supra* note 69, at 160–61, 163–64.

[80] *See, e.g.*, McGowan v. Maryland, 366 U.S. 460, 461, 463–66 (1961); Everson v. Board of Educ., 330 U.S. l, 8–16 (1947); Cover, *supra* note 29, at 26–29 (quoting and discussing amicus briefs filed on behalf of Mennonites in Bob Jones Univ. v. United States, 461 U.S. 574 (1983), and on behalf of the Amish in Wisconsin v. Yoder, 406 U.S. 205 (1972)); *cf.* Rawls, *supra* note 25, at 225, 228–29, 240–42, 249 (arguing thusly to *us, now*); Cover, *supra* note 29, at 4–5 ("For every constitution there is an epic . . . ").

[81] *See* Cornell, *Institutionalization of Meaning, Recollective Imagination, and the Potential for Transformative Legal Interpretation*, 136 U. PA. L. REV. 1135, 1171–72 (1988).

[82] Hanna Pitkin endorses this view: "We are human selves, capable of choice and action, precisely insofar as we are part of a human culture which has, in our time and in us, a specific, determinate form that cannot be wished away but must be recognized if we are to act." H. PITKIN, *supra* note 31, at 279 (offering "republican interpretation" of thought of Machiavelli); *see also* M. SANDEL, LIBERALISM AND THE LIMITS OF JUSTICE 179–83 (1982) (affirming relation between moral freedom and socially and historically situated nature of self).

[83] Cornell, *supra* note 81, at 1204.

[84] *See* R. DWORKIN, LAW'S EMPIRE 348 (1986) ("Hercules interprets not just the statute's text but its life, the process that begins before it becomes law and extends far beyond that moment."); *cf.* B. FAY, *supra* note 69, at 174:

> The understanding which we can have of ourselves is always 'in the middle of the way': there are no absolute beginnings and absolute endings. . . . This is because we are always interpreting ourselves 'in the light of anticipation, of what we will do and what the outcomes of this activity will be, and because we are always interpreting our deeds and thoughts in light of our present understandings-understandings which themselves are always changing in the course of our own and others' history.

commitment to "consistency in principle" in its treatments of its members, and of law as the "personification" of the community itself (that is, as the institutional manifestation of the political community's existence and identity as such) all emphasize law's historical aspect.[85] They all present law as the institutionalized form of self-consciousness on the part of community members about their situatedness in a common past, required by a conception of personal and political freedom that involves our continuing to be ourselves even as we reconsider what we are and ought to be about. At the same time, Dworkin's insistence on the bottomlessly interpretive nature of law, on the pervasively political character of legal interpretation, and on the necessity of political-moral choice that befalls judges adjudicating "hard" cases, reminds us of law's self-revisionary aspect, echoing the self-critical dimension of moral and political freedom.[86] Perhaps it should come as no surprise that what appears under the name of politics in this essay's republican-inspired account of the validity of law should appear under the name of law in another's study of political legitimacy from the standpoint of jurisprudence. We already knew, after all, that republican constitutionalism implied a politics of law.[87]

So what began as pluralist constitutional explanation has now ended by returning us to the indispensable premise of Publian history: that Americans once rose to the republican achievement of popular self-creation—of recollecting themselves as a people—through a politics of partial self-transcendence and of law.

Once, however, is hardly enough.

III. POPULAR AUTHORITARIANISM

A. Founders and Citizens: Of Constitutional Time and Alienated Authority

1. FOUNDERS

"Proclaiming its desire to 'secure the Blessings of Liberty to ourselves and our Posterity,' the Constitution took the liberty of speaking for that posterity."[88] Such authoritarian posturings by American founders and their reflection, on occasion, by a respectful judicial posterity are, on one view of the tradition, a classical republican reminiscence. For there is no denying that the tradition has its authoritarian side, symbolized by the classical republican figure of the heroic Founder or Legislator:[89] the historically singular figure who by extraordinary force of intellect, will, and personality has succeeded in imposing upon a turbulent and endangered country a political regime, in the form of a constitution, so designed that faithful adherence to its precepts will tend to reproduce the civic virtue

---

[85] See R. DWORKIN, supra note 84, at 93–96, 164–75, 189–90, 211–15, 219–28.

[86] See id. at 62–68 (interpretive nature of law), 73–76 (political character of legal interpretation), 87–93 (political choices), 189 (self-revisionary aspect), 359–60 (interpretive nature of law), 413 (describing law's role in constructing new community by helping old community revise itself); see also Dworkin, Law as Interpretation, 60 TEX. L. REV. 527 (1982) (political character of legal interpretation). Cornell's critique of Dworkin helps us retrieve this reminder from partial obfuscation by the lingering remnant of authoritarianism (or "positivism") in Dworkin's jurisprudence. See Cornell, supra note 81, at 1141. Lipkin, Conventionalism, Pragmatism, and Constitutional Revolutions, 21 U.C. DAVIS L. REV. 645, 731–32, 753, 757–60 (1988) denies the compatibility of Dworkin's theory of law as integrity with the transformative aspect of constitutional adjudication as Cornell and I both conceive of it. See infra notes 145–47 and accompanying text.

[87] See supra text accompanying notes 39–43.

[88] Leubsdorf, Deconstructing the Constitution, 40 STAN. L. REV. 181, 188 (1987).

[89] See, e.g., H. PITKIN, supra note 31, at 52–55, 68–69; J. SHELAR, MEN AND CITIZENS: A STUDY OF ROUSSEAU'S SOCIAL THEORY 165–69 (1969).

required to sustain that very adherence.[90] The myth of the Founder apparently describes an ideal history of the republic in which there was and will be only one act of political-moral originality; in which all the political freedom belongs for all time to a single heroic individual, or perhaps generation;[91] and in which the only act of political valor or worth remaining to the denizens of posterity is, from time to time, when by fault of corruption things threaten to fall apart, to assert a grip on themselves and, in the Machiavellian formula,[92] return the country to its origins by rededicating themselves to the founding principles.

2. THE QUESTION OF CONSTITUTIONAL DURATION

Consider, now, the American founders' debate over the permanence of their own foundations.[93] Restaging that debate, it is tempting to cast Jefferson as Pluralist, playing opposite Madison's Republican.[94] Jefferson's protest against the inter-generational tyranny of constitutional permanence seems most compelling on a view of constitution-making as just another round of pluralist politics-as-usual, while Madison's protest against the disruptive effects of repeated future constitution-making might be taken to valorize *the* Constitution—"*this* Constitution"[95]—as the exceptionally meritorious product of a peculiarly virtuous historical event.

Consider, however, a somewhat different interpretation of the dispute. We have seen that for pluralist political science—based as it is on a political psychology that cannot entertain the possibility of jurisgenerative politics—the only form of discursive validation available for a constitution is the metaphysical-not-political appeal to rationality or natural law: that is, the appeal to that constitution's just being, as a demonstrable matter of objective reason, *the right* constitution for a country such as ours is fated to be, populated by folk such as we by nature are.[96]

---

[90] *See* H. PITKIN, *supra* note 31, at 75–77; *see also* Appleby, *The American Heritage. The Heirs and the Disinherited,* 74 J. AM. HIST. 798–801 (1987); *cf.* Pennell v. City of San Jose, 108 S. Ct. 849, 864 (1988) (Scalia, J., dissenting) ("The fostering of an intelligent democratic process is one of the happy effects of the constitutional prescription [of compensation for property taken]—perhaps accidental, perhaps not."); R. EPSTEIN, *supra* note 63, at 344–46.

[91] See H. PITKIN, *supra* note 31, at 79:

The Founder . . . must generate in his "sons" . . . piety toward his initiative. He must be the very opposite of a parricide because he must embody filial piety for them to emulate. And he must slay his sons because if they sought to be fully alive and autonomously follow his example, no lasting institution would be constructed by him.

This is Pitkin's rendition of the lesson drawn by Machiavelli from Livy's account of the public execution of the rebellious sons of Junius Brutus, founder of the Roman republic, over which their father presided. See *id.* at 59–61; N. MACHIAVELLI, DISCOURSES ON THE FIRST TEN BOOKS OF TITUS LIVY 392–94 (B. Crick ed. 1970) (bk. III, ch. 3). *But see infra* notes 101–02.

[92] *See, e.g.,* N. MACHIAVELLI, *supra* note 91, at 385–90 (bk. II, ch. 1).

[93] *See* A. KOCH, JEFFERSON AND MADISON: THE GREAT COLLABORATION 62–96 (1950). *Compare* T. JEFFERSON, NOTES ON THE STATE OF VIRGINIA 62–96 (W. Peden ed. 1955) (proposing constitutional conventions whenever called for by any two of the three branches of the government) *with* THE FEDERALIST No. 49 (J. Madison) (arguing against such easy access to constitutional revision).

[94] This would be, of course, a reversal of the usual tendency to contrast the obvious republican affinities of Jeffersonian agrarianism with Madison's prescience, if not parentage, of modern pluralist political science. *See, e.g.,* D. McCoy, THE ELUSIVE REPUBLIC: POLITICAL ECONOMY IN JEFFERSONIAN AMERICA (1980) (Jefferson); R. DAHL, A PREFACE To DEMOCRATIC THEORY (1956) (Madison). *But see* G. WILLS, EXPLAINING AMERICA: THE FEDERALIST xv–xxii, 254–70 (1981) (Madison); Appleby, *What is Still American in the Political Philosophy of Thomas Jefferson,* 39 WM. & MARY Q. 287 (1982) (Jefferson). Perhaps such reversability just signifies the intimate embrace in which the two visions are locked in American political thought.

[95] *See* Van Alstyne, *Interpreting* This *Constitution: The Unhelpful Contributions of Special Theories of Judicial Review,* 35 U. FLA. L. REV. 209 (1983).

[96] *See supra* text accompanying notes 62–71. By "discursive validation" I mean reasons for re-specting the Constitution as law other than the brutely positivistic reason that the Constitution *just is* the law in force. *See supra* notes 30, 53.

On this view of the matter, Madison's sense of the Constitution's exceptionality, inspiring his defense of its permanence, would rest not on its special provenance in jurisgenerative politics but on its special conformity to right reason. For insofar as a law's special authority is felt to derive from its informing reason, that law presumably ought to be left unmolested until, if ever, it is determined (by whoever or whatever we imagine determining these things) that that informing reason is vitiated by error. (Perhaps nature turns out different from what we had thought. Perhaps the canons of reason themselves undergo change.)[97]

Conversely, to trace a constitution's validity as the people's law to its republican political origins would evidently imply that constitution's impermanence. For we have seen that the requisite context of jurisgenerative political conversation is a prior deposit of normative references composing the imprint of a people's history as a normatively self-directing political community, and of course the history of a contemporary people can never have been completely contained in the history of an ancestral generation.[98] A constitution cannot retain its claim to republican validity without changing in response to historical change in the people's composition and values, its identity and "fate as a People."[99]

3. CITIZENS

Taken as a self-sufficient emblem of the republican constitution, the figure of the once-and-future Founder would thus be both puzzling and disheartening—an epitome of both alienated authority and political-moral stasis, in both respects antithetical to a modern sense of personal and political freedom. Happily, the tradition's figurative vocabulary supplies the additional component needed for a more satisfactory view in its image of the Citizen.

Granted, the traditional republican image of the Citizen contains its own ambiguity.[100] But from a modern standpoint, it seems a disservice both to republican thought and to ourselves—it seems our failure to extract from that thought the best it has to offer us—to regard the Machiavellian doctrine of return to origins as

---

[97] Madison expressed himself on this point with an easy and elusive ambiguity—nicely echoed in David Richards' reprise of Madison's view. *See* Richards, *supra* note 2, at 818–20. In THE FEDERALIST No. 49, Madison presented three arguments, in ascending order of importance, against Jefferson's proposal for constitutional conventions upon the call of any two of the three branches of the central government. *See* T. JEFFERSON, *supra* note 93. First, frequent proposals for repairing the Constitution would imply its imperfection and thereby tend to undermine its veneration by public opinion. "In a nation of philosophers. . . . [a] reverence for the laws would be sufficiently inculcated by the voice of an enlightened reason. . . . [I]n every other nation, the most rational government will not find it a superfluous advantage to have the prejudices of the community on its side." THE FEDERALIST No. 49, *supra* note 23, at 315 (J. Madison). Second, the successful round of constitution-making recently completed in America occurred in conditions of emergency that tended to suppress the worst of public passions and stimulate civically virtuous devotion to the work—a set of conditions that may not attend future constitution-making. *Id.* Third, "the decisions which would probably result from such appeals would not answer the purpose of maintaining the constitutional equilibrium of the government." *Id.* For various reasons, Madison expected that "the passions, . . . not the reason, of the public would sit in judgment. But it is the reason, alone, of the public, that ought to control and regulate the government. The passions ought to be controlled and regulated by the government." *Id.* at 317 (emphases in original).

[98] *See* B. FAY, *supra* note 69, at 173:

> The narratives intent on illuminating human lives are historically sensitive in that their nature changes in relation to the historically changing circumstances of both the narrators and the narratees. This historical sensitivity means that the ideal of a perfectly dear self-knowledge deriving from knowing 'the genuine narrative of one's life' is not compelling. Who humans are and what roles they play are continually shifting because of their ever-changing location in history and because of the ever-changing perspective of those trying to tell their story.

[99] Ackerman, *supra* note 11, at 1180; see Brennan, *supra* note 28, at 438; Lipkin, *supra* note 86, at 706–11.

[100] *See, e.g.*, J. SHKLAR, *supra* note 89, at 180–83 (presenting Rousseau's image of citizenship as epitomizing motivation to abide by founding principles).

attributing distinct and complementary kinds of republican virtue to the founder inventing the social order and to the citizens reciprocally submitting. The more challenging reading, recently clarified by Hanna Pitkin's probing of Machiavelli's own thoughts on the matter, sees citizens as founders, corruption as alienation of authority, and virtue as the spirit of constitutional renovation.[101] The republican images of founder and citizen may in this way be used to express the generative tension of political freedom. Foundership stands for freedom as security—the security of the people, of their lives and of their society, against annihilation by enemies external and internal: domination, corruption, entropy, chaos. A founding unifies, invents *ex nihilo*, thrives as authority, requires submission, succeeds by endurance. Citizenship stands for freedom as activity: the constant redetermination by the people for themselves of the terms on which they live together. Citizens are a plurality, appeal argumentatively to available reasons, thrive on contestation, require mutuality, succeed by self-recollection. In sum, the dialectic of foundership and citizenship may be taken as republicanism's traditional, figurative expression of what I have presented as American constitutionalism's problematic and dynamic core—that is, its endless interplay between the principles of legality (entailing respect for historical commitment) and self-government (entailing respect for the human capacity for self-renewal).[102]

---

[101] Pitkin writes:

Perhaps one should construe the forgetfulness that gradually corrupts a composite body as reification: a coming to take for granted as "given" and inevitable what is in fact the product of human action. Thus people may come to consider their civic order beyond their choice or control and, therefore, beyond their responsibility, secure without any special effort on their part. Then each may feel free to poach on the public spirit . . . of others, behaving as if someone else were in charge and losing touch with his own stake in public life, [perhaps succumbing to) . . . the existential fear inherent in recognizing the full extent of human responsibility, the fragility of human order and its dependence on our commitment. From that perspective, the return to origins would be a return not to the initial institutions but to the spirit of origins, the human capacity to originate. . . . As Strauss says, Machiavelli eventually reveals that "foundation is, as it were, continuous foundation" and is carried on jointly by many.

. . . From this perspective, believing in the superhuman Founder and seeking to imitate him by dutiful obedience rather than by discovering one's own capacity to found are not merely failures to recognize the actual origins of one's community and its tradition, but also failures in self-knowledge.

H. PITKIN, *supra* note 31, at 276–78.

[102] Again, Pitkin finds the makings of this view in the republican thought of Machiavelli:

[I]f the discovery of this capacity in ourselves [to create and sustain civilization) is a self-recognition, it is accompanied by a simultaneous discovery of our particular, historically shaped selves, and the particular, historically shaped way of life of our community. . . .

The community, like the choosing self, already exists in its historical particularity. Both can be changed, and some changes will be an enhancement of the self, a return to fundamental principles. Becoming aware that one has a choice about one's habits and commitments need not mean abandoning them but may equally well lead to their reendorsement, to holding the same commitments in a new way.

Id. at 279.

Pitkin suggests that in a certain equivocation in Machiavelli's account of the history of Florence—between the city's origin as a colonial outpost under Caesarist imperial auspices and its earlier origin as an indigenous Tuscan creation—there is a lesson to be read about an important avenue for self-recollection by citizens: "Perhaps it would be enough-would in important ways even be preferable—to be merely Tuscan and Florentine rather than Roman, to be oneself rather than bound to a mythical hero?" *Id.* at 95; *see also id.* at 259–62. In other words, citizens can redefine their political community by discovering or remembering new or different founders and founding moments. See *infra* text accompanying notes 117–23, 150–56; *see also* Minow, *supra* note 10, at 1877:

The civil rights movement . . . created a legacy of meanings for the Fourteenth Amendment, reflecting the commitment of civil rights activists and the officials persuaded by them to incorporate elements of the movement into the formal legal system. Invocation of . . . that history can add to the persuasive force [of] rights discourse even when that discourse depends on nothing beyond current and future human choices.

B. Periodic Citizenship

One all-conditioning, prepossessing fact—the fact of history, or temporality—invites us to use sequential alternation to preserve both principles of the republican constitutionalist antithesis. Nothing, it seems, could be simpler: From time to time refoundings occur, and in the wake of each follows a period of law-abiding citizenship.[103]

Insofar as our own Constitution expressly contemplates anything like occasional refoundings, it does so in article V. But article V seems, upon consideration, decidedly *not* a license to refound. If article V seems from one standpoint the Constitution's admission of its own alterability,[104] from another standpoint article V seems the Constitution's presumption of its own entrenchment. We might, indeed, regard article V as the epitome of the founding arrogance: the arrogance not just of qualified entrenchment of the founders' ideas about constitutional-legal content, but absolute entrenchment of their ideas about constitutional-legislative process.[105]

Bruce Ackerman's elaboration of Publian popular-sovereignty theory is commendable for its special sensitivity to such an encroachment by article V on the preserve of republican citizenship.[106] Out of that sensitivity comes Ackerman's *insistence* upon judicially cognizable constitutional alteration whenever a civically aroused constitutional majority of the people and their leaders have found a way to adapt—or bend, or stretch—the Constitution's institutional forms, especially those providing for the separation of powers (whose use for this constitutional-legislative purpose may bear no more than a remote analogical resemblance to the procedures prescribed for the same purpose by article V) to the conduct of what Ackerman calls constitutional, and I call republican and jurisgenerative, politics: the mobilization, formation, and expression of a public-regarding, popular determination to legislate a "decisive break with [the country's] constitutional past."[107] Ackerman's is the most deeply popularist, and genuinely republican, constitutional theory now going. In its popularism lies its appeal; but therein also lies, I am afraid, its danger from the standpoint of a concern about the excessively authoritarian jurisprudence of *Bowers v. Hardwick*. From that standpoint, the objection to deep popularism as a validating constitutional premise is that when translated into the form of a historical sequence, that premise finds expression—at least in the current Ackermanian version—as authoritarian constitutional jurisprudence.

Let us consider what motivates Ackerman's inquiry into the possibility of nonformal, "structural" amendment of the people's Constitution. Ackerman asks how one might justify historic Supreme Court decisions that have given effect to constitutional change in what he takes to be a progressive direction. Specifically, he seeks a way of justifying these decisions by arguments that maintain the republican sense of the validity of constitutional law not only as popularly self-given but also as always above and prior to arbitrary, personal will or preference. Accordingly, he

Frank Michelman

---

[103] Pitkin argues that such a sequential deployment of the images risks losing touch with citizen-ship, for reasons that recall the familiar Thayerite objection to activist judicial review. *Compare* H. Pitkin, *supra* note 31, at 97–98 with J. THAYER, JOHN MARSHALL 106–07 (1901). *See infra* note 127 and accompanying text.

[104] *See* Schneiderman v. United States, 320 U.S. 119, 137 (1943) (relying on Article V to "refute the idea that . . . one who advocates radical changes" in the Constitution cannot honestly swear loyalty to it); S. LEVINSON, *supra* note 28, at 135–38.

[105] *See* Ackerman, *supra* note 5, at 1059–60.

[106] *See id.* at 1057–63.

[107] Ackerman, *supra* note 11, at 1172, *see also* Ackerman, *supra* note 5, at 1053–56.

demands arguments that steer clear of the "legal nihilism" courted by readings of constitutional text and precedent that purport to be interpretations but are so "fast and loose" that they smack of interpretative fraud.[108]

Without assistance from the notion of informal amendment, Ackerman believes, we cannot explain the legitimacy of judicial revolutions like the New Deal Court's wholesale rejection of *Lochner*-era jurisprudence in favor of judicial affirmation of the constitutional rectitude of the welfare state, and the Warren Court's detection of thitherto unrecognized meanings in "the equal protection of the laws." This is so, in Ackerman's view, because only the people speaking in their higher law-making modality—only the legislative utterance of a "mobilized constitutional majority"—can authorize a sharp judicial departure from a prior constitutional-legal understanding that itself must be taken, for the sake of its own some-time legitimacy, as having emanated from the still prior law-making pronouncements of a civically mobilized citizenry.[109] Without an actual, intervening event of jurisgenerative popular politics, Ackerman can see no solution to what he perceives as an otherwise insoluble problem of legitimacy: the legitimacy, that is, of the judicial creativities of both the New Deal and the Warren Courts, which he believes must, without his solution of recognizing intervening constitutional amendments authored by the people informally, stand condemned as constitutionally unauthorized judicial usurpations of democratic authority.

Now consider what Ackerman's position says about how the Supreme Court should dispose of *Bowers v. Hardwick*. Straightforwardly, it implies that *the judiciary* can never take upon itself the instigation of a constitutional moment by proposing, in the form of a renovative judicial decision, a "decisive break" with the people's prior pronouncements on political morality. In Ackerman's theory, the judiciary is cast as the agent of our constitutional past. What is more to the point, Ackerman, evoking the nihilist menace, leaves us to infer that as the faithful agent of our past the judiciary cannot also be a spontaneous agent of our future.[110] The judiciary appears in the theory as the specially entrusted agent and organ of the people's past law-giving, as such the special guardian of the very principle of legality—of its credibility—against corrosion by suspicious interpretation or pseudo-interpretation. It would seem that a court outspokenly "recollecting" the authorities with a conscious eye on the future would be dangerously consorting with "legal nihilism." From that it would seem to follow that the judiciary's role in the process of constitutional change can only be benedictory, never prophetic.[111] A justice conscientiously committed to that theory must have, so far

---

[108] *See* Ackerman, *supra* note 5, at 1070.

[109] *Id.* at 1053, 1070–71.

[110] My appraisal of Ackerman's constitutional theory in this respect parallels Drucilla Cornell's appraisal of the jurisprudence of Ronald Dworkin. *See* Cornell, *supra* note 81, at 1140–42. Dworkin too links futurism with nihilism through his jurisprudential category of legal "instrumentalism." See R. DWORKIN, *supra* note 84, at 95, 98, 152–53, 160–62, 318.

[111] In Ackerman's New Deal paradigm of structural amendment, the Court's crucial role is precisely that of putting up a very public and articulate defense of the old order against the futuristic pretensions of the political branches—a barrier of resistance for the political branches to overcome, if they can, by successfully evoking a decisive popular endorsement of their assault on the Court's guardianship of the hitherto established understanding. Only after such a popular mandate has been delivered does the acquiescent Court officiate over the final consolidation of the change. *See* Ackerman, *supra* note 5, at 1153–57; Ackerman, *supra* note 11, at 1174. When Ackerman does expressly contemplate the possibility of "*Court-led*" constitutional transformation," he restricts that possibility to the case in which an already successfully consummated series of "transformative" judicial appointments has disclosed a popular will in favor of change, leaving us to puzzle over what he means in this context by judicial leadership. See Ackerman, *supra* note 11, at 1172 n.11 (emphasis in original).

as I can see, a hard time escaping the authoritarian logic of Justice White's majority opinion in *Bowers*. Moreover, that condition must last until, if ever, there occurs a nationally organized, popular political mobilization that can fairly be said to have resolved the issue of political morality presented in that case. Hardwick must abide an historically concrete occasion of constitutional politics, articulated in highly visible and contentious official (or better, for Ackerman's theory, debatably official) acts of the legislative and executive branches (perhaps enriched and propelled by backward-looking judicial reactions thereto), capable of engaging a decisive popular response to his appeal to political freedom.[112]

In his perception that the judicial creativities of the New Deal and Warren Courts present a legitimacy problem otherwise insoluble, Ackerman stands on common ground with Robert Bork. He shares Bork's insistence on the authoritarian character of the law—on the anteriority to the case and exteriority to the judge of the arguments that determine judicial action. Ackerman shares with Bork the view that judicial power cannot be legitimate unless its exercise consists, in the final analysis, of the translation of directions uttered in the past by someone else—the people acting in a suitably organized and galvanized jurisgenerative political modality.

As we know, actual episodes of such constitutional politics—of republican popular mobilization—have been and probably must forever be rare on the national scale. In effect, then, Ackerman seems to condemn the history of the country's normative

---

[112] Ackerman declines to suggest that the events surrounding the Senate's rejection of President Reagan's nomination of Robert Bork to a seat on the Supreme Court might amount to that occasion, rather construing the Bork nomination as a *failed* occasion of *conservative* constitutional transformation. *See id.* at 1178.

Against my pessimistic appraisal of Ackerman's theory's implications for the *Bowers* case, it might be urged that the relevant values endorsed by American constitutional moments past are not limited to the homophobic and moral-majoritarian values inspiring the majority and concurring opinions in that case, but include also the libertarian, tolerationist, and anti-arbitrariness values inspiring the dissents. I certainly agree that the tradition *can* actively be read to contain all of these values. *See infra* text accompanying notes 175–80. The difficulty remains, however, that Ackerman has presented his constitutional theory as specifically meant to dissuade judges from challenging currently prevailing constitutional-legal common sense with intellectually strenuous readings of the constitutional past.

It seems that such dissuasion must be what Ackerman intends by his insistence on the extraordinary and episodic character of "transformative" or "constitutional" politics, and on the need for finding such an extraordinary constitutional-political event intervening between (say) Lochner v. New York, 198 U.S. 45 (1905), and West Coast Hotel v. Parrish, 300 U.S. 377 (1937), in order to justify the decision in *West Coast Hotel* as properly judicial. *See* Ackerman, *The Storrs Lectures, supra* note 5, at 1070. It seems no less true of the actual decision in *West Coast Hotel* than of a hypothetical opposite decision in *Bowers* that (quite apart from any New Deal "structural amendment") the American constitutional past contained ample argumentative resources with which to justify that decision and its reversal of Lochnerian conventional wisdom. *See,* e.g., Holmes, *Liberal Guilt,* in RESPONSIBILITY, RIGHTS AND WELFARE: THE THEORY OF THE WELFARE STATE (J. Moon ed. 1988); Michelman, *supra* note 39. What is, however, also plainly true of both the constitutional arguments favoring the Court's actual result in *West Coast Hotel (pace* structural amendment) and the arguments favoring an opposite result in *Bowers* is that these arguments ran or would run strongly counter to contemporarily regnant, conventional constitutional-legal wisdom. They were or are experienced as hard arguments—elaborate, venturous, "fancy." It must be just such a perception of *West Coast Hotel* that prompts Ackerman to say that, without help from structural amendment, any attempts to justify the result in that case must be invitations to legal nihilism. But then it is quite unclear how this would be any less true (assuming there is any truth in it) as applied to a hypothetical opposite result in *Bowers.*

In order to dispel my inference about what his position implies regarding the correct judicial decision in *Bowers,* Ackerman would at the very least have to speak to the questions of (1) whether and how a "re-collective" (or comparably strenuous) judicial approach to constitutional interpretation might avoid or control the damage consisting of destruction of public confidence in the principle of legality, and (2) how much, if any, risk of such damage is acceptable as the accompaniment of (otherwise welcome) venturous constitutional adjudication. Perhaps Ackerman will in due course address these questions successfully. Or perhaps it will turn out, when he does address them, that he has thus far been too hasty in naming legal nihilism—rather than, say, legal authoritarianism, the equation of legality with instruction—following-as the enemy his theory aims to slay.

contention to the pattern once imposed by Thomas Kuhn (on what I suppose may be called the vulgar reading of Kuhn's view) on the history of science: we have extended periods of normal practice punctuated by occasional moments of revolutionary upheaval.[113] Kuhn's normal science is Ackerman's popular-authoritarian law; Kuhn's paradigm shift is Ackerman's "transformative" moment of civically aroused popular politics.

The comparison suggests what is troubling about Ackerman's theory. Kuhn's original statement came in for strong criticism on the ground of its excessively authoritarian rendition of the proprieties of normal-scientific practice, as too unquestioningly deferential to the regnant paradigms. [114] As Kuhn himself has acknowledged,[115] normal-scientific consensus is always in some degree spurious, and normal-scientific practice is always in some degree nurturing the development of its own impending transformation. Science, on this more sensitive account, includes the work of what might be called marginal or deviant practitioners aimed at undermining rather than shoring up the currently dominant worldview. A shift from pre- to post-transformation practice is more like a movement from margin to center—a shift of attention—than it is like the total replacement of one "world" by another.[116] Through the critique of Kuhn, we reach an appreciation of scientific practice as cherishing all moments as potentially transformative, so that it would be anti-scientific to exclude marginal or deviationist investigators, as such, from the precincts of science.

Of course, where Kuhn's topic is the career—not to say the progress—of scientific understanding, Ackerman's is that of political freedom. Whatever difference this makes seems unlikely to help Ackerman. It will not be less strongly said of political freedom than of scientific understanding that all moments are potentially transformative, so that the only way to tell is to try.

To try is precisely to take leave of prior authority and of authoritarian jurisprudence. If Michael Hardwick's case leaves the matter in doubt, Linda Brown's should settle it. Although I suppose one could strain to describe the series of judicial decisions from *Brown*[117] to *Loving*[118] as reactively marking and consolidating the "final victory" of a constitutional transformation already effectively wrought by the people,[119] that is not how we best describe these events. Surely the Court's role in them was more prophetic—even if equivocal—than benedictory.[120]

---

[113] *See* T. KUHN, THE STRUCTURE OF SCIENTIFIC REVOLUTIONS (2d ed. 1970). Lipkin, *supra* note 86, at 734–50, similarly insists on a sharp differentiation between "revolutionary" constitutional adjudication, involving a reversal of some "foundational" constitutional-legal precept, and "normal," intra-paradigmatic constitutional adjudication, and on the impossibility of explaining or justifying revolutionary adjudications—Brown v. Board of Educ., 347 U.S. 483 (1954), is the chief example—without appeal to normative resources "extrinsic to the Constitution" such as a "critical-cultural" or an "abstract" moral-political theory. For this essay's alternative account of *Brown*, see *infra* text accompanying notes 117–22, 148–56.

[114] *See, e.g.*, Feyerabend, Consolations for the Specialist, in CRITICISM AND THE GROWTH OF KNOWLEDGE 197 (1. Lakatos & A. Musgrave eds. 1970); Popper, *Normal Science and its Dangers*, in *id.* at 51.

[115] *See* T. KUHN, THE ESSENTIAL TENSION: SELECTED STUDIES IN SCIENTIFIC TRADITION AND USAGE (1977).

[116] See, e.g., Feyerabend, *supra* note 114, at 207–10.

[117] Brown v. Board of Educ., 347 U.S. 483 (1954).

[118] Loving v. Virginia, 388 U.S. 1 (1967).

[119] *See* Ackerman, *supra* note 11, at 1173.

[120] For equivocation, see *Broom*, 347 U.S. at 494–95 (declining to overrule Plessy v. Ferguson, 163 U.S. 537 (1896), thereby arguably sanitizing *Plessy*). Perhaps we should say that by this equivocation the *Brown* opinion augured (as it by the same token recalled) an unfinished emancipation. See, e.g., Crenshaw, *supra* note 10, at 1332–33, 1333 n.3; Cornell, *supra* note 81, at 1176–70 (criticizing *Brown* on this ground as insufficiently prophetic).

The Court did not, of course, prophesy in a vacuum, but rather in a context of changes in self-understanding pursued over the years by Black Americans.[121] Black Americans, however, were not tantamount to "the people," and there is no telling how long it would have taken for their new foundations to have risen to the level of constitutional *significance* for a Court following Ackerman's argument. Rather, they were, as of 1954, still the marginalized and deviationist cultivators of transformative potential, a potential that both had been developed[122] and would come to such partial fruition as it has in part through the willing enlistment of the Court. If we imagine the *Brown* Court acting in accordance with the understanding (to which Ackerman and I are both committed) of constitutional adjudication as always proceeding from within an ongoing normative dialogic practice, then that Court's willingness to be thus enlisted must signify its grasp of the enlisters and their work as lying within the bounds, if away from the center, of our then constitutional practice. Thus informed, the *Brown* Court spoke in the accents of invention, not of convention; it spoke for the future, criticizing the past; it spoke for law, creating authority; it engaged in political argument. In Hardwick's case the Court did the opposite. It thus did, I have felt bound to suggest, what Ackerman's theory apparently would have it do.[123]

IV. TOWARDS DIALOGIC CONSTITUTIONALISM

A. *Republican Process and Judicial Role*

I launched this essay by suggesting two reasons for trying to refocus constitutional vision on a republican notion of jurisgenerative politics as the crux of political freedom: first, that such a notion would fortify constitutional adjudicators against a liberty-deferring, authoritarian stance towards constitutional law;[124] and, second, that American constitutionalism requires such a notion to redeem its problematic, dual promise of popular self-government and a government of laws.[125] I then developed a certain conception of jurisgenerative politics as an historically situated, recollective process of normative contention; noticed the close resemblance between that idealized account of politics and Dworkin's idealized account not of politics but of adjudication; and contended that no appreciation of jurisgenerative political possibility will drive out constitutional-legal authoritarianism without a further commitment to political jurisgenesis as a constant, not an episodic, activity.[126] How, then, does my work-up of these implications of republican constitutionalism not end by subverting the entire practice of judicial review—implying its total subordination to popular politics—rather than by emboldening the independent spirit in which that practice sometimes is carried on?

Frank Michelman

---

[121] *See, e.g.*, E. RUDWICK, W.E.B. DuBOIS: VOICE OF THE BLACK PROTEST MOVEMENT (1982); BLACK LEADERS OF THE TWENTIETH CENTURY (J. Franklin & A. Meier eds. 1982); A. MEIER, NEGRO THOUGHT IN AMERICA 1880–1915 (1963); *see also infra* notes 150–56 and accompanying text.

[122] *See* McLaurin v. Oklahoma State Regents, 339 U.S. 637 (1950); Sweatt v. Painter, 339 U.S. 629 (1950); Sipuel v. Board of Regents, 332 U.S. 631 (1948); Missouri *ex rel.* Gaines v. Canada, 305 U.S. 337 (1938).

[123] In his entertaining the possibility of "court-led . . . transformation," there is indication that Ackerman himself does not accept the attribution of such an implication to his theory. *See supra* note 111.

[124] *See supra* text accompanying notes 1–5.

[125] *See supra* text accompanying notes 29–30.

[126] *See supra* text accompanying notes 78–88, 101–23.

Certainly I have ventured far from the haven of *Federalist No. 78*. Publius envisioned, and Ackerman still explains, the judiciary adjudicating constitutional cases as the vicariate of We The People, the founding authority, during Our long vacations. If now we are to spread founding moments over continuous political time, and if now we are to locate the political virtue of a republically self-governing citizenry in its constant cultivation of revisionary potential, then it seems that not only have we lost the explanation for judicial review we thought we had, we have also activated a heavy count against it: the Thayerite objection is now upon us with a vengeance.[127]

The work of John Ely points the way toward one line of response. If republican constitutional possibility depends on the genesis of law in the people's ongoing normative contention, it follows that constitutional adjudicators serve that possibility by assisting in the maintenance of jurisgenerative popular engagement. Republican constitutional jurisprudence will to that extent be of the type that Laurence Tribe calls (and criticizes as) "process-based,"[128] recalling Ely's well-known and controversial justification of judicial review as "representation reinforcing."[129]

There will, however, remain a difference of substance between Ely's process-based theory of judicial review and the one I have in mind, reflecting the difference between the conceptions of political possibility respectively informing our two accounts— pluralist in Ely's case, republican in mine.[130] Ely's theory would attack Georgia's morality-based justifications for its discriminatory sodomy law on the ground that homosexuals as a group are victimized by societal prejudice denying to their special interests a fair shake in the rounds of give-and-take comprising pluralist politics.[131] That argument has nothing to say against outright rejection of its pluralist premises by justices disposed—on occasion—toward a republican conception of law as an expression of public values springing from the historically conditioned, normative persuasions of "the people."[132] Such a disposition always lurks in American constitutional sensibility; witness *Bowers v. Hardwick*. Only a constitutional jurisprudence that takes it seriously can hope to provide effective defense against its popular-authoritarian excesses and perversions. But what, then, would a process-based, republican-not-pluralist constitutional jurisprudence be like?

For the beginning of an answer, we must return finally to the challenge of reclaiming the idea of jurisgenerative politics from its ancient context of hierarchical, organicist, solidaristic communities for the modern context of equality of respect, liberation from ascriptive social roles, and indissoluble plurality of perspectives.[133]

---

[127] "[T]he tendency of a common and easy resort to (judicial review is] to dwarf the political capacity of the people, and to deaden its sense of moral responsibility" that comes from "righting the question out in the ordinary way." J. THAYER, *supra* note 103, at 106–07.

[128] Tribe, *The Puzzling Persistence of Process Based Constitutional Theories*, 89 YALE L. J. 1063 (1980); *see* Michelman, *supra* note 5, at 42 n. 223.

[129] See J. ELY, *supra* note 63; Monaghan, *Our Perfect Constitution*, 56 N.X.U. L. Rtzv. 353 (1981) (commending Ely's account); Parker, *The Past of Constitutional Theory—And Its Future*, 42 OHIO ST. L. J. 223, 239–57 (1981) (urging rejection of Ely's account).

[130] *See, e.g., J.* ELY, *supra* note 63, at 77–84, 151–53 (presenting Ely's pluralism).

[131] *See id.* at 162–64.

[132] *See* L. TRIBE, CONSTITOTIONAL CHOICES 16–17 (1985):

Legislators may see homosexuals as "different" not out of [prejudice], but on . . . the basis of a morality that treats certain sexual practices as repugnant to a particular view of humanity. . . . Such legislation can be rejected only on the basis of . . . a [substantive] view of what it means to be a person. . . .

[133] See *supra* text accompanying note 32.

B. Plurality: Public Vice to Public Virtue

Start again with the basal requirement for republican jurisgenerative politics: that both the process and its law-like utterances must be such that everyone subject to those utterances can regard himself or herself as actually agreeing that those utterances, issuing from that process, warrant being promulgated as law.[134] Given the modern supposition of pre-political dissensus, it seems that no set of procedural conditions—no "ideal speech situation"—can suffice to guarantee the requisite validation.[135] Or rather, to speak more carefully, this impossibility obtains as long as we suppose that all of the participants' pre-political self-understandings and social perspectives must axiomatically be regarded as completely impervious to the persuasion of the process itself.[136] Given plurality, a political process can validate a societal norm as self-given law only if (i) participation in the process results in some shift or adjustment in relevant understandings on the parts of some (or all) participants, and (ii) there exists a set of prescriptive social and procedural conditions such that one's undergoing, under those conditions, such a dialogic modulation of one's understandings is not considered or experienced as coercive, or invasive, or otherwise a violation of one's identity or freedom, and (iii) those conditions actually prevailed in the process supposed to be jurisgenerative.[137]

Of these three stipulations, the crucial and obviously problematic one is stipulation (ii). To imagine that stipulation (ii) might be satisfied is not, I want now to suggest, necessarily to imagine the possibility of dissolving to the bottom rational (and passionate) disagreements attendant upon perspectival differences.[138] Perhaps such a final dissolution of difference is not required in order to meet the validity condition that everyone subject to a law-like utterance can actually agree that the utterance warrants being promulgated as law. In speaking of dialogic "modulation" of participants' pre-political understandings, I have meant to allow—as the American constitutional tradition evidently enjoins us to allow—for the possibility of cases in which validation occurs when participants, rather than "abandoning" their commitments, come to "hold the same commitments in a new way."[139]

If gaining a secure grasp on such a possibility stretches to the limits our powers of comprehension, it may help to recall how we have come to be making the attempt. I undertook in this essay to clarify certain conditions of republican constitutionalism's possibility in a modern, liberal society—to uncover certain beliefs we must hold regarding ourselves, our social relations, and specifically (as it turns out) our capacities for dialogic self-modulation, as long as we profess commitment to both popular self-government and a government of laws. Rather than claiming to

---

[134] *See supra* text accompanying notes 30, 69–71.

[135] An "ideal speech situation" is a setting in which everyone, free of domination and false consciousness, speaks out, listens, gives and is given reasons to and by everyone else. *See, e.g.,* J. HABERMAS, LEGITIMATION CRISIS 107–08 (T. McCarthy tr. 1975); T. MCCARTHY, THE CRITICAL THOUGHT of JURGEN HABERMAS 305–07 (1978).

[136] *See* S. BENHABIB, *supra* note 30, at 309–14.

[137] *See id.* at 312–16.

[138] *See id.* at 230 (accepting limitations on possibility of eliminating disagreements about justice).

[139] H. PITKIN, *supra* note 31, at 279; *see also* Schneiderman v. United States, 320 U.S. 119 (1943), discussed *supra* note 104. As an example of this possibility, consider Rawls' distinctions among three grounds for commitment to a constitutional principle of freedom of conscience—(i) adherence to a particular sect's tolerationist doctrine, (ii) adoption of a "comprehensive liberal moral doctrine such as those of Kant and Mill," and (iii) belief that such a principle "expresse[s] political values that, under the reasonably favorable conditions that make a more or less just constitutional democracy possible, normally outweigh whatever other values may oppose [it]"—and his discussion of the difference it makes which ground is operative. *See* Rawls, *Overlapping Consensus, supra* note 68, at 9–15; *see also* H. Pitkin, *supra* note 31, at 102 (Machiavelli's equivocation between founders suggests how individuals can experience shift in perspective on their traditions or values without being disloyal to those traditions or values).

establish unconditionally that republican constitutionalism is possible for us, or that we can coherently hold to both commitments, my strategy has been to start with the actual, problematic experience of the dual commitments (I trust that the experience is widely shared by readers) and from it derive a normative idea of dialogic constitutionalism as consistent, at least, with this problematic experience.[140] That derivation is now essentially complete, and its crucial result is stipulation (ii). But stipulation (ii), then, does not occupy the status of an independent assertion, standing on its own bottom so to speak, about actual or possible experience. Its status is rather that of an inference about what we have to regard as possible as long as we do not give up the historic American idea of constitutionalism.

What stipulation (ii) apparently describes is a process of personal self-revision under social-dialogic stimulation. It contemplates, then, a self whose identity and freedom consist, in part, in its capacity for reflexively critical reconsideration of the ends and commitments that it already has and that make it who it is.[141] Such a self necessarily obtains its self-critical resources from, and tests its current understandings against, under-*standings* from beyond its own pre-critical life and experience, which is to say communicatively, by reaching for the perspectives of other and different persons.[142] If my argument to this point has held together, then these dialogic conceptions of self and freedom are implications of the republican—the American—ideal of political freedom in a modern liberal state.[143] Thus might a modern republican conception of political freedom make a virtue of plurality.[144]

C. The Dialogic Forum: Law and Politics, State, and Society

The legal form of plurality is indeterminacy—the susceptibility of the received body of normative material to a plurality of interpretive distillations, pointing toward differing resolutions of pending cases and, them, toward differing normative

---

[140] *See supra* text accompanying notes 48–49.

[141] *See* S. BENHABIB, *supra* note 30, at 332–33; M. SANDEL, *supra* note 82, at 179.

[142] *See* S. BENHABIB, *supra* note 30, at 333–34, 348–49.

[143] *Cf.* Cornell, *supra* note 81, at 1220–24 (explaining personal identity and freedom via law as grounded in interpersonal "dialogic reciprocity").

[144] *See* S. BENHABIB, *supra* note 30, at 348–49:

By "plurality" I . . . mean . . . that our embodied identity and the narrative history that constitutes our selfhood give us each a perspective on the world, which can only be revealed in a community of interaction with others. . . . A common, shared perspective is one that we create insofar as in acting with others we discover our difference and identity, our distinctiveness from, and unity with, others. The emergence of such unity-in-difference comes through a process of self-transformation and collective action.

Through such processes we learn to exercise political and moral judgment. We develop the ability to see the world as it appears from perspectives different from ours. Such judgment is not merely applying a given rule to a given content. In the first place it means learning to recognize a given content and identifying it properly. This can only be achieved insofar as we respect the dignity of the generalized other, who is our equal, by combining it with our awareness of his or her concrete otherness. What we call content and context in human affairs is constituted by the perspectives of those engaged in it.

At any point in time, we are one whose identity is constituted by a tale. This tale is never complete: the past is always reformulated and renarrated in the light of the present and in anticipation of a future. Yet this tale is not one of which we alone are the authors. Others . . . often tell our stories for us and make us aware of their real meaning. . . . The interpretive indeterminacy of action arises from the interpretive indeterminacy of a life-history.

Benhabib's notion of plurality is strongly reminiscent of the linked ideas of plurality and natality derived by Hannah Arendt from her reflections on ancient republicanism, *see, e.g.,* H. ARENDT, *supra* note 31, at 8–9, although distinctly marked by Benhabib's emphasis on "concrete other-ness"—our immediate experiences of encounter with the specific people who happen to belong to our particular communities.

futures.[145] Legal indeterminacy in that sense is the precondition of the dialogic, critical-transformative dimension of our legal practice variously known as immanent critique, internal development, deviationist doctrine, social criticism, and recollective imagination.[146]

But the generative indeterminacies are not just *there* as secrets awaiting random discovery. Rather they are products of action, the creations of motivated acts of perception and cultivation.[147] Action by whom, then? Most likely, it would seem, by those who enter the conversation—or, as we may sometimes feel, seek to disrupt it—from its margins, rather than by those presiding at the center.[148] So the suggestion is that the pursuit of political freedom through law depends on "our" constant reach for inclusion of the other, of the hitherto excluded—which in practice means bringing to legal-doctrinal presence the hitherto absent voices of emergently self-conscious social groups.[149]

Take for example the indeterminacy (as it became for a crucial moment of time) of the American constitutional-legal principle of "equal protection of the laws" in its application to separate-but-equal public facilities or formally neutral interracial sex and marriage laws.[150] That indeterminacy arose along with the rise in American legal culture of belief (always contested) in such factors as the social construction of race, the subordinative motivations and meanings built into that construction, the efficacy of subordinative cultural meaning as race-specific harming, and the

---

[145] *See* R. DWORKIN, *supra* note 84, at 413; Cornell, *supra* note 81, at 196–98,1201–04; *cf.* B. FAY, *supra* note 69, at 169–73; *id.* at 168: "[T]he narrative of a person's life can never be settled because the causal repercussions from it will continue indefinitely into the future, and because the story which ought to be told about this life will be deeply affected by these repercussions."

[146] *See, e.g.,* R. UNGER, *supra* note 2, at 15–19; M. WALZER, INTERPRETATION AND SOCIAL CRITICISM 20–22, 25 (1987); Cornell, *supra* note 81, at 1204–06.

[147] *See* Cornell, *supra* note 81, at 1202–04.

[148] *See supra* text accompanying notes 113–16 (critique of Kuhn); B. HOOKS, FEMINIST THEORY: FROM MARGIN TO CENTER ix (1984):

> To be in the margin is to be part of the whole but outside the main body. . . . Living as we did—on the edge—we developed a particular way of seeing reality. We looked both from the outside in and from the inside out. . . . This mode of seeing reminded us of the existence of a whole universe, a main body made up of both margin and center. Our survival depended on an ongoing public awareness of the separation between margin and center and on ongoing private awareness that we were a necessary, vital part of that whole. This sense of wholeness . . . provided us an oppositional world view—a mode of seeing unknown to most of our oppressors, that sustained us . . . in our struggle to transform poverty and despair, strengthened our sense of self and our solidarity.

Cf. Brennan, Reason, Passion, and *the "Progress of the* Lam," 42 REC. A.B. CITY N.Y. 960–61, 970 (1987):

> How do we arrive at a new concept such as [the positive liberty of genuine opportunity, as opposed to the negative liberty of absence of restraint]? Although we might get there by a process of abstract philosophical reflection, most of us would initially take a different route. The concept of positive liberty is easily arrived at by considering the plight of an employee whose one "choice" is between working the hours the employer demands and not working at all. . . . . Only by remaining open to the entreaties of reason and passion, of logic and experience, can a judge come to understand the complex human meaning of a rich term such as "liberty". . . . . If due process values are to be preserved in the bureaucratic state of the late Twentieth Century, it may be essential that officials possess passion—the passion that puts them in touch with the dreams and disappointments of those with whom they deal.

[149] *See* Minow, *supra* note 10, at 1867 ("cognizance of rights . . . is . . . knowledge of the process by which hurts that once were whispered or unheard have become claims, and claims that once were unsuccessful have persuaded others and transformed social life"); *see also* Hartog, *The Constitution of Aspiration and "The Rights That* Belong *to Us All"*, 74 J. AM. HIST. 1013, 1014–17, 1024 (1987).

[150] *See, e.g.,* McLaughlin v. Florida, 379 U.S. 184 (1964); Sweatt v. Painter, 339 U.S. 629 (1950). Perhaps the best memorial of the moment of indeterminacy is Wechsler, *Toward Neutral Principles of Constitutional Law*, 73 HARV. L. REV. 1 (1959).

injustice of a legal order (including legal doctrines of formal equality) sustaining and reproducing the constructions and meanings that wreak such harms.[151]

How does such a new slant on the world penetrate the dominant consciousness? Without belaboring the point, does anyone doubt the primary and crucial role in this instance of the emergent social presence and self-emancipatory activity of Black Americans?[152] Does anyone doubt that their impact on the rest of us has reflected their own oppositional understandings of their situation and its relation to our (and increasingly their) Constitution[153]—developed, in part, through conflict within their own community,[154] in a process that both challenged and utilized such partial citizenship as the Constitution granted and allowed them[155] (and left its clear imprint on constitutional law both within and beyond the topical area of race[156])? Does anyone doubt that the judicial agents of the challengers' accumulating citizenship drew on interpretive possibilities that the challengers' own activity was helping to create?

The full lesson of the civil rights movement will escape whoever focuses too sharply on the country's most visible, formal legislative assemblies—Congress, state legislatures, the councils of major cities—as exclusive, or even primary, arenas of jurisgenerative politics and political freedom. I do not mean that those arenas are dispensable or unimportant. Rather I mean the obvious points that much of the country's normatively consequential dialogue occurs outside the major, formal channels of electoral and legislative politics, and that in modern society those formal channels cannot possibly provide for most citizens much direct experience of self-revisionary, dialogic engagement. Much, perhaps most, of that experience must occur in various arenas of what we know as public life in the broad sense, some nominally political and some not: in the encounters and conflicts, interactions and debates that arise in and around town meetings and local government agencies; civic and voluntary organizations; social and recreational clubs; schools public and private; managements, directorates and leadership groups of organizations of all kinds; workplaces and shop floors; public events and street life; and so on. Those

[151] See, e.g., 1 G. MYRDAL, AN AMERICAN DILEMMA (1944); Colker, Anti-Subordination Above All. Sex, Race, and Equal Protection, 61 N.Y.U. L. REV. 1003 (1986); Fiss, Groups and the Equal Protection Clause, 5 PHIL. & PUB. AFF. 107 (1976); Freeman, Legitimizing Racial Discrimination Through Antidiscrimination Law: A Critical Review of the Supreme Court's Doctrine, 62 MINN. L. REV. 1049 (1978); Lawrence, The Id, The Ego, and Equal Protection: Reckoning With Unconscious Racism, 39 STAN. L. REV. 317 (1987). But see Thomas, Toward a "Plain Reading" of the Constitution—The Declaration of Independence in Constitutional Interpretation, 30 HOW. L.J. 691 (1987) (recognizing but deploring influence of such matters of "sensitivity" (as opposed to "justice") on recent directions in constitutional-legal treatment of race).

[152] See, e.g., R. KLUGER, SIMPLE JUSTICE (1975); G. MCNEIL, GROUNDWORK: CHARLES HAMILTON HOUSTON AND THE STRUGGLE FOR CIVIL RIGHTS (1983); J. WILLIAMS, EYES ON THE PRIZE: AMERICA'S CIVIL RIGHTS YEARS 1954–65 (1987); Davis, In Commemoration of the Bicentennial Celebration: Blacks and the Constitution, 30 HOW. L. J. 915 (1987).

[153] See Lawrence, Promises to Keep: We are the Constitution's Framers, 30 HOW. L.J. 645 (1987).

[154] See, e.g., Norwalk CORE v. Norwalk Bd. of Educ., 423 F.2d 121 (2d Cir. 1970) (involving conflict between cause of desegregation and concern for educational effectiveness and minority control in community schools); D. BELL, RACE, RACISM AND AMERICAN LAW 424–31 (2d ed. 1980) (recounting arguments in this conflict and citing authorities).

[155] See Crenshaw, supra note 10, at 1364–65 ("Blacks' assertion of their rights constituted a serious ideological challenge to white supremacy. . . . In asserting rights, Blacks defied a system which had long determined that Blacks were not and should not have been included."); see also id. at 1381–82.

[156] See, e.g., NAACP v. Claiborne Hardware Co., 458 U.S. 886 (1982); Gibson v. Florida Legislative Investigation Comm., 372 U.S. 539 (1963); Edwards v. South Carolina, 372 U.S. 229 (1963); NAACP v. Button, 371 U.S. 415 (1963); NAACP v. Alabama, 357 U.S. 455 (1958); Burnham, Reflections on the Civil Rights Movement and the First Amendment, in A LESS THAN PERFECT UNION 335 (J. Lobel ed. 1988); cf. Bell v. Maryland, 378 U.S. 226 (1964).

are all arenas of potentially transformative dialogue.[157] Understandings of the social world that are contested and shaped in the daily encounters and transactions of civil society at large are of course conveyed to our representative arenas. They also, obviously, enter into determinations of policy that occur within nominally private settings but that can affect people's lives no less profoundly than government action. Those encounters and transactions are, then, to be counted among the sources and channels of republican self-government and jurisgenerative politics. They are arenas of citizenship in the comparably broad sense in which citizenship encompasses not just formal participation in affairs of state but respected and self-respecting presence—distinct and audible voice—in public and social life at large.

Such a non–state centered notion of republican citizenship is, of course, both historically American[158] and congenial to a characteristic strain in contemporary civic revivalism.[159] My argument in this essay leads to it by way of two distinct but related considerations. One is that a notion of republican dialogue not exclusively and immediately tied to the coercive exercise of centralized majoritarian power can help make credible for contemporary Americans the idea of social and procedural conditions[160] under which communicative revision of a citizen's normative understandings escapes condemnation as oppression.[161]

The other is that by noticing how some of the well-springs of republican politics are separated from the ultimate political process—by locating them in extra-governmental social processes that state law, therefore, may either nurture or suppress—we obtain a non-Publian but still republican rejoinder to the Thayerite objection to judicial review. The Court helps protect the republican state—that is, the citizens politically engaged—from lapsing into a politics of self-denial. It challenges "the people's" self-enclosing tendency to assume their own moral completion as they now are and thus to deny to themselves the plurality on which their capacity for transformative self-renewal depends.[162]

---

[157] *See* Minow, *supra* note 10, at 1861–62. In what follows I continue in the spirit of Bruce Ackerman's urging of an anti-formalist understanding of constitutional "conventions," only carrying it further. *See supra* text accompanying notes 105–109. I also offer some vindication for Laurence Tribe's superficially implausible assertion that we are all constantly engaged in "constitutional choices." *See* L. TRIBE, *supra* note 132, at vii.[158] *See* A. DE TOCQUEVILLE, DEMOCRACY IN AMERICA (G. Lawrence trans. 1969).

[159] *See, e.g.,* Frug, *supra* note 5.

[160] *See supra* text accompanying notes 138–44 ("Stipulation (ii)").

[161] *See, e.g.,* Cover, *supra* note 29, at 11–19, 40–44 (comparing "jurisgenerative" local and voluntary communities with "jurispathic" central, court-administered law); Cover, *Violence and the Word*, 95 YALE L. J. 1601, 1628 (1986) (warning against "exaggerating the extent to which any interpretation rendered as part of a state act of violence can ever constitute a common and coherent meaning"). Consider American Booksellers Ass'n v. Hudnut, 771 F.2d 323, 332 (7th Cir. 1985) (holding anti-pornography ordinance violative of First Amendment), *aff'd per curiam*, 475 U.S. 1001 (1986), where Circuit Judge Easterbrook, writing for the Seventh Circuit panel, accepted the city's argument that pornography, like other communication, can affect its readers' attitudes and behaviors in ways that are harmful to others, but reasoned from this premise to an anti-censorship conclusion: "Change in any complex system ultimately depends on the ability of outsiders to challenge accepted views and the reigning institutions. Without a strong guarantee of freedom of speech, there is no effective right to challenge what is." *See* Baker, *The Process of Change and the Liberty Theory of the First Amendment*, 55 S. CAL. L. REV. 293 (1982). Judge Easterbrook unfortunately offered only an authoritarian response *(see Booksellers*, 771 F.2d at 325, 327) to the argument that in some circumstances too strong—too absolute—a free-speech guarantee can itself result in denial of an effective right to challenge what is. *See* C. MACKINNON, *Frances Biddle's Sister: Pornography, Civil Rights, and Speech*, in FEMINISM UNMODIFIED: DISCOURSES ON LIFE AND LAW 163, 192–95 (1987); Fiss, *Why the State?*, 100 HARV. L. REV. 781 (1987); Sunstein, *Pornography and the First Amendment*, 1986 DUKE L. J. 589, 618–24.

[162] "The Constitution demands the full measure of all our human capacities, not merely from judges, nor from rulers, but from our ultimate sovereign—the people." Brennan, *supra* note 148, at 975.

To allay any possible misunderstanding, I do not mean to be offering here a complete or exhaustive theory of judicial review, in which counter-action against popular self-enclosure is all there is for the Court to do—anymore than even Ely can plausibly claim that "representation-reinforcement" exhausts the meaning of the Constitution. *See* J. ELY, *supra* note 63, at 88–101; Brennan, *supra* note 28, at 437.

All the components of the republican constitutional argument for an opposite result in *Bowers v. Hardwick* are now before us. The argument construes Hardwick's complaint as, in essence, one of unjustified denial of due citizenship (or is it due foundership?) by reason of denial of liberty, and specifically of that aspect of liberty we have come to know as privacy; its text is section 1 of the Fourteenth Amendment.[163] The argument accepts without question Georgia's explanation of the meaning and purpose of its challenged law: the meaning is to brand and punish as criminal the engagement by homosexual partners, but not heterosexual partners, in certain forms of sexual intimacy, and the purpose is to give expression and effect to a legislative majority's moral rejection of homosexual life.

Such a purpose is deeply suspect under the modern republican commitment to social plurality. In the circumstances of contemporary society, homosexuality has come to signify not just a certain sort of inclination that "anyone" might feel, but a more personally constitutive and distinctive way, or ways, of being.[164] Homosexuality has come to be experienced, claimed, socially reflected and—if ambiguously—confirmed as an aspect of identity demanding respect.[165] What is more, by its very emergence as an aspect of ways of living and not just an inclination or taste, homosexuality challenges established orders.[166]

It seems very likely that among the effects of a law like Georgia's on persons for whom homosexuality is an aspect of identity is denial or impairment of their citizenship, in the broad sense which I have suggested is appropriate to modern republican constitutionalism: that of admission to full and effective participation in the various arenas of public life.[167] It has this effect, in the first place, as a public expression endorsing and reinforcing majoritarian denigration and suppression of homosexual identity.[168] It also—and for my purposes more interestingly—denies citizenship by violating privacy.

---

[163] It reads:

All persons born or naturalized in the United States, and subject to the jurisdiction thereof, are citizens of the United States and of the State wherein they reside. No State shall make or enforce any law which shall abridge the privileges or immunities of citizens of the United States; nor shall any State deprive any person of life, liberty, or property, without due process of law; nor deny to any person within its jurisdiction the equal protection of the laws.

U.S. CONST. amend. XIV, § 1; *see* Karst, The *Supreme Court 1976 Term Foreword. Equal Citizenship Under the Fourteenth Amendment*, 91 HARV. L. REV. 1 (1977).

[164] *See Law, Homosexuality and the Social Meaning of Gender, 1988* WIS. L. REV. 1, 15, 24–26; Richards, *supra* note 2, at 854; Note, *The Constitutional Status of Sexual Orientation: Homosexuality as a Suspect Classification*, 98 HARV. L. REV. 1285, 1304–05 (1985).

[165] *See* Law, *supra* note 164, at 20–31.

[166] Sylvia Law writes:

Lesbians and gay men pose a formidable threat to the classic gender script. They deny the inevitability of heterosexuality. . . .

[W]hen homosexual people build relationships of caring and commitment, they deny traditional belief and prescription that stable relations require the reciprocity of male/female polarity. In homosexual relationships, authority and hierarchy cannot be premised on the traditional criteria of gender. For this reason lesbian and gay couples who create stable loving relationships are indeed more threatening to conservative values than mere isolated violators of the ban on non-marital sex.

Id. at 24, 31–32; *see also* Note, *supra* note 164, at 1307.

[167] *Cf.* Karst, *Paths to Belonging. The Constitution and Cultural Identity*, 64 N.C.L. REV. 303 (1986) (developing similar conception of constitutional citizenship rights for members of ethnoculturally identifiable groups).

[168] *See* Law, *supra* note 164, at 4, 6–8; *cf.* Lawrence, *supra* note 151 (explaining injurious impacts of laws' "cultural meanings" in racial contexts).

The Bork nomination hearings have made clear that "privacy" (in a sense directly implicated by Hardwick's claim) enjoys broad popular support as a constitutional value. Yet the notion remains suspect, for differing reasons, among constitutional commentators of widely differing persuasions. Conservative originalists of course condemn it as illegitimate judicial invention. What is more striking is that some strong supporters of women's rights of choice in regard to child-bearing have cogently criticized the Supreme Court's decisions[169] affirming such rights for basing them on a constitutional principle of privacy.[170] The core of the criticism is that the privacy rationale conceptually separates this aspect (and by implication others) of the problem of women's subordination from the domain of public or political concern. The privacy rationale, it is argued, implies that the choice, or the problem, is, precisely, the individual woman's own concern—an implication that has untoward political and doctrinal ramifications, one of which is the unconditional release of the state (that is, the political public at large) from any responsibility for assuring or supplying resources needed by poor women to make practically effective their putative choices for abortion.[171]

In somewhat similar fashion it has been argued that a constitutional privacy principle would be a poor basis on which to ground judicial invalidation of laws, such as Georgia's, penalizing homosexual sex. To base such a decision on privacy, it is said, would be to reinforce the idea "that homosexuality is merely a form of [bedroom] conduct . . . rather than a continuous aspect of identity" demanding public expression; it would be to fail to recognize that freedom to have impact on others—to make the "statement" implicit in a public identity—is central to any adequate conception of the self. Such a decision would do little to allay "pervasive discrimination against gays" in public society; it would not itself contribute, nor would it directly empower its beneficiaries to contribute, to "heightening public awareness of homosexuality and thus broadening public acceptance of gay lifestyles." To the contrary, it would burden homosexuality with the stigma of the quarantine.[172]

These critiques of constitutional privacy doctrine reveal the dangers of reliance on such a doctrine as long as privacy stands for an attitude of hostility towards public life and a need for refuge from and protection against public power. This way of valorizing a legally protected, private realm, as the counter to a state regarded solely as a dangerous instrumentality whose tendencies to overreach must be curbed even at some significant cost in policy goals foregone, has been salient in American constitutional thought. By contrast to this oft-used strategy of carving a private space to defend against the public, a republican slant on the same issues produces a reoriented understanding: not only an appreciation of the active state's potential as an affirmative friend to effective liberty as political freedom,[173] but an appreciation of privacy as a political right.

Frank Michelman

---

[169] *See, e.g.*, Roe v. Wade, 410 U.S. 113, 152–53 (1972).

[170] *See* MacKinnon, *Privacy v. Equality. Beyond Roe v. Wade*, in C. MACKINNON, *supra* note 161, at 93; *cf.* Tribe, *The Abortion Funding Conundrum: Inalienable Rights, Affirmative Duties, and the Dilemma of Dependence*, 99 HARV. L. REV. 330, 338 (1985) (suggesting that Court's description of its holding as based on privacy inadequately conveys true ground of decision).

[171] *See* Harris v. McRae, 448 U.S. 297 (1980); Maher v. Roe, 432 U.S. 464 (1977).

[172] *See* Note, *supra* note 164, at 1290–91 (quoting L. TRIBE, AMERICAN CONSTITUTIONAL LAW § 15-1, at 888 (1st ed. 1978)).

[173] Such appreciations are manifest in Fiss, *supra* note 161, and Tribe, *supra* note 170, although not linked by either author to republican credentials.

Just as property rights—rights of having and holding material resources—become, in a republican perspective, a matter of constitutive political concern as underpinning the independence and authenticity of the citizen's contribution to the collective determinations of public life,[174] so is it with the privacies of personal refuge and intimacy.[175] Justice Blackmun's dissenting opinion in *Bowers* at least begins to articulate this republican appreciation of the political significance of privacy, both by itself explaining the value of intimate association as formative and supportive of personal identity, of self-understanding, and thus of diverse ways of life,[176] and by its reference[177] to the Court's earlier rumination, in *Roberts v. United States Jaycees*,[178] on the "central(ity] to our constitutional scheme" of a protected sphere of intimate association.[179] This cross-fertilization of the constitutional-legal notion of autonomy—simple personal liberty—by the first-amendment inspired value of freedom of association[180] nicely represents the republican penchant for rights that bridge the personal and the political.

The argument also nicely illustrates the re-collective aspect of constitutional-legal interpretation. The argument realigns our accustomed sense of the relation between privacy and political freedom by regarding privacy not only as an end (however controversial) of liberation by law but also as such liberation's constant and regenerative-jurisgenerative-beginning. The argument forges the link between privacy and citizenship. It attacks the Georgia law for denying or impairing citizenship by exposing to the hazards of criminal prosecution the intimate associations through which personal moral understandings and identities are formed and sustained.[181]

Doubtless an argument along these lines involves a degree of reinterpretation, or reorientation, of constitutional history. It involves, for example, a definitive decoupling of rights of "privacy" and "intimate association" from a certain "traditional" cult of the family. The argument re-collects the authorities and recasts

---

[174] *See, e.g.*, Michelman, *Possession vs. Distribution, supra* note 39, at 1329.

[175] See *supra* notes 43 & 142 and accompanying texts. Such an understanding of the political significance of privacy seems to have been deep in ancient, classical republicanism, although institutionalized in a way repellant to us: that is, in the idea of the *oikos*, the dominated household to which the independent citizen retired for service (by noncitizens) to his bodily needs for sustenance and release, and his spiritual need for replenishment (by the daily experience of his domestic mastership) of his sense of independent self-direction. *See* Michelman, *supra* note 5, at 29–30 n.138.

[176] *See supra* note 38.

[177] *See Bowers*, 478 U.S. at 204 (Blackmun, J., dissenting).

[178] 468 U.S. 609 (1984).

[179] Justice Blackmun explains:

[W]e have noted that certain kinds of personal bonds have played a critical role in the culture and traditions of the Nation by cultivating and transmitting shared ideals and beliefs; they thereby foster diversity and act as critical buffers between the individual and the power of the State.

Id. at 618–19; *see also* Heymann & Barzelay, *The Forest and the Trees: Roe v. Wade and Its Critics*, 53 B.U.L. REV. 765, 772–73 (1973).

[180] *See, e.g.*, NAACP v. Alabama, 357 U.S. 449, 462–63 (1958) (granting constitutional protection to "freedom to engage in association for the advancement of beliefs and ideas [as] an inseparable aspect of the 'liberty' assured by the Due Process Clause of the 14th Amendment," against regulation that would "affect adversely the ability of [the NAACP] and its members to pursue their collective effort to foster beliefs which they admittedly have the right to advocate").

[181] *See* Karst, *The Freedom of Intimate Association*, 99 YALE L. J. 624, 635–37 (1980); Law, *supra* note 164, at 38–40; Richards, *supra* note 2, at 843–45, 852–53, 855–56. For a defense of a decisional-privacy rationale for permissive abortion rights resting on a contractarian argument that starts with the idea of such privacy as a pre-political moral right of any individual—an aspect of the individual's right to equal respect and concern—but also adverts to the instrumental relation between privacy and citizenship, see Allen, *supra* note 70, at 462, 473 & *passim*.

the tradition along the axes of self-formation and diversity rather than those of dominant social expectation and conformity.

Such a re-collective form of argument is, of course, not in the least foreign to ordinary American constitutional-legal practice; the example I have just presented is, after all, drawn in part from justice Blackmun's *Bowers* dissent. Thus, in appropriating for "republican" constitutional theory Cornell's idealization of that practice as the exercise of "recollective imagination," I do not mean to be describing or prescribing a novel set of legal-doctrinal operations, by which lawyers and judges would refer to different kinds of sources, or say different kinds of things about them, than they now do. What is rather at issue is one's comprehension of the "point" of the practice[182]—one's sense of an underlying "best theory of law"[183]—that gives shape and orientation to these familiar operations.

My work-up of the republican case for Hardwick's right thus exhibits the disputatious activity of constitutional interpretation as a Machiavellian practice of return-to-the-founding-principles in which the first principle of the founding— the "point" of the practice—turns out to be just that of the constant value of (re)foundation (renewal, renovation) itself. In the larger frame of history, the ascription of such a "point" to American constitutionalism can hardly be called non-interpretive. I have presented the argument as motivated by a republican commitment to social plurality, but the larger contention of this essay has been that the same commitment is implicit in American constitutionalism's most basic professions of attachment to both self-government and a government of laws. In that sense, I claim, republican inspiration enters the privacy-based argument for a reversal of *Bowers* along with the deepest, organizing premises of American constitutional discourse. Precisely because it is a problem, not a solution, that those premises construct—and because, further, it is the problematic character of that central constitutional construct that allows the Constitution to ground our identity as a political community by also inviting us to self-revision through debate over its meaning—there is no demonstrating that the republican-inspired, process-based, reverse-Bowers argument I have presented is what the Fourteenth Amendment has always meant or always will mean, or is all and only what it means today.[184] All that I, or anyone, can offer is an argument, not a demonstration, about the Constitution's meaning in this context, now, as both *ours* and *law*.

The difficulty remains of explaining how it can be right to address such a non-demonstrative argument about the impermanent meaning of the people's law to any body other than the People. Judges perhaps enjoy a situational advantage over the people at large in listening for voices from the margins.[185] Judges are perhaps better situated to conduct a sympathetic inquiry into how, if at all, the readings of history upon which those voices base their complaint can count as interpretations of that history—interpretations which, however re-collective or

[182] *See* R. DWORKIN, *supra* note 84, at 58–59, 87–88.
[183] *See* R. DWORKIN, TAKING RIGHTS SERIOUSLY 106–07 (1977).
[184] *See* Hartog, *supra* note 149, at 1032.
[185] *See* Minow, *supra* note 50, at 74–95; Minow, *supra* note 10, at 1880–81:

> The interpretive approach construes a claim of right, made before a judge, as a plea for recognition of membership in a community shared by applicant and judge . . . The use of rights discourse affirms . . . a community that acknowledges and admits historic uses of powers to exclude, deny, and silence—and commits itself to enabling suppressed points of view to be heard, to make covert conflict overt.

even transformative, remain true to that history's informing commitment to the pursuit of political freedom through jurisgenerative politics. Still, a judicial constitutional convention is not equivalent—indeed, it is contrary—to actual democracy. That difficulty, too, must yield (if at all) to a pragmatic consideration: Actual democracy is not all there is to political freedom, and Hardwick is before us, appealing to law's republic.

Identity Politics

Catharine A. MacKinnon

Catharine A. MacKinnon

CATHARINE MACKINNON has been the most significant feminist voice in the American legal academy for more than twenty-five years. Her two short articles in the journal *Signs* mark the entrance of feminist theory into American legal thought. In them, MacKinnon harnessed emerging traditions from legal and social theory that were critical of both liberalism and Marxism to the project of developing a specifically feminist legal theory. The ideas MacKinnon develops in these articles about the relationship between law and society and the nature of social and legal power have been significant far beyond the community of scholars and activists who identify with feminist or left politics.

During the 1970s, when these articles were conceived, many legal scholars criticized "liberalism" as the dominant frame for thinking about law and legal reform. The criticisms they developed were as diverse as their definitions of "liberalism." At the same time, no author in the Canon breaks as sharply and self-consciously from the broad liberal tradition of postwar American legal scholarship as MacKinnon. As we have seen, the word "liberalism" is used by American legal thinkers in a wide variety of ways. It can refer generally to the politics of the center-left, and be used as a loose synonym for the positions of the Democratic Party, for progressive or reformist initiatives, or for ideas that might in other countries be termed "social-democratic." It can refer more particularly to legal reform projects that seek either to moderate the impact of market power on weaker parties or defend the rights of marginal or stigmatized groups—perhaps modeled on those that emerged from the Civil Rights Movement and the Great Society programs of the 1960s. The term liberalism is also routinely used by legal scholars to refer generally to a body of ideas borrowed from social and political theory—individualism, rationalism, a sharp distinction between the civil society of right-bearing individuals and the public authority of the state and the ideal of limited government—all of which have been used to defend political projects ranging from laissez-faire to social democracy.

In the 1970s and '80s, "liberalism," in one or another sense, was attacked from both the left and right. As a set of welfare-state style regulatory interventions, "liberalism" was attacked by scholars from the law and economics movement. As an encouragement for judicial activism to cushion the impact of markets on the weak, "liberalism" would be undermined by the emergence of neo-formalist ideas about the appropriate role for the judge. The left also attacked liberal reforms for failing to go far enough, for attending only to the exceptional case of unequal bargaining power or market injustice, rather than addressing more fundamental or structural relationships of domination in American society. Outside the legal academy, black nationalist groups had challenged the "liberalism" of the Civil Rights Movement, with its focus on integration, individual rights, and equality rather than group cohesion and power.

In the broader academy, variants of Marxist thought had remained the dominant framework for left-wing criticism of liberalism in the broader philosophical sense through the 1960s. Few traces of these ideas remain in the Canon, although many in the Law and Society and the Critical Legal Studies movements would have described themselves in these terms. In the 1970s, however, a generation of scholars entered the legal academy who were critical of mainstream liberal thinking from the left, and self-consciously opposed to much of what they took to be the Marxist tradition. For many white male scholars in this position, the emerging Critical Legal Studies movement provided a social, scholarly, and political community. Scholars associated with CLS developed a range of doctrinal, historical, and theoretical accounts for what they took to be the general limitations of liberalism in law. Many of the arguments analyzing the limits of liberal legal reform initiatives in MacKinnon's two articles have parallels in these other critical legal traditions.

Feminist legal thought not only originated many moves that would eventually become part of the broader tradition of critical thinking about law; it was also the first tradition to link post-Marxist criticisms of liberalism with the interests and perspectives of groups other than white men in theoretical terms. What CLS and other contemporary critics of legal liberalism took to be liberalism's *general* limitations were, from a feminist viewpoint, the limitations most apparent to some men. Women's experiences, in feminist analysis, would foreground other limits. Feminist theory also presented a new standpoint from which to think about legal, political, and social life—the standpoint from women's experience. In this, feminist theory aspired to offer an account of social life and social hierarchies as fundamental as that of Marxism—for MacKinnon, one predicated on sexual subordination and the sex "differences" that flow from it, rather than on the division of labor and the subordination of labor to capital. Other critical theories of law tended not to share the ambition of providing an account of legal injustice that was also an account of society-wide injustice of a fundamental kind. Indeed, their rejection of Marxism often began with a rejection of precisely what they saw as this kind of grand theoretical ambition. Although they might have been equally critical of liberalism in law, their criticisms were mounted in a more case-by-case manner, rooted in the repeated experience of disappointment with liberalism and in the search for a broader range of pragmatic reform ideas than liberalism seemed to offer. In this light, it is interesting to note the range of specific law reform initiatives that have been inspired by MacKinnon's analysis in the ensuing years. It might well be argued that, if anything, the conceptual shift wrought by her analysis has been more significant in the real world of policy, for good or ill, than the law reform initiatives associated with more conventional liberal efforts to secure equal treatment for women in American society.

MacKinnon graduated from Smith College in 1969, and from Yale Law School in 1977. She received a PhD in political theory from Yale in 1987. Involved in the black Civil Rights Movement and the women's movement from the early 1970s, MacKinnon has been active in litigation, legislative initiatives, and policy development in the field of women's rights for three decades. After law school, she worked as a founding attorney in the New Haven Law Collective for three years while at the same time beginning law teaching. She pioneered the theory that sexual harassment is a form of sex discrimination. Her 1979 book *Sexual Harassment of Working Women*, in draft and as published[1], has provided the foundation both for legislation and judicial decisions recognizing sexual harassment as sex-based discrimination worldwide. Beginning in 1983, MacKinnon worked with feminist writer and activist Andrea Dworkin on a series of legislative initiatives to recognize specific harms of pornography as violations of civil rights. MacKinnon has also been active in international women's rights efforts, particularly in establishing rape as a form of genocide under international law. She has taught at many law schools in the United States and Canada, has been a long-term visitor at the University of Chicago Law School, and has taught at the University of Michigan Law School since 1990, where she is currently the Elizabeth A. Long Professor of Law teaching constitutional law, international law, and a range of courses on the theory and practice of sex equality and women's rights.

In the 1970s, students encountered women in the law school curriculum in a variety of ways. Women often figured as plaintiffs or victims in the fact patterns of cases illustrating doctrinal exceptions—excusing contract performance by widows or housewives who could be presumed not to have understood what they were getting into, for example. Specific statutory regimes purporting to protect women might be part of employment law, criminal law, or the law of evidence. There were also courses in legal fields thought to be of concern to women—family law most prominently. At the same time, courses in private law or constitutional law that stressed the progressive historical development of their fields might well mention efforts to expand the suffrage to include women, or to abolish property, contract, and family law regimes that denied women equal status to engage in commercial transactions or to own and freely dispose of property. Taken together, women were presented both as a social group with particular interests—in family law, in rape-shield laws, in employment—and as individuals long denied, but increasingly afforded, equal treatment—in constitutional law, property or contract law. In the classroom, faculty (almost all of whom were male) sometimes depicted women as needing special treatment and sometimes as needing equal treatment, depending upon whether the laws involved were thought to affect women in their particularity as women or in their general identity as citizens. This polarity continues to be felt in many law school classrooms. Legal reform efforts to address issues of gender justice through a combination of "equal" and "special" treatment have also continued to dominate constitutional and statutory litigation in the field of women's rights. Taken together, these approaches are often referred to as the projects of "liberal feminism," in part because MacKinnon criticized them as "liberal." In the articles included here, MacKinnon criticizes John Stuart Mill's petition for women's suffrage as representative of this broad liberal tradition. In MacKinnon's view, even the best of the liberal tradition interprets women's interests and viewpoint from a male point of view, encouraging special treatment when women are not "like men," and equal treatment when they are.

MacKinnon aims to develop an alternative theory of society and law grounded in the experience and viewpoint of women. Women, as a category, are not simply individuals who remain subject to "inequalities inaccurate or dubious, inefficient, and therefore unjust."[2] Women are not properly defined as being *like men*, except insofar as they are subject here and there to prejudice and injustice, and they are not properly defined as being *unlike men* either. Women's distinctive experience and perspective are products of their social subordination. It is important to understand that for MacKinnon, the central fact is social subordination. She has suggested that being a woman, in the most significant sense, is not being biologically female but being socially subordinated like women distinctively are. For example, when asked about the relationship between her proposed legal definition of pornography and the exploitation of men through rape or pornographic representation, MacKinnon responded:

> The second part of the definition [of pornography] spells out that men, children, or transsexuals who are used in the place of women also have a cause of action, so that what is made through their use is pornography. This design is actually a new legal approach to the question of inequality in general, and of sexual inequality in particular. It is both sex-specific and gender-neutral. It is sex-specific because it defines pornography as pornography is. It defines pornography in terms of what it does to women, but it acknowledges that what pornography does is make inequality sexy—it reflects an understanding that *whoever* is on the bottom is *the girl*, regardless of whether that person be a woman, a man, a transsexual, or a child. If you look at what happens in gay male rape and talk to those male victims, they know that they have been treated like women. It is part of the insult. If you look at what happens with rape in prison, you know that the one who gets repeatedly raped is the *girl*. You understand that what it is to be female is to be targeted and stigmatized on the basis of your sexuality; you can tell it is a stigma and not just your identity by the fact that when it is transferred to somebody who does not share your biology everybody knows it is an insult.[3]

Sexual inequality, moreover, is *relational*—women are what they are made to be as social subordinates by men's domination, and their experience "as women" is an experience of subordination to and by men. For feminist theory, according to MacKinnon, the structural fact of social life to be analyzed is domination of women by men. The central fact is not an original or aspirational human equality with men that can be either recognized, fought for and achieved, or denied:

> [T]he molding, direction, and expression of sexuality organizes society into two sexes—women and men—which division underlies the totality of social relations.[4]

As a result, one "becomes a woman" in Simone de Beauvoir's terms, in a relationship to what men do with their power, and what men understand as knowledge about reality. To be a woman in the male-dominant sense of social reality is to be sexually desirable to men, to be subjugated by men, and to be known by men through institutions and ideas designed from a male point of view. Indeed, male dominance is constitutive of women as such, making it (almost) impossible to develop an alternative women's point of view:

> Feminism criticizes this male totality without an account of our capacity to do so or to imagine or realize a more whole truth. Feminism affirms women's point of view by revealing, criticizing, and explaining its impossibility. This is not a dialectical paradox. It is a methodological expression of women's situation, in which the struggle for consciousness is a struggle for world: for a sexuality, a history, a culture, a community, a form of power, an experience of the sacred.[5]

Consequently, an immediate and urgent project for feminism is theoretical and methodological: to develop a mode of seeing, thinking, and experiencing up to the challenge of "male totality":

> Feminism has not been perceived as having a method, or even a central argument, with which to contend. It has been perceived not as a systematic analysis but as a loose collection of factors, complaints, and issues which, taken together, describe

rather than explain the misfortunes of the female sex. The challenge is to demonstrate that feminism systematically converges upon a central explanation of sex inequality through an approach distinctive to its subject yet applicable to the whole of social life, including class.[6]

Or later:

The practice of a politics of all women in the face of its theoretical impossibility is creating a new process of theorizing and a new form of theory.[7]

MacKinnon could hardly have proposed a more ambitious intellectual project. Looking back across the Canon, it is difficult to identify a project of parallel scope launched *within* the field of American legal thought. For MacKinnon, to overcome the subordination of half the human race required an intellectual project larger than understanding or reforming the operations of America's existing legal institutions. Other legal scholars have tended to import their general theories from the existing intellectual disciplines of philosophy, or sociology, or psychology, or economics—all of which, for MacKinnon, were as male as law. For MacKinnon, however, legal norms and legal ordering are a primary site for male power and male modes of knowledge requiring a new paradigm if necessary change for women is to occur.

It is important to note the range of themes separating MacKinnon from mainstream liberal legal thought. Each theme would become familiar in anti-liberal criticism and reform efforts in areas other than feminism—just as each would be questioned by legal scholars interested in women's rights who did not share MacKinnon's anti-liberal methodological and other commitments. MacKinnon expresses her rejection of legal liberalism expansively, rejecting the "individualist, naturalist, idealist, moralist structure of liberalism."[8] In MacKinnon's description, liberals think of society as composed of individuals, associating with one another on the basis of common interests, against a background legal and political structure which *aims*, even if unsuccessfully, to remain neutral among them. For MacKinnon, by contrast, groups—notably men and women—are constitutive of the individuals who are their members. Men and women differ not only in their interests, but in their experience, hence standpoint and relation to the society as a whole.

The incommensurability of the experiences of groups in hierarchies results from the fact that society is not a terrain upon which interest groups contend equally, but a structure of domination, of women by men, among others. As a result, to see incidents of sexism as aberrations, women's inequalities as defects in otherwise sensible and equitable social orderings, is to see things like a man—and to deny the reality of women's experience of subordination:

Where liberal feminism sees sexism primarily as an illusion or myth to be dispelled, an inaccuracy to be corrected, true feminism sees the male point of view as fundamental to the male power to create the world in its own image, the image of its desires, not just as its delusory end product.[9]

Rather than neutral referees in the struggle between interest groups, the law and the state are instruments and products of male domination—institutionalizing a male point of view as normal, even as they offer to treat women equally here and to give them "special" treatment there. Feminism is a "theory of power and its distribution," offering an account of "how social arrangements of patterned disparity can be internally rational yet unjust."[10]

In liberal moments the state is accepted on its own terms as a neutral arbiter among conflicting interests. The law is actually or potentially principled, meaning predisposed to no substantive outcome, thus available as a tool that is not fatally twisted. Women implicitly become an interest group within pluralism, with specific problems of mobilization and representation, exit and voice, sustaining incremental gains and losses. . . . Applied to women, liberalism has supported state intervention on behalf of women as abstract persons with abstract rights, without scrutinizing the content of those notions in gendered terms.[11]

The idea that hierarchy is central to the organization of social life and to what it means to be a woman has led many to describe MacKinnon as a "dominance" or "subordination" feminist. The significance of this conclusion is readily visible in MacKinnon's treatment of consent as the mark of women's autonomy and freedom. For liberal feminists, one goal of legal reform is often to promote legal respect for the autonomy of women in the market and in the home. They should have the capacity to say yes to market transactions, to own and dispose of their own property, for example, and to say no to unwanted intimacy and sex. When they say no, in the sexual context, they should be believed—they mean it—and their wishes, and their bodies, should be respected. MacKinnon's work focuses more on why they are not believed, as well as on the deeper issues of how desires are socially determined as they are.

If what it means to be a woman is to be subordinated, for example, woman's "consent" will be difficult to trust or interpret. For example, if women submit to sexual intercourse required as the price of a job they need, the law of rape considers that "consent" to sex; for MacKinnon, it provided part of the origins of the law of sexual harassment. At a minimum, her approach could expand the range of harms which would need recompense to include harms to which women had given their "consent" as the law interprets it; perhaps a great many sexual encounters to which individual women have "consented," meaning acquiesced in silently or without dissent, lacking options or reasonably fearing the consequences of resistance, are, in a larger sense, the product of male domination. Women's own desires may well also be shaped by such forces, MacKinnon observes, from sexual abuse in childhood to sex-based poverty and unavailable employment options. MacKinnon's legal initiatives for civil and human rights therefore seek to expand women's capacity to assert rights they want, in resistance to forces of male dominance, without assuming that every woman in the same situation holds the identical view.

In one sense, MacKinnon's analysis is reminiscent of the skepticism of legal reliance on the autonomy of private actors in a market that we have seen since at least Hale. If bargains are a reflection of legal powers and are struck in the shadow of legal arrangements, for Hale, it is meaningless to treat the principle of "autonomy" as the basis for justifying those rules. Autonomy is structured by legal authority. The analysis is far more difficult, and significant, however, if one class of people are subordinate to another as a matter of social knowledge and power—before they ever get to the legal rules. It might seem possible, following Hale, simply to remove legal restrictions that incapacitate women by treating them differently. Removing legal discrimination would leave women and men bargaining in the shadow of the same law. For MacKinnon, however, this simply ignores the fact that women and men, standing in the shadow of the same law are not equal or the same—women are subordinate to men. Capacitating women, freeing them from discrimination in the narrow sense, is not to liberate them from this subordination.

MacKinnon also rejects the liberal commitment to the distinction between public and private realms. For women, she argues, the private has not been a realm separated from politics—quite the contrary. It has been in the private realm that women have distinctively experienced the politics of their subordination on the basis of sex. MacKinnon also rejects the liberal distinction between objective and subjective knowledge:

> Having been objectified as sexual beings while stigmatized as ruled by subjective passions, women reject the distinction between knowing subject and known object—the division between subjective and objective postures—as the means to comprehend social life. . . . women's interest lies in overthrowing this distinction itself.[12]

It would be some time before it would become clear what it meant to "reject" ideas like the public/private or objective/subjective distinctions. Although their significance runs through the fabric of law, they had certainly been criticized before. The legal examples MacKinnon develops in the field of rape in the last portion of the second article share a great deal with critical ideas we have seen elsewhere in the Canon—perhaps most strikingly in the essays by Robert Hale and Felix Cohen. Nevertheless, the feminist insistence that the "personal is the political" sought to bring these criticisms of public and private, objective and subjective, together in a new way:

> The personal as political is not a simile, not a metaphor, and not an analogy. It does not mean that what occurs in personal life is similar to, or comparable with, what occurs in the public arena. It is not an application of categories from social life to the private world, as when Engels (followed by Bebel) says that in the family the husband is the bourgeois and the wife represents the proletariat. Nor is it an equation of two spheres which remain analytically distinct, as when Reich interprets state behavior in sexual terms, or a one way infusion of one sphere into the other, as when Lasswell interprets political behavior as the displacement of personal problems into public objects. It means that women's distinctive experience as women occurs within that sphere that has been socially lived as the personal—private, emotional, interiorized, particular, individuated, intimate—so that what it is to *know* the *politics* of woman's situation is to know women's personal lives.[13]

Moreover, the feminist practice of "consciousness raising," developed in the 1960s and 1970s, offered a novel image of what feminist knowledge—neither subjective nor objective—might look like. It was neither critical reflection to separate the chaff of error and prejudice from the wheat of truth, nor was it a social process of persuasion, criticism, or enlightenment which could rid one of prejudices or ideological deformations. While important, both are too rationalist and individualized to capture the epiphanal and collective aspects of what MacKinnon has in mind. As MacKinnon sees it, through consciousness raising, women have glimpsed the near-totality of their situation as the product of male power as well as the difficulty and necessity of changing it—the new feminist theoretical project powerfully evoked by MacKinnon's prose. Consciousness raising is not the translation of personal narratives into policy—it is a project of knowledge that grounds a more far-reaching political project and perspective:

> Although feminism emerges from women's particular experience, it is not subjective or partial, for no interior ground and few if any aspects of life are free of male

power. Nor is feminism objective, abstract, or universal. It claims no external ground or unsexed sphere of generalization or abstraction beyond male power, nor transcendence of the specificity of each of its manifestations.[14]

As in many other post-Marxist critical theories, the goal is as much epistemological as political—to reject the gap between knowledge and power—in MacKinnon's case, to expose the absence of a gap between male knowledge and male power. Scholars influenced by this aspect of MacKinnon's work—or by parallel arguments in the philosophy of Michel Foucault, which was being translated into English in the same years—have analyzed forms of knowledge as modes of domination, and modes of domination as forms of knowledge. The institutions or social practices they have analyzed have varied—the family, warfare, contract, the prison, and more. For MacKinnon, the analysis of sexuality is key. Men are taught to experience masculinity as dominance and to eroticize that. Women are taught to experience femininity as subordination, and to eroticize that. In this way, what is sexuality for women becomes what men desire in women. Sexuality in men is at once a form of power, experienced ideologically as desire, and a form of knowledge about who a man is, what a man likes, and what women are and are for:

> Men create the world from their own point of view, which then becomes the truth to be described. This is a closed system, not anyone's confusion. Power to create the world from one's point of view is power in its male form.[15]

MacKinnon's goal in these two articles is primarily theoretical—to sketch the parameters for what she proposes will become feminist theory. She harnesses legal examples to illustrate the behavior of the male state through specific legal doctrines—most significantly, doctrines in rape law:

> Attempts to reform and enforce rape laws, for example, have tended to build on the model of the deviant perpetrator and the violent act, as if the fact that rape is a crime means that society is against it, so law enforcement would reduce or delegitimize it. Initiatives are accordingly directly toward making the police more sensitive, prosecutors more responsive, judges more receptive, and the law, in words, less sexist. This may be progressive in the liberal or the left senses, but how is it empowering in the feminist sense? Even if it were effective in jailing men who do little different from what nondeviant men do regularly, how would such an approach alter women's rapability? Unconfronted are *why* women are raped and the role of the state in that.[16]

MacKinnon's own practical work on sexual harassment, pornography, rape, and genocide has consistently had a heuristic as well as a practical import. She devoted several years to the effort to assist in adopting ordinances at the municipal, state, and international levels that would give individual women a civil right of action to sue pornographers they could prove had harmed them in a variety of concrete ways. These efforts were enormously controversial, for their potential impact on free speech and for what many observers interpreted as an inattention to the sexual desires and pleasures of many actual women. MacKinnon surely intended the statutes to be effective in limiting pornography and in remedying real injuries to women. She insisted that no woman who was not harmed by pornography would have a legal claim under her proposed laws—and that many of those who were would gain a remedy, once they had proven their injuries.

Catharine A. MacKinnon

Even where they were not enacted, MacKinnon's proposals were powerful illustrations of what it would mean to take seriously her critique of women's subordination in all its forms.

Although MacKinnon sees parallels between the reform proposals of liberals and leftists, she also sees important parallels between feminism and Marxism. Both are theories of society as a whole, rooted in domination and inequality. Both focus on the experience of a subordinated group as a source of authority and insight. Both see their theoretical work as itself political. The possible homology between Marxism and feminism—and the aspiration that feminism offer a theory as comprehensive as Marxism—was made famous by MacKinnon's opening paragraphs:

> Sexuality is to feminism what work is to marxism: that which is most one's own, yet most taken away. Marxist theory argues that society is fundamentally constructed of the relations people form as they do and make things needed to survive humanly. . . . Class is its structure, production its consequence, capital its congealed form, and control its issue. Implicit in feminist theory is a parallel argument. . . . Sexuality is that social process which creates, organizes, expresses and directs desire, creating the social beings we know as women and men, as their relations create society. As work is to marxism, sexuality to feminism is socially constructed yet constructing, universal as activity yet historically specific, jointly comprised of matter and mind. As the organized expropriation of the work of some for the benefit of others defines a class—workers— the organized expropriation of the sexuality of some for the use of others defines the sex, woman. Heterosexuality is its structure, gender and family its congealed forms, sex roles its qualities generalized to social persona, reproduction a consequence and control its issue.[17]

At the same time, MacKinnon, like many legal critics of liberalism on the left during the 1970s and '80s, is also critical of the Marxist tradition—in her case primarily because of the degree to which Marxism leaves women out. Marxists, she argues, assimilate women's experience to class experience—ignoring the specificity of women's subordination as resolutely as does liberalism. Commenting on Rosa Luxembourg, a leading Marxist thinker and activist of the interwar period, MacKinnon notes, "Women as women, across class distinctions and apart from nature, were simply unthinkable to Luxembourg, as to most Marxists."[18] In MacKinnon's view, "women's struggles, whether under capitalist or socialist regimes, appear to feminists to have more in common with each other than with leftist struggles anywhere."[19]

There is no question that MacKinnon remains the most significant American feminist legal theorist. She has had an enormous impact on the theoretical and practical work of others seeking to work outside the liberal and Marxist traditions, just as she has had a tremendous impact on the thinking and practice of feminists. Her writing has also influenced legal thought more broadly—indeed, these two articles are among the handful of most cited scholarly works in the legal field. This is, if anything, all the more noteworthy given their publication in *Signs*—a journal on "women, culture and society." The voice and style of these articles precluded their publication in law journals at the time. In this, MacKinnon's articles changed not only what one could write about, but how one could write legal scholarship.

MacKinnon remains an extremely controversial figure. Her anti-pornography work was a lightning rod for civil libertarians and other liberals who responded to her attack on liberal legal values and presuppositions. It also divided her from some feminists for whom an affirmation of some women's sexual autonomy and pleasure outweighed concern about the impact of pornography on the practices of coercion, force, assault, and trafficking her proposed law aimed to address by establishing a right of action that included the pornography they were coerced into making, assaulted as a direct result of, or that trafficked in subordination. Since these articles were written, the number of women in the legal academy has grown exponentially, as has the diversity of ideas about how best to think about gender, sexuality, and the empowerment of women. Over the ensuing years, legal feminists developed a wide range of alternative strands of feminist legal theory. It is striking how many of the traditions define themselves by differentiation from one or another element in MacKinnon's thought. MacKinnon had termed her approach "feminism," and distinguished it from "liberalism" and "Marxism." As legal feminism split to include "liberal feminism," "socialist feminism," "cultural feminism," "equality feminism" and more, MacKinnon continued to insist, as did the exponents of each of these theories, that her own vision was feminism— for MacKinnon, "feminism unmodified." Other feminists responded by continually recharacterizing MacKinnon's approach. Those who thought MacKinnon had identified significant issues for feminist work, but did not share her aspiration to analyze society and law as a whole in gendered terms or for breaking with the liberal tradition, often labeled her work "radical feminism." Many feminists take the view that women share a unique cultural perspective and experience, but associate it with caring, sharing, and nurturing, as opposed to male norms of competition and judgment, or with practical intuition rather than male abstract reason. They often termed MacKinnon's approach "subordination feminism" or "domination feminism" to stress her focus on the persistence and significance of a structural relationship of domination. In turn, these feminists were often termed "difference" feminists, to distinguish them from liberal feminists more focused on "equality." They might also be termed "cultural feminists" for their focus on the significance of culturally constructed gender and sexual identities.

MacKinnon repeatedly differentiated herself from these "difference" feminists by stressing the significance of power and politics to her feminism. In 1985, she said at a conference:

> In my opinion, to take the differences approach is to take a moral approach, whereas to criticize hierarchy is to take a political approach. To take a differences view is also to take a liberal view (although that view, of course, included conservatism as well), and to take the view that we are dealing with a hierarchy is to take a radical approach. I also think that to make issues of gender turn on the so-called gender difference is, ultimately, to take a male perspective. I therefore call the differences approach masculinist. The position that gender is first a political hierarchy of power is, in my opinion, a feminist approach.[20]

Some feminists have shared MacKinnon's focus on power and subordination, but do not see sexuality as key to it. Others have shared her focus on sexuality, but do not feel women's sexuality is defined primarily by subordination to men. Such feminists were often termed "sex-positive" or "sex-affirmative" feminists, and tend to see MacKinnon's feminist critique of violence against women as a form of cultural conservatism. Others thought that MacKinnon identified important instances of inequality, but do not share her sense for the structural nature of that subordination. Still others have shared MacKinnon's desire for a more complete break with the liberal and Marxist traditions, but do not share her sense for the cohesiveness or distinctiveness of *women's* social experience.

Debates about MacKinnon's ideas have been particularly significant for feminists who have continued the search for an anti-liberal, anti-Marxist approach to domination in the diverse traditions of critical race theory, lat-crit theory, and queer theory. MacKinnon's post-Marxist and non-liberal legal theory, grounded in the viewpoint of a stigmatized social group, would be the model for much work produced by black, latino, and gay scholars over the ensuing years. In the 1980s and '90s, scholars rethinking the liberal tradition of civil rights from a non-Marxist left position would find a home in critical legal studies and in the emerging Critical Race Theory movement. Indeed, we might see efforts of Derrick Bell's pioneering work on the limitations of the civil rights legacy and the need for a more thoroughgoing understanding of the role of race in American law as parallel to MacKinnon's work in the same period. In the late 1980s, a network of "Lat-Crit" scholars emerged seeking to rethink United Statesean law from the perspective of Hispanic minority experience. In the 1990s, scholars seeking distance from the liberal "gay rights" tradition would develop parallel themes under the banner of Queer Theory. (For many of these initiatives, however, MacKinnon's aspiration for unifying structural theory focused on sexual subordination would seem equally unsatisfying.) Their theoretical work developed against the background of competition *among* stigmatized groups and decreasing confidence in the unity or particularity of the experience of women. They did not see gender as ordering social power as definitively and crucially as does MacKinnon.

DAVID KENNEDY

Notes

1. Catharine MacKinnon, *Sexual Harassment of Working Women: A Case of Sex Discrimination* (New Haven: Yale University Press, 1979).

2. Catharine MacKinnon, "Feminism, Marxism, Method, and the State: An Agenda for Theory," 7 *Signs: Journal of Women in Culture and Society* 3 (1982): 519. (Hereafter "An Agenda for Theory.")

3. Catharine MacKinnon. "Feminist Discourse, Moral Values, and the Law—A Conversation," 34 *Buffalo Law Review* 35 (1985).

4. "An Agenda for Theory," 516.

5. Catharine MacKinnon, "Feminism, Marxism, Method, and the State: Toward a Feminist Jurisprudence," 8 *Signs: Journal of Women in Culture and Society* (1983), 637. (Hereafter "Toward a Feminist Jurisprudence.")

6. "An Agenda for Theory," 528.

7. "Toward a Feminist Jurisprudence," 38.

8. Ibid., 640.

9. Ibid.

10. "An Agenda for Theory," 516.

11. "Toward a Feminist Jurisprudence," 642.

12. "An Agenda for Theory," 536.

13. Ibid., 534–5.

14. "Toward a Feminist Jurisprudence," 638.

15. "An Agenda for Theory," 537 (emphasis removed).
16. "Toward a Feminist Jurisprudence," 643.
17. "An Agenda for Theory," 515–16.
18. Ibid., 521.
19. Ibid., 523.
20. MacKinnon, "Feminist Discourse, Moral Values, and the Law—A Conversation," 34 *Buffalo Law Review* 21–2 (1985).

Bibliography

Catharine MacKinnon

MacKinnon has written numerous books and articles, including a casebook *Sex Equality* (New York: Foundation Press, 2001), and two collections of essays: *Women's Lives, Men's Laws* (Cambridge, Mass.: Harvard University Press, 2005), and *Feminism Unmodified: Discourses on Life and Law* (Cambridge, Mass.: Harvard University Press, 1987). Her two *Signs* articles became the basis for *Toward a Feminist Theory of the State* (Cambridge, Mass.: Harvard University Press, 1989), which also develops her criticism of liberalism in more detail.

Her law reform initiatives in the fields of sexual harassment, pornography, and rape law have also yielded significant publications. See *Sexual Harassment of Working Women: A Case of Sex Discrimination* (New Haven: Yale University Press, 1979); *Directions in Sexual Harassment Law*, edited with Reva Siegel (New Haven: Yale University Press, 2004); *Only Words* (Cambridge, Mass.: Harvard University Press, 1993); *Pornography and Civil Rights: A New Day for Women's Equality* with Andrea Dworkin (Minnesota: Organizing Against Pornography, 1988); "Pornography as Defamation and Discrimination," 71 *Boston University Law Review* 793 (1992); "Reflections on Sex Equality Under Law," 100 *Yale Law Journal* 1281 (1991). Her 2005 *Women's Lives, Men's Laws* collects and extends her more significant writing on each of these topics.

Commentary

MacKinnon's work has generated a tremendous amount of comment. Reviews and explications of her work which focus on the ideas developed in these two essays include: Frances Olsen, "Feminist Theory in Grand Style, Review of Feminism Unmodified," 89 *Columbia Law Review* 1147 (1989)(containing excellent references to feminist work influenced by and departing from MacKinnon); Janet Halley, *Split Decisions: How and Why to Take a Break from Feminism* (Princeton, 2006) (acknowledging the parallel between Halley's orientation to Queer Theory and the early MacKinnon of the *Signs* articles); Dan Danielsen, Book Review, *Feminism Unmodified* 23:2 *Harvard Civil Rights Civil Liberties Law Review* 611 (1988); Christine Littleton, "Book Review: Feminist Jurisprudence: The Difference Method Makes, Reviewing *Feminism Unmodified*," 41 *Stanford Law Review* 751 (1988–89); Katherine Bartlett, "MacKinnon's Feminism: Power on Whose Terms? Review of *Feminism Unmodified*." 75 *California Law Review* 1559 (1987); Drucilla Cornell, "Sexual Difference, the Feminine, and Equivalency: A Critique of MacKinnon's *Toward a Feminist Theory of the State*," 100 *Yale Law Journal* 2247 (1990–91); Lucinda Finley, "The Nature of Domination and the Nature of Women:

Reflections on Feminism Unmodified" Book Review of *Feminism Unmodified*," 82 *Northwestern Law Review* 352 (1987–88); Cass Sunstein, "Feminism and Legal Theory, Book Review of *Feminism Unmodified*," 101 *Harvard Law Review* 826 (1987–88); Kathryn Abrams, "Sex Wars Redux: Agency and Coercion in Feminist Legal Theory," 95 *Columbia Law Review* 304 (1995) (tracing opposition to "dominance feminism" in the decade after MacKinnon's *Signs* articles appeared and proposing an "agency-based" approach to feminist theory and practice).

For feminisms by other authors in the Canon, see Kimberle Crenshaw, "Demarginalizing the Intersection of Race and Sex: A Black Feminist Critique of Antidiscrimination Doctrine, Feminist Theory and Antiracist Politics," 1989 *University of Chicago Legal Forum* 139; Duncan Kennedy, *Sexy Dressing* (Cambridge, Mass.: Harvard University Press, 1993). For a fascinating analysis of the presence of women in a commonly used contracts case book, illustrating the modes of understanding women available in the law, see Mary Joe Frug, *Postmodern Legal Feminism* (New York: Routledge, 1992), chapter 4, "A Feminist Analysis of a Casebook? An Introductory Explanation," in Mary Joe Frug, *Postmodern Legal Feminism* (New York Routledge, 1992). See also Babcock, Freedman, Norton, Ross, *Sex Discrimination & The Law: Causes and Remedies* (Boston: Little, Brown, 1975).

There is now an enormous corpus of feminist theoretical writings. Our take on the most significant, several of which might also have been candidates for canonical treatment, includes:

Hilary Charlesworth, Christine Chinkin, and Shelley Wright, "Feminist Approaches to International Law," 85 *American Journal of International Law* 613 (1991).

Clare Dalton, "An Essay in the Deconstruction of Contract Doctrine," 94 *Yale Law Journal* 997 (1985).

Martha Fineman, "Challenging Law, Establishing Differences: The Future of Feminist Legal Scholarship," 42 *Florida Law Review* 25 (1990).

Mary Joe Frug, *Postmodern Legal Feminism*. New York and London: Routledge, 1992.

Katherine Franke, "What's Wrong With Sexual Harassment?" 49 *Stanford Law Review* 691 (1996–1997).

Janet Halley, *Split Decisions: How and Why to Take a Break from Feminism* (Princeton, 2006).

Angela Harris, "Race and Essentialism in Feminist Legal Theory," 42 *Stanford Law Review* 581 (1989–90).

Christine Littleton, "Reconstructing Sexual Equality," 75 *California Law Review* 1279 (1987).

Martha Minow, "Foreword: Justice Engendered," 101 *Harvard Law Review* 10 (1997–1988).

Frances Olsen, "The Family and the Market: A Study of Ideology and Legal Reform," 96 *Harvard Law Review* 1497 (1983).

Frances Olsen, "Statutory Rape: A Feminist Critique of Rights Analysis," 63 *Texas Law Review* 387 (1984).

Elizabeth Schneider, "Describing and Changing: Women's Self-Defense Work and the Problem of Expert Testimony on Battering," 9 *Women's Rights Law Reporter* 195 (1986).

Reva Siegel, "Why Equal Protection No Longer Protects: The Evolving Forms of Status-Enforcing State Action," 49 *Stanford Law Review* 1111 (1996–97).

Reva Siegel, "Home as Work: The First Women's Rights Claims Concerning Wives' Household Labor, 1850–1880," 103 *Yale Law Journal* 1073 (1993–94).

Reva Siegel, "Reasoning from the Body: A Historical Perspective on Abortion Regulation and Questions of Equal Protection," 44 *Stanford Law Review* 261 (1991–92).

Vicki Schultz, "Telling Stories About Women and Work: Judicial Interpretations of Sex Segregation in the Workplace in Title VII Cases Raising the Lack of Interest Argument," 103 *Harvard Law Review* 1749 (1989–90).

Robin West, "The Difference in Women's Hedonic Lives: A Phenomenological Critique of Feminist Legal Theory," 3 *Wisconsin Women* 81 (1987).

Robin West, "Jurisprudence and Gender," 55 *University of Chicago Law Review* 1 (1988).

There are numerous anthologies of feminist theory. An excellent recent anthology is Nancy Down and Michelle S. Jacobs, *Feminist Legal Theory: An Anti-Essentialist Reader* (New York: New York University Press, 2003).

Earlier useful anthologies, in reverse chronological order, include:

Frances Olsen, ed., *Feminist Legal Theory I: Foundations and Outlooks* (New York: New York University Press, 1995) and Frances Olsen, ed. *Feminist Legal Theory II: Positioning Legal Theory Within the Law* (New York: New York University Press, 1995).

Susan Sage Neinzelman and Ziporah Batshaw Wiseman, *Representing Women, Law, Literature and Feminism* (Durham, N.C.: Duke University Press 1994).

Patricia Smith, ed. *Feminist Jurisprudence* (New York: Oxford University Press, 1993).

D. Kelly Weisberg, ed., *Feminist Legal Theory, Foundations* (Philadelphia: Temple University Press, 1993). Weisberg and Olsen's contributions are reviewed and situated historically in the emergence of successive "waves" of legal feminism by Adelaide Willmoare, "Feminist Jurisprudence and Political Vision," 24 *Law and Social Inquiry* 443 (1999).

Katherine T. Bartlett and Rosanne Kennedy, eds., *Feminist Legal Theory: Readings in Law and Gender* (San Francisco: Westview Press, 1991).

Martha Fineman and Nancy Thomadsen, eds., *At the Boundaries of Law: Feminism and Legal Theory* (New York: Routledge, 1991).

For a general overview of feminist legal theory, see Martha Chamallas, *Introduction to Feminist Legal Theory* (New York: Aspen Law and Business, 1999) (analyzing MacKinnon's "dominance feminism" at 53 and following).

A variety of casebooks and coursebooks for teaching feminist jurisprudence are now on the market. Particularly significant recent examples include:

Mary Joe Frug, Judith Greenberg, Martha Minow, Dorothy Roberts, eds., *Women and the Law* (New York: Foundation Press, 1998).

Mary Becker, Cynthia Grant Bowman, and Morrison Torrey, *Feminist Jurisprudence: Taking Women Seriously: Cases and Materials*, 2d ed. (St. Paul: West Publishing, 2001).

Numerous law journals have devoted symposia volumes to feminist theory, often focused at least in part on MacKinnon's work. Among the most significant, in reverse chronological order:

"The Future of Intersectionality and Critical Race Feminism," 11(2) *Journal of Contemporary Legal Issues* 677–936 (2001).

"Feminist Jurisprudence," 24 *Georgia Law Review* 759–1044 (1999).

"Feminist Jurisprudence and Political Vision," 24 *Law and Social Inquiry* 443 (1999).

"InterSEXionality Interdisciplinary Perspectives on Queering Legal Theory," 75 *Denver University Law Review* 1321 (1998).

"Feminism and the Law," 1994 19–4 *Signs: Journal of Women in Culture and Society* 816–1083.

"Feminist Theory and Legal Strategy," 20(1) *Journal of Law and Society* (1993).

"Symposium: Gender and Law," 46 *University of Miami Law Review* 503–854 (1992).

"Symposium Issue: Recent Work in Feminist Legal Thought," 59 *Tennessee Law Review* 441–616 (1991–92).

"Symposium: The Voices of Women," 77 *Iowa Law Review* 1–199 (including a selective bibliography of feminist legal writing) (1991).

"Sexual Difference," 1(2) *Law and Critique* 131–248 (1990).

"Papers from the 1986 Feminism and Legal Theory Conference," 3 *Wisconsin Women's Law Journal* 1 (1987).

"Feminism, Marxism, Method, and the State: An Agenda for Theory"

7 Signs: Journal of Women in Culture and Society 3 (1982)

Sexuality is to feminism what work is to marxism: that which is most one's own, yet most taken away. Marxist theory argues that society is fundamentally constructed of the relations people form as they do and make things needed to survive humanly. Work is the social process of shaping and transforming the material and social worlds, creating people as social beings as they create value. It is that activity by which people become who they are. Class is its structure, production its consequence, capital its congealed form, and control its issue.

Implicit in feminist theory is a parallel argument: the molding, direction, and expression of sexuality organizes society into two sexes—women and men—which division underlies the totality of social relations. Sexuality is that social process which creates, organizes, expresses, and directs desire,[1] creating the social

---

Dedicated to the spirit of Shelly Rosaldo in us all.

The second part of this article, which will appear in a forthcoming issue of *Signs* as "Feminism, Marxism, Method, and the State: Toward Feminist Jurisprudence," applies the critique developed here to theories of the state and to legal materials. Both articles are parts of a longer work in progress. The argument of this essay on the relation between marxism and feminism has not changed since it was first written in 1973, but the argument on feminism itself has. In the intervening years, the manuscript has been widely circulated, in biannual mutations, for criticism. Reflecting on that process, which I hope publication will continue (this *is* "an agenda for theory"), I find the following people, each in their way, contributed most to its present incarnation: Sonia E. Alvarez, Douglas Bennett, Paul Brest, Ruth Colker, Robert A. Dahl, Karen E. Davis, Andrea Dworkin, Alicia Fernandez, Jane Flax, Bert Garskoff, Elbert Gates, Karen Haney, Kent Harvey, Linda Hoaglund, Nan Keohane, Duncan Kennedy, Bob Lamm, Martha Roper, Michelle Z. Rosaldo, Anne E. Simon, Sharon Silverstein, Valerie A. Tebbetts, Rona Wilensky, Gaye Williams, Jack Winkler, and Laura X. The superb work of Martha Freeman and Lu Ann Carter was essential to its production.

I have rendered "marxism" in lower case and "Black" in upper case and have been asked by the publisher to explain these choices. It is conventional to capitalize terms that derive from a proper name. Since I wish to place marxism and feminism in equipoise, the disparate typography would weigh against my analytic structure. Capitalizing both would germanize the text. I also hope feminism, a politics authored by those it works in the name of, is never named after an individual. Black is conventionally (I am told) regarded as a color rather than a racial or national designation, hence is not usually capitalized. I do not regard Black as merely a color of skin pigmentation, but as a heritage, an experience, a cultural and personal identity, the meaning of which becomes specifically stigmatic and/or glorious and/or ordinary under specific social conditions. It is as much socially created as, and at least in the American context no less specifically meaningful or definitive than, any linguistic, tribal, or religious ethnicity, all of which are conventionally recognized by capitalization.

[1] "Desire" is selected as a term parallel to "value" in marxist theory to refer to that substance felt to be primordial or aboriginal but posited by the theory as social and contingent. The sense in which I mean it is consonant with its development in contemporary French feminist theories, e.g., in Hélène Cixous, "The Laugh of Medusa: Viewpoint," trans. Keith Cohen and Paula Cohen, *Signs: Journal of Women in Culture and Society* 1, no. 4 (Summer 1976): 875–93; and in works by Gauthier, Irigaray, LeClerc, Duras, and Kristeva in *New French Feminisms: An Anthology*, ed. Elaine Marks and Isabelle de Courtivron (Amherst: University of Massachusetts Press, 1980). My use of the term is to be distinguished from that of Gilles Deleuze and Felix Guattari, *Anti-Oedipus: Capitalism and Schizophrenia* (New York: Viking Press, 1977); and Guy Hocquenghem, *Homosexual Desire* (London: Allison & Busby, 1978), for example.

EDITORS' NOTE: *Central to feminist theory and feminist method, as Catharine A. MacKinnon shows, is consciousness raising. Through this process, feminists confront the reality of women's condition by examining their experience and by taking this analysis as the starting point for individual and social change. By its nature, this method of inquiry challenges traditional notions of authority and objectivity and opens a dialectical questioning of existing power structures, of our own experience, and of theory itself.*

beings we know as women and men, as their relations create society. As work is to marxism, sexuality to feminism is socially constructed yet constructing, universal as activity yet historically specific, jointly comprised of matter and mind. As the organized expropriation of the work of some for the benefit of others defines a class—workers—the organized expropriation of the sexuality of some for the use of others defines the sex, woman. Heterosexuality is its structure, gender and family its congealed forms, sex roles its qualities generalized to social persona, reproduction a consequence, and control its issue.

Marxism and feminism are theories of power and its distribution: inequality. They provide accounts of how social arrangements of patterned disparity can be internally rational yet unjust. But their specificity is not incidental. In marxism to be deprived of one's work, in feminism of one's sexuality, defines each one's conception of lack of power per se. They do not mean to exist side by side to insure that two separate spheres of social life are not overlooked, the interests of two groups are not obscured, or the contributions of two sets of variables are not ignored. They exist to argue, respectively, that the relations in which many work and few gain, in which some fuck and others get fucked,[2] are the prime moment of politics.

What if the claims of each theory are taken equally seriously, each on its own terms? Can two social processes be basic at once? Can two groups be subordinated in conflicting ways, or do they merely crosscut? Can two theories, each of which purports to account for the same thing—power as such—be reconciled? Or, is there a connection between the fact that the few have ruled the many and the fact that those few have been men?

Confronted on equal terms, these theories pose fundamental questions for each other. Is male dominance a creation of capitalism or is capitalism one expression of male dominance? What does it mean for class analysis if one can assert that a social group is defined and exploited through means largely independent of the organization of production, if in forms appropriate to it? What does it mean for a sex-based analysis if one can assert that capitalism would not be materially altered if it were sex integrated or even controlled by women? If the structure and interests served by the socialist state and the capitalist state differ in class terms, are they equally predicated upon sex inequality? To the extent their form and behavior resemble one another, could this be their commonality? Is there a relationship between the power of some classes over others and that of all men over all women?

Rather than confront these questions, marxists and feminists have usually either dismissed or, in what amounts to the same thing, subsumed each other. Marxists have criticized feminism as bourgeois in theory and in practice, meaning that it works in the interest of the ruling class. They argue that to analyze society in terms of sex ignores class divisions among women, dividing the proletariat. Feminist demands, it is claimed, could be fully satisfied within capitalism, so their pursuit undercuts and deflects the effort for basic change. Efforts to eliminate barriers to women's personhood—arguments for access to life chances without regard to sex— are seen as liberal and individualistic. Whatever women have in common is considered based in nature, not society; cross-cultural analyses of commonalities in women's social conditions are seen as ahistorical and lacking in cultural specificity.

---

[2] I know no nondegraded English verb for the activity of sexual expression that would allow a construction parallel to, for example, "I am working," a phrase that could apply to nearly any activity. This fact of language may reflect and contribute to the process of obscuring sexuality's pervasiveness in social life. Nor is there *any* active verb meaning "to act sexually" that specifically envisions a woman's action. If language constructs as well as expresses the social world, these words support heterosexual values.

The women's movement's focus upon attitudes and feelings as powerful components of social reality is criticized as idealist; its composition, purportedly of middle-class educated women, is advanced as an explanation for its opportunism.

Feminists charge that marxism is male defined in theory and in practice, meaning that it moves within the world view and in the interest of men. Feminists argue that analyzing society exclusively in class terms ignores the distinctive social experiences of the sexes, obscuring women's unity. Marxist demands, it is claimed, could be (and in part have been) satisfied without altering women's inequality to men. Feminists have often found that working-class movements and the left undervalue women's work and concerns, neglect the role of feelings and attitudes in a focus on institutional and material change, denigrate women in procedure, practice, and everyday life, and in general fail to distinguish themselves from any other ideology or group dominated by male interests. Marxists and feminists thus accuse each other of seeking (what in each one's terms is) reform—changes that appease and assuage without addressing the grounds of discontent—where (again in each one's terms) a fundamental overthrow is required. The mutual perception, at its most extreme, is not only that the other's analysis is incorrect, but that its success would be a defeat.

Neither set of allegations is groundless. In the feminist view, sex, in analysis and in reality, does divide classes, a fact marxists have been more inclined to deny or ignore than to explain or change. Marxists, similarly, have seen parts of the women's movement function as a special interest group to advance the class-privileged: educated and professional women. To consider this group coextensive with "the women's movement" precludes questioning a definition of coalesced interest and resistance[3] which gives disproportionate visibility to the movement's least broadly based segment. But advocates of women's interests have not always been class conscious; some have exploited class-based arguments for advantage, even when the interests of working-class *women* were thereby obscured.

For example, in 1866, in an act often thought to inaugurate the first wave of feminism, John Stuart Mill petitioned the English parliament for women's suffrage with the following partial justification: "Under whatever conditions, and within whatever limits, men are admitted to suffrage, there is not a shadow of justification for not admitting women under the same. The majority of women of any class are not likely to differ in political opinion from the majority of men in the same class."[4] Perhaps Mill means that, to the extent class determines opinion, sex is irrelevant. In this sense, the argument is (to some persuasively) narrow. It can also justify limiting the extension of the franchise to women who "belong to" men of the same class that already exercises it, to the further detriment of the excluded underclass, "their" women included.[5]

This kind of reasoning is confined neither to the issue of the vote nor to the nineteenth century. Mill's logic is embedded in a theoretical structure that underlies much contemporary feminist theory and justifies much of the marxist critique. That women should be allowed to engage in politics expressed Mill's concern that the state not restrict individuals' self-government, their freedom to develop talents for their own growth, and their ability to contribute to society for the good of humanity.

---

[3] Accepting this definition has tended to exclude from "the women's movement" and make invisible the diverse ways that many women—notably Blacks and working-class women—have *moved* against their determinants.

[4] John Stuart Mill, "The Subjection of Women," in *Essays on Sex Equality*, ed. Alice S. Rossi (Chicago: University of Chicago Press, 1970), pp. 184–85.

[5] Mill personally supported universal suffrage. As it happened, working-class men got the vote before women of any class.

As an empirical rationalist, he resisted attributing to biology what could be explained as social conditioning. As a utilitarian, he found most sex-based inequalities inaccurate or dubious, inefficient, and therefore unjust. The liberty of women as individuals to achieve the limits of self-development without arbitrary interference extended to women his meritocratic goal of the self-made man, condemning (what has since come to be termed) sexism as an interference with personal initiative and laissez-faire.

The hospitality of such an analysis to marxist concerns is problematic. One might extend Mill's argument to cover class as one more arbitrary, socially conditioned factor that produces inefficient development of talent and unjust distribution of resources among individuals. But although this might be in a sense materialist, it would not be a class analysis. Mill does not even allow for income leveling. Unequal distribution of wealth is exactly what laissez-faire and unregulated personal initiative produces. The individual concept of rights that this theory requires on a juridical level (especially but not only in the economic sphere), a concept which produces the tension between liberty for each and equality among all, pervades liberal feminism, substantiating the criticism that feminism is for the privileged few.

The marxist criticism that feminism focuses upon feelings and attitudes is also based on something real: the centrality of consciousness raising. Consciousness raising is the major technique of analysis, structure of organization, method of practice, and theory of social change of the women's movement.[6] In consciousness raising, often in groups, the impact of male dominance is concretely uncovered and analyzed through the collective speaking of women's experience, from the perspective of that experience. Because marxists tend to conceive of powerlessness, first and last, as concrete and externally imposed, they believe that it must be concretely and externally undone to be changed. Women's powerlessness has been found through consciousness raising to be both internalized and externally imposed, so that, for example, femininity is identity to women as well as desirability to men. The feminist concept of consciousness and its place in social order and change emerge from this practical analytic. What marxism conceives as change in consciousness is not a form of social change in itself. For feminism, it can be, but because women's oppression is not just in the head, feminist *consciousness* is not just in the head either. But the pain, isolation, and thingification of women who have been pampered and pacified into nonpersonhood—women "grown ugly and dangerous from being nobody for so long"[7]—is difficult for the materially deprived to see as a form of oppression, particularly for women whom no man has ever put on a pedestal.

[6] Feminists have observed the importance of consciousness raising without seeing it as method in the way developed here. See Pamela Allen, *Free Space: A Perspective on the Small Group in Women's Liberation* (New York: Times Change Press, 1970); Anuradha Bose, "Consciousness Raising," in *Mother Was Not a Person*, ed. Margaret Anderson (Montreal: Content Publishing, 1972); Nancy McWilliams, "Contemporary Feminism, Consciousness-Raising, and Changing Views of the Political," in *Women in Politics*, ed. Jane Jaquette (New York: John Wiley & Sons, 1974); Joan Cassell, *A Group Called Women: Sisterhood & Symbolism in the Feminist Movement* (New York: David McKay, 1977); and Nancy Hartsock, "Fundamental Feminism: Process and Perspective," *Quest: A Feminist Quarterly* 2, no. 2 (Fall 1975): 67–80.

[7] Toni Cade (now Bambara) thus describes a desperate Black woman who has too many children and too little means to care for them or herself in "The Pill: Genocide or Liberation?" in *The Black Woman: An Anthology*, ed. Toni Cade (New York: Mentor, New American Library, 1970), p. 168. By using her phrase in altered context, I do not want to distort her meaning but to extend it. Throughout this essay, I have tried to see if women's condition is shared, even when contexts or magnitudes differ. (Thus, it is very different to be "nobody" as a Black woman than as a white lady, but neither is "somebody" by male standards.) This is the approach to race and ethnicity attempted throughout. I aspire to include all women in the term "women" in some way, without violating the particularity of any woman's experience. Whenever this fails, the statement is simply wrong and will have to be qualified or the aspiration (or the theory) abandoned.

Marxism, similarly, has not just been misunderstood. Marxist theory *has* traditionally attempted to comprehend all meaningful social variance in class terms. In this respect, sex parallels race and nation as an undigested but persistently salient challenge to the exclusivity—or even primacy—of class as social explanation. Marxists typically extend class to cover women, a division and submersion that, to feminism, is inadequate to women's divergent and common experience. In 1912 Rosa Luxemburg, for example, addressed a group of women on the issue of suffrage: "Most of these bourgeois women who act like lionesses in the struggle against 'male prerogatives' would trot like docile lambs in the camp of conservative and clerical reaction if they had the suffrage. Indeed, they would certainly be a good deal more reactionary than the male part of their class. Aside from the few who have taken jobs or professions, the bourgeoisie do not take part in social production. They are nothing but co-consumers of the surplus product their men extort from the proletariat. They are parasites of the parasites of the social body."[8] Her sympathies lay with "proletarian women" who derive their right to vote from being "productive for society like the men."[9] With a blind spot analogous to Mill's within her own perspective, Luxemburg defends women's suffrage on class grounds, although in both cases the vote would have benefited women without regard to class.

Women as women, across class distinctions and apart from nature, were simply unthinkable to Luxemburg, as to most marxists. Feminist theory asks marxism: What is class for women? Luxemburg, again like Mill in her own context, subliminally recognizes that women derive their class position, with concomitant privileges and restrictions, from their associations with men. For a feminist, this may explain why they do not unite against male dominance, but it does not explain that dominance, which cuts across class lines even as it takes forms peculiar to classes. What distinguishes the bourgeois woman from her domestic servant is that the latter is paid (if barely), while the former is kept (if contingently). But is this a difference in social productivity or only in its indices, indices which themselves may be products of women's undervalued status?[10] Luxemburg sees that the bourgeois woman of her

---

[8] Rosa Luxemburg, "Women's Suffrage and Class Struggle," in *Selected Political Writings,* ed. Dick Howard (New York: Monthly Review Press, 1971), pp. 219–20. It may or may not be true that women as a group vote more conservatively than men, on a conventional left-right spectrum. The apparently accurate suspicion that they do may have accounted for left ambivalence on women's suffrage as much as any principled view of the role of reform in a politics of radical change.

[9] Ibid., p. 220.

[10] This question is most productively explored in the controversy over wages for housework. See Margaret Benston, "The Political Economy of Women's Liberation," *Monthly Review,* vol. 21, no. 4 (September 1969), reprinted in *From Feminism to Liberation,* ed. Edith Hoshino Altbach (Cambridge, Mass.: Schenckman Publishing Co., 1971), pp. 199–210; Peggy Morton, "Women's Work Is Never Done," in *Women Unite* (Toronto: Canadian Women's Educational Press, 1972); Hodee Edwards, "Housework and Exploitation: A Marxist Analysis," *No More Fun and Games: A Journal of Female Liberation,* issue 4 (July 1971), pp. 92–100; and Mariarosa Dalla Costa and Selma James, *The Power of Women and the Subversion of the Community* (Bristol: Falling Wall Press, 1973). This last work situates housework in a broader theoretical context of wagelessness and potential political power while avoiding support of wages for housework as a program; its authors have since come to support wages for housework, deducing it from the perspective presented here. See also Sylvia Federici, *Wages against Housework* (Bristol: Falling Wall Press, 1973); Wally Seccombe, "The Housewife and Her Labor under Capitalism," *New Left Review* 83 (January–February 1974): 3–24; Carol Lopate, "Women and Pay for Housework," *Liberation* 18, no. 9 (May–June 1974): 11–19; Nicole Cox and Sylvia Federici, *Counter-Planning from the Kitchen—Wages for Housework: A Perspective on Capital and the Left* (Bristol: Falling Wall Press, 1975); Wendy Edmond and Suzi Fleming, eds., *All Work and No Pay: Women, Housework and the Wages Due* (Bristol: Falling Wall Press, 1975); Jeanette Silveira, *The Housewife and Marxist Class Analysis* (Seattle, Wash.: By the author, 1975) (pamphlet available from the author, P.O. Box 30541, Seattle, Wash. 98103); Jean Gardiner, "Women's Domestic Labor," *New Left Review* 89 (January–February 1975): 47–55; Beth Ingber and Cleveland Modern Times Group, "The Social Factory," *Falling Wall Review,* no. 5 (1976), pp. 1–7; Joan Landes, "Wages for Housework: Subsidizing Capitalism?" *Quest: A Feminist Quarterly* 2, no. 2 (Fall 1975): 17–30; Batya Weinbaum and Amy Bridges, "The Other Side of the Paycheck: Monopoly Capital and the Structure of Conscription," *Monthly Review* 28, no. 3 (July–August 1976): 88–103.

time is a "parasite of a parasite" but fails to consider her commonality with the proletarian woman who is the slave of a slave. In the case of bourgeois women, to limit the analysis of women's relationship to capitalism to their relations through men is to see only its vicarious aspect. To fail to do this in the case of proletarian women is to miss its vicarious aspect.

Feminist observations of women's situation in socialist countries, although not conclusive on the contribution of marxist theory to understanding women's situation, have supported the theoretical critique.[11] In the feminist view, these countries have solved many social problems, women's subordination not included. The criticism is not that socialism has not automatically liberated women in the process of transforming production (assuming that this transformation is occurring). Nor is it to diminish the significance of such changes for women: "There is a difference between a society in which sexism is expressed in the form of female infanticide and a society in which sexism takes the form of unequal representation on the Central Committee. And the difference is worth dying for."[12] The criticism is rather that these countries do not make a priority of working for women that distinguishes them from nonsocialist societies. Capitalist countries value women in terms of their "merit" by male standards; in socialist countries women are invisible except in their capacity as "workers," a term that seldom includes women's distinctive work: housework, sexual service, childbearing. The concern of revolutionary leadership for ending women's confinement to traditional roles too often seems limited to making their labor available to the regime, leading feminists to wonder whose interests are served by this version of liberation. Women become as free as men to work outside the home while men remain free from work within it. This also occurs under capitalism. When woman's labor or militancy suits the needs of emergency, she is suddenly man's equal, only to regress when the urgency recedes.[13] Feminists do not argue that it means the same to women to be on the bottom in a feudal regime, a capitalist regime, and a socialist regime; the commonality argued is that, despite real changes, bottom is bottom.

---

[11] These observations are complex and varied. Typically they begin with the recognition of the important changes socialism has made for women, qualified by reservations about its potential to make the remaining necessary ones. Delia Davin, "Women in the Countryside of China," in *Women in Chinese Society,* ed. Margery Wolf and Roxane Witke (Stanford, Calif.: Stanford University Press, 1974); Katie Curtin, *Women in China* (New York: Pathfinder Press, 1975); Judith Stacey, "When Patriarchy Kowtows: The Significance of the Chinese Family Revolution for Feminist Theory," *Feminist Studies* 2, no. 2/3 (1975): 64–112; Julia Kristeva, *About Chinese Women* (New York: Urizen Books, 1977); Hilda Scott, *Does Socialism Liberate Women? Experiences from Eastern Europe* (Cambridge, Mass.: Beacon Press, 1974); Margaret Randall, *Cuban Women Now* (Toronto: Women's Press, 1974) (an edited collation of Cuban women's own observations); and *Cuban Women Now: Afterword* (Toronto: Women's Press, 1974); Carollee Bengelsdorf and Alice Hageman, "Emerging from Underdevelopment: Women and Work in Cuba," in *Capitalist Patriarchy and the Case for Socialist Feminism,* ed. Zillah Eisenstein (New York: Monthly Review Press, 1979).

[12] Barbara Ehrenreich, "What Is Socialist Feminism?" *Win* (June 3, 1976), reprinted in *Working Papers on Socialism and Feminism* (Chicago: New American Movement, n.d.). Counterpoint is provided by feminists who have more difficulty separating the two. Susan Brownmiller notes: "It seems to me that a country that wiped out the tsetse fly can by fiat put an equal number of women on the Central Committee" ("Notes of an Ex-China Fan," *Village Voice,* quoted in Batya Weinbaum, *The Curious Courtship of Women's Liberation and Socialism* [Boston: South End Press, 1978], p. 7).

[13] Stacey (n. 11 above); Janet Salaff and Judith Merkle, "Women and Revolution: The Lessons of the Soviet Union and China," *Socialist Revolution* 1, no. 4 (1970): 39–72; Linda Gordon, *The Fourth Mountain* (Cambridge, Mass.: Working Papers, 1973); Richard Stites, *The Women's Liberation Movement in Russia: Feminism, Nihilism, and Bolshevism* (Princeton, N.J.: Princeton University Press, 1978), pp. 392–421.

Catharine A. MacKinnon

Where such attitudes and practices come to be criticized, as in Cuba or China, changes appear gradual and precarious, even where the effort looks major. If seizures of state and productive power overturn work relations, they do not overturn sex relations at the same time or in the same way, as a class analysis of sex would (and in some cases did) predict.[14] Neither technology nor socialism, both of which purport to alter women's role at the point of production, have ever yet equalized women's status relative to men. In the feminist view, nothing has. At minimum, a separate effort appears required—an effort that can be shaped by revolutionary regime and work relations—but a separate effort nonetheless. In light of these experiences, women's struggles, whether under capitalist or social ist regimes, appear to feminists to have more in common with each other than with leftist struggles anywhere.

Attempts to create a synthesis between marxism and feminism, termed socialist-feminism, have not recognized the depth of the antagonism or the separate integrity of each theory. These juxtapositions emerge as unconfronted as they started: either feminist or marxist, usually the latter. Socialist-feminist practice often divides along the same lines, consisting largely in organizational cross-memberships and mutual support on specific issues.[15] Women with feminist sympathies urge attention to women's issues by left or labor groups; marxist women pursue issues of class within feminist groups; explicitly socialist-feminist groups come together and divide, often at the hyphen.[16]

Most attempts at synthesis attempt to integrate or explain the appeal of femi nism by incorporating issues feminism identifies as central—the family, house work, sexuality, reproduction, socialization, personal life—within an essentially

[14] See Fidel Castro, *Women and the Cuban Revolution* (New York: Pathfinder Press, 1970); but compare Fidel's "Speech at Closing Session of the 2d Congress of the Federation of Cuban Women," November 29, 1974, *Cuba Review* 4 (December 1974): 17–23. Stephanie Urdang, *A Revolution within a Revolution: Women in Cuinea-Bissau* (Boston: New England Free Press, n.d.). This is the general position taken by official documents of the Chinese revolution, as collected by Elisabeth Croll, ed., *The Women's Movement in China: A Selection of Readings, 1949–1973,* Modern China Series, no. 6 (London: Anglo-Chinese Educational Institute, 1974). Mao Tse-Tung rec ognized a distinctive domination of women by men (see discussion by Stuart Schram, *The Political Thought of Mao Tse-Tung* [New York: Praeger Publishers, 1969], p. 257), but interpretations of his thought throughout the revolution saw issues of sex as bourgeois deviation (see Croll, ed., pp. 19, 22, 32). The Leninist view which the lat ter documents seem to reflect is expressed in Clara Zetkin's account, "Lenin on the Woman Question," excerpted as appendix in *The Woman Question* (New York: International Publishers, 1951), p. 89. Engels earlier traced the oppression of women to the rise of class society, the patriarchal family, and the state, arguing that woman's status would be changed with the elimination of private property as a form of ownership and her integration into public production (Friedrich Engels, *Origin of the Family, Private Property and the State* [New York: International Publishers, 1942]).

[15] Sheila Rowbotham, *Hidden from History: Rediscovering Women in History from the Seventeenth Century to the Present* (New York: Random House, 1973); Mary Jo Buhle, "Women and the Socialist Party, 1901–1914," in Altbach, ed. (n. 10 above); Robert Shaffer, "Women and the Communist Party, USA, 1930–1940," *Socialist Review* 45 (May–June 1979): 73–118. Contemporary attempts to create socialist-feminist groups and strategies are exemplified in position papers: Chicago Women's Liberation Union, "Socialist Feminism: A Strategy for the Women's Movement," mimeograph (Chicago, 1972) (available from Women's Liberation Union, Hyde Park Chapter, 819 W. George, Chicago, Ill. 60657); Berkeley-Oakland Women's Union, "Principles of Unity," *Socialist Revolution* 4, no. 1 (January–March 1974): 69–82; Lavender and Red Union, *The Political Perspective of the Lavender and Red Union* (Los Angeles: Fanshen Printing Collective, 1975). Rosalind Petchesky, "Dissolving the Hyphen: A Report on Marxist-Feminist Groups 1–5," in Eisenstein, ed. (n. 11 above), and Red Apple Collective, "Socialist-Feminist Women's Unions: Past and Present," *Quest: A Feminist Quarterly* 4, no. 1 (1977): 88–96, reflect on the process.

[16] Many attempts at unity began as an effort to justify women's struggles in marxist terms, as if only that could make them legitimate. This anxiety lurks under many synthetic attempts, although feminism has largely redirected its efforts from justifying itself within any other perspective to developing its own.

unchanged marxian analysis.[17] According to the persuasion of the marxist, women become a caste, a stratum, a cultural group, a division in civil society, a secondary contradiction, or a nonantagonistic contradiction; women's liberation becomes a precondition, a measure of society's general emancipation, part of the superstructure, or an important aspect of the class struggle. Most commonly, women are reduced to some other category, such as "women workers," which is then treated as coextensive with all women.[18] Or, in what has become near reflex, women become "the family," as if this single form of women's confinement (then divided on class lines, then on racial lines) can be *presumed* the crucible of women's determination.[19] Or, the marxist meaning of reproduction, the iteration

[17] While true from a feminist standpoint, this sweeping characterization does minimize the wide varieties of marxist theories that have produced significantly different analyses of women's situation. Juliet Mitchell, *Woman's Estate* (New York: Random House, 1971); Sheila Rowbotham, *Women, Resistance and Revolution: A History of Women and Revolution in the Modern World* (New York: Random House, 1972); Zillah Eisenstein, "Some Notes on the Relations of Capitalist Patriarchy," in Eisenstein, ed. (n. 11 above); Eli Zaretsky, "Socialist Politics and the Family," *Socialist Revolution* 19 (January–March 1974): 83–99; Eli Zaretsky, "Capitalism, the Family and Personal Life," *Socialist Revolution* 3, nos. 1 and 2 (January–April 1973): 69–126, and no. 3 (May–June 1973): 19–70; Virginia Held, "Marx, Sex and the Transformation of Society," in *Women and Philosophy: Toward a Theory of Liberation,* ed. Carol C. Gould and Marx W. Wartofsky (New York: G. P. Putnam's Sons, 1976), pp. 168–84; Mihailo Markovic, "Women's Liberation and Human Emancipation," ibid., pp. 145–67; Hal Draper, "Marx and Engels on Women's Liberation," in *Female Liberation,* ed. Roberta Salper (New York: Alfred A. Knopf, Inc., 1972), pp. 83–107. No matter how perceptive about the contributions of feminism or sympathetic to women's interests, these attempts cast feminism, ultimately, as a movement *within* marxism: "I want to suggest that the women's movement can provide the basis for building a new and authentic American socialism" (Nancy Hartsock, "Feminist Theory and the Development of Revolutionary Strategy," in Eisenstein, ed. [n. 11 above], p. 57). Attempts at synthesis that push these limits include Gayle Rubin, "The Traffic in Women: Notes on the 'Political Economy' of Sex," in *Toward an Anthropology of Women,* ed. Rayna R. Reiter (New York: Monthly Review Press, 1975), pp. 157–210; Sheila Rowbotham, *Women's Liberation and the New Politics,* Spokesman Pamphlet, no. 17 (Bristol: Falling Wall Press, 1971); Annette Kuhn and AnnMarie Wolpe, "Feminism and Materialism," in *Feminism and Materialism: Women and Modes of Production,* ed. Annette Kuhn and AnnMarie Wolpe (London: Routledge & Kegan Paul, 1978); Ann Foreman, *Femininity as Alienation: Women and the Family in Marxism and Psychoanalysis* (London: Pluto Press, 1977); Meredith Tax and Jonathan Schwartz, "The Wageless Slave and the Proletarian," mimeograph (1972) (available from the author); Heidi I. Hartmann, "Capitalism, Patriarchy, and Job Segregation by Sex," *Signs: Journal of Women in Culture and Society* 1, no. 3, pt. 2 (Spring 1976): 137–69, and "The Unhappy Marriage of Marxism and Feminism: Towards a More Progressive Union," *Capital and Class* 8 (Summer 1979): 1–33; advocates of "wages for housework" mentioned in n. 10 above: and work by Linda Gordon, *Woman's Body, Woman's Right: A Social History of Birth Control in America* (New York: Grossman Publishers, 1976), pp. 403–18. Also see Linda Gordon, "The Struggle for Reproductive Freedom: Three Stages of Feminism," in Eisenstein, ed. (n. 11 above). Charlotte Bunch and Nancy Myron, *Class and Feminism* (Baltimore: Diana Press, 1974) exemplifies, without explicitly articulating, feminist method applied to class.

[18] This tendency, again with important variations, is manifest in writings otherwise as diverse as Charnie Guettel, *Marxism and Feminism* (Toronto: Canadian Women's Education Press, 1974); Mary Alice Waters, "Are Feminism and Socialism Related?" in *Feminism and Socialism,* ed. Linda Jenness (New York: Pathfinder Press, 1972), pp. 18–26; Weather Underground, *Prairie Fire* (Underground, U.S.A.: Red Dragon Collective, 1975); Marjorie King, "Cuba's Attack on Women's Second Shift, 1974–1976," *Latin American Perspectives* 4, nos. 1 and 2 (Winter-Spring 1977): 106–19; Al Syzmanski, "The Socialization of Women's Oppression: A Marxist Theory of the Changing Position of Women in Advanced Capitalist Society," *Insurgent Sociologist* 6, no. 11 (Winter 1976): 31–58; "The Political Economy of Women," *Review of Radical Political Economics* 4, no. 3 (July 1972). See also Selma James, *Women, the Unions and Work, or What Is Not to Be Done* (Bristol: Falling Wall Press, 1976). This is true for "wages for housework" theory in the sense that it sees women as exploited because they do work—housework.

[19] Engels (n. 14 above); Leon Trotsky, *Women and the Family,* trans. Max Eastman et al. (New York: Pathfinder Press, 1970); Evelyn Reed, *Woman's Evolution: From Matriarchal Clan to Patriarchal Family* (New York: Pathfinder Press, 1975); Lise Vogel, "The Earthly Family," *Radical America* 7, nos. 4–5 (July–October 1973): 9–50; Kollontai Collective, "The Politics of the Family: A Marxist View" (paper prepared for Socialist Feminist Conference at Yellow Springs, Ohio, July 4–6, 1975); Linda Limpus, *Liberation of Women: Sexual Repression and the Family* (Boston: New England Free Press, n.d.); Marlene Dixon, "On the Super-Exploitation of Women," *Synthesis* 1, no. 4 (Spring 1977): 1–11; David P. Levine and Lynn S. Levine, "Problems in the Marxist Theory of the Family," photocopied (Department of Economics, Yale University, July 1978). A common approach to treating women's situation as coterminous with the family is to make women's circumstances the incident or focus for a reconciliation of Marx with Freud. This approach, in turn, often becomes more Freudian than marxist, without

Catharine A. MacKinnon

854

of productive relations, is punned into an analysis of biological reproduction, as if women's bodily differences from men must account for their subordination to men; and as if this social analogue to the biological makes women's definition material, therefore based on a division of *labor* after all, therefore real, therefore (potentially) unequal.[20] Sexuality, if noticed at all, is, like "every day life,"[21] analyzed in gender-neutral terms, as if its social meaning can be presumed the same, or coequal, or complementary, for women and men.[22] Although a unified theory of social inequality is presaged in these strategies of subordination, staged progression, and assimilation of women's concerns to left concerns, at most an uneven combination is accomplished. However sympathetically, "the woman question" is always reduced to some other question, instead of being seen as *the* question, calling for analysis on its own terms.

Socialist-feminism stands before the task of synthesis as if nothing essential to either theory fundamentally opposes their wedding—indeed as if the union had already occurred and need only be celebrated. The failure to contain both theories on equal terms derives from the failure to confront each on its own ground: at the level of method. Method shapes each theory's vision of social reality. It identifies its central problem, group, and process, and creates as a consequence its distinctive conception of politics as such. Work and sexuality as concepts, then, derive their meaning and primacy from the *way* each theory approaches, grasps, interprets, and inhabits its world. Clearly, there is a relationship between how and what a theory sees: is there a marxist method without class? a feminist method without sex? Method in this sense organizes the apprehension of truth; it determines what counts as evidence and defines what is taken as verification. Instead of engaging the debate over which came (or comes) first, sex or class, the task for theory is to explore the conflicts and connections between the methods

---

yet becoming feminist in the sense developed here. Juliet Mitchell, *Psychoanalysis and Feminism: Freud, Reich, Laing and Women* (New York: Pantheon Books, 1974); Eli Zaretsky, "Male Supremacy and the Unconscious," *Socialist Revolution* 21, no. 22 (January 1975): 7–56; Nancy Chodorow, *The Reproduction of Mothering: Psychoanalysis and the Sociology of Gender* (Berkeley: University of California Press, 1978). See also Herbert Marcuse, "Socialist Feminism: The Hard Core of the Dream," *Edcentric: A Journal of Educational Change*, no. 31–32 (November 1974), pp. 7–44.

[20] Sometimes "reproduction" refers to biological reproduction, sometimes to the "reproduction" of daily life, as housework, sometimes both. Political Economy of Women Group, "Women, the State and Reproduction since the 1930s," *On the Political Economy of Women*, CSE Pamphlet no. 2, Stage 1 (London: Conference of Socialist Economists, 1977). Family theories (n. 19 above) often analyze biological reproduction as a part of the family, while theories of women as workers often see it as work (n. 18 above). For an analysis of reproduction as an aspect of *sexuality*, in the context of an attempted synthesis, see Gordon, "The Struggle for Reproductive Freedom: Three Stages of Feminism" (n. 17 above).

[21] Henri Lefebvre, *Everyday Life in the Modern World* (London: Penguin Books, 1971); Bruce Brown, *Marx, Freud and the Critique of Everyday Life: Toward a Permanent Cultural Revolution* (New York: Monthly Review Press, 1973).

[22] Herbert Marcuse, *Eros and Civilization: A Philosophical Inquiry into Freud* (New York: Random House, 1955); Wilhelm Reich, *Sex-Pol: Essays, 1929–1934* (New York: Random House, 1972); Reimut Reiche, *Sexuality and Class Struggle* (London: New Left Books, 1970); Bertell Ollman, *Social and Sexual Revolution: Essays on Marx and Reich* (Boston: South End Press, 1979); Red Collective, *The Politics of Sexuality in Capitalism* (London: Red Collective, 1973). This is also true of Michel Foucault, *The History of Sexuality*, vol. 1, *An Introduction* (New York: Random House, 1980). Although Foucault understands that sexuality must be discussed at the same time as method, power, class, and the law, he does not systematically comprehend the specificity of gender—women's and men's relation to these factors—as a primary category for comprehending them. As one result, he cannot distinguish between the silence about sexuality that Victorianism has made into a noisy discourse and the silence that has *been* women's sexuality under conditions of subordination by and to men. Lacan notwithstanding, none of these theorists grasps sexuality (*including desire itself*) as social, nor the content of its determination as a sexist social order that eroticizes potency (as male) and victimization (as female).

that found it meaningful to analyze social conditions in terms of those categories in the first place.[23]

Feminism has not been perceived as having a method, or even a central argument, with which to contend. It has been perceived not as a systematic analysis but as a loose collection of factors, complaints, and issues which, taken together, describe rather than explain the misfortunes of the female sex. The challenge is to demonstrate that feminism systematically converges upon a central explanation of sex inequality through an approach distinctive to its subject yet applicable to the whole of social life, including class.

Under the rubric of feminism, woman's situation has been explained as a consequence of biology[24] or of reproduction and mothering, social organizations of

[23] Marxist method is not monolithic. Beginning with Marx, it has divided between an epistemology that embraces its own historicity and one that claims to portray a reality outside itself. In the first tendency, all thought, including social analysis, is ideological in the sense of being shaped by social being, the conditions of which are external to no theory. The project of theory is to create what Lukáacs described as "a theory of theory and a consciousness of consciousness" (Georg Lukáacs, "Class Consciousness," in *History and Class Consciousness: Studies in Marxist Dialectics* [Cambridge, Mass.: MIT Press, 1968], p. 47). Theory is a social activity engaged in the life situation of consciousness. See Jane Flax, "Epistemology and Politics: An Inquiry into Their Relation" (Ph.D. diss., Yale University, 1974). In the second tendency, theory is acontextual to the extent that it is correct. Real processes and thought processes are distinct; being has primacy over knowledge. The real can only be unified with knowledge of the real, as in dialectical materialism, because they have previously been separated. Nicos Poulantzas, *Political Power and Social Classes* (London: Verso, 1978), p. 14. Theory as a form of thought is methodologically set apart both from the illusions endemic to social reality—ideology—and from reality itself, a world defined as thinglike, independent of both ideology and theory. Ideology here means thought that is socially determined without being conscious of its determinations. Situated thought is as likely to produce "false consciousness" as access to truth. Theory, by definition, is, on the contrary, nonideological. Since ideology is interested, theory must be disinterested in order to penetrate myths that justify and legitimate the status quo. As Louis Althusser warned, "We know that a 'pure' science only exists on condition that it continually frees itself from ideology which occupies it, haunts it, or lies in wait for it" (*For Marx* [London: Verso, 1979], p. 170). When this attempt is successful, society is seen "from the point of view of class exploitation" (Louis Althusser, *Lenin and Philosophy* [New York: Monthly Review Press, 1971], p. 8). A theory that embraced its own historicity might see the scientific imperative itself as historically contingent. (On the objective standpoint, see text, pp. 537–42.) The problem with using scientific method to understand women's situation is that it is precisely unclear what is thought and crucial what is thing, so that the separation itself becomes problematic. The second tendency grounds the marxist claim to be scientific; the first, its claim to capture as thought the flux of history. The first is more hospitable to feminism; the second has become the dominant tradition.

[24] Simone de Beauvoir, *The Second Sex* (New York: Alfred A. Knopf, Inc., 1970). Her existential theory merges, in order to criticize, social meaning with biological determination in "anatomical destiny": "Here we have the key to the whole mystery. On the biological level a species is maintained only by creating itself anew; but this creation results only in repeating the same Life in more individuals. But man assures the repetition of Life while transcending Life through Existence; by this transcendence he creates values that deprive pure repetition of all value.... Her misfortune is to have been biologically destined for the repetition of Life when even in her own view Life does not carry within itself its reasons for being, reasons that are more important than life itself" (p. 59). She does not ask, for example, whether the social value placed upon "repetition of life," the fact that it is seen as iterative rather than generative, or the fact that women are more identified with it than are men, are themselves social artifacts of women's subordination, rather than existential derivations of biological fiat. Shulamith Firestone substitutes the contradiction of sex for class in a dialectical analysis, but nevertheless takes sex itself as presocial: "Unlike economic class, sex class sprang directly from a biological reality; men and women were created different, and not equally privileged.... The biological family is an inherently unequal power distribution" (*The Dialectic of Sex: The Case For Feminist Revolution* [New York: William Morrow & Co., 1972], p. 3). Her solutions are consistent: "The freeing of women from the tyranny of their reproductive biology by every means available, and the diffusion of childbearing and the childrearing role to the society as a whole, men as well as women" (p. 206). Susan Brownmiller (in *Against Our Will: Men, Women and Rape* [New York: Simon & Schuster, 1976]) expresses a biological theory of rape within a social critique of the centrality of rape to women's subordination: "Men's structural capacity to rape and woman's corresponding structural vulnerability are as basic to the physiology of both our sexes as the primal act of sex itself. Had it not been for this accident of biology, an accommodation requiring the locking together of two separate parts, penis and vagina, there would be neither copulation nor rape as we know it.... By anatomical fiat—the inescapable construction of their genital organs—the human male was a natural predator and the human female served as his natural prey" (pp. 4, 6). She does not seem to think it necessary to explain why women do not engulf men, an equal biological possibility. Criticizing the law for confusing intercourse with rape, she finds them biologically indistinguishable, leaving one wondering whether she, too, must alter or acquiesce in the biological.

biology;[25] as caused by the marriage law[26] or, as extensions, by the patriarchal family, becoming society as a "patriarchy";[27] or as caused by artificial gender roles and their attendant attitudes.[28] Informed by these attempts, but conceiving nature, law, the family, and roles as consequences, not foundations, I think that feminism fundamentally identifies sexuality as the primary social sphere of male power. The centrality of sexuality emerges not from Freudian conceptions[29] but from feminist practice on diverse issues, including abortion, birth control, sterilization abuse, domestic battery, rape, incest, lesbianism, sexual harassment, prostitution, female sexual slavery, and pornography. In all these areas, feminist efforts confront and change women's lives concretely and experientially. Taken together, they are producing a feminist political theory centering upon sexuality: its social determination, daily construction, birth to death expression, and ultimately male control.

Feminist inquiry into these specific issues began with a broad unmasking of the attitudes that legitimize and hide women's status, the ideational envelope that contains woman's body: notions that women desire and provoke rape, that girls' experiences of incest are fantasies, that career women plot and advance by sexual parlays, that prostitutes are lustful, that wife beating expresses the intensity of love. Beneath each of these ideas was revealed bare coercion and broad connections to woman's social definition as a sex. Research on sex roles, pursuing Simone de Beauvoir's insight that "one is not born, one rather becomes a woman,"[30] disclosed an elaborate process: how and what one learns to become one. Gender, cross-culturally, was found to be a learned quality, an acquired characteristic, an assigned status, with qualities that vary independent of biology and an ideology that attributes them to nature.[31] The discovery that the female archetype is the feminine stereotype exposed "woman" as a social construction. Contemporary industrial society's version of her is docile, soft, passive, nurturant, vulnerable, weak, narcissistic, childlike, incompetent, masochistic, and domestic, made for child care, home care, and husband care. Conditioning to these values permeates the upbringing of girls and the images for emulation thrust

[25] Adrienne Rich, *Of Woman Born: Motherhood as Experience and Institution* (New York: W. W. Norton & Co., 1976); Chodorow (n. 19 above); Dorothy Dinnerstein, *The Mermaid and the Minotaur: Sexual Arrangements and Human Malaise* (New York: Harper & Row, 1977); Suzanne Arms, *Immaculate Deception: A New Look at Women and Childbirth in America* (Boston: Houghton Mifflin Co., 1975).

[26] I take Mill's "The Subjection of Women" (n. 4 above) to be the original articulation of the theory, generalized in much contemporary feminism, that women are oppressed by "patriarchy," meaning a system originating in the household wherein the father dominates, the structure then reproduced throughout the society in gender relations.

[27] In her "notes toward a theory of patriarchy" Kate Millett comprehends "sex as a status category with political implications," in which politics refers to "power-structured relationships, arrangements whereby one group of persons is controlled by another. . . . Patriarchy's chief institution is the family" (*Sexual Politics* [New York: Ballantine Books, 1969], pp. 32, 31, 45).

[28] Sandra L. Bem and Daryl J. Bem, "Case Study of Nonconscious Ideology: Training the Woman to Know Her Place," in *Beliefs, Attitudes and Human Affairs*, ed. D. J. Bem (Belmont, Calif.: Brooks/Cole, 1970); Eleanor Emmons Maccoby and Carol Nagy Jacklin, *The Psychology of Sex Differences* (Stanford, Calif.: Stanford University Press, 1974); and Shirley Weitz, *Sex Roles: Biological, Psychological and Social Foundations* (New York: Oxford University Press, 1977).

[29] Nor does it grow directly from Lacanian roots, although French feminists have contributed much to the developing theory from within that tradition.

[30] De Beauvoir (n. 24 above), p. 249.

[31] J. H. Block, "Conceptions of Sex Role: Some Cross-cultural and Longitudinal Perspectives," *American Psychologist* 28, no. 3 (June 1973): 512–26; Nancy Chodorow, "Being and Doing: A Cross-cultural Examination of the Socialization of Males and Females," in *Women in Sexist Society*, ed. V. Gornick and B. K. Moran (New York: Basic Books, 1971); R. R. Sears, "Development of Gender Role," in *Sex and Behavior*, ed. F. A. Beach (New York: John Wiley & Sons, 1965).

upon women. Women who resist or fail, including those who never did fit—for example, black and lower-class women who cannot survive if they are soft and weak and incompetent,[32] assertively self-respecting women, women with ambitions of male dimensions—are considered less female, lesser women. Women who comply or succeed are elevated as models, tokenized by success on male terms or portrayed as consenting to their natural place and dismissed as having participated if they complain.

If the literature on sex roles and the investigations of particular issues are read in light of each other, each element of the female *gender* stereotype is revealed as, in fact, *sexual*. Vulnerability means the appearance/reality of easy sexual access; passivity means receptivity and disabled resistance, enforced by trained physical weakness; softness means pregnability by something hard. Incompetence seeks help as vulnerability seeks shelter, inviting the embrace that becomes the invasion, trading exclusive access for protection . . . from the same access. Domesticity nurtures the consequent progeny, proof of potency, and ideally waits at home dressed in saran wrap.[33] Woman's infantilization evokes pedophilia; fixation on dismembered body parts (the breast man, the leg man) evokes fetishism; idolization of vapidity, necrophilia. Narcissism insures that woman identifies with that image of herself that man holds up: "Hold still, we are going to do your portrait, so that you can begin looking like it right away."[34] Masochism means that pleasure in violation becomes her sensuality. Lesbians so violate the sexuality implicit in female gender stereotypes as not to be considered women at all.

Socially, femaleness means femininity, which means attractiveness to men, which means sexual attractiveness, which means sexual availability on male terms.[35] What defines woman as such is what turns men on. Good girls are "attractive," bad girls "provocative." Gender socialization is the process through which women come to identify themselves as sexual beings, as beings that exist for men. It is that process through which women internalize (make their own) a male image of their sexuality *as* their identity as women.[36] It is not just an illusion. Feminist inquiry into women's own experience of sexuality revises prior comprehensions of sexual issues and transforms the concept of sexuality itself—its determinants and its role in society and politics. According to this revision, one "becomes a woman"—acquires and identifies with the status of the female—not so much through physical maturation or inculcation into appropriate role behavior as through the experience of sexuality: a complex unity of physicality, emotionality, identity, and status affirmation. Sex as gender and sex as sexuality are thus defined in terms of each other, but it is sexuality that determines gender, not the other way around. This, the central but never stated insight of Kate

Catharine A. MacKinnon

[32] National Black Feminist Organization, "Statement of Purpose," *Ms.* (May 1974): "The black woman has had to be strong, yet we are persecuted for having survived" (p. 99). Johnnie Tillmon, "Welfare Is a Women's Issue," *Liberation News Service* (February 26, 1972), in *America's Working Women: A Documentary History, 1600 to the Present,* ed. Rosalyn Baxandall, Linda Gordon, and Susan Reverby (New York: Vintage Books, 1976): "On TV a woman learns that human worth means beauty and that beauty means being thin, white, young and rich. . . . In other words, an A.F.D.C. mother learns that being a 'real woman' means being all the things she isn't and having all the things she can't have" (pp. 357–58).

[33] Marabel Morgan, *The Total Woman* (Old Tappan, N.J.: Fleming H. Revell Co., 1973). "Total Woman" makes blasphemous sexuality into a home art, redomesticating what prostitutes have marketed as forbidden.

[34] Cixous (n. 1 above), p. 892.

[35] Indications are that this is true not only in Western industrial society; further cross cultural research is definitely needed.

[36] Love justifies this on the emotional level. Firestone (n. 24 above), chap. 6.

Millett's *Sexual Politics*,[37] resolves the duality in the term "sex" itself: what women learn in order to "have sex," in order to "become women"—woman as gender—comes through the experience of, and is a condition for, "having sex"— woman as sexual object for man, the use of women's sexuality by men. Indeed, to the extent sexuality is social, women's sexuality *is* its use, just as our femaleness *is* its alterity.

Many issues that appear sexual from this standpoint have not been seen as such, nor have they been seen as defining a politics. Incest, for example, is commonly seen as a question of distinguishing the real evil, a crime against the family, from girlish seductiveness or fantasy. Contraception and abortion have been framed as matters of reproduction and fought out as proper or improper social constraints on nature. Or they are seen as private, minimizing state intervention into intimate relations. Sexual harassment was a nonissue, then became a problem of distinguishing personal relationships or affectionate flirtation from abuse of position. Lesbianism, when visible, has been either a perversion or not, to be tolerated or not. Pornography has been considered a question of freedom to speak and depict the erotic, as against the obscene or violent. Prostitution has been understood either as mutual lust and degradation or an equal exchange of sexual need for economic need. The issue in rape has been whether the intercourse was provoked/mutually desired, or whether it was forced: was it sex or violence? Across and beneath these issues, sexuality itself has been divided into parallel provinces: traditionally, religion or biology; in modern transformation, morality or psychology. Almost never politics.

In a feminist perspective, the formulation of each issue, in the terms just described, expresses ideologically the same interest that the problem it formulates expresses concretely: the interest from the male point of view. Women experience the sexual events these issues codify[38] as a cohesive whole within which each resonates. The defining theme of that whole is the male pursuit of control over women's sexuality—men not as individuals nor as biological beings, but as a gender group characterized by maleness as socially constructed, of which this pursuit is definitive. For example, women who need abortions see contraception as a struggle not only for control over the biological products of sexual expression but over the social rhythms and mores of sexual intercourse. These norms often appear hostile to women's self-protection even when the technology is at hand. As an instance of such norms, women notice that sexual harassment looks a great deal like ordinary heterosexual initiation under conditions of gender inequality. Few women are in a position to refuse unwanted sexual initiatives. That consent rather than nonmutuality is the line between rape and intercourse further exposes the inequality in normal social expectations. So does the substantial amount of male force allowed in the focus on the woman's resistance, which tends to be disabled by socialization to passivity. If sex is ordinarily accepted as something men do *to* women, the better question would be whether consent is a meaningful concept. Penetration (often by a penis) is also substantially more central to both the legal definition of rape and the male definition of sexual intercourse than it is to

---

[37] Millett's analysis is pervasively animated by the sense that women's status is sexually determined. It shapes her choice of authors, scenes, and themes and underlies her most pointed criticisms of women's depiction. Her explicit discussion, however, vacillates between clear glimpses of that argument and statements nearly to the contrary.

[38] Each of these issues is discussed at length in the second part of this article "Toward Feminist Jurisprudence"), forthcoming.

women's sexual violation or sexual pleasure. Rape in marriage expresses the male sense of entitlement to access to women they annex; incest extends it. Although most women are raped by men they know, the closer the relation, the less women are allowed to claim it was rape. Pornography becomes difficult to distinguish from art and ads once it is clear that what is degrading to women is compelling to the consumer. Prostitutes sell the unilaterality that pornography advertises. That most of these issues codify behavior that is neither countersystemic nor exceptional is supported by women's experience as victims: these behaviors are either not illegal or are effectively permitted on a large scale. As women's experience blurs the lines between deviance and normalcy, it obliterates the distinction between abuses *of* women and the social definition of what a woman *is*.[39]

These investigations reveal rape, incest, sexual harassment, pornography, and prostitution as not primarily abuses of physical force, violence, authority, or economics. They are abuses of sex. They need not and do not rely for their coerciveness upon forms of enforcement other than the sexual; that those forms of enforcement, at least in this context, are themselves sexualized is closer to the truth. They are not the erotization *of* something else; eroticism *itself* exists in their form. Nor are they perversions of art and morality. They *are* art and morality from the male point of view. They are sexual because they express the relations, values, feelings, norms, and behaviors of the culture's sexuality, in which considering things like rape, pornography, incest, or lesbianism deviant, perverse, or blasphemous is part of their excitement potential.

Sexuality, then, is a form of power. Gender, as socially constructed, embodies it, not the reverse. Women and men are divided by gender, made into the sexes as we know them, by the social requirements of heterosexuality, which institutionalizes male sexual dominance and female sexual submission.[40] If this is true, sexuality is the linchpin of gender inequality.

A woman is a being who identifies and is identified as one whose sexuality exists for someone else, who is socially male. Women's sexuality is the capacity to arouse desire in that someone. If what is sexual about a woman is what the male point of view requires for excitement, have male requirements so usurped its terms as to have become them? Considering women's sexuality in this way forces confrontation with whether there is any such thing. Is women's sexuality its absence? If being *for* another is the whole of women's sexual construction, it can be no more escaped by separatism, men's temporary concrete absence, than eliminated or qualified by permissiveness, which, in this context, looks like women

Catharine A. MacKinnon

---

[39] On abortion and contraception, see Kristin Luker, *Taking Chances: Abortion and the Decision Not to Contracept* (Berkeley: University of California Press, 1975). On rape, see Diana E. H. Russell, *Rape: The Victim's Perspective* (New York: Stein & Day, 1977); Andrea Medea and Kathleen Thompson, *Against Rape* (New York: Farrar, Straus & Giroux, 1974); Lorenne N. G. Clark and Debra Lewis, *Rape: The Price of Coercive Sexuality* (Toronto: Women's Press, 1977); Susan Griffin, *Rape: The Power of Consciousness* (San Francisco: Harper & Row, 1979); Kalamu ya Salaam, "Rape: A Radical Analysis from the African-American Perspective," in his *Our Women Keep Our Skies from Falling* (New Orleans: Nkombo, 1980), pp. 25–40. On incest, see Judith Herman and Lisa Hirschman, "Father-Daughter Incest," *Signs: Journal of Women in Culture and Society* 2, no. 1 (Summer 1977): 735–56. On sexual harassment, see my *Sexual Harassment of Working Women* (New Haven, Conn.: Yale University Press, 1979). On pornography, see Andrea Dworkin, *Pornography: Men Possessing Women* (New York: G. P. Putnam's Sons, 1981).

[40] Ellen Morgan, *The Erotization of Male Dominance/Female Submission* (Pittsburgh: Know, Inc., 1975); Adrienne Rich, "Compulsory Heterosexuality and Lesbian Existence," *Signs: Journal of Women in Culture and Society* 5, no. 4 (Summer 1980): 631–60.

emulating male roles. As Susan Sontag said: "The question is: *what* sexuality are women to be liberated to enjoy? Merely to remove the onus placed upon the sexual expressiveness of women is a hollow victory if the sexuality they become freer to enjoy remains the old one that converts women into objects. . . . This already 'freer' sexuality mostly reflects a spurious idea of freedom: the right of each person, briefly, to exploit and dehumanize someone else. Without a change in the very norms of sexuality, the liberation of women is a meaningless goal. Sex as such is not liberating for women. Neither is more sex."[41] Does removing or revising gender constraints upon sexual expression change or even challenge its norms?[42] This question ultimately is one of social determination in the broadest sense: its mechanism, permeability, specificity, and totality. If women are socially defined such that female sexuality cannot be lived or spoken or felt or even somatically sensed apart from its enforced definition, so that it *is* its own lack, then there is no such thing as a woman as such, there are only walking embodiments of men's projected needs. For feminism, asking whether there is, socially, a female sexuality is the same as asking whether women exist.

Methodologically, the feminist concept of the personal as political is an attempt to answer this question. Relinquishing all instinctual, natural, transcendental, and divine authority, this concept grounds women's sexuality on purely relational terrain, anchoring women's power and accounting for women's discontent in the same world they stand against. The personal as political is not a simile, not a metaphor, and not an analogy. It does not mean that what occurs in personal life is similar to, or comparable with, what occurs in the public arena. It is not an application of categories from social life to the private world, as when Engels (followed by Bebel) says that in the family the husband is the bourgeois and the wife represents the proletariat.[43] Nor is it an equation of two spheres which remain analytically distinct, as when Reich interprets state behavior in sexual terms,[44] or a one-way infusion of one sphere into the other, as when Lasswell interprets political behavior as the displacement of personal problems into public objects.[45] It means that women's distinctive experience as women occurs within that sphere that has been socially lived as the personal—private, emotional, interiorized, particular, individuated, intimate—so that what it is to *know* the *politics* of woman's situation is to know women's personal lives.

---

[41] Susan Sontag, "The Third World of Women," *Partisan Review* 40, no. 2 (1973): 180–206, esp. 188.

[42] The same question could be asked of lesbian sadomasochism: when women engage in ritualized sexual dominance and submission, does it express the male structure or subvert it? The answer depends upon whether one has a social or biological definition of gender and of sexuality and then upon the content of these definitions. Lesbian sex, simply as sex between women, does not by definition transcend the erotization of dominance and submission and their social equation with masculinity and femininity. Butch/femme as *sexual* (not just gender) role playing, together with parallels in lesbian sadomasochism's "top" and "bottom," suggest to me that sexual conformity extends far beyond gender object mores. For a contrary view see Pat Califia, *Sapphistry: The Book of Lesbian Sexuality* (Tallahassee, Fla.: Naiad Press, 1980); Gayle Rubin, "Sexual Politics, the New Right and the Sexual Fringe," in *What Color Is Your Handkerchief: A Lesbian S/M Sexuality Reader* (Berkeley, Calif.: Samois, 1979), pp. 28–35.

[43] Engels (n. 14 above); August Bebel, *Women under Socialism*, trans. Daniel DeLeon (New York: New York Labor News Press, 1904).

[44] Reich (n. 22 above). He examines fascism, for example, as a question of how the masses can be made to desire their own repression. This might be seen as a precursor to the feminist question of how female desire *itself* can become the lust for self-annihilation.

[45] Harold Lasswell, *Psychoanalysis and Politics* (Chicago: University of Chicago Press, 1930).

The substantive principle governing the authentic politics of women's personal lives is pervasive powerlessness to men, expressed and reconstituted daily *as* sexuality. To say that the personal is political means that gender as a division of power is discoverable and verifiable through women's intimate experience of sexual objectification, which is definitive of and synonymous with women's lives as gender female. Thus, to feminism, the personal is epistemologically the political, and its epistemology is its politics.[46] Feminism, on this level, is the theory of women's point of view. It is the theory of Judy Grahn's "common woman"[47] speaking Adrienne Rich's "common language."[48] Consciousness raising is its quintessential expression. Feminism does not appropriate an existing method—such as scientific method—and apply it to a different sphere of society to reveal its preexisting political aspect. Consciousness raising not only comes to know different things as politics; it necessarily comes to know them in a different way. Women's experience of politics, of life as sex object, gives rise to its own method of appropriating that reality: feminist method.[49] As its own kind of social analysis, within yet outside the male paradigm just as women's lives are, it has a distinctive theory of the *relation* between method and truth, the individual and her social surroundings, the presence and place of the natural and spiritual in culture and society, and social being and causality itself.

Having been objectified as sexual beings while stigmatized as ruled by subjective passions, women reject the distinction between knowing subject and known object—the division between subjective and objective postures—as the means to comprehend social life. Disaffected from objectivity, having been its prey, but excluded from its world through relegation to subjective inwardness, women's

[46] The aphorism "Feminism is the theory; lesbianism is the practice" has been attributed to TiGrace Atkinson by Anne Koedt, "Lesbianism and Feminism," in *Radical Feminism,* ed. Anne Koedt, Ellen Levine, and Anita Rapone (New York: New York Times Book Co., 1973), p. 246. See also Radicalesbians, "The Woman Identified Woman," ibid., pp. 24–45; TiGrace Atkinson, "Lesbianism & Feminism," *Amazon Odyssey: The First Collection of Writings by the Political Pioneer of the Women's Movement* (New York: Links Books, 1974), pp. 83–88; Jill Johnston, *Lesbian Nation: The Feminist Solution* (New York: Simon & Schuster, 1973), pp. 167, 185, 278. This aphorism accepts a simplistic view of the relationship between theory and practice. Feminism reconceptualizes the connection between being and thinking such that it may be more accurate to say that feminism is the epistemology of which lesbianism is an ontology. But see n. 56 below on this latter distinction as well.

[47] Judy Grahn, *The Work of a Common Woman* (New York: St. Martin's Press, 1978). "The Common Woman" poems are on pp. 61–73.

[48] Adrienne Rich, "Origins and History of Consciousness," in *The Dream of a Common Language: Poems, 1974–1977* (New York: W. W. Norton & Co., 1978), p. 7. This means that a women's movement exists wherever women identify collectively to resist/reclaim their determinants as such. This feminist redefinition of consciousness requires a corresponding redefinition of the process of mobilizing it: feminist *organizing.* The transformation from subordinate group to movement parallels Marx's distinction between a class "in itself" and a class "for itself." See Karl Marx, *The Poverty of Philosophy* (New York: International Publishers, 1963), p. 195.

[49] In addition to the references in n. 1, see Sandra Lee Bartky, "Toward a Phenomenology of Feminist Consciousness," in *Feminism and Philosophy,* ed. Mary Vetterling-Braggin et al. (Totowa, N.J.: Littlefield, Adams & Co., 1977). Susan Griffin reflects/creates the process: "We do not rush to speech. We allow ourselves to be moved. We do not attempt objectivity. . . . We said we had experienced this ourselves. I felt so much for her then, she said, with her head cradled in my lap, she said, I knew what to do. We said we were moved to see her go through what we had gone through. We said this gave us some knowledge" (*Woman and Nature: The Roaring Inside Her* [New York: Harper & Row, 1978], p. 197). Assertions such as "our politics begin with our feelings" have emerged from the practice of consciousness raising. Somewhere between mirror-reflexive determination and transcendence of determinants, "feelings" are seen as both access to truth—at times a bit phenomenologically transparent—and an artifact of politics. There is both suspicion of feelings and affirmation of their health. They become simultaneously an inner expression of outer lies and a less contaminated resource for verification. See San Francisco Redstockings, "Our Politics Begin with Our Feelings," in *Masculine/Feminine: Readings in Sexual Mythology and the Liberation of Women,* ed. Betty Roszak and Theodore Roszak (New York: Harper & Row, 1969).

interest lies in overthrowing the distinction itself. Proceeding connotatively and analytically at the same time, consciousness raising is at once common sense expression and critical articulation of concepts. Taking situated feelings and common detail (common here meaning both ordinary and shared) as the matter of political analysis, it explores the terrain that is most damaged, most contaminated, yet therefore most women's own, most intimately known, most open to reclamation. The process can be described as a collective "sympathetic internal experience of the gradual construction of [the] system according to its inner necessity,"[50] as a strategy for deconstructing it.

Through consciousness raising, women grasp the collective reality of women's condition from within the perspective of that experience, not from outside it. The claim that a sexual politics exists and is socially fundamental is grounded in the claim of feminism *to* women's perspective, not from it. Its claim to women's perspective *is* its claim to truth. In its account of itself, women's point of view contains a duality analogous to that of the marxist proletariat: determined by the reality the theory explodes, it thereby claims special access to that reality.[51] Feminism does not see its view as subjective, partial, or undetermined but as a critique of the purported generality, disinterestedness, and universality of prior accounts. These have not been half right but have invoked the wrong whole. Feminism not only challenges masculine partiality but questions the universality imperative itself. Aperspectivity is revealed as a strategy of male hegemony.[52]

"Representation of the world," de Beauvoir writes, "like the world itself, is the work of men; they describe it from their own point of view, which they confuse with the absolute truth."[53] The parallel between representation and construction should be sustained: men *create* the world from their own point of view, which then *becomes* the truth to be described. This is a closed system, not anyone's confusion. *Power to create the world from one's point of view is power in its male form.*[54] The male epistemological stance, which corresponds to the world it creates, is objectivity: the ostensibly noninvolved stance, the view from a distance and from no particular perspective,

[50] Fredric Jameson, *Marxism and Form* (Princeton, N.J.: Princeton University Press, 1971), p. xi. Jameson is describing dialectical method: "I have felt that the dialectical method can be acquired only by a concrete working through of detail, by a sympathetic internal experience of the gradual construction of a system according to its inner necessity."

[51] This distinguishes both feminism and at least a strain in marxism from Freud: "My self-analysis is still interrupted and I have realized the reason. I can only analyze my self with the help of knowledge obtained objectively (like an outsider). Genuine selfanalysis is impossible, otherwise there would be no [neurotic] illness" (Sigmund Freud, Letter to Wilhelm Fleiss, #71, October 15, 1887, quoted in Mitchell, *Psychoanalysis and Feminism: Freud, Reich, Laing and Women* [n. 19 above], pp. 61–62, see also p. 271). Given that introspection is not analytically dispositive to Freud, the collective self-knowledge of feminism might be collective neurosis. Although it is interpersonal, it is still an insider to its world.

[52] Feminist scholars are beginning to criticize objectivity from different disciplinary standpoints, although not as frontally as here, nor in its connection with objectification. Julia Sherman and Evelyn Torton Beck, eds., *The Prism of Sex: Essays in the Sociology of Knowledge* (Madison: University of Wisconsin Press, 1979); Margrit Eichler, *The Double Standard: A Feminist Critique of Feminist Social Science* (New York: St. Martin's Press, 1980); Evelyn Fox Keller, "Gender and Science," *Psychoanalysis and Contemporary Thought* 1, no. 3 (1978): 409–33. Adrienne Rich, "Toward a Woman-centered University," in *Woman and the Power to Change*, ed. Florence Howe (New York: McGraw-Hill Book Co., 1975).

[53] De Beauvoir (n. 24 above). De Beauvoir had not pursued the analysis to the point I suggest here by 1979, either. See her "Introduction," in Marks and de Courtivron, eds. (n. l above), pp. 41–56.

[54] This does not mean all men *have* male power equally. American Black men, for instance, have substantially less of it. But to the extent that they cannot create the world from their point of view, they find themselves unmanned, castrated, literally or figuratively. This supports rather than qualifies the sex specificity of the argument without resolving

apparently transparent to its reality. It does not comprehend its own perspectivity, does not recognize what it sees as subject like itself, or that the way it apprehends its world is a form of its subjugation and presupposes it. The objectively knowable is object. Woman through male eyes is sex object, that by which man knows him-self at once as man and as subject.[55] What is objectively known corresponds to the world and can be verified by pointing to it (as science does) because the world itself is controlled from the same point of view.[56] Combining, like any form of power, legitimation with force, male power extends beneath the representation of reality to its construction: it makes women (as it were) and so verifies (makes true) who women

---

the relationship between racism and sexism, or the relation of either to class. Although historically receiving more attention, race and nation are otherwise analogous to sex in the place they occupy for, and the challenge they pose to, marxist theory. If the real basis of history and activity is class and class conflict, what, other than "false consciousness," is one to make of the historical force of sexism, racism, and nationalism? Similarly, positing a supra-class unit with true meaning, such as "Black people," is analytically parallel to positing a supra-class (and supra-racial) unit "women." Treating race, nation, and sex as lesser included problems has been the major response of marxist theory to such challenges. Any relationship *between* sex and race tends to be left entirely out of account, since they are considered parallel "strata." Attempts to confront the latter issue include Adrienne Rich, "Disloyal to Civilization: Feminism, Racism and Gynephobia," in *On Lies, Secrets and Silence: Selected Essays, 1966–1978* (New York: W. W. Norton & Co., 1979); Selma James, *Sex, Race and Class* (Bristol: Falling Wall Press, 1967); R. Coles and J. H. Coles, *Women of Crisis* (New York: Dell Publishing Co., Delacorte Press, 1978); Socialist Women's Caucus of Louisville, "The Racist Use of Rape and the Rape Charge" (Louisville, Ky., ca. 1977); Angela Davis, "The Role of Black Women in the Community of Slaves," *Black Scholar* 3, no. 4 (December 1971): 2–16; The Combahee River Collective, "A Black Feminist Statement," in Eisenstein, ed. (n. 11 above); Karen Getman, "Relations of Gender and Sexuality during the Period of Institutional Slavery in the Southern Colonies" (working paper, Yale University, 1980); E. V. Spelman, "Feminism, Sexism and Racism" (University of Massachusetts, 1981); Cherrie Moraga and Gloria Anzaldúa, eds., *This Bridge Called My Back: Writings of Radical Women of Color* (Watertown, Mass.: Persephone Press, 1981).

[55] This suggests a way in which marxism and feminism may be reciprocally illuminating, without, for the moment, confronting the deep divisions between them. Marxism comprehends the *object* world's *social* existence: how objects are constituted, embedded in social life, infused with meaning, created in systematic and structural relation. Feminism comprehends the *social* world's *object* existence: how women are created in the image of, and as, things. The object world's social existence varies with the structure of production. Suppose that wherever the sexes are unequal, women are objects, but what it means to be an object varies with the productive relations that create objects as social. Thus, under primitive exchange systems, women are exchange objects. Under capitalism, women appear as commodities. That is, women's sexuality as object for men is valued as objects are under capitalism, namely as commodities. Under true communism, women would be collective sex objects. If women have universally been sex objects, it is also true that matter as the acted-upon in social life has a history. If women have always been things, it is also true that things have not always had the same meaning. Of course, this does not explain sex inequality. It merely observes, once that inequality exists, the way its dynamics may interact with the social organization of production. Sexual objectification may also have a separate history, with its own periods, forms, structures, technology, and, potentially, revolutions.

[56] In a sense, this realization collapses the epistemology/ontology distinction altogether. What is purely an ontological category, a category of "being" free of social perception? Surely not the self/other distinction. Ultimately, the feminist approach turns social inquiry into political hermeneutics: inquiry into situated meaning, one in which the inquiry itself participates. A feminist political hermeneutics would be a theory of the answer to the question, What does it mean? that would comprehend that the first question to address is, To whom? within a context that comprehends gender as a social division of power. Useful general treatments of hermeneutical issues (which nevertheless proceed as if feminism, or a specific problematic of women, did not exist) include Josef Bleicher, *Contemporary Hermeneutics: Hermeneutics as Method, Philosophy and Critique* (London: Routledge & Kegan Paul, 1980); Hans-Georg Gadamer, *Philosophical Hermeneutics*, trans. David E. Linge (Berkeley: University of California Press, 1976); Rosalind Coward and John Ellis, *Language and Materialism: Developments in Semiology and the Theory of the Subject* (London: Routledge & Kegan Paul, 1977). Mary Daly approaches the ontological issue when she says that ontological theory without an understanding of sex roles can not be "really ontological" (*Beyond God the Father: Toward a Philosophy of Women's Liberation* [Boston: Beacon Press, 1973], p. 124). But both in this work, and more pervasively in *Gyn/Ecology: The Metaethics of Radical Feminism* (Boston: Beacon Press, 1978), the extent of the *creation* of women's *reality* by male epistemology, therefore the extent and nature of women's damage, is slighted in favor of a critique of its lies and distortions. Consider her investigation of suttee, a practice in which Indian widows are supposed to throw themselves upon their dead husband's funeral pyres in grief (and to keep pure), in which Daly focuses upon demystifying its alleged voluntary aspects. Women are revealed drugged, pushed, browbeaten, or otherwise coerced by the dismal and frightening prospect of widowhood in Indian society (Daly, *Gyn/Ecology*, pp. 113–33). Neglected—both as to the women involved and as to the implications for the entire diagnosis of sexism as illusion—are suttee's deepest victims: women who want to die when their husband dies, who volunteer for self-immolation because they believe their life is over when his is. See also Duncan Kennedy, "The Structure of Blackstone's Commentaries," *Buffalo Law Review* 28, no. 2 (1979): 211–12.

Catharine A. MacKinnon

"are" in its view, simultaneously confirming its way of being and its vision of truth. The eroticism that corresponds to this is "the use of things to experience self."[57] As a coerced pornography model put it, "You do it, you do it, and you do it; then you become it."[58] The fetish speaks feminism.

Objectification makes sexuality a material reality of women's lives, not just a psychological, attitudinal, or ideological one.[59] It obliterates the mind/matter

[57] Dworkin (n. 39 above), p. 124. Explicitness is the aesthetic, the allowed sensibility, of objectified eroticism. Under this norm, written and pictured evocations of sexuality are compulsively literal. What it is to arouse sexuality through art is to recount events "objectively," i.e., verbally and visually to re-present who did what to whom. On the "dynamic of total explicitness" as stylization, explored in the context of the "foremost insight of the modern novel: the interweaving, the symbolic and structural interchange between economic and sexual relations," see George Steiner, "Eros and Idiom: 1975," in *On Difficulty and Other Essays* (New York: Oxford University Press, 1978), p. 100: "Chasteness of discourse [in George Eliot's work] acts not as a limitation but as a liberating privacy within which the character can achieve the paradox of autonomous life" (p. 107). This connects the lack of such liberating privacy for women—in life, law, or letters—with women's lack of autonomy and authentic erotic vocabulary.

[58] Linda Lovelace, *Ordeal* (Secaucus, N.J.: Citadel Press, 1980). The same may be true for class. See Richard Sennett and Jonathan Cobb, *The Hidden Injuries of Class* (New York: Alfred A. Knopf, Inc., 1972). Marxism teaches that exploitation/degradation somehow necessarily produces resistance/revolution. Women's experience with sexual exploitation/degradation teaches that it also produces grateful complicity in exchange for survival and self-loathing to the point of the extinction of self, respect for which makes resistance conceivable. The problem here is not to explain why women acquiesce in their condition but why they ever do anything but.

[59] The critique of sexual objectification first became visibly explicit in the American women's movement with the disruption of the Miss America Pageant in September 1968. Robin Morgan, "Women Disrupt the Miss America Pageant," *Rat* (September 1978), reprinted in *Going Too Far: The Personal Chronicle of a Feminist* (New York: Random House, 1977), pp. 62–67. The most compelling account of sexual objectification I know is contained in the following description of women's depiction in art and the media: "According to usage and conventions which are at last being questioned but have by no means been overcome, the social presence of a woman is different in kind from that of a man. . . . A man's presence suggests what he is capable of doing to you or for you. By contrast, a woman's presence expresses her own attitude to herself, and *defines what can and cannot be done to her*. . . . To be born a woman has been to be born, within an allotted and confined space, into the keeping of men. The social presence of women has developed as a result of their ingenuity in living under such tutelage within such a limited space. But this has been at the cost of a woman's self being split into two. A woman must continually watch herself. She is almost continually accompanied by her own image of herself . . . she comes to consider the surveyor and the surveyed within her as the two constituent yet always distinct elements of her identity as a woman. She has to survey everything she is and everything she does because how she appears to others, and ultimately how she appears to men, *is of crucial importance for what is normally thought of as the success of her life*. Her own sense of being in herself is supplanted by a sense of being appreciated as herself by another. One might simplify this by saying: men act; women appear. *Men look at women. Women watch themselves being looked at*. This determines not only most relations between men and women but also the relation of women to themselves. The surveyor of woman in herself is male: the surveyed, female. Thus she turns herself into an object—and most particularly an object of vision: a sight" (John Berger, *Ways of Seeing* [New York: Viking Press, 1972], pp. 46, 47 [my emphasis]). All that is missing here is an explicit recognition that this process embodies what the sexuality of women is about and that it expresses an inequality in social power. In a feminist context, aesthetics, including beauty and imagery, becomes the most political of subjects. See Purple September Staff, "The Normative Status of Heterosexuality," in *Lesbianism and the Women's Movement*, ed. Charlotte Bunch and Nancy Myron (Baltimore: Diana Press, 1975), pp. 79–83, esp. pp. 80–81.

Marxist attempts to deal with sexual objectification have not connected the issue with the politics of aesthetics or with subordination: "She becomes a sexual object only in a relationship, when she allows man to treat her in a certain depersonalizing, degrading way; and vice versa, a woman does not become a sexual subject simply by neglecting her appearance. There is no reason why a women's liberation activist should not try to look pretty and attractive. One of the universal human aspirations of all times was to raise reality to the level of art. . . . Beauty is a value in itself" (Markovic [n. 17 above], pp. 165–66). Other attempts come closer, still without achieving the critique, e.g., Power of Women Collective. "What Is a Sex Object?" *Socialist Woman: A Journal of the International Marxist Group* 1, no. 1 (March/April 1974): 7; Dana Densmore, "On the Temptation to Be a Beautiful Object," in *Toward a Sociology of Women*, ed. G. Safilios-Rothschild (Lexington, Mass.: Xerox Publication, 1972); Rita Arditti, "Women as Objects: Science and Sexual Politics," *Science for the People*, vol. 6, no. 5 (September 1974); Charley Shively, "Cosmetics as an Act of Revolution," *Fag Rag* (Boston), reprinted in *Pink Triangles: Radical Perspectives on Gay Liberation*, ed. Pam Mitchell (Boston: Alyson Publication, 1980). Resentment of white beauty standards is prominent in Black feminism. Beauty standards incapable of achievement by any woman seem to fulfill a dual function. They keep women buying products (to the profit of capitalism) and competing for men (to be affirmed by the standard that matters). That is, they make women feel ugly and inadequate so we need men and money to defend against rejection/self-revulsion. Black women are further from being able concretely to achieve the standard that no woman can ever achieve, or it would lose its point.

distinction that such a division is premised upon. Like the value of a commodity, women's sexual desirability is fetishized: it is made to appear a quality of the object itself, spontaneous and inherent, independent of the social relation which creates it, uncontrolled by the force that requires it. It helps if the object cooperates: hence, the vaginal orgasm;[60] hence, faked orgasms altogether.[61] Women's sexualness, like male prowess, is no less real for being mythic. It is embodied. Commodities do have value, but only because value is a social property arising from the totality of the same social relations which, unconscious of their determination, fetishize it. Women's bodies possess no less real desirability—or, probably, desire. Sartre exemplifies the problem on the epistemological level: "But if I desire a house, or a glass of water, or a woman's body, how could this body, this glass, this piece of property reside in my desire and how can my desire be anything but the consciousness of these objects as desirable?"[62] Indeed. Objectivity is the methodological stance of which objectification is the social process. Sexual objectification is the primary process of the subjection of women. It unites act with word, construction with expression, perception with enforcement, myth with reality. Man fucks woman; subject verb object.

The distinction between objectification and alienation is called into question by this analysis. Objectification in marxist materialism is thought to be the foundation of human freedom, the work process whereby a subject becomes embodied in products and relationships.[63] Alienation is the socially contingent distortion of that process, a reification of products and relations which prevents them from being, and being seen as, dependent on human agency.[64] But from the point of view of the object, objectification *is* alienation. For women, there is no distinction between objectification and alienation because women have not authored objectifications, we have been them. Women have been the nature, the matter, the acted upon, to be subdued by the acting subject seeking to embody himself in the social world. Reification is not just an illusion to the reified; it is also their reality. The alienated who can only grasp self as other is no different from the object who can only grasp self as thing. To be man's other *is* to be his thing. Similarly, the problem of how the object can know herself as such is the

---

[60] Anne Koedt, "The Myth of the Vaginal Orgasm," in Koedt et al., eds. (n. 46 above), pp. 198–207; TiGrace Atkinson, "Vaginal Orgasm as a Mass Hysterical Survival Response," in *Amazon Odyssey* (n. 46 above), pp. 5–8.

[61] Shere Hite, *The Hite Report: A Nationwide Study of Female Sexuality* (New York: Dell Publishing Co., 1976), "Do you ever fake orgasms?" pp. 257–66.

[62] Jean-Paul Sartre, *Existential Psychoanalysis,* trans. Hazel E. Barnes (Chicago: Henry Regnery Co., 1973), p. 20. A similar treatment of "desire" occurs in Deleuze and Guattari's description of man as "desiring-machine," of man in relation to the object world: "Not man as the king of creation, but rather as the being who is in intimate contact with the profound life of all forms or all types of beings, who is responsible for even the stars and animal life, and who ceaselessly plugs an organ-machine into an energy-machine, a tree into his body, a breast into his mouth, the sun into his asshole; the eternal custodian of the machines of the universe" (Deleuze and Guattari [n. 1 above], p. 4). Realizing that women, socially, inhabit the object realm transforms this discourse into a quite accurate description of the feminist analysis of women's desirability to man—the breast in his mouth, the energy machine into which he ceaselessly plugs an organ machine. Extending their inquiry into the extent to which this kind of objectification of woman is specific to capitalism (either as a process or in its particular form) does little to redeem the sex blindness (blind to the sex of its stand-point) of this supposedly general theory. Women are not desiring-machines.

[63] Peter Berger and Stanley Pullberg, "Reification and the Sociological Critique of Consciousness," *New Left Review,* vol. 35 (January-February 1966); Herbert Marcuse, "The Foundation of Historical Materialism," in *Studies in Critical Philosophy,* trans. Joris De Bres (Boston: Beacon Press, 1972); Karl Klare, "Law-Making as Praxis," *Telos* 12, no. 2 (Summer 1979): 123–35, esp. 131.

[64] Istvan Meszaros, *Marx's Theory of Alienation* (London: Merlin Press, 1972); Bertell Ollman, *Alienation: Marx's Conception of Man in Capitalist Society* (London: Cambridge University Press, 1971); Marcuse, *Eros and Civilization* (n. 22 above), pp. 93–94, 101–2.

Catharine A. MacKinnon

same as how the alienated can know its own alienation. This, in turn, poses the problem of feminism's account of women's consciousness. How can women, as created, "thingified in the head,"[65] complicit in the body, see our condition as such?

In order to account for women's consciousness (much less propagate it) feminism must grasp that male power produces the world before it distorts it. Women's acceptance of their condition does not contradict its fundamental unacceptability if women have little choice but to *become* persons who freely choose women's roles. For this reason, the reality of women's oppression is, finally, neither demonstrable nor refutable empirically. Until this is confronted on the level of method, criticism of what exists can be undercut by pointing to the reality to be criticized. Women's bondage, degradation, damage, complicity, and inferiority—together with the possibility of resistance, movement, or exceptions—will operate as barriers to consciousness rather than as means of access to what women need to become conscious of in order to change.

Male power is real; it is just not what it claims to be, namely, the only reality. Male power is a myth that makes itself true. What it is to raise consciousness is to confront male power in this duality: as total on one side and a delusion on the other. In consciousness raising, women learn they have *learned* that men are everything, women their negation, but that the sexes are equal. The content of the message is revealed true and false at the same time; in fact, each part reflects the other transvalued. If "men are all, women their negation" is taken as social criticism rather than simple description, it becomes clear for the first time that women *are* men's equals, everywhere in chains. Their chains become visible, their inferiority—their inequality—a product of subjection and a mode of its enforcement. Reciprocally, the moment it is seen that this—life as we know it—is not equality, that the sexes are not socially equal, womanhood can no longer be defined in terms of lack of maleness, as negativity. For the first time, the question of what a woman *is* seeks its ground in and of a world understood as neither of its making nor in its image, and finds, within a critical embrace of woman's fractured and alien image, that world women have made and a vision of its wholeness. Feminism has unmasked maleness as a form of power that is both omnipotent and nonexistent, an unreal thing with very real consequences. Zora Neale Hurston captured its two-sidedness: "The town has a basketfull of feelings good and bad about Joe's positions and possessions, but none had the temerity to challenge him. They bowed down to him rather, because he was all of these things, and then again he was all of these things because the town bowed down."[66] If "positions and possessions" and rulership create each other, in relation, the question becomes one of form and inevitability. This challenges feminism to apply its theory of women's standpoint to the regime.[67]

Feminism is the first theory to emerge from those whose interest it affirms. Its method recapitulates as theory the reality it seeks to capture. As marxist method is dialectical materialism, feminist method is consciousness raising: the collective critical reconstitution of the meaning of women's social experience, as women live through it. Marxism and feminism on this level posit a different relation

[65] Rowbotham, *Women's Liberation and the New Politics* (n. 17 above), p. 17.

[66] Zora Neale Hurston, *Their Eyes Were Watching God* (Urbana: University of Illinois Press, 1978). pp. 79–80.

[67] In the second part of this article, "Feminism, Marxism, Method, and the State: Toward Feminist Jurisprudence" (forthcoming in *Signs*), I argue that the state is male in that objectivity is its norm.

between thought and thing, both in terms of the relationship of the analysis itself to the social life it captures and in terms of the participation of thought in the social life it analyzes. To the extent that materialism is scientific it posits and refers to a reality outside thought which it considers to have an objective—that is, truly nonsocially perspectival—content. Consciousness raising, by contrast, inquires into an intrinsically social situation, into that mixture of thought and materiality which is women's sexuality in the most generic sense. It approaches its world through a process that shares its determination: women's consciousness, not as individual or subjective ideas, but as collective social being. This method stands inside its own determinations in order to uncover them, just as it criticizes them in order to value them on its own terms—in order to *have* its own terms at all. Feminism turns theory itself—the pursuit of a true analysis of social life—into the pursuit of consciousness and turns an analysis of inequality into a critical embrace of its own determinants. The process is transformative as well as perceptive, since thought and thing are inextricable and reciprocally constituting of women's oppression, just as the state as coercion and the state as legitimizing ideology are indistinguishable, and for the same reasons. The pursuit of consciousness becomes a form of political practice. Consciousness raising has revealed gender relations to be a collective fact, no more simply personal than class relations. This implies that class relations may also be personal, no less so for being at the same time collective. The failure of marxism to realize this may connect the failure of workers in advanced capitalist nations to organize in the socialist sense with the failure of left revolutions to liberate women in the feminist sense.

Feminism stands in relation to marxism as marxism does to classical political economy: its final conclusion and ultimate critique. Compared with marxism, the place of thought and things in method and reality are reversed in a seizure of power that penetrates subject with object and theory with practice. In a dual motion, feminism turns marxism inside out and on its head.

To answer an old question—how is value created and distributed?—Marx needed to create an entirely new account of the social world. To answer an equally old question, or to question an equally old reality—what explains the inequality of women to men? or, how does desire become domination? or, what is male power?—feminism revolutionizes politics.

STANFORD LAW SCHOOL
Stanford University

Catharine A. MacKinnon

868

CATHARINE A. MACKINNON

"Feminism, Marxism, Method, and the State: Toward a Feminist Jurisprudence"

8 *Signs: Journal of Women, Culture, and Society* (1983): 635

I

Feminism has no theory of the state. It has a theory of power: sexuality is gendered as gender is sexualized. Male and female are created through the erotization of dominance and submission. The man/woman difference and the dominance/submission dynamic define each other. This is the social meaning of sex and the distinctively feminist account of gender inequality.[1] Sexual objectification, the central process within this dynamic, is at once epistemological and political.[2] The feminist theory of knowledge is inextricable from the feminist critique of power because the male point of view forces itself upon the world as its way of apprehending it.

The perspective from the male standpoint[3] enforces woman's definition, encircles her body, circumlocutes her speech, and describes her life. The male perspective is systemic and hegemonic. The content of the signification "woman" is the content of women's lives. Each sex has its role, but their stakes and power are

For A. D. and D. K. H. In addition to all those whose help is acknowledged in the first part of this article, "Feminism, Marxism, Method, and the State: An Agenda for Theory," *Signs: Journal of Women in Culture and Society* 7, no. 3 (Spring 1982): 515–44 (hereafter cited as part 1), my students and colleagues at Yale, Harvard, and Stanford contributed profoundly to the larger project of which both articles are parts. Among them, Sonia E. Alvarez, Jeanne M. Barkey, Paul Brest, Ruth Colker, Karen E. Davis, Sharon Dyer, Tom Emerson, Daniel Gunther, Patricia Kliendienst Joplin, Mark Kelman, Duncan Kennedy, John Kaplan, Lyn Lemaire, Mira Marshall, Rebecca Mark, Martha Minow, Helen M. A. Neally, Lisa Rofel, Sharon Silverstein, Dean Spencer, Laurence Tribe, and Mary Whisner stand out vividly in retrospect. None of it would have happened without Lu Ann Carter and David Rayson. And thank you, Meg Baldwin, Annie McCombs, and Janet Spector.

Marxism appears in lower case, Black in upper case, for reasons explained in part 1.

[1] Much has been made of the distinction between sex and gender. Sex is thought the more biological, gender the more social. The relation of each to sexuality varies. Since I believe sexuality is fundamental to gender and fundamentally social, and that biology is its social meaning in the system of sex inequality, which is a social and political system that does not rest independently on biological differences in any respect, the sex/gender distinction looks like a nature/culture distinction. I use sex and gender relatively interchangeably.

[2] This analysis is developed in part 1. I assume here your acquaintance with the arguments there.

[3] Male is a social and political concept, not a biological attribute. As I use it, it has *nothing whatever* to do with inherency, preexistence, nature, inevitability, or body as such. It is more epistemological than ontological, undercutting the distinction itself, given male power to conform being with perspective. (See part 1, pp. 538–39, n. 56.) The perspective from the male standpoint is not always each man's opinion, although most men adhere to it, nonconsciously and without considering it a point of view, as much because it makes sense of their experience (the male experience) as because it is in their interest. It is rational for them. A few men reject it; they pay. Because it is the dominant point of view and defines rationality, women are pushed to see reality in its terms, although this denies their vantage point as women in that it contradicts (at least some of) their lived experience. Women who adopt the male standpoint are passing, epistemologically speaking. This is not uncommon and is rewarded. The intractability of maleness as a form of dominance suggests that social constructs, although they flow from human agency, can be less plastic than nature has proven to be. If experience trying to do so is any guide, it may be easier to change biology than society.

not equal. If the sexes are unequal, and perspective participates in situation, there is no ungendered reality or ungendered perspective. And they are connected. In this context, objectivity—the nonsituated, universal standpoint, whether claimed or aspired to—is a denial of the existence or potency of sex inequality that tacitly participates in constructing reality from the dominant point of view. Objectivity, as the epistemological stance of which objectification is the social process, creates the reality it apprehends by defining as knowledge the reality it creates through its way of apprehending it. Sexual metaphors for knowing are no coincidence.[4] The solipsism of this approach does not undercut its sincerity, but it is interest that precedes method.

Feminism criticizes this male totality without an account of our capacity to do so or to imagine or realize a more whole truth. Feminism affirms women's point of view by revealing, criticizing, and explaining its impossibility. This is not a dialectical paradox. It is a methodological expression of women's situation, in which the struggle for consciousness is a struggle for world: for a sexuality, a history, a culture, a community, a form of power, an experience of the sacred. If women had consciousness or world, sex inequality would be harmless, or all women would be feminist. Yet we have something of both, or there would be no such thing as feminism. Why can women know that this—life as we have known it—is not all, not enough, not ours, not just? Now, why don't all women?[5]

---

[4] In the Bible, to know a woman is to have sex with her. You acquire carnal knowledge. Many scholarly metaphors elaborate the theme of violating boundaries to appropriate from inside to carry off in usable form: "a penetrating observation," "an incisive analysis," "piercing the veil." Mary Ellman writes, "The male mind . . . is assumed to function primarily like a penis. Its fundamental character is seen to be aggression, and this quality is held essential to the highest or best working of the intellect" (*Thinking about Women* [New York: Harcourt, Brace, Jovanovich, 1968], p. 23). Feminists are beginning to understand that to know has meant to fuck. See Evelyn Fox Keller, "Gender and Science," *Psychoanalysis and Contemporary Thought* 1, no. 3 (1978): 409–33, esp. 413; and Helen Roberts, ed., *Doing Feminist Research* (London: Routledge & Kegan Paul, 1981). The term "to fuck" uniquely captures my meaning because it refers to sexual activity without distinguishing rape from intercourse. At least since Plato's cave, visual metaphors for knowing have been central to Western theories of knowledge, the visual sense prioritized as a mode of verification. The relationship between visual appropriation and objectification is now only beginning to be explored. "The knowledge gained through still photographs will always be . . . a semblance of knowledge, a semblance of wisdom, as the act of taking pictures is a semblance of wisdom, a semblance of rape. The very muteness of what is, hypothetically, comprehensible in photographs is what constitutes their attraction and provocativeness" (Susan Sontag, *On Photography* [New York: Farrar, Straus & Giroux, 1980], p. 24). See part 1, pp. 539–40, n. 59.

[5] Feminism aspires to represent the experience of all women as women see it, yet criticizes antifeminism and misogyny, including when it appears in female form. This tension is compressed in the epistemic term of art "the standpoint of all women." We are barely beginning to unpack it. Not all women agree with the feminist account of women's situation, nor do all feminists agree with any single rendition of feminism. Authority of interpretation—the claim to speak as a woman—thus becomes methodologically complex and politically crucial for the same reasons. Consider the accounts of their own experience given by right-wing women and lesbian sadomasochists. How can patriarchy be diminishing to women when women embrace and defend their place in it? How can dominance and submission be violating to women when women eroticize it? Now what is the point of view of the experience of all women? Most responses in the name of feminism, stated in terms of method, either (1) simply regard some women's views as "false consciousness," or (2) embrace any version of women's experience that a biological female claims as her own. The first approach treats some women's views as unconscious conditioned reflections of their oppression, complicitous in it. Just as science devalues experience in the process of uncovering its roots, this approach criticizes the substance of a view because it can be accounted for by its determinants. But if both feminism and antifeminism are responses to the condition of women, how is feminism exempt from devalidation by the same account? That feminism is critical, and antifeminism is not, is not enough, because the question is the basis on which we know something is one or the other when women, all of whom share the condition of women, disagree. The false consciousness approach begs this question by taking women's self-reflections as evidence of their stake in their own oppression, when the women whose self-reflections are at issue question whether their condition is oppressed at all. The second response proceeds as if women are free. Or, at least, as if we have considerable latitude to make, or to choose, the meanings if not the determinants of our situation. Or, that the least feminism can do, since it claims to see the world through women's eyes, is to validate the interpretations women choose. Both responses arise because of the unwillingness, central to feminism, to dismiss some women

Catharine A. MacKinnon

The practice of a politics of all women in the face of its theoretical impossibility is creating a new process of theorizing and a new form of theory. Although feminism emerges from women's particular experience, it is not subjective or partial, for no interior ground and few if any aspects of life are free of male power. Nor is feminism objective, abstract, or universal.[6] It claims no external ground or unsexed sphere of generalization or abstraction beyond male power, nor transcendence of the specificity of each of its manifestations. How is it possible to have an engaged truth that does not simply reiterate its determinations? Disengaged truth only reiterates *its* determinations. Choice of method is choice of determinants—a choice which, for women as such, has been unavailable because of the subordination of women. Feminism does not begin with the premise that it is unpremised. It does not aspire to persuade an unpremised audience because there is no such audience. Its project is to uncover and claim as valid the experience of women, the major content of which is the devalidation of women's experience.

This defines our task not only because male dominance is perhaps the most pervasive and tenacious system of power in history, but because it is metaphysically nearly perfect.[7] Its point of view is the standard for point-of-viewlessness, its particularity the meaning of universality. Its force is exercised as consent, its authority as participation, its supremacy as the paradigm of order, its control as the definition of legitimacy. Feminism claims the voice of women's silence, the sexuality of our eroticized desexualization, the fullness of "lack," the centrality of our marginality and exclusion, the public nature of privacy, the presence of our absence. This approach is more complex than transgression, more transformative than transvaluation, deeper than mirror-imaged resistance, more affirmative than the negation of our negativity. It is neither materialist nor idealist; it is feminist. Neither the transcendence of liberalism nor the determination of materialism works for us. Idealism is too unreal; women's inequality is enforced, so it cannot simply be thought out of existence, certainly not by us. Materialism is too real; women's inequality has never not existed, so women's equality never has. That is,

---

as simply deluded while granting other women the ability to see the truth. These two resolutions echo the object/subject split: objectivity (my consciousness is true, yours false, never mind why) or subjectivity (I know I am right because it feels right to me, never mind why). Thus is determinism answered with transcendence, traditional marxism with traditional liberalism, dogmatism with tolerance. The first approach claims authority on the basis of its lack of involvement, asserting its view independent of whether the described concurs—sometimes because it does not. It also has no account, other than its alleged lack of involvement, of its own ability to provide such an account. How can some women see the truth and other women not? The second approach claims authority on the basis of its involvement. It has no account for different interpretations of the same experience or any way of choosing among conflicting ones, including those between women and men. It tends to assume that women, as we are, have power and are free in exactly the ways feminism, substantively, has found we are not. Thus, the first approach is one-sidedly outside when there is no outside, the second one-sidedly inside when someone (probably a woman) is inside everything, including every facet of sexism, racism, and so on. So our problem is this: the false consciousness approach cannot explain experience as it is experienced by those who experience it. The alternative can only reiterate the terms of that experience. This is only one way in which the object/subject split is fatal to the feminist enterprise.

    [6] To stress: the feminist criticism is not that the objective stance fails to be truly objective because it has social content, all the better to exorcise that content in the pursuit of the more truly point-of-viewless viewpoint. The criticism is that objectivity is largely accurate to its/the/a world, which world is criticized; and that it becomes more accurate as the power it represents and extends becomes more total. Analogous criticisms have arisen in the natural sciences, without being seen as threatening to the "science of society" project, or calling into question that project's tacit equation between natural and social objects of knowledge. What if we extend Heisenberg's uncertainty principle to social theory? (Werner Heisenberg, *The Physical Principles of the Quantum Theory* [Chicago: University of Chicago Press, 1930], pp. 4, 20, 62–65). What of the axiomatic method after Gödel's proof? (See Ernest Nagel and James R. Newman, *Gödel's Proof* [New York: New York University Press, 1958].)

    [7] Andrea Dworkin helped me express this.

the equality of women to men will not be scientifically provable until it is no longer necessary to do so. Women's situation offers no outside to stand on or gaze at, no inside to escape to, too much urgency to wait, no place else to go, and nothing to use but the twisted tools that have been shoved down our throats. If feminism is revolutionary, this is why.

Feminism has been widely thought to contain tendencies of liberal feminism, radical feminism, and socialist feminism. But just as socialist feminism has often amounted to marxism applied to women, liberal feminism has often amounted to liberalism applied to women. Radical feminism is feminism. Radical feminism—after this, feminism unmodified—is methodologically post-marxist.[8] It moves to resolve the marxist-feminist problematic on the level of method. Because its method emerges from the concrete conditions of all women as a sex, it dissolves the individualist, naturalist, idealist, moralist structure of liberalism, the politics of which science is the epistemology. Where liberal feminism sees sexism primarily as an illusion or myth to be dispelled, an inaccuracy to be corrected, true feminism sees the male point of view as fundamental to the male power to create the world in its own image, the image of its desires, not just as its delusory end product. Feminism distinctively as such comprehends that what counts as truth is produced in the interest of those with power to shape reality, and that this process is as pervasive as it is necessary as it is changeable. Unlike the scientific strain in marxism or the Kantian imperative in liberalism, which in this context share most salient features, feminism neither claims universality nor, failing that, reduces to relativity. It does not seek a generality that subsumes its particulars or an abstract theory or a science of sexism. It rejects the approach of control over nature (including us) analogized to control over society (also including us) which has grounded the "science of society" project as the paradigm for political knowledge since (at least) Descartes. Both liberalism and marxism have been subversive on women's behalf. Neither is enough. To grasp the inadequacies for

[8] I mean to imply that contemporary feminism that is not methodologically postmarxist is not radical, hence not feminist on this level. For example, to the extent Mary Daly's *Gyn/Ecology: The Metaethics of Radical Feminism* (Boston: Beacon Press, 1978) is idealist in method—meaning that the subordination of women is an idea such that to think it differently is to change it—it is formally liberal no matter how extreme or insightful. To the extent Shulamith Firestone's analysis (*The Dialectic of Sex: The Case for Feminist Revolution* [New York: William Morrow & Co., 1972]) rests on a naturalist definition of gender, holding that women are oppressed by our bodies rather than their social meaning, her radicalism, hence her feminism, is qualified. Susan Griffin's *Pornography and Silence: Culture's Revolt against Nature* (San Francisco: Harper & Row Publishers, 1982) is classically liberal in all formal respects including, for instance, the treatment of pornography and eros as a distinction that is fundamentally psychological rather than interested, more deeply a matter of good and bad (morality) than of power and powerlessness (politics). Andrea Dworkin's work, esp. *Pornography: Men Possessing Women* (New York: Perigee Books, 1981), and Adrienne Rich's poetry and essays, exemplify feminism as a methodological departure. This feminism seeks to define and pursue women's interest as the fate of all women bound together. It seeks to extract the truth of women's commonalities out of the lie that all women are the same. If whatever a given society defines as sexual defines gender, and if gender means the subordination of women to men, "woman" means—is not qualified or undercut by—the uniqueness of each woman and the specificity of race, class, time, and place. In this sense, lesbian feminism, the feminism of women of color, and socialist feminism are converging in a feminist politics of sexuality, race, and class, with a left to right spectrum of its own. This politics is struggling for a practice of unity that does not depend upon sameness without dissolving into empty tolerance, including tolerance of all it exists to change whenever that appears embodied in one of us. A new community begins here. As critique, women's communality describes a fact of male supremacy, of sex "in itself": no woman escapes the meaning of being a woman within a gendered social system, and sex inequality is not only pervasive but may be universal (in the sense of never having not been in some form) although "intelligible only in . . . locally specific forms" (M. Z. Rosaldo, "The Use and Abuse of Anthropology: Reflections on Feminism and Cross-cultural Understanding." *Signs: Journal of Women in Culture and Society* 5, no. 3 [Spring 1980]: 389–417, 417). For women to become a sex "for ourselves" moves community to the level of vision.

Catharine A. MacKinnon

women of liberalism on one side and marxism on the other is to begin to comprehend the role of the liberal state and liberal legalism[9] within a postmarxist feminism of social transformation.

As feminism has a theory of power but lacks a theory of the state, so marxism has a theory of value which (through the organization of work in production) becomes class analysis, but a problematic theory of the state. Marx did not address the state much more explicitly than he did women. Women were substratum, the state epiphenomenon.[10] Engels, who frontally analyzed both, and together, presumed the subordination of women in every attempt to reveal its roots, just as he presupposed something like the state, or state-like social conditions, in every attempt to expose its origins.[11] Marx tended to use the term "political" narrowly to refer to the state or its laws, criticizing as exclusively political interpretations of the state's organization or behavior which took them as sui generis. Accordingly, until recently, most marxism has tended to consider political that which occurs between classes, that is, to interpret as "the political" instances of the marxist concept of inequality. In this broad sense, the marxist theory of social inequality has been its theory of politics. This has not so much collapsed the state into society (although it goes far in that direction) as conceived the state as determined by the totality of social relations of which the state is one determined and determining part—without specifying which, or how much, is which.

In this context, recent marxist work has tried to grasp the specificity of the institutional state: how it wields class power, or transforms class society, or responds to approach by a left aspiring to rulership or other changes. While liberal theory has seen the state as emanating power, and traditional marxism has seen the state as expressing power constituted elsewhere, recent marxism, much of it structuralist, has tried to analyze state power as specific to the state as a form, yet integral to a determinate social whole understood in class terms. This state is found "relatively autonomous." This means that the state, expressed through its functionaries, has a definite class character, is definitely capitalist or socialist, but also has its own interests which are to some degree independent of those of the ruling class and even of the class structure.[12] The state as such, in this view, has a specific power and

---

[9] See Karl Klare, "Law-Making as Praxis," *Telos* 12, no. 2 (Summer 1979): 123–35; Judith Shklar, *Legalism* (Cambridge, Mass.: Harvard University Press, 1964). To examine law as state is not to decide that all relevant state behavior occurs in legal texts. I do think that legal decisions expose power on the level of legitimizing rationale, and that law, as words in power, is central in the social erection of the liberal state.

[10] Karl Marx, *Capital, Selected Works*, 3 vols. (Moscow: Progress Publishers, 1969), 2:120, 139–40; *The German Ideology* (New York: International Publishers, 1972), pp. 48–52; *Introduction to Critique of Hegel's Philosophy of Right*, ed. Joseph O'Malley, trans. Annette Jolin (Cambridge: Cambridge University Press, 1970), p. 139; Marx to P. V. Annenkov, 1846, in *The Poverty of Philosophy* (New York: International Publishers, 1963), pp. 179–93, 181.

[11] I am criticizing Engels's assumptions about sexuality and women's place, and his empiricist method, and suggesting that the two are linked. Friedrich Engels, *Origin of the Family, Private Property and the State* (New York: International Publishers, 1942).

[12] Representative works include Fred Block, "The Ruling Class Does Not Rule: Notes on the Marxist Theory of the State," *Socialist Revolution* 33 (May–June 1977): 6–28; Ralph Miliband, *The State in Capitalist Society* (New York: Basic Books, 1969); Nicos Poulantzas, *Classes in Contemporary Capitalism* (London: New Left Books, 1975), and *Political Power and Social Classes* (London: New Left Books, 1975); Goran Therborn, *What Does the Ruling Class Do When It Rules?* (London: New Left Books, 1978); Norberto Bobbio, "Is There a Marxist Theory of the State?" *Telos* 35 (Spring 1978): 5–16. Theda Skocpol, *States and Social Revolution: A Comparative Analysis of France, Russia and China* (Cambridge: Cambridge University Press, 1979), pp. 24–33, ably reviews much of this literature. Applications to law include Isaac Balbus, "Commodity Form and Legal Form: An Essay on the Relative Autonomy' of the Law," *Law and Society Review* 11, no. 3 (Winter 1977): 571–88; Mark Tushnet, "A Marxist Analysis of American Law," *Marxist Perspectives* 1, no. 1 (Spring 1978): 96–116; and Klare (n. 9 above).

interest, termed "the political," such that class power, class interest expressed by and in the state, and state behavior, although inconceivable in isolation from one another, are nevertheless not linearly or causally linked or strictly coextensive. Such work locates "the specificity of the political" in a mediate "region"[13] between the state as its own ground of power (which alone, as in the liberal conception, would set the state above or apart from class) and the state as possessing no special supremacy or priority in terms of power, as in the more orthodox marxist view.

The idea that the state is relatively autonomous, a kind of first among equals of social institutions, has the genius of appearing to take a stand on the issue of reciprocal constitution of state and society while straddling it. Is the state essentially autonomous of class but partly determined by it, or is it essentially determined by class but not exclusively so? Is it relatively constrained within a context of freedom or relatively free within a context of constraint?[14] As to who or what fundamentally moves and shapes the realities and instrumentalities of domination, and where to go to do something about it, what qualifies what is as ambiguous as it is crucial. Whatever it has not accomplished, however, this literature has at least relieved the compulsion to find all law—directly or convolutedly, nakedly or clothed in unconscious or devious rationalia—to be simply bourgeois, without undercutting the notion that it is determinately driven by interest.

A methodologically post-marxist feminism must confront, on our own terms, the issue of the relation between the state and society, within a theory of social determination adequate to the specificity of sex. Lacking even a tacit theory of the state of its own, feminist practice has instead oscillated between a liberal theory of the state on the one hand and a left theory of the state on the other. Both treat law as the mind of society: disembodied reason in liberal theory, reflection of material interest in left theory. In liberal moments the state is accepted on its own terms as a neutral arbiter among conflicting interests. The law is actually or potentially principled, meaning predisposed to no substantive outcome, thus available as a tool that is not fatally twisted. Women implicitly become an interest group within pluralism, with specific problems of mobilization and representation, exit and voice, sustaining incremental gains and losses. In left moments, the state becomes a tool of dominance and repression, the law legitimizing ideology, use of the legal system a form of utopian idealism or gradualist reform, each apparent gain deceptive or cooptive, and each loss inevitable.

Applied to women, liberalism has supported state intervention on behalf of women as abstract persons with abstract rights, without scrutinizing the content of these notions in gendered terms. Marxism applied to women is always on the edge of counseling abdication of the state as an arena altogether—and with it those women whom the state does not ignore or who are, as yet, in no position to ignore it. Feminism has so far accepted these constraints upon its alternatives: either the state, as primary tool of women's betterment and status transformation, without analysis (hence strategy) for it as male; or civil society, which for women has more closely resembled a state of nature. The state, with it the law, has been either omnipotent or impotent: everything or nothing.

---

[13] Poulantzas's formulation follows Althusser. Louis Althusser and Etienne Balibar, *Reading Capital*, trans. Ben Brewster (London: New Left Books, 1968). For Poulantzas, the "specific autonomy which is characteristic of the function of the state . . . is the basis of the specificity of the political" (*Political Power and Social Classes* [n. 12 above], pp. 14, 46). Whatever that means. On structural causality between class and state, see p. 14.

[14] See Ernesto Laclau's similar criticism of Miliband in *Politics and Ideology in Marxist Theory* (London: New Left Books, 1977), p. 65.

Catharine A. MacKinnon

The feminist posture toward the state has therefore been schizoid on issues central to women's survival: rape, battery, pornography, prostitution, sexual harassment, sex discrimination, abortion, the Equal Rights Amendment, to name a few. Attempts to reform and enforce rape laws, for example, have tended to build on the model of the deviant perpetrator and the violent act, as if the fact that rape is a crime means that the society is against it, so law enforcement would reduce or delegitimize it. Initiatives are accordingly directed toward making the police more sensitive, prosecutors more responsive, judges more receptive, and the law, in words, less sexist. This may be progressive in the liberal or the left senses, but how is it empowering in the feminist sense? Even if it were effective in jailing men who do little different from what nondeviant men do regularly, how would such an approach alter women's rapability? Unconfronted are *why* women are raped and the role of the state in that. Similarly, applying laws against battery to husbands, although it can mean life itself, has largely failed to address, as part of the strategy for state intervention, the conditions that produce men who systematically express themselves violently toward women, women whose resistance is disabled, and the role of the state in this dynamic. Criminal enforcement in these areas, while suggesting that rape and battery are deviant, punishes men for expressing the images of masculinity that mean their identity, for which they are otherwise trained, elevated, venerated, and paid. These men must be stopped. But how does that change them or reduce the chances that there will be more like them? Liberal strategies entrust women to the state. Left theory abandons us to the rapists and batterers. The question for feminism is not only whether there is a meaningful difference between the two, but whether either is adequate to the feminist critique of rape and battery as systemic and to the role of the state and the law within that system.

Feminism has descriptions of the state's treatment of the gender difference, but no analysis of the state as gender hierarchy. We need to know. What, in gender terms, are the state's norms of accountability, sources of power, real constituency? Is the state to some degree autonomous of the interests of men or an integral expression of them? Does the state embody and serve male interests in its form, dynamics, relation to society, and specific policies? Is the state constructed upon the subordination of women? If so, how does male power become state power? Can such a state be made to serve the interests of those upon whose powerlessness its power is erected? Would a different relation between state and society, such as may pertain under socialism, make a difference? If not, is masculinity inherent in the state form as such, or is some other form of state, or some other way of governing, distinguishable or imaginable? In the absence of answers to such questions, feminism has been caught between giving more power to the state in each attempt to claim it for women and leaving unchecked power in the society to men. Undisturbed, meanwhile, like the assumption that women generally consent to sex, is the assumption that we consent to this government. The question for feminism, for the first time on its own terms, is: what is this state, from women's point of view?

As a beginning, I propose that the state is male in the feminist sense.[15] The law sees and treats women the way men see and treat women. The liberal state coercively and authoritatively constitutes the social order in the interest of men

---

[15] See Susan Rae Peterson, "Coercion and Rape: The State as a Male Protection Racket," in *Feminism and Philosophy*, ed. Mary Vetterling-Braggin, Frederick A. Elliston, and Jane English (Totowa, N.J.: Littlefield, Adams & Co., 1977), pp. 360–71; Janet Rifkin, "Toward a Theory of Law Patriarchy," *Harvard Women's Law Journal* 3 (Spring 1980): 83–92.

as a gender, through its legitimizing norms, relation to society, and substantive policies. It achieves this through embodying and ensuring male control over women's sexuality at every level, occasionally cushioning, qualifying, or de jure prohibiting its excesses when necessary to its normalization. Substantively, the way the male point of view frames an experience is the way it is framed by state policy. To the extent possession is the point of sex, rape is sex with a woman who is not yours, unless the act is so as to make her yours. If part of the kick of pornography involves eroticizing the putatively prohibited, obscenity law will putatively prohibit pornography enough to maintain its desirability without ever making it unavailable or truly illegitimate. The same with prostitution. As male is the implicit reference for human, maleness will be the measure of equality in sex discrimination law. To the extent that the point of abortion is to control the reproductive sequelae of intercourse, so as to facilitate male sexual access to women, access to abortion will be controlled by "a man or The Man."[16] Gender, elaborated and sustained by behavioral patterns of application and administration, is maintained as a division of power.

Formally, the state is male in that objectivity is its norm. Objectivity is liberal legalism's conception of itself. It legitimizes itself by reflecting its view of existing society, a society it made and makes by so seeing it, and calling that view, and that relation, practical rationality. If rationality is measured by point-of-viewlessness, what counts as reason will be that which corresponds to the way things are. Practical will mean that which can be done without changing anything. In this framework, the task of legal interpretation becomes "to perfect the state as mirror of the society."[17] Objectivist epistemology is the law of law. It ensures that the law will most reinforce existing distributions of power when it most closely adheres to its own highest ideal of fairness. Like the science it emulates, this epistemological stance can not see the social specificity of reflection as method or its choice to embrace that which it reflects. Such law not only reflects a society in which men rule women; it rules in a male way: "The phallus means everything that sets itself up as a mirror."[18] The rule form, which unites scientific knowledge with state control in its conception of what law is, institutionalizes the objective stance as jurisprudence. A closer look at the substantive law of rape[19] in light of

---

[16] Johnnie Tillmon, "Welfare Is a Women's Issue," *Liberation News Service* (February 26, 1972), in *America's Working Women: A Documentary History, 1600 to the Present*, ed. Rosalyn Baxandall, Linda Gordon, and Susan Reverby (New York: Vintage Books, 1976), pp. 357–58.

[17] Laurence Tribe, "Constitution as Point of View" (Harvard Law School, Cambridge, Mass., 1982, mimeographed), p. 13.

[18] Madeleine Gagnon, "Body I," in *New French Feminisms*, ed. Elaine Marks and Isabelle de Courtivron (Amherst, Mass.: University of Massachusetts Press, 1980), p. 180. Turns on the mirroring trope, which I see as metaphoric analyses of the epistemological/political dimension of objectification, are ubiquitous in feminist writing: "Into the room of the dressing where the walls are covered with mirrors. Where mirrors are like eyes of men, and the women reflect the judgments of mirrors" (Susan Griffin, *Woman and Nature: The Roaring Inside Her* [New York: Harper & Row Publishers, 1979], p. 155). See also Mary Daly, *Beyond God the Father: Toward a Philosophy of Women's Liberation* (Boston: Beacon Press, 1975), pp. 195, 197; Sheila Rowbotham, *Women's Consciousness, Man's World* (Harmondsworth: Pelican Books, 1973), pp. 26–29. "She did suffer, the witch/trying to peer round the looking/ glass, she forgot/ someone was in the way" (Michelene, "Reflexion," quoted in Rowbotham, p. 2). Virginia Woolf wrote the figure around ("So I reflected . . ."), noticing "the necessity that women so often are to men" of serving as a looking glass in which a man can "see himself at breakfast and at dinner at least twice the size he really is." Notice the doubled sexual/gender meaning: "Whatever may be their use in civilized societies, mirrors are essential to all violent and heroic action. That is why Napoleon and Mussolini both insist so emphatically upon the inferiority of women, for if they were not inferior, they would cease to enlarge" (*A Room of One's Own* [New York: Harcourt, Brace & World, 1969], p. 36).

[19] Space limitations made it necessary to eliminate sections on pornography, sex discrimination, and abortion. For the same reason, most supporting references, including those to case law, have been cut. The final section accordingly states the systemic implications of the analysis more tentatively than I think them, but as strongly as I felt I could, on the basis of the single substantive examination that appears here.

such an argument suggests that the relation between objectification (understood as the primary process of the subordination of women) and the power of the state is the relation between the personal and the political at the level of government. This is not because the state is presumptively the sphere of politics. It is because the state, in part through law, institutionalizes male power. If male power is systemic, it *is* the regime.

II

Feminists have reconceived rape as central to women's condition in two ways. Some see rape as an act of violence, not sexuality, the threat of which intimidates all women.[20] Others see rape, including its violence, as an expression of male sexuality, the social imperatives of which define all women.[21] The first, formally in the liberal tradition, comprehends rape as a displacement of power based on physical force onto sexuality, a pre-existing natural sphere to which domination is alien. Thus, Susan Brownmiller examines rape in riots, wars, pogroms, and revolutions; rape by police, parents, prison guards; and rape motivated by racism—seldom rape in normal circumstances, in everyday life, in ordinary relationships, by men as men.[22] Women are raped by guns, age, white supremacy, the state—only derivatively by the penis. The more feminist view to me, one which derives from victims' experiences, sees sexuality as a social sphere of male power of which forced sex is paradigmatic. Rape is not less sexual for being violent; to the extent that coercion has become integral to male sexuality, rape may be sexual to the degree that, and because, it is violent.

The point of defining rape as "violence not sex" or "violence against women" has been to separate sexuality from gender in order to affirm sex (heterosexuality) while rejecting violence (rape). The problem remains what it has always been: telling the difference. The convergence of sexuality with violence, long used at law to deny the reality of women's violation, is recognized by rape survivors, with a difference: where the legal system has seen the intercourse in rape, victims see the rape in intercourse. The uncoerced context for sexual expression becomes as elusive as the physical acts come to feel indistinguishable.[23] Instead of asking, what is the violation of rape, what if we ask, what is the nonviolation of intercourse? To tell what is wrong with rape, explain what is right about sex. If this, in turn, is difficult, the difficulty is as instructive as the difficulty men have in telling the difference when women see one. Perhaps the wrong of rape has proven

---

[20] Susan Brownmiller, *Against Our Will: Men, Women and Rape* (New York: Simon & Schuster, 1976), p. 15.

[21] Diana E. H. Russell, *The Politics of Rape: The Victim's Perspective* (New York: Stein & Day, 1977); Andrea Medea and Kathleen Thompson, *Against Rape* (New York: Farrar, Straus & Giroux, 1974); Lorenne M. G. Clark and Debra Lewis, *Rape: The Price of Coercive Sexuality* (Toronto: The Women's Press, 1977); Susan Griffin, "Rape: The All-American Crime," *Ramparts* (September 1971), pp. 26–35; Ti-Grace Atkinson connects rape with "the institution of sexual intercourse" (*Amazon Odyssey: The First Collection of Writings by the Political Pioneer of the Women's Movement* [New York: Links Books, 1974], pp. 13–23). Kalamu ya Salaam, "Rape: A Radical Analysis from the African-American Perspective," in *Our Women Keep Our Skies from Falling* (New Orleans: Nkombo, 1980), pp. 25–40.

[22] Racism, clearly, is everyday life. Racism in the United States, by singling out Black men for allegations of rape of white women, has helped obscure the fact that it is men who rape women, disproportionately women of color.

[23] "Like other victims, I had problems with sex, after the rape. There was no way that Arthur could touch me that it didn't remind me of having been raped by this guy I never saw" (Carolyn Craven, "No More Victims: Carolyn Craven Talks about Rape, and about What Women and Men Can Do to Stop It," ed. Alison Wells [Berkeley, Calif., 1978, mimeographed]), p. 2.

so difficult to articulate[24] because the unquestionable starting point has been that rape is definable as distinct from intercourse, when for women it is difficult to distinguish them under conditions of male dominance.[25]

Like heterosexuality, the crime of rape centers on penetration.[26] The law to protect women's sexuality from forcible violation/expropriation defines the protected in male genital terms. Women do resent forced penetration. But penile invasion of the vagina may be less pivotal to women's sexuality, pleasure or violation, than it is to male sexuality. This definitive element of rape centers upon a male-defined loss, not coincidentally also upon the way men define loss of exclusive access. In this light, rape, as legally defined, appears more a crime against female monogamy than against female sexuality. Property concepts fail fully to comprehend this,[27] however, not because women's sexuality is not, finally, a thing, but because it is never ours. The moment we "have" it—"have sex" in the dual sexuality/gender sense—it is lost as ours. This may explain the male incomprehension that, once a woman has had sex, she loses anything when raped. To them we *have nothing* to lose. Dignitary harms, because nonmaterial, are remote to the legal mind. But women's loss through rape is not only less tangible, it is less existent. It is difficult to avoid the conclusion that penetration itself is known to be a violation and that women's sexuality, our gender definition, is itself stigmatic. If this is so, the pressing question for explanation is not why some of us accept rape but why any of us resent it.

The law of rape divides the world of women into spheres of consent according to how much say we are legally presumed to have over sexual access to us by various categories of men. Little girls may not consent; wives must. If rape laws existed to enforce women's control over our own sexuality, as the consent defense implies, marital rape would not be a widespread exception,[28] nor would statutory rape proscribe all sexual intercourse with underage girls regardless of their wishes. The rest of us fall into parallel provinces: good girls, like children, are unconsenting, virginal, rapable; bad girls, like wives, are consenting, whores, unrapable. The age line under which girls are presumed disabled from withholding consent to sex rationalizes a condition of sexual coercion women never outgrow. As with protective labor laws for women only, dividing and protecting the most

---

[24] Pamela Foa, "What's Wrong with Rape?" in Vetterling-Braggin, Elliston, and English, eds. (n. 15 above), pp. 347–59; Michael Davis, "What's So Bad about Rape?" (paper presented at Annual Meeting of the Academy of Criminal Justice Sciences, Louisville, Ky., March 1982).

[25] "Since we would not want to say that there is anything morally wrong with sexual intercourse per se, we conclude that the wrongness of rape rests with the matter of the woman's consent" (Carolyn M. Shafer and Marilyn Frye, "Rape and Respect," in Vetterling-Braggin, Elliston, and English, eds. [n. 15 above], p. 334). "Sexual contact is not inherently harmful, insulting or provoking. Indeed, ordinarily it is something of which we are quite fond. The difference between ordinary sexual intercourse and rape is that ordinary sexual intercourse is more or less consented to while rape is not" (Davis [n. 24 above], p. 12).

[26] Sec. 213.0 of the *Model Penal Code* (Official Draft and Revised Comments 1980), like most states, defines rape as sexual intercourse with a female who is not the wife of the perpetrator "with some penetration however slight." Impotency is sometimes a defense. Michigan's gender-neutral sexual assault statute includes penetration by objects (sec. 520a[h]; 520[b]). See *Model Penal Code*, annotation to sec. 213.1(d) (Official Draft and Revised Comments 1980).

[27] Although it is true that men possess women and that women's bodies are, socially, men's things, I have not analyzed rape as men treating women like property. In the manner of many socialist-feminist adaptations of marxian categories to women's situation, that analysis short-circuits analysis of rape as male sexuality and presumes rather than develops links between sex and class. We need to rethink sexual dimensions of property as well as property dimensions of sexuality.

[28] For an excellent summary of the current state of the marital exemption, see Joanne Schulman, "State-by-State Information on Marital Rape Exemption Laws," in *Rape in Marriage*, Diana E. H. Russell (New York: Macmillan Publishing Co., 1982), pp. 375–81.

Catharine A. MacKinnon

vulnerable becomes a device for not protecting everyone. Risking loss of even so little cannot be afforded. Yet the protection is denigrating and limiting (girls may not choose to be sexual) as well as perverse (girls are eroticized as untouchable; now reconsider the data on incest).

If the accused knows us, consent is inferred. The exemption for rape in marriage is consistent with the assumption underlying most adjudications of forcible rape: to the extent the parties relate, it was not really rape, it was personal.[29] As the marital exemptions erode, preclusions for cohabitants and voluntary social companions may expand. In this light, the partial erosion of the marital rape exemption looks less like a change in the equation between women's experience of sexual violation and men's experience of intimacy, and more like a legal adjustment to the social fact that acceptable heterosexual sex is increasingly not limited to the legal family. So although the rape law may not now always assume that the woman consented simply because the parties are legally one, indices of closeness, of relationship ranging from nodding acquaintance to living together, still contraindicate rape. Perhaps this reflects men's experience that women they know meaningfully consent to sex with them. That cannot be rape; rape must be by someone else, someone unknown. But *women* experience rape most often by men we know.[30] Men believe that it is less awful to be raped by someone one is close to: "The emotional trauma suffered by a person victimized by an individual with whom sexual intimacy is shared as a normal part of an ongoing marital relationship is not nearly as severe as that suffered by a person who is victimized by one with whom that intimacy is not shared."[31] But women feel as much, if not more, traumatized by being raped by someone we have known or trusted, someone we have shared at least an illusion of mutuality with, than by some stranger. In whose interest is it to believe that it is not so bad to be raped by someone who has fucked you before as by someone who has not? Disallowing charges of rape in marriage may also "remove a substantial obstacle to the resumption of normal marital relations."[32] Depending upon your view of normal. Note that the obstacle to normalcy here is not the rape but the law against it. Apparently someone besides feminists finds sexual victimization and sexual intimacy not all that contradictory. Sometimes I think women and men live in different cultures.

Having defined rape in male sexual terms, the law's problem, which becomes the victim's problem, is distinguishing rape from sex in specific cases. The law does this by adjudicating the level of acceptable force starting just above the level set by what is seen as normal male sexual behavior, rather than at the victim's, or women's, point of violation. Rape cases finding insufficient force reveal that acceptable sex,

[29] On "social interaction as an element of consent," in a voluntary social companion context, see *Model Penal Code*, sec. 213.1. "The prior *social* interaction is an indicator of consent in addition to actor's and victim's *behavioral* interaction during the commission of the offense" (Wallace Loh, "Q: What Has Reform of Rape Legislation Wrought? A: Truth in Criminal Labeling," *Journal of Social Issues* 37, no. 4 [1981]: 28–52, 47). Perhaps consent should be an affirmative defense, pleaded and proven by the defendant.

[30] Pauline Bart found that women were more likely to be raped—that is, less able to stop a rape in progress—when they knew their assailant, particularly when they had a prior or current sexual relationship ("A Study of Women Who Both Were Raped and Avoided Rape," *Journal of Social Issues* 37, no. 4 [1981]: 123–37, 132). See also Linda Belden, "Why Women Do Not Report Sexual Assault" (City of Portland Public Service Employment Program, Portland Women's Crisis Line, Portland, Ore., March 1979, mimeographed); Diana E. H. Russell and Nancy Howell, "The Prevalence of Rape in the United States Revisited," in this issue; and Menachem Amir, *Patterns in Forcible Rape* (Chicago: University of Chicago Press, 1971), pp. 229–52.

[31] Answer Brief for Plaintiff-Appellee at 10, People v. Brown, 632 P.2d 1025 (Colo. 1981).

[32] Brown, 632 P.2d at 1027 (citing Comment, "Rape and Battery between Husband and Wife," *Stanford Law Review* 6 [1954]: 719–28, 719, 725).

in the legal perspective, can entail a lot of force. This is not only because of the way specific facts are perceived and interpreted, but because of the way the injury itself is defined as illegal. Rape is a sex crime that is not a crime when it looks like sex. To seek to define rape as violent, not sexual, is understandable in this context, and often seems strategic. But assault that is consented to is still assault; rape consented to is intercourse. The substantive reference point implicit in existing legal standards is the sexually normative level of force. Until this norm is confronted as such, no distinction between violence and sexuality will prohibit more instances of women's experienced violation than does the existing definition. The question is what is *seen as* force, hence as violence, in the sexual arena. Most rapes, as women live them, will not be seen to violate women until sex and violence are confronted as mutually definitive. It is not only men convicted of rape who believe that the only thing they did different from what men do all the time is get caught.

The line between rape and intercourse commonly centers on some measure of the woman's "will." But from what should the law know woman's will? Like much existing law, Brownmiller tends to treat will as a question of consent and consent as a factual issue of the presence of force.[33] Proof problems aside, force and desire are not mutually exclusive. So long as dominance is eroticized, they never will be. Women are socialized to passive receptivity; may have or perceive no alternative to acquiescence; may prefer it to the escalated risk of injury and the humiliation of a lost fight; submit to survive. Some eroticize dominance and submission; it beats feeling forced. Sexual intercourse may be deeply unwanted— the woman would never have initiated it—yet no force may be present. Too, force may be used, yet the woman may want the sex—to avoid more force or because she, too, eroticizes dominance. Women and men know this. Calling rape violence, not sex, thus evades, at the moment it most seems to confront, the issue of who controls women's sexuality and the dominance/submission dynamic that has defined it. When sex is violent, women may have lost control over what is done to us, but absence of force does not ensure the presence of that control. Nor, under conditions of male dominance, does the presence of force make an inter- action nonsexual. If sex is normally something men do to women, the issue is less whether there was force and more whether consent is a meaningful concept.[34]

To explain women's gender status as a function of rape, Brownmiller argues that the threat of rape benefits all men.[35] She does not specify in what way. Perhaps it benefits them sexually, hence as a gender: male initiatives toward women carry the fear of rape as support for persuading compliance, the resulting appearance of which has been called consent. Here the victims' perspective grasps what liberalism applied to women denies: that forced sex as sexuality is not exceptional in relations between the sexes but constitutes the social meaning of gender: "Rape is a man's act, whether it is male or a female man and whether it is a man relatively permanently or relatively temporarily; and being raped is a woman's experience, whether it is a female or a male woman and whether it is a woman relatively permanently or relatively temporarily."[36] To be rap*able*, a posi- tion which is social, not biological, defines what a woman *is*.

Catharine A. MacKinnon

[33] Brownmiller (n. 20 above), pp. 8, 196, 400–407, 427–36.

[34] See Carol Pateman, "Women and Consent," *Political Theory* 8, no. 2 (May 1980): 149–68.

[35] Brownmiller (n. 20 above), p. 5.

[36] Shafer and Frye (n. 25 above), p. 334. Battery of wives has been legally separated from marital rape not because assault by a man's fist is so different from assault by a penis. Both seem clearly violent. I am suggesting

Most women get the message that the law against rape is virtually unenforce-able as applied to them. Our own experience is more often delegitimized by this than the law is. Women radically distinguish between rape and experiences of sexual violation, concluding that we have not "really" been raped if we have ever seen or dated or slept with or been married to the man, if we were fashionably dressed or are not provably virgin, if we are prostitutes, if we put up with it or tried to get it over with, if we were force-fucked over a period of years. If we probably couldn't prove it in court, it wasn't rape. The distance between most sexual violations of women and the legally perfect rape measures the imposition of someone else's definition upon women's experiences. Rape, from women's point of view, is not prohibited; it is regulated. Even women who know we have been raped do not believe that the legal system will see it the way we do. We are often not wrong. Rather than deterring or avenging rape, the state, in many victims' experiences, perpetuates it. Women who charge rape say they were raped twice, the second time in court. If the state is male, this is more than a figure of speech.

The law distinguishes rape from intercourse by the woman's lack of consent coupled with a man's (usually) knowing disregard of it. A feminist distinction between rape and intercourse, to hazard a beginning approach, lies instead in the *meaning* of the act from women's point of view. What is wrong with rape is that it is an act of the subordination of women to men. Seen this way, the issue is not so much what rape "is" as the way its social conception is shaped to interpret particular encounters. Under conditions of sex inequality, with perspective bound up with situation, whether a contested interaction is rape comes down to whose meaning wins. If sexuality is relational, specifically if it is a power relation of gender, consent is a communication under conditions of inequality. It transpires somewhere between what the woman actually wanted and what the man comprehended she wanted. Instead of capturing this dynamic, the law gives us linear statics face to face. Nonconsent in law becomes a question of the man's force or the woman's resistance or both.[37] Rape, like many crimes and torts, requires that the accused possess a criminal mind (mens rea) for his acts to be criminal. The man's mental state refers to what he actually understood at the time or to what a reasonable man should have understood under the circumstances. The problem is this: the injury of rape lies in the meaning of the act to its victims, but the

---

that both are also sexual. Assaults are often precipitated by women's noncompliance with gender requirements. See R. Emerson Dobash and Russell Dobash, *Violence against Wives: A Case against the Patriarchy* (New York: Free Press, 1979), pp. 14–20. Nearly all incidents occur in the home, most in the kitchen or bedroom. Most murdered women are killed by their husbands, most in the bedroom. The battery cycle accords with the rhythm of heterosexual sex (see Leonore Walker, *The Battered Woman* [New York: Harper & Row Publishers, 1979], pp. 19–20). The rhythm of lesbian S/M appears similar (Samois, eds., *Coming to Power* [Palo Alto, Calif.: Up Press, 1981]). Perhaps most interchange between genders, but especially violent ones, make sense in sexual terms. However, the larger issue for the relation between sexuality and gender, hence sexuality and violence generally, including both war and violence against women, is: What *is* heterosexuality? If it is the erotization of dominance and submission, altering the participants' gender is comparatively incidental. If it is males over females, gender matters independently. Since I see heterosexuality as the fusion of the two, but with gender a social outcome (such that the acted upon is feminized, is the "girl" regardless of sex, the actor correspondingly masculinized), battery appears sexual on a deeper level. In baldest terms, sexuality is violent, so violence is sexual, violence against women doubly so. If this is so, wives are beaten, as well as raped, *as women*—as the acted upon, as gender, meaning sexual, objects. It further follows that all acts *by anyone* which treat a woman according to her object label "woman" are *sexual* acts. The extent to which sexual acts are acts of objectification remains a question of our account of our freedom to make our own meanings. It is clear, at least, that it is centering sexuality upon genitality that distinguishes battery from rape at exactly the juncture that both the law, and seeing rape as violence not sex, does.

[37] Even when nonconsent is not a legal element of the offense (as in Michigan), juries tend to infer rape from evidence of force or resistance.

standard for its criminality lies in the meaning of the same act to the assailants. Rape is only an injury from women's point of view. It is only a crime from the male point of view, explicitly including that of the accused.

Thus is the crime of rape defined and adjudicated from the male standpoint, that is, presuming that (what feminists see as) forced sex is sex. Under male supremacy, of course, it is. What this means doctrinally is that the man's perceptions of the woman's desires often determine whether she is deemed violated. This might be like other crimes of subjective intent if rape were like other crimes. But with rape, because sexuality defines gender, the only difference between assault and (what is socially considered) noninjury is the meaning of the encounter to the woman. Interpreted this way, the legal problem has been to determine whose view of that meaning constitutes what really happened, as if what happened objectively exists to be objectively determined, thus as if this task of determination is separable from the gender of the participants and the gendered nature of their exchange. Thus, even though the rape law oscillates between subjective tests and more objective standards invoking social reasonableness, it uniformly presumes a single underlying reality, not a reality split by divergent meanings, such as those inequality produces. Many women are raped by men who know the meaning of their acts to women and proceed anyway.[38] But women are also violated every day by men who have no idea of the meaning of their acts to women. To them, it is sex. Therefore, to the law, it is sex. That is the single reality of what happened. When a rape prosecution is lost on a consent defense, the woman has not only failed to prove lack of consent, she is not considered to have been injured at all. Hermeneutically unpacked, read: because he did not perceive she did not want him, she was not violated. She had sex. Sex itself cannot be an injury. Women consent to sex every day. Sex makes a woman a woman. Sex is what women are *for*.

To a feminist analysis, men set sexual mores ideologically and behaviorally, define rape as they imagine the sexual violation of women through distinguishing it from their image of what they normally do, and sit in judgment in most accusations of sex crimes. So rape comes to mean a strange (read Black) man knowing a woman does not want sex and going ahead anyway. But men are systematically conditioned not even to notice what women want. They may have not a glimmer of women's indifference or revulsion. Rapists typically believe the woman loved it.[39] Women, as a survival strategy, must ignore or devalue or mute our desires (particularly lack of them) to convey the impression that the man will get what he wants regardless of what we want. In this context, consider measuring the genuineness of consent from the individual assailant's (or even the socially reasonable, i.e., objective, man's) point of view.

Men's pervasive belief that women fabricate rape charges after consenting to sex makes sense in this light. To them, the accusations *are* false because, to them, the facts describe sex. To interpret such events as rapes distorts their experience. Since they seldom consider that their experience of the real is anything other than

---

[38] This is apparently true of undetected as well as convicted rapists. Samuel David Smithyman's sample, composed largely of the former, contained self-selected respondents to his ad, which read: "Are you a rapist? Researchers Interviewing Anonymously by Phone to Protect Your Identity. Call . . ." Presumably those who chose to call defined their acts as rapes, at least at the time of responding ("The Undetected Rapist" [Ph.D. diss., Claremont Graduate School, 1978], pp. 54–60, 63–76, 80–90, 97–107).

[39] "Probably the single most used cry of rapist to victim is 'You bitch . . . slut . . . you know you want it. You *all* want it' and afterward, 'there now, you really enjoyed it, didn't you?'" (Nancy Gager and Cathleen Schurr, *Sexual Assault: Confronting Rape in America* [New York: Grosset & Dunlap, 1976], p. 244).

Catharine A. MacKinnon

reality, they can only explain the woman's version as maliciously invented. Similarly, the male anxiety that rape is easy to charge and difficult to disprove (also widely believed in the face of overwhelming evidence to the contrary) arises because rape accusations express one thing men cannot seem to control: the meaning to women of sexual encounters.

Thus do legal doctrines, incoherent or puzzling as syllogistic logic, become coherent as ideology. For example, when an accused wrongly but sincerely believes that a woman he sexually forced consented, he may have a defense of mistaken belief or fail to satisfy the mental requirement of knowingly proceeding against her will.[40] One commentator notes, discussing the conceptually similar issue of revocation of prior consent (i.e., on the issue of the conditions under which women are allowed to control access to their sexuality from one time to the next): "Even where a woman revokes prior consent, such is the male ego that, seized of an exaggerated assessment of his sexual prowess, a man might genuinely believe her still to be consenting; resistance may be misinterpreted as enthusiastic cooperation; protestations of pain or disinclination, a spur to more sophisticated or more ardent love-making; a clear statement to stop, taken as referring to a particular intimacy rather than the entire performance."[41] This equally vividly captures common male readings of women's indications of disinclination under all kinds of circumstances.[42] Now reconsider to what extent the man's perceptions should determine whether a rape occurred. From whose standpoint, and in whose interest, is a law that allows one person's conditioned unconsciousness to contraindicate another's experienced violation? This aspect of the rape law reflects the sex inequality of the society not only in conceiving a cognizable injury from the viewpoint of the reasonable rapist, but in affirmatively rewarding men with acquittals for not comprehending women's point of view on sexual encounters.

Whether the law calls this coerced consent or mistake of fact, the more the sexual violation of women is routine, the more beliefs equating sexuality with violation become reasonable, and the more honestly women can be defined in terms of our fuckability. It would be comparatively simple if the legal problem were limited to avoiding retroactive falsification of the accused's state of mind. Surely there are incentives to lie. But the deeper problem is the rape law's assumption that a single, objective state of affairs existed, one which merely needs to be determined by evidence, when many (maybe even most) rapes involve honest men and violated women. When the reality is split—a woman is raped but not by a rapist?—the law tends to conclude that a rape *did not happen*. To attempt to solve this by adopting the standard of reasonable belief without asking, on a substantive social basis, to whom the belief is reasonable and why—meaning, what conditions make it reasonable—is one-sided: male-sided. What is it reasonable for a man to believe concerning a woman's desire for sex when heterosexuality is compulsory? Whose subjectivity becomes the objectivity of "what happened" is a matter of social meaning, that is, it has been a matter of sexual politics. One-sidedly erasing

[40] See Director of Public Prosecutions v. Morgan, 2411 E.R.H.L. 347(1975); Pappajohn v. The Queen, 11 D.L.R. 3d 1 (1980); People v. Mayberry, 15 Cal. 3d 143, 542 P.2d 1337 (1975).

[41] Richard H. S. Tur, "Rape: Reasonableness and Time," *Oxford Journal of Legal Studies* 3 (Winter 1981): 432–41, 441. Tur, in the context of the Morgan and Pappajohn cases, says the "law ought not to be astute to equate wickedness and wishful, albeit mistaken, thinking" (p. 437). In feminist analysis, a rape is not an isolated or individual or moral transgression but a terrorist act within a systematic context of group subjection, like lynching.

[42] See Silke Vogelmann-Sine et al., "Sex Differences in Feelings Attributed to a Woman in Situations Involving Coercion and Sexual Advances," *Journal of Personality* 47, no. 3 (September 1979): 420–31, esp. 429–30.

women's violation or dissolving the presumptions into the subjectivity of either side are alternatives dictated by the terms of the object/subject split, respectively. These are alternatives that will only retrace that split until its terms are confronted as gendered to the ground.

Desirability to men is commonly supposed to be a woman's form of power. This echoes the view that consent is women's form of control over intercourse, different but equal to the custom of male initiative. Look at it: man initiates, woman chooses. Even the ideal is not mutual. Apart from the disparate consequences of refusal, or openness of original options, this model does not envision a situation the woman controls being placed in, or choices she frames, yet the consequences are attributed to her as if the sexes began at arm's length, on equal terrain, as in the contract fiction. Ambiguous cases of consent are often archetypically referred to as "half won arguments in parked cars."[43] Why not half lost? Why isn't half enough? Why is it an argument? Why do men still want "it," feel entitled to "it," when women don't want them? That sexual expression is even framed as a matter of woman's consent, without exposing these presuppositions, is integral to gender inequality. Woman's so-called power presupposes her more fundamental powerlessness.[44]

III

The state's formal norms recapitulate the male point of view on the level of design. In Anglo-American jurisprudence, morals (value judgments) are deemed separable and separated from politics (power contests), and both from adjudication (interpretation). Neutrality, including judicial decision making that is dispassionate, impersonal, disinterested, and precedential, is considered desirable and descriptive. Courts, forums without predisposition among parties and with no interest of their own, reflect society back to itself resolved. Government of laws not men limits partiality with written constraints and tempers force with reasonable rule following. This law aspires to science: to the immanent generalization subsuming the emergent particularity, to prediction and control of social regularities and regulations, preferably codified. The formulaic "tests" of "doctrine" aspire to mechanism, classification to taxonomy. Courts intervene only in properly "factualized" disputes,[45] cognizing social conflicts as if collecting empirical data. But the demarcations between morals and politics, the personality of the judge and the judicial role, bare coercion and the rule of law,[46] tend to merge

---

[43] Note, "Forcible and Statutory Rape: An Exploration of the Operation and Objectives of the Consent Standard," *Yale Law Journal* 62 (1952): 55–56.

[44] A similar analysis of sexual harassment suggests that women have such "power" only so long as we behave according to male definitions of female desirability, that is, only so long as we accede the definition of our sexuality (hence, ourselves, as gender female) to male terms. We have this power only so long as we remain powerless.

[45] Peter Gabel, "Reification in Legal Reasoning" (New College Law School, San Francisco, 1980, mimeographed), p. 3.

[46] Rawls's "original position," for instance, is a version of my objective standpoint (John Rawls, *A Theory of Justice* [Cambridge, Mass.: Harvard University Press, 1971]). Not only apologists for the liberal state, but also some of its most trenchant critics, see a real distinction between the rule of law and absolute arbitrary force. E. P. Thompson, *Whigs and Hunters: The Origin of the Black Act* (New York: Pantheon Books, 1975), pp. 258–69. Douglas Hay argues that making and enforcing certain acts as illegal reinforces a structure of subordination ("Property, Authority, and the Criminal Law," in *Albion's Fatal Tree: Crime and Society in Eighteenth Century England*, D. Hay et al., eds. [New York: Pantheon Books, 1975], pp. 17–31). Michael D. A. Freeman ("Violence against Women: Does the Legal System Provide Solutions or Itself Constitute the Problem?" [Madison, Wis., 1980, mimeographed], p. 12, n. 161) applies this argument to domestic battery of women. Here I extend it to women's situation as a whole, without suggesting that the analysis can *end* there.

in women's experience. Relatively seamlessly they promote the dominance of men as a social group through privileging the form of power—the perspective on social life—feminist consciousness reveals as socially male. The separation of form from substance, process from policy, role from theory and practice, echoes and reechoes at each level of the regime its basic norm: objectivity.

Consider a central example. The separation of public from private is as crucial to the liberal state's claim to objectivity as its inseparability is to women's claim to subordination. Legally, it has both formal and substantive dimensions. The state considers formal, not substantive, the allocation of public matters to itself to be treated objectively, of private matters to civil society to be treated subjectively. Substantively, the private is defined as a right to "an inviolable personality,"[47] which is guaranteed by ensuring "autonomy or control over the intimacies of personal identity."[48] It is hermetic. It means that which is inaccessible to, unaccountable to, and unconstructed by anything beyond itself. Intimacy occurs in private; this is supposed to guarantee original symmetry of power. Injuries arise in violating the private sphere, not within and by and because of it. Private means consent can be presumed unless disproven. To contain a systematic inequality contradicts the notion itself. But feminist consciousness has exploded the private. For women, the measure of the intimacy has been the measure of the oppression. To see the personal as political means to see the private as public. On this level, women have no privacy to lose or to guarantee. We are not inviolable. Our sexuality, meaning gender identity, is not only violable, it *is* (hence we are) our violation. Privacy is everything women as women have never been allowed to be or to have; at the same time the private is everything women have been equated with and defined in terms of *men's* ability to have. To confront the fact that we have no privacy is to confront our private degradation as the public order. To fail to recognize this place of the private in women's subordination by seeking protection behind a right to that privacy is thus to be cut off from collective verification and state support in the same act.[49] The very place (home, body), relations (sexual), activities (intercourse and reproduction), and feelings (intimacy, selfhood) that feminism finds central to women's subjection form the core of privacy doctrine. But when women are segregated in private, one at a time, a law of privacy will tend to protect the right of men "to be let alone,"[50] to oppress us one at a time. A law of the private, in a state that mirrors such a society, will translate the traditional values of the private sphere into individual women's right to privacy, subordinating women's collective needs to the imperatives of male supremacy.[51] It will keep some men out of the bedrooms of other men.

Liberalism converges with the left at this edge of the feminist critique of male power. Herbert Marcuse speaks of "philosophies which are 'political' in the widest sense—affecting society as a whole, demonstrably transcending the sphere

---

[47] S. D. Warren and L. D. Brandeis, "The Right to Privacy," *Harvard Law Review* 4 (1890): 193–205.

[48] Tom Gerety, "Redefining Privacy," *Harvard Civil Right-Civil Liberties Law Review* 12, no. 2 (Spring 1977): 236.

[49] Harris v. McRae, 448 U.S. 287 (1980), which holds that withholding public funds for abortions does not violate the federal constitutional right to privacy, illustrates. See Zillah Eisenstein, *The Radical Future of Liberal Feminism* (New York: Longman, Inc., 1981), p. 240.

[50] Robeson v. Rochester Folding Box Co., 171 NY 538 (1902); Cooley, *Torts*, sec. 135, 4th ed. (Chicago: Callaghan & Co., 1932).

[51] This argument learned a lot from Tom Grey's article, "Eros, Civilization and the Burger Court," *Law and Contemporary Problems* 43, no. 3 (Summer 1980): 83–99.

of privacy."[52] This does and does not describe the feminist political: "Women both have and have not had a common world."[53] Isolation in the home and intimate degradation, women share. The private sphere, which confines and separates us, is therefore a political sphere, a common ground of our inequality. In feminist translation, the private is a sphere of battery, marital rape, and women's exploited labor; of the central social institutions whereby women are deprived of (as men are granted) identity, autonomy, control, and self-determination; and of the primary activity through which male supremacy is expressed and enforced. Rather than transcending the private as a predicate to politics, feminism politicizes it. For women, the private necessarily transcends the private. If the most private also most "affects society as a whole," the separation between public and private collapses as anything other than potent ideology. The failure of marxism adequately to address intimacy on the one hand, government on the other, is the same failure as the indistinguishability between marxism and liberalism on questions of sexual politics.

Interpreting further areas of law, a feminist theory of the state will reveal that the idealism of liberalism and the materialism of the left have come to much the same for women. Liberal jurisprudence that the law should reflect society and left jurisprudence that all law does or can do is reflect existing social relations will emerge as two guises of objectivist epistemology. If objectivity is the epistemological stance of which women's sexual objectification is the social process, its imposition the paradigm of power in the male form, then the state will appear most relentless in imposing the male point of view when it comes closest to achieving its highest formal criterion of distanced aperspectivity. When it is most ruthlessly neutral, it will be most male; when it is most sex blind, it will be most blind to the sex of the standard being applied. When it most closely conforms to precedent, to "facts," to legislative intent, it will most closely enforce socially male norms and most thoroughly preclude questioning their content as having a point of view at all. Abstract rights will authoritize the male experience of the world. The liberal view that law is society's text, its rational mind, expresses this in a normative mode; the traditional left view that the state, and with it the law, is superstructural or epiphenomenal expresses it in an empirical mode. Both rationalize male power by presuming that it does not exist, that equality between the sexes (room for marginal corrections conceded) is society's basic norm and fundamental description. Only feminism grasps the extent to which the opposite is true: that antifeminism is as normative as it is empirical. Once masculinity appears as a specific position, not just as the way things are, its judgments will be revealed in process and procedure, as well as adjudication and legislation. Perhaps the objectivity of the liberal state has made it appear "autonomous of class." Including, but beyond, the bourgeois in liberal legalism, lies what is male about it. However autonomous of class the liberal state may appear, it is not autonomous of sex. Justice will require change, not reflection—a new jurisprudence, a new relation between life and law.

UNIVERSITY OF MINNESOTA LAW SCHOOL

Catharine A. MacKinnon

[52] Herbert Marcuse, "Repressive Tolerance," in *A Critique of Pure Tolerance*, ed. Robert Paul Wolff, Barrington Moore, Jr., and Herbert Marcuse (Boston: Beacon Press, 1965), pp. 81–117, esp. p. 91.

[53] Adrienne Rich, "Conditions for Work: The Common World of Women," in *Working It Out: Twenty-three Women Writers, Artists, Scientists, and Scholars Talk about Their Lives and Work*, ed. Sara Ruddick and Pamela Daniels (New York: Pantheon Books, 1977), pp. xiv–xxiv, esp. p. xiv.

Kimberlé Crenshaw, Neil Gotanda, Gary Peller, and Kendall Thomas

Kimberlé Crenshaw, Neil Gotanda, Gary Peller, and Kendall Thomas

RACE HAS BEEN part of American law from the birth of the Republic, embedded in our public and private law at the national, state, and international levels. Slavery was a legal institution, governed by private, public, national, state, and international law. The abolition of slavery and the process of Reconstruction after the Civil War were written in law. The system of racial separation and subordination known as "Jim Crow" in the South, and the segregation of housing, education, and civic life throughout the nation were legal regimes. Native American lands became subject to federal plenary power through law. The reservation system and the system for recognition of tribal identities are legal regimes, as are immigration and naturalization which have authorized racial exclusions and regulated racial identity at the border. The wartime internment of Japanese and other Asian citizens was a legal regime. At the same time, the struggle to overcome racial exclusion, segregation, discrimination, and inequality have also been carried forward in legal terms.

Given the ubiquity of race in American life and law, it is surprising how infrequently racial issues have preoccupied those who have contributed to the development of American Legal Thought. The focus on private law and the role of judges in common-law adjudication may be partly responsible—for more than a century, race has been considered primarily a matter of public or constitutional law, despite the significance of slavery for American private law. Issues of race enter the Canon first in the early years of the Civil Rights Movement, in the mixed feelings legal process scholars experienced in response to the Supreme Court's decision in *Brown v. Board of Education*. There is no question that scholars associated with law and society, with the public law scholarship of the Great Society era, with the liberal reconstruction of rights, and with critical modes of legal analysis in the years after 1970 were influenced by the revolution in American law and society let loose by the Civil Rights Movement. Many legal scholars wrote powerfully in defense of the civil rights project, and many more participated in its struggles in courts and elsewhere in government.

But it remains surprising how few of the most significant theoretical contributions in the Canon mention race. Felix Cohen had worked and written extensively, and often critically, about Federal Indian Law, but his canonical criticism of "transcendental nonsense" in legal reasoning makes no mention of it. Similarly, Llewellyn's anthropological study of the Cheyenne legal system, written with Adamson Hoebel, makes scant appearance in his legal theory work. Surely Marc Galanter was thinking about race when we wrote about the "haves" and "have-nots" in American society—he had been studying the legal and social implications of caste in India for decades—but he does not mention it in his contribution to the Canon. The new public-law litigation Abe Chayes championed in his contribution to the Canon was often concerned, in fact, with responding to racial segregation or inequality, but this remained in the margins of his argument, one application among many of his general idea. The "hard cases" Dworkin envisioned included many centering on race—indeed, his theory of rights could easily be read as a defense of the "Herculean" Warren Court, but again, race is but an example of the kind of social conflict that can give rise to particularly hard cases. Robert Cover had written a book about the judicial enforcement of fugitive slave laws, and Duncan Kennedy would go on to write about affirmative action and contribute significantly to the effort to develop more race-conscious legal scholarship. Indeed, as individuals, most of the postwar authors contributing to the Canon were strong supporters of the civil rights struggle. But when they came to write about legal theory, race slipped from the page.

It is difficult not to interpret this, in some sense, as a function of the fact that all the authors in the Canon have so far been white. Although African American and other minority lawyers have long been active in American public life, the elite sites where American legal thought has been produced remained largely white throughout the postwar period. That began to change only with the expansion of law faculties in the late 1970s and '80s, and the arrival of a generation of minority law students. Their arrival coincided with an explosion of identity consciousness in the American intelligentsia more generally. The Civil Rights model was reinvented and reinstitutionalized by numerous groups—Hispanics, Asian Americans, women, as well as gays, lesbians, and other gender minorities. These were the years of identity nationalism, cultural diversity, multiculturalism.

The numerous attorneys, black and white, who had worked on race issues at the national and federal levels in the decades after the Second World War had by and large shared the dominant theoretical vernaculars of the time—legal process, law and society, liberal rights theory. At the level of grassroots organizing, in the labor movement, in community organizing networks, there were, of course, more radical voices speaking the vernaculars of black nationalism, communism, socialism, as well as a variety of religious approaches to emancipation and empowerment. But the Civil Rights Movement, as it was seen from the heights of the American legal profession, was scripted in terms familiar from earlier contributions to the Canon.

The arrival of larger numbers of minority scholars in the legal academy in the late 1970s and early 1980s coincided with a broader disenchantment with the civil rights struggle, and with many of the social welfare projects associated with the Great Society of the 1960s. Results had been mixed, and the litigation and organizational strategies that had worked in the early years were running into resistance and backlash. The election of Ronald Reagan brought an administration to power that seemed intent on reducing the power of liberal judges and of public interest lawyers more broadly.

It was in this context that a group of legal scholars began to search for new ways of thinking about race in American law. By the mid-1980s, their collective efforts had come to be known as "Critical Race Theory." No single article originated and set the agenda for Critical Race Theory in the way that many other articles in the Canon did for the approach they represent. The best overall statement of the ideas they developed remains the Introduction to a volume collecting the work of more than two dozen scholars, published in 1995 under the title *Critical Race Theory: The Key Writings That Formed the Movement*. The essay presents itself as an overview of other articles—but it was also itself a powerful intervention in the debate about what Critical Race Theory might become. Indeed, it has become something of an intellectual manifesto and road-map for understanding the broader Critical Race Theory movement.

Critical Race Theory was very much a collaborative production. No single figure—parallel perhaps to Catharine MacKinnon—emerged as the dominant voice. The Introduction was itself jointly authored by Kimberlé Crenshaw, Neil Gotanda, Gary Peller, and Kendall Thomas, and recounts the history of the collaborative struggles among critical race theorists which accompanied the emergence of their most significant intellectual contributions. At the same time, just as MacKinnon did not speak for all feminists, so critical race theory, taken collectively, has not spoken for all—or even most—of the minority scholars and lawyers active over the last decades. Lawyers and scholars interested in racial justice, like those interested in gender justice, have by and large continued to work in the theoretical vernaculars developed by others in the Canon. But like MacKinnon's work, Critical Race Theory has provided a unique and powerful theoretical contribution to American legal thought.

Precisely because Critical Race Theory has been a collaborative enterprise, it is difficult to summarize the points of agreement—certainly difficult to do so more succinctly than the Introduction included here. In several broad ways, Critical Race Theory developed themes parallel to those advanced by MacKinnon's feminism, reflecting the joint participation of their authors in the broader academic left at the time. For both, modes of analysis developed in Critical Legal Studies scholarship would provide a point of departure. Each of the four authors of the Introduction had been an active participant in Critical Legal Studies.

One way to understand MacKinnon's project would be to say that she sought to place the experience of women at the center of a critical theory of law. Critical Race Theory scholars sought to do something similar—place race at the center of their own understanding of American law. Race would, in their view, no longer be treated as one among many social issues amenable to conventional legal analysis and reform. Focusing on race distanced critical race theorists from other critically minded scholars for whom the goal was more likely to be analytic tools, methods, and theories useful in critical projects cutting across a range of issues. The feminist focus on sex and gender had raised a similar issue: were these scholars pursuing a special interest *within* the broader critical—or liberal—project, or did the focus on race and gender promise a new approach to law, legal theory, or critical practice altogether?

The authors of the Introduction described their objective in political terms— as a complex "intervention" in two different ongoing scholarly projects:

> In short, we intend to evoke a particular atmosphere in which progressive scholars of color struggled to piece together an intellectual identity and a political practice that would take the form both of a left intervention into race discourse and a race intervention into left discourse. (p. xix)

Critical Race Theory was not to be another "school of thought"—it was to be a platform of ideas and a social network for progressive scholars to intervene in ongoing discussions about racial justice—most of which were conducted in the liberal terms of the Civil Rights Movement—and in the scholarly debates of critical legal studies—for most of which race did not play a central role. Placing race at the center of the analysis would, they thought, permit both. A race-conscious scholarship would at once be a departure from the race-neutral or color-blind habits of liberal civil rights discourse, and from critical work that remained unspecific about its potential constituency or ignored the specificity of race in American society.

That said, placing race "at the center of analysis" meant a variety of things. In part, it meant demonstrating the salience of race in places where its significance had been overlooked in American law, often by mainstream and left scholars alike. Derrick Bell, generally celebrated as the originator of Critical Race Theory, focused attention on what he termed the "permanence of racism" in American society and its correlative significance for law. He reinterpreted the broad history of American constitutional law as an engagement with American racial attitudes and politics. For Bell, race had an across-the-board impact on the development of constitutional law, affecting doctrines and institutional arrangements that did not seem to be overtly concerned with race. Moreover, he argued, compromises over slavery in the early days of American constitutional history established a pattern in American political life of sacrificing the interests of blacks in compromises among divergent white interests, and through which the losers in struggles among whites could feel compensated by their systemically guaranteed superiority to blacks.

For Bell, focusing on the significance of race also meant highlighting the many ways in which American law had enforced racial differences and racial subordination. Shared in one or another way by most Critical Race Theorists, this dystopic view of American law as a vehicle for racial domination—and of white supremacy as a *legal regime* rather than as an unfortunate condition in society to be redressed by law—set Critical Race Theory apart from the liberal mainstream of American legal scholarship at the time. It was not enough to call America to return to its high constitutional traditions and ideals—that constitutional order had been conceived and developed through racial exclusion and domination.

Indeed, as minority voices began to be heard in legal scholarship, many challenged what had become firm and important commitments for liberal lawyers committed to the legacy of the Civil Rights Movement. The editors of the Introduction speak of "a deep dissatisfaction with traditional civil rights discourse" (p. xiv). Throughout his work, Bell highlights the symbolic and social significance of civil rights landmarks—from the Emancipation Proclamation through the Civil Rights Acts of the 1960s—as redemptive, but unfulfilled, promises.

It is difficult to recapture how dramatic this idea seemed in the legal academy of the 1980s. In 1976, Derrick Bell wrote critically about the work of public interest lawyers pursuing school desegregation claims after Brown—their work, he argued, often pursued values and objectives, including integration, that were shared in the elite communities of public interest lawyers with more fidelity than they pursued objectives more widely shared by their black clients, who often preferred better schools to desegregated schools. The article was immediately infamous, not so much for his analysis of the professional responsibility norms applicable in school desegregation cases, as for the fact that an elite black scholar, at the time a professor at Harvard Law School, had staked out a position to the left of—and critical of—the civil rights legacy.

In 1978, Alan Freeman, himself a founder of the Critical Legal Studies movement, published "Legitimizing Racial Discrimination Through Anti-Discrimination Law: A Critical Review of Supreme Court Doctrine," arguing that through doctrinal oscillation among competing visions of racial equality, the judiciary had de-radicalized the civil rights promise and been largely ineffective in reducing racial inequality.

Crenshaw, Gotanda, Peller, Thomas

Freeman blamed the tendency of judges to focus on the perspective of the perpetrator of racial discrimination—what did he intend, what did he do—rather than on the perspective of the victim—in what ways do legal arrangements impede his freedom. For Freeman, the result was to normalize the "conditions" of racial inequality and reinforce the notion that most Americans were innocent of participating in racial injustice—the problem lay with a small group of prejudiced individuals acting with discriminatory intent.

In 1980, Bell followed up with an assessment of Brown—and a response to Wechsler's skepticism about the neutrality of the principles underlying the Brown decision. For Bell, Brown had brought a revolution in consciousness about race, and transformed the power of blacks in American political life—but, he noted, as a result of housing patterns, white flight, and a judicial inability or unwillingness to effect the social change necessary to transform racial inequality, "today most black children attend public schools that are both racially isolated and inferior." The problem, he argued, lay in the failure to develop a convergence of interest between whites and blacks on the need for social change—most whites simply did not accept the necessity for changes in their own lives to bring about racial justice. In this broader social and political struggle, the legal frame developed by Brown may have done more harm than good. Wechsler had found it difficult to develop a "neutral principle," applicable to whites and blacks alike that would sustain Brown. For Bell, the insight had meaning on a political level—the civil rights legacy had generated no broad-based perception of common interest between whites and blacks. In 1980, it was remarkable for a leading civil rights scholar to embrace any part of Wechsler's analysis. As Bell noted, "most of us ignored [Wechsler's] observation openly and quietly raised a question about the sincerity of the observer." But Bell's reassessment of the Brown legacy would become far more common in the following years. On the fiftieth anniversary of Brown, more than two decades after Bell wrote, a list of leading black legal scholars produced books critical in one way or another of the *Brown* legacy.

For the emerging Critical Race scholars, Bell's challenge to civil rights orthodoxy was emboldening. As they looked back at the civil rights era, they found it "amazing . . . how very little actual social change was imagined to be required by the 'civil rights revolution'" (p. xvi). In their view, the

> "legislation" of the civil rights movement and its "integration" into the mainstream commonsense assumptions in the late sixties and early seventies were premised on a tragically narrow and conservative picture of the goals of racial justice and the domains of racial power.

By 1991, Derrick Bell reviewed the fate of the 1964 Civil Rights Act in the hands of an increasingly conservative judiciary and offered a kind of dystopian heuristic—given the ubiquity of discrimination in American society and the disappointments of various legislative remedies, perhaps we should give up on legislation and litigation as tools for achieving racial justice and simply license discrimination for payment of a fee, as for many other permitted social harms, and put the money to good use. For thirty years, Bell has offered a similarly provocative and often bleak assessment of the use of law as a tool for achieving racial justice, attacking the "myth" of reliance on a liberal Supreme Court, and highlighting the dark sides of all manner of legal remedies for racial discrimination, including affirmative action.

The dissatisfaction had several elements. In part, it reflected a general loss of faith in the efficacy of judicial solutions and redress, a chastened realism about what could be achieved through public interest litigation, and about the resilience of racial hierarchy in American life almost three decades after *Brown v. Board of Education*. A similar disenchantment had led law and society scholars to focus on alternate strategies—community organizing, changing the "parties rather than the rules."

This broad disenchantment with the civil rights legacy led critical race scholars to reexamine the theoretical premises of liberal reform, in a manner parallel to MacKinnon's reexamination and ultimate rejection of liberal approaches— "equality" and "special treatment"—to women's emancipation and empowerment. Like MacKinnon, critical race scholars saw subordination and power hierarchy as fundamental facets of American life, supported in numerous ways by apparently neutral legal regimes. For critical race scholars, white supremacy in America was less a matter of individual discrimination or conscious racial bias than it was an embedded system of domination. Like MacKinnon, they sought to expose that domination by attending to the perspective of the victim—asking what held the victim of racial domination back, rather than what the "perpetrator" of racism did or intended. As a result, critical race theorists, beginning with Alan Freeman, tended to see even those parts of the legal order aimed at the remediation of civil rights violations as part of the problem—part of a broader structure of racial subordination precisely because they focused attention on the lone prejudiced perpetrator of discrimination and reinforced the notion that the broader society was basically an egalitarian one, rather than offering tools for understanding and dismantling legally reinforced patterns of racial disadvantage.

Central to their departure from the liberal civil rights tradition was a critique of "color-blindness" as a norm for American society and law. Gary Peller, among others, developed the argument that a focus on color-blindness had hampered the ability of the Civil Rights Movement to address racial subordination, leading, in the words of the Introduction's editors, to the "deradicalization of racial liberation movements" (xv). The color-blindness idea, Peller argued, reinforced the sense that, absent race-conscious discrimination, the society would be egalitarian. More importantly, for Peller, the color-blindness norm delegitimated race-conscious remedies, offering defenders of the status quo a potent argument against efforts to change the background rules of social life that inhibited black progress. Peller interpreted the color-blindness ideal as part of a successful effort to demobilize and marginalize black nationalism and race-conscious antidotes for white supremacy. By equating black nationalism with intentional white discrimination, the color-blindness idea effectively cut off inquiry into the structural subordination that seemed so significant to critical race scholars more generally, and offered strong arguments for opponents of efforts to reverse racial subordination by means targeting the victims. In this, putting race at the center of the analysis meant affirming the potential for *race consciousness* in legal discourse and political practice.

Although those who developed these Critical Race Theory intuitions had been influenced by their association with the traditions of Critical Legal Studies and Feminism, they also departed quite self-consciously from each. They tended to be more ambivalent than MacKinnon about the exact nature of their theoretical ambition. They generally did not present "race consciousness" or the "victim's perspective" as promising a complete or total alternative legal theory, in the sense that MacKinnon offered Feminism as a complete theory of law and society, parallel to Marxism, rooted in "women's point of view" and the "experiences" of women discovered through consciousness raising. Nor did critical race theorists tend to treat subordination as the lexical equivalent of racial identity. Where MacKinnon often insisted that to be a woman *is* to be subordinated—and to be subordinated *sexually*—critical race theorists were more ambivalent in their presentation of the relationship between racial identity and racial subordination.

Critical race theorists described their approach to racial identity as "anti-essentialist." The word "anti-essentialism" suggested a variety of related ideas—as the word suggests, it is far easier to state the ideas about identity it rejects than those it affirms.

In one sense, anti-essentialism implied a rejection of the idea that identity, whether racial, ethnic, or sexual, was *determined* by social structures, or underlying economic and political dynamics. The authors of the Introduction explicitly reject what they term the "narrow, and frequently unsatisfying theory in which complex phenomena are reduced to and presented as a simple reflection of some underlying 'facts'" (p. xxiv). They thus challenge more conventional "theoretical accounts of racial power that explain legal and political decisions which are adverse to people of color as mere reflections of underlying white interest" (p. xxiv). This position distanced Critical Race Theory from some left or Marxist accounts of race.

Critical race theorists were equally skeptical, however, of the vision of liberals who often seemed to share a parallel idea about the relationship between law and underlying social or economic struggle, in which the "legal system is . . . simply or mainly a biased referee of social and political conflict whose origins and effects occur elsewhere." Treating law as the reflection—biased or not—of a struggle carried out elsewhere, ratifier of the gains made by winners in struggles that took place outside of and prior to law, was to make the same mistake about law that Marxists made about racial identity. Both are cultural forms, influenced by social struggle and constitutive of the terms in which social struggle occurs.

Although racial subordination was ubiquitous, critical race theorists did not present it as the core or essence of racial identity. Racial identity had some autonomy beyond being an effect of subordination. To be black was to be black—not to be subordinated as black. That came later. People of color had a shared history—but it was not all subordination, it was not a monolithic experience for all people of color, and it was not the core or essence of their identity.

Similarly, although struggles of power and interest were everywhere written into law, the law was also an autonomous site of cultural power. Law, they insisted, has a "*constitutive force*" . . . "in constructing the rules of the game, in selecting the eligible players, and in choosing the field on which the game must be played" (p. xxv). Moreover, the relationship between law and racial identity was similar—law in some sense "*constructed* race" (p. xxv). In their insistence on the socially productive role of law and identity, Critical race theorists shared more with their allies in Critical Legal Studies than with MacKinnon's Feminism. At the same time, however, they were often frustrated that white critical legal studies scholars showed so little interest in applying these jointly developed methodologies in the context of race.

Critical race scholars emphasized two further differences from Critical Legal Studies. First, a different attitude about rights—or, about the "critique of rights." The criticisms of the Civil Rights Movement developed by critical race scholars paralleled the analyses of other rights-based reform projects of the postwar era analyzed by Critical Legal Studies scholars. Indeed, both groups borrowed critical analytic moves from across the Canon of American Legal Thought to uncover the ambivalence, the deductive errors and exaggerations of reform projects based on the interpretation of legislative or judicial pronouncements. Nevertheless, critical race scholars seemed continually to suspect that their Critical Legal Studies allies would throw out the baby with the bath water. The social assertion of rights had more vitality—and had been more significant for the African American community—than was suggested by critical work analyzing the weak linguistic or logical force of arguments from rights.

Second, many critical race scholars worried that the tendency in many Critical Legal Studies circles to focus on the linguistic and socially constructed nature of identity categories would lead to an insensitivity to the hardships of living within those categories. The Introduction editors refer to this tendency in some "post-modern" critical work as "vulgar anti-essentialism"—a tendency whose "upshot . . . seemed the same" as more conventional liberal thinking:

> an abiding skepticism, if not outright disdain, toward any theoretical or political project organized around the concept of race. Where classical liberalism argued that race was irrelevant to public policy, these crits argued that race simply didn't exist. (p. xxvi)

We might understand the Critical Race Theory project as situated directly on this problem: how to affirm a race-conscious frame of analysis against liberal color-blindness, while embracing an anti-essentialist conception of racial identity. One way of engaging this issue has been to focus on the personal and political dilemmas of diverse, multiple, and overlapping identities: on conflicts within the American black community, on ambivalences within members of every social identity group about what their identity signifies, and on the conflicts posed for individuals and social movements by the fact that individuals inhabit multiple identities—black, female, young, and so on.

Kimberlé Crenshaw, among the editors of the Introduction, is most associated with this set of issues, which she explored under the term "intersectionality." The experience of black women, in her view, is not simply the sum of being black and being female; it is a unique set of conflicts and affiliations that make it easy for the experience of black women to seem invisible when law focuses on one or the other identity category. Crenshaw, writing in 1989, chronicled the ways in which anti-discrimination doctrine could overlook the oppression of black women by finding, for example, that there were sufficient (white) women and black (men) in an employment pool to make discrimination claims by black women unsustainable. Intersectionality offered one way to affirm identity consciousness without essentializing identity—there were more than one.

Nevertheless, the relationship between "race-consciousness" and "anti-essentialism" remains a central site for debate and theoretical innovation among critical race scholars. Often, they have used the reactions to popular controversies, such as the O. J. Simpson verdict or the testimony by Anita Hill during the Clarence Thomas confirmation hearings, to explore this set of issues. While seeking to rehabilitate the tradition of race nationalism, the authors of the Introduction express scorn for the "erroneous view that racial interests would be advanced by the appointment of *any African-American to the Supreme Court*." Discussing debates within the black community over the appointment of Clarence Thomas, Crenshaw, among others, made clear her conviction that unconditional support for Thomas's appointment could only be sustained by treating issues of gender subordination as irrelevant to the black community. Nevertheless, to the extent color-blindness is the only alternative to this kind of race nationalism, Crenshaw, like most critical race theorists, finds herself leaning toward race-conscious modes of understanding and activism.

Like most of the other contributors to the tradition of American legal thought, critical race theorists have taken the ideas and conflicts within the legal academy seriously. Debates over "race-consciousness" or the "critique of rights" have seemed as significant as debates about the relative priority of "policies," "purposes," and "principles" in judicial work had once seemed to Legal Process scholars. Like other legal theorists, critical race theorists write passionately about their ethical and political commitments, their vision of the good society and their hopes for American law and society. Unlike most other scholars, however, they have often done so in a very personal style, mobilizing their own experiences to illustrate their arguments, and presenting their own institutional struggles as emblematic for their theoretical propositions. In this, they share a great deal with many scholars influenced by both critical legal studies and feminism. The authors of the Introduction do so as well, recounting a history of the development of Critical Race Theory that foregrounds their own experiences as law students and teachers. Other critical race theorists—perhaps most famously, Patricia Williams—have expanded this narrative approach to a wide range of legal and political issues. In the same spirit, critical race theorists have mobilized a range of other innovative scholarly styles, including fictional narrative and other literary devices to develop and present their ideas.

Critical Race Theory remains a relatively young contribution to American legal thought—barely twenty years old. Although scholars have sought to apply its central ideas in a variety of different legal fields, it is too early to be confident about its impact on legal reasoning. The idea that there could be a race-conscious alternative to the liberal civil rights tradition, and the fact that there exist creative minority voices within the American legal academy developing the analytic tools to place race at the center of legal analysis, have already energized and mobilized a generation of law students and young legal scholars. The future of Critical Race Theory, like that of the Canon as a whole, remains to be written.

DAVID KENNEDY

BIBLIOGRAPHY

Anthologies of Critical Race Theory Writing

Kimberlé Crenshaw, Neil Gotanda, Gary Peller, and Kendall Thomas, *Critical Race Theory: The Key Writings that Formed the Movement* (New York: The New Press: 1995), whose introduction is included here, provides the broadest access to works in the field.

Richard Delgado *Critical Race Theory: The Cutting Edge.* (Philadelphia: Temple University Press, 1995); 2d ed., Richard Delgado and Jean Stefancic (2000).

Francisco Valdes, Jerome McCristal Culp, and Angela Harris, ed., *Crossroads, Directions, and a New Critical Race Theory* (Philadelphia: Temple University Press, 2002).

Useful annotated bibliographies include:

Richard Delgado and Jean Stefancic, "Critical Race Theory: An Annotated Bibliography," 79 *Virginia Law Review 461* (1993).

Richard Delgado and Jean Stafancic, *Critical Race Theory: An Introduction* (New York: New York University Press, 2001).

A number of critical race theorists have written accounts of the movement's development and major ideas.

Kimberlé Crenshaw updates the story begun in the Introduction and responds to criticism of the Critical Race Theory movement in Kimberlé Crenshaw, "The First Decade: Critical Reflections, or 'A Foot in the Closing Door'" 49 *UCLA Law Review* 1343 (2001–2).

Crenshaw has also taped an interview with Canon editor William Fisher developing her account of the Critical Race Theory tradition. The interview is available at HTTP://www.cyber.law.HARVARD.EDU.

Sumi Cho and Robert Westley offer an account that foregrounds the social and political context within which Critical Race Theory developed, focusing on the role of student activism and other "actual resistance movements" rather than on the "agency of individual scholars." See Sumi Cho and Robert Westley, "Performing Latcrit: Critical Race Coalitions: Key Movements that Performed the Theory," 33 *U.C. Davis Law Review* 1377 (Summer 2000).

For an interesting account of the effort to introduce a "concentration" in Critical Race Studies at the UCLA law school, see Cheryl Harris, "Critical Race Studies: An Introduction," 49 *UCLA Law Review* 1215 (2001–2).

Richard Delgado has written forcefully against what he sees as a split from the "realist" and "materialist" roots of Critical Race Theory in favor of "idealist approaches and discourse analysis"; see Richard Delgado, "Book Review Essay, Crossroads and Blind Alleys: A Critical Examination of Recent Writing About Race," 82 *Texas Law Review* 121 (November 2002). He concludes that "the volume of Critical Race Theory should consider that race is not merely a matter for abstract analysis, but for struggle" (p. 151). See also Richard Delgado, "Two Ways to Think About Race: Reflections on the Id, the Ego, and Other Reformist Theories of Equal Protection," 89 *Georgetown Law Journal* 2279 (2001).

Ken Mack has chronicled the salience of alternative minority voices during the civil rights era in Ken Mack, "Rethinking Civil Rights Lawyering and Politics in the Era Before Brown," 115 *Yale Law Journal* 256 (2005).

The Critical Race Theory movement has experienced a number of divisions, and has spawned a number of spin-off efforts to develop the Critical Race Theory approach to other racial, ethnic, and sexual forms of subordination. The most significant have been the LATCRIT movement and the development of Queer Theory in the legal academy.

For an analysis of the debate between Critical Legal Studies and Critical Race Theory over the significance of "rights," see Daria Roithmayr, "Left (Over) Rights," 2001 5 *Law Text Culture* 407, focusing particularly on the significance of Duncan Kennedy's *Critique of Adjudication: Fin de Siecle* (Cambridge, Mass.: Harvard University Press, 1997).

Significant Articles and Books

There is now an enormous corpus of Critical Race Theory writings. Many civil rights activists and judicial figures have contributed to retrospective, and often bitter, evaluations of American law and race, including during the civil rights era. Perhaps most well known is Thurgood Marshall's harsh article in the *Harvard Law Review* on the occasion of the bicentennial. "Reflections on the Bicentennial of the United States Constitution," 101 *Harvard Law Review* 1 (1987).

Our take on the most significant scholarly articles, several of which might also have been candidates for canonical treatment, would include:

DERRICK BELL

"Serving Two Masters: Integration Ideals and Client Interests in School Desegregation Litigation," 85 *Yale Law Journal* 470 (1975–76).

"*Brown v. Board of Education* and the Interest Convergence Dilemma," 93 *Harvard Law Review* 518 (1980).

"An American Fairy Tale: The Income Related Neutralization of Race Law Precedent," 18 *Suffolk University Law Review* 331 (1984).

And We Are Not Saved: The Elusive Quest for Racial Justice (New York: Basic Books, 1987).

"Foreword: The Final Civil Rights Act," 79 *California Law Review* 597 (1991).

Derrick Bell, *Faces at the Bottom of the Well: The Permanence of Racism* (New York: Basic Books, 1992).

"Racial Realism," 24 *Connecticut Law Review* 363 (1992).

Bell reflects on his own life and career in *Ethical Ambition: Living a Life of Meaning and Worth* (New York : BLOOMSBURY, 2002).

Race Racism and American Law (Boston: Little, Brown, 1973; 5th edition 2004).

Works by the Authors of the Introduction

KIMBERLÉ CRENSHAW

"Race, Reform and Retrenchment: Transformation and Legitimation in Antidiscrimination Law," 101 *Harvard Law Review* 1331 (1988).

"Demarginalizing the Intersection of Race and Sex: A Black Feminist Critique of Antidiscrimination Doctrine, Feminist Theory and Antiracist Politics," 1989 *University of Chicago Legal Forum* 139.

"Foreword: Toward a Race-Conscious Pedagogy in Legal Education," *National Black Law Journal* 11(1): 1–14 (1989).

"Mapping the Margins: Intersectionality, Identity Politics and Violence Against Women of Color," 43 *Stanford Law Review* 1241 (1990–91).

(with Gary Peller), "Real Time/ Real Justice," 70 *Denver University Law Review* 283 (1992–93).

(with Gary Peller), "The Contradictions of Mainstream Constitutional Theory," 45 *UCLA Law Review* 1683 (1997–98).

NEIL GOTANDA

"Other Non-Whites" in American Legal History: A Review of *Justice at War*, 85 *Columbia Law Review* 1186 (1985).

"A Critique of 'Our Constitution Is Color-Blind,'" 44 *Stanford Law Review* 1 (1991).

"Race-Consciousness," 1990 *Duke Law Journal* 758.

(with Kimberlé Crenshaw), "Real Time/ Real Justice," 70 *Denver University Law Review* 283 (1992–93).

(with Kimberlé Crenshaw), "The Contradictions of Mainstream Constitutional Theory," 45 *UCLA Law Review* 1683 (1997–98).

KENDALL THOMAS

"A House Divided Against Itself: A Comment on Mastery, Slavery, and Emancipation," 10 *Cardozo Law Review* 1481 (1989).

Kendall Thomas, "Rouge et Noir Reread: A Popular Constitutional History of the Angelo Herndon Case," 65 *Southern California Law Review* 2599 (1992).

OTHER LEADING WRITINGS

Regina Austin, "Sapphire Bound!" 1989 *Wisconsin Law Review* 539.

Richard Delgado, "The Imperial Scholar: Reflections on a Review of Civil Rights Literature," 132 *University of Pennsylvania Law Review* 561 (1984).

Richard Delgado, "Rodrigo's Chronicle," 101 *Yale Law Journal* 1357 (1992).

Richard Delgado and Jean Stefancic, eds., *The Latino/a Condition: A Critical Reader* (New York: New York University Press, 1998).

Richard Ford, "The Boundaries of Race: Political Geography in Legal Analysis," 107 *Harvard Law Review* 1891 (1994).

Alan Freeman, "Legitimizing Racial Discrimination through Antidiscrimination Law: A Critical Review of Supreme Court Doctrine," 62 *Minnesota Law Review* 1049 (1978).

Alan Freeman, "Antidiscrimination Law: The View from 1989," 64 *Tulane Law Review* 1407 (1990).

Carole Goldberg, "Descent into Race," 49 *UCLA Law Review* 1373 (2001–02).

Linda Greene, "Race in the 21st Century: Equality Through Law?" 64 *Tulane Law Review* 1515 (1990).

Lani Guinier, "The Triumph of Tokenism: The Voting Rights Act and the Theory of Black Electoral Success," 89 *Michigan Law Review* 1077 (1991).

Lani Guinier, *The Miner's Canary: Enlisting Race, Resisting Power, Transforming Democracy* (Cambridge, Mass. : Harvard University Press, 2003).

Angela Harris, "Race and Essentialism in Feminist Legal Theory," 42 *Stanford Law Review* 581 (1990).

Cheryl Harris, "Whiteness as Property," 106 *Harvard Law Review* 1709 (1993).

Duncan Kennedy, "A Cultural Pluralist Case for Affirmative Action in Legal Academia," 1990 *Duke Law Journal* 705 (1990).

Charles Lawrence, "The Id, the Ego, and Equal Protection: Reckoning with Unconscious Racism," 39 *Stanford Law Review* 317 (1987).

Gerald Lopez, "The Idea of a Constitution in the Chicano Tradition," 37 *Journal of Legal Education* 162 (1987).

Mari Matsuda, "Looking to the Bottom: Critical Legal Studies and Reparations," 22 *Harvard Civil Rights–Cilvil Liberties Law Review* 323 (1987).

Mari Matsuda, "Pragmatism Modified and the False Consciousness Problem," 63 *Southern California Law Review* 1763 (1990).

Joseph Singer, "Property and Coercion in Federal Indian Law: The Conflict Between Critical and Complacent Pragmatism," 63 *Southern California Law Review* 1821 (1990).

Giradeau Spann, "Pure Politics," 88 *Michigan Law Review* 1971 (1990).

Gerald Torres, "Critical Race Theory: The Decline of the Universalist Ideal and the Hope of Plural Justice—Some Observations and Questions of an Emerging Phenomenon," 75 *Minnesota Law Review* 993 (1991).

Gerald Torres, "Local Knowledge, Local Color: Critical Legal Studies and The Law of Race Relations," 25 *San Diego Law Review* 1043 (1988).

Gerald Torres and Kathryn Milum, "Translating "Yonnondio" by Precedent and Evidence: The Mashpee Indian Case," 1990 *Duke Law Journal* 625.

Francisco Valdes, "Queers, Sissies, Dykes and Tomboys: Deconstructing the Conflation of 'Sex,' 'Gender,' and 'Sexual Orientation,' in Euro-American Law and Society," 83 *California Law Review* 1 (1995).

Patricia Williams, *The Alchemy of Race and Rights* (Cambridge, Mass.: Harvard University Press, 1991).

Robert Williams, *The American Indian in Western Legal Thought: The Discourses of Conquest* (New York : Oxford University Press, 1990).

Robert Williams, "Columbus's Legacy: The Rehnquist Court's Perpetuation of European Cultural Racism Against American Indian Tribes," 39 *Federal Business News and Journal* 358 (1992).

Commentaries

Kenneth Karst wrote a useful comparative review of the two leading anthologies of Critical Race Theory writings, as well as of Richard Delgado's *The Rodrigo Chronicles*. See Kenneth Karst, "Book Review: Integration Success Story: A Review of Three Recent Books on Critical Race Theory," 69 *Southern California Law Review* 1781 (1006). Karst highlights the distinction between Critical Race scholars and Critical Legal Studies, praising critical race theory for a range of proposals for legal reform produced by scholars "who have not abandoned the civil rights quest," including:

> Kimberle Crenshaw's call for recognition in Title VII cases of the particular kinds of discrimination that black women confront at the "intersection" of racial discrimination and sex discrimination; Charles Lawrence's call for a reconsideration of the "purpose" requirement for finding racial discrimination in equal protection cases; Richard Delgado's proposal that racial insults be redressed by tort damages; Mari Matsuda's argument that accent discrimination should be redressed under Title VII; and Lani Guinier's argument for a strong form of group representation principle as the proper interpretation of the Voting Rights Act of 1965. All these proposals are argued within the framework of what a CLS writer might call liberal legalism. (Karst at 1786)

For a critique of Derrick Bell, Mari Matsuda, Richard Delgado, and others for promoting a race-conscious scholarship, see Randy Kennedy, "Racial Critiques of Legal Academia," 102 *Harvard Law Review* 1745 (1989).

Richard Delgago responded to commentary on Critical Race Theory by Scott Brewer and Randall Kennedy in "Brewer's Plea: Critical Thoughts on Common Cause," 44 *Vanderbilt Law Review* 1 (1991), and in "Mindset and Metaphor," 103 *Harvard Law Review* 1872 (1990).

KIMBERLÉ CRENSHAW, NEIL GOTANDA, GARY PELLER,
AND KENDALL THOMAS, EDS.

"Introduction," *Critical Race Theory: The Key Writings that Formed the Movement*

(New Press, May 1996)

This volume offers a representative, though by no means exhaustive, compilation of the growing body of legal scholarship known as Critical Race Theory (CRT). As we conceive it, Critical Race Theory embraces a movement of left scholars, most of them scholars of color, situated in law schools, whose work challenges the ways in which race and racial power are constructed and represented in American legal culture and, more generally, in American society as a whole. In assembling and editing these essays, we have tried both to provide a sense of the intellectual genesis of this project and to map the main methodological directions that Critical Race Theory has taken since its inception. Toward these ends, the essays in the first few parts are arranged roughly in the chronological order of their publication. The remaining parts, however, are devoted to the most important methodological strands of Critical Race Theory today. We have chosen to present the substance of the original essays rather than small portions of a greater number of works, in the interest of providing the reader with texts that retain as much of their complexity, context, and nuance as possible.

As these writings demonstrate, there is no canonical set of doctrines or methodologies to which we all subscribe. Although Critical Race scholarship differs in object, argument, accent, and emphasis, it is nevertheless unified by two common interests. The first is to understand how a regime of white supremacy and its subordination of people of color have been created and maintained in America, and, in particular, to examine the relationship between that social structure and professed ideals such as "the rule of law" and "equal protection." The second is a desire not merely to understand the vexed bond between law and racial power but to *change* it. The essays gathered here thus share an ethical commitment to human liberation—even if we reject conventional notions of what such a conception means, and though we often disagree, even among ourselves, over its specific direction.

This ethical aspiration finds its most obvious concrete expression in the pursuit of engaged, even adversarial, scholarship. The writings in this collaboration may be read as contributions to what Edward Said has called "antithetical knowledge," the development of counter-accounts of social reality by subversive and subaltern elements of the reigning order. Critical Race Theory—like the Critical Legal Studies movement with which we are often allied—rejects the prevailing orthodoxy that scholarship should be or could be "neutral" and "objective." We believe that legal scholarship about race in America can never be written from a distance of detachment or with an attitude of objectivity. To the extent that racial power is exercised legally and ideologically, legal scholarship about race is an important site for the construction of that power, and thus is always a factor, if "only" ideologically, in the economy of racial power itself. To use a phrase from the existentialist tradition, there is "no exit"—no scholarly perch outside the social dynamics of racial power from which merely to observe and analyze. Scholarship—the formal production, identification, and organization of what will be called "knowledge"—is inevitably political. Each of the texts in this volume seeks in its own way not simply to explicate but also to intervene in the ideological contestation of race in America, and to create new, oppositionist accounts of race.

The aspect of our work which most markedly distinguishes it from conventional liberal and conservative legal scholarship about race and inequality is a deep dissatisfaction with traditional civil rights discourse. As several of the authors in this collection demonstrate, the reigning contemporary American ideologies about race were built in the sixties and seventies around an implicit social compact. This compact held that racial power and racial justice would be understood in very particular ways. Racial justice was embraced in the American mainstream in terms that excluded radical or fundamental challenges to status quo institutional practices in American society by treating the exercise of racial power as rare and aberrational rather than as systemic and ingrained. The construction of "racism" from what Alan Freeman terms the "perpetrator perspective" restrictively conceived racism as an intentional, albeit irrational, deviation by a conscious wrongdoer from otherwise neutral, rational, and just ways of distributing jobs, power, prestige, and wealth. The adoption of this perspective allowed a broad cultural mainstream both explicitly to acknowledge the fact of racism and, simultaneously, to insist on its irregular occurrence and limited significance. As Freeman concludes, liberal race reform thus served to legitimize the basic myths of American meritocracy.

In Gary Peller's depiction, this mainstream civil rights discourse on "race relations" was constructed in this way partly as a defense against the more radical ideologies of racial liberation presented by the Black Nationalist and Black Consciousness movements of the sixties and early seventies, and their less visible but intellectually subversive scholarly presentations by people such as James Turner, now a teacher in black studies at Cornell. In the construction of "racism" as the irrational and backward bias of believing that someone's race is important, the American cultural mainstream neatly linked the black left to the white racist right: according to this quickly coalesced consensus, because race-consciousness characterized both white supremacists and black nationalists, it followed that both were racists. The resulting "center" of cultural common sense thus rested on the exclusion of virtually the entire domain of progressive thinking about race within colored communities. With its explicit embrace of race-consciousness, Critical Race Theory aims to reexamine the terms by which race and racism have been negotiated in American consciousness, and to recover and revitalize the radical tradition of race-consciousness among African-Americans and other peoples of color—a tradition that was discarded when integration, assimilation and the ideal of colorblindness became the official norms of racial enlightenment.

The image of a "traditional civil rights discourse" refers to the constellation of ideas about racial power and social transformation that were constructed partly by, and partly as a defense against, the mass mobilization of social energy and popular imagination in the civil rights movements of the late fifties and sixties. To those who participated in the civil rights movements firsthand—say, as part of the street and body politics engaged in by Reverend Martin Luther King, Jr.'s cadres in town after town across the South—the fact that they were part of a deeply subversive movement of mass resistance and social transformation was obvious. Our opposition to traditional civil rights discourse is neither a criticism of the civil rights movement nor an attempt to diminish its significance. On the contrary, as Anthony Cook's radical reading of King's theology and social theory makes explicit, we draw much of our inspiration and sense of direction from that courageous, brilliantly conceived, spiritually inspired, and ultimately transformative mass action.

Of course, colored people made important social gains through civil rights reform, as did American society generally: in fact, but for the civil rights movements' victories against racial exclusion, this volume and the Critical Race Theory movement generally could not have been taught at mainstream law schools. The law's incorporation of what several authors here call "formal equality" (the prohibition against explicit racial exclusion, like "whites only" signs) marks a decidedly progressive moment in U.S. political and social history. However, the fact that civil rights advocates met with some success in the nation's courts and legislatures ought not obscure the central role the American legal order played in the deradicalization of racial liberation movements. Along with the suppression of explicit white racism (the widely celebrated aim of civil rights reform), the dominant legal conception of racism as a discrete and identifiable act of "prejudice based on skin color" placed virtually the entire range of everyday social practices in America—social practices developed and maintained throughout the period of formal American apartheid—beyond the scope of critical examination or legal remediation.

The affirmative action debate, which is discussed in several essays in this volume, provides a vivid example of what we mean. From its inception, mainstream legal thinking in the U.S. has been characterized by a curiously constricted understanding of race and power. Within this cramped conception of racial domination, the evil of racism exists when—and only when—one can point to specific, discrete acts of racial discrimination, which is in turn narrowly defined as decision-making based on the irrational and irrelevant attribute of race. Given this essentially negative, indeed, dismissive view of racial identity and its social meanings, it was not surprising that mainstream legal thought came to embrace the ideal of "color-blindness" as the dominant moral compass of social enlightenment about race. Mainstream legal argument regarding "race relations" typically defended its position by appropriating Dr. King's injunction that a person should be judged "by the content of his character rather than the color of his skin" and wedding it to the regnant ideologies of equal opportunity and American meritocracy. Faced with this state of affairs, liberal proponents of affirmative action in legal and policy arenas—who had just successfully won the formal adoption of basic antidiscrimination norms—soon found themselves in a completely defensive ideological posture. Affirmative action requires the use of race as a socially significant category of perception and representation, but the deepest elements of mainstream civil rights ideology had come to identify such race-consciousness as racism itself. Indeed, the problem here was not simply political and strategic: the predominant legal representation of racism as the mere recognition of race matched the "personal" views of many liberals themselves, creating for them a contradiction in their hearts as well as their words.

Liberal antidiscrimination proponents proposed various ways to reconcile this contradiction: they characterized affirmative action as a merely "exceptional" remedy for past injustice, a temporary tool to be used only until equal opportunity is achieved or a default mechanism for reaching discrimination that could not be proved directly. Separate but related liberal defenses of affirmative action hold that its beneficiaries have suffered from "deprived" backgrounds that require limited special consideration in the otherwise fully rational and unbiased competition for social goods, or that affirmative action promotes social "diversity," a value which in the liberal vision is independent of, perhaps even at odds with, equality of opportunity or meritocracy.

The poverty of the liberal imagination is belied by the very fact that liberal theories of affirmative action are framed in such defensive terms, and so clearly shaped by the felt need to justify this perceived departure from purportedly objective findings of "merit" (or the lack thereof). These apologetic strategies testify to the deeper ways civil rights reformism has helped to legitimize the very social practices—in employment offices and admissions departments—that were originally targeted for reform. By constructing "discrimination" as a deviation from otherwise legitimate selection processes, liberal race rhetoric affirms the underlying ideology of just desserts, even as it reluctantly tolerates limited exceptions to meritocratic mythology. Despite their disagreements about affirmative action, liberals and conservatives who embrace dominant civil rights discourse treat the category of merit itself as neutral and impersonal, outside of social power and unconnected to systems of racial privilege. Rather than engaging in a broad-scale inquiry into why jobs, wealth, education, and power are distributed as they are, mainstream civil rights discourse suggests that once the irrational biases of race-consciousness are eradicated, everyone will be treated fairly, as equal competitors in a regime of equal opportunity.

What we find most amazing about this ideological structure in retrospect is how very little actual social change was imagined to be required by "the civil rights revolution." One might have expected a huge controversy over the dramatic social transformation necessary to eradicate the regime of American apartheid. By and large, however, the very same whites who administered explicit policies of segregation and racial domination kept their jobs as decision makers in employment offices of companies, admissions offices of schools, lending offices of banks, and so on. In institution after institution, progressive reformers found themselves struggling over the implementation of integrationist policy with the former administrators of segregation who soon regrouped as an old guard "concerned" over the deterioration of "standards."

The continuity of institutional authority between the segregationist and civil rights regimes is only part of the story. Even more dramatic, the same criteria for defining "qualifications" and "merit" used during the period of explicit racial exclusion continued to be used, so long as they were not directly "racial." Racism was identified only with the outright formal exclusion of people of color; it was simply assumed that the whole rest of the culture, and the de facto segregation of schools, work places, and neighborhoods, would remain the same. The sheer taken-for-grantedness of this way of thinking would pose a formidable and practically insurmountable obstacle. Having rejected race-consciousness in toto, there was no conceptual basis from which to identify the cultural and ethnic character of mainstream American institutions; they were thus deemed to be racially and culturally neutral. As a consequence, the deeply transformative potential of the civil rights movement's interrogation of racial power was successfully aborted as a piece of mainstream American ideology.

Crenshaw, Gotanda, Peller, Thomas

Within the predominantly white law school culture where most of the authors represented in this volume spend professional time, the law's "embrace" of civil rights in the Warren Court era is proclaimed as the very hallmark of justice under the rule of law. In our view, the "legislation" of the civil rights movement and its "integration" into the mainstream commonsense assumptions in the late sixties and early seventies were premised on a tragically narrow and conservative picture of the goals of racial justice and the domains of racial power. In the balance of this introduction, we describe as matters both of institutional politics and intellectual inquiry how we have come to these kinds of conclusions.

In his essay on the Angelo Herndon case, Kendall Thomas describes and pursues a central project of Critical Race scholarship: the use of critical historical method to show that the contemporary structure of civil rights rhetoric is not the natural or inevitable meaning of racial justice but, instead, a collection of strategies and discourses born of and deployed in particular political, cultural, and institutional conflicts and negotiations. Our goal here is similar. We hope to situate the strategies and discourses of Critical Race Theory within the broader intellectual and social currents from which we write, as well as within the specific work place and institutional positions where we are located and from which we struggle.

The emergence of Critical Race Theory in the eighties, we believe, marks an important point in the history of racial politics in the legal academy and, we hope, in the broader conversation about race and racism in the nation as a whole. As we experienced it, mostly as law students or beginning law professors, the boundaries of "acceptable" race discourse had become suddenly narrowed, in the years from the late sixties to the late seventies and early eighties, both in legal institutions and in American culture more generally. In the law schools we attended, there were definite liberal and conservative camps of scholars and students. While the debate in which these camps engaged were clearly important—for example, how the law should define and identify illegal racial power—the reigning discourse seemed, at least to us, ideologically impoverished and technocratic.

In constitutional law, for example, it was well settled that government-sanctioned racial discrimination was prohibited, and that legally enforced segregation constituted such discrimination. That victory was secured in *Brown v. Board of Education* and its progeny. In the language of the Fourteenth Amendment, race is a "suspect classification" which demands judicial strict scrutiny. "Race relations" thus represent an exception to the general deference that mainstream constitutional theory accords democratically elected institutions. Racial classifications violate the equal protection clause unless they both serve a compelling governmental interest and further, are no broader than necessary to achieve that goal. Within the conceptual boundaries of these legal doctrines, mainstream scholars debated whether discrimination should be defined only as intentional government action . . . or whether the tort-like "de facto" test should be used when government actions had predictable, racially skewed results . . . or whether the racial categories implicit in affirmative action policy should be legally equivalent to those used to burden people of color and therefore also be subject to strict scrutiny . . . and then whether remedying past social discrimination was a sufficiently compelling and determinate goal to survive strict scrutiny . . . and so on.

In all these debates we identified, of course, with the liberals against the intent requirement established in *Washington v. Davis*, the affirmative action limitations of *Bakke* (and later *Croson*), the curtailment of the "state action" doctrine resulting in the limitation of sites where constitutional antidiscrimination norms would apply, and so on. Yet the whole discourse seemed to assume away the fundamental problem of racial subordination whose examination was at the center of the work so many of us had spent our college years pursuing in Afro-American studies departments, community mobilizations, student activism, and the like.

The fact that affirmative action was seen as such a "dilemma" or a "necessary evil" was one symptom of the ultimately conservative character of even "liberal" mainstream race discourse. More generally, though, liberals and conservatives seemed to see the issues of race and law from within the same structure of analysis—namely, a policy that legal rationality could identify and eradicate the biases of raceconsciousness in social decision-making. Liberals and conservatives as a general matter differed over the degree to which racial bias was a fact of American life: liberals argued that bias was widespread where conservatives insisted it was not; liberals supported a disparate effects test for identifying discrimination, where conservatives advocated a more restricted intent requirement; liberals wanted an expanded state action requirement, whereas conservatives wanted a narrow one. The respective visions of the two factions differed only in scope: they defined and constructed "racism" the same way, as the opposite of color-blindness.

In any event, however compelling the liberal vision of achieving racial justice through legal reform overseen by a sympathetic judiciary may have been in the sixties and early seventies, the breakdown of the national consensus for the use of law as an instrument for racial redistribution rendered the vision far less capable of appearing even merely pragmatic. By the late seventies, traditional civil rights lawyers found themselves fighting, and losing, rearguard attacks on the limited victories they had only just achieved in the prior decade, particularly with respect to affirmative action and legal requirements for the kinds of evidence required to prove illicit discrimination. An increasingly conservative judiciary made it clear that the age of ever expanding progressive law reform was over.

At the same time that these events were unfolding, a predominantly white left emerged on the law school scene in the late seventies, a development which played a central role in the genesis of Critical Race Theory. Organized by a collection of neo-Marxist intellectuals, former New Left activists, ex-counterculturalists, and other varieties of oppositionists in law schools, the Conference on Critical Legal Studies established itself as a network of openly leftist law teachers, students, and practitioners committed to exposing and challenging the ways American law served to legitimize an oppressive social order. Like the later experience of Critical Race writers vis-à-vis race scholarship, "crits" found themselves frustrated with the presuppositions of the conventional scholarly legal discourse: they opposed not only conservative legal work but also the dominant liberal varieties. Crits contended that liberal and conservative legal scholarship operated in the narrow ideological channel within which law was understood as qualitatively different from politics. The faith of liberal lawyers in the gradual reform of American law through the victory of the superior rationality of progressive ideas depended on a belief in the central ideological myth of the law/politics distinction, namely, that legal institutions employ a rational, apolitical, and neutral discourse with which to mediate the exercise of social power. This, in essence, is the role of law as understood by liberal political theory. Yet politics was embedded in the very doctrinal categories with which law organized and represented social reality. Thus the deeply political character of law was obscured in one way by the obsession of mainstream legal scholarship with technical discussions about standing, jurisdiction and procedure; and the political character of judicial decision-making was denied in another way through the reigning assumptions that legal decision-making was—or could be—determined by preexisting legal rules, standards, and policies, all of which were applied according to professional craft standards encapsulated in the idea of "reasoned elaboration." Law was, in the conventional wisdom, distinguished from politics because politics was open-ended, subjective, discretionary, and ideological, whereas law was determinate, objective, bounded, and neutral.

This conception of law as rational, apolitical, and technical operated as an institutional regulative principle, defining what was legitimate and illegitimate to pursue in legal scholarship, and symbolically defining the professional, businesslike culture of day-to-day life in mainstream law schools. This generally centrist legal culture characterized the entire post-war period in legal education, with virtually no organized dissent. Its intellectual and ideological premises had not been seriously challenged since the Legal Realist movement of the twenties and thirties—a body of scholarship that mainstream scholars ritually honored for the critique of the "formalism" of turn-of-the-century legal discourse but marginalized as having "gone too far" in its critique of the very possibility of a rule of law. Writing during the so-called liberty of contract period (characterized by the Supreme Court's invalidation of labor reform legislation on the grounds that it violated the "liberty" of workers and owners to contract with each other over terms of employment) the legal realists set out to show that the purportedly neutral and objective legal interpretation of the period was really based on politics, on what Oliver Wendell Holmes called the "hidden and often inarticulate judgments of social policy."

The crits unearthed much of the Legal Realist work that mainstream legal scholars had ignored for decades, and they found the intellectual and theoretical basis for launching a fullscale critique of the role of law in helping to rationalize an unjust social order. While the Realist critique of American law's pretensions to neutrality and rationality was geared toward the right-wing libertarianism of an "Old Order" of jurists, crits redirected it at the depoliticized and technocratic assumptions of legal education and scholarship in the seventies. Moreover, in the sixties tradition from which many of them had come, they extended the intellectual and ideological conflict they engendered to the law school culture to which it was linked.

By the late seventies, Critical Legal Studies existed in a swirl of formative energy, cultural insurgency, and organizing momentum: It had established itself as a politically, philosophically, and methodologically eclectic but intellectually sophisticated and ideologically left movement in legal academia, and its conferences had begun to attract hundreds of progressive law teachers, students, and lawyers; even mainstream law reviews were featuring critical work that reinterpreted whole doctrinal areas of law from an explicitly ideological motivation. Moreover, in viewing law schools as work-places, and thus as organizing sites for political resistance, "CLSers" actively recruited students and leftleaning law teachers from around the country to engage in the construction of left legal scholarship and law school transformation. CLS quickly became the organizing hub for a huge burst of left legal scholarly production and for various oppositional political challenges in law school institutional life. Several left scholars of color identified with the movement, and, most important for the eventual genesis of

Critical Race Theory a few years later, CLS succeeded in at least one aspect of its frontal assault on the depoliticized character of legal education. By the late seventies, explicitly right-wing legal scholarship had developed its own critique of the conventional assumptions, just as the national mood turned to the right with the election of Ronald Reagan. The law school as an institution was, by then, an obvious site for ideological contestation as the apolitical pretensions of the "nonideological" center began to disintegrate.

Critical Race Theory emerged in the interstices of this political and institutional dynamic. Critical Race Theory thus represents an attempt to inhabit and expand the space between two very different intellectual and ideological formations. Critical Race Theory sought to stage a simultaneous encounter with the exhausted vision of reformist civil rights scholarship, on the one hand, and the emergent critique of left legal scholarship on the other. Critical Race Theory's engagement with the discourse of civil rights reform stemmed directly from our lived experience as students and teachers in the nation's law schools. We both saw and suffered the concrete consequences that followed from liberal legal thinkers' failure to address the constrictive role that racial ideology plays in the composition and culture of American institutions, including the American law school. Our engagement with progressive-left legal academics stemmed from our sense that their focus on legal ideology, legal scholarship and the politics of the American law school provided a language and a practice for viewing the institutions in which we studied and worked both as sites of and targets for our developing critique of law, racism, and social power.

In identifying the liberal civil rights tradition and the Critical Legal Studies movement as key factors in the emergence of Critical Race Theory, we do not mean to offer an oversimplified genealogy in which Critical Race Theory appears as a simple hybrid of the two. We view liberal civil rights scholarship and the work of the critical legal theorists not so much as rudimentary components of Critical Race Theory, but as elements in the conditions of its possibility. In short, we intend to evoke a particular atmosphere in which progressive scholars of color struggled to piece together an intellectual identity and a political practice that would take the form both of a left intervention into race discourse and a race intervention into left discourse. To better capture the dynamics of these trajectories, we now turn to two key institutional events in the development of Critical Race Theory as a movement. The first is the student protest, boycott, and organization of an alternative course on race and law at Harvard Law School in 1981—an event that highlights the significance of Derrick Bell and the Critical Legal Studies movement to the ultimate development of Critical Race Theory, and symbolizes Critical Race Theory's oppositional posture vis-à-vis the liberal mainstream. The second is the 1987 Critical Legal Studies National Conference on silence and race, which marked the genesis of an intellectually distinctive critical account of race on terms set forth by raceconscious scholars of color, and the terms of contestation and coalition with CLS.

As Richard Delgado states in "The Imperial Scholar," quite bluntly, the study of civil rights and antidiscrimination law in the mainstream law schools in which we found ourselves in the eighties was dominated by a group consisting almost entirely of white male constitutional law professors. Derrick Bell was one of the few exceptions; he went to Harvard after a distinguished record as a litigator in the civil rights movement, becoming one of only two African-American professors on the large Harvard faculty. In his course and book *Race, and Racism and*

American Law, Bell developed and taught legal doctrine from a race-conscious viewpoint. Implicitly repudiating the reigning idea of the color-blindness of law, pedagogy, and scholarship, he used racial politics rather than the formal structure of legal doctrine as the organizing concept for scholarly study.

It is important to understand the centrality of Bell's coursebook and his opposition to the traditional liberal approach to racism for the eventual development of the Critical Race Theory movement. A symbol of his influence is his inclusion as the first page of his book of a photograph of Thomas Smith and John Carlos accepting their Olympic trophies at the 1968 Mexico City Summer Games. In the foreground are balding white men in suits, apparently Olympic officials of some kind; rising behind them are Smith and Carlos, standing on the raised platforms in sleek warmup suits, at the height of their competitive achievement. In one hand, the victorious athletes hold their gold and silver medals; Smith and Carlos defiantly hold their other hand over their heads in the clinched fist of the Black Power salute. This symbolic action, staged during the playing of the National Anthem, spawned an enormous controversy in the United States; patriots charged that Smith and Carlos embarrassed the country and privileged their racial identity over their more important identity as Americans.

To those of us who were then law students and beginning law teachers, Bell's inclusion of the Smith-Carlos photograph as a visual introduction to his law school casebook suggested a link between his work and the Black Power movements that most of us "really" identified with, whose political insights and aspirations went far beyond what could be articulated in the reigning language of the legal profession and the legal studies we were pursuing. Although we could not then fully articulate the nature and basis of this connection, we were able to recognize that Derrick Bell's position within legal study bore a family resemblance to the oppositional stance that Smith and Carlos had taken in Mexico City. Just as Carlos and Smith participated on behalf of their nation in the Olympic competition, Bell had chosen to enter the arena of American legal scholarship instead of eschewing it and taking the path of total separation. Similarly, just as Carlos and Smith refused to allow American nationalism to subsume their racial identity, Bell insisted on placing race at the center of his intellectual inquiry rather than marginalizing it as a subclassification under the formal rubric of this or that legal doctrine. In a subtle way, Bell's position within the legal academy—an arena that defined itself within the conventional legal discourse as neutral to race—was akin to putting up his fist in the black power salute.

As his articles in the first part of this volume demonstrate, Bell provided some of the earliest theoretical alternatives to the dominant civil rights vision we have described. In the face of the hegemony of racial integration as the ideal of reform in the seventies, he argued in "Serving Two Masters," the essay that opens this collection, that the exclusive focus on the goal of school integration responded to the ideals of elite liberal public interest lawyers rather than to the actual interests of black communities and children. In "The Interest-Convergence Dilemma," Bell sketched a full-scale structural theory to account for the ebb and flow of civil rights reform in America, according to the political machinations of whites themselves.

In 1980, Bell left Harvard to become dean of the University of Oregon Law School and one of the first African-Americans to head a mainstream American law school. Student activists, particularly students of color, demanded that Harvard hire a teacher of color to replace him and to teach his courses in constitutional law and minority issues. The liberal white Harvard administration responded to student protests, demonstrations, rallies and sit-ins—including a takeover of the Dean's office—by asserting that there were no qualified black scholars who merited Harvard's interest. Harvard's response was structured around two points produced from within liberal race discourse which Critical Race Theory would ultimately contest. First, they asked why the students wouldn't prefer an excellent white professor over a mediocre black one—that is, at a conceptual level, they posited the particular liberal epistemology that associated color-blindness with intellectual merit. Second, the Harvard administration, skeptical about the pedagogical value of a course devoted to racial topics, asserted that no special course was needed when "those issues" were already covered in classes devoted to constitutional law and employment discrimination thus, to our minds, failing to comprehend the significance of Bell's projects. Instead, Jack Greenberg and Julius Chambers, both important and distinguished civil rights litigators, were hired to teach a three-week mini-course on civil rights litigation.

It was in the midst of this kind of institutional struggle, played out in one form or another at mainstream law schools around the country, that many of us now writing in the Critical Race Theory genre began to elaborate what we took to be the limitations of traditional race analysis and argument. After all, in a context such as Harvard, administrators saw themselves as racially enlightened: they were liberals who were against racial discrimination—indeed, Harvard wanted to honor a heroic litigator of the school desegregation era with a visiting professorship. Clearly, the cool, technocratic and business-like culture of mainstream law schools was hostile at all points to raw "prejudice"—these were not institutions in which a hardcore, "Bull Conner" type racist would receive a warm welcome. Although those of us who were agitating for hiring teachers of color knew we didn't accept the kinds of justifications the Harvard administrators offered, we also knew that we lacked an adequate critical vocabulary for articulating exactly what we found wrong in their arguments. It was out of this intellectual void that the impetus for a new conceptual approach to race and law was based. Our critique of ideas like "color-blindness," "formal legal equality," and "integrationism" are linked to their institutional manifestations as a rhetoric of power in the schools we attended and the work-places we now occupy.

In the local Harvard confrontation, student organizers decided to boycott the mini-course offered by the administration and organized instead "The Alternative Course," a student-led continuation of Bell's course which focused on American law through the prism of race. Taught by scholars of color from other schools who were each asked to speak about topics loosely organized to trace the chapters of Bell's *Race, Racism and American Law* book, the course simultaneously provided the means to develop a framework to understand law and racial power and to contest Harvard's deployment of meritocratic mythology as an instance of that very power.

The Alternative Course was in many ways the first institutionalized expression of Critical Race Theory. With the aid of outside funding and sympathetic Harvard teachers (many of them white crits who provided encouragement, strategic advice, and independent study credit to enable students to attend the classes) the course brought together a critical mass of scholars and students, and focused on the need to develop an alternative account of racial power and its relation to law and antidiscrimination reform. Among the guest speakers were Charles Lawrence,

Linda Greene, Neil Gotanda, and Richard Delgado, all of whom were already in law teaching. Mari Matsuda, then a graduate law student, was a participant in the Alternative Course, and Kimberlé Crenshaw one of its main organizers.

The Alternative Course is a useful point to mark the genesis of Critical Race Theory for many reasons. First, it was one of the earliest attempts to bring scholars of color together to address the law's treatment of race from a selfconsciously critical perspective. There had been some race-conscious organizing in law schools in the preceding years. For example, within the Association of American Law Schools, (AALS) the professional association of law teachers, a minority section had been established which Ralph Smith of the University of Pennsylvania and Denise Carty-Bennia of Northeastern University used as a vehicle for intellectual development. However, the AALS group neither provided a basis for sustained dialogue, nor openly identified itself within the profession as intellectually oppositional and politically left-progressive. Recognizing these inherent institutional limitations, legal academics of color created an informal network of support for law students and teachers of color, whose existence was enormously important in developing a critical mass of law teachers of color. These were efforts, though, that carried no direct implications for scholarship and theory.

Second, the Alternative Course exemplified another important feature of the Critical Race Theory movement, namely, the view—shared with the Critical Legal Studies movement—that it is politically meaningful to contest the terrain and terms of dominant legal discourse. In one sense, the importance of mainstream law school discourse to Critical Race Theorists flows from the view that power is implicated in, say, the privileging of certain topics and viewpoints as worthy of being curricular entries at mainstream law schools. The idea here, in essence, is that knowledge and politics are inevitably intertwined. As an influential site for indoctrination and propagation, the ideology of law schools helps in turn to shape and give substance to the broader legal and social ideologies about race and legitimacy. In another sense, the focus on the law school and legal scholarship as a terrain worth contesting is based on a view of law schools in left terms as work-places in which we find ourselves as part of a productive enterprise, the "production of knowledge." This perspective helps to explain an important difference with earlier conceptions of race reform, which looked to law schools and other legal institutions as places to gather tools to deploy in political struggles that occurred "out there" in the South, the ghetto, or some other place besides law schools or courtrooms themselves. Against this view, we take racial power to be at stake across the social plane—not merely in the places where people of color are concentrated but also in the institutions where their position is normalized and given legitimation. The Alternative Course reflected—as well as helped to create—the sense that it was meaningful to build an oppositional community of left scholars of color within the mainstream legal academy.

Finally, the Alternative Course embodied one of the key markers of Critical Race Theory—the way in which our intellectual trajectories are rooted in a dissatisfaction with and opposition to liberal mainstream discourses about race such as those presented by the Harvard administration.

We turn now to the Critical Legal Studies conferences of the mid-eighties and the general engagement with the white left in and outside of the legal academy both of which were crucial in the development of the Critical Race Theory project. If the Alternative Course symbolizes the trajectory of Critical Race Theory as a left intervention in conventional race discourse, then the Critical Legal Studies

Conferences during the mid-eighties can be equally useful in situating Critical Race Theory as a raceconscious intervention on the left.

At its inception in the late seventies, Critical Legal Studies (CLS) was basically a white and largely male academic organization. By the mid-eighties, there was a small cadre of scholars of color who frequented CLS conferences and summer camps. Most were generally conversant with Critical Legal Theory and sympathetic to the progressive sensibilities of Critical Legal Studies as a whole. Unlike the law school mainstream, this cadre was far from deterred by CLS critique of liberal legalism. While many in the legal community were, to put it mildly, deeply disturbed by the CLS assault against such ideological mainstays as the rule of the law, to scholars of color who drew on a history of colored communities' struggle against formal and institutional racism, the crits' contention that law was neither apolitical, neutral, nor determinate hardly seemed controversial. Indeed, we believed that this critical perspective formed the basic building blocks of any serious attempt to understand the relationship between law and white supremacy. However, while the emerging "race crits" shared this starting position with CLS, significant differences between us became increasingly apparent during a series of conferences in the mid-eighties.

Our discussions during the conferences revealed that while we shared with crits the belief that legal consciousness functioned to legitimize social power in the United States, race crits also understood that race and racism likewise functioned as central pillars of hegemonic power. Because CLS scholars had not, by and large, developed and incorporated a critique of racial power into their analysis, their practices, politics and theories regarding race tended to be unsatisfying and sometimes indistinguishable from those of the dominant institutions they were otherwise contesting. As race moved from the margins to the center of discourse within Critical Legal Studies—or, as some would say, Critical Legal Studies took the race turn—institutional and theoretical disjunctures between critical legal studies and the emerging scholarship on race eventually manifested themselves as central themes within Critical Race Theory.

One of the most significant institutional manifestations of CLS's underdeveloped critique of racial power occurred during the 1986 CLS conference. The 1986 conference, organized by a group of women who worked in feminist legal theory, marked the zenith of the feminist turn within CLS. Having placed feminism and its critique of patriarchy squarely within the discourse of and about CLS, the "fem-crit" conference organizers asked scholars of color to facilitate several concurrently held discussions about race. Drawing on a central CLS tenet that power is not, ultimately, "out there," but in the very institutions and relation-ships that shape our lives, the handful of scholars of color attending this conference designed the workshop to uncover and discuss various dimensions of racial power as manifested within Critical Legal Studies. Though the practice of uncovering and contesting power within law school institutions was a standard feature of CLS politics, the attempt to situate this practice within CLS as a "white" institution drew a surprisingly defensive response. The pitched and heated exchange that erupted in response to our query, "what is it about the whiteness of CLS that discourages participation by people of color?" revealed that CLS's hip, cutting edge irreverence toward establishment practices could easily disintegrate into handwringing hysteria when brought back "home." Of course, not all crits were resistant to this dialogue and it is only fair to point out that those who did find the query to be unnecessarily adversarial probably held a good faith belief that CLS marked a sphere of activity completely distinct from both law schools and society at large. Since "we" were joined as allies rather than adversaries within the law school arena, crits troubled by our workshop no doubt believed that critical energies would be best directed at tearing down institutional practices at our workplace rather than bringing these disruptive interventions "home." But feminists had already problematized the conceptualization of "home" that seemed to ground this view, revealing such spaces to be a site of hierarchy and power as well. Moreover, as the race crits experienced it, despite some points of convergence, some of the racial dynamics of CLS as an institution were not entirely distinct from the law school cultures "we" had set out to transform.

Another point of conflict and difference between white crits and scholars of color revolved around the widely debated critique of rights. According to other scholars of color at the 1987 conference, another dimension of the failure of CLS to reflect the lived experience of people of color could be glimpsed in the CLS critique of rights. Crits tended to view the idea of legal "rights" as one of the ways that law helps to legitimize the social world by representing it as rationally mediated by the rule of law. Crits also saw legal rights—like those against racial discrimination—as indeterminate and capable of contradictory meanings, and as embodying an alienated way of thinking about social relations.

Crits of color agreed to varying degrees with some dimensions of the critique—for instance, that rights discourse was indeterminate. Yet we sharply differed with critics over the normative implications of this observation. To the emerging race crits, rights discourse held a social and transformative value in the context of racial subordination that transcended the narrower question of whether reliance on rights could alone bring about any determinate results. Race crits realized that the very notion of a subordinate people exercising rights was an important dimension of Black empowerment during the civil rights movement, significant not simply because of the occasional legal victories that were garnered, but because of the transformative dimension of African-Americans re-imagining themselves as full, rights-bearing citizens within the American political imagination. We wanted to acknowledge the centrality of rights discourse even as we recognized that the use of rights language was not without risks. The debate that ensued in light of this different orientation engendered an important CRT theme: the absolute centrality of history and context in any attempt to theorize the relationship between race and legal discourse.

A third ideological difference emerged in a series of critiques of early attempts by scholars of color to articulate how law reflects and produces racial power. Most of these critiques were articulated at the next 1987 CLS conference, "The Sounds of Silence," sponsored by Los Angeles area law schools. Although the terms of the debate were not fully clear, and at the time, there were few key words or concepts on which our analysis could then focus, we have come to articulate the central criticism by crits to be that of "racialism." By racialism, we refer to theoretical accounts of racial power that explain legal and political decisions which are adverse to people of color as mere reflections of underlying white interest. To phrase this critical model in more contemporary terms, we might say that racialism is to power what essentialism is to identity—a narrow, and frequently unsatisfying theory in which complex phenomena are reduced to and presented as a simple reflection of some underlying "facts." Specifically, the "sin" of racialism is that it presumes that racial interests or racial identity exists somewhere outside of or prior to law and is merely reflected in subsequent legal decisions adverse to nonwhites.

Such an approach struck crits as far too instrumental to be a useful account of race and power. During the eighties, crits had been debating the issue of "instrumentalist" and "irrationalist" accounts of law; most agreed with the problematic character of what came to be called "vulgar Marxism." Briefly stated, in traditional Marxist analysis, law appears as merely an instrument of class interests that are rooted outside of law in some "concrete social reality." In sum, law is merely an "ideological reflection" of some class interest rooted elsewhere. Many critics—echoing the late sixties New Left—sought to distinguish themselves from these "instrumentalist" accounts on the grounds that they embodied a constricted view of the range and sites of the production of social power, and hence of politics. By defining class in terms of one's position in the material production process, and viewing law and all other "superstructural" phenomena as merely reflections of interests rooted in social class identification, vulgar Marxism, crits argued, ignored the ways that law and other merely "superstructural" arenas helped to constitute the very interests that law was supposed merely to reflect. Crits such as Freeman, Duncan Kennedy, and Karl Klare (to name a few) developed non-instrumentalist accounts of law and its relationship to power that focused on legal discourse as a crucial site for the production of ideology and the perpetuation of social power. First, Critical Legal theorists developed a genealogical account of the relationship between law and social interests. Noting the degree, for example, to which political struggles in the U.S. are conducted in the language and logic of the law, crits argued that social interests, and the weight they are accorded, do not exist in advance of or outside the law, but depend on legal institutions and ideology for both their content and form. Second, the crits provided a detailed inventory of the ideological practices by which the legal order actively seeks to persuade those who are subject to it that the law's uneven distribution of social power is nonetheless "just." Third, in their account of legal consciousness, critical legal theorists demonstrated the precise mechanisms by which legal institutions and ideology obscure and thus legitimize their productive, constitutive social role. The crits argued that the law does not passively adjudicate questions of social power; rather, the law is an active instance of the very power politics it purports to avoid and stand above. In brief, the crits revealed in often dizzying detail the cunning complexity of legal texts which traditional Marxists simply dismissed as "capitalist ideology."

One consequence of this particular intellectual genealogy is that in their engagement with orthodox and scientistic forms of Marxist thought on the left, CLS scholars had already developed a critique of the kinds of instrumentalist analyses that were presented in the language of race. To critics of racialism, prevailing theorizations of race and law seemed to represent law as an instrumental reflection of racial interests in much the same way that vulgar Marxists saw the legal arena as reflecting class interests. Just as the white left had learned, by the eighties, that a one-dimensional class account was too simplistic for legal analysis, they interpreted racialist accounts as analogous to class reductionism.

To be sure, some of the foundational essays of CRT could be vulnerable to such a critique, particularly when read apart from the context and conditions of their production. Yet, when read as interventions against a liberal legalist tradition that viewed law as an apolitical mediator of racial conflict, it becomes clear that by articulating a structural relationship between law and white supremacy, these essays dislodged an entrenched pattern of viewing racial out-comes as merely the random consequences of aracial legal processes. These early essays thus constituted a critical first step in identifying the operation of racial power within discursive traditions that had been widely accepted as neutral and apolitical. By legitimizing the use of race as a theoretical fulcrum and focus in legal scholarship, so-called racialist accounts of racism and the law grounded the subsequent development of Critical Race Theory in much the same way that Marxism's introduction of class structure and struggle into classical political economy grounded subsequent critiques of social hierarchy and power.

At the same time, the critique of racialism did help clarify what was "critical" about our race project. As we noted earlier, their dissatisfaction with the narrow instrumentalist view of law had moved CLS scholars to elaborate a theory of the constitutive form of legal ideology. The crits challenged the understanding of social and political interests that instrumentalist portrayals of law had viewed as simply given. The crits' more dynamic and dialectical model revealed the constitutive force of law, the ways legal institutions constructed the very social interests and relations that cruder instrumentalist accounts of law thought it merely regulated and ratified. For our purposes, the chief theoretical advantage of this anatomy of the constitutive dimensions of law was that it made it possible to argue that the legal system is not simply or mainly a biased referee of social and political conflict whose origins and effects occur elsewhere. On this account, the law is shown to be thoroughly involved in constructing the rules of the game, in selecting the eligible players, and in choosing the field on which the game must be played.

Drawing on these premises, we began to think of our project as uncovering how law was a constitutive element of race itself: in other words, how law *constructed* race. Racial power, in our view, was not simply—or even primarily—a product of biased decision-making on the part of judges, but instead, the sum total of the pervasive ways in which law shapes and is shaped by "race relations" across the social plane. Laws produced racial power not simply through narrowing the scope of, say, of antidiscrimination remedies, nor through racially-biased decision-making, but instead, through myriad legal rules, many of them having nothing to do with rules against discrimination, that continued to reproduce the structures and practices of racial domination. In short, we accepted the crit emphasis on how law produces and is the product of social power and we cross-cut this theme with an effort to understand this dynamic in the context of race and racism. With such an analysis in hand, critical race theory allows us to better understand how racial power can be produced even from within a liberal discourse that is relatively autonomous from organized vectors of racial power.

If the foregoing critique clarified at least one dimension of our project that grew from a shared theoretical investment with CLS, it also revealed subtle, but crucial theoretical divergences between CLS and CRT. Despite the sophistication of the crits' understanding of how law constituted social interests and legal identity, they were, for the most part, unable to transpose these insights into an analysis of racial power and law. Our point here is not that the crits committed the typical Marxist error of subsuming race under class. Rather, our dissatisfaction with CLS stemmed from its failure to come to terms with the particularity of race, and with the specifically racial character of "social interests" in the racialized state. For some, their lack of critical thinking about race was a reflection of intellectual interest. With respect to other crits, however, our divergence produced a much sharper conflict. While we were straining to strengthen our understanding of racial power, it appeared to us that some crits were deploying racialist critiques from a position on race that was close if not identical to the liberalism we were otherwise joined in opposing. To be sure, these crits positioned themselves in a discourse far removed from liberalism—a certain post-modern critique of identity. Yet the upshot of their position seemed to be the same: an abiding skepticism, if not outright disdain, toward any theoretical or political project organized around the concept of race. Where classical liberalism argued that race was irrelevant to public policy, these crits argued that race simply didn't exist. The position is one that we have come to call "vulgar anti-essentialism." By this we seek to capture the claims made by some critical theorists that since racial categories are not "real" or "natural" but instead socially constructed, it is theoretical and politically absurd to center race as a category of analysis or as a basis for political action. This suggested to us that underlying at least some of the critiques from the left was not simply a question about the *way* we represented racial power, but instead, a more fundamental attack on the very possibility of our project. In short, this position constituted an attack on "color-consciousness" which differed from the conservative assault only in its rhetorical politics.

Many of us did, of course, accept the more complicated notions of power and identity implicated by both the anti-instrumentalist and anti-essentialist positions. Yet in our view, neither was inconsistent with the project of mapping the domain of law and racial power. It was obvious to many of us that although race was, to use the term, socially constructed (the idea of biological race is "false"), race was nonetheless "real" in the sense that there is a material dimension and weight to the experience of being "raced" in American society, a materiality that in significant ways has been produced and sustained by law. Thus, we understood our project as an effort to construct a race-conscious and at the same time anti-essentialist account of the processes by which law participates in "race-ing" American society.

Perhaps prophetically, the conference was also occasioned by a prototype of an assault launched against critical race theory from a position firmly situated within the very paradigm we sought to criticize. The highlight of the 1987 conference was a plenary in which numerous scholars of color articulated how institutional practices and intellectual paradigms functioned to silence insurgent voices of people of color. Responding to the critique, another scholar of color shared with the audience his impression that the absence of much of minority scholarship was attributable to its poor quality, and to the lack of productivity of minority scholars. Scholars of color were urged to stop complaining and simply to write. Of course, the discussion that followed was animated. But more important than what was said was what was assumed—namely, that the arena of academic discourse was functionally open to any scholar of merit who sought to enter it. Yet the very point that the speakers were trying to reveal (perhaps too subtly, in retrospect) was that the notions of merit that were so glibly employed to determine access and status within the intellectual arena were themselves repositories of racial power. This exchange, and the subsequent incarnation of this conflict in the pages of the *Harvard Law Review*—provides one of the clearest points of demarcation between critical and liberal race discourses.

The 1986 and 1987 CLS conferences thus marked significant points of alignment and departure, and should be considered the final step in the preliminary development of CRT as a distinctively progressive critique of legal discourse on

race. As a political and intellectual matter, the upshot of this engagement with
CLS can best be characterized as "coalition." We see CLS and CRT as aligned—
in radical left opposition to mainstream legal discourse. But CRT is also different
from CLS—our focus on race means that we have addressed quite different concerns, with distinct methodologies and traditions that we honor.

We have argued that the institutional and ideological antecedents of CRT can
be usefully grounded in two historical sites: the Harvard boycott, and the CLS
conferences of the mid-eighties. These roughly parallel the duality of CRT as both
a progressive intervention in race discourse and a race intervention on the left.
Yet, while we have identified these moments and will trace the trajectory of
these themes into the writings that appear in this volume, it would be remiss for
us to leave the impression that CRT subsequently developed as a disembodied,
abstracted, and autonomous intellectual formation. In the first place, we believe
that this image of scholarship is simply false—intellectual work is always situated, reflective to varying degrees of the cultural, historical, and institutional
conditions of its production. Second and most importantly, this view of scholarship obscures the shared difficulties that insurgent scholars must negotiate and
the importance of developing collective strategies to write about racial power
from within the institutions central to its reproduction. A thorough mapping of
Critical Race Theory, then, must include a discussion of the role of community-
building among the intellectuals who are associated with it, particularly in light
of the challenging conditions under which insurgent scholarship is produced.

During the mid-eighties, many of us met in smaller groups, before and after
larger law school conferences and conventions, first at the fringes of and then as
a caucus within Critical Legal Studies meetings, and so on. Shared experiences at
the margins of liberal institutional policies and critical legal studies provided
some basis for a collective identity. Yet the process of recognizing ourselves as a
group with a distinct intellectual project was gradual. Our ad hoc meetings prior
to and during various conferences provided an occasional opportunity to discuss
our views; however, the key formative event was the founding of the Critical Race
Theory workshop. Principally organized by Kimberlé Crenshaw, Neil Gotanda,
and Stephanie Phillips, the workshop drew together thirty five law scholars who
responded to a call to synthesize a theory that, while grounded in critical theory,
was responsive to the realities of racial politics in America. Indeed, the organizers coined the term "Critical Race Theory" to make it clear that our work locates
itself in intersection of critical theory and race, racism and the law. To be sure,
while we have emphasized throughout the liberal and critical poles against which
Critical Race Theory developed, in experience, such dialectical relations produce
less of a sharp break, and more of a creative and contestatory engagement with
both traditions. This is true not only of the content of Critical Race Theory, but
is true as well of the workshop's participants. Indeed, both liberal race theorists
and critical legal theorists have been deeply engaged in critical race discourse. For
example, among the range of scholars who were attracted to the workshop and
who contributed to the development of Critical Race Theory were scholars who
had written squarely within the liberal paradigm. The workshop itself was underwritten by a grant provided by David Trubek, a founding member of the Critical
Legal Studies Conference and a law professor at the University of Wisconsin,
Madison. Finally, as this volume attests, we consider the work of members of
CLS conference to represent a crucial contribution to the Critical Race Theory
literature.

In the opening pages of this introduction, we argued that Critical Race Theory does not simply seek to understand the complex condominia of law, racial ideology, and political power. We believe that our work can provide a useful theoretical vocabulary for the practice of progressive racial politics in contemporary America. The need for an oppositional vision of racial justice becomes particularly acute in light of the Supreme Court's radical movement toward a jurisprudence which not only accepts but affirms the current racial regime.

As this volume goes to press, the U.S. Supreme Court has issued a series of decisions which effectively repeal the ideological "settlement" struck during the civil rights era. In *Adarand Constructors v. Pena*, the Supreme Court extended its 1989 decision in *City of Richmond v. J.A. Croson* to categorically require strict judicial scrutiny whenever government, at any level, considers race in its decisionmaking process. In the last few years, the Supreme Court had all but foreclosed the adoption of race-conscious responses to racial inequity by state and local governments. In a cramped conception of the scope of national power under the Fourteenth Amendment, the *Adarand* Court has pressed further and formally forbidden even the federal government from taking race explicitly into account in addressing societal-wide discrimination. In *Missouri v. Jenkins*, the Supreme Court held that racially-concentrated public schools could no longer be deemed presumptively unconstitutional, even in the presence of a history of formal segregation. As to any continuing racial segregation in these schools, the *Jenkins* opinion concluded that the courts could not address the problem of racial concentration if it could plausibly be said that a public school district was making a "good faith" effort to achieve desegregation "to the extent practicable." The court has thus effectively mandated the withdrawal of the federal judiciary from continued involvement in the effort to achieve racial desegregation in the nation's public schools. Finally, in *Miller v. Johnson*, the Supreme Court retreated from its longstanding enforcement of the historic Voting Rights Act, erecting rigid new barriers to the federal government's effort to increase the participation and representation of racial minorities in the political process.

Reading these decisions, one cannot help but notice the degree to which they deploy traditional liberal racial principles. The current Court has effectively conscripted liberal theories of race and racism to wage a conservative attack on governmental efforts to address the persistence of societal-wide racial discrimination. This harsh reality confirms the need for a critical theory of racial power and an image of racial justice which reject classical liberal visions of race as well as conservative visions of equal citizenship.

We believe that core concepts from Critical Race Theory can be productively used to expose the irreducibly political character of the current Court's general hostility toward policies which would take race into account in redressing historic and contemporary patterns of racial discrimination. We might, for example, draw on Critical Race Theory's deconstruction of color-blindness to show that the current Supreme Court's expressed hostility toward race-consciousness must be deemed a form of raceconsciousness in and of itself. As Neil Gotanda has cogently argued, one cannot heed the newly installed constitutional rule that forbids raceconscious approaches to racial discrimination without always first taking race into account. Similarly, Critical Race Theory helps us understand how race-consciousness implicitly informs the current Court's paradoxical insistence that the norm of color-blindness requires a voting rights regime which effectively deprives racial minorities of political advantages that are accorded to other organized social interests.

Critical Race Theory indicates how and why the contemporary "jurisprudence of color-blindness" is not only the expression of a particular color-consciousness, but the product of a deeply politicized choice. The current Court would have us believe that these decisions are the product of an ineluctable legal logic. Critical Race Theory tells us rather that the Court's rulings with respect to race may more plausibly be deemed a result of a tactical political choice among competing doctrinal possibilities, any one of which could have been legally defensible. The appeal to color-blindness can thus be said to serve as part of an ideological strategy by which the current Court obscures its active role in sustaining hierarchies of racial power. We believe that Critical Race Theory offers a valuable conceptual compass for mapping the doctrinal mystifications which the current Court has developed to camouflage its conservative agenda.

The preceding discussion has focused on the possible uses to which Critical Race Theory might be put in understanding and intervening in the politics of racial jurisprudence. However, since discussions about race and rights in the U.S. have always overrun the narrow institutional confines of the law, we want to conclude this introduction to Critical Race Theory by suggesting some of the implications our work as legal scholars holds for broader national conversations about racial politics. In our history of the development of Critical Race Theory, we have highlighted the ways in which our work is a record of our engagement with what we saw as limitations of liberal, leftist and racialist accounts of racial power in law. The similar limitations of recent liberal defenses of affirmative action, left-liberal discourses on globalization, and racialist responses to post-civil rights retrenchment suggest that Critical Race Theory may provide new and much needed ways to think about (and challenge) the contemporary politics of racial domination.

We turn first to the vexed question of liberal discourse in the current national disputations regarding affirmative action. Earlier in this introduction we noted how the liberal defense of affirmative action has been stymied from its inception by a decidedly ambivalent attitude toward the matters of race and racial power. To be sure, liberals are generally willing to concede that racism continues to be an "obvious and boring fact" of American life (as the liberal pundit Michael Kinsley rather remarkably put it in a recent article). What liberal proponents of affirmative action seem unwilling to do is to move toward a direct critique of the hidden racial dimensions of the meritocratic mythology that their conservative opponents have so deftly used to control the terms of the current debate.

This ambivalence toward race-consciousness is best understood as a symptom of liberalism's continued investment in meritocratic ideology and its unacknowledged resistance to reaching any deep understanding of the myriad ways racism continues to limit the realization of goals such as equal opportunity. This liberal ambivalence is particularly manifested in today's debates, particularly about affirmative action. But it is also reflected in the lukewarm liberal defense of the Great Society programs of the 1960s and other policies which were adopted to address contradictions between American ideals and historical realities. Like the Harvard Law School administration's response to the demand for a course focused on race and the law, the liberal position reflects an abiding uncertainty about the value of such projects, and a lingering, wistful sense that if we could just agree to abandon race-consciousness, racism and racial power would somehow recede from the American political imagination.

Critical Race Theory is instructive here in that it uncovers the ongoing dynamics of racialized power, and its embeddedness in practices and values which have been shorn of any explicit, formal manifestations of racism. Critical Race Theory thus provides a basis for understanding affirmative action as something other than "racial preference" (a notion whose implicit premise is that affirmative action represents a deviation from an otherwise non-racial neutrality). Critical Race Theory understands that, claims to the contrary notwithstanding, distributions of power and resources which were racially determined before the advent of affirmative action would continue to be so if affirmative action is abandoned. Our critiques of racial power reveal how certain conceptions of merit function not as a neutral basis for distributing resources and opportunity, but rather as a repository of hidden, race-specific preferences for those who have the power to determine the meaning and consequences of "merit." We have shown that the putatively neutral baseline from which affirmative action is said to represent a deviation is in fact a mechanism for perpetuating the distribution of rights, privileges, and opportunity established under a regime of uncontested white supremacy. Critical Race Theory recognizes accordingly that a return to that so-called neutral baseline would mean a return to an unjust system of racial power. Finally, Critical Race Theory fully comprehends that the aim of affirmative action is to create enough exceptions to white privilege to make the mythology of equal opportunity seem at least plausible. In fact, a defense of affirmative action premised upon CRT rather than liberal ambivalence would neither apologize for affirmative action nor assume it to be a fully adequate political response to the persistence of white supremacy. Rather, Critical Race Theory supports affirmative action as a limited approach which has achieved a meaningful, if modest measure of racial justice.

A second discussion to which we believe Critical Race Theory might bring a useful perspective is liberal and left debate in the U.S. over the proliferation of economic, political, social relations across national borders which has come to be known as globalization. Like Critical Legal Studies in the mid-1980s, the left-liberal approach to globalization has yet to generate an adequate account of the connections between racial power and political economy in the New World Order. Instead, generalized references to the "North" and "South" figure as a metaphorical substitute for serious and sustained attention to the racial and ethnic character of the massive distributive transformations that globalization has set in motion. Abstract allusions to "rich" and "poor" nations simply fail to yield an adequate vocabulary for analyzing the precise processes that produce globalized racial stratification. As the Nigerian scholar Claude Ake has argued, globalization enacts a "hierarchization of the world" and the "crystallizing of a domination." While that domination may be essentially *constituted* by economic power, it is essentially *legitimized* by racial power or, to use Ake's term, by ideologies of "political ethnicity." Critical Race Theory would thus focus on the degree to which the effects of globalization in the (so-called) Third World demand analysis as an instance of what Arjun Makhijani calls "economic apartheid."

This general indifference to questions of racial ideology and power also informs liberal and left efforts to explain the political significance of global economic processes within the U.S. For the most part, liberal and left analysis of this question has focused on the impact of globalization on U.S. class structure and politics. To the extent these debates *do* consider the role of race in the age of globalization, they do so only in the context of conversations about the "cultural pathologies" of the "underclass" (in liberal circles), or (on the left) in terms of a "class" of subordinated racial groups whose vulnerable economic position is the product of past, but not current, dynamics of racial power. The particularities of race and its persistent presence as an explicit rationalization of structural stratification in the current economy seem hardly to warrant discussion. One would think that the racial composition of the communities which have been chosen to bear the sharp edge of economic dislocation is altogether irrelevant. However, even a cursory review of current national discourses about public education, unemployment, education, immigration and welfare reform (to take a few examples) demonstrates the degree to which questions of race and racial ideology stand at the very center of today's debates. These developments defy explanation in terms of liberal accounts of poverty and social equality, on the one hand, or leftist formulations about the historical class relations between labor and capital, on the other.

A CRT-grounded response to these developments would intersect contemporary critical discourses concerning the domestic social transformations wrought by globalization and critical theories of race and power to better understand the "racial economy" of this transition. This CRT-informed investigation of the "South in the North" would examine the way a certain brand of racial politics has been mobilized to buffer the massive upward distribution of resources and opportunity within the United States, or explore the way racial ideologies have been used to justify relatively open border policies toward our Northern neighbors, even as we close off our borders to those from the South. Just as Critical Race Theory introduced racial ideology as a necessary component of hegemony in the wake of the Critical Legal Studies emphasis on legal consciousness, so too must contemporary social theory fully incorporate notions of racial power as a way of understanding (and contesting) changing economic relations.

A third and final aspect of contemporary politics on which Critical Race Theory might be brought to bear is the struggle within communities of color over the future direction of anti-racist politics. The difficulties critical race scholars faced in attempting to push the analysis of law and racial politics beyond the narrow boundaries of racialism may all be seen at work in contemporary political debates among people of color. The emergence of powerful voices of racialism is particularly evident within the African American community, in which contemporary racial crisis is frequently represented as a reflection of unmediated white power. Although the message of racialist politics speaks to a broad range of disaffected African-Americans, it is also the source of debilitating contradictions within black political life. Indeed, as a mode of political analysis and action, racialism has ironically facilitated ideological attacks on black America that are now simplistically represented as coming from "out there"—that is, from outside the African-American community.

To take one example, racialists rightly identify the right-wing decisions of the current Supreme Court as part of the panoply of assaults directed against black Americans. What they all too often fail to note is that this same racialist politics helped secure the radical right's crucial fifth vote on the Supreme Court, in the person of Clarence Thomas. At the time of his nomination, Thomas had left little doubt about his political commitments. Despite a clearly manifested ideological agenda from which one could fully predict his role in consolidating the conservative wing of the Supreme Court, Thomas was nonetheless able to garner crucial support across the spectrum of African-American political formations. Narrow notions of racial solidarity led African-Americans to rally behind a figure who, though black, had been and would continue to be an eager participant in the evisceration of the post-civil rights coalition.

Another dimension of the racialism that led black Americans to support the Thomas nomination was deeply gendered in its determination. The erroneous view that racial interests would be advanced by the appointment of *any African-American to the Supreme Court* was compounded by a misguided racialist belief that questions of gender power were irrelevant (if not antagonistic) to the interests of the "larger" black American community. During our earlier discussion of racialism, we argued that one of the chief problems with the racialist account of social power and struggle lies in the tendency to "essentialize" the racial communities with which it represents the social world. In black racialist circles, the felt necessity to articulate a stable vision of group identity and interest has underwritten a "representational politics" in which the experience of one segment of black America is taken to be representative of black experience *tout court*. As a result, black racialism yields a flat, fixed image of racial identity, experience and interest, which fails to capture the complex, constantly changing realities of racial domination in the contemporary U.S.

The concrete implications of this crude essentialism became painfully apparent in the subordinating gender politics to which black racialist support for the Thomas nomination gave rise. As Kimberlé Crenshaw has argued, the black racialist account proffers a vision of racism which portrays racial power primarily through its impact on African-American males. Because it is unwilling or unable to apprehend the ways in which racial identities are lived within and through gendered identities, racial essentialism renders the particular experiences of black females invisible. Black racialist politics thus effectively denies the struggle against racialized gender oppression a place on its anti-racist agenda. A final recent example will suffice to show how black America continues to be held hostage to racialism's essentialist politics. Although much of the rhetoric supporting a proposed "Million Man March" is grounded in the need for a black American response to Supreme Court decisions, the March's proponents not only fail to problematize the racialist politics that installed Clarence Thomas, but effectively reproduce those politics by promoting gender exclusivity, with its concomitant subordination of the irreducibly gendered dimensions of black women's racial oppression.

Because there is no currently viable alternative to an ambivalent liberal vision of race, on the one hand, and an inadequate vision of racialism, on the other, many progressive voices in the black community tend to gravitate toward the racialist view. For all its faults, racialism at least acknowledges the persistence of racism (albeit in an essentialist and exclusionary way). Without a counter vision of race that does not fall into the nebulous world of liberal ambivalence and apology, the dangers of racialist politics for communities of color will continue to go unheeded, even in light of the deep contradictions that such politics produces.

Historians of American racial politics may rightly remember the final years of the twentieth century as the "Age of Repudiation." All the evidence suggests that the 1990s mark the rejection of the always fragile civil rights consensus and the renunciation of by federal, state and city authorities (indeed, of the American people themselves) that government not only can but must play an active role in identifying and eradicating racial injustice. The ideological offensive against civil rights reform (not to mention deeper social change) has consolidated what we have called a new common sense regarding race and racism in the United States. Although the new racial common sense defies both reason and contemporary reality, this fact has not deterred makers of public policy and public opinion in the post-reform era from using it to justify their indifference or outright hostility toward those who continue to struggle for racial justice and multicultural democracy in the United States. In the 1980s, the architects of the new racial common sense provided an ideological foundation for dismantling many of the key reforms and programs adopted during the civil rights period. In the 1990s, the apologists for racial reaction have deepened and extended their attack to include the very principle of racial antidiscrimination. Emboldened by the successes of the 1980s, right-wing legal academics such as Richard A. Epstein now openly decry laws forbidding racial discrimination on the grounds that they are economically inefficient and morally indefensible. And in a deliberate distortion of the 1954 *Brown* decision, Supreme Court Justice Clarence Thomas has cynically described the *Brown* court's historically-based claim that racial segregation was "inherently" unequal as itself an example of white racism. The power of new racial common sense may be seen, too, in the felt necessity of Democratic President Bill Clinton to qualify his already compromised defense of affirmative action with a neo-liberal nod toward the "angry white males" who, against all the evidence, have positioned themselves as the chief "victims" of contemporary racial politics.

The task of *Critical Race Theory* is to remind its readers how deeply issues of racial ideology and power continue to matter in American life. Questioning regnant visions of racial meaning and racial power, critical race theorists seek to fashion a set of tools for thinking about race that avoids the traps of racial thinking. Critical Race Theory understands that racial power is produced by and experienced within numerous vectors of social life. Critical Race Theory recognizes, too, that political interventions which overlook the multiple ways in which people of color are situated (and resituated) as communities, subcommunities, and individuals will do little to promote effective resistance to, and counter-mobilization against, today's newly empowered right. It is our hope that the writings collected here will prove to be a useful critical compass for negotiating the treacherous terrain of American racial politics in the coming century.